A HISTORY OF LITERARY CRITICISM
IN THE ITALIAN RENAISSANCE

A HISTORY *of* LITERARY CRITICISM IN THE ITALIAN RENAISSANCE

VOLUME I

By Bernard Weinberg

THE UNIVERSITY OF CHICAGO PRESS

Library of Congress Catalog Number: 60–5470
The University of Chicago Press, Chicago 37
The University of Toronto Press, Toronto 5, Canada
Published 1961
ALL RIGHTS RESERVED
*Made and printed in Great Britain by
William Clowes and Sons, Limited, London and Beccles*

To

RONALD CRANE

RICHARD McKEON

ELDER OLSON

PREFACE

THE HISTORY OF LITERARY CRITICISM in the Italian Renaissance has been written several times. It is the subject of a volume by Ciro Trabalza entitled *La Critica letteraria (Dai primordi dell'Umanesimo all'Età nostra)* and published in Milan (1915) in the series "Storia dei generi letterari italiani." Inside and outside Italy the most widely read and influential treatment of the subject is to be found in Joel Elias Spingarn's *History of Literary Criticism in the Renaissance* (New York: Macmillan, 1899), published in Italian in a somewhat expanded form in 1904. The various works of Marvin T. Herrick have provided much useful information on the development of the theory of the genres during the Renaissance.

The present attempt to rewrite that history has two justifications. The first of these lies in the limited bibliography upon which the earlier histories were based. Spingarn discussed, in the briefest fashion, only some thirty documents in the original edition, a few more in the Italian translation. Trabalza and Herrick dealt with a considerably larger number of documents, but they fell far short of an adequate representation of the numerous texts that actually constitute the vast bibliography of literary criticism in the Italian Renaissance. This bibliography comprises, besides the major printed works, a great quantity of manuscript materials preserved in the libraries of Italy; these were left untouched by the earlier historians. It also includes many texts that are "minor" only in the sense that they are short or relatively unknown; they are frequently "major" because of their ideas or because of the contribution they have made to the development of literary criticism.

The second, and more important, justification derives from the way in which Spingarn and Trabalza used their materials. Their methods were those of the literary historians of an earlier generation. They tended rather to summarize texts than to analyze them, rather to disrupt texts (by isolating terms and passages) than to discover their structures, rather to construct chronologies than to write histories. What one learns from them, essentially, is the order and the content of a certain number of works; but even here one cannot be sure, since the content as they state it is often philosophically unconvincing. One cannot be sure, from the evidence they present, that their reading is a proper one. Such cautions, of course, attach to any reading of any text; the only recourse for the reader is his own reading of the text, and the only hope for the historian is that his reading, through its consistency and through the citations that support it, will convince others that it is a tenable hypothesis about the particular text.

In a sense, what I have attempted is an experiment in the writing of intellectual history. What is experimental is not the extension of the bibliography through the addition of hundreds of items not hitherto considered: this is merely the normal effect of the growth of bibliographical knowledge and the continued pursuit of the subject. It is rather the organization of the materials and the elaboration of the historical statement. I have not sought to follow any author through his career or any term or concept through the century. Instead, I have tried to distinguish the main intellectual traditions of the century as they relate to literary criticism and to trace them, year by year and text by text, up through the sixteenth century to the final, arbitrary date of 1600. These traditions were of two kinds: they were ways of regarding the art of poetry (a theoretical approach) and ways of judging poetic works (a practical approach). This distinction accounts for the two major divisions of my book.

With respect to the theoretical traditions, it has seemed to me useful to distinguish and identify them as developments and continuations of three great critical positions of the classical past: those of Plato, Aristotle, and Horace. These were the positions that provided Italians of the Renaissance with the greater part of their ideas on the art of poetry. It is rare, of course, that any one of them appears, purely and simply, in any single text; the Renaissance was not a period of intellectual purity and orderliness. But any individual text, taken in its entirety, should be classifiable under one or another of the major traditions; or at least its major tendencies may be expected to bear some resemblance to one of the major tendencies of the century—unless it is a completely eclectic work. It is only through the reading of the texts, indeed, that we discover the existence of those tendencies.

A consideration of each of the texts in its entirety should constitute another of the experimental aspects of my approach. It is, at least, one of the first principles of that approach. I have attempted, in the reading of each work, to discover its essential position; to discern what, basically and peculiarly, it was saying about the art of poetry or about a particular poem; to determine the methodological and the logical bases for its statements; to define its terms in relation to the whole complex of terms and concepts present in the work. I should point out that what I have said about any individual text is not intended to represent the totality of its contents; I have no more tried to report every idea than I have tried to account for every failure or inconsistency. My aim has been rather to state, with the greatest possible economy, its central position, to give an epitome of its premises and its conclusions, and to discover the method by which it passed from premises to conclusions. I have not undertaken to provide a substitute for the reading of any text but, instead, a guide to that reading.

Given the nature of the texts themselves, I have frequently found it necessary to discuss certain of them at two or three or four points in my study. A commentary on Aristotle's *Poetics*, for example, might also make a significant contribution to the study of Horace's *Ars poetica*, another to the development of Platonic ideas, still another to the criticism of a contemporary author. For the most part, though, each work is given major consideration only once. In a few cases I have had to deal with texts whose main subjects were not directly pertinent to my inquiry—broad philosophical treatises, works on other arts—but which did contain useful materials. Here I have been obliged, contrary to my general practice, to isolate passages or sections rather than to study entire texts.

I have limited my inquiry to literary criticism in the Italian Renaissance. The temptation was present, constantly, to associate with literary criticism such related fields as rhetorical theory and the criticism of the other arts, for the problems are the same or nearly so, and the documents themselves readily lead from one discipline to another. But I have had to resist this temptation sternly. The materials on literary criticism are themselves so abundant that to add others to them would have made the subject completely unmanageable. Moreover, the virtues of limitation to a single line of inquiry seemed to me obvious. Hence, the reader will find here no history of the important rhetorical documents of the century, even though there is much discussion of rhetorical ideas which appear in the treatises on poetry. Nor will he find any discussion of the quarrel over the Italian language, of the theory of painting or sculpture or architecture, in spite of the many resemblances of this theory to literary theory.

I have taken "Italian" in a fairly broad sense, including the works not only of Italians publishing in Italy but of foreigners publishing there and of Italians publishing abroad; the criterion for inclusion is the direct relationship of any given document to the Italian tradition. On the other hand, I have given to the term "Renaissance" a highly restricted meaning: I have limited it to the sixteenth century, except for those few cases in which I have found it necessary to trace a movement back into the Quattrocento. Here again, the decision was determined by the nature of the materials. The Cinquecento was the century of major development and full realization, both in poetic theory and in practical criticism; the Quattrocento, for all its overwhelming importance in other phases of the Renaissance, provided only a minor impetus in the domain of literary criticism, and the Seicento did little more than repeat and reorder the ideas of the preceding century. By 1600, the renaissance in criticism had run its full course, and at that date I have ended my investigation.

A word about the translations included in my text. In order to provide as nearly as possible a continuous text in one language, I have translated all quoted passages from Latin or Italian into English. The effort to make the translations both accurate and literate has been a task full of difficulties. Because in sixteenth-century usage many terms had multiple meanings and because syntax and construction, in both the Italian and the Latin texts, are frequently loose and inaccurate, it has been necessary at every point to decide upon the particular meaning intended. I present these translations with the usual reservations of the translator, urging the reader—if he thinks that I may have gone astray or if he wishes to follow the terminology in the original languages—to check them against the original texts, given in the footnotes. Among other technical matters, I have sometimes provided subheadings within the chapters for authors or subjects; but this is not done consistently for every text—merely from time to time in order to help with the chronology and to call attention to the most important documents. I have regularly reproduced original texts exactly, in spite of obvious errors; only rarely have I thought it necessary to make emendations.

As far as the source materials are concerned, I have attempted in all cases to consult the best manuscripts and the earliest printed editions. All documents are listed in a single Bibliography, arranged alphabetically by author; where more than one edition of a given work is described, I have indicated the edition used for study and citation. There is virtually no secondary bibliography. Except for light on bibliography itself and on the dating of works, I have chosen to discuss works themselves rather than the interpretations of those works by others. I was convinced that the only possibility of a fresh history of the subject lay in the rereading of all the pertinent materials (or at least of as many as I could find), by a single reader, and according to a constant method of analysis. My history, therefore, excludes some of the approaches common in the writing of intellectual and literary history. It is not concerned with sources and influences in the usual sense, with the discovery of where and how a given writer obtained his ideas. Rather, it tries to show how those ideas are related to the developing currents of Renaissance thought. I have consulted freely such bibliographical instruments as the lists of R. C. Williams and W. L. Bullock, the Cooper-Gudeman bibliography of Aristotle's *Poetics*, the bibliographies found in earlier histories of the subject; and I have also made use of various biographies and separate studies concerning the authors themselves.

I have many debts to discharge, both to those institutions which have subsidized and furthered my work over a period of some twenty-five years and to those individuals who have counseled and helped me. I can discharge them only through the simplest kind of thanks: to Washington University, to Northwestern University, and to the University of Chicago for grants in aid of my research; to the John Simon Guggenheim Memorial Foundation and the administrators of the Fulbright Program for generous fellowships; to the Institute for Advanced Study at Princeton for its hospitality. Many friends have been unsparing of time, wisdom, and

PREFACE

material assistance; I would thank especially Donald Bryant, Ronald Crane, Phillip DeLacy, Edward Kaufmann, Paul Kristeller, and Peter Riesenberg for their reading of parts or all of the manuscript and for useful suggestions; Mrs. Anne McDonnell Heisler, for help in the preparation of the manuscript; and colleagues at the University of Chicago, too numerous to name, for the generous giving of their erudition and advice. I should wish also to thank many librarians for their kind co-operation, above all those at The University of Chicago Libraries, the Newberry Library, the Harvard University Library, the British Museum, the Bibliothèque Nationale in Paris; all the Biblioteche Nazionali in Italy, but mostly that in Florence; the other great Florentine libraries and the Vatican; and provincial libraries all over Italy.

CONTENTS

PART ONE: POETIC THEORY

I. The Classification of Poetics among the Sciences / *1*
II. The Methodology of the Theorists / *38*
III. The Tradition of Horace's *Ars poetica:* I. The Earliest Commentaries / *71*
IV. The Tradition of Horace's *Ars poetica:* II. The Confusion with Aristotle / *111*
V. The Tradition of Horace's *Ars poetica:* III. The Application to Practical Criticism / *156*
VI. The Tradition of Horace's *Ars poetica:* IV. The Return to Theory / *201*
VII. Platonism: I. The Defence of Poetry / *250*
VIII. Platonism: II. The Triumph of Christianity / *297*
IX. The Tradition of Aristotle's *Poetics*: I. Discovery and Exegesis / *349*
X. The Tradition of Aristotle's *Poetics:* II. The First Theoretical Applications / *424*
XI. The Tradition of Aristotle's *Poetics:* III. The Vernacular Commentaries / *478*
XII. The Tradition of Aristotle's *Poetics:* IV. The Effect of the Literary Quarrels / *564*
XIII. The Tradition of Aristotle's *Poetics:* V. Theory of the Genres / *635*
XIV. The New Arts of Poetry / *715*
XV. Conclusions on Poetic Theory / *797*

PART TWO: PRACTICAL CRITICISM

XVI. The Quarrel over Dante / *819*
XVII. The Quarrel over Dante (Concluded) / *877*
XVIII. The Quarrel over Speroni's *Canace* and Dramatic Poetry / *912*
XIX. The Quarrel over Ariosto and Tasso / *954*
XX. The Quarrel over Ariosto and Tasso (Concluded) / *991*
XXI. The Quarrel over Guarini's *Pastor Fido* / *1074*
XXII. Conclusions on Practical Criticism / *1106*
Bibliography / *1113*
Index / *1159*

PART ONE
POETIC THEORY

CHAPTER ONE. THE CLASSIFICATION OF POETICS AMONG THE SCIENCES

A RENAISSANCE PROFESSOR, beginning a series of lessons on a topic or a text, almost invariably devoted the first lecture—the prolusio—to explaining his subject's place in the whole scheme of arts and sciences. This was not merely an academic gesture. It fulfilled an intellectual expectation of his auditors which had been passed on to them by their medieval and humanist forebears. For some centuries, it had been customary to regard each art or science as a part of the great complex of Philosophy. The individual science was defined or delimited by distinguishing it from its neighboring sciences; its ends and its means and its possibilities were discovered by determining to what faculty of the mind it belonged, what human need it served, under which of the major branches of human activity it was to be subsumed. All subsequent thinking about the science flowed from these initial and fundamental presuppositions.

To be sure, by the time of the Cinquecento the logical tightness of these systematic attitudes had been considerably weakened. The stern syllogistic discipline of the Schools had in some cases been openly attacked, in others it had been allowed to degenerate—almost imperceptibly—into the rhetorical loquacity of the universities. The academies, attracting as they did great numbers of aristocrats and bourgeois and providing them with an essentially lay instruction, frequently replaced the old severity of method by fostering enthusiasm for new fields of study and by a questioning, even a disparaging, approach to the traditional modes of thought. Nevertheless, the old framework continued to supply the usual points of reference, and the old habits of thinking continued to inform the major part of philosophical discussion. Perhaps it would be correct to say that the habit of a systematic approach to the sciences was still cultivated at a time when the instruments of analysis were no longer adequate to the task of pursuing classification to its last consequences and distinction to its final implications.

For the science of poetics, one of the old sciences made new by a fresh interest, a practical need, and the rediscovery of ancient texts, this was as true as for other sciences. Perhaps it was especially true. For poetics, formerly considered an auxiliary of grammar and rhetoric—an auxiliary whose particular concern was with versification and figures of speech—but now given new dignity as a guide to the greatest of the arts, had special need of justification. Witness the "defenses of poesy" which, from the fourteenth century on, were a standard form of literary expression. One of the most effective means of supplying that justification was to place the science in a position of dignity, honor, and utility among all the others. But even where justification was not the motive, the theorists followed the traditional pattern of exposition and somewhere—in the prolusio or later

—provided for poetics its proper place among the other sciences. The family to which poetics was assigned might be large or small, incomplete or complete, depending upon the cast of mind of the theorist or the necessities of his argument. But always it was of sufficient magnitude to throw upon the "science" or the "art" the kind of light which, for a man of the Cinquecento, could come only from classification and distinction.

Much of what a theorist was later to say about poetics would of necessity derive from his original classification of it. Hence the great importance of this initial step in the critical process. If, for example, he were to classify it with rhetoric as one of the instrumental disciplines, then his tendency would be to consider poems in terms of their probable specific effects upon specific audiences. He would, if he were an Aristotelian rhetorician, think of poems in terms of poet–poem–audience relationships; if he were a Ciceronian, in terms of invention, disposition, and elocution, and of what the poet must do to gain the acclaim of his listeners. On the other hand, should he begin by defining poetry as a branch or an instrument of moral philosophy, then his whole theory must be oriented toward the ability of the poet to produce or of the critic to judge the desired ethical effect. Any change in classification brings with it a consequent shift in the whole conception of the poetic art. The relationship of the parts within the poem, the criteria for its beauty or goodness or success, the hierarchy of the various poetic genres—all these varied with the place assigned to poetics in the total family of sciences.

THE ARTS OF DISCOURSE

The Cinquecento inherited from the immediate past a method of classifying poetry which we may characterize as the traditional system. Poetics took its place, according to this method, among the arts of discourse. Since poetry used words as its medium, it belonged with all the logical disciplines—with logic, dialectic, rhetoric, and sophistic—and with such arts as grammar and history, all of which also used words. This meant that poetry was joined on the one hand to the trivium (or to Aristotle's group of instrumental sciences), on the other hand to history. Renaissance theorists in a sense never abandoned this classification, although the sciences associated with poetry appear in different groupings and combinations. Throughout the sixteenth century we find systems modeled on this essentially medieval pattern.

For some Renaissance theorists (such as Bartolomeo Lombardi), the source and authority for so classifying poetry was Averroës. In Averroës they found poetry grouped with demonstrative logic, dialectic, rhetoric, and sophistic, and arranged with them in a hierarchy on the basis of their relationship to the truth.[1] This placed it definitely among the discursive

[1] I have found no single passage in Averroës making this complete association and hierarchy of the various arts mentioned. But in various scattered places individual arts are so combined; cf. the "Prooemium in libros posteriorum," in the Venice edition of Aristotle, trans. Mantinus (Iuntas, 1574), I, Pt. IIA, 9–9v: "Ad reliquas vero quinque artes se habet verè, veluti dominus

sciences. Such early humanists as Coluccio Salutati had also, in passing, placed it among these sciences; in his *De laboribus Herculis*, begun between 1383 and 1391 and left unfinished at his death in 1406, Salutati characterized poetics as a "sermocinalis philosophie pars," a part of the branch of philosophy concerned with words.[2] By the time we come to the later humanists, this particular branch has been fitted into more comprehensive views of the whole of philosophy. Thus Angelo Poliziano in the *Panepistemon*, printed in the *Opera* of 1498, sets out to find a general scheme for the sciences treated in Aristotle's works. He divides all doctrine into three kinds, the inspired (theology), the invented (philosophy), and the mixed (divination). Philosophy is then subdivided in the following way:

Spectativa	*Actualis*	*Rationalis*
De Anima	Mores	Grammatica
Mathematicae	Ethica	Historia
Arithmetica	Economica	Dialectica
Musica	Politica	Rhetorica
Geometria	Agricultura	Poetica
Sphaerica	Pastio	
Calculatoria	Venatio	
Geodesia	Architectura	
Canonice	Grafice	
Astrologia	Coquinaria	
Optica	Teatricae	
Mecanica	Etc.	

In this system, the contemplative ("spectativa") science is one which considers a given "res" or "materia," the practical ("actualis") is one which leads to useful activity, and the rational ("rationalis") is one which "iudicat, narrat, demonstrat, suadet, oblectat." Apparently one is to take the "oblectat" as referring specifically to "Poetica." Insofar as poetics is concerned, two things need to be noted: first, it is dissociated from other "creative" arts such as music (which comes under mathematics) and architecture and "graphics" (which belong to the practical sciences); and,

---

ad suos subiectos & proportio illius, cui subministratur ad ipsum seruum, adinuentae enim sunt illae artes vt inseruiant scientiae demonstratiuae, quam hęc pars nobis tradit: nempe, quod per persuasionem dialecticam, vel rhetoricam persuadetur, aut per fictionem poeticam fingitur." Also the commentary on Bk. I in the same edition, p. 13: "Potest tamen haec enuntiatio complecti quinque artes logicas, ac genera definitionum, & partes definitionum": and the *In libros rhetoricorum Aristotelis paraphrases*, trans. Balmes, same edition, II, 73v; "manifestum est quòd in vnoquoque istorum generum orationis sit species rhetorica, species topica, & species demonstratiua, & species sophistica: qui sicut reperiuntur in his artibus inductio & syllogismus, sic in rhetorica reperiuntur exemplum & enthymema." A 1522 volume of Averroës' paraphrases of logical works by Aristotle, containing also Abram de Balmes' translation of the Averroës paraphrase of the *Poetics* (Venice: De Sabio), is followed by a separate section (dated 1523) devoted to the *Epithoma Auerroys omnium librorum logice*. After treating other logical works, the *Epithoma* passes to a section entitled "De orationibus poeticis" (p. 26).

[2] *De laboribus Herculis*, ed. B. Ullman, I, 17; also Introduction, pp. vii–viii.

second, it is associated with the three members of the medieval trivium—logic, grammar, and rhetoric—and with history. In a later passage, Poliziano places the poet close to the orator: "For the poet is very close to the orator (as Cicero says); just as he is more restricted in rhythms, so is he freer in the choice of words."[3]

At a somewhat later date another formal philosopher, Agostino Nifo (*De iis qui apte possunt in solitudine vivere*, 1531), proposed a similar classification. He divided the "contemplative intellect" into two sections, thus:

Partes principes	Partes subministrae, aut organicae
Physica	Grammatica
Mathematica	Analytica
Astrologia	Topica
Perspectiva	Sophistica
Musica	[Rhetorica]
Theologia	[Poetica]

Of the "auxiliary and instrumental parts," analytics (or logic) is the instrument of natural philosophy and rhetoric the instrument of moral philosophy. In the text, however, the connection between rhetoric and poetics is not completely clear, and the place of the latter is left ambiguous: "Though rhetoric is the instrument of moral philosophy as analytics of natural philosophy, nevertheless it is useful in all forms of discourse in which we are accustomed to express ourselves before listeners. Moreover, poetry was invented (as Aristotle suggested in the book which he wrote on poetics) for purposes both of pleasure and utility."[4] Here again, as with Poliziano, music and poetry retain their essentially medieval positions. The implication is that poetry is merely one of those "forms of discourse in which we are accustomed to express ourselves before listeners," distinguished from the others by the combined ends of utility and pleasure which it pursues.

The documents cited so far have not been specifically concerned with the art of poetry. But we find the same basis of classification in a lecture which must have been one of the first public expositions of Aristotle's *Poetics*. Around 1541, according to the testimony of Vincenzo Maggi, Bartolomeo Lombardi addressed to the Accademia degl'Infiammati at Padua the exordium of a series of lectures on the *Poetics*; Lombardi died soon thereafter, and the series was given by Maggi; but the first lecture was printed by Maggi as a preface to his and Lombardi's *In Aristotelis librum de poetica communes explanationes* (1550; p. *ij). Lombardi took Averroës as

---

[3] In *Opera* (1498), fols. Yix–Yixv and Zvi: "Quippe finitimus oratori poeta est (ut Cicero inquit). Sicut numeris astrictior. ita uerbis licentior" (quoted from Cicero, *De Oratore*, I, xvi).

[4] (1535 ed.), p. 89: "Rhetorica licet moralis philosophię sit instrumentum, ut Analytica naturalis philosophię: tamen utilis est in omnibus dicendi generibus: in quibus dicere solemus coram auditoribus. Poetica autem inuenta est (ut Aristoteles auctor est in eo Libro, quem de poetica scripsit) & ad delectandum, & ad conferendum."

his authority for placing poetry among the logical and rational sciences; it shares with demonstrative logic, dialectic, sophistic, and rhetoric certain common qualities:

... neither do they have a specific thing as their subject matter, but only words and discourse, nor do they consist in one specific genus but introduce themselves into all. These are their common characteristics. As for the particular and distinct ones, demonstration and its two companions, dialectic and sophistic, are called logical faculties, since their major and more common use is in arguments and they effect what they set out to do by means of certain concise points and in a brief and strict fashion, and if I may say so, they exist exclusively as syllogistic forms.... Rhetoric and poetic, on the other hand, are not called logical faculties in a true and proper sense, and hardly ever use the syllogism, but they use rather the example and the enthymeme, which are, so to speak, popular devices. Their products, insofar as they are of this kind, are orations and poems, and for the most part they are concerned with political subject matters.[5]

The use of words and discourse and the cultivation of a universal rather than a particular subject matter are thus the bases for classifying poetics along with these other sciences.

In a much less systematic document, Sperone Speroni (*Dialogo della rhetorica*, 1542) again conjoins poetry and rhetoric, but for entirely different reasons. Speroni is not concerned with the whole system of the sciences, but only with the arts, which he classifies as useful (or mechanical) and pleasurable; the latter are subdivided into the arts which delight the body and those which delight the spirit:

Body	*Spirit*
Painting (eyes)	Rhetoric
Music (ears)	Poetry
Perfumery (nose)	
Cooking (taste)	
Heating (touch?)	

Poetry and rhetoric are arts of words, which are the instruments of the mind. They are distinguished by their ends: poetry aims only to please, rhetoric wishes both to please and to persuade. As a result, the orator's art is more difficult, since he must produce a much tighter rhythmic structure (pp. 138, 154–54v).

[5] *Explanationes* (1550), p. 8: "quòd neque materiae loco res habeant: uerba tantum & orationem. neque in certo uno genere uersentur: sed in omnia insinuant sese. haec communia. illa propria atque distincta; quòd Demonstratiua, & eius duae comites Dialectica & Sophistica logicae ipsae appellantur: quòd harum maior quidam usus & communior in dissertationibus & quibusdam quasi punctis concisa breuiter admodum atque strictim quod proposuerunt, efficiunt, & ut ita loquar, syllogisticae prorsus existunt.... Rhetorica, Poeticáque contra: quòd non adeò uerè ac propriè Logicae appellantur, neque syllogismo ferè, sed exemplo atque enthymemate, rationibus quasi popularibus utuntur: atque harum quà huiusmodi sunt, extant opera, orationes atque poemata, plurimumáque in politicis occupantur argumentis."

[5]

With Francesco Robortello's *In librum Aristotelis de arte poetica explicationes* (1548) we return to the position of Lombardi (whose preface was published two years later); the classification is the same, although some of the reasons are different. Robortello's point of view is stated in his own preface, before the commentary on Aristotle actually begins:

> Discourse is placed under the poetic faculty as its material, as it is placed under all the others which concern themselves with discourse. These are five in number, demonstrative (for so it is proper to call apodeictic discourse), dialectic, rhetoric, sophistic, poetic. ... All these have discourse as their matter; indeed, since discourse assumes a different force and form, both from the kind of things which it treats and from the person who uses it to set forth or prove something, for that reason it is necessary that every discourse be different in some way. The most proper and genuine function of discourse is to express what is true. ... Insofar as discourse of any kind departs from truth, to that same degree it moves nearer to what is false. Between truth and falseness, in a kind of interval between the two, are placed τὸ ἔνδοξον, τὸ πιθανὸν, τὸ φαινόμενον which may be expressed in Latin as the *probabile* [the probable], the *suasorium* [the persuasive], and the *apparens verum*; *seu probabile quod videtur* [the apparently true, or that which seems probable]. From among these each separate faculty seizes upon one kind: demonstration, upon the true; dialectic, upon the probable; rhetoric, upon the persuasive; sophistic, upon that which has the appearance of probability, but in the sense of verisimilitude; poetics, upon the false or the fabulous.[6]

The traditional classification, on the basis of the use of words as a medium, still prevails here.

A different kind of approach seems to be present in the thinking of Benedetto Varchi. But if to an original statement by Varchi, which antedates Robortello, is added a later one, his ultimate position turns out to be essentially the same as Robortello's. The first document is a "Lezzione della maggioranza dell'arti," delivered before the Florentine Academy in the spring of 1546. Varchi here addressed himself not so much to the problem of the place of poetics among the sciences as to the more general problem of the place of all the arts among human activities. He admittedly took as his point of departure the *Nicomachean Ethics*, especially Book VI. His division of the soul gives the following schema:

---

[6] *Explicationes* (1548), p. 1: "Subiicitur tanquàm materies poëticę facultati oratio, sicuti et aliis omnibus, quae circa orationem uersantur. Eae autem sunt quinque numero, Demonstratoria (sic enim ἀποδεικτικὴν licet appellare) dialectice. rhetorice. sophistice. poëtice. ... Omnes hae subiectam sibi habent orationem; Verùm, quoniam oratio diuersam accipit uim, & formam, tùm ex genere rerum, quas tractat; tùm ab eo, qui ipsa vtitur ad aliquid edisserendum, & probandum; ideò diuersam quoque omnium oportet esse orationem; Orationis maximè proprium, & genuinum munus est, proferre id, quod verum est. ... Quantum autem orationis quodque genus à vero recedit, tantò propius accedit ad id, quod est falsum. Inter verum sanè, & falsum medio quodam interuallo posita sunt, τὸ ἔνδοξον, τὸ πιθανὸν, τὸ φαινόμενον; quę sic libet Latinè proferre; probabile, suasorium; & apparens verum; seu probabile quod videtur. Ex his quaelibet facultas vnum arripit genus, Demonstratoria verum. Dialectice probabile. Rhetorice suasorium. Sophistice id, quod probabilis, sed verisimilis habet speciem. Poëtice falsum, seu fabulos[u]m."

POETICS AMONG THE SCIENCES

Anima

Ragione particolare	Ragione universale
intenzioni individuali	intenzioni uniuersali
cose particolari, generabili, & corruttibili	cose private d'ogni materia, spogliate da tutte le passioni, & accidenti materiali
= cogitativa	cose ingenerate, et incorrutibili

Ragione superiore	Ragione inferiore
intelletto specolativo, contemplativo	intelletto pratico, attivo
= conoscere, intendere	= fare, operare
Habiti contemplativi	Habiti pratichi
intelletto	agibile
sapienza	fattibile
scienza	

All the arts fall under the second of the "practical habits."[7] Varchi gives examples of the kinds of arts included under each category: horsemanship, dancing, singing, playing musical instruments under the "attiva;" architecture, painting, and sculpture (and "infinite others") under the "fattiva." Presumably, poetry is one of the "infinite others"; although poetry is not specifically mentioned here, the last section of the lecture is devoted to a detailed comparison of poetry and painting (pp. 68, 72). The major purpose of the lecture is to establish a hierarchy among the arts according to their nobility; and since the dignity of the end is set up as the criterion, and since warfare, medicine, and architecture occupy the highest positions in the hierarchy, the place assigned to poetry will be relatively humble.

These views of Varchi's are to be supplemented and perhaps corrected by those expressed, in a fuller and more careful way, in another lecture delivered to the Florentine Academy, in October, 1553. This time—referring again to the Aristotelian system but including the *Poetics*, which had been absent from the earlier materials—Varchi does offer a complete system of the sciences. He begins by dividing philosophy into "real" philosophy and "rational" philosophy:

Reale		*Rationale*
(*cose*)		(*parole*)
Contemplativa	Pratica	Loica giudiziale
Specolativa	Attiva	Dialettica
Metafisica		Topica
Fisica	Agibile	Sofistica
Matematiche	Etica	Tentativa

[7] In *Due lezzioni* (1549), pp. 58–59.

	Reale (*cose*)		*Rationale* (*parole*)
Aritmetica	Economica	Rettorica
Musica	Politica	Poetica
Geometria	Fattibile	Storica
Astrologia	Arti meccaniche	Gramatica

In the commentary on this scheme, Varchi specifically states that poetry, coming as it does in the group of disciplines dealing with words, cannot be considered either an art or a science but merely a faculty. If it is sometimes called an art, this is only because it has been reduced to precepts and rules.[8] Moreover, its position in fourth place among the instrumental sciences shows its rank according to nobility; it is inferior not only to all the sciences but also to the disciplines above it in the same group. In a sense, it is indistinguishable from those disciplines. "It is indeed true that dialectic, logic, and poetics are almost the same thing, not being different substantially but only in accidents, and thus the dialectician, the rhetorician, and the poet may be placed at the same level of nobility and of honor."[9]

How poetics is related to the other rational faculties is indicated in another classification of these faculties in which Varchi assigns to each a subject matter and a corresponding instrument among the instruments of discourse:

Rational Faculty	*Subject*	*Part of Discourse*
loica, dimostrativa	vero	[demonstrative syllogism]
dialetica, topica	probabile	[topical syllogism]
sofistica	pare probabile, ma non è	[sophistical syllogism]
retorica	persuasivo	[enthymeme]
poetica	finto, favoloso	[example]

Once again, poetics, whose instrument is the "least worthy of all the others," is placed in a very inferior position.[10]

But this is not Varchi's final word. One must, he says later, take into consideration two things with respect to poetry: first, the host of wonderful things which become the objects of its imitation; second, the magnificent end which it serves, that of making men good, virtuous, and happy, that of perfecting the human soul. When these qualities are taken into account, poetry emerges as the greatest of all human activities:

Since poetics, then, treats of all things divine as well as human, of so sublime, desirable, and worthy an end, and in the most beautiful, useful, and delightful way, because it is language it comes to contain in itself necessarily all the sciences,

---

[8] In *Lezzioni* (1590), pp. 571–72.

[9] *Ibid.*, p. 572: "Ben'è vero, che la dialettica, la loica, e la poetica sono quasi vna medesima cosa, non essendo differenti sostanzialmente, ma per accidente, e così il dialettico, il retore, e il poeta si posson mettere in vn medesimo grado di nobiltà, e d'honore."

[10] *Ibid.*, p. 573.

all the arts, and all the faculties at once, whence it is more noble, more delightful, and more perfect than each one of them in itself; thus it is deserving without any doubt of greater marvel as a faculty, and greater praise as an art, and greater honor as a science, than all the other faculties, arts, and sciences.[11]

One senses, in this last phase of the argument, a desire to break out of the restrictions imposed by the system, to elevate poetry above its systematic rank as one of the lowest of the rational faculties.

In the dedication to his *Dialogi della inventione poetica* (1554) Alessandro Lionardi allies poetics once more with rhetoric and history, although there are no traces of a more complete philosophical system. He begins by stating that the two most necessary and useful human activities are speaking and doing:

... neither the one nor the other of these actions can be completely and properly done without a knowledge of history, of orations, and of poems, as those things which teach us to do, to say, and to deliberate what is required in this life in every manner of state, of age, and of condition, showing us in actions and in discourse what is to be imitated and what avoided. ...

Poetry contains the other two within itself, and hence is the most worthy of study. It will be noted that here, again, there is an effort to ennoble the art of poetry, and that part of the process consists in assigning to poetry an important function in teaching men how to live.[12]

For Giovanni Battista Pigna (*I romanzi*, 1554), the reason for classifying poetry with rhetoric and dialectic under logic is to permit the explanation of its universality of subject matter; like the other instrumental sciences, it has no fixed subject: "... just as rhetoric and dialectic, since they are under logic, have had no definite subject matter on which to fix themselves, so poetry, which falls under the same, will not be restricted to any specific branch of human activity. Whence it is common to say that the poet participates in every science."[13]

A division of the sciences which again presents itself as traditional, but which proceeds on a somewhat different basis, is offered by Antonio Sebastiano Minturno in his *De poeta* (1559). He groups all sciences under

[11] *Ibid.*, p. 592: "Trattando dunque la poetica di tutte le cose così diuine, come humane tanto sublime desiderato, e degno fine e nel piu bello vtile, e diletteuole modo per esser prosa viene à conteneder in se necessariamente tutte le scienze tutte l'arti, e tutte le facultà insieme, donde è più nobile piu piaceuole, e piu perfetta di ciascuna di loro di perse; dunque merita senza alcun dubbio maggior merauiglia, come facultà, e maggior lode, come arte e maggiore honore come scienza, di tutte quante l'altre facultà arti, e scienze."

[12] *Dialogi* (1554), p.3: "nè l'una nè l'altra di queste due attioni potersi compiutamente, & conueneuolmente fare senza la cognitione dell'istoria, dell'orationi, & de' poemi, come quelli, che ci insegnano à fare, à dire, & à deliberare cioche à questa uita in ogni maniera di stato, di età, & di conditione si richiede, mostrandoci nelle operationi, & ne' parlamenti quel che si ha da imitare, & da fuggire."

[13] *I romanzi* (1554), p. 19: "come la Rhetorica & la Dialettica, perche sono sotto la Logica, alcun certo soggetto su che si fermino, hauuto non hanno; cosi la Poesia, che cade sotto la medesima, ad alcuna certa professione non sarà astretta. La onde dir si suole che il poeta è d'ogni scienza partecipe."

four major headings: (1) those which are concerned with "knowing the nature and the causes of things" and with a "contemplation of divine things"; (2) those concerned with "instructions for good living"; (3) those belonging to the "faculty of discussing and speaking"; (4) mathematics.[14] Poetics, of course, belongs in the third category, along with grammar, rhetoric, logic, and history. Minturno introduces this distinction at a point where he is estimating the contribution of each of the other sciences to poetry; but the fact that it is fundamental in his thinking about poetry emerges from an analysis of his work as a whole.[15]

Alessandro Piccolomini, who wrote commentaries both on the *Rhetoric* and the *Poetics* of Aristotle, considered himself an Aristotelian and found justification for his views on the philosophical position of poetics in the works of Aristotle themselves. Thus he defends the affiliation between rhetoric and poetics as follows; he is explaining why he expects to work on the *Poetics* after he finishes his labors on the *Rhetoric* (*Piena parafrase nel terzo libro della Retorica d'Aristotele*, 1572):

... for the reason that these two faculties, rhetoric and poetics, are so closely linked together in kinship that a great many of the subjects they treat can and should be equally useful in the one and the other faculty. Thus it is that Aristotle, knowing this, in order not to repeat the same things in both [treatises] when he was writing about the one and the other, made a choice of the aforementioned common materials in such wise as to put in one faculty those considerations which were closest to it and most conjoined with it; then, writing about the other, he referred to the first when necessary.[16]

In the subsequent work on the other "faculty," *Annotationi nel libro della Poetica d'Aristotile* (1575), Piccolomini indicates his basic position by referring directly to the *Ethics*. All arts, he says, aim at "some honest utility and convenience for human life"; hence poetry will also seek as its end some such usefulness, "since poetry also is a habit of the practical intellect relevant to things which can be made, and since it may consequently be called an art, and since it is most honored among all the other habits of this kind and in nobility very close to civil prudence, which is that art to which all others are subordinated." The notion that civil prudence (a paraphrase for politics) is the "architectonic" science will gain

[14] *De poeta* (1559), p. 87: "partem in cognoscendo rerum naturam, causasque posuerunt, atque cum ea rerum diuinarum perspicientiam coniunxerunt; partem in bene uiuendi institutione uersari, partem in disserendi ac loquendi ratione, partem in Mathematicis uoluerunt."

[15] *Ibid.*, p. 92; cf. my article, "The Poetic Theories of Minturno," in *Studies in Honor of Frederick W. Shipley* ("Washington University Studies" [St. Louis, Mo., 1942]), pp. 101–29.

[16] *Parafrase* (1572), p. *2v: "Percioche essendo queste due facultà, la Retorica, & la Poetica tanto congiunte di parentela insieme, che moltissime lor considerationi possono, & debbon communemente seruir' all'una, & all'altra: di qui è che, sì come Aristotele conoscendo questo, per non replicar' in scriuer dell'una, & dell'altra, le stesse cose in amendue; fece delle dette communi consideratione vna scelta in modo, che quelle, ch'alquanto fusser più vicine, & congiunte all'una, ch'all'altra di dette facultà, in quella poneua, & a quella scriuendo dell'altra, si rimetteua."

currency later in the century, and poetry will with increasing frequency be subsumed under it.[17]

Piccolomini's approach presupposes a purview of the Aristotelian system which extends beyond poetics and rhetoric and includes at least one other science in a different category, politics. A system which extends still farther beyond, and which really returns to the universal classifications of the first part of the century, is proposed by Federico Ceruti in a work which he presents as anonymous but which is probably his own, the *De re poetica libellus incerti auctoris* of 1588. Indeed, Ceruti outlines two possible complete schemata of the sciences. The first would be divided as follows:

Theoretice	*Practice*	*Logice*	*Mecanice*
theologia	ethice	rhetorice	lanificium
mathematica	oiconomice	grammatice	res militares
arithmetice	politice	historia	navigatio
musice		poetice	agricultura
geometria			venatio
astronomia			medicina
physice			pictura
			tectonica
			architectonica
			fabrilis

A second and somewhat different division would proceed as follows:

Theoretice	*Practice*	*Poietice*	*Instrumentales*
mathematice	de moribus	ars militaris	logice
metaphysice	de ciuili	nautica	grammatice
phisice	gubernatione	pictura	rhetorice
etc.	de legibus	musica	poetice
	etc.	etc.	historia

Whichever of these systems one adopts, says Ceruti, the place of poetics is clear. In both, in fact, it is linked with the same cognate disciplines, although in the first it is subsumed under grammar, which in turn is subsumed under logic, whereas in the second all five instrumental sciences are on the same plane. What is not clear is why a group of "poetical" arts, which for the most part make things by hand ("quae manibus vt plurimum fiunt"), should not include "poetics" itself. Apparently for Ceruti the traditional place of poetry is so firmly established that even the close etymological proximity of the terms does not raise any questions for him.[18]

Two years later—and very close to the end of the century—Gabriele Zinano (or Ginani) presents another such system of the sciences in his *Il*

---

[17] *Annotationi* (1575), p. ††6v: "qualche honesto giouamento, & commodo dell'humana vita. . . . essendo la poesia anch'ella vn'habito dell'intelletto prattico intorno à cose fattibili; & per conseguente potendosi chiamar' arte; & essendo trà tutti gli altri così fatti habiti honoratissima, & in nobiltà alla ciuil prudentia, architetonica di tutte l'arti, vicinissima."

[18] *De re poetica* (1588), chap. ix, pp. 10–11.

sogno, overo della poesia (1590). Zinano claims that the one he offers is Aristotelian:

SCIENCES

Speculative	Practical	
Metaphysics	Internal	External
Physics	Operations	Operations
Mathematics	(mind)	(words, deeds)
Geometry		
Arithmetic	will: moral philosophy	
Astrology	ethics	grammar — military art
Music	economics	rhetoric — agriculture
	politics	poetry — navigation
	intellect: dialectic	history — wool-making
	memory:	etc.
	art of remembering	

Grammar, among the practical sciences dealing with words, is concerned with "il ben dire"; rhetoric, with "l'ornato dire." As for poetry, it soon breaks out of its assigned compartment and becomes a universal science encompassing all the others; this is so because all the others furnish it with subject matter, because it teaches the lessons of all the others, and because through its allegory—moral or natural or divine— it contains the essential doctrines of all the others.[19]

The last important document, among those examined, to insist on the grouping of poetics with logic, grammar, and rhetoric is Gioseppe Malatesta's *Della poesia romanzesca* (1596). This is a sequel to an earlier dialogue of 1589, *Della nuova poesia*, in which Malatesta had not raised the question of the classification of poetry. In the present one, he does hazard a general system. He divides all the sciences into five groups: the natural sciences, the metaphysical sciences, the rational faculties, the liberal arts, and the mechanical arts. The rational faculties are arts of discourse which have no specific subject matter; they include logic and grammar. They might also include poetics:

In this group and of this kind is also poetry, to which by its nature no specific subject matter was given, but which rather remained free to treat of as many

[19] *Il sogno* (1590), pp. 19–21: "Le scienze, & l'arti in prattica, & in speculativa si diuidono, come vuole Aristotile nel primo della Metafisica, & questa divisione è presa dal fine, perciò che la speculatiua consiste in contemplatione, la prattica in operatione: l'vna contempla tutte le cose dell'vniuerso, l'altra quelle, che sono soggette all' arti, l'vna considera il vero, l'altra il buono, & di qui hanno origine l'intelletto speculatiuo, & prattico, ò più tosto le sopradette cose da lui origine hanno. Non si contenta il Peripatetico d'hauer cosi nel primo le scienze, & l'arti diuise, che ancora considerando le scienze esser varie secondo la qualità de gli enti, le subdiuide nel sesto [of the *Metaphysics*]. La speculatiua in Metafisica, in Fisica, & in Matematica subdiuide. . . . La prattica, versando circa l'operationi, secondo l'operationi si diuide. Del'operationi altre sono esterne, & altre interne. L'operationi interne prouengono dalla mente, & sono di tre sorti, di uolontà, d'intelletto, & di memoria. Nella volontà consiste la filosofia morale, che si diuide in Etica, in Economia, & in Politica." Cf. also pp. 21–31.

things as it might wish and to enter everywhere. . . . And therefore it would have been very proper for Aristotle, when he compared rhetoric to dialectic, to have added as a third, poetics, which no less than the other two occupies itself with things which can in a certain sense be understood by anyone, which does not recognize any definite or limited subject matter, and in which every subject finds itself in some way a participant by the goodness of Nature.

In this analysis, the basis of classification is uniquely the subject matter, since the initial assumption is that sciences are differentiated one from another solely on the basis of differences in subject matter.[20]

Beginning with the humanistic period—which had inherited it from the Middle Ages—and extending throughout the sixteenth century, there is thus a strong tradition that associates poetry with logic, grammar, rhetoric, and history as one of the discursive or instrumental sciences. Poetry belongs with the others as a discursive science because it uses words (or "discourse") as its means. One consequence of this association is that the resultant theories will tend to emphasize problems of language, the special kind of diction which differentiates poetry from the other discursive sciences, the matter of rhythm and rhyme, the figures and tropes which are regarded as peculiar to poetic expression. Another consequence is that, since words are symbols for things and represent meanings to the person for whom signification is intended, theories of this kind will hesitate or oscillate between emphasis on the things themselves and attention to the kinds of meanings associated with the words by the readers. Poetry is regarded as an instrumental science because it is thought to have no fixed subject matter and hence to resemble logic, grammar, and rhetoric. Resulting theories will stress on the one hand the universality of its subject and will compile long lists of the kinds of things it treats; on the other hand, they will consider its quality *qua* instrument and the ends which it achieves. This latter activity will bring such theories into close contact with another set of theories based specifically on conceptions of the end of poetry, especially those which consider it as an instrument of moral and civil philosophy, i.e., of ethics and politics.

HISTORY

A special place must be made for those classifications which include history among the discursive or instrumental sciences related to poetry. History, too, uses words, and it may be thought of as serving ethical or political ends. But it also presents other possibilities of comparison with

---

[20] *Poesia romanzesca* (1596), pp. 27–28: "In questo numero, & di questa conditione, è ancora la Poesia, a cui non fù dalla natura sua prescritto niun soggetto particolare, anzi venne libera di poter trattare di quante cose volesse, & di ingerirsi per tutto. . . . Et per tanto non saria stato se non molto conueniente che quando Aristotele proportionò la Rethorica, alla Dialettica, hauesse aggiunta per terza la Poesia, la quale non meno che l'altre due si essercita sopra cose che ponno in certo modo capirsi da ciascuno, non riconosce materia definita, ò limitata, & ognuna se ne troua in qualche modo partecipe dal benefitio della Natura."

poetry; these may be boiled down to the essential fact that history, like so many forms of poetry, presents a "narration." One may thus apply to it (albeit equivocally) such common terms of the critical vocabulary as action, character, thought, episode, and so forth; one may discover in it such common features as descriptions of places and persons, speeches, great deeds of kings and heroes. These further possibilities of comparison led another group of theorists to set up a separate classification of poetry as a kind of history; they constitute in a sense a cognate strain of classification, beginning again with the humanists and continuing—although much less frequently—throughout the sixteenth century. It is appropriate at this point, in order to fill out the picture of this kind of classification, to examine the position of a group of theorists representing this cognate strain.

Giovanni (or Gioviano) Pontano, in a dialogue entitled *Actius de numeris poeticis et lege historiae* and written toward the end of the fifteenth century, attempted to relate poetry to such divers activities as prophecy, history, oratory, and painting; but the comparison developed most extensively is the one with history. The following bases of similarity are discovered: both relate ancient and remote deeds; both describe places, peoples, nations; both condemn vices and praise virtues; both partake of the demonstrative and deliberative types of oratory, as shown by the orations which they introduce; both treat the unexpected and accidental events which happen so frequently in life. The comparison continues in these terms, then is supplemented by a series of contrasts demonstrating in what ways the two arts differ. Finally, sets of criteria for both arts are derived from their common characteristics.[21]

The same tendency to pair poetry with history is developed at some length in an anonymous *Dialogue on History* found in MS Vat. Lat. 6528, whose date is probably around 1560–65. In this dialogue the main expositor, Hieronimo Zabbarella, claims to be presenting and defending the theory of Pomponazzi on history. He starts with the assertion of the existence of a four-way "chiasmus," a division of narration into four subordinate parts:

Poema: narration of a single action of a single man
Historia: narration of a single action of many persons
Vita: narration of many sayings and actions of a single man
Sermone: narration of many and various actions of many men

Poetry differs from history, first, in the character of the action narrated and, second, in the use of verse and a special kind of language. Both "poetry" and "history" are used in very broad senses, and the whole discussion has an essentially analogical quality (fols. 142v, 151).

Julius Caesar Scaliger's point of view, in the *Poetices libri septem* of

[21] In *I Dialoghi*, ed. Previtera, pp. 193–227.

1561, puts him into both categories of critics, those who classified poetry as a part of "oratio" and those who considered it a form of narration. He begins with a general division of "oratio" according to its ends, as follows:

End	Type of Expression	Audience
veritas	necessitas	philosophi
prudentia	vtilitas	cives
voluptas	delectatio	theatra

The third type of expression, "delectatio," uses the common form of narration, accompanied by ornate language. It is subdivided into history and poetry: history which "by a sure belief professes and produces truth, spinning its discourse in a simpler thread," poetry which "either adds fiction to truth, or imitates true things by means of false, but in any case with greater splendor." As is the case for history, the final end of poetry is also to teach: "This end [of imitation] is intermediate to another which is final, and which is to teach with pleasure."[22]

In a work which is essentially a treatise on history, the *De ratione scribendae historiae* of 1574, Uberto Foglietta spends a certain amount of time in drawing a comparison between history and epic poetry. Both are narrations (the essential basis for the comparison), both treat events which have actually happened. But history is different insofar as it depends upon truth and cannot exist without it, and insofar as it may dispense with the various ornaments and decorations which are required in poetry. In his discussion of the component graces of history, Foglietta indicates that these are the ones commonly cultivated by the poet. Indeed, such a document as this is more interesting for its assumption that the internal procedures of the two arts of history and poetry are the same than for its theoretical statements about them.[23]

For Lionardo Salviati, the last of this group of theorists, the two arts are related not so much because they are forms of narration as because they serve a common end, instruction by means of pleasure. His dialogue, *Il Lasca* (1584), raises the whole issue of the relationship of poetry to history. Unlike earlier theorists, he admits the possibility of history which tells not the truth but what is commonly believed, and which may even tell lies when these would be useful. Its usefulness is to "render prudent those who read it or hear it, so that . . . they may know how to govern the community well, if it is a public history, and themselves and their houses if it is a private history";[24] this end is achieved through the means of the pleasure inherent

---

[22] *Poetice* (1581 ed.), p. 2: "Differunt autem, quòd alterius fides certa verum & profitetur & prodit, simpliciore filo texens orationem: altera aut addit ficta veris, aut fictis vera imitatur, maiore sanè apparatu. . . . Hic enim finis est medius ad illum vltimum, qui est docendi cum delectatione."

[23] *De ratione*, ed. with Bodin (1576), pp. 947–48, 963.

[24] *Il Lasca* (1584), p. 8: "Ch'ella sia vtile, cioè faccia prudente quei, che la leggono, o che l'ascoltano, si che, e in pace, e in guerra sappiano ben gouernare il comune, s'ella sia storia pubblica: se priuata lor medesimi, e le lor case."

in the reading. Such views, of course, bring history very close to the common conception of poetry, and Salviati sees between them the following differences (pp. 11–13):

Poetry	History
forma: imitazione	forma: narrazione
soggetto: verisimile	soggetto: quel che si crede
fine: purgar gli animi renderci ben costumati	fine: prudenza
stromento: verso, melodia, ballo	stromento: favellare sciolto

"For which reasons," he goes on to say, "poetry may in a way be made subordinate to the philosophy of conduct, and history to that of government; nevertheless, as far as the end is concerned there might be occasion to argue to the contrary, that is, that it is the same both in history and in poetry."[25] As the dialogue continues, however, Salviati argues that poetry achieves these ends less well than history, since it is not believed and has as a result no lasting moral effect, and hence is to be considered an inferior art.

Most of these texts, classifying poetry with all the rest of the discursive or instrumental sciences or with history singled out from among them, fall within the first sixty years of the century. The few which come later do little more than continue a tradition dating back to the humanist period. Not all of them, indeed, give so restricted a role to poetry as the mere process of classification might indicate. At times, out of the conviction that poetry is really something more than an instrument, that it serves higher purposes in a more particular way, there is an effort, not to assign it to another position, but to find some supplementary way of regarding it which will make it transcend its companion arts. This effort, as with Varchi, results in the affirmation that poetry is a universal science, a recipient of all the riches of philosophy, whose function is to contribute to the highest welfare of mankind. During the rest of the century, while the old classification continues to appear from time to time, the essential position of poetics will be one rather more in keeping with its exalted functions, that is, as a part or as an instrument of moral philosophy.

MORAL PHILOSOPHY

This position is first assigned to poetics, among the documents studied, by Scipione Ammirato in *Il Dedalione overo del poeta dialogo*, dated 1560. The work is essentially a rebuttal of Plato's banishment of the poets. Ammirato divides philosophy into two main branches, the contemplative and the active:

[25] *Ibid.*, p. 11: "Per laqual cosa la Poesia in qualche modo sotto la filosofia de' costumi: La Storia ridur potrassi sotto quella della città, tuttauia quanto è il fine, ci sarebbe forse da disputare in contrario, cioè, che fosse, e nella storia, e nella poesia il medesimo."

Contemplative	Active
Natural	"morale costumatezza" (= Ethics)
Supernatural	"domestica, familiare" (= Economics)
Mathematics	"civile" (= Politics)

Poetics is subsumed under civil philosophy: "If civil philosophy concerns the good of our minds and of our bodies, it will really concern both these arts, that is, poetics and medicine; but let us take the matter in a larger sense and say that it concerns equivocally both the one and the other medicine, that of the soul and that of the body."[26] The poet bears the same relationship to the physician as the legislator does to the surgeon, and the "end of poetry is to induce virtue into the soul by driving vice out of it."[27]

This is essentially the point of view of Antonio Posio, whose aim in the pertinent section of his *Thesaurus* (1562) is to summarize the order and the contents of Aristotle's works. The *Poetics* would fall into the sequence "Dialectica–Rhetorica–Poetica–Ethica" for the reasons given below:

Rhetoric in fact is the instrument of the moral philosopher, an instrument with which good laws are proposed and which is used in the senate for the best deliberations about the observance of the laws, of divine worship, of peace, of charity, of justice, and of all the other things that are necessary to a state. To it indeed is added poetics, which must not be rejected from a perfect state, whatever Plato seems to want to do with it in the eighth book of the *Republic*. In fact, the poet, using a certain sweetness of language, purges the soul of evil passions and brings great utility through the action and great pleasure through the imitation. Those have not been lacking, even, who have maintained that it is part of rhetoric. I leave to others to decide whether this be true. Moreover, the same poetics serves the state as an art of discourse, since the poet must arouse anger, fear, hope, and the other passions. These books having been placed as first handmaidens to moral and civil philosophy, to them were added immediately the books on ethics dedicated to Nicomachus.

Poetics remains, here, an associate of dialectic and rhetoric, maintaining its function as a discursive science; but the whole group to which it belongs becomes "ancillary" to moral and civil philosophy, and poetry itself is distinguished by the pleasure and the utility which it affords.[28]

[26] In *Opuscoli* (1642), p. 386: "Se la ciuile riguarda il bene degli animi nostri & de corpi, veramente ella riguarderà amendue questi, cioè la poetica & la medicina; ma prendiamo la cosa più larga & diciamo ch'ella riguarda equiuocamente l'vna & l'altra medicina dell'anima & del corpo."

[27] *Ibid.*, "il fine della poetica è indur nell'anima la virtù discacciandone il vizio."

[28] *Thesaurus* (1562), fol. *5v: "Rhetorica enim est instrumentum moralis philosophi, quo bonae proponuntur leges, optimaeque fiunt in senatu deliberationes ad obseruandas leges, cultum diuinum, Pacem, pietatem, Iustitiam, & caetera quae Reipub. sunt necessaria. Accedit vero Poetica, quae ab optima Repub. non est abiicienda. Quicquid videatur velle Plato in octauo de Repub. Poeta enim cum quadam sermonis suauitate, animum malis affectibus purgat, magnamque actione vtilitatem, & imitatione delectationem affert. Non defuerunt autem, qui partem Rhetorices eam esse putauerint. An id verum sit, aliorum nunc sit iudicium seruit autem ipsa Poetica Reipublicae tanquam sermocinalis facultas, cum debeat poeta commouere iram, timorem, spem, caeterosque affectus. His praepositis ciuili, ac morali philosophiae ancillis, libri ad Nicomachum de moribus statim adiecti sunt."

[17]

The next statement is neither so systematic nor so explicit, since it relates poetry to moral philosophy without specifying the nature of the relationship. It is found in Jacopo Mazzoni's *Discorso in difesa della Comedia del divino poeta Dante* (1572, under the pseudonym of Donato Rofia), which devoted its first chapter to the proposition "that it is not improper for philosophers to discuss poets." Mazzoni here makes only the bald statement: "... elsewhere we have sufficiently clearly proved that poetry is a part of moral philosophy" (p. 3). The assertion is neither developed nor supported later in the text, nor are we told how poetry serves the end of moral philosophy. I have found no earlier text by Mazzoni to which he might be referring.

Concern with the "dignity" of the art is really the primary characteristic of a work which made public its conclusions four years later, in 1576. Just as Varchi in 1546 had been concerned with the "maggioranza dell'arti," so Lorenzo Giacomini in 1576 proposed the topic *Della nobiltà delle lettere e delle armi* for three lectures to be read in the Florentine Academy. Under letters he included moral philosophy, the art of logic, rhetoric, poetics, history, medicine, and architecture. In his final arrangement, Giacomini seems to divide letters into two subgroups: the first, the "scienzie contemplative," is superior to arms; the second, made up of moral philosophy and other forms of knowledge, is inferior to arms, since it merely supplies the doctrine which leads to action. Action itself is more noble than doctrine. Although it is not so stated, poetry presumably falls into the last category; instruction in the literary arts will include "rhetoric and poetics, which furnish us with the means to explain moral subjects for our own benefit and that of others, and music also, which like poetry used to be used for four ends, for formation of character, for the purgation of the passions, for rest from our affairs, and for recreation in our studies."[29]

By this date, 1576, the position of poetics as related to moral philosophy is firmly established; there will be very few dissenters later on. But a new question now arises: is it a part or an instrument of moral philosophy? The distinction is sometimes not clear, but much debate centers upon it, especially in a large group of documents relating to the quarrel over Dante. It will be remembered that, five years earlier, Jacopo Mazzoni had initiated the discussion in his defense of Dante with the statement that "poetry is a part of moral philosophy." Sometime between 1573 and 1576–77 Bellisario Bulgarini of Siena wrote his *Alcune considerazioni sopra'l discorso di M. Giacopo Mazzoni, fatto in difesa della Comedia di Dante*, published only in 1583. Since Bulgarini set out to counter Mazzoni on every possible point, he did not fail to take issue with him on this statement. Poetry, he insisted,

---

[29] MS B.N. Paris, Fonds italien 982, fols. 62v–63: "impareremo ... la Rettorica, et la Poetica le quali ci danno il modo di spiegare i suggetti morali in benefizio nostro et d'altrui. et la Musica ancora, la quale si come la Poesia per quattro fini soleua vsarsi, per il costume, per purgazione degli affetti, per riposo da i negozij, et per diporto negli studij."

could not be considered a part of moral philosophy because it was an art; Aristotle and Horace should be taken as authorities for this. Moreover, if it were a part of philosophy it would belong to the rational and discursive branches, not to the practical group in which moral philosophy falls.

Nor do I see, at best, how one can say anything else about it except that it might be an instrument of moral philosophy, in the way in which (by those who know best) logic is held to be an instrument of philosophy in general: and this also according to the opinion of those who claim that the principal end of this same poetics is not to delight—as is maintained by many and not without reason —but to profit.[30]

In a sense, Bulgarini's thesis is an attempt to liberate poetry from the domination of moral philosophy; to do so, he returns it to its place as an instrumental science; but he implies meanwhile that it really should be considered an independent art whose end is only to give pleasure.

The passage cited from Bulgarini was answered directly by Orazio Capponi in his manuscript *Risposte alle prime cinque particelle delle considerazioni di Bellisario Bulgarini* (1577). In reality, there are no adequate reasons given for the opposition; the following text largely illustrates a wish to retain poetry in its currently established place:

... it would not at all be an improper thing to say that poetry, insofar as it is useful to human life, as we see clearly considering it in its parts, some of which purge us of the excess of those passions which are found in us, and it teaches us good modes of conduct distinguishing them from the bad and many other such things useful for arriving at human happiness—insofar, then, as poetry can bring about this effect [it is not improper to say] that it is a part of moral philosophy whose only purpose is to direct us along the road which may lead us to happiness.[31]

Capponi does go on to say that, even according to Aristotle, there is no objection to calling an art a part of philosophy.

Bulgarini's reply came two years later in his *Repliche alle Risposte del sig. Orazio Capponi*, published in 1585 (but the work is dated at the end "Di Siena, il di 20. di Maggio 1579"). In it, he asserted the same position but at somewhat greater length: poetry is not a part of moral philosophy but an instrument of it, bearing to it the same relationship that logic bears to

---

[30] *Alcune considerazioni* (1583), pp. 14–15: "Nè so veder, che di lei, al più, altro si possa dire, se non ch'ella sia istromento della moral filosofia; nella maniera, che da' più intendenti, è tenuta la Logica, per istromento, della filosofia in vniuersale: e questo anco per l'opinion di quelli, che voglion ch'il fin principale di essa Poetica sia non il dilettare, come da molti, non senza ragion si tiene; ma il giouare."

[31] MS Bibl. Com. Siena G.IX.54, fol. 14v: "non sarebbe cosa del tutto sconcia il dire, che la Poesia in quanto è utile alla vita humana, come si uede manifesto risguardando nelle sue parti, alcuna delle quali ci purga dal souerchio di quelli affetti, che si trouano in noi, e ci fà conoscere i buoni costumi distinguendoli da rei, e molte delle si fatte cose utili a peruenire alla felicità humana, Inquanto dunque, che la poesia può questo effetto cagionare, sia parte della filosofia morale, laquale altro non fa, che indrizzarci per la strada, che possa conduci alla felicità."

philosophy in general. He would suggest, with respect to logic and poetics, that

the one and the other of them should perhaps be placed among the arts, or we might say sciences (taking science in a broad sense) which are called rational or discursive; and that just as logic, agreeing in this with rhetoric, has no fixed subject matter about which it operates, almost the same thing happens with respect to poetics, and particularly with relationship to the human actions that it undertakes to imitate; so that, not being confined to speaking or treating exclusively of such or such human actions, it may have free choice with respect to any and all, with one or another kind of poem. Add to this the fact that just as logic was invented primarily to serve philosophy in general as its particular instrument, so poetry perchance [was invented] to serve the moral philosophies, occupying itself with the subject matters of these latter; whence it will come to be also in a certain way their instrument, since they use it to bring profit and to form better (by means of the pleasure which it always carries with it) the moral characters of men, directing them toward practical happiness, which is the most immediate end of the moral philosopher.[32]

It would be improper, however, to consider poetry an instrument of natural science, since verse compositions treating the latter are not really poems. Bulgarini repeats, finally, his notion that, if all arts are divided into the speculative, the practical, and the instrumental, logic and rhetoric and poetics belong to the last of these; poetics cannot thus possibly be considered a part of such a practical science as moral philosophy.

Bulgarini's manuscript of this last work came to the attention of Lelio Marretti, who wrote an answer in the form of *Avvertimenti*, presumably around 1579–80; the manuscript is to be found with most of the others in this interchange in the Biblioteca Comunale at Siena. Marretti's notes are confused and show a misunderstanding of some of Bulgarini's ideas. He begins with the thesis that poetry is subordinate to politics insofar as the politician must judge of the possible moral effects of a poem. Still, it would not be proper to call it an instrument of moral philosophy, since it does not teach the principles of that science; it teaches only "how to live well, to ignorant men."[33] It is an instrument only in a special sense: "It seems to me that one might say that poetry was an instrument of the moral

[32] *Repliche* (1585), pp. 27–28: "l'vna, e l'altra di loro sia forse da riporsi infra l'arti, ò vogliam dire scienze (pigliando la Scienza in largo modo) che razionali, ò sermocinali si chiamano; e che, si come la Logica, conforme in ciò alla Retorica, non ha alcuna determinata materia, intorno alla quale s'esserciti; quasi, che questo medesimo interuiene alla Poetica, e particolarmente intorno alle azzioni vmane, ch'ella si prende ad imitare: conciosiacosa che, non essendo ristretta à dire, ò à trattar di queste, ò di quelle vmane azzioni solamente, habbia l'elezzion libera intorno à tutte quante, con' vna, ò con' vn' altra sorte di Poemi. Aggiungasi à questo, che si come la Logica è stata principalmente trouata, per seruire alla Filosofia in vniuersale, come suo proprio stromento; così la Poesia, per auentura, per seruir' alle Morali, venendo ad essercitarsi intorno alle materie di esse. Iaonde verrà ad esser' anco in vn certo modo loro stromento; seruendosi quelle di lei, per giouare, e formar meglio, per mezzo della dilettazione, che ella porta tuttauia seco, i costumi de gli huomini, indirizzandoli alla felicità pratica; la qual' è il fin più propinquo del moral Filosofo."
[33] *Avvertimenti*, fol. 438: "ma sol il ben viuere à gl'huomini rozzi."

philosopher, since he uses it to give proper moral character to men, rather than an instrument of moral philosophy, since the latter teaches us man's end in life and how to achieve it, for which teaching neither poetics nor poetry is useful to us. I suspect that there is considerable equivocation about this word 'instrument.'"[34] This stand rather leads Marretti to take sides with Capponi: "The opinion of Capponi seems to me quite probable, that poetry is rather a part than an instrument of moral science, since it does exactly what that science does, bringing in its own way happiness to the ordinary man."[35] As for Bulgarini's classification of poetry among the rational disciplines, Marretti will have none of it: "If poetry could be called a part of philosophy, without doubt it could not be placed anywhere else than under the branch of moral philosophy, both because it deals with the very same matter and because it concerns the very same end."[36]

During the years 1573–80, then, the Bulgarini-Capponi-Marretti controversy revolved about the designation of poetry as a part or as an instrument of moral philosophy. Some of the difficulty of decision arose from the inability of the theorists to decide to which of the Aristotelian branches of science the art of poetry belonged. They hesitated between the practical and the instrumental. About the same period, a formal philosopher, Francesco Patrizi, was concerning himself with the same question. In Book VIII of Volume I of his *Discussiones peripateticae* (1571), devoted to a division of Aristotle's works ("Aristotelicorum librorum extantium per genera distributio"), he first distinguishes eight groups of works: "Logicum, De Ente, De Sapientia, Mathematicum, Naturale, Medicum, Morale, Artificiale." Each is then subdivided, and under the group "Morale" come these treatises: *Ethics, Politics, Economics, Poetics, Rhetoric*, and sections 18, 27, 28, and 29 of the *Problemata*. The assignment of the *Poetics* to the group of moral sciences is justified by reference to Book VIII of the *Politics* and by the argument that, along with music, poetics is useful for the instruction of the young. The authority of Plato is cited in support. In Book IX of the same volume ("Aristotelicorum librorum in singulis generibus distributio"), Patrizi insists that the *Poetics* was really meant to be the last book of the *Politics*.[37]

For Jacopo Zabarella, as for several previous theorists, poetry is at one

---

[34] *Ibid.*, fol. 438v: "Più tosto par à me si potrebbe dire, che la Poetica fusse istromento del filosofo morale, seruendosi d'essa per render costumati gli huomini, che istromento della filosofia morale insegnandoci questa il fine dell'huomo, et il modo d'acquistarlo, al che non ci serue, ne la poetica, ne la poesia. Dubbito, che non s'equiuochi assai intorno à questa parola istromento."

[35] *Ibid.*, fol. 438v: "Parmi assai probabile l'oppinion del Capponi, che la poesia sia piu tosto parte, che istromento del morale, facendo il medesimo appunto, che fa la scientia inducendo con il suo modo felicità nell'huomo ordinario."

[36] *Ibid.*, fols. 439–439v: "Se la poetica se potesse chiamar parte di filosofia senza dubbio non potrebbe porsi, se non sotto il membro della morale e perche la si raggira intorno alla medesima materia, e perche la riguarda 'l medesimo fine."

[37] *Discussionum peripateticarum tomi primi* (1571 ed.), pp. 66–66v, 82.

and the same time related to the rational sciences and to moral philosophy. It should be noted that the work in which he discusses the problem is a work on logic, his *De natura logicae libri duo* of 1578; the specific chapters devoted to the discussion are in Book II, chapter 13, "De Rhetorica, & Poetica quòd philosophiae contemplatiuae instrumenta non sint"; chapter 14, "Quòd Rhetorica, & Poetica neque artium, neque moralis philosophiae instrumenta sint"; and chapter 15, "Quòd Rhetorica, & Poetica solius ciuilis disciplinae instrumenta sint, & quomodo." The relationship to logic, the association with rhetoric, are thus initial assumptions. The point at issue is specifically what branch of philosophy is served by poetry as an instrument. Zabarella argues first that poetry and rhetoric do not serve contemplative (or speculative) philosophy, since the latter is concerned only with knowledge whereas the two sister faculties are concerned with action: "... their usefulness is related to action rather than to contemplation; they deal with things in action."[38] Next, he argues that they are not instrumental to moral philosophy, which has as its function to teach each man how to improve himself, but rather to the "civil discipline," by which each man attempts to improve others. Both are thus the tools of the politician. The distinction is made clear in the following passage:

> The moral man is he who does right; the citizen, however, causes others to do right; for the moral man wants to make himself good, whereas the citizen wants to make others good. ... Rhetoric and poetics are thus instrumental faculties which the citizen employs for action, namely, to make his fellow citizens good; with this distinction, however, that he uses rhetoric through his own means, but poetics by means of other persons.[39]

In later chapters Zabarella contends that they are a part of particular rather than of universal logic, and that poetics is a part of logic insofar as it uses one of the means of logic, the example. Example is taken in the broad sense of actions, characters, and passions presented to the audience for imitation or rejection.

Some expansion and clarification of the point of view of Lionardo Salviati, who has already appeared as one of those classifying poetry with history, may be seen in his *Commentary on Aristotle's Poetics*, written in 1585–86. Salviati considers the opinions of such other commentators as Maggi, Piccolomini, and Castelvetro. He decides that "with respect to the end of the poem, which is relative to moral character, the operation of the poet will have its place within moral philosophy." As for history, he rejects Castelvetro's theory that a treatise on poetry presupposes a treatise

---

[38] *De natura logicae* (1578), pp. 53–57, esp. p. 53: "ad actionem potius, quàm ad contemplationem vtilitas ipsarum pertinet."

[39] *Ibid.*, p. 55: "moralis ipse est, qui bene agit, ciuilis verò facit vt alii bene agant; moralis enim uult seipsum bonum reddere, ciuilis autem alios. ... Sunt igitur Rhetorica, atque Poetica facultates instrumentales, quibus homo ciuilis ad agendum vtitur, idest ad ciues bonos efficiendos, cum hoc tamen discrimine, quòd arte Rhetorica per semetipsum vtitur, Poetica uerò per alios."

on history. Even though the poet must know something about truth, "to the knowledge of truth, in what pertains to things that have happened, not a treatise on the writing of history but history itself is required. ... And without reading histories the truth about things which happen may rather be derived from experience."[40] Salviati's approach is not basically systematic, and these statements show rather a preoccupation with current problems than an orderly attempt at solving them.

A much more orderly treatment is seen in Bernardino Baldino's *Discorso breve intorno all'utilità delle scienze et arti* (1586); but the order here is derived less from philosophical principle than from moral conviction. That conviction is briefly put at the outset: "... poetry by its essence can and must blame misdeeds, no less than certain other disciplines and arts."[41] As a result, all branches of philosophy are transformed into types of moral philosophy. All sciences are divided into speculative and practical. The speculative exist in order "to heal the soul"; theology, which presumably belongs in this group, "provides medicine against our sins." So for the practical: the moral disciplines "heal the mind of its vices," and medicine contributes to "the health of human bodies." If everything thus is analogized in medical terms, the medical science involved is specifically curative rather than preventive. Poetry, along with rhetoric, falls within the class of liberal arts, those which pertain to the soul.[42] Its curative functions are stated thus:

... it also, like the other noble arts, came into being to enrich our spirit with salutary and honorable precepts. But it is different from the other disciplines in this, that the others come unveiled and bear openly their bitterness and their whip, with which they freely touch and beat the hearts of the harmful and the vicious; whereas poetry with masks, and with sharp words but covered with honey, proposes as do the other doctrines to attack the guilty and scold faults and errors, and bring health to sick minds corrupted by spots and rottenness, just as the clever doctor sweetens bitter medicines. ... And this they do to attract young people to study its works, which are full of teachings and remedies against misdeeds and crimes.[43]

---

[40] MS BNF II, II, 11, fols. 13–13v: "risguardando al fine del poema, il quale è intorno a' costumi, l'esercizio del poeta tra la moral filosofia harà luogo ..."; "alla cognizion del uero, in cio che all' auuenute cose appartiene, non il trattato dello scriuer la storia, ma essa storia è richiesta. ... E senza legger le storie il uero dell'accadenti cose dall'esperienzia eziandio puo ritrarsi."

[41] *Discorso* (1586), p. A2v: "la poesia di sua ragione può & deue biasimare i misfatti; non meno ch'alcune altre discipline, & arti."

[42] *Ibid.*, pp. B4–B4v.

[43] *Ibid.*, p. B3: "anch'essa come l'altre nobili arti, e venuta in luce, per arricchire l'animo nostro de precetti salutari, & horreuoli. In ciò questa e differente dall'altre discipline, che l'altre vengono scoperte, & portano palese l'amarezza & la sferza; conche liberamente toccano, & flagellano i cuori de i nocenti, e vitiosi; doue la poesia con maschere, & con parole pungenti, ma coperte di mele dissegna come le altre dottrine mordere i diffettosi, & riprendere le diffalte, & errori, & sanare gl'animi amalati, & corrotti dalle macchie, e magagne. come il medico auueduto ch'adolcisce le medecine amare. ... E ciò fanno per allettare i giouani a studiare l'opere sue piene di documenti, e remedij contra i misfatti, e delitti."

Baldino's little treatise, with its extreme moralizing tendency, is representative of a certain kind of thinking found with some frequency in the latter decades of the century.

The last of the documents in the Dante quarrel to concern itself specifically with the classification of poetry is Jacopo Mazzoni's *Della difesa della Comedia di Dante*, a voluminous work in two parts completed about 1585. Part I was published in 1587, Part II not until 1688. The argument by which Mazzoni arrives at his conclusion is very complex. He begins with the statement that the arts and sciences are distinguished from one another by the differences in the objects of which they treat. As for the meaning of "objects," he interprets it according to the opinion of the Peripatetics: "... sciences and arts derive their true and real distinction from their objects, not insofar as these are things, but insofar as they are knowable things and, if one might say so, things makable by art."[44] In the Aristotelian system, the considerations of rhetoric are all directed to the "persuasible," of poetics to the "imitable," of moral philosophy to—the phrase is untranslatable—the "beatificabile humano." For clarification of the idea of imitation he turns to Plato, *Republic*, Book X, to the three-way distinction of objects as Ideas (which are contemplated), Works (which are made), and Images (which are made by imitation). Poetics falls among the arts which deal with the last of these; all kinds and forms of poetry form images or Idols (secs. 9–10). The genus being thus established, Mazzoni differentiates the species by a determination of the means, which are harmony, rhythm, and meter; and of the subject matter, which is the credible (rather than the false or the possible). At this point, finally, comes the classification: since it deals with the credible, poetry "must properly be placed under that rational faculty which was called sophistic by the ancients."[45] But this is an incomplete classification; the complete one is given shortly afterward:

... the poetic art may be considered in two ways, that is either as it considers the rightness of the poetic Image, or as it makes and forms the latter. In the first way, I say that it should be called poetics, and in the second, poetry. In the first it is an art which controls and uses the Image, and is a part of the civil faculty. . . . In the second way it is an art which forms and makes the Image, and is a species under the rational faculty.[46]

Since he had previously stated that the means were exclusively productive of pleasure, Mazzoni can now summarize thus his reasons for placing

[44] *Della Difesa*, Pt. I (1587), "Proemio," Sec. 7: "le scienze, e l'arti prendano la sua vera, e reale distintione da gli oggetti, non inquanto, che sono cose: ma inquanto, che sono. . . . Scibili, e se cosi si potesse dire, artificiabili."
[45] *Ibid.*, Sec. 53: "si deue drittamente collocare sotto quella facultà rationale, che fù da gli antichi Sophistica nominata."
[46] *Ibid.*, Sec. 54: "l'arte poetica si può prendere in due modi, cioè, o secondo, ch'ella considera la drittura dell'Idolo poetico, o secondo, che lo fabbrica, e lo forma. Nel primo modo, dico, ch'ella si deue nomare Poetica, e nel secondo Poesia. Nel primo è arte imperante, & vsante l'Idolo, & è parte della facoltà Ciuile. . . . Nel secondo modo è arte formante, e fabbricante l'Idolo, & è specie della facoltà rationale."

poetry under the rational faculty: "Poetry is a sophistic art because of imitation, which is its proper genus, and of the credible, which is its subject, and of pleasure, which is its end; since by being under that genus, by concerning itself with that subject, and by seeking that end, it is frequently constrained to admit the false."[47] The role of the civil faculty is explained as a kind of higher justification of the art: poetry is a game, a cessation or privation of serious activity, the most noble of them all. Thus it may be said that "the civil faculty should be divided into two highly important parts, one of which considers the proper form of activity, and was called by the general name of politics, or the civil faculty. The other considers the proper form of the cessation of activity or the proper form of the activity of games, and was called poetics."[48] Therefore, the *Poetics* should properly be considered as the ninth book of the *Politics*. This argument, for all its diffuseness, is remarkable for two points: first, Mazzoni insists that the end of poetry is pleasure exclusively; second, even when he places poetry under politics he does not do so because he wishes to assign to it a pedagogic end or an ethical purpose.

In Part II, the first book of which is devoted to "character" in poems, Mazzoni reopens the discussion of the relationship of poetry to politics. He emphasizes the difference between the positions of Aristotle and Plato; Aristotle, who considers poems as poems, admits both "good" and "bad" characters in poetry, whereas Plato, whose approach is ethical, admits only the "good":

> Reason is on the side of Plato; for if poetry is a part of philosophy, as has been shown above, it follows that poetic pleasure must be regulated and so to speak qualified by moral philosophy; and therefore good character will necessarily be conjoined with poetics and in such a way that bad character will not be admitted in it, since it would destroy moral goodness. But the practice of the poets is on the side of Aristotle.[49]

The divergence between the two philosophers is explained by the types of governments in terms of which they spoke: Plato of the ideal republic in which only a special kind of poetry would be useful, Aristotle of a practical government in conformity with the habits of mankind in which poetry is

---

[47] *Ibid.*, Sec. 60: "la Poesia è arte Sophistica, e per l'imitatione, che è il suo genere proprio, e per lo credibile, che è il suo soggetto, e per lo diletto, che è il suo fine, poiche per esser sotto quel genere, per esser intorno a quel soggetto, e per rimirare quel fine, viene astretta molte volte a dar luogo al falso."

[48] *Ibid.*, Secs. 66–67: "la facoltà ciuile si deua diuidere in due principalissime parti, l'vna delle quali considera la rettitudine dell' operationi, e fù nomata col nome generale Politica, cioè Ciuile. L'altra considera la rettitudine della cessatione o la rettitudine delle operationi de' giochi, e fù nomata Poetica."

[49] *Difesa*, Pt. II (1688), p. 2: "a Platone è fauoreuole la ragione; percioche se la Poetica è parte della Philosophia, come si è di sopra dimostrato, segue, che il diletto Poetico debba esser regolato, e per cosi dire qualificato dalla morale Philosophia. . . . Ma ad Aristotele è fauoreuole l'vso de Poeti."

admissible as a form of entertainment. When the two theories are so seen, the contradiction between them disappears (pp. 3–4). Similarly, the difficulty over the classification of the art is solved if one realizes, again, that there are two ways of looking at it:

> Poetry may be considered in two ways, that is, in itself insofar as it is an art having the pleasure of man as its aim, in such wise that by means of pleasure it restores the energies grown weary in serious occupations; and when so considered it has no other function but to imitate human actions in a way to delight those who listen to them or who read them. . . . One may, in the other way, consider poetry insofar as it is regulated and ordered by the civil faculty in operation. . . .[50]

Mazzoni, for the most part, considers poetry in the first way and addresses himself to problems of structure and artistry; but he never completely loses sight of the second, and there are constantly evidences of a preoccupation with moral problems and values.

The remaining documents in this group belong to another of the great literary polemics of the century, that waged over Battista Guarini's *Pastor Fido*. The central issue, whether the pastoral and the tragicomedy were legitimate forms of the literary art, led to many auxiliary questions, and one of these was the end of poetry and its classification as an art. The first document is a treatise by Giason Denores (1586) whose title itself is highly significant: *Discorso intorno à que' principii, cause, et accrescimenti, che la comedia, la tragedia, et il poema heroico ricevono dalla philosophia morale, & civile, & da' governatori delle republiche*. In accordance with this announced intention, Denores throughout seeks the contribution of philosophers and rulers to the invention and development of the various kinds of poems. Poetry sprang from natural causes; but it was soon directed by wise men to serve the purposes of the state, "to generate good principles of conduct in their republics and to direct them towards happiness . . . since poetry, as is also rhetoric, is subordinate to moral and civil philosophy, and owes to it every one of its most regulated productions."[51] The end of delight is intermediate to the more important end of utility; it should never be pursued for its own sake. Denores concludes where he had begun:

> . . . let us conclude that it does not belong to any other part of philosophy except politics. . . . everything that we have dealt with in relation to such compositions remains within the province of the moral and civil philosopher, whose duty it is

---

[50] *Ibid.*, p. 6: "la Poetica si può in due modi considerare, cioè in se stessa inquanto ch'ella è vn'arte, che rimira il diletto humano, accioche per mezo di quello ella ristori le forze affaticate nelle graui occupationi, & in questo modo ella non hà altro officio, che di assomigliare le attioni humane in modo ch'elle dilettino quelli che le ascoltano, e che le leggono. . . . Si può nell'altro modo considerare la Poetica in quanto ch'ella è retta, & ordinata dalla facolta ciuile operante."

[51] *Discorso* (1586), p. 2: "per generar buoni costumi nelle loro republiche & per inuiarle alla felicità. . . . essendo la poetica, come è ancho la rhetorica, soggetta alla philosophia morale, & ciuile; & da essa riceuendo ogni sua piu regolata produttione."

to direct all arts and all doctrines to their true and proper end, that is public utility and benefit.[52]

Two years later, in 1588, Denores returned to a discussion of the same genres in his *Poetica nella qual si tratta secondo l'opinion d'Arist. della tragedia, del poema heroico, & della comedia*. The second work adds little to the theories of the first, except for certain emphases not formerly present. One of these is the claim of the superiority of poetry to politics; poetry

> in part is equal to moral and civil philosophy, in part is superior to it. It is equal insofar as both attend with every care to the two most noble actions already mentioned [the purgation of the passions, the inculcation of virtue]. It is superior insofar as the other proceeds by means of laws, penalties, and punishments, while this produces the same result with the greatest enjoyment and recreation of the spirit.[53]

Another such is the insistence that Aristotle in the *Poetics* treated only three genres—tragedy, comedy, and epic—because these were the three commonly recited in public gatherings and hence the only ones capable of exerting a moral influence in the state. "With the greatest perspicacity, as a moral and civil philosopher, he refused to accept as parts of the poetic art all such compositions in verse as did not receive their rules and their principles from Moral and Civil Philosophy, from the rulers and legislators of states ordered to the common weal."[54] To each of these genres Denores assigns a special ethical function, for a specific audience in specific circumstances. Finally, he insists that the poet must not only be fully instructed in ethics and politics but must be himself the kind of man he undertakes to praise in his works. This is a far cry from the early notions of the poet as a rhetorician; it is even farther from the more recent conception of him as a sophist. Poetry has become one with moral philosophy, and the poet is identified both with Cicero's ideal orator and with the Philosopher, or the Good Man.

In neither of these works would there seem to be any controversial materials, especially for the last decades of the century. But Battista Guarini saw in the first of them an attack upon his manuscript *Pastor Fido*, and in reply to this attack he wrote *Il Verrato, ovvero difesa di quanto ha scritto M. Giason Denores contra le tragicomedie, et le pastorali, in un suo*

[52] *Ibid.*, pp. 43–43v: "concluderemo, che non aspetti ad altra parte della philosophia, che alla politica. . . . tutto quel, che habbiamo trattato di tai componimenti, non è fuor della profession del philosopho morale, & ciuile, a cui aspetta dirizzar tutte le arti, & tutte le dottrine al loro uero, & proprio fine, cioe alla utilità, & al beneficio publico."

[53] *Poetica* (1588), p. ✠2v: "è parte vguale, parte è superiore alla philosophia Morale, & Ciuile. E vguale, inquanto che ambedue con ogni studio attendono alle predette due nobilissime attioni. E superiore, in quanto che quella procede con leggi, con pene, con castigamenti, & questa opera il medesimo con sommo godimento, & ricreation d'animo."

[54] *Ibid.*, p. ††: "egli, come Philosopho Morale, & Ciuile con sommo auedimento non si curò di ridur tutti i componimenti, fatti in verso, come parti dell'arte Poetica, che non riconosceuano le loro regole, & i loro principii dalla Philosophia Morale, & Ciuile, da' gouernatori, & da' legislatori delle Republiche a beneficio commune. . . ." See also p. 67.

discorso di poesia (1588). Guarini's stand on the classification of poetry is directly opposed to Denores':

> How can you hold that poetics, which is an art and therefore a habit of the speculative intellect, can take its principles from ethics, which is a habit of the active intellect? You will tell me that from ethics it derives notions of character; and I say to you that it gets them rather from rhetoric, which is much different from ethics in the definition of the virtues. But even granted that it does get them from ethics, I insist that it does so not to teach them but solely to imitate them. ... You will add further that it serves politics insofar as the legislator does or does not permit the people to have a given poem, depending upon whether it demonstrates good or bad mores. That is true; but it does not follow from that that it takes its principles from politics. ... depending upon the form of the republic, poetry has more or less freedom. ... And in this only is it placed under the politician; but as for its intrinsic and formal principles, it has nothing to do with politics, but is a member of sophistic and rhetoric.[55]

From this general position, Guarini passes to a point-by-point denial of Denores' argument: Aristotle's intention in the *Poetics*, the status of the minor poetic genres, the nature of the poet. But he does not completely rule out a relationship between poetry and politics or ethics, as the above quotation shows. Instead, he distinguishes for each of the dramatic genres two separate ends, an instrumental end (which for all dramatic genres is the imitation of an action) and an architectonic end (which for each genre is a special kind of purgation: for comedy, the purgation of sadness through laughter; for tragedy, the purgation of pity and fear, which are moderated in a way to induce virtue; for tragicomedy, the purgation of melancholy). This theory of Guarini's will be developed and reinforced as the polemic with Denores continues.

Denores replied in 1590, in an *Apologia contra l'auttor del Verato*. Much of the essay is devoted to specific problems of the tragicomedy and the pastoral. On the matter of the classification of poetry Denores does little more than reaffirm his earlier convictions. The nature of the repetitions will be indicated by this passage on Aristotle's intention in the *Poetics*:

> ... as a moral and civil philosopher, he was not concerned with speaking of any such form of poetry as did not receive its rules and its principles from moral and civil philosophy and from the rulers and legislators of republics designed for the common good, but only of those forms which, receiving them [from these sources]

[55] *Il Verrato* (1588), pp. 39v–40: "Come volete, che la Poetica la quale è arte, & però habito dello 'ntelletto speculatiuo prenda i suoi principi dalla morale, ch'è habito dell'attiuo. Voi mi direte, che dal morale prende i costumi. & io vi dico, che anzi dal ritorico, il quale è molto diferente dal morale nelle difinizioni delle virtù. ma posto, che pur gli prenda dal morale. vi dico, che ciò non fà per insegnargli, ma solo per imitargli... soggiugnerete ancora, che serue al politico in quanto il legislatore la concede al popolo & nò, secondo ch'ella è di buoni, e di cattiui costumi. Egli è vero. ma non per tanto non seguita, che dal Politico prenda i principi ... della poetica, la quale secondo le forme delle Republiche ha più & meno licenza. ... E'n questo solo è sottoposta al politico, ma quanto ai suoi principi intrinsechi, & formali non ha che fare con esso lui, ma è membro della sofistica, e della ritorica." See also pp. 20–27.

could generate good principles of conduct or not so receiving them could generate bad principles of conduct in the minds of the citizens in general.[56]

The general contention is, again, that tragedy, comedy, and the epic have as their function to exert a moral influence on the masses assembled to hear them, and that any kind of poem which does not fulfil this function is not worthy of consideration as poetry.

Although Guarini finished his answer in the following year, 1591, it was not published until 1592 (according to the colophon) or 1593 (according to the title page). He entitled it *Il Verato secondo ovvero replica dell'Attizzato accademico ferrarese in difesa del Pastor Fido*. In it, Guarini first reconsidered the whole question of the subordination of poetry to politics. Certain new principles appear at the outset; first, the achievement of the end of poetry is not necessary to the achievement of the end of politics:

If then the end of moral and civil philosophy is none other than public or individual happiness, what need does it have, in order to make man happy, of fables? Man acquires his happiness through the exercise of the virtues, which are rational and true operations; fictional works for the most part, since they are false and lying, will rather harm than aid the achievement of this end.

But what about purgation as a means to moral betterment?

I answer that, in order to subordinate poetry to morality, it is not sufficient that it should be useful for the purgation of the passions, but it would have to be necessary to the acquisition of virtue; for the superior art cannot obtain its end without the operation of the inferior art. ... man can purge the passions of terror and pity through other and better means than that of tragedy. And moral and civil philosophy has its own laws and private and public expedients for the achievement of this end.[57]

In sum, whatever moral profit may attach to poetry is merely an auxiliary accompaniment to the contemplation of pleasurable objects. What is more, there is no foundation anywhere in Aristotle for the subordination of poetry to politics. The end of the poet is not a utilitarian one but an aesthetic one: "His end is then not to imitate the good, but to imitate well, whether he imitate good or bad moral character; and if he imitates what is

---

[56] *Apologia* (1590), p. 2v: "egli, come philosopho morale, & ciuile, non si curo di fauellar di ogni forma di poesia, che non riceuea le sue regole, & i suoi principii dalla philosophia morale, & ciuile, & da' gouernatori, & legislatori delle Repubbliche ad utilità commune, ma solamente di quelle, che, riceuendogli, poteuano generar buoni costumi, ò non riceuendogli poteuano generar cattiui costumi ne gli animi de' Cittadini in uniuersale."

[57] *Il Verato secondo* (1593), p. 63: "Se dunque il fine della morale, e ciuile Filosofia non è altro, che la felicità o publica, ò priuata, che bisogno ha ella, per far felice l'huomo, di fauole? il qual' huomo acquista la sua felicità con l'esercizio della vertù, che son opere ragioneuoli, e vere, al qual suo fine possono, per lo più, l'opere fauolose, come false, e mentite, anzi nuocere. ... Rispondo, che per esser subalternata alla morale, non basta che sia gioueuole alla purgazion degli affetti, ma bisogna che sia necessaria all'acquisto della vertù, perciochè l'arte superiore non può, se non con l'opera della 'nferiore, ottenere il suo fine. ... può ben l'huomo, per altra, e molto miglior maniera, purgar gli affetti del terrore, e della compassione, che per quella della Tragedia. E la Filosofia morale, e ciuile ha di ciò le sue leggi, ed ha per questo fine le sue priuate, e pubbliche cure."

good poorly, he will not be a good poet, but he may be called a good poet if he imitates well what is bad."[58] Indeed, all the important questions to be asked about a poem lie exclusively in the realm of poetics itself:

> Furthermore, what does the poet have to do with the laws of the city? To whom must he give an accounting as to whether his plots are pathetic, or ethical, or sententious, or ridiculous, or complex, or simple, or single, or double, or with happy ending, or with turbulent ending, which are the essential parts of poetry; with respect to which, from whom does he get the rules, from legislators or from poets?[59]

Guarini also now develops two points made earlier, that touching the relation of poetry to rhetoric and that on the existence of the instrumental and architectonic ends. The poet derives from rhetoric, rather than from ethics, the notions of moral character which he uses. Like the rhetorician, he must consider the nature of his audience if he would achieve his architectonic end, since it is a form of persuasion; different audiences in different times require more or less violent tragic effects, purgation of a more or less vigorous kind. But in any event, this rhetorical end is a secondary one; the primary one still remains the artistic end proper to the art:

> ... the poet is not concerned with purging more or less, but with imitating well that subject—even though it may be little useful for purgation—which he undertakes; so that, if in a subject with a happy ending he will do his job well with a good imitation, with the required unity, with artful recognition, with judicious sententiae, with appropriate character, and (what is more proper to him than all the rest) with splendor of diction, he will without doubt avoid being charged with that mediocrity which Horace blames.[60]

This is as close as Guarini comes—or as any of his contemporaries come—to developing a theory of poetry as an independent art, subordinated neither to the rational disciplines nor to the ethical sciences and achieving its own special ends by following principles which are specifically its own.

There is a definite philosophical relationship between the large group of texts which classified poetry as an instrument or a part of moral philosophy and that earlier group which placed it among the rational or discursive or

---

[58] *Ibid.*, p. 66: "Non è dunque suo fine d'imitare il buono, ma di bene imitare, o buono o cattiuo che sia il costume: e'l buono, male imitando, non sarà buon poeta, ma imitando [bene] il cattiuo buon poeta potrà chiamarsi" (the original text reads "imitando male il cattiuo," but this must be an error).

[59] *Ibid.*, p. 90: "Del resto, che ha da fare il poeta con le leggi della città? A cui ha egli da render conto, se le sue fauole son patetiche, o morate, o sentenziose, o ridicole, o rannodate, o piane, o semplici, o doppie, o con fin lieto, o con fin turbulento, che sono le parti essenziali di poesia, delle quali, da chi prende le regole, da' legislatori, o pur da' poeti?"

[60] *Ibid.*, p. 118: "il ... poeta non ha riguardo di purgar più, e meno, ma di bene imitar quel soggetto, quantunque poco purgante, che si propone, per modo, che se in soggetto di lieto fine farà bene la parte sua con la buona imitazione, con la debita vnità, con l'artifizioso riconoscimento, con la prudente sentenza, col conueneuol costume, e quello ch'è più suo proprio di tutto 'l resto, con lo splendor della locuzione, fuggirà, senza fallo, la nota di quella mediocrità, che biasima Orazio."

instrumental sciences. If the earlier group insisted upon the character of poetry as useful for serving some final purpose through its means as variously considered—words, which have powers of signification; arguments, which have powers of persuasion or conviction—the later group insisted upon the kinds of usefulness provided. If poetry was discursive, its discourse concerned itself with moral activity, ethical or civil or political. If poetry was instrumental, it served as an instrument for the achievement of moral ends—for supplying examples of good and bad conduct, for administering praise and blame, for persuading to activity or inactivity. The second group thus comes to constitute a kind of specification of the first, a pushing of assumptions to further conclusions; the earlier critics are concerned with the problem of instrumentality, the later ones with the ends for which the instrument is used. The change in concern accounts for the change in classification of the art.

ECLECTIC CLASSIFICATIONS

It should not be surprising that, among all these attempts to decide in favor of moral philosophy or history or logic or rhetoric as the closest relative of poetry among the sciences, there should be at least a few works in which all seem to occupy an equal position. Such is the case with Agnolo Segni, for whom the frames of reference are both philosophy and history. The following passage from his *Ragionamento sopra le cose pertinenti alla Poetica* (written in 1576 as a revision of lectures given in 1573; published in 1581) states the essence of his position, which is basically Platonic in its assumptions:

... we may consider the difference manifest among these three faculties of history, philosophy, and poetry and among their forms of discourse. For since there are two extreme species of objects, one, the things in our world with their imperfections, the other, their perfect forms which we call Ideas, the latter make up philosophy and the former history, each of the two being separate from the other; but the one and the other conjoined generate poetry. History, residing in things past and present, expounds and narrates them as different from their Ideas, just as they are or were in themselves. Philosophy rises to the Ideas of things different from the things themselves, and these she contemplates as they are in their perfect nature. Poetry joins the one part and the other, recounting things past or present, not as they are or were, but similar to their Ideas, and showing the Ideas not in themselves, but in things which have been and things which are. Whence history and philosophy, which are at the pure extremes, are each completely true; poetry, which tries to combine them, since they remain uncombined is in part true and in part false: true for the Ideas which she expresses, and false for the things in which she puts these Ideas, and because she makes things similar to these Ideas whereas they are really different. And therefore poetry is intermediate between philosophy and history because it participates in these two extremes; and insofar as it participates in philosophy and in her objects, it is better than history; but because of its participation in history and in the particular sensible things which are the objects of history, to this extent it is below philosophy, and the poet is of lesser dignity than the philosopher.[61]

Another eclectic document, and perhaps a more extreme one, is Torquato Tasso's *Discorsi del poema heroico* [1594]. Poetry, for Tasso, serves the traditional ends of pleasure and utility; but utility is foremost, pleasure auxiliary. Hence the role of the moral philosopher:

Therefore it is the task of the political philosopher to consider what poetry is to be prohibited and what pleasure, so that the pleasure ... should not produce the effect of an infectious poison, or should not keep the mind occupied in idle reading. ... poetry is a first philosophy which from our earliest years teaches us principles of conduct and the ways of life.[62]

But insofar as poetry achieves political ends it is subordinate to a higher art and is considered in terms of that art; considered in itself, it seeks only pleasure as its end:

If the poet as a poet pursues this end, he will not err far from that goal to which he must direct all his attention ...; but as a political person and part of the city, or at least insofar as his art is subordinated to that art which is queen of all the others, he seeks some profit, and rather that which is honest than useful. Thus of the two ends which the poet envisages, one is proper to his own art, the other to the superior art.[63]

When one comes to consider the subject matter of poetry, the classification again changes abruptly; the poet, treating the probable and the verisimilar, is a kind of dialectician, as is the rhetorician. "Without doubt

[61] *Ragionamento* (1581), pp. 65–66: "si può contemplare da noi la differenza tra queste tre facultà manifesta, historia, filosofia, & poesia, & tra le loro orazioni. che essendo due spezie estreme, vna le cose tra noi co' loro difetti, l'altra le loro perfezzioni, che noi chiamiamo Idee, queste fanno la filosofia, & quelle l'historia, ciascuna delle due parti da se: ma l'vna parte & l'altra congiunte insieme generano la poesia. L'historia stando nelle cose, nelle passate, & nelle presente, l'espone & le narra dalle loro Idee diuerse, così com'elle sono ò furono in se stesse. La filosofia s'alza all'Idee delle cose diuerse dalle cose, & quelle contempla com'elle sono nella natura loro perfette. La poesia congiugne l'vna parte & l'altra, narrando cose state ò presenti, non come sono ò furono, ma simili all'Idee, & mostrando l'Idee non in se, ma nelle cose state & nelle presenti. Onde l'historia & la filosofia, che stanno nelle pure estremità, è tutta vera l'vna & l'altra: la poesia, che congiugner le vuole, non essendo congiunte, è parte vera, & parte falsa: vera per l'Idee, le quali ella esprime: & falsa per le cose, doue ella le pone, et le cose fa simili à loro, essendo diuerse. Et però è mezzana tra la filosofia & l'historia la poesia, perche participa di que' due estremi: & in quanto participa della filosofia, & de suoi oggetti, è migliore dell' historia: ma per la participazione dell'historia, & de' particolari sensibili dell'historia oggetto, per questo è sotto la filosofia, & di minor degnità del filosofo il poeta."

[62] *Poema heroico* [1594], p. 7: "Però al Politico s'appartiene di considerare, quale poesia debba esser prohibita, e qual diletto; accioche il piacere ... non facesse effetto di pestifero veleno, ò non tenesse occupati gli animi in vana lettione. ... la poesia ... è vna prima Filosofia, la qual sin dalla tenera età, ci ammaestra ne costumi, e nelle ragioni della vita."

[63] *Ibid.*, p. 8: "Se'l Poeta dunque in quanto Poeta hà questo fine, non errerà lontano da quel segno, alquale egli deue dirizzare tutti i suoi pensieri ...; ma in quanto è huomo ciuile, e parte della Città, ò almeno in quanto la sua Arte è sottordinata à quella, ch'è Regina delle altre, si propone il giouamento, il quale è honesto più tosto, che vtile. de due fini dunque, i quali si prepone il Poeta, l'vno è proprio dell'arte sua, l'altro dell'arte superiore."

poetry is placed in order under dialectic, along with rhetoric. ... the probable insofar as it is verisimilar belongs to the poet, for the poet uses proofs less effectively than does the dialectician."[64] Or the poet may be regarded as a kind of logician, if one attends now to the kinds of proofs he uses. If there are three kinds of logic, so there are three kinds of poetry (or parts of poetry), each of which employs different proofs (p. 28):

Logic	Poetry
Demonstrative	"dimostrando co' Filosofi, e usando il Filosofema"
Probable	"seguendo il verisimile, & seruendosi dell'essempio, e dell'enthimema"
Sophistic (or apparent probable)	"equiuoco, fallaci argomenti"

Poetry is then a part of moral philosophy if one looks at its external or "superior" end, a part of dialectic according to its subject matter, a part of logic on the basis of the arguments it uses; it is also a part of logic, but related to grammar and rhetoric, as a result of its use of "poetic diction":

... poetry is an art subordinated to logic, or really a part of it, not only because it is an art of discourse which seeks to produce pleasure, just as grammar produces regulated speech and rhetoric persuasion, but because in poetic diction, which is not without imitation, there is a kind of tacit proof which is frequently most effective; for one cannot imitate without the simile and the example, but in the example and in everything which appears verisimilar there is a kind of proof.[65]

These shifts in Tasso's position are interesting not only as they represent in one work a kind of epitome of all the theories of the century but as they demonstrate some of the characteristics and the deficiencies of the methods of thinking used by the critics. I shall have occasion to speak of them again in the following chapter.

ARISTOTELIAN CLASSIFICATIONS

From the thinking of Tasso as from that of most theorists of the century one type of classification is strikingly absent, the one we might call Aristotelian in the strict or proper sense. Of this type there were, among the documents examined, really only two examples: that of Lionardo Salviati, a very slight one, and that of Francesco Buonamici, a much more considerable one. For Lionardo Salviati, in his *Trattato della poetica*,

---

[64] *Ibid.*, p. 27: "senza dubio la poesia è collocata in ordine sotto la dialettica insieme con la rhetorica ... il probabile inquanto egli [è] verisimile appertiene al Poeta: percioche il Poeta vsa le proue men efficacemente che non fà il dialettico."

[65] *Ibid.*, p. 129: "la poesia, è vn'arte subordinata alla logica, ò veramente vna sua parte, non solamente perch'ella è arte dell'oratione, laqual cerca il diletto, non altrimente che la Grammatica il regolato parlare, e la Rhetorica, la persuasione. ma perche nel parlar poetico, il quale non è senza imitatione, è vna tacita proua; e molte volte efficacissima: perche non si può imitare senza similitudine, e senza essempio, ma nell'essempio, & in ogni cosa, che paia verisimile è la proua."

Lezzion prima (1564), the problem is less to relate poetry to other arts than to establish the fact that it is an intellectual habit and hence susceptible of cultivation. He is replying to Plato, to the assertion that poetry is merely a furor. The skeleton plan which he suggests is essentially Aristotelian: all habits are either moral or intellectual; the intellectual are either active (inducing perfection in the operator) or factitive (inducing perfection in some external matter); poetry belongs in the latter group.[66] Salviati, it is clear, is not establishing an Aristotelian system of the sciences but is merely inquiring into the kind of activity involved in the production of poetry.

This is not the case with Francesco Buonamici, who wrote a treatise in which he set out to restore to Aristotle's *Poetics* whatever glory and authority may have been removed from it by such critics as Castelvetro. He called it *Discorsi poetici nella Accademia fiorentina in difesa d'Aristotile* (1597). He thought that he could solve some of the difficulties of the text by presenting an elaborate system of the sciences in which the place of poetics would explain some of the operations of the "art." But the system so presented is itself confused, difficult to follow, and lacking in examples; I offer the following schematic reduction only with reservations. The first step is clear enough: all knowledge is divided into two kinds, one of which seeks truth and contemplates the nature of things (the speculative sciences), the other of which seeks truth for purposes of applying it later to some activity (the practical sciences). Poetics is among the latter, which perhaps may be represented as follows:

Practical Sciences

(with specific subject matters)		(with no specific subject matters)
Doing	Making	Instrumental
(*activities*)	(*works*)	Sciences
(πράττειν)	(ποιεῖν)	
Politics	Poetics	Logic
Medicine		Dialectic
		Rhetoric

Each of the subgroups under the practical sciences has itself a theoretical and a practical phase: there is a theory of medicine which affords precepts and a practice which applies them, a theory of poetry (the *Poetics*) and an application of this theory in the writing of poems, a theory of logic and its use in every other science. Moreover, in each of the main divisions there is one master science, from which all the others derive. In the contemplative or speculative sciences, this is metaphysics; in the practical sciences, it is politics (pp. 10–12).

It is perhaps worthy of note that a century which considered itself Aristotelian in poetic matters should have waited until its very last years to produce a text, such as Buonamici's, showing some comprehension of

[66] MS BNF, Magl. VII, 307, fol. 29.

Aristotle's general system of the sciences and of the place of poetry among them. Buonamici lists poetry neither among the instrumental sciences nor among the parts or instruments of moral philosophy. He sees it as specifically a "poetic" science whose function is to make poems. Along with the rest of his contemporaries, however, he continues to regard it, in a broader view, as auxiliary to politics; its artistic end is intermediate to a larger "architectonic" end, that of contributing to man's happiness. It would be possible, of course, so to regard poetry without ceasing to be a good Aristotelian; everything would depend upon how, in general, one interprets the text of the *Poetics* in relation to the other sciences. I reserve that analysis and that judgment for a later chapter.

CONCLUSIONS

Although there may seem to be a certain amount of similarity among the various theories proposed during the century—one might even say monotony—a close questioning of the reasons for the predominant classifications leads rather to an impression of diversity. Let us take, for example, the earliest and most persistent classification, where poetry is assigned to the group constituted by logic, grammar, rhetoric (with the occasional addition of dialectic, sophistic, and history). This assignment may be made, first, because all the arts in the group use language as their medium or material; they are all "discursive" sciences. Second, it may be made because poetry is regarded, along with the others, as neither an "art" nor a "science" but a "faculty" of the mind; hence it will belong with the others in the family of rational faculties. Or it may, third, result from a consideration of the subject matter of poetics, which deals not with the truth (as do certain other sciences) but with one of the variations of the probable or the false or the verisimilar; this will relate it to sophistic on the one hand and to rhetoric on the other. Or, fourth, the whole group may be composed of those disciplines which could be classified as "instrumental sciences," since in themselves they produce no knowledge or activity but are useful only as means of investigating, expounding, or presenting for persuasion the materials of some other science.

It is easy to see how the reason for the assignment of position will in each case predetermine the emphasis which the critic will give to his theory of the poetic art (unless, contrariwise, the classification proceeds from the emphasis). If poetry is a discursive science, then the important thing to investigate is its qualities as language, how these differ from the language of the other discursive sciences, how its language may be made to conform to the special norms established. If it is a rational faculty, one will wish to know about the peculiarities of its operation as a faculty, about what special characteristics of the mind are manifested in its products. If it is an art determined by its subject matter—the false, the probable, or the verisimilar—whether or not it is acceptable will depend upon the total philosophical outlook of the theorist; moreover, the plots to be used, the traits to be attributed to the characters, the handling of situation and story, will all depend upon this conception of subject matter. If it is an instrumental science, finally, its uses will vary with the sciences which it is made to serve and the ends which it is made to seek; it will be caught inextricably between the principles of the architectonic science and the devices required for achieving the purposes of that science. Thus although the classification "logic, rhetoric, poetic" may seem to be simple enough and traditional enough, it is susceptible of a broad range of interpretations and may produce a whole gamut of diverging theories of the poetic art.

The same is true of the classification of poetry as a part or an instrument of moral philosophy. This may result, for example, from the observation that poetry deals with the moral characters of persons, with their conduct, just as does the science of ethics; both would then have the same subject matter. The principles of behavior established in the theorist's ethics would have to be reflected in poems produced according to his poetics. Or it may result from a conviction with respect to the ends of the sciences: if ethics has as its end to produce happiness in the individual and politics to produce happiness in the state, then poetics belongs to both, since it offers examples of how happiness is achieved or lost by various kinds of persons in various situations. It must therefore offer these examples in such a way that the right moral lessons will be taught and the proper effect produced. But even within these limits there is a fair breadth of possibilities. The poet may be regarded as completely subservient to the moral philosopher or the politician, using his art to achieve the ends of the other. Or he may be on a par with the other, achieving ethical or political ends (determined by himself) by using the resources of his own art. Or he may be completely independent of the other, functioning as an artist who merely happens to cross the path of the moral philosopher when he touches upon character and conduct. According as this theory varies, politics or ethics will be considered as being the "architectonic" science for poetry, or as belonging to the same family, or as having merely a slight and accidental resemblance.

Several explanations might be offered for this great divergency of opinion over the classification of poetics. The most obvious one, of course, would be the nature of the antecedent philosophical tradition and the character of the texts which were being explained or paraphrased or commented upon. Of this, much will be said in subsequent chapters. Another one, and more germane to the present discussion, would be the method of classification itself. Any art may, in the abstract, be considered from a multiplicity of points of view; one may look at it from innumerable external positions, consider it in a large variety of contexts. But these possibilities of discussion need not affect its essence as an art or its place in a total system of philosophy; these may remain firm and fixed if the system itself provides constant principles of classification. For the critics and philosophers of the Cinquecento, two things happened, one dependent upon the other. First, they used each of the many points of view as a basis for classification: if poetry may be considered in the light of the principles of ethics, it is an ethical science; if it uses words as its means, it is a discursive science; and so on. Second, the philosophical systems into which they fitted poetics were incompletely or improperly understood. Various systems which claimed to be Aristotelian resulted in widely different conceptions of the poetic art and of its relationship to the rest of the parts of philosophy. So for those which were admittedly Platonic. The critic might begin with principles which he thought satisfactory for the classification of the sciences; but he might pursue them imperfectly, or he might abandon them without realizing it and pass into an entirely different context of analysis. Such insufficiencies will be found frequently in the documents to be studied. Perhaps this is because the large majority of the men writing on literary matters were not philosophers but critics, not specialists in the formal disciplines of analysis but critics and poets curious about the literary art. This was not always true, however, and in no event should be taken as an explanation or an exculpation.

One may ask, also, whether any change or progress or evolution in the theories of classification is perceptible through the century. This question is difficult to answer. It should be clear that the major theories exist simultaneously throughout the century. Perhaps in the early years the tendency to occupy oneself with complete philosophical systems is more prevalent than in the later. Perhaps also the classification as a discursive science or rational faculty is more prominent in the first part of the century, whereas the classification as a relative of moral philosophy is more frequent in the second part; the "rhetorical" approach gradually gives way to the "ethical." It may also be that only in the last decades of the century do we find any insistence that poetry has the right to be considered an art in itself, that it might be approached from an "artistic" or "aesthetic" point of view. But this is at best a very mild insistence and might almost pass unperceived among the dominant tendencies of the century.

CHAPTER TWO. THE METHODOLOGY OF THE THEORISTS

THE PROBLEM of literary criticism in the Cinquecento was largely a problem in aesthetics. This would, of course, be true of criticism in any place and in any period. But it is true in sixteenth-century Italy in a very special way and for two special reasons. Perhaps more than in any other time and place, the problem of criticism was essentially a theoretical problem. The major effort of the critics was to develop a theory of the literary art; even when they were engaged in practical criticism, their preoccupation was primarily with theory and with the possibilities of applying theory to the judgment of specific works. At all times, they were aware of theoretical cruxes, theoretical difficulties, theoretical modes of approach. Perhaps nowhere else in the intellectual history of the West can one find so continual, so abundant, and so diverse a centering of attention upon problems of literary theory. Moreover, and this is the second reason, the literary aesthetics of the Cinquecento did not develop independently as a free and indigenous flowering. Instead, it was transplanted from Greece and Rome and the European soils of the Middle Ages. It must therefore manifest at all times two concerns, concern with fidelity to the borrowed tradition which it pretended to continue and concern with the usefulness of this tradition for a new age and a new literature.

For the theorist, the task was thus extremely complex. He must discover, first, the meaning of the ancient text or texts which he had set out to interpret—and this at a time when the texts themselves were imperfectly established. The texts, moreover, were difficult ones, which are still subject to much uncertainty and diversity of interpretation. Next, he must decide whether it was possible to reach a satisfactory reading of the text by remaining within the *données* and the arguments of the text itself, or whether he must seek assistance by reference to another of the available ancient texts. Then, when he proceeded to develop his own theory, he must choose between the alternative possibilities of basing it upon a single ancient author or upon a conflation of several ancient authors. Finally, he must see to it that his theory not only fitted the text out of which it grew but that it accounted for and explained and permitted him to judge more recent works by his countrymen and his contemporaries. We should not assume that these problems were posed and solved in a deliberate and conscious fashion by all theorists; they are merely the problems which, somewhere or other in the process of developing a theory, must be considered and resolved.

For the practical critic, the procedure was only slightly less complicated. He, too, had to find a theoretical basis for his criticism, whether he developed his own theory or borrowed one from a contemporary or an ancient philosopher. He had to be versed in the literature of a long and diversified critical tradition. Most important of all, he had to convert the theoretical statements from which he started into guides for the reading of poems, into criteria for the judging of poems, into norms for the admission or exclusion of new literary types, into weapons for current controversy. Perhaps he had also to reconcile the findings of his intellectual explorations with the promptings of his sensitivity, his enthusiasms with contrary theoretical conclusions, his dislikes with the acceptances of a long tradition.

Both the theorist and the practical critic stood at a crucial point in the history of Western criticism, that point at which the doctrines of classical antiquity were transformed into something new and different, which in its turn became the basis of modern literary criticism. From their point of view, the critical process looked essentially backward: it attempted to extract from classical and medieval traditions the lessons needed for the solution of contemporary critical problems. From our point of view, the whole process had consequences for the future of even greater significance; at four centuries' remove, the specific nature of the transformation, the exact character of the new orientations become matters of considerable importance in intellectual history.

It is in the light of these last considerations that the matter of method or methodology becomes vital in the history of Renaissance criticism. Given a limited number of ancient texts; given a medieval tradition in which these texts, when not forgotten, had already suffered a certain transmutation; given a desire to find in these ancient and medieval materials a new critical apparatus: what results from this desire operating on these materials will depend in large part upon the way in which theorists and critics go about the solution of their problems. If the individual theorist comes to his problem with one set of intellectual habits, with one discipline for the reading and interpretation of texts, with one attitude toward the procedures of his predecessors, the theory that he himself propounds will be of one kind. Another habit, another discipline, another attitude might produce an entirely different kind of theory.

In such a situation there are really no constants. The basic texts themselves change from reader to reader; the mode of procedure of each critic will differ in some way from those of all the others; no two of the resulting theories will be exactly identical. Hence the tremendous variety and complexity of critical thought in the Cinquecento. In a sense, the only valid statements one can make are statements about individual authors and individual texts. Nevertheless, there was such a thing as a general current of intellectual discipline through the century. There was a fairly constant formation of habits of mind in the schools, a fairly definite tradition about how certain subjects were to be treated, a relatively widespread assumption with respect to the conduct of an argument. This general tendency—always with variations—formed the basis of the method employed by the individual writer in his theorizing or in his criticism. It is this general method which I wish to describe in the present chapter, as a means to aiding the reader in his understanding of subsequent textual analyses.

CLASSIFICATION AMONG THE SCIENCES

The first characteristic of this method has already been described: the tendency to preface discussion of the poetic art by indicating its position with reference to the other arts and sciences. This effort at classification might take one of several forms: that of situating poetics in the whole family of the components of philosophy; that of relating it to a smaller group of cognate arts such as logic and rhetoric, or to a single sister art such as history; that of transforming it, by a kind of analogy, into a universal art encompassing all other branches of philosophy. The first of these forms has already been studied as symptomatic of a general philosophical approach which in its essence was systematic; the same approach, but reduced in the scope of its intention, is apparent in the second. Of the third and fourth, something further needs to be said.

Let us take, to illustrate how poetics was assimilated to another art, several examples of the relating of poetics to history throughout the century. The problem here, as distinguished from that of the preceding chapter, is not so much to discover the fact or the basis of classification as to determine what methodological approaches are involved in the coupling of the two arts. An early case, from the fifteenth century, is Rodolphus Agricola's *De inventione dialectica*. Here, the two arts are compared, since both of them use words to narrate an order of events which have happened. But whereas history, bent upon representing the truth, gives events in the "natural" order in which they actually occurred, poetry may permit itself an "artificial" order. The typical case is that of the beginning "in medias res" with a later summation of antecedent happenings. As far as method is concerned, Agricola's consists in seeking a factor common to the two arts and in using this factor as a means to comparison and differentiation. Any other features of the arts are left out of consideration.[1]

The procedure of Dionigi Atanagi in his *Ragionamento de la eccellentia et perfettione de la historia* (1559) is much more complex. Atanagi wishes essentially to characterize the art of history; he adopts as the best expedient a lengthy set of likenesses and differences between history and poetry, which incidentally provides a complete theory of poetry. The important

[1] *De inventione dialectica* (Louvain: Martin, 1515), Liber Tertius, fol. b viv: "Est tamen differentia poetice dispositionis ab historia vel maxima: quod poeta solum quantum ad ipsius: hoc est ad narrantis personam pertinet: in speciem tantum. sequitur temporum ordinem. quantum autem est ex rerum gestarum natura: plerunque perturbat eas atque a mediis orditur rebus: deinde quae primae fuerant earum: posterius personae colore alicuius aut alio quouis commento infert mentionem. [Example of *Aeneid*.] Sin vero res ipsas respicimus non personas quibus dat orationem poeta: iam videmus contrarium naturali: id est artificialem ordinem esse. . . . Historie cuius prima laus est veritas: naturalis tamen ordo conuenit. . . ."

difference is not between the use of prose and the use of verse (since some poems are also found in prose), but between the use, or not, of imitation. The differences may be summarized thus:

History	*Poetry*
1. No imitation	Imitation
2. Many actions of many men	Single action of one man
3. Treats the particular, things as they are	Treats the universal, the pure Idea of things
4. Narrates things done as they were done	Narrates things as they should be done, according to necessity, verisimilitude, and probability
5. Presents characters as they were, varied, unstable, etc.	Maintains constancy of character
6. Uncertain and confused order, following events themselves	Certain order, subordinating all events to central plot
7. Natural order, as events happened	Artificial order; beginning "in medias res"
8. Limited by the materials, the truth of the facts	Not limited by facts; extensive additions to produce the marvelous, the stupendous, the delightful
9. Invents speeches attributed to men; real art consists in writing dialogues, orations	Also makes men speak as they should speak
10. Rarely introduces gods or uses personifications	Introduces gods, uses personification, at will
11. Restricted in use of words, sententiae	Freer in use of words, sententiae
12. Literal meanings only for words	Allegorical meanings hidden under literal meanings

The points of likeness or similarity may also be summarized briefly:

1. Both use "proposition" and "narration," but only poetry uses "invocation"
2. Both use the "demonstrative" and the "deliberative" types of rhetoric
3. Both use the "judicial" type, which is, however, more proper to history
4. Both observe prudence and decorum
5. Both seek to teach, to delight, to move, and to bring profit; history especially seeks utility
6. Both use ancient and distant subjects, describe places, peoples, laws, customs, etc.
7. Both use sudden and unexpected accidents, changes of fortune, leading to a wide variety of emotions
8. Both use digressions, amplifications, variety

9. Both use numbers, figures of speech, although different ones
10. Both must represent things in so graphic a way as to make them visible to the eye

What was for Agricola the whole basis of comparison becomes for Atanagi only one of many points of contact between the two arts. His method is to multiply such points of juxtaposition as far as his ingenuity will permit. Each additional point further circumscribes the material or the operation of the art. One ends up with a conception of what poetry is not—as compared to history—and of what it is. What it is is not determined by discovery of a definition (inductively) and by derivation of the consequences of that definition; rather, it comes from an accumulation of isolated descriptive statements, generated dialectically by considering how it resembles and differs from something else. Moreover, the topics which give rise to these statements are themselves significant of a method of thinking about poetry. Roughly, the topics are these: the genus, kind of action, relation to truth and probability, character, order, factualness, dialogue, use of the supernatural, diction, literalness, type of rhetoric, decorum, ends, ornaments, nature of plot, figures, numbers, visual qualities. Presumably, a poem which satisfied all the conditions established by consideration of these topics would be a good poem, whether or not it conformed to such other artistic demands as might be required by a more systematic approach.[2]

A similar approach, but again fairly restricted, is that of the anonymous *Dialogue on History* in MS Vat. Lat. 6528, which I have dated roughly around 1565. As, however, the principal protagonist claims to be maintaining the point of view of Pomponazzi, the ideas would belong to the early part of the century. Here, as we have seen in the preceding chapter, both history and poetry are species of the genus narration, differentiated by the fact that poetry narrates a single action of one man whereas history narrates a single action of many men. The various poetic genres spring from a single source, historical annals: these give rise to the epic through the selection of one exceptionally great man and one of his exceptionally great actions; from the epic springs tragedy; and so on for the rest. Once the poet has dedicated himself to treating the exceptional, he must find a decorum and a style and a diction appropriate to it; thence come into being the various "modes" of poems, the use of verse and of poetic diction, allegory, and prosopopoeia. The procedure is once more to select a single common factor—the narration of an action—to seek a basis of differentiation, and from the single elementary difference so discovered to construct a whole theory of the poetic art.[3]

Giovanni Antonio Viperano, in the first of two treatises on history, the *De scribenda historia* of 1569, also uses as his starting point the genus

[2] *Ragionamento* (1559), pp. 3v–6.
[3] MS Vat. Lat. 6528, fols. 142v, 150v–151.

narration. Within this genus he finds three species, history, poetry, and oratory. (Oratory is included because, according to currently accepted rhetorical doctrines, "narration" was one of the component parts of any speech: "Habet quoque Orator narrationes suas.") Further distinctions sometimes include oratory, sometimes do not. History and poetry differ in the kinds of actions they represent, history using only "res gestas" and poetry "res fictas." Each of the three species has a separate end; indeed, each seems to have several ends, one serving the other. History tries immediately to "narrate well," ultimately to teach proper modes of action and to form character; it is also useful to the other arts, by supplying examples and materials, and should be accompanied by pleasure. Poetry tries immediately to "invent what is proper to each character," finally to bring pleasure through its narration. For oratory, the immediate end is to praise and to blame, but it too seeks to please through narration. Finally, while history guides the mind, poetry arouses and calms the passions. What is interesting in this method is the kind of equivocation by which oratory falls into the same genus as history and poetry and the multiple distinctions applied to these arts.[4]

Viperano's second work, *De scribendis virorum illustrium vitis* (1570), applies the general ideas of the first to the more specific field of biography. The general ideas are not repeated. Instead, biography is discussed in such a way as to indicate that the trilogy history–poetry–oratory is still present in the author's mind. For example, the main task of biography is to present the character of the hero; this will be done properly if all the topics of decorum—age, sex, condition, nation, and so forth—are treated in the way prescribed by the best rhetorical tradition and practised by the best poets.[5]

One final example: A position similar to that of the anonymous *Dialogue on History* is found in Sperone Speroni's *Dialogo dell'historia*, to which I have not been able to assign a date (published 1596). For Speroni also, history and poetry are kinds of narration; poetry narrates one action of one man, history one action of many men. But he goes beyond the *Dialogue* when he introduces the question of truthfulness of subject matter; contrary to what is commonly believed, he says, both poetry and history treat the truth. If one takes three such forms as the annal, history, and poetry, the following distinctions apply: "the annal is true, history is true and worthy, poetry is true and worthy and marvelous." The truth of poetry is changed into something higher and more wonderful through the process of treating it "as it should be" according to necessity and probability; it is this that makes of poetry an imitation. Thus, although poetry is like history in treating the truth, it is unlike it, since it transforms the particular of history into the universal; hence it is a higher and more noble art.[6]

[4] *De scribenda historia* (1576 ed.), esp. pp. 845–48.
[5] *De scribendis vitis* (1570), esp. pp. B4–B4v, Cv.
[6] In *Dialoghi* (1596 ed.), esp. pp. 376, 394–403, 411–412.

What is involved, essentially, in these multiple comparisons of the art of history to the art of poetry is not classification but delimitation. The critic is faced with the problem of explaining the nature of one art. He finds that it is like another art in some salient respect—the use of language, the narration of an action, the treatment of the truth—and he proceeds to search for other points of agreement or disagreement. The more such points he can find, the more complete will be his comparison of the two arts, and hence the more satisfactory will be his description of either one. For poetry, the comparison may be with history or with rhetoric or with painting or with logic; the resulting delineation of the poetic art will be more or less adequate as the other art is ill or well chosen or as the initial point of comparison is appropriate or inappropriate. The potential danger in the method is that the original basis of equivalence may be some aspect of the poetic art which is not really of the essence of the art, and that the whole resulting discussion may therefore deal with auxiliary or incidental or accidental features of the art. Its distinguishing characters as an art may thus never be apprehended. Such a method may also result merely in a collection of traditional statements about the art, of commonplace pros and cons relative to the central topics, with no attempt to examine the art in itself in a systematic way.

The method by which poetry becomes a universal science, containing and transcending all others, is not too different. Once again the critic selects for consideration a single aspect of the poetic art; this is always the same one, the subject matter—or rather the subject matters—of poetry. Subject matters are here taken in the broadest sense: not "human action" or "character" or "the verisimilar," but all the infinite variety of things about which a poet may speak in a poem. If he speaks of the stars, he encompasses astronomy; if he describes a battle, he applies his knowledge of the military art; the wanderings of Odysseus display Homer's expertness in geography; and so forth without end. This is the kind of thinking about poetry which, in the late Greek world, gave rise to such a document as the pseudo-Plutarchian *De Homeri poesi*, which made of Homer the "ocean" of all knowledge. In the Quattrocento, the *De Homeri poesi* was copied in large part by Angelo Poliziano in his *Oratio in expositione Homeri*.[7] In the Cinquecento the same ideas were expressed in such texts as Varchi's *Lezzioni della poetica* (already referred to), Giacopo Grifoli's *Oratio de laudibus poetarum* (1557),[8] Bernardino Parthenio's *Della imitatione poetica* (1560),[9] and numerous others. If, by using this method, it is possible to make of poetry a universal science, it is because that aspect of poetry singled out for attention, its "subject matters," is in no way a distinguishing feature of the art. How the method came to have a degree of authority in

[7] See ed. Lyon, Gryphius (1527–28), *Alter Tomus Operum Angeli Politiani*, pp. 339–75.
[8] In *Orationes* (1557); see p. 48.
[9] See pp. 3–5.

the Renaissance is easily understood. For the systematic philosopher, every science had its specific subject matter, which separated it from all others; but poetry rather than having a single subject matter included all the materials of all the other sciences; hence it must be a universal science and preferable to all the others. The ambiguities involved here in the use of the term "subject matter," the misconceptions with respect to the definition of sciences by their subject matters, the imperfections of the systems which could permit such a logical impossibility, will be immediately apparent.

GLOSSES AND COMMENTARIES

All the procedures involved in classification and in assimilation of poetry to another art were procedures which came to the Renaissance as a part of the antecedent intellectual tradition. The principal method of treating a text, that of the gloss or the extended commentary, was another such heritage from the recent past; as applied to the chief critical texts of antiquity, it constituted one of the standard ways of approaching problems of criticism during the Cinquecento. The method was fairly constant, although as the century progressed some variants were introduced and some refinements added. One took a small section of the text—a short paragraph if it was in prose, or a small number of verses—and printed after it a section of commentary, long or short. Sometimes a marginal notation summarized the content of the commentary. Then the same was done for the next section of the text, and so on to the end. Sometimes at the end, by way of conclusion, a digest or a summary of the comments was given. If the text was in Greek, usually a Latin translation followed it, and after this the commentary; later in the century, the same procedure was followed for vernacular translations and commentaries. Certain authors chose to provide further enlightenment by inserting a paraphrase between translation and commentary, so that the order would be text–translation–paraphrase–commentary. Thus, as time went on, the whole apparatus became more complicated and the commentary much longer. What is important for the student of criticism, of course, is what was said in the commentaries and how they were conceived. A few examples should suffice to illustrate this method.

Pomponio Gaurico's *Super Arte poetica Horatii* was the earliest of the Cinquecento commentaries on the *Ars poetica*; it was written shortly before 1510. Gaurico himself claims in his dedicatory epistle to Francesco Pucci that it is a new kind of commentary, not written "grammaticorum more" as were the earlier ones. Instead of writing a grammatical gloss on the separate words of the text, Gaurico does a continuous prosification of the epistle, in which he attempts to distinguish and clarify Horace's meaning. At intervals corresponding to sections of the text, he reduces that meaning to concise precepts and these precepts (some forty in all) are collected together in a brief final section of the commentary. There is little in the way of explanation, although occasionally examples from ancient art or literature are added. A commentary of this type does little more than extract the barest meaning from the *Ars poetica* and isolate a given number of critical ideas. It makes no attempt to discover the philosophical structure of the work, the reasons for the order of presentation of ideas, the conception of the poetic art contained within it. The later edition of Gaurico, published in 1541, intercalates the commentary among passages of the text, divided into thirty-seven sections; in this form, both text and commentary are fragmented, and any semblance of synthesis is destroyed. Indeed, such fragmentation may prevent the reader from seeing the work as a whole; and if it is badly done, if the points of separation are badly chosen, a totally false conception of the meaning of the text may result.

A much more highly developed form of the same method is found in Giovanni Battista Pigna's *Poetica Horatiana* of 1561. Once the text has been divided into sections—there are eighty in Pigna's division—and the "precept" stated for each fragment, the commentator proceeds to an elaborate exposition of the ideas of the text. He cites supporting or illustrative passages from innumerable other theorists—Cicero, Quintilian, Aristotle, Plutarch, Donatus, Plato—from miscellaneous philosophical texts on other sciences, finally from many poets who demonstrate Horace's principles. He goes into lengthy discussions of individual words and phrases, citing the authority of previous expositors of the text and seeking clarification from other texts. Sometimes this leads to the most astonishing results: the first four lines of the *Ars poetica* are made to refer, for example, to the four genres distinguished by Aristotle, with the "caput humanum" standing for the epic, the "ceruicem equinam" for tragedy, the "collatas plumas" for the dithyramb and the lyric, and the "atrum piscem" for comedy. Moreover, certain distinctions from other sciences are made to bear upon the text; in an introduction, Pigna insists that the work must be studied in the light of "res" and "verba" (an essentially grammatical distinction) and these in turn in their relationship to "invention, disposition, and elocution" (an essentially rhetorical distinction). Thus, in spite of his contention that all of Horace's precepts are linked in a tight chain, the work becomes more confused as he expounds it, and all sense of an orderly development is lost.[10]

Some of the same characteristics—not to say vices—of procedure are apparent in Pietro Vettori's extensive commentary on the *Poetics*, his *Commentarii in primum librum Aristotelis de arte poetarum* (1560). Here the approach is much more carefully philological; the Greek text is closely studied, useful emendations are suggested, better translations are proposed. But there is still no comprehensive interpretation of the text as a whole. At best, there are certain general notions which determine the interpretation of specific passages: the idea that all poetry must be in verse, the idea that

[10] *Poetica Horatiana* (1561); see p. 3.

the treatment of the poem must be such as to assure the persuasion and the pleasure of the audience. Unfortunately, these ideas are such as to lead to a warping rather than to a clarification of Aristotle's meaning, and they are not capable of binding into an organized whole the multiple passages into which the text has been broken.

Even so few examples as these—and many others will be examined in detail in later chapters—are sufficient to illustrate the disruptive effect of the consistent use of the textual gloss. Such a gloss was frequently helpful from the linguistic or philological standpoint, and the Cinquecento contributed considerably to the accuracy and the intelligibility of the critical texts involved. From the philosophical standpoint, it was almost always disadvantageous. It inculcated and promoted the habit of regarding texts as collections of fragments and hence as collections of isolated precepts; contrariwise, it prevented any effort to see over and beyond the single line or paragraph to the total philosophical form of the work. It encouraged a miscellaneous citing of parallel or similar passages from other works and a kind of frantic search for outside "authorities" of no matter how different a general philosophical tendency. As a result, Horace ceased to be Horace and Aristotle never became Aristotle; each grew, instead, into a vast monument containing all the multiform remains of the literary past.

SCHOLASTIC APPROACHES

I have characterized this use of the textual commentary as a method which came to the Cinquecento from the antecedent literary tradition; I might have called it frankly a "scholastic" method. Certain other approaches could also be described, somewhat loosely, as remains of the scholastic tradition. One such approach would be the use of a fairly standard formula for the introduction of any subject. After the prolusio, in which the author indicated the place of his particular subject among the other sciences, he might well indicate how he meant to go about treating it. For many authors, the pattern would be the same. In the prefatory materials to his great commentary on Aristotle (1548), for example, Francesco Robortello says that he means to discuss "what the poetic faculty is, and what effect it has; what end it proposes for itself; what is the subject matter out of which it makes its product."[11] Similarly, the "Prolegomena" to Vincenzo Maggi's *In Aristotelis librum de poetica communes explanationes* (1550) contains a program for Maggi's own treatment of the Aristotelian text. He will discuss, in order, the "subject, its usefulness, the title, in what order the author should be read, the divisions of the text, the method of instruction, and under what faculty the latter falls."[12] In the field of practical

---

[11] *In librum Aristotelis de arte poetica explicationes* (1548), p. 1: "Qualis sit poëtica facultas, & quam habeat uim; Quem finem propositum; Quam materiem subiectam, ex qua opus suum conficiat."

[12] *Explanationes* (1550 ed.), p. 13: "scriptionis Propositum, Vtilitas, Inscriptio, Quo ordine auctor legi debeat, Diuisio, Doctrinae uia, Quamque haec sub facultatem cadat."

criticism, Marcantonio Maioragio applies to the analysis of Book IV of the *Aeneid* a set of eight topics which he admittedly borrows from Averroës; the text is Preface VIII of the *Orationes et praefationes*, written around 1550, published in 1582; the topics are, respectively, "the purpose, the utility, the order, the division, the proportion, the method of instruction, the name of the book, the name of the author."[13] Such programs as these made for a semblance of order in the handling of a subject, providing as they did a kind of advance outline for the consecutive discussion of a number of important points relevant to the materials. They came into being, indeed, as a means of assuring the consideration of these points somewhere in the course of the discussion. But as is the case with many rules of thumb, they tended to replace active thinking about poetics by routine answering of a set of questions. The various parts of the outline were considered as isolated topics, without the necessary illumination of any one of the topics by the answers found for the others.

For the same advantages of order and completeness, theorists and critics used another such fixed system for organizing their ideas on the poetic art. It was one which had very ancient and very firm philosophical bases and which had contributed to the later Middle Ages and to the humanistic period a mold for their intellectual procedures: namely, the method of the "four causes." In the Cinquecento, the mold was sometimes used in a much reduced form, sometimes fully developed and realized. An example of the former type might be found in Maggi's *Explanationes* (1550), where he points out first that the end of poetry is, "by imitating human actions through pleasant language, to ennoble the mind," and later that its material is the "human mind, which it proposes to refine with the best principles of conduct";[14] another would be Alessandro Lionardi's *Dialogi della inventione poetica* (1554), where—almost in passing—the author remarks that "every oration and speech consists in the form, which is eloquence, in the matter, which is the thing proposed, and in the end, which is the listener."[15] Here there is obviously only a vague reflection of the method and little comprehension of it. As employed by Filippo Sassetti in his marginalia to Piccolomini's *Annotationi* (1575), the form is still abbreviated; he merely says that "one might say that the efficient cause of poetry was the poet himself, the formal cause the imitation, the material cause the verse, and the final cause pleasure."[16] In spite of its brevity, this statement is revela-

---

[13] *Orationes et praefationes* (1582), p. 178: "intentionem, utilitatem, ordinem, diuisionem, proportionem, uiam doctrinae, nomen Libri, nomen authoris."

[14] *Explanationes* (1550 ed.), p. 13: "actiones humanas imitando, suaui sermone animum excultum reddere"; and "animus scilicet humanas: quem ... optimis moribus sibi expoliendum proponit."

[15] *Dialogi* (1554), p. 15: "nella forma che è l'eloquenza, nella materia, che è la cosa proposta, et nel fine, che è l'uditore, consiste ogni oratione & parlamento."

[16] BNF Postillati 15, p. 65: "si potrebbe dire, che la causa efficiente della Poesia fusse lo stesso Poeta la formale l'imitatione la materiale il uerso, e la finale il diletto."

tory of the whole theory of poetics held by Sassetti; it indicates the usefulness of the method for concentrating the attention on certain central problems of the art and for eliciting definite pronouncements about those problems.

All four of the causes are present in Julius Caesar Scaliger's *Poetices libri* (*septem* 1561), but in a strange way; they are introduced at a point where Scaliger is making the traditional distinction among the terms poesis, poema, and poeta. "Poema," he says, "is the work itself, the matter ... which is made. But poesis is the reason and the form of the poem"; poeta is of course the poet. Then he concludes his argument: "Thus you have three causes, the material, the formal, and the efficient; and in the preceding commentary the final, that is, imitation, or the ultimate end, instruction." What is strange is the assigning of the meanings of poema and poesis to the first two causes (to say nothing of the interpretations given the other two) and the attempt to combine this analysis with the traditional definitions.[17]

Lionardo Salviati, in his *Commentary on Aristotle's Poetics*, 1585–86, exploits the method to a much fuller extent, actually basing upon it a good deal of his preliminary discussion of the *Poetics*. In a section entitled "Agente, materia, forma, fine, e difinizione del poema," he interprets the causes thus: "The cause of the poem, that cause I say which is called acting or efficient, is the soul of the poet operating through habit or disposition or moved by the divine spirit as the case may be. ... The matter of the same poem is indeed the verisimilar expressed through ornamented speech. ... The form is the flawless disposition." The final cause, "which concerns moral character," is treated only much later, when Salviati finally decides that the special and ultimate final cause of poetry is "to profit and delight by imitating with verse." Since the major part of the work is, however, a running commentary on Aristotle, the method is soon abandoned and does not in any sense inform the rest of the treatment.[18]

In various other texts—for example, Niccolò Rossi's *Discorsi intorno alla tragedia* (1590, p. 21v) and Jacopo Mazzoni's *Della difesa della Comedia di Dante* (1587; pp. 63 ff.)—all or several of the causes appear incidentally in the course of the development. Indeed, it is because, essentially, the method is employed as incidental to some other frame of discussion, because it is never fully exploited in its own right as capable of producing a total and exhaustive analysis, that it fails to contribute as

---

[17] *Poetice* (1581 ed.), p. 13: "Poema est opus ipsum: materia ... quae fit. Poesis autem, ratio ac forma Poematis ..." and "Ita habes causas tres, Materiam, Formam, Efficientem: & in superiori commentario Finem, id est, Imitationem, siue vlteriorem finem, doctionem ..."

[18] MS BNF II, II, 11, fols. 9–9v: "La cagione del poema, la cagione dico, la quale agente, o uero efficiente è chiamata, è l'anima del poeta, o habituata, o disposta, o mossa da diuino spirito, ch'ella si sia. ... La materia del medesimo poema si è il uerisimile espresso col fauellar condito. ... La forma è la disposizione senza fallo"; fol. 13, "il quale è intorno a' costumi"; fol. 151v: "Giouare e dilettare imitando col uerso."

completely as it might to a clarification of critical ideas. The eclectic tendency, the wish to amalgamate all possible methods of approach within a single treatise, easily led to the nullification of the best characteristics of the best methods. Moreover, knowing of the existence of a method and something about its general nature did not assure that it would be properly applied; the few examples cited here, with the variety of solutions proposed, should suffice to suggest that there was, in this century, no sure grasp on the logical instruments that would have been needed to make of the device of the four causes a valid basis for discussion of the poetic art.

In the field of practical criticism, one of the favorite devices was the full-scale "Sposizione" of a text. Since it wished to be full-scale, it operated most readily on shorter texts such as the sonnet. There are, throughout the Cinquecento, as there had been in the Quattrocento, innumerable lectures, discourses, epistles which take the form of the "Exposition"; mostly, they concern themselves with sonnets of Petrarch. The intention in this form is usually to develop and expound the ideas contained in the poem. After a paraphrase of the sonnet and a restatement of its principal idea, the author usually proceeds to a discussion of the idea itself, its philosophical backgrounds and implications, its validity and usefulness for human conduct. The poem, in a sense, provides the text for a sermon or a philosophical disquisition that soon leaves the poem entirely out of consideration. Rarely do these expositions make any reference to the artistic structure and qualities of the poem or attempt to evaluate it as a work of art. Such documents belong rather to the history of some other branch of philosophy than aesthetics in the Cinquecento, and I have hence omitted them almost entirely from the materials to be considered in the present work.

FOUR CHARACTERISTIC METHODS

All that the Italian sixteenth century did in the way of method was not, however, a piecemeal and imperfect combination of approaches inherited from its recent past. Writers of the century developed, as the years went by, a set of characteristic methods that were their own—which had, to be sure, many ties with the past, which had been practiced before and which have been practiced since, but which nevertheless may be studied as representing the predominant modes of development and presentation of ideas. As the first among these, we may examine the method of imitation of a single ancient text. Theorists who wished to develop a theory of a literary genre which had not been satisfactorily treated in antiquity— comedy, say, or the romance of chivalry—would take as their model some ancient theoretical text. The rules for the new genre would merely be the old rules transposed to fit the special circumstances of subject matter or end or manner of the genre in question. The ancient text most frequently used as the model was, of course, Aristotle's *Poetics*; hence the production of a large number of "Aristotelian" theories of the minor or the recent literary genres—or, in fact, of any genre which Aristotle himself had not completely explored.

We may take, as an example of this methodological phenomenon, Giovanni Battista Pigna's *I romanzi* (1554), which is a lengthy study of the "romance" form as practiced by Italian poets. Pigna himself, at the end of Book I, which is devoted to the general theory of the romance, confesses his indebtedness to Aristotle:

> This is what I have thought proper to say about the romance considering it in general. Although I have never mentioned Aristotle while speaking about it, that does not mean that I have not used the whole of his *Poetics*, making use of every part of its. And just as this same Aristotle gave us light on the subject of the duel, which he had never seen, so here he has been our guide on the subject of romances, even though he had never spoken of them.

The way in which Aristotle is "used" is of the highest interest. The skeleton outline of Book I, called "Argomento del primo libro," shows in brief how the framework of the *Poetics* is transferred in part to the discussion of the new form:

> First words and subject matters are treated generally. And then the epic is taken up, which is considered with respect to the plot; and thence springs the conclusion that imitation and narration are practically opposites; and then the role of truth and of verisimilitude, and how the action may be made illustrious and how it may be made one. Similarly we derive the plot of one and of two kinds, and the simple, complex, passionate, and ethical types of plot. Under the complex type come the six kinds of recognition, and reversal; which last contains the question as to whether good poets should be banned from the republic. Under the ethical type the four requirements for character are expounded. And all of this discussion concerns the qualitative parts. With respect to the quantitative parts there is the matter of composition, and the introduction of beginnings without going back to the first origins of the story; and in giving the reason for this we then discuss why tragedy is greater than epic. And then there is the resolution, which brings with it the treatment of the "deus ex machina" and of the Fates. Next come the episodes both good and bad, which are divided into "epangelia" [those narrated] and "amaprattomena" [those actually acted], under which fall the cantos and the knights errant and the paladins, all of which are explained. . . .

This outline is followed fairly closely in Book I, although many other ideas intervene and there are lengthy digressions; moreover, at many points not referred to in the outline, Aristotle is called upon for distinctions and clarification. Thus the initial distinction between poetry and history (p. 2) is from *Poetics* 1451b5; the definition of plot as imitation (p. 15) from 1450a4; the differentiation of imitations according to object, manner, and means (p. 15) from 1447a15; and so on down the line. All this does not mean, however, that Pigna agrees with Aristotle on all points or even that he accepts the general body of Aristotelian doctrine. It merely means that

POETIC THEORY

he borrows from the *Poetics* a relatively complete schematism for the handling of the genre.[19]

Francesco Robortello appended to his commentary on Aristotle's *Poetics* (1548), a short treatise on comedy, in which the method is again the imitation of the procedures of the basic text. The treatise is very short (less than ten folio pages); hence it presents a kind of epitome of all that Aristotle said about tragedy translated into terms of comedy. All of Aristotle's direct statements about comedy are of course included, and to them are added whatever materials Robortello could find in such supplementary sources as Donatus, Vitruvius, and Cicero. A brief outline of the contents will show how the method works. Robortello begins with a statement of the end of poetry. He then differentiates imitations according to means, object, and manner, indicating in each case which are used by comedy. There follows (as in Aristotle) a brief history of the origins of the genre; then the causes for its invention—man's instinct to imitate, and so forth; then the growth and development of the form, and the time of its invention as compared with that of tragedy. For a long section on the types of comedy, he draws heavily on Donatus; but his imitation of Aristotle on tragedy is apparent. In the discussion of the qualitative parts, he paraphrases or transposes Aristotle, making almost identical statements about plot, the kinds of recognition, knot, and solution; about the four requirements for character (with some parallels taken from Horace); about sententiae and diction. For what he has to say about apparatus or spectacle, however, he rests upon Vitruvius, and for the quantitative parts he refers directly to Donatus. The final statements about the limitation to five acts and the number of interlocutors are ascribed to Horace and Donatus. In spite of these supplementary borrowings, however, the core of the work still follows the outline of the *Poetics*.[20]

A clear statement of the intention to imitate a single text is found in the prefatory section of Antonio Riccoboni's *De re comica*, which is itself an

[19] *I romanzi* (1554), p. 65: "Questo è quello che intorno al Romancio m'è paruto di dire, generalmente considerandolo. del quale mentre ho fauellato, quantunque d'Aristotile mai mentione fatto non habbia; non è stato però che di tutta la sua Poetica seruito non mi sia, tutta maneggiandola. Et come in tutto il Duello non mai da lui veduto, lume ne diede esso Aristotile; cosi quiui ne Romanzi è stato la nostra guida: benche egli mai non ne parlasse"; p. a2: "Prima delle parole, & delle materie generalmente si tratta. Et pigliasi l'Epopeia: la quale è considerata in quanto alla fauola. & cosi ne nasce, come l'imitare & il narrare sieno quasi contrarij: & la parte del uero & del uerisimile. & come l'attione sia illustre: & come una. ne nasce parimente la fauola d'un genere & di due: & il genere semplice, il composto, il perturbato & il costumato. sotto il composto sono sei agnitioni, & la peripetia: che contiene la quistione, che è, se i poeti da una buona republica si scaccino. sotto il costumato i quattro decori si espongono. & tutto cio intorno alla qualità. Nella quantità euui il comporre: & l'introducimento de principij senza la prima origine. & nel render la cagione di cio, segue perche da piu sia la Tragedia che la Epopeia: & ui è lo sciorre: che con seco porta il trattare della machina, & delle Fate. Vengono gli Episodij & i uitiosi & i buoni, che diuisi sono in epangelia & in amaprattomena. sotto i quali cadono i canti & i cauaglieri erranti & i paladini: che tutti si dichiarano...."

[20] Part II of the *In librum Aristotelis de arte poetica explicationes* (1548), pp. 41–50.

[52]

appendix to his translation of the *Poetics* (1579). The full title is "De re comica ex Aristotelis doctrina," and the purpose is summarized thus:

> ... with respect to comedy, on the one hand to collect together everything that is found in that most authoritative philosopher, on the other hand also, in imitation of those things which have been written down about tragedy and the epic, to devise some precepts which will in no way disagree with the Aristotelian theory, and by means of which comedy may be created in a laudable fashion. We shall do this in such a way as to investigate first the origin of comedy; then what comedy is; in the third place what qualitative parts it has; in the fourth place, what quantitative parts; finally, what kinds of ridiculous things they are that serve the purposes of comedy.

The program here outlined is virtually a complete listing of the later chapter headings, except for such additions as the chapters for the various "parts."[21]

Such imitative treatises, long or short, constituted a large part of the theoretical effort of the century. They will be examined, along with the theories they produced, in later chapters.

The second of the characteristic methods of the Cinquecento was the systematic comparison or combination of two different texts of classical antiquity. The method was most constantly applied to Horace's *Ars poetica*, which presented to the commentators grave problems of understanding and interpretation; therefore, they sought clarification in a point-by-point paralleling of the text with Aristotle's *Poetics*. The initial assumption was that the two works said essentially the same things about the poetic art and that if one sought carefully one could find identical statements in both. Moreover, since the order of the *Poetics* was clearer, it was even thought that the same order was followed by Horace. If, then, order and ideas were generally the same, Horace could be easily understood as a kind of Latinization of the Greek *Poetics*. Such indeed is the point of view of Vincenzo Maggi in his *In Q. Horatii Flacci de arte poetica librum ad Pisones, Interpretatio*, appended to his 1550 commentary on the *Poetics*. His statement could not be more specific:

> Since indeed those two parts of this little book which we have declared the fundamental ones were written almost entirely in imitation of Aristotle's *Poetics*, I believed that it would be useful if, after having explained all matters pertinent to the *Poetics* of Aristotle, ... I were able to demonstrate that those things which

---

[21] In *Aristotelis ars poetica* (1579 ed.), pp. 433-34: "tum de Comoedia ea colligere omnia, quaecunque apud grauissimum philosophum reperiuntur: tum uero ad imitationem eorum, quę de Tragoedia, & de Epopoeia tradita sunt, praecepta quaedam conformare, ab Aristotelica doctrina non abhorrentia, quibus confici Comoedia laudabiliter possit. Quod ita faciemus, vt primum originem Comędiae inuestigemus: deinde quid sit Comoedia: tertio loco quas partes habeat qualitatis: quarto quas quantitatis: postremo cuiusmodi sint ridicula illa, quae rei comicae seruiunt." The 1587 ed., p. 140, substitutes the following sentence: "ut naturam eius inuestigemus ex genere, & differentijs Poesis: ex ipsius origine: ex similitudine, & dissimilitudine, quam habet cum alijs Poesibus, & imitationibus: ex definitione: ex partibus qualitatis: ex partibus quantitatis: ex pulcherrima constitutione."

are found in Horace are already found in Aristotle, as in a spring from which he made this book flow like a small river.

In the treatise that follows, Maggi's only interest is to demonstrate the conformity between the two texts. The first thirteen lines of Horace, for example, are equivalent to what Aristotle has to say about plot; no less than five passages in Aristotle—referred to by the numbers earlier assigned by Maggi in his commentary on the *Poetics*—are adduced as parallels. Lines 14–23 refer to episodes; compare passages from Aristotle on episodes. The same procedure continues for the whole of the Horatian text. Wherever Maggi is unsuccessful in finding a comparable text in Aristotle, he declares that the passage in the *Ars poetica* is a digression; for example, most of the final section on the poet, lines 412 ff. to the end, is so labeled. Besides the indication of the parallels, there is little of interest for the theory of poetry in the Maggi text.[22]

Sometimes the search for parallels is less dogged and unimaginative. At the very end of the century, for example, in 1599, Antonio Riccoboni published his *De Poetica Aristoteles cum Horatio collatus*. In the course of the work he cited all the *Ars poetica*, broken up into small sections and rearranged according to the needs of his outline. That outline itself was very simple, containing the following general headings: On the nature of poetry; On the causes of poetry; On the kinds of imitations and poems; On the qualitative parts; On the quantitative parts; On faults and their excuse. Under each of these headings he placed a prose passage meant to summarize the doctrine of Aristotle relevant to that heading; then followed the passages from Horace which he thought pertinent. Riccoboni's approach differs from Maggi's insofar as he seeks correspondence only between the doctrine of Aristotle and the passages from Horace, not between passage and passage.

A variant on this technique, which really constitutes a third method characteristic of the century, is the conflation of one text with several others. Rather than limiting himself to a Horace-Aristotle comparison, the theorist introduces a triple or a quadruple analogy, thereby enriching his commentary and making his interpretation more complex. This is the procedure of Giacopo Grifoli in the *In Artem poeticam Horatii interpretatio* (1550). An initial statement in the introduction makes the point that, whereas Horace treats the same materials as Aristotle, he does so in a different order:

> Seeing then that in Aristotle's opinion tragedy is composed of plot, character, thought, diction, spectacle, and melody, he decided to discuss the constitution of

---

[22] *Interpretatio* (1550), esp. p. 328: "Quoniam uero partes illae duae libelli huius, quas praecipuas esse diximus, totae ferè ad Poetices Aristotelis imitationem conscriptae sunt: non inutile futurum existimaui, si postquam ea, quae ad Aristotelis Poeticam attinebant, explicauimus; cuius ratione omnis mihi fuerat susceptus labor; quae hic ab Horatio habentur, in Aristotele, uelut in fonte demonstrarem, à quo uelut riuulum, librum hunc deduxit."

THE METHODOLOGY OF THE THEORISTS

the plot first since it contains the basis for the imitation of the whole object; then, since character and thought are expressed through words, he began to elaborate on style immediately after plot. In this he did not follow either the order or the plan of Aristotle; for the latter treated character after plot, then thought, then diction, and he handled all of these in detail. But Horace, seeing that, although it is said that a play is "acted", there is no place in thought or character (that is, περὶ διανοίας, ἢ περὶ μύθου) which is not treated by means of speech, believed that by discussing speech, even changing the order of Aristotle and omitting all those points over which there is no controversy, he could most conveniently progress in both to those places to which he might wish to come. And so in the second place he spoke of diction. . . .[23]

This analysis of Horace's attitude toward the text of Aristotle prepares the way for the second of the fundamental analogies in Grifoli's text. This is an implicit one. The order suggested in the passage above—plot, then diction—brings to mind the traditional divisions of Ciceronian or pseudo-Ciceronian rhetoric, i.e., invention, disposition, and elocution. It is not long before Grifoli specifically sees these divisions as supplying the ordering principle of at least certain parts of Horace's text. Thus the passage in the commentary on verses 32–45:

And at the same time he touches upon the three points which belong to the orator's faculty, invention, elocution, and disposition. And because he had used a turned-about order, placing elocution before disposition (a thing which he did for a reason, since he here is treating of language proper to the matter and this is the right place for language), and then speaking lightly and in passing about disposition, nevertheless returning to his order, after having said a little about disposition he now comes back to elocution . . . .[24]

To the first assumption that Horace is following Aristotle's division into six qualitative parts is added, then, a second assumption that he is following the commonplace three-way rhetorical distinction. Grifoli's commentary will, therefore, shift back and forth between these two analyses, although the comparison with Aristotle remains the dominant one.

The situation is in a sense reversed in the commentary of Giason

[23] *Interpretatio* (1550), esp. pp. 11–12: "Videns igitur Aristotelis iudicio Tragoediam constare fabula, moribus, sententia, dictione, apparatu, & melodia; primum de constitutione fabulae disserendum esse statuit, nam rei totius imitandae rationem ea continet: deinde, cum mores, & sententiae verbis explicentur, orationem statim post fabulam coepit expolire; in quo non est secutus nec ordinem, nec rationem Aristotelis, nam hic post fabulam mores, tum sententiam, post dictionem explicauit, atque de his omnibus omnia diligenter executus est. Videns autem Horatius, quamuis agi fabula dicatur, tamen nullum esse locum aut de sententia, aut de more idest περὶ διανοίας, ἢ περὶ μύθου qui non tractetur oratione, existimauit de ea disserendo, etiam mutata Aristotelis dispositione, ac omissis ijs omnibus de quibus nulla est controuersia, se posse quàm commodissimè ad quos vellet vtriusque locos peruenire. Itaque secundo loco de oratione dixit. . . ."

[24] *Ibid.*, pp. 24–25: "Atque simul tres partes attigit quae sunt in oratoris vi sitae. Inuentionem, elocutionem & dispositionem. Et quia praepostero vsus erat ordine, praeponens elocutionem dispositioni, quod tamen cum causa fecit, cum de oratione hic apta rei tractet, & proprius orationis sit hic locus. Et de dispositione casu, & obiter loquatur, tamen in ordinem hęc suum redigens, vbi pauca de Dispositione dixit, ad Elocutionem redijt. . . ."

Denores, *In epistolam Q. Horatij Flacci de arte poetica* (1553). Here the major point of reference is the invention—disposition—elocution schema, as Denores indicates at the beginning: "... in this same epistle to the Pisos are collected together by Horace, who chose them from various works by many authors, the points which seemed to him to be essential for the judging of the writings of poets or for the formation of our taste with respect to every rule of invention, disposition, and elocution in every type of poetry."[25] Denores follows this schematism faithfully throughout. The first lines of the *Ars poetica*, he says, concern invention; lines 24-31 make distinctions relative to elocution; lines 32-41 are on disposition, as are lines 42-45; lines 46-72 treat certain problems of elocution; and so forth. However, from the very beginning the parallels with Aristotle are presented either implicitly or explicitly. So Denores' first remark about invention is that it is the "anima" of poetry: the term comes directly from Aristotle's characterization of plot. Figurative language (*in re* lines 46-72) is pleasurable because of the imitation involved, and imitation itself is enjoyable because it is a source of knowledge; compare Aristotle. In a similar way, Denores constantly brings in from the *Poetics* statements or comparisons which illuminate his essentially rhetorical interpretation.

Such a method is among the most dangerous of those used by theorists of the Cinquecento: dangerous in the sense that it must inevitably result in hopeless deformation of the texts involved. The mere fact that it should have been practiced so widely is symptomatic of the philosophical naïveté of its users. They discovered certain obvious parallels or similarities between texts; this led them to seek other less obvious agreements, to the point where the texts became totally equivalent. What they did not realize was that two texts having occasional similarities may, in their essence, present completely different theories of the poetic art. Aristotle and Horace do touch upon a certain number of common topics; but the one is essentially concerned with the internal structures of poems as these become beautiful objects of contemplation, the other with the making of poems which will have a specific effect upon a given audience at a particular time. To generalize from the accidental similarities to an identity of doctrine in the *Poetics* and the *Ars poetica* is to indicate complete failure to understand either text. To read Horace as if he were Aristotle or Aristotle as if he were Horace is to eliminate all possibility of ever arriving at a proper interpretation of either. This error on the part of the Cinquecento was of course correlative to other errors already noted, especially the tendency to reduce texts to series of isolated fragments, thereby destroying their basic philosophical integrity.

[25] *In epistolam* (1553), p. 5v: "in hac ipsa ad Pisones uel de poetarum scriptis diiudicandis, uel communiter de nostris ingenijs ad omnem inuentionis, dispositionisque, ac elocutionis rationem in quocunque poematum genere formandis, quae praecipua uidebantur, ex uarijs multorum libris excerpta diligentissime ab Horatio colliguntur."

A fourth characteristic approach of critics in this century was the constant attempt to reconcile divergent positions. When "authorities" were recognized as equally valid, differences of opinion between them must be explained away and ultimate agreement must be discovered. Perhaps the central figure in such discussions was Plato, whose attacks upon poetry in the *Republic* needed to be reconciled on the one hand with his own defences of it in other dialogues and on the other hand with the numerous "apologies" by other "authorities" and with such a position as Aristotle's. The passages in the *Republic* on the banishment of the poets were at the center of attention and controversy all through the humanistic period and the Cinquecento. One of the favorite arguments in the attempt to reconcile Plato with himself was to insist that he banished, after all, only those poets whose writings contained undesirable moral teachings. That is the point of view of such a writer as Lodovico Ricchieri (Caelius Rhodiginus) in his *Lectionum antiquarum libri XXX* (1516):

> But with respect to these [fables for the young] we must note carefully that the poets are not condemned outright by Plato; since to the degree in which he holds that they should be rejected when they disturb the state and invent shameful things, to that same degree he embraces them and kisses them tenderly when they exhort to moral improvement, celebrating elegantly and eloquently in their praises of heroes or their hymns to the gods.[26]

After this statement, Ricchieri goes on to cite others of the *Dialogues* in which Plato praises poets and poetry. Giacopo Grifoli's opinion, in the *Oratio de laudibus poetarum* (1557), is similar: despite all that might be said in favor of poets, Plato banished them because of their wicked doctrines:

> In truth we must believe that that famous philosopher condemned the teachings of poets, even though he himself had called them the fathers of all wisdom; or that he banished them because they were harmful, even though he himself had declared that they were the go-betweens of the gods; and although he held that their poems are not human inventions but gifts of the gods, he ordered that they should be driven from the territory of his state because they were wicked.[27]

This type of analysis of the various Platonic texts does one of two things: it concludes that good poets remain acceptable in the state while bad ones are excluded, or it decides that only poems with undesirable moral tendencies are the objects of Plato's attack. What it does not do is discover that different conclusions about poetry are reached in different texts because of the fact that the problems posed and the contexts established are themselves

---

[26] *Lectionum* (1516), p. 158: "Sed in iis illud impense animaduertendum, non damnari prorsum à Platone Poetas, Siquidem quantum, ubi perturbant, aut turpia fingunt, reiiciendos putat, tantundem amplexatur, exosculaturque, si ad bonam frugem hortentur, laudibus heroum aut Deorum hymnis eleganter, facundeque concelebratis."

[27] In *Orationes* (1557), p. 59: "est vero credendum illum philosophum doctrinam damnasse poetarum, qui eosdem ipse sapientiae patres appellarit, aut tanquam perniciosos exclusisse, quos idem interpretes deorum testetur esse, & quorum poemata non hominum inuenta, sed munera coelestia esse ducat, hos tanquàm impios arcendos à finibus ciuitatis suae statuisse."

different. Plato is seeking answers to widely divergent questions in the *Symposium* and the *Republic* and the *Laws*; hence, what he has to say about poetry will in each case be influenced by the special context in which he is considering it. That this was not realized, or was realized rarely, by the critics of the Renaissance is again explained by their general method: fragmentation and the concentration on the isolated passage did not lead to an awareness of the total philosophical meaning of texts and of the relationship of any individual passage to that meaning. At times, of course, this kind of awareness was present. We may take as an example Marcantonio Maioragio's statement in the "Oratio XXIV: De arte poetica" of the *Orationes et praefationes* (ca. 1550):

The fact that Plato led the poets out of his state is no argument against them, especially since in many other places Plato himself praises them to the skies with almost divine commendations and admires them to a most extraordinary degree. Indeed, just as in that state, where nobody is sick at all but all are healthy and sound of body, there is no need for doctors, so Plato, since he was inventing a state most blessed and most wise in all things, removed the poets from it, because for that state, which had already achieved the highest end, there seemed to be no further need for any teachers of living, for any instructions, for any precepts of conduct, for in itself it was ready for good and blessed living.[28]

Here Maioragio realizes that, within the assumption of the *Republic* that all things are considered with reference to the achievement of justice within the state, poetry is unnecessary or undesirable as a means to that justice. But such a realization, along with the making of distinctions that it involves, is relatively rare in the Cinquecento.

It was this wish to explain away Plato's banishment of the poets which led, to a large degree, to the most common construction put upon the "purgation" clause in Aristotle's *Poetics*. Here we are confronted not so much with an attempt to reconcile two contradictory texts as with the interpretation of one text in the light of the other, on the grounds that both are talking about the same thing. Plato had banished the poets because of their undesirable moral effects; Aristotle, who wished in all things to contradict Plato, said that their moral effect was desirable; it consisted precisely in the "purgation" of pity and fear. So runs the argument. One variation of it is found in Lodovico Castelvetro's *Chiose intorno al libro del comune di Platone* (ca. 1570); Castelvetro argues that whereas Plato assumes that the examples found in poems must be followed by their readers, Aristotle answers that they may be either followed or rejected:

[28] *Orationes et praefationes* (1582), p. 147v: "quod autem è ciuitate sua Plato poetas eduxerit, id quidem nullum est contra illos argumentum. cum praesertim alijs in locis plurimis idem Plato propè diuinis in cęlum laudibus eosdem efferat, & mirandum in modum admiretur. Verum quemadmodum in ea ciuitate, ubi nullus omnino sit aegrotus, sed omnes bene ualentes, & corpore bene constituto, nihil medicis opus est, ita Plato cum omnium beatissimam & sapientissimam fingeret ciuitatem, ex ea poetas eduxit, quoniam ei ciuitati, quae iam optimum finem esset consecuta, nullis uitae magistris, nullis institutionibus, nullis morum praeceptis amplius opus esse uidebatur, cum per se contenta esset ad benè beateque uiuendum."

THE METHODOLOGY OF THE THEORISTS

In this passage [*Rep.* III, 395] Plato supposes that poetry was invented for no other reason than to teach by means of examples and that whatever is found in poetry, be it good or bad, can and must of necessity be followed by others. This is false; for what is contained in poetry is proposed, before we wish that it should teach, as a matter for careful consideration, and so that we may have examples of all kinds—to frighten the wicked, and to console the good, and to learn about the nature of men and women. And therefore Aristotle said that tragedy, through fears and injustices, drove out fears and injustices from the heart of the men who listened to it, contradicting what Plato says in this passage.[29]

Another variation is presented by Girolamo Frachetta's *Dialogo del furore poetico* (1581). Frachetta's general thesis is that Aristotle assigns to poetry only the single end of pleasure, never that of instruction. Why then should he include purgation, with its pedagogical intent, in the definition of tragedy?

He does this because he was always eager to contradict Plato, so much so that we might almost say that at times he went about begging and borrowing the occasions to do so. Wherefore seeing that he [Plato] forbids in his Republic the horrible and pitiable subjects of the poets, which in his opinion make us fearful and full of pity, and consequently of low and poor heart; and wishing to correct him on this matter, he [Aristotle] said in defining tragedy that by means of pity and of fear it frees our minds of such passions.[30]

Lorenzo Giacomini's opinion on the matter is stated in his academic discourse *Sopra la purgazione della tragedia*, delivered to the Accademia degli Alterati in 1586; his general position is, again, that Aristotle develops his theory of purgation as an answer to Plato's banishment of poets and poetry. He ascribes it to tragedy specifically because of the nature of the audience, the circumstances of performance, and the special kind of utility which the genre is meant to have.[31]

In all these variations of the same argument, what is never questioned is the assumption that catharsis, in the *Poetics*, is a pedagogical device or an instrument to moral improvement. That assumption itself is in part the

---

[29] In *Opere varie critiche* (1727), pp. 215-16: "561. *Nihil aliud agere, vel imitari oportet.* In questo luogo presuppone Platone, che la Poesia non sia trovata per altro, se non per insegnare per Esempio, e ciò, che si truova in Poesia, o bene o male che sia, altri lo possa, o debba seguire. Il che è falso; perciocchè è proposta, prima che vogliamo che insegna, per materia da farvi pensamenti sopra, & acciocchè abbiamo esempj d'ogni maniera e da spaventare i rei, e da consolare i buoni, e da conoscere la natura de gli uomini, e delle donne. E perciò diceva Aristotele, che la Tragedia con le paure, e con le ingiustizie scacciava le paure, e le ingiustizie dal cuore de gli uomini ascoltanti, riprovando quello, che dice Platone in questo luogo."

[30] *Dialogo* (1581), p. 92: "ciò fà perche egli fu sempre uago di contradire a Platone, intantoche si può dir per poco, ch'egli sia andato alle uolte limosinando, & accattando le occasioni. La onde ueggendo ch'egli diuieta nella sua Republica le cose de poeti horribili, & compassioneuoli, perciò, che a suo parere ci fanno paurosi, & pieni di misericordia, & conseguentemente di stremo, & pouero cuore. & uolendol di cio ripigliare; disse in definendo la tragedia, che ella per la compassione, & per lo spauento ci libera l'animo da cotai passioni."

[31] In *Orationi e discorsi* (1597), pp. 29-52.

result of reading Platonic intentions into Aristotle. For Plato, in the *Republic*, the "effect" of poetry is a pedagogical or a moral one; therefore, in Aristotle, the "effect" of tragedy must also be pedagogical or moral. The two texts are more than reconciled; the second is read as if its premises, its procedures, and its conclusions were the same as those of the first.

These, then, would seem to be the four characteristic methods or approaches of Cinquecento critics: (1) the imitation of a single text for the development of new theories; (2) the conflation of one text with another; (3) the conflation of several texts; (4) the reconciliation of divergent positions. If we would explain certain of the difficulties of Renaissance criticism, two auxiliary problems must be considered: the problem of terminology and the meanings of words and the problem of the procedure of argumentation.

TERMINOLOGY AND MEANINGS

The matter of terminology and meanings is in a sense related to the subject just discussed, the attempt to reconcile differing texts. For if one tried to reconcile the major ideas one also had to try to reconcile the terms of the discussions; the latter attempt was a concomitant of the former. Perhaps the best example of the multitude of meanings—and hence the confusion of meaning—associated with a single term is the case of "imitation." One sense of the word not subject to confusion was the "Ciceronian" meaning of the imitation of earlier poets—the use of a model for matters of language, expression, style. This meaning, as it is found in Giovambattista Giraldi Cintio's *Super imitatione epistola ad Coelium Calcagninum* (dated 1532), or in Celio Calcagnini's *Super imitatione commentatio* (1532), or in Bernardino Parthenio's *Della imitatione poetica* (1560), is clear and remains distinct from the others. Indeed, Parthenio states the difference between two major kinds of imitation:

> ... it seems to me reasonable and necessary to recall that there are two kinds of poetic imitation. One, which consists in expressing in an excellent fashion the nature and characters of those persons whom we undertake to imitate. And this is the end of poetry.... But leaving this type of imitation to Aristotle, we shall treat only the other one, which consists in words and in figures of speech.[32]

It is the second of these, which might be called "rhetorical" imitation—the type that the "Ciceronians" were talking about and that interested such a theorist as Du Bellay in the *Deffence et illustration de la langue française*—that was free of confusion and ambiguity. The difficulty arises when we wish

---

[32] *Della imitatione poetica* (1560), pp. 92–94: "mi pare ragioneuole, et douuto ricordar, due esser le sorti della Imitatione poetica. Vna, laquale consiste nell'esprimere eccellentemente le nature et i costumi di quelle persone, che ci proponiamo d'imitare. Et questo è il fine della poesia.... Ma di queste sorti di imitationi lasciando la cura ad Aristotele, solamente tratteremo dell'altra, laquale consiste nelle parole, et ne modi di dire."

to consider the meaning of "poetic" imitation. And the difficulty springs from two causes: first, the variety of meanings assigned to the term in the various dialogues of Plato; and, second, the superimposition of several or all of these meanings upon the term as it is used in the *Poetics*.

Perhaps the single passage in Plato which led to the greatest uncertainty was the discussion in Book III of the *Republic* (Steph. 392–93) where Socrates distinguishes three "styles" of poetry: the narrative, in which the poet speaks in his own person; the imitative, in which the poet takes the person of another, whom he thus "imitates"; and the mixed, in which the two other styles are combined. Now critics of the Renaissance saw in this passage an exact parallel to *Poetics* 1448a19, on the manners of imitation. They thus saw also an equivalence between Plato's διὰ μιμήσεως (for the second style) and Aristotle's πράττοντας καὶ ἐνεργοῦντας (for the second or "dramatic" manner). The next step in reasoning was the basis of the later confusion: if Aristotle here uses "dramatic" as equivalent to Plato's "imitative," then when he himself uses "imitative" or "imitation" he means "dramatic." This assumption led to interminable discussion of the meaning of "imitation" in Aristotle and of related problems: Is the lyric an imitation, and does it come within the categories of poetry considered by Aristotle? Or are tragedy and comedy the only true imitations? To what extent is the epic an imitation? If a narrative poem is not an imitation, does it need to have unity? And so on, into manifold ramifications.

Echoes of these doubts and uncertainties and misunderstandings are to be found in such texts as Pigna's *I romanzi* (1554). The following passage may be taken as an example:

... there are three ways of imitating: the first is the imitation of one single thing through different kinds of imitation, as would be the case if a horse were represented by art, by means of lines and colors by the painter, by descriptions in words by the poet. The second is the imitation of things which differ from one another, through one kind of imitation, as if I were to represent beautiful things in verse alone and ugly things in verse alone. The last is the imitation of one single thing through one kind of imitation, but in a different manner, as is the case with the epic and the tragic poet, who treat of heroes in poetry; but the latter introduces persons in action on the stage, the former narrates how they accomplish their actions. And this epic procedure is also appropriate to our own [writers of romance], since these relate how matters stand, and when the opportunity presents itself to them, they quote the conversations that have taken place between one person and another, which, the more frequently it is done, the more the poet imitates, since introducing the actors themselves so that they may speak together is a way of making the action come more directly before our eyes. And therefore tragic and comic plots are called dramatic, because of the events which are seen and not merely heard. And it is said that these compositions come closest to being true imitations, in the same way as paintings are truly praised when they really come close to life itself. Therefore since the word "poet" means nothing else but "imitator," the more we introduce people in conversation the more will we be

POETIC THEORY

worthy of that name. Nevertheless it would seem to be better to avoid this kind of imitation and to use narration more continuously.[33]

I quote the text at such length because it is important to see how the shift in terminology takes place. Pigna begins with a distinction of the three kinds of imitation (which he calls "modi"), paraphrasing *Poetics* 1447*a*16. The third distinction, that of manner, leads him to use "imitation" as equivalent to "dramatic" and as opposed to "narrative." Follow all the consequences of the use of the term in this Platonic sense.

Another document which involves such a progression of meanings, not only of "imitation" but also of "fable," is a fragment in MS Laurenziana Ashb. 531. The fragment is anonymous, but I attribute it to Lorenzo Giacomini, whose translation of the *Poetics* it follows in the manuscript. Giacomini is attempting to arrive at a definition of poetry; once more, the passage is such as to merit lengthy quotation:

In the Third book of the *Republic*, Plato says that to imitate is to make one thing resemble another, and that poetic imitation exists when the poet speaks in the person of another. In the Tenth, differentiating imitation as a whole, he says that it is a fabrication, that is a making of idols, that is of images, and that the imitator is a fabricator and maker of idols, that is of images . . . whence he is led to say also that poetic imitation is a fabrication of idols. But surely it is not necessary to fabricate idols only by speaking in the person of another, but this can be done in another way. But since the proper instrument of the poet with which he imitates is speech, it follows that poetic imitation is a fabrication of idols with speech. But that form of speech which fabricates idols and images of things is none other than fable and mythology. Aristotle, therefore, when he says that all poetry is imitation means not that first imitation of the Third book of Plato, but this second one of the Tenth, that is, mythology and fable. And this is clear, furthermore, because Aristotle himself applies to imitation the same division with which Plato in the Third book divides mythology; for Plato assigns three kinds to mythology, and Aristotle three kinds to imitation, and the same ones. But when Aristotle says that poetry is an imitation, meaning by imitation mythology, he agrees with Plato, who in the Third book conjoins poetry with mythology and

[33] *I romanzi* (1554), pp. 15–16: "tre sono i modi dell'imitare. L'uno in vna istessa cosa di genere diuersa; come nell'esprimere con l'arte vn cauallo: il quale mostrato sarà dal dipintore con lineamenti & con colori, & dal poeta con descrittion di parole. l'altro in cose tra se diuerse d'un genere istesso: come s'io in versi solo le belle cose rappresentar voglia: & in versi solo le sozze. L'ultimo in vna cosa medesima d'un medesimo genere, ma di diuerso modo: come l'Epico & il Tragico, che poeticamente de gli heroi trattano. ma questi in su la scena le persone induce à negociare: & quegli narra come i fatti loro trattino. Et tale tutta uia con i nostri si confà: conciosia cosa ch'essi dicono come le cose stiano: & quando l'opportunità loro s'offre, riferiscono i parlamenti corsi tra l'una parte & l'altra. il che quanto piu si frequenta di fare, tanto maggiormente s'imita: essendo che l'introducere i proprij negociatori insieme à fauellare, è far che piu la cosa dinanzi à gli occhi ci venga. & perciò Dramatiche si chiamano le Tragiche & le Comiche fauole da gli affari che non vditi, ma veduti sono. Et dicesi che cotesti componimenti piu alla imitatione s'accostano: nel modo che le dipinture, le quali veramente lodate sono, quando al viuo veramente s'appressano. Adunque perche la voce di poeta altro non suona che imitatore, di tal nome degni tanto piu saremo, quanto piu i parlamenti induceremo. Con tutto ciò pare che meglio sia fuggir questa sorte d'imitatione, & essere nel narrar piu continouo."

the poet with the mythologist, that is, the teller of fables. If then poetry is an imitation, and the poet an imitator, and to imitate is to feign and compose fables, it follows that the poet can imitate even if he speaks in his own person. . . . There being then two kinds of imitation, these two authors mean now the one, now the other; but in the definition of poetry Aristotle means that broader one, that is, mythology, that is, fable-telling speech.

Besides, it seems that fable has two meanings according to the aforementioned two authors, because Plato in the Second book of the *Republic* says that fable generally is a lie; later he takes it for discourse which is lying and tells fables. But Aristotle in the poetic art, taking the "fable" as a part of tragedy or of the epic, means by fable the actions themselves, feigned and false; whence fable has a double meaning, that is, false discourse and false action. When therefore we say that poetry is mythology, we mean the first kind of fable, that is, lying dicourse. . . . Poetry is thus a feigned and mendacious form of speech, which by means of narrated discourses not true in themselves, and with a certain lying and falseness, imitates true actions and real things.[34]

This is not an extreme case of the errors produced by careless or unintelligent handling of terms; such procedures are common in much of the critical writing of the Cinquecento.

PROCEDURES OF ARGUMENTATION

To this matter of terminology is also related the even more important question of argumentation. For if the theorist's use of terms is shifting and

[34] MS Laur. Ashb. 531, fols. 39–39v: "Nel terzo libro de la Rep^a Platone dice lo imitare essere assimigliare una cosa ad unaltra, et la imitazion poetica essere quando il poeta parla in persona d'altri. Nel X ponendo la differenza di tutta l'imitazione dice lei essere fabricamento, cio è facimento di idoli cio è di imagini et lo imitatore essere fabricatore et facitore di idoli cio è di imagini . . . onde viene a dire ancora che l'imitazione poetica sia fabricamento di idoli. ma certo è che non è necessario fabricare idoli parlando in persona d'altri, ma che questo si puo fare ancora in altro modo. ma essendo il proprio instrumento del poeta col quale egli imita l'orazione seguita la poetica imitazione essere fabricamento di idoli con orazione. ma l'orazione la quale fabrica gli idoli et le imagini de le cose altro non è che la favola et la mythologia. Aristotile adunque quando dice ogni poesia essere imitazione intende non quella prima del terzo libro di Platone, ma questa seconda del X, ciò è mythologia et favola. et questo è manifesto ancora, perche esso Aristotile divide l'imitazione con la divisione medesima con la quale Platone nel 3 divide la mythologia, perche tre modi à la mytologia assegna Platone, et tre Aristotile al imitazione, et i medesimi. Ma dicendo Aristotele la poesia essere imitazione, et per imitazione intendendo mytheologia convien con Platone, il quale nel terzo con la poesia congiunge la mithologia, et col poeta il mythologo, cio è il favoleggiatore. Se adunque la poesia è imitazione, et il poeta imitatore, et l'imitare è fingere et comporre favole seguita che il poeta puo imitare parlando ancora in propria persona. . . . essendo adunque due l'imitazioni, ora questa, et ora quella intendono questi due autori, ma ne la diffinitione de la poesia Aristotile intende quella piu larga, cio è la mythologia, cio è l'orazione fauolosa.

"Ancora pare che la fauola sia doppia secondo i due autori predetti, perche Platone nel secondo de la Republica dice la favola generalmente essere mendacio dipoi la piglia per orazione mendace et favolosa. Ma Aristotile nel arte poetica pigliando la favola per una parte de la tragedia et del epopeia intende la favola essere l'azzioni stesse finte et false, per la qual cosa la favola è doppia, cio è l'orazion falsa, et l'azzione falsa. quando adunque diciamo la poesia essere mythologia intendiamo il primo genere de la favola, cio è l'orazion mendace. . . . E adunque la poesia orazione finta et mendace, la quale con l'orazioni non vere da se narrate, et con qualunque mendacio et falsità imita le vere azzioni et le cose veraci."

uncertain, he can with difficulty pursue an orderly argument or achieve a convincing demonstration. Among critics of the Cinquecento the two deficiencies, of terminology and of argumentation, were sometimes concomitant, sometimes separate. That weakness in logical method should appear is not surprising, given the wilful rejection of the Aristotelian logic of the schools, the failure to discover the essence of Plato's method of dialectic, and the unawareness of the art of considering and analyzing texts as complete and consistent philosophical documents.

The best way to illustrate these deficiencies or peculiarities of argumentation is, of course, to analyze some work or works in entirety. Since I shall be doing that frequently and repeatedly in the later chapters, perhaps it will be sufficient at this point—in order to avoid repetition—to study a section of a work which presents a typical example. Let us take the sections of Francesco Patrizi's *Della poetica: La deca disputata* (1586) in which he attacks Aristotle's proposition that poetry is an imitation. Patrizi is a reputable philosopher; much of his philosophy was based upon a wish to controvert the theories of Aristotle; his method in controverting them must have been the best he could find and the object of careful attention and consideration. This particular attack begins with Book III. Starting with the objection that Aristotle had nowhere defined the term imitation, Patrizi collects six passages from Aristotle in which the term μίμησις has six different meanings, two from the *Rhetoric* and four from the *Poetics*. For several of these passages the meaning is found by consulting texts of Plato. Patrizi concludes that these are six separate meanings, with distinct definitions. Asking, then, whether individually these meanings supply a proper definition for poetry, he concludes that they do not: (1) If poetry is an imitation because words are imitations (*Rhet.* III, I, 8; cf. *Cratylus*, 423), then all forms of discourse would be poetry. (2) If imitation means "enargia" or vivid description (*Rhet.* III, XI, 2; cf. Hermogenes, καὶ τὸ μέγιστον ποιήσεως, μίμησιν ἐναργῆ), then only some parts of poetry would contain imitation, which would also be found in rhetoric and history. (3) If imitation means "favola" (plot, or fable, or mythology; *Poetics* 1450*a*3), then two propositions must necessarily follow: every poem will be a "favola," and every "favola" will be a poem. Leaving the first of these propositions for discussion in Book IV, Patrizi demonstrates that the second is false, for the ancients wrote many "favole" (here, fables) which were not poems because they were in prose, and many ancient authorities made a careful distinction between poetry and mythology. Moreover, he says, if we reduce Aristotle's argument to the following syllogism:

> Every poem is an imitation
> Every "favola" is an imitation
> Therefore every "favola" is a poem,

we obtain a conclusion which is in accord neither with the first premise nor with the facts. (4) If by imitation is meant a dramatic representation, as in comedy and tragedy (*Poetics* 1449*b*24; cf. *Rep*. III, 394), then it would admit neither epic nor dithyrambic poetry, but it would include both comedy and dialogues in prose. (5) If imitation does include the epic and the dithyramb (*Poetics* 1447*a*13), then Aristotle contradicts himself when he later says (1460*a*5) that many epic poets "imitate" very little because they speak constantly in their own persons; and imitation consists in speaking in the person of another. (6) If imitation is constituted by auletic, citharistic, syringic, and orchestic poetry, which would be equivalent to encomia, hymns, blames, and gnomes (*Poetics* 1447*a*15, 25, –48*a*9), then it is not poetry at all, for these are not forms of poetry; if these are taken, metaphorically, as forms of poetry, then they will be imitations only when they are represented on the stage. Patrizi summarizes thus:

> All six "imitations," therefore, have different meanings; of which some are not appropriate to poetry, others are common to other writings also and not proper to poetry, others make the compositions of writers both poetry and non-poetry, and others make all of them non-poetry. And none of them is sufficient to provide the genus for all poems.[35]

The weaknesses of this argument are immediately apparent. Not only are all the terms from the *Poetics*—"poetry, imitation, plot"—given meanings which are not justified by the context in Aristotle or which are directly excluded by that context, but these terms and others shift their meaning as Patrizi passes from stage to stage in the argument. Moreover, there is a kind of pseudological analysis of the propositions being attacked, which is itself very unsure; e.g., his treatment of the proposition (itself incorrectly derived) that "every 'favola' is a poem." The careful reader, working his way through such a series of arguments, feels himself driven to a point of complete confusion where words no longer have fixed meanings and demonstration has no validity. Perhaps Patrizi felt that he was following the example of the Platonic dialectic; instead, he was violating the very principles of that dialectic, in which change of meaning is accompanied by redefinition, justified by context, and submitted always to searching analysis and careful distinction.

These remarks on the methodology of the critics have been, I fear, fairly damaging. They would seem to point to a degree of philosophical incompetence, both in the reading and interpretation of earlier texts and in the development of new theories. I have ventured to make them for two reasons: first and primarily, so that they might serve as a partial explanation of how the ancient theories came to be interpreted as they were and

[35] *Della poetica* (1586), pp. 59–74; v. p. 74: "Tutte adunque le sei imitazioni, hanno tra loro significati differenti. De quali altri a poesia non conuengono. Altre sono communi ad ad [*sic*] altri scrittori, e non proprie de poeti. Altre che fanno le composizioni altrui, e poesie, e non poesie. e altre del tutto non poesie. E niuna bastante ad essere genere alle poesie tutte."

how the new theories came to assume the form that they did; second, so that the reader might be more acutely aware, as he reads the subsequent chapters, of what is taking place in the individual texts analyzed. He should not, however, conclude from these remarks either that method was universally bad or that the theorists never succeeded in making consistent sense in their treatises. There were examples of good method; there were cases of solid contribution to theory; there were completely consistent and well developed documents.

Perhaps we may thus analyze the situation with respect to the procedure of the best of the theorists. A given critic has developed, let us say, a clearly thought out and perfectly self-contained poetics. He may undertake, then, to write a commentary on Aristotle's *Poetics*. The peculiarities or the deficiencies of his general philosophical method permit him to read his own theory into the text of Aristotle, even though the two may be worlds apart. Or he may set out to write an art of poetry which will expound his own theory. The peculiarities or the deficiencies of his general philosophical method permit him to cite in support of his doctrine a whole set of miscellaneous texts which might, taken separately, be entirely irreconcilable with it. In either situation, it is essentially the interpretation of the ancient text or texts which suffers; his own theory remains undamaged except insofar as the proofs offered may appear at places to be inadequate or inappropriate. By way of illustration of such procedures, I wish to summarize briefly my findings (published previously) on four of the most prominent of Cinquecento critics, Robortello, Scaliger, Minturno, and Castelvetro.

Francesco Robortello published in 1548 the first extensive commentary on Aristotle's *Poetics* in his *In librum Aristotelis de arte poetica explicationes*.[36] But far from approaching his basic text without prior suppositions about the poetic art and with the intention of interpreting the text only in and for itself, he brought to the text a completely worked out theory of poetics. He had derived this theory from his reading of Horace's *Ars poetica* and the Greek and Roman rhetoricians; hence it was essentially rhetorical in character. Robortello conceived of poetry as written for the purpose of producing certain effects of pleasure and of utility on a given audience. The audience was composed of an elite of wise men of good moral character, who would be persuaded only if certain kinds of actions and characters were presented to them; persuasion was a necessary antecedent of both utility and pleasure. The work itself would produce a variety of utilities and pleasures, not as a whole, but through different parts and elements. For example, certain lessons about human destiny would be learned from watching the action of a tragedy develop on the stage, certain lessons about character from the observation of characters in poems; certain truths would be demonstrated by the sententiae, and on the

[36] "Robortello on the *Poetics*," in R. S. Crane *et al., Critics and Criticism: Ancient and Modern* (Chicago: University of Chicago Press, 1952), pp. 319–48.

basis of these the audience would be moved to undertake action or to refrain from it. With respect to pleasure, again it would be produced by separate parts of the poem: that related to imitation would come from the plot itself, that associated with the *difficulté vaincue* from successful treatment of unpleasant subjects, that ascribable to admiration from certain kinds of episodes, from diction, from various ornaments.

Now this is a completely conceived system of poetics, which Robortello could defend upon philosophical or pragmatic grounds. But when he proceeds to read Aristotle as if this were Aristotle's theory, too, he completely deforms the meaning of his basic text. What happens to Aristotle may be summarized thus:

... what emerges is a poetic method essentially different from Aristotle's. The fundamental alteration comes in the passage from a poetic to a rhetorical position, from a position in which the essential consideration is the achievement of the internal and structural relationship which will make the poem beautiful to one in which the main problem is the discovery of those devices which will produce a desired effect upon a specified audience. I do not mean that in Aristotle no consideration is given to the effect of the poem upon the audience; indeed, at every crucial point in the *Poetics* the relationship of object of contemplation to contemplator is maintained constant. Such concepts as the pleasure derived from imitation, the "effect" proper to a given species, the pity and fear of tragedy and their "purgation," the "likeness" of hero to audience among the requisites of character are integral to the argument; they are fundamental if the work of art is to fulfil its function of giving a certain kind of artistic pleasure to the men who see it or hear it. But herein lies the basic departure of Robortello: the effect produced is no longer one of artistic pleasure resulting from the formal qualities of the work, but one of moral persuasion to action or inaction, in which the pleasure involved is merely an accompaniment or an instrument; and the audience is composed of men capable of yielding to this persuasion rather than of men capable of enjoying this pleasure.

This means that the problem for the poet is no longer to compound out of the constitutive parts an artistic whole which, as a whole, will produce the desired aesthetic effect, but rather to insert into the work such parts as will, by themselves, produce multiple utilities and pleasures, each part producing a separate utility or a separate pleasure. The bases for the inclusion of any given part is its capacity, by itself, to awaken in a highly specified audience a given reaction of persuasion or of pleasure. This means, in turn, that the artistic unity and integrity of the work disappear as part of the problem: "plot" may be removed from among the poetic elements of a work and may be transferred to its specifically histrionic functions. Only the vaguest notions of a unifying and ordering structure for the work need be retained; these are not vital. On the other hand, such elements as diction and the means by which diction is made ornate assume great importance.

Moreover, since the sense of the total poetic structure is lost, there is no longer any possibility of deriving from such a structure the criteria for the appropriateness, for the goodness or badness, of individual parts. Instead, criteria for each separate part will be separately derived by a reference to the character of the audience as it specifically affects that part and in the light of the utility or the pleasure which that part should produce. At each step, there will be reference outside the poem. The poem becomes, as a result, a collection rather than a unit. From it the audience derives utility of a moral character and pleasure of a nonaesthetic kind, since it is not related to the structure or the form of the work as a whole.[37]

Julius Caesar Scaliger, who died in 1558, left behind him the completed manuscript of his *Poetices libri septem,* which was published in 1561.[38] Unlike Robortello's work, this is an original art of poetry; it presents in an orderly and highly systematic fashion Scaliger's theory of the art. Indeed, so orderly and systematic is the presentation that this work might well be taken as an example of a "good" method employed by a Renaissance theorist. The theory as a whole might be described as a grammatical one, in the sense that Scaliger is essentially preoccupied with poetry as an art of discourse. Poetry is conceived primarily as language. As language, it must enter into two distinct relationships: (1) the relationship with the things which are signified by the words employed and (2) the relationship with the audience for whom the signification is intended. Scaliger will thus concern himself with things as they are in nature—or in Vergil's *Aeneid,* which represents perfectly the norm of nature—and with the effects of pleasure and utility produced in the audience. Both nature and the needs of the audience impose conditions upon poetry, which has no conditions or principles of its own except those that are purely prosodic. Such a system is, of course, diametrically opposed to that of Aristotle; and Scaliger recognizes this fact when he takes direct issue with Aristotle on such points as the definition of tragedy, its constituent parts, the end of poetry, and the internal economy of the poem. This does not prevent him, however, from using the *Poetics* constantly as a source of definitions, distinctions, and arguments.

The *De poeta* of Antonio Sebastiano Minturno (1559), almost exactly contemporary with Scaliger's work, is much less successful in achieving order and system.[39] It draws heavily upon a wide variety of works—Plato's *Republic, Laws, Ion,* etc., Aristotle's *Poetics* and *Rhetoric,* Horace's *Ars poetica,* Quintilian, Cicero's *Orator, De oratore, De optimo genere oratorum, Topica.* Such works as the *Poetics* and the *Ars poetica* are almost completely incorporated into Minturno's treatise; others contribute more or less extensive developments. But from these disparate elements no single, central approach emerges. Not only does Minturno fail to apply certain of his distinctions consistently, but there are whole groups of concepts—the rules

---

[37] *Ibid.,* pp. 346–47.
[38] "Scaliger versus Aristotle on Poetics," *Modern Philology,* XXXIX (1942), 337–60.
[39] "The Poetic Theories of Minturno," in *Studies in Honor of Frederick W. Shipley* ("Washington University Studies," [St. Louis, Mo., 1942]), pp. 101–29.

and precepts for the specific genres, for example—which do not in any way derive from the more general concepts of the work. Even among these more general ideas, a complete ordering to a central problem is lacking. Some of them relate to the poet himself, to his faculties and his character as a good man; some of them to the audience with its desire for pleasure and its need for moral improvement; some of them to the poem as an imitation composed of qualitative and quantitative parts. But no one of these analyses is complete; each is presented in a fragmentary form and Minturno passes rapidly from one context to another. Insofar as there is an ordering of ideas, it is an ordering to rhetorical principles. For the various chains of relationships established within the work there is, at one end of each chain, an effect upon the audience; at the other end, some faculty of the poet capable of producing that effect; in the middle, the poem serving as a means or instrument. This arrangement is essentially rhetorical and is vaguely reminiscent of Aristotle's system in the *Rhetoric*, in which the nature of the audience, the character of the orator, and the proofs presented in the speech itself must all be taken into consideration. In the detail of the treatment, however, Minturno's system is really Ciceronian, and most of the discussion in specific passages comes from one or another of Cicero's rhetorical works. Here again, the lack of order, the lack of discipline, the failure to arrive at a synthesis or to impose a central organization upon a mass of irreconcilable materials are evident.

Lodovico Castelvetro's *Poetica d'Aristotele vulgarizzata et sposta* (1570) is, like Robortello's work, a commentary on the *Poetics*.[40] Unlike Robortello, however, Castelvetro sets out to refute Aristotle and to suggest his own theories instead. He begins with the basic assumption that poems are written for a specific audience, the ignorant multitude, which has no knowledge, no imagination, no memory, and which demands that its comfort be respected. In order to please this audience—and pleasure is the only end—the poet must above all seek credibility or verisimilitude in combination with the marvelous: credibility so that the unimaginative audience will believe, the marvelous so that it will find pleasure in the uncommon and the extraordinary. These two factors determine the nature of plots, episodes, character, the choice of materials; they make of poetry a kind of history which differs from history only in the use of verse. The audience's demand for comfort introduces the requirement of a "unity" of time, its lack of imagination adds the "unity" of place; the unity of action (which Castelvetro does not really consider essential, even though it is the only one of the three required by Aristotle) comes as an adjunct to the unities of time and place; it serves as an additional ornament and shows the excellence of the poet. Moreover, the audience will impose upon the work a whole set of special conditions which will be codified in the rules and precepts which the poet must follow. Such a system as this, in which every-

[40] "Castelvetro's Theory of Poetics," in R. S. Crane *et al.*, *op. cit.*, pp. 349–71.

thing results from the necessity of pleasing a specific audience, is rhetorical in a sense; besides, it is historical to the degree that it concerns itself with credibility. It is, of course, clearly distinct from Aristotle's conception of poetics; and what is amazing from the point of view of methodology is that the vehicle for its presentation should be a commentary on the *Poetics*. Little light will be thrown on the *Poetics* in the course of the commentary, but much illumination of Castelvetro's own doctrine will result.

These four documents are representative, in their general outlines, of the results produced by application of the methods that I have described in this chapter. An examination of the details of discussion would show other procedures at work. We should not, of course, expect to find all the methods exemplified in any single work, all the faults and failings epitomized by any one theorist, who would thus become the arch-sinner of Renaissance critical theory. Rather, we should expect that the various habits of intellectual approach, the major difficulties, the characteristic ways of solving those difficulties, would manifest themselves variously and in varying combinations in the numerous documents which constitute the body of critical materials of the Cinquecento. If we are concerned not only with what the theoretical and the practical critics said in their writings, but with why they said what they did, we should anticipate that a constant awareness of methodological factors will enable us both to understand and to judge their writings. The problem of reading Renaissance critical texts is complex, not only because of the complexities of the critical situation itself but because of our distance from it in time and in intellectual habits. By constantly asking what virtues or vices of method are present in a given document, we shall without doubt be able to discover some simplicity in complexity and some clarity in confusion.

CHAPTER THREE. THE TRADITION OF HORACE'S *ARS POETICA*: I. THE EARLIEST COMMENTARIES

THIS CHAPTER and the three succeeding ones will be concerned with tracing through the course of the sixteenth century in Italy the intellectual fortunes of Horace's *Ars poetica*. Of all theoretical documents relative to the art of poetry in classical antiquity, this was the only one which had some currency during the Middle Ages and which came to the humanistic period and the Renaissance as a part of their more immediate intellectual heritage.[1] Throughout both periods, it continued to be a dominant text in the molding of critical opinion and in the formation of new doctrines. Horace's work represented, in addition to the specific recommendations of the text itself, a general way of thinking about poetry which was highly acceptable to the Renaissance mind and which continued to dominate critical thinking in spite of the emergence of such new points of view as that contained in Aristotle's *Poetics*.

Essentially, the *Ars poetica* regards poems in the context of the society for which they are written. It considers above all the dramatic forms, in relation both to nature and to their capacity to please and to instruct an audience of a given kind that would see them in a given age under given circumstances. What goes into the making of any poem will be determined in large part by the expectations, the requirements, the taste of this particular audience. Translated into terms of the poem, these requirements become certain precepts for its ordering and unification (the audience dislikes disorder and laughs at disunity), certain conventions for its superficial forms (the audience expects that plays will have five acts and a limited number of interlocutors), certain recommendations for the decorum of its characters (the audience has fixed notions both about types and about traditional heroes), and certain generalizations about diction (the audience associates specific kinds of diction and styles of writing with each of the literary genres). Moreover, since the various age groups and the divers social sectors in the audience make different demands upon the poem, it will have to provide a proper combination of pleasurable and profitable elements.

The fact that, in Horace's theory, the internal characteristics of the poem are determined largely, if not exclusively, by the external demands of the audience brings his theory very close to specifically rhetorical approaches. In theories of this kind, the determining factor in the production of the work is not an internal principle of structural perfection, but rather an acceptance of the assumption that all those elements are included in the work that will be susceptible of producing the desired effect upon the

---

[1] For the scattered appearances of Aristotle's *Poetics* during the medieval period, see below, chap. ix, p. 352.

audience envisaged, arranged in an order calculated to achieve the maximum degree of that effect. However, in proper and complete rhetorical approaches, one essential element—absent from Horace—enters at all times into consideration: the character of the orator (or poet) as it really is (Quintilian) or as it is made to appear to be (Aristotle's *Rhetoric*). If Horace's thesis is a rhetorical one, it is incomplete rhetoric because it omits this essential aspect.

For theorists and critics of the Renaissance, the rhetorical tendency of Horace's *Ars poetica* was perhaps its most appealing characteristic. Indeed, as we have already seen in Chapter I, their own thinking about poetry inclined most frequently toward considering it as a kinsman of rhetoric or as an instrumental science serving the ends of moral philosophy. Whatever doubts they may have had about how specific passages in Horace's text were to be interpreted, they seem to have sensed immediately to what extent the whole corresponded to their favorite ways of looking at the art of poetry. Perhaps they merely continued in the paths of their medieval ancestors, for many of whom poetry was an adjunct to rhetoric and for whom the *Ars poetica* provided occasional ideas for the arts of poetry (which were otherwise largely arts of rhyming) and for passing allusions to the broader aspects of poetry.

Horace's verse epistle may thus be taken—and in fact was so taken by Renaissance critics—as the epitome of an essentially rhetorical approach to the art of poetry. Indeed, this is true to such an extent that it is frequently difficult to distinguish a predominantly "Horatian" text of the Cinquecento from one which sprang primarily from Cicero or Quintilian transmuted into an authority on the art of poetry. The details of the treatment, the specific ideas, might be different; but the basic assumptions, the fundamental ways of considering the poetic art, would be the same. For this reason, I shall include in the present chapter and the following ones not only those works which are commentaries upon Horace but all such works as are related to it in a secondary way, insofar as they represent the kind of approach indicated. As I stated in the Preface, I do not mean to trace through the Cinquecento the history of the rhetorical documents themselves, since that in itself would be a vast and complex undertaking. But a treatment of poetic theory in the period would be incomplete if cognizance were not taken of the impact of rhetorical theory upon poetics; and since this rhetorical theory is most closely associated, in the Renaissance, with the interpretation of Horace's *Ars poetica*, the present series of chapters seems to be the logical place for its treatment.

THE LATE-CLASSICAL COMMENTATORS: ACRON AND PORPHYRION

The *Ars poetica* did not come to the Renaissance as a naked text for which the simplest and most elementary interpretations had to be provided. The earliest printed editions were accompanied by two commentaries of the late Roman period, that attributed to Helenius Acron (second century A.D.) and that of Porphyrion (third century A.D.).[2] Moreover, these printed editions continued an ancient manuscript tradition (extant manuscripts date back to the ninth and tenth centuries) in which the same commentaries accompanied the Horatian text.[3] To these were added, before 1500, the commentary of Cristoforo Landino, and, around 1500, the commentary of Iodocus Badius Ascensius; and although Badius' annotations were for a number of years printed only in Paris editions, they ultimately were added to the earlier commentaries in Italian editions.[4] By the time, then, that the major Cinquecento studies of the text were made, all four glosses were a standard part of the available editions, and critics and theorists took them as a point of departure for their own interpretations.

Much of what Acron has to say in his commentary is essentially grammatical or explanatory in character. He explains the meanings of words, word order, matters of syntax; sometimes, when the sense is particularly obscure, he gives a paraphrase. He provides classifications for the various figures of speech used by Horace, cites parallels from other poets, explains legends and allusions, brings to the text a kind of grammatical and historical *explication*. However, for numerous passages he makes remarks—in a sentence or sometimes in a single word—which suggest an interpretation of the basic work, and these remarks taken together constitute a fairly complete theory of poetry as Acron discovers it in Horace. One thing that he does (and I presume that he was the first to do it for this particular text) is to distinguish a series of precepts, definitely labeled as such, in the *Ars poetica*. He prefaces these indications with a statement at the very beginning of his commentary: "De inaequalitate operis loquitur, et dat praecepta scribendi poema. Et primum praeceptum est de dispositione et conuenientia carminis."[5] Subsequently, some dozen or more precepts of this kind are pointed out. At a few other places, although he does not specifically call his remark a "praeceptum," he uses some such word as "docet" to show that he is thinking in essentially the same terms. This procedure is not without importance for the subsequent history of Horace's text. It establishes a precedent for reducing the text to a set of fixed rules for the writing of poetry, a precedent which Renaissance commentators were to follow constantly.

More important still, however, was the general orientation which Acron

---

[2] E.g., the *editio princeps*, the so-called "editio Romana," printed by Bartholomew Guldinbeck around 1475; the edition of Milan, 1474; of Venice, 1481; and so forth.

[3] For a list of the manuscripts, see the edition by Ferdinand Hauthal, *Acronis et Porphyrionis commentarii in Q. Horatium Flaccum* (Berlin, 1864), I, iii; also II, 574, 648, 649, and 665.

[4] See the Index, s.v. Badius Ascensius, of *Quintus Horatius Flaccus: Editions in the United States and Canada* (Mills College, California, 1938); the earliest Italian edition listed here as containing the Badius commentary is Item 85, Milan, 1518.

[5] Ed. Hauthal, cited in note 3 above, II, 575. All subsequent references to Acron will be to this volume; comments not specifically located by page will be found under the line number indicated.

gave to the *Ars poetica* in his reading of it. This was an essentially rhetorical orientation which, if it did not introduce any new ideas, emphasized and exaggerated tendencies latent in the Horatian text. One such tendency is to consider poetry in terms of the conventional rhetorical distinction of invention, disposition, and elocution. The passage previously cited ("primum praeceptum est de dispositione") already shows this intention. The other two terms of the trilogy appear in the commentary on line 40: "if one selects a subject matter which he is capable of fulfilling, neither inventions nor eloquence can be lacking to him."[6] The term "dispositio" appears in close conjunction in the gloss on the following line. But the three-way distinction is little more than suggested and does not constitute the major effort of the commentary.

If one were to attempt to find a guiding principle for Acron's whole reading of the text, it would probably be a principle of appropriateness. Everywhere, the attempt is made to reduce all matters to questions of "propriety," of "fittingness" of this to that. This attempt is apparent, again, in the first precept already cited, "et primum praeceptum est de dispositione et *conuenientia* carminis." From then on, one hardly ever loses sight of the central principle. The second precept restates it: "Praecipit, poetam *conuenientiam* seruare debere"; here, it is Acron's summation of the meaning of the first three lines of the text (p. 576). So does the third: "Docet, *non inportune* inducendam esse parabolam aut descriptionem" (p. 577). The same organizing concept is invoked in the commentaries on line 20 ("Ita ergo qui scribit, nisi *opportune* scribat..."), line 31 ("Docet hic, non esse indulgendum eloquentiae, *quae careat arte et ratione*, ne quis incidat in opinionem *inepti et superflui*"), lines 35–37 ("... ita enitor omni parte poeta uideri, *nulla in parte ab alia discrepans*"), lines 47–48 ("si tota uerba *opportune* et *proprie* ponantur"); and so on through innumerable passages. The principle is in itself vague, since no criterion for appropriateness is presented. When one has said that the style must fit the subject, the diction must fit the characters, the conception of characters must fit the notion of decorum, the end must fit the beginning, one has made a rule whose application depends almost exclusively upon the sensitivity of the poet, upon his sense of what is right in a given relationship. But the principle is no more vague than it was in the Horatian text itself; the only difference is that Acron sees it as operating in many places where the original text of Horace seems not to imply it at all. For example, lines 125–27 of the *Ars poetica*—

> Siquid inexpertum scaenae committis et audes
> personam formare novam, servetur ad imum,
> qualis ab incepto processerit, et sibi constet

—undoubtedly contain a recommendation that character be kept constant

[6] *Ibid.*, p. 581: "qui eligit materiam, quam possit inplere, huic nec inuentiones, nec eloquentia deesse possunt."

or consistent throughout a work; but Acron's gloss on "sibi constet" is as follows: "Let the material finish within itself, nor should it pass on to something else. Do not pass to anything else before you have finished it."[7] The idea is generalized and is made into another expression of the central notion of "fittingness" or "belongingness."

That central notion itself provides in effect a rhetorical rather than a poetic basis of organizing and constructing a work. I do not mean that a norm of "appropriateness" does not or could not apply to poetic works. But in such a document as Aristotle's *Poetics*, the relationship between one part and another of the poem is stated in other terms: in terms of the hierarchical interdependence of such component parts as plot, character, thought, and diction, or in terms of the specifically poetic devices which link the parts together, necessity and probability. That is, a given element (a word or an action or a passion) is "appropriate" to the whole work in a special way determined by the total unity and the total order of the given work itself. But for Acron (following and simplifying Horace), the principle of appropriateness is general rather than specific; it applies in the same way to all works, regardless of their particular natures; it involves such diverse kinds of appropriateness as that of meters to subject matters and of traits of character to historical personages. If it is thus unspecified, it is because, in the last analysis, appropriateness is not determined from within the work, but is at all times judged from without by the particular audience. In this resides its peculiarly rhetorical quality.

As Acron interprets Horace, the constant search for the appropriateness of all elements within a poem is a part of the constant search to please the audience. This is, of course, a Horatian principle; but Acron extends it and states it much more explicitly. For example, the "commendare" of line 225 clearly means "to render acceptable to the public"; Acron expands the statement, applied originally to satiric drama, into a general statement about all poetry: "... nam omnia, quae dicimus, placere desideramus, ac per hoc uidentur conmendare, quae dicimus, auribus auditorum. Omnia enim, quae dicuntur a poetis, ita debent dici, ut conmendari uideantur, id est, ut libenter adspiciantur." In a similar way, Horace's emphasis on the audience is everywhere pointed up by Acron. The "semper ad euentum festinat" of line 148 is the occasion for the gloss: "Considering the possible distaste of the reader, he hastens to the end of the work."[8] In explaining the "in medias res" beginning (line 148) he goes on to say: "... the good poet leads his listener immediately to known things"; and then, for the next line, "... the good poet excludes those things which cannot please, that is, he passes over those things which are not agreeable in the treatment."[9]

[7] *Ibid.*, p. 598: "In se finiatur materia, nec ad aliud transeat. Ne transeas ad aliam, antequam illam finias."
[8] *Ibid.*, p. 601: "Cogitans fastidium lectoris ad exitum operis properat."
[9] *Ibid.*, p. 602: "adducit bonus poeta auditorem [suum] quasi ad nota" and "bonus poeta relinquit ea, quae placere non possunt, hoc est, praeterit ea, quae in tractatu ingrata sunt."

Line 153 is elucidated thus: "... what I and the people might desire, that is, what all would willingly listen to...."[10] For "omne tulit punctum" in line 343 he provides this explanation: "He alone obtains the votes and the [favorable] judgment of the people who writes a poem in a useful and pleasant fashion and who can both profit and delight."[11]

The general thesis is stated in connection with the phrase "Ut pictura poesis" in line 361: "indeed, an excellent poem pleases even when frequently repeated."[12] Within this audience, various segments must be pleased in special ways: Acron again emphasizes Horace's ideas. Part of the audience is low, ignorant, and wicked, and it must be pleased by special kinds of poetic fare; so the commentary on lines 213-14: "He indicates the cause for the increase of licence: because of the ignorance of the people and because there was no difference between the good and the bad," and "because the people was uneducated."[13] Another segment consists of grave persons, officials and noblemen, who will be offended by anything dishonorable; the commentary on line 248 reads: "The meaning is this: The Roman knights and senate fathers, who have great wealth and hence are noble and enjoy honorable reputation, are offended if anything shameful is expressed before them."[14] Some of the audience are young and will find delight in light things, some are old and want serious materials (commentary on line 342): "The meaning is this: Old men are pleased by the gravity of the verse and the weight of the diction, young men do not like austere and grave things."[15] The introduction to the same gloss shows that the pleasure of poetry is intended for the young, its profit for the old: "The poem must be properly tempered, so that through its pleasure it will serve the younger men and through its severity it will satisfy the older."[16] Apparently, the insistence upon moral precepts, philosophical arguments, and the arousing of the passions—because these are "grave" matters—is intended especially for the older men. The effort to find everywhere both pleasure and utility may account for the somewhat startling construction put on line 99—

> Non satis est pulchra esse poemata: dulcia sunto

—when, after the gloss "Therefore, let those poems which are morally

---

[10] *Ibid.*, p. 602: "quid ego et populus desideret, id est, quid libenter audiant omnes...."

[11] *Ibid.*, p. 632: "Solus suffragia et iudicium populi tulit, qui utile et dulce poema scripsit et qui prodest et delectare potest."

[12] *Ibid.*, p. 634: "probum uero poema placet etiam saepe repetitum."

[13] *Ibid.*, p. 611: "Dicit autem causam, per quam creuit licentia; propter inperitiam populi, et quia nulla erat differentia inter bonos et malos" and "quia indoctus erat populus."

[14] *Ibid.*, p. 619: "Sensus est: Equites Romani et patres senatores, quibus sunt substantiae magnae, ac per hoc nobiles et honestate gaudentes, offenduntur, si aliquid coram eis inhonestum fuerit prolatum."

[15] *Ibid.*, p. 631: "Sensus est: Senes grauitate carminis et dictionis pondere delectantur, iuuenes austera et grauia non amant."

[16] *Ibid.*, p. 631: "Poema debet temperari, et ut uoluptati seruiat iuniorum, et seueritati satisfaciat seniorum."

recommendable have beauty as well and carry the mind of the auditor wherever they will, either to pity or to indignation," the phrase "dulcia sunto" is translated by the formula "Ethica sint," which I take to mean "having moral implications."[17] In any case, the pleasure-profit distinction comes to be crossed with another grammatical and rhetorical one, the "res-verba" juxtaposition; cf. the gloss on line 320:

> He shows only to what extent is important the consideration of customs, saying that sometimes a story through the suitableness of the persons introduced and the expression of the mores, even though it may be without art, without beauty, without gravity of sententiae, pleases more than high-sounding verses which are lacking in the observation of the mores. Things without ornament can please more than poems adorned with words without substance.[18]

One special aspect of Acron's conception of the role of the audience is his interpretation of "nature" as it figures in Horace's work. Clearly, if for many things in a poem the precise way of judging "appropriateness" is not made apparent, for some at least the judgment is possible through a reference to nature. The audience is the custodian of a certain conception of nature, and it uses this conception as its criterion; what nature *is* does not count, but what the audience thinks it to be does. This is of course true in Horace, and the laughter of the spectator in the first lines indicates that the monster he sees does not conform to his notion of nature. Acron merely states the idea more explicitly. Thus for line 23—

> Denique sit quod vis, simplex dumtaxat et unum

—he adds a highly significant phrase: "Quiduis scribe, simplex ut sit *et ueri simile*." Similarly, the "specie recte" of line 25 is interpreted as "imagine boni, dum praeferimus imaginem ueritatis." The whole series of comments on lines 108 ff. is interesting in the same connection. The "intus" of line 108 is glossed as follows: "We have all passions within our souls by nature, and they are moved singly whenever they see their own images in others."[19] For the "iuvat aut impellit ad iram" of line 109 he says this: "Nature delights us when we see it charmingly presented. For through nature we become angry, we feel pleasure, we have pity."[20] The "angit" of line 110 is explained as meaning that "Nature herself [troubles] the spec-

---

[17] *Ibid.*, p. 593: "Habeant ergo haec, quae sunt probata, etiam uenustatem, et, quocumque uoluerint, animum auditoris trahant, siue ad misericordiam, siue ad indignationem."

[18] *Ibid.*, p. 629: "Ostendit modo, quantum prodest consideratio consuetudinis, dicens, quod interdum fabula opportunitate personarum inductarum et expressione morum, quamuis sit sine arte, sine uenustate, sine grauitate sententiarum, plus placet quam uersus bene quidem sonantes, sed morum obseruatione carentes. Magis possunt delectare res sine ornatu, quam ornata poemata uerbis sine rebus."

[19] *Ibid.*, p. 594: "adfectus omnes habemus in animis nostris ex natura, et singuli mouentur, cum imagines suas uiderint in aliis."

[20] *Ibid.*, p. 594: "Delectat nos natura, cum delicata uidemus. Nam natura irascimur, delectamur, miseremur."

POETIC THEORY

tator."[21] The commentary on line 111 is essentially the same in intent.[22] Finally, the distinction between historical and newly invented subjects is transformed by Acron into a distinction between the true and the verisimilar; for line 119 he says: "Si ergo certam scribis, famam sequere, aut si *fingis*, habeat artem et uerisimilitudinem figmentum tuum. Aliud praeceptum: aut notam historiam scribe, aut uerisimilia finge." In all these passages, the introduction of the term "verisimilitude," the insistence upon nature, the indication of the interaction between nature and the spectator, are signs of an approach to poetry in which the role of the audience is even more emphatically stressed than in Horace himself.

In such an approach, the goal pursued by the poet must also be related to the audience. Acron begins with the "applause" or the "laughter" of the audience and extends it to mean "fame, glory," something very close to the Ciceronian "victory." "Whoever writes, unless he write appropriately, will not obtain glory for himself" (on line 20).[23] The single word "finis" in line 406 (which Acron apparently mistakes as referring to the "end" of poetry) is translated by "laudatio," and several comments on line 412—

> Qui studet optatam cursu contingere metam

—insist that the goal is glory: "Qui studet ad gloriam uenire ..."; "*Optatam* ergo *metam* dicit gloriam, quia finis istiusmodi uitae parit gloriam sempiternam"; "Id est, propositi finem, gloriam."

If I have insisted at such length on so ancient a commentator as Acron, it is because his remarks, for readers of the Cinquecento, are in a sense contemporary both with the text of Horace and with themselves. They accompany that text in all scholarly and critical editions, are read along with it almost as if they had been written by Horace himself. Moreover, Renaissance students of the text have these remarks constantly in mind, cite them when they need support or authority for their own ideas. Finally, the salient tendencies of Acron's commentary—the reduction to precepts, the emphasis upon rhetorical elements, the attention to the role of the audience—enter bodily into the thinking of later critics about the Horatian text and in large measure determine their orientation.

As compared with the commentary of Acron, that of Porphyrion is brief, pedestrian, and relatively unimportant. It repeats a certain amount of material from Acron; but this is usually material of the grammatical or explanatory type, which constitutes the bulk of Porphyrion's contribution. The major emphases of Acron are lacking, save perhaps that upon the reduction of the work to a series of precepts. Only a few points are worthy of special mention here. As with Acron, the basis for judging appropriate-

---

[21] *Ibid.*, p. 594: "Ipsa natura spectatorem."

[22] *Ibid.*, pp. 594–95: "Id est: natura, quae me deiecit rerum miseratione, extollit prosperitate, et modo deducit ad humanitatem, modo ad iracundiam."

[23] *Ibid.*, p. 578: "qui scribit, nisi opportune scribat, non sibi conparat gloriam."

ness—and hence for assuring the audience's approval—is by reference to nature. The reason that the audience laughs, says Porphyrion, is "quod contra naturam omnia faciat."[24] Poets should choose subjects equal to their strength not (as we presume Horace to have meant) so that they can complete all parts of the work properly, but so that they may please the audience: "ut eam materiam eligant, qua possint placere" (p. 651). In the gloss on line 119—

> Aut famam sequere aut sibi conuenientia finge

—Porphyrion states a precept different from that of Acron: "For the poet who is going to write must either describe something according to the common opinion of men, or if he does not wish to handle a dry history, as it were, he must introduce known things in a proper way."[25] The distinction here is not between history and what is invented in a verisimilar way, but between a known history and some other known fact. The "res-verba" distinction again appears in connection with lines 319–20 in terms very similar to those of Acron. These few ideas, insofar as they corroborate or insist upon those of Acron, made of the commentary of Porphyrion an addendum to that of Acron which was not without its influence upon critics of the Cinquecento.

CRISTOFORO LANDINO (1482)

Acron, second century, Porphyrion, third century: between them and the critics of the Cinquecento there is a long gap. This gap is filled in part by the late-classical grammarians, Donatus and Diomedes, in part by the humanists of the fifteenth century. Both groups enter the Horatian tradition through the intermediary of two commentators who stand at the threshold of the sixteenth century, Cristoforo Landino and Badius Ascensius.

Landino's commentary on the *Ars poetica* appeared first, as far as I know, in the edition of Horace's *Opera* which he published in Florence in 1482. By way of incorporating into his remarks typical medieval thinking about poetic matters, he introduced lengthy quotations from Diomedes; by way of taking cognizance of the humanist contribution, he quoted Plato, cited Aristotle, called frequently upon Cicero, and in a long prefatory section presented a defence of poesy in the fashion of Boccaccio. Moreover, he referred to his own dialogue on poetry in his edition of Vergil. Landino's defence comprises the arguments which were already traditional: the poet is a creator inspired by the divine furor; no other writer equals him in wisdom and eloquence; he exerts a civilizing influence, is an instrument of religion, has always been held in high esteem by kings

---

[24] In the comment on the first line, p. 649 of the Hauthal edition, which is cited throughout for Porphyrion as for Acron.

[25] *Ibid.*, p. 655: "Nam poeta scripturus aut secundum hominum consensum debet aliquid describere, aut si historiam tamquam tritam non uult adtingere, debet conuenienter notam inducere."

and rulers. Great philosophers have always praised him, especially Plato in the *Ion* and Aristotle—"et ipse de facultate poetica duos: de poetis autem tres libros elegantissime scripserit." One passage in this preface indicates clearly how Landino conceives of the art of poetry and of its allegorical uses:

> Indeed its matter [is] much more divine than that of other writings; for embracing all of them, and bound together by varied rhythms, and circumscribed by separated measures, and adorned in short by various ornaments and various flowers, it embellishes with admirable fictions whatever men have heretofore done, whatever they have accomplished, whatever they have known and contemplated with a divine genius; and for fear that they cannot be understood except through allegories perceived by us, it transposes completely into things of different kinds. For when it most appears to be narrating something most humble and ignoble or to be singing a little fable to delight idle ears, at that very time it is writing in a rather secret way the most excellent things of all, and which are drawn forth from the fountain of the gods.[26]

In the commentary itself, Landino goes far beyond Acron by way of interpreting Horace in terms of invention, disposition, and elocution. His gloss on the first words of the text reads as follows: "Because in the writing of a poem the first thing to be investigated is invention, disposition, and elocution, at the very beginning he explains immediately those things which relate to invention and disposition." In this regard Landino points out how close poetry is to rhetoric; the precepts for elocution are common to both (cf. Cicero), whereas the differences occur in the other two parts. He then proceeds to subdivide the text according to these distinctions: after the lines in which the relationship of the subject matter to nature and to decorum is treated, Horace passes on to disposition (beginning with line 41, "lucidus ordo"), then to elocution (beginning with line 46, "In verbis").[27] A cognate rhetorical distinction, that of the "three styles," is introduced in an interesting fashion. If subject matters (which are invented) divide themselves into three groups, the "high," the "middle," and the "low," then the types of poems used to develop them and the kinds of diction used to express them must also fall into the same three groups. Vergil's three major poems, the *Aeneid*, the *Georgics*, and the *Bucolics*, may serve as examples of proper adaptation.

[26] *Opera* (1482 ed.), pp. clviv–clvii: "Verum rem esse multo illis diuiniorem quę illas omnes amplectens uariisque numeris colligata: distinctisque pedibus circumscripta: ac uarias denique luminibus uariisque floribus illustrata quęcunque hactenus homines fecerint; quęcunque egerint: quęcunque cognouerint: ac ingenii diuinitate contemplati fuerint admirandis figmentis exornat: et ne nisi allegoriis a nobis perceptis intelligi possint in diuersas omnino species traducit. Nam cum ostendat se aliud quippiam longe humilius ignobiliusque narrare aut fabellam ad ociosas aures oblectandas canere tunc res omnino egregias et a diuinitatis fonte exhaustas occultius scribit."

[27] *Ibid.*, p. clvii: "Quoniam in poemate scribendo inuentio dispositioque atque elocutio in primis inuestiganda est: statim a principio quę ad inuentionem dispositionemque spectant exequitur"; also pp. clviii–clviiii.

As far as Horace is concerned, the principle is intimated in lines 86 ff., "Descriptas servare vices, etc." Elocution thus fits invention, always within the framework of one of the three "figures," and a mixing of styles becomes as impossible as a mixing of matters: "neither may we write a tragedy about comic matters nor a comedy about tragic ones."[28] This fittingness of style to genre to subject matter is expressed in the general term decorum, which for Landino is one of the concerns most "proper" to poets. As for invention itself, subjects must be natural, verisimilar, but "feigned" or created; this is because the end of poetry is to please or delight—"Nos enim delectare uult"—and there is no delight without belief. The false, the ridiculous, the monstrous will cause laughter or disdain because they are not representations of nature, and one of the fundamental notions about poetics is that every art imitates nature—"omnis ars naturam imitetur."[29] The same end of delight necessitates the cultivation of variety: "The major virtue is to distinguish the poem by much variety; for by variety we delight the soul of the listener, and render him attentive, and remove him from all boredom." It will be noted to what extent these remarks depend upon a rhetorical conception of the audience, which is either to be given pleasure or to be moved—"ut auditores in quemcunque affectum mouere possit"; and although Landino makes the appropriate comments on Horace's demands for moral utility, he emphasizes much more in his commentary elements of pleasure and feeling. The audience itself, however, is superior to that for rhetoric, being more erudite and having more time to engage in reading and rereading of the work. Hence, in disposition, for example, the poet may use an artificial order, whereas the orator is restricted to a natural one.[30] In Landino, all circles close in this same consistent fashion, and whether we start with the audience, or the elements of invention, disposition, and elocution, or the three styles, we end with some other of these factors or with all of them. A totally self-consistent rhetorical system is imposed bodily upon the Horatian poetic, and made to coincide with it at every point.

BADIUS ASCENSIUS (1500)

With the publication of the commentary of Iodocus Badius Ascensius in 1500, the interpretation of the *Ars poetica* takes another step forward. Not only is Badius' discussion much longer and more complete than any of the earlier ones, but it is enriched by a vast quantity of materials brought in from new sources. Acron, Porphyrion, and Landino are of course quoted. To them are added the grammarians who figured so importantly in the

---

[28] *Ibid.*, pp. clxv and clxi: "ne de re comica tragediam: aut de tragica comediam scribamus."

[29] *Ibid.*, p. clviiv; see also p. clxiiv.

[30] *Ibid.*, p. clviiiv: "Virtus maxima est poema multa uarietate distinguere. Animum enim auditoris ex uarietate delectamus: et attentum reddimus: et ab omni fastidio remouemus"; p. clxii and p. clviiii.

medieval conceptions of poetry, Diomedes, Donatus, and Priscian. There are also references to Plato.[31] But most significant of all, Badius calls constantly upon the *Institutes* of Quintilian and upon the various rhetorical works of Cicero for explanations, clarifications, and examples of Horace's ideas. In a sense, then, the commentary of Badius at once bridges the gap between the late-classical period and the Renaissance by incorporating the principal "medieval" sources, and it relates Horace specifically to the chief Latin rhetoricians.

Badius is a lover of divisions and a maker of distinctions almost in the scholastic fashion. Hence in a prologue to his commentary he indicates that the *Ars poetica* is divided into five sections: "Item quarum prima inquiunt poeta vitia extirpat. In secunda verbi decorum instituit. In tertia rerum qualitatum & personarum decora & discrimina. Item poematos genera & inuentores demonstrat. In quarta actores: formam agendi & quomodo consummata fuit docet. Et in quinta ad diligentem castigationem cohortatur" (fol. II*v*). In the ideas of the work, Badius sees almost everywhere three-way distinctions: "Pro descriptione poetice subnotandum est triplicem esse materiam scribentium, triplicem stylum, triplex potissimum decorum, triplicem qualitatem, triplicem finem & his similia" (*ibid.*). The three "matters" so distinguished are the true (which supplies the facts for history), the verisimilar (which supplies the arguments for comedy), and the fictional, which is neither true nor verisimilar (and which supplies the fables for poetry). It should be noted that the distinction is made as a gloss upon the "materiam" of line 38 and that it is derived from the *Rhetorica ad Herennium*, at that time ascribed to Cicero. But Badius goes on to say that there is another three-way division of matters, into the "sublime" or elevated, which involves gods, heroes, and kings; the "mediocre" or middling, which consists of the scientific information exploited in didactic poetry; and the "humble" or low, containing pastoral and trivial subjects. To each of these is adapted a style and a form of verse: result, a three-way distinction of styles (also called "characteres, figurae, genera dicendi") and of meters. This is of course the commonplace rhetorical division of the Middle Ages, epitomized in the "wheel of Vergil."[32] The three "decorums" are of things, of words, and of persons; the three "qualities" of verse correspond to the three styles, the elevated, the middle, and the low; the three kinds of poems are the narrative, the dramatic, and the mixed; the three ends of the poet are to bring profit, to please, or to do both at the same time (fol. VIII*v*).

It is significant that the first statement of this set of trilogies should come in the author's preface to his commentary and that the second, expanded

---

[31] I quote Badius passages from the edition of Paris, Gerlier, 1500, the earliest edition that I know; all references are to this edition.

[32] *Ibid.*, fols. VIII–VIII*v* (on the "wheel of Vergil," cf. E. Faral, *Les Arts poétiques du XIIe et du XIIIe siècle* [Paris: Champion, 1923], p. 87).

statement should appear very early in his remarks on the text. For the schematism is in every sense prior to his interpretation of Horace. His standard procedure will be to wait for some point in the text where a key word (such as the "materiam" of line 38) gives him the opportunity to exploit one of his distinctions and then to develop it fully in connection with that word. Thus the "In *verbis* etiam *tenuis*" of line 46 becomes the occasion for expatiating on the "low" style and for citing what Cicero has to say about it: "De hac re ita dicit Cicero in de oratore" (fol. X). And the passage beginning with line 112—

Si dicentis erunt *fortunis* absona dicta

—leads to a long development on the decorum of persons, prefaced by the remark "Quia decorum personarum imprimis obseruandum est ostendit quo pacto id seruabitur," and continuing to the discussion of the fortune or condition of life of various kinds of characters, their age, and their country (fol. XIX*v*).

This matter of decorum is indeed central to the whole conception of the work, even more so than it is in Horace. For if Badius separates his ideas on poetry into small groups of three, he must find some device for collecting them together again into larger units, and that device is precisely the principle of decorum. Decorum accepted in this broader sense is really little more than a principle of appropriateness, similar to that which we have seen in Acron. Once again, Badius' ideas fall into a major group of three, as he sees all things dividing themselves according to the major distinction of the "elevated," the "middle," and the "low." One may represent these relationships in a rough tabular form as follows:

	Elevated	*Middle*	*Low*
Matters:	gods, heroes, kings	information	shepherds
Styles:	*sublime*	*mediocre*	*humile*
	altisonum		*tenue*
Meters:	hexameter	pentameter	iambic
Genres:	epic, tragedy	didactic	comedy, pastoral

The table is inexact and incomplete, since certain subsequent refinements of the ideas necessitate a crossing over from column to column. But it does represent the fundamental concept in Badius' thinking: a "high" genre such as the epic or tragedy will present persons of a certain kind, each of whom has the proper traits of character (hence the decorum of persons), speaking or spoken of in a style fitted to them (hence the decorum of words), in verse suited to them both in its general rhythmic patterns and in the structure of its sounds. Moreover, these persons will engage in actions appropriate to their characters and stations (hence the decorum of things). All but two of the smaller trilogies (manner of representation and end of the poet) are combined in this set of major relationships.

The *Ars poetica* is thus read as if it were part of the classical-medieval rhetorical tradition, which culminated in the rigorous hierarchy of the literary types as it is symbolized in the "wheel of Vergil." What is more, Badius introduces other essentially rhetorical distinctions which complete the transformation of the Horatian text. As the above table shows, the "res-verba" division is made to apply in a very real way, "matters" being the "res" and "styles" the "verba." Such a statement as the following, offered as explanation of lines 310–11—

> Rem tibi Socraticae poterunt ostendere chartae:
> Verbaque provisam rem non invita sequentur

—may be cited in corroboration: "Poema enim constat ex re & oratione. Res autem ex philosophia originem trahit vt praecepta contineat. Oratio in grammatica & rhetorica dicitur" (fol. XXXVI*v*). There is, thus, no separate art of poetry, merely a combination of philosophy, grammar, and rhetoric. The rhetorical categories of invention, disposition, and elocution are introduced at the very outset, in the conclusion to the first set of remarks: "Three things are therefore necessary at first: The careful consideration and invention of the whole matter; an economy or disposition fitted with deliberation, for the events to be narrated will be placed otherwise in a poem than in a history; and their embellishment ("exornatio") in accordance with their arrangement."[33] As for the rhetorical ideas of Cicero and Quintilian, they are introduced whenever Badius can find a plausible reason for bringing them in. For example, the requirement of unity stated in line 23 elicits the following remark: "Apta autem digressio tribus modis fieri ex quarto Quintiliani colligitur"; and Quintilian's enumeration follows (fol. V). Where Horace speaks of the danger of falling into obscurity when brevity is sought (lines 25–26), Badius finds the antidote in Cicero: "De apta tamen breuitate non nihil dicemus de qua Cicero in rhetorice veteri de enarratione loquens ita inquit ..."; and the quotation follows (fol. VII).

As for the medieval ideas incorporated into the commentary, those of Diomedes and Donatus (which I call "medieval" since they were the standard sources of ideas about poetry throughout the Middle Ages), they frequently come into the discussion even when there is no justification in the Horatian text itself. Badius opens his prologue with a number of general matters, among them the title, "Quinti Horatii Flacci ad Pisones de arte poetica institutio"; "to understand this," he goes on to say, "let us listen to Diomedes. Poetics, he says, is a metrical structure of narration of true and false things, composed in proper rhythm or meter, suitable for pleasure

---

[33] *Ibid.*, fol. IIII*v*: "Tria ergo primum sunt necessaria. Materiae totius excogitatio atque inuentio. Excogitate apta oeconomia seu dispositio. aliter enim in poemate: aliter in historia locabuntur res narrande & disposite exornatio: in qua elegantie & decori habenda est ratio."

or utility."[34] Much later, after he has finished his gloss on lines 189–201, he adds: "Since we have promised to speak of the decorum of comedies and tragedies a little later, let us now set forth a few things about their description and parts, taken from Diomedes"; and he writes over three full pages, collecting together all of Diomedes' dicta about the dramatic forms, which, essentially, have nothing to do with Horace.[35] Similarly, after his remarks on lines 275 ff., treating the history of tragedy and comedy, he adds what Donatus has to say on the same subject: "With respect to the invention of satires, tragedies, and comedies, let us recite a few things found in the grammarian Donatus. . . ."[36] Obviously, the intention is no longer merely to provide elucidation for Horace's text, but to use the commentary as a repository for everything that Badius knew or could find about the art of poetry, to transform it into a vade mecum of the kind which the Renaissance found so useful.

One final remark: The tendency found in Acron and Porphyrion to reduce Horace to a set of precepts is here carried to its inevitable conclusion. For whereas the earlier commentators had only occasionally labeled their remarks as "precepts," Badius constantly and invariably supplies a "regula" at the end of each section of the commentary. There are twenty-five such rules corresponding to the first twenty-five of the twenty-six portions of the text. Were one to assemble them in the order in which they are given, one would have a complete epitome of Badius' interpretations of the *Ars poetica*.

The net result of the addition of these four pre-Cinquecento commentaries to the text of Horace was to make of that text something very special for Cinquecento readers. The latent rhetorical characteristics of the *Ars poetica* had been made explicit and stated overtly by the two earlier commentators. The two later ones had produced as further evidence of its rhetorical character a number of parallel quotations from classical rhetoricians and had completed the rhetorical distinctions. Moreover, they had made of their commentaries compendiums of all knowledge about the poetic art, so that Horace's work was no longer a theory of poetry, but the theory of poetry, the summum of all useful ideas about the art. Text and commentaries, taken together as they always were, provided for the Cinquecento reader an initiation to poetics—which was, let it not be forgotten, an initiation of a very special kind.

[34] *Ibid.*, fol. II*v*: "Pro quo intelligendo audiamus Diomedem. Poetica inquit est ficte vereque narrationis congruenti rythmo vel pede composita: metrica structura ad vtilitatem voluptatemque accommodata."

[35] *Ibid.*, fol. XXV*v*: "Quia de comoediarum & tragoediarum decoro paulo post loqui polliciti sumus. Nunc de ipsarum descriptione & partibus pauca praemittemus ex Dyomede. . . ."

[36] *Ibid.*, fol. XXXIII*v*: "Circa inuentionem satyrarum tragoediarum & comoediarum pauca ex Donato grammatico recitabimus. . . ."

QUATTROCENTO THEORISTS

During the Quattrocento, evidences that this Horatian-rhetorical mode of thinking about poetry was common are found in various documents. I shall cite here only a few cases, which are not in themselves directly related to the Horatian text but which show the continuation, into the humanistic period, of the standard medieval distinctions about the art of poetry. A brief example is found in the *In errores Antonii Raudensis adnotationes* of Lorenzo Valla (d. 1457). Antonio had provided the following definition: "Clamare, deinde mouere tragoedias, est mouere exclamationes & exclamare." To which Lorenzo objects thus:

> And he cites the example of Quintilian; but neither in Quintilian nor in Cicero is it found in this sense. Rather, [it means] to make things more terrible and shameful by the use of the right words, which is the function of the writers of tragedy, who always speak of sad and terrible things; just as, on the contrary, to make comedies or *comoediari* is used by Aristophanes and certain other Greeks to mean "to speak ridiculously or bitingly."

To Antonio's remarks on comedy he offers these corrections:

> The author seems not to know that the "toga" is the dress of the Romans just as the "pallium" is the dress of the Greeks; and that the "togatae" were comedies which were not translated from the Greek but composed by Romans and Latins. ... Indeed, all or nearly all the works of the best comic writers, Caecilius, Plautus, and Terence, were translated from the Greek; and therefore Antonio should not have have said that Plautus was the greatest "inventor" of comedies, ... for certainly Afranius and others like him are much more properly called "inventors" than Caecilius, Plautus, and Terence, since they themselves invented and did not translate.

What is significant here is the reference to Quintilian and Cicero, the simple distinction between tragedy and comedy, and the meaning attached to the rhetorical term "invention."[37]

In the *De regno et regis institutione, libri IX* of Francesco Patrizi, Bishop of Gaeta (d. 1494), Horatian notions of the pleasure and utility of poetry are crossed with Platonic ideas of moral criteria. The utility of comedy is also made to comprise its usefulness for teaching of the language, another medieval conception. The pertinent passage occurs in Book II, chapter IX,

---

[37] In *Opera* (1543 ed.), p. 399: "Affertque exemplum Quintiliani, sed neque apud Quintilianum, neque apud Ciceronem in hanc significationem inuenitur. Imò rem uerbis atrocem magis, & indignam efficere, quale est opus tragicorum de rebus atrocibus semper, moestisque loquentium: sicut e contrario, comoedias agere, siue comoediari, pro ridicule, ac dicaciter loqui apud Aristophanem, & alios nonnullos Graecorum"; and p. 400: "Autor uidetur nescire togam esse uestem Romanorum, ut pallium, uestem Graecorum. Et togatas esse comoedias, non è Graeco traductas, sed à Romanis, Latinisque compositas. ... Etenim omnes, aut ferè omnes summorum comicorum libri è Graeco traducti sunt, Caecilij, Plauti, Terentij: eoque non fuit Raudensi dicendum, fuisse Plautum maximum fabularum inuentorem, nam . . . certe Afranius, & alij similes magis inuentores, quàm Caecilius, Plautus, Terentius dicendi sunt, qui ipsi inuenerunt non transtulerunt."

"A Futuro Rege Qui Scriptores Legendi Discendique sint, quíue negligendi":

It is not without utility that one may also read tragedies, if morality is respected in them; for they carry weight, and have elegance of expression and gravity of thought, especially Euripides. . . . In the same way the writers of comedy are also to be read. For they nourish everyday conversation, and by the propriety and the elegance of their words they make the art of speaking more polished and richer. But to conclude briefly, individual poets, even if they are read with a certain pleasure, have certain virtues of their own, and a certain wonderful grace which is not at all unsuitable to the dignity of a king.

Obscene poets must be absolutely rejected, because they corrupt good mores and imbue the soul with wickedness. . . . But let us listen to Plato, who orders the poets to write those things which will make men good and will teach them that the good are happy and the bad are unhappy even if they are rich and lucky.[38]

A much more complete representation of this Horatian-rhetorical point of view is contained in Giovanni Pontano's dialogue, *Actius*, already mentioned as one of those documents which classified poetry with history. On the one hand, the dialogue is full of rhetorical distinctions applied to poetry: both history and poetry fall within the deliberative and demonstrative categories of oratory; each proposes as its ends "ut doceat, delectet, moveat"; the functions of both are divided into invention, disposition, and elocution; the personal goal of "victory" for the orator is very similar to that of "fame" or "glory" for the poet. On the other hand, differences between poetry and either history or rhetoric are usually explained in terms of distinctions found in Horace or in his commentators: poetry is more studied and elegant in its vocabulary and rhythms, especially in the use of new words; history is restricted to the truth, whereas poetry treats as well "probabilia, ficta," and sometimes things which are in no wise "veri similia"; history follows a natural order of narration, while poetry cultivates the "in medias res" beginning. The language of the orator is fitted to the forum and the senate; that of the poet must display a special kind of magnificence, elevation, and excellence:

The end of both orater and poet is to move and carry away the listener. Indeed to what end, I ask, to what end is directed this capacity to move and to carry away and the extraordinary attention that both men give to it? The orator

[38] *De regno* (1567 ed.), pp. 56v–57: "Non sine vtilitate etiam leguntur Tragoedi, si mores in tuto fuerint, habent enim pondus, ac nitorem verborum, & sententiarum grauitatem, pręcipuè Euripides. . . . Eodem etiam modo Comici legendi sunt. Alunt siquidem quotidianum sermonem, & proprietate elegantiáque verborum eloquentiam nitidiorem uberiorémque reddunt. Sed vt breuiter concludam, singuli poëtae, si cùm delectu quodam leguntur, proprias quasdam virtutes habent, & mirificam quandam gratiam, quae à regia dignitate nequaquam aliena est. . . . Obscoeni poëtae omnino negligendi sunt, bonos enim mores corrumpunt, & animum nequitiis imbuunt. . . . Nos autem Platonem audiamus, qui ea poëtas scribere iubet, quae viros bonos efficiant, doceantque bonos beatos esse, malos verò miseros, etiam si fortunati ac diuites essent."

clearly wishes to persuade the judge, the poet wishes to obtain the admiration of the listener and the reader, since the first strives for victory, the second for fame and glory.... The poet will be completely cheated of his end unless he has aroused and impressed admiration in the soul of the listener or the reader, by means of which he will acquire fame and reverence.

Such a passage as this is almost completely Ciceronian in tone; taken together with the other ideas of the text, it demonstrates to what extent rhetoric and poetics were combined under the aegis of Horace.[39]

What Pietro Ricci (Petrus Crinitus) had to offer in the way of theoretical statements in his *Libri de poetis Latinis* (1505) was very slight. His work is a series of notices on the Latin poets, containing brief remarks on the poets' place and time of birth, family, studies, protectors and friends, the genres which they practiced, their characters, lists of their works, some ancient opinions about them. If it has any interest at all for us, it is because for each poet passing estimates of his work are offered, usually in the form of epithets or concise critical formulas. In these occasional attempts at practical criticism, the standards of judgment remain essentially the same as those of the Middle Ages, reflecting the tradition which I am here discussing. Plautus excelled, he says, "scribendi elegantia & salibus"; Pacuvius cultivated the "amplum ac sonorum dicendi genus"; Terence was perfect "sermonis elegantia & proprietate," and moreover, according to the opinion of Donatus, "he controlled the emotions in such a way that he neither swells to the magnitude of tragedy nor descends to the level of simple history." Sextus Turpilius is praised for his "senarii de officio & ratione uiuendi," Publius Syrius for his "sententiarum grauitatem atque singularem elegantiam" (a standard formula used also for other writers), Horace because "plenus est iucunditatis & gratiae." The Horatian ends appear in such a phrase as this, applied to Manilius: "ut magis instruere: ac docere uideatur: quam delectare."[40] Brief though they may be, statements of this kind are indicative of the current ways of thinking about poetic works and of the persistence, into the sixteenth century, of older orientations toward the art.

POMPONIO GAURICO (1510)

The earliest formal commentary on the *Ars poetica* in the Cinquecento, as far as I have been able to discover, was that of Pomponio Gaurico

---

[39] In *I Dialoghi*, ed. Previtera (1943), pp. 193–94, 202, 232; and p. 233: "Utriusque etiam, oratoris ac poetae officium est movere et flectere auditorem; verum quonam, quo, inquam, haec et commotio et flexio et maximum utriusque in hoc ipso studium? Oratoris scilicet ut persuadeat iudici, poetae ut admirationem sibi ex audiente ac legente comparet, cum ille pro victoria nitatur, hic pro fama et gloria.... poeta fine omnino defraudabitur suo nisi in audientis ac legentis animo pepererit infixeritque admirationem, per quam sit famam venerationemque assecuturus."

[40] *De poetis Latinis* (1505), pp. Aiii, Aiv, Av, Avv: "ita temperauit affectus ut neque ad tragicam magnitudinem intumescat: neque abiciatur ad historicam," Avi, Bv, D2.

(*ca.* 1482–1530). Published with the text of Horace in 1541 under the title *Pomponius Gauricus super Arte poetica Horatii*, the commentary alone had been previously printed as the *De Arte poetica* in an undated edition which must go back to about 1510.[41] Gaurico declares in his dedication to Francesco Pucci that he does not wish to give a word-for-word gloss on the text in the fashion of the grammarians, but to "collect together the precepts themselves and to tell what he himself [Horace] had warned against."[42] Nevertheless, he does not reduce the text to a set of precepts as certain of his predecessors had done. Instead, what he gives is little more than a running paraphrase or prosification of the original text. In that paraphrase, little is added to the ideas of the text, little that might be said to be the contribution of Gaurico. What he does contribute follows the lines previously indicated in this chapter. He emphasizes what he thinks to be the most important ideas by putting brief formulas in the margin, such as "De speciebus concipiendis," "De totius operis aequabilitate," "De proposito," "De stilo." These provide a kind of outline for his reading of Horace. For lines 38 ff., the marginalia read "De Inuentione," "De Dispositione," "De Elocutione," indicating that Gaurico is once again effecting the conflation between Horace and the standard rhetorical approach. Other significant remarks are found in such formulas as "Numeros ad materiam accomodandos," "De Comoediae Tragoediaeque decoro," "De optima Ratione compositionis," and "Quid in Comoedia Tragoediaque necessarium." In the text itself, Gaurico tends to reduce all Horace's suggestions to a universal principle of appropriateness. Frequently, this "appropriateness" is to a norm of nature; thus the comment on the first lines: "as for what is said about poets and painters, that they may do what they please, this is valid to the extent that they do not depart from nature."[43] Or the remarks on style relevant to lines 24 ff.: "That style turns out to be the best which will imitate the nature of the thing treated."[44] A somewhat longer passage, on the "Sumite materiam uestris" of line 38, further circumscribes this "nature" and indicates the essential orientations of the commentary:

> You will have to find a subject matter of this kind: not absurd, not difficult, not far removed from daily usage, but appropriate, susceptible of ornament, and such that you will know it thoroughly and be capable of sustaining it to the very end. If it is such, you will understand better in what manner the disposition is to

---

[41] The *De Arte poetica*, the first edition, prints on page Biv*v* a "Sanctio" given by Pope Julius II; since Julius was Pope between 1503 and 1513, this would presumably be the ten-year period during which the edition was printed.

[42] *De Arte poetica* (*ca.* 1510 ed.), p. A: "sed tantummodo praecepta ipsa colligerem: & quid ille commonuerit: enarrarem."

[43] *Ibid.*, p. A*v*: "Nam quod aiunt Pictoribus ac Poetis licere quod uelint: eatenus licet: quatenus a natura non recedant."

[44] *Ibid.*, pp. A*v*–Aii: "optimum illum uideri stilum: qui eius rei de qua agitur naturam imitabitur."

be treated and you will be able to express the matter in words much more appropriately.[45]

At other times, "appropriateness" merely means following the norms of decorum; for example, the use of comic verse for a tragic subject would be like an impropriety of dress (p. Ai*v*). A few isolated passages are worthy of attention: (1) the "prodesse" of line 333 is explained as meaning "ad institutiones uitaeque praecepta referamus," thus putting the emphasis upon moral teaching (p. B*v*); (2) the pendant "delectare" is made to depend upon verisimilitude, "if we invent things which make for pleasure, the things invented must appear as similar to the truth as possible; lest by chance you may suppose that you must invent things which cannot be in any way believed to have happened";[46] (3) the end of the lyric is also made one of utility, in the following terms: "ut hominibus uiam ad uirtutem significaremus: Regum gratiam aucuparemur" (p. Biii). The main directions of Gaurico's development of the Horatian text would thus seem to be toward a pointing up of the rhetorical tendencies of the *Ars poetica* and their association with Ciceronian rhetorical principles, toward an extension or even exaggeration of the idea of appropriateness, and toward an insistence upon the conception of nature held by the audience addressed.

During the same years, Vittore Fausto published his brief *De comoedia libellus* (1511). He declares that it will be an expansion upon Donatus and Diomedes, and it soon becomes clear that this expansion will take the form of a few references to Aristotle and some crossing with the rhetorical mode. The *Ars poetica* does not enter directly into cause, but some of the positions of the earlier commentators are approximated. For example, the "res-verba" distinction is present in the following statement, in which Fausto is telling how the goals of comedy may be achieved: "Since poets used to try to bring this about with things and with words, they will have two ways of doing so...." The two ways refer to types of plot. For the rest, Fausto's treatise is concerned with the seven kinds of words which cause laughter, with the importance of stage action and apparatus, with the appropriateness of intonation to action, and with historical matters.[47]

Le selvette of Niccolò Liburnio (1513) is a collection of short dialogues on sundry matters. In the first one, the art of poetry is discussed in what is essentially another defence of poesy. The poet is said to require great

---

[45] *Ibid.*, p. Aii: "Inuenienda uero uobis scribendi materia erit: non absurda: non aspera: non longius a cotidiana consuetudine remota: sed que conueniat: que ornamenta suscipiat: quam et uos pulcherrime cognitam habeatis et constanter substinere ualeatis. Sic enim quemadmodum dispositio tractanda sit melius intelligetis: et rem ipsam multo conuenientius eloqui poteritis."

[46] *Ibid.*, p. Bii: "si que ad uoluptatem faciunt confingemus: hec que confingentur ueri similima uideri debebunt: ne forte putetis fingenda uobis: ea que facta fuisse: nullo modo credi possunt."

[47] *De comoedia libellus* (1511), p. AA3: "Quandoquidem illud in primis poetae rebus, & uerbis efficere conabantur, ipsa quidem re bifariam...."

erudition, especially in Greek literature; he must be adept in language (acquired through art) and in subject matters (acquired through extensive reading). To achieve perfection in a work he must combine art, nature, and diligence. Horace's precepts for the comportment of the poet are cited, and various models for the writer are proposed, including Dante, Petrarch, Antonio Tibaldeo, Sannazaro, and Bembo. Follows at last a long series of the conventional arguments in defence of the art. The "Selvetta terza" urges the poet to imitate earlier models, as Dante imitated Vergil and Vergil imitated Homer. Both "materia" and "stile" may benefit from such imitation. The ends of all poetic writing, as in Horace, are to profit and to please: "for the first of these it is necessary to read ... a great mass of ancient authors; for the second, in whatever you write, it is necessary to weave so lovely and elegant a garland of varied flowers that whoever is tricked into assaying it with the eyes of the mind may derive from it pleasure and utility, in a way which will teach good and happy living."[48]

As a matter of record, it should be pointed out that Matteo Bonfini's *In Horatianis operibus centum et quindecim annotationes* appeared at about this time, although the exact date is unknown. Bonfini's annotations on the *Ars poetica* are, however, disappointing, since they are exclusively grammatical and lexicographical in character and throw no light upon the interpretation of the text as a theoretical document.

In the 1517 Aldine edition of Terence there appeared for the first time a prefatory letter entitled "In Terentium epistola," which has since been attributed to Andrea Navagero.[49] It is an interesting letter because it judges Terence in terms of the criteria supplied by Horace and is thus a kind of essay in practical Horatian criticism. The author proceeds on the basis of a comparison between Terence and Plautus, indicating throughout the reasons for Terence's superiority. In language, first Terence excels in "elegantia," is "cultior," "limatior." These are the standard terms of rhetorical criticism. In the general construction of his comedies, Terence satisfies all the requirements of Horace:

The comedies of Plautus often gape at the seams and do not have sufficient cohesion. Those of Terence are all so well woven within themselves, make so complete a unity out of all the elements, that nothing could be more completely realized than those compositions, nothing more perfect. And this is precisely the thing in which all poets and writers must principally excel, and which demands the greatest art—if indeed there be any others. For that decorum which is to be so carefully observed in all things, if it be not observed in dramatic compositions,

---

[48] *Le selvette* (1513), pp. 9–14v and pp. 33v–34: "alla prima fa di mestieri leggere ... selue d'authori antichi; alla seconda, in cio tu iscriui, bisogna de fiori uarii tessere si uaga & pulita ghirlanda; che chiunque s'inueschi d'assagiarla co gli occhi dello'ntelletto, posse dillettatione & utilita sciugharne, con modo maestreuole al buono & beato viuere."

[49] For the basis of the attribution, see Navagero, *Opera omnia* (Padua: Volpi-Camino, 1718), p. 427. On the 1517 ed., see A. Firmin-Didot, *Alde Manuce et l'Hellénisme à Venise* (Paris: Firmin-Didot, 1875), pp. 465–66.

where everything must be contrived appropriately to each personage, then nothing at all is accomplished.[50]

Furthermore, of the two possible types of humor, that of actions and that of words, Terence cultivates the former and hence appeals to a superior audience.

GIOVANNI BRITANNICO DA BRESCIA (1518)

To approximately the same period belongs another extensive commentary on the *Ars poetica*, that of Giovanni Britannico da Brescia (Ioannes Britannicus Brixianus). Britannico flourished toward the end of the fifteenth century and produced commentaries on various Latin authors; the standard biographical dictionaries give the date of his death as 1510, but Tiraboschi (Venice, 1796 ed., VI³, 992) cites a document by him dated November 26, 1518. I do not know when the commentary on Horace was written or first appeared; but since the first edition that I have been able to discover is that of Milan, Scinzenzeler, 1518 (*Q. Horatij Flacci poemata*), I am discussing the commentary at this chronological position. It is a conventional commentary in every respect, frequently calling, as did others of the time, upon Acron, Porphyrion, Diomedes, and Donatus. It makes no mention of Badius and may possibly be earlier than his exegesis. It goes beyond most other early glosses, however, in the extent of its references to a multitude of classical writers; Plato, Cicero, Quintilian, Pliny, Valerius Flaccus, Vitruvius, Vergil, and Homer are called upon frequently for examples and explanations. One realizes that the whole richness of humanistic erudition is being brought to bear upon the explanation of the *Ars poetica*. What emerges is in a sense disappointing, since few new critical orientations are discovered. Britannico continues to make a systematic reduction of the Horatian text to a series of precepts, and most of these precepts repeat the traditional rhetorical admonitions. The undercurrent of thinking in terms of invention, disposition, and elocution rises to the surface at the proper places: when, for example, he wishes to provide remarks on the "Rem" of line 310—

Rem tibi Socraticae poterunt ostendere chartae

—he says: "Thus he indicates that the invention of the materials is necessary above all else in the poet." Or with respect to the "ordinis" of line 42 he defines: "for order is the disposition and distribution of the materials which shows what is to be put in each place." The "verba" of line 311 (following the "rem" of line 310) provides the occasion for a definition of elocution: "for elocution (as Cicero teaches in the *Rhetorica*) is the fitting

---

[50] (1517 ed.), p. a2: "Hyant nonnunquam, neque satis cohaerent Plauti Comoediae. ita omnia Terentij inter se nexa: ita ex omnibus unum quoddam conficitur: ut nihil aptius illius fabulis, nihil magis fieri ad unguem possit. atqui hoc id est, quod praecipue praestari & ab poetis, & ab scriptoribus omnibus debeat: ac maximam, si aliud quippiam, artem exigat. iam decorum illud, quod in omnibus tantopere custudiendum rebus est: in fabulis uero, ubi congrua unicuique personae effingenda sunt omnia: nisi seruetur, nihil prorsus fiat."

of proper words and of sententiae to the invention."[51] What Britannico says in the sentences immediately following shows that he is also making the usual association of these elements with the "res-verba" distinction: "For every poem," he says, "consists of words and things. The things are these same moral precepts, and the words are the diction itself."[52]

What is perhaps a more distinctive contribution on Britannico's part is his development of a dichotomy between the parts of poems providing pleasure and utility to the audience. Pleasure is a product of both "verba" and "res": of "verba," insofar as pleasantness and elegance of language are delightful in themselves (of the "dulci" in line 343 he says: "iucunditatem, elegantiamque sermonis intelligit: quae multum delectat," after which he states that it is another expression of the "delectare" in line 333); of "res," insofar as a "natural" and "verisimilar" representation of objects is pleasurable. The conditions here imposed are important; for if Horace's monster is ridiculous rather than pleasurable, it is because it is "contra naturam," and however fictional and imaginary the ornaments of a poem may be, they must nevertheless be like the truth. Another principle is really involved here: that part of "res" which is imitated from nature— e.g., the characters assigned to people according to decorum—must actually be faithfully copied from nature in a consistent and appropriate way; whereas that part which is "feigned" or created by the poet must be "like" nature. Both the real and the fictional must impress the audience as being true if they are to give it pleasure. Utility, however, is a product of "res" only. It consists in the lessons to be learned by the audience from the moral precepts and the moral examples presented by the poet. Hence, it is not sufficient for the poet to imitate the mores of men; he must limit himself to the imitation of "good" mores. Britannico interprets "morataque recte" of line 319 not as meaning "having correct mores" but as meaning "quae bonis moribus sit instructa: quae a turpitudine sit aliena."[53]

Into this central scheme Britannico has no difficulty in fitting the standard elements of Horatian theory and of the traditional interpretations. Simplicity or unity of plot is merely a reflection of the natural oneness of the materials imitated (v. pp. CXIIIv–CXIV). In the same way, the universal principle of appropriateness is merely a transposition into literary terms of the notion that things of the same kind are assorted by nature and that such things as would not be put together by nature must not be

[51] *Poemata* (Milan, 1518 ed.), p. CXXXVI: "sicque ostendit in poeta necessariam imprimis esse rei inuentionem"; p. CXVIv: "Est autem ordo dispositio & distributio rerum: qui demonstrat: quid quibusque locis sit collocandum," and cf. p. CXXXIv: "Per seriem igitur intellige ordinem & rerum dispositionem, quae distribuit quid quibusque locis sit collocandum"; and p. CXXXVI: "est enim elocutio: ut docet Cicero in rhetoricis idoneorum uerborum & sententiarum ad inuentionem accommodatio."

[52] *Ibid.*, p. CXXXVI: "omne enim poema rebus & uerbis constat: res enim sunt ipsa praecepta: uerba uero ipsa oratio."

[53] *Ibid.*, p. CXXXVIIv; pp. CXIV–CXVv, especially the last page: "debet enim fictio artificiosa naturam imitari"; p. CXXXVI.

combined by art. Therefore the three styles, each of which assembles coherent and consonant elements, and the interdiction against crossing or mixing them: literary "species" are as distinct and discrete as natural species. The theory of the literary genres is rounded out by prescription of the subject matters and of the meters for each. Thus, as compared with earlier or with contemporary commentators, Britannico would seem to place greater emphasis on the relationships between poetry and nature, although he by no means decreases the time and attention devoted to rhetorical matters.

The *Epistola* of Andrea Navagero, cited a few pages back, had been dedicated to Pietro Bembo. In 1525, Bembo himself published his *Prose della volgar lingua*. This is essentially a linguistic document, as its title indicates; but it belongs to the present inquiry in two ways: first, because it was the earliest important document in the quarrel over Dante which raged later in the century, and second, because when he speaks of the relationship between language and poetry, Bembo does so in terms of the current Horatian tradition. In Book II, for example, Bembo discusses the choice and disposition of words to be used for any given subject matter by referring to the three styles:

If one is speaking of a high subject matter, the words to be chosen should be grave, elevated, sonorous, clear, luminous; if of a low and vulgar subject matter, they should be light, plain, humble, popular, quiet; if of a subject midway between these two, one should speak with middling and temperate words and ones which tend to move as little as possible in the direction of the one or the other extreme. It is necessary, nevertheless, to use discretion in the observance of these rules, and above all to avoid satiety by varying occasionally both grave words with temperate ones and temperate words with light ones. ... Nevertheless, a most general and universal rule is that, in each one of these manners and styles, we must choose the purest, the cleanest, the clearest, the most beautiful and agreeable words possible and bring them to our compositions.[54]

In Bembo's linguistic theory, styles and words exist in self-determined categories, with the only reference to an external context being to the general types of subject matters which they express. As for his dicta on Dante, they will be treated in the appropriate chapter.

Like Navagero's *Epistola*, Mario Equicola's *Libro de natura de amore* of 1525 may serve as an example of an application in practical criticism of the

[54] *Prose* (1525 ed.), p. xxiiiv: "Da scieglere adunque sono li uoci; se di materia grande si ragiona; graui, alte, sonanti, apparenti, luminose: se di bassa et uolgare; lieui, piane, dimesse, popolari, chete: se di mezzana tra queste due: medesimamente con uoci mezzane et temperate, et lequali meno all'uno et all'altro pieghino di questi due termini che si puo. È di mestiero nondimeno in queste medesime regole seruar modo, et schifare sopra tutto la satieta uariando alle uolte et le uoci graui con alcuna temperata, et le temperate con alcuna leggiera. ... Tuttafiata generalissima et uniuersale regola è in ciascuna di queste maniere et stili le piu pure, le piu monde, le piu chiare sempre, le piu belle et piu grate uoci scieglere et arrecare alle nostre compositioni, che si possa."

Horatian and rhetorical principles which are here occupying us. The occasion for such an application comes in the first book, where Equicola is discussing the poets who have treated of love. In his remarks on Guittone d'Arezzo he speaks of the pleasure afforded by poets through the use of music and rhythms, and Guido Cavalcanti is praised for the everyday flavor of his diction. Petrarch seems to occupy his high position in Italian poetry largely because he added to Tuscan many words from other regions of Italy, and Boccaccio because (like Lucian and Apuleius) he wrote poetically in prose and "embraced delightful poetry and beautiful materials." Most of Equicola's critical remarks, though, concern the work of Jacopo Calandra of Mantua, in connection with whom he states a number of critical principles. He speaks of the difficult task of the poet who must "delight and move with ornamented language" and of the remarkable talent required to "discover, and to take care to dispose and order well, whatever he invents." Even if invention and disposition are provided by nature, the poet will fail to delight and move unless he be a master of diction; and this requires erudition, study, labor, art. "The invention may be as beautiful as you please; without ornament it is a mass of gold that does not shine." To achieve ornament, the poet must know many things, cultivate exquisite sententiae, tend to the propriety of words; above all, he must choose words in common usage and those which will please the ear. All these qualities are found in Calandra. In his *Aura* he observes the decorum of persons throughout; above all, his style displays great virtues: words purely and properly derived from Latin, well-chosen diction, a great impression of naturalness and perfect rhythms.[55] In the last analysis, all of Equicola's criteria reduce to matters of language, and he is almost as exclusively concerned with the "volgar lingua" as was Bembo.

Another work essentially linguistic in character is Niccolò Liburnio's *Le tre fontane* of the following year, 1526. Liburnio studies the language of Dante, Petrarch, and Boccaccio, after having made a preliminary statement to the effect that for the poet as for the orator language is fitted to materials on the basis of the three styles. He debates at length—as the commentators on Horace had so frequently done—the question of art versus nature in the work of the poet, citing Plato's *Ion* and Cicero's *Pro Archia* on the side of nature. Of the five parts of oratory which he distinguishes—invention, disposition, elocution, memory, and pronunciation—he accords most time to elocution. The reasons are clear, for this is the part which is most admirable, which is involved in the three styles, and which demands the greatest application. Of the three styles, Vergil is cited as the consummate master; the opinion of the Middle Ages endures. The advice to young writers is to learn thoroughly all Tuscan words and to cultivate all the best authors of the past, who will provide them with invention as well as with

[55] *Libro de natura de amore* (1525), pp. 3v–5v, 39: "la inuentione quanto uoi bella, senza ornamento e una massa d'oro che non risplende."

elocution. Cicero and Quintilian and Horace are cited as authorities for this opinion.[56]

In the light of these last documents, it is perhaps not fortuitous that Giovan Giorgio Trissino should have published his Italian translation of Dante's *De vulgari eloquentia* in 1529. Clearly, we are in a period of intense interest in problems of language and especially the problem of the Italian language. Dante's *De la volgare eloquenzia* comes appropriately just a few years after Bembo's *Prose della volgar lingua*. Moreover, for readers of the time, it was a contemporary document. Many of them believed that Trissino himself had written it—no version of Dante's text had previously been printed—and was merely trying to gain authority for his ideas by assigning them to Dante. What Dante had to say, besides, sounded so much like what writers in these years were saying that it did not fall at all strangely upon the ears of contemporaries. The basis of Dante's treatment of poetry is a division of language into three levels, the "illustre," the "mediocre," and the "humile," which conform to three kinds of subject matter, the tragic, the comic, and the elegiac. It should be noted that these are kinds of materials, not literary genres, and that the meanings attached to the terms are different from the conventional ones. The tragic style, for example, is adapted to poems about war, about love, and about virtue:

It appears certain that we use the tragic style when the gravity of the sententiae and the loftiness of the verse and the elevation of the constructions and the excellence of the words all are assorted to one another; but because ... it has already been proved that the highest things are worthy of the highest, and this style, which we call the tragic, seems to be the highest of the styles, therefore those things which we have already distinguished as demanding to be sung in the highest manner must be sung in this style only: that is, safety, love, and virtue.[57]

Poetry itself is defined as "a rhetorical fiction [or invention] set to music"; it may be written in any language, but that composed in the "regulated" classical languages is the best, and that composed in the vulgar tongues will achieve excellence to the degree to which it imitates the other. This way of thinking in terms of the three styles and of the subject matters to which they belong, this tendency to regard poetry as a kind of rhetoric whose problems are essentially linguistic, would of course sound very familiar to the reader of the 1520's.

AULO GIANO PARRASIO (1531)

To the same decade of the twenties should probably be attributed Aulo Giano Parrasio's *In Q. Horatii Flacci Artem poeticam commentaria*, pub-

[56] *Le tre fontane* (1526), pp. *iiv, 46, 64v.

[57] *De la volgare eloquenzia*, trans. Trissino (1529), pp. b viii-c and cv: "Appare certamente, che noi usiamo il stilo tragico, quando e la gravità de le sentenzie, e la superbia de i versi, e la elevazione de le construzioni, e la excellenzia de i vocabuli si concordano insieme; ma perche ... gia è provato, che le cose somme sono degne de le somme, e questo stilo, che kiamiamo tragico, pare essere il sommo de i stili, però quelle cose, che havemo gia distinte doversi sommamente cantare, sono da essere in questo solo stilo cantate; cioè la salute, lo amore, e la virtù" (spelling modified; I have replaced Trissino's omegas by conventional o's).

lished posthumously by Bernardino Martirano in 1531. This is another full-scale commentary that was to be incorporated frequently into later editions of the Horatian text.[58] Parrasio's position is essentially the same as that of his predecessors, but there are certain notable departures that show some forward movement in the thinking about Horace's epistle. Before beginning his study of the text, Parrasio writes a lengthy introduction, which is in itself a kind of miniature *ars poetica*. He develops, on the basis of Plato, the theory of the divine origin of poetry, of the divine furor, of the poet as prophet. He may be alluding indirectly to Averroës' paraphrase of the *Poetics* when he insists that harmony and rhythm are natural or instinctive in man, that poetry was used originally for purposes of praising virtue and attacking vice, that the poet must form in advance a complete conception of the poem before beginning to write it.[59] From Quintilian he derives not only the idea that the poet must be a good man, but also that he must be "peritus" in an infinity of subjects. Both of these ideas are developed in passages which are interesting because they are so frequently re-echoed in later critical writing of the century. On the "goodness" of the poet: "First of all it is essential that the poet himself be a wise man, that he understand what things are proper to a good man. This he will not be able to do unless he be a good man himself, unless he himself abound in all the virtues, unless he have absorbed the whole of poetry, that is of wisdom, unless he lack all vices."[60] And on his infinite "knowledge":

It is necessary then that every poet be an expert on all matters, so that he may be able to speak copiously about everything. He must know well the customs of the various peoples, the usages, the laws, the details about maritime and inland cities, the descriptions of places, agriculture, the military art, the sayings and the acts of illustrious men; let him be expert with the stylus, erudite in geometry, learned in architecture and music, experienced as well in natural and moral science as in the art of writing, not ignorant of medicine. He must remember the opinions of lawyers, have certain knowledge of astrology and astronomy. But above all a knowledge of histories and of myths is necessary, and of everything that is related to grammar.[61]

[58] For references to some of these editions, see the Index to the Mills College check-list (note 4 above), s.v. Parrhasius, Aulus Janus. The date of Parrasio's death is commonly given as 1534 in the standard biographical dictionaries; but note that the dedication to the 1531 edition, by Martirano, refers to him as already dead.

[59] *Commentaria* (1531), pp. 1, 2, 6v; cf. Averroës (1481 ed.), p. f2v, p. f ("Omne itaque poema & omnis oratio poetica aut est uituperatio aut est laudatio"), p. gv.

[60] *Ibid.*, pp. 3–3v: "Ante omnia oportet ipsum poetam esse sapientem, quae boni uiri sint intelligat. quod non faciet, nisi ipse sit bonus, nisi omnibus abundet uirtutibus, nisi poeticam omnem, id est sapientiam imbiberit, careat uitijs"; cf. Quintilian, Bk. XII, ch. I.

[61] *Ibid.*, pp. 2v–3: "Quemcunque autem poetam rerum omnium peritum esse oportet, ut de una quaque re possit copiose dicere. Mores populorum, consuetudines, iura, terrestrium, maritimarumque cognitiones urbium, locorumque descriptiones, agriculturam, rem militarem, clarorum uirorum dicta factaque pernoscat, graphidos peritus sit, geometriae eruditus, architecturam edoctus, musicam sciat, scientiam cum naturae & morum, tum disserendi calleat, medicinae non ignaris, iurisconsultorum responsa teneat, astrologiam, coelique rationes compertas habeat. Nam historiarum, fabularumque cognitio, quaeque grammaticae copulantur, in primis sunt necessaria"; cf. Quintilian, Bk. I, ch. X.

Parrasio's introduction contains, moreover, other elements that reveal his attitudes toward poetry. He conceives of the end of poetry as being both rhetorical and moral: rhetorical insofar as it must "inflame the souls of men, extinguish wrath, arouse hate and sorrow, or lead them away from these same passions to gentleness and pity"; moral insofar as it must "invite men to good living by means of examples and reasoning, teach character and the passions, prescribe in a pleasant way what things are to be done."[62] The insistence, in the above paragraph concerning knowledge, on a mastery of grammar and, in this last citation, on the "pleasant way" is explained by Parrasio's stand on diction. For whereas most of his remarks so far have pertained to the poet and the effect of the poem upon the audience, when he actually does speak about the poem itself, he speaks of it largely in terms of diction. "Nothing," he says, "is as poetic as the diction." This emphasis will be apparent in the commentary itself; it is also prominent in the concluding section of the introduction, where he outlines Horace's general procedure. This procedure consists in dividing the work into two parts, the function of the first being to show what things are to be avoided ("uitanda ostendere") and of the second to prescribe what things are to be done ("sequenda praecipere"). Five precepts contain the essence of the first: (1) admit nothing inappropriate, lest there be discrepancies in the invention and a lack of total harmony; (2) avoid placing things where they do not belong, or introducing digressions or superfluous ornaments; (3) do not pursue the various kinds of style ("dicendi figuras") to the point of falling into the opposite vices; (4) in the search for variety, so important to the poet, refrain from the excessive cultivation of mythology, the excessive desire for eloquence, for superfluous and inappropriate ornament; (5) never depart from the most important matters. For the second, there seem to be seven brief precepts: (1) know how to provide a fitting order for the whole work; (2) narrate elegantly; (3) write beautifully; (4) cultivate variety constantly; (5) attend to the perfection of the whole; (6) start from an advance idea of the structure of the total poem; (7) achieve a tight correspondence of beginning, middle, and end. It is in the set of negative precepts especially that the emphasis on style is found.[63]

In the commentary itself, Parrasio develops and expands the notions epitomized in his precepts. As he does so, certain of the distinctions now so familiar—invention, disposition, and elocution, "res" and "verba," the three styles, nature, art, and practice in the poet—come to light and are exploited. These cross one another in interesting ways: "res" becomes equivalent to invention, "verba" to elocution; the three styles all belong to elocution, which is more important than invention ("poetis maiori obser-

---

[62] *Ibid.*, p. 3: "inflammare animos hominum, & extinguere iram, odium, dolorem incendere, aut ab his ijsdem ad lenitatem & misericordiam reuocare"; and p. 4v: "ad bene uiuendum rationibus exemplisque inuitare, mores, affectionesque docere, res gerendas cum iocunditate praecipere."

[63] *Ibid.*, p. 3: "Nihil tam est poeticum, quam eloquutio"; pp. 6–6v.

uanda diligentia," p. 12) since it depends more completely upon genius (or nature) than upon art, which is sufficient for invention and disposition. The further distinction of pleasure and utility is also related, because in a general way utility comes from the "res" and pleasure from the "verba." One might reduce his argument in connection with Horace's line 333 as follows:

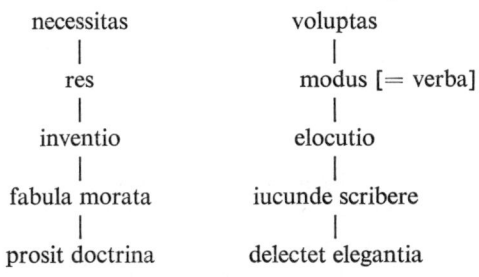

```
        necessitas              voluptas
            |                       |
           res                  modus [= verba]
            |                       |
         inventio                elocutio
            |                       |
       fabula morata           iucunde scribere
            |                       |
       prosit doctrina         delectet elegantia
```

Furthermore, a kind of distinction among genres seems to be made on the same basis: tragedy aims primarily at utility, comedy at pleasure.[64] The principle of decorum applies to both "res" and "verba." With respect to "res," it involves a correspondence between the things imitated in the work of art and things in nature; this is the most important thing for the poet to observe. "Not only in our lives but also in speech nothing is more difficult than to perceive what is proper, what the Greeks call πρέπον and we call *decorum*. . . . We must pay due attention to appropriateness, so that we imitate what really happens in nature and do not disturb its order."[65] With respect to "verba," the principle of decorum involves an appropriateness of words to things; all words must be chosen and placed "in a way fitting and proper to the dignity of the things."[66] Considerations of "nature" enter prominently in the commentary, not only in connection with decorum but as related to the origins of poetry (there are again strong echoes of Averroës in the statement that imitation is instinctive in man[67]), to the definition of poetry as an "imitatio naturae" (p. 78), to the genius of the poet. In a general way, all matters of "res" are referred to criteria of nature insofar as they involve verisimilitude and decorum, and to the audience insofar as they must persuade and move through credibility. On

[64] *Ibid.*, pp. 69v, 72: "habent inter se nonnullam similitudinem uescentes & scribentes, ut quibusdam utantur ad uoluptatem, quibusdam ad necessitatem. Docendi necessitas, in rebus est constituta, delectatio uero, in modo, quo docemus. Prosumus autem, cum morata recte est fabula. delectamus cum iucunde scribimus. . . . Laus poetae est ut prosit doctrina, delectet elegantia"; and p. 38.

[65] *Ibid.*, p. 7: "non solum in omni uita, sed etiam in oratione nihil est difficilius quam uidere quid deceat, πρέπον Graeci uocant, nostri decorum. . . . Est & suus conuenientiae labor adhibendus, ut quae in naturam cadunt fingantur, illius ordo non perturbetur."

[66] *Ibid.*, p. 12v: "ad rerumque dignitatem apte & decore."

[67] *Ibid.*, p. 68v: "Nihil enim aliud est poesis nisi imitatio uitae & morum, quae hominis propria est, facitque ut uel hac una differat a caeteris animalibus"; with which cf. Averroës (1481 ed.), p. f2v: "Prima quidem quum in homine existit naturaliter a prima sua natiuitate assimilatio rei ad rem: . . . & istud proprium est homini respectu ceterorum animalium."

the other hand, all matters of "verba" are referred to art, which consists essentially in the proper exploitation of the three styles according to the usual rhetorical precepts.

These interrelationships of distinctions perhaps indicate in Parrasio a more tightly knit conception of the art of poetry than was present in earlier commentators. He provides just as many disconnected remarks on isolated passages as did his predecessors, refers to as many different authorities. But over and above these, one senses some fairly definite orientations in his thinking: toward seeing a system in what had hitherto been independent sets of distinctions; toward emphasizing diction as the really poetic element and as the product of a special talent furthered by a special art; toward analyzing more searchingly the relationships of the poem to nature, to the poet, and to the audience.

In connection with line 128 of the *Ars poetica*, "Difficile est proprie communia dicere ... ," Parrasio had developed his ideas on another kind of "imitation," that of other writers whom the poet might take as his models; he had previously recommended Vergil as the model to be followed unfailingly for all three styles (pp. 43–43*v*, 20). These were not, of course, new ideas, and they had before this appeared in conjunction with the Horatian text. But their timeliness here is indicated by the fact that they appear almost contemporaneously with the writing of two letters on the subject of imitation by Giovambattista Giraldi Cintio and by Celio Calcagnini. Giraldi's letter to Calcagnini, dated 1532, is concerned exclusively with the art of oratory and with what it may gain from proper imitation; but so completely, by this time, has the Horatian tradition assimilated the standard language of the rhetoricians that Giraldi's statements bear close resemblance to the commentaries on the *Ars poetica*. I cite the following passage, in which Giraldi is praising Cicero, in the original so that it may be compared with similar ones in the commentators:

... quis ad animos uel ad iram, uel ad odium, uel dolorem incitandos uegetior? quis ab ijsdem permotionibus ad amorem, ad lenitatem, ad misericordiam reuocandos aptior? quis uerborum copia locupletior? quis sententiarum pondere grauior? quis figuris iucundior? quis trallationibus magnificentior? quis totius orationis serie magis elaboratus? quis in dicendo candidior.[68]

Giraldi's letter is occupied with the debate between those who insist that many different authors should be imitated and those who maintain that the best results are obtained by imitating a single model. The subject of this "imitation" is exclusively diction: choice of words, figures of speech, rhythms and harmonies. Giraldi decides in favor of the single model, who for Latin must be Cicero, and he speaks of the components of imitation in terms long familiar in the Horatian-rhetorical tradition.

[68] In *Poematia* (1540 ed.), pp. 202–3.

Celio Calcagnini, to whom the letter had been addressed, answered in the same year in another letter entitled *Super imitatione commentatio*. In it, he defended the necessity of practicing imitation, especially for modern Italians who wished to rise out of barbarism. Then, basing his discussion on the three elements of invention, disposition, and elocution, he pointed out that the first of these is inherent in the material itself, the second is within the power of the writer, the third comes entirely from without. That is, the ability to handle language in an excellent manner is learned from the teacher or the models; it is here that imitation plays its part. The greatest lesson taught by proper imitation is the proper fitting of words to things ("uerba inuenire rei propositae accommodata"), a phrase which is almost the battle cry of the Horatians (p. 217).

Two other favorite ideas of the Horatians, the interpretation of poetry as an allegory concealing moral lessons and the insistence upon the necessity of verse, are the main points of emphasis in a short critical document of the following year, 1533. This is Alessandro Vellutello's letter to the readers printed as a preface to Agostino Ricchi's *I tre tiranni*. With respect to the first, Vellutello argues that the principal requirement of comedy is, "under the veil of joyous and pleasant discourse, to hide always some useful and appropriate morality." He then interprets the allegory or "senso mistico" of Ricchi's play. He defends Ricchi's use of verse on the basis of the whole history of comedy, the usage of the Greeks and the Romans, the authority of Aristotle in the *Poetics*. Poetry is verse, and as such is opposed to prose: "... everything that is true history or a rhetorical oration, or any part of them, belongs to prose; but the fictional fables of the poets never do. Since we do not believe that to the same things one can equally well adapt verse or write them in prose, we think that when this happens it must rather be attributed to lack of judgment than to an oversight." He admits blank verse as closer to everyday speech than rhymed verse—which would be "contra al naturale, et al uero"—and goes as far as to accept the use of prose in comedies with a modern subject, alive in themselves and necessitating no "imitation."[69]

In 1535, Lodovico Dolce published his translation of the *Ars poetica* into Italian verse; it was accompanied by a dedication to Pietro Aretino in which Dolce raises the practical question of the usefulness of Horace's precepts in the present day. His first argument is itself Horatian. Starting from the premiss that the poet depends both upon nature and upon art for the excellence of his work, he suggests that the mediocrity against which Horace had warned may be avoided only by the practice of art; and the

---

[69] In Ricchi, *I tre tiranni* (1533), p. Aijv: "sotto uelo di lieto, et piaceuole discorso sempre nascondere utile et accomodata moralità"; p. Aiij; p. Aiijv: "tutto quello che è fidele Historia, o uero Oration rethorica, o parte di loro, appartiene a la prosa, ma le finte fauole de i Poeti non mai. A le quali cose non considerando, potendosi nel medesimo modo adattare al uerso, et scriuere in Prosa, pensiamo che sempre questo ci saria piu tosto attribuito a mancamento di giuditio, che a trascuraggine."

Ars poetica is the best source of wisdom on all phases of the art. "He composed a book in which he collected together, wonderfully in a small space, everything that a good poet needs."[70] Dolce feels that such a work is especially needed today, when poets are ignorant of the basic elements of their art:

> And this comes to pass because, writing today for the most part in the vulgar tongue (since we are born and grow up in it), we think that, having studied Petrarch, we can with little effort write some verse or sonnet that will give off a perfect odor of poetry. And we do not understand that this same Petrarch, and in our own century Sannazaro, Bembo, and also Ariosto, from all of whom not a little splendor has come to our language, all spent all their time, not without labor, in studies.[71]

Dolce does not fail to include Aretino himself among the distinguished writers of the century, praising him for the purity and appropriateness of his diction, for the felicity of his invention, for the art of his disposition, for his judgment in observing decorum, for the pleasantness and gravity of his thoughts—all of them Horatian qualities. Nor does he fail, in passing, to make a brief defence of poetry.

Like Giraldi and Calcagnini, Bartolomeo Ricci is concerned with the imitation of models, but in a more complete and in a more philosophical way than they had been. His *De imitatione libri tres* (1541) is a Horatian document in several respects. It justifies "imitation" as the ingredient of art that must be added to nature; it maintains that a writer imitates the invention, disposition, and elocution of his model; it selects and classifies models according to the genres that they represent; and it provides a certain number of precepts for each of the more important genres. Ricci recognizes the existence of two theories of imitation (and of a current debate over their respective merits). The first proposes that any writer imitate only his own nature, with no help at all from outside; the second proposes that he devote himself exclusively to the imitation of another. Both positions, thinks Ricci, are extreme, for the first neglects the contribution that art can make to nature, while the second unnecessarily restricts the writer to a single model. The best solution consists in supplementing nature with art, in correcting one's genius by adding to it the experience of a variety of other authors. "I therefore believe this: that in imitation as in other matters artifice is of great benefit to nature as nature is to artifice, and that each one needs

---

[70] *Poetica d'Horatio* (1535), pp. A2v–A3: "vn Libro compose; in cui tutto quello, che a buon Poeta è necessario, in breue campo mirabilmente racolse."

[71] *Ibid.*, p. A3: "E questo auiene; che scriuendosi hoggidi per la maggior parte nella lingua volgare; per esser noi nati e cresciuti in essa; ci pare, che hauendo il Petrarcha studiato; con poca fatica si possa dettare alcun verso o Sonetto, che renda perfetto odore di Poesia: e non comprendemo; che esso Petrarcha, e nel secol nostro il Sannazaro, il Bembo, e l'Ariosto anchora; da i quali n'è vscito non poco splendore alla lingua; hanno tutto il lor tempo, non senza fatica, consumato ne gli studi."

entirely the help of the other."[72] By this process, the deficiencies of the individual's talent will be compensated by the experience of his predecessors.

Such a procedure, says Ricci, merely follows the normal patterns of nature. All the arts derive ultimately from nature; one may take rhetoric as an example: "Indeed, in the universal art of speaking, what else do the rhetoricians propose than to adapt all their precepts to Nature herself?"[73] Just as any art is a reduction of nature to precepts, so the activity of any artist should consist in reducing his own nature to the satisfactory modes of artistry, and for this purpose the best device is imitation. "Thus will my imitator do: he will preserve carefully the many natural gifts with which he may be endowed; but if any then are lacking . . . , he will have to obtain them from elsewhere by his study, through the imitation of the good writers."[74] The problem then becomes one of selecting the best models, those which will best complement one's native genius. Late in Book I, Ricci indicates that his criteria for the choice of models are essentially their invention and elocution; but some of his discussions of the narrative and dramatic genres reveal that he also accords some importance to disposition.

Since his greatest concern is with Latin eloquence, Ricci surveys the whole field of Latin poetry and selects those poets who may best serve as models in each of the genres. This involves, of necessity, criteria for the genre and for poetry in general. For comedy, only Plautus and Terence are acceptable; Plautus is better for continuous comedy and laughter (but one must beware of triviality), Terence for seriousness and decorum. Seneca is the only model for tragedy. He satisfies the requirements of excellence in the arousing of suspense, in the conduct of the action, and in its denouement; with respect to the latter, he makes his endings sufficiently sad, whether they be related in words or enacted on the stage (following Horace's distinction). His whole conduct of the tragedy, in the serious action, in the royal personages, in the grave words is such as to achieve the desired goal of applause for the poet: "The more a tragic writer arouses pity in the spectator, the more he makes the subject cruel and terrible, the more will he elicit a greater applause for himself from the spectator, the more will he obtain for himself a merited esteem."[75] In this discussion of

---

[72] *De imitatione* (1545 ed.), pp. 12*v*–13: "Ego igitur sic sentio, & naturae artificium, & artificio naturam, ut in caeteris rebus, sic in imitatione plurimum prodesse, atque alterum alterius auxilio omnino indigere."

[73] *Ibid.*, p. 4*v*: "In uniuersa uero dicendi arte quid aliud Rhetores attendunt, quàm ut eius praecepta omnia ad naturam ipsam accommodentur?"

[74] *Ibid.*, p. 14: "ita meus faciat imitator, cui naturae bonum plurimum affuerit, id diligenter conseruabit, si quae uero desiderabuntur . . ., ea suo studio aliunde bonorum imitatione comparare debebit."

[75] *Ibid.*, p. 22*v*: "Quanto tragoediae scriptor magis misericordiam auditori commouebit, quanto rem crudeliorem, ac magis atrocem faciet, tanto ab hoc maiorem sibi plausum excitabit, tanto eius gratiam inibit aequiorem."

tragedy, Ricci's sources and orientations become apparent. Horace is accompanied by some allusions to Aristotle; Cicero provides the general rhetorical goal; moreover, the old medieval conception of the genre still serves as a basis. Similar recommendations are made for the other forms: Tibullus is first among the elegiac poets, Horace for the lyric and hexameter, Martial for the epigram, Vergil for the epic.

Books II and III of the *De imitatione* treat the practical rules for imitation. Once again, Ricci declares that one may imitate the invention and disposition of a work as well as elocution. He authorizes the copying or translation of whole passages and points to the great achievements of modern imitators. Yet there are important theoretical statements. In his insistence that the moderns can equal the ancients, that Nature has been as generous to us as to men of the classical past, he presents an idea that was soon to be exploited by Sperone Speroni and then by Du Bellay. He distinguishes natural from artificial order in the development of a plot, discerns a rhetorical order of parts (demonstration, narration, and so forth) in the poems and cantos of Vergil. On the purely practical side, all Book III is devoted to a consideration of language. Ricci's treatise, as a whole, represents a bridge between works of rhetorical theory and works of poetic theory, at a time when the latter were just beginning to come into prominence.

Imitation in the Giraldi-Calcagnini sense is again the subject of two treatises by Giulio Camillo Delminio, although only one of them is formally called a treatise on imitation. The work is his *Due trattati: l'uno delle materie, che possono uenir sotto lo stile dell'eloquente: l'altro della imitatione*, published in 1544. The first of these, on eloquence, is strictly rhetorical in character and derives its materials and its basic theses rather from Cicero than from Horace. The second is more remote from Horace than the letters on imitation already studied, largely because its approach is almost exclusively linguistic and it evinces no higher rationale in terms of the effects of language upon a potential audience. Camillo distinguishes language as literal, or as figurative, or as "topically figurative," and concludes that one author may borrow the first two types from another without engaging either in imitation or in plagiarism. The third provides the occasion for true imitation, and hence is the special prerogative of the poet, although the orator may also use it at times. Cicero is, as usual, held up as the sole model for imitation in Latin, and the ways in which proper imitation may be achieved are outlined.

In 1545, Lilio Gregorio Giraldi published his long *Historiae poetarum dialogi*, which belongs to the Horatian tradition by virtue not only of its numerous borrowings from the *Ars poetica* itself but also of its reflection of many of the ideas added by the expositors. In the course of the ten dialogues, certain of which are devoted to a mere biographical account of poets practicing the separate genres, Giraldi finds occasion to discuss a number of theoretical matters. The first dialogue, especially, is a full-scale defence of the art and a statement of its principles. In it, he finds it useful to call not only upon the witness of the standard commentators but also upon such ancient authorities as Plato, Strabo, Maximus of Tyre, and Theophrastus. Moreover, he patterns certain sections closely after Aristotle's *Poetics*, as I shall indicate in a subsequent chapter. In connection with his defence of poetry, he cites the recent apologies of Petrarch, Boccaccio, Budé, and Pontano. The defence itself follows the traditional lines: the early esteem in which poetry was held as a kind of first theology and first philosophy; its civilizing function; its uses in sacred writings. In connection with these, Giraldi insists upon the hidden meanings of all poetry, upon the mysteries concealed beneath its literal statements, upon its essentially allegorical nature: "it seems that generally in the art of poetry one thing is said whereas another is meant, and that the meaning is hidden, so to speak, under a veil."[76] The defence also requires an answer to Plato's ban and a demonstration of the usefulness of the art—topics long familiar to the Horatians. For the first, Giraldi declares that Plato had exiled only poets who lied about the gods; he quotes Petrarch to the effect that only scenic poets had been excluded from the Republic. For the second, he discusses the arguments of Eratosthenes (that poetry need only delight), of Strabo (that it need only instruct), and of Horace (that it must both "prodesse" and "delectare"). His own conclusion would seem to be that instruction is necessary and that it takes several forms. For one thing, as Cicero pointed out, poetry offers us in fictional guise an image of our daily lives: "Indeed these things have been feigned by the poets in such wise that we see our own characters represented in other persons, and we see expressed in them our image of daily life."[77] For another, specific moral lessons are contained in such genres as tragedy and comedy; in tragedy:

... this is the opinion of the comic poet Timocles, who says that in tragedy are found the models and the teachings for all of life and for every human condition. ... thus from some writers you will learn to bear with equanimity certain things, and from other writers how to bear other things; indeed, the sum of all misfortunes is greater than those which any one person suffers, and the man who has observed that they have befallen others, has become accustomed to bear his own more easily and more imperturbably.[78]

Giraldi's general notions of tragedy and comedy are derived from the

[76] *Historiae poetarum* (1545), p. 9: "in poëtica enim unum plerunque dici uidetur, aliud ueró significatur, & sensus quodam, ut ita dicam, uelamine occultatur."

[77] *Ibid.*, pp. 81, 72, 10: "Haec enim ... conficta sunt à Poëtis, ut effictos nostros mores in alienis personis, expressamque imaginem nostram uitae quotidianae uideamus."

[78] *Ibid.*, p. 676: "idque ex Timocle Comico, qui ait, apud Tragoediam totius uitae & conditionis esse exempla, atque documenta. ... & sic ab alijs alia aequo animo ferre disces: omnia enim maiora quàm quiuis patitur infortunia, qui alijs accidisse contemplatus, suas ipsius calamitates aequius faciliusque ferre consueuit."

medieval-Horatian school, and this in spite of the fact that he cites definitions and discussions from Aristotle. Dialogue VI is devoted to tragedy. He defines the genre thus: "Tragoedia est heroicae fortunae in aduersis comprehensio, ut nostri definiunt" ("*nostri*" being critics writing in Latin, such as Diomedes); then, after citing Theophrastus' definition in Greek, he paraphrases it in Latin: "Tragoedia est fortunę heroicae calamitas, seu infortunium. tragoediae enim propria est tristia, & luctus." Aristotle is cited on the antiquity of tragedy, and then Giraldi remarks that "in prouerbium Tragoedia exiuit, de re turbulenta, & molestiae plena." I cite these passages as samples of the continued use by Giraldi of traditional ideas and formulas.[79] When he comes to compare tragedy and comedy, he again does so in terms familiar to readers of Donatus and Diomedes:

> In comedy indeed the ordinary fortunes of men, the minor shocks and perils, are represented, and the ends of the actions are happy. In tragedy everything is the opposite: imposing personages, great fears, calamitous outcomes. In the former, unsettled events at the beginning, calm ones at the end; whereas in tragedy things transpire in the opposite order. Then in tragedy life is represented in such a way as to make us wish to flee it, in comedy so as to make us desire it. Finally, every comedy is derived from subjects invented by the poet, but tragedy frequently springs from historical truth.[80]

Similarly, his definition of the poet himself is a composite of elements derived from various accepted sources: "Perhaps one would not be wrong if he were to define the poet as a man who, moved by the divine afflatus, speaks nobly and appropriately of great things in such a way as to arouse admiration. If to this definition verse is added as an equal element, everything will seem to be plainly included in it."[81] In his treatment of the details of poetic composition—the handling of the three styles, the five acts in comedy and its various kinds, the histories of the genres, the definitions of the minor types—Giraldi refers directly and specifically to Horace and to the various expositors who, by the Renaissance commentators, were integrated into the corpus of "Horatian" ideas.

CONCLUSIONS

The gradual emergence of references to Aristotle's *Poetics* and the appearance in Lilio Gregorio Giraldi of formal definitions and discussions

---

[79] *Ibid.*, pp. 671–74; for the formulas, cf. Isidore, *Etymologiae*, VIII, vii; Evanthius, ed. Wessner, IV. 2; Diomedes, ed. Keil, I, 487; Donatus, ed. Wessner, V. 1.

[80] *Ibid.*, p. 681: "In Comoedia quidem mediocres fortunae hominum, parui impetus, periculaque, laetique sunt exitus actionum: at in Tragoedia omnia contraria, ingentes personae, magni timores, exitus funesti habentur, & illic turbulenta prima, tranquilla ultima, in Tragoedia contrario ordine res aguntur. tum in Tragoedia fugienda uita, in Comoedia capessenda exprimitur, postremò omnis Comoedia de fictis argumentis, Tragoedia saepe de historica fide petitur."

[81] *Ibid.*, p. 86: "non malè fortasse is dixerit, qui poëtam ita definierit, hominem esse, qui spiritu afflatus magna egregiè appositeque cum admiratione loquatur. . . . cui definitioni si par carmen addatur, omnia planè comprehensa uidebuntur."

derived from Aristotle indicate the arrival at a turning point in the Horatian tradition. The next text to be studied will be the first in a long series of texts which effect an intermingling of Horace's theories with those of Aristotle, and which produce in the end a complete confusion of Horace with Aristotle. Before proceeding to that study, however, it will be well to estimate the effects of the growth of the Horatian tradition in Italy up to about the year 1545.

In the first place, there is what we might call the material growth of the tradition. By that I mean the gradual accretion to the text of Horace of a host of other texts, which first become attached to it and then become inseparably identified with it. The earliest of these would be the ancient commentators, who persist with the text throughout the Middle Ages and bring to it an initial interpretation. Next would come the commentators of the end of the fifteenth century, who add not only their own glosses and their own ideas but who incorporate as well relevant materials from the late-classical grammarians and from the Latin rhetoricians. To some degree, also, these writers bring into the tradition the growing humanist knowledge of ancient texts, including both theoretical documents and various kinds of poems. Finally, the commentators of the first half of the sixteenth century expand the number of Greek and Latin theorists who are considered to have said things relevant to the interpretation of the *Ars poetica*. Plato, Aristotle, and Averroës are called upon increasingly, as well as many minor writers on poetic and rhetorical theory. There is another sense in which we may perceive a material growth of the tradition: to formal commentaries on the Horatian text are added, first, independent theoretical statements in other contexts or in separate works, and, second, essays in practical criticism in which principles belonging to the tradition are applied to poems of one kind or another. Not only are more things added to the text of the *Ars poetica*, but it is constantly applied to more things.

In the second place, we discern what might be called a methodological growth of the tradition. The earliest form of commentary is essentially a grammatical commentary, in which the exegesis of the text as a linguistic document is the primary problem. To be sure, philosophical interpretation is already present, but it is present in a secondary way. This type of grammatical commentary will continue throughout the later phases, but will gradually be subordinated to other types. To it is added, in the fifteenth century, more and more interpretation of a philosophical and literary character. At the outset, this kind of interpretation is applied to separate lines or passages in the text, for which analogues or explanations are found in other texts and for which illustrations are found in the poets. But already, because of the character of the documents which are cited as analogues, a totality of interpretation (which, as we have seen, is a rhetorical one) is present. In the sixteenth-century commentaries, the large body of disparate distinctions brought into the tradition in connection with one passage or another is organized into a set of related distinctions, and systematic interpretations of Horace appear with some frequency. None of the earlier forms of gloss is abandoned, and the increasing length and complexity of the commentaries is a reflection of the greater number of things done with the text and their greater diversity.

In the third place, and by far the most important, the tradition presents evidences of considerable doctrinal growth. Two words of caution are necessary about the meaning given to "growth" at this point. For one, it should not be thought that during the period under consideration there was any notable change in the over-all understanding of the Horatian epistle, any appreciable shift from one way of regarding the text to another. Throughout these years, the *Ars poetica* was read as a kind of rhetoric that indicated how certain effects of utility or pleasure could be brought about in a specific audience by treating nature in certain ways and by making certain kinds of adaptations of words to subject matter. For another, "growth" should not be understood as meaning necessarily that the later documents were more sophisticated or more complicated philosophically, or that they contained a larger and richer body of ideas. What doctrinal growth there was must be sought in the tradition as a whole, in the sum of doctrine during the later years as compared with the sum during the middle years as compared with the sum during the early years. Here there is substantial progress. If we see the general process of development as consisting of a more and more complete identification of Horace with the rhetorical tradition, then the first stages would be present in the simplest assimilation of the invention-disposition-elocution analysis to Horace's statements. This assimilation will grow as the division is made to correspond more and more completely with parts of the *Ars poetica*. At the same time appears another way of looking at the text, its main point being the emphasis upon the necessity of appropriateness in all poetic matters—of character traits to character or to type or to historical conceptions, of diction to subject matter, of style to genre, of social station to genre, of verse to material or genre, and so forth. The canon of appropriateness will likewise be enlarged and expanded as the tradition grows. Consonant with the increasing complexity of the rhetorical associations of the text, critics will tend to orient their thinking more definitely toward the audience and its requirements and to develop theories fitting to such an orientation. The end of poetry with respect to the audience, that of pleasing or instructing or both, is clarified by explanations and examples. At times one of these ends is emphasized as the only one (as pleasure with Landino); at times all are said to be achieved through separate parts of the work; at times each one is sought for some special segment of the audience. The constantly greater attention to moral considerations is a part of this manner of considering the ends.

For certain other relevant distinctions, one needs to go back again to the earliest commentators and from them trace a widening and diversified set of ramifications. This would be the case for the insistence, with respect to Horace, upon the "res-verba" dichotomy, an essentially grammatical distinction which comes to belong to all the arts of discourse. It would be the case, again, for the three styles; especially in the postmedieval years, these styles are called upon to provide a basis of organization for nearly all of the ideas connected with the text. To them is also related the matter of diction, and in an interesting way. For if all poetic concerns may be reduced to the three styles, then they may also be reduced to questions of diction; one of the ways of considering poetry, which will never lose its popularity during the Renaissance, will be to consider it exclusively in terms of words or expression or style. If there are thus several separate approaches of a verbal character, there are also several which spring from preoccupations with "res." The most prominent of these is the reading of Horace essentially as a document centered about a principle of decorum, a reading which reaches complete expression in Badius. Such an interpretation is of course related to those which were insistent upon appropriateness, but in a specialized way. Similarly, the persistent return to considerations of nature and verisimilitude is a facet of the theorists' attention to "res." One special phase of this is the insistence, in certain writers, that when the poet deals with historical matters he must be true, whereas when his subjects are feigned or invented it is sufficient for him to be verisimilar.

Still another direction of doctrinal growth is discerned in what we may characterize as the transforming of the *Ars poetica* into a "total poetics." Horace himself had treated a large number of matters pertinent to the art of poetry: the internal order of poems, the appropriateness of diction, the history and the materials of certain genres, the behavior of the poet, the function of the critic, and so forth. All these matters are developed in great detail by the commentators, either through the addition of examples or through the expansion of the ideas. Moreover, other developments occur. The transformation of the text into a set of rules or precepts would probably be one of these. Horace's fairly fluid organization of materials is made more solid and substantial by the declaration that every statement constitutes a "praeceptum" (as for Acron) or a "regula" (as for Badius). At times, this effort results in the discovery of dogmas for which there is actually no basis in the Horatian text itself. The aggregation of the defence of poetry to the Horatian tradition expands and enriches it to a notable degree, since it soon involves the crossing with other traditions and the appeal to other authorities. A part of this defence consists in the allegorical interpretation of poetry, where again both a renewed Platonism and a continued medievalism enter into the sum of "Horatian" ideas. Finally, the commentators introduce a large number of concepts relevant to the character of the poet: his inspiration through divine furor, his essential goodness, the universality of his knowledge, his capacities as a seer and a prophet. Through such accretions as these, the *Ars poetica*—with its attendant glosses—becomes a repository for everything that was being thought about poetry in the humanistic period and during the Renaissance up to about 1545.

In the following years, another impulse to material and methodological and doctrinal growth is given to the Horatian tradition, and in such a way as to merit separate and detailed study. This impulse comes from the text and the interpretation of Aristotle's *Poetics*.

CHAPTER FOUR. THE TRADITION OF HORACE'S *ARS POETICA*: II. THE CONFUSION WITH ARISTOTLE

IT WOULD BE ERRONEOUS to believe that in the years before 1545 work on Horace's *Ars poetica* had been done exclusively by persons who did not know Aristotle's *Poetics*. The passing allusions and references to the *Poetics* mentioned in the preceding chapter would disprove such a belief. A more correct statement would be that although these scholars knew Aristotle's treatise or knew of it, such knowledge did not fundamentally affect their general reading and interpretation of the Horatian text. They read it in the same way as did their colleagues who lacked this knowledge; and allusion and reference were incidental to an interpretation which had nothing to do with the *Poetics*. In the years that we shall now be studying, however, a number of theorists brought Horace's work into clear juxtaposition to and explicit comparison with Aristotle's, and in some cases at least, a new analysis of Horace resulted. What happened to Aristotle will be treated in a later section.[1]

Nor should it be thought that the comparison with Aristotle produced a revolution in the interpretation of Horace. We shall increasingly discover commentators and theorists who make the assimilation of the Greek to the Roman; but we shall also continue to meet—and perhaps more frequently—writers who persist in the earlier tradition. Both in theory and in practical criticism, it may be that the "un-Aristotelians" or the "non-Aristotelians" constitute the dominant element in the Horatian tradition of the later years as they did in the earlier. To determine the proportion, to weigh the importance of the two trends, will be one of the problems of this and the succeeding chapters.

FRANCESCO FILIPPI PEDEMONTE (1546)

The first of the Cinquecento commentaries on the *Ars poetica* to make extensive use of Aristotle was Francesco Filippi Pedemonte's *Ecphrasis in Horatii Flacci Artem poeticam*, published by his pupil Puresius in 1546. In some respects this is a conventional commentary, but in others it presents notable innovations. For example, Pedemonte follows the usual routine of dividing Horace's text into small sections, with a commentary for each section; but he varies the technique by giving a heading to each section. Thus lines 1–13 are preceded by "De Idea Concipienda," lines 14–23 by "Non esse à materia discedendum," and so on. These headings themselves indicate the direction of the interpretation. But the great innovation con-

---

[1] The same subject with respect to Horace is treated by Marvin T. Herrick in *The Fusion of Horatian and Aristotelian Literary Criticism, 1531–1555* (Urbana: University of Illinois Press, 1946); but since Herrick proceeds by a fragmentation of texts and an arrangement according to critical ideas, he does not achieve the kind of historical statement of the development which I am here seeking.

sists in the use made of Aristotle. Let us see how this is done in several typical passages. In the first passage, lines 1–13, Pedemonte sees an expression of Plato's theory that Ideas precede forms; from this theory he derives Horace's contention that "it is necessary that the artist have a preconceived notion of the things which are made by him before putting his hand to them, and that he see in advance in his mind's eye the Form according to the model of which he may give form to every work." This is the procedure, he goes on to say, in all the arts, and "especially in the arts of painting, molding, and sculpturing, which indeed seem to Aristotle to proceed in the same way of imitation as does poetry." Thus Aristotle's theory of imitation is made equivalent to Plato's theory of the imitation of Forms and to Horace's initial statements in the *Ars poetica*. Later in the same passage, when he is speaking of the impossibility of unity when disparate elements are combined, Pedemonte again quotes Aristotle: "the first parts of the poem will not fit with the last, and the poem as a whole, which (as Aristotle says) consists of a beginning, a middle, and an end, will in no way be complete." Here, Aristotle's principle of unity is identified with Horace's principle of appropriateness. Finally, Horace's recommendations that nature must be followed are said to be corroborated by Aristotle's insistence that Homer be taken as the best model, since he best taught how a "lie" (which would be something out of nature) should be told. In each of these cases, a new light is shed upon the Horatian passage by the reference to Aristotle.[2]

Pedemonte's procedure is similar in his commentary on lines 92–107, headed "De decoro, atque affectibus exprimendis. quae res ad actionem pertinere uidetur." After an initial sentence about the importance of observing decorum, he quotes Aristotle (I have been unable to locate the passage), thus making Horace's "quid deceat" equivalent to Aristotle's τὸ πρέπον. As the Horatian passage goes on to the effects produced by the poem—

>Non satis est pulchra esse poemata: dulcia sunto,
>et quocumque volent animum auditoris agunto

—Pedemonte first cites Cicero on the closeness of the poet to the orator and the necessity for both to sway their audiences, then both Cicero and Aristotle on the need for the poet to feel the passions that he is portraying; the reference to Aristotle is to *Poetics* 1455a31. At the end of the com-

---

[2] *Ecphrasis* (1546), p. 3v: "necesse enim est artificem earum rerum, quae à se fiunt, priusquam manum admoueat, precognitam habere notitiam; animoque praeuidere formam, cuius exemplo opus quodque informet. sic itaque in omni arte, pingendi maxime, fingendi, atque sculpendi; quae quidem eodem imitationis tramite cum poesi Aristoteli incedere uidentur"; p. 4: "poematis prime partes cum postremis non conuenient; miniméue totum ipsum, quod (ut inquit Aristoteles) ex principio, medio ac fine constat, absoluetur"; also pp. 4v, 16. I use the name "Pedemonte" rather than "Filippi" since he was called Pedemonte by his own pupil, Puresius, and by the whole tradition of scholars up to and including Tiraboschi (Venice, 1796 ed., VII¹, 235).

mentary—and for reasons difficult to discern—he quotes Aristotle on the beautiful animal and on the proper magnitude of a poem (1450b35).

These passages in the *Ecphrasis* are typical. For an indication of the extent to which Pedemonte seeks parallels in Aristotle, a simple list of the texts involved will suffice:

Ars poetica	*Poetics*
1–13	1447a18, 1450b27, 1460a18
42–45	1459b31
46–72	1458b31
73–88	1459b31, 1448b32, 1459a11
89–91	1449b9, 1448a16
92–107	1455a31, 1450b35
128–34	1448b35, 1460b16
149–52	1451a32
179–88	1448a36, 1449b21, 1448a30, 1449b4, 1449a31, 1451a16, 1453b3, 1453b19
189–92	1451a9
193–95	1456a25
202–19	1455b32
220–24	1449a21
234–39	1458b31, 1456a20
275–80	1449a9
281–84	1449a36
338–40	1451a36
457–69	1447b19

As compared with earlier commentators, the extent of these references is considerable; but the study of later commentators will show that we have here only the beginning of an important tendency.

What is important, however, is not the fact of reference, but the degree to which such reference causes a change in the interpretation of the text of Horace. A careful reading of Pedemonte's commentary shows that while several new ideas are added to the Horatian tradition as the result of the parallel with Aristotle, none of the old ideas is in any way modified; the process is one of accretion rather than change. I have already referred to several of these new ideas: Aristotle's theories of imitation and of the magnitude of beautiful poems compared to that of beautiful animals. Other added elements are the notion of necessary order, in which no part of a poem may be moved or removed without destroying the total structure; the definition of tragedy and the explanation of the various components of that definition; the insistence that unity of plot is not provided by unity of hero; the declaration that tragedy should attain its effect even in the reading, through the constitution of the plot rather than through stage spectacle; the distinction of four kinds of plot; and the statement that the domain of poetry is the presentation of things as they should be, according to necessity and probability. In connection with this last, it should be noted that both the idea of the "verisimile" and the idea of "things as they should be" had appeared in earlier commentators (cf. Acron on the first and Parrasio on the second); Pedemonte's contribution consists in grouping them together and in adding to them the notion of necessity, which he does not explain.

The addition of these Aristotelian concepts does not mean, however, that any of the old components of the Horatian theory are lost or diminished. The work is still read in the light of Cicero, Quintilian, Acron, and Donatus, and the essentially rhetorical interpretation still obtains. Thus, lines 38–72 of the *Ars poetica* are divided into three sections, entitled respectively "De Inventione," "De Dispositione," and "De Vocabulorum compositione"; and as he passes on to the next section Pedemonte remarks: "So far we have abundantly discoursed about poetic invention, disposition, and the artistry of elocution."[3] Similarly, when he speaks of comedy, Pedemonte insists: "It is not sufficient to have invention, but it is also necessary to understand disposition and elocution and to fashion the poem itself according to the rules."[4] The related "res-verba" distinction appears in a somewhat special form, since the "verba" are replaced by "rhythmi" and these in turn are called "colores" (contrary to the usual practice, which reserved the term "colores" for figures of speech). The distinction is formulated thus: "So in poetry two principal things are considered, namely the material of the things which are taken by the poet for treatment, and the numbers from which this material receives its form and is made distinct by its own colors."[5]

With respect to the ends of poetry, Pedemonte seems to remain undecided between the two rival positions most commonly held by his predecessors, that which maintained that the end was pleasure and that which declared that pleasure must be mingled with utility. Commenting on the "variare" of line 29 of the *Ars poetica*, he insists on the necessity of variety in the poetic work, "for otherwise it will by no means produce admiration and pleasure, which are the poets' aim."[6] Much later, however, when he discusses line 333 ("Aut prodesse volunt, aut delectare poetae"), he is obliged by the text itself to consider the dual end, and he does so in these terms:

Yet since poetry seems to have been invented in part to give pleasure and in part also to be of utility, lest someone might think that it was entirely alien to

[3] *Ibid.*, p. 12v: "Hactenus de inuentione poetica, dispositione, elocutionisque artificio abunde disseruimus."

[4] *Ibid.*, p. 40v: "Non enim satis est inuentionem habere, uerum etiam dispositionem, ac elocutionem callere oportet; ipsumque poema rite intexere."

[5] *Ibid.*, p. 14v: "Ita in poesi duo praecipua considerantur; rerum uidelicet, quae tractandę à poeta sumuntur, materia; ac numeri, à quibus informatur, efficiturque suis coloribus distincta."

[6] *Ibid.*, p. 6: "cum alioquin admirationem, oblectationemque, qui poetarum est scopus, nequaquam praebeat."

pleasure he [Horace] felt it necessary to remove such a concern from men's minds by making a universal distinction among all poets. [The three kinds of poets distinguished.] Those provide utility, I say, who communicate in verse the precepts of the disciplines and of the arts, especially the precepts which are called moral, and who teach the norm of proper living.... These poets [Empedocles, Lucretius, Aratus, etc.] seem to have created many things in their poems for purposes of pleasure, in addition to moral portraits and a sculptured image of life which they include under the appearance of fiction. In fact, those very ancient poets who first invented poetic lies seem to have set for themselves that same purpose: to envelop, in the wrappings of fables, doctrinal mysteries and moral instructions and a way of life.[7]

By such a statement as the last one, Pedemonte allies himself with those theorists who had seen the chief utility of poetry as residing in an allegorical function. Moreover, he indicates in the passage that his whole conception of the ends of poetry is unaffected by his study and his citation of Aristotle.

As for the actual production of utility, it seems to be brought about almost entirely by the introduction of proverbs or sententiae. In connection with lines 202–19, Pedemonte insists that ethical philosophy "filled tragedy and comedy with most weighty sententiae, apposite to the teaching of right living."[8] There appears to be, in the same passage, some connection between poems offering such sententiae and the "moral" type of plot distinguished by Aristotle (*Poetics* 1456a1). The same position with respect to sententiae is present in the commentary on lines 309–22 where, among other related things, Pedemonte says this: "Indeed, unless all comedies and tragedies derived their seriousness from precepts and sententiae pertaining to everyday life, what would we say they were other than a dry discourse and a sterile matter?"[9] At the end of the same commentary, Pedemonte gives priority to this kind of utility over pleasure itself: "A poem faithfully reflecting mores, adorned with philosophical passages, or containing useful matter, even if it is without the seduction of beauty, or grandeur of words, or cleverness of construction, will better delight and hold the public than a poem with the most highly embellished verses if no wisdom or knowledge

---

[7] *Ibid.*, pp. 51–51v: "cum tamen poesis ad oblectandum partim, partim uero ad iuuandum inuenta uideatur, ne aliquis existimaret omnino à uoluptate eam esse alienam, uatum omnium uniuersali distinctione eiusmodi scrupulum euellere ex animis necessarium duxit.... Prosunt inquam qui disciplinarum praecepta, artiumúe, tum praesertim quę moralia uocantur, carminibus tradunt, rectéque uiuendi normam edocent.... multa enim ab illis oblectationis causa efficta uidentur, alioquin expressos mores, insculptamque uitae imaginem sub falsitatis umbra continent. Nam & uetustissimi illi, qui ab initio poetica mendacia excogitarunt, illud sibi scopum proposuisse uidentur; ut sub fabularum inuolucris doctrinarum mysteria, mores, uiuendíque modum inuoluerent."

[8] *Ibid.*, p. 36: "quae tragoedias comoediasque grauissimis sententijs, & ad recte uiuendum appositis repleuit."

[9] *Ibid.*, p. 49v: "comoedias omnes, tragoediasque, ni pondus à praeceptis, ac sententijs ad quottidianam uitam spectantibus accepissent, quid aliud esse, quàm ieiunum sermonum, sterilemque materiam diceremus?"

supports it." The position is of course that of Acron and later commentators;[10] it would not be that of Aristotle at any point in the *Poetics*. A little later, Horace's dictum on brevity (1. 335) is expanded to refer specifically to these moral precepts: "He advises us to make every possible effort toward brevity, which indeed is held to be particularly suitable for teaching the mind, and to stray as little as possible from the line of profiting and teaching; so that the learners may more easily grasp the precepts and may keep them as long as possible locked within the storehouse of the memory."[11]

We have already examined the tenor of Pedemonte's discussion of decorum in connection with *Ars poetica* 92–107; as in the Horatian text, decorum will be throughout one of the commentator's primary concerns. It should be pointed out further, relative to the above passage, that Pedemonte tends to make a proper observance of decorum one of the conditions both of sound teaching and of audience attention. Two sentences show this: "All of those who have undertaken the task of writing poetry, let them pay attention especially, according to their powers of judgment, to what is decorous, so that the proper qualities be attributed to each person; and let them observe decorum itself, through ignorance of which offense results, not only in life but most frequently in poetry and in speeches"; and "Furthermore, the writer who fails to give to each personage speech that is in keeping with character will by no means obtain the attentive minds or the open ears of his listeners."[12] Decorum also provides one of the bases for distinguishing poetry from history; for whereas the historian treats what is true, the poet pays attention "only to those things which can be treated with decorum, or which seem likely to confer splendor upon the work."[13] The treatment of the decorum of ages follows Horace with no significant additions.

Aside from these major emphases, what Pedemonte adds to the text of Horace had already been added by his predecessors. The basic principle of unity is stated in the conventional terms: "unum," "simplex," "congruens"

[10] *Ibid.*, p. 50: "poema bene moratum, locisqúe philosophicis ornatum, utilemúe continens materiam, sine tamen uenustatis lenocinio, aut uerborum maiestate, aut constructionis artificio, melius spectantem populum oblectat, detinetqúe, quàm exornatissimis uersibus, nulla subiecta sententia, neque scientia"; cf. Acron, ed. Hauthal, II, 629: "dicens, quod interdum fabula opportunitate personarum inductarum et expressione morum, quamuis sit sine arte, sine uenustate, sine grauitate sententiarum, plus placet quam uersus bene quidem sonantes, sed morum obseruatione carentes."

[11] *Ecphrasis*, pp. 51v–52: "quae quidem ad docendos animos admodum idonea habetur, maxime studendum esse monet; minimeqúe à iuuandi ac praecipiendi linea errandum; ut discentes praecepta facilius comprehendant, memoriaeqúe thesauro recondita quamdiutissime seruent."

[12] *Ibid.*, p. 15v: "Omnes qui poeticam prouinciam susceperint, pro suo iudicio maxime quid deceat animaduertant, ut unicuique personę suę partes tribuantur; ipsumqúe decorum obseruent; cuius ignoratione non modo in uita, sed sępissime in poemate, & in oratione peccatur"; and p. 16: "Praeterea qui personae cuique congruentem orationem nequaquam tribuet, nullo pacto attentos animos, patentesúe aures habebit."

[13] *Ibid.*, p. 24v: "sic Poeta non omnia, sed ea tantummodo attendere debet, quae tractari cum decoro possint, quaeúe splendorem operi allatura uideantur."

ARS POETICA: CONFUSION WITH ARISTOTLE

(p. 5). For each of the "simple" styles, Vergil may be taken as the model (p. 5v). But lest simplicity cloy, one introduces variety into the poem—always keeping appropriateness in mind—and in so doing one follows the example of nature; "for poetry and numerous noble arts follow nature as their guide, and nature, indeed, rejoices to an astonishing degree in variety."[14] The "following of nature" is one of the kinds of imitation; but in addition to the Platonic and Aristotelian meanings assigned to the term, the text also uses it to mean the adaptation of old plots and the following of models. Hence the section of the commentary on lines 128 ff. ("Difficile est proprie communia dicere") is entitled "De imitatione atque convertendis fabulis," and the general thesis is stated in this way: "Finally, the poem which we undertake to imitate must be as a model and a sort of image, in whose likeness everyone should execute his own work; he should, I say, make the sum total and not merely separate parts conform to this image."[15] Finally, the poet who executes such works, if he is to excel and exert a proper moral influence, must himself be a good man: "castum decet esse pium poetam" (p. 56v).

In its main lines, then, Pedemonte's *Ecphrasis* of 1546 adds to the tradition of commentary on Horace a sizable amount of reference to the *Poetics*. This reference adds some new ideas to the corpus of interpretation, and at times it results in changes in that interpretation. But for the most part the construction put upon the *Ars poetica* remains unaltered, and Pedemonte merely adds another document to the series which by this time had established a standard reading for the text.

A similar alliance of Aristotelian and rhetorical elements is found in a letter by Claudio Tolomei to Marcantonio Cinuzzi, dated July 1, 1543, but published in 1547. Once more, the rhetorical elements are predominant. Tolomei is discussing Cinuzzi's translation of Claudian's *Rape of Proserpine*; he praises the three books of the work because they are "ingenious in invention, clear in disposition, elevated in their great sentiments, terse in selected words, lovely through their varied ornamentation"; he finds that the translation is distinguished by its clarity, the kind of clarity which derives both from the words and from their ordering.[16] This insistence on clarity may in itself be a reference to Aristotle (*Poetics* 1458a18), although not necessarily so; what is directly from Aristotle is the discussion of the hexameter: "I remember what Aristotle says in the *Poetics* [1459b31], who praises greatly the hexameter verse appropriate to the heroic style, since

---

[14] *Ibid.*, p. 6: "Nam poetica & artes quamplurimae nobiles naturam tanquam ducem sequuntur; quae quidem mirum in modum uarietate gaudet."

[15] *Ibid.*, p. 21: "Poema denique, quod imitandum suscipimus, debet esse exemplar & imago quasi quaedam; ad cuius similitudinem opus suum quisque effingat; totum inquam corpus, & non partes singulas conformet."

[16] *Delle lettere* (1547), p. 8: "son ingegnosi per inuenzione, chiari per disposizione, alti per gran sentimenti, tersi per iscelte parole, uaghi per uario ornamento"; also p. 9.

that kind of verse does not as easily happen in the speech of men at all times as do six-syllable verses and other similar forms."[17] Here again, critical elements of all kinds are slight and commonplace; they are assembled from various sources with no systematic readjustments.

ROBORTELLO (1548) AND MAGGI (1550)

Continuing the lead of Pedemonte, although to a lesser degree, Francesco Robortello seeks to establish parallels between Horace and Aristotle in his *Paraphrasis in librum Horatii, qui vulgo de arte poetica ad Pisones inscribitur* (1548); this is one of the appendices to Robortello's commentary on the *Poetics*. As his title promises, he limits himself almost exclusively to paraphrasing Horace's epistle, and there is little if any doctrinal value in Robortello's statements. If a paraphrase is necessary at all, it is because—so he says—the order of Horace's treatise is obscure and many points need expansion and clarification. Indeed, Horace's work is not an "art" of poetry at all, but merely a "sermo" touching upon all current errors in the writing of poetry. The expositor's function will therefore be to distinguish what order is perceptible and to expand and clarify the text. In the course of his paraphrase, Robortello finds occasion to cite a number of passages from the *Poetics* which (he claims) say the same things as Horace does and thus corroborate his opinions. These are the parallels established:

Horace	*Aristotle*
42–45	1460a5 (Homer's narration)
73–74	1459b31 (hexameter for epic)
79	1449a23 (iambic)
82	(no definite passage; necessity of meter)
101–13	1454a16 (mores)
125–27	1453a17, 1451b11 (few families)
	1454a25 (ὁμαλίαν)
151–52	1460a18 (παραλογισμός)
191–92	1454a37 (deus ex machina)
193–201	1456a25 (chorus)
220 ff.	1449a19 (tragedy from satire)
281–88	1449a2 (old comedy)
317–20	1456a1 (ethical plot)

A mere listing of the comparisons shows, first, the kinds of subject matters for which Robortello was interested in juxtaposing the two texts (metrics, ethics and decorum, certain rules for the handling of narration, and historical considerations) and, second, the miscellaneous character of these problems. Robortello goes to Aristotle for scattered details which resemble

---

[17] *Ibid.*, p. 8v: "mi souuiene di qvel che dice Aristotile ne la poetica, ilqval loda molto il uerso Hesametro atto a lo stile Heroico: percio che qvella sorte di uerso, non cade cosi ageuolmente nel parlar che l'hvom fa a tvtte l'hore, come i uersi senarii, e alcvne altre simili forme."

isolated remarks in Horace, not for any consistent or particularized theory of poetry.

In this series of the early "comparers" of Horace to Aristotle, the first to read Horace in the light of the Aristotelian text was Vincenzo Maggi, who appended to his commentary on the *Poetics* an *In Q. Horatii Flacci de arte poetica librum ad Pisones, Interpretatio* (1550). I have already referred to this text in Chapter II and quoted Maggi's assumption that the important sections of Horace's work "were written almost entirely in imitation of Aristotle's *Poetics*" and his intention "to demonstrate that those things which are found in Horace are already found in Aristotle."[18] But the text merits more complete and more intensive study. Maggi discovers three separate purposes in Horace: (1) to teach the laws for the proper making of poems; (2) to treat of poetry itself; (3) to criticize, satirize, and render ridiculous.[19] Only the first two are essential to the work, and all materials belonging to them derive from Aristotle; anything concerning the third is labeled a digression and promptly dismissed. Since lla fundamental parts of the work have their source in Aristotle, their meaning can be clarified by a citation of the parallel Aristotelian text, and Maggi is for the most part satisfied with the discovery and adducing of parallels. This is clearly stated in the introduction, where Maggi declares that he will not repeat the explanations of others but merely treat of those things "quae huic nostro cum Aristotele communia sunt." The procedure is not novel, of course; but what is new is Maggi's *parti pris* to begin with Aristotle and work forward to Horace rather than following the usual, inverse process.

An example of this method of reading is found in the commentary on the very first section of the Horatian text, lines 1–13. Maggi quotes five separate texts from the *Poetics*, all relating to the distinction between plot and episode and to the importance of plot itself. Then he goes on to say:

Therefore, since from all these texts it may be clearly concluded that Aristotle himself divided Homer's poetry into two parts, that is, plot and episodes, and that plot is so to speak the soul of poetry, that is, the thing which is most important of all, it seems to me reasonable that Horace should have given at the beginning of this work the precepts for the proper making of the plot, so that he evidently treats at once and on the very threshold of his work what is first and foremost in poetry; especially since there is no other place in Horace's *Ars poetica*, except this one, which explicitly deals with the plot, that is to say, the composition of events.[20]

---

[18] See above, p. 53.

[19] *In Aristotelis librum de poetica communes explanationes* (1550), p. 328: "partim leges rectè Poesim conficiendi docere, partim de Poesi ipsa tractare, partim criminari, ac perinde ut satyricum mordere, irrideréque.

[20] *Ibid.*, pp. 329–30: "Quare cùm ex omnibus his locis plane colligi possit, Aristotelem ipsum Homeri Poesim in duas diuisisse partes, fabulam inquam, & episodia; & fabulam esse ueluti Poeseos animam, hoc est, quiddam omnium maximum: rationi consentaneum esse mihi uidetur, Horatium praecepta, quibus recte fabula confici posset, in operis huius initio tradidisse, ut quod in Poesi primum & potissimum est, in ipso statim libri limine tractare uideretur: cùm praesertim nullus in tota Horatii arte Poetica locus sit, hoc excepto, qui de fabula, id est rerum constitutione ex instituto pertractet."

He then asks whether the precepts for plot suggested by the two theorists are the same and concludes that they are, with Aristotle's requirements of necessity and probability corresponding to Horace's insistence upon the properly constituted animal. Plainly, the argument runs this way: Horace is imitating Aristotle; he finds in Aristotle precepts for the proper constitution of the plot, the most important part of any poem; he introduces at the beginning of his treatise an equivalent set of precepts. As far as the interpretation of Horace is concerned, this means that lines 1–13 will be read as a section on the proper organization of poetic plot.

In general, Maggi's procedure is to seek for each passage in Horace as many equivalents in Aristotle as he can possibly discover. We may take as an example his treatment of lines 312 ff., on the general subject of decorum; Maggi's references to the "particulae" of the *Poetics* are to his own divisions of the text in the commentary preceding. He has this to say:

... mihi uidetur Horatius intelligere, poetam oportere rectè actiones exprimere personis congruas. quae pars desumpta esse uidetur ex .II.VIII. et .IX. particulis [= 1447a13, 1447b13–24]: in quibus dicitur Poesim necessario imitari. Illud autem: Respicere exemplar uitae, ex .LXXX. particula [= 1454b8] Aristotelis sumptum uidetur: siquidem ibi ait: [translation of Aristotle quoted]. Pars uero illa:
   Interdum speciosa iocis: morataque rectè,
ubi Horatius uerba cum rebus confert, docetque multo maiorem in rebus ipsis, quàm in uerbis curam esse adhibendam: particulae Poetices Aristotelis .XLI. [= 1450a29] proportione respondere uidetur. fabulam enim eo loco cum moribus, dictionibus, et sententiis conferens, principatum ac praecipuum locum in Poesi obtinere docuit. ita Horatius illum imitatus, res uerbis comparans, ipsas primas sibi uendicare asserit. Verba autem Aristotelis sunt haec. [translation of Aristotle quoted] (p. 360).

It can readily be seen how such a determination will lead, at times, to the discovery of parallels that are very farfetched indeed. A case in point is the remark on lines 38–41, where Horace advises the poet to select a subject matter suited to his own genius in order to achieve "facundia" and "ordo"; for Maggi, this "seems to correspond" to *Poetics* 1450a35, in which Aristotle insists upon the greater difficulty of treating plot than character or diction (p. 334). But Maggi is unaware of any such discrepancies. Indeed, he finds it possible to justify, as clever imitations, all of Horace's departures from the order or the doctrine of the Aristotelian text. Horace follows his own precept "Nec uerbum uerbo curabis reddere fidus/Interpres" (1. 133); "In fact, he made the *Poetics* his own, which had already been made generally known and public by Aristotle, handing it down in a different order and not translating it word for word."[21] Thus Horace "dissimulated" his borrowings by treating epic first instead of

---

[21] *Ibid.*, p. 345: "nam uulgatam iam, communemque factam ab Aristotele, propriam Poeticam effecit, alio eam ordine tradens, nec uerbum uerbo reddens."

tragedy, as Aristotle had done (p. 335), and by introducing his counsels on new words in connection with the epic rather than with tragedy, since the epic demands high-sounding speech (p. 336).

This generous conception of parallelism leads Maggi to find equivalent passages in Aristotle for almost all sections of the *Ars poetica* except those which he characterizes as satirical digressions. A complete listing follows:

Horace	*Aristotle*
1–13 (plot)	1455b12, 1450a3, 1450a15, 1450a38, 1451b27, 1451a23, 1451a36
14–23 (episodes)	1451b33, 1456a25, (last two above)
24–31 (diction)	1458a18
32–37	(digression)
38–41 (genius: subject)	1450a33
42–45 (epic)	1460a1, 1459a29
46–59 (new words)	1458b31–1459a16
60–72	(digression)
73–85 (meters)	1460a1, 1448b28, 1449a21
86–88	(digression)
89–95 (tragic, comic verse)	1448a14
96–103 (passions, pity)	1455a31, 1456a33
104–11 (diction)	1456b8
112–18 (decorum)	1454a15, 1461b9
119–27 (old, new characters)	1453b21, 1454a15
128–35 (imitation of poets)	1456a7, 1448b34
136–45 (epic beginning)	(no equivalent; but cf. 1462b3)
146–50 (epic plot)	1459a29
151–52 (true and false)	1460a18–33
153–78 (decorum of age)	1454a33; also *Rhetoric*
179–88 (incredible)	1460a11, 1453b1, 1461b26
189–92 (plot)	1452b14
192 (3 interlocutors)	1449a14
193–201 (chorus)	1456a25
201–19	(digression; but cf. 1458b31)
220–33 (satire and tragedy)	1449a19, 1451a6
234–43 (satire)	(no equivalent)
244–50 (rustic audience)	(„ „)
251–59 (iamb)	1449a21, 1459b31
260–74	(digression)
275–84 (tragedy, old comedy)	1448a29, 1449a14
285–94	(digression)
295–308	(„)
309–16 (wisdom)	(no equivalent)
317–22 (imitation)	1447a13, 1447b13–24, 1454b8, 1450a29
323–32	(digression)
333–46 (utility, pleasure)	1449b21, 1453a1, 1453b11 (also *Rhetoric* on brevity)
347–60 (defences)	1460b6 ff.

Horace	Aristotle
361–65 (poetry and painting)	1454b8
366–78	(digression)
379–90	(,,)
391–407 (natural origins)	1448b4
408–11 (nature vs. art)	1461b26
412–18	(digression)
419–44	(,,)
445–52 (meter and poetry)	1456b24
453–76	(digression)

Maggi's initial thesis that Horace was versifying Aristotle and his demonstration of the parallelism of the two texts did not fail to produce changes in the interpretation of the *Ars poetica*. Not only are all traces of the late-classical and the humanistic commentators removed (this had already been accomplished in Robortello's *Paraphrasis*), but certain new orientations in the reading of the text are introduced. And these concern really important poetic matters. Horace's somewhat vague distinction between "res" and "verba" becomes the much more specific division of plot and diction. The general admonition to make all parts of the poem cohere is read as equivalent to the organizing principles of necessity and probability. Horace's digressions are identified with Aristotle's episodes. The vices of diction pointed out by the Roman are found to be the opposites of the virtues of diction extolled by the Greek. The "dulcia sunto" of Horace (l. 99), long since identified by the commentators with the arousing of the audience's passions, is now related to Aristotle's pity; similarly, "prodesse" is taken as an exemplification of the arousal of pity, fear, and τὸ φιλάνθρωπον, while "delectare" becomes synonymous with the pleasure produced by imitation. Horace's mixture of truth with falsehood is traced back to Aristotle's παραλογισμός and the impossible probable. Notions of imitation, which had already been related by earlier commentators to a copying of nature, are, by Maggi, more definitely connected with Aristotles' conception of action. Finally, Maggi follows his predecessors in associating Horace's precepts on decorum with Aristotle's recommendations for character. All in all, this is not an inconsiderable reorientation of the reading of Horace, and Maggi becomes a kind of pioneer in this respect.

GRIFOLI (1550)

Some of the same credit for pioneering may also be accorded to Giacopo Grifoli, who in the same year of 1550 published his *In Artem poeticam Horatii interpretatio*.[22] For Grifoli also rereads the *Ars poetica* in the light of the *Poetics*. Two factors, however, decrease his originality: first, he

---

[22] There is no indication in the Grifoli volume as to whether it was published early or late in the year; the same is true for the Maggi volume. But since the dedication of the latter is dated September, 1549, I am assuming that it was published fairly early in 1550 and hence antedated Grifoli.

came after Maggi and probably knew his *Interpretatio*; second, in certain senses, his "rereading" reverts to a much earlier tradition. Grifoli's commentary is long and complete; it follows the usual pattern of citing a passage of the text, giving a general interpretation of the passage, and then providing a line-for-line or word-for-word gloss. Its total position is a very curious one. The basic assumption is that Horace in the *Epistle* is imitating Aristotle and adopting, paraphrasing, and reorganizing Aristotle's central ideas. This is clear from such statements as the one found in the dedication to Fabio Mignanelli, Bishop of Lucera: "This certainly I do not hesitate to affirm, that I have expounded the passages in Horace and that this work was culled almost entirely from Aristotle's *Art of Poetry*," and others in the body of the text proper: "Seeing then that in Aristotle's opinion tragedy consists of plot, characters, thought, diction, spectacle, and melody, he decided that the first thing to discuss was the construction of the plot"; "nor does he follow any the less here than elsewhere the teaching of Aristotle."[23] Starting from this assumption, he seeks a way of explaining Horace's organization in terms of the *Poetics*. He finds, first, that Horace is concerned essentially with tragedy, just as Aristotle was, and that he treats the epic only insofar as it has characteristics in common with tragedy (p. 11). Second, he believes that Horace has ordered his work around the six qualitative parts of tragedy, altering, however, the sequence of treatment. Thus lines 1–23 are devoted to plot, lines 114–18 and 319–22 to character, lines 93–113, 114–18, and 319–22 to thought, lines 24–31, 32–45, 114–18, and 319–22 to diction, and lines 179–83 and 275–80 to spectacle and melody. But there is much uncertainty, as the overlappings and repetitions indicate; this is a result of the corruption of the original assumption by other positions derived from other systems.

I have already pointed out in Chapter II how Grifoli adds to the system just outlined the set of rhetorical distinctions of invention, disposition, and elocution, thereby introducing a third layer of meanings. What Horace says is read not only under the influence of preconceptions about the *Poetics* but also as a representation of well-known rhetorical topics. This makes it possible to attach to given passages a variety of associated meanings. In lines 32–45, for example, Horace is speaking of the necessity of choosing a subject fitted to one's genius; if this is done, eloquent words and a proper order will ensue. Grifoli sees in the lines "things more abstruse than most people suspect." First, he paraphrases and quotes Aristotle on the two types of errors in poems, those ascribable to the poetic art and those ascribable to some other art (*Poetics* 1460b15); a craftsman like the one Horace mentions sins in the poetic art when he

[23] *Interpretatio* (1550), p. 7: "Illud certe affirmare non dubito, ostendisse me locos Horatianos, ac totum ferè hoc opus ex Aristotelis Arte poetica decerptum"; p. 11: "Videns igitur Aristotelis iudicio Tragoediam constare fabula, moribus, sententia, dictione, apparatu, & melodia; primum de constitutione fabulae disserendum esse statuit"; p. 39: "neque nunc minus, quàm vnquam alias praeceptionem Aristotelis secutum."

undertakes a task superior to his capacities. Next (for ll. 38–41), Grifoli states that Horace is here beginning a new section of the work: after having expounded the proper composition of the plot, he now indicates how beauty may be achieved through diction. We shall see that this division between plot and diction is fundamental in the commentary. Finally, Horace's statement about "facundia" and "ordo" leads Grifoli to draw a parallel between the poet and the orator: the proper choice of subject matter is equivalent to invention, "ordo" to disposition, and "facundia" to elocution (see the passage quoted above in Chapter II). The general rhetorical preoccupations of the work are confirmed by Grifoli's frequent references to Cicero, Quintilian, and other masters of the art.

A further distinction is necessary, however, in order to understand completely what is going on in Grifoli's commentary. In his introduction, Grifoli twice insists that, in speaking about tragedy (and incidentally the epic), Horace was concerned essentially with the matter of appropriateness: "quaecunque ad rerum *congruentiam*, & *decorum* attinent, ea diligenter est persecutus" (p. 11) and "Constat igitur hic libellus ex ijs praecipuè rebus, in quibus maxime *quid deceat* apparet" (p. 12). In his effort to reconcile this emphasis with the Aristotelian system that he sees in the work, Grifoli arrives at this solution: The major form of appropriateness in a poetic work is of words to things. Of Aristotle's six qualitative parts, therefore, the two most important are μῦθος or "fabula" and λέξις or "oratio," and the *Ars poetica* thus divides its time between these two parts. Thus lines 1–23 concern "fabula," but the section of commentary on lines 24–31 begins with "Transit ad alteram partem, quae λέξις nominatur" (p. 17), and the commentary on line 280 starts thus: "ad λέξιν redit. supra quoque: & tulit eloquium insolitum" (p. 82). But what of the other four parts? The answer is fairly simple: spectacle and melody are dismissed as belonging to the instruments of poetry, and character and thought are in a sense collapsed with diction. Already in the introduction, Grifoli has declared that there is no point concerning sententiae or mores that is not treated by means of diction; moreover, "since speech is the translator of the mind and this is the indicator of character, in speaking of its decorum one has also spoken of the decorum of the rest."[24] Without consideration of language it would hardly be possible to know if the "officium, proprietas, similitudo, constantia" of character are properly observed or not (under these four terms are hidden Aristotle's requisities for character). The same idea is made even more explicit later:

Although the subject discussed is περὶ τῆς λέξεως, nevertheless nature and character are here treated, from which diction normally derives. Otherwise it will not be appropriate, and from the beginning we have warned that whenever the poet spoke about diction, he would be speaking in the proper places about

[24] *Ibid.*, p. 12: "quoniam oratio est interpres mentis, & haec est morum index, de illius decoro dicendo de reliquorum quoque decoro dixit."

sententia and character, as he does here [*A.p.*, ll. 119–135] and in what follows.[25]

For these reasons, when Grifoli comes to assign the six qualitative parts to object, manner, and means (p. 97), the three belonging to object of imitation are identified as diction, thought, and character, the two belonging to means as spectacle and melody, and the one belonging to manner as plot. From his explanation of this last assignment, it is apparent that he gives to "imitation" the meaning of "representation": "Since plot is the composite of the events in a tragedy, let it be imitated both in that way and in that sequence in which the plot itself has been composed."[26]

Horace, thus, in the last analysis, reduces Aristotle to the old "res-verba" dichotomy—and then in turn reduces it to "verba" alone. For if the object of imitation is character, thought, and diction, and if diction contains the essence of the other two, then one treats all of the essential problems of poetry when one speaks about language. Grifoli's analysis is, in fact, largely a reduction of Horace's poetics to linguistic problems. In the list of parallel passages following, I shall indicate for the most significant passages how this is true:

Horace	Aristotle	
1–23	1451a16	Horace's "natural" corresponds to Aristotle's "necessary and probable." Unity of action, which does not even result from having a single hero, cannot possibly come from mixed subjects. Unity and simplicity are required, mixture of styles and genres is condemned.
24–31	(none)	λέξις; in passing, spectacle and melody. In language, as in character, vices exist which imitate virtues. Of the three styles, Horace here is treating the middle. Cross references to rhetorical works. Excess of ornament in *diction* creates a monster comparable to the monster in *plot* of ll. 1–23.
32–45	1460b16	First, proper choice of subject to avoid artistic error. Then, return to λέξις; beauty of diction after beauty of plot. Invention, disposition, and elocution.
73–85	1459b32	Epic verse.
	1449a23	Iamb and daily speech; in tragedy, produces admiration.
86–92	(none)	Diction adapted to "quod decet"; the "color" of the iamb adapted to the quality of persons in tragedy or comedy.
93–113	1449b27	Language adapted to characters, situation, etc.
	1455a31	Arousal of passions in the audience; cf. the orator. In comedy, pleasure; in tragedy, "metus, misericordia, horror."

[25] *Ibid.*, p. 41: "Quamuis enim περὶ τῆς λέξεως disputetur, tamen natura, & mores exprimuntur, & ab his ea emanare solet. alioqui decorum suum non habebit, & nos à principio monuimus, cum de Oratione dissereret poëta, de Sententia, & Moribus suis locis eum dicturum, vt hic, & in sequentibus cum dicit."

[26] *Ibid.*, p. 97: "cum fabula sit compositio rerum omnium in tragoedia, & eo modo, & ordine imitandum sit, quo composita sit ipsa fabula."

POETIC THEORY

Horace	Aristotle	
114–18	1454a16	Language appropriate to persons: Aristotle's τὸ ὅμοιον.
	1454a33	Horace's equivalents for Aristotle's four requisites of character: line 312 for τὰ χρηστά; line 156 for τὰ ἁρμόττοντα; line 114 for τὸ ὅμοιον; line 119 for τὸ ὁμαλόν. Differences in λέξις from differences in character.
119–35		In new characters, τὸ ὁμαλόν.
136–52	1448a25 [1460a20]	Epic characters insofar as they resemble tragic; mixture of the true and the false.
153–78		Decorum of age; τὰ ἁρμόττοντα.
179–83	1452b19 1455b24 1453b1 1449b27	Parts of tragedy; on- and off-stage action.
189–201	1454a37	Deus ex machina.
202–19	1447a22	Spectacle and melody. Horace's primitive audience.
220–43	1456b2	The diction of satire. Cicero against the mixing of genres. Sententiae and "verba" as appropriate to "res"; reference to the rhetoricians.
275–80	1450a13	ὄψις. Spectacle and melody as instruments of imitation; cf. action and memory in rhetoric. λέξις again.
295–308	(none)	Art vs. nature. Horace's double intention: (1) precepts for poem, (2) precepts for the end of poetry, i.e., for "delectatio" and "utilitas."
309–18	1454b8	Imitation of Platonic Ideas and Forms.
319–22	1450a7 1454a16 1450a25 1451b27 1453b11	Six parts of tragedy (distributed as indicated in discussion above). Diction from character and thought. Diction as deriving its meaning from character, and meaningless without it. Pleasure from the "fabula morata," from pity and fear in tragedy. For affecting the audience, necessity of properly constituted plot and decorum.
323–32	(none)	Both diction and materials must be great. Nature and art.
333–60	(none)	Utility and pleasure; need of "brevitas" for the first and "natura, verosimilia" for the second. Utility: "quae doceant, corrigant, moueant." Appeal to the young through pleasure, to the old through utility.
366–78	1448b4	Two natural causes of poetry. Imitation as a source of pleasure, which in turn leads to utility.
391–407	(none)	Pleasure as leading to utility.

As far as Grifoli's general interpretation of Horace is concerned, then, it is a strange combination of an attempt to read Horace as an imitator of Aristotle and a reversion to the rhetorical approaches of earlier years. Aristotle is soon made subject to the rhetoricians, and rhetoric itself is reduced to its minimal term, the study of language and all its problems.

ARS POETICA: CONFUSION WITH ARISTOTLE

That these were the ideas about poetry still most current is indicated by such a work as Lodovico Dolce's *Osservationi nella volgar lingua* (1550), whose first three books are exclusively linguistic and grammatical but whose fourth book deals with poetry. Here again, a few ideas are borrowed from Aristotle: poetry is an imitation; not all writers of verse are poets. But the main body of doctrine is in the old Horatian-rhetorical tradition. Immediately after the statement that poetry is an imitation, Dolce says: "for the function of the poet is to imitate the actions of men, and his end, under lovely veils of useful and moral inventions, to delight the soul of him who reads."[27] The poet must possess not only wisdom, but also invention, order, artifice, and words; of these, the most important are the last two. The real poetic gift is that of expressing the invented materials by means of "beauties and ornaments," in order to delight the reader, to arouse his passions. The whole position of Dolce, which is not too distant from that of Grifoli, is contained in the following passage:

> Nevertheless, since verses and words are the brush and the paints of the poet with which he shades and colors the canvas of his invention to make so marvelous a portrait of nature that the minds of men are ravished by it, he must devote his greatest attention and industry to composing them in this way, and with words so beautiful and so appropriate to the matter of which he treats that that end, sought and desired by him who reads, will be achieved; without which all his labors are exerted and consumed in vain.[28]

Lilio Gregorio Giraldi's *Dialogi duo de poëtis nostrorum temporum* (1551) is even more backward looking in its few passages relevant to poetics. Essentially the work is a catalogue of recent and contemporary poets of various European countries. The listing is summary, providing merely names, an occasional fact, and, for each poet, a conventional bouquet. The complimentary phrases that Giraldi accords the poets he admires sound for all the world like those used by Pietro Ricci at the beginning of the century; the epithets applied in 1505 to Latin poets are now applied to modern poets writing in Latin or in the vulgar tongues. So Pico della Mirandola is praised for his "ingenium, doctrina," for his "facilitas, affectus"; Pontano is "doctus, elegans, absolutus, enucleatus, exquisitus"; Sadoleto has as his qualities "grauitas, modestia," Bembo's poems are "dulcia, mollia, delicata"; Sannazaro has created "ingenij exquisita monumenta," and Calcagnini is noteworthy for "eruditio, doctrina."[29]

---

[27] *Osservationi* (1550), p. 87v: "percioche l'ufficio del Poeta è di imitare le attioni de gli huomini: e il fine sotto leggiadri ueli di morali & utili inuentioni dilettar l'animo di chi legge."

[28] *Ibid.*, p. 88v: "Non di meno, perche i uersi e le parole sono il pennello, & i colori del Poeta, con che egli ua adombrando e dipingendo la tauola della sua inuentione per fare un ritratto cotanto marauiglioso della natura, che ne stupiscano gli intelletti de glihuomini; dee porre ogni suo principale studio e diligenza in comporgli tali, e con uoci cosi belle & appartinenti alla materia, di che egli tratta, che ne riesca quel fine ricercato e desiderato da chi legge; e senza ilquale ogni sua fatica è posta e consumata in darno."

[29] *Dialogi duo* (1551), pp. 16-20, 40.

These epithets indicate no more than certain kinds of knowledge on the part of the poet and certain qualities of style in his writing; they do not presuppose any poetic theory beyond the simplest rhetorical preconceptions.

DENORES (1553)

After Grifoli's fairly complex and experimental commentary, that of Giason Denores in his *In epistolam Q. Horatij Flacci de arte poetica Interpretatio* (1553) seems like a return to the patterns and the procedures of an earlier generation. Indeed, Denores takes frequent issue with the interpretations of both Maggi and Grifoli, claiming that he is reflecting instead the lectures of Trifon Gabriele on Horace, as he had heard them and as he had summarized them even before Gabriele's death in 1549. Gabriele's ideas, if they are accurately represented here, are very close to those of Giovanni Britannico and Parrasio. For Denores organizes the whole of the Horatian text around the invention–disposition–elocution distinction, and in a way even more systematic than that of his predecessors. Almost all the precepts he states—and he returns also to the preceptive form—are concerned with one of the three terms. The initial statement that he intends to follow this pattern is found in connection with the first lines of the *Ars poetica*, when he affirms that one of Horace's aims is "the formation of our taste with respect to every rule of invention, disposition, and elocution in every type of poetry."[30] Lines 1–23, he says, are concerned with invention, which is the "soul" of poetry. To explain the subsequent passages, he calls upon the rhetorical division into three parts of elocution itself: "genus" or "ratio dicendi" or "character" (the particular kind or quality of style), "verba," and "numeri" (meters or verses). Lines 24–31 treat the first of these, "character." General notions of disposition appear in lines 32–41, and the more particular problem of natural versus artificial order in lines 42–45. The second part of elocution, "verba," figures in lines 46–72, and the third part, "numeri," in lines 73–88. Lines 89–98 make special applications of the rules for "character" and "verba" to tragedy and comedy. Then, after long sections on other matters, Horace returns to the distinction in lines 220–50, pointing out that it is disposition and elocution, rather than invention, that give quality to commonplace materials. Lines 251–74, on the verse of tragedy and comedy, treat its "numeri" (rounding out the materials of lines 89–98). Finally, when Horace speaks of "sapere" and Socratic philosophy in lines 309–32, he is returning to the problem of invention. In all, somewhat over a third of the text is made to fit into this general scheme. As for the rest of it, Denores sees the long central section as devoted primarily to problems of arousing the audience's emotions, of decorum, and of conventions for the stage; but even here the major dis-

---

[30] *In epistolam* (1553), p. 5v; see above, chap. II, p. 56 and n. 25 for the full text.

tinction is sometimes applicable. For example, if the poet wishes to arouse the passions, he must attend to "ornaments" and "figures" (ll. 99–113); if he uses old, traditional characters, he exercises no invention, but he makes these characters his own through proper disposition and elocution (ll. 119–30). The last part of the text (aside from the recommendations for the behavior of the poet) seems to be of interest to Denores mostly for the discussion of utility and pleasure as the ends of poetry.

Throughout the *Ars poetica*, although in comparatively small number, Denores finds analogies to the Aristotelian poetics. Sometimes these are merely implied, with no direct reference to Aristotle—as, for example, the characterization of invention as the "anima" of poetry (ll. 1–23), or the suggestion that the five-act magnitude of dramas is related to the proper size of animals (ll. 189–90), or the inclusion of "timor" and "misericordia" among the passions to be aroused by the poet (ll. 99–113). Elsewhere, the references are explicit and the text is cited: Aristotle on the pleasure derived from imitation, in connection with Horace's remarks on the choice of words and figures (ll. 46–72); on the difference between poetry and history, relevant to Horace's "res gestae" (ll. 73–88); on history and verisimilitude, apropos of Horace's three types of narrative (ll. 131–52); on the necessity of producing pity and fear by plot rather than by spectacle, in connection with Horace's precept on off-stage action (ll. 179–88); on purgation, as a means of producing Horace's "prodesse" (ll. 333–46); and on artistic and nonartistic errors (ll. 347–60). The list of parallels is not long, and it will be readily seen that they merely indicate an association of Aristotle's text with Horace's, without any important influence upon the interpretation of the latter.

For Denores' reading of Horace remains essentially rhetorical. This is true not only because of his persistence in applying the invention–disposition–elocution terminology to so large a portion of the text, but also because other rhetorical tendencies are evident. The whole conception of the relationship of audience to work and to poet is in the Ciceronian tradition: the poet, like the orator, seeks to induce the audience to admiration (in part for his own genius) and to awaken in it a wide variety of passions (ll. 46–113). To do so, he must pay particularly close attention to the decorum of persons, just as the orator does and just as Aristotle recommends in the *Rhetoric* (ll. 114–18, 153–78). Such arousing of the passions is itself merely a means to a further end, that of correcting and directing its lives by providing moral precepts and examples. It is interesting in this connection to note that Denores insists that "delectare" does not mean "oblectare" but rather "movere" and that pleasure itself is thus a form of utility; pleasure operates on the will of the audience as utility concerns its mind, and the two together produce the desired moral effects (ll. 333–46). Many details of the construction of poems are determined by this desire to produce stated effects on audiences by means of rhetorical devices.

LOVISINI (1554)

As compared with Denores, the Aristotelian flavor of Francesco Lovisini's *In librum Q. Horatii Flacci de arte poetica commentarius* (1554) is much more considerable. This results in part from the generous citation of the *Poetics* to explain passages in the *Ars poetica*, in part from the numerous references to various other works of Aristotle, especially the *Nicomachean Ethics* and the *Rhetoric*. Indeed, the whole impression of erudition is much greater; Lovisini brings into his commentary on Horace every possible quotation from Greek and Latin literature that seems to him to have some relevance to the words or the lines in question. Much of this erudition, however, turns out to be historical in content—very like that of the expositors at the beginning of the century—and adds little to the meaning of the text as an art of poetry. For Lovisini's interpretation of Horace, the most significant references are those to rhetorical treatises, primarily Aristotle's *Rhetoric*, but also Cicero, Quintilian, Demetrius, Hermogenes, and others. These sources, plus all the others he invokes, enable him to contest and correct the older commentators such as Acron and Porphyrion and the more recent ones such as Maggi, Grifoli, and Denores; but these corrections concern points of detail rather than any general reading of the text. This is also true of the majority of the texts cited from the *Poetics* as parallels to Horace, a list of which follows:

Horace		*Aristotle*	
1–13	(congruous subject)	1447b13	(poet from imitation)
		1450a38	(plot as soul)
		1448a4	(poetry and painting)
14–23	(simplicity, unity)	1451b33	(episodic plot)
		1451a19	(unity not from hero)
24–31	(vices in style)	(none)	
32–37	(total excellence)	(none)	
38–41	(choice of subject)	(none)	
42–45	(order of epic)	(none)	
46–51	(elocution)	1456b20	(diction)
52–59	(new words)	(none)	
60–72	(usage)	(none)	
73–85	(meters for genres)	1460a1	(mixture of meters)
		1447a15	(poetic genres)
		1459b34	(epic meter)
		1448b31	(iamb)
		1449a21	(iamb in tragedy)
		1449a26	(iamb in daily speech)
86–88	(poetic styles)	(none)	

ARS POETICA: CONFUSION WITH ARISTOTLE

Horace		*Aristotle*	
89–92	(trag. and comedy)	1448a16	(trag. and comedy)
		1453a18	(Thyestes)
93–95	(style of tr., com.)	1453b1	(pity and fear)
96–103	(speech of tragedy)	1453a21	(tragic families)
		1453b1	(pity and fear)
	(audience emotion)	1455a30	(emotion of poet)
		1452a4	(sources of emotion)
104–13	(action and speech)	(none)	
114–18	(decorum of speech)	(none)	
119–27	(old, new heroes)	1460a35	(improbabilities in *Odyssey*)
		1453b22	(traditional plots)
		1454a20	(τὰ ἁρμόττοντα)
		1454a22	(τὸ ὅμοιον)
		1454a25	(τὸ ὁμαλόν)
128–35	(old subjects)	1448b38	(Homeric subjects)
136–39	(epic beginning)	(none)	
140–45	(,, ,,)	(none)	
146–52	("in medias res")	1451a36	(necessary, probable)
	(true, false)		
153–57	(decorum of age)	(none)	
158–60	(child)	(none)	
161–65	(youth)	(none)	
166–68	(adult)	(none)	
169–74	(old man)	(none)	
175–78	(traits for each)	(none)	
179–88	(on-, off-stage)	1453b1	(emotions from spectacle)
189–90	(five acts)	1450b35	(magnitude)
		1449b12	(time of tragedy, epic)
191–92	("deus ex machina")	1454b2	("deus ex machina")
193–201	(chorus)	1452a15	(parts of tragedy)
		1456a29	(choral songs)
202–7	(melody, music)	1450a7	(qualitative parts)
		1450b18	(melody)
		1447a23	(harmony, rhythm)
208–19	(licence, vulgarity)	1447a26	(,, ,,)
220–24	(satyrs in tragedy	1449b27	(pity and fear)
		1449a19	(satyric tragedy)
		1451b37	(dramatic contests)
		1462b11	(tr. superior to epic)
225–33	(decorum of satyrs)	(none)	
234–39	(satyric diction)	(none)	
240–43	(satyric invention)	(none)	

[131]

POETIC THEORY

Horace		*Aristotle*	
244–50	(speech of satyrs)	1449a35	(αἰσχρόν, φθαρτικόν)
251–59	(iamb and spondee)	(none)	
260–69	(Gk. *vs.* Lat. poets)	1454a28	(Euripides' errors)
270–74	(Plautus censured)	(none)	
275–80	(history of tragedy)	1448a29	(origins of tragedy)
		1449a15	(Aeschylus' additions)
281–84	(old comedy)	1449a31	(definition of comedy)
		1449a37	(chorus in comedy)
285–94	(Latin poets)	(none)	
295–301	(art and nature)	1455a33	(talent, poetic furor)
301–8	(poetic problems)	1447a13	(imitation as "officium")
309–16	(knowledge)	(none)	
317–22	(life as model)	1447a15	(poetry as imitation)
		1449b7	(qualitative parts)
323–32	(Roman avarice)	(none)	
333–46	(ends of poetry)	1451a36	(necessary, probable)
347–60	(errors of poet)	1460b15	(two kinds of errors)
		1454a29	(errors of Homer)
361–65	(poetry, painting)	1454b9	(poetry, painting)
		1450a38	(,, ,,)
366–73	(no mediocrity)	(none)	
374–78	(poetry for delight)	(none)	
379–85	(ignorant poets)	(none)	
386–90	(correction)	(none)	
391–99	(civilizing role)	(none)	
400–7	(praise of poetry)	1447a24	(music and poetry)
408–11	(nature, art)	(none)	
412–18	(advice to poet)	(none)	
419–25	(flatterers)	(none)	
426–33	(friends)	(none)	
434–37	(,,)	(none)	
438–44	(true critic)	(none)	
445–52	(role of critic)	(none)	
453–63	(mad poet)	(none)	
463–69	(,, ,,)	(none)	
470–76	(,, ,,)	(none)	

I have given this list in such detail, respecting all of Lovisini's divisions of the Horatian text, for several reasons. First, it is interesting to see to what an extent the text is now subdivided—Lovisini's divisions number sixty-eight—and what topics are indicated as the subject-matter of each division. Second, the list shows how many passages from the *Poetics* are brought

[132]

into association with the text, and to what ideas in Horace they are said to be parallel. It is easy to see how commentators and critics, finding so many recurrences of ideas in the two documents, might be strengthened in their conviction that Horace was merely imitating or paraphrasing Aristotle and that the two theorists were saying essentially the same things. But a close study of the parallels in the above list shows that the resemblances are largely topical; in some cases they concern purely historical matters, such as the identity of Thyestes or Aeschylus' additions to the tragic form; in others they show that the two theorists were writing about the same topics, but do not indicate conclusions by any means similar. For example, to take a case of "multiple reference," three passages from Aristotle are cited as parallel to lines 1–13 of the *Ars poetica*. In the first of these Aristotle states that the poet is a poet by reason of his imitation, and not because he writes in verse; in the second, that plot is the soul of tragedy; in the third, that poets represent characters as better or worse than we, or as like us, just as painters do. Now the first is cited in support of the general idea, attributed to these lines in Horace, that the poet follows fantasy rather than opinion; the second, to show that it is proper for Horace to treat, at the very beginning, the "constitution of the argument and the plot"; the third, because Horace had drawn the comparison "pictoribus atque poetis...." This juxtaposition of passages neither indicates a clear conception of Aristotle's theory of imitation or of his definition of plot, nor, for that matter, does it throw any additional light on the comprehension of Horace's lines. Or for another such example: five passages from Aristotle are fitted to lines 119–27, in which Horace says that when traditional characters are introduced they must be handled in keeping with the tradition and that when new ones are used, they must be made to be self-consistent. Aristotle is first quoted to show that traditional materials must be followed exactly, no matter how improbable they may be; second, that traditional plots must not be modified; third, that τὰ ἁρμόττοντα is equivalent to "sibi conuenientia"; fourth, that τὸ ὅμοιον means similarity to historical or traditional character, such as the "honoratum ... Achillem"; fifth, that τὸ ὁμαλόν states a principle of consistency identical with that of Horace. These parallels, interesting as they may be for Lovisini's interpretation of Aristotle, add little to the interpretation of Horace—unless it be a certain number of irrelevant and inappropriate considerations.

Finally, I have produced the complete list above to demonstrate what passages in Horace, at this stage of scholarship, were still regarded as independent of Aristotle. These, it will be seen, largely concern Latin poetry and certain practical counsels to poets which Aristotle's theoretical position did not admit.

Out of all this elaborate commentary and this extensive juxtaposition of texts, there emerges very little that might be called Lovisini's interpretation of Horace. Erudition and the conventional explanations have taken the

POETIC THEORY

place of independent reading. Lovisini assigns the usual passages to invention, disposition, and elocution, makes the usual comparisons between poetry and rhetoric, insists as did his predecessors on the decisive role of the audience in determining the nature of poems. A few points that he makes are, however, original enough to deserve special mention. For one, he seems to be more of a Platonist than many of his forerunners; in the first section of commentary, he quotes the *Symposium* to the effect that all artisans and artificers are poets in a sense, and the *Apology* on the divine furor; he identifies Horace's "exemplar vitae" (l. 317) with the "Idea which, as Plato says in the *Parmenides*, contains all particular things and is separate from them."[31] Moreover, many passages are quoted from Plato in connection with incidental matters. For another, Lovisini emphasizes certain ideas about the relationship between poetry and nature. From his comments on lines 14–23 it is clear that he thinks of probability as natural probability, for he defends the Dido episode in the *Aeneid* in this way: "that episode is not completely inconsistent with the matter at hand, but rather produces pleasure through the variety of materials; frequently, in fact, voyagers driven by storms have arrived at the outermost lands."[32] The fact that a thing may happen in nature is taken as justification for a particular happening in a specific poem. Lastly, Lovisini expands Horace's notions about utility and pleasure as the ends of poetry. He quotes Theon on the ends proposed by Homer: in the *Iliad*, that he might inspire men to justice, in the *Odyssey*, to exhort us to bear adverse fortune with equanimity.[33] He sees the "prodesse" as resulting from allegory in plots, "which teach us wisely and thoroughly what is best in life," and from the representation of character, which teaches us our duty.[34] Utility and pleasure are expanded into the triple "ut doceret, ut delectaret, ut moueret" of Cicero, with the third member of the trilogy making the other two effective (p. 24v).

Lovisini's commentary of 1554 was the last of a series of five formal expositions of the *Ars poetica* which appeared in the short space of six years: Robortello's in 1548, Maggi's and Grifoli's in 1550, Denores' in 1553, Lovisini's in 1554. The next such formal discussion will not be published for seven years, in 1561, when Pigna produces his *Poetica Horatiana*. But in the intervening years, many documents in the "Horatian mode" were written and published, and the tradition was by no means interrupted.

---

[31] *Commentarius* (1554), p. 63v: "Idaea, quae, ut ait Plato in Parmenide, singularia omnia continet, & ab ijs seiuncta est."

[32] *Ibid.*, p. 7v: "res illa à re proposita non penitus abhorret, quin potius rerum uarietate delectationem affert: nauigantes enim saepe in ultimas terras tempestate appulsi peruenerunt."

[33] *Ibid.*, p. 4v: "ut homines ad iustitiam inflammet, in Odyssaea ad ferendam aequo animo aduersam fortunam nos cohortatur."

[34] *Ibid.*, p. 66: "fabularum allegoria, quibus, quid optimum in uita sit, prudenter edocent" and "moribus etiam nos ad officium poetae boni inflammant."

In fact, during the last two of these six years, while the formal commentaries were being published, Benedetto Varchi was delivering a series of lectures to the Accademia Fiorentina which reflected, in part at least, the same Horatian ideas. The lectures, dated 1553 and 1554, were not published until 1590. As we shall see later, Varchi's point of departure was specifically the text of the *Poetics*; but most of the *Lezzioni della poetica* move rapidly away from Aristotle in the direction of Horace. In a sense, he ascribes the same movement to Horace himself, since he speaks of the *Poetics* as the text "from which Horace drew his own art" ("dal quale cauò Horazio la sua," p. 677). With Horace, also, Varchi insists that the knowledge of the art, derived from arts of poetry ancient or modern, is insufficient without the poet's natural gifts; to both art and nature must be added a firm knowledge of several languages and of the poets who have written in them. This emphasis upon knowledge of various kinds finds authority in Cicero, whom Varchi cites, and brings Varchi's position into close contact with that of the rhetoricians.

Cicero is the authority, as well, for Varchi's declaration that the qualities requisite for the poet are three in number: eloquence, goodness, and knowledge. All three are required if the ends of poetry are to be achieved. As Varchi explains the relationship between qualities and ends, he produces an extremely interesting statement, one in which, to a degree, certain distinctions are lost. The ends, as Horace would wish them, are utility and pleasure. We discover, in the following sentence, an initial dependence of ends from qualities, in which utility springs from goodness and knowledge, and pleasure from eloquence: "It is therefore necessary . . . that good and perfect poets should be eloquent, virtuous, and erudite; otherwise we could never derive and learn from them either delightfulness of words, or goodness of behavior, or knowledge of things."[35] But pleasure, we are soon told, is not only of the sensual kind which comes from the harmonies of poetry, but also of the intellectual kind and of a kind combining the two others. For this reason, utility itself will be a source of pleasure for the soul:

. . . because pleasure is of three sorts, of the mind (which we shall call intellectual pleasure), of the body (which we shall call sensual pleasure), and of the soul and the body together (which we shall call mixed or common pleasure), we must know that in the poets alone, or surely more so in the poets than in all other writers, all these three kinds of pleasures are found together. For the harmony of the words which are heard . . . delights properly the body; and the utility of the things which are understood delights properly the mind; but because words cannot be separated from things . . . and things cannot be expressed without words, it

---

[35] *Lezzioni* (1590 ed.), p. 630: "Bisogna dunque . . . che i poeti buoni, e perfetti siano eloquenti, virtuosi, e dottrinati, altramente mai da loro trarre, o imparare non si potrebbe ne leggiadria di parole, ne bontà di costumi, ne scienza di cose."

POETIC THEORY

comes to pass that the soul as well as the body, at the very same time, are delighted by words through things and by things through words.[36]

In these passages, an additional distinction has been introduced. It is the distinction between "res" and "verba," taken both as components of the poem and as causes of its effects. All in all, some such schematism as the following results:

Qualities of the poet	Parts of the poem	Ends or effects
goodness	things	utility, pleasure
knowledge	things	utility, pleasure
eloquence	words	pleasure

Much of what Varchi has to say, in this Horatian context, relates to the end of utility, which he sees as essentially a form of teaching. What is taught is primarily lessons for ethics, secondarily information pertaining to all branches of knowledge: the rewards of virtue, the punishments for vice, the elements of the sciences (p. 576). On the basis of their success or failure in this kind of teaching, one will classify poets as good or bad: "Those alone merit all praise who remove men from the vices and inspire them to the virtues; then the others, as they do this more or less, are to be more or less praised and held in esteem."[37] Those who do the opposite should be punished. Among them, Varchi distinguishes four separate classes: (1) The plebeian poets, "all those who without art, or judgment, or knowledge write only to please the common people and to make the crowd laugh." Examples are the authors of the *Morgante* and the *Girone Cortese*. (2) The ridiculous poets, "all those poets who write for the sake of nonsense and of plays on words." Examples: Burchiello, Antonio Alamanni, Berni. (3) The obscene poets, such as Ovid and Catullus; these especially should be punished. (4) The satirical poets, who "through their wicked nature, or through hatred, or because they have been besought or paid, or merely for the joy of it, speak ill of others." These, in keeping with Plato's recommendation, should be banished.[38]

[36] *Ibid*., pp. 631–32: "perchè il diletto è di tre ragioni, d'animo, il quale chiameremo intellettuale; di corpo, il quale chiameremo sensuale; e d'anima, e di corpo insieme, il quale chiameremo misto, ouero comune, deuemo sapere, che ne' poeti soli, o certamente piu ne i poeti, che in tutti gli altri scrittori, si ritrouano tutte e tre queste maniere di diletti insiememente, percioche l'armonia delle parole, che s'odono, . . . diletta propriamente il corpo, e l'vtilità delle cose, che s'intendono diletta propiamente l'animo; ma perche le parole non possono separarsi dalle cose . . . e le cose non possono senza le parole sprimersi, quinci è, che l'vne per l'altre, e l'altre per l'vne dilettano à vn medesimo tempo, cosi l'animo, come il corpo."

[37] *Ibid*., p. 585: "quegli soli meritano tutte le lodi, i quali rimuouono gli huomini da' vizij, o gl'accendono alle virtù, gli altri poi, secondo, che piu, o meno cio fanno, deono essere piu, o meno lodati, e tenuti in pregio."

[38] *Ibid*., pp. 585–87: "tutti quegli, che senza arte, o giudizio, o dottrina scriuono solo per piacere alla Plebe, e far ridere il Volgo"; "tutti quei poeti, che scriuono per ciancia, e da motteggio"; "o per loro cattiua Natura, o per odio, o per preghi, o per danari, o per sollazzo scriuono male d'Altrui."

There are, in Varchi's lengthy *Lezzioni*, a number of miscellaneous borrowings from the *Ars poetica*. The recommendations for the proper use of decorum (p. 583) are derived specifically from Horace, as is the demand for the hexameter as the correct epic verse (p. 616). But these, by 1553, are completely commonplace and make very little contribution to the development of the Horatian mode.

The "Horatian mode" is clearly present in Alessandro Lionardi's *Dialogi della inventione poetica* of 1554. The set of two dialogues represents a kind of converse of the commentaries of the preceding years, for instead of introducing rhetorical distinctions into a basically Horatian exposition, it introduces Horatian elements into a basically rhetorical treatise. The treatise is rhetorical in spite of the fact that its title refers to "poetical invention." Lionardi begins with a consideration of three associated arts—rhetoric, history, and poetry—which belong together not only because they are arts of discourse but also because they serve the same practical ends of teaching men how to speak and to act. Of these arts, poetry is the most excellent because it embraces the other two, which serve it as auxiliaries and instruments. All three make use of invention, disposition, and elocution, of which invention is the most important for various reasons: it requires the greatest and most special talent; it is most directly responsible for the teaching of speaking and action; it is the equivalent of imitation in poetry (to which Aristotle had given primacy over other elements). If these things be true about poetry and invention, then the poet must be above all else a man possessed of various kinds of knowledge. He must be a natural and moral philosopher in order to describe nature and contrive plots, an orator in order to write speeches and deliberations for his personages and to move the passions of his audience, a historian so that he may know the virtuous and vicious actions of great men and the pertinent facts about countries and peoples. Moreover, he must be erudite in astrology (presumably because of the relationships between the constellations and the myths about the gods) and in numerous other arts not needed by the historian or the orator.

His art, as well as his information, includes the arts of the historian and the orator and goes beyond them. It is here that invention is predominant. For the poet takes the true materials provided by the historian, imposes upon them an artificial order, expresses them in a special kind of language, and treats them in verse. His inventive powers are manifested, besides, in the transformation of truth into verisimilitude. From the rhetorician he obtains his knowledge of the passions, of actions and their causes, of necessity and probability, of how to argue in various circumstances; these are all matters which pertain to invention. From the rhetorician, also, he learns such aspects of disposition and elocution as the proper ordering of various kinds of speeches and the many figures of speech by which language is made more ornate. From both of these he obtains the means for achieving

POETIC THEORY

his ends of teaching men how to live and speak properly; he will argue with the reasons they provide him, persuade with the truth, move with the passions, and delight with the eloquent diction.

Into this context, many Horatian ideas are readily incorporated. This is done not so much by way of the citation of corroborating arguments as by the casual use of formulas borrowed directly from the *Ars poetica*. Thus at the very beginning of Dialogue I, Lionardi says that one of the main tasks of the poetic art is so to operate "that common materials become one's own" (p. 7); later in the same dialogue he treats decorum and natural versus artificial order in terms which suggest Horace's (pp. 16–18); at the end of it, the phrase "it is proper to the poet to delight and profit" reflects line 333 of the *Ars poetica*. In Dialogue II, the passing discussion of the "in medias res" beginning is again reminiscent of Horace (p. 67). In spite of such allusions, however, Lionardi's work belongs in the present series rather because of its associations with the rhetorical tradition now currently attached to the Horatian text than because of the direct textual reference. It is also significant of current trends that there is perhaps an even larger number of citations of the *Poetics* and of other Aristotelian works. Lionardi cites the *Poetics* on the distinction between poetry and history (p. 14), on poetry as deriving its essence not from verse but from imitation (p. 14), on the necessary and the probable (p. 15), on Nature as the source of imitation, rhythm, and harmony (p. 51), on the possibility of plot without character (p. 58), on the impossible probable (p. 67), and on other subjects. He also calls upon various Platonic texts for support of his ideas: on the *Republic* and the *Phaedo* for the requisites of the poet (p. 62), on the *Republic* for the condemnation of the arousing of certain passions (p. 76) and for the distinction between narration and "imitation," as also for the division between the passions banned and those permitted (p. 80)—all this in connection with a defence of the utility of poetry. I cite these various borrowings not for their own sake but as an indication of the extent to which the divers intellectual traditions are by this time mixed and confused. For Lionardi, the essential approach is a rhetorical one; but poetic elements of a formal character from Aristotle and moral elements from Plato are intermingled to serve the purposes of the discussion.

A similar mixture of other elements into a basically rhetorical analysis is found in Book II of Matteo San Martino's *Osservationi grammaticali e poetiche della lingua italiana* (1555), for it is Book II that contains the poetical observations. It begins with a defence of poesy in the standard fashion; nothing of interest is present here. Then comes an expanded definition of poetry, which merits quotation:

> Poetry is nothing else but an imitation of human actions accompanied by wonder on the part of the listener. ... perhaps I might be so bold as to say that poetics is a lovely fiction which, restricted within harmonized rhythms, imitating human actions, brings profit along with delight to him who listens; so that

imitation is its secondary, not its principal part. . . . it is certain that an imitation cannot be made unless the invention with which one imitates is prepared first. And as for the function of the poet and the end toward which he should tend, I say that in the poems he must investigate things which can profit and delight, and in such wise that they really do profit and delight (else he is not worthy of the name of poet), constantly filling the reader with joy and with wonder, ever feigning new things, so that with such novelty he may delight, mixing true things with false, that is not as they were, but as they should be; in such a way that neither the beginning will be in discord with the middle nor the middle with the end.[39]

One begins, in such a definition, with Aristotle, continues with Cicero, passes on to Horace, encounters nameless rhetoricians, and concludes with a final statement in which all are lumped together in the most helter-skelter fashion. The same kind of confusion prevails in other parts of the work. There are, for example, five statements on the role, or the function, or the main concern of the poet; all are different. In the passage just quoted, the function and end are to "giovar e dilettare"; a few pages later, the principal part of poetry is said to be the "fittione" or "inventione" (p. 133); farther on, "the final intention of the poets is in the imitation"—almost in direct contradiction to the passage above (p. 135); still later, a longer text of considerable interest in which the poet is said to need "persuasion, in which consists the principal strength of the intent of the poet, which is to acquire belief for his incitements; for which purpose, in order to profit through delight, he strives to move or to placate others under the veil of his fictions" (p. 178); finally, his activities are directed toward "teaching, delighting, and profiting readers at the same time" (p. 180). There is, through all these texts, a certain concentration upon the end of poetry as instructing and giving pleasure; but there is at the same time an unwillingness to make a clear subordination of any one source document to another.

As he operates in the making of poems, the poet for San Martino is essentially a rhetorician; he must be provided with precepts for invention, disposition, and elocution. But really there are no precepts for the first, since the number of subjects is infinite and the poet has free choice among them (p. 133). However, San Martino provides the usual suggestions for

---

[39] *Osservationi* (1555), pp. 129–31: "la Poesia altro non è che imitatione delle humane attioni con merauiglia di chi l'ascolta. . . . temerario forse mi mouero a dire, che la Poetica sia una uaga fittione che fra harmonizzati numeri ristretta, imitando l'humane attioni, con diletto gioui a chi l'ascolta; Si che la imitatione è sua parte secondaria, e non principale. . . . certo è non potersi far imitatione, che prima non si prepari la inuentione con cui si imitti. Et quanto a lo officio del Poeta, & al fine oue tender debbia, dico che nei Poemi de inuestigar cose che giouar possano e dilettare, e si che in effecto giouino e dilettino, o che degno non è di tal nome, di continuo riempiendo il lettor di giocondita e merauiglia, nuoue cose sempre fingendo, si che con simil nouita diletti, le cose uere con le false mescolando, cioè non quali furono, ma quali esser deueano; per maniera che ne'l principio dal mezzo ne questo dal fine si discordino."

what he calls "the six parts of invention," i.e., exordium, narration, division, confirmation, confutation, and conclusion; the poet's invention is thus the same as the orator's (p. 159). Disposition, or the "ordinatione" of the materials, largely concerns words; Horace is called upon for many of the precepts here. As for elocution, the largest part of San Martino's treatment is devoted to it; for words constitute the "materia" of poetry (p. 159) and if they are properly chosen and arranged, "from them will result in the minds of the readers a most sweet harmony adorned with inconceivable loveliness" (p. 179). For all these elements, the counsels are those which might be found in any of the standard rhetorics. To them are added generous materials from the *Ars poetica*—incorporated in the way exemplified in the long quoted passage—and occasional borrowings from Aristotle and Plato. These remain, however, auxiliary and subsidiary, and they are introduced only as they furnish additional authority for points in the rhetorical system, which is unchanged by their accretion.

Giovambattista Giraldi Cintio's *Letter to Bernardo Tasso*, dated October 10, 1557, is more limited in scope than the preceding document in two ways: first it deals only with epic poetry, since Giraldi is defending his practice in his *Ercole*; and second, it is Horatian almost solely in the conception of the ends of poetry. Giraldi takes as his point of departure the thesis—by no means original—that poetry is a kind of "first philosophy"; hence, of the two ends of pleasure and utility proposed for it, utility is indisputably the more important. The theory is expounded in the following passage:

I strove, insofar as wit was granted to me to do so, to see to it that the whole work was composed in the light of the useful and the honest, since it seemed to me that this must be the end of the poet, and not pleasure alone. For, if we believe what the ancient writers have to say about it, poetry is nothing else but a first philosophy which, like a schoolmistress of life working secretly, proposes to us under poetic covering the image of a civilized and praiseworthy life drawn from the fountain of that philosophy; to which life, as to an assigned goal, we must direct our actions—as Horace showed us when he said:

Rem tibi Socraticae poterunt ostendere chartae.[40]

The utility proposed is thus exclusively moral. The poet must seek to represent behavior which is appropriate to "honest and honorable living, to praiseworthy actions, and to the whole scale of social procedures."[41]

[40] In *Lettere di XIII. huomini illustri* (1565 ed.), p. 871: "usai, quanto meglio mi fu concesso l'ingegno, perche l'opera tutta fusse composta all'utile, & all'honesto, parendomi che questo debba essere il fine del Poeta, & non il diletto solo. Però che, per quanto ne dicono gli auttori antichi; La Poesia non è altro, che una prima filosofia, la quale, quasi occulta maestra della uita, sotto uelame poetico, ci propone la imagine di una ciuile, & lodeuole uita tratta dal fonte di essa filosofia, alla qual uita, quasi a proposto segno, habbiamo a drizzare le nostre attioni, il che ci mostrò Horatio, quando disse.
Rem tibi Socraticae poterunt ostendere chartae."
[41] *Ibid.*, p. 872: "che si conuiene alla uita honesta, et honorata, alle lodeuoli attioni, & alla uarietà delle cose ciuili."

Applying this theory in his own poem, Giraldi has depicted the life of a man who was an example of praiseworthy and honorable actions (p. 868); he has universalized the illustrious actions, making sure that honesty was everywhere respected (p. 874); he has tried to arouse compassion and move his audience (*ibid.*); above all, he has attended to morality, "by praising the virtues, condemning the vices, and giving wherever necessary the rewards to the former and the punishments to the latter, in order to instruct persons of various ranks, according to their station, in the praiseworthy life."[42]

Pleasure is a means to the achievement of this utility. "I saw that, in order to make this utility enter into the mind of the reader with greater efficacy, a very wide pathway could be made by pleasure, whence I sought to make of it a companion to the profit, and I did not wish to take it as my primary object."[43] Pleasure is produced by writing the work "poeticamente," that is, by stopping at given places to intercalate ornaments and by devising entertaining digressions (p. 873). These add beauty to the composition and make the reader follow it with greater attention. Even the ugly may be rendered beautiful (as Aristotle and Horace have pointed out) if it is treated with the proper decorum, and it then becomes an additional source of pleasure. Similarly the use of the pagan gods, acceptable in an ancient subject such as the *Ercole*, may increase the marvelous of the poem and hence its possibilities for delight (p. 882). Finally, verse itself is an additional ornament which, when it is allied with appropriate diction, serves the purposes of both utility and pleasure (p. 888).

Giraldi's conception of the poem, made to conform to these requirements, clearly involves no notion of the unity of artistic structure. Indeed, he specifically rejects the need for unity of action and replaces it by unity of hero (p. 868). The life of Hercules is the only unifying element—unless one take into consideration the general moralizing intent or the prevailing concern with decorum. Around this life, Giraldi has gathered many "actions," some of them taken from ancient poets, some of them invented by himself. Since the subject is ancient, he has treated it in the manner of the ancients, except for the addition of such modern devices as transitions from one canto to another in order to hold the interest of his readers (pp. 879–80). Everything that he does, he insists, is calculated to please and instruct the specific audience that he has in mind. This is not an audience of the "vulgo"—no poet worthy of praise ever wrote in order to give pleasure to this vulgar crowd, or made of it his judges—but of the "best

[42] *Ibid.*, p. 881: "con lodare le uirtù, biasimare i uitij, & dare, oue è stato bisogno, a quelle il premio, a queste la pena, per formare persone di uarie qualità, secondo la loro conditione alla lodeuole uita."

[43] *Ibid.*, p. 872: "uidi ch'a fare, che con maggiore efficacia questo utile entrasse nell'animo a chi leggeua, ui poteua fare assai ampia strada il diletto, onde cercai ch'egli al giouamento fussi compagno, & no'l uolli prendere per primo oggetto."

judges," those who know why the poem pleases them and are capable of evaluating its artistic excellences (pp. 876–78).

In these ways, the Horatian conception of the ends of poetry comes to inform Giraldi's whole theory of the poetic art. Almost everything in it is subordinated to the wish to instruct, and even the devices for pleasure are ancillary to this. In its general supposition of the work and of a certain effect upon that audience as the goal proposed, it again falls into broadly rhetorical patterns. But much of the detailed treatment of diction, the figures, and the styles present in the more ambitious treatises is absent here, as are the numerous cross references to ancient theorists.

Similar ideas about the poetic art are at work, in an even briefer compass, in Girolamo Ruscelli's dedication to his *Fiori delle rime de' poeti illustri* of 1558—similar, that is, in the general application of rhetorical criteria to poetry. Ruscelli starts out with a defence, not of poetry in general, but of Italian poetry, declaring that in spite of the prejudice in favor of Greek and Latin literature, there is a possibility that Italian will soon come to equal them "both in delight and in profit." Ariosto has already proved this in the epic and Petrarch in the lyric, others in elegiac verse. One may judge for oneself: "This may easily be discovered by those who, having the art and the judgment to be able to know entirely the degrees and the places of perfection in invention, in disposition, in style and in all the other parts of elocution, will consider those compositions of Bembo, of Guidiccioni, of Sannazaro, of Molza, of La Pescara."[44] The proof, in a word, will be found in Ruscelli's anthology of poetry, "in which one may see the true portrait of all the beauties of poetry, where one finds the examples of every splendor and of every ornament that a language is capable of receiving, and where there are subjects and cases of history, of philosophy, of spiritual things, and almost of as many other subjects as all of the sciences are able to furnish to poetry."[45]

Although the passages in Cristoforo Rufo's *Antexegemata* (1559) which are of interest for poetic theory largely concern the *Poetics*, there are several commentaries on lines of Horace and a few places where a rhetorical interpretation is applied to Aristotle. This is not true everywhere, however; in connection with *Poetics* 1452b11, for example, he takes issue with Robortello's interpretation of πάθος as referring to the audience and insists that it refers rather to the plot (p. I3). The work is a collection of isolated

---

[44] *Fiori delle rime* (1558), p. *iij$v$: "Ilche ... possono ageuolmente conoscer coloro, che hauendo arte & giudicio da poter conoscere interamente i gradi e i luoghi di perfettione, nella inuentione, nella dispositione, nello stile, & in tutte l'altre parti della elocutione, haueranno considerati quei componimenti del Bembo, del Guidiccioni, del Sannazaro, del Molza, della Pescara." "La Pescara" is Vittoria Colonna.

[45] *Ibid.*, p. *vij: "oue si vede il vero ritratto di tutte le bellezze della Poesia, oue sono gli essempi d'ogni candidezza & d'ogni ornamento, che vna lingua possa riceuere, & oue si hanno soggetti & occasioni d'istorie, di filosofia, di cose spirituali, & quasi di tanti altri soggetti, quanti alla Poesia ne possono somministrar tutte le scienze."

remarks on passages selected by Rufo because he disagrees with previous commentators. On *Poetics* 1456*b*8, disagreeing with Maggi's reading, he maintains that the writer of tragedy may derive arguments from the same topics as does the rhetorician, since both seek to arouse the emotions; but the poet must do so in a hidden way, whereas the orator's devices are apparent. On 1456*b*3, adding to "pity and fear" the additional effects of "amplification, proof, and persuasion," he again points out that these must be sought in the appropriate topics. For the *Ars poetica*, he provides commentary on two lines, on line 1 (where he disagrees with Maggi's gloss) to insist that the initial passage does not refer to plot alone but to the combination of plot and episodes, and on line 132 (rejecting Maggi again) to clarify the proper manner of adapting borrowed materials.[46] On the whole, however, the document is more interesting as it relates to the history of the *Poetics*, and I shall discuss it again later in that context.

In the same year, 1559, Lodovico Dolce appended to his translation of the satires, epistles, and *Ars poetica* of Horace a set of three short discourses, one for each of the works. In the first, *Origine della satira*, he traced also the origins of tragedy and of comedy, emphasizing above all the moral purposes for which they were invented: tragedy to demonstrate "how much the condition of human frailty is different from that of divine felicity and beatitude," comedy "to scold men for their vices."[47] In the second, *Discorso sopra le epistole*, he said that the satires and the epistles had complementary functions: "In the satires it was his intention to remove the vices from the breast of men, and in these [the epistles] to plant there the virtues."[48] The third, the *Discorso sopra la poetica*, is by far the most important; since it gives a brief *summa* of what Dolce considered to be the salient points of Horace's text, I translate it below almost in its entirety:

This little book composed by Horace on the art of poetry may be divided into five parts. For he demonstrates first the vices that the poet must flee; then he speaks of the appropriateness that must be observed in words; in the third place he touches on the quality of materials and persons, and on the differences that are present in them. In the fourth he treats of actions, and in the fifth he counsels poets to correct diligently their compositions, submitting them to the judgment of those who know. The reader will thus learn from the notes that Horace gives us in this brief but most useful work of his, to consider first very carefully all the material that these poets have proposed to write about; then to dispose it, that is to order it and to give it such form that there will not be in it anything discordant or contrary, but that everything will be in conformity and appropriate. From this it results that when poets have begun or promised to write serious things, they should not descend to low ones, or to describe others that are lovely

---

[46] *Antexegemata* (1559), pp. G6, G5–G5v, H, and H8 respectively.

[47] In *I dilettevoli sermoni* (1559), p. 313: "quanto la conditione della fragilità humana fosse differente dalla felicità e beatitudine Diuina" and "per riprendere i uitij de gli huomini."

[48] *Ibid.*, p. 316: "Nelle Satire fu la sua intentione di leuare i uitij dal petto de gli huomini, & in queste di piantarui le uirtù."

and delightful but not pertinent, to show that they are clever. And in this, as in every other aspect, Ariosto merits infinite praise. Also, when we need to pass from one subject to another, we should do it in such a way that the composition will not resemble a monster. Nor, fleeing one vice, should we fall into another; but taking upon ourselves a burden equal to our strength, we should see to it that the end corresponds to the beginning and the middle; and although we may treat divers things, and although the parts be varied, it should be a single body which is not discordant in any of its parts. And as for the order, they should begin from the middle or after the middle of the subject, as Homer, Vergil, and our Ariosto did.[49]

Such a summary as this indicates what points in the *Ars poetica* seemed, to a vulgarizer like Dolce, to be worthy of emphasis. It will be noted that invention and disposition are clearly intimated and that the dominant principle of appropriateness appears again as it had in the earliest Horatian exegesis.

Girolamo Ruscelli, who only the year before had published his *Fiori delle rime*, published in 1559 a work called *Del modo di comporre in versi nella lingua italiana*; this was really a combination of two works: a treatise on verse, comprising also a fairly complete poetics; and a very lengthy rhyming dictionary. In the section on poetics, Ruscelli is most concerned with two problems, the superiority of poetry over other forms of expression and the superiority of verse over prose. He regards all forms of speech as having the function of persuading, delighting, and moving. But whereas other forms are written to appeal only to contemporaries, poetry has added beauties which give it eternal life and bring glory to its author. Hence its excellence. These beauties—if one is to respect the basic dichotomy of his analysis—are both of material and of words. For the subject matter of poetry must itself be of a special kind. It may well be false, "invented" by the poet; if so, it must be handled in such a way as to produce belief on the part of the reader. If it is true (as a historical subject is), it is rendered more

[49] *Ibid.*, pp. 317–18: "Si puo diuidere questo libricciolo composto da Horatio sopra l'arte della Poetica in cinque parti. Percioche egli prima dimostra i uitij, che dee fuggire il Poeta: dipoi fauella della conueneuolezza, che si conuien serbare nelle parole: nel terzo luogo tocca la qualità delle materie, e delle persone, e le differenze, che ui entrano. Nel quarto tratta dell'attioni; e nel quinto conforta i Poeti a corregger diligentemente le lor compositioni, rimettendole al giudicio di coloro, che sanno. Il lettore adunque apparerà da i ricordi, che ci da Horatio in questa sua brieue, ma utilissima fatica, di considerar primieramente molto bene tutta la materia, che essi hanno proposto di scriuere: poi disponerla, cioè ordinarla, e darle una cotal forma, che non u'habbia in lei cosa discordante, e contraria, ma tutto sia conforme e corrispondente. Onde hauendo i Poeti cominciato, o promesso di scriuer cose graui, non discendano alle basse, ouero a discriuere alcune uaghe e dilettueoli, ma impertinenti, per dimostrarsi ingeniosi. Et in questa, come in ogni altra parte, merita infinita lode l'Ariosto. Douendo anco passar d'uno in altro soggetto, ci facciano in guisa, che'l componimento non sia simile a un Mostro. Ne schifando un uitio, incorriamo in un'altro: ma prendendo peso eguale alle nostre forze, procuriamo, che'l fine corrisponda al principio & al mezo: e se ben trattiamo diuerse cose, quantunque le membra siano diuerse, sia un solo corpo, ilquale punto nelle sue parti non discordi. E, quanto all'ordine, debbono cominciar dal mezo, o dopo il mezo della materia; come fece Homero, Virgilio, e'l nostro Ariosto."

perfect by the kind of selection and rearrangement which are the prerogative of the poet, and all the imperfections of reality are removed. In either case, it must be something that is "pleasing, lovely, gay, grave, or pleasant, and that in the end will delight or profit, or better still, that will profit and delight at the same time."[50] The words are the "beautiful dress" in which the subject is clothed. Great attention must be paid to the purity of language, the placing or organizing of the words, the qualities of style—all things which constitute the virtues of elocution. Disposition, it is clear, is an element to be watched closely by the poet in connection with both words and things.

Even if all these precepts be followed, however, the ultimate in perfection will not be achieved unless verse is added. For verse adds harmony, and harmony is an additional source of persuasion and of arousal of the passions. The sequence of events in the soul of the reader is as follows: the beauty of verse, added to all the other beauties of poetry, gives increased delight; this delight leads the reader to have a higher estimate of the poet's genius; the work thereby becomes more credible and more capable of producing its utilitarian effects; the profit that results is hence greater. As in so many of these texts, the end term in the argument as developed is that of utility. Indeed, the same is true for the argument about subject matter: "much greater utility, to say nothing of the pleasure, . . . will be obtained from the same event narrated by a poet than if told by a historian,"[51] and the point about the perfecting of reality is made in substantiation. This exaltation of poetry and of verse leads Ruscelli to write a "defence" of the most extravagant kind, one feature of which is the declaration that Italian is superior to all other languages for verse and that Petrarch and more recent Italian poets may be used as models.

PARTHENIO (1560)

A number of the literati whose names had appeared in recent years in connection with Horatian criticism appear again as interlocutors in Bernardino Parthenio's lengthy dialogue, *Della imitatione poetica*, of 1560. Trifon Gabriele, Giovan Giorgio Trissino, Paolo Manuzio, Francesco Lovisini, and Parthenio himself gather together to discuss the matter of poetic imitation and how it differs from rhetorical imitation. In so doing, they pretend to be supplementing the work of Aristotle and Horace, who spoke only of tragedy and the epic and of plot and character in connection with those genres; their own concern will be broader, since they will treat

[50] *Del modo di comporre* (1559), p. xix: "cosa grata, uaga, leggiadra, graue, ò piaceuole, & che finalmente ò diletti, ò gioui, ma molto più, che ella gioui et diletti unitamente."

[51] *Ibid.*, pp. xi–xii: "molto più utilità, per tacer la dilettatione . . ., si trarrà da un fatto stesso narrato da un poeta, che da uno istorico, percioche all'istorico si conuiene di narrarlo ueramente come sia seguito, ò bene ò male che sia stato in tutto, ò in parte. Là oue il poeta lo finge, & lo forma nelle parti non buone, quale douerebbe essere stato per esser buono, & perfetto nell'esser suo."

of words, figures of speech, and *sententiae* (which are common to all genres) and of such general subjects as invention and the universal topics. In his preface, Parthenio defends poetry not only by adducing the customary arguments but by pointing out the multitude of kinds of knowledge which one may derive from such a poet as Homer (the *De Homeri poesi* is echoed here). Besides the knowledge that he imparts, Homer teaches lessons in morality—"What philosopher teaches us better what prudence, what fortitude, what discretion we should use in every slightest action, than in his poems? He makes us wise, prudent, modest, strong, patient, constant, just, good, religious, and holy"[52]—and he shows orators how to write expositions, beginnings, confirmations, amplifications, and so forth. These, then, will be the ends that the poet must pursue. But he will not achieve them if he does not pay attention to the delight that comes from excellence in verse and elocution. It is the latter of these that constitutes Parthenio's central subject.

Parthenio does not wish us to be misled by his title, *On Poetic Imitation*, and insists that he means to present all the precepts of the art not already exhausted by Aristotle and by Horace, "who seems to have kept his feet fixed in the very footsteps of that same Aristotle" (p. 6). But he soon limits his scope by excluding one of the two types of imitation which he distinguished; he will not here treat that kind of imitation which seeks to represent "that certain force, or faculty, that we bear in our soul, that they call Idea,"[53] but rather that other kind which consists in representing the Ideas and the Forms of others. In a word, he is interested in the imitation of other poets, taken as models. A further restriction appears when he makes still another subdivision of poetic imitation. The poet may, on the one hand, imitate the natures and the characters of the persons whom he undertakes to represent; "and this is the end of poetry, which intends to express human actions, and with that expression to instruct and inform the soul, which is its subject and its matter."[54] Imitation of this kind is left by Parthenio to Aristotle. On the other hand, the poet may imitate the words and the figures of speech already used by other poets, and to the problem of how this is properly accomplished Parthenio addresses himself. The major part of the dialogue is devoted to suggestions about how the poet, by long practice, may ultimately come to express himself in a way very similar to that of the model without actually copying or plagiarizing him; and to detailed analysis of the numerous rhetorical "topics" distinguished

---

[52] *Della imitatione poetica* (1560), p. 3: "Qual de' Filosofi meglio ci insegna, qual prudenza, qual fortezza, qual discritione habbiamo da usare in ciascuna minima attione, che ne i suoi poemi? Questo ci fa saggi, prudenti, modesti, forti, patienti, costanti, giusti, buoni, religiosi, & Santi."

[53] *Ibid.*, p. 11: "quella certa forza, o uero facultà, la quale portiamo nell'animo, che chiamano idea."

[54] *Ibid.*, p. 93: "Et questo è il fine della poesia; laquale intende esprimer le attioni humane, & con quello amaestrare, & informare bene l'animo, che è suo soggetto, & materia."

by Giulio Camillo Delminio, proposed as devices to guide the poet in his imitation.

Throughout Parthenio's treatise, the assumption is implicit that the really important thing about poetry is the diction that it uses. Poetic diction, in fact, is different from that of oratory in several respects. The words used by the orator "must be such that they may be understood by the people and must be drawn from common usage, from that usage which the writers of comedy and the orators have established. Those [used by the poets] must be highly ingenious—I almost said 'bizarre'—and completely alien from habitual use."[55] They must be selected for their qualities of sound as well as of sense (full-sounding words containing "a" and "o" are to be preferred), and compound or complicated words are better than simple ones (p. 80). As he proceeds with this analysis, Parthenio comes closer and closer to the kind of teaching that would be found in the section on diction in almost any standard rhetoric.

It is interesting to note that, in spite of the elaborateness of such a theory as the one just outlined, when its author is called upon to engage in practical criticism he talks in ancient commonplaces. At one point in Book II of the dialogue, Trifon Gabriele, after having refused to comment on living poets, agrees to pass judgment on certain recent Italian poets now dead. This is what he says about Sannazaro: "I have always prized him, and he has always seemed to me grave and sonorous, to have had a fine selection of words, to be of a great and truly poetic nature...." And of Pontano: "Pontano is also very sublime"; and of Fracastoro: "Most ornate and most polished is Fracastoro, and excellent in imagining fables." Navagero is "polished, charming, elegant and full of new, light poetic thoughts, varied and versatile."[56] Such comments as these are consistent with the theory behind them insofar as they bear almost exclusively on diction; but in their effort to characterize the genius of the poet they hark back to a much earlier time, to the days of Pietro Ricci (Petrus Crinitus) or of Lilio Gregorio Giraldi.

A document closely related to the preceding one (through the person of its author and through its rhetorical associations) is Giulio Camillo Delminio's *Discorso sopra l'idee di Hermogene*, published posthumously in 1560. It is a brief treatise which, after a comparison of Cicero's three styles with Hermogenes' types of oratory—the judicial, the deliberative, and the

---

[55] *Ibid.*, p. 34: "Questi deono esser tali, che dal popolo possano esser intesi, & esser tratti dalla communanza, quello, che i Comici & gli Oratori hanno fatto. Quelli hanno da essere ingeniosissimi, & quasi, che non dissi bizarri, & del tutto estratti dalla consuetudine."

[56] *Ibid.*, p. 85: "l'ho sempre prezzato, & emmi sempre paruto graue, & sonoro, hauer hauuta bella elettione di parole, esser di natura grande & ueramente poetica. . . . Molto sublime altresi è il Pontano"; p. 86: "Ornatissimo, & politissimo è il Fracastoro, & eccellente nel finger fauole"; p. 87: "Il Nauaiero polito, & uago, & elegante & pieno di pensieri poetici, noui, & leggiadri, uario, & uersatile."

panegyric—goes on to a brief summation of the various "senses" found in Hermogenes. Only one short section is of interest for poetic theory, a section entitled "Panegirica in Metro," which discusses poetry as a versified type of panegyric oratory; the classification itself is significant. Camillo's notions of poetry are simple and, at the same time, somewhat confused; he says that it is an "imitation of all things," that it contains pleasure and greatness, that it involves the use of verse. Its proper materials are myths about the gods, the supernatural and the superhuman, impossible and incredible actions. Its procedures are the narration of events simply and in detail, the invocation of the muses, and the use of special kinds of words and of figures; the latter it shares with panegyric oratory in general.[57]

Francesco Patrizi would have disagreed with Camillo's classification of poetry as panegyric; for although, in his *Della historia* (1560), he, too, classifies poetry under oratory, he assigns it to the demonstrative and deliberative branches. His dialogue concerns history, and when he classifies poetry, he is expounding Pontano's views on the relationship of poetry to history. According to these views, history is a kind of poetry, but in prose. Both arts treat the same kind of materials, praise and blame their actors, belong to the same branches of oratory; as parts of oratory, they employ similar procedures, "they arouse the passions, they do things with decorum." Their ends are the same: "Both teach, delight, move, profit, adorn, elevate, lower." Their differences are those between truth and probability, prose and verse, natural order and artificial order. Patrizi does not need to identify his sources (or Pontano's) to indicate to what kind of intellectual tradition he belongs; traces of both Horace and the rhetoricians are manifest in his statements. The verbs collected together to define the ends of the two arts provide all the necessary links.[58]

Some of the same principles, applied to a specific literary genre, are operative in Francesco Sansovino's *Discorso in materia della satira* (1560). The dedication presents a brief defence of poetry; then this statement: "the end of poetry consists in nothing else than in withdrawing men from vice, whence it is a gift of God, directing them according to the good orders of nature, His servant, so that they will know their own minds; hence it is that certain poets, wishing to achieve such an end, have written precepts of human life under various forms of verse."[59] Of these divers genres, satire is always a favored one, since it scolds men for their evil-doing. The *Discorso* proper differentiates satire from the other forms on several bases:

[57] In *Il secondo tomo dell'opere di M. Giulio Camillo Delminio* (1560), pp. 119–21.

[58] *Della historia* (1560), pp. 5–5v: "muouono gli affetti, fanno le cose con decoro"; "insignano, dilettano, muouono, giouano, adornano, inalzano, abbassano." Patrizi undoubtedly knew Camillo's work, since he edited Vol. II of Camillo's *Opere* (1560).

[59] *Discorso* (1560), p. *3: "il fin della Poesia non consiste in altro, ch'in ritrar gli huomini dal vitio, ond'ella è dono di Dio, indirizzandoli a i buoni ordini della natura sua ministra, accio ch'essi riconoschino la mente loro, di qui è ch'alcuni volendo conseguir cotal fine, hanno scritto precetti della vita humana sotto varie forme di versi."

style (satire uses the humble, low style, rather than the high or the middle), subject matter (which is humble and low, not high and magnificent), the kinds of persons depicted (who are humble, such as servants and sinners, not great), the nature of the imitation (in satire, nature is imitated directly, without adornment or artifice). It will be readily seen that the opposite term in each case is tragedy or the epic, and Sansovino points up the contrast wherever possible. Once again, the insistence is upon diction; this must not differ from the language of prose, must contain neither ornament nor grace, must be instead simple, sharp, witty, and direct. Such a method of describing and delimiting a literary genre by its style, its subject matter, its characters, and its form of imitation (taken in a special sense) falls readily within the context of the tradition that I have been tracing, and Sansovino's little *Discourse* serves as an epitome of many tendencies (pp. *6v–*7).

As a final sample in the present chapter, we may examine those few paragraphs in Benedetto Varchi's *Hercolano* which concern poetry. The dialogue, one of the important documents in the "question of the language," is almost wholly linguistic in content; although it was published only in 1570, posthumously, it was written around 1560, during the years of the Caro-Castelvetro controversy. As might be anticipated, Varchi's approach to poetics is here colored by this specific concern. In one of the pertinent paragraphs (p. 51), he notes that the two components of "poetare" or "poeteggiare" are verse and a certain kind of language present in "fauellare poeticamente." In the second (p. 123), he remarks that whereas other writers practice only one form of eloquence, the poet practices all forms; hence his divinity. The third (pp. 219–20), more extensive, distinguishes seven kinds of poetry by naming the authors who practiced them; the basis of the distinction is not clear, but it would seem that Varchi is merely classifying according to verse forms. The last passage (p. 269), in addition to declaring again that verse is necessary in poetry, contains the following passage:

> The poet, in addition to well-composed and sententious verse, has a greatness, a majesty more divine than human, and not only teaches, delights, and moves, but engenders admiration and wonder in the minds of the listeners, if they are noble and gentle, and in all those who are naturally disposed, for imitation and consequently poetry is (as Aristotle shows in the *Poetics*) most natural for man.[60]

These passages hardly constitute a theory of poetry; at best they display a few common, current preconceptions: poetry is verse, it uses a special kind of language, and it seeks ethical and rhetorical ends.

---

[60] *Hercolano* (Florence, 1570), p. 269: "Il Poeta oltra il verso ben composto, e sentenzioso ha vna grandezza, e maestà più tosto diuina, che humana, e non solo insegna, diletta, e muoue, ma ingenera ammirazione, e stupore negli animi, o generosi, o gentili, e in tutti coloro, che sono naturalmente disposti, perche l'imitare, e conseguentemente il poetare è (come ne mostra Aristotile nella Poetica) naturalissimo all'huomo."

CONCLUSIONS

The materials contained in this chapter have covered a span of approximately fifteen years, from 1546 to 1560, and have included, besides six formal commentaries on the *Ars poetica*, a wide variety of shorter documents on miscellaneous literary subjects. The common basis for their inclusion was the fact that they belonged, in one way or another, to a tradition of poetic theory that I have called the Horatian-rhetorical tradition. The center of this tradition is the text of the *Ars poetica*; but allied to it and mingled with it are a multitude of ideas derived, for the most part, from classical treatises on oratory or on style.

By this period at midcentury, critics and theorists and commentators had developed what might be termed a standard reading of Horace. I do not mean that everybody read him in precisely the same way, but merely that certain interpretations recur with great frequency and that from the maze of suggestions and theories and precepts contained in the *Ars poetica*, a certain number seem to be the favorites of readers and to be cited most constantly. Of these, perhaps the most signally "Horatian" of all is the notion that poetry has as its dual ends to profit and delight. There is no major commentator who does not emphasize this as one of the characteristic features of the Horatian system, and in many cases shorter texts are identified with this tradition basically because of their insistence that "prodesse" and "delectare" constitute the ends of poetry. Indeed, the statement becomes so much a commonplace that it probably has, at times, no really direct connections with the text of Horace itself. This may be one reason why the formula "aut prodesse aut delectare" is so readily expanded to include additional goals (such as the Ciceronian "admiratio") or is crossed with similar statements from other theorists (such as Cicero's "docere, delectare, mouere"). Such expansion and augmentation accounts, in part, for the conflation of Horace with the purely rhetorical treatises, and in part explains the confusion attaching to the purposes of the poetic art. Nevertheless, the predominant tendency is to regard the really important purpose as that of bringing some profit to the reader, and that profit is invariably said to be a moral one. By using sententiae and aphorisms, by demonstrating the common fate of man and the rewards and punishments attached to virtues and vices, by presenting charming allegories which hide eternal truths, the poem teaches man all the lessons he needs to know for proper living. Sometimes, the pleasure resulting from the imitation, or from diction, or from ornaments and episodes retains its full status as a partner or accompaniment of the utility; but more usually it is reduced to the role of a means or instrument for the achievement of that utility. As a device for stirring the emotions of the reader and persuading him through examples, pleasure makes him amenable to the moral teachings that are the real end of the poet.

Certain of the internal components of poems are, according to this standard reading of Horace, in direct relationship to the ends proposed. The whole matter of decorum is extremely important if moral lessons are to be conveyed; in fact, the observance of decorum is itself a form of teaching, since the proper behavior for persons of all kinds should be deducible from the characters and their actions. This is a positive contribution to the achievement of the ends. Most of the components, though, operate indirectly through the pleasure which they afford. Thus the central principle of unity and appropriateness—the two elements are indistinguishable for the Horatians—is a *sine qua non* for the production of pleasure; it is the counterpart, for artistic elements, to decorum, for moral elements. Similarly, imitation is a source of pleasure, but only if it is correctly accomplished and if the object as represented is recognized to be "true."

The other habitual ways of reading Horace consist in the application of a number of distinctions by midcentury universally associated with the text. First and foremost of these is, of course, the trilogy of invention, disposition, and elocution. Certain sections of the *Ars poetica* are now regularly identified as treatments of these three "parts," and when in practical criticism a work is singled out for comment, that comment will almost always revolve about the same three parts. A second trilogy, that of the three styles, is almost equally prominent. It is connected with what Horace says about the vices of diction, becomes the main device for assuring the integrity of the separate literary genres, and is often regarded as auxiliary both to decorum and to appropriateness. That is, a given "style" will entail the speech proper to persons of given social status and to their actions and characters, and it will require figures and ornaments in keeping with the general nature of the subject matter. Finally, the "res-verba" distinction, according to which all considerations relevant to poetry are classified as belonging to the subject matter or to the expression, continues to be applied just as it had been in the earliest Horatian criticism.

A parallel inquiry of equal usefulness for understanding the criticism of the period would be an inquiry into the kind of rhetorical doctrine that was ordinarily associated with Horace. We have already seen some of its constituents, especially with respect to the ends; for if the Ciceronian ends of "admiratio" directed toward the orator himself and of "docere, delectare, and mouere" directed toward the audience are the ones proposed, then a special brand of rhetoric results. It can be seen, strictly in terms of the moral bias of Horace's interpreters and of the construction which they put upon his text, why this type of rhetoric rather than variant possibilities should have been related to him. Cognate ends are the "arousing of the passions" found in so many of the critics (sometimes as an intermediate end) and the imparting of all kinds of miscellaneous information. In fact, just as the conception of the ends is frequently the basis for calling a document Horatian, so the specific nature of the ends is often, in the minds of the critics, the primary reason for developing extended rhetorical parallels. As for the rest of the rhetorical system involved, it is usually of a linguistic character, with the main stress on diction, on figures and styles, and on the "topics" which are curiously transformed into stylistic procedures. Thus of the three traditional parts, elocution is the one accorded the greatest amount of attention and importance—a tendency also notable in the late-classical rhetoricians. When one compares the set of ideas belonging to the reading of Horace with those composing the rhetorical tradition, one finds very close resemblances if not complete identity; one may begin within the text of Horace, as critics of this period did, and end within the context of a standard rhetoric; or one may reverse the process and pass from the *Rhetorica ad Herennium* or from the *De oratore* or from the *Institutes* into the *Ars poetica*. The two traditions are in many very real senses indistinguishable.

But what of Aristotle? This is the period, as I have indicated, when the first persistent attempts are made to connect the *Ars poetica* with the *Poetics*. Especially in the formal commentaries, Aristotle tends to replace the older authorities as a source of illumination and elucidation of the text. The belief becomes current that Horace knew Aristotle's work, used it as his source and guide, meant to do no more than paraphrase it in verse. Of necessity, the ideas in the two works must be the same. This is the basis for the increasing vogue of citing parallels between the two texts; from modest beginnings in Pedemonte, this fashion attains its full expression in such commentators as Maggi, Grifoli, and Lovisini. By the time of Lovisini, parallels are available for almost every passage in Horace that specifically concerns the art of poetry or the composition of poems. If we compare the various lists of parallel passages suggested by the successive commentators, we discover a number of revealing facts. First, certain passages in Aristotle become permanently assigned to given lines in Horace as each expounder borrows from his predecessors. For example, to the opening lines of the *Ars poetica* (ll. 1–23) three passages from the *Poetics* are equated, 1450a38 (on plot as the soul of the poem), 1451b33 (on episodic plots), and 1451a19 (on the fact that unity of plot does not result from unity of hero); to lines 73–88, suggesting styles and meters for various genres, three passages again, 1459b31 on epic meter and 1448b31 and 1449a21 on iambic verse. The same lines in Horace will sometimes suggest other parallels in Aristotle; but certain basic comparisons recur in the glosses of a large number of the writers. There thus comes to be a body of traditional cross references for each section of the Horatian text; to this body, each commentator adds such other parallels as his ingenuity can devise, and indeed one has the impression, occasionally, that the parallels have as their only merit this display of ingenuity.

From this cultivation of parallelism certain advantages accrue to the interpretation of Horace. These are mostly in the form of an enrichment of the understanding of isolated sections of the text. If we take, as a case in point, the first section of Horace's text (ll. 1–13) and compare the glosses of Badius Ascensius and Francesco Lovisini, we may estimate what advance in interpretation has been made during the fifty-year period separating the two commentaries. Badius takes the passage as being, first, a warning against the errors of "soresmos," that is, "mala accumulatione seu aggregatione," and of "coinismos," that is, "vitiosa communicatione, seu commixtione sermonis." Positively, it recommends symmetry, measure, economy, decorum, insistence upon the proper "color" and the integrity of each genre. Badius reduces the meaning to the following "regula":

For any work that is to be composed or written, the poet must so invent the whole subject, so dispose what is invented, so decorate what is disposed that nothing in it will be like a monster or incongruous, but all things will be similar and in agreement among themselves.

Three things thus are necessary at first: The careful consideration and invention of the whole matter; an economy or disposition fitted with deliberation to the materials invented, for the things to be narrated will be placed differently in a poem and in a history; and their embellishment in accordance with their arrangement, in which regard must be had to elegance and decorum.[61]

Lovisini, seeing in the text the problem of limiting the free play of the poet's imagination, begins with Aristotle's distinction (in the *De anima*) between fantasy and opinion; the poet, he says, follows fantasy, "for the poets adopt for themselves the name of poet not because of the verse, but because of the plot and the fiction, as Aristotle testified in the *Poetics*."[62] Horace, he goes on to say, permits the use of figments only to the extent to which "prudence" is observed; the monstrous is never tolerated. "Let all things in a poem therefore harmonize, agree, correspond; let them all regard the aim and the end; let nothing be inconsistent, nothing unsuitable"; so it is that nothing in the *Aeneid* is unfitting to a "summus Imperator," and all things in the *Iliad* and the *Odyssey* serve the moral purposes envisaged.[63] Then, after referring to Quintilian on "coinismos" and drawing a comparison between a mixture of Greek dialects and a mixture of sublime and humble styles, Lovisini compliments Horace for having chosen this as his first precept: "Nor is it by chance that he taught first what the construction of the argument and the plot should be, for, as

[61] Ed. Paris, Gerlier, 1500, p. IIIIv: "Compositurus seu cumscripturus quodlibet opus sic rem omnem excogitabit, excogitatam disponet, dispositam ornabit vt nihil monstri simile aut repugnans in eo sit sed omnia sui similia, atque inter [se] quadrantia.

"Tria ergo primum sunt necessaria. Materiae totius excogitatio atque inuentio. Excogitate apta oeconomia seu dispositio. aliter enim in poemate: aliter in historia locabuntur res narrande & disposite exornatio: in qua elegantie & decori habenda est ratio."

[62] *Commentarius* (1554), p. 4: "quia poetae nomen sibi asciscunt non propter carmen, sed propter fabulum, & fictionem, ut in poetice testatum relinquit Aristoteles."

[63] *Ibid.*, p. 4v: "omnia igitur in poemate sibi conueniant, consentiant, respondeant, scopum, ac finem omnia spectent, nihil abhorreat, nihil alienum sit."

Aristotle established in the *Poetics*, the plot is the soul of the poem."[64] He then proceeds to the word-for-word explanation of the passage. It is clear that, whereas Badius' gloss is purely linguistic and rhetorical in character, speaking only of matters of diction and invention, Lovisini's passes beyond to considerations of the poetic imagination and of the importance of plot in the total poetic structure.

As another case, we may juxtapose the readings of Badius and Grifoli on *Ars poetica* 114–18. Badius, largely concerned with textual problems, sees in these lines only a formulation of the principle of decorum and how it is to be observed; this is solely a question of fitting the proper speech to personages of different ages, stations, countries, sexes, and so forth. The statement of the rule is brief: "Seruandum est igitur studiose decorum personarum pro sua cuiusque fortuna, aetate, ac patria" (p. XX*v*). Grifoli starts with this point, stating that Horace here as always is interested in the decorum of persons and in fitting words to people as well as to things. But he expands these ideas by bringing into consideration Aristotle's four requisites for character, all of which Horace treats in the *Ars poetica*; Grifoli cites the passages in which each of the four is adumbrated. With respect to all of them, he says, necessity and verisimilitude must be observed —and he cites *Poetics* 1454*a*32. For one who reads the Horatian passage accompanied by Grifoli's remarks, the passage carries with it all the overtones of Aristotle's theories of character and of necessity and probability and hence (whether or not these associations be correct for the text here studied) is richer and more suggestive than it was for Badius.

Other passages might be cited to exemplify the claim that through the cultivation of parallelism with the *Poetics* of Aristotle, critics gave to those passages a more extensive and a more complex meaning than they had had for commentators of the preceding generation. But the enrichment stops at the level of the individual passage. It would not be possible, I believe, to state that any general change in the interpretation of Horace takes place, that the total approach to the *Ars poetica* is any different from what it was previously. The close ties with the rhetorical tradition, the persistence of basically rhetorical distinctions, the survival of the construction put upon the text by the earliest commentators, and the fundamental nature of the text itself prevented any such change from taking place. Moreover, as later chapters of this study will demonstrate, certain modes of approach to intellectual problems and certain habits of method practically assured the continuation of the older approaches. These same modes and habits were responsible for the fact that, throughout all this extensive comparison and equation of the *Poetics* and the *Ars poetica*, there was no slightest intimation of the true state of affairs with respect to these two texts: the fact that

[64] *Ibid.*, pp. 4*v*–5: "nec temere primum docuit, qualis esse debeat argumenti, & fabulae constitutio, quia, ut in poetice auctor est Aristoteles, fabula poematis anima est."

they address themselves to essentially different problems, that they use widely different methods, and that they produce statements of a completely different nature about poetry. For theorists of this period, only the accidental—and sometimes the forced—resemblances between the two were discovered; their real opposition was not even suspected. So it was that Horace could be said to be an imitator of Aristotle, that many lines of his text could be identified with Aristotle, and at the same time the whole of the text could be read much as it had been before Aristotle was brought into the discussion.

CHAPTER FIVE. THE TRADITION OF HORACE'S *ARS POETICA*: III. THE APPLICATION TO PRACTICAL CRITICISM

So FIRMLY ENTRENCHED an intellectual tradition as the tradition of Horace's *Ars poetica* would not be apt to change with the change of the decades. The habits of interpretation were by 1560 so firmly established that little modification could be expected. Even the way of coupling Aristotle's text with Horace's was a fairly unimaginative procedure. Yet we are not to suppose that the succeeding decades add nothing and modify nothing, nor that the remaining documents to be considered are merely repetitions of the earlier ones. For one thing, the major effort of the century to provide formal commentaries to the *Ars poetica* seems, from this date on, to taper off; and although there will still be some important glosses to the text, they will occur less frequently from now until 1600 than they had in the decade of the fifties. In their place, we shall have to deal usually with shorter treatises, many of which will apply Horatian principles to literary works of current interest.

As a matter of fact, the first two works to be discussed in this chapter are formal commentaries on the *Ars poetica*. One of them is undated, and I include it at this point merely because its author's literary activity fell approximately around 1560. It is an unpublished manuscript, MS BNF II.IV.192, fols. 153²–161v, entitled *Petri Angelii in Quintij Horatij de arte poetica librum annotationes*; its author was Pietro Angeli, who also called himself Petrus Bargaeus. The manuscript is exactly what it pretends to be, a set of miscellaneous notations on Horace's work rather than a complete and thoroughgoing treatment of it. In a number of these notations, Angeli indicates parallels with Aristotle, just as his predecessors had done:

Horace	*Aristotle*
1	1451*a*22
14	
34	1456*a*9
38	1460*b*15
42	1451*a*34
82	1449*a*27
105	1455*a*23
146	1459*a*33
150	1451*a*36
179	1460*a*11
259	1460*a*1
333	1449*b*26
338	1451*b*1
347	1460*b*16
465	

The briefness of the list is explained not only by the fragmentary character of Angeli's notes, but also by the fact that he seeks such parallels only incidentally, not as a major intention. In fact, he takes pains to point out how Aristotle differs from Horace on such matters as the history of tragedy and comedy and how superior Aristotle is on such subjects as verisimilitude (fol. 160). For the rest, his annotations are limited to paraphrasing the text, to pointing up the major ideas (such as unity and simplicity of plot or the necessity of deriving the denouement from internal elements rather than from a "deus ex machina"), or to emphasizing certain original interpretations. Among these latter, we might note his distinction (*in re* l. 179) between τὸ πάθος, produced by what is shown on the stage, and τὸ θαῦμα, produced by what is narrated; and his insistence that the five-act division of drama is a means to the resting and refreshing of the audience. He also declares (on l. 318) that the poet, as an imitator, must direct his attention to the general rather than the particular and that this involves a close observance of decorum. He equates Horace's ends of profit and delight (l. 333) with Aristotle's end of "mitigating the perturbations and movements by which the soul is violently affected."[1]

PIGNA (1561)

The second work, Giovanni Battista Pigna's *Poetica Horatiana* of 1561, is not only a full-scale commentary; it is one of the lengthiest and most detailed of the century. Its author apparently starts from the premise that although various of his predecessors had sought a principle of organization for the Horatian text, no one of them had found it. In fact, those who had used the rhetorical terms of invention, disposition, and elocution (such as Pedemonte) had explained successfully the first seventy-two lines of the *Ars poetica*, but then had been obliged to start again with some other system. Pigna sees the whole of the work as organized on another basis:

> The poetics of Horace was written in such a way as to expound first the whole of poetry, treated as still unknown; then to continue with it, after having divided it into its species, to the point where the necessary parts of these same species would be completely analyzed; finally, collecting together these separate elements, to touch again upon the whole of poetry, but treated now as fully known. As not yet known, it must be considered according to matter [rem], words [verba], and the combination of the two [compositionem]. To the matter belong invention and disposition, and the same two also to words. To the composition belong the whole form of the poem and the entire power of the poet. . . . [2]

[1] MS BNF II.IV.192, fol. 159v: "poëticae finem uidetur statuisse perturbationum ac motuum, quibus animi uehementer afficiuntur mitigationem."

[2] *Poetica Horatiana* (1561), p. 1: "Poetica Horatij ita est conscripta, vt poesim totam, prout est ignota, primo suscipiat: deinde illam in sua genera partitam eo vsque perducat, quousque ipsorum generum necessariae particulae sint absolutae: postremò ex singulis collectis totam rursus poesim perstringat, sed prout iam cognoscitur. Vt tota ignota, consideranda est secundum rem, verba, & compositionem. Rei sunt inuentio, & dispositio: verborum idem pariter. compositionis sunt poematis integra forma, & poetae integrae vires. . . ."

POETIC THEORY

The first half of the preceding paragraph gives the general outline of the *Ars poetica* as Pigna analyzes it; the second half establishes the methodological framework into which he will fit a large part of the text. The "res-verba" distinction, which had been for all commentators (as for Horace himself) an incidental aspect of the total structure, becomes for Pigna the central element of Horace's methodology; even invention and disposition, as the quotation shows, are made subordinate to it.

Pigna organizes most of the text around this "res-verba" distinction. He divides it into sections of a few lines each—the number of divisions has now grown to eighty—and states a precept in summary of each section. The first precept (ll. 1–13) concerns the "inventio rei"; the second (ll. 14–24), the "dispositio rei"; the third (ll. 25–28), the invention and disposition of the words ("de uerbis agit, eodem modo inueniendo, ac disponendo"); the fourth (ll. 29–31), the same with respect to the mixture of styles. The fifth precept (ll. 32–37), on the "poematis forma integra," combines all these elements—invention and disposition of things and words—and proceeds on the basis of an analogy with life; just as the happy life results from the proper admixture of reason and prudence (cf. the *Ethics*), so the perfect poem effects a proper combination of invention (equivalent to reason) and disposition (equivalent to prudence). The analysis continues in this fashion, with a consistent application of the same set of terms. It is not until the twelfth precept (ll. 73–76) that the element of "composition" enters into play, and we discover then that it refers to metrical form rather than to any other kind of "composition": "quae non est elocutio ab Oratore consideranda, sed est carmen" (p. 32); this element accounts for Horace's treatment of the verse forms appropriate to the various genres. For lines 220–50, the forty-first to forty-fifth precepts treat both "res" and "verba" with respect to satyric drama. Precept fifty-four (ll. 309–10), on moral philosophy as supplying the "materia" of poetry, obviously belongs to the same set of distinctions, as do many other precepts throughout the analysis.

One result of Pigna's consistent application of this method is the reduction of almost all of Horace's poetics to a theory of the genres. If material, words, and verse are to be fitted together, some principle of fittingness must be established; this may be the vague notion of appropriateness employed by so many of the commentators, or the more restricted notion of appropriateness involved in appropriateness to genre. Pigna uses the latter principle. This becomes apparent as early as the first precept, which insists that "the different forms of poetry should not be joined together," and it is developed at length in the second, which "refers to the choice of a single *genus* of poetry."[3] Indeed, Pigna forces the Horatian text in order to make it include the four genres distinguished by Aristotle ("caput humanum" representing the epic, "ceruicem equinam" tragedy, "collatas plumas"

[3] *Ibid.*, p. 2: "vt diuersę poeseos formae simul coniungi non debeant" and "ad solum poeseos genus eligendum refertur."

[158]

dithyrambic and lyric poetry, and "atrum piscem" comedy) and to justify this statement of principle: "it is to be understood that those four kinds of poetry can never be brought together in one poem and, in fact, that there is no different method that would be appropriate to all of them."[4] Hence it is, he says, that Horace lays the groundwork for poetry in general in the first lines of his epistle and then passes rapidly to treatment of the individual genres: to the epic with line 42, to the lyric with line 77, to tragedy and comedy with line 89, to satyric drama with line 220, and so forth, in each case considering "res" and "verba" in their relationships to invention and disposition and then "compositio" in connection with all.

A concomitant of this general approach will of necessity be a theory of decorum. Arriving at precept twenty-one (ll. 114–18), Pigna makes and explains the transition:

> Up to this point, I think, we have discussed plot and diction; now comes character ... which is not expressed for itself but in order to make the plot one which has character. And just as mores are derived from the plot, so are the passions, because when the diction contains character and passion, so too does the subject-matter.[5]

The line of reasoning may not be very clear here, but Pigna apparently means that character and thought (the Aristotelian qualitative parts are referred to here) must depend upon the nature of the plot, and that when they are seen to be proper in the diction, it is a sign that they are correct in the material itself. That is, "oratio morata et perturbata" will be a reflection of "fabula morata et perturbata"—"verba," of "res." When he discusses character, Pigna develops a fairly original and interesting theory. He starts with Aristotle's four requisites for character, which he proceeds to rebuild into a system of his own. All four requisites, he says, are forms of the verisimilar, which itself is of two types: (1) the "easy" verisimilar (because it is easily believed), applicable to well-known persons, and for which "quod decet" is sufficient; (2) the "difficult" verisimilar, applicable to less well-known persons, and for which some kind of "similitudo" is required. Under each type, a personage may be considered by himself or in comparison with others; and the four resulting kinds correspond to the four requisites, thus:

	verisimile		
facile		difficile	
per se	in collatione	per se	in collatione
τὰ χρηστά	τὰ ἁρμόττοντα	τὸ ὁμαλόν	τὸ ὅμοιον

[4] Ibid., p. 3: "sciendum est, quatuor illa Poeseos genera nunquam in vnum poema posse reduci: etenim nulla esset diuersa ratio illis consentanea."

[5] Ibid., pp. 44–45: "Mea est interpretatio hucusque actum esse de fabula, & de dictione: nunc de moribus.... qui non absolute traduntur sed vt fabulam moratam efficiunt. & quemadmodum ex ipsa suscepti sunt mores, ita etiam perturbationes: quia vt oratio est morata, & perturbata, ita quoque materia."

Further statements show that τὰ χρηστά is merely a theoretical type of mores and is never really considered in a poem, since no person's actions are of interest of and by themselves; that τὰ ἁρμόττοντα refers to type characteristics, differentiating persons according to station, age, profession, nation; that τὸ ὁμαλόν or "conuenientia" is essentially a principle of self-consistency and is useful especially in comedy; that τὸ ὅμοιον is a matter of opinion or "fama," demanding that known persons be presented in keeping with their reputations, and is proper to both epic and tragedy. Pigna is, of course, completely faithful to his theory of literary genres when he conceives of separate kinds of mores for the separate genres.

To the question of mores (character and decorum) is closely allied, for Pigna, the question of the moral ends of poetry, and this leads him to a seemingly contradictory position. Commenting on lines 311–18 (on the uses of philosophy in poetry), he had approved of Horace's insistence that "the whole of poetry rests upon mores."[6] But a little later, speaking of the "prodesse" and "delectare" of line 333, he argues against the frequent assumption that delight is merely a handmaiden of utility, and he presents a long argument to prove, contrariwise, that the real end of poetry is pleasure. The reconciliation of this conflict is found, I believe, in the notion of the "verisimile." For Pigna, the primary end of poetry is pleasure, but it is accompanied by utility. In order that there may be pleasure, the audience must be convinced of the credibility of the persons and actions involved in the poem, and this credibility is assured by moral verisimilitude. "For if things were treated which were completely alien from truth and which could not really happen, no credibility would attach to them nor would they be followed by that pleasurable remembrance";[7] in support of which Aristotle is cited on the impossible probable. Such credibility is guaranteed by the "fabula morata" (p. 74).

We have seen that, in various places, Pigna calls upon the authority of Aristotle to sustain his arguments. That is, in general, Aristotle's role in his commentary, rather than as an inspirer of the whole Horatian theory. But Pigna does not resist the current fashion of citing parallels; I give the list for the record:

Horace	Aristotle
1–13	1448a4, 1447a14
14–23	[gen.: "Duo sunt, quae ex Aristotelis poetica illis competunt, tum vt ex subiecta materia consistant, tum vt nexu congruenti coniungantur," p. 5.]
	1456a30
	[gen.: "neque enim Hesiodus sub aliquo poeseos genere ab Aristotele reponitur," p. 8.]
	1451b15, 1453a12

[6] Ibid., p. 72: "poesim totam positam in moribus."
[7] Ibid., p. 79: "Quòd si à uerò prorsus aliena: & quae accidere non possint tractarentur, nulla eis fides adhiberetur: neque subsequeretur iucunda illa recordatio."

ARS POETICA: PRACTICAL CRITICISM

Horace	Aristotle
24–28	1458a18
29–31	1460b3, 1458a18, 1458a21
32–37	1450b34, 1460b17, 1456a18
	[gen.: "Homerum ab Aristotele excusatum," p. 18]
38–41	1460b2
42–45	1447a14, 1449b23, 1448a19(?), 1454a26(?)
46–50	1457b1
52–59	1457b2
73–76	1449a21, 1448a21
79–82	1449a25
83–85	1447a15
89–92	1448a16, 1453a20
93–98	1455b25, 1453a12
104–13	1462a4
114–18	1450a8, 1454a16
119–27	1454a16
128–30	1454a16
136–45	1451a22
149–50	1451a24
153–60	1454a21, 1453a33
179–88	1452b12, 1453b2
189–90	1450b37
191	1452b17, 1454b19, 1454b2
192	1449a16
202–19	1449b7
220–24	1449a19
244–50	[?: "Aristoteles enim Agathonem reprehendit, quòd eius fabulae vulgarium hominum sententiae potius satisfacerent, quam prudentum," p. 67]
260–74	1458b20
275–80	1448a29, 1449a16
295–301	1455a34
333–34	1449b26, 1451b5, 1460b6, 1460a18
338–42	1460a26, 1451a38
347–50	1460b16
351–60	[?: A. on Homer: many virtues, few faults, pp. 80–81]
361–65	1448a4
453–69	1455a34

Although the presence of Aristotle is considerable (less considerable, perhaps, than it might seem, since many of the passages are quoted several times), it has little effect upon the total view of the *Ars poetica*. Pigna seems rather to build his interpretation about the "res-verba" distinction, about a theory of the genres, and about the standard rhetorical notion of the "verisimile." However, he objects to another rhetorical approach, via invention, disposition, and elocution, as a means of discovering the order

[161]

of Horace's text. His own proposed order is more consistent with his own system. It does not prevent him, nevertheless, from effecting a fragmentation of the text into a number of passages and precepts even greater than that proposed by earlier commentators.

BARTOLOMEO MARANTA (1561)

These positions of Pigna and the even more traditional ones of Robortello and Maggi are attacked openly in a set of six lectures delivered by Bartolomeo Maranta to the Accademia Napoletana, meeting in the convent of San Pietro a Maiella, in 1561. A Latin summary of the first lecture and the actual notes for the other five (in Italian) are now in the Ambrosian Library in Milan, MSS R. 118. Sup. and R. 126. Sup.[8] Maranta devotes all six of his lectures to the first two "precepts" of Horace, the materials contained in lines 1–24—obviously a very extended discussion and one which could not help but bore its listeners; Maranta admits that it did and that he has rewritten the last two lectures to give a more succinct presentation. In fact, the discourses are hopelessly long-winded and repetitious, but they are not without merit. Their initial premiss is itself noteworthy for its time: Maranta declares that the distinction of invention, disposition, and elocution, so universally applied by earlier commentators on the *Ars poetica*, is in no wise appropriate to the poetic art and should not be brought into consideration. Instead, "we believe it necessary that he who wishes to analyze poetics should seek a proper basis of division which would not be applicable to any other art or science."[9] He finds this proper division in Aristotle's *Poetics*, where kinds of poems are differentiated by their means of imitation, and where each poem is divided into qualitative and quantitative parts. Moreover he believes (as others had before him) that Horace set out to treat the same six qualitative parts that Aristotle had distinguished, albeit in a different order, and that "he borrowed from Aristotle almost all the precepts, and especially those which are of greatest importance."[10]

These distinctions from Aristotle enable Maranta to make the point which he regards as his original contribution to Horatian exegesis: the first precept concerns the choice of plot and the unifying of plot, and the second precept is devoted to episodes. Just as Aristotle, according to Maranta, had named three kinds of false unity (unity of person, unity of time, unity of a single war), so Horace gives examples of three kinds of false unity: the multiplex monster, the vision of the man in fevered sleep, and the mixture

---

[8] The manuscripts are anonymous. For my attribution of them to Maranta and a general discussion of the problem, see "Bartolomeo Maranta: Nuovi Manoscritti di Critica Letteraria," *Annali della Scuola Normale Superiore di Pisa*, Serie II, XXIV (1955), 115–25.

[9] MS R. 118. Sup., fol. 117v: "Oportere autem eum qui poeticam partiri cupiat propriam, et quae nulli praeterea arti aut scientiae conueniat, diuisionem quaerere existimauimus."

[10] *Ibid.*, fol. 118v: "ipsa tamen praecepta fere omnia, et praesertim quae maioris sunt momentj ab Aristotele mutuatus est."

of wild and tame beasts. The first of these corresponds to the manifold actions of a single man, which do not constitute unity; the second, to successive but disconnected events, which do not constitute unity; the third, to contemporary but unrelated events, equally without unity. Aristotle's three kinds are thus found exemplified in Horace (fols. 120–23). The second precept, on episodes, demands the major part of the treatment after the first lecture. Maranta decides, on the basis of Aristotle, that the episode must be a quantitative part whose function is to give greater volume to the poem. It is thus never a part of the unified plot, but something added to it and integrated with it. Certain difficult problems arise as a result: How can a quantitative part be integrated with a "formal" or qualitative part? Can extraneous elements appear in the prologue and exode as well as in the "episodes"? How does one distinguish episode from plot itself in such genres as the epic? To such considerations as these Maranta devoted most of his time before the Accademia Napoletana.

It may seem that the debate is trivial, and it is certain that the discussion is too long. But for Maranta the subject warranted all the time and reflection that he could give it, since it was the central problem in any theory of poetics: the constitution of the central, unifying element in the poem—the plot—and the relationship of other parts of the action to it. Maranta apparently believed that if he could decipher Horace's meaning with respect to this problem, he would have the key to the rest of the text. The way in which he uses Aristotle in seeking the solution is in a sense original, for he does not merely cite parallel passages, he does not merely call upon an additional authority; he attempts, rather, to apply the method of Aristotle, as he understood it, to the Horatian text, and this constitutes a considerable innovation. The recognition that rhetorical distinctions do not supply answers to poetic questions and that a specifically poetic method must be used marks a notable departure from the thinking of his contemporaries.

Another unpublished manuscript, this one undated as well, has both theoretical and practical pertinence to the Horatian mode. It is perhaps of even greater interest as an early estimate of Torquato Tasso's *Rinaldo*. This is MS 985 (M.8) of the Biblioteca Comunale at Perugia, and I have assigned it an approximate date of 1561; it is entitled *Tractatus de tragoedia* and is in the form of a dialogue involving such celebrated interlocutors as Cardinal Ranuzio Farnese, Jacopo Sadoleto, Pietro Bembo, Bernardo Tasso, and Annibale Caro.[11] On the theoretical side, the prologue and the dialogue itself touch upon four points in connection with tragedy: the

---

[11] The list of names raises some question about anachronism in the text: both Sadoleto and Bembo died in 1547, at which time Torquato Tasso was only three years old. Such anachronism suggests the possibility that the treatise may have been written at a much later date than that assigned, by somebody whose knowledge of the earlier years of the century was very imperfect.

effect produced, the ends, the pleasure derived from imitation, and the educative function of poets. The following passage demonstrates the attitude with respect to the effect and, to some extent, with respect to the ends:

> For what else are we to say of the fact that we very willingly give applause to a mournful poem? that we follow with a pleasant sense of grief the horrible destruction of the most prosperous of princes? that we behold without satiety their unexpected vicissitudes and reversals of fortune? that we are reduced to pity by the pretended complaint of the actors, very pleasurably albeit with pain? that we fill up our eyes with gloomy images? that we cannot satisfy our grief with weeping? that, lastly, we are so regaled by fictional deaths, bereavements, grief, wailing, ruin? if not that we have already accustomed ourselves to wretchedness and failings in the most catastrophic way in the natural course of events, and we have grown so hardened to the sensation of our own calamity, after the pain has healed, that to have the wound now aggravated by one's own hand when it is rough to the touch produces a very agreeable sensation, ameliorated by habit itself. Last of all, so you may not fail to be aware of the ultimate state of the most calamitous exile, there is great pleasure in weeping when a moral man has been overwhelmed by misfortunes that inspire tears.[12]

The effect is here a pleasurable participation in the woes of others (a thesis, incidentally, that explains much of the characteristic quality of Renaissance tragedy), the end is to harden the soul to misfortune and suffering. But the pleasure results also from the artifice of the poet and even more from the fact that the poem is an imitation; things which are disagreeable in life become agreeable through imitation (fols. 103v–104v). "Quanto sunt illa iucundiora ficta quam facta?" (fol. 104v). Because of the presence of such pleasure, the lessons taught by poetry are willingly received—compare the sugar-coated pill—and the utility results, in an almost automatic fashion. Hence the author of the *Tractatus* takes issue with Plato's banishment of the poets and with the severe condemnations of Proclus and of Maximus of Tyre and prefers to adopt instead the opinion of Plato in Book II of the *Laws*. His arguments on the role of poets as educators are the ones commonly used in the defences of poetry.

On the practical side, the author gives extravagant praise to the adolescent Torquato Tasso's *Rinaldo*, of which he has heard a reading. His

[12] Perugia, Bibl. com., MS 985 (M.8.), fol. 96v: "Quid enim aliud dicamus esse, quod lamentabili carmini libentissime plausum damus. quod horribiles exitus Principum florentissimorum iucunda conquestione prosequimur? quod inopinatas uicissitudines rerumque conuersiones sine satietate spectamus? quod ad misericordiam actorum ficta querimonia iucundissime quamuis dolenter incondimur? quod oculos moestis imaginibus explere? quod dolorem lacrymis satiare non possumus? Quod denique simulatis funeribus, orbitatibus, luctibus, eiulationibus, vastitatibus tantopere delectamur? nisi quod aerumnosissime natura miserijs ac uitijs iam insueuimus, et ad sensum nostrae calamitatis obducto dolore sic obduruimus, ut sua manu vulnus asperum tactu iam exulcerari iucundissimum sit, ipsa consuetudine mitigatum? Demum vt exilij calamitosissimi conditionem ultimam non ignores, mortali flebilibus aerumnis obruto flere magna uoluptas est. . . ." In referring to this MS, I use the new folio numbers penciled into the codex, which numbers stop at "99"; after that, I have supplied numbers myself.

ARS POETICA: PRACTICAL CRITICISM

remarks center largely around the genius of the young poet, his faculties and his knowledge, his familiarity with all poetry and all branches of philosophy. But he also comments on "how diligently he seeks out whatever will please, how acutely he discerns what will teach," and he gives special attention to Tasso's style; such epithets and descriptions as "copious, varied, unhampered, free, sententious, grave, elegant" will sound familiar to the reader who knows the tradition that we have been tracing. Some modicum of the theory—the reference to the ends, for example—pierces through in the practical criticism; but for the most part the latter is satisfied with the facile adjectives for genius and style that had for so long been in vogue.

Sebastiano Erizzo likewise effects a combination of theoretical and practical criticism in his *Espositione nelle tre canzoni di M. Francesco Petrarca* (1562), except that in his case there really is a close relationship between theory and practice. Since he wishes to speak later of Petrarch the poet as having achieved such-and-such effects in his poems, he states all his theoretical ideas in terms of the requisites for the poet rather than in terms of the nature of the poem. His starting point is the statement, from Horace, that mediocrity is not sufferable in a poet; rather must he have a divine and superhuman genius, the components of which will be a natural gift, a knowledge of many things, and the ability to combine the right words in verse. These are all needed if the poet is "to teach and move the listener, and then give pleasure, and awaken in him admiration with his poem."[13] For the natural gift there are no precepts to be given; but on the score of knowledge, Erizzo has much to say. It is essentially knowledge of the natural sciences and of philosophy and, within the latter, of moral philosophy:

... it is necessary that he learn the precepts of all the best arts, for since he has to treat of any subject whatsoever, he should show himself most well versed in that art which treats of the causes of things, of the vices of men, of the pleasures, of pain, of death, of the passions and all the perturbations of the soul, of the honest, of the true good, of all the virtues, of life, of mores, all of which things are contained under moral science.[14]

Its content of moral wisdom makes poetry excellent among all the arts, and the same excellence is found also in its capacity to give pleasure. Pleasure results from the "various ornaments," from the "beauty of the diction," from the harmony of verse. Nor does Erizzo neglect the standard

---

[13] *Espositione* (1561), p. 1v: "insegnare, & commouere l'uditore, & appresso dilettare, & indurlo à marauiglia col suo poema."

[14] *Ibid.*, p. 2: "fa mestieri, che egli apprenda i precetti di tutte le ottime arti, perche douendo di qualunque cosa trattare, in quella peritissimo si dimostri, cio è delle cagioni delle cose, de i uitij de gli huomini, de i piaceri, del dolore, della morte, de gli affetti, & di tutte le perturbationi dell'animo, dell'onesto, del uero bene, di tutte le uirtù, della uita, de i costumi, le quai cose tutte sotto la scientia morale si contengono."

[165]

7§

distinctions in his enumeration of its sources; the poem must be of rare and exquisite invention and must have a choice of delightful words.

Before passing on to the discussion of Petrarch, Erizzo attempts a theory of the genre in which he is specifically interested, lyric poetry. Distinguishing, first, three general kinds of poetry, the expository and narrative (I take it that he has didactic poetry in mind), the fictional, and the mixed, he places lyric poetry in the third category. He then proceeds to definitions of the lyric in general and of the elegy, both of which have a decidedly Aristotelian ring. Of the lyric, "at times it is an imitation of a grave and honest action, and sometimes of a joyous and light one, composed in verses which are not bare, but adorned with rhythm and harmony, so that with its sweetness it may at the same time profit and delight"; of the elegy, "it is for the most part love poetry which revolves about the passions of the soul, and it is an imitation of a complete lamentable action which, feigning the action in [the poet] himself or in another, expresses a melancholy effect."[15] The Aristotelian ring has, at times, Horatian overtones. Lyric poetry is said to be the most pleasing and delightful of all the types because of the elegance of its diction and its special musical qualities.

Petrarch belongs among the lyric and elegiac poets because of his treatment in a modest style of amorous subjects. The weeping and lamenting tone of his poems, the tears and sighs, make him an elegiac. After the classification, the praise; and it contains at once many of the traditional epithets, rhetorical criteria, and Horatian elements. (1) Petrarch's ideas are noble and full of wisdom, his sentiments grave, his style easy and full of an abundance of ornate words. (2) He equals Pindar in greatness, gravity, nobility of spirit, choice of words, and splendor of style and is unique in the imitation of the passions of love. (3) His invention shows the workings of nature and of art, "so abundant, in his style, was the natural facility, so rich, so sweet and full of gayety and loveliness, so rich in figures like precious jewels, and of the most beautiful and most necessary in poems of this kind."[16] (4) His verse is rhythmical and harmonious. (5) The moral sententiae throughout his poems show his mastery of moral philosophy, and the natural philosophy shows his indebtedness to Plato.

Such practical criticism as this shows some progress over the earlier varieties, insofar as some attempt is made to bring into operation the conclusions of the antecedent theoretical thinking. But the progress is still not very great.

[15] *Ibid.*, pp. 3v–4: "alle uolte è una imitatione di attione graue, & onesta, & alcune uolte di giocosa, & lieue, che si compone di uersi non nudi, ma di numero, & di armonia ornati, accioche colla sua dolcezza gioui parimente, & diletti" and "è in gran parte poesia amorosa, che si riuolge intorno alle passioni dell'animo, & è una imitatione di perfetta attione lamenteuole, la quale ò fingendola in se stesso il P. ouero in altrui, esprime malinconioso effetto."

[16] *Ibid.*, p. 4v: "tanto fu larga del suo stile la uena, ricca, dolce, & piena di leggiadria, & uaghezza, copiosa di figure à guisa di care gioie, & delle più belle, & necessarie à sì fatti poemi."

ORAZIO TOSCANELLA (1562)

In the realm of the purely theoretical, again, a document of some interest is Orazio Toscanella's *Precetti necessarii sopra diverse cose pertinenti alla grammatica, poetica, retorica, historia, loica, et ad altre facoltà* (1562). And the interest does not derive from the author's originality; quite the contrary. For Toscanella aims only to simplify other works for beginners and students of his time; in the field of poetics, therefore, he gives reductions and paraphrases of Donatus, Horace, Aristotle, and a section of Minturno. His claim to do so, though, is not completely accurate, for he does not stick very closely to the text that he is treating. For example, much material from Horace, not identified as such, is incorporated into the section entitled "Auertimenti della Comedia da Donato." Such a schoolboy's version of the classics of criticism is interesting in that it represents a kind of vulgate of critical thinking. What such a popularizer as Toscanella chooses to emphasize, what he singles out for quotation or expansion, is significant for estimating the state of criticism at the time.

In the Donatus section, Toscanella collects all of his ideas about comedy —and comedy is taken in the broadest sense of dramatic representation. After a preliminary statement that "comedy was first discovered so that people might moderate their desires through the examples of others and might become better,"[17] Toscanella goes on to such headings as "What persons are introduced in comedy," "What is the subject of comedy," "On sounds (or music)," "On vocal sections," "Why they are called acts," and "How many persons may speak in each scene." Most of these concern the kind of mechanics with which Donatus was occupied, but there are digressions and excursions which add considerably to the richness of the materials. For example, in connection with the subject of comedy he adds a note on the "in medias res" beginning and on the development of suspense in the spectator. When speaking of acts in drama, he gives his conception of imitation: "Comedy consists in imitation, and one who plays the part of a servant imitates as much as he can the comportment of a servant, one who represents a lover imitates a man who is really in love."[18] Like the expositors of the *Ars poetica*, he cites Aristotle (1453*b*1) in reference to Horace's lines on off-stage action. A long section, still in this paraphrase of Donatus, is devoted to the decorum of persons, with extended passages on "convenevolezza," "similitudine," and "egualità," and another to the verisimilitude to be observed in narration. Here, again, several texts from Aristotle are cited as parallel. Clearly, all this is very far from Donatus's text, and it is obvious that the latter has merely been used

---

[17] *Precetti Necessarii* (1562), p. 12v: "La Comedia primieramente fù ritrouata, accioche le persone moderassero i loro desiderij con lo essempio di altri, & si facessero migliori."

[18] *Ibid.*, p. 15v: "la Comedia consiste nella Imitatione; & uno, che fa la parte del seruo, imita quanto può gli andamenti del seruo; Vno che rappresenta lo innamorato, imita uno, che sia ueramente innamorato."

as a starting point for the development of a complete collection of statements on poetics, with special reference to the dramatic forms.

In a later section on poetics in general ("Che cosa sia poetica," pp. 57v ff.), Toscanella defines the art in a way which reveals the eclecticism of his method: "Poetics is a structure of feigned art and true narration, composed in fitting rhythm, or rather in metric feet."[19] Then, after the division of poems into the narrative, the dramatic, and the mixed, he defines tragedy: "Tragedy is an embracing of the heroic condition in a state of misfortune." (Toscanella is having difficulty in translating Diomedes' "Tragoedia est heroicae fortunae in adversis conprehensio.") "The subject and the material of tragedy are sufferings, tears, hate, murders, poisonings, burnings, bitternesses, poverty, heartaches, sobbings, sighs, dismemberments of small children, downfalls of great houses; movements to madness, betrayals, arms, violence, fury, wrath, etc."[20] In an identical fashion, the definition of comedy is translated from Diomedes and the subjects listed are those which had appeared traditionally in the medieval descriptions of the genre. So for the other genres. What pretends to be a theory of poetics turns out to be merely a compendium of the commonplaces on the art.

Most of what Toscanella gives in the section on Horace is merely a translation of selected lines from the *Ars poetica* strung together to make a fairly continuous exposition. This is preceded by a brief statement of five precepts, which apparently are to be taken as the salient aspects of the text; they all refer to the general principles of composition contained in the first few lines of Horace's epistle. A paragraph on style contains recommendations on invention, disposition, and elocution. When he reaches the point at which he must discuss the ends of poetry, Toscanella presents one of the "tabular reductions" of which he was so fond and which figure so prominently throughout his little manual. I reproduce a part of it here:

On the functions of the poet.
The function of the poet is to:

Delight—		*Profit*—
He who wishes to delight must not depart too much from the truth, but must stand firm within the limits of verisimilitude. In a word, he must mix together:		He who wishes to profit with his poem must be brief and treat only as much as he knows will suffice to make the listener understand what is being treated.[21]
The useful. So that the poem may delight grave persons, such as mature men, old men, etc., who take delight in utility.	*The sweet.* So that the poem may delight the young, who take delight in pleasant things, etc.	

[168]

It can hardly be said that here or elsewhere Toscanella offers any interpretation of his basic text; he summarizes, codifies, simplifies, outlines, but that is all. (I shall discuss his treatment of Aristotle's *Poetics* in a later chapter.)

An effort at practical criticism that involves incidental pronouncements on theory was made by Sperone Speroni in his *Discorsi sopra Virgilio*, most of which he probably wrote around 1563-64 but which was still incomplete in 1581, and was published only posthumously.[22] Speroni's central intention is to attack the reputation of Vergil and to prove his inferiority as a poet, both absolutely and in comparison with Homer. To do so, he examines Vergil's performance in the areas of invention, disposition, and elocution. Speroni insists first on the importance of the first of these, which he identifies with plot, and he cites Aristotle on plot as the soul of the poem. Here he finds Vergil at fault in several ways: he does not *invent* anything at all, but borrows both the plot and its disposition from Homer; there are many errors and insufficiencies in the handling of plot and character, which Speroni points out at length and for some of which he suggests corrections. The matter of the poem is itself so slight that one wonders whether Vergil might not have foregone imitation entirely in favor of the cultivation of beauties which were essentially "extra fabulam." In this connection, Speroni proposes his theory on the unity of plot:

[19] *Ibid.*, p. 57v: "La Poetica è una struttura d'arte finta, & di uera narratione; composta di numero conueneuole: ouero di piede metrico."

[20] *Ibid.*, p. 58v: "La Tragedia è uno abbracciamento della conditione heroica in stato di disauentura. . . . Il soggetto, & la materia della Tragedia, sono i dolori, le lagrime, l'odio, gli ammazzamenti, ueleni, incendij, amaritudini, pouertà, cordogli, singulti, sospiri, sbranamenti di membra di figliuoli, disgratie di case: mouimenti a pazzia, tradimenti, arme, uiolenza, furore, ira, &c."

[21] *Ibid.*, p. 76:

De gli uffici del poeta.
Vfficio del poeta è
Di

Dilettare,	*Giouare*.
Bisogna, che colui che uuol dilettare, non si parta troppo dal uero: ma stia saldo ne i termini del uerisimile. In somma bisogna, che mescoli insieme	Bisogna che sia breve, colui, che intenda di giouare col suo poema, & tanto tratti, quanto conosca che basti per fare intendere allo ascoltante cio che tratta.
L'utile.	*Il dolce.*
Accioche diletti il poema le persone graui: come gli huomini fatti, i uecchi, &c. che dell'utilità prendono diletto.	Accioche il poema diletti i giouani, che di cose dolci si dilettano, &c.

[22] The date of *ca.* 1563-64 is suggested by Speroni's biographer, Francesco Cammarosano, *La vita e le opere di Sperone Speroni* (Empoli, 1920), p. 164; a letter of 1581 from Speroni to Felice Paciotto, dated 1581, states that the discourses are still incomplete (*Opere* [1740], V, 280-81). The *Discorsi* were first published in the Venice ed. of 1740, IV, 419-579.

Hence it is that the poem must consist of one single action, as Aristotle said, not only because any imitation must imitate one single thing just as any science concerns one subject, but also because if a poem consists essentially in redundant and superfluous ornament, if a poet were to undertake to imitate poetically more than one action, the poem in order to be complete would grow to infinite size.[23]

As for Vergil, Speroni concludes that "Vergil did not possess the poetic art; because with respect to invention, in which the art consists, he does not dare to break away from Homer; for just as the art of oratory resides in invention, so does that of poetry."[24] Without Homer, he says, Vergil would have been nothing at all in plot and in disposition.

Vergil's merit, therefore, is exclusively in elocution. But it is not an absolute merit. Speroni, as we have seen, places the whole essence of poetry in ornament. Another passage may be cited in confirmation: "That poetry consists entirely of ornament may be seen in its figurative modes of speech, which are not used by orators or by historians or even by the art of grammar; it is seen in the sweetness of verse, in the restrictions which it imposes."[25] This leads him to place a premium on two qualities, "ornateness" and "floridity," both of which he finds in Homer, both of which are lacking in Vergil. Vergil's error lies in the fact that he "was concerned with brevity, in which the poet should take no delight if he wishes to delight the reader; for brevity cannot be ornate, and consequently is not pleasurable."[26] The comparison between the two poets is concluded thus:

I return to speak again of the brevity of Vergil and the floridity of Homer. The latter delights properly, pleasantly ornamenting and amplifying his subjects, whence he always abounds in epithets; but Vergil delights through the marvelous, speaking as he does with so much brevity and precision and without affectation. But from the delightfulness of Homer is born joyfulness and gaiety, from that of Vergil is born astonishment and melancholy, which is not proper to the poet but rather to the historian.[27]

[23] In *Opere* (1740), IV, 438–39: "di qui nasce che'l poema dee essere di una azione sola, come disse Aristotile, non solo perchè di una imitazione debba essere una cosa sola imitata, come di un soggetto una scienzia; ma anche perchè se'l poema è ornamento redundante e superfluo, se'l poeta togliesse a imitar più di una azione poeticamente, il poema a volere esser perfetto cresceria in infinito." The argument is repeated on p. 534.

[24] *Ibid.*, p. 571: "L'arte poetica non era in Virgilio: però quanto all'invenzione, ove l'arte consiste, non osa scostarsi da Omero. che come l'arte oratoria è nella invenzione, così è la poetica."

[25] *Ibid.*, p. 534: "Che la poesia sia tutta ornamento, si vede per li suoi modi figurati di dire non usati dalli oratori, e dalli istorici, e dall'arte istessa della gramatica: si vede per la soavità del verso, per li suoi obblighi."

[26] *Ibid.*, p. 438: "Fu studioso di brevità, della quale non si de' dilettare il poeta, se vuol dilettar i lettori; perchè la brevità non può essere ornata, e per conseguente non è dilettevole."

[27] *Ibid.*, p. 439: "Torna a parlar della brevità di Virgilio, e floridità di Omero. Costui propriamente diletta ornando ed amplificando gentilmente le cose sue; onde sempre abbonde di epiteti: ma Virgilio diletta con la meraviglia, parlando con tanta brevità, e così assegnatamente, come fa, senza affettazione. ma dalla dilettazion di Omero nasce allegria ed ilarità; da quella di Virgilio nasce stupore e melanconia: il che non è proprio del poeta, ma anzi dell'istorico."

So that whereas Vergil may be praised for his brevity and his diction for certain rhetorical effects, these are not qualities which necessarily make of him a great poet. He is likened, indeed, to the "Asiatic" poets whose decoration is not appropriate to their subject matter.

From this process of applying a method of invention, disposition, and elocution there results a fairly consistent poetic. The plot, from invention, must be single and simple (but not too brief) so that a proper amount of ornamentation may be added. The diction must be ornate, but not too much so, lest it be in excess of what is demanded by the materials. If the poet strikes a proper balance between invention and elocution, as Homer did, then he is a great poet and worthy of the highest praise; if he fails in either of these aspects, much as he may be admired for other qualities, he ranks as an inferior poet, as Vergil did. Speroni's insistence upon ornament, upon the florid style, shows that his total approach is rhetorical in its conception of diction as well as in its tripartite division of elements.

MARANTA (1564)

If we had any evidence that Speroni knew Bartolomeo Maranta's *Lucullianae quaestiones* (1564), we might almost think that his discourses on Vergil were written in reply to Maranta. For Maranta's position is the exact opposite of Speroni's, and in the five dialogues contained in the work (so called after Colantonio Caracciolo's villa at Lucullo, near Naples, where the dialogues are set), we find nothing but the most fulsome praise for every aspect of Vergil's work. The interlocutors (they include Scipione Ammirato, Alfonso Cambi, Girolamo Colonna, Giovanni Villani, Gian Pietro Ciccarello, and other members of the Accademia Napoletana) talk most about the beauties produced by Vergil's studied assortments of sounds, about the appropriateness of certain sounds to certain ideas, about effects of onomatopoeia. Their second major concern is with figures of speech and the use of words in general; Girolamo Colonna's original proposal is to defend Vergil on the basis of his diction. For all these matters, an elaborate theory is presented as the conversations develop; the classical rhetoricians are cited in authority, especially Cicero, Hermogenes, and Dionysius of Halicarnassus. Other classical writers are quoted for parallel uses of figures or sounds.

In each of the five dialogues, however, some attention is paid to theoretical matters of broader import, since Maranta apparently wishes to develop a complete theory of the epic—even though much of the generalized material is never applied specifically to Vergil. At least some of the conclusions so presented are reached by comparing the epic with tragedy and comedy, and as a result the theoretical scope of the *Quaestiones* is considerably widened. Aristotle and Horace are the main authorities here, with Plato being used incidentally. The theory evolved is based in large part upon the comparison between the poet and the orator. At times, Maranta states the comparison explicitly, as in Book V: "We are not now comparing oratorical matters with poetic ones; but observing certain rules in the former, as in the very fountainhead, we then apply them to poetic matters, with due respect to the differences."[28] But more usually it is implicit in statements made exclusively about poetics, as in this sentence praising Vergil:

> Indeed, to say nothing about the vehemence and the greatness that we see in his sententiae; and how variedly—and always wherever he wishes—he draws away the souls of men, inflames, calms, teaches, impels, excites, diverts, discourages them; and how distinctly and clearly and abundantly and luminously he writes, with respect both to content and to expression; and how also, without ever neglecting brevity, to both matter and form he so adapts all things that if you were to add, or change, or remove anything it would be wholly faulty and less perfect; I shall address myself to the discussion of diction.[29]

The string of verbs describing the effect upon the audience, the "res-verba" distinction, the general terms of praise for the style are all such as would properly belong to a conventional rhetorical estimate.

The poet, as we have seen, is like the orator in the ends he seeks. Maranta insists upon this in Book III also: "The poet proposes as his principal goal to arouse the different passions of the soul and whichever ones he wishes, and to generate them in the souls of those who listen or read. . . . Therefore, as far as this is concerned, the poet and the orator are very close together. . . . Each of them must thus, in the things which are common to both, have recourse to the same devices in order to achieve the goal."[30] Furthermore, the poet shares with the orator the end of admiration, although this is most properly attributed to the epic poet: "the marvelous is more proper to the epic than to tragedy, but it nevertheless belongs to both kinds of poems. . . . Among the principal aims of the poet is to arouse admiration from whatever source he can."[31] From these statements of the ends, the familiar "prodesse" and "delectare" are notably absent; Maranta, here as elsewhere, is

---

[28] *Lucullianarum quaestionum libri quinque* (1564), p. 364: "Nos nunc non conferimus oratoria poeticis: sed regulas in illis obseruantes, quasi in proprio fonte proportione seruata, ad res poeticas deinde accommodamus."

[29] *Ibid.*, p. 15: "Nam ut omittam, quantam in eius sententijs uehementiam ac magnitudinem uideamus, ac quàm uariè & semper quocunque uult, animos hominum distrahat, incendat, leniat, doceat, impellat, concitet, reflectat, deterreat: ac quàm distinctè & explicatè, & abundanter, & illuminatè, & rebus & uerbis scribat: & cum his quoque breuitatis haud immemor, ita res omnes temperet, ut quicquid aut addideris, aut mutaueris, aut detraxeris, uitiosius & deterius omnino sit futurum: ad orationem meipsum conuertam."

[30] *Ibid.*, p. 179: "Poeta pręcipuum scopum sibi proponit, ut uarias, & quas uult affectiones animi concitet, atque generet in animis eorum qui se uel audiunt, uel legunt. . . . Igitur quantum ad hoc attinet, Orator & Poeta maximè conueniunt. . . . Debet igitur in re communi utrisque, ad eadem uterque confugere, ut scopum attingant."

[31] *Ibid.*, p. 88: "ut admirabilitas magis Epopoeiae conueniat, quàm Tragoediae: tametsi utriusque poematis propria est. . . . Inter praecipuos poetae scopos illud est, ut admirationem undique pariat."

ARS POETICA: PRACTICAL CRITICISM

closer to the rhetoricians themselves than to Horace. For similar ends, similar means. The poet will have to pay particular attention to the "proposition" of his poem, which must be simple and unornate and must stand in proper relationship to the plot, just as the orator will use poetic diction in his exordium (p. 179). Both must study the proper handling of "res" and "verba." Maranta equates two rhetorical elements (and he may have in mind two of Aristotle's qualitative parts), sententiae and "oratio," with "res" and "verba" respectively: "The words produce the diction and the things themselves the sententiae. The latter cannot exist without language, that is without words; but the words can exist without sententiae."[32] It is these, indeed, in which he is primarily interested, and he sacrifices the other parts in favor of an abundant discussion of the multiple aspects of words. Like the orator, again, the poet in any given poem works within the framework of one of the three styles; he chooses the proper style for the genre and then the proper words and figures for that style (Book V). Finally, one may analyze a poet's work, as one does an orator's, in terms of invention, disposition, and elocution, and Maranta does not fail to pay passing tribute to Vergil's invention and disposition (p. 96).

There is one lengthy discussion in the work, however, which is specifically germane to the poet, and that relates to truth and verisimilitude and the kinds of plots proper to the epic and to tragedy. Maranta assumes, as we have seen, that one of the ends of the poet is to stir the reader to admiration and that this is done through the use of the marvelous. The marvelous is produced by actions which are "unheard of, new, and completely unexpected."[33] At the same time, however, the poet must be sure never to tax the credulity of his audience; a delicate balance must be maintained between the marvelous and the verisimilar. It is here that a difference arises between tragedy and the epic. For the reader will accept certain things as credible which will be rejected by the spectator, and the spectator will sometimes be more deeply moved by what is narrated than by what is enacted. Therefore, "it is certain that the marvelous, especially when it attaches to those things which cannot really happen, cannot be represented in the same way in drama and in simple discourse where there is no representation of actions."[34] The epic poet may thus cultivate the extraordinary and incredible more freely than the tragic poet, and the latter must take care to relegate certain violent actions ("death itself, massacres, the cooking and eating of human flesh, and others of this kind"[35]) to narrative

---

[32] *Ibid.*, pp. 17–18: "Verba orationem conflant, res ipsae sententias. Hae sine oratione, hoc est sine uerbis esse non possunt: at uerba sine sententijs possunt."

[33] *Ibid.*, p. 89: "inaudita, ac noua, & praeter expectationem."

[34] *Ibid.*, p. 91: "Constat igitur admirabilitatem, praesertim ueró earum rerum quae fieri nequeunt, non aequè posse in dramatibus effingi, atque in sermone nudo: ubi nulla est actionum repraesentatio."

[35] *Ibid.*, p. 90: "Mors ipsa, trucidatio, membrorum humanorum coctio, comestio, & id genus caetera."

passages; in these, however, the "imitative" actions of the messenger or other narrator, his gestures and pronunciation, may considerably enhance the emotional effect. Clearly, all this is an expansion and explanation of Horace's line 179—

> Aut agitur res in scaenis aut acta refertur

—but the explanation involves certain ideas about the nature of the audience which bring the analysis close to rhetorical theories. The audience is defined, in this connection, as being made up of "selectissimi viri" whose judgment would be more discerning than that of the "vulgus." It is this audience that sets the standards of credibility and verisimilitude, whose eyes will believe a limited number of actions and through whose ears the proper emotions of tragedy may be aroused and purged.

On the whole, then, Maranta's position remains a rhetorical one. The praise of Vergil which he so generously bestows has as its object the various excellences of Vergil's diction, although compliments are offered in passing to his invention and disposition. Curiously enough, Speroni also admitted in a general way the merit of the diction, but refused all worth and all poetic quality to the other two elements of the trilogy. In Maranta, whatever expansion of theory in the direction of a more complete poetics may be found is left without application to the text of Vergil itself; in Speroni, it is just such an expansion that leads to the denial of Vergil's right to the name of poet.

An even more restricted application of the same principles, with Ariosto as the poet studied, is presented by Lodovico Dolce's *Modi affigurati e voci scelte et eleganti della volgar lingua, con un discorso sopra a mutamenti e diuersi ornamenti dell'Ariosto* (1564). This is really not a treatise at all, but a collection of examples of "selected and elegant words" and of metaphors ("modi affigurati") cited as demonstrations of Ariosto's artistry. The only theoretical statements appear in the preface "A I Lettori," where Dolce says, "Everybody who wishes his compositions to be read willingly and praised by judicious and learned men must without fail try to write in a regulated, ornate, figurative, and artful manner," and where he insists upon the necessity of following the rules. He admits that both ornate and figurative writing find their rules in rhetoric and cites Bartolomeo Cavalcanti's *Retorica* and the *Modi affigurati* as providing examples and suggestions.[36]

To these specimens of practical criticism of the epic and the romance we may add two discussions of comedy, Lodovico Castelvetro's *Giuditio delle*

---

[36] *Modi affigurati* (1564), p. 1: "Ciascuno, che disidera, che i suoi componimenti siano uolentieri letti e lodati da gli huomini giudiciosi e dotti, dee senza fallo procacciar di scriuer regolatamente, ornatamente, figuratamente & artificiosamente."

comedie di Terentio and his *Parere sopra ciascuna comedia di Plauto*.[37] Both of these are undated, and I have assigned them arbitrarily to *ca.* 1565. The *Giuditio* consists of scattered remarks on specific words or lines of the various comedies of Terence. Castelvetro's main concern is with the problem of verisimilitude. He reproaches Terence with having neglected to present the true and the verisimilar, and in all cases these terms refer to natural rather than artistic probability. For example, it is not "verisimile" that Pamphilus in the *Andria* should walk from the forum to his house in complete silence and then begin to shout as he approaches the house,[38] nor is the line "Ex ara hinc sume verbenas" acceptable since it is not common to find, on the public streets, altars covered with sacred boughs (p. 170). These would be, I presume, sins against nature; the remainder of Castelvetro's strictures apply to sins against art: telling the story in the prologue, since the comedy should be completely self-contained and have no need of prior explanation; committing "sconvenevolezze" by assigning to persons or situations speeches or actions not appropriate to them; narrating briefly what should be told at length, and vice versa. Rarely Terence is applauded for a proper solution, as in his introduction of the parasite in the *Eunuch*; such persons may be used in comedy only as companions to sons of good family whose fathers are far away or to vain and spendthrift soldiers (p. 174). The tendency of all these remarks is to set up three criteria—nature, decorum, and the strict rules of art—as guides to the practicing poet.

The situation is much the same in the *Parere* concerning the comedies of Plautus. More rules are added by implication: an actor must not address the audience (p. 8); the stage must not remain empty (p. 9); the "deus ex machina" ending is not desirable (p. 9), nor is the double ending, which brings happiness to some and unhappiness to others (p. 14). For the most part, Castelvetro talks about the plots of the comedies and criticizes details of construction, again usually in terms of natural probability. On this score, several new points are made. Of the *Amphytrion* Castelvetro says: "Next, this action involves kings and gods; but it is not known through history or through legend; hence it is not a poetic subject"[39]—the implication being the familiar one that, in poems, kings and gods may figure only in actions already known to the audience. Moreover, Castelvetro raises moral objections to certain of the actions in the *Asinaria*, indicates the possibility of sad endings for comedy and happy endings for tragedy. All these criticisms belong strictly to the Horatian tradition which I have been

---

[37] The author of the *Parere* is identified in the title of the manuscript (Vat. Lat. 5337) only as "L. C."; but the editor of the text, Giuseppe Spezi (Bologna, 1868), argues for the attribution to Castelvetro.

[38] In *Opere varie critiche* (1727), p. 168.

[39] *Parere, ed. cit.*, p. 8: "Appresso questa azione è reale e divina, nè appare per historia, o, per fama; dunque non è soggetto poetico."

tracing, and there are only the slightest reflections of the Aristotelian *Poetics*. This is surprising indeed for one of the century's principal commentators on Aristotle. It may be explained either by assuming that these criticisms were written before Castelvetro began his work of textual exegesis, or by concluding that even a professional Aristotelian theorist could operate, in the domain of practical criticism, in complete independence of the *Poetics*.

Torquato Tasso, himself a sonneteer, provides us with an example of criticism of the sonnet in the same mode. It is his *Lezione sopra un sonetto di Monsignor Della Casa*, written in his youth and recited before the Accademia Ferrarese; I have assigned to it a tentative date of 1565.[40] After a preliminary discussion of nature and art in the poet (Tasso gives precedence to art and indicates how the poet must combine the imitation of models with the following of precepts), he chides the imitators of Casa with having failed to reflect his greatest qualities. "What is marvelous in him, the choice of words and of sententiae, the novelty of the figures and especially of the metaphors, his strength, greatness and majesty, they either do not try to express or are unable to do so in any degree."[41] Tasso will attempt to explain these elements in his lecture. Since they refer exclusively to matters of style, he prefaces his remarks by a distinction of the various styles as seen by Demetrius, by Hermogenes, and by Cicero; then, placing this sonnet in the "magnificent, grand, and sublime" style, he defends Casa's use of this style in the sonnet. Dante's objections are overridden, since if grave and magnificent matters may be used in the sonnet, why not words of the same kind? Tasso here applies the rhetorical distinction between concepts and words: "It is clear that the concepts are the end and consequently the form of discourse, and the words and the composition of the verse are the material or the instrument."[42] Casa's concepts are then analyzed in terms of Demetrius' criteria—with passing reference to Book III of the *Rhetoric* and to Cicero's *Orator*—and the general question of the proper subjects for poetry is raised.

This was a moot question at the time. Tasso shares the position of those who held that profound philosophical and scientific concepts, especially when expressed in proper philosophical terms, are not acceptable in poetry. He praises Petrarch for having reduced Plato's philosophy to terms that were comprehensible to the reader. Two basic conceptions relative to the

[40] Guasti, who edited the *Lezione* in the *Prose diverse* (1875), II, 111–34, gives no indication of its date. According to Solerti, *Bibliografia delle opere minori in versi di Torquato Tasso* (Bologna, 1893), pp. 12–13, the lecture was first published in *Delle rime* (Venice, 1582).

[41] In *Prose diverse*, ed. Guasti, II, 117: "quel che è in lui maraviglioso, la scelta delle voci e delle sentenze, la novità delle figure, e particolarmente de' traslati, il nerbo, la grandezza e la maestà sua, o non tentano, o non possono pur in qualche parte esprimere."

[42] *Ibid.*, p. 119: "chiara cosa è, che i concetti siano il fine e conseguentemente la forma dell'orazione; e le parole, e la composizione del verso, la materia o l'instromento."

poetic art are present here: first, the poet must delight; second, his audience is made up primarily of the common people. With respect to the first:

... since the poet must delight, either because pleasure is his end, as I believe, or because it is a necessary means to bring about utility, as others judge, he is not a good poet who does not delight, nor can he delight with those concepts which bring with them difficulty and obscurity; for a man must weary his mind in order to understand them, and since fatigue is contrary to human nature and to pleasure, wherever fatigue is present no pleasure can in any way be found.[43]

And to the second: "The poet speaks not only to the learned but to the people, as the orator does, and therefore let his concepts be popular; I mean by popular not those which the people uses ordinarily, but such as are intelligible to the people."[44] Judged by these standards, Casa receives a high rating; the concepts in this sonnet are "clear, pure, easy, but of a clearness that is not ordinary, a purity that is not low, an ease that is not ignoble."[45] From these bases, Tasso goes on to an appreciation of Casa's versification, of the sounds he uses, of the figures of speech and their appropriateness to the kind of style employed. The approach remains restricted to various levels of language—to elocution and versification—and never inquires into the possibility of other types of poetic structure and excellence. For this reason, it is related to the Horatian-rhetorical trend, which in the sonnet (where "plot" and "characters" in the strictest sense are lacking) could produce no other kind of interpretation or judgment.

With Benedetto Grasso's *Oratione contra gli Terentiani* (1566) we return to comedy and to Terence. Like Castelvetro's criticism, Grasso's is negative; but it is more severe and it is based on essentially different grounds. Perhaps the starting point for Grasso is his comparison of the poet and the orator. He sees them as having different ends and different procedures:

... just as the orator follows the wide road and goes wandering through the spacious fields of eloquence, never departing from common usage so that at the same time he may show the happy abundance of his speech, so also he tries with every art and diligence to obtain the desired victory. The poet, since he moves toward a different end, issues forth from the common usage of men and in this way he becomes admirable, giving pleasure and attracting the souls of the listeners with the beauty of the words, the sweetness of the rhymes, the variety and the floridity of the figures, in such wise that with the happy representation of charac-

---

[43] *Ibid.*, p. 124: "dovendo il poeta dilettare, o perchè il diletto sia il suo fine, come io credo, o perchè sia mezzo necessario ad indurre il giovamento, come altri giudica; buon poeta non è colui che non diletta, nè dilettar si può con quei concetti che recano seco difficoltà ed oscurità: perchè necessario è che l'uomo affatichi la mente intorno a l'intelligenza di quelli; ed essendo la fatica contraria a la natura degli uomini ed al diletto, ove fatica si trovi, ivi per alcun modo non può diletto ritrovarsi."

[44] *Ibid.*, p. 124: "Parla il poeta non a i dotti solo, ma al popolo, come l'oratore; e però siano i suoi concetti popolari: popolari chiamo non quai il popolo gli usa ordinariamente, ma tali, che al popolo siano intelligibili."

[45] *Ibid.*, p. 125: "chiari, puri, facili, ma d'una chiarezza non plebea, d'una purità non umile, d'una facilità non ignoble."

ters, gestures, and actions at one and the same time he gives us pleasure, and giving us pleasure he so attracts us that, as if beside ourselves, we are intent upon nothing else but considering the loveliness and perfection of that poem.[46]

According to this statement, the poet produces a kind of Platonic rapture, largely by means of extraordinary diction but also through the proper imitation of actions and characters. The statement is incomplete, however, as far as the ends are concerned; for elsewhere Grasso expands it by introducing the formula "insegna, deletta, e moue" (p. 6) and by citing Plutarch on the uses of poetry in curbing violent passions and in teaching men to bear with equanimity the excesses of adverse or propitious fortune (p. 35). But his real meaning becomes apparent only when he proceeds to condemn Terence for the immorality and the obscenity of his comedies. Quoting Horace on the civilizing function of the earliest poets, who were priests and philosophers, he declares that it was through a desire to please the masses that later poets fell into decadence and that the reading of such poets can produce only blushes and contempt. Terence is one of these: "poets such as this, with the sweetness of their rhymes and the beauty and smoothness of their words, at first delight us; but they leave our souls infected and poisoned by the corruption of their enormous vices and their immoral stories."[47]

On the basis of the quality of the imitation, says Grasso, Terence is again open to criticism. His deficiencies are dual: in the lack of originality and in the nature of the imitation itself. Grasso equates imitation with invention, but only in the narrow sense of "imitation" as borrowing from other poets. To justify his attack on Terence, he develops an elaborate theory of this kind of imitation, which may take any one of three forms: (1) simple translation; (2) the use of different words; (3) an entirely new treatment, different in subject, words, and other ornaments. The last of these itself has three subdivisions: (a) the use of other names, general outline, means and ends, as in Vergil's use of Homer and Cicero's of Demosthenes; (b) the use of the same argument, but with different words, sententiae, and figures, as in Horace's imitation of Vergil's descriptions of rustic life; (c) the use, but in a changed form, of topics, sententiae, and words only, as in

---

[46] *Oratione* (1566), p. 7: "si come l'Oratore abbracia la strada larga, e ua uagando per li spaciosi campi di eloquentia non partendosi dalla consuetudine ciuile, a ciò ad un' tempo dimostri la felice copia del suo fauelare. Così ancora tenta con ogni arte, e studio acquistare la desiderata vittoria: el poeta come tende ad un'altro fine, così esce fuori della consuetudine delli huomini, & per questo admirabil' resta, dilettando, e tirando li animi delli ascoltanti con la vaghezza delle parole, la dolceza delle rime, la varietà e la floridezza delle figure, in modo che con la felice representatione delli costumi, gesti, & attioni alle volte in tal modo ci diletta, e dilettando ci tira, che come alienati da noi medesimi ad altro non siamo intenti, quanto che a considerar' la legiadria & felicità di quel poema." Cf. also p. 17 for a restatement.

[47] *Ibid.*, p. 38: "questi tali poeti con la dolcezza delle rime vaghezza, & lisci di parole al primo ci dilettano, ma lasciano gl'animi infettati, & auelenati dalla corruttela delli vitij enormi, e dishoneste suoe narrationi."

Vergil's borrowings from Lucretius and Ariosto's and Petrarch's borrowings from ancient authors. All the latter forms constitute the perfect art of imitation; but Terence did not possess this art, being a mere translator or at best a borrower of plots without the beauty and excellence that should accompany them. He can thus be credited with no talent for invention. (We may remember Speroni's similar strictures on Vergil.) This deficiency is related to Terence's failings in the other kind of imitation, that which consists in the representation of the actions, lives, and characters of men. The criterion here is resemblance: "one poet comes to be called more excellent than another insofar as he comes closer to what is natural, and this talent of expressing actions and characters and, in describing them, of representing faithfully the nature of things and their decorum, gives life, soul, and eloquence to the poet."[48] But Terence's imitations do not resemble nature, largely because of their immorality and obscenity.

These failures in invention are accompanied by unsatisfactory performance in elocution. Grasso concedes that Terence's diction is familiar and in the low style proper to comedy, that the words and sentences are good (albeit somewhat licentious), but not that he is a truly eloquent writer. For true eloquence demands a diction above and beyond that of the people: "It must use more choice and more beautiful words so that, by delighting with the diction, it will hold with wonder the minds of the listeners; and this thing simple and plebeian speech, because it is lacking in ornament and grace, cannot do."[49] One may wonder how Grasso would reconcile his requirement of florid and eloquent language with his notions about the proper style for comedy; but the problem is neither suggested nor solved. One sees at work, throughout Grasso's analysis, the traditional categories of invention and disposition, the rhetorical ends of teaching, delighting, and moving (accompanied by pleasure, admiration, and a kind of rapture), the moral goals of proper instruction and exemplification, and the current notions about imitation taken in its various senses.

GIOVANNI FABRINI (1566)

In 1566, when most Horatians seemed to be devoting themselves exclusively to practical criticism, Giovanni Fabrini da Fighine published a complete commentary in Italian on the *Opere* of Horace. The final section contained the *Ars poetica* "col comento vulgare" and is remarkable on two scores: it is the first commentary written in Italian and the only one in Italian to be published during the Cinquecento. Since Fabrini is writing his gloss in the vulgar tongue, and since he wishes to make "the two languages

---

[48] *Ibid.*, p. 6: "vn' poeta viene esser chiamato piu eccellente del altro quanto che piu s'accosta al naturale, & questa virtu d'esprimer i gesti, costumi, & descriuendo accostarsi alla Natura delle cose, e il decoro da vita, anima, eloquenza del poeta."

[49] *Ibid.*, p. 16: "& vsi parole piu scielte, & leggiadre, aciò con la dolcezza del dir' delettando, tienni ancora con marauiglia gl'animi dell'ascoltanti. La qual cosa non puo il parlar' plebeio & semplice, per esser priuo d'ornamento, & legg adria, operare."

explain each other," he spends much of his time on simple translation or paraphrase of the original; by piecing together the equivalents suggested for each word, one would have a continuous translation of the epistle. Otherwise, he provides the usual identification of historical persons, citation of authorities, and quotation of illustrative examples. Fabrini states at the outset what he thinks to be the content of Horace's treatise: "first it seems to me that in this epistle . . . he teaches the laws of poetry, second that he treats of poetry itself, and finally that he blames and scoffs at those who do not observe in poetry what should be observed by good and true poets."[50] The laws of poetry, he insists, are the same as those taught by Aristotle:

> It seems that Horace in this passage [ll. 1–13] imitated Aristotle, or rather, that poetics is one single art which has only one single path from the beginning to the end, and that he who has perfect knowledge of it, wishing to discourse about it, can discourse about it only in one way; for in truth it is seen that Aristotle and Horace have, from the beginning to the end, proceeded at the same pace, with the same order, and with the same arrangement.[51]

The statement that Horace imitated Aristotle is repeated later: "If you wish to see how Horace means that one should proceed [in imitation], place before yourself this poetics of his and the poetics of Aristotle, which it is clear to see that he imitated, and you will know what is to be done."[52] Convinced, as had been so many of his predecessors, that Horace was copying directly the *Poetics*, Fabrini could not fail to point out numerous parallels between the two texts:

Horace	*Aristotle*
1–13	1450*a*38, 1455*b*12
14–23	1451*b*33, 1451*a*16, –*a*23
24–31	1456*a*25
38–41	1450*b*35
42–45	1459*a*29, 1460*a*1
60–76	1459*b*34, 1460*a*1
90–95	1448*a*14
96–103	1455*a*30, 1456*a*33

[50] *L'Opere d'Oratio* (1566), p. 355: "primieramente mi pare, che in questa epistola . . . egli insegni le leggi de la poesia; secondariamente, che tratti de la poesia, e finalmente biasima, e si ride di coloro, che ne le poesie non osseruano quello, che da buoni, e ueri poeti dee essere osseruato." Much of the pagination in this edition is erroneous, and where errors occur I give first the wrong number as printed and then the correct number.

[51] *Ibid.*, p. 355v: "Pare, che Oratio in questa diuisione habbia imitato Aristotile, ouero, che la Poetica sia un'arte, la quale habbia un solo camino dal principio al fine, e che ragionandosene da chi n'ha perfetta cognitione, non se ne possa ragionar, se non in un modo: perche inuerità si uede, che Aristotile, & Oratio hanno dal principio al fine proceduto con pari passo, col medesimo ordine, e con la medesima dispositione."

[52] *Ibid.*, p. 372v [=368v]: "chi ben uuol uedere, come Oratio intende, che si faccia; mettasi innanzi questa sua poetica, e la poetica d'Aristotile, che manifestamente si uede, che egli hà imitato, e conoscerà, come si dee fare."

Horace	Aristotle
104–13	1457a31(?)
119–27	1453b22, 1454a15
146–52	1459a29
153–65	1454a33
179–92	1460a11, 1453b1, 1450b35, 1454a33
193–201	1456a25
347–60	1460b13
361–65	1454b8

In comparison with some of the commentators of the preceding decade, this is a modest list indeed, and it is more significant for the general statement that it seeks to prove than for its own size.

Fabrini's ideas on the Horatian text itself show the curious eclecticism which by this date is commonplace in Italy. Some of these ideas are merely reflections of the old rhetorical tradition. For example, in his preliminary remarks he points out (quoting Aristotle) that the poet is a poet by reason of invention rather than because he uses rhyme; in connection with lines 42–45, that proper disposition is imperative if the audience is to be pleased; on lines 46–59, that elocution may be made more striking by certain devices. Others show a resemblance to more recent emphases on the part of the commentators; he holds (as Maranta had done) that Horace's main concern is with the distinction between plot and episodes, that in fact this division is the basis for Horace's organization of his *Ars poetica* (p. 355v). Elsewhere, he finds solutions in the ancient philosophers. In his gloss on lines 309–22, where Horace is speaking of the poet's wisdom, Fabrini develops the thesis that this wisdom will consist rather in a knowledge of Ideas than in a knowledge of realities:

> For example, if one wishes to write about the duties of a prince, he should not set before his eyes any individual prince as the example from which he would derive the precepts that a prince should observe; for no single prince is so good that he does not have some fault. But Horace wishes that he should have in mind the example or the Idea of the true prince, and that he should write how a prince ought to be according to that Idea or rather that example. . . . his end is to write how a prince should be, even though it is found that no real prince has ever been that way.[53]

There is a strange mixture here of Horace's ideas on decorum, Aristotle's ideas on the universal, and Plato's ideas on Ideas as seen, probably, through Cicero's *Orator*. Cicero's *Brutus* is quoted on the subject of

---

[53] *Ibid.*, pp. 384v [=380v]–381: "Vno uerbigratia uuole scriuere de l'uffitio d'un Principe. questo tale non si dee proporre innanzi a gli occhi per essempio, donde egli caui i precetti, che dee osseruare un principe: perche nessun principe è tanto buono, che non habbia qualche mancamento: ma uuole, che egli si proponga l'essempio, ouero la idea del uero principe: e scriua, come dee essere un principe, secondo quella idea, ouero quello essempio. . . . il fin suo è di scriuere, come principe dee essere, se bene non si troua, che nessuno mai sia stato tale."

decorum, and Fabrini expands the usual list of topics to include "fortune, age, sex, profession, parentage, nation, and place" (p. 371[=367]); he also makes decorum an equivalent of Aristotle's necessity and probability (p. 375[=371]). Here and there, Fabrini expresses fairly original ideas, as when he finds that tragedy and comedy are comparable in their use of the iambus and in their interchange of styles in certain circumstances (p. 368[=364]); or when, in the perennial controversy on nature versus art, he decides unhesitatingly for the primacy of nature (pp. 383v[=379v], 386); or when he interprets line 128 ("Difficile est proprie communia dicere") in the following way:

> Those matters are called "common" which have never been written down by anybody, for they are in the common domain and anybody can help himself to them. . . . and he speaks the truth, for common material is material without any artificial form whatsoever, in which it is much more difficult to introduce an artificial form than it is to introduce it in a matter which already has some artificial form.[54]

The conception of form and matter provides an illumination (although a questionable one) of this particular passage.

On one subject, the relationship of poems to their audience, Fabrini makes numerous statements which delimit his whole approach to poetry. He apparently has no specific conception of the nature of this audience, for at one place he says that it is composed of both "dotti" and "indotti" (p. 374[=370]), at another—following Horace very closely—of both old and young persons (p. 381v), at still another that the poet has in mind the "popolo" when he writes. But he does have definite ideas about the kinds of things that will affect the audience and what it will believe. It will be more moved by what it sees than by what it hears, but it will reject as incredible certain actions that might be shown to it on the stage. The basis of credibility is again dubious. If, for example, a poet wished to show a mother murdering her children (Medea, obviously), the audience would refuse belief for two reasons: (1) it would not accept the possibility that a mother could actually commit this crime; and (2) it would know that the children so murdered on the stage were of paper, and no belief would ensue (p. 372[=368]). These objections presuppose (1) certain fixed expectations with respect to human behavior and (2) an incapacity, through a lack of imagination, to accept representation for reality. If the same event were narrated, however, the audience would readily give it credence. Without such belief there can be no pleasure for the audience, and hence the "vero" or the "verisimile" is a prerequisite to delight and profit. It is for

---

[54] *Ibid.*, p. 372 [=368]: "Comuni si chiamano quelle materie, che non sono mai state scritte da nessuno: perche sono del comune, & ciascuno se le puo appropriare. . . . e dice la uerità: perche la materia comune è una materia senza alcuna forma artifitiale, doue è molto piu difficile introdurre una forma artifitiale, che non è introdurla in una materia, che hauesse qualche forma artifitiale."

ARS POETICA: PRACTICAL CRITICISM

this reason especially that the poet must observe decorum with the greatest care; if he does, he will please "the educated, because they will recognize the artistry of the writer and will derive pleasure from it; the uneducated, because even if these latter do not know the artistry of the composition, nevertheless they will have pleasure from it because nature in itself, without art, causes things to please whoever sees them whenever they are done with decorum and appropriately."[55] The audience will also find pleasure in the kind of decorations which episodes add to a plot (p. 361v[=357v]) and generally in anything that gives variety to the work: "Variety is a necessary thing and is a great virtue in a poet; for with variety, great delight is given to the listener, and he is made attentive, and he is prevented from being annoyed."[56] Thus, like Horace, although to a greater extent, Fabrini makes much of what may happen within a poem depend upon the likes and the capacity for belief of the audience.

In 1557, Luca Antonio Ridolfi had published at Lyons a *Ragionamento sopra alcuni luoghi del Cento novelle del Boccaccio*, in which Alessandro degli Uberti discussed with Claude d'Herberé various linguistic problems connected with the text of Boccaccio. Some years later (probably around 1567) Lodovico Castelvetro and Francesco Giuntini exchanged letters relating to this *Ragionamento*, which have some bearing on the critical tradition we are here discussing. Castelvetro's *Lettera del Dubioso Academico* answered some of Ridolfi's linguistic objections before passing on to more general remarks on Boccaccio; in these, Castelvetro considerably broadened the whole basis of discussion, making it include both literary and moral issues. On the literary side, his strictures are of two kinds. He objects to a certain number of Boccaccio's stories because in them verisimilitude—and he means exclusively natural verisimilitude—is not properly observed. Everybody knows, for example, that young ladies of good family are carefully guarded by their parents; yet Boccaccio frequently has them meeting with men and he does not tell how this surveillance had been circumvented. Next, Boccaccio does not do all that he might in order to "arouse greater pity in the minds of the readers";[57] he should have treated the sacrament of confession when he was discussing the plague, as a means to awakening in the readers greater compassion for the victims. This objection is closely related to the one which he raises on moral, or rather religious, grounds. He criticizes Boccaccio for his neglect of other sacraments in various of the stories, for attributing to priests actions unbecoming to their office, and

[55] *Ibid.*, pp. 374–74v [=370–70v]; "a dotti: perche conosceranno l'artifitio de lo scrittore, e n'haranno piacere; a gl'indotti: perche se bene essi non conoscono l'artifitio de la compositione; nondimeno n'haranno piacere: perche la natura da per lei senza l'arte fa, che le cose piacciono sempre a chi le uede quando elle son fatte con decoro, & conueneuolmente."
[56] *Ibid.*, p. 358v: "il uariare è cosa necessaria, & è una gran uirtu in un poeta: perche con la uarietà si dà gran dilettatione a l'uditore, e si fa stare attento, e si fa, che non gli rincresce."
[57] *Lettera*, undated ed., p. 12: "& muouere compassione maggiore ne gli animi de Lettori."

for similar offences. These criticisms are essentially outside the limits of the Horatian mode as we have defined it. In his *Risposta* to Castelvetro, Giuntini asserts that although Boccaccio's style has many faults, it may nevertheless be defended against some of Castelvetro's attacks. Then he adds objections of his own, all based, again, on violations of natural verisimilitude. In a lengthy discussion of *Decameron* I, 5, he indicates how some of the objections may be met and how solutions favorable to Boccaccio may be found.[58] Both these critics present, in their practical criticism, contacts with the Horatian tradition in their concern with style, with natural probability, and with effects produced by the work on its readers.

Torquato Tasso returns to this series of practical criticisms with his *Considerazioni sopra tre canzoni di M. Gio. Battista Pigna intitolate Le tre sorelle*, to which Pier Antonio Serassi assigned the date of 1568.[59] The little treatise is largely devoted, as so many of these "lezioni" on sonnets were, to the philosophical content of the work studied, here the conception of love found in Pigna's canzoni. But in several excursions Tasso manifests an interest in theoretical matters. At one point, he compares the canzone as a form with the epic; the shorter poem is less perfect than the longer, but it has its own parts corresponding to those of the epic. Both of them are alike in having a "proposition," an "invocation," and a "narration"; the rhetorical source of these terms is at once apparent. In his comparison of Petrarch and Pigna, he again applies criteria derived from the same source. The comparison revolves around the topics of subject matter, language, versification, and "concetti." Petrarch may seem to be superior on the basis of variety of subject matter; but this, says Tasso, is merely an accident of fortune (the death of Laura having provided him with a new body of materials). Petrarch is more prudent in the choice of his subjects, selecting only those which will clearly lend themselves to "ornament and poetic splendor"; whereas Pigna sometimes chooses sterile subjects and overcomes their difficulties through the strength of his genius. In language, Petrarch is more sparing, Pigna bolder since he is striving for grandeur and majesty; the older poet is more apt to expand and dilate his ideas, while Pigna usually confines his to a brief turn of phrase. Petrarch is clear, Pigna sometimes obscure—but gracefully so. The former puts his words together and organizes his rhythms in a delicate fashion, the latter, more roundly and fully. In the variety of "concetti," "drawn from the innermost fountains of the sciences," Pigna is definitely superior; all in all, his poems are like Horace's paintings, which, when seen at close range, give even more pleasure to the viewer than when seen at a distance.[60] Choice and variety of subject matter, paucity or richness in diction, clarity and obscurity, the

---

[58] *Risposta del Giuntino*, in Castelvetro, *Lettera del Dubioso* (undated), pp. 23-30.
[59] See Guasti, *Prose diverse*, prefatory note to this treatise, II, 73.
[60] *Ibid.*, pp. 81-82, 109-110.

general effect of the versification, these are problems and solutions familiar to the practicing rhetorician.

On the purely theoretical side, Tommaso Correa's *De toto eo poematis genere, quod epigramma vulgo dicitur Libellus* (1569) is different from most of the documents that we have seen thus far in that it develops its theory not with respect to poetry in general but in relation to one of the minor genres, the epigram. A total theory is implicit, but what is said is partial and specific. Correa is much preoccupied with the ends served by the poem and the effects produced by it; and perhaps because of the peculiar character of the epigram as a genre, he sees three different types of relationship between the poem and persons concerned with it. The epigram serves an end, first, with respect to the poet, to whom it brings praise and glory (p. 19), and he must keep in mind these goals when he composes it. Second, it is meant to influence in some way the persons who are its subjects and at whom its praise or blame is directed. At this point more general principles of poetry intervene, in the form of the Horatian idea that the poem must both be useful and give pleasure (p. 22); the utility of the epigram, stated in a general way, consists in the "laus" or the "vituperatio" which it metes out to the persons it treats. This is a part of its very definition: "The epigram is simply a short poem which makes a straightforward mention of something, whether a person or an action; either it is a declaration drawn from what has been stated, in commendation of something, or an expression of censure."[61] The formula appears again in such a series as this: "ad laudem, uituperationem, irrisionem, cauillationem, criminationem" (p. 22).

In order to provide the specific utility for which it exists, the epigram "must show that there is a great baseness present in the vices, an almost divine glory in the virtues; with one single effort it must both moderate the feelings of the soul and render the mores more honest."[62] Third, and perhaps most prominently, it produces an effect upon its general audience, those who merely read about the actions of others but are not involved in them. For this effect Correa has many descriptions, and he repeats them on various occasions. Just as any speech or any poem would presumably do, the epigram "affects and almost seizes upon the most intimate feelings of the soul."[63] The feelings so aroused are ones of pleasure ("voluptas," "delectatio"), of wonder and admiration ("admiratio"), of joy ("gaudio," "laetitia"), and the poem which produces them is pleasant, delightful, praiseworthy ("iucundus," "dulcis," "laudabilis").[64] All these effects are

---

[61] *Libellus* (1569), pp. 25–26: "Epigramma enim nihil est aliud quam breue poema cum simplici rei cuiuspiam indicatione uel personae, uel facti; seu est contestatio deducta ex propositis in commendationem rei alicuius, seu detestationem."

[62] *Ibid.*, p. 23: "demonstret in uitijs summam inesse turpitudinem, prope diuinam gloriam in uirtutibus: una denique, eademq́ue opera & sensus animi leniter afficiat, & mores cohonestet."

[63] *Ibid.*, p. 19: "intimos animi sensus afficiat, ac pene capiat."

[64] See esp. pp. 21, 23, 32, 39, 98.

such as might result from any form of poetry. But they are produced in a special way by the specific qualities of the epigram; its universal and particular qualities are combined in such a passage as the following:

In fact, if it is beautiful, well proportioned and unified, polished and perfect, so that its parts cohere and harmonize among themselves in such a way as to express clearly, briefly, sharply and elegantly any thought, it arouses admiration and produces an extraordinary pleasure. It requires great art, wit, sharpness of talent, becoming brevity, and a certain dexterity and discernment.[65]

Horace's vague recommendations for cohesion and appropriateness are contained in the first sentence, the peculiar characteristics of the epigram in the second. The latter, in combination with the effects they produce, are repeated and expanded a little later: "But in the epigram the brevity delights us, the sharpness arouses us, the harmony seizes us, the thought remains with us, the humor pervades our mind with an incredible pleasure."[66]

Such broad descriptions as these apply to all forms of the epigram; for it is not a single genre, but has many subforms related to it, such as the epitaph, the "naenia, epicedium, monodia, threnus, elogium, aenus, palinodia." These in turn fall into three categories as they conform to one or another of the three kinds of oratory; that is, there are judicial epigrams, deliberative epigrams, and epideictic epigrams (p. 45). In a general way, there are as many different kinds of epigrams as there are subject matters treated in the form: "Tot enim epigrammatum sunt genera, quot et rerum, de quibus texitur" (p. 50). Correa establishes, for each of the kinds, a principle of appropriateness that is merely an application of his general theory: each subject matter will demand a special style (one of the three) and a special verse form (all verses are admissible in the genre).

In true Renaissance fashion, Correa does not fail to include, along with his dicta on the ends of the epigram and the means by which they are achieved, indications about the particular genius of the poet necessary to produce poems in the genre. His initial assumption is Horatian: the poet needs both nature and art to produce the perfect poem. This is translated into two substitute terms which reveal his meaning, "iudicium" and "imitatio." About the first, naturally acquired, he has little to say; about the second, artificially developed, he has many suggestions. Imitation is the imitation of ancient poets; unnecessary for the ancients, it is indispensable for moderns, and no contemporary poet can succeed without it. It operates in this manner:

[65] *Ibid.*, p. 19: "Nam illud si uenustum, aptum connexumque sit, teres, & rotundum, ut inter se ita partes cohaereant, & congruant, ut distincte, breuiter, acute, et ornate sententia exprimatur, & admirationem mouet, & uoluptatem affert, non uulgarem. Multa arte opus est; sale, ingenij acumine, breuitate decora, dexteritate quadam, & iudicio."

[66] *Ibid.*, p. 21: "Sed in epigrammate breuitas delectat, acumen excitat, concinnitas capit, haeret sententia, lepor uoluptate incredibili animum perfundit." For other similar statements, see pp. 23, 24, 25, 32, 39, 49.

We must therefore consider carefully in what way the old poets expressed the feelings of the soul, what they judged to be poetic and what they judged not to be poetic; in accordance with what order, ornaments and figures, what rhythms, length, method, even in particulars, we should adapt our own epigram. . . . In order that we may more easily and properly compose a perfect epigram and more diligently polish it to perfection, it will be very useful for us to compare the various ways in which other poets treated the same subject, so that we may understand in what way these poets achieved proper form, and in what respect another failed; thus we shall become more prudent through the errors of others and by the trials of others we may make trial of our own talent.[67]

Such qualities and procedures as these might of course be assigned to poets practicing in any genre; the argument so far remains general. The epigrammatist must possess in addition the peculiar capacities necessary for his art: cleverness, wittiness, artistry, judgment, and the ability to estimate the nature of the subject matter (p. 23). A particular kind of poetic talent thus becomes the basis for the correct assorting of matter, style, and prosodic form.

Correa's little treatise is an interesting example of the adaptation of the Horatian mode to a specific literary type. Its conceptions of the ends of poetry, of the principles of internal organization, of the poet's talent and method are closely related to the *Ars poetica*. But at every point, and above all in its notions of the three styles, the "res-verba" relationship, the effects produced in the audience, and the personal glory sought by the poet, it extends beyond the basic text and makes contact with the broader rhetorical tradition.

The latter tradition far outweighs the purely Horatian elements in Pietro Pagano's *Discorso sopra il secondo sonetto del Petrarca*, an undated manuscript in the British Museum (Additional MS 33,470), to which I have given an arbitrary date of about 1570. Pagano's main intention is to provide a running commentary on the text, with special attention to the effects produced by words and figures. But he begins with the customary statements about the poet's model (here, Euripides' *Hippolytus*), about the reasons why poets invoke the gods or the muses, about the nature of the action and the classification of the poem. He finds that the action is a single one but not a simple one since it is accompanied by passions. As for the classification, it is derived from Aristotle's *Rhetoric*: "And since every discourse and composition falls, according to the opinion of Aristotle, under one of the three types, demonstrative, or deliberative, or judicial, we shall

---

[67] *Ibid.*, pp. 82, 85–86: "Videndum igitur diligenter est, quomodo ueteres animi sensa exposuerint, quae poetica iudicarint, quae non: quo ordine, quibus luminibus, & figuris, quibus numeris, qua longitudine, qua ratione, & in singulis accommodemus epigramma nostrum" and "Quo facilius, & commodius perfectum epigramma componere queamus, & diligentiam expoliendi adhibere erit utilissimum conferre rem eandem a diuersis poetis explicatam, ut quomodo his assequatur decorum, qua in re ille fuerit mancus, intelligamus: ut in alienis erroribus cautiores efficiamur, et aliorum periculis faciamus de nostro ingenio peri-

say that this sonnet belongs to the judicial kind, and in that part of the assumptive juridical constitution which is called translation of the fault, where guilt is transferred to another person."[68] In the treatment of this kind of subject matter, Petrarch uses the form of expression called by Hermogenes σεμνότης, or the "grave," and his sonnet belongs to the highest level of this form since it speaks of the action of a powerful god. The effect produced is admiration, resulting from an unexpected event (fol. 6v). When Pagano passes from generalities of style to the individual passages of Petrarch's sonnet, he cites Book II of the *Rhetoric* on the figures of speech and points out Petrarch's conformity to the teachings of the rhetoricians. Finally, he indicates how Petrarch achieves the ends of poetry:

> And since poets must delight and profit, we might say that he delights with the poetic fiction, supposing that a powerful god has wounded him with a mortal blow; that he profits, next, because he teaches man that he should take heed not to allow himself to be vanquished by vain and carnal love, lest he should have happen to him what happened to Petrarch; for man can never disentangle himself from that knot. But the profit would be much better shown if one were to give the poem an allegorical and a Christian explanation.[69]

Whereupon Pagano proceeds to offer such an interpretation of the sonnet. The rhetorical tone of Pagano's whole approach is evident, and it is crossed in an interesting fashion with certain medieval practices, such as this closing allegorical interpretation.

What Pagano meant by "the highest level of the grave form" is explained fully in another contemporary document, the *Commentarius in Longinum*, attributed to Franciscus Portus and probably dating from around 1570.[70] The commentary is important since it brings, as it were, a new dimension into the critical tradition that we are here discussing. We have seen throughout the development of this tradition an emphasis upon the three styles and various kinds of relationship established between Horace's theories and this conception of the styles; in more recent years, we have seen the

---

[68] MS BM Add. 33,470, fols. 5–5v: "Et perche ogni ragionamento, et componimento, casca, secondo l'opinione d'Aristotele, sotto uno delli tre genere, ó Demonstratiuo, ó Deliberatiuo, ó Giudiciale, diremo, che questo sonetto uersa nel genere Giudiciale, et in quella parte della constitutione giuridiciale assontiua, che si chiama translatione del mancamento, quando si transferisce la colpa in altra persona."

[69] *Ibid.*, fol. 15: "Et perche li Poeti deuono dilettare, et giouare, potressimo dire, che diletta con la fictione poetica, con fingere, che un Dio potente l'habbia ferito di colpo mortale; che gioua poi, perche insegna all'huomo, che auertisca che non si lascia uincere d'Amore uano, et lasciuo, che non gli intrauenga quello, che á lui è auenuto, che l'huomo non puo mai suilupparsi da tal nodo. Ma molto piu si mostrarebbe il giouamento, quando si uolesse allegoricamente dichiarare, et christianamente."

[70] On the reasons for the attribution and the objections to it, see "Translations and Commentaries of Longinus, *On the Sublime*, to 1600: A Bibliography," *Modern Philology*, XLVII (1950), 149. I have since found confirmation for the attribution in the existence of Modena Estense MS y.S.3.18, Parte II[a], fols. 1–87. This MS of the *Commentarius* bears Portus' name.

four forms or Ideas of Hermogenes associated with the same theories, giving somewhat more variety and flexibility to critical discussion. What Portus does is to interpret Longinus, now, as a treatise on Hermogenes' "sublime, magnificent, and grave form of expression." Longinus' *On the Sublime* lends itself, of course, to such an interpretation, given its emphasis on the effects produced by diction and figures of speech. Thus, Portus' initial statement in the commentary is a distinction of the four subtypes of the grave style, highest of which is the one that speaks truly of God or the gods. Just as Longinus himself had done, he selects examples indiscriminately from the sciences and the various branches of philosophy, and Aristotle or Cicero may serve to exemplify a given style as well as Homer or Horace. The significant consideration everywhere is the nature of the subject matter treated. Portus also distinguishes three methods for handling the grave or sublime style: clearly and unambiguously, allegorically, and secretly or mysteriously. He comes closest to poetic theory, however, when he states his ideas on words, which come to belong to the sublime form either through their sound or because they are used metaphorically. The poet, who otherwise has much in common with the orator, is distinguished from him on this basis:

They [the poets] may doubtless be freer and more audacious in using words figuratively; orators must be much more diffident. Among poets, the tragic, lyric, and dithyrambic poets are more daring than all the others; to be sure, they seem to aim and strive to make their verse inflated and turgid. Tragic poets achieve this most easily because the persons they introduce are above the ordinary in station; of course, they present on the stage kings and princes, so that, taking the persons into account, the verse must be elevated and more sublime.[71]

At other places, as in the remarks on section 7 of Longinus (p. 293), Portus extends his comparison of poets and orators. This he does on the assumption that the sublime may appear either in prose or in poetry ("sive in soluta oratione, sive in poësi") and that in either case it represents a certain kind of state of soul and produces a similar effect in the audience. His contention with respect to audience is that it should judge not as the ignorant masses do but as serious and wise men do ("non plebeiorum & imperitorum more, sed ut solent graves & sapientes homines," p. 339), that is, in terms of the virtues rather than of the defects of the work. Perhaps one should say rather "the defects of the passage," since nowhere in Portus is there any consideration of works other than as assemblages of passages.

---

[71] Ed. Pearce (Amsterdam, 1733), p. 282: "Sunt nimirum liberiores, & audaciores in verbis transferendis: Oratores multo verecundiores. Inter Poëtas, Tragici, Lyrici, & Dithyrambici audent prae caeteris: illud nimirum spectare, affectareque videntur, ut carmen sit inflatum & turgidum. Tragici facilius id obtinent, quòd personae quas inducunt, habent non mediocrem dignitatem. inducunt nimirum reges, & principes in scenam, ita ut habita personarum ratione necessario tollatur carmen, & fiat sublimius."

He remains close to the text he is explaining, and his poetic theory is limited to a theory of styles, diction, and effects.

The *Lettione [sulla favola]* which Baccio Neroni prepared for delivery to the Accademia degli Alterati around 1571 is also restricted, but in a different way; it attacks the proposition, defended by Carlo Rucellai in an earlier lecture, that every plot does not need to comprise recognition and reversal. Hence, it deals solely with aspects of plot. Aristotelian though the problem would seem to be from its statement, it nevertheless is attacked from a Horatian point of view by Neroni. His premises for the discussion are a mixture of the two authorities:

> Plots having been ordered and composed, as are all other things, to some end, undoubtedly those which will be organized in such a way that they achieve the end to which they are directed will be the only ones worthy to be called plots, and the others will not even be taken into account.... And it is a certain thing that poets in composing plots have as their end either to profit or to delight, and that for no other reason do they put themselves to this trouble than to be of some usefulness to men. Wherefore when they compose either tragedies or comedies or epic poems they have their eye on this end, and in order to achieve it they use those means which best lead them to it. To do this, reversal and recognition are powerful above all the other parts that are found in these poems, since they are those which are more apt than the others to move the passions, and they seize upon the souls of persons, either delighting them or moving them to disdain or to compassion according to the action that is being represented.[72]

In pursuing his argument, Neroni cites Aristotle's definitions of the two parts; but for the rest, he argues almost exclusively by citing examples from such poets as Homer, Vergil, Sophocles, Euripides, and Terence. His conclusion is that since all genres display the use of recognition and reversal, they are necessary in all genres. Neroni's Horatianism in this lecture is limited to his conception of the ends of poetry.

As an adjunct to Lodovico Dolce's translations of Homer and Vergil, Andrea Menechini published in 1572 an oration *Delle lodi della poesia, d'Omero, et di Virgilio*, a highly inflated and bombastic discourse, which repeats most of the sixteenth-century commonplaces in praise of poetry. It belongs to theoretical criticism insofar as it makes general statements about the ends served by the art, to practical criticism in the later pages where it

---

[72] MS Laur. Ashb. 559, fol. 1: "Essendo le fauole state ordinate et composte, si come tutte le altre cose, à qualche fine, quelle senza dubbio che in tal modo saranno disposte, che quel fine conseguitino, al quale son indiritte, saranno solamente da essere chiamate fauole, et dell'altre non sara da tenerne conto alcuno.... Et è cosa per certa, che i poeti nel comporre le fauole hanno per fine, o di giouare, o dilettare, et che per altro non si muouono ad affaticarsi se non per essere di qualche utilita agli huomini, Onde componendo essi, ò tragedie, ò comedie, ò poemi Heroici in tuttj hanno l'occhio à tal fine, per il quale conseguir adoperano que mezzi, che meglio uegli conducono, alche fare sopra tutte le parti che si trouano in tali poemi sono potentissime la Peripetia. et la recognitione, come quelle che sono piu che altro atte à muouere gli affetti, et pigliano gli animi delle persone, ò dilettando, ò mouendo à sdegno, ò à compassione secondo il fatto. che allora si rappresenta."

gives appreciations of Homer and Vergil. The ends, as we might expect, are utility and pleasure. Concerning utility, rather than develop a reasoned argument (since that is neither his method nor his tone), Menechini accumulates in a haphazard fashion as many kinds of usefulness as he can think of. Some of these are historical, such as the civilizing function of poetry in its early days and its use by religion (p. a iv); some are remote from everyday life, such as the everlasting fame or infamy bestowed upon the good or the wicked by the poet (p. b). In a more immediate and more present way, poetry is the "corrector of our life" (p. a ij*v*), largely through the examples which it furnishes us of monstrous things that we must avoid and of desirable things that we must follow. Examples of these kinds are deduced from the actions narrated by the poet, which are much more effective than those told by the historian since they are relieved of dross and imperfection (p. b ij). Through its delineations of characters, poetry will teach us the duties and functions of every kind of man and woman in every phase of life. Especially, it will lead us into paths of virtue, making us chaste and simple, and this it will do better than any other discipline. And so we may ask, thinking of Vergil's excellence:

What philosopher ever taught us more graceful behavior? what orator ever persuaded us more ardently to follow the road to the virtues? what jurist ever ordered us to treat with greater prudence the affairs of state? to regulate with greater wisdom our magistrates? to take more holy counsel in high matters? to help the fatherland with hotter zeal?[73]

All these things it does because of its superior capacity to persuade and because it is accompanied by pleasure.

Menechini does not specify the nature of this pleasure, but he does point out its manifold sources. Principal among them, perhaps, is the imitation contained in poetry, which fills us with incredible delight (how or why we do not know). More directly, we derive pleasure from such technical elements as harmony, rhyme, diction, and maxims; Menechini collects these sources in the following apostrophe to poetry:

Shall I be silent about the delight that is derived from you, when there is no harmony that more sweetly strikes our minds? For what ordered discourse, what eloquent language can be more sweet and more pleasant than a lovely sound and a pure concord of harmonious verses felicitously unrolled? What more elegant and adorned speech can generate in us as much joy as a high composition of beautiful and chosen rhymes, all full and resounding? What is more ingenious and full of greater marvel than a very beautiful subject developed with very ornate

---

[73] *Delle lodi* (1572), p. e iv*v*: "Qual Filosofo ci insegnò più gratiosi costumi? qual' Orator ci persuase più ardentemente d'incaminar' alle Virtù? qual Giureconsulto ci diede ordine di trattar con maggior prudenza le cose publiche? di regger con più rara Sapienza i Magistrati? di consigliar più santamente gli alti affari? di aiutar la Patria con più caldo zelo?"

and very lovely words, adorned with the splendor of wise and most grave maxims, sung according to the perfect rule of Music?[74]

Finally, we presumably are pleased at the discovery, within a good poem, of the riches and the treasures of all the arts, sciences, and disciplines.

On the side of practical criticism, the same considerations will of course be prominent. Vergil is praised, for example, for the vehemence, the carefulness, the felicity of his diction, for his abundance of words and their correctness; from these, one obtains the pleasures proper to poetry. I suppose that the same would be true for the gravity of his maxims and the artful disposition of his materials. He would also make profitable reading since he teaches all the lessons that the good poet should teach and since he displays every imaginable kind of knowledge. In every other aspect he is excellent, approaching as close to perfection as any man may do. These judgments of Menechini's are vague and general in character, making no specific reference to texts or parts of them. They come from the application of a small number of topics which belong, almost entirely, to the tradition of the Horatians.

Franciscus Portus, who died in 1581, left behind him (in addition to the *Commentarius in Longinum* already discussed) a number of other unpublished works. Two of these, the *Prolegomena* to Sophocles' tragedies and the *Orationes*, were published together by his son Aemilius in 1584; I presume them to have been written about 1575. Both contain materials pertinent to the present analysis. The title-page of the *Prolegomena* announces that the work contains as well a section on the comparison of tragedy and comedy and another on the relative merits of Sophocles and Euripides. And from Portus' early statement that tragedy and comedy both derive from nature through imitation, one is led to expect some fairly original ideas on the subject. But the hope is soon dashed, for it becomes clear that Portus has in mind no mimetic theory of poetry, but wishes merely to differentiate between tragedy and comedy on the basis of the different kinds of "life" they represent. Man's life is divided into fortunate and unfortunate events; comedy treats the first, tragedy the second. From then on, the distinctions are such as might have been found in Donatus or Diomedes or any of their medieval continuators:

... in comedy, the fortunes of men are moderate, their fears [for their safety] are small, the dangers small, the endings are happy; in tragedy, on the other hand, the persons are of great importance, their fears are great, the endings are fatal; in the former the first events are agitated, the last ones calm; in tragedy, contrari-

---

[74] *Ibid.*, p. e iij: "Tacerò il diletto, che da te si prende, non ui essendo armonia, che più addolcisca l'intelletto nostro? perciò che qual' ordinato parlare, qual' eloquente lingua può esser più dolce, ò più soaue, che un leggiadro suono, & puro concento di armoniosi uersi felicissimamente spiegati? Qual' oratione più culta, & più adorna può generar' in noi tanta gioia, che un' alto componimento di uaghe, & scielte rime, tutte piene, & risuonanti? Qual cosa è più ingeniosa, & piena di maggiore stupore, che un bellissimo soggetto spiegato con ornatissime, & leggiadrissime parole, illustrato con splendor di saggie, et grauissime sentenze, cantato con perfetta ragion di Musica?"

ARS POETICA: PRACTICAL CRITICISM

wise, the beginnings are joyous and peaceful, the endings disturbed and fateful; and in tragedy the life to be avoided is expressed, in comedy the life to be sought. Finally, comedy invents its subjects, tragedy frequently borrows them from historical truth.[75]

In the comparison between Euripides and Sophocles, the criteria are largely rhetorical. Euripides is said to be less pretentious, hence close to oratory and more acceptable to the popular ear. He is more useful to those who wish to learn how to act, since he is full of maxims and commonplaces. In the arousing of the emotions he is, to quote Aristotle, the most tragic poet of all. Sophocles is always grave, tragic, sublime, grandiloquent; but he tempers gravity with joy, tragic severity with poetic sweetness, and as a result produces great delight through the arousing of pity and admiration, the two feelings proper to tragedy (p. 13).

The second of the *Orationes* is subtitled "Qua Historia, & Historici laudantur." I cite it here not only because it contains, along toward the end, a comparison of history and poetry, but because the terms in which it praises history are almost identical with those familiar in the defences of poetry. Were one to substitute the word "poetry" for the word "history" in the discussion, the rest would be acceptable as an oration on the uses of poetry. The historians, Portus tells us, "set before us examples of lives, characters, exploits, deliberations, and events, upon all of which posterity when it gazes as if at certain pictures, may easily take counsel for both its public and its private affairs."[76] All things in life and in nature are recorded by history, so that we have before our eyes "the things that we must avoid and those that we must follow" (p. 60). We also learn from the reading of history how to form our own characters so that we may ultimately become men, shunning the vices that we see in some, imitating the virtues of others. These effects are not purely intellectual in their origins; we are swayed, moved, impressed by the way in which the history is written: "Who indeed does not take delight in the skilful descriptions of places and regions? Who in reading is not kept attentive by the variety of epochs, the vicissitudes of fortune, the great and important deeds accomplished by various illustrious heroes and placed by the historian almost under the eyes and before the face of everybody?"[77] Aware of the argument that the same things might

[75] *Prolegomena* (1584), p. 12: "in Comoedia mediocres fortunae hominum, parui metus, parua pericula, exitus laeti sunt. In Tragoedia contrà ingentes personae, magni metus, funesti sunt exitus: in illa, turbulenta prima, tranquilla postrema: in Tragoedia contrà, principia laeta & pacata, exitus turbulenti, & funesti: & in Tragoedia vita fugienda, in Comoedia vita expetenda exprimitur. Denique Comoedia fingit argumenta. Tragoedia saepe ab historica fide petit."

[76] *Ibid.*, p. 59: "exempla vitae, morum, factorum, consiliorum, atque euentuum proponunt, in quae omnis posteritas tanquam in tabulas quasdam inspiciens, & publicis rationibus, & priuatis rebus facilè consulat."

[77] *Ibid.*, p. 62: "Quem enim non delectent locorum ac regionum scitae descriptiones? quem in legendo non retineant temporum varietates, fortunae vicissitudines, res maximae grauissimaeque à clarissimis quibúsque viris gestae, ac sub oculos, aspectúmque omnium penè ab historico subiectae?"

be said about poetry or oratory, Portus answers it by declaring the superiority of history to both arts. Poetry is less effective since it relates falsehoods or incredible actions and hence loses the confidence of the reader; the more closely it resembles true history, the better it is. Oratory exaggerates its effects, thereby alienating certain listeners, or it sins by excess of any one of the numerous passions which it seeks to awaken. Philosophy itself, when it wishes to argue effectively on matters of individual character and public affairs, must borrow from history a host of supporting examples. I have previously pointed out (Chapter I, pages 13–16) that a large group of theorists associated history with poetry as a sister art, and the reader may remember that the points of contact indicated were precisely those which Portus here claims for history alone.

ALDO MANUZIO (1576)

After a lapse of ten years, from 1566 (date of Giovanni Fabrini da Fighine's Italian commentary) to 1576, we come again to a formal commentary on the *Ars poetica*, this one in Latin and the work of Aldo Manuzio the Younger. It does not have much new to offer. Most of the remarks on individual passages are the same as the ones made earlier, and frequently they do not go beyond simple paraphrase. In an introductory section, called the "Prolegomena," Manuzio gives initial definitions of poetry, deriving his materials largely from Aristotle (four different texts from the *Poetics* are quoted, 1447a13, 1451b27, 1447a29, 1447b26). He seems to be most intent, here, upon establishing the nature of verisimilitude and the roles of truth and falsehood in poetry. In the body of the commentary itself, the references to Aristotle are slight; the list below gives them all:

Horace	*Aristotle*
1–23	1451b27
73–88	1449a24, 1459a11, 1459b8, 1460a1, –a5
89–113	1455a31, 1455a27, 1456a2
113–27	1454a15, 1454a30
128–52	1451b27
191–219	1454a37, 1452b16
220–33	1449a19, 1453a4
234–43	1449a19
275–94	1449a15
295–308	1455a33
347–65	1454a30

It will be noted that even in this short list, several of the texts appear twice; one of them, *Poetics* 1451b27, is used three times in all. They are all very general in nature ("Poetry is an imitation," "The poet is a poet by virtue of the imitation and not because he uses verse") and show neither a thorough knowledge of Aristotle nor an intention to make of him a source or a counterpart of Horace.

On the other hand, there are almost as many references to the rhetorical works of Cicero. But here again they are miscellaneous in character and do not go together to make up a rhetorical theory. Manuzio follows the lead of almost all his predecessors in pointing out a parallel between Horace's theories and the oratorical divisions of invention, disposition, and elocution; yet he does so only in passing, in the following sentence: "The sixth precept treats of eloquence in diction; for in the first place he gave his precepts on invention when he said: 'Cui lecta potenter erit res,' then on order, finally on elocution; this the rhetoricians also do."[78] The sixth precept, deduced from lines 46–72, is the last so named; for although Manuzio had begun with an orderly enumeration and stating of precepts, after this one he abandons the method. We shall probably be forced to conclude that in this as in other aspects his commentary is imperfect and haphazard. There is no attempt to distinguish any plan in Horace's work, to impose a general interpretation upon it; the commentary remains a collection of isolated glosses. These tend, for the most part, to be very simple, much simpler than those of the preceding generation of scholars. Sometimes this is an advantage, since unwarranted subtleties are avoided; but at other times the meat of Horace's meaning is missed. For example, the first twenty-three lines are said to contain two precepts: the first, the poet should stick to the subject that he has undertaken; the second, he should avoid descriptions since they would not be in keeping with his serious subject matter. In only a few cases does Manuzio offer interesting readings, as when he declares (against the major part of the antecedent tradition) that the "communia" of line 128 means materials which have already been used by another poet and are hence available for imitation (rather than unused materials open to all comers); or as when he insists, in connection with line 151, that truth is necessary for the poet (else where would the imitation be?), that if he treats only the truth he becomes a historian, and that hence truth must be tempered by falsehood. These few passages relieve only slightly the mediocrity of the text; one misses here the enthusiasm, the scholarship, and the imagination of some of the earlier commentaries.

CONCLUSIONS

Manuzio's commentary is perhaps an unfortunate work on which to end the present chapter, for it leaves an impression of disappointment and a sense of the decadence of a tradition. Perhaps this is in itself significant. For the fifteen-year period under consideration has been distinguished less for its illuminations of the Horatian text than for its expansion and application of the Horatian mode independent of the text itself. While there have been three extensive commentaries, the bulk of the progress in theory has

---

[78] *In Q. Horatii Flacci librum de arte poetica Commentarius* (1576), p. 10: "Sextum praeceptum, de facundia. nam de inuentione primo loco, cum dixit, *Cui lecta potenter erit res*, tum de ordine, postremo de elocutione praecipit: quod etiam rhetores faciunt."

been made in the shorter theoretical articles or incidentally to practical criticism. In the field of practical criticism, this period has contained the first sizable body of pertinent materials and has permitted us to see in what way contemporary critics translated their theory into actual appreciations of works.

Of the specifically Horatian ideas, the one most constantly repeated, developed, and modified by the theorists is the notion of utility and pleasure as the ends of poetry. In a sense, this becomes the hallmark of the mode. Many writers who seem to know little else of the *Ars poetica* emphasize the importance of "prodesse" and "delectare," of the "utile dulci," as the ends to be sought. In these particular years, the stress is probably stronger on utility; writers are concerned with the moral implications of poems and are insistent that they must contribute to the betterment of the individual or of society. They relate to this their preoccupations with truth and verisimilitude; for the general assumption is that moral effects will be properly accomplished only if the audience believes what it sees or reads, and that this belief depends upon the correct admixture of the true or the seeming-true into the ingredients of the poem. The need for the marvelous, the strange, the extraordinary (both to capture the attention of the audience and to give it pleasure) is a complicating factor, and many critics debate the relationship between truth and falsehood, the credible and the incredible. In these debates, the character of the audience enters as a consideration, since the capacity for believing is recognized as varying from group to group. Here, the ground has shifted somewhat from Horace's old man or young man, senator or nut-eating farmer, to the wise against the ignorant, the elite against the masses. It is difficult to see a preference, for Tasso will declare just as loudly in favor of the common people as Maranta does for the "selectissimi viri." For the most part, though, critics at this time seem to have in mind an audience educated at least in two special fields, the rules and requirements of the art of poetry and the eternal laws of decorum.

Considerations of the audience lead us away from the Horatian text strictly interpreted and into the broader rhetorical tradition of which it is by this time an integral part. The explicit comparison between the poet and the orator still serves a number of theorists as a starting point for developing their ideas about the poetic art; for some, the historian replaces the orator or becomes a third writer in the comparison. The more complete these comparisons are, the more nearly the theories propounded take on a special flavor. Thus for many writers there is little perceptible difference between their theories of poetry and the usual doctrine of the rhetorics. They talk constantly about invention, disposition, and elocution; they organize their materials around "res" and "verba"; they construct elaborate systems on the basis of decorum. Only rarely, as in the case of Maranta, does anybody warn against the basic impropriety of such a procedure for the discussion of poetry. One of the most persistent forms of rhetorical approach is via the notion of the effects produced in the audience, and in the years from 1560 to 1567 an even wider variety than had previously existed is introduced into the conception of these effects. Poetry, of course, must move the passions of the audience; but it must also arouse admiration, it must produce a kind of rapture, it must inspire to virtue and create an abhorrence of vice. Thinking of this sort in terms of rhetorical ends was bound to lead to thinking in terms of rhetorical means, and hence we have a growing desire to speak of such parts of a poem as the proposition, the narration, the exordium, and to classify poems as belonging to one or another of the known types of oratory.

Special note must be taken of the attention paid to two sets of ideas, the notion of the fixed styles and the theory of the fixed genres. The first of these goes back to ancient rhetoric, but it was enriched by medieval theorists of poetry; then these Cinquecento critics add certain refinements. As a result, a "style" is now no longer merely a form of diction or discourse; it involves as well certain kinds of actors or personages, certain kinds of actions, a special variety of "thoughts" or maxims, and corresponding effects in the reader or listener. Any poetic genre falls within one of the styles (the traditional Ciceronian three or the four of Hermogenes) and is circumscribed by it from the outset. To the ideas of Donatus and Diomedes concerning the subject matter, the meter, and some of the mechanics of individual genres, critics now bring more subtle conceptions of the style, the kind of figures, the sententiae, the qualitative and quantitative parts, and the specific reactions aroused in the audience. Consequently, these more and more restrict the freedom of the poet as he operates within a given genre, especially if he must at the same time practice the form only as he finds it exploited in the works of his model.

Throughout this theorizing, Aristotle enters much less prominently as a source than he had done in the earlier years. There are still commentators who insist that Horace used Aristotle as his exemplar—Maranta and Fabrini are examples—but there are fewer than previously. For the most part, references to the *Poetics* are scattered and incidental, centering about standard parallels and obvious resemblances, and the main body of theory proceeds independently of them. On the contrary, there is probably somewhat greater use of Plato (this matter will be investigated in later chapters), and we have even seen one reference to Longinus—indications, even if inconsiderable ones, of a broadening of the critical horizon. A few citations of Demetrius' *On Style* and an almost faddish use of Hermogenes would tend to confirm this supposition.

In the domain of practical criticism, the proliferation of documents in these years affords us an opportunity of estimating the state of opinion with respect to a number of literary types and a number of authors, both ancient and modern. We have evaluations not only of the epic, tragedy, and comedy (represented by Homer and Vergil, Sophocles and Euripides, and Terence), but also of such newer forms as the sonnet (Petrarch and Giovanni della Casa) and the verse "romanzo" (Ariosto). It must be said immediately that some of this criticism represents no advance over earlier periods and might have been written at any time during the previous one hundred years; I mean here on the one hand the compliments to the poet's genius, to his faculties and knowledge, to the divine furor as it operates within him; on the other hand, the repetition of those time-worn epithets that had constituted the only evaluative apparatus of a Pietro Ricci or a Lilio Gregorio Giraldi. Most of these epithets refer to style. But this "criticism by epithets" is now a secondary tendency; primarily, writers are making some application—through intention or habit—of the theoretical positions evolved. Frequently they begin, as the theorists did, with a comparison of their author to the orator or the historian and derive judgments from the comparison; Benedetto Grasso affords an example of such an approach.

With even greater frequency (undoubtedly because they regard it as more important) they speak of poets in terms of the ends achieved, remarking upon the peculiar qualities of the delight procured or the effectiveness with which the utility is achieved. This leads some critics (such as Grasso and Castelvetro) to make severe moral judgments, the "utility" here being a negative one and involving improper or unacceptable moral lessons. At times, the objections are on religious grounds; but I believe that these belong rather to the Platonic mode, which I shall be discussing later. For such enthusiastic judges as Menechini, the chief value of the poetry they were considering was in its positive contribution to the moral improvement of its readers. The old medieval justification by allegory still serves as an auxiliary to the discussion of the utilitarian ends of poetry; certain poems whose moral lessons are not immediately discernible are endowed with them by means of an allegorical interpretation.

Just as for the theorists, the problem of verisimilitude was of primary importance for the practical critics. They asked constantly whether the actions and persons represented in a poem were "true to life"; the answer depended upon several criteria: for actions, upon their conceptions of Aristotle's necessity and probability; for persons, upon the laws of decorum. It should be pointed out, again, that for such men as Castelvetro and Giuntini probability was always natural, never artistic; that is, an action was probable because they thought of life as producing actions in the same way, not because it had been made probable by the prior conditions and preparations of the poem itself. As for decorum, the requirements seem to grow more stringent from year to year, until one wonders how a poet, once he had elected to treat a given kind of character, could have done otherwise than to copy in detail the treatments of his predecessors.

Sperone Speroni and Bartolomeo Maranta on Vergil may serve as examples of another typically rhetorical procedure in practical criticism, that is, the inquiry into the invention, disposition, and elocution of their subject poet. Others, of course, did the same, making judgments upon the originality of the poet or upon his skill as an imitator of other poets (both related to invention), upon his arrangement of the parts of his poem, and especially upon his handling of diction. It is sometimes difficult to distinguish treatments of invention, disposition, and elocution from treatments of such qualitative parts as plot and character (associated with invention) and thought and diction (associated usually with elocution); for, as we have seen, theorists and practical critics alike effected a conflation of the two sets of terms. Once again, Speroni supplies us with a typical discussion here, examining in detail Vergil's deficiencies in plot construction and in character development and giving a half-hearted approval to his handling of diction.

I must emphasize the extent to which considerations of sententiae and of diction dominate the practical criticism of this period. The use of epithets describing style was not an accident, for one of the tendencies of rhetorical approaches was to reduce all critical questions to questions of figures of speech and ornaments of diction. Maranta's long *Lucullianae quaestiones* presents an extreme case of analysis and praise of all aspects of style, but there were many others in which the intention was the same even if the results were not so monumental. The whole matter of prosodic excellence is linked to this same brand of criticism, since the sounds of words become as much a subject of investigation as their sense. The position of sententiae, again, is a special one. The seeker after moral usefulness, the lover of philosophical wisdom, the student of mores and character, all found in the little "pearls of wisdom" contained in these maxims one of the most satisfying parts of the poems they read. Hence the praise so frequently bestowed upon the gravity, the variety, the truth of a given author's sententiae. Such statements would, of course, have been equally appropriate to maxims found in orations, in histories, in philosophical writings, or anywhere else; this the critics realized and admitted, but the realization did not deter them. Poems rarely existed for them as complete works of art; in the main, they were content to separate from them this or that component and to judge it independently of the rest.

A final result of the application of rhetorical theories to practical criticism was the habit of judging on the basis of rules and conventions and on the basis of the three (or four) styles. Horace himself had set the pattern for the habit by his remarks on the five-act division of drama, on the three interlocutors, on the "deus ex machina." Critics of the Cinquecento developed and expanded it, and in a writer like Castelvetro we find a multiplicity of rules applied to the comedies of Plautus and Terence. It should not be thought, however, that anywhere nearly so elaborate a procedure is involved here as was later to flourish in French neo-classical criticism; but this is certainly a formative period for that later development. Judgment by asking whether the appropriate style was practiced and exploited in the right way was also popular, and it furnished another compartment into which the practicing critic could neatly fit his remarks and asseverations.

CHAPTER SIX. THE TRADITION OF HORACE'S *ARS POETICA*: IV. THE RETURN TO THEORY

THE LAST GENERATION of critics working in the Horatian mode, covering approximately the last twenty years of the sixteenth century, reverses the tendency of the preceding generation and returns largely to the cultivation of poetic theory. The materials for the present chapter include only a few documents in the field of practical criticism, and these all concern themselves with the sonnet. The theoretical materials, moreover, are still only secondarily devoted to commentary on the *Ars poetica*; only three—possibly four—treatises belong in this category. Instead, theorists produce a large number of short treatises on particular genres—the madrigal, the sonnet, the elegy, comedy, the verse romance—in which they apply Horatian principles to these special forms; they write, besides, on miscellaneous poetic problems and on the relationship of the art to other arts. A partial explanation of the decline in practical criticism may be found in the fact that much of the critical energy of the period was being turned toward the major literary quarrels then raging, and it is only because I have chosen to treat those quarrels separately that materials for this chapter seem so one-sided.

BONCIANI AND PINO DA CAGLI (1578)

One of the miscellaneous poetic problems, that of prosopopeia or personification, forms the object of Francesco Bonciani's *Lettione della prosopopea*, read before the Accademia Fiorentina in 1578.[1] But Bonciani so expands the treatment as to make of his lecture a poetics in little, of which the fundamental principles are simple and few in number. All speech persuades and moves, especially when it is accompanied by such ornaments as verse, harmony, and figures of speech; of the last, prosopopeia is one of the most effective. For it is an imitation and hence marvelous. Bonciani gives several ways in which this figure is an imitation: (1) insofar as animals, inanimate objects, or incorporeal beings are represented as speaking, the poet is imitating because he is not speaking in his own person (Plato's distinction is here being applied); (2) imitation occurs whenever one represents the form, habit, and action of any thing whatsoever (Aristotle's *Rhetoric* is cited in justification).[2] Of the four categories of objects which may be so imitated—the true, the false, the verisimilar, and the impossible —prosopopeia imitates those false objects that are neither verisimilar nor possible; hence it is that the special effect of admiration is added to the persuasion and the moving ordinarily produced by speech. If one ask how

---

[1] On the attribution and the MSS, see my article "Nuove Attribuzioni di manoscritti di critica letteraria del Cinquecento," *Rinascimento*, III (1952), 249–50.

[2] MS Ricc. 1539, fols. 132–34v.

it is feasible to imitate things which do not exist, the answer is that we assemble into a nonexistent whole parts which we know from nature: "since we have known various things, our fancy sometimes confuses the natures of these things, making of them a new nature different from all the others as far as the whole is concerned, but similar in the parts."[3] Since the object of imitation is thus something which has never been and cannot be, the audience marvels at it; and because this marvel is accompanied by a process of learning what it had not known before, the audience experiences an extreme pleasure.

Bonciani is quoting Aristotle when he mentions the pleasure which accompanies learning; but he is really preparing the way for the development of an idea that has nothing to do with Aristotle, namely, that the triple end of prosopopeia is to instruct, to delight, and to persuade. When the figure takes the form of animal apologues, as it did in Hesiod and Aesop, it transmits to the ignorant lessons which they need but would be incapable of understanding in any more recondite form. Pleasure, insofar as it graces these stories, is merely a means and an instrument for the achievement of the utilitarian ends. A more philosophical poet, like Dante, will use the figure to express abstract and divine ideas for which no proper words exist in the language. Some poets employ it solely for purposes of delight, but in so doing they incompletely fulfil the purposes of their art; whereas the orators who exploit prosopopeia in order to persuade— through apologues and the invention of supposed persons—are making a much more proper use of it. Poet, orator, and philosopher alike must follow the prime rule of appropriateness in their handling of prosopopeia: all attributes must conform to the nature of the object to which they are assigned; if a place or dwelling is imagined for a person, it must be in keeping with his station; and to each person only such speeches and actions may be given as are in conformity with his character. "This above all is to be observed in every one of our discourses, that evil mores shall not be introduced, and that we should speak with due reverence of things belonging to religion so that these will not supply us with matter for ridicule."[4] In general, the verisimilitude of prosopopeia is comparable to any other, once the initial impossibility has been granted.

Concerning the figure which he is treating (and it has been seen that this figure may sometimes provide the basis for a whole poem), Bonciani thus starts from a general theory of diction, passes on to one of imitation, establishes the relationships of the imitation to nature, indicates the ends for which the imitation is made, and offers recommendations for the

[3] *Ibid.*, fol. 135*v*: "hauendo noi uarie cose conosciute la fantasia nostra confonde talhora le nature d'esse formandone una quanto al tutto da ogni altra differente, ma simile nelle parti."

[4] *Ibid.*, fol. 139: "questo sopr'ogni cosa è da osseruarsi in ogni nostro parlare, che rei costumi non s'introducano, e delle cose alla religione pertinenti con la debita riuerenza si fauelli, in guisa che elle non ci somministrino materia da cauarne il ridicolo."

internal organization of the work or the part of the work involved. At almost every one of these points, except perhaps the theory of diction, we find him in complete agreement with the many theorists who preceded him in the Horatian-rhetorical tradition.

That popular literary exercise, the defence of poetry, takes the special form of defence of comedy in the *Discorso intorno al componimento de la comedia de' nostri tempi*, which, in 1578, Bernardo Pino da Cagli published as an adjunct to Sforza d'Oddo's *Erofilomachia*; the discourse itself is dated 1572. Pino feels that he must justify comedy against the opinion currently held:

Today, this composition should either be abandoned altogether or else treated with much care and diligence, for it has come to such a state in the opinion of the masses that for the most part they regard it as a simple tale, vain and without profit, and as the work of a low mind, considering not the true artifice present in it and the utility that is had from it, when it is prudently written and treated, but the baseness of certain authors. . . . This results from no other thing than from the false opinion that is held with respect to the end of that type of work; whereas this should be to profit by means of the ridiculous, on the contrary the ridiculous is proposed as the end, to give pleasure alone by means of obscenity and ugliness.[5]

If the masses err in this way, erudite men and certain poets err in another, by a faulty interpretation of Aristotle's remarks on comedy; for the scholars read the *Poetics* as justifying the imitation of low and vile persons, the poets take it as permitting the imitation of vice. The antidote to these positions is obviously the restatement of the proper ends and the correct construction of the Aristotelian text. The ends are Horatian: to give pleasure and profit by means of laughter and without harm to the spectators (p. a10v). These ends require a reinterpretation of Aristotle, for vice could under no circumstances generate pleasure, and abject and immoral persons could not possibly provide acceptable moral lessons. Instead, Aristotle meant that the personages of comedy are less noble and less exalted than those of tragedy, being gentlemen and private citizens rather than kings and princes (we return to the medieval differentiation of genres by the station of the actors); and the ugliness he spoke of excluded immorality, dishonesty, and obscenity and referred only to deformity and disproportion. In fact, the vices, sins, and actions of comedy are less reprehensible than those of tragedy, where the really monstrous deeds of wickedness occur.

[5] *Discorso* (1578), pp. a6–a6v: "al dì d'oggi tal componimento si douerebbe ò a fatto lasciare, ò con molto studio, & diligenza trattare, poiche è venuto in tal conditione, & opinione del volgo, che di piu l'hanno per simplice fauola, vana & infruttuosa, & per opera da vile ingegno; considerando non il vero artifitio d'esso, o l'utile, che se ne prende, quando è prudentemente scritto & trattato, ma la bassezza d'alcuni autori. . . . Il che non prouiene da altro, che da la falsa opinione, che si ha del fine di cotal opera: il quale si come douerebbe essere il giouare, col mezzo del ridiculo, cosi per contrario si mette per fine il ridiculo, per piacer solo col mezzo della dishonestade, & della brutezza."

Since it is an imitation of life, says Pino, comedy will change as life changes, but only with respect to its materials. That is, new times will present to the comic poet new mores and new actions as his subjects. But the form will at all times remain the same: "Comedy is a kind of composition which, retaining always the same form, changes from time to time its matter; so that it always had five acts, always its complication and its denouement in order to be good."[6] Its immutable rules for form are found, it would seem, almost entirely in Horace: rules for the handling of the chorus, rules for diction, rules for decorum. The latter are really of two kinds, since they involve the proper "circumstances" for any given action and the proper behavior for any given person. In both, the spectator must have the impression of seeing nature herself represented; and the principal wisdom of the poet will consist in his knowledge of decorum and "circumstances." Indeed, Pino's generalization upon them almost constitutes a definition of comedy: "the whole body of comedy, if we wish to consider it carefully, is nothing else but the matter of divers passions, thoughts, and actions treated in familiar conversations."[7] Each person presented on the stage must be made to speak according to his condition, "with proverbs, maxims, sayings, and ways of speaking" that will be apposite both to the condition of the person addressed and to the circumstances. Finally, all these matters must be expressed in beautiful language, preferably of a metaphorical turn. An Aristotelian of 1578 would have noted in this discussion of the rules an enumeration of the four qualitative parts of comedy, plot, character, thought, and diction; but he also would have noted that the other three are really transformed into functions of thought, that the hierarchy of the parts is destroyed, and that what remains is a moralistic theory of comedy in which the most important thing is the utilitarian value of what is said.

In the same year, 1578, Giason Denores published a short treatise which in a sense reversed the tendencies that I have been discussing. It was entitled *Introduttione sopra i tre libri della Rhetorica di Aristotile*, and since it dealt with the *Rhetoric* rather than the *Poetics*, it might seem not to belong at all in a history of poetic theory. But whereas most of the theorists I have analyzed heretofore had effected an assimilation of poetics to rhetoric, Denores in the present work detaches one whole part of rhetoric from that science and attaches it to poetics. The part at issue is the materials contained in Book III of the *Rhetoric*, which Denores summarizes as including action (by which he means histrionics), elocution, and disposi-

[6] *Ibid.*, p. a7v: "E la comedia vna sorte di componimento, che ritenendo sempre la medesima forma muta di tempo in tempo la materia: si che haueua sempre cinque atti, sempre il suo nodo, e'l suo scioglimento per essere bona."
[7] *Ibid.*, p. b7v: "non essendo altro tutto il corpo della Comedia, se vogliamo bene considerarla, che materia di diuersi affetti, di pensieri & attioni, trattata con ragionamenti famigliari."

tion. He maintains that, according to Aristotle's conception, only those elements which contribute directly to persuasion—namely, proper and common propositions, examples, and enthymemes—belong to rhetoric; the elements treated in Book III are hence not substantial, and the book really should have been placed elsewhere in the Aristotelian corpus. Why not, then, placed with the *Poetics*? Since action, elocution, and disposition contribute nothing to rhetorical proof, be it demonstrative, ethical, or pathetic, and since they have as their sole purpose to give pleasure, to add beauty, to beguile the listener, their affiliation is clearly much closer with poetics than with its sister art; in fact, they belong primarily to poetics, and their use in rhetoric is accidental. The implication is that the specific domain of poetry is the pleasurable, the amusing, the idle, and that it is not concerned with more serious purposes.[8]

After this case of inverse method, we return to what is an almost perfect example of the rhetoricizing of poetry in Giovanni Andrea Gilio's *La topica poetica* of 1580; the title itself shows that its author wishes to discover rhetorical topics in the art of poetry. In fact, this is the main endeavor of the work: Books II, III, and IV are devoted to a listing of topics (by which he means arguments, passions, bases of demonstration), of figures of speech, and of figures of thought, respectively. More general materials, including a justification of this approach, appear in the dedication and in Book I. In the former, the commonplaces in the defence of poetry are once again collected together, and there is no need to retail them. In Book I, the whole principle of the work is stated: Everything that one says falls under one or several of the three kinds of discourse, the consultative or deliberative, the demonstrative, and the judicial; of these, the first two are more proper to the poet, the third to the orator. It would therefore be well for the poet to know in which type he is going to write, but it is not absolutely necessary; even if he does not, his compositions may be "lovely, and beautiful, ornamented by figures, by topical passages, by beautiful and graceful style, and by the other parts appropriate to well regulated poetry."[9] Clearly, there is no consideration of any "parts" above and beyond diction and possibly thought. There is, however, one prior step that the poet must take before beginning the task of expression; he must discover the materials to be expressed, and he does so through invention, which is, in a way, the most important aspect of poetry. "And when the invention is beautiful, and well conceived, well ordered, and well clothed and well ornamented with words, with figures, with topical passages, and with a beautiful style, it may be said to be not only perfect but perfect in the highest degree."[10]

[8] *Introduttione* (1578), pp. bv, b4–c, g3v–g4.

[9] *Topica poetica* (1580), p. 1: "vaghi, e belli, ornati di figure, di luoghi topici, di bello e vago stile, e d'altre parti conueneuoli a ben regolata poesia."

[10] *Ibid.*, p. 4v: "E quando la inuentione è bella, e bene intesa, ben ordinata, e ben vestita e bene ornata di parole, di figure, di luoghi Topici, e di bello stile: Si potrà dire non solo perfetta ma perfettissima."

Invention itself is a product of imitation, either of nature, art, or fortune, or of earlier poets taken as models; imitation, in turn, applies to disposition and elocution as well as to invention.

Throughout Gilio's treatise, the Horatian references are numerous, but they are always altered in the direction of a more purely rhetorical approach. For example, Horace's statement of the ends of poetry is expanded from two to four: to delight, to profit, to move or persuade, and to be sweet or agreeable (referring to the "dulcia sunto" of line 99). All would seem to be achieved when words are correctly suited to matter. The subject of variety leads to a discussion of the mixture of styles and of the three styles in general. The quantitative parts distinguished are the proem, the narration, and the invocation. Decorum boils down to the "proportion, correspondence, or conformity that style has with subject matter."[11] All roads thus lead to diction and to the specific topics which Gilio is treating. He shows how the demonstrative, deliberative, and judicial types are used by Dante and Petrarch, how Petrarch and Ariosto may be used as models of style, how native and foreign words may be properly mixed. This limitation of the examples to Italian poets is an interesting feature of the work.

From the dual ends of pleasure and instruction, Torquato Tasso derives as much of the theory of epic poetry as he presents in the *Allegoria del poema* printed with the 1581 edition of the *Gerusalemme Liberata*. The whole passage merits quotation:

Heroic poetry, like an animal in which two natures are conjoined, is composed of imitation and of allegory. With the former it attracts the minds and the ears of men to itself and delights them in a wonderful way; with the latter it instructs them in the virtues or in knowledge, or in both together. And just as epic imitation is never anything else but a resemblance and image of human action, so the allegory of the epic poets is wont to be for us a figuration of human life. But imitation concerns the actions of man which are subject to the external senses, and laboring mainly over these, it tries to represent them with effective and expressive words and ones apt to place clearly before the physical eyes the things represented; nor does it consider characters or passions or the discoursings of the mind insofar as these are intrinsic, but only insofar as they issue forth and accompany action by manifesting themselves in speech and in actions and in deeds. Allegory, on the contrary, concerns passions and opinions and characters not only insofar as these are apparent, but mainly in their intrinsic being; and it signifies them more obscurely, with what one might call mysterious notes, and which can be fully understood only by those who know the nature of things.[12]

---

[11] *Ibid.*, p. 10: "quella proportione, corrispondenza ò conformità c'ha lo stile co'l soggetto."

[12] *Allegoria*, ed. Perchacino (1581), pp. **1–**1v: "L'Heroica Poesia, Quasi Animale, in cui due Nature si coniungano, d'imitatione, & d'Allegoria è composta, con quella alletta à se gli animi, & gli orecchi de gli huomini, & marauigliosamente gli diletta, con questa nella Virtù, ò nella scienza, ò nell'una, [e] nell'altra gli amaestra, et si come l'Epica imitatione altro giamai non è, che somiglianza, & imagine d'attione humana, cosi suole, l'Allegoria de gli Epici, dell'humana Vita esserci figura. Ma l'imitatione riguarda l'attioni dell'huomo, che

Furthermore, Tasso states that since the epic wishes to represent all life, some of its works will depict the life of the soul, or the contemplative life, others the life of the body, or the civil life; the *Odyssey* and the *Divina Commedia* are examples of the former, the *Iliad* and the *Aeneid* of the latter. The whole dichotomy may be figured graphically in the following way:

                            Epic poetry
    imitation   allegory
  attracts, delights   teaches virtue
external actions, appearance   passions, opinions, characters
 clear presentation   obscure presentation
    (all men)   those who know nature of things
                       (soul)   (body)
                contemplative life   civil life
                    Odyssey   *Iliad*
                      Dante   *Aeneid*

Several points are significant in this analysis: first, the importance placed upon the allegorical interpretation of literature, equal to its importance in the Middle Ages; second, the restricted conception of imitation, which comes to mean a literal and simple portrayal of external actions; third, the division of the functions of the two parts of a poem providing pleasure and utility.

When Tasso was speaking of the epic (as well as writing it), he was occupying himself with the genre that many Renaissance theorists considered the most important of all. When Filippo Massini delivered his lecture, *Del madrigale*, to the Accademia degli Insensati at Perugia in the same year, 1581, he admitted with becoming modesty that he was about to treat the smallest and weakest of all Tuscan verse forms. The object of his lecture was to contest the assertions of Ruscelli and Minturno that the madrigal was a "regulated" poem, to deny the limitations placed upon the form by them, and to indicate how it might be thought of as belonging to the other category of "free" poems. "Regulation," for Massini, involves fixity of subject matter, of style, of metrical pattern; for the madrigal, this means exclusive use of rustic materials (as recommended by Bembo and Minturno), treated in a low style, in eleven or twelve lines rhyming in a set way. Massini contends, on the contrary, that the madrigal is free in all these respects. His authority, in a general fashion, is Aristotle's statement in *Poetics* 1447*b*13, which he paraphrases thus: "the quality of the verse does not distinguish the poem substantially, to use this term; the poem takes its

---

sono à i sensi esteriori sottoposte, & intorno ad esse principalmente affaticandosi, cerca di rappresentarle con parole efficaci, & espressiue, & atte à por chiaramente dinanzi à gli occhi corporali le cose rappresentate; nè considera i costumi, ò gli affetti, ò i discorsi dell'animo inquanto essi sono intrinseci; ma solamente in quanto fuori se n'escono, & nel parlare, & ne gli atti, & nell'opere manifestandosi accompagnano [l]'attione. L'Allegoria all'incontro rimira le passioni, & le opinioni, & i costumi, non solo inquanto essi apparino; ma principalmente nel lor essere intrinseco, & piu oscuramente le significa con note (per cosi dire) misteriose, & che solo da i conoscitori della Natura delle cose possono essere à pieno comprese."

form and its quality from the quality of the plot or of the thought that one undertakes to write about."[13] Since he thinks of the madrigal as admitting any subject matter, it may thus admit any one of the styles, high, middle, or low. There are, however, preferable practices all along the line. The best subjects are the light ones, "since pleasantness is without any doubt more proper and more fitting to the very agreeable nature of this composition, which however is not at all incapable of gravity."[14] The style should be distinguished, no matter which one it may be:

> I should wish then above all else that the madrigal should contain some rare and ingenious thought, and that its elocution should be very pure and artful, and that both thought and elocution in the graver madrigals should be such that they would produce honesty, dignity, majesty, magnificence, and greatness, and in the more amusing ones, grace, suavity, loveliness, sweetness, jokes, and playful expressions.[15]

In the verse form, the poem is "free" to the extent that it does not have a fixed number of lines, that some unrhymed lines are permitted, and that "mezzi versi" may be intermingled with "versi interi." But Massini nevertheless sets up certain rules: it must not contain fewer than five lines and preferably should not have more than twenty; rhymes should not be more than five lines apart. By way of conclusion, he states that, like the canzone, the madrigal is essentially a free form, but that it may be regulated in one of two ways: (1) by accepting and following the form practiced by some other poet, or (2) by evolving one's own rules and then following them consistently (pp. 173–74, 185).

Massini's analysis represents an attempt at liberation from the rule-of-thumb poetizing which had given substance to the late medieval and early Renaissance prosodic treatises; in a broader sense, it belongs to the general contention over freedom and regulation (extending far beyond prosodic matters) which was a permanent concern of Cinquecento theory. We shall meet many other examples of it as we go along. In a minor way, this attempt may be a reaction against some of Horace's specific prescriptions for the drama. But one breaks away from Horace here only to join the ranks of the rhetoricians associated with him in current thinking. The three styles, invention and elocution, the principle of appropriateness of thought and diction, specific effects to be produced by the diction, all these are part of the contemporary tradition.

[13] In *Lettioni* (1588), pp. 168–69: "La qualità del verso non qualifica, per vsar questo termine, sostantialmente il Poema, il quale prende la forma, e qualità sua dalla qualità della fauola, e del concetto, che s'imprende à scriuere."

[14] *Ibid.*, p. 173: "essendo la piaceuolezza, senz'alcun dubbio, più propria, e più proportionata alla natura piaceuolissima di questo componimento, non incapace però affatto . . . di grauità."

[15] *Ibid.*, p. 181: "Desidererei poi sopra 'l tutto, che'l Madrigale hauesse 'l concetto raro, & ingegnoso, e l'elocution purissima, & artifitiosa, e che questa, e quello, nei Madrigali più graui, fossero tali, che producessero, l'honestà, la dignità, la maestà, la magnificenza, e la grandezza, e nei più piaceuoli, la gratia, la soauità, la vaghezza, la dolcezza, gli scherzi, e i giochi."

In the same year, 1581, the Plantin press published an edition of **Cicero's** *De optimo genere oratorum*, with a commentary containing several pages of remarks specifically devoted to poetics; it was written by Giovanni Antonio Viperano, who had published his *De poetica* just two years before. It should be pointed out that the passage at the beginning of Cicero's treatise to which these remarks refer had been used repeatedly by writers on poetry, especially those who were intent upon establishing airtight divisions between the genres, and by scholars working on the text of Horace. Viperano also uses it to set up a system of genres, but in a somewhat different way; indeed, he attacks previous divisions as incorrectly established. His own solution is a strange cross between Aristotle and the rhetoricians. Poetry, he says, is an imitation of human actions, and human actions are of two sorts. Either they are good and virtuous and merit praise, or they are bad and vicious and merit blame. Hence one may classify poems as they provide "laus" for the former or "vituperatio" for the latter. This is, of course, an accurate reflection of Averroës' system. To the laudative poems belong the melic (or lyric) and its derivatives, the epic and tragedy; to the vituperative, comedy. Having thus classified the genres, Viperano then indicates for each one its subject matter (usually persons of a given station in life), its kind of action (happy at the beginning, unhappy at the end, and so forth), its style (a combination of sententiae and diction) and its meter (iambic, hexameter). Unfortunately, most of the materials here are the time-worn ones from Donatus and Diomedes, with occasional additions from Horace, and there is nothing new to be learned from studying them.

As he continues his gloss on Cicero, Viperano takes occasion to insist upon the meaning of the sentence, "Itaque & in tragoedia comicum uitiosum est, & in comoedia turpe tragicum." He argues that, although all poems belong to the genus poetry, they are so distinct one from another that they can under no circumstances be mixed:

... of the forms of poetry, one cannot be associated with another, given the fact that they have a separate and distinct nature. Since then, tragedy imitates the actions of illustrious men and comedy those of humble men, it is improper and faulty and contrary to the nature of either one if comic and humorous matters are brought up in a tragedy, or in a comedy tragic upheavals are employed...
Nor do comedy and tragedy differ only in the diverse imitation of illustrious and ordinary actions, but also in diction. For tragedy uses a grave and sublime diction, comedy instead descends to the familiar usage of almost pure talk.[16]

---

[16] *In Ciceronis de optimo genere oratorum commentarius* (1581), p. 12: "poëticae formarum altera in alterius consociationem venire non potest, vt quae propriam habeant distinctamque naturam. Quando igitur virorum illustrium actiones tragoedia imitatur, & comoedia humilium, indecorum est, ac vitiosum, repugnansque cuiusque naturae, si aut comicae res & iocosae in tragoedia excitentur, aut in comoedia tragicae perturbationes adhibeantur ... neque solùm diuersa actionum illustrium & humilium imitatione comoedia & tragoedia differunt, sed etiam oratione. Nam tragoedia graui & sublimi oratione vtitur, comoedia verò ad vsitatam ferè puri sermonis consuetudinem sese dimittit."

As elsewhere in his thinking, Viperano does not feel that the distinction is complete until he has added "verba" to "res"; this conclusion is borne out by the commentary on the following sentence in Cicero, where he assigns to each of the genres—earlier distinguished on the basis of subject matter—a certain kind of words having a specific and separate tonal effect.

With Roberto Titi's *Locorum controversorum* (1583) we return briefly and fragmentarily to the text of Horace. Titi's work treats a large number of "disputed points" from many ancient authors, pretending to improve upon earlier interpretations, and included are two texts from the *Ars poetica*. The first is lines 408 ff., "Natura fieret laudabile carmen an arte ...," which treats the general question of art and nature in the poet. Titi's original contribution is his insistence that even the combination of art and nature is not sufficient and that the poet must possess also "effort, love, exercise, opportunity, time, judgment."[17] The second remark concerns lines 128 ff., "Difficile est proprie communia dicere ...," on the use of new and borrowed materials. Titi extends the meaning to a general theory of imitation, with special emphasis on the parts of a model which the poet should imitate. He sees imitation as concerning both "materia" and "verba." The particular passage in Horace refers to "materia" only and (according to Titi) makes the point that the poet should select those passages for imitation which are splendid and noble, which will enable the poet to be brilliant; on the other hand, he should avoid all such as are low and nondescript. The fact that the example chosen to illustrate "low" passages is Catullus leads one to suspect that the criterion being applied is again a moral one.

In 1583, also, Giraldi Cintio's tragedies were collected and published by his son, Celso, and thus the verse "Prologues" to the various tragedies were printed for the first time. They had probably been written many years earlier, but it is impossible to assign exact dates to them. Although there are five prologues containing reflections on poetic theory, the doctrine found in them is consistent and unified and may be reduced to a few major points: (1) The laws of poetry are not immutable, but change with the times, with audiences, with the wishes of the patrons who order them, and with the subject matters that are different from age to age (Prologue to *Altile*, pp. 7–8). An example of such change would be his use of a prologue in each of his tragedies, a practice unknown to the ancients, who used prologues only in comedy. (2) Tragedy does not need to have a tragic ending, but may end happily; when, after turmoil and sadness, a happy ending ensues, the play may be called a tragicomedy. This is the case with his own *Altile* (Prologue, pp. 8–9). (3) The ends of tragedy are to give pleasure and to provide utility, with the emphasis decidedly on the latter. This is the one point most insistently repeated in the various prologues,

---

[17] *Locorum controversorum* (1583), bk. II, ch. xxiii, p. 56: "sumptus, Amor, exercitium, opportunitas, tempus, Iudicium." For the second passage, cf. bk. VIII, ch. xxii, pp. 219–20.

the kind of utility varying from prologue to prologue. In *Altile*, for example:

>Vedrete adunque in questa nostra Altile
>. . .
>Quanta inconstanza è ne l'humane cose.
>E che per mal' oprar mai non gioisce
>Vn animo maluagio, e che conuiene
>. . .
>Ch'auenga quel, ch'è statuito in Cielo
>Dal supremo Motor, che il tutto regge,
>Con quella sua ineffabil prouidenza (p. 9).

The lessons: the inconstancy of human affairs; the wicked are never happy; the will of God, expressed through Providence, will be done.

In *Didone*, the same moral as the one taught by the ancient poets who borrowed subjects from Homer:

>E l'esposero in scena, a gli occhi altrui,
>Per purgar l'humane alme col terrore,
>E, con compassion de gli altrui casi,
>Da la vana ridurle à miglior vita (p. 7).

The utility: through purgation of pity and terror, to lead men to a better life.

In the Prologue to *Cleopatra* a statement first about the dual end of dramatic poetry:

>Fra le cose trouate da gli antichi,
>Per insegnare i buon costumi al Mondo,
>Nulla ue n'hà, che piu diletti, e gioui,
>Che le fauole, ben condutte in scena,
>E benche d'esse sian varie le sorti,
>Fra quelle nondimen di maggior loda
>Ottiene la Tragedia il primo luoco (p. 7).

Then the specific moral of this tragedy: that wealth and power are nothing unless accompanied by virtue.

In *Arrenopia*:

>Hor qui vedrete, spettatori, quanto
>Ci apporti danno il non vedere il vero,
>Et il lasciarsi à l'appetito in preda
>E che il non vbedire a suoi maggiori,
>E cagione di scandali, ch'à guerra,
>Inducon spesso i piu potenti Regi (pp. 9–10).

The conclusions: one must see the truth, resist the promptings of appetite, obey one's superiors.

POETIC THEORY

From the Prologue to *Selene*:

> Perche ueggendo indi gli spettatori
> Varie sembianze d'huomini, e di donne,
> Di uarij vffici, & qualità diuerse,
> E di varij costumi, & varie leggi
> Sortir diuersi fini, & uarie sorti;
> Fatti acuti, sapesser da se in tanta
> Varietà di genti, & di costumi,
> Seguir la loda, & ischiuare il biasmo,
> Et ueder, che chiunque uirtù segue,
> Giunge à buon fine, & chi'l mal segue, à reo (p. 9).

The purpose: to demonstrate, via the divers kinds of men and women in the world and the ends they come to, that virtue leads to happiness and vice to unhappiness; and through the demonstration, to make the spectators wary and wise.

There can be little doubt here as to the kind of utility involved and how it is achieved. The stage is a place for examples, in both characters and actions, of proper kinds of behavior—to be followed—and improper kinds —to be shunned. Giraldi, as he enumerates these examples, gives some indications as to how they should be presented—brief remarks on decorum, on the fitting of actions and the general tone to the dignity of the persons, on the inclusion of the action within a single day, on the audience, which is made up of "thousands of people" and must be spoken to in terms accessible to it. Giraldi's own precepts are accessible in this way and show what elements of Horatian theory (with a smattering of Aristotle) he deemed it possible and worth while to address to the pit and the boxes.

TORQUATO TASSO (1584)

From the subtitle of Torquato Tasso's dialogue, *La Cavaletta, overo della poesia toscana* (written in 1584, published in 1587),[18] one is led to expect an illuminating treatment of poetry in the vernacular; and this expectation is further aroused when one discovers that Tasso means to proceed in a practical and deductive fashion by comparing two sonnets, one by Francesco Coppetta and one by Giovanni della Casa. Some illumination, indeed, is provided. But it is a light out of the past, coming largely from two medieval theorists, Dante and Antonio da Tempo, supplemented by Hermogenes' Ideas and the truisms of classical rhetoric.

Tasso's starting point is Dante's definition of poetry as "a rhetorical fiction set to music" ("una fintione Retorica posta in musica"),[19] for which he finds corroboration in Plato's statement from the *Gorgias* that

---

[18] On the date, see Solerti, *Vita di Torquato Tasso* (Torino, Roma, 1895), I, 396.

[19] *De vulgari eloquentia*, II.iv.2. In the edition of P. Rajna (Florence, 1896), p. 129: "fictio rethorica . . . in musicaque posita." In the Trissino translation of 1529, p. c: "una fizione rettorica, e posta in musica."

tragedy is "a deceit in which the deceivers are better than those who do not deceive, and the deceived are wiser than those who are not deceived." Poets, rhetoricians, musicians, actors are all "dissimulators." Aristotle would have called them imitators (except for the rhetorician), but it is clear that Tasso does not mean to speak in the same way as Aristotle. Dissimulation involves, among other things, the hiding of the effects of art itself: "Thus, to hide the deceit, and so to speak the dissimulation of the art, is the highest artistry."[20] Tasso develops at some length the comparisons of the poet with the orator and the musician. Unlike the logician, who uses induction and the syllogism as his forms of argument, the orator uses the enthymeme and the example, and these are the same forms employed by the poet. Generally, anybody who imitates imitates some "example" and hence in a sense argues; even though the argument may not be formally stated, it exists. In poetry, the argument is concealed in some fictional form, and this makes it all the more effective as far as persuasion is concerned. For the poet, like the orator, wishes to persuade; "in truth, through reading of the poets I have been greatly persuaded to honor, to glory, and to virtue, and almost more than by the philosophers themselves."[21] Furthermore, certain kinds of poems are parallel with certain kinds of arguments; the canzone is a reflection of the "divisive" argument, the sonnet of the "compositive" (p. 36v). Finally, both arts are compounded of sententiae and of elocution, of which the latter is the more important in poetry. As for music, it is associated only accidentally with poetry, since the latter may dispense with it; indeed, some of the highest genres do not need it at all, and the fact that some of the lower ones must have it as an additional ornament is a sign of their weakness. Dante's definition is thus now fully explained, and Tasso is able to conclude with respect to poetry in general that "its genus and as it were its matter will be the fiction and its forms will have rhetoric and music."[22] The practicing poet still remains a poet, though, and he must avoid indulging both in sophistic subtleties, which would bring him too close to the rhetoricians, and in excessive and intemperate musical ornament.

With special reference to the sonnet, Tasso holds that it has various forms (by which he means various rhyme schemes) and that each of these is capable of any of the "Ideas" or "characters" of diction. The determining factor in every case is the nature of the subject matter. Thus Coppetta's sonnet, which has a "very noble subject" and a "very grave texture" will require the "most noble" form or character of discourse. In any given sonnet, the style may be mixed, but there will be one dominant style, which

[20] In *Rime e prose*, Vol. VI (1587), p. 31: "Il nasconder dunque l'inganno, e per cosi dire, la dissimulatione dell'arte, è sommo artificio."
[21] *Ibid.*, p. 36: "Veramente leggendo i Poeti, molto sono stato persuaso all'honore, alla gloria, & alla virtù, e quasi piu che da filosofi stessi."
[22] *Ibid.*, p. 37: "il genere suo e quasi la materia sarà la fintione e sue forme aranno Rethorica, & Musica."

will set the tone. The poem must end on the dominant, toward which there should be steady progression throughout. The musical terminology is not amiss here, since Tasso has in mind effects of tone—"high-sounding" and "low-sounding" words, and so forth—and their development through the sonnet. In his comparison of the two sonnets, it is largely these effects that he discusses, to the advantage of Casa because he builds properly toward the concluding sonorities, to the discredit of Coppetta because he does not. In this part of the discussion, at least, Tasso is closer to the art of prosody than to the art of poetry; and when he remains within the art of poetry, he is also astride the art of rhetoric.

Girolamo Frachetta attacks directly the problem of the difference between poetry and prosody in his *Spositione sopra la canzone di Guido Cavalcanti, Donna mi prega, &c.* (1585). In spite of its title, the "exposition" is of greater interest as a theoretical than as a practical document; for the sections referring directly to Cavalcanti's poem are, like so many similar works of the century, concerned exclusively with the philosophical content and with detailed speculations on the meaning. Frachetta's thesis is that Cavalcanti's canzone should not be rated as a poem at all, and the demonstration of this thesis leads him into various theoretical questions. He finds it necessary to distinguish, first, between poetry and prosody, and he does so on the basis of their "materia": the matter of poetry is made up of things which can happen, sometimes of things which have happened; whereas the matter of prosody is syllables, vowels, and consonants, combined to make verse. Verse is the form of the work as viewed prosodically and constitutes its internal end; its external end is pleasure. When he raises the question as to whether either of these arts can exist without the other, he finds himself at variance with the opinion of Castelvetro, who had maintained that they cannot. Frachetta's own stand is that the art of poetry cannot exist without versification, but that the art of prosody can exist without poetry. To justify the first of these statements, he interprets Aristotle's text (*Poetics* 1451b27) as meaning that the poet is a poet *more* by virtue of imitation than of verse—but that verse is nevertheless necessary. This is in keeping with the nature of the poet and his ends: "the poet, who wishes to be considered by the masses as surpassing the condition of other men (as the ancients especially wished him to be), must speak in that manner which is more exquisite than all the rest, and precisely in the one in which the oracles used to give their answers; and this is without any doubt the manner of verse."[23] In support of the second statement, he declares that since versification is an instrumental science having no essence of its own, it may be attached to other forms besides poetry.

[23] *Spositione* (1585), p. 3: "il poeta, che uuole essere stimato dal popolo trapassar la conditione de gli huomini, come massimamente uoleuan gli antichi, dee fauellare in quella maniera, che è piu isquisita dell'altre, & in quella appunto nella qual si soleuano dar le risposte da gli Oracoli: & questa è senza fallo niuno la maniera del uerso."

The upshot of this argument is that there may be compositions in verse that are not poems, even whole verse genres that are not poetry. The canzone as practiced by early poets was of this kind. How, then, would one distinguish a canzone that was a poem from another that was not? The answer is double: from the style and from the matter. Lyric poems contain matters of various kinds, but above all commendations of one sort or another and amorous themes. But they must not approach commendatory orations or philosophical disquisitions on love in difficulty or subtlety, "because poems were invented to give recreation to men's minds, and not to weary them."[24] Moreover, as compared with these nonpoetic forms, poems have a special kind of style: "they are distinguished mainly by the transformation of the material, which depends upon additions; by metaphors, by allegories, by hyperboles, and by similar colorings and embellishments."[25] Cavalcanti's canzone is not a poem because its subject matter is too obscure, and if Frachetta has undertaken to explain it, it is not because he wished to expound a poem, but merely to shed light upon an obscure work (p. 7).

TOMMASO CORREA (1587)

Tommaso Correa, known to us through his treatise on the epigram, in 1587 published his *In librum de arte poetica Q. Horatij Flacci explanationes*. It was the first of the three complete commentaries on Horace to appear during this "last generation" of Horatian criticism. The immediate impression is one of simplification of the whole approach to the text, as compared with the great complexity of earlier exegeses. This results in part from the reduction in the number of divisions of the text and of accompanying precepts. Whereas Pigna had seen eighty separate rules in Horace, Correa subdivides into only twenty-five sections; instead of Pigna's four separate precepts for lines 73–85, he gives only one, and instead of the six for lines 275–308, one again. The consequence is a sense of more closely knit and better organized exposition. Besides, some of the promiscuous citing of authorities is eliminated; Plato and Cicero are cited a few times each, Donatus with some frequency, and the parallels with Aristotle are whittled down to the following modest list:

Horace	Aristotle
1–23	1450a38, 1451a16, 1450b24
42–45	1450a38, 1449b12
73–85	1449a24, 1459b31
275–308	1450a12
309–32	1447a16

[24] *Ibid.*, p. 7: "percioche le poesie sono state trouate per ricrear gli animi, & non per affaticargli."
[25] *Ibid.*, p. 6: "si seperano principalmente per l'alteratione della materia, laqual depende dalle aggiunte; per le tralationi; per le allegorie; per le hiperboli; & per somiglianti coloramenti, & abbeglimenti."

If these passages be consulted, it will be noted that they contain only the most familiar commonplaces of the Aristotelian text: "The poet is an imitator," "The plot is the soul of the poem," "The plot must be one," and so forth. But these changes do not mean that Correa wishes to make wide departures from the antecedent tradition; rather, he preserves much of the rhetorical machinery which had for so long been a standard feature of the interpretations of the text.

In part, at least, Correa organizes the *Ars poetica* according to the elements of invention, disposition, and elocution. He thinks that the first precept (ll. 1–23) concerns invention and disposition and that the second one (ll. 24–31) treats elocution. Later, the fourth precept (ll. 42–45) returns to disposition. To these three elements he adds, in at least one passage, the rhetorical parts of pronunciation and action (in connection with ll. 99–111). Crossed with this set of distinctions is its constant concomitant, the "res-verba" distinction; but here the treatment is more interesting and more original. For the group of terms appears not only as explicitly stated, but also under various disguises. When he is discussing lines 46–72, where Horace touches upon the invention of new words, Correa indicates that the text here passes from "res" to "verba," "since a poem, like a speech, consists of things and of words."[26] Earlier, in connection with the second precept (already identified as belonging to elocution), the opposition had taken the various forms of "res : verba," "res : dictio," "res : oratio"; later, the sixth precept states it as modified to "res : versus." Clearly, what Correa has in mind is a major juxtaposition of "matter" to "form" and the problem of suiting the latter to the former. The question of decorum, as we shall see, arises in connection with both matter and form.

Alongside these fairly conventional approaches, Correa presents a certain number of personal ideas, which constitute modifications to the standard theory. He seems to regard the materials of poetry as circumscribed and determined in a number of ways. First, as in Horace, by nature: the poet may not mix in his poem parts and elements which are separate in nature, "so that his poem will not resemble a monster made up of various natures in conflict with one another."[27] Second, as in Plato, by the conventions of society: the poet does not have complete freedom of invention since he must not say things which are contrary to the institutions and customs of society (p. 6); for this restriction Correa uses the term "conuenientia." Third, by the rules of the style in which the poet is writing: these are equivalent to a second "nature" whose requirements are as strict as those of the first. Basically, the style should be adapted to the materials; but by a kind of inverse action, certain types of persons, actions, and

---

[26] *Explanationes* (1587), p. 28: "Quoniam poema, vt oratio constat rebus & verbis. . . ."

[27] *Ibid.*, p. 3: "vt non videatur monstrum aliquod ex diuersis inter se pugnantibus naturis conflatum."

thoughts come to be associated invariably with each style. For example, the sublime style:

> The highest style contains important personages and excellent actions, to which are to be fitted choice sententiae, which must be expressed with choice words and adorned by rhythmic grouping, as if you were to speak of God or describe heroes, kings, military leaders, governments; but if others are mixed in, such as charioteers, sailors, merchants, artisans and others of that kind, it is done so that human society may constitute a kind of complete body. Excellent matters are such things as wars for peace, deliberative councils, trials for selection, the virtues useful for the regulation of life, and great actions. Choice sententiae are those which are remote from common usage, choice words those which are not trite; a rhythmic grouping is one which, through its sounds, almost depicts the thing itself.[28]

Fourth, by the fixed subjects prescribed for the individual genres; this is, in a sense, a refinement and specification of the preceding. Not only is the type of action recommended for each genre ("In tragedy incredible and most horrible actions are related, in comedy actions from the average and common life of men and from their usual behavior"[29]), but for some genres very definite content—largely from traditional sources—is proposed. Thus, in tragedy the plots will revolve about "great and horrible actions, the murders of kings, hopeless situations, exiles, parricides, burnings, armed contests, weepings, wailings, laments, funerals, burial hymns";[30] in the New Comedy, about "loves, marriages, girls sold into slavery who are later found to be free and are recognized by their father, their mother, their brother, their nurse."[31] If to all these limitations one adds the typification of personages imposed by the laws of decorum, characters as well as action become set and almost invariable parts of the work. Indeed, the whole hemming in of the "matter" of poetry is equivalent to a kind of super-law of decorum.

The poet, circumscribed in these ways with respect to his subject matter, finds his great field of activity in the form which he imposes upon it. If one were to ask Correa what the distinguishing characteristics of poetry were, his answer would undoubtedly include primarily those elements

---

[28] *Ibid.*, pp. 14–15: "Genus summum personas graues, & res excellentes continet, quibus lectę sententie accommodandae sunt, & illae proferendae verbis lectis, & numerosa collocatione illustrandae; vt si de Deo loquaris, Heroas describas, Reges, Duces, Ciuitates, quòd si alia admisceantur, vt Aurigae, Nautae, Mercatores, fabri, & huiusmodi id adeo fit, quòd Hominum societas quasi quoddam corpus efficiat. Res excellentes sunt bella propter pacem, Concilia ad deliberandum, Iudicia ad eligendum, virtutes ad vitam constituendam, & actiones. Sententiae lectae, ab vsu remotę communi, lecta verba, quae non sunt trita: numerosa collocatio quae quasi rem ipsam suo sono depingit."

[29] *Ibid.*, p. 41: "In Tragędijs atrocissim[ę] res exponuntur, & incredibiles, in Comoedijs res sumptę de media & communi hominum vita, & moribus."

[30] *Ibid.*, p. 93: "Res Tragicae grandes, atroces, cędes Regum, desperationes, exsilia, parricidia, incendia, pugnae, fletus, vlulatus, conquestiones, funera, Epicedia."

[31] *Ibid.*, p. 95: "In Comoedia noua vt plurimum amores, nuptiae, virgines venditae, quae liberae inueniantur, cognoscuntur a patre, matre, fratre, nutricę."

which he regarded as belonging to the form. Verse would be one of them, inseparably and inescapably connected with any conception of poetry. Therefore, to each type of subject matter the proper verse must be matched. Some genres have verse as their only poetic property; if one were to remove verse from the satire, for example, one would no longer have a poem (p. 79). Another required feature would be a special kind of language or diction. In fact, one reason why the satire is so unstable a poetic genre is that its language is not different from that of everyday usage. The real poet is one who writes metaphorically, who cultivates the figures and the tropes, even though he must not do so to excess or in an inappropriate way (pp. 28–29). Again, poetry is distinguished by the use of an artificial order in place of the natural order found in history and in the narrations of the orator.

The greatest merit of the poet consists in the fact that he departs considerably from the laws of history and disregards the natural order of narration, if one consider the succession of events; for sometimes he passes over the things prescribed by the natural order, pursues those things which it provides, places elsewhere those which it seemed ought to be said in the present. Nor is that law imposed upon him which would make him write a kind of history and collect all things in an orderly fashion. He may of course choose the events, express and embellish some of them, pass over others which he does not deem worthy of mention.[32]

In all this answer, Correa would have little to say about imitation, except for a passing remark about the requirement that the imitation should follow the thing imitated (p. 18) and another indicating that the poet imitates when he introduces other persons who speak for themselves (p. 35). No special essence is contributed to poetry through the fact that it is an imitation; it is merely a particular kind of rhetoric or history.

In keeping with this conception, Correa devotes much of his time to matters of style. He takes pains to define what is meant by the terms "Idea," "character," "stilus," so common in critical parlance, and he does so as follows:

A "character," then, is a diction similar to the thing which it designates, or else it is the effigy and image of the thing, for speech expresses the thing just as colors do in painting. Just as one obtains from wax, when a seal is applied to it, an image in every respect similar to the thing of which the seal is a representation, so the Idea of the thing is expressed in speech; and therefore the form of diction is called "genus" or "stilus," for the word "phrasis" is used to refer to a plain,

---

[32] *Ibid.*, p. 23: "Poetę summa laus est à legibus Historię longe abscedere & naturalem narrandi ordinem negligere, si series rerum spectetur, quoniam, quę naturalis ordo prescribit, interdum negligit, quę fert prosequitur ac quae in pręsentia dicenda videbantur, in alium locum traducit, neque illi ea lex imponitur, vt quasi Historiam scribat, omnia ordine colligat. Habeat sanè delectum rerum, & alia dicat, & ornet, alia prętereat, quę non esse dicenda iudicauerit."

or elegant, or a strange and foreign diction, whereas "stilus" or "character" or "forma dicendi" indicates the general conformation of the diction.[33]

Correa then proceeds to a description of each of the three styles, to an indication of the subject matters to which each is appropriate, and to a statement of the general principle of decorum operative in all matters of style. When, later, he gives his definitions of comedy and tragedy, they are compounded of these elements; he himself says that they differ in three ways, in "the social status of the personages, the manner and quality of the affairs and destinies, and finally in the ending." And then he adds, immediately, a fourth difference: "This being the case, they must necessarily differ in style also."[34] Applied to tragedy, these distinctions lead to the following definition: "Tragedy, then, is an imitation by means of action of an illustrious destiny, with an unhappy ending, and in the grave style";[35] and to comedy, this: "Comedy, then, is a dramatic poem full of activity, with a happy ending, and in the humble style."[36] The elaborate apparatus of distinctions thus produces definitions which are not notably more sophisticated than those of Diomedes and the whole medieval school.

To these questions of matter and of form we may relate what Correa has to say about the audience for which the poem is intended and about the poet who writes it. Audience considerations are not prominent, but they are important beyond their number. The ends of poetry are stated in terms of the audience, in several ways: as the instruction and pleasure of men ("hominum institutio, & voluptas," p. 18); as admiration, admonishment, delight, teaching ("vt spectator admiretur, ... vt admoneatur, delectetur, doceatur," p. 93). The nature of these ends determines certain characteristics both of matter and of form. Of the many available subjects, the poet chooses those which are most outstanding and excellent, since these will be of greatest interest to his audience (p. 24); he will retain this interest by introducing the greatest possible variety into the materials. No two deaths will occur in the same way, no two cities will be besieged and conquered according to the same pattern, and so forth (p. 40). Moreover, if the "institutio" is to be accomplished, materials must be verisimilar and

[33] *Ibid.*, p. 13: "Est autem character dictio similis illi rei, quam notat: siue est rei effigies, & imago, quoniam oratio rem exprimit, vt in pictura colores. Ex cera, vt addita nota exprimitur effigies persimilis ei rei, cuius nota est; sic oratione rei Idea exprimitur, & ideo dicend forma, aut genus, aut stilus dicitur, quoniam phrasis ad elocutionem planam, elegantem, aut peregrinam, & barbaram refertur; stillus, siue character, aut forma dicendi conformationem orationis indicat."

[34] *Ibid.*, p. 91: "Differt Tragędia a comoedia tribus potissimum rebus, personarum condicione, negotiorum, & fortunarum modo, & qualitate, atque tandem exitu. Haec cum ita sint stilo etiam differant, necesse est."

[35] *Ibid.*, p. 92: "Est autem Tragędia imitatio Illustris fortunae per actione[m] exitu infoelici, oratione graui."

[36] *Ibid.*, p. 94: "Est autem Comoedia poema dragmaticum, negotiosum, exitu laeto, stylo humili."

self-consistent (note the references to nature and to decorum); and if the "voluptas" is to accompany it, variety must be cultivated (p. 18). As for form, the great reason for the necessity of artificial order is that by means of it the poet creates suspense. The passage cited previously on artificial order continues thus: "In fact, since the poet makes an effort to detain the auditor as it were against his will and in suspense, he makes his poem varied throughout by the arrangement of the events.... For the highest praise of the poet is to hold the listener as if he were a captive."[37] Finally, the pleasure so provided is itself an aid to the achieving of the utility, and the utility involved makes the pleasure more acceptable and more memorable (p. 107).

That Correa is independent of certain parts of the current tradition is attested by his discarding of the notion, in connection with the poet, of the poetic furor. He treats the subject when he is discussing lines 309 ff. ("Scribendi recte sapere est et principium et fons"). "So far," he says, "is the poet from being mad that nobody can write well unless he is wise. Indeed, every good and proper discourse must derive from the knowledge of things."[38] The knowledge in question concerns, for the poet, the rules of decorum—especially with reference to character—and human nature. Since the poet is an imitator, he must express the essence of nature ("exprimit naturae uim," p. 103); this is the opinion of both Plato and Aristotle. For Correa, this knowledge is obtained by study of rules and does not come as a form of inspiration. The poet must of course have an "ingenium" or "facultas" suited to the genre which he means to practice, but even more so must he have such virtues as "prudentia, varietas, efficacia, suauitas" (p. 18). These, translated into terms of his activity, have to do largely with disposition and elocution—with the proper handling of the elements constituting form.

Thus, the major orientations in Correa's commentary are probably more definitely toward the internal relationships of "res" and "verba" than toward the more specifically rhetorical factors so common in the present tradition. These latter are all developed, and in a way only slightly divergent from the ordinary; but the emphasis is elsewhere. One feels, after studying the commentary, that its main preoccupations are with problems of matter and form rather than with the devices and expedients for swaying, influencing, and arousing the audience. Since it is a commentary on Horace, it must of necessity make all the centrifugal movements that are found in the text itself—toward nature, toward conventions, toward the poet, toward the audience. But it manages, in a fairly consistent way, to reverse the

---

[37] *Ibid.*, pp. 23–24: "Nam cum poeta in eo elaboret, vt vel inuitum detineat auditorem, & suspensum, in finem vsque variat poema collocatione rerum. . . . Nam poetę illa summa laus, vt auditorem quasi captiuum detineat."

[38] *Ibid.*, p. 102: "Tantum verò abest, vt furiosus poeta sit, vt bene scribere nemo possit, nisi sapiens. Omnis enim oratio bona, & apta ex cognitione rerum promanet necesse est."

motion of all these and bring them into contact with the central problem of the text as Correa interprets it.

NICOLA COLONIO (1587)

The second of the complete commentaries to appear in this last period was published in the same year as Correa's, 1587. It is Nicola Colonio's *Methodus de Arte poetica*, and its principal distinction is its claim that it perceives—as had never been done before—the true order or "method" of the *Ars poetica*. In his dedication (p. iiiv), Colonio boasts that he has for long years studied Aristotle's "analytic method," and his intention in the present work is to apply what he has learned to the analysis of Horace's epistle. He believes that, by such an application, he has discovered what Horace's principal subject matter is and how it is presented:

> I confess that I was first impelled by this to consider more attentively the subject; then, pondering the particular matters not only carefully but fastidiously—namely, what he teaches, and in what way, and in what order—with the whole method frequently and thoroughly examined in the fashion of an army most beautifully drawn up in order, it seems to me that I have seen that Horace wanted to explain, in this *Epistle to the Pisos*, the universal nature of the poetic faculty (insofar as the law of metrical expression would permit), which he himself, as an especially great poet and adorned with the greatest learning, held contained within his own mind.[39]

What he discovers is that Horace treats the "universal nature of the poetic faculty" not in terms of the general nature of the art, but in terms of the four main genres: epic, tragic, comic, and satiric. Moreover, since the major problem with respect to any genre is the handling of plot, Colonio sees the largest section of the *Ars poetica* as devoted to this problem. His summary to the first two hundred and fifty lines makes this clear:

> To this point, the principal matters of the method of poetics adopted have been explained: whatever the imitation may be, expressing man's life in invented fables, it has four fixed species of plot, and these are the epic, tragic, comic, and satiric plots. He treated these singly, and first of the constitution of the epic plot, which is the most difficult of all because it is composed of many episodes contrived by the poet's genius. And so he taught, in that plot in which one may most easily fail, that unity of plot, which is common to any plot, is what is to be worked on above all else.... Along with the fact that what is required especially in a plot is that it be one, he taught briefly both about its order and its language.... Just

---

[39] *Methodus* (1587), p. 2: "Hac me fateor primo compulsum, vt rem attentius considerarem; deinde singulis rebus non diligenter modo, sed fastidiose expendendis, quidnam scilicet, & quomodo, quoue ordine doceret, tota Methodo instar exercitus pulcherrime instructi saepius perlustrata, vidisse mihi videor, Horatium vniuersam vim Poeticae facultatis, quam ipse magnus in primis Poeta, & magnis excultus doctrinis, animo comprehensam tenebat, in hoc libello ad Pisones, quantum lex carminis pateretur, explicare voluisse."

as he did for the epic plot, so he treated with respect to the comic and the tragic in what way they differ in matter, diction, and style.[40]

Consistent with this discovery of the general lines of Horace's development, Colonio gives a detailed interpretation of the first part of the *Ars poetica* as a treatise on epic plot. Lines 1–9 treat of plot and episodes, 9–18 of the objects of epic imitation (with the indication, in 14–18, that digressions are a vice and that when they appear, as in the *Orlando Furioso*, they must be condemned). Line 23 is devoted to epic unity, 24–31 to excessive variety as a source of error, 32–37 to knowledge as the source of epic plot. After pausing, in 38–40, to make the essential division into invention, disposition, and elocution, Horace goes on (in 42–45) to discuss epic disposition and the artificial order and then (in 46–56) its elocution. The relationship to epic plot of epic meter is outlined in 73–82, of epic diction in 83–92; the latter problem involves the principle of decorum, and this is applied to elocution in 93–109, to character in 114–18. Horace then speaks of the epic hero (ll. 119–30), of the distinction between old and new epic plots, of the objects of imitation, and once again of epic order; he concludes with further remarks on the juncture of episodes. "To this point," says Colonio after expounding line 152, "[he has treated] of the whole circle of the epic and of composing, distributing, treating, and writing the epic matter and plot."[41] There then follow, according to Colonio, similar sections—albeit abbreviated—on comedy, on tragedy, and on satire.

Within each of these sections, it is clear that Colonio is thinking largely in terms of invention, disposition, and elocution. The reference is explicit in his remark on lines 38–40: "He makes the transition from invention and from composition of the plot to order and to poetic elocution. What could be more consequent than these things and indicate better that they are propounded in a methodical way?"[42] At lines 55–56 he adds: "This is the first part of the method, common to all those who write of poetic invention, disposition, and elocution."[43] But others of the familiar rhetorical distinctions are also present, sometimes in a striking way. So for the "res-

---

[40] *Ibid.*, pp. 39–40: "Hactenus exposita sunt, quae sunt praecipua susceptae Methodi de Poetica: quae cum sit imitatio, exprimens hominum vitam fictis fabulis, certas habet species fabularum quatuor; & sunt fabula Epica, Tragica, Comica, Satyrica. De singulis tractauit, ac primum de constitutione Epicae fabulae, quę est omnium difficillima, quoniam constat ex multis Episodijs, ingenio poetae excogitatis. Itaque, quod commune est omni fabulae vt sit vna, hoc praecipue elaborandum esse docuit in ea fabula, in qua facilius peccari possit.... Cum eo, quod in fabula maxime postulatur vt sit vna, docuit breuiter, & de ordine, & de elocutione.... Sicut fecit de fabula Epica, sic tractauit de Comica, & Tragica, quomodo differant materia, oratione, & stylo."

[41] *Ibid.*, p. 31: "Hactenus de orbe Epico & materia fabulaque Epica componenda, distribuenda, tractanda, & scribenda."

[42] *Ibid.*, p. 13: "parit transitum ab inuentione, & compositione fabulae ad ordinem & elocutionem Poeticam: quibus rebus quid potest esse magis consequens, & magis indicare haec methodice tradi?"

[43] *Ibid.*, p. 18: "Haec est Methodi prima pars communis omni Scribenti de Poetica inuentione, dispositione, & elocutione."

verba" distinction. Colonio sees it as equivalent to Aristotle's object and means, as the "quas imitantur" and the "quibus imitantur"; the three kinds of things which poets imitate are expressed in the three kinds of language or style (see p. 21 on ll. 83–85). The close relationship between "verba" and "res" is supplied by Nature herself: "So easily in an abundance of subjects Nature herself, without anybody to lead her, if only she is practiced, will glide into the ornaments of speech; moreover, if there is decency in the things themselves that are written, there emerges from the nature of the things even a certain splendor in the words."[44] He does not fail to use, when he wishes to designate the language or style appropriate to a given matter, the rhetorical term "character."

The early statement of an Aristotelian intention prepares us for the discovery, throughout the treatise, of the same kinds of parallels with the *Poetics* which Colonio's predecessors had used; but he cites them in the moderate way current in this latter part of the century. The list follows:

Horace	Aristotle
1–9	1450a34, 1450a38, 1451a4, 1451b27, 1455b34, 1456a12, 1459b28
9–10	1448a5
23	1451a29
24–31	1459b34
73–74	1448b34
79	1448b31
80–82	1449a22
132	1455b15
134	1451b27
140	1451a22
146	1451a20
189–90	1450b25, 1449b12
193–95	1456a26
202–3	1449b28
241–43	1457b6
275–77	1448b34
278–80	1449a15
338–40	1461b11

Except for repeated praise of Homer and certain details in the histories of the genres, Colonio refers to Aristotle mostly on matters of unity, of plot in its relationship to episodes, and of imitation—rather than verse—as constituting the essence of poetry. These are, as we have seen in earlier commentators, the stock topics on which the Horatians sought the authority of the Aristotelians or of Aristotle himself. They do not show any special command of Aristotle's "method" or any particular penetration into the essence of the *Poetics*.

[44] *Ibid.*, p. 48: "Ita facile in rerum abundantia ad orationis ornamenta, sine duce, natura ipsa, si modo est exercitata, labetur. praeterea si est honestas in rebus ipsis, quae scribuntur, existit ex rerum natura quidam etiam splendor in verbis."

POETIC THEORY

Nor are Colonio's claims to having made original discoveries with respect to the "method" of the *Ars poetica* substantiated by his commentary. In reality, all that he does is to declare that Horace treated four poetic genres separately rather than poetry in general, and to find an order in the succession of these four treatments. Otherwise, when talking about individual passages, he gives interpretations very similar to those of his predecessors. His finding of the basic analogies in rhetorical theory and of occasional parallels in Aristotle in no way distinguishes him from the common breed of Horatians.

In the year of these two commentaries on Horace, we find, in this period, the first real effort at practical criticism. It is Giovanni Talentoni's *Lettione sopra'l principio del Canzoniere del Petrarca*, read before the Accademia Fiorentina on September 13, 1587, and published in the same year. Like so many other practical essays of the time, it attempts to apply well-stated theoretical criteria to an individual work and to derive evaluative conclusions. It goes beyond the implications of the short title, for the complete title indicates that it will treat the beginning, narration, and conclusion of all kinds of poems, and it touches upon all these in dealing with Petrarch. This same title demonstrates at once the general approach and the general method: an approach via the traditional parts of an oration, a method of deducing from the practice of the ancients a standard of judgment for moderns. Talentoni's investigation will therefore consist of three steps: (1) a discovery of the principles underlying the use of such parts as prologue, invocation, proposition, narrative, and epilogue; (2) an examination of the treatment of these parts by Greek and Latin poets; and (3) a study of Petrarch's *Canzoniere* to see whether or not it conforms to their usage. Since the parts distinguished are rhetorical parts, Talentoni will naturally think of them in reference to their effects upon a prospective audience. In their prologue, for example, the ancient poets "strove to make the listener favorable, to make him attentive to them and aware, and finally to make him well disposed to understand what they say, in the way taught by the rhetoricians."[45] Book III of Aristotle's *Rhetoric* is cited in support. Epic, tragic, and comic poets used prologues for a slightly different purpose—to give the reader or spectator a foretaste of the plot so that he might anticipate what was coming, whereas philosophers used them to prepare their readers for the instruction that they meant to give. Similar reasons are adduced for the cultivation of such other "preliminary" parts as the invocation and the proposition.

Since Petrarch is a lyric poet, Talentoni must analyze some ancient examples of that genre before determining the correctness of Petrarch's

[45] *Lettione* (1587), pp. A*v*–A2: "s'affaticauano in farsi l'uditor fauoreuole, in farselo attento, & auuertito, e finalmente in farselo ben disposto a comprendere il lor parlare, con quella maniera, che c'insegnano i Retori."

procedures; the cases he chooses are Pindar and Horace. He finds that sometimes Pindar wrote merely a "gay proem," and that this was justified by the "demonstrative kind" in which he was writing; Horace sometimes used invocation, dedication, and proposition, sometimes omitted them. As for Petrarch, he "did not depart from this practice of the lyric poets, ... since once in his canzoni he also merely proposed the subject ... ; sometimes, he both proposed and invoked; at other times he did neither the one nor the other."[46] The content and the effect of his beginning (Talentoni is speaking of the first sonnet, "Voi ch'ascoltate ...") are also acceptable, since through his confession of error and his apology for his varied style, "he makes himself known as a good man of high morals, and thus he makes the reader docile, that is, disposed to understand what is treated later."[47] The whole series of sonnets may be considered as a single narration having the following order of materials: the efficient cause of his love, the final cause, the manner, its state of being, its time, place, and name (p. F3). Its epilogue is found in the canzone "Vergine bella," where he warns us not to follow the example of his life.

In the course of this discussion, Talentoni seeks justification for his remarks (and for Petrarch's poems) in more general principles of the art. The end of poetry, he says, is essentially to profit the audience "by introducing into our souls, as Aristotle taught, good mores and by withdrawing them from bad ones."[48] Plato is the second authority for this end; his banishment of the poets was meant to apply only to those who sought pleasure alone, and he gave highest praise to those who taught good behavior and the proper ways of life. Pleasure, to be sure, is to be sought by the poet, but only as an instrument to the working of utility. On this score, also, Petrarch merits praise, for in his epilogue "he makes clear to us that in his rhymes we should enjoy only the sweetness and take from them that utility which is taken from lyric poems, but that we should beware of attaching ourselves to that life which, as he passed through it, caused him to write them."[49] In fact, the moral lessons taught and the subject matter from which they arise constitute a superiority of Petrarch over his compeers—the superiority of the Christian over pagans. The Italian surpasses all Greek and Latin lyricists in the decency ("onestà") of his words and his actions; he speaks as a Christian poet, avowing his shame and confessing his errors in the most proper terms. It will be noted that

[46] *Ibid.*, pp. E–Ev: "Da questa vsanza de' Lirici non si scostò il Petrarca, come uero Lirico, impercioche alcuna volta anch'egli nelle sue canzoni solamente propose il soggetto. . . . Alcuna volta propose, e inuocò. . . . Alcuna volta ancora non fece ne l'vn ne l'altro."

[47] *Ibid.*, p. Fv: "si da a conoscere per huomo costumato, e buono, e perciò si rende l'auditor docile, cioè, disposto a comprender quel, che poi si tratta."

[48] *Ibid.*, p. E4v: "l'introdur negli animi nostri, come uolle Aristotile, costumi buoni, e ritrargli da' rei."

[49] *Ibid.*, "ci viene a significare, che dobbiamo delle rime sue sol goder la dolcezza, e da quelle prendere quell'vtilità, che si prende dalle poesie liriche: ma che guardiamo di non ci appigliare a quella vita, per la quale camminando egli hebbe a comporle."

this "honesty" is one both of matter (Petrarch's emotions and experiences) and of form (his words); in a larger sense, the latter also refers to prosodic form, the sonnet, the canzone, and so forth.

In connection with the larger genres, such as tragedy, comedy, and the epic, Talentoni raises another general question: to what extent are verisimilitude and credibility observed by the poet? The conditions governing these change with the subject matter. They would be widely different for tragedy and comedy, and thus the latter admits a separate prologue, whereas in the former the prologue (which we should call the "exposition") must be made an integral part of the drama.

Credibility involves a believing audience, and Talentoni points out that three matters are to be considered here. First, even the popular audience of comedy recognizes that the play is an imitation and a representation, and that the actors are not real people. Second, it lends credence more readily to tragedy because the events are known through history or legend, whereas the plots of comedy are made up of whole cloth by the poet. Third, the decorum of each of the genres must be respected. In these latter considerations Talentoni comes very close to the commentators on Horace, and the former ones relate him directly to the purest strain of rhetoricians.

FEDERICO CERUTI (1588)

There is a question as to whether Federico Ceruti's *Paraphrasis in Q. Horatii Flacci librum de arte poetica,* published in 1588, should be called a "major" commentary on the Horatian text. For the volume itself is very slight and follows a plan somewhat different from that of its predecessors, printing the complete text first and then adding the *Paraphrase,* which occupies about twenty pages. Besides, much of the material is, in actuality, no more than paraphrase of the original. Yet if the crucial questions be asked—Is there something here in the way of an original interpretation of Horace? Is there a theory of poetry that goes beyond Horace or at least shows a special orientation?—the affirmative answers indicate that the little work at least merits careful consideration. Ceruti does have a theory of poetry, and if it is not complete, it at least contains fairly substantial ideas on what makes good poetry. These ideas are all related to a conception of the audience as the ignorant populace which must be amused, entertained, kept interested, pleased. Essentially, then, a good poem will cultivate those ornaments and those devices susceptible of appealing to such an audience. First of these will be, in such a genre as the epic, the episodes. Ceruti thinks of the central plot of an epic, provided by history and long familiar to the reader, as of minimum importance:

> The epic material, which is like a subject placed at the disposal of all, can be made the writer's own if the epic poet does not dwell on the exact history of the subject proposed, which has practically no importance in the poem; but, disregarding that historical cycle containing what is true in the plot to be treated, he

will seek grandeur and dignity for the poem in those fictitious things called episodes.[50]

What is really important, then, is the unreal material added to the basic story by way of amplification and decoration; this comes from the poet's inventiveness and is a sign of his genius. But if the episodes constitute the "laus Epicae fabulae" (p. 17), they also introduce the primary danger: for the poet, in his eagerness to provide that delight which episodes afford, may invent too many or ones which are not fitting. The monstrous product results. An ornament of another kind is found in the inverted, unnatural, unhistorical order in which the poet narrates his materials; the "exordium," especially, consisting of something which should be said much later but is transferred to the beginning, gives light and luster to the order (p. 18). Still another ornament is contributed by meter and diction. The criterion for the former is appropriateness to the specific genre for which it is used, and hence to the kind of subject matter typical of the genre; for the latter, the same appropriateness to genre and subject. Both, in fact, are regulated by a special kind of decorum: "Materia igitur quęque suo carmine, & proprio cum decoro tractetur" (p. 20). All these ornaments, if re-examined, will be found to distribute themselves among the three parts of composition—plot and episodes under invention, artificial order under disposition, meter and style under elocution. This is intentional with Ceruti, who writes in the margin of his remarks on lines 38 ff., "Inuentio fabulae, Dispositio fabulae, Elocutio fabulae."

A good poem, however, is not one which merely pleases its popular audience; the other end—utility—must be served simultaneously. Ceruti believes that the utilitarian purpose of leading men to virtue will be most directly achieved through the introduction of the right kind of sententiae into the work, ones which are brief enough to be easily learned and long remembered (p. 29). Presumably, some instruction in virtue is also contained in the examples presented by perfect heroes, since the poet "expresses the ideal essence of the perfect man."[51] In some genres, also, utility may derive from the development of the plot itself. This may be the case with Old Comedy, which was written "above all for its usefulness in correcting mores,"[52] although Ceruti does not specifically identify the instrumentality of moral correction. Nor does he indicate with precision whether the primordial qualities of unity, self-consistency, verisimilitude, and credibility, each of which is treated in connection with the usual passage in the *Ars poetica*, are related to either or both of these ends. He seems

---

[50] *Paraphrasis* (1588), p. 22: "Materies epica, quae quasi res omnium usui exposita est; effici propria scribentis poterit; si Epicus poeta non immorabitur in propria rei propositae historia, quae nullam ferè habet in poemate dignitatem: sed circulo illo historiae, continente quod uerum est tractandae fabulae, tamquàm uili neglecto, in rebus fictis, quae Episodia uocantur, amplitudinem, & poematis dignitatem quaesierit."

[51] *Ibid.*, p. 29: "perfecti hominis idęam exprimere."

[52] *Ibid.*, p. 27: "ad mores emendandos adprime utilem."

rather to accept them as a part of the standard doctrine, without attempting to integrate them with his own notions on good poetry. In the same way he accepts the dogma of the decorum of character and the idea that plot is primary in a work as concepts necessarily present in any Horatian commentary, regardless of their pertinence to the commentator's own philosophy of poetry.

Like Massini's lecture on the madrigal earlier in the same decade, Vicenzo Toralto's *La Veronica, o del sonetto* of 1589 deals with one of the shorter, lyric genres. But Toralto would be the last to admit that he was discussing a minor form; rather, he declares that the sonnet is the most difficult of all forms to write, surpassing even the tragedy. The occasion for his treatise is a sonnet by an academician whose pseudonym was "Il Risvegliato," and he spends a portion of his time (and the whole center section of his work) in interpreting this sonnet and others by the same author. The practical criticism involved, however, is concerned exclusively with expounding the hidden meanings to be found in the sonnets, and the treatise remains interesting only for the theoretical positions which it espouses. The matter of hidden meanings is important for Toralto, since he regards every good sonnet as having two sets of meanings, one for the person addressed (this an easy and superficial one), another for the learned and wise reader (this a secret and recondite one). The necessity of combining the two in a single, brief sonnet constitutes the first and perhaps the major difficulty. The second one consists in the prosodic restrictions: limitation to fourteen lines, to fixed rhyme schemes, and so forth. The third, in the necessity of choosing an "easy" subject, since the aim of poetry is to please and there can be no pleasure in grave matters. Among other criteria for the sonnet, Toralto would include the verisimilitude of language, by which he means language such as the person speaking might use to express the emotion involved. That is, a very sorrowful man should speak only in proper terms, not figurative ones, since the latter would not occur to him in his sorrow; but a "grave" sonnet would require metaphorical language, precisely in order to differentiate it from everyday speech. In fact, most of Toralto's preoccupations seem to be linguistic. When he metes out praise to Petrarch, it is because of his variety, and this is in style: "now he raised his style, then lowered it, now made it sorrowful, then pleasant."[53] Variety as a criterion applies to the total work of a poet, not to an individual sonnet, and Toralto demonstrates its presence in Petrarch by citing selected sonnets, each of which represents a different style. One prosodic matter comes in for special attention, and in a way which illustrates a curious effort to relate versification to states of soul; this is the run-on line, or enjambment:

[53] *La Veronica* (1589), p. 19: "hora egli inalzò, hora abbassò lo stile, hora il fece doloroso, hora piaceuole."

... our nature abhors corruption, and on the contrary loves and desires eternity. Thus when we read a sonnet in which every verse represents for us an end [by being end-stopped], that is, corruption, our intellect suffers; and on the contrary, when we read another which has its verses running on into one another, it takes pleasure, for from them it derives an indefinable promise of eternity.[54]

The difficulties of the tragedy are of other kinds. Mostly they concern the invention of the plot and its disposition; from the extent of the treatment, the former would seem to be by far the more important. Invention is circumscribed by many factors. The plot must be true, and it must therefore be historical in origin; but the history must itself be incomplete so that the poet may be free to add episodes of his own contriving, and this he must do without contradicting the history itself. It is only in this one respect that tragedy might be said to be more difficult than the sonnet. The plot, again, should be "magnificent" and "royal" in its personages, "sorrowful" and "fearful" in its effect—the latter apparently a counterpart of Aristotle's pity and fear. Finally, a tragedy must achieve an impression of extreme gravity, and this too has its difficulties.

Toralto has little to say about more general poetic matters. He uses the term "imitation" only for the imitation of models, sees the use of metaphors and other figures as the feature which distinguishes poetry from prose, and insists upon the necessity of both divine inspiration and acquired knowledge for the poet. In passing, he discusses Tasso's works, finding his sonnets inferior to the *Gerusalemme* since they do not imitate as well; in Tasso's heroic poem, the principal qualities are in the diction used to express the borrowed materials.[55]

Another of the shorter lyric genres, the elegy, is the object of Tommaso Correa's inquiry in his *De elegia* (1590). His approach here, however, is broader and more general than in his earlier treatise on the epigram (1569) and proceeds on a somewhat different basis. Before actually beginning the discussion of the elegy, he indulges in a number of generalizations about poetry, and these concern almost equally the poet, the poem, and the audience. Indeed, there is so free a passage from one to another of these topics that at times it is difficult to discover which is being treated. One might state the nearly circular relationship in this way: The poet seeks admiration and praise. He must have, to obtain them, qualities supplied by both art and nature—genius and judgment, precepts and prudence. These qualities will manifest themselves in the poem, both in its over-all structure and in the details. And the poem, when properly constructed, will produce the proper effect upon its erudite and elite audience, which will accord to the poet its praise and admiration. Since this set of relation-

---

[54] *Ibid.*, p. 23: "la natura nostra abborrisce la corruttione; e per lo contrario ama, e desidera l'eternità; leggendo adunque vn sonetto, ch'in ogni verso ci rappresenti il fine, ciò è la corruttione, l'intelletto nostro patisce, ed all'incontro leggendone vn'altro, c'habbia i versi entranti l'vno nell'altro, gode, perche da quelli si promette non sò che di eternità."

[55] The principal passages in Toralto are to be found on pp. 10–30, 37, and 78.

ships obtains, any aspect of a poem may be discussed in itself or with reference to the poet or the audience. Correa does all three, alternately or simultaneously. The following passage on the good poet may serve as an example:

> Since indeed the poet seeks admiration and that praise which derives from admiration itself, he must certainly strive to see to it that his poem is admirable, that the artifice is extraordinary, the composition elegant and praiseworthy; and when the reader examines it, he approves the devices, praises the invention, commends the joining of words and rhythms, extols the wit, whatever features it may set forth; he admires the thoughts, expressed in a proper and harmonious manner, and learns to appreciate fully the greatness and excellence of the artifice.[56]

The audience, in this analysis, is the direct opposite of the ignorant crowd, the "plebecula," the "turba inscia et imperita." It is made up rather of men who would be like the ancients in sound judgment, like the poet himself in knowledge of the art. In fact, the best audience would be composed of poets: "That man cannot judge appropriately nor react properly who does not have genius, art, practice and familiarity in poetry, and who is not himself a good poet."[57]

As for the poem itself, it is to be made according to Horace's prescriptions. The three elements to be successfully combined are "res," "verba," and "numeri," and their correct handling is taught by art: "It teaches what subject matter is appropriate, what words, what rhythms, and it sees what connection of words and rhythms is required."[58] The terms "appropriate" and "connection" give the key to Correa's whole conception of poetry. For on the one hand he insists everywhere on the necessity of decorum—in character, in actions, in words, in rhythms—and on the other hand he emphasizes the importance of conjoining things which are compatible by nature and of achieving by their combination a uniform tone and effect. When, after these preliminary matters, he comes to the elegy, he applies the principles enunciated earlier. In a definition which apes Aristotle he says: "The elegy is an imitation of a lamentable action expressed in verses with unequal rhythmic intervals."[59] But the definition would be incomplete for Aristotle, since only "object" and "means" are touched upon, with no reference to "manner" and no equivalent of the purgation (or "effect") clause. The "lamentable action" is part—but only part—of

[56] *De elegia* (1590), pp. 20–21: "Cum enim poeta admirationem quaerat, & laudem, quae ex ipsa admiratione comparatur; eniti certe debet, vt admirabile sit eius carmen, singulare artificium, laudabilis & ornata coagmentatio; quam cum introspicit lector, probat consilia, laudat inuentionem, commendat connexionem verborum, & numerorum, extollit acumen, quaecumque lineamenta praedicat; sententias apte, & concinne conclusas admiratur, artificij magnitudinem, & praestantiam penitus cognoscit."

[57] *Ibid.*, p. 22: "Iudicare congrue non potest, neque honeste sentire is, in quo non sit ingenium, non ars, non exercitatio poetica, & vsus, non sit bonus ipse poeta."

[58] *Ibid.*, p. 6: "Docet quod argumentum conueniat, quae verba, qui numeri, quae verborum, & numerorum coagmentatio requiratur, videt."

[59] *Ibid.*, p. 25: "Elegia quidem est querebundae actionis imitatio, versibus numerorum disparibus interuallis expressa."

the "res"; it comprises such things as the commiserations of lovers, funeral lamentations, and letters. "Res" includes as well the persons concerned in the actions—with all their characteristics and attributes—and nonpersonal elements such as divine providence and fate; I suspect that it also includes the sententiae or thoughts uttered by the characters. Correct development of these matters demands, on the part of the poet, a knowledge of economics and politics, so that he may distinguish public from private affairs, of the characters to be assigned to various types of persons, and of the activities to be attributed to the various kinds of life, the urbane, the rustic, the military. This is, essentially, a knowledge of divers kinds of decorum. Since the elegy belongs to the "low" or simple style, its diction must be "most tender and delicate"

... so that the reader may take delight and admire, and may judge that the most essential feelings have been set forth, and we may be caught by that bright and pure simplicity. In the words, one must strive for a sure and fit propriety of diction, and the words themselves should be varied and elegant, capable of arousing grave, magnificent, noble, distinguished, new and agreeable feelings, and ones which will flow easily into the souls of the readers.[60]

Verse, for Correa, is an essential accompaniment of all poetry, and in the elegy it is even more necessary than elsewhere; it endows the poem with a special essence, makes it admirable and worthy to be read, gives it honor and the assurance of glory for its author. Rhythm is the soul of poetry (p. 54). Correa summarizes his requirements for all poetry, and for the elegy in particular, with a string of nouns: "Varietas, Perspicuitas, Cultus, Proprietas, Venustas, Numerus"; and his estimate of what the effect of the elegy should be with an even more formidable string of adjectives: "candidam, elegantem, laeuem, aequabilem, tersam, mollem, perspicuam, rectam, plenam, rotundam, dulcem, lepidam, puram, venustam, concinnam, variam, floridam, tenui ... et simplicissimo filo perfectam, ... ingenuam" (pp. 29, 43). Matter, diction, and versification must be so combined as to produce a work answering these requirements. From both sets of terms, it would seem that Correa is really more concerned with the poem itself than with its effect upon an audience or with the faculties of the poet. His approach is Horatian in the broadest sense, with the rhetoricians called upon mostly for their distinction of styles and for their teachings on diction and versification.

RICCOBONI (1591)

In 1591, Antonio Riccoboni published three separate works dealing with the art of poetry; two of them concerned Horace's *Ars poetica*. In the first,

[60] *Ibid.*, pp. 29–30: "vt & oblectetur lector, & admiretur, & simplicissime exposita sensa mentis esse iudicet, atque illa simplicitate candida, & munda capiatur. In verbis spectetur dictionis secura, & legitima proprietas, atque verba ipsa sint varia, & ornata, quae sensus gignant graues, magnificos, nobiles, praeclaros, nouos, suaues, & qui facile influant in animos lectorum."

entitled *Dissensio de epistola Horatii ad Pisones*, Riccoboni takes issue with an anonymous "vir doctus" who had declared that Horace's work displayed a complete confusion of subject matters, with no organization or order. Riccoboni counters with the thesis that although the epistle may not show a clear order (it need not, since the epistolary form permits of passage in a random way from one topic to another), it does have a method and an organization. Its ideas, if rearranged, would compose a complete and thoroughgoing dissertation on the art of poetry. Ideally, Riccoboni believes that such an art should have been organized as follows:

... first poetry had to be praised, just as Aristotle praised rhetoric before giving its precepts and as many others have similarly done. And since praise for the poet can derive either from nature or art, or from both, this is the reason why such an inquiry had to be broached; and at the same time those should be reproved who wish to seem to be struck by madness, among whom Horace did not wish to be counted. Next, it must be made clear that the work of the poet and his poetry, or the poem, must be something excellent, and that the poet himself should not excel in one single part of the poem, but in the whole work; and that excellence of this kind in invention, in elocution, and in poetic decorum must be sought from philosophy; moreover, that the Greeks were more capable of achieving excellence in poetic matters than the Romans. Further, the end of the poet had to be revealed, the kinds of poems listed. After having explained these latter in general, following the lead of Aristotle, it was necessary, if not for each and every poetic genre, at least for some of the major ones, to examine carefully now the constituent parts, which are six in number: plot, characters, sententia, diction, melody, spectacle, even though all are not proper to all poetic genres. Next the quantitative parts, which are four in number: prologue, episode, exode, choral song, which similarly are not appropriate to all genres. And just as Aristotle at the end of his book treated of the censures brought against poets and the excuses for them, so at the end it would have been necessary to show which errors of the poets should be pardoned and which not, and in what way a sincere judgment of poetic works should be sought and how the bad poets should be avoided by the wise ones.[61]

[61] *Dissensio* (1591), p. D4v: "Etenim primum Poetica erat laudanda, ut ab Arist. laudatur Rhetorica ante praecepta, & similiter fit ab aliis multis: quoniamque laus poetae potest prouenire aut à natura, aut ab arte, aut ab utraque, idcirco talis quaestio erat aperienda: simulque reprehendendi illi, qui uolunt uideri furore perciti, in quorum esse numero Horatius nolebat. Deinde ostendendum, poetae opus, & poesim, seu poema rem quandam excellentem esse oportere: ipsumque poetam non in una parte poematis, sed in toto opere excellere debere: atque huiusmodi excellentiam in inuentione, in elocutione, in decoro poetico à philosophia petendam esse: in re autem poetica magis Graecos, quam Romanos excellere potuisse. praeterea erat aperiendus finis poetae: enumerandaque poematum genera. Quibus uniuerse explicatis ad imitationem Aristotelis, si non in singulis poematum generibus, at certe in praecipuis quibusdam oportebat perpendere tum partes conformantes, quae sunt sex, fabula, mores, sententia, dictio, melopoeia, apparatus, quamuis non omnes omnibus conuenientes: tum partes quantitatis, quae sunt quattuor, prologus, episodium, exodus, choricum, non omnibus itidem congruentes; & quemadmodum in fine libri sui Arist. egit de reprehensionibus, & excusationibus poetarum, sic denique ostendendum erat, quibus poetarum erroribus esset ignoscendum, & quibus non ignoscendum, ac quomodo de poematibus syncerum iudicium sit requirendum, malique poetae à prudentibus fugiantur."

This program for an art of poetry in part follows Aristotle's order in the *Poetics*, in part adds sections from other works and from the popular defences of poetry.

Riccoboni then proceeds to cut the Horatian text into small pieces and to rearrange the pieces according to the topics outlined in the above plan. For each topic, he indicates parallels with Aristotle wherever warranted. By the time he finishes, every line of the Horatian epistle has been accounted for, and the parallelism with Aristotle is complete. Since this rearrangement itself constitutes a valuable interpretation, I give it below in brief outline form:

		Horace	Aristotle
I.	The praise of poetry art and nature divinity of poet natural causes	391–418 295–308	1455a33, 1448b4, 1451a22
II.	The necessity of excellence moral philosophy	361–385 32–41 309–332 285–294	1456a3, 1456a9, 1454b8
III.	The ends of poetry "delectare" primarily "prodesse" accidentally the genres	333–334 341–346 73–85	1448a25
IV.	The plot in various genres	275–280 220–233 281–284	
	Aristotle's requirements for plot:		
	(1) order	42–45	
	(2) magnitude	146–152	
	(3) unity	1–13	[General]
	(4) possible	338–340 128–135	1460a26
	(5) not episodic	14–23	
	(6) admirable, marvelous	136–145	
	(7) simple or complex	[none]	1452a12 1452b30
	(8) pathetic	[none]	
V.	Character	119–127 114–118 153–178	1453b22
VI.	Sententia	333–337 96–113	1456a34

[233]

		Horace	*Aristotle*
VII.	Diction	86–95	
		270–274	
		234–250	
		251–269	
		24–31	
		46–72	
VIII.	Melody	202–219	
IX.	Spectacle	179–188	
X.	Quantitative parts	189–201	1452b19
XI.	Errors of the poets	347–360	[1460b6]
		386–390	
		419–476	

Aside from the mechanical redistribution of segments, Riccoboni has little of interest to offer on the *Ars poetica*. In a preliminary section on epic poetry, he controverts Aristotle's assertion that tragedy is superior to the epic, maintaining instead that since the epic plot is longer and more difficult, it may be considered preferable (p. D2). His insistence that the primary end of poetry is to give pleasure is exceptional, especially in this last decade of the century. So, too, is his wish to find in Aristotle a basis for the organization of ideas about poetry, rather than merely a set of isolated parallels with Horace—a wish infrequently entertained or exploited by the Horatian critics.

Riccoboni's second work of 1591, published three months later in July, is a reply to Nicola Colonio's *Methodus de Arte poetica* (1587); he had either come to know it only after publishing the first or preferred to withhold his rebuttal of Colonio until after he had stated his own position. In his *Defensor seu pro eius opinione de Horatij epistola ad Pisones*, he discusses with Colonio, in dialogue form, the question of the order of the *Ars poetica*. The dialogue does little more than reiterate the positions of the *Dissensio* in a brief and general way. Riccoboni states his stand thus at the beginning of the dialogue:

> I have demonstrated that from him [Horace], as from the inexhaustible fountainhead of all doctrine, one may draw if not all the things that pertain to poetry, at least many, which are transmitted in a methodical fashion. . . . I say that not everything is contained in the *Epistle to the Pisos* part for part, but that everything is present there in a general sense, so that it seems that Horace in some way touched upon everything that Aristotle treated.[62]

Colonio's contention that Horace had not treated of plot in general, but

---

[62] *Defensor* (1591), pp. 11–12: "ostendi ex eo, tamquam ex uberrimo omnis doctrinae fonte, si non omnia, quae attinent ad Poeticam, ac certe multa, quae Methodice traduntur, hauriri posse. . . . dico non omnia quidem comprehendi in Epistola ad Pisones secundum partem, sed omnia contineri vniuersè, ut omnia quaecunque egerit Aristoteles, quodammodo attigisse Horatius videatur."

only of the plot in specific genres, leads to a long argument over plots and episodes and their interrelationship, in which the opinions of Castelvetro are cited. A long section near the end of the *Defensor* is devoted to an interpretation of line 128, "Difficile est proprie communia dicere," and Riccoboni recommends that the poet should not only prefer materials already exploited by others, but that he should treat them in such a way that their universal applications—in causes, in effects, in modalities of action—will be manifest. By so doing, he will give the greatest possible pleasure to the audience (pp. 31–32).

Five short treatises on literary problems by Giulio Cortese, a Neapolitan poet and academician, were published in 1591 and 1592; they are now usually found with the 1588 or 1592 editions of his *Rime*. Two of them, the *Regole per fuggire i vitii dell'elocutione* (1592) and the *Regole per formare epitafii* (1591), are exclusively rhetorical in content. But the other three, *Avertimenti nel poetare*, *Dell'imitatione e dell'inventione*, and *Delle figure* (all of 1591), contain theories of poetry and advice for their application to the practice of the art. The *Avertimenti nel poetare* is, in its own way, a very significant document. For it affords us our first encounter, in the present tradition, with a theory of the literary conceit and with the notions of Marinism, gongorism, and euphuism which were to be so prominent in these last years of the century. Cortese distinguishes three elements as important in any kind of poetry, the "concetto," the words, and the sounds. The first of these is defined as "that meditation which the spirit makes upon some object offered to it, of what it means to write about."[63] "Concetto" is thus different from "subject"; the subject is the general material chosen for treatment—arms, love, beauty, madness—whereas the "concetto" is a development of some particular aspect of this subject, through meditation or cogitation, in such a way as to permit expression in words. So considered, the conceit is the soul of poetry. In fact, certain verse genres which do not contain conceits, such as narratives of events, should not be called poetry at all, but rather historical or "casual" verse. Even some lyrics are to be denied the title, such as Petrarch's second and third sonnets, which do not engender any conceit in the mind (p. 2). Basically, the materials for conceits are furnished by the sciences, and hence the poet must be erudite in order to enrich and embellish his poetry. But two dangers attend him here: that of making his conceit too obscure to be understood by the reader (Giulio Camillo's cabalistic poems would be examples of such obscurity), and that of presenting scientific materials in bare, proper terms. Rather, "the conceit will be so drawn from the sciences as not to obfuscate or confuse the eye of the soul, but to instruct and illuminate it, so that the reader will know what it said and not have to guess at what it was trying

[63] *Avertimenti* (1591), p. 1: "quella meditatione che lo spirito fa sopra alcuno obietto che se gli offerisce di quello, c'ha da scriuere."

to say."[64] The principle for the other two elements is a simple one. The words must be appropriate to the conceit and the sounds to both. The poet must take particular care to see that the words are adapted to the style in which he is writing and that the sounds are at once fitting to the thought and harmonious among themselves.

In the second treatise, *Dell'imitatione e dell'inventione*, the conceit comes to be, by implication at least, synonymous with imitation. Cortese distinguishes in general two ways of writing, by words which signify directly the intended meaning and by phrases or paraphrases which describe, instead, the action. The first of these he calls simple narration (note the parallelism with the distinction concerning "concetti") and the second, imitation. It is imitation in the sense that the description of an action follows, somehow, the procedure of nature herself in establishing the law governing the action. Simple narration may be used to signify an action which is not immediate to the end of the poet; imitation will be used for one which is proximate to that end. Invention, also, has two meanings, since it refers on the one hand to the discovery of new things, new ways, new usages, on the other hand to the production of artificial things in semblance of natural things. In the latter category Cortese places all epic and dramatic plots (which resemble history), all lyric discoursings, with respect not only to the subject matter but also to such ornaments as episodes and epithets. "For," he says, "to invest a substance with a new accident congruous with it, containing a reason or a cause or an explanation, will constitute a very noble invention, and herein reside the riches of poetic compositions."[65]

The very brief *Delle figure*, in addition to a high-flown theory of figures and rules for their use, makes some statements about the reasons for the invention and use of these same figures. Cortese believes that they were invented out of necessity and to give pleasure, the necessity being to make certain ideas understandable, the pleasure being that which the human spirit customarily derives from literary works. In all three treatises, what is notable is a philosophy of linguistics that goes far beyond the usual theories of the styles or of diction, a theory of the conceit, which attempts to distinguish it from its materials in nature, and in general a curious wrestling with the problem of the difference between objects in nature and those same objects as the substance of literary expression.

Some time after 1592, Cesare Crispolti delivered to the Accademia Insensata of Perugia his *Lettione del sonetto*, now found in manuscript in the Biblioteca Comunale of that city. His lecture is a kind of amalgam of materials earlier developed by others. He derives his definition of the

---

[64] *Ibid.*, p. 7: "Sarà dunque il concetto tirato dalle scienze tale che non offuschi, ò ingarbugli l'occhio dell'anima; ma che l'erudisca, & l'illumini, accioche il lettore conosca quello, c'habbia detto, & non quello c'habbia uoluto dire."

[65] *Dell'imitatione* (1591), p. 5: "poiche uestire una sostanza di accidente nuouo congruente, che contenga ragione, ò cagione, ò esplicatione, sarà assai nobile inuentione, & quì stanno le ricchezze delle poesie."

sonnet from Minturno's *Arte poetica Thoscana*, his ideas on its style from Bernardino Tomitano, general notions on the fitting of style to matter from Aristotle's *Rhetoric*, Bembo's *Prose*, and Patrizi's *Retorica*. He also considers and rejects Dante's classification of lyric poetry under the low style, maintaining that a sonnet on a grave matter would demand the grave style. The sonnet, for Crispolti, is the most beautiful and the most difficult of the Tuscan poetic genres; its difficulty results primarily from its small size, in which—as in a small painting—every slightest defect can be seen. In long poems the situation is otherwise:

> In long compositions the poets, no matter how mediocre they may be, usually put many things which, with their beauty and their grace, compensate for other things which are less beautiful and less grave. In this composition, if the thought is happily developed, it moves, arouses, and ravishes the reader as if with a secret miracle. If other compositions must have many parts, this one seeks clarity of style and to join together gravity and pleasantness of diction.[66]

This description of the effect upon the reader has Longinian overtones. The sonnet differs from the epigram in the general tone achieved, and from the canzone in the absence of digressions and ornaments which give to the latter an epic majesty. It shares the subject matter of the other lyric genres —gods, heroes, and loves—and has the same ends as the canzone: to narrate, to pray, to comfort, to praise, and to blame. For all matters, internal construction as well as external effects, Petrarch is to be taken as the model, for his usage is everywhere marvelous. Crispolti's approach is thus essentially traditional. He thinks of the sonnet in terms of subject matter and the styles, of prosodic form and the ends with respect to the reader, of diction and sounds. His solutions for many of these problems come from the rhetoricians.

For Frederico Ceruti, the problem of the available sources is again an important one in his *Dialogus de comoedia* (1593). Since Horace had had little to say specifically about comedy and since Aristotle gave only suggestions, Ceruti was obliged to turn to the perennial source of information on the genre, Donatus. From him he borrowed a definition and the distinction of narrative, dramatic, and mixed manners. His use of Aristotle, however, is of some interest. From him, Ceruti takes the division of qualitative and quantitative parts, and although he desists from a full treatment of the former, he does point out that not only is the poet concerned with supplying them to the poem, but also the actor, the musician, and the architect. Aristotle also furnishes a model for Ceruti's description of the comic protagonist and the comic action: "It [the plot] will then imitate

[66] MS Bibl. Com. Perugia 1058 (N. 10), fol. 64v: "Ne i longhi componimenti i Poeti, per mezzani che siano, sogliono porre molte cose, che con la uaghezza, e gratia loro, l'altre men belle, e graui ricompensano. In questo se il concetto è felicemente spiegato, muoue, risueglia, e rapisce altrui, quasi con occulto miracolo. Se gl'altri componimenti deuono molte parti hauere. Questo ricerca la chiarezza dello stile, e che siano insieme accoppiate la grauità, e la piaceuolezza del dire."

only a single action, very agreeable in tone, suitably amusing, concerning private citizens who are neither entirely good nor entirely bad, but who through some imprudence or error (such as happen to men in private life) not unproductive of laughter, pass from a troublesome situation into one where they achieve happiness."[67] Other passages, such as a hint on the nature of the ridiculous (p. 27) and a reference to the dance as a form of imitation (p. 33), may also be traced to Aristotle. For the rest, such recent writers as Pontano, Maggi, and Riccoboni are called upon to authorize and illustrate an essentially rhetorical point of view. The tastes and the pleasure of the audience and the effect which the comedy will have upon it are paramount for Ceruti. He states as the end "to profit through delight and laughter" (p. 15) and sees comedy as a great school for providing examples of ways of life to be followed or to be eschewed. With those who hold that comedy might exert a corrupting influence on the young he disagrees heartily, especially since he sees in his century actors capable of expurgating obscene passages and of pointing up the moral. Many structural features of comedy are determined by the audience. The prologue, peculiar to comedy, exists as a means of obtaining the attention and the good will of the spectators; yet it must not reveal the denouement lest it spoil the suspense. The handling of all aspects of the plot must make it seem credible, even though the audience knows that it has been invented by the poet. Comedies are divided into acts to help the playgoer's memory and to provide intervening periods of relaxation, and the five-act length seems to be naturally adapted to the faculties and the capabilities of the audience. Songs and dances are provided in the *entr'actes* so that no spectator, even the most ignorant who would not understand the goings-on on the stage, will be deprived of some form of entertainment during the performance.

In 1597, Giovanni Talentoni attempted to solve a problem that had long been puzzling his predecessors in the field of poetic theory. Many of them had indicated the marvelous as one of the effects to be produced by the art in general and by the epic in particular and had spoken of the "admiration" which the poem must arouse in its audience. Talentoni's *Discorso sopra la maraviglia*, delivered as a lecture before the Accademia degli Inquieti of Milan, inquired into the nature of the marvelous and the conditions for achieving it; its point of departure was the passage at the beginning of Canto IV of the *Purgatorio*. The approach is only incidentally Horatian; but insofar as it seeks to analyze the effect as one of the passions of the soul, it belongs to the rhetorical tradition so constantly present in the Cinquecento. After an initial statement that the end of poetry is "by

[67] In *Dialogi duo* (1593), pp. 24–25: "imitabiturque duntaxat actionem vnam, perplacidam, & risu dignam hominum priuatorum, eorumdemque nec prorsus bonorum, nec prorsus malorum; sed eorum, qui imprudentia aliqua & errore (vt hominibus priuatis solet accidere) non sine risu ex molestia aliqua foelicem statum consequuntur."

means of pleasure to attract men and to lead them into ways of good living" and that the poets do this (according to Strabo) solely by the use of the marvelous,[68] Talentoni indicates that his treatment of the subject will have three parts,

... in the first of which we shall show that admiration is a passion, and to what kind of passion and appetite it should be reduced; in the second, coming much closer to its nature, we shall discover its form, and the subject and the cause from which it springs, and from these things we shall assemble its definition; we shall show that the species into which it is divided are five, and on the occasion of the third we shall treat of laughter and of ridiculous things. Since we shall classify astonishment under some of these species, we shall also speak of it. Having sufficiently explained in this way in the aforesaid two parts its nature and its essence, in the third we shall come to speak of the effects which it produces in those who receive it . . . , and finally to inquire into its qualities, that is, whether it be a good or a bad thing.[69]

After having established in the first part that admiration is a passion which, like others, dominates and tyrannizes the soul, Talentoni examines its causes, finding that it springs basically from the unexpected, the unknown, from whatever the patient is ignorant of. In tragedy and comedy, its sources include peripeteia, but exclude accidental events for which no cause may be discovered by the reader or the spectator. The four kinds of the marvelous are related to the four kinds of objects producing it: (1) the inanimate, (2) the animate but nonrational, (3) the animate and rational operating through chance, and (4) the animate and rational operating with intent. As for the effects, Talentoni sees some of them as physiological, especially a kind of helpless amazement in which the functions of both soul and body are arrested. It is important to note for poetics that this sensation is accompanied by pleasure and that hence the poem is capable of effecting its final goal of moral admonition.

One of the few exercises in practical criticism performed by this "last generation" of Horatian critics was Pietro Cresci's *Discorso sopra un Sonetto in lode del celebre luogo di Valchiusa* (1599), delivered to the Accademia degli Uranici in Venice. The sonnet in question was by Marco Cavallo. After preliminary remarks in praise of the sonnet as a genre, emphasizing the perfection achieved in so brief a form, Cresci proceeds to

[68] *Discorso* (1597), p. 5: "col piacer allettar gli huomini, e tirargli al ben viuere, nelle fauole sue."

[69] *Ibid.*, p. 6: "nella prima delle quali mostreremo, che la marauiglia è affetto, & à quale specie d'affetto, e d'appetito si debba ridurre: nella seconda, accostandoci molto più alla natura sua, scuopriremo la forma sua, il soggetto, e la cagione, ond'ella nasce, e da queste cose raccoglieremo la sua diffinitione; mostreremo, che le sue specie, nelle quali elia si diuide son cinque, e per cagion della terza tratteremo del riso, e delle cose ridicolose. Ad alcune di quelle, perche ridurremo lo stupore, di lui parimente fauelleremo. Spiegata à bastanza in questa guisa nelle dette due parti la natura, & essenza sua, verremo nella terza à parlar de gli effetti, ch'ella produce in quei, che la riceuono . . .; e finalmente à ricercar le sue qualitadi, cioè, s'ella sia cosa buona, ò ria."

a full analysis of Cavallo's sonnet. He does so by discussing in order its invention, its disposition, and its elocution. What he means by these is made clear by his essential statements under each heading. Under invention:

... invention, which is nothing other than an imagination of things which are either true or verisimilar, or we might say possible, and which is the main pillar of the great structure of imitation, the base and foundation of the whole poetic art since it is concerned with those same three objects upon which imitation, as if upon its proper seat, rests—that is, imitating nature, or art, or fortune.

Under disposition:

[The author of the sonnet] has, then, so well disposed all things, appropriately placed the words, used the attributes at the right time, developed the thoughts in a beautiful order, scattered the ornaments and the figures with moderation, and has so well observed variety and decorum (essential parts of disposition) that he has certainly achieved its designated end of giving pleasure and of renewing in the minds of the listeners and of the readers the graceful memories of those delightful places.

Under elocution:

And he has similarly succeeded with much felicity in elocution, having judiciously chosen words which are sonorous, grave, clear, proper, circumscribed, and figurative ... and he has at the same time elegantly filled the whole sonnet with gravity, with clarity, with purity, and with sweetness.[70]

The total critique of the sonnet revolves about these three topics. It is interesting to note, by way of general commentary on the procedure, that the same set of statements might have been made about almost any other work; only the examples or the citations would need to be changed, the judgments would remain the same. This is a characteristic feature of the rhetorical method of analysis in the sixteenth century.

RICCOBONI (1599)

Antonio Riccoboni, who had figured so prominently as an expositor of Horace in the early years of the decade, appears again at its very end with his *De Poetica Aristoteles cum Horatio collatus* of 1599; the work may,

[70] *Discorso* (1599), pp. B5–B5v: "l'inuentione, la quale altro non è, ch'vna imaginatione di cose, ò vere, ò verisimili, ò vogliam dir possibili, & ch'è colonna principale della gran machina dell'immitatione, base, e fondamento di tutta l'arte Poetica; versando ella intorno quei tre oggetti medesimi, sopra i quali l'immitatione, come in suoi proprij seggi si riposa, cioè, ò Natura, ò Arte, ò Caso immitando.... Ha poi cosi ben disposto le cose, collocato conueneuolmente le parole, vsato à tempo gli attributi, disteso con bell'ordine i concetti, sparso con misura gli ornamenti, e le figure, & hà cosi ben seruata la variatione, & il decoro, parti essentiali della dispositione, che certamente n'hà conseguito il dissegnato fine di dilettare, & di rinouellar ne gli animi de gli vditori, ò de' lettori la gratiosa memoria di quei diletteuoli luoghi.... Et è con molta felicità parimente riuscito nell'elocutione, hauendo giuditiosamente scelto voci sonore, graui, chiare, proprie, circonscritte, e traslate ... e hà insieme di grauità, di chiarezza, di purità, e di dolcezza tutto il Sonetto elegantemente ripieno."

[240]

indeed, be contemporary with the ones already discussed.[71] In these, Riccoboni had suggested the possibility of reordering the *Ars poetica* according to a more scientific arrangement. In the new work he does just that. Under a number of section headings, which are those of the major divisions of the poetic art, he first places prose passages which are presumably summations of Aristotle's positions, then he quotes *in extenso* the passages from Horace which he deems pertinent. Once again, the whole of the Horatian text passes into the rearrangement. The kind of order which Riccoboni proposes for a scientific treatise on the art of poetry is perhaps of greater significance than the parallelisms between Aristotle and Horace, most of which were by this time completely conventional. I give below the section headings in Latin, a summation of the "Aristotelian" doctrine stated in the prose passages, and the numbers of the lines quoted from the *Ars poetica*:

	Horace
De Natura Poesis	
Poetry as imitation; object, manner, and means. The poet must excel in all parts of the poem.	361–85
Poetry and history, the universal and the particular; imitation through embellishment.	309–32
Ends: profit and pleasure; purgation of pity and fear as the proper pleasure of tragedy.	333–34, 341–46
De Caussis Poesia	
Divine cause: the divine furor.	391–407
Human cause: art and nature.	408–18, 295–308
Natural cause: imitation and harmony. Historical origins and development of tragedy and comedy	275–80, 220–33
Origins of comedy.	281–94
De Generibus Imitationum, & Poesium	
The arts as imitations; definitions of epic, tragedy, comedy.	73–85
De Partibus Qualitatis	
De Fabula. Eight requirements for plot:	
(1) completeness	32–45
(2) magnitude	146–52
(3) unity	1–13
(4) possible (necessity, verisimilitude)	338–40
(5) non-episodic	14–23
(6) marvelous	136–45
(7) simple, complex	[none]
(8) pathetic	[none]
De fabulis non immutandis, aut conuenienter fingendis.	
Traditional plots.	119–35

---

[71] R. C. Williams, "Italian Critical Treatises of the Sixteenth Century," *Modern Language Notes*, XXXV (1920), 506–7, lists a *Praecepta Aristotelis cum praeceptis Horatii collata* under the date of 1592, but I have been unable to find a copy of this work.

De Partibus Qualitatis	*Horace*
De Moribus. Characters for the main genres; decorum.	114–18, 153–78
De Sententia. Cf. the *Rhetoric.* The parts of thought. Persuasion.	335–37, 96–113
De Dictione. Kinds of words; two qualities of style; words for each genre.	24–31, 46–72, 86–95, 234–74
De Melopoeia.	202–19
De Apparatu. Not part of the poetic art. Effect from plot, not apparatus.	178–88
De Partibus Quantitatis	
Of tragedy, comedy, epic	189–201
De reprehensionibus, & excusationibus poetarum	
Five sources of blame, three types of excuse.	346–60, 386–90, 419–76

Elements of theory contained in Riccoboni's prose passages are more specifically pertinent to Aristotle than to Horace, and they will be treated subsequently in the appropriate chapter.

In the same year, perhaps even as early as 1598, Camillo Pellegrino wrote his treatise *Del concetto poetico,* returning thus to a subject which had been treated only recently by Giulio Cortese. The latter's discussion, however, seems more philosophical and more sophisticated, even though one of the interlocutors in Pellegrino's dialogue is Giambattista Marino. Pellegrino begins with a conventional position, the distinction of the three styles, which he equates at various places with Hermogenes' Ideas; the different styles are appropriate to different poetic genres. Differences in style, he says, depend upon "subject matter, conceits, words, the disposition of the latter and the colors of the figures."[72] Since this might sound like a description of diction, he finds himself obliged first to define style ("a quality which results from the putting together of the words and the thoughts"[73]) and to distinguish between diction and style: "the former is nothing but the choice and the placing of the words which are images of the thoughts, the latter is a quality which results from the combination of the words and the thoughts."[74] Taken in its broadest sense of "thought," "concetto" is synonymous with "senso, sentimento, sentenza"; it may be defined as "a thought formed by the intellect as an image or resemblance of a real thing, signified by these latter."[75] The specifically poetic "con-

---

[72] In Borzelli, *Il Cavalier Giovanbattista Marino* (Naples, 1898), p. 328: "si cagiona dalla materia, da' concetti, dalle voci, dalla disposizione di quelle e da' colori delle figure."

[73] *Ibid.,* p. 328: "una qualità che risalta dalla composizione delle voci e dai concetti."

[74] *Ibid.,* p. 329: "quella altro non è che scelta e collocazione delle voci, che sono immagini de' Concetti, e questa è una qualità, che risulta dal Composto delle voci e dai concetti insieme."

[75] *Ibid.,* p. 331: "un pensamento formato dall'Intelletto imagine e somiglianza di cosa reale, intesa da quelle."

cetto" is defined in significantly altered terms: "a thought of the intellect, an image or resemblance of true things and of things which resemble the truth, formed in the fantasy."[76]

The poetic "concetto" is defined in this way in order to include the peculiar characteristics of the art. The image produced may be of verisimilar things, since verisimilitude is the proper field of operation of the poet, as compared with the orator, whose province is the true. Besides, the fantasy rather than the intellect is the productive faculty since the poet wishes to give pleasure, not to persuade, and the same imaginative powers involved in the invention of plot are concerned with the formation of "concetti." Indeed, there is a kind of analogy between plot-making and "concetto"-making: just as in tragedy, comedy, and the epic the digressions must bear a necessary and probable relationship to the plot, so in the lyric (which is its preferred genre) the "concetto" must have its roots in the main argument of the poem. This same imagination differentiates the conceit of poetry from that of prose: "Prose in expressing conceits uses pure forms of expression, proper words, and when it uses metaphors and figurative language it uses them rarely and with moderation; whereas verse, with greater liberty and sometimes with excessive boldness expresses its conceits with figures and metaphors distant from literal meanings."[77] The faculty of inventing such conceits springs from nature rather than from art (which is at the basis of ordinary diction) and in this respect is superior to the talent for prose; and (to continue the same analogy) nature is responsible also for the invention which makes plots. Thus Pellegrino is able to say, adapting Aristotle's dictum, that the "concetti" "are the soul and the form of a composition."[78]

We have seen, earlier, Pellegrino's statement that the end of poetry is to give pleasure. This he reiterates at various points; but he does not fail to make a concession which was current in these last years of the century: "considered in itself as an imitation and as a maker of images, poetry has no other end than delight; but as qualified by the civil faculty it will have besides as its end utility and profit, which in any case must make itself felt through the intermediary of the pleasure."[79] The immediate end of pleasure is best served by the diction and the "concetti," which, in a poem, depict the object or the action as if it were before our eyes. In a practical way,

[76] *Ibid.*, p. 332: "un pensamento dell'Intelletto, imagine e simiglianza di cose vere e di cose simili al vero formato nella fantasia."

[77] *Ibid.*, p. 336: "la prosa nello esprimer de' concetti usa modi di dir puri, voci proprie ed usando le metafore, ed i traslati il fa con riguardo e di rado, la dove il verso con più libertà ed alle volte con troppo ardire spiega i suoi concetti con traslati e metafore lontane dal proprio."

[78] *Ibid.*, p. 340: "sono anima e forma di un componimento."

[79] *Ibid.*, p. 340: "la Poesia considerata per se stessa, come Imitazione e facitrice degli Idoli non abbia altro fine che il diletto, ma qualificata dalla Civile facoltà avrà eziandio per suo fine l'utile e il giovamento, il quale in ogni modo converrà che si senta per mezzo del diletto."

these "concetti" seem to be no more than figures of speech; in a series of examples taken from Petrarch, Pellegrino points out how they belong to the general argument of the sonnet, how appropriate they are and how in keeping with decorum, how they correspond to the various Ideas of Hermogenes, and to what extent they contribute beautiful and splendid ornamentation to the poem.

The concluding year of the century presents two works pertinent to the Horation tradition, one of them on a general topic and the other more specific, and both of them by the same writer, Paolo Beni. The first, his *De humanitatis studiis oratio*, is concerned with the broad problem of literary studies and only incidentally discusses the work and the role of the poet. In addition to a conventional praise of the art, he indicates that its usefulness resides in the various precepts and meanings hidden under the fictional veil. But he says nothing about the nature of these precepts or about how the fiction containing them is to be constructed. For Beni, the greatest problem for the poet seems to be that of style—how to provide the just measure of ornamentation so that the style is neither unadorned nor overwrought. Three arts—of rhetoric, of history, of poetry—are involved here, and the poet must see to it that he cultivates his own proper style and not those of the other two:

> Since indeed many things must frequently be taken over into poetry from history and oratory, and not a few in fact from poetry into oratory, it is certainly difficult to retain a just measure in all of them without the utmost degree of care and vigilance, so that the poem does not reproduce the popular exuberance of the orators or the restraint of history, and the speech will not be colored at times excessively by the stylistic colors and pigments of the poets.[80]

The less general treatise is Beni's *Disputatio in qua ostenditur praestare comoediam atque tragoediam metrorum vinculis soluere*, also of 1600, one of the principal documents in the quarrel over verse which achieved such prominence in the last years of the century. Beni's contention is that prose is better than verse for the dramatic genres, and in order to sustain it he develops a fully realized theory of poetry. This theory, in its broadest aspects, is Horatian to the extent that it insists upon pleasure and utility as the ends of poetry, that it places the audience in a determining position with respect to works of art, and that it establishes a central principle of decorum.

Of the two Horatian ends, Beni declares that the really important one is utility, and he sees utility as consisting of moral instruction. The statements are unequivocal. "The function of the poets is to prescribe for man certain

---

[80] *Oratio* (1600), p. 5: "Cum enim multa saepè ad Poesim ex historia & eloquentia, ad eloquentiam verò ex Poesi non pauca sint referenda; difficile profectò est sine summa quadam industria & vigilantia modum seruare in omnibus, ita ut nec popularem Oratorum vbertatem, siue etiam historiae verecundiam, referat poema, nec Poetarum coloribus ac pigmentis nimis interdum coloretur oratio."

ideal forms and models in relation to the variety of life itself and in a sense place them before his eyes, from which he may regulate his behavior and arrange his life."[81] Or again: "In fact, this is the end proposed by tragedy and comedy, that the spectators may leave them more circumspect, and, learning thoroughly the duties of life, may order their own conduct and may be capable of rendering themselves useful to themselves, to their friends, and finally to the whole country."[82] To such instruction, pleasure serves only as an instrument, the honeyed glass with which the skilful physician makes the bitter potion palatable (p. 4v). In order that the end of moral instruction may be achieved, the poem must possess certain qualities. Above all, it must be completely clear, credible, and verisimilar, and it must observe the laws of decorum; if it does not, the audience will not believe, and where there is no belief there can be no persuasion to emulation or to avoidance of the actions presented. On the side of pleasure, the poet must make sure that attractiveness of the pleasurable aspects of his poem does not grow to such an extent as to constitute an end in itself, to overshadow the utility or even to create an opposite effect. The question of credibility and verisimilitude is related, for Beni, to the peculiar nature of poems as imitations of human actions. This he takes in its narrowest sense of a direct and unaltered representation of life as it really is. For example, since people naturally speak in prose, a poet who made them speak in verse would be departing from nature: "These, therefore, do not follow nature as a guide, they do not observe the law of decorum and of verisimilitude; but they depart from nature and disturb both decorum and verisimilitude."[83] The close relationship of nature (or external reality), decorum (or internal features of the poem), and verisimilitude (which results from a comparison of the poem to nature), is significant.

It is in the light of both ends, utility and pleasure, that Beni makes his case against the use of verse in tragedy and in comedy. We have already seen the essential argument on the score of utility: if verse is unnatural to people speaking among themselves, then the audience hearing them so converse will deny credence to the drama in which they appear. Moreover, the use of verse will so obscure the meaning that the proper lessons will not readily be learned: "since verse may be very difficult to understand, both in itself and because of its unfamiliarity, the result is of course that the audience not only does not take in the total structure and composition of the plot, or even its fictitious characters or the reversal, but it does not even

---

[81] *Disputatio* (1600), p. 1v: "Poetarum munus est homini pro vitae varietate certas quasdam Ideas ac formas praescribere, & tanquam ante oculos ponere, vnde & mores componere possit & vitam instituere."

[82] *Ibid.*, p. 3v: "Finis enim Tragoediae Comoediaéque propositus ille est, ut Auditores inde euadant cautiores, ac vitae officia perdiscentes, componant mores, ac sibi, amicis, Patriae denique vniuersae prodesse valeant."

[83] *Ibid.*, p. 2v: "non Naturam Ducem sequantur isti: non decorum ac verisimile tueantur: sed a Natura discedant: decorum perturbent ac verisimile."

understand the thought and the diction."[84] On the score of pleasure, verse is undesirable in two ways: it dispels all thought of utility, swaying its ignorant audience through the constant use of rhythm and song; and it so softens the souls of the audience that they become immoral and effeminate. In these ideas, Beni comes very close to Plato in certain passages of the *Republic*, which indeed he cites. The whole condemnation of verse with respect to the ends of poetry is related to a conception of the audience as ignorant, weak, and uncouth—the audience of the vulgar crowd in the pit.

If Beni is willing to admit verse in the nondramatic genres, it is precisely because he conceives of them as addressed to a different audience. The epic poet, he says, writes essentially for himself and the Muses, or "for those who have been exceptionally well educated in the liberal arts" (p. 11*v*). For such as these, the verse is not only a source of a refined enjoyment, but it also helps the reader remember the poem. The case of the lyric is similar. Composed not for the crowd or tumultuous performance, but resulting rather from careful meditation, it may without violating either decorum or verisimilitude cultivate such an additional grace as verse. But for the dramatic genres, given the nature of the audience and the circumstances of performance, only prose is an acceptable medium. All the best features of the dramatic art are enhanced by the use of prose:

... in comedy and in tragedy we imitate human actions properly with prose, less properly—nay, even absurdly—when bound by the limits of verse. Therefore prose is to be practiced, verse rejected, ... since poetry is an imitation of human actions either as they actually were done or as they should have been done, neither of which can be achieved in comedy and tragedy through an imitation bound down by verse.[85]

If prose is used, the audience will understand the events and the thoughts presented, will derive the appropriate lessons from them, and will experience a suitable and a moderate pleasure. Beni's position in the dispute over verse is thus determined entirely by broader considerations of the poetic art.

CONCLUSIONS

It would be futile to reiterate, by way of concluding this chapter, the various ways in which the theorists and the practicing critics of the "last generation" manifested in their writings the standard features of the Horatian-rhetorical tradition. These features should by now be clear, and their appearance in the individual writers has been pointed out in each case.

[84] *Ibid.*, p. 4: "cum enim carmen tum per se tum propter insolentiam sit ad intelligendum perdifficile, fit sanè vt populus non modò vniuersam fabulae structuram & constitutionem aut etiam effictos mores peripetiamue non percipiat animo, sed ne sententiam quidem atque dictionem."

[85] *Ibid.*, p. 2: "in Comoedia & Tragoedia humanas actiones oratione soluta, rectè, carminibus adstricta, minùs rectè, immo praeposterè imitamur. Soluta itaque oratio retinenda, adstricta repudianda est.... Siquidem Poesis est imitatio humanarum actionum vel prout gestae sunt, vel certè prout geri debuerunt: quorum neutrum in Comoedia aut Tragoedia efficere potest imitatio adstricta numeris."

It would perhaps be more useful to study in what ways these last years of the century differ from earlier periods, what new directions and what new tendencies may be discerned, what innovations seem to bear the promise of a reorientation of critical thinking.

The existence, in this period, of so many new treatises on individual genres—Pino and Ceruti on comedy, Tasso on the epic, Massini on the madrigal, Correa on the elegy, Talentoni, Toralto, and Crispolti on the sonnet—would seem to indicate the nature of one of these new tendencies. Theorists apparently now feel that what needed to be said about the text of Horace had already been said by earlier generations, that the exegesis and explication of the *Ars poetica* had reached a satisfactory stage; hence the very limited number of such formal commentaries during these years. But what now needed to be done was to discover how the general principles of poetics contained in Horace could be applied to other genres not treated by him or treated only incompletely. If poetics was to be made practical, its theoretical basis must be transformed into clear precepts for the composition of the currently popular genres. To be sure, not only Horatian principles would be so transferred, and we shall see at a later time that many strongly Aristotelian treatises were written during this part of the century.

Under the stimulus of this necessity, the conception of the various genres grows and develops considerably. Thinking about literature in terms of the rules or precepts for specific genres had, of course, long been a standard approach. Some of it is already found in Horace, its tendencies are accentuated in the earliest commentators, and during the Middle Ages it produces such schematizations as the "wheel of Vergil," in which each of the genres involved a specific kind of subject matter, a type of personage, and a style—with all the ramifications inherent in the conception of style. Such a way of thinking is, of course, closely related to the notion of decorum, not as it concerns the behavior of types of personages compared with their counterparts in reality, but as it involves internal relationships within the poem, a notion central in the whole Horatian doctrine. Development of theories of the genres along these lines will thus be a natural outcome of the age-old approaches to the Horatian text.

What particularly characterizes theorizing about the genres in the last quarter of the sixteenth century is the attempt to relate the rules for the specific genre to the audience for which it is intended and the ends which it is meant to serve. Here, again, the tendencies hark back to earlier approaches; but they are now more fully realized and exploited. If the theorist thinks of a type as addressed to a "grave" audience—say the epic or the sonnet—he will associate with it all the multiple qualities by now linked almost automatically with the "grave" style. And they will consist not only of subject matter, persons, and style, but as well of a host of rules and conventions, of prosodic recommendations (the late medieval prescriptions for verse are now aggregated to the other rules for the genre), of descriptions of the general effect to be achieved, and of statements of the ends. For the ends, also, will be adapted to the character of the audience. The major ends of pleasure and instruction are still predominant in the minds of the theorists, with persuasion sometimes added as an auxiliary or a means. Perhaps in these later years the preoccupation with moral instruction is greater than previously. For each genre, now, the problem will be to decide whether its audience is such as to demand utility or delight or both, and what brand of either of these will be acceptable to it. That is, the general theories about the ends of poetry are particularized as the "art of poetry" becomes the "art of the comedy," and so forth. Insofar as the internal workings of the poem are thus brought into relationship with the audience and with audience-oriented ends, this is Horatianism in the best tradition.

If we consider theorizing about the genres as a refinement upon antecedent approaches, then other new directions during these years will be seen to be closely related to it. Throughout the century, for example, the problem of style and of language had been a central one in this rhetorical mode of criticism. Not only had each theory of a genre involved extensive treatment of the particular "style" appropriate to it, but whole theories of poetry had been constructed about differentiations among the three or four styles as they had been found in the analogous rhetorical treatises of Cicero or of Demetrius or of Hermogenes. Now, in these late years, further refinements take place. We have already seen, for example, how Giason Denores would transfer to the realm of poetics all those aspects of rhetoric which had to do specifically with diction; this resulted from his conviction that language, differing in this from the other rhetorical elements whose function was persuasion, had as its peculiar domain the arousing of the passions and the providing of pleasure. This is symptomatic of a growing tendency to regard the distinctive features of poetry as verse and as a special kind of language. Thus Correa saw fit to reverse the usual subordination of style to materials and to see instead an adaptation of materials to the kind of style being cultivated. Perhaps it would not be an exaggeration to say that the emphasis shifts, during this period, from "res" to "verba," that theorists tend more and more to concern themselves with linguistic aspects of the poetic art.

A special manifestation of this tendency is discernible in the preoccupation with the "concetto" as a peculiarly poetic form of expression. Giulio Cortese's theory of the "concetto" as the central organizing element of a poem is the best example. Insofar as he conceives of it as the "soul of poetry," he displaces the emphasis from the Aristotelian "plot" or the "character" of the moralists or the "thought" of the pure rhetoricians. To be sure, the conceit is not a purely linguistic element in poetry, and Cortese, for one, thinks of it as a device for organizing all the materials pertinent to a given feeling or idea. But others, less philosophical in their approach, see it only as a figure of speech and consider it frankly at the level of diction. Indeed, some of the stress upon matters of diction may spring from the fact that theorists believe that the larger matters of poetic form have been satisfactorily solved—or on the other hand that they are insoluble, and hence the poet can do no better than to attend to the virtuoso handling of his medium. I should point out that there is no single statement to this effect and that the tendency is not even implicit in very many documents. But directions and occasional signs in critical thinking lead one to believe that such a hypothesis is tenable.

Such thinking may account for the raising of the question, this time overtly, as to whether the poetic genres are "regulated" or "free." The thesis of regulation, predominant in the early years of the century, when critics were eager to discover exact rules for the composition of each literary type, seems now to be under attack, in part because of the current literary quarrels, which had introduced doubts about such major forms as the epic and tragedy, in part because contemporary poets were practicing successfully a large variety of kinds sometimes in violation and frequently in variation of the accepted rules. Hence, some theorists are willing to propose a doctrine in which genres are broadly characterized by a category of subject matter and a general effect, and to permit great liberty in the working out both of internal poetic structure and prosodic detail. Here, again, the tendencies are little more than incipient, and it should not be thought that Italian critics are about to abandon a "classical" position in favor of the freedoms and excesses of "romanticism." They might, indeed, have done so, had not the influence of French classicism in the following century brought about a reversal of trends. On the whole, these last years of the century mark a broadening, within the Horatian tradition, of the scope of critical inquiry, some loosening of tight systematic distinctions, and occasional prying into the psychological and linguistic factors that underlie a theory of diction.

CHAPTER SEVEN. PLATONISM: I. THE DEFENCE OF POETRY

UNLIKE THOSE RENAISSANCE CRITICS who attached themselves to Horace's *Ars poetica* or to Aristotle's *Poetics* as the basis for their critical thinking, the Platonic critic was essentially a man without a text. I mean by this that he was unable, as were his compeers, to derive his critical doctrine point by point from a central text, to concentrate his efforts of exegesis and commentary and interpretation upon that text, to discover within it all the answers to a host of artistic and technical questions. For there is no Art of Poetry by Plato, no single treatise (the notion of "treatise" is itself alien to the Platonic approach) in which one might find collected the total theory of the philosopher with respect to this specific art, in all its ramifications and all its ultimate deductions. Lacking such a document, the Platonic critic of the sixteenth century was obliged to base his Platonism upon scattered dicta in various dialogues. These dicta were such that they provided a set of general principles about literature without examining in detail their implications for the practice of the art, and the critic who used them possessed rather an all-inclusive attitude toward poetry than a firm body of precepts and rules.

Plato himself had seen the art of poetry not in itself but in relationship to various contexts which required consideration of it. He was interested not in the practice of the art or in the means by which it achieved the beautiful poem, but in how it was related to truth, or to the needs of education in a real or an ideal society, or to the divine forces of inspiration. As these contexts changed, Plato's ideas on poetry—and sometimes his total evaluation of the art—expanded or contracted, became more positive or more negative, took on new orientations. This was, of course, entirely in keeping with his general method. Rather than establishing a separation among the sciences and treating each one in terms of the principles proper only to itself, he chose to preserve at all times the manifold relationships present within an undifferentiated and unanalyzed reality, or at least as many of them as were pertinent to his inquiry of the moment.

Of Plato's various dicta on the art of poetry, the critics of the Renaissance were interested primarily in the following ones:

The divine furor. In several passages of the *Phaedrus* (245A, 265B) and the *Ion* (534), and in a lesser way in other dialogues, Plato had declared that the poet produces not by art but by divine inspiration, that he is moved by the Muses to a state of frenzy, and that when he speaks it is really the voice of the gods and not his own voice that speaks within him. The poet thus mad or possessed is really more than a man, and his works "are not human, or the work of man, but divine and the work of God" (*Ion*, 534). It is for this reason that he is able to bestow immortality upon those whose deeds he sings. The poet who lacks such inspiration and who attempts to write merely according to the rules of art is doomed to failure.

Imitation. Of the various ways in which the term imitation was used by Plato, two especially were found to be eminently useful in Renaissance criticism. First, in Book III of the *Republic* (394 ff.), Plato had divided narration into three types, simple narration, imitation, and a mixture of the two. In the first, the poet spoke only in his own voice, telling a story; in the second, he assumed the person of one or another of his characters, and spoke through the voice of that character; in the third, he alternated between the two procedures. Otherwise stated, imitation in this sense is the equivalent of a dramatic form of presentation. Second, in Book X of the *Republic* (595 ff.), Plato had developed the argument that the poet, as an imitator of appearances rather than of those realities which he calls Ideas, is at several removes from the truth, that he has neither knowledge nor right opinion of the object which he imitates, that hence his imitation is "merely a kind of play or sport" (602). These ideas were used by the Renaissance on the one hand to describe the relationship between imitation and reality, on the other hand to discredit the imitative process.

The banishment of the poets. Since in the *Republic* Plato was primarily concerned with the relationships of poetry to the education of the future citizens and guardians of the State, he had examined the various ways in which the art might be harmful or beneficial as an instrument of instruction. He had concluded that since poetry teaches false tales about the gods, since it tends to render the soul effeminate through its use of soft strains and rhythms, since it is at many removes from the truth through its very nature as an imitation, since it feeds the passions of the soul by providing the occasion for their expression, it should not be granted admission to the ideal State. Rather should the poets, except those who write hymns to the gods and praises of famous men, be banished (Books II, III, X). The point of view is specifically pedagogical and moral, considering as it does the ultimate effects of poems upon the moral fiber of the young. These ideas became in the Renaissance (as they had been at times in the Middle Ages) one of the principal sources of the attack on poetry, and all Renaissance theorists felt themselves obliged to deal with Plato's banishment of the poets, either by way of accepting it or—much more frequently—by way of rejecting it on the basis of other criteria. The defence of poetry in the Cinquecento is largely a reply to Plato.

What the Renaissance frequently failed to realize about Plato's varied positions with respect to poetry was that they do not necessarily represent inconsistencies. Hence much effort was spent in the attempt to reconcile ideas that are irreconcilable only when they are torn from their context of reference and placed in bare juxtaposition to one another. Returned to their contexts, seen in the light of the presuppositions and the conditions which surround them, they are perfectly understandable, consistent, and "true." But it was not in the spirit of Renaissance intellectual method to see ideas in this way, and critics proceeded here as elsewhere by way of fragmentation, separation, and isolation. They were content with the individual dictum—sometimes merely derived from the oral tradition without any reference to the original texts—and with an acceptance or rejection of the dictum by itself. This fact, added to the absence of a central basic text, accounts for the extreme fluidity of the Platonic position in Renaissance criticism. The position is found joined and combined with all other possible attitudes, introduced as an accompaniment or an addendum; when it provides the point of departure for a given theorist, it trails off into some other mode as generalization gives way to the details of the poetic art. In a very real sense, there are hardly any true Platonists among literary theoricians or practising critics of the sixteenth century. And when they are found, they are Platonist in their total philosophical outlook, and this reflects itself in their total approach to poetry.

In the case of Horace, Renaissance critics inherited a tradition of interpretation which had begun in the late-classical period and had persisted, with some additions, through the Middle Ages. For Plato, this was not true. Whereas there had been some use made of his strictures on poetry by churchmen of the medieval period, for the most part his writings became significant documents for literary discussion only with the rise of the great Platonic commentators and philosophers of the Quattrocento. As compared with Horatianism, then, Platonism is a relatively new force in literary theory, relatively unencumbered by an ancient reading, and relatively free for the inquiring lucubrations of the Renaissance mind. Many of the theorists and critics who will appear in the following discussion were not truly Platonists, nor was Plato their immediate source. They belong in the tradition only because they manifest a critical mode or position related to the central problems of Platonism in literature.

QUATTROCENTO DOCUMENTS

Although our concern in the present study is exclusively with Platonism in the Cinquecento, it would perhaps be instructive to examine two typical documents of the Quattrocento, so that we may have some appreciation of the state to which thinking of this kind had advanced before 1500. The first of these is the *De institutione reipublicae* of Francesco Patrizi, Bishop of Gaeta, who died in 1494; the work contains, in Book II, chapter 6, a discussion "De Poetis et eorum virtutibus, & qui legendi, quique ex theatris exigendi sint." Like Plato in the *Republic*, Patrizi is here considering poetry in the general framework of the state, in its possible moral effects on the young. But he tends to disagree with Plato about the banishment of the poets. Citing Cicero and Strabo in support of his thesis, he points out the multiple utilities of the art: The poet, like a first philosopher, leads men to a proper way of life, teaches them what they need to know about the

PLATONISM: DEFENCE OF POETRY

passions and customs of men. He provides the grammarian with the best examples of all kinds of language, especially that which is elegant and ornate and beautiful. Unlike other disciplines, which derive from art, doctrine, and precepts, the functioning of the poet depends upon nature and upon divine inspiration, and hence he is able to combine human and divine matters in his works.

From this general defence of poetry, Patrizi passes to a consideration of the separate genres and their relative usefulness. First, the drama:

> Fictional inventions, which exist partly for utility but partly also for pleasure, are by no means to be repudiated. Children must be taught, and those things which otherwise they could with difficulty conceive, they accept through the enticements of fictions, and they easily bring them to mind, and they allow themselves to be led to virtue much more readily by their meaning. [The story of Hercules.] Stories of this kind instruct the young and make them more disposed to desire praise. . . . However, I do not wish to assume the defence of fictions to the extent of praising all types of them. Indeed, almost all tragedy should be excluded from the best city. . . . It is not without reason that tragedy should be hissed off the stage from every civil spectacle; for it has within it a certain excessive violence mixed with despair which readily changes stupid men into madmen and drives the unstable to frenzy.[1]

Nor does comedy come off much better:

> It does not please me either that comedy should be performed in public spectacles. For it corrupts the mores of men, and makes them effeminate, and drives them towards lust and dissipation. . . . For the plots of comedy for the most part concern adultery and rapes, and the habit of seeing them affords to the spectator the license for changing for the worst.[2]

Comedy may be read by scholars in the privacy of their studies—and essentially for the linguistic interest rather than for the actions represented. Epic poetry, on the other hand, is highly recommended, since it presents the figures of great heroes, with all the virtues they represent. As for satire, it is found to be generally desirable, since it praises virtue and blames vices; but a caution must be expressed in regard to the scabrous and even obscene language which it sometimes uses. In each case, the criterion to which the genre is referred is specifically an ethical one.

---

[1] *De institutione reipublicae* (1534 ed.), pp. xxviv–xxvii: "Fabularum inuentio partim ad vtilitatem, partim autem ad delectationem neutiquam repudienda est. Docendi sunt pueri, & quę vix alioqui cogitare possent, fabularum illecebris accipiunt, & facile in memoriam redigunt, earumque sensu ad virtutem longe magis diriguntur. . . . Eiusmodi fabulae adolescentes instituunt, & promptiores ad optandam laudem reddunt. . . . Non tamen fabularum vsque adeo patrocinium suscipere volo, vt omnes laude afficere velim. Nam tragoedia pene omnis extrudenda est ab optima ciuitate. . . . Nec immerito explodenda est ex omni ciuili spectaculo tragoedia. Habet enim in se violentiam quandam nimiam mistam desperationi, quae facile ex stultis insanos reddat, & leues in furorem compellat. . . ."

[2] *Ibid.*, p. xxvii: "Comoediam . . . in spectaculis etiam recitari non placet. Corrumpit nanque hominum mores, eosque effoeminatos reddit, & ad libidinem, luxuriamque compellit. . . . Comoediarum nanque argumenta, magna ex parte adulteria, & stupra continent, quocirca spectandi consuetudo, mutandi etiam licentiam facit."

One peculiar feature of Patrizi's remarks is his defence of the ancient poets against their banishment by Plato and against their exclusion by Christian apologists. From the point of view of the Christian, the ancient poets rendered a real service to the cause of the true religion by deriding and humiliating the false gods of the pagans: "... they ridiculed, by making sport of them in their stories, the very stupid opinions of the people about the gods and their vain and foolish superstitions."[3] Moreover, the wish of the Christian apologist to exclude them as heretical is unfounded, for before the coming of Christ, God was unknown to all men, and the philosophers erred as much as the poets in their ignorance of Him. For these reasons the poets of antiquity should be forgiven their errors and men should be allowed to read them. As we shall discover later, the point of view of the Christian apologist is frequently very close to that of the Platonist and represents a similar approach to literary problems.

Also in the fifteenth century, Antonio Mancinelli published his *De poetica virtute, et studio humanitatis impellente ad bonum.* This is really not a treatise on poetry at all, but a collection of quotations from Greek and Latin poets. Yet the order and arrangement of these quotations is in itself significant, and the prefatory materials state a typical attitude toward the art. The dedicatory epistle quotes the customary ancient authorities on the role of poetry in the betterment of mores—Theophrastus, Strabo—and then defends it against Catholic accusations:

> The poets seem, therefore, to be wrongfully damned by certain people, especially on the grounds that they draw away from the Catholic faith those who are unwary. I shall truly show this to be false by the words of the selfsame poets. For we shall find in them the ten commandments of the law, and we shall see that they damn and prohibit the seven deadly sins, and that they likewise teach many of the finest things...[4]

A subsequent section on the "Poetarum Laus" insists on the divine inspiration of poets and the reverence in which they should be held; it also repeats the time-honored examples of the esteem in which certain poets, especially Homer, were held by all antiquity. If they were so regarded, it was because of the contribution that they had made to the civilizing of man; poetry was the first philosophy:

> The ancients, in fact, say that poetry is a kind of first philosophy, which brings us from youth to the art of living, which teaches the mores and the passions, which in a pleasant way teaches us our duty. Later writers declare that only the poet is a wise man. For these reasons the cities of the Greeks from the very earliest

---

[3] *Ibid.*, p. xxv: "stultissimas gentium de dijs opiniones, vanasque, ac fatuas superstitiones fabularum ludibrio contempserunt."

[4] *De poetica virtute* (*ca.* 1490), pp. aiiv–aiii: "Iniuria igitur a quibusdam damnari videntur: praesertim quod a catholica fide remoueant eis inuigilantes. Id equidem ego falsum eorundem poetarum uerbis ostendam. Decem nanque legis praecepta in ipsis reperiemus; septem quoque mortalia uitia illos & damnare & prohibere videbimus. Plurima item quam optima edocere. . . ."

times instructed their children in poetry, assuredly not for its gross pleasure but for its chaste moderation.[5]

Other uses of poetry are adduced in support of the argument. Mancinelli's position is essentially moralistic, placing whatever emphasis it can on the utility of poetry rather than on its pleasure. (It will be noted that the Horatian "utile dulci" is inextricably mingled with the thinking of the Platonists.) When he arrives at the anthology which is the main purpose of his work, he provides a series of headings—religious and ethical for the most part—under which he gives brief prose introductions (themselves quotations from ancient authors) and then pertinent selections from the ancient poets. The ten commandments, the seven deadly sins, and other similar categories furnish the basis of organization for the passages quoted. Clearly, it is the "sententious" quality of poetry that alone is of concern to the editor.

Two distinguished humanists, whose lives span the turn of the century, may serve as a transition to the criticism of the Cinquecento proper. They are Giovanni Francesco Pico della Mirandola and Battista Mantovano. Pico, in a pair of works which date from the late Quattrocento, expresses a point of view which is violently antipoetic in the best neo-Platonic tradition. The first work is his *De studio divinae et humanae philosophiae*. In Book I, chapter VI, he discusses the relationship of the various kinds of ancient writings to divine philosophy, and finds that whereas physics, logic, and metaphysics have some affinity to divine scripture, geometry, arithmetic, and poetry have much less. He cites his own experience, which parallels that of many others: a love of poetry in childhood and early manhood, followed by satiety and complete rejection—

But after I had devoted myself to philosophy and sacred letters I so completely renounced the delights of poetry that I scarcely opened the books of the poets three times in five years, because I was drawn away from them and felt my soul to be softened by them. But what is more detestable is that most poets mixed into their verses the greatest wickednesses and impurities, which are not only not to be touched by a Christian but are to be utterly expelled by him. You will not easily find many poems, otherwise beautiful, which are not made foul by filthiness and obscenities; for which reason Isidore writes that Christians are forbidden to read the fancies of the poets, because through the delights of their plots they excite the mind to the provocations of lust.[6]

---

[5] *Ibid.*, p. aivv: "Antiqui ueró poeticam primam philosophiam quandam esse perhibent: quae ab ineunte nos aetate ad uiuendi rationes adducit: que mores: que affectiones edoceat: quae res gerendas cum iucunditate precipiat. Posteriores uero solum poetam ipsum sapientem esse asseruerunt. Quamobrem graecorum ciuitates ab ipso primordio eorum liberos in poetica erudierunt: non nude utique uoluptatis sed caste moderationis gratia."

[6] In *De rerum praenotione* (1506–7), pp. fv–fii: "Sed postquam ad philosophiam & sacras litteras me contuli adeo illis remisi nuncium ut nec poetarum libros toto quinquennio ter forte aperuerim: quandoquidem ab illis trahi: animum & emolliri sentiebam: Sed quod est detestabilius plerique poetarum turpitudines maximas & obscenitates suis uersibus immiscuerunt. Quae christiano homini non modo attrectanda sed prorsus eliminanda: Nec temerè multos inuenies qui pulchra alioquin poemata spurcitijs libidinibusque non foedauerint: Quare scribit Isidorus ideo christianis prohiberi legere figmenta poetarum quia per oblectamenta fabularum excitant mentem ad incentiua libidinum."

Pico sees in this same corrupting influence of poetry the reason why Plato banished the poets from his republic. In the following chapter, Pico explains why in the early days of Christianity certain very holy men not only made use of pagan literature themselves but recommended its use to others. The circumstances, however, are not now the same, and one should prefer Christian poetry on religious themes; this will have the greatest possible superiority over pagan poetry—the superiority of subject matter— and may be equally eloquent in its language.

The same question is examined again, but in a somewhat different light, in Pico's *Examen vanitatis doctrinae gentium, & veritatis disciplinae Christianae*. In Book III, chapter III of this work, Pico answers the claim that poetry, along with history and grammar, is "useful" for life and leads to happiness. The statement, he believes, is false in its premises and its conclusions:

> ... for men derive from the poets occasions for evil not less significant for vice than for virtue, since the poets wrote in different ways, and at one time they let loose the reins of the vices, at another they held them in check, as is easy to see for anyone who takes them in hand; although one may be more prone to virtue than another, and another may be more inclined to narrating or praising the vices.[7]

In order to distinguish poet from poet and passage from passage, the reader must appeal to the philosopher, so that for Pico the whole art of poetics is specifically subordinated to philosophy. In the statement that he is challenging, Pico finds no clear definitions of utility and of happiness, and hence he believes that it is impossible to judge properly of poetry's contribution to either. What he does know is that the poets have frequently, in the past, provided examples for undesirable activity:

> ... many believe that Epicurus drew from Homer his idea that the greatest good lies in pleasure, that many found the excuse for irreligion in Euripides, that many sought in Alcaeus and Anacreon instigation to impure and lewd loves and to lives of drunkenness, and there are some who hold that precepts of anger were imbibed from Archilochus and Hipponax; and it would take a long time to enumerate the particular cases in which some foolhardy men have fallen on account of those things which they had falsely learned from the poets.[8]

Ethical and religious criteria are inextricably mingled in Pico's judgments

---

[7] In *Opera omnia* (1573 ed.), II, 938: "non minores enim malorum occasiones ex Poëtis, ad uitia quam ad uirtutes trahunt homines, ut qui & uariè scripserunt, & modò uitijs habenas laxarunt, modò eas compescuerunt, ut facilè est uidere si quis eos in manus sumpserit, tametsi alio alius ad uirtutem propensior, & alius alio sit inclinatior in uitia uel narranda, uel extollenda."

[8] *Ibid.*, II, 939: "multi existiment Epicurum ex Homero traxisse summum bonum esse in uoluptate, ex Euripide multos impietatis habuisse occasionem: Impuri & obscoeni amoris, & ebriosae uitę fomenta ab Alcaeo & Anacreonte multos petisse: Iracundiae praecepta ab Archilocho & Hipponacte bibisse, sunt qui uelint, & longum esset percensere singula quibus aliqui praecipites inierunt ob ea quae apud Poëtas perperam didicissent."

of the art of poetry, and, hence, those judgments bear almost solely upon the implications of subject matter for the lives of the reader.

About 1505, Battista Mantovano wrote a letter to Pico in praise of one of his poems; the terms of praise show a clear critical position:

> Since you have written a poem in a scrupulous, eloquent, and learned fashion, I can neither praise nor admire it sufficiently. For it has wit and charm without effeminacy and lewdness, and it gives pleasure not as Flora does, but as Diana; not as Venus, but as Minerva; combining, in the way prescribed by Horace, utility and beauty with pleasure. Obscene and lewd poems, in my opinion, bear the same relationship to true poems as do wanton prostitutes to honest matrons. I, indeed, do not deem a poem to be a true poem and one capable of withstanding every censure unless it be serious, pure, and holy. . . . Nor should we listen to the soft and effeminate poets, for whom nothing is savoury if it is not base, impure, corrupt, and malodorous. . . . This poem of yours is like a river which grows as it flows along, and which the more it advances the more beautiful, the more pleasant, the more grand it appears, which is a sign of a very great talent. It is, I say, the sign of a very great talent, such as does not weaken with exercise, but gathers strength from effort.[9]

Moral and religious considerations are uppermost; but there is also respect for the pleasure to be combined with utility and for the artistic strength of the work, which represents the poet's genius. It is significant that in one of the passages not quoted here Battista cites the verse of Horace (*Ars poetica* 310: "rem tibi Socraticae poterunt ostendere chartae") that indicates that the poet is to use the philosopher as his source.

CINQUECENTO HUMANISTS

In contrast with Pico's passionate abuse of the art of poetry, Lodovico Ricchieri (Caelius Rhodiginus) presents a moderate estimate in his *Lectionum antiquarum libri XXX* of 1516. Book IV of the work is devoted to a defence and discussion of poetry. The defence is made in terms almost identical with those used by Mancinelli: poetry as a first philosophy, as a teacher to youth of a way of life. But Ricchieri also insists on the character of the poet as a good and wise man and makes a case for the priority of verse over prose. In his effort to discern the major usefulness of the art, he develops at length the power of allegory as a pedagogical device; this insistence upon allegorical interpretation relates him at once to a long line of medieval expositors and to his fellow Platonists:

[9] In G. F. Pico della Mirandola, *Epistolarum libri quattuor* (1506–7), p. Fv*v*: "Poema quod religiose, eloquenter & docte conscripsisti, neque laudare, neque admirari satis possum: Habet enim sine mollitie & impudicitia, salem ac leporem, & delectat non ut Flora, sed ut Diana: non ut Venus, sed ut Minerua miscens, quemadmodum praecipit Horatius dulcedini utilitatem ac pulchritudinem. Poëmata obscoena & impudica sunt iudicio meo inter uera poemata, quales inter probas matronas, fornicariae meretrices. Ego enim poema uerum, & quod omne punctum ferre possit esse non puto nisi sit graue castum, ac sanctum. . . . Nec audiendi sunt poetae molles & effoeminati, quibus nihil sapit nisi turpe, impurum, purulentum, & olidum. . . . Poema hoc tuum simile fluuio, qui currendo crescit quo magis procedit uidetur uenustius, dulcius, grandius, quod est indicium fortioris ingenij. Fortioris inquam ingenij quod exercitio non flacescat, sed laborando uires acquirat."

But if profound matters are veiled and concealed in the outward covering of the fictions, and hidden as in the most secret sanctuaries, you must know that this is invention proper to poetry and among the ancients also that habit of fanciful invention has long since grown strong.... With such fictions as these, it seems to me, we should from the start form and, so to speak, "delineate" our youth from tenderest childhood. For this animal, prudent and wise and possessed of reason, whom we call man, wishes, through a kind of internal drive, to know, and is hungry for knowledge; and the poetic fiction is the first stimulus to such learning, especially since it remains unexpressed and vague and seems always to suggest some other matter. Thus all of us, spurred on to it by a kind of natural force, are most avid for what is new, which is experienced by us as most sweet and pleasant and is not lacking in the marvelous.[10]

For all of us, thus, poetry provides a ready and delightful answer to this thirst for knowledge, and especially in youth it may give us the roots of all arts and disciplines. Ricchieri demonstrates his point by giving an allegorical interpretation of the *Aeneid*, insisting on the lessons to be learned from it in this way.

The dangers of such a use of poetry are of course apparent to Ricchieri. If the fictional envelope contains wicked or reprehensible actions, and if the spectator, through youth or ignorance, is unable to penetrate within to the allegorical meanings, what will be the result? Obviously, an undesirable moral conclusion. To prevent it, he says, care must be taken to see that only virtuous plots are presented to the young, and it was such a concern that lay behind Plato's banishment of the poets. But here Ricchieri makes a distinction that became a commonplace among the apologists for poetry:

But with respect to these we must note carefully that the poets are not condemned outright by Plato; since to the degree in which he holds that they should be rejected when they disturb the state and invent shameful things, to that same degree he embraces them and kisses then tenderly when they exhort to moral improvement, celebrating elegantly and eloquently in their praises of heroes or their hymns to the gods.[11]

Plato's ban thus is a limited one, affecting not the whole of the art of poetry but only those practices of it which would lead to undesirable consequences for the state. With these restrictions upon the activity of the poet Ricchieri

---

[10] *Lectionum* (1516), p. 156: "Quod si fabularum inuolucris res profundae conuelantur, obtegunturque, & ferè Sanctariis secretioribus reconduntur, id scire conuenit, esse poetices germanum. Et Veteribus quoque illum irroborasse pridem, confingendi morem.... iis uero imprimis tenerior aetas formanda, delineandaque, ut sic dicam, uidetur, Quoniam animal hoc prouidum, & sagax, ac rationis compos, quem uocamus hominem, intimo quodam impetu scire desyderat, estque cognationis auidum, Cuius fomentum primum fabula est, eo imprimis argumento, quod indicta inscitaque alias profert. Sumus autem, ad id nos prouehente naturali quadam ui, nouitatis omnes perauidi, quod praedulcis haec sentiatur, & iucunda, nec admiratione careat."

[11] *Ibid.*, p. 158: "Sed in iis illud impense animaduertendum, non damnari prorsum à Platone Poetas, Siquidem quantum ubi perturbant, aut turpia fingunt, reiiciendos putat, tantundem amplexatur, exosculaturque, si ad bonam frugem hortentur, laudibus heroum aut Deorum hymnis eleganter, facundeque concelebratis."

would agree, and he sees two agencies as capable of exercising the control, the church and the philosopher. The church, through its canonical decrees, for example, has declared that the good Christian should not read too frequently the fictions of the poets, since through them he becomes stimulated to seek pleasure and, in a sense, is made to "sacrifice to the demons" (p. 160). In a more general way, the writing of the poet and the interpreting of his works should be under the watchful supervision of the philosopher:

> ... one must have recourse to those who are skilled in philosophy, who administer an antidote, having explained by allegory the outer cloaks of the fables and having used the curative powers of their precepts, by which means (as if by a brake) the enticements of the pleasures are restrained and at the same time the violence of the passions is diminished—which, excited for the most part by reading as by a living example placed before it, forces itself upon the very reason and after having trod upon it succeeds in extending its dominion even farther.[12]

The ideal solution would be a combination of philosophy and poetry, one in which poets were philosophers and philosophers were poets.

Ricchieri's ideas on poetry, moreover, extend beyond the simple consideration of the moral ends to be served. He attacks the problem of imitation and discovers that there are really two types: one in which everything is invented and there is no representation of truth; a second in which the truth is represented in the garb of a fictional narrative. The second is called "narratio fabulosa" and may be treated in either of two ways, by treating profound subjects completely acceptable on philosophical and religious grounds or by admitting reprehensible matters. Once again, the distinction is that between two kinds of subject matter, and obviously the philosopher-critic will tolerate only the first kind (p. 158).

In connection with imitation, Ricchieri does not fail to call attention to the pleasure which we find in accurate representations, even of ugly objects (he is apparently following Aristotle here), a statement to which he adds the warning that we must not allow this kind of admiration to deceive us into accepting everything that we find in poems. He follows Aristotle again in his solution of the problem of art versus nature in the poet and of the differentiation of poets according to their characters; Ricchieri believes in divine inspiration, but he also believes that the characters of men, good or bad, determine what kind of poetry they will write. He reduces questions of art to the types of rhythms used in various genres and to the elements of style proper to poetry. In the latter connection he cites Horace, Cicero, and such rhetoricians as Dionysius of Halicarnassus. On the whole, Ricchieri's position is much more eclectic than that of the other Platonists whom we

---

[12] *Ibid.*, p. 160: "... decurrendumque ad Philosophiae non ignaros, Qui antipharmacum propinent, explicatas per allegorias fabulamentorum uelaminibus, adhibitaque praeceptorum salubritate, quibus Voluptatum adlubentia quodam, uelut sufflamine reprimatur, atque item deferuescat perturbationum impetus, qui lectione tanquam exemplo proposito, plerunque concitatior ingerit sese rationi, & illa exculcata latius affectat dominari."

have studied thus far. He goes beyond the usual praise or blame of poetry; but when he does so he finds himself largely outside the Platonic context and is obliged to appeal to other masters.

In his *De incantationibus* (1520), Pietro Pomponazzi displays a much more restricted view of the whole problem of poetics, but one which is essentially favorable to the art. His concern is with two questions, that of the divine furor and that of allegory. For the first, he accepts fully all the ancient statements about the divine inspiration of the poet, about the essential opposition between reason and poetry—the poet really does not *know* what he is writing—about the poets as instruments and interpreters of the gods. For the second, he starts from the assumption that there are important truths hidden under the fables of the poets: "... they invent those fables to lead us to the truth and so that we may instruct the uneducated masses, who must be led to the good and drawn away from evil just as children are led and drawn by the hope of reward and the fear of punishment."[13] Poetry has the particular virtue of instructing in abstract matters through the use of material images. It may thus be used or quoted as a supplementary device whenever it is necessary to persuade, because of its capacity "to fortify and caress the minds of the listeners" ("ad firmandum, & animos demulcendum," p. 297). The rhetorical bias of Plato is here very close to the usual theory of the Horatians.

Gasparo Contarini's *De officio episcopi* (which belongs roughly to this period, although its exact date is unknown) is concerned with the role that a bishop should assign to poetry in the education of the young. And the churchman finds that the very rhetorical attractions of which Pomponazzi had spoken constitute the greatest dangers resident in poetry. It is because the poet is divinely inspired, because his works are full of charms and enticements, that he is able to sway the souls of his readers whichever way he will. Hence the young reader, incapable of resisting these influences, should not be allowed to read him. Contarini finds that especially in his own time men err in allowing youth full access to the works of the poets: "he [the bishop] should absolutely not permit the minds of the young, from childhood on, to be corrupted by the lascivious writings of poets and other writers of this kind; for if they drink them in in their tender years, it will be next to impossible for them, in their mature age, to be called back to better moral behavior; in which matter our own time ... sins greatly."[14] Contarini can see some profit in the reading of certain poets, especially Vergil, but on the whole he deems it better for all men to read Christian

---

[13] In *Opera* (1567), p. 201: "nam illa fingunt, ut in ueritatem ueniamus, & rude uulgus instruamus, quod inducere oportet ad bonum, & à malo retrahere, ut pueri inducuntur & retrahuntur, scilicet spe pręmij, & timore poenae."

[14] In *Opera* (1571), p. 425: "non permittat statim ab ineunte aetate puerorum animos corrumpi poetarum, coeterorumque huiusmodi auctorum lasciuiis: quas si à teneris annis imbiberint; impossibile prope erit, vt in maturiori ętate ad meliorem frugem reuocentur, qua in re nostris temporibus ... magnopere peccatur."

writings. Presumably, as so frequently with these antagonists of the art, the term "poet" refers specifically, if not exclusively, to the pagan poets of antiquity, and some, at least, of the objection to them is on theological grounds.

The *Libro de natura de amore* of Mario Equicola (1525) has been studied in connection with Horace's *Ars poetica*. It should be mentioned again, briefly, because of several passing references to Plato's ban on the poets and to exceptions that Equicola would make to the general interdict. Dante, for one, fits the category of those poets who, according to Plato, "draw the ignorant multitude to a knowledge of high matters" (p. 5v). The high matters taught by Dante in his hendecasyllables are "what punishment follows the guilt of those confirmed in vice, how one ascends purged to the true glory of beatitude, then the perfect life" (*ibid.*). Another poet whom Plato would have admitted to his republic is Battista Mantovano, who represents the divine nature of the poet required by such theorists as Cicero and Democritus, combined with art as demanded by Horace (p. 37v).

If the attack upon poetry and its defence is one of the essential features of the Platonic tradition in criticism, then Francesco Berni's *Dialogo contra i poeti* (1526) in some way fits into the tradition. This may seem a strange classification of the joking and satirical dialogue. But it will be less strange when we realize that Berni proceeds, at least in part, by upholding the contrary of the arguments usually used in the defence; perhaps this might be called reverse-Platonism. The interlocutors make fun of the self-styled madness of the poets, of their overbearing claim to divine inspiration. They should rather be charged with heresy, uselessness, complete lack of substance and solidity; they are venal and obsequious, malicious and immoral, unashamed plagiarists; they are worthy of punishment rather than of praise. Only when they are "good" for something other than the writing of verses should they be tolerated, and even then it is their quality as men and not as poets that is to be appreciated. Berni suggests such punishments as making the poets themselves undergo the adventures which they attribute to their heroes. One should bear in mind, in reading the *Dialogo*, the jocular tone and the satirical intent and make compensatory allowances; but nevertheless a certain serious animus against poets, and on grounds not too dissimilar from those of the unjesting writers, is evident.

Rather than emphasize the moral consequences of the reading of poetry, as most of his contemporaries seemed to be doing, Giovanni Bernardino Fuscano chose to indulge in elaborate praise of the art because of its divine origins. His short treatise, *De la oratoria et poetica facolta*, was really an introduction to the *Stanze sovra la bellezza di Napoli* and was published with the *Stanze* in 1531. Fuscano begins with a general description of the virtues of eloquence, which is a part of poetry, extolling its capacity to seize upon the soul and to confer life upon the dead past. When to eloquence are added the beauties of poetry, especially verse, it achieves its most marvelous form. This is because poetry, unlike all other forms of eloquence and indeed unlike all other arts and sciences, is divine rather than human in inspiration. The poet is like an unconscious instrument in whom and through whom speaks the voice of God; without this voice, the poet is mute. Poetry is defined by Fuscano in this way:

> Poetry is that art which, embracing all other arts, marvelously expresses through definite rhythms, through measured feet, and through grave maxims all that men have done, all that they have ever said and known, under marvelous veils, illuminated by clear ornaments and at the same time adorned by variegated flowers, not without delighting the ears and bringing profit to the mind.[15]

In a separate development he treats of the relationship between the poet and God, implying that it is specifically of the Christian poet that he speaks. He begins with an analogy: God Himself is a poet and all creation is His poem. Of all creatures the poet is most like God in his powers, and this resemblance carries with it a responsibility: the poet must devote all of his God-given powers to the glory, service, and honor of God: "... tempering his voices with the harmony of all the corporeal senses, he must at all times give Him thanks in verses and in hymns, and all the gifts which come to him from His bounty, he must use, spend, and consume in the cult of His glory and in the honor of His majesty; for all that time which is spent otherwise than in thinking of Him must be accounted as lost."[16] Thus it is that the poet always invokes God at the beginning of his compositions, that he is closely akin to the prophet, and that his name itself means to make or to create. Fuscano's approach is still Platonic, and although it emphasizes another of Plato's ideas rather than the idea of the moral utility of poetry, it concludes with a Christianization of the doctrine.

Since he employs the form of the dialogue in his *De liberis recte instituendis liber* of 1533, Jacopo Sadoleto is able to present in a lively way both sides of the argument on the banishment of the poets. Sadoleto himself upholds the affirmative, using proofs that by now have become fairly standard: the divine inspiration of the poets, which causes their works to operate in an irresistible fashion upon the souls of the listeners; their resultant capacity to orient the soul toward good or evil; the necessity, therefore, that they should be supervised by the state and if necessary banished from its walls. On these points Sadoleto is answered by the other interlocutor, Paolo Sadoleto, who declares that he cannot imagine any

[15] *De la poetica facolta* (1531), pp. Biij–Biijv: "la Poesia è quella che abbracciando tutte l'arti con diffiniti numeri, con misurati piedi, et con graui sententie, quanto l'homini han fatto quanto han mai detto, et conosciuto, sotto merauigliosi uelamenti, da chiari lumi illustrati, et di uarij fiori parimente ornati, non senza dilettar l'orecchi, & giouar l'animo, mirabilmente exprime."

[16] *Ibid.*, p. Biijv: "temprando sue voci con l'Harmonia di tutti corporali sensi darli ogn'hor gratie in versi & Cantici, & tutti doni, che da sua larga bontà li ueneno deue per lo colto di sua gloria, & per l'honore di sua Maestà usarli, spenderli, & consumarli, peròche tutto quel tempo, che a non pensar di lui fia speso, indubitatamente se può tener perduto."

reading more useful or more delightful than that of Homer and of Vergil; in Homer, especially, all wisdom and doctrine are to be found, and all other poets have derived from him as rivers from a fountainhead. He extends this toleration of the poets to include even writers of comedy, especially Terence: "What you yourself frequently say, that comedy is the schoolmistress of private life and of social behavior, makes me believe that you do not repudiate these poets either."[17] Terence is not only a model for diction and language but may serve as an example of good judgment itself; whereas Plautus is to be recommended solely on linguistic grounds. Paolo concludes that there is some good in every poet and that all should be admitted to the educative process. Jacopo's own conclusion is that, if they are to be admitted, the poets must observe faithfully the proper ethical code, and those who prefer to write trivial, corrupt, or scurrilous verse are by no means to be tolerated. The "good" poets may, along with musicians and those who cultivate the other liberal arts, participate in the education and indoctrination of the young.

If one reduces the general defence of poetry to a defence of a single author, one finds essentially the substance of Nicolò Franco's dialogue, *Il Petrarchista* (1539). In addition to much biographical and anecdotic detail, the dialogue on Petrarch contains a passage presenting the reasons why Petrarch should be imitated. What is said about language and style is not especially pertinent here; it could just as well have occurred in a document in the Horatian mode. But Petrarch is to be admired for his substance as well as for his style, and indeed for his character as a man:

And he should so much the more be always in our hands that he contains within him all knowledge, that every science has some place in his verses. And who can say how many and how great thoughts of divine and human philosophy are hidden in his rhymes? how modest (oh, immortal God!) he is? how clean and pure of every stain of lowness? how gay without lewdness? how religious in his thoughts? how chaste in his mind? how Platonic in his love? . . . In a word there is nothing in him which does not belong to the divine virtues, to the celestial beauties, to angelic mores, to the most honest love, to the highest humanity, and to ineffable courtesy.[18]

Two remarks: first, there is nothing in this praise that might not also have been found in a typically Horatian document; second, the qualities singled

[17] *De liberis* (1533), p. 108: "Nam quòd comoediam saepe affirmas priuatae uitae & ciuilis consuetudinis esse magistram, speciem habet, ut ego arbitror, hos quoque poëtas non repudiantis."

[18] *Il Petrarchista* (1539), p. 12v: "E tanto piu per le mani si deue hauere, quanto e poi in lui tanta dottrina; che ogni scienza ne i suoi uersi ha qualche luogo. E chi puo dire quanti e quali sentimenti de la diuina, e de la humana philosophia si stieno ascosi ne le sue rime? Quanto e egli (o Dio immortale) modesto? quanto terso, e netto d'ogni lasciua ruggine? Quanto senza lasciuia leggiadro? Quanto e religioso ne i pensieri? Quanto e casto ne la mente? Quanto e Platonico nel suo amore? . . . Niente in somma e in lui; che non sia di diuine uirtuti, di celesti bellezze, d'angelici costumi, d'honestissimo amore, di somma humanitate, e d'ineffabile cortesia."

out, breadth of knowledge, godliness, and morality, are precisely the same ones that would make a poet acceptable even in Plato's republic.

Mario Equicola presents us, in his *Institutioni al comporre in ogni sorte di rima della lingua volgare*, with a much more completely Platonic work than his *Libro de natura de amore*. Published in 1541, the posthumous treatise is concerned above all with prosodic recommendations for the various lyric forms, for which it leans heavily on the old treatise of Antonio da Tempo. But as a prelude to such discussion, it develops the history of poetry, a lengthy comparison between poetry and painting, a defence of the art, and a praise of both Dante and Petrarch. In almost all phases of this prelude the source is Plato. So for the distinction made, close to the beginning, among the various kinds of verse: the active (under which Equicola classifies tragedy, comedy, bucolic, and satire), the narrative (history, maxims, philosophy, and mathematics), and the mixed (heroic, lyric, and elegiac poetry). So also for the insistence upon divine inspiration. On the matter of the banishment of the poets, however, Equicola disagrees, declaring that it came about only in the *Republic* and only because that work designed a state entirely outside the bounds of human possibility. Elsewhere, he says, Plato praised the poets, and Equicola joins in the praise here: for the delight which they bring to our ears, for the way in which "from our earliest years they invite us, by means of fables, to praiseworthy and great actions" (p. B), for their incitement to virtue. Poetry "teaches us to adorn ourselves with good mores and to hold our passions in check; intent as it is upon giving pleasure and enjoyment and utility to men, it makes accessible for our use the examples of many things, setting before us in a most diligent fashion and with delight the glory of the ancient virtues."[19] More specifically, poetry shows us the fortunes of kings and heroes, indicates how we may temper our passions; thus the fact that it uses myths or fictions is no more to be condemned than a similar use in religious mysteries and parables, and the bad moral examples which it sometimes provides are no worse than those found constantly in life, in history, in the laws. Equicola's comparison of poetry with painting points out that both arts may legitimately "invent" or "feign," provided that in so doing they observe the laws of decorum. His conclusion that poetry is superior to painting is based on two reasons: poetry makes its appeal to the mind rather than to the body, and its products are less subject to destruction. The brief discussion of Dante and Petrarch employs the terms and the attitudes commonplace in Horatian criticism.

TOMITANO (1545)

The *Ragionamenti della lingua toscana* of Bernardino Tomitano (1545) represents the first nearly complete "art of poetry" in the present series of

[19] *Institutioni* (1541), p. B: "Ornarne di buon costumi, & rifrenar gli affetti ne insegna. studiosa di far piacere, & dar volutta, & vtile a' mortali, di molte cose gli essempij à nostro vso riduce, diligentissimamente con giocondità delle antiche virtù ne propone la gloria."

PLATONISM: DEFENCE OF POETRY

Platonic treatises; it also represents the most eclectic and in a sense the most typical studied thus far. If one were to read the three books of the *Ragionamenti* in reverse order, one would find in the third all the detailed treatment of the more particular aspects of the art, a treatment resting largely on Horace's *Ars poetica* and on the rhetoricians but deriving certain essential ideas from Aristotle. The second book deals largely with oratory, but even here the application of oratorical principles to poetry is constantly traced and all the examples are taken from poets; once again, the classical rhetoricians provide the distinctions and the rules. But in the first book, where Tomitano wishes to lay the philosophical foundations for all the art of writing, his source is Plato. And it is Plato appealed to on a much broader basis than was done by most of Tomitano's contemporaries. For rather than begin with one of the favorite dicta (which I have outlined at the beginning of this chapter), he takes as his starting point Plato's general concept of Ideas. Like the painter, the poet and the orator attempt to represent in the medium of their arts some perfect concept or Idea; Ideas are "those simple and spiritual forms ... which mean nothing else but examples and norms of those things which are born naturally or made artificially, which are absolutely eternal and durable just as all others are born perishable and mortal and may be said to be subject to constant mutation."[20] If the poet is to succeed as a poet, he must therefore be something of a philosopher so that he may know the truths which he is going to imitate.

The relationship of poetry to philosophy is indeed a complicated one. The business of philosophy is the discovery of truth; the business of poetry is the imitation of truth through the medium of fictions. But poetry does not imitate all truth, nor does it serve its ultimate ends in every part of its imitation. Of its two ends, pleasure and utility, it is the latter which involves philosophy. For the utility is both moral and intellectual in character, and it is found in moral and intellectual precepts scattered throughout the work. In order to write such precepts properly, Tomitano insists, the poet must know the philosophical truths from which they spring: "These precepts then will either teach us how to live well and happily, or else they will merely render us wise through some intellectual habit; the latter ones are called contemplative just as the former are called moral, and both kinds are a necessary part of philosophy."[21] Does this mean that the poet must have exact and complete knowledge of all matters, both human and divine? Or does he speak without knowledge and run the risk of Platonic con-

---

[20] *Ragionamenti* (1545), p. 8: "quelle semplici & spiritali forme, ... che altro non importano che essempi & norme di quelle cose, che nascono naturalmente, ò artificiosamente si fanno: lequali sempiterne del tutto & dureuoli sono, si come tutte l'altre cose nascenti mancheuoli & mortali, & a mutatione di continuo soggiacenti si possono addomandare."

[21] *Ibid.*, pp. 42–43: "Questi precetti adunque ouero ci insegneranno uiuer bene & beatamente, ò che ci renderanno solamente per alcun habito intellettuale saputi, liquali contemplatiui si addomanderanno, come quegli altri morali: gli uni & gli altri de quali sono parte necessaria della philosophia."

demnation on that score? Tomitano takes a middle position: The poet must have knowledge, and the more he knows the more successfully will he write; but it need not be profound and thorough knowledge. "I tell you that the orator and the poet must possess so pure and simple a knowledge of things pertaining to philosophy, that when he remains silent about them he will show that he knows them; and aside from this they will be a guide and norm to him from which he may derive more pleasant and more solid maxims and may give to all that he writes or speaks a greater splendor."[22] Indeed, if the poet cultivates philosophy to an excessive degree, he thereby becomes less good a poet. Tomitano's remarks on Dante clarify his whole position:

> I hold therefore that that man is a better and graver poet who with the aid of philosophy will be able to render his compositions more beautiful and more grave, but not that he should for this reason dispute or talk about philosophy. And therefore it is not conceded to you that Dante, although he may be a better philosopher, succeeds in being a greater poet than Petrarch. For Petrarch understood that minimum amount of philosophy which was sufficient to give spirit and solidity to his rhymes; whereas in the matter of beautiful diction, from which the poet derives his name, . . . he was better than Dante.[23]

To this matter of philosophy, also, is related the problem of allegory. The poet knows a basic collection of truths, but instead of expounding them directly he dresses them in the outward fashion of a myth or a fiction. If the reader would derive full benefit from the poem he must penetrate, by means of allegorical interpretation, to the truths within the fable. Tomitano shows how this is done by interpreting the myth of Parnassus and giving an analysis of Petrarch's madrigal "Perch' al viso d'amor portava insegna."

If the poet, as a philosopher in disguise, can be useful to the lives of men, then clearly he should not be expelled from any state. Tomitano meets Plato's ban by two counterproposals: first, the works of the poet should at all times be subjected to the examination and the censorship of the philosophers; second, the poet must both be possessed of knowledge of the truth and must be a man of high moral character. From such a poet, so supervised, no harmful or reprehensible works need be feared (pp. 34, 141–42). He may even tell lies—a practice for which Plato blamed the

---

[22] *Ibid.*, pp. 94–95: "dicoui, l'oratore & il poeta douer una cognitione cosi schietta & semplice ritenere delle cose alla philosophia appartenenti, lequali egli tacendole mostrera di saperle, & oltre di questo gli seranno una guida & norma, onde egli piu uaghe & sode sententie ne diriui, & maggior splendore doni à tutto quello, onde egli scriue ò parla."

[23] *Ibid.*, p. 240: "Voglio adunque che miglior poeta sia quello & piu graue, che con l'aiuto della philosophia sapra render i suoi componimenti piu belli et piu graui, ma non per questo che egli di philosophia tenzoni ò parli. Et per questo non ui si concede, che Dante quantunque sia maggior philosopho; uenga ad esser piu gran poeta del Petrarca. Percioche il Petrarca quel tanto di philosophia intese, che a recar spirito et fermezza alle sue rime bastaua: la doue che poi nella bella elocutione, dallaquale si denomina il Poeta, come piu à basso ui dirò, fu di Dante migliore."

poets—provided that he avoid the "fraudulent lie," which has no virtue in it, and practice only the "artful lie," which masks a hidden truth. Only in passing does Tomitano mention the divine furor and its manifestations in the poet; apparently he regarded this as an incidental aspect of theory.

In these various remarks on poetry, Tomitano frequently associates it with oratory. The two arts are very closely allied for him as they were for theorists of the rhetorical school. He sees them both as having a similar relationship to Ideas, as seeking the same ends of pleasure and profit, as finding their utility largely in the inclusion of moral precepts, as sharing the same qualitative parts of invention, disposition, and elocution, and as using identical figures of speech. They differ, however, in various respects: oratory tends to emphasize utility, poetry gives more attention to pleasure; the orator uses persuasion as his means of achieving his ends, the poet uses imitation; whereas the one writes in prose, the other writes in verse; and the poet alone makes use of fables and fictions. These theoretical differences do not prevent Tomitano from citing passages from poems as examples of all the rhetorical devices which he discusses; in fact, he tends more and more throughout the treatise to find all his demonstrative materials in Petrarch alone. This means that, in the last analysis, he reduces all the arts using language to a single one, and finds their most interesting and important feature in the language which they use. It is at this point that he comes into closest contact with certain theorists of the Horatian-rhetorical school.

ANTONIO MARIA DE' CONTI (CA. 1550)

To this same period, roughly the middle of the century, must be assigned a group of works by Antonio Maria de' Conti, who called himself professionally Marcantonio Maioragio. Since he died in 1555 and the major part of his career as professor at Milan fell in the preceding ten years, the works published in the *Orationes et praefationes* of 1582 would seem to belong to the period around 1550. On the subject of poetry, Conti has two contributions to make, a theoretical statement in the form of a *De arte poetica* and a number of practical applications in the "prefaces" which were really "praelectiones" to courses of academic interpretation of various texts. Conti's oration *De arte poetica* is not an art of poetry at all, since it makes no inquiry into the nature of the art or into the devices by which poetic excellence is achieved; instead, it offers praise of poetry in fairly conventional terms. Poetry is the most excellent and the most divine of all the arts, since it provides man with a knowledge of things both human and supernatural. Its prime function is educative; as Maximus of Tyre and Strabo have pointed out, it is a first philosophy "which from earliest childhood leads us to an honest way of life, which instructs us in good mores, which calms and rules the disturbed movements of the soul, which teaches, in the most pleasurable fashion, what things are to be done."[24] The terms of praise are all old and familiar. As for the Platonic eviction, there are two great arguments against it: First, one may find in every poet the most saintly moral maxims, since good poets are also good men and are the preceptors of life. Second, such great pillars of religion as Augustine, Jerome, and Ambrose were great readers of poetry and cited it constantly. Moreover, even Plato argues against himself, since in other works (where he is not concerned with the perfect state) he insists upon the divinity of poetry and praises it to the skies. Follows Conti's own extravagant praise: "By the immortal gods, what sweetness do we not find in the language of poetry? what harmony? what charm? what loveliness, what cleverness of invention? what proportion of composition? what gravity of maxims? what majesty in all kinds of style?"[25] As is so frequently the case, the praise here given resolves itself into matters of diction and sound, and what might be considered to be more distinctly poetic qualities are not even intimated.

A similar set of principles is found applied in the "praelectiones." The two prefaces to Homer are typical. Homer is, of course, the ocean from which all knowledge and all literary skill have been derived. He has taught kings how to be kings, has given the foundations of all the arts and sciences, and has surpassed even the historians in those lessons which are the proper contribution of history. His use of mythological tales, blamed by so many, is to be defended as a device for the presentation of serious materials; properly interpreted, these tales contain within themselves all kinds of hidden knowledge. They are the means by which Homer attracts and captivates the "rudes" and the "imperitos," teaching them the greatest mysteries in the guise of frivolous myths. In so doing, he uses the method of the theologians, who "frequently use parables and similes for divine matters, by means of which untutored minds are easily raised from known things which are apparent to the senses to those which are unknown and sublime."[26] In so doing, also, he serves the ends of poetry as established by Horace, providing useful instruction in mores and in the good life.

The second preface, devoted to the *Odyssey* (as the first had been to the *Iliad*), stresses what is to be learned from the work about eloquence and about all the arts; it also quotes Plutarch to the effect that the *Iliad* teaches

[24] *Orationes et praefationes* (1582), p. 145: "quae nos ab ineunte aetate ad honestas uiuendi rationes adducit, quae bonis moribus instruit, quae motus animi turbidos placat, ac regit, quae res gerendas summa cum iucunditate praecipit."

[25] *Ibid.*, p. 148: "Proh Dij immortales, quę suauitas poeticae locutionis? quae concinitas? qui lepos? quae uenustas? quod inuentionis acumen? quae compositionis harmonia? qui uerborum splendor? quae sententiarum grauitas? quae denique generum omnium dicendi maiestas?"

[26] *Ibid.*, p. 154v: "sicut etiam Theologi nostri parabolis ac similitudinibus in rebus diuinis frequenter utuntur, quo rudes animi facilius à cognitis & sub sensum cadentibus rebus ad incognitas & sublimes extollantur."

above all strength of body and the *Odyssey*, strength of soul (p. 157v). In his remarks on Hesiod's *Works and Days*, Conti rests upon the praise given the poet by the greatest philosophers and rhetoricians, sharing their admiration for the precepts and for the apt handling of the "middle" style (pp. 158v–162).

Two fairly lengthy prefaces are devoted to Vergil, one to the *Georgics* and the other to the *Aeneid*. The first work is compared with Hesiod and is found to be superior, largely because of the elegance and the clearness of its diction but also because of its erudition. For the *Aeneid*, Conti concentrates on the fourth book. He finds that, if the general aim of the poem is to present Aeneas as the exemplar of piety and fortitude, the particular function of Book IV is to show the evil power of love, the errors and catastrophes to which it leads, so that we may avoid it. For the rest, one may see in the life of Aeneas every virtue in its highest form, presented as a living example and through action rather than description. In a more general way, Vergil is praised for his incredible erudition, for his admirable style and versification, for his use of a poetic rather than a natural order of treatment, and for his proper exploitation of all the rhetorical devices. Once again, as soon as Conti passes from general remarks on subject matter and on the end of poetry to particular consideration of poetic techniques, his text becomes the *Ars poetica* and his method Horatian (pp. 173v–177v, 178–183v).

In another of his works, his *In tres Aristotelis libros, de arte rhetorica explanationes* (posthumous, 1572), Conti reflects other aspects of the current Platonic doctrine. He explains the special sense in which Plato uses "imitation" to describe the representation of things by words (p. 347A) and cites the *Ion* on the divinity of poets (p. 381A). These remarks are found in a context of a commentary on Aristotle and are frequently coupled with similar remarks from Horace. They demonstrate once more the eclectic nature of Conti's approach and the extent to which he uses Plato for a number of purposes.

Sperone Speroni, in his *Discorso in lode della pittura* (undated), is incidentally concerned with the broader meaning of imitation and with Plato's distinction between narrative and dramatic imitation in poetry. He also establishes a hierarchy of nobility on the basis of the subjects imitated and the prosodic means:

... all the imitative arts are more or less noble not only according to the thing imitated, which is common to all arts and sciences, but also according to the means and the manner of imitating. Thus if the epic and tragedy and comedy all imitate, as far as the thing imitated is concerned the first two are nobler than the third; but as for the mode or instrument of imitation, tragedy and comedy are not unlike since the one and the other imitates with the iamb. But the epic is indeed different from these because it imitates with the hexameter, a most noble verse. It is quite true that the epic does not imitate as well, speaking absolutely about imitation, as do the other two which are dramatic.[27]

In such a statement as this, of course, there are strong echoes of the distinctions made by Aristotle in chapter 3 of the *Poetics*; but perhaps the assigning of "nobility" on various scores is more specifically Platonic in its implications.

The Platonic element is decidedly secondary in the *In Aristotelis librum de poetica communes explanationes* of Maggi and Lombardi (1550). This is, of course, one of the major Aristotelian commentaries of the century, and it will be treated in detail later on. But Plato appears both as a source for certain ideas in the commentary and as an earlier theorist whose ideas Aristotle either combatted or developed. The latter position is stated clearly in connection with the distinction between narrative and dramatic imitation; Maggi cites Book III of the *Republic* at length "so that we may more easily discover how wisely Aristotle, using the precepts of his teacher Plato, has improved upon them."[28] Occasionally, Aristotle's ideas are seen as being in opposition to those of Plato, as when (in connection with *Poetics* 1460*b*33) Aristotle is said to be answering Plato's attacks on Homer in Books II and III of the *Republic*. Again, in the last lines of his treatise Aristotle is said to be using Plato's argument that the end of poetry is pleasure, although elsewhere Aristotle goes beyond when he states that the end is rather utility through purgation (pp. 277, 299). Most frequently, though, the commentators wish to find parallels and influences. In Maggi's *Prolegomena*, which treats the standard topics relative to any work, one point of investigation is the end of poetry. Insofar as Aristotle holds that the end is, "by imitating human actions, and through pleasurable language, to ennoble the soul," he is spanning the tradition of both Plato and Plutarch, who saw its end as the education of youth.[29] Plato's condemnation of the poets who seek only "voluptas" is thus a limited one, applying to bad poets who would corrupt youth; his general conclusion, like that of Aristotle and Horace, would be that poetry is useful as an educative instrument.

In connection with specific passages of the *Poetics*, the commentators cite Plato's definition of beauty (p. 123), they establish a parallel between the παράδειγμα of *Poetics* 1454*b*13 and Plato's Ideas ("siue natura secun-

[27] In *Opere* (Venice, 1740), III, 443–44: "tutte le arti imitative sono più o men nobili non solo quanto alla cosa imitata, il che è comune a tutte le arti e scienzie, ma quanto allo instrumento e modo dello imitare. però se la epopeja, e la tragedia imitano, e la commedia, quanto alla cosa imitata le due prime sono più nobili della terza; ma quanto al modo o istrumento dello imitare non son diverse la tragedia della commedia, imitando l'una e l'altra col jambo: ma sì è diversa la epopeja da esse, perchè imita collo esametro nobilissimo verso. è ben vero che non imita così bene, assolutamente della imitazione parlando, come imitano le altre due, le quali sono drammatiche. . . ."

[28] *Explanationes* (1550), p. 67: "ut facilius deprehendi possit, quàm doctè placitis Platonis sui praeceptoris Aristoteles utens, in melius ea reformet."

[29] *Ibid.*, p. 13: "actiones humanas imitando, suaui sermone animum excultum reddere."

dum se consyderata, non ut in hoc, aut in illo reperta," p. 175), and of course they refer to Plato on the divine furor as antecedent to Aristotle's ideas on the sources of poetic inspiration (p. 187). In all this, it would be very difficult to distinguish anything that might be termed an underlying Platonic position. The text is interesting because of its assumption that Plato is frequently present as a source for Aristotle's ideas and that, contrariwise, Aristotle is frequently concerned with a development or a refutation of his master's poetic theories.

A distinctly Platonic position is indeed visible in a much shorter text of approximately the same time (I date it roughly in the decade 1550–1560), found in several manuscripts: Giovanni Giacomo Leonardi's *Discorso qual sia piu utile al mondo ò l'historia ò la poesia*. Leonardi takes issue with the usual assumption that poetry is more useful than history because it presents ideal models rather than imperfect realities. History, according to this conception, might well incite men to imitate the errors of the great. Leonardi's own opinion is directly opposed:

... I always was and still am of the opinion that History is of much greater usefulness to the world than Poetry, since it seems to me that in all things truth carries with it a certain admiration, an impression upon men which gives them a much greater desire to imitate it than do fiction and lies. ... this does not come to pass with invented things, since as fables they give of themselves from the very beginning an impression of the impossible, and one does not heed them with the same attention as the true. Besides the poet, who in large part is desirous of giving pleasure, pays so much attention to this end that at times he forgets to pursue that which he has proposed as his end, that is, utility ... and it results that men, as those who do not understand the secret, or whether what the poet was trying to say is found in the verse, on the surface and in the pleasure, or whether in things difficult to discover, leave aside the intention hidden within the poetry.[30]

Three essentially Platonic ideas are present here: (1) truth is preferable to fiction as a means of teaching men; (2) the poet tends to seek pleasure rather than utility and hence is to be condemned; (3) the meanings contained under the allegorical exterior may not be readily apparent to the reader. Leonardi goes on to say that only good and rare intellects will perceive the hidden meanings, and he concludes with a summation of the various lessons to be learned from history.

[30] MS BNF II. III. 384, fols. 133v–134: "Io nondimeno sempre fui, et sono in opinione che l'Historia torni al Mondo utile molto maggiore che la Poesia, parendomi, che la uerità habbia in tutte le cose una certa admiratione, un' impression negli huomini, che doni loro molto maggiore studio d'imitarla, che la fittione, et la bugia. ... cosi non auuiene nelle cose finte, percioche come fauole danno di se nel principio un' impressione dell'impossibile, et non s'attendono con quella attentione come le uere. Il Poeta poiche è uolto a dilettare in buona parte mira tanto questo che si scorda alle uolte di proseguir quello, che s'hà posto per fine che è l'utile ... fà che gli huomini come quelli che non intendono il secreto, ne quel che habbia uoluto dire il Poeta se ne stia nel uerso, nella superficie, et nella dilettatione, oueramente come di cose difficili à saper l'intention nascosa nella poesia la lascia da un lato. ..."

POETIC THEORY

A letter written by Girolamo Fracastoro to Girolamo Amalteo in 1551 indicates that at that date it was still necessary to protest against a common opinion that poetry was a "madness" ("una pazzia") and that poetic genius was inconsistent with disciplined intellectual activity. Fracastoro declares that, had he been able to live according to his own wishes, he would have chosen to know only philosophy and poetry, since "only these two fields of knowledge with their related materials seem to me to be worthy of man."[31] He quotes Navagero to the effect that without poetic genius, a man cannot indeed be excellent in the mechanical arts nor can he appreciate their beauty. As a case in point, he cites his own works, showing how they combine both scientific and poetic compositions. Fracastoro's argument belongs to the larger position of the anti-Platonists who felt it necessary to defend the art against the charge of madness and irresponsibility.

PATRIZI (1553)

On the other hand, the *Discorso della diversità dei furori poetici* of Francesco Patrizi (1553) lies entirely within a framework of Platonic presuppositions. The problem which Patrizi poses is to discover why different poets excel in different genres. To answer it, he inquires into the various sources of poetic excellence, concluding that to achieve it the poet must possess both the Horatian "ingenium" and the Platonic "furor." Art, in these matters, is of little use, since it will not help to make the poet "rich in all the beautiful images and in all the perfections which can exist in an eloquent man."[32] For "ingenium" two definitions are given: " 'Ingegno' is properly used for an attitude and a readiness of our mind to learn and to discover. ... In still another way, 'ingegno' is taken for a certain disposition and inclination which at times is found in a given man and which makes him incline toward one thing rather than toward another." This is apparently a natural gift in man. "Furor," however, contains certain supernatural elements: " 'Furor' ... as Plato teaches us in the *Phaedrus*, is either natural or supernatural; or, we might say, human and divine ... what is divine descends from Heaven and raises us above the human, and makes us almost semiangels."[33] After having developed at some length the relationship of God, the planets, and the muses to human genius, Patrizi discourses on the possibility that the soul may take certain impressions

---

[31] In *Raccolta*, ed. Calogerà, II, 263: "solo queste due cognizioni con li suoi annessi mi parono degne dell'uomo."

[32] *Discorso* (1553), pp. 45–45v: "ricco di tutti i bei concetti, & di tutte le perfettioni, che possano cadere in huomo eloquente."

[33] *Ibid.*, p. 45v: "ingegno propriamente si dice, una attitudine, & una prontezza della nostra mente, all'imparare, & al ritrouare. ... In un' altro modo ancora, si prende l'ingegno, per una certa affettione & inclinatione, che tal'hora si troua in alcun' huomo, che lo fa ad una cosa piu che ad un'altra inchinato"; and "Il furore, ... secondo che Platone ci insegna nel Fedro, è ò naturale, ò sopranaturale, ò uogliamo dire, humano, et diuino. ... il diuino, descende da Cielo, & sopra all'esser humano ci inalza, & quasi semiangeli ci rende."

from the planets and that the poetic faculty may be one of the impressions so derived. This assumption leads to the solution of the specific problem:

> ... the writing of poetry, then, rather on one subject than on another results from the disposition which the soul, in descending through the other heavens, takes more from this planet than from that. And according as it is more illuminated by the rays of Phoebus or of Venus than by Mars or Mercury, it is more given to sing of amorous matters and the liberal arts than either of war or of the mechanical arts.[34]

This, then, is the source of "ingegno," of the inclination toward a special subject matter. "Furor" is a developed state of the same, whose copiousness and abundance results from additional gifts by the muses. A final problem remains, that of the relationship between these natural or divine gifts and the purely artificial or acquired powers of learning and practice of the art. These are regarded as relieving the soul of earthly darkness and permitting it to see the divine light: "... each hour they purify the soul a little more from its earthly shadow and cause it to be exposed to that heavenly light."[35] In general, then, for Patrizi the divine furor is necessary if the poem is to be anything but "cold and stupid" (p. 50v); the particular kind of poem practised by the poet will depend upon his special gifts; and even the kind of verse used by him for treating a given matter will be a function of his inspiration.

I have already had occasion to analyze Alessandro Lionardi's *Dialogi della inventione poetica* of 1554 (cf. Chapter IV above, pp. 137–38) and to suggest how both Aristotelian and Platonic elements exist as incidental accompaniments to an essentially rhetorical theory. The borrowings from Plato are typical of the period. Thus Lionardi calls upon Plato for the special meaning of "imitatione" as dramatic representation, as against "enuntiatione" or narrative representation (p. 76). He calls upon the *Republic*, the *Phaedo*, and the *Ion* for the qualities of the poet, which are said to consist in "copiousness of diction, readiness to discover knowledge [defined as "perfect erudition and wisdom"], and art [defined as "a judgment reduced to rules for knowing how to invent and imitate well, and at the same time adorn and enrich the matter"]."[36] Since this definition involves a conception of knowledge, Lionardi also refers to Plato when he comes to discuss the kinds of knowledge that the poet must have (p. 82).

---

[34] *Ibid.*, p. 48v: "il Poetare poi piu in una materia, che in un' altra, uiene dall'affettione, che nel discendere per gli altri Cieli, prende piu da questo Pianeta che da quello. Et secondo che è illuminata piu da i raggi di Febo, ò di Venere, che di Marte ò di Mercurio, è piu data à cantare delle cose amorose, & dell'arti liberali, che ò della guerra, ò delle mecanice."

[35] *Ibid.*, p. 50v: "ogni hora uanno piu disgombrando l'anima dall' ombra terrena, et à quel celeste lume la fanno esposta."

[36] *Dialogi* (1554), p. 62: "uena del dire, prontezza del ritrouare dottrina [perfetta eruditione & scienza], arte [un regolato giudicio di saper ben fingere & imitare, & insieme adornare et arricchire la materia]."

Finally, he makes the usual references to Plato when moral questions or questions of the lessons taught by poetry are at issue; Book III of the *Republic* is cited for the opposition to the moving of the passions by poetry (p. 76), and Plato's real meaning is interpreted thus:

> Plato does not condemn those passions from which come honest and virtuous desires and effects, but only those which induce vicious longings and activities. This does not mean that the poet should not narrate that which is harmful and to be avoided, since it is necessary for him to relate as well the causes of wicked deeds and blameworthy as of the good and praiseworthy ones.[37]

It would seem, here, that the Platonic criticism is tempered by a theory of the right—even the moral duty—of the poet to treat the whole gamut of the passions. This is a kind of defence of poetry against Plato.

Platonic elements are again secondary in Giovanni Battista Pigna's *I romanzi* of 1554. The work has as its aim the development of a theory for a new genre, the romanzo, and it founds this theory essentially upon the pattern of the *Poetics*. But when, for example, Pigna speaks of "imitatione" as equivalent to "parlamenti" and of the poet as fulfilling most completely his role of imitator when he presents men conversing (p. 16), he is obviously following the current Platonic tradition. Likewise, when religious preoccupations lead him to condemn the use of classical mythology and recommend instead a moderate application of the Christian marvelous, he is at once reflecting the Platonic concern with "a true and proper presentation of the gods" and the later Christian prejudice (itself an outgrowth of Platonic modes of thought) against representation of the pagan gods (pp. 40–41). At other times, however, Pigna places himself in opposition to Plato. His discussion of the true, the false, and the verisimilar results in the conclusion that the poet may feign untrue things, such as the passions of the gods, that certain genres indeed are based upon untrue materials, and that the use of "lies" may even be recommended because of the truths that they may conceal: "So that a lie told by a good poet carries buried within it every form of truth."[38] Plato's ban on the poets is explained rather as a condemnation of certain audiences than of certain poets: "I believe that the reading of the poets is not forbidden to everybody, but only to people who are not capable of perceiving their meanings or of understanding their secrets, such as is the common and ignorant people. . . . For this reason the poets are sent out of the city . . . , since the greater part of the people are not apt for the understanding of poetry." After explaining the four "lies" contained in poetry, Pigna concludes that "these are held to be completely incredible by the ignorant and the material-minded; and

---

[37] *Ibid.*, p. 80: "Platone non riprende quegli affetti, onde ne uengono desiderij & effetti honesti, & uirtuosi, ma quelli, che à uitiose uoglie, & operationi inducono; non però che quello che è noceuole & da fuggirsi, il poeta narrar non debba, essendoli necessario riferir le cause così de' fatti maluagi, & uitupereuoli, come de' buoni, & laudeuoli."

[38] *I romanzi* (1554), p. 22: "Tal che vna bugia d'un buon poeta ogni verità sepellisce."

among those who are judicious they pass as being beautiful and good."[39]

To his essentially Horatian and rhetorical approach Matteo San Martino adds, in his *Osservationi grammaticali e poetiche della lingua italiana* (1555), two arguments springing from Platonic sources. These concern the defence of poetry and the character of the poet. Aside from the usual praise of poetry, based on its englobing of all other arts and sciences, its civilizing function, its antiquity, and its religious uses, San Martino singles it out as the one art devoted to the worship of God and to the betterment of political life. A part of its praise, to be sure, consists in the fact that—of all sciences—poetry alone is of divine origin since it requires the presence of the divine furor (pp. 124–25). At this point, the defence of poetry and the description of the character of the poet are identical. For the distinguishing feature of the poet is that he depends upon a special kind of divine inspiration, without which he cannot possibly excel in his art (pp. 128–29). Indeed, San Martino himself seems to be moved by a basically Platonic aim, since his purpose in writing is to present to future poets: "a simple intellectual form or Idea of the perfect poet, and a solid norm for arriving, by observing it, at such perfection as perhaps nobody could ever achieve."[40]

GRIFOLI (1557)

As its title indicates, Giacopo Grifoli's *Oratio de laudibus poetarum* (1557) is again a praise and a defence of poetry. But it has a special character insofar as it concludes with the Platonic necessity of imposing philosophical restrictions upon poetry. Grifoli's first premiss is that all arts must provide both utility and pleasure and that any art is judged great according as it satisfies both ends. By this standard, poetry is the greatest, since it excels all others in these respects. The utilities of poetry are to be divided into those which it claimed in the past (this is the commonplace allegation of a civilizing function) and those which it may still serve; the latter would seem to be largely political and ethical:

... since the poets so taught us not only the duties of private citizens and those common to the general condition of all men, but also the functions of magistrates, of military leaders, of kings, that no part of human life seems to have been neglected by them; since moreover they bring profit to the human race in many ways and through a multiplicity of actions, in no way did they ever offer us more ample service than in preventing either the virtues of men, or distinguished exploits, or the deeds of the brave from dying in any way. ... now, in fact, the poets

---

[39] *Ibid.*, p. 31: "mi penso che ad ognuno non sia vietato il leggere i poeti: ma solo alla gente che ne de i sensi loro è capace, ne intendente de i loro secreti; quale è la plebeia, & la ignorante. ... La onde si mandano fuori i poeti della città ...: essendo in esso i piu non atti all' intelligenza della poesia"; and "le quali in tutto per incredibili tenute sono da i rozzi & materiali: & passano per belle & buone tra i giudiciosi."

[40] *Osservationi* (1555), pp. 127–28: "una simplice spirital forma o Idea del sommo Poeta, & una salda norma di peruenir osseruandola a tal perfettione, alla qual forse non fia mai chi arriui."

POETIC THEORY

not only write of the exploits virtuously accomplished by others, but they also teach the offices of virtue and instruct men to do those things which will be the ornaments of the centuries.[41]

This conception of the aim of poetry may also serve as a means of distinguishing among poets; Horace, for example, would be second only to Vergil and would be preferred to Lucretius "because he attends to what is true and proper and is entirely concerned with leading men to a proper life and to true virtue."[42]

If these utilities be present in poetry, why then should Plato have excluded the poets from his perfect state? Grifoli recognizes that for Plato himself there would seem to be contradictions:

> Indeed we must believe that that philosopher condemned the teachings of the poets although he himself had called them the fathers of wisdom, or else that he had excluded them as dangerous although he himself affirms that they are the go-betweens of the gods, and while he holds that their poems are not the inventions of men but the gifts of heaven, he nevertheless legislated that they were to be kept, as wicked men, outside the borders of his State.[43]

Grifoli further maintains that, far from being a source of corruption for youth, poems may be used to advantage as a pedagogical device for the imparting of knowledge that would be otherwise inaccessible. The danger lies in the fact that at an early age, readers may be insufficiently wise to interpret the hidden meanings of poetry and may hence be led into error by the trumperies of the superficial statements. The solution lies in the joining of philosophy, which would provide correct interpretations, to the poetry itself:

> Thus poetry brings us many sweets by means of which our native abilities may be nourished, but no fewer which—if the best training were not ready at hand—would disturb the mind and would lead it away from proper modes of thinking. Therefore poetry united to philosophy gives pleasure and profit like wine diluted with water.... Let this then be the function of the poets, to charm the minds of men with pleasant fables; for it is their business to make known the most famous exploits and to imitate convincingly the characters of all men, so that whoever

---

[41] In *Orationes* (1557), pp. 53, 54–55: "quoniam non modo priuatorum officia, & omnium communis conditionis hominum, sed magistratuum, ducum, regumque munera ita docuerunt, vt nulla pars vitae ab ijs neglecta esse videatur, cum autem multis hi rebus, multiplicique industria iuuent humanum genus, nulla tamen in re commodiores se nobis praebuerunt, quàm quod neque virtutes hominum, neque praeclaros labores, neque fortium gesta vllo pacto mori patiuntur"; and "iam vero poetae non de rebus aliorum modo cum virtute gestis scribunt, sed etiam docent officia virtutum, atque homines instituunt, vt ea faciant, quae sint ornamenta saeculorum."

[42] *Ibid.*, p. 56: "qui verum, & decens curat, & totus in eo est occupatus, vt ad rectam vitam & ad ueram virtutem homines perducat."

[43] *Ibid.*, p. 59: "est vero credendum illum philosophum doctrinam damnasse poetarum, qui eosdem ipse sapientiae patres appellarit, aut tanquam perniciosos exclusisse, quos idem interpretes deorum testetur esse, & quorum poemata non hominum inuenta, sed munera coelestia esse ducat, hos tanquàm impios arcendos à finibus ciuitatis suae statuisse."

reads or hears them will not only know with the greatest clarity what things are to be done and what ones avoided, but will also be filled with a most joyful feeling of pleasure.[44]

All difficulties thus disappear if the teacher or the philosopher be present to extract the lesson from the poet; the poets are readmitted to the state, where they serve a special purpose because of the pleasurable elements which accompany their art.

The problem of truth, sometimes central in Platonic discussions of poetry, is treated in passing by Annibale Caro in his *Apologia degli Academici di Banchi di Roma* (1558)—his famous reply to Castelvetro's famous attack. In both documents the argument is largely linguistic; but at one point in his reply, Caro has Predella speak thus on the subject of poetic license:

> Don't you know, nevertheless, that where opposite opinions exist the poets may attach themselves to one of them, whether it be the better or the worse? and that in different places they may use now the one, now the other? Don't you know, further, that they may follow not only the opinion of the wise but also the errors of the common people, as when they say that the rainbow drinks? ... The license of the poets is such that they may use not only opposite opinions, but those which are clearly false and ridiculous, without being blamed for so doing.[45]

Two things are notable here: first, that the poet is not held to logical consistency or to philosophical soundness; second, that the criterion of truth is not necessarily applied to his works.

AMMIRATO (1560)

A still more complete examination of the same questions—of truth, of knowledge, of the ban—forms the subject of Scipione Ammirato's dialogue, *Il Dedalione overo del poeta dialogo*. The dialogue was written in 1560 and presents two interlocutors, Dedalione (identified in the manuscript as Francesco Maria Giordano) and Tiresia (Marino Cosentino); both were members of the Accademia dei Trasformati, which Ammirato founded at

---

[44] *Ibid.*, pp. 60, 62–63: "ita poesis dulcia quidem multa tradit, quibus vegetentur ingenia, at non pauciora, quae, nisi praesto sit optima institutio, perturbent animum, & à recta ratione deducant. quare vt vinum aqua temperatur, ita poesis cum philosophia prodest, & delectat.... sit igitur poetarum iucundis fabulis mentes hominum delinire, quorum est & res praeclarae gestas illustrare, atque verisimili poemate cuiusvis mores imitari, vt quicunque legit, aut audit eos, non modo quae sequenda, quaeque fugienda sint apertissime cognoscat, sed iucundissima quoque voluptate capiatur."

[45] *Apologia* (1558), p. 83: "Non sapete uoi nondimeno, che doue sono diuerse openioni, i poeti si possono attaccare à una d'esse, ò migliore, ò peggiore ch'ella sia? & seruirsi anco in diuersi lochi hora di questa, & hora di quella? Non sapete ancora, che non solamente possono seguir l'openione de i dotti; ma gli errori ancora del uolgo? come dicendo, che l'Arcobaleno beua. ... la licenza de' poeti, è tale; che si possono ualere, non pur de le diuerse openioni; ma de le espressamente false, & de le ridicole; senza meritarne riprensione."

Lecce in 1558–59.[46] There are several sections in the dialogue, corresponding to the various aspects of the problem of poetry; all of them, it will be noted, concern the generalities about poetry with which Platonic discussion was exclusively occupied. As Grifoli had done, Ammirato starts from the apparent contradiction in Plato between the praise of poetry and the banishment of the poets. He sees the banishment as depending upon two things, the incapacity of listeners rather than the vice of poets, the special conditions of the *Republic*. For in the latter work the aim is to consider poetry not in general but rather in its effects upon the education of the youths who will ultimately become the leaders of the state. Now it is at this early age that men are especially unqualified to "understand and penetrate" the lessons concealed beneath poetic expression. The relative character of Plato's ban is to be appreciated in contrast with the absolute ban on sophists:

> Truly Plato drives out all the sophists and from every place; not all the poets, but only those who feign ugly things about the gods and who go about imitating in an intense way disturbed minds. And not from every place, but from the city, that is from the mass of the ignorant and the young, who easily fall into disturbances and who do not penetrate the allegorical meaning of the poets.[47]

This weakness of the audience should not itself be entirely condemned; for it accounts for the fact that, in the Bible, God and the angels are spoken of in certain ways. This is entirely acceptable because of "our small capacity, which is more readily moved to the knowledge of high things through material and common examples than through abstract and subtle ones."[48] The assumption here, apparently, is that the devices of poetry are necessary for the communication of certain ideas to men, young or old; but some safeguards must be offered so that men, young or old, will put the proper construction upon poems and will not be led astray by false interpretations.

The second problem is that of knowledge. Plato had included among his charges against poetry the fact that poets really did not know the subjects about which they wrote, that their poems were at several removes from the truth. Ammirato answers thus: "... the poets know nothing about the

---

[46] The dialogue exists in manuscript in MS Bibl. Naz. Florence, Magl. VII, 12 and was published in Ammirato's *Opuscoli* (Florence, 1642), III, 353–94. On the Accademia dei Trasformati, see Eustachi d'Afflitto, *Memorie degli Scrittori del Regno di Napoli* (Naples, 1782), p. 308. On Ammirato's later associations with the Accademia degli Alterati in Florence, see my "Argomenti di discussione letteraria nell'Accademia degli Alterati (1570–1600)," *Giornale Storico della Letteratura Italiana*, CXXXI (1954), 177–78.

[47] In *Opuscoli*, III, 359: "Veramente discaccia Platone i sofisti tutti, & da ogni luogo; i poeti non tutti, ma coloro che degli Dij brutte cose fingono, & gli animi perturbati intensamente vanno imitando. Nè da ogni luogo, ma dalla città, cioè dalla turba de giouani e ignoranti, i quali di leggieri nelle perturbazioni discorrano, & l'allegorico sentimento de Poeti non penetrano."

[48] *Ibid.*, p. 361: "la picciola capacità nostra, la quale più ageuolmente si muoue alla cognizione delle cose alte con gli esempi materiali & comuni, che con gli astratti & sottili."

PLATONISM: DEFENCE OF POETRY

things about which they write, and still they [are] full of knowledge and wisdom. ... speaking in terms of the art, he [the poet] really knows nothing as a poet, writing and developing materials under the influence of the divine furor."[49] This divine furor itself, however, constitutes a kind of knowledge, and one which, in the long run, is superior to that obtained through science. That is to say, God and the muses, speaking through the voice of the poet, infuse into his works a kind of superhuman truth which the mind of man alone would be incapable of discovering.

The third problem is that of the ends of poetry. The Horatian assumption of the "utile dulci" is at the basis of the discussion, which revolves about the specific character of the usefulness. Ammirato sees both the body and the soul as suffering ills and as needing remedies. Those of the body are provided by the doctor. Those of the soul are supplied by the legislator, the orator, and the poet. For both body and soul, some device is necessary to make the remedy palatable—the sugar-coating of the doctor's pills, the examples of the orator, the fables and the verse of the poet. It is this that gives the special quality to poetry:

... as it was said above that the philosopher in general is concerned with the health of the soul, let us say that when he condescends to minister to it with sweetness, he becomes a poet as distinguished from the other cures. ... Whence it is necessary to point out that the delight is not to be considered here as a companion to the profit, making two ends for the poet according to which he would truly be held to profit and delight, but it is a consequence of the profit; for the poet wishes first and absolutely to profit, but since he cannot do so without the accompaniment of pleasure, he uses it as a servant of the first.[50]

The poet is thus a philosopher who uses a special instrument to attain the same end: "The philosopher who uses poetry in order to be able to profit does not thereby alter and change his end, even though he takes another means and other ways necessary and appropriate to what he intends to do, but he still follows his principal end, which is to profit."[51]

These various considerations lead Ammirato on the one hand to classify poetry under philosophy and on the other to distinguish the specific uses of the various poetic genres. Philosophy is divided into the contemplative and the active, which subdivide respectively into the natural and the super-

[49] Ibid., p. 364: "i poeti delle cose che scriuono nulla sanno, & pur tuttauia esser pieni dl dottrina & di sapienza. ... secondo l'arte parlando, egli veramente niuna cosa sà inquanto poeta, scriuendo & trattando da diuino furore commosso."

[50] Ibid., p. 377: "come di sopra si disse il filosofo in genere riguarda la sanità dell'anima, diciamo che quando egli discende à curarla con dolcezza diuenta poeta à differenza dell'altre curazioni. ... Oue bisogna auuertire, che il diletto non si hà da porre quì per compagno del giouamento, onde s'habbiano à far due fini del poeta, ch'egli veramente sia tenuto di giouare & dilettare, ma và egli in conseguenza del giouamento; perciòche vuole primieramente e assolutamente il poeta giouare, ma non potendo farlo senza la congiunzione del diletto il prende per ministro del primo." Cf. p. 383 on fable and verse.

[51] Ibid., p. 378: "il filosofo che per poter giouare prende la poesia, non per questo altera & cangia il suo fine, se ben piglia altro mezzo e altre vie necessarie & proporzionate à quel che intende di fare, ma segue il principal suo, ch'è di giouare."

natural sciences and mathematics (for the contemplative) and into ethics, domestic or family economy, and civil philosophy (for the active). Poetry belongs under the last of these: "If civil philosophy concerns the good of our minds and of our bodies, truly it will concern both of these arts, poetry and medicine; but let us take the matter in a broader sense and say that it concerns equivocally the one and the other medicine, that of the soul and that of the body."[52] The poet here stands in the same relationship to the physician as the legislator does to the surgeon, and "the end of poetics is to introduce virtue into the soul by driving vice out of it."[53] This is done separately by the separate genres. Tragedy ministers to the public person of society, comedy to the private person of the individual. For comedy alone teaches ethics, economics, and perhaps even politics. Such final statements as these constitute Ammirato's ultimate defence of poetry against the Platonic ban. In so doing, it is significant that they remain within the essential presuppositions of Plato's approach, although they find a contrasting answer.

Bernardino Parthenio's *Della imitatione poetica* of 1560 was, as we have seen (Chapter IV, p. 145, a document belonging primarily to the Horatian tradition, since it took "imitation" in the specific sense of imitation of models and developed the techniques for the approximation of another poet's style. It contains, incidentally, two passages related to Platonic modes of thought about poetry. The first is a sequel to the extravagant praise of Homer and the other poets and constitutes a formal defence of the art. Parthenio speaks of the antiquity of poetry, of how it preceded prose, of its invention by the gods; the poets, moreover, are beloved of the gods and inspired by them. If we wish an additional proof, we need only look at the heavens:

... if we wish to know that God, wise above all others and prudent above all others, loves poetry, we may understand it either from the harmony of those most holy celestial choirs, which with that ineffable sweetness make sweet the heavens and the divine mind, or from the harmony which we know arises from the most orderly movement of the spheres of heaven, which the divine wisdom wished to be tempered with numbers and with poetic arrangement, joining together to form among themselves such harmony as might calm within us the power of hearing.[54]

[52] *Ibid.*, p. 386: "Se la ciuile riguarda il bene degli animi nostri & de corpi, veramente ella riguarderà amendue questi, cioè la poetica & la medicina; ma prendiamo la cosa più larga & diciamo ch'ella riguarda equiuocamente l'vna & l'altra medicina dell'anima & del corpo."
[53] *Ibid.*: "il fine della poetica è indur nell'anima la virtù discacciandone il vizio."
[54] *Della imitatione poetica* (1560), p. 5: "se uogliamo conoscere, che Dio solo sapientissimo, & solo prudentissimo ama la poesia, comprendiamolo dalla harmonia ouero di quelli beatissimi chori celesti, i quali con quella ineffabile dolcezza addolciscono il cielo, & la mente diuina; ouero dal concento, che sappiamo nascer dal ordinatissimo mouimento delle sfere del cielo, le quali la sapienza diuina uolle, che con numeri, & con ragione poetica temperate fossero tra loro accordandosi in creare tal harmonia che in noi la uirtù del sentire addormenta."

Such a passage as this is doubly significant; it shows the persistence of a habit of regarding poetry in the vaguest analogical terms, as a kind of superior harmony, and at the same time it limits the essence of poetry to rhythm and to musical qualities. In a second passage, Parthenio distinguishes the imitation of which he is speaking from that considered by Plato, so that he may exempt his own from Plato's ban. Plato's imitation, he says, was that of the passions and, hence, involved all kinds of perils as far as truth, religion, and moral education were concerned. His own is merely that of other poets, and far from being blameworthy it satisfies in us our natural instinct to imitate and the delight we take in the process (pp. 15–16).

Two years after the writing of his *Dedalione*, Scipione Ammirato returned, in 1562, to the subject of poetry in *Il Rota, overo delle imprese dialogo*. The particular circumstances of the dialogue explain in part the orientation toward poetry. For poetry enters into the discussion because of a basic similarity with "imprese" (heraldic devices containing a hidden meaning); this is explained by the Bishop of Potenza, one of the interlocutors:

It was an ancient usage among all the wise men to keep, with every care and device, from revealing to all persons the most important doctrines and sciences, so that they would not come to be profaned by the vulgar crowd. And this was the reason why the imaginary fables were invented, under whose outer surface were hidden, by those ancient wise men, all the secrets of the speculative sciences and of the things of nature and all the useful and necessary forms of knowledge which pertain to man. In this way, the ignorant man had the pleasure of the fable and the wise man, penetrating farther within, gathered the fruit contained within it. And since poetry and painting are sisters both born at one delivery, just as poetry began to explain these fictions with words, so also afterwards painting began to depict many things which seemed monstrous but which under these fictions contained many fine secrets.[55]

In the development of these ideas, however, Ammirato passes on to other sources. He finds that both arts need to seek the marvelous—"what rarely happens and is outside the nature of other, ordinary things" (p. 30)—in order to make the proper appeal to their audience. In poetry, the marvelous of subject matter has its justification in Aristotle ("for it presents men as good or bad with greater virtue or vice than ordinary men have"), while that of form is justified by the rhetoricians ("for it uses the figurative, the new, the old, the foreign, the improper, the abbreviated, the extended, and

---

[55] *Il Rota* (1562 ed.), pp. 14–15: "Fu antica osseruanza di tutti i saui guardarsi con ogni studio & ingegno di non palesar le belle dottrine & scienze à tutte le persone in guisa, ch'elle si venissero à profanare dal volgo. Et questa fù la cagione, che si ritrouassero i fingimenti delle fauole: sotto le cui scorze si ricopriuano da quelli antichi saui tutti i segreti delle scienze speculatiue, & delle cose della natura, & tutte le vtili & necessarie cognitioni, che appartengono all'huomo. Di modo che all'ignorante restaua la piaceuolezza della fauola, & il sauio ne raccoglieua, penetrando più à dentro, il frutto di essa. Et perche la poesia & la pittura sono sorelle tutte nate in vn parto; si come la poesia con le parole cominciò à spiegare queste fintioni; così cominciò susseguentemente la pittura à pigner di molte cose, che pareuano mostruose: le quali però sotto esse rinchiudeuano molti belli segreti."

other figures in greater number than does ordinary speech").[56] Horace supplies the basis for the warning against excess in any particular style (p. 31). A final comparison between the "impresa" and poetry concerns their audiences; both must be accessible to the ignorant and pleasurable to the wise, and they must thus be based on common materials which will be readily intelligible. In this sense, comedy is of all poetic genres the one closest to the "impresa" (p. 33).

I have already mentioned, in connection with the *Tractatus de tragoedia* (MS 985 [M.8], Biblioteca Comunale, Perugia, about 1562) how the author's convictions with respect to the utility present in poetry led him to reject the condemnations of such philosophers as Plato. He insists upon the impropriety of regarding either pleasure or utility as the sole end of poetry and considers that both Plato and Aristotle saw the pleasure as serving the utility: "From which it follows that poetry, since it is a diversion, as both Aristotle and Plato hold, is agreeable to those for whom it is employed, and that the technique of the poets has been brought into use as a pleasure, to delight the mind, either to contemplate it as perfect, or at least as next to perfect and as it were mingled with the perfect."[57] It is this function of pleasure as intermediary to utility that constitutes the main defence of poetry, and even Plato himself admits it in Book II of the *Laws*. In essence, poets are educators, and that is their main justification.

One of the interlocutors in the preceding dialogue, Bernardo Tasso, is the author of a *Ragionamento della poesia* delivered before the Accademia Veneziana in 1560 and published in 1562. The *Ragionamento* is a fairly complete Platonic document, touching upon all the main points of current interest. It does not fail to answer those Platonists who interpret the master as having banished the poets; this is sheer ignorance:

He does not exclude poetry in general, but in particular those poets who, by means of the harmony and sweetness of their verses, aroused and inflamed the tender souls of young people to lascivious and voluptuous actions, and by means of the example and of imitation rendered them soft, effeminate, and entirely useless for the good and the improvement of the republic. Nor is this a fault of poetry but of the poet, who like a wicked doctor gives poison instead of medicine.[58]

[56] *Ibid.*, p. 30: "percioche fa gli huomini o buoni, o cattiui in maggior uirtù, o vitio, che non son gli ordinarij; e nelle parole; percioche vsa il traslato, il nuouo, il vecchio, lo straniero, l'improprio, l'accorciato, l'allungato, & l'altre figure in maggior numero, che non fa l'oratione pedestre."

[57] Perugia, Bibl. Com., MS 985 (M.8), fol. 103v: "Ex quo consequitur, poesim siquidem ludus est, ut Aristoteli placet et Platoni, iucundam esse quibus adhibeatur, et oblectandis animis artificium poetarum accersitum uoluptatem, uel intueri semper ut ultimum, uel certe tamquam ultimo proximum, quasique cum ultimo temperatum."

[58] *Ragionamento* (1562), p. 10: "non la Poesia in uniuersale, ma in particolare que Poeti esclude, i quali con l'armonia, e dolcezza de loro uersi commoueuano, et infiammauano i teneri animi de giouenetti a cose lasciue, e uoluttuose: e con l'essempio, e con l'imitatione gli rendeuano molli, effeminati, e del tutto inutili al benifitio, et a la essaltatione de la republica. Ne questo è difetto de la Poesia, ma del poeta: ilquale a guisa di maluagio medico da il ueleno in uece de la medicina."

PLATONISM : DEFENCE OF POETRY

The proper function of the poet is indeed the opposite: "by imitating human actions through the delightfulness of plots, through the sweetness of the words arranged in a most beautiful order, through the harmony of the verse, to adorn human souls with good and gentle characters, and with various virtues."[59] This moral and social usefulness is the main element in the defence of poetry, and Tasso finds it both in times past and in times present. He makes the usual statements about the contributions of the poets to the advance of civilization and their present favors. In summary, he asks: "Oh venerable science, which brings pleasure and profit to every kind of person, to every age, to every sex, to every nation, and in every season and in every time, who could ever praise you properly and to the extent to which you merit praise?"[60]

According to Tasso, the poet excels all other men through two qualities, the divine furor and the universality of his knowledge. The first is indispensable and is the sign of the poet's dependence upon God:

... without this extraordinary gift of nature, even though a man may have knowledge of all doctrines; even though through long study he may have learned the law and the art of perfect writing; even though he may have long experience of the things of the world; still it will be impossible that he should turn out to be a good poet. There is no doubt whatsoever but that the perfection of this science has something divine about it, and that for this same reason it should be placed before all others.[61]

Both Plato and Cicero are cited on the necessity of divine inspiration. This does not mean, however, that the poet may rely upon his natural gifts. Tasso develops at length the kinds of knowledge which the poet must possess—all arts and sciences are his prerogative—and cites the cases of Homer and Vergil as the most extraordinary in this respect. This erudition may also be found in the Italian poets (example, Petrarch) and is especially to be appreciated when it is hidden under an allegorical exterior (example, Dante). Probably because a part of this wisdom consists in an understanding of the passions, the poets are able to produce a great emotional effect in their readers, and this is the source of their power both as entertainers and as teachers (pp. 7–8).

It is perhaps interesting that the separate elements of Tasso's theory,

---

[59] *Ibid.*, p. 12: "imitando l'humane attioni con la piaceuolezza de le fauole, con la soauità de le parole in bellissimo ordine congiunte, con l'armonia del uerso gli humani animi di buoni, e gentili costumi, e di uarie uirtù adornare."

[60] *Ibid.*, pp. 15–15v: "O uenerabile scienza: che ad ogni qualità di persone, ad ogni età, ad ogni sesso, ad ogni natione, et in ogni stagione, in ogni tempo porti piacere e benefitio; chi fie giamai che degnamente, e quanto tu ben meriti lodar ti possa?"

[61] *Ibid.*, p. 12v: "senza questo singolar dono di natura, ancor che altri di tutte le dottrine habbia cognitione; ancor che con lungo studio habbia imparata la legge, e l'arte del perfettamente scriuere; ancor che lunga esperienza habbia de le cose del mondo; impossibil tuttauia sarà, che riesca buon poeta. non è dubbio alcuno, che la perfettione di questa scienza non partecipi di diuinità: e che per questo anco non sia da essere antiposta a tutte l'altre."

taken one by one, are almost identical with the essential doctrines of the Horatian-rhetorical creed: the ends of poetry as pleasure and utility; the complicity of art and nature; the importance of erudition; the moving of the passions. This does not mean eclecticism, but merely current modes of thinking about poetry that are so deeply imbedded that they tend to determine the interpretation put upon any doctrinal source. There is, to be sure, some eclecticism in Tasso: his definitions of the various genres, derived from all the classical and medieval sources, may serve as a case in point. When, however, he wishes to argue the superiority of the epic to tragedy, he returns to Plato, declaring that tragedy appeals only to the people and merely gives delight, whereas the epic gives both pleasure and virtuous instruction to men of mature judgment and dignity (p. 5). Aristotle's arguments for the superiority of tragedy are cited to complete the presentation.

Around 1564, Sperone Speroni, a frequent participator in the literary quarrels of the century, wrote a short fragment on imitation; its editor called it *Dialogo sopra Virgilio: Fragmento*. Two things are noteworthy about this fragment, first its special use of the word "imitation," second its attack upon Aristotle and the intention of the *Poetics*. After reviewing the various meanings assigned to the word, Speroni indicates that it may be applied in an extraordinary way to such a work as the *Poetics*. Nature, let us say, is the first object of imitation, and such poems as the *Iliad* and the *Odyssey* are imitations of it. These poems themselves become objects of imitation, but in two ways: for one, a philosopher may imitate them in an "art," and this is what Aristotle has done in the *Poetics*; for the other, another poet may imitate them, and this is what Vergil has done in the *Aeneid*. The first process, says Speroni, is much less to be praised than the second, which produces "true poetic effects," whereas Aristotle is incapable of practising what he teaches (p. 358). As a practical matter, then, the poet should devote himself to the study of other poets—his models—and should not concern himself with the "rules." Speroni also furnishes a criterion for imitation: that imitation is best which is most like Nature. Thus, if he is to choose between two depictions of a voyage to the Underworld, he will say: "This is now and always has been my judgment, that of these two the better poet ... was the one who made his inferno worse; for evil must be made evil, just as it is, and must not be made good, which it is not."[62] On the whole—and he comes close to a Platonic position here—Speroni disdains imitation and ranks it as inferior to art: "It is a clear fact that imitation is not proper to man, as art is. Therefore art is always conjoined with reason, and imitation is not always so; it is a thing not proper to us, but to rooks and monkeys. ... One can see with a single eye how much

---

[62] In *Opere* (1740), II, 360: "Questo è ora e sempre fu il mio giudicio, quello esser stato miglior poeta di questi due ... che fe piggiore il suo inferno: perciocchè 'l male si dee far male come è, e non far bene come non è."

more worthy art is than either usage or imitation."[63] This last passage indicates that the Platonic opposition to imitation is accompanied by a specific attack on Aristotle's notion that imitation is proper to man.

Lionardo Salviati, who in his abundant critical activity included a translation and commentary of the *Poetics*, shows a strong anti-Platonic bias in his *Trattato della poetica, Lezzion Prima* (1564). Plato's whole philosophy is attacked by Salviati, since his doctrine "does not have as its end, in his works, to teach about Nature . . . , but referring to God the major part of our important actions and the most noble, it tries to fill our minds with pure religion."[64] In the specific realm of poetry, this tendency leads Plato to propose the doctrine of the divine furor and to deny that the poetic faculty is a habit of the mind. It is this denial which Salviati wishes to refute in his lecture before the Florentine Academy. He discusses one by one the arguments offered by the Platonists. First, they claim that the poets write about things which they do not really understand; but all men do this, and it is particularly excusable for the poets because of the brevity of their expression and because of the licenses accorded them. Second, they argue that occasionally a bad poet or a bad painter may produce a single good work, thus demonstrating the power of inspiration; but this may merely show the operation of chance or accident. Third, they contend that the best-trained minds are frequently incapable of writing verse; but just as frequently they are, and in any case all kinds of other influences—the humors, the planets, weather, food and drink—affect the individual's capacities as a poet, in general or at any given time. In conclusion to these rebuttals Salviati says: "I think that I have sufficiently shown so far that poetry is a habit, having demonstrated that from it derive certain operations which usually are regulated and ordered, and which could not in this way, being what they are, derive from anything but a habit."[65]

The affirmative aspect of Salviati's argument is developed further by a classification of the habits. Of the two general kinds, moral and intellectual, the latter subdivides into active and productive, according as it operates within the person acting or within some external matter. This series of distinctions leads to a definition of poetry as "a habit of operating in an external subject, through the reason";[66] no other definition than this is

---

[63] *Ibid.*, II, 365–66: "chiara cosa è, la imitazione non esser propria dell' uomo, siccome è l'arte, però l'arte è sempremai con la ragione congiunta, non già sempre la imitazione: la quale è cosa non pur da noi, ma da cornacchie e da scimie. . . . si può discernere da ciascuno occhio, tanto esser l'arte più gentil cosa, che non è l'uso o l'imitazione."

[64] *Trattato*, MS BNF Magl. VII, 307, fol. 23: "non ha per fine nelle sue opere lo insegnare la Natura . . .; ma riducendo a Dio la maggior parte, e le piu nobili delle azzioni principali, studia di riempiere gli animi di pura relligione."

[65] *Ibid.*, fol. 28: "Assai mi credo io infino a hora hauer mostro la Poesia essere habito, hauendo dimostrato, che da essa deriuano alcune operazioni, che le piu uolte sono regolate, e con ordine, e che da altro, che da habito in cotal guisa, e cosi fatte deriuare non potrebbono."

[66] *Ibid.*, fol. 29: "habito d'operare in subietto esteriore con ragione. . . ."

needed to classify poetry as an art. If further proof be required, Salviati finds it in the exhaustive enumeration of all human actions as resulting from nature, art, violence, intellect, fortune, or chance (the source of the enumeration is said to be Aristotle's *Metaphysics*, Book VIII). He eliminates all of these sources except art, which must thus be the origin of poetry. The anti-Platonic position thus leads him, as he pursues his argument, to adopt what he considers to be an essentially Aristotelian point of view toward poetry and the poet (see below, Chapter XI, pp. 494–97).

An amusing attitude toward the whole idea of the poetic furor is expressed by Lodovico Castelvetro in his *Parere sopra l'ajuto che domandano i poeti alle Muse*; the fragment is undated, but I presume it to be from around 1565. Castelvetro states frankly that the philosophers have never believed in the fiction of the Muses and of the divine furor and that the poets themselves have merely used it as a fraud to impose themselves upon the public: "In truth, Poetry never had its beginning, or its middle, or its end in a divine furor infused by the Muses or by Apollo in the poets, except in the opinion of the vulgar crowd . . .; but the poets,to render themselves marvelous and worthy of attention in the eyes of men, helped and augmented this opinion, calling upon that divine aid and pretending to have obtained it."[67] Given this basic fact about the divine furor (so contrary in its assumptions to Plato's central theory), Castelvetro adopts a realistic attitude toward the conditions and circumstances in which the Muses may properly be invoked by the poet. This leads him to several interesting distinctions with respect to the poetic art. He first divides written works into three pairs: verse and prose, long and short, narrative and dramatic. The Muses will be called upon only in long narrative poems in verse: ". . . the miraculous favor of the Muses, as far as the form is concerned, consists only in helping the writer to make such verses as would be thought impossible, by the masses, as productions simply of human effort, either because of the power of their meaning or because of their beauty."[68] A similar three-way division of subject matters provides these couples: historical and argumentative, invented and observed, difficult and easy. The poet will invoke the Muses only for historical, invented and difficult materials. By "historical" Castelvetro means "that material which we believe to have occurred, or which we give the appearance of believing that it occurred, merely on the basis of the words presented to us by the author, without any other proof." "Invented" materials are those which come "from the mind of the writer," and "difficult" materials,

[67] In *Opere varie critiche* (1727), p. 90: "veramente la Poesia non ebbe mai principio, o mezo, o fine da Furore divino infuso dalle Muse, o da Apollo ne' Poeti, se non secondo l'opinione del Volgo . . .; la quale i Poeti per rendersi maravigliosi, e riguardevoli nel cospetto degli uomini, ajutavano, & accrescevano, domandando quel divino soccorso, e facendo sembiante d'averlo impetrato."

[68] *Ibid.*, p. 88: "il miracoloso favore delle Muse, quanto alla forma, consiste solamente in ajutare lo Scrittore a far versi tali, che l'umana industria non sia creduta dal Volgo atta per se a farli, o per efficacia della significazione, o per riguardo della vaghezza."

those which "contain things which, either because of their past time or for some other reason, it is not verisimilar that the writer could know or understand."[69] In summary, then, the poet may be expected to use the device of the Muses whenever either his form or his subject matter is so extraordinary as to tax the credulity of his audience; invocation of divine assistance will then presumably create a kind of verisimilitude. Such invocation must be used only in a limited way, by poets and for poems that merit it.

GRASSO AND GIRALDI (1566)

As in the case of so many other theorists of this period, it is difficult to distinguish in Benedetto Grasso between the Horatian and the Platonic strains. I have already spoken at some length of his *Oratione contra gli Terentiani* (1566) in connection with the Horatian tradition (Chapter V, p. 177). Perhaps in the present case the distinction could be properly made in this way: as far as the ends of poetry are concerned, the simple assigning of the dual function of pleasing and instructing is essentially Horatian, whereas the condemnation of the art or of specific poets for unsatisfactory serving of the utilitarian end is specifically Platonic. This means, really, that the objection to poetry on moral grounds is taken to have Platonic origins, and Grasso's objections are exclusively moral. He declares that Terence "is not worthy to be read publicly in the schools, since he carries with him ... a poisonous plague, by which the minds of tender youths, bewitched, become infected and poisoned in the sewer of the vices."[70] Such results are not necessary concomitants of poetry. Grasso sees two factors as producing them, first, the inherent capacity of poetry to dominate the souls of men (something of the Platonic chain of inspiration and the communication of madness is present here), and second, the wilful appeal of poets to the vulgar crowd. In an earlier, more noble age the poets used their art for its highest purposes, addressing themselves as priests and philosophers to the wise men of the community. But later, reflecting a decadence in the art, they tried only "to give amusement to the crowd and to licentious ears."[71] This tendency accounts for Plato's ban, which Grasso endorses wholeheartedly. For the effects produced by Terence's poetry, which should certainly fall under the ban, are like those accompanying a lewd picture:

... just as painting, the more close to nature it is, the more it delights the spectators and holds them bound with marvel, so each time it represents for them lasci-

[69] *Ibid.*, p. 89: "quella Materia, la quale noi crediamo essere avvenuta, o facciamo vista di credere, che sia avvenuta per le parole sole rappresentateci dallo Scrittore senz'altra prova"; and "dall'ingegno dello Scrittore"; and "che contiene cose, le quali o per tempo passato, o per altro rispetto non è verisimile, che lo Scrittore possa sapere, o comprendere."

[70] *Oratione* (1566), p. 5: "non essere degno publicamente nelle Scuole si legge, portante seco ... vnà venenosa peste, dalla quale l'animi de teneri fanciulli affascinati nella sentina de vitij s'infettano ed auelleneno."

[71] *Ibid.*, p. 33: "per dar' spasso al volgo, & alle licentiose orecchie."

vious acts, obscene objects, dirty and ugly actions, it moves in us an honest blushing and arouses an unwillingness to look at them. And even if we do look at them, it is rather because we are moved by the artifice of the painter than by the beauty or the novelty of the painting.[72]

Poets and painters, then, will fall into two categories: those who use their art for the proper ends of honest instruction and those who corrupt it to the improper ends of dishonest pleasure. The former are to be accepted and praised, the latter are to be rejected and banished.

Grasso's attack was answered immediately by Lucio Olimpio Giraldi in a *Ragionamento in difesa di Terentio* (1566). I shall not here go into the whole of Grasso's argument, already treated in Chapter V, but shall discuss only the materials pertinent to the present discussion. Giraldi regards Terence as the greatest of comic poets, especially because he is "so excellent a demonstrator of customs and of daily life that nowhere else may one have a more useful and a clearer image of the ordinary way of life, both civil and popular."[73] This general statement provides Giraldi, later, with the basis for his refutation of Grasso's moral strictures. He admits that a poet offering obscene and lewd images would be a dangerous influence upon the young; but he denies that Terence ever does so:

> I deny that Terence should be excluded from the schools for having proposed anything less than what was useful for private life; for he was never anything but the most modest writer and representative of every kind of person, and he was so careful that no clever sailor ever avoided the rocks as carefully, while sailing, as he fled from lascivious and obscene words—even though he had before him Plautus, who was very licentious.[74]

Giraldi cites the authority of Sadoleto, who also praised Terence for his avoidance of improper language. Apparently, the critic here is considering only the dangers of language. As for the actions themselves, he believes that even when they seem to be vicious, they contain hidden lessons and precepts and are hence acceptable: "in the comedies of Terence we find examples of honest behavior and of honorable citizens, which teach the reader what is proper to the praiseworthy life and through whose example may be known how much blame is deserved by those who have given them-

---

[72] *Ibid.*, p. 31: "si come la pittura quanto piu s'acosta al naturale, tanto piu gli diletta, e tiene legati, con marauiglia gli riguardanti: Cosi ogni volta gli r'apresenta atti lasciui, figure inhoneste, sporche, & laide attioni, muoue in noi un' honesta erubescentia, & genera un' sdegno di mirarle: Et se pur le mirano, piu presto mossi dal' artificio del pittore, che dalla vaghezza ò nouità della pittura."

[73] *Ragionamento* (1566), pp. 2–3: "così vago dimostratore de costumi, et della vita ciuile, che altronde non si puo hauere di lei piu vtile, ne piu espressa imagine del viuere commune, ciuile & popolaresco."

[74] *Ibid.*, p. 55: "niego, che Terentio sia, da scacciar delle schuole, perche egli proponga cosa meno, che utile alla uita ciuile, perche non fù mai il più modesto scrittore, & rappresentatore di ogni qualita di gente, & fù cosi schifo, che non schiuò mai tanto accorto nocchiero, lo scoglio, nel nauicare, quanto questi ha fuggito (quantunque hauesse hauuto Plauto inanzi molto licentioso) le parole lasciue, & dishoneste."

PLATONISM: DEFENCE OF POETRY

selves over to a vicious way of life."[75] Indeed, it is of the essence of comedy to provide lessons of this kind; and, rather than being dangerous to youth, it is an indispensable part of early education. Plato's ban on the poets is thus to be considered only as applying to those who displayed wicked acts and words and who created an improper image of the gods; other poets were exempted from it.

Examining Terence's plays, Giraldi finds in them numerous examples of both kinds of actions, wicked ones to be avoided, good ones to be imitated:

> Terence's intention was to show the ugliness of foul things so that men would abstain from them, not so that they would follow them; and to propose to them the praiseworthy and virtuous and honest ones so that they might embrace them and adorn themselves with them. Just as tragedy purges men's minds, through terror and pity, and induces men to abstain from acting wickedly, so comedy, by means of laughter and jokes, calls men to an honest private life.[76]

In sum, then, Terence may serve as a teacher of the very essence of good living. It should be pointed out that, for Giraldi, the position remains definitely Platonic, insofar as the same moral criteria continue to be applied to comedy. He differs from his opponent only in the conclusions which he derives from application of these criteria to Terence. But the difference itself is significant; it shows a much broader moral outlook and an initial tendency to justify rather than to condemn poetic works.

The *Osservazioni sopra Virgilio* of Orazio Toscanella (1566) has little to offer except a conventional defence of poetry in the usual terms; such defences continued to be produced throughout the century and were especially frequent in the works of vulgarizers and popularizers such as Toscanella. The present little treatise is nothing more than a list of the subject matters treated by Vergil, in alphabetical order, with examples of each subject and appropriate citations. In the dedication, he proposes first to indicate why poetry "surpasses all other disciplines in goodness and in dignity" and offers two reasons: "one of which is that from her, as from a mother, all the other sciences issued forth . . .; and the other, that she alone of all the rest of the arts is learned through the divine furor."[77]

---

[75] *Ibid.*, p. 58: "nelle Comedie di Terentio, si hanno essempi, di honesti costumi, & di honorate persone, ciuili, lequali dittano à lettori, quello, che conuiene alla lodeuole vita, coll' essempio delle quali si conoscano di quanto biasimo, siano degni quelle, che à vitioso modo di vita, si son date."

[76] *Ibid.*, p. 65: "intentione di Terentio è stata, il far uedere la brutezza delle cose sozze, perche gli huomini se ne astengano, non perche le seguitino: & . . . hà proposto loro, le lodeuoli, & virtuose, & honeste, perche le abbraccino, & di esse si adornino, & . . . come la Tragedia purga gli animi col terrore, & colla commiseratione, & induce gli huomini, ad astenersi dal mal operare, cosi il riso, & le beffe nelle Comedie . . . chiama gli huomini alla honesta vita ciuile."

[77] *Osservazioni* (1566), pp. *ij–*ijv: "l'una delle quali è, che da lei, come da madre quasi tutte l'altre scienze uscirono . . .; l'altra, che essa sola fra tutto il rimanente dell' arti, per diuin furore s'apprende."

Follow the well-known arguments: all knowledge is to be found in Homer and Vergil—not only fine doctrines, but the most practical suggestions for the conduct of life and for mechanical operations; poetry had early religious uses and was highly honored in antiquity. Consequently, "it is a very fine thing that every elevated mind should devote itself to poetry, in order to acquire the most noble and precious doctrine that may be obtained among mortals, and to ascend to the level of everlasting fame."[78]

In the following year, the same Toscanella published a treatise on the *Arte metrica*, concerned with problems of metrics and extolling the art of writing in verse. Verse is considered to be a necessary part of all poetry, because of the "incredible pleasure" which it affords and because of its power of moving the human passions. As for poetics itself, "it is that art which teaches the decorum, the characters, the style, the way, the passions, and the order which the poet must observe, and in sum, all the artifice that belongs to the best poet."[79] It is hard to see in this anything but the traditional definition of the poetic art, and the emphasis upon decorum and the passions is technical rather than moralistic.

With Frosino Lapini's *Letione nella quale si ragiona in universale del fine della poetica*, we encounter a type of text which will become increasingly prominent during the last third of the sixteenth century, a text combining traditional Platonism with official Christian ethics. The *Letione*, a commentary on Petrarch's sonnet "Lasciato hai, morte, senza sole il mondo," was delivered before the Accademia Fiorentina on May 1, 1567, and the theoretical considerations precede the commentary proper. Lapini starts from the principle that all the arts and faculties have as their end the perfection of man. But since they depend from man's free will, they may be used either to achieve this end or to achieve its contrary, the destruction of man. So with poetry the proper end is "with its delightful and verisimilar fictions presented to us, to profit us much more than would be done if it narrated as does the historian or if it warned and advised us as the moral philosopher does."[80] Tragedy, for example, benefits us by purging our souls of all passions. Thus Sophocles and Euripides always ended their tragedies with useful warnings about human life; thus Aristotle insisted that—among its other requisites—character must be "good." And Vergil intimated, in Book VI, that the divine furor was given the poets so that they might bring to the attention of men many things useful for their lives.

[78] *Ibid.*, p. *iiijv: "ottimamente stà, che ciascuno ingegno eleuato, in essa studio ponga, per fare acquisto della più nobile, & pregiata dottrina, che s'acquisti fra i mortali; & per poggiare à grado di nome sempiterno."

[79] *Arte metrica* (1567), p. 1v: "Poetica è quella, che insegna il decoro, i costumi, lo stile, la strada, gli affetti, & l'ordine, che deue osseruare il poeta; & in somma, tutto quello, che d'artificioso pertiene all'ottimo poeta."

[80] *Letione* (1567), p. Bivv: "con le sue diletteuoli e uerisimili fintioni à noi rappresentate molto meglio giouare, che in raccontando come Historico, o amonendo come moral Filosofo non si farebbe."

PLATONISM: DEFENCE OF POETRY

Such artists and philosophers as these shared a proper conception of the poetic art.

On the other hand, there have always been those artists whose only aim has been "to give pleasure to people, not without damage and harm not only for public and private life, but also for the reverence that is due religion, since they frequently make fun of the things they should revere and exalt."[81] These artists are sometimes read for the elegance of the treatment and the pleasure which men take in imitation (Aristotle is cited as authority here), sometimes for their sensuous appeal. A work of the latter kind

... will please and delight, indeed, not because of the power or the art of the poetry, but because of the delight it gives to the appetite eager for such sensuality; by which such appetite is not only not removed and regulated and dominated, as would be done by the good poet who writes to benefit men, but by means of such examples it is called to life and inflamed and invited to do evil and to plunge into vice through imitation and through the evil example observed in others.[82]

Nor is the private life of the poet, which presumably may be purer than his works, any justification; his words, written or spoken, have a power of influence and expansion that renders them dangerous. It is such poets as these whom Plato wished to banish, and justifiably. It is such poetry as this, also, that notable Christian writers have condemned, Saint Paul and Saint Augustine and Savonarola among others. The last of these, for example, distinguishes between the poetry to be prohibited and that to be permitted, and establishes the conditions for the latter:

... having damned and driven out of the Christian republic such ruin and pestilential vanity [i.e., poetry intended for pleasure alone], he nevertheless leaves its place, nor does he take away from it its due praises, to that poetry which, following its true end, attends only to the profit of its readers. If this profit is concerned with human and moral matters, he shows that the poetry cannot properly use ornament and other poetic colors which would render it graceful and pleasing. But if it treats high and sublime and divine matters, such as the Christian religion and its mysteries, he affirms that such ornaments (as in truth we see) appear puerile and ridiculous, since high subjects of this kind cannot stand such ornamentation, in itself a weak and vain thing.[83]

---

[81] *Ibid.*, p. D*v*: "altro fine non è che dar' piacere alla gente, non senza nocumento, e danno, non solo del uiuer politico e ciuile, ma della reuerentia che alla Religione si debbe, pigliandosi eglino bene spesso in scherzo e in gioco le cose, che reuerire et esaltar douerebbero."

[82] *Ibid.*, p. Dij*v*: "piacerà pure, e diletterà non per la virtù, et per l'arte della Poesia, ma per la delettatione dell' appetito vago di tali sensualità, dalle quali non solo non è rimosso, e regolato, e ribattuto, come il uero Poeta farebbe che per giouare ha scritto . . ., ma con tali esempli ne inanimisce & ne infiamma, & ne inuita à comettere il male, & attuffarsi nel vitio per la imitatione e per il malo esempio scorto in altrui."

[83] *Ibid.*, pp. Div–Div*v*: "dannata e scacciata dalla Christiana rep. tale rouina, e pestilentiale uanità, lascia pur il suo luogo, ne toglie à quella Poesia le sue douute lodi, la quale seguendo il suo uero fine, all' utile solo attende de suoi lettori; il qual utile se è intorno a cose morali et humane, mostra egli non disconucnirglisi l'ornato, et altri colori Poetici, che gratiato e piaceuole lo rendino; ma se si tratta di cose alte, e sublimi, e diuine, come della Christiana legge, e de' suoi misterij, afferma tali ornamenti apparire (come in verità si vede) cose puerili e ridicole, non patendo tali soggetti alti si fatt'ornamento, per se cosa debile, e uana. . . ."

Lapini recognizes the fact that part, at least, of the blame for the success of "pleasurable" poetry lies with the audience, which is more prone to follow the easy way of its pleasure than the hard way of the utility that it might possibly derive. The end thus comes to lie outside the poet himself and to depend upon those to whom his poem is addressed: "... all the blame must be assigned to those who do not allow themselves to be persuaded, because of their wicked disposition in which all good teaching is completely lost."[84]

Lapini's position is thus a curious and a mixed one. Platonic insofar as it starts with a subordination of the art of poetry to moral principles, it becomes strangely rhetorical when it places the effectiveness of poetry in the natural dispositions of the audience and when it undertakes consideration of the poet's life and character. Moreover, these elements are complicated by an essentially Christian severity towards poetic ornament and all artistic elements which might be pleasurable, and by a preference for a kind of poetry whose subject matter might be divine and whose uses would be essentially religious.

The miscellaneous short treatises on critical matters of Lodovico Castelvetro, left in manuscript at his death and published in the *Opere varie critiche* of 1727, contain certain materials of a Platonic character. These treatises were probably written between 1565 and 1571. One of them, entitled *Che cosa abbia la scienza comune, o differente con l'arte*, is generally interesting for its distinction between the sciences and the arts and incidentally displays a tendency (which might also be Horatian) to ascribe moral values and social usefulness to the arts:

Science has two things in common with art and two which are different. It has in common first the solidity of the proofs, because the one and the other proceed by means of demonstrative proofs. Next it has in common the order of the teachings, which in the one and in the other must be complete and perfect. On the other hand, science has this which is different from art, first, that science takes as its subject things which although they may be known do not necessarily lead to action; but Art does not take for its subject things which, when they are known, cannot much more easily lead to action. It has also this that is different, that science tolerates every material, whether it be decent, or useful, or dishonest, or harmful to the world; but art does not tolerate any subject which is not decent and useful to the world.[85]

---

[84] *Ibid.*, p. E: "tutta la colpa è di quelli, che persuader non si lasciano per la mala dispositione loro, nella quale si perde ogni buono ammaestramento."

[85] In *Opere varie critiche* (1727), p. 124: "la Scienza ha due cose comuni con l'Arte, e due differenti. Ha comune premieramente la fermezza delle prove, perciocchè l'una, e l'altra procede con prove dimostrative. Ha poi comune l'ordine de gl'insegnamenti, il quale dee nell'una, e nell'altra essere compiuto, e perfetto. Ha dall'altra parte la Scienza questo differente dall'Arte, prima: Che la Scienza si prende per soggetto cose le quali per sapersi non si possono far venire all'atto; ma l'Arte non si prende cose per soggetto, le quali non possano molto più agevolmente risapendosi venire all'atto. Ha ancora differente questo: Che la Scienza si tollera d'ogni cosa o onesta, o utile, o disonesta, o dannosa, ch'ella sia al Mondo; ma l'Arte non si tollera di cosa, che non sia onesta, & utile al Mondo."

PLATONISM: DEFENCE OF POETRY

The notion of the arts as necessarily "honest" and "useful" is a first step in the direction of a Platonic subordination of poetry to politics.

A more direct consideration of questions raised by Plato himself is found in the *Chiose intorno al libro del Comune di Platone*, which Castelvetro states to be posterior to his redaction of the commentary on Aristotle's *Poetics*. Here again, as in the following statement, a "usefulness" is assumed for poetry: "Here we see that the utility or the harm that is derived from the epic is the same one that is derived from history, that is, the example."[86] But the whole question is argued in a later passage, and Plato's own solution is rejected; the reference is to the passage beginning "Nihil aliud agere, vel imitari oportet."[87]

In this passage Plato presupposes that poetry was not invented for any other reason than to teach by way of example and that what is found in poetry, whether it be good or evil, can or must be followed by the reader. This is false; for we wish, not that it should teach, but that it should present matters that we can think about and that we may have examples of every kind before us: to frighten the wicked and to console the good, and to give knowledge of the nature of men and women. And for this reason Aristotle said that tragedy, by means of fears and injustices, drove fears and injustices from the hearts of men who heard it, rejecting what Plato says in this passage.[88]

Thus, for Castelvetro Plato's theory would seem to demand that the reader follow, unwittingly and unwillingly, all the examples presented to him by the poet; whereas Aristotle's theory would permit the reader choice and reflection, or rather choice following upon reflection. The basic principle of moral instruction remains, in both, the same; but Castelvetro sees the reader as a more independent and a more intelligent man and the poet as having a greater scope of activity.

CONCLUSIONS

To interrupt this analysis of the "Defence of Poetry" at the present chronological point, about 1570, is not to imply that there was any such interruption in the thinking and writing upon the subject. The defence continues throughout the century, using for the most part the same arguments; so does the attack. But on the one hand, by this date the essential elements of both attack and defence have been established and amply

---

[86] *Ibid.*, p. 209: "Ecco che l'utilità, o il danno, che si trae dell'Epopea, è quella stessa, che si trae dell'Istoria, cioè l'essempio."

[87] Trans. Ficino (Basel, 1546), p. 561.

[88] *Ibid.*, pp. 215–16: "In questo luogo presuppone Platone, che la Poesia non sia trovata per altro, se non per insegnare per Esempio, e ciò, che si truova in Poesia, o bene o male che sia, altri lo possa, o debba seguire. Il che è falso; perciochè è proposta, prima che vogliamo che insegna, per materia da farvi pensamenti sopra, & acciocchè abbiamo esempj d'ogni maniera e da spaventare i rei, e da consolare i buoni, e da conoscere la natura de gli uomini, e delle donne. E perciò diceva Aristotele, che la Tragedia con le paure, e con le ingiustizie scacciava le paure, e le ingiustizie dal cuore de gli uomini ascoltanti, riprovando quello, che dice Platone in questo luogo."

illustrated; on the other hand, after 1570 an increasing number of documents adopt an antipoetic attitude because of their strong Christian bias. This means that while the problem remains the same during the last years of the century, some of the solutions become more extreme and more violent.

This identity of the problem constitutes the principal unifying element for the numerous texts that I have examined so far. Let me state it, briefly, in this way: Should the art of poetry be admitted to society because its products contribute to the good of the state, or should it be proscribed because its works are essentially harmful? Whether the critics take the position favorable to poetry or its opposite, they remain within the same framework of discussion, within the basic assumption that it is proper to consider poetry in this light.

The opponents of poetry start from certain premises which are not always clearly stated and which are sometimes mutually contradictory. They assume that one reason why poetry is dangerous is that it exercises upon the reader or hearer a kind of irresistible power, a superior rhetorical force which sways his passions and imposes upon him the teachings of the poem. The causes of this power are partly divine, partly human. In terms of the ancient poetic of pagan times, the divine cause lies within the gods and the Muses; in terms of a modern Christian theory, within God and the natural talents or inspirations with which he endows certain men. As for the human causes, they consist almost entirely in those pleasurable adornments by means of which the poet beautifies his poem and makes it attractive to his audience. Such an assumption of "irresistibility" would seem to indicate that all men, young or old, wise or foolish, should fall prey equally to the blandishments of the poetic art. Yet a second basic assumption denies this. It holds that poetry, written under the conditions indicated, is dangerous only for certain groups—for the young men and women to whose education it might contribute, for the ignorant masses, for those men who are morally predisposed to wickedness and vice. Others are quite capable of resisting, and hence are out of danger—mature and adult persons already formed by a sound education, the sages of the city who have extraordinary faculties of discrimination, all those men who are morally disposed to goodness and virtue. The differentiating factor here is intelligence; the young and the ignorant cannot understand the true meanings of poetry and are led astray by its false appearances, whereas the old and the wise pierce beneath the illusory surface to the salutary teachings contained within. This involves a third assumption, that all poetry—even the comedies of Terence—is essentially allegorical in character, that what is visible to the eye and audible to the ear is but an imperfect representation of a hidden truth perceptible only by the intellect. The young and the foolish see only the surface and cannot "resist" the pleasurable enticements which it presents; the old and the wise, blessed with intelligence, refuse to be duped by appearances and extract from the core of poetry the most abstruse and recondite teachings.

Because of the dangers presented by the art of poetry to the young and the foolish, several alternatives for combatting these dangers are suggested by critics and philosophers. The most obvious is to forbid, to banish, to condemn poetry entirely. This is Plato's extreme solution in the *Republic*, and it has adherents throughout the years we have been studying. A second solution is to make a choice among poets and poems, admitting some and rejecting others according as they do or do not satisfy accepted standards of a pedagogical, ethical, political, or religious nature. This involves a third possibility, that of placing the whole art under the jurisdiction of a body of arbiters. These might be the elders of the city, and they would then apply political standards; or philosophers, who would see poetry in its relationships with the totality of human behavior; or priests, whose judgments would be based on theological principles involving also an ethical code; or those of the citizens themselves who would be capable of the proper kind of discrimination. Of these groups, it is probably the philosophers who enjoy the greatest favor with Cinquecento theorists, and this is undoubtedly because of the Platonic origins of this point of view and because of the vogue of the notion of the philosopher-king.

Whatever the particular group chosen to hold sway over poets and poetry, the principle of subordination of the art to another discipline is constant throughout and constitutes one of the distinguishing features of the Platonic approach during this century. I have already pointed out, however, that the central assumption of a pedagogical potential is very close to the Horatian notion of utility, whereas the recognition of the corrupting force of sweet ornament takes into account Horace's pleasure. The "utile dulci" is thus present for both lines of critics, as a statement of ends for the Horatians, as a statement of dangers for the Platonists. And while the former debated which of the ends should be predominant or how one might serve the other, the latter sought means of reducing the effectiveness of the pleasure and of directing the application of the utility. A special case must be made for the extreme Christian apologists, such as Lapini, for they tend to admit certain religious uses for certain kinds of poetry, provided that these be carefully limited and circumscribed—as regards both the pleasurable ornaments and the doctrines taught—in the light of firm theological premises.

The critics who defend poetry—not the anti-Platonists, but rather the Platonists who come to opposite conclusions—are concerned with the same basic problem. But they tend to see the circumstances in a different way. As far as they can discover through their historical researches, through their appeal to other authorities such as Cicero, Plutarch, and Strabo, through their own observations, the teachings of poetry are highly desirable and should be encouraged by every society. The testimony of the ancients, historians and philosophers alike, convinces them that in the remote ages of mankind the first contributions to civilization were made by the poets; as a result, poetry became the first of the arts and the sciences and mother of all the rest. They support this opinion on the one hand by citing a restricted number of historical and philosophical texts, on the other hand by pointing to the wealth and diversity of knowledge found in such poets as Homer and Vergil. They themselves seem to recognize in men they have known—and perhaps in their own characters—the softening influences of an art that appeals to men through all kinds of refinements and demands of its audience subtlety both of spirit and of sensibility. They thus argue, as a corollary, that the pleasures of poetry, deriving from its use of verse, a special kind of language, and all the ornaments, should be sought rather than avoided—for their own sake as well as for the contribution that they make to an ultimate utility.

How shall we explain these differences between two groups of men who approach the same problem, on the basis of the same general system of reference, and still come forth with contradictory conclusions? One answer, I believe, lies in the attitude of each group toward the men who constitute the audiences of the poets. The defenders of poetry tend less than their opponents to look upon mankind as corrupt and corruptible. They are willing to admit that the reader or the spectator has enough intelligence to perceive whatever hidden meanings there may be, enough moral stability to be moved or amused by examples of vice without necessarily undertaking to imitate them immediately, enough common sense to recognize that the works of poetry are (after all) fictions. Perhaps they recognize thus in the audience a measure of artistic sensitivity which enables it to enjoy the pleasure of the work without becoming a victim of it and to discern what parts of the work are valid guides to life. Another answer, I suggest, is that the defenders of poetry have, on the whole, a less definitely ethical and political approach to poetry than do their opponents. Although they consent to argue the matter on the grounds proposed by the Platonists, they really do not put much stock in the moral mission of the poet or in the educative function of poetry. They affirm, but without conviction or enthusiasm. Primarily, they are interested in the work of art as work of art, in the problems of its technique and its perfection, rather than in the ulterior ends it might serve. If they argue about these ends, it is because they are driven to do so by the vehemence and the persistence of the attacks; and they argue largely by affirming the contrary of what their opponents had declared. Perhaps a third answer should also be intimated: the defenders of poetry are much less prone to adopt toward their art the official position of the church or the usual suppositions of Christian theology and ethics. They remain to a greater extent within the context of the arguments of classical antiquity, and their loud proclaimings of the beauties and the delights and the educative virtues of poetry constitute, in a way, the triumph of paganism.

CHAPTER EIGHT. PLATONISM: II. THE TRIUMPH OF CHRISTIANITY

During the last thirty years of the Cinquecento, the principal Platonic ideas on poetry, pro and contra, continue as before. There is little contraction or expansion of the arguments, little diversification of the standard approaches to the problem. At best, one may note an increase in the number of critics and theorists who display an ultra-Catholic attitude toward questions of literature. Some of these are churchmen, and they undoubtedly reflect the conclusions of the successive meetings of the Council of Trent—conclusions which tended to place stringent limitations on the practice and uses of poetry. One may perhaps note this as a general development in the century, a repentance over the pagan excesses of the earlier years and a wish to rival, if not overtake, the strait-laced Puritanism of the reformed churches. In the literary world itself, some such turnabout may be detected in the case of Tasso—there was a modicum of madness connected with it—who first imposed an allegorical interpretation upon his masterpiece, then proceeded to the disastrous "purification" of the *Gerusalemme Liberata* into the *Gerusalemme Conquistata*. Such a purification was in complete keeping with the wishes of those few theorists of whom I shall be speaking.

VIPERANO (1570)

The first of the theorists to be considered in this chapter, Giovanni Antonio Viperano, belongs rather to the defenders of poetry. Or, more specifically, his *De scribendis virorum illustrium vitis* (1570) is a kind of "art of biography," which praises the biographer because he serves the same ends as the poet and describes the techniques common to both. "Of all the arts which teach," says Viperano, "the study of the historians and the poets seems to me to be divine and admirable; for with an almost heavenly power they rescue the deeds of great men from oblivion and from the damage of time, and at the same time sow them far and wide in the memory of all peoples."[1]

The major pedagogical value of history and biography, for Viperano, is in the instruction of princes; but it will be remembered that this was frequently assumed to be the case for certain poetic genres. For both, the education to virtue and the stimulation to glorious actions result from the proper depiction of character, and practically the whole art of biography consists in knowing how to present characters. The ingredients of such a presentation are the ones familiar to the rhetoricians and the Horatians:

[1] *De scribendis vitis* (1570), p. A3v: "inter cetera doctrinarum genera historicorum praecipue studium & poëtarum mihi diuinum, & admirabile videtur: qui coelesti quadam vi clarorum hominum res gestas ab obliuione, & uetustatis iniuria vindicant, simulque in omnium gentium memoriam disseminant."

age, sex, fortune, profession, place of birth, all the others. They must be presented clearly and vividly; *ut pictura historia*: "And just as the painter, in shaping the features of a face, in which the movements of thought shine out, uses all of his powers, so the good writer in expressing the characteristics of the soul, from which the way of life of the person is perceived, will put into such expression all his care and diligence."[2] It would seem, however, that the actions accomplished by the hero of history or of poetry are also important, for the ends are stated, partially at least, in terms of the lessons to be learned from deeds and acts: "Men should be taught to maintain a constancy of spirit in every vicissitude of fortune, not to allow themselves to be carried away by good fortune or to be depressed by misfortune; that there is no dishonor that does not come from wickedness, nor any praise that does not flow from the springs of honor."[3] Such lessons may also be learned, in both arts, from apothegms. History differs from poetry in that it is obliged on all occasions to tell the truth, whereas poetry invents all kinds of fictions (and rhetoric may indulge in expansion and exaggeration). The whole point of view of Viperano is Platonic not only in the assignment of a pedagogical function to the various arts discussed, but, in a more subtle way, in the breaking down of the barriers among these arts and the crediting of all with common ends and common means.

There is little to be added to what has already been said (in Chapter V) about Andrea Menechini's oration *Delle lodi della poesia, d'Omero, et di Virgilio* (1572). It may serve admirably as an example of the close companionship between the Horatian and the Platonic attitudes toward the ends of poetry, and also as a witness to the continuation of the vogue of the "defences of poetry." Menechini cites Plato frequently, in praise of poetry, on the divine furor and the prophetic gift of the poets. He emphasizes especially the superiority of verse over prose in harmony, in persuasive power, in imitative capacity. Imitation itself (and it will be remembered that this is one of the central concepts of the Platonists) constitutes the major effectiveness of poetry: "... it excites the movements of our souls, takes possession of our minds, frightening us with examples of monstrous things and delighting us with the image of those things which we desire with every warmth of passion."[4] It is through this capacity to possess the souls of its listeners that poetry achieves its usefulness, that it works miracles, that it arouses men to the contemplation of the general and the universal and frees them from the singular and the particular. Thus it

[2] *Ibid.*, p. Cv: "Itaque vt pictor in conformandis lineamentis oris, in quo motus animorum elucent, summam operam consumit, sic bonus scriptor in exprimendis animi moribus, e quibus vitae ratio perspicitur, omne studium suum & diligentiam ponet."

[3] *Ibid.*, pp. Dijv–Diij: "Doceanturq́ue homines in omni fortuna constantem animum tenere, nec in secundis rebus se efferre, nec in aduersis demittere: ac nullam esse ignominiam, quae a turpitudine non proficiscatur, nec laudem vllam quae non ab honestatis fonte emanet."

[4] *Delle lodi* (1572), p. a iv–ivv: "eccita i mouimenti de gli animi, s'insignorisce delle menti, spauentandoci con essempij di cose monstruose, & rallegrandoci con l'imagine di quelle, che noi desideriamo con ogni caldo affetto."

[298]

becomes the mistress of all the sciences. These various powers are the consequences of the divinity of poetry: "The divinity of poetry is understood from this fact, that nobody can achieve success in it without celestial breath or inspiration."[5] From the poet, the divine spirit passes to the reader or the listener, making of him a person closer to the gods in his perfection:

> Oh holy Poetry! oh highest of divine inspirations! for by purging us of every stain, making us pure and simple, you make our soul shine with its own splendor, and through its proper and natural strength, as also through its intelligence which is the chief and pilot of that same soul, you cause it to obtain from the angels in a single moment whatever it desires.[6]

The praise continues in this tone, now general, now applied to Homer and Vergil—a tone which recalls that of Plato in the dialogues dealing with inspiration and enthusiasm.

The same problem of imitation, but approached from a more intellectual standpoint, is the subject of a brief fragment by Lorenzo Giacomini Tebalducci Malespini; it is without title, and I shall call it *On the Definition of Imitation*. The fragment follows Giacomini's translation of Aristotle's *Poetics* in MS Laurenziana Ashb. 531, and is likewise in the hand of Giorgio Bartoli, and I presume it to be of the same date, 1573. Its content is also related to the text of the *Poetics*, since Giacomini is here trying to distinguish between the definitions of imitation offered by Plato and by Aristotle. By combining the definitions in Books III and X of the *Republic*, Giacomini produces a somewhat strange interpretation of Plato; I have already cited the passage in extenso in Chapter II (p. 62). He assumes that all the uses of the term "imitation" in Plato are identical or at least similar and hence that various meanings can be combined into a single one. This leads him to equate imitation with fable or mythology, to raise the question of whether a fable need be told "in the person of another," to decide that it need not, and to concoct a curious definition of poetry in which various senses of "imitation" and of "fable" are hopelessly confused. Giacomini belongs in the Platonic tradition in the sense that he continues the discussion of one of the main ideas associated with that tradition by contemporary theorists and that he presents a kind of commentary or interpretation of the text of Plato.

AGNOLO SEGNI (1573)

In fact, Giacomini's little passage on imitation (if indeed it be his) may be more closely indebted to another work of 1573 than to his own translation of the *Poetics*. That work is a set of lectures delivered by Agnolo Segni

---

[5] *Ibid.*, p. b ijv: "Et di qui si comprende la diuinità della Poesia, imperò che alcun non può conseguirla senza fiato, ò inspiration celeste."

[6] *Ibid.*, p. b iijv: "Ò santa Poesia, ò ben somma inspiration diuina; poiche purgandoci da ogni macchia, rendendone casti, & semplici, rilucer fai l'anima col proprio splendore, & per la natural, & propria diligenza sua, come ancor per la sua mente, che è capo, & auriga di essa anima, in un subito momento la fai conseguir da gli Angeli ciò, che ella disidera."

to the Accademia Fiorentina; in their original form they were six in number, although Segni reduced them to four in 1576. The original lectures are now to be found in the Biblioteca Laurenziana, MS Ashb. 531 (the one which contains Giacomini's works); the published form appeared posthumously in 1581.[7] In keeping with the traditions of the Accademia, Segni must limit himself to a discussion of Petrarch, and he chooses to speak of the canzone (No. CXXVII) beginning "In quella parte dove Amor mi sprona." But only a few paragraphs of the lengthy *Lezioni* are devoted to the poem; the rest is an essay on imitation, on Platonic principles, meant to serve as prolegomena to the analysis of Petrarch. In itself, the essay is one of the most extensive, most thoroughgoing, and most valuable Platonic documents of the century.

Seen in its narrowest sense, Segni's group of lectures may be taken as an attempt to justify lyric poetry as a proper genre and Petrarch as a poet. But in its broadest sense, this justification requires a complete theory of poetry, of imitation, and of all the literary genres, and it is to that theory that Segni addresses himself. The first lezione establishes a general Platonic system, involving the need for the search, in any field of knowledge, for the "highest good," discovering that in most disciplines it is found in the intellect but that in poetry it is found in the divine furor, asserting that the genus of poetry is imitation. The second lezione defines imitation, establishes its relationships to false discourse ("orazione falsa") and to fable ("favola"), and inquires into the objects of such an imitative fable. The third studies the kinds of imitation, both without and within poetry, and explains in what sense Plato found imitation bad and why he banished the poets from the Republic. The fourth investigates the instruments of imitation, including the necessary instrument of verse, and arrives at preliminary definitions of poetry, poetics, and poem. In the fifth, seeking to discover the ends of poetry, Segni examines the various kinds of arts (with respect to their ends), the faculties to which they are addressed, and the various ends which might be assigned to poetry. Finally, in the sixth (after a lengthy summary of the preceding five lezioni), he reaches the discussion of Petrarch; but since this immediately involves him in an elementary theory of the lyric, little if anything is said about the poem in question.

Segni's first definition of poetry (in the fourth lecture) is: "An imitation of human and divine things, by means of fable-making discourse, in verse, according to the divine furor." In the last lecture, this definition is expanded and completed by the addition of the formula "to the end of purging human minds of their emotions."[8] A gloss on this definition will reveal Segni's main ideas about the art of poetry. He means, by imitation, a

[7] See my "Nuove Attribuzioni di manoscritti di critica letteraria del Cinquecento," *Rinascimento*, III (1952), 247–49.

[8] MS Laur. Ashb. 531, fol. 74v: "Immitazione de le cose humane, et de le divine con orazione favolosa in versi secondo il furor divino"; and fol. 88: "à fine di purgare gli animi humani da loro affetti."

number of things. He does not exclude the simplest Platonic meaning of "to speak in the person of another" (fol. 53); but this is too limited a meaning and it would eliminate most of the writings of the lyric poets—for example, Petrarch. It indicates an accident of poetry, not an essential differentia. In its most general meaning, to "imitate" is to make one thing resemble another (fol. 54), to fabricate one thing—an "idolo," an "immagine," a "fantasma"—in likeness of another which is its "essempio" or "essemplare." The "idolo" gives an appearance, a representation of its object, and poetry is concerned with the making of such images. As an art of imitation, poetry enters into the whole broader schematism of imitation which Segni borrows from Plato. Since it uses discourse, its words imitate concepts just as its concepts imitate things (fol. 86v). The general process of imitation is found everywhere in the world: God imitates himself in man (see Scripture), nature imitates the world of ideas, art imitates nature, men imitate each other (fols. 32–33). In a word, the whole Platonic chain of relationships—from universal Ideas to particular concepts or objects to representations of those concepts or objects—is constituted by a series of imitations.

The particular realm of poetry involves imitations of special kinds and many cautions with respect to them. Its materials are not "true" things, such as those which go into the making of history and science and the arts, but rather "false" things; for it imitates things which, without being true in themselves, create a semblance or a likeness of truth. These are called "fabula" by the Latins, "favola" by the Italians, "mythology" by the Greeks. Segni, in this analysis, apparently collapses the materials of poetry with the instrument of their expression. As he himself states (attributing the distinction to Plato), it is the language (the "orazione") of poetry which is false, and hence poetry is a false imitation:

Of these two kinds of language, the true, which narrates the truth of things exactly as they were done or are done or as they are, does not belong to poetic imitation or to poetry, but it is proper either to history or to one or another of the sciences. Hence, the other part remains for poetic imitation and for poetry: to make images out of false language and out of fable; and consequently poetry is this—false language which makes images, that is, which makes false things and things invented by itself in resemblance to the true, which language is called mythology by the Greeks and "favola" by us and by the Latins.[9]

In another context, however, he distinguishes false plot from false speech: "The fable is thus always lying and falseness, but it is divided into two; one

---

[9] *Ibid.*, fol. 56: "Di queste due orazioni la vera, la quale narra la verità de le cose appunto come sono state fatte ò si fanno ò come elle sono, questa non appartiene à la poetica immitazione, ne à la poesia, ma è propria ò del istoria, ò d'una ò d'un altra scienza: adunque l'altra parte resta al'immitazione poetica et à la poesia, il far idoli con l'orazione falsa et con la favola; et diremo la immitazione poetica essere il far idoli con la orazione falsa et con la favola; et conseguentemente la poesia essere questo, orazione falsa la quale fa idoli, cio è fa le cose false e finte da lei somiglianti à le vere, la quale orazione mithologica è chiamata da Greci, et da noi favola et da Latini."

is the false language, as Plato says . . . , which contains within itself false things, whatever they may be; the other is those false things themselves and particularly false actions, not true but invented."[10] Segni thinks that herein lies the difference—or one of the differences—between Aristotle and Plato on imitation: Aristotle considered the actions themselves, not the words, as the plot or "favola."

In a general way, Segni attributes to Aristotle the same meanings for imitation as to Plato. He argues that because Aristotle divided imitation into three manners—narrative, dramatic, and mixed—and because these were the three manners which Plato had given to "mythology," then imitation and mythology must be the same thing. Aristotle is made the authority for the statement that the objects of imitation are not restricted to human actions but include characters, passions, and thoughts as well (fol. 59), while Plato indicates that the gods also may be treated. Segni feels that these statements are necessary, first to justify the inclusion of lyric poetry (which has no actions), second to permit the kind of loose description of the object, in his definition, as "human and divine things." In that same definition, the means of imitation are said to be "fable-making discourse" (a concept which we have already examined) and verse. Verse is demanded by the common conception of poetry, by Plato (explicitly) and by Aristotle (implicitly); it is the "necessary matter" for the realization of the "form":

> Thus poetry is a composite of imitation and of verse, in which the imitation is its essence and not the verse; but not for this reason can it be poetry without verse, which is necessary to it as its proper matter, just as a body is necessary to man, and not just any body, but a particular body and a particular matter: but to the soul and to the form corresponds, in poetry, the imitation, just as the language corresponds to the body and to a certain kind of body, and not any language whatsoever but this fixed one, that is, metrical language or language made in verse.[11]

The last member of Segni's original definition—"according to the divine furor"—is meant to indicate the main efficient cause of poetry. Nature and art are also efficient causes; but nature, in the Platonic system, is identifiable with divine inspiration, and art is secondary because it is powerless without nature. For Segni, it is the presence or absence of the divine furor which accounts for the goodness or badness of poetry.

When, in order to complete his definition, Segni adds the formula "to the end of purging human minds of their passions," he is providing his

[10] *Ibid.*, fol. 57: "È adunque sempre menzogna la favola et falsità, ma si divide in due, una è la orazione falsa come dice Platone . . ., la quale contiene in se cose false, qualunque elle si sieno: l'altra è le stesse cose false, et particolarmente l'azzioni false non vere ma finte."

[11] *Ibid.*, fol. 72v: "Cosi la poesia è il composto di immitazione et di verso, dove la immitazione è l'essenza di lei, et non il verso, ma non pero puo essere poesia senza il verso, il quale è necessario à lei come propria sua materia, si come al huomo è necessario il corpo, et non qualunque corpo, ma un corpo tale, et una materia tale, ma al anima et à la forma risponde ne la poesia la immitazione, si come al corpo, et tale corpo risponde l'orazione, et non qualunque orazione, ma questa determinata, ciò è l'orazione metrica, ò fatta in versi."

statement of the final cause. This may seem to be a nod to Aristotle; but the formula is much more than a paraphrase of the purgation clause in Aristotle's definition of tragedy. For Segni, working in a Platonic context, the ends of poetry are varied and complex. As an imitative art, it appeals to the senses, which are both deceived and satisfied by it; it does not appeal to the reason. If there is another part of the soul to which imitation is germane, it is the appetitive faculty, for the appetite transforms itself into the object of its desire. In a word, poetry addresses itself to the irrational and hence the inferior parts of the soul. According to Plato, the end of poetry is to alter the appetite and to fill it with passions; if these are good, the poem will be good, and vice versa. But according to Aristotle, the end is just the opposite: to remove the passions from the soul by means of purgation. After lengthy examination of the nature of this effect, Segni concludes that it consists in the removal, not of pity and fear themselves, but of their opposites, and that a similar purgation of opposites takes place in the other genres. He states that the end of poetry is "the purgation from the mind of various noisome and blameworthy passions, brought about through the means of other better passions" ("la purgazione del animo da diversi affetti noiosi et biasimevoli col mezzo d'altri affetti migliori condotta à fine," fol. 82). He does not, however, fail to take into account other suggestions of the possible ends: Aristotle's, that it is the plot; Horace's, that it is pleasure and utility; Proclus', that it is similarity to the original. In a final summation, he attempts to distinguish among these rival ends and to admit all of them into a total conception of poetry:

We have explained several ends for poetry: the plot as the form and soul and the end of the other parts: the moving of the passions and purgation as operations of the whole; the passions that are moved and the purgation, ends insofar as they are works which remain as made. Pleasure as an accident of the end is also called an end and is placed among the ends. But because when one speaks about the end, one means that end which is the end of the whole and not of the parts of the thing proposed, and because also the works made by the operations are an end and purgation is an end of the passions previously aroused, it follows that the true and ultimate end of poetry and of the poem is the purgation of our minds of their passions, as we said above according to Aristotle. And I mean always by this name of purgation not the operation of purging which is in the agent, but that of the patient and of the subject purged.[12]

---

[12] *Ibid.*, fols. 83–83v: "Habbiamo esplicati piu fini de la poesia, la favola come forma et anima, et fine del altre parti: il mover gli affetti et il purgare come operazioni del tutto: gli affetti mossi et la purgazione, fini come opere che rimangano fatte: il piacere come accidente del fine, ancora egli fine s'appella et si pone tra' fini. Ma perche quando e' si ragiona del fine, e' s'intende di quello che è fine del tutto et non de le parti de la cosa proposta: et perche ancora l'opere de le operazioni sono fine et la purgazione è fine de gli affetti mossi inanzi: seguita che de la poesia et del poema il fine vero et ultimo è la purgazione degli animi nostri da loro affetti, come noi dicevamo disopra secondo Ar.e et intendo sempre per questo nome purgazione, non l'operazione del purgare la quale è ne lo agente, ma quella del paziente et del suggetto purgato."

The seeming duality of approach, involving an admixture of an incidental Aristotelianism to a basic Platonism, is present throughout the work. We have seen it in the concept of imitation, in the insistence on verse, in the idea of purgation. At times, Segni thinks that the two ancient philosophers are in precise agreement; at others, when they disagree, he finds the means of reconciling them by a more inclusive theory which embraces both. Occasionally, where Aristotle fails to define a term, Segni assumes that he adopts and shares Plato's use of it. When Aristotle says (*Poetics* 1454*b*11) that the tragic poet's portrayals must represent men as more remarkable than they really are, Segni interprets this as calling for a representation of Platonic Ideas of character and the passions (fol. 63). The distinction of poetry into four species, epic, tragic, comic, and lyric, is found in both philosophers, and it depends upon the division of the three manners of imitation: the epic is mixed, tragedy and comedy are dramatic, the lyric is narrative. (It is a further division of lyric poetry that permits Segni to discover the proper classification of Petrarch as a writer of encomia and of threnes.) From Aristotle Segni borrows the notion that poetry is superior to history because it is more universal; from Plato, the judgment that it is inferior to philosophy because of its very particularity (fol. 90). On the whole, the general structure of ideas and the framework of reference in Segni are Platonic: poetry exists in a Platonic world of imitations, it is made possible by the presence of the divine furor, it pursues a goal of moral betterment for the spectator.

At the beginning of his discussion of the utility of poetry in his *Apologia dei dialogi*, written around 1574–75,[13] Sperone Speroni seems to be espousing a position opposite to Plato's in the *Republic*. For he answers Plato by pointing out the political usefulness of the art:

> If it is a good thing to purge the errors of a single man through repentance, it is undoubtedly much better to connect in their natural order our particular arts with that general art of the state, and to subordinate the former to the latter, as is proper. For from the preservation of that order arises the determination not only to do no evil . . . , but to refrain from any actions which might appear legitimate to this or that individual, but which are in opposition to the best behavior of the whole body of the citizenry.[14]

It is this notion of a social usefulness, according to Speroni, which led Aristotle to include the purgation clause in the definition of tragedy. We note here that although Speroni sees virtues in the use of poetry for social instruction, he nevertheless wishes to subordinate the art to the higher art

---

[13] See Speroni, *Opere* (1740), V, 209, 364, 365, for letters useful in dating the *Apologia*.

[14] In *Opere* (1740), I, 355: "se egli è bene purgar gli errori di un uomo solo per penitenza; è senza dubbio assai meglio tener congiunte nel loro ordine naturale le nostre arti particolari colla comune della repubblica, e quelle a questa, come è ragione, subordinare. con ciò sia cosa che da questo ordine conservato nasce il consiglio, non solamente di non far male . . . ma di astenersi d'alcune vili operazioni, che pajon lecite a questo e quello, ma son diverse al decoro della adunanza cittadinesca."

of politics. When he goes on to discuss specific genres, especially comedy, he discovers that such forms may do as much harm as good—that they may be "schools of vice" as well as "schools of virtue." He must therefore conclude that the state should restrict the kinds of poetry that it allows men to write and to publish, and that essentially all public or political poetry should have a religious intention:

> It is the duty of every well-ordered city to portray in verse, as elegantly as it knows how and without admitting any other fables, all of the favors that God has granted it . . . ; to praise the deeds of the citizens who were victorious in just wars . . . ; and to sorrow over the death of those who did not merit death. . . . If it does so, its poems will not turn out to be comedies, or tragedies, or epics, but hymns, canticles, and psalms, useful, decent, and religious. If these poems are accompanied artistically in the presentation by music, song, and dance . . . , there is no woman or child who, having heard them one single time, will not retain them pleasurably in the memory for the rest of his life.[15]

The conclusion is that of Plato; it reflects the general circumstances and tone of the *Apologia*, a work written in old age as a repentance for youthful sins. Perhaps some of the religious afterthought of which I have been speaking is already present here.

LORENZO GAMBARA (1576)

The next two documents are definite examples of such public repentance. The first is the *Tractatio de perfectae poëseos ratione* of Lorenzo Gambara (1576); its subtitle is in itself significant: "tum ostenditur, cur abstinendum sit à scriptione poëmatum turpium, aut falsorum Deorum fabulas continentium. Ac quàm late pateat campus ad pulcherrima alia poëmata edenda." Gambara admits that he had spent his youth in the writing of profane poetry and that he was now determined to the necessity of burning these same poems. For they had served neither of the two ends legitimate for poetry: the singing of the glory of God and the salvation of man's soul. Instead, they had merely been manifestations of his own desire for worldly fame (one is reminded of the conversations between St. Augustine and Petrarch in the *Secretum meum*). In writing them, he had been pursuing false appearances, false gods and lying muses, because the only real truth had not yet been apparent to him. The misguided Gambara is here like the poet of Plato, who represents semblances only and is never able to see Truth. He thus agrees with the banishing of the poets by the pagan philosophers (Plato, Dio, Suetonius, and Plutarch are cited) and with the con-

---

[15] *Ibid.*, p. 357: "egli è officio di ogni cittade bene ordinata ritrarre in versi quanto più sappia elegantemente, senza altre favole, tutte le grazie che le son fatte dal Signor Dio . . .; lodar le geste de' cittadini in guerre giuste vittoriosi . . .; e condolersi alla morte di chi era degno di non morire. . . . ciò facendo, riusciranno li suoi poemi non commedie, non tragedie, non epopeje, ma inni, cantici, e salmi, utili, onesti, e religiosi. li quai poemi, accompagnandosi con bella arte nelli spettacoli al suono, al canto, ed al ballo . . ., non sarà donna o fanciullo, che quelli uditi una sola volta, volentieri tutta sua vita non li abbia sempre in memoria."

demnation by the church fathers (Clement of Alexandria and Basil, for example) of any works which introduced heresy, magic, or moral wickedness.

Gambara himself will base the whole discussion of the art of poetry on the foundation of Christian theology. Seen in this light, the obscene and wicked fables of the poets and the licentious images of the painters are the work of Satan, designed to make men revolt against reason and develop the habit of sin. Moreover, the poet who adds to a Christian poem either the myths of antiquity or improper moral actions creates a work as ridiculous as Horace's monster:

> But if he who joined a human head to a horse's neck ought to be laughed at, certainly he who joins to a Christian neck, that is a poem, a hydra's head in the form of a vile conflux of filthy wantonness is greatly to be lamented, for his salvation, along with the salvation of many others, is either already to be deplored or is fast approaching the point where it will have to be deplored. And indeed the hydra's head and all other prodigies and chimeras were invented by us according to our powers, since we filled our writings with so many monstrosities, that even if there were no peril for our honor and decency, there certainly would derive from them a considerable peril for our faith so long as our minds were darkened when submerged in these shadows, and distracted completely from heavenly things to the constant pursuit of vanities.[16]

If the writing of such works is reprehensible, the reading of them is full of dangers: our senses are depraved, we are excited to vice, or if we have already sinned we are moved to sin again rather than to repent our former errors. The ultimate consequence is heresy. Hence, there is no doubt that the Christian reader should avoid all the literary monuments of antiquity, in spite of the fact that certain church fathers may seem to have authorized them.

In place of these monuments, the Christian poet will provide works representing not only a new theology and a new ethic, but also a new poetics. For Aristotle's *Poetics* based on Homer and Horace's *Ars poetica* based on Vergil can be of no use to him; they merely provide rules for the imitation of unacceptable models. Gambara is willing to admit, with St. Augustine, certain beauties of art and of style in the ancient poets; but their content is such as to render them inadmissible to the Christian state. If the wise ancient philosophers who wrote arts of poetry based them upon these works, it is only because they had not yet had the privilege of seeing the light of Truth:

[16] *Tractatio* (1576), pp. 11–12: "Quod si . . . qui humano capiti ceruicem equinam adiungeret ridendus esset, sane qui Christianę ceruici, hoc est poëmati caput hydrę, faedarum nempe libidinum colluuiem apponit, magnopere deflendus est, cuius salus, cum salute plurimorum aut deplorata sit, aut non procul est, cum sit deploranda. Et hydrę quidem caput, ceteraque portenta, & chimera[e] pro viribus effingebantur à nobis, cum scripta tot monstris oppleremus, vt nisi honestati periculum ac pudicitię fuisset, certe fidei non leuis erat iactura dum mens nostra his tenebris offusa cęcabatur, atque à cęlestibus ad inania celebranda curuabatur omnino."

... but although they have understood that poetry has been instilled in us by nature, and that it therefore resides in the imitation of truth, still, when once the fountain of nature had been troubled and their vision was overcast by a cloud of error, because they had not achieved the greatest virtue in poetry, they chose finally what seemed right to themselves.[17]

The Truth that was lacking to them was of course that of Christian revelation, and without it they could not possibly discover the truth about poetry:

> Now, since they were neither enlightened by the light of faith, nor so lived by the light of nature as to give glory to God; and since, moreover, sin had introduced into the world the errors of the false gods and the many common ideas about them; and since indeed they had neither read nor understood the holy Scriptures, nor had they read or understood something in them would they have believed them, or even had they believed something in them would they have dared to make it public out of fear; and finally, since they did not see among their countrymen absolutely anybody endowed with those virtues which even the light of nature requires in the formation of a perfect man, they themselves invented certain men for whom descendance from the gods or their exploits or the supposition that they were numbered among the gods won a certain esteem, stimulating others to imitate them. But we have already indicated with what manifold error![18]

The new poetry, the Christian poetry, must have principles essentially different from the old. Perhaps, in a sense, the ends will be the same, since it too will seek to delight and profit; "imitation" and "doctrine" are the two ends proposed for poetry, and it is the function of the poetic faculty "to see whatever is appropriate to the imitation of each action, passion, character, by means of beautiful language, in order to improve life and to live well and happily."[19] But whereas the old poetry was content, for its subject matter, with the necessary and the probable (following Aristotle's recommendation), the new poetry must content itself with nothing less than the truth. Whereas the old pagan poets derived their model of the perfect man from error, through invention and fiction, the new poets will find theirs in truth, through pious meditation and the teachings of theology.

---

[17] *Ibid.*, p. 22: "quod & si, à natura Poësim nobis inditam, ac proinde in veritatis imitatione sitam esse intellexerunt, naturę tamen fonte turbato, & caligine errorum oculis offusa, quod in Poesi rectissimum erat, non assequuti, quod sibi tandem rectum visum est, elegerunt."

[18] *Ibid.*, p. 22: "Cum enim nec fidei lumine illustrarentur, neque pro naturalis luminis ratione ita viuerent, vt Deo gloriam tribuerent; falsorum autem Deorum errores, promiscuasque de illis opiniones peccatum inuexisset in Mundum; nec vero Diuinas scripturas legissent, aut intellexissent: nec si quid legerant, aut intellexerant credidissent, aut tamen si quid crederent, auderent propter metum pronunciare: denique cum apud suos neminem ijs omnino virtutibus prędeitum cernerent, quas ipsum etiam naturę lumen requirit in homine perfecto efformando, ipsi per se aliquos effinxere: quibus vel ortus ex Dijs, vel res gestę, vel in Deorum numerum conficta relatio illis quidem existimationem conciliarent, ceteris autem adderent calcar ad imitandum. Sed quam multiplici errore, iam diximus."

[19] *Ibid.*, p. 24: "vt poëtica facultas sit videndi quodcunque accommodatum sit ad imitationem cuiusque actionis, affectionis, moris, suaui sermone ad vitam corrigendam, & ad bene beateque viuendum."

Thus the old criteria of "prudentia, varietas, efficacia, suavitas," will be replaced by two only, "modestia" and "veritas," sufficient in themselves to assure the achievement of the ends. The strength of the word of God will be more efficacious than all the rhetorical devices and all the prodigies of the ancient poets and their modern imitators. The lives and deeds of the martyrs will supply materials having all the required characteristics; using them, one may write

> ... the epic without adulation and without damage to the truth; tragedy presenting the praise of the Christian religion; satire without bitterness, permitting the poets to inveigh against heresy and against the vices with the greatest sincerity, but without violating charity. A vast field is thus opened for writing all kinds of poems without falsehood, without ineptitudes, without causticness, without foulness, but with faith, majesty, graveness, penetration, charity.[20]

To a degree the new poetry has already been attempted. But Gambara condemns those who have chosen sacred subjects only to mix them with profane matters and to treat them in profane meters; Marot, Beza, Buchanan come under the ban for this reason. Only those poems devoted to the spreading of the faith, to the publishing of holy crusades, to the conquest of Jerusalem, will be found acceptable and will be admitted to the Christian Republic.

I have dwelt at some length on Gambara's theories for two reasons: First, they represent the complete Christianization of the Platonic point of view. The Republic having been transformed into the Christian Republic, everything that Plato had said about poetry in relation to the former is restated in terms of the latter. The treatment of the gods or of God, the relationship to truth or to Truth, the role in education, all these come in for consideration. Second, these theories are an early statement of a doctrine which was to be developed at some length in the following century, not only in Italy but in France as well, the doctrine of the Christian epic. Gambara adumbrates, in 1576, the characteristics of that new literary genre.

It must have been shortly after its publication that Cardinal Sirleto sent a copy of Gambara's treatise to Francesco Panicarola, for in 1576 Panicarola wrote a letter to Sirleto thanking him for the work and adding his own remarks to the discussion; the letter is preserved in MS Vat. Lat. 6531 and is dated "Di Bologna li .8. di Settembre 1576." Panicarola reveals an interesting filiation among writers sharing the same point of view toward poetry; he speaks of Gambara as his friend and states that his master was Antonio Possevino, who in 1593 was to write a treatise *De poësi et pictura*

---

[20] *Ibid.*, p. 27: "epopeia sine assentatione, aut veritatis damno; Tragica cum Christianae religionis commendatione; satyrae sine amarulentia, dum in haeresim, vitiaque Poetę sincerissimi salua charitate inuehuntur. Ad cetera denique Poemata scribenda latissimus patet campus, sine falsitate, sine ineptijs, sine mordacitate, sine faeditate, sed cum fide, maiestate, grauitate, acumine, charitate."

ethnica. All three writers were Jesuits and reflected the teaching of the order; Panicarola makes specific reference to the decree of the twenty-fifth session of the Council of Trent, 1563, condemning obscene works of art. He is enthusiastic over Gambara's burning of his own poetry and hopes that other poets—and especially painters and sculptors—will destroy their works. The whole tenor of his letter is that he wishes to see Gambara's principles for poetry applied to the other arts; it is especially important that painting and sculpture should be subjected to control and censorship since the images they present affect the senses even more violently than do those of poetry. On the thesis of the close similarity between poetry and painting, which he finds stated by the best philosophers, he proposes that just as an Index has been established for books, so also one should be set up for works in the other arts. What he is most eager to insure is the limitation of any works which might be obscene or libidinous in their materials. The principles upon which such restriction would rest are suggested by Panicarola, who calls upon the authority of the ancient saints and upon the suggestions made in the Decree of the Council of Trent. Clearly, the letter has no pretentions of being an exhaustive treatment of its subject; it merely extends Gambara's arguments to the other arts. It is useful as an illustration of the spreading of this ultra-Christian point of view, as a representation of the kind of thinking current within a certain restricted milieu.

When, in 1576, Agnolo Segni revised for publication his set of lectures to the Accademia Fiorentina, he made those excisions necessary to reduce the series from six to four lectures. He died in the same year, and the *Ragionamento sopra le cose pertinenti alla poetica* was not published until 1581. A comparison of the two texts[21] shows no really essential differences in poetic theory. Although he cuts out some of the basic philosophical material (such as the general outlines of a Platonic theory of the "summo bene" at the beginning of the first lecture) the general position does not change. Nor does it differ as a result of curtailment of some passages presenting specific arguments. In its broad lines, the point of view toward the art is the one outlined earlier in this chapter. At certain points there are significant alterations of the text; but their importance should not be overstressed. Thus the addition to the definition of poetry of the words "and spirit"—"it is an imitation of human and divine things, by means of fable-making discourse, in verse, according to the divine furor and spirit"[22]— merely brings in another of the terms which had been frequently used in the original version. The expansion, at a later place, of the final clause of this definition so that it reads "to the end of purging human minds of their emotions and of harmful passions,"[23] may be intended only to stress a

[21] See my "Nuove Attribuzioni di manoscritti di critica letteraria del Cinquecento," *Rinascimento*, III (1952), 247–49.
[22] *Ragionamento* (1581), p. 44: "ella è imitazione delle cose humane, & delle diuine con orazione fauolosa in versi secondo il furore, & spirito diuino."
[23] *Ibid.*, p. 58: "à fine di purgare gli animi humani da' loro affetti, & dalle passioni nociue."

utilitarian end which had always been recognized. In any case, the gloss upon the total definition need not be revised, nor was it by Segni, in the light of these alterations. His general vision of poetry as an art intermediate between philosophy and history[24] still obtains, and Plato remains the dominant master, who explains and complements the terse and elliptical Aristotle.

Some of Segni's ideas were certainly known to Lorenzo Giacomini by 1576, for he had a copy made of the original lectures of 1573. Yet it is difficult to see any direct reflection of them in his own lectures *Della nobiltà delle lettere e delle arme*, read to the Accademia Fiorentina in 1576. His problem in the three lectures is to discover the relative worth of letters and of arms; early in the first lecture he outlines his procedure: "... it will be necessary ... to discuss virtue in general, both active and contemplative, and, since the virtues are habits of the soul, to discuss the soul and its capabilities; and moreover happiness, for the virtues are the causes of happiness."[25] This outline describes the general character of the discussion, which throughout remains vague and abstract and only occasionally approaches the specific problem of literature and of poetry. I have indicated in Chapter I its general conclusions: those branches of "letters" which constitute the contemplative sciences would be superior to arms, whereas the ones which merely lead to the kind of action represented by arms would be inferior to them. The general supposition is that philosophical disciplines which determine the ends and the modes of action take precedence over it, whereas ancillary sciences—including poetry—which merely serve the ends of action are less meritorious. Giacomini, remaining within his generalizations and considering poetry only in terms of the ends served, represents one of the typical Platonic attitudes toward the art.

The Accademia Fiorentina also heard, two years later, in 1578, Francesco Bonciani's *Lettione della prosopopea*. (I have analyzed its Horatian elements in Chapter VI.) From Plato Bonciani borrowed above all certain ideas on imitation. He sees imitation in the broader sense as any representation of a person or object; in the more specific sense, "when anybody, in his speech, introduces a third person who speaks in his own person ... , there is nobody who does not know that this is an imitation. One imitates also in relating partially the form and the character and the action of any person whatsoever."[26] These preliminary distinctions allow him to classify the figure in which he is interested, prosopopeia, as an imitation. Along

---

[24] See above, chap. i, p. 31 and n. 61.

[25] MS B.N. Paris, Fonds italien 982, fol. 2: "sarà necessario ... ragionare della virtù in vniuersale, et della attiua, et della contemplatiua: et poiche le virtù sono habiti dell'anima, ragionare dell'anima et delle sue potenzie; et della felicità ancora; poiche sono cause della felicità." See also above, chap. i, p. 18 and n. 29, for an earlier discussion.

[26] MS Ricc. 1539, fol. 132v: "quando altri nel suo ragionamento introduce un terzo, che'n sua persona fauelli ... niuno è che non sappia questa essere imitatione: Imitasi ancora nel riferire partitamente la forma, e l'abito, e l'attione di che che sia."

with other Platonists, he defends poetry on the basis of its civilizing function in antiquity; but he makes the argument specific by insisting that one of the devices used by the wise men of early times to educate and domesticate primitive peoples was the animal apologue, a form of prosopopeia. This form seems to him to fit ideally the requirements for poetry, since it presents a pleasurable exterior—an imitation—under which is concealed a serious lesson useful to the audience.

In a short passage of a very considerable work, the *Uniuersales institutiones ad hominum perfectionem*, Filippo Mocenigo considered briefly the problem of the regulation of the arts. The work was first published in 1581, and the passage in question is Contemplatio V, Pars II, Cap. XIIII, entitled "De artium omnium, ac de Magistratuum, qui artibus praeficiuntur, fontibus." Starting from a division of the arts into the perfect ones and the imperfect ones, the former being those which create, by means of the artistic activity, a product which remains, the latter being limited only to the activity, Mocenigo sees the imperfect arts as having as their sole end an appeal to one or several of the senses. They may be productive of no effect beyond that upon the senses, or they may be applicable to some further use. In some cases, the appeal to the senses may result in pleasure for a spectator rather than for the person engaging in the activity, or in addition to the latter's pleasure. Such arts as the dance, choral singing, singing and instrumental playing, belong to the latter category, whereas tragedy, comedy, and other poetical works combine such pleasure of the spectator with a higher function. This would seem to be the building of character and of moral strength. Both the pleasurable aspects of art and its educative possibilities demand that the magistrates of the city intervene to control it; they must "drive out the useless and indecent arts, as well as the indecent uses of the arts, according as will be established by the laws."[27] Plato's suggestions in the *Republic* are here echoed in an incidental way.

GIROLAMO FRACHETTA (1581)

In the same year, 1581, Girolamo Frachetta published a work which enters much more fully into the Platonic current than the last few which I have been discussing; this was his *Dialogo del furore poetico*, whose interlocutors were Frachetta himself, Giovan Battista Pona, Prospero Bernardo, and Luigi Prato. The problem of the dialogue is double: to discover whether Plato's theory of the divine furor is reconcilable with other things which Plato himself has to say about poetry, and to ask whether the theory itself is tenable. Two interpretations of Plato are presented in connection with the first problem, one asserting that all Plato's statements about the art of poetry are consistent, the other insisting that it is impossible to accept at the same time the doctrine of the divine furor and the banishment

---

[27] *Institutiones* (1581), p. 529: "expellere inutiles, ac inhonestas artes, necnon inhonestos artium vsus, prout legibus sancitum erit."

of the poets. Pona is the champion of the affirmative, and his argument may be summarized in this way: Plato does believe completely the theory of the divine furor; the poet writes not through natural causes but through a divine inspiration coming to him from God via the muses. If at the same time he banishes the poets from his Republic, it is because of the special conditions of the Republic and because of certain characteristics of poetry. When the poet speaks under the influence of the furor he can speak only the truth, and this should be desirable in any state; but he may speak this truth in the guise of an allegory which, because it is not intelligible to the young and the ignorant, would thus not be desirable. The Republic, accepting only what is perfect and wishing to use poetry for pedagogical purposes, could not admit poetry of this kind. But poets also speak, at times, for themselves, on the basis of their purely human capacities; and at such times they may err and may introduce lies into their poems. They may seek the pleasure of their audience, especially through such forms as tragedy and comedy, and in so doing they may depart from the mission assigned to them by the state. Any of these contingencies would disqualify them from participation in the labors of the Republic. Pona insists that Plato's statements are to be taken absolutely: the ban affects all poets and all poetry, it was necessary in the conception of the Republic, and it is entirely defensible in the light of a belief in the divine furor.

Through most of the *Dialogo*, Frachetta himself takes the negative position. He cites Castelvetro and other scholars to the effect that Plato could not really have believed in divine inspiration. For divine inspiration would mean truth and truth would mean good poetry, and good poetry could not possibly be excluded. The ban, however, applies only to bad poets and certain fictions and lies that must be considered bad poetry; these things were not only not true, they were not even verisimilar, and neither Plato nor his readers accepted them as such at the time. Being bad and false, they could not result from the divine furor; hence, either the ban is unjustified or the divine furor is itself a fiction. Frachetta chooses the latter alternative. Throughout this argument, he contrasts the position of Aristotle with that of Plato, using the former in support of his own points of view. In the later pages of the dialogue, other interlocutors intervene and carry the major part of the conversation, and they conclude by stating that Aristotle's theories of poetry not only are more acceptable to the reason but are also more in keeping with Christian theology and the views of a Christian reader. (I shall treat these discussions of Aristotle in a later chapter.)

In addition to its comparison of poetry and history, already studied (Chapter I, p. 15), Lionardo Salviati's dialogue *Il Lasca* (1584) is interesting for its attack upon the art of poetry from a Platonic point of view. The comparison of the two disciplines, which begins innocently enough, ends with a condemnation of poetry on all scores; the attack, indeed, springs from principles stated in the first stages of the argument. Among other distinctions, poetry and history are differentiated on the basis of their ends: that of poetry is to "purge our souls of the passions and assure that our behavior will be proper"; that of history is "prudence."[28] But there is some doubt about this difference, for the epic poem seems also to have "prudence" as its goal:

> It seems necessary to admit that the proper end of epic poetry, which is commonly conceded to be the most magnificent form, is equally prudence and the good of the state; and I said the "proper" end because the other forms of poetry, just as all the arts, are governed in some way or other by the needs of the city. . . . But in such cases it is a secondary or derivative end. . . . Whereas it seems that the work of the epic poet concerns the good of the republic by primary intention . . . by purging the passions and by correcting manners it makes itself useful to the city, but accidentally and not through primary concern.[29]

The essence of the argument here is that, in the special case of the epic, poetry serves accidentally an end which falls in the domain of ethics and essentially an end which falls in the domain of politics. The important question, and the one upon which the attack will later be founded, is this: Is poetry capable of properly serving its end, whether it be ethical or political?

Il Deti, the interlocutor who is responsible for presenting the argument, believes that poetry is incapable of so serving its end. As compared with history, it has the weakness of not carrying conviction: "For history is believed as true, and poetry is held to be a fiction. . . . the poem moves us more than history does, but the emotion ends with the reading. History on the contrary does not by any means arouse us so much as poetry does, but it leaves us persuaded, a thing which, in my personal belief, is not brought about by a poem."[30] As for the pleasure involved in poetry, it is brief, passing, and costly in the sense that it involves a great loss of time. Worse still, it is accompanied by a corrupting influence on character and behavior:

> When poetry puts forward the virtues, no benefit results; for since we quickly recognize them as false, we do not found our actions upon those good examples.

---

[28] *Il Lasca* (1584), p. 11: "il fine il purgar gli animi dagli affetti, e renderci ben costumati"; and for history, "il fine la prudenza."

[29] *Ibid.*, pp. 11–12: "del poema eroico, che per lo piu magnifico si reputa comunemente, par da concedere, che il diritto fine sia la prudenza altresì, ed il ben esser del comune. e ho detto il diritto: imperciochè anche l'altre guise di poesia, si come tutte l'arti, sono ordinate per alcuna delle maniere de' beni della città. . . . Ma il cotale si è fine conseguente. . . . Ma l'opera dell'Eroico il ben della repubblica par che riguardi di prima intenzione. . . . col purgarsi le passioni, e col dirizarsi i costumi, si fa vtile alla città, ma per conseguente, non di primo riguardo. . . ."

[30] *Ibid.*, p. 31: "Perchè la Storia si crede cosa vera, ed il poema si tien per finzione. . . . il poema ci commuoue piu, che la Storia: ma il commouimento cessa con la lettura: La Storia per lo contrario non ci sollieua a gran pezza quanto la Poesia, ma lasciaci persuasi: cosa che dal poema, secondo che credo io, non s'adopera."

On the contrary, by showing us vice the poet frequently does us much harm. For vice is completely the prey of the passions, and these passions constitute properly the power of the poem: it excites them, it works upon them, it exercises its force over them, it is with respect to them that poetry excels. Nor is damage of this kind compensated by blame or punishment of vice [within the poem]; for our desire, without wishing to hear out the argument, seizes suddenly upon what pleases it and accepts it for true; but when unpleasant things are involved, it has recourse to reason and says, "These are mere stories, what's the use of thinking about them?" The pleasure is in the imitation, the beauty of the verse, the sweetness of the song, the excitement of the dance; all these are sulphur and pitch which augment the fire and the flame; all are ready to harm.[31]

It will be noted that if the presentation of the virtues is inefficacious while that of the vices is capable of producing undesirable effects, it is because of inherent weaknesses of the audience, which tends to be led by its appetites rather than by its reason. Another weakness of this same audience consists in its inability to reason about what it sees; hence the relationship of the false objects of poetry to truths of reality, through verisimilitude, escapes it, and it does not learn the intended lessons. Such a conception of the audience—the young and the ignorant—is common among the Platonists, but Salviati generalizes it in such a way as to lead to a complete condemnation of the art of poetry. The state as such is not involved in the same way as it is in the *Republic*—a special kind of commonwealth with specific functions reserved for poetry—but the governing disciplines of politics and ethics are brought to bear upon the judgment of the art of poetry. In the light of these disciplines, Salviati decides (through his interlocutor, Il Deti) that one should completely abandon poetry in favor of the superior art of history.

Since Torquato Tasso himself had indicated, in the *Allegoria del poema* affixed to the 1581 edition of his *Gerusalemme Liberata*, that he meant the allegorical aspects of his poem to have an educative function (see Chapter VI, p. 206), his critics and commentators were not long in applying such criteria to his epic. One commentator, Scipione Gentili, made a few remarks of this character in his *Annotationi sopra la Gierusalemme Liberata di Torquato Tasso* (1586). As a result, his commentary on stanza I presents the following theory of the ends of poetry:

[31] *Ibid.*, pp. 39–40: "La Poesia del metterne auanti la virtù, niun guadagno ne puo lasciare: conciosia che per falsa riconoscendola noi prestamente, sopra quei buoni esempli non facciam fondamento. Per lo contrario, col dimostrarne il vizio, spesse fiate ci nuoce assai il Poeta. Perocchè il vizio è in tutto in preda agli affetti: e questi affetti sono propriamente lo sforzo del poema: quelli eccita, quiui s'adopera, in quelli esercita la sua possanza, in questa parte sormonta la Poesia. Ne col biasimo, ne col gastigo si fatto danno si puo ricompe[n]sare: poscia che l'appetito senza voler vdire il discorso, subitamente, prende quel, che gli piace, e come vero il riceue: ma verso lo spiaceuole ricorre alla ragione: e dice, queste son fauole: che fa luogo il pensarci? Il piacere della imitazione, la vaghezza del verso, la dolcezza del canto, il solleuamento del ballo, son tutti zolfo, e pece, che crescono lo'ncendio, e la vampa: tutti stanno per nuocere."

But what is more important is the fact that the true and proper end of the poet is no other that to profit by introducing the virtues and extirpating the vices from the souls of the citizens. He brings this about by purging them of those passions from which a great proportion of adverse events are born and depend. This purgation was indeed known and praised by Plato, who called it καθαρμόν; to say nothing of Aristotle, who put it in his definition of tragedy as the proper final cause of the latter.[32]

The conflation of Plato and Aristotle, so familiar in the century, is here presented in a highly abbreviated form.

The whole theory of purgation is developed at great length by Lorenzo Giacomini in his *Sopra la purgazione della tragedia* (1586); but since much of the text concerns the interpretation of Aristotle, I shall treat it at a later time. There is, however, one sense in which the discussion is pertinent in the present context, and that is insofar as purgation, for Giacomini, is related to the utilitarian ends of poetry. Indeed, he sees the introduction of the purgation clause in Aristotle's definition of tragedy as a direct answer to Plato, an attempt to counteract the banishment of tragedy and the tragic poets. Giacomini distinguishes two ends for poetry: one, which we might call Aristotelian, is the making of the poem according to the principles of the art; the second, which is "Platonic" in a vague way, is the use of the poem for other purposes, "whose consideration with respect to their causes belongs to the politician who forms the state or who governs it."[33] When, therefore, he forms his own definition of poetry, he includes in it two phrases which state these ends, "made according to the poetic art" and "proper for purging, for teaching, for giving recreation or noble diversion."[34] And when he seeks to identify the four causes of poetry, he sees the final cause (according to Aristotle) as including "purgation, teaching, rest from the cares and from the affairs of life, and finally the diversion of the mind in the intelligent man, which is found in the perfect and joyous knowledge of the excellence of the work."[35] (The same ends are also applicable to painting and sculpture.)

These distinctions provide Giacomini with a satisfactory solution to the debate about pleasure and utility; his is a compromise position:

... we say that poetry should be used not for one single end but for many,

---

[32] *Annotationi* (1586), p. 3: "Ma cio che piu importa, s'è che il vero e dritto fine del poeta non è altro, che di giouare inserendo le virtu, e sterpando gli vitij dagli animi de' cittadini. Il che conseguisce col purgargli di quelle passioni, che gran parte dalle cose auuerse nascono e dipendono. La quale purgatione fu etiandio cognosciuta e lodata da Platone, dimandandola καθαρμὸν. per tacere di Aristotile, il quale la mise nella definitione della Tragedia, come per causa finale di essa propriamente."

[33] In *Orationi e discorsi* (1597), p. 33: "la consideratione de quali per le loro cagioni pertiene al politico."

[34] *Ibid.*, p. 33: "fatta secondo l'arte poetica" and "atta a purgare, ad ammaestrare, a dar riposo, o nobile diporto."

[35] *Ibid.*, pp. 33–34: "la purgatione, l'ammaestramento, il riposo da le molestie, e da negotii de la vita, e finalmente il diporto del animo nel huomo intendente, che è gioconda, e perfetta cognitione del eccellenza del opera."

according to the different kinds of poems and of listeners, all of which ends we include under the name of profit; for the rest and relaxation of the mind from its affairs and labors, and the noble diversion of the mind through the knowledge of the exquisiteness of the work—along with Aristotle we classify these as profit, along with purgation and teaching. Those first two ends are common to all kinds of poetry, but one of them belongs to intelligent men, the other indeterminately to everybody. The last two are proper to special kinds of poetry, since purgation takes place only where strong passions are expressed, and it is certain that some poems do not have the power to benefit virtue and to improve character.[36]

Some indication of the specific ways in which the last kinds of utility are effected is found later in the discourse, where Giacomini points out that we see, in poetry, how calamity falls to the lot even of the great and that we learn wherein true happiness is to be found (p. 46). For all these reasons, he concludes that the politician, far from exiling the poets, "should accept tragedy as profitable to the city if it is used properly and at the right time and in moderation; for if it were used too frequently it would not effect purgation, or else it would bring about a purgation that was neither useful nor necessary."[37] Once again, within the framework of Platonic presuppositions, Giacomini arrives at conclusions divergent from those of his opponents, conclusions that he considers to be integral to the philosophy of Aristotle.

GIASON DENORES (1586)

The juxtaposition of Plato and Aristotle, or rather their fusion and confusion, is again characteristic of Giason Denores' *Discorso intorno à que' principii, cause, et accrescimenti, che la comedia, la tragedia, et il poema heroico ricevono dalla philosophia morale, & civile, & de' governatori delle republiche* (1586).[38] But more striking still in this text is the extent to which the whole art of poetry is reduced to the service of its utilitarian ends. Whereas most theorists are content to make general statements about these ends, Denores insists upon seeing in every part and every feature of the poem a specific device for the achievement of these ends, in each case determined by them. His final summary makes his point clear: " ... we have already clearly shown that most of the parts of tragedy, of comedy,

---

[36] *Ibid.*, p. 34: "diciamo essa douersi vsare non per vn fine solo, ma per molti secondo la diuersità de poemi, e deli vditori, i quali fini tutti comprendiamo sotto nome di giouamento, poiche & il riposo, e l'allentamento del animo da negozij, e da le fatiche, e'l nobile diporto de la mente per la conoscenza de la esquisitezza del opera, con Arist. al giouamento riduciamo, si come anco la purgatione, e l'ammaestramento. quei due primi fini sono a tutte le poesie comuni, ma vno pertiene a gli huomini intelligenti, l'altro indeterminatamente a ciascuno; gli altri due s'appropriano a speziali poesie, poiche la purgatione non ha luogo, se non doue si esprimono gagliardi affetti, & alcuni poemi è certo non hauer forza di giouare alla virtù, e di migliorare il costume."

[37] *Ibid.*, p. 51: "douere il Politico accettare la Tragedia come gioueuole a la Città, se conueneuolmente, & a tempo, e con misura è adoperata: perche il troppo frequente vso, o non purgherebbe, o farebbe purgatione non vtile, ne necessaria."

[38] See above, chap. i, p. 26, for a brief discussion of this text.

and of the heroic poem—change of fortune, reversals, recognitions, character, thought—practically serve no other purpose than this utility."[39] The general statement is, of course, present—present on almost every page of the work—and it takes various forms in various contexts. It is present in the discussion of the origins of poetry, where certain men of high genius directed the art, after its natural beginnings, "to the public benefit and utility, to which according to reason and according to the sayings of the wise all the arts and the professions of men who lead civilized lives in the cities must be directed."[40] Present, necessarily, in the definition of poetry, a definition modeled on Aristotle's definition of tragedy and containing this final clause: "... in order to purge them [the listeners], by means of pleasure, of the most important passions of the soul, and to direct them to good living, to the imitation of virtuous men, and to the conservation of good republics."[41] Present, in a modified way, in the definitions of the various kinds of poetry. The modification comes about through the assignment of each genre to a specific audience, in a special kind of state, and needing a particular kind of indoctrination. Thus, comedy will have as its end "to purge the spectators, by means of pleasure and the ridiculous, of those troubles which disturb their peace and their tranquillity through the falling in love of wives, daughters, and sons, through the deceit and treachery of servants, pimps, nurses, and others of their kind; and to cause them to love private life and to wish to preserve that well-regulated popular republic in which they live."[42] Tragedy will seek "to purge the spectators, by means of pleasure, of terror and of pity, and to make them abhor the life of the tyrants and of the most powerful men."[43] And the heroic poem will have as its goal "to inflame the listeners to the love and the desire to imitate the magnanimous and glorious exploits of great persons and of good and legitimate princes, and to make them content to live under their state, and to abhor the dominion of tyrants and to wish to preserve that well-regulated monarchy in which they live."[44]

---

[39] *Discorso* (1586), p. 43: "gia habbiamo apertamente fatto uedere, le piu parti della tragedia, della comedia, & del poema heroico, la tramutation di fortuna, le peripetie, le agnitioni, il costume, la sentenza non tender quasi ad altro, che alla utilità."

[40] *Ibid.*, p. 1v: "al beneficio, & alla vtilità publica, alla quale per ragione, & per sentenza de' sauii deono hauer la mira tutte le arti, & profession d'huomini, che uiuono accostumatamente nelle città."

[41] *Ibid.*, p. 36: "per purgargli col mezzo del diletto da' piu importanti affetti dell'animo, & per indrizzargli al ben viuere, alla imitation degli huomini virtuosi, & alla conseruation delle buone republiche."

[42] *Ibid.*, p. 36v: "per purgar gli spettatori col mezzo del diletto, & del ridicolo da que' trauagli, che turbano la loro quiete, & tranquilità per gl'inamoramenti delle mogli, delle figliole, de' figlioli, per gl'inganni, & tradimenti de' seruitori, de' ruffiani, delle nutrici, & di altri simili, & per fargli inamorar della vita priuata a conseruation di quella tal ben regolata republica populare, nella quale si troueranno."

[43] *Ibid.*, p. 36v: "per purgar gli spettatori per mezzo del diletto dal terrore, & dalla misericordia, & per fargli abhorrir la uita de' tiranni, & de' piu potenti."

[44] *Ibid.*, p. 37: "per accender gli ascoltanti all'amor, & al desiderio d'imitar l'imprese magnanime, & gloriose de' gran personaggi, & de' buoni, & legitimi principi, & per fargli contentar di viuere sotto il loro stato, & abhorrir la Signoria de' tiranni a conseruation di quella tal ben regolata monarchia, nellaquale si troueranno."

Since each of the genres has a special message for a separate group of people, its content and its construction will be determined by that message. For example, the heroes of the epic, because they are presented as models to be admired and imitated, must be perfect in every respect; but those of tragedy and comedy, because their vices and failings are to be punished as warnings to the spectator, should be midway between the absolutely good and the absolutely bad. Denores develops at length the reasons why, in these characters, absolute goodness or absolute badness would defeat the purposes of poetry. Similarly, the materials of poetry must be presented in such a way as to engender the marvelous, for this brings about pleasure and pleasure is the instrument of utility. In tragedy and comedy, the marvelous is achieved through the accomplishment of the change of fortune within the brief period of time (twelve hours) allotted to the poet. The rapidity of the change in itself provides lessons:

Who then of the spectators would not be inflamed to a desire for private living, seeing many times in these plays that in so brief a period of time every trouble of private citizens may be changed into the greatest happiness? and who would not hate the tyrannical life of the more powerful, seeing and considering that every form of their greatness almost in the blinking of an eye may be turned into extreme ruin, into exile, death, and murder?[45]

The more leisurely adventures of the epic hero show that even the life of the perfect man is full of uncertainties and hence less to be desired than a private existence; they also serve to illustrate even more vividly his numerous virtues. Thus the episode, the particular form which the marvelous takes in the epic, is itself a pedagogical device. So also, in all forms, are the other constituents of plot as Aristotle distinguishes them: recognition and reversal. Both help to produce the marvelous and both enable the poet to bring about the reward of the good and the punishment of the wicked. A perfect plot will combine all these elements in such a way as to communicate a simple and intelligible moral and political lesson (Denores illustrates his meaning by showing how excellent epics or tragedies could be drawn from Boccaccio's tales about the Conte d'Anversa, Gismonda, and Rosciglione). One requisite for perfection will always be the capacity of the materials to "riceuere ... la moralità" (p. 29v).

Following Aristotle's order in the *Poetics*, Denores then passes on to the other qualitative parts. Character, with which he associates decorum, was introduced into all forms of poetry "especially to generate in the minds of the spectators or of the listeners a knowledge and experience of human actions. ... for who will ever say that it is not also useful to him to understand all these qualities and conditions of men, and to distinguish the good

[45] *Ibid.*, p. 17: "Chi è dunque de' spettatori, che non si accenda al desiderio della vita priuata, riguardando spessissime volte in queste rappresentationi, che in cosi breue giro di tempo ogni trauaglio de' priuati si riuolga in somma letitia, & che non abhorisca la vita tirannica de' piu potenti, vedendo, & considerando, che ogni loro grandezza quasi in vn batter d'occhio si possa riuolger in estrema ruina, in essilio, in morte, in vccisioni?"

from the bad, in order to know himself and the ways of human life?"[46] This is a separate end, served by a separate part of the poem. Thought, which he translates by "sententia" and "discorso," has (curiously enough) a utility of a different kind, insofar as it may be of service to those of the citizenry who devote themselves to the study of eloquence. Diction and verse, finally, contribute to the production of the marvelous; besides, when they are properly adapted to the character and the station of the personages, they enhance the verisimilitude and hence the power of persuasion of the work.

Every part of a good poem will therefore be included in the poem because it makes a contribution to its utility; it may serve either the general end of moral instruction or some particular end peculiar to itself. Moreover, the handling of each part by the poet will be judged proper or improper as it corresponds or fails to correspond to the needs of the lesson. All the criteria for the poem will necessarily be linked to ethical and political considerations. Indeed, Denores insists that "as a good moral and political philosopher" Aristotle treated only those forms of poetry which derived their principles from moral and civil philosophy. He himself, applying the same principles, declares that such forms as the tragicomedy and the pastoral are not worthy of attention since they are monstrous as artistic compositions and, more damaging still, they cannot possibly teach the kinds of lessons which are the province of poetry. Their authors are not poets; at best, since they seek only the pleasure of their audience and not its profit, they are like sophists who pursue a false and deceptive form of their art. Throughout this analysis, Denores holds tenaciously to his principle of the social usefulness of poetry, never doubting it to be true, never seeking to answer those who had raised doubts about it. The principle is axiomatic, no defence is needed. He applies it to every aspect of the art and every part of the poem; and since he does so within the skeleton of the arrangement of Aristotle's *Poetics*, he achieves a kind of complete Platonization of the latter document, limited only by the limits of the problem: the usefulness of poetry in the state.

TOMMASO CORREA (1586–87)

In contrast to Denores' work, Tommaso Correa's *De antiquitate, dignitateque poesis & poetarum differentia* (1586), is entirely conscious of its Platonism and seeks a position that will at once explain Plato's favorable statements about poetry and justify his banishment of the poets. It begins with a defence of poetry composed of all the traditional elements: its ancient dignity, its noble rank among the arts, its status as a first philosophy bringing wisdom and manners to uncouth peoples. But immediately,

---

[46] *Ibid.*, pp. 30–30*v*: "per generar specialmente negli animi de' spettatori, & degli ascoltanti cognition, & esperienza delle attioni humane. ... chi dira mai, che non gli sia anchora utile il comprender tutte queste qualità, & condition d'huomini, & distinguer le buone dalle cattiue, per cognoscer se stesso, & la prattica del uiuer nostro."

a distinction: not all poets are worthy of such praise. It belongs only to those poets whom Plato called "the ministers and interpreters of the gods" and should be denied to those who sing vacuous verses appreciated only by the vulgar crowd. To explain these differences among poets, Correa appeals to a metaphysical principle of the three levels of existence in the human soul. The highest of these is celestial and divine, representing the existence of God in man, removed from all corruption by the senses and the body. The middle level is the peculiarly human one, representing a combination of the highest and the lowest things in man's nature, of the divine and the bestial; it is the realm of the mind, of reason, of knowledge. The lowest level is the dark region of the body and the senses, where man is close to the lower animals; it is dominated by visions, phantasies, appearances. To each of these levels, says Correa, corresponds a category of poetry and a kind of poet.

The divine furor is responsible for the first and most excellent class of poetry. It denotes the presence of God in man and is the expression of his highest capacities. This is that furor or afflatus of which Plato spoke. From it comes all such poetry as celebrates the great deeds of our ancestors and serves to render us and our progeny more perfect. The poetry of the prophets and the seers, that of sacred letters and religious writings, belongs in this category:

In this kind of poetry were active almost all those holy prophets whose works we have in sacred letters, who in part predicted many future things, in part revealed to mortals many things about God and about heavenly matters, in part celebrated excellent deeds, in part exhorted men by divine warnings to religion and to the other virtues, in part deterred them from vices. All these things those men have done, inspired and impelled by a heavenly spirit, and deservedly these things are referred to this first kind of poetry.[47]

The second species, inferior in many ways to the first, is the product of the human faculties of reason: "... it knows the nature of things, and takes delight in honest deeds and sayings, and concerns finite things."[48] It is a kind of philosophical and moral poetry, providing knowledge, admonitions to virtue, warnings against vice; examples of it are furnished by Tyrtaeus, Theognis, Empedocles, Nicander, and Lucretius.

To the lowest form, dark and ignoble because it springs from opinion and visions, belongs all such poetry as has its basis in imitation. Aristotle devoted his *Poetics* exclusively to this type, and Horace most of his *Ars poetica*. Imitation itself is divided into two kinds:

[47] *De antiquitate* (1586), p. 679: "In hoc genere poeticae versati sunt omnes fere illi sacri vates, quorum monumenta in sacris litteris habemus, qui partim futura multa prędixerunt; partim de Deo, rebusque celestibus multa mortalibus aperuerunt: partim excellentia facta exornarunt; partim monitis diuinis ad religionem, caeterasque virtutes adhortati sunt, partim à vitijs deterruerunt. Quae omnia illi afflati, & instincti caelesti numine fecerunt, & merito, ad hoc primum poeticae genus referuntur."

[48] *Ibid.*, p. 682: "cognoscit naturam rerum, & honeste factis, & dictis delectatur, & res in numerum includit."

... a kind of true and exact imitation which renders each and every thing exactly as it is; the second, contrived and invented, expresses each thing, not as it actually is, but as it appears to be, or else can appear to the many. From this there arises one form of poetry which has rested upon opinions about true things, and, by putting forth a likeness very close to those [things] and distinct, is completely adapted to the imitation of the truth. The second form, which, by following only that which seems and appears to be, sets before their eyes not the true likeness, but a kind of simulated appearance of the likeness, is completely adapted to pleasure. The former alters nothing by imitation, the latter inflates slight defects to huge dimensions, restores the listeners by the kind of language and the variety of harmony, completely changes the feelings of men and the nature of things, because it renders them by imitation not as they actually are but as they can seem to be, since it is a kind of sketchy outline, not a finely wrought conception of things.[49]

Correa goes on to say that the first two types are not only approved but are highly recommended by Plato; whereas the third is accepted insofar as its first subdivision is concerned, rejected and excluded and banned in its second subdivision. For the end of the first two categories is instruction; but the end of the third is pleasure. Correa seems to accept these distinctions as he sees them in Plato, and to see in them an adequate explanation of Plato's "contradictions."

The same Correa published, in 1587, his *In librum de arte poetica Q. Horatij Flacci explanationes* (already analyzed in Chapter VI, p. 215). Since his purpose here obviously was to provide a commentary on Horace, the problems of poetry are seen from a special point of view; Plato enters only incidentally and in an illustrative capacity. There are, however, several points of interest with respect to Plato, and perhaps even one modification of the theory presented in the *De antiquitate*. Plato is first called upon in connection with the remarks on *Ars poetica* 1–23, where Correa sees above all a principle of propriety or "conuenientia." This propriety is of various kinds, and among them there is a "Platonic" kind: "Indeed Plato also in Book IV of the *Republic* affirms that the poets are not permitted to say whatever they wish, but he teaches that they must observe the law of propriety. There exist in fact certain circumscribed limits beyond which they may not pass, lest things be said contrary to the accepted norms of life and

---

[49] *Ibid.*, pp. 682–83: "Imitatio quaedam vera & recta quę talem vnamquamque rem effingit, qualis ipsa est; altera simulata, & ficta vnamquamque rem exprimit, non qualis ipsa est, sed qualis videtur, aut multitudini videri potest. Hinc existit vna forma poeticę, quae veris de rebus opinionibus nixa est, & germanam illarum, & expressam similitudinem proponens tota ad imitationem veritatis accommodatur. Altera, quae sequens id tantum quod videtur, & apparet, non similitudinem veram, sed quamdam simulatam speciem similitudinis ante oculos ponit, ac tota ad voluptatem comparatur. Illa nihil immutat imitando, hęc ad ingentem magnitudinem extollit exigua mala, auditores verborum genere & concentus varietate recreat, commutat animos hominum, & naturam rerum, quia non quales sunt, sed quales videri possunt effingit imitando, cum sit adumbratio quaedam, non subtilis rerum cognitio."

of mores."[50] Correa seems to imply that in the Horatian context the preoccupations of Plato, largely religious and ethical, are reduced to a political and social level. So in his statement of the ends of poetry the Platonic elements of instruction of the young and formation of character are attenuated to the traditional rhetorical "vt admoneatur, delectetur, doceatur" (p. 93). But he passes from attenuation to denial when he discusses the subject of the poetic furor. It will be remembered that in the *De antiquitate* Correa had situated the operation of the poetic furor in the highest reaches of poetic activity, as a manifestation of the presence of God in those poets who wrote religious and prophetic poetry. In the present work, however, he all but denies the existence of such divine intervention. Commenting on lines 309–10, where Horace is speaking of the necessity for knowledge, Correa writes:

> Since he had touched upon the argument that, according to the opinion of Democritus, the poet became a poet through nature and through a kind of furor, in this twentieth precept he declares whence springs every praiseworthy poem having decorum. Knowledge, he says, just as it is the mother, the fountain, and the origin of all things meriting praise, is also the nurse of poetry. And so far is it from the truth that the poet is "furious," that nobody can write well unless he has knowledge. In fact it is essential that every good and proper form of writing should derive from a knowledge of things.[51]

The difference between this text and his own treatise is undoubtedly explained by the fact that in the latter he had denied the existence of the furor in the second and third levels of poetry and had asserted that Horace himself was concerned only with the lowest of these levels. But part of the explanation may also be found in the circumstance that Correa is here no longer in the realm of the purely theoretical; he is providing a commentary on what he regards as an essentially practical treatise.

LORENZO GIACOMINI (1587)

As its title indicates, Lorenzo Giacomini's oration *Del furor poetico*, delivered before the Accademia degli Alterati in 1587, is also devoted to the problem of poetic inspiration. And in a sense it reaches the same practical conclusion as had Correa in the *Explanationes*, and for the same reasons. For Giacomini recognizes immediately the practical consequences of assuming that the divine furor exists: if it does, then art and principles and practice are useless; if it does not, then the poet must address himself to his

---

[50] *Explanationes* (1587), p. 6: "Nam etiam Plato in iiij. de Rep. negat permitti poetis dicere, quicquid voluerint, sed spectandam esse conuenientiam docet. Nam quidam sunt circunscripti termini, vltra quos egredi, fas non est, ne aliena à vitae institutis, & moribus dicantur."

[51] *Ibid.*, pp. 101–2: "Quia natura, & quasi quodam furore poetam fieri attigerat ex sententia Democriti hoc xx. precepto declarat vnde efflorescat laudabile & decorum carmen. Est inquit sapientia, vt omnium laudandarum rerum mater fons, & origo, sic etiam est poetae altrix. Tantum verò abest, vt furiosus poeta sit, vt bene scribere nemo possit, nisi sapiens. Omnis enim oratio bona, & apta ex cognitione rerum promanet necesse est."

art with greater seriousness and application. After presenting the conventional arguments for the divinity of poetry, Giacomini points out that this theory involves a separation of poetry from the other arts; for, whereas all the other arts would have particular principles and fixed subjects, poetry would have neither. He sees no reason for making this distinction. Poetry, he says, may be defined simply as "a fable expressed in verse," and both fable (or plot) and verse may be produced separately. Moreover, the concept of divinity destroys all art, all merit and praise for the poet. If not by the furor, how then are poems produced? Giacomini's answer is simple; it involves instead a theory of the humors:

The man who wishes to rise to the heights of poetry or of eloquence or of philosophy has need of temperate spirits, inclining rather towards the cold ones, in order to think, investigate, discourse, and judge . . . ; to continue in such operations, he seeks an abundance of humors neither weak nor easily dissipated, but stable and firm, which move through vigorous and powerful imaginations; but in order to execute well in conformity with the idea conceived within himself, he needs warmth so that the expression may be effective.[52]

These latter "heated" spirits are the ones that give the effect of "estasi, rapimento, furore, smania"; it is because of them that the soul, "fixed and intent upon an operation, forgets every other object, and does not even remember itself or what it is doing."[53] Such concentration by the poet may in a sense be called a furor and divine:

. . . if by furor we mean that fixation of the soul upon the Idea, or if we denote that internal incitement and movement, born not of individual reasoning and judgment but of the natural disposition of the instrument to which it is united, then there will be furor in the poet, and it will be called divine not without reason since it proceeds from Nature, which is the daughter of God, and from an excellent Nature: I mean the human soul combined with a subject having that temperament.[54]

But this furor has nothing to do with an individual act of inspiration on the part of God, with a special favor accorded to given men (and only the poets) at given moments in their lives.

The mechanism of poetry is thus essentially a natural one for Giacomini.

[52] In *Orationi e discorsi* (1597), pp. 59–60: "l'huomo che al altezza de la Poesia o del Eloquenza, o de la Filosofia dee salire, per pensare, inuestigare, discorrere, e giudicare, ha bisogno di spiriti temperati, che inclinino nel freddo . . .; per continuare in queste operationi, ricerca copia di spiriti non deboli, ne facili a risoluersi, ma stabili, e fermi, che muouon con vigorosi, e potenti fantasmi, ma per bene eseguire secondo l'idea in se concepúta, ha bisogno di calore, accioche con efficacia esprima."

[53] *Ibid.*, p. 60: "affisata & intenta ad vna operatione di ogni altro oggetto si scorda, ne pure si ricorda di se stessa, ne quello che faccia."

[54] *Ibid.*, p. 61: "se per furore intendiamo quel affisamento del anima del Idea, o vero se denotiamo quel incitamento, e mouimento interno, nato non da proprio discorso, e giudizio ma da naturale proprietà del instrumento al quale è vnita, harà luogo il furore nel poeta, e sarà non senza ragione detto Diuino, poiche procede da la Natura, che è figliuola di Dio, e da Natura eccellente dico dal anima humana a soggetto di tal temperamento congiunta."

He explains the power that the art has over its listeners or spectators not by an appeal to supernatural intervention but by two natural causes. One is sympathy, that movement of the soul by which men identify themselves with the passions of others. In the case of poetry, this identification is favored and augmented by a second cause, the delight which comes to men, through their senses, from imitation. The poet wishing to produce these effects operates on the basis of principles (the ends proposed) and upon a special subject matter (the words and ideas employed in the construction of the poem). His is a work of art rather than of nature; the poet possessing completely the principles of his art will succeed better than one who has merely a natural inclination or instinct toward it. This is true for all the arts, and the fact that a man of talent becomes a poet rather than something else is a result of various circumstances and accidents. In some cases, and only for short poems in the minor genres, precept and principle may be replaced by imitation (which I take to mean imitation of the works of others). But this can never be a sufficient means of achieving perfection in the major poetic forms. In order to become an excellent poet a man must possess "those natural virtues of the soul, intelligence, judgment, docility, and memory";[55] besides, he must know everything about all subjects, and Giacomini presents a long list of the sciences in which he must be expert, including the whole range of arts and disciplines.

Giacomini thus occupies a very special place in the ranks of those who discussed the inevitable Platonic question of the divine furor. He does not believe in it; there were others who did not. But he sees in poetry the kinds of effects usually attributed to such a furor and investigates them in order to find some other explanation. That explanation is a completely natural one in which the innate qualities of the poet, supplemented by what he has learned about his own art and about others, and taking into account the natural capacity of the audience to be moved by poetic means, produce the pleasurable excitement and enthusiasm which result from poetry. It is also an "artistic" explanation in the sense that it tends to ascribe all causes and their effects to the art of the poet rather than to the accidents of divine intervention.

JACOPO MAZZONI (1587)

The two parts of Jacopo Mazzoni's *Della difesa della Comedia di Dante*, written around 1585 and published respectively in 1587 and 1688, are in a sense complementary to Giacomini's oration insofar as their Platonic elements are concerned. For whereas Giacomini had centered his attention upon the question of the divine furor, Mazzoni is interested in the other two major Platonic problems: the definition of imitation and the ends of poetry, the latter involving the banishment. I have already discussed at some length (Chapter I, pp. 24–26) those aspects of Mazzoni's work that relate to his

[55] *Ibid.*, p. 70: "quelle naturali virtù del anima Ingegno, Giudicio, Docilità, e Memoria."

PLATONISM: TRIUMPH OF CHRISTIANITY

classification of poetry. It springs in part from a distinction which he finds in Book X of the *Republic*, concerning the three kinds of objects that lend themselves to the activity of the arts. These are Ideas (which are contemplated), Works (which are made), and Images (which are made by imitation). In this connection, Mazzoni finds it necessary to define imitation, and the first attempt produces this statement:

> Since, then, we see that the artifice of the arts of making [i.e., those which produce an object, such as the bit of the bit-maker] is directed toward something other than mere representation or mere resemblance, therefore we shall say that they cannot be called imitative. But those arts which have as their object the Image ["idolo"], have an object that has no other end, in its artifice, than to represent and to resemble; therefore they were properly called imitative.[56]

The kind of image or idol imitated by poetry "has its origin in our artifice and is born of our fancy and of our intellect through our choice and our will."[57] This statement immediately raises the question of Plato's seeming use of the term "imitation" to mean only a dramatic representation. Mazzoni concludes, after due analysis, that Plato also admitted other forms of representation as imitations, but that he wished to indicate the superiority of dramatic representation to narrative; imitation is thus the genus for all poetry.

To Plato also Mazzoni ascribes a correlative principle: imitation is correct and proper when it represents things exactly as they are, and it is an error of the poetic art to imitate them in any other way or with dissimilarity.[58] A further restriction upon the imitative arts is introduced at a later point in the discussion, and this is the unity of the object that leads to the unity of the work:

> ... the proper nature and the excellence of the Image ["idolo"] which is the object of the imitative arts is that it should be of one thing and only one thing; this is not true either of the Work or of the Idea. ... The Image which is their object will be all the more worthy and excellent as it represents better that one thing in imitation of which it is made. ... They limit themselves only to the representation of the unity of the thing which they wish to resemble.[59]

---

[56] *Della difesa*, Pt. I (1587), sec. 10: "Perche adunque veggiamo, che l'artificio dell'arti facitrici viene indirizzato ad altro, che al solo a [sic] rappresentare, & al solo rassomigliare, però diremo, ch'elle non si poteano nomare imitatrici. Ma quell'arti, c'hanno per oggetto l'Idolo, hanno vn'oggetto, che non hà altro fine nel suo artificio, che di rappresentare, e di rassomigliare, però furo debitamente imitatrici appellate."

[57] *Ibid.*, sec. 15: "hà l'origine dall'artificio nostro, la quale suol nascere dalla nostra phantasia, e dal nostro intelletto mediante l'elettione, e la voluntà nostra."

[58] *Ibid.*, secs. 20–28; also secs. 45–46. The same ideas are discussed again in chaps. 1 and 58 of Book III.

[59] *Ibid.*, pp. 644–45: "la propria natura, e l'eccellenza dell'idolo oggetto dell'arti imitanti è, ch'egli sia d'vna cosa sola d'vno, il che non auuiene dell'opera, ne dell'idea. ... l'Idolo oggetto loro sia tanto più degno, e più eccellente, quanto che rappresenterà meglio quella cosa sola a imitatione della quale è fatto. ... si ristringono solamente a rappresentare l'vnità della cosa, che vogliono rassomigliare."

These notions with respect to imitation stand in close relationship, for Mazzoni, to Plato's ideas about the ends of poetry. If, ideally, poetry should have as its object only the truth, practically it is also required to imitate the false, the possible, and the credible, and the latter is indeed its best object. For poetry appeals to an audience of common and ignorant men and cannot hope to present to them the same materials as would the sciences, or in the same way. It is thus that Mazzoni classifies the art under the rational faculty of sophistics: "Poetry is a sophistic art because of imitation, which is its proper genus, and because of the credible, which is its subject, and because of pleasure, which is its end; since being under that genus, and concerning that subject, and because it seeks that end, it is frequently constrained to admit what is false."[60] One should, however, distinguish this "sophistic" from another one which has no relationship to the truth and to true philosophy, and which deliberately engages in the telling of lies. To this latter kind belongs a species of poetry which is not real poetry and which has no place in the state; this is the kind that Plato banished. For in addition to its end of pleasure, springing from good and perfect imitation, poetry also serves another end, that of relaxation from labor; since it does, it also falls under the civil faculty and under the jurisdiction of politics. When this second end is improperly satisfied, the philosopher has the right to expel poetry from the state. The two ways of considering poetic pleasure are distinguished as follows:

In the first way, pleasure is the end of that poetry which was placed under the blameworthy type of sophistic, for it is such as brings disorder to the appetite through excessive delight, making it in every way rebellious to reason and bringing at the same time harm and danger to virtuous living.... But qualified by the civil faculty, we shall necessarily have to say that that kind of poetry which was placed under the praiseworthy type of sophistic, that is, under that which orders and subordinates appetite to reason, and considered as a game authorized by the civil faculty, has utility as its end.[61]

Plato, says Mazzoni, recognizes this kind of utility in the *Laws*, and, indeed, we may interpret the *Republic* as distinguishing three kinds of poetry as bringing separate utilities to three classes of people: epic poetry, which teaches virtue and glory to soldiers through the examples of great heroes; tragedy, which presents to princes and magistrates and men of

[60] *Ibid.*, sec. 60: "la Poesia è arte Sophistica, e per l'imitatione, che è il suo genere proprio, e per lo credibile, che è il suo soggetto, e per lo diletto, che è il suo fine, poiche per esser sotto quel genere, per esser intorno a quel soggetto, e per rimirare quel fine, viene astretta molte volte a dar luogo al falso."

[61] *Ibid.*, secs. 73–74: "Nel primo modo [il diletto] è fine di quella Poesia, che fù collocata sotto alla Sophistica degna di biasmo, poich'ella è tale, che disordina l'appetito con smoderato diletto rendendolo in tutto ribello dalla ragione, e recando insieme nocumento, e danno al viuere virtuoso.... Ma se si considera questo diletto, inquanto ch'egli è regolato, e qualificato dalla facoltà ciuile, ci bisognerà necessariamente dire, ch'egli sia indirizzato all'vtile, e conseguentemente, che quella specie di Poesia, che fù riposta sotto la Sophistica lodeuole, cioè sotto quella, ch'ordina, e sottopone l'appetito alla ragione, considerata come gioco qualificato dalla facoltà ciuile habbia per fine l'vtile."

power the terrible cases of the fallen great, so that they may seek moderation and remain submissive to the laws; and comedy, which consoles the middle and lower classes for their mediocre fortune by showing them actions which end happily (sec. 80).[62] These various types of utility are achieved through the arousing of the passions, and hence the further question arises as to whether it is legitimate to proceed in this fashion. Plato condemns all arousal of the passions in Books II and III of the *Republic*, as does Proclus. But Mazzoni contends that the method of poetry is acceptable here, provided that the proper passions be properly moved; and he says that Plato's true intention was to condemn the stimulation of certain passions while allowing others to be exploited in the proper circumstances. Book VII of the *Laws* is cited in support of the latter contention.

Part II of the *Difesa* repeats many of these ideas, develops some of them, and seeks to apply them practically to the defence of the *Divina Commedia*. The whole argument over imitation, for example, is reopened and expanded. New distinctions are added: The poet does not imitate when he speaks in his own voice—or, if he does, it is to an inferior degree. But imitation is nevertheless present whenever events are related that did not really happen, since verisimilitude is an imitation of the truth (pp. 133–34). Mazzoni treats the question of the passions, of virtue and vice, at great length in Book IV, where he is discussing mores and character in Dante's poem. He sets up a contrast between the position of Plato, who does not admit any representation of wickedness or of bad character, and that of Aristotle, who admits the whole range of passions. Both seem to him to be "right"; for Plato's point of view is supported by reason and Aristotle's by the practice of the poets (see Chapter I, p. 25 for a translation of the passage). The difference between the two is explainable to Mazzoni (as I have already noted) by the fact that Plato is speaking in terms of an ideal republic where there is no need for the poets "since its citizens learned everything that was necessary in the civil education instituted by him, and moreover lived with the obstinate wish not to allow any kind of pleasure to enter into that Republic, knowing that pleasures are linked together in such a way that one necessarily draws another after it."[63] Whereas Aristotle's state was a practical one following the common practice of men. As for those critics who attempt to defend poetry on the basis of allegorical interpretations, Mazzoni rejects their argument:

... this defence should not be admitted as a good one, since there is too great danger that honest things will come to be expressed in ugly and dishonest words. Without doubt, appetite, by its nature inclined to evil, would stop at the outer

---

[62] The usefulness of tragedy and comedy is discussed later in Bk. II, chap. 9.

[63] *Della difesa*, Pt. II (1688), p. 5: "essendoche i suoi Cittadini imparauano tutto quello ch'era necessario nella educatione ciuile instituita da lui, e nel resto viueuano ostinati di non voler lasciar entrare in quella Republica sorte alcuna di piacere, sapendo, che i diletti sono di modo insieme concatenati, che vno si tira dietro l'altro necessariamente."

covering as at a thing adapted to its pleasure, and in this way it would rather receive harm from the apparent meaning than benefit from the hidden one.[64]

There is everywhere in Mazzoni's lengthy work a consciousness of the moral problems raised by the art of poetry, undoubtedly because these were the problems raised by some of the critics of Dante. And his appeals to Plato for answers to some of these questions are a part of his determination to seek, in any source whatsoever, the means of defending Dante. I shall indicate the particular character of that defence at the appropriate time.

The range of Platonic "topics" is somewhat extended in the *De re poetica libellus incerti auctoris* (1588), which I have attributed to Federico Ceruti (see Chapter I, p. 11). For not only does Ceruti touch upon such matters as the furor, the defence of poetry, the ban, and the kinds of imitation; he also appeals to Plato for assistance in his classification of the art, which is indeed one of the most interesting contributions of his little treatise. He declares that Plato divides poetry into two kinds:

... one which he calls θεωρική, the other πρακτική; the former treats of God, of the celestial creatures, of heaven, of the constellations, of the stars, and of divine things; the latter, instead, of men, of animate beings, of countries, cities, mores, laws, in a word, of all things human insofar as it is proper and possible to do so. From which division we conclude readily that the material of poetry is very vast and extends everywhere, and that it undertakes to treat in verse all human and divine matters.[65]

Ceruti's willingness to accept the inclusion of divine matters among the subjects of poetry indicates his general position: he is a defender and an apologist, and he selects from Plato those texts and passages which provide praise for the art of poetry. Thus in his first chapter, "De poetices vtilitate ac dignitate," he includes Plato among the writers who have declared poetry to be "not only pleasant and useful for young people, but indeed necessary," and he cites the *Minos* on the poets as "interpreters of the gods, so long as they use poetry chastely and modestly to direct the minds of the young to every virtue."[66] The art itself is divine, and Ceruti traces its

---

[64] *Ibid.*, p. 22: "Ma questa difesa non si si deue ammettere per buona, essendoche troppo gran pericolo è dell'honesta, ch'ella venga dichiarta [sic] con brutte, e dishoneste parole. E senza dubbio l'appetito inclinato per sua natura al male si fermarebbe nella scorza di fuori, come in cosa appropriata al suo diletto, e in questo modo più tosto riceuerebbe nocumento dal senso manifesto, che giouamento dall'occulto."

[65] *De re poetica* (1588), pp. 9–10: "vna, quae θεωρική altera, quae πρακτική vocatur; illa de Deo, de coelitibus, coelo, syderibus, astris, rebusque diuinis; haec autem, de homine, de animantibus, regionibus, ciuitatibus, moribus, legibus, denique de rebus omnibus humanis, quoad licet, & fieri potest, pertractat. Ex qua diuisione facile colligimus, poetices materiam amplissimam esse, & per omnia vagari; & quae res diuinas, & humanas carmine tractandas suscipiat."

[66] *Ibid.*, p. 1: "non modo iuuenibus iucundam, & vtilem; sed etiam necessariam esse ducant" and "interpretes deorum appellat, modo poeticen castè, & pudicè ad formandos animos ad omnem honestatem, iuuenibus tradant."

origins to Moses, Noah, Abraham, and other holy men who used it for religious purposes. In fact, the term "divine" appears in almost every description of the poet or of the content of the art offered by Ceruti (v. p. 6 for several examples). It follows almost necessarily that the ends of the art will be useful ends, and Ceruti multiplies his statements of its utility. In Chapter VII, "Quod sit poetae officium, et quis finis," he states the ends thus: "to teach men by means of precepts and instructions, to bring them to wisdom, to drive the shadows of ignorance from the minds and souls of men is a difficult and sublime thing which requires labor and industry."[67] The formulation is more specific in Chapter XI, "Quantum ex poetices facultate emolumentum percipiatur" (I give the chapter titles because they reveal so much about the general approach):

Two extremely important things happen to those who are taught by poetry: for first, indeed, it serves by that restraint of the soul and it teaches that no man should accuse his own fortune harshly and boldly; and, on the other hand, it opens the way to magnanimity, by means of which you may so prepare your mind against all the accidents of fortune that you will not be dejected, or perturbed, or excessively moved by anything.[68]

Earlier in the same chapter Ceruti points to the special efficacy of poetry in this kind of instruction, since its pleasurable aspects have a ready appeal to the young. For these reasons, he believes that poetry is eminently useful to the state (v. Plato in Book II of the *Laws*) and that far from being banned from the state, it should be encouraged and cultivated. If one ask why Plato should have condemned it in the *Republic*, the answer is that he condemned only evil and wicked poets, not the art as a whole (p. 16). In order to escape such blame, the poet must praise virtue, decry vice, follow decorum, and provide the kinds of instruction which will serve its ends.

The other topics are treated in a fairly perfunctory manner. It is notable that when Ceruti discusses the nature of the poet in Chapter VI ("Poeta naturane, an arte, an vtraque fiat"), he makes no mention of the divine furor, putting the question rather in terms of the Horatian art-versus-nature. He mentions the divine afflatus only in Chapter IX, where he uses it to explain the powerful effect which poetry has upon the minds of its audience. As for imitation, he reflects the Platonic tradition only in the distinction of narrative, dramatic, and mixed representation; but he does so in such a way that he might easily be reflecting Aristotle or the ancient, anonymous tradition of the rhetoricians. In general, he is a theorist who

[67] *Ibid.*, p. 8: "pręceptis, & institutis homines docere, ad sapientiam erudire, ignorantiae tenebras ex hominum mentibus, atque animis depellere, arduum quiddam, & sublime est, & quod magnum requirit studium, atque industriam."

[68] *Ibid.*, p. 17: "Duo pręclara illis contingunt, qui poetica instituuntur: primum enim ea moderatione animi famulatur, docetque, nulli moleste, ac temere fortunam exprobandam; alterum viam struit ad magnanimitatem, qua ad omnes fortunę casus ita componas animum, vt non deijciaris, ac conturberis, nihilque commouearis."

has Plato's writings fairly constantly in mind, but who selects from them those dicta that would seem to rank him with the anti-Platonist defenders of poetry rather than with the Platonic objectors.

Giovambattista Strozzi (the Younger) concerns himself with a much more restricted subject in his paper *Se sia bene il servirsi delle favole delli antichi*, delivered before the Accademia Fiorentina in 1588. For the "favole" of which he speaks are the ancient myths concerning the gods, and his inquiry centers about the possibility or the desirability of Christian poets' using these myths in modern times. The work thus belongs to the literature that considers poetry from a religious point of view. Strozzi's first care, therefore, is to summarize the arguments of those who would deny the use of that mythology. These men, he says, argue that no religion can permit the publication of myths contrary to its own beliefs, that the Christian religion especially outlaws all fables, that these fables cannot possibly produce the effects desired by poetry because they are known to be false and incredible, and that they cannot but have a harmful effect upon the ignorant multitude. But such arguments, Strozzi insists, do not carry conviction, and critics like Castelvetro have already refuted them. He himself proceeds to counter them. First, he says, the Christian religion does not specifically ban the use of fables and even admits such mythical personages as nymphs and fates. Second, even though these myths are recognized as being entirely false, they may still be effective in poetry, and not only because they give pleasure, but also because they may arouse a whole variety of emotions. This comes about because the actions represented are what move the audience, not the names of the persons performing the actions. Third, the multitude remains in no danger from contact with these pagan tales; for no Christian, however simple, will ever take the pagan gods to be true and real, and hence his religious beliefs will not be imperiled. Since these myths are now so widely disseminated as to be known by all, it would be ridiculous and impossible to try to exclude them. Hence, Strozzi finds it expedient to establish norms for their proper use. They should be introduced only into nonreligious poems, whether their subject be ancient or modern; in religious poems they are presumably replaced by God, the angels, and other supernatural beings. He concludes: "... let us use the myths and the mythical personages not as principal subjects for poems but as intercalation, as ornament, as passing reference in the descriptions of times, in comparisons, in examples, in order to delight, to give recreation to the minds, to cause men to marvel; and let us always direct the whole to our own profit and that of others."[69]

It is perhaps stretching a point to include within the Platonic tradition

---

[69] In *Orazioni et altre prose* (1635), pp. 137–38: "servianci delle fauole, e de fauolosi non per suggetto principale, ma per framesso, per condimento, per passaggio nelle descrittioni de tempi, nelle comparationi, negl'esempli, per dilettare, per recrear gl'animi, per eccitar marauiglia, e'l tutto indrizziamo sempre à giouamento nostro, e altrui."

Giovanni Mario Verdizzotti's treatise *Della narratione poetica* (1588). It might perhaps have been just as well classified among the rhetorical documents studied in Chapter VI. I have placed it here since it belongs (vaguely perhaps) in the long series of discussions about the kinds of imitation and their subdivisions. Verdizzotti is not interested, as were Plato and so many others, in the major classification of narrative, dramatic, and mixed modes of representation; he is concerned exclusively with narration. This he divides into four kinds: the direct ("retta"), the semidirect ("quasi retta"), the oblique ("obliqua"), and the semioblique ("quasi obliqua"). In direct narration the poet himself relates events with all their accompaniments; in semidirect narration, he introduces another person who relates such events, as, for example, when Aeneas tells his story in Books II and III of the *Aeneid*. In oblique narration, things are said to have been said by a third person who is not himself introduced as a speaker. And in semioblique narration no person at all is introduced, but stories are told by means of depictions in painting, sculpture, embroidery, and so forth. Alongside this classification, Verdizzotti makes a number of remarks which indicate clearly his conception of the art of poetry. The method of direct narration is that of the historian or orator; but poetry differs from these

... in the manner of discourse, which is in verse, with a greater and freer abundance of figures, of thought as well as of words, than is found in either of the other two; and in the excess in quality of the virtues and of the vices and of all the other things which he explains and demonstrates in the actions of the persons introduced in his poem, as for example an excessive strength, an excessive wickedness, an excessive prudence, an excessive madness, love, beauty, of places or of persons, and other things of this kind meant to arouse the marvelous which accompanies the particulars.[70]

Semidirect narration is peculiarly poetic in quality, since it is "all imitation" —so much so that it may not be used by the historian or the orator. So also for the semioblique form, purely poetic since it is imitative. It is such narratives as these that give the poet his particular character and his works their special charm. Verdizzotti cites the case of Vergil's summary, at the beginning of the *Aeneid*, of what was to take place:

... this is a kind of artistic narration and one which is completely poetic since it is proper to the poet alone; for he is not allowed to pass beyond the limits of the single action which he proposes to treat. If he observes this rule, the action will be treated by him as a poet, not as an historian. For this manner of proceeding is the only thing which distinguishes him from the historian and the orator; and

---

[70] *Della narratione poetica* (1588), pp. 5–6: "per la maniera di dire, che è in verso, con maggior e piu licentiosa copia di figure, sì di sentenze, come di parole, che non ha lo stile di questo, ò di quello: & per l'eccesso in qualità delle virtù, e de i vitij, & di tutte l'altre cose, che egli spiega, e dimostra nelle attioni delle persone introdotte nel suo poema: come sarebbe à dire, vna eccessiua fortezza, una eccessiua viltà, vna eccessiua prudenza, vno eccessiuo furore, amore, bellezza, di luoghi, ò di persone, & altre cose di questa sorte per far nascer la merauiglia accessoria de i particolari."

through this way of proceeding we may learn how to constitute the true definition of the poetic art.[71]

The poetic art would thus seem to consist, for Verdizzotti, in four qualities: imitation, the representation of a single action, an abundance of figures and ornaments (including verse), and a superior or excessive degree of all the characteristics represented by the poet. Such a definition as this, as I have already intimated, is very close to the formulations of the rhetoricians and of the Horatian theorists.

GIOSEPPE MALATESTA (1589)

Although it belongs primarily to the documents concerning the dispute over Ariosto, Gioseppe Malatesta's *Della nuova poesia* (1589) is sufficiently involved in the discussion of the ends of poetry to merit treatment here. Through much of the dialogue, the main interlocutor, Sperone Speroni, insists so constantly that the end of poetry is delight alone that one wonders whether other possible ends will be considered at all. He defines the subject matter of poetry as "all pleasurable things treated through imitation" and explains the "dilettabili" in this way: ". . . although Poetry with a generous hand takes of all things, nevertheless these are useful to her or not to the extent to which they are pleasurable or not."[72] Art must direct all its dogmas and precepts toward the achieving of this pleasure (p.110), and "the end of poetry, if we are to speak the truth, is nothing else but delight."[73] Monsignor Dandino, however, raises the question of utility, and this leads to a full-scale consideration of the ends of poetry. Speroni recognizes the possibility of three solutions: (1) utility as the end, served by pleasure; (2) utility and pleasure as joint and equal ends; (3) pleasure alone as the end. To the first he objects that "giovare" would not be an end peculiar to poetry since it would be shared by other arts; that this would presuppose the possibility of poetry without delight, whereas no such exists; and that the presence of imitation, the form and soul of poetry, necessarily involves the presence of pleasure. To the second he objects that it is impossible for a single thing to have more than one end. The third solution is thus the proper one, and he contends that all the means of poetry are proportioned to the end of pleasure. Aristotle, Quintilian, and Cicero, he says, all support this theory.

---

[71] *Ibid.*, pp. 11–12: "questa è vna specie di narratione artificiosa, & tutta poetica: come solo propria del Poeta; alquale non è lecito passar i termini dell'vnica da lui proposta attione. Laquale esso così facendo vien da lui trattata, come poeta, non come historico. Percioche questa maniera di fare è quella sola, per laquale egli si distingue dall'historico & dall'Oratore: & per questa via di procedere si uiene in conoscimento di constituire la vera diffinitione dell' arte poetica."

[72] *Della nuova poesia* (1589), pp. 109–10: "tutte le cose dilettabili trattate con imitatione" and "se ben la Poesia con ampia mano piglia da tutte le cose, nondimeno elle tanto fanno, ò non fanno per lei, quanto sono delettabili, ò non sono."

[73] *Ibid.*, p. 119: "il fin della Poesia, secondo il vero parlando, non è altro, che la dilettatione." See also p. 150.

Does this mean that the end of utility is to be completely denied to the art of poetry? In the course of the discussion, Malatesta admits not only that useful ends may be served, but also that they are desirable. He first admits that "giovamento" or "documento" may be an accidental concomitant of the pleasure, all the while insisting that a poet may do harm and still be a good poet. The second admission is more serious: at times, he says, arts may have two ends, one intrinsic and the other extrinsic; so for poetry, "which proposes for itself, indeed, a proper end, which is to imitate elegantly in order to delight; but frequently another extrinsic end follows this one, namely that of profit."[74] The poet achieves his proper end through pleasure only; but he may also participate in the general end proposed by Aristotle for all the arts, that is, to help men to achieve human happiness:

> Whence Poetry, which is not the least among the arts, wished to have a part along with the others in this happiness of ours, and, therefore, resolved to bring profit to the human species insofar as that was possible, she conceived the idea of directing that pleasure of hers in some way to our utility and profit; and thus by means of imitation, of fiction, and of verse, which naturally delight us, she tried to unroll before us such things and subjects as might bring us a considerable utility. . . . under the outer bark of the fables are hidden and covered many mystical and allegorical meanings, all directed toward our good and instruction.[75]

Follows a conventional praise of poetry—with a caution, however, that the poet should not allow such concerns to take precedence over his primary end, which is to give pleasure. Inevitably, before the conclusion of the dialogue, the question is asked why Plato should have banished the poets if they are useful in the ways indicated. Scipione Gonzaga undertakes the explanation. After examining the usual arguments, he presents his own conclusion about Plato: ". . . his intention is not to wish that the poets should be exiled and driven out absolutely as poets, but only with respect to the guardians."[76] The fault is thus in the weakness of the audience, not in the poetic art; and the passage ends with a long defence of the latter. Malatesta's position thus develops from one in which there would seem to be no evidence of Platonism, through one in which the Horatian thesis is essentially approved (as interpreted by certain theorists, at least), to one in which Plato himself is made to be a defender of the utility of the art.

---

[74] *Ibid.*, p. 189: "la qual si propon bene un fin proprio, che è di imitare acconciamente; per dilettare, ma a questo segue molte uolte un' altro fine estrinsico, che è del giouamento."

[75] *Ibid.*, p. 190: "Onde la Poesia, che pur trà le Arti non è infima, volle auer parte, come le altre, in questa beatitudine nostra, & perciò risoluta di giouare, in quanto per lei si potesse, alla specie humana, imaginossi d'indrizzare in qualche modo quella sua dilettatione all'vtilità, & giouamento nostro, & così con la imitatione, con la fintione, & col verso, che naturalmente ci dilettano, si sforzò di andarci spiegando cose, & soggetti tali, che potessero apportarci non picciola utilità. . . . sotto alla scorza delle fauole stanno uelati, & coperti molti sensi mistici, & allegorici tutti indrizzati a nostro prò, & ammaestramento."

[76] *Ibid.*, p. 256: "animo suo non è di uoler, che i Poeti siano fuggiti, & discacciati assolutamente come Poeti, ma solo per rispetto delli custodi."

POETIC THEORY

Unlike his fellow Jesuits, Gambara and Panicarola, Francesco Benci spoke out in praise of poetry in two of his *Orationes,* published in 1590, Numbers VI and VII, both entitled "De laudibus poëticae." He does not understand how anybody can attack an art which is "mother of all the virtues and all the arts, sole parent and mistress of our duties and our mores."[77] Rather would he praise it for its service to mankind in the past—"it taught men to moderate their passions, restrain their desires, control their impulses; to hate the vices and embrace the virtues; to have knowledge and wisdom of all things"—and for the ends which it still pursues; for the poets

> ... are totally dedicated to the praise of good deeds and the blame of bad ones, by the magnification of any glory and infamy whatsoever; and by doing these things they both introduce the virtues into the souls of men and draw out of them the vices, to their very roots; and they produce men wholly lacking in greed, and wholly deserving of every honor and praise.[78]

The effectiveness of poetry, ascribable to its pleasurable accompaniments and to the ease with which it is remembered, is enhanced in certain cases by the knowledge that the events recounted are true—so for the Old and the New Testaments, which have religious as well as ethical uses. For all these reasons, Benci believes that Plato's ban was meant to affect only false poets who used the art as a disguise for their wickedness and that Plato himself recognized and recommended the pedagogical possibilities of the art.

In the *Oratio VII,* Benci passes on to a comparison of poetry with its sister arts of painting, music, and divination. As compared with the first, poetry is definitely superior: painting merely gives a visual image of things, to which poetry adds character, attitudes, disposition, and the deeds, words, and counsels of men, as well as the sound of the actions presented (p. 110). Music moves the passions; but poetry does so better, since its verses not only move the soul but "impel men to every kind of virtue, deter them from vice, and are very efficacious in exercising and sharpening their minds."[79] Poetry is thus itself a kind of divine force, as useful for the inculcation of piety and religious observance as for the direction of our mundane lives. Benci's praise of the art is thus complete and unreserved, and indeed he commends it warmly for that quality which its Platonic opponents most frequently denied it, its service of religion.

[77] *Orationes* (1590 ed.), p. 88: "in procreatricem illam virtutum omnium & artium, in vnicam officiorum morumque parentem & magistram contumeliose inuehuntur."
[78] *Ibid.,* pp. 89, 94: "coërcere cupiditates, impetus frangere, detestari vitia, amplexari virtutes, rerum denique omnium ... cognitionem ac scientiam tenere"; and "Toti sunt in benefactorum commendatione, maleficiorum vituperatione, gloriae cuiuslibet atque infamiae amplificatione: quod cum faciunt, & virtutes in animis inserunt, & vitia radicitus extrahunt: & homines omni carentes cupiditate, omni honore ac laude dignissimos efficiunt."
[79] *Ibid.,* p. 112: "homines ad omne virtutum genus impellunt: deterrent à vitio, & in excitandis acuendisque ingenijs nimium quantum valent."

ANTONIO POSSEVINO (1593)

With Antonio Possevino's *Tractatio de poësi et pictura ethnica, humana, et fabulosa collata cum vera, honesta, et sacra*, we rejoin the ultra-Catholic, Jesuit tradition of Gambara and Panicarola, and we encounter one of those documents which, if they do not dominate the last years of the Cinquecento, at least give them a special character. The treatise, published in 1593, is also in a sense a reply to Benci, whom it mentions. And while it contradicts Benci, refusing to accept his praise of the Greek and Latin poets (the ones whom Possevino calls "ethnic"), it does not go so far as Gambara and Panicarola in their condemnation of the whole art of poetry. Possevino's position is simply stated: he approves of the art because of its potential utility; but this must be manifested always in glorification of Christianity, which means that only Christian poetry is acceptable; thus all the poetry of pagan antiquity is condemned and discarded. Although he begins with a statement of his intention to treat both poetry and painting (announced also in the title), Possevino devotes himself almost exclusively to poetry, only the last six chapters bearing upon the ends and techniques of painting. The two arts, he says, are alike in their ends, different in their means:

> The whole effect of poetry and of painting is reduced to two things, teaching and delighting; and what poetry achieves by means of narrations, episodes, eulogies, tropes, and other such means, painting also achieves, which by using colors, catches the ideas from things themselves, or else as these should be, [and] by which ideas it imitates lines, light, dark, and background.[80]

Of these two ends, the primary one is instruction, and to it the poet should bend all his effort; pleasure is secondary. The specific lessons taught are variously stated:

> ... through a knowledge of natural things and of mores, and through a demonstration of the virtues, men are made in some unknown way to be greater and more excellent; and ... from both of these things are derived a greatness of soul against adversity and against the weaknesses inherent in human affairs, strength against the fear of death, temperance against lustful desires, constancy in the Catholic religion against all heresies.[81]

From Lucretius one may learn lessons "on the contempt for death, on avoiding love, on controlling the desires, on calming the emotions and achieving tranquillity of the soul; about sleep, about the rising and setting

---

[80] *Tractatio* (1593 ed.), p. 1v: "tota vis Poeseos, atque Picturae duobus absoluitur docendo, & delectando; quodque, Poesis efficit narrationibus, episodijs, encomijs, tropis, & eiusmodi alijs; idem Pictura facit; quae coloribus vtens, ex ipsis rebus, aut quales hae esse deberent, capessit notiones, quibus lineamenta, lucem, vmbram, recessus imitatur." (Page numbers represent my own counting.)

[81] *Ibid.*, p. 3v: "è rerum naturalium cognitione, morumque, ac virtutum explicatione homines efficiantur, nescio quo modo, maiores, atque elatiores: & ... ex vtraque re animi magnitudo contra aduersa, rerumque humanarum imbecillitatem, fortitudo contra mortis timorem, temperantia contra libidinem, constantia Catholicae Religionis contra haereses comparetur."

of the stars, about the eclipses of the sun and the moon"—and so forth.[82] Man will therefore learn from poetry divers lessons which fall into the general categories of ethical, religious, and scientific.

The fact that the lessons are of so many kinds leads Possevino to a conception and a classification of poetry that are not conventional for his century. In the first place, he rejects the idea that imitation is necessary for poetry. Rather than accepting the authority of Aristotle, he turns to Lambin, who declares that the distinguishing features of poetry are not only imitation, but also rhythm, figures, certain kinds of extraordinary words, and the divine genius of the poet. The purpose of Possevino's rejection of imitation is to permit the inclusion, among the kinds of poetry, of compositions in verse which are not necessarily imitations but which serve the ends already noted. Possevino proceeds to his classification by two steps. First, he cites Plato's division of poetry into true and false, the true poetry being that which delights by teaching decent things and which has a laudable subject matter, the false being that which insinuates obscene and wicked things by means of its attractions. It is this latter kind, incidentally, which Plato is said to have banished from his *Republic* (p. 3). True poetry then subdivides into the following categories: (1) divine, of which Moses and David may be proposed as the best examples; (2) natural, represented by Empedocles, Lucretius, and Fracastoro; and (3) moral, exemplified by Phocylides and Pythagoras. The last category also includes economic and political poetry and all such genres as tragedy, comedy, the epic, the lyric, and the epigram when they are made to lead to virtue and to exclude vice (p. 3). It will be noted that this is a mixed classification, based partly upon subject matter and partly upon effect.

Obviously, the only poetry which Possevino cares to condone is the true, and his preferred category is the religious. Sacred poetry is the best of all: Moses, David, the Psalmists.

> ... the other poems, which consist only of fanciful wrappings, are fables rather than poems.... Moreover, the utility of every honest form of poetry is great and great its advantage for learning things, so that he spoke true who called it the nurse and the teacher of the minds of the young. Certainly the very movement and rhythm of the verses, since it attracts the soul, so impresses itself upon the memory, making the mind receptive through its diversified charm, that it causes the mind almost never to forget what it has perceived so well. Moreover, it also incites to the praise of God's work and is a great solace for setting aside one's cares.[83]

---

[82] *Ibid.*, p. 11: "de morte contemnenda, de amore fugiendo, de coercendis cupiditatibus, de sedandis animorum motibus, de mentis tranquillitate comparanda, de somno, de ortu, obituque syderum, de Solis, & Lunae defectu...."

[83] *Ibid.*, p. 3v: "vt reliqua Poemata, quae tantum ex fabulosis inuolucris constant, fabulae potius sint, quàm Poemata.... Ceterum honestae omnis Poeseos ingens vtilitas est, atque ad res ediscendas percommoda: vt vera dixerit, qui eam adolescentis animi nutricem, & alumnam vocauit. Certè ipse carminum flexus, & numerus, vt animum allicit, sic memoriae

Possevino is hard put to it to find modern examples of the kind of poetry which he recommends; but he nevertheless cites and quotes a number of sacred poems, songs, epigrams, elegies, and epics written in recent times. Above all he admires, in the category of epics, the *Triumphus Christi ascendentis in caelum* of Macarius Mutius, which he reprints *in toto* as an example to future poets.

It will be remembered, however, that Possevino's primary interest in this treatise is in "ethnic" or pagan poetry, and hence he does not fail to inquire to what extent that poetry is acceptable and useful to Christians. He finds in the ancient poets certain passages stating that there is only one God and rejecting the numerous pagan gods; these would be useful. He finds it possible, through allegorical and Christological interpretations, to discover in the Greeks and Romans certain adumbrations of the Christian mysteries and to transform an ode of Pindar or a song of Sappho into a religious poem. Most of all, he extracts from the works of antiquity innumerable passages—proverbs, "centones," speeches—which contain the kind of moral instruction of which he approves.

This procedure, by selection, by extraction, by interpretation, exemplifies what Possevino states theoretically to be the proper use of the ancient poets. In Chapter IV, "Usus qualis, ac fructus è poetis ethnicis. Adduntur cautiones," he outlines that theory, introducing it thus:

> In truth we must say first that from most of the pagan poets may be learned many things which pertain to the investigation of natural phenomena and to the forming of character. Similarly, from them may be derived the style and the correct use of words either of Greek and Latin or of the other languages. But one must know how to choose and apply generally cautions which were taught by the pagans themselves, but still more profoundly and solidly by the church fathers, with respect to this matter.[84]

The theory is stated in a number of precepts: (1) one must choose carefully the authors to be read; (2) one must be prepared to resist the false teachings of the pagan poets, to remove their errors, to turn them to our own purposes; (3) rather than translate the obscene poets and surround them with critical apparatus, one should expurgate them and publish selections only; (4) from the good poets one should select passages on such useful matters as descriptions of wars, comparisons, honest and grave sententiae. In a general way, the criteria are religious orthodoxy and moral acceptability: whatever would seem to praise or even recognize the pagan gods is

---

haeret, variaque iucunditate mentem permulcens facit, ne penè vnquam ea, quae rectè percipit, obliuiscatur. Quin & incitat ad laudanda Dei opera, magnoque est ad remissionem curarum leuamento."

[84] *Ibid.*, p. 3v: "Id vero ante omnia fatendum est, è plerisque Poetis Ethnicis multa intelligi posse, quae ad rerum naturas vestigandas, & ad mores efformandos pertinent: Stylum item, ac verborum proprietatem siue Graecae, ac Latinae; siue aliarum linguarum ex ijs posse comparari: delectum tamen eorum habendum, & cautiones omnino adhibendas, quas ipsimet Ethnici, sed altius, atque solidius Patres hac de re docuerunt."

to be excluded, whatever might seem to prophesy Christianity may be retained; whatever is lewd, obscene, demoralizing must go, whatever tends to inculcate the proper moral lessons may remain. Two lesser criteria are also present: we may read those parts of ancient works which contain useful linguistic and stylistic models and those which impart information about the natural world. In terms of these criteria, Possevino makes a rapid examination of the principal writers of antiquity and provides for each a criticism and a commentary.

These latter ideas demand a modification of my original statement that "all the poetry of pagan antiquity will be condemned and discarded." Condemnation and discard will apply only to the poems as wholes, or to certain poets from whom nothing may be salvaged. For most works, carefully selected sections or lines will be salvable and what Possevino proposes is a kind of anthology or *morceaux choisis* of Greek and Roman writings. A few works may be totally conserved, but only when surrounded by the proper commentaries, which will assure correct interpretation. In a word, those remnants of ancient literature which correspond to the doctrinal, ethical, scientific, and stylistic principles of the Christian critic—who is also a Christian theologian—will be permitted the modern reader. The basic Platonism of the approach is apparent; indeed, this fundamental way of looking at poetry in a context of theological and ethical standards is much more significant, in the case of Possevino, then the fact that he occasionally refers to the divine furor. It is also apparent in his review of ancient and modern writings on the art of poetry itself, in which he lauds or condemns theorists on the basis of their conformity to his own standards.

Allegorical interpretation of the kind suggested by Possevino for religious reasons and by other defenders of poetry for other reasons is judged to be entirely inexcusable by Fabrizio Beltrami in his *Sopra l'allegoria del poeta nella sua favola*. The treatise, found in manuscript in MS D. VII, 10 of the Biblioteca Comunale of Siena and accompanied by a letter dated June 22, 1594, is an answer to statements made by Francesco Patrizi and Jacopo Mazzoni on the subject of allegory. The denial of all allegory by Beltrami is based upon several simple premisses: poetry is written specifically for the common people, who would be incapable of penetrating beneath the surface to seek out hidden meanings; allegory supposes an impossible external action and a possible internal action, whereas the general theory of poetry admits only the possible; the admission of allegory involves permission of a plurality of actions, which is against the poetic art. Plato is cited as the authority for the first of these premisses; in the *Gorgias*, says Beltrami, Plato declared that "Poesia est res popularis," and similar statements are to be found in the *Phaedo* and in Book X of the *Republic*. In Book II of the latter, moreover, Plato prohibited all things said in the form of fictions, either allegorically or nonallegorically. The reasons are clear: not only will no two men ever come to the same interpretation of a given work, but rarely will anybody be found who will have the necessary intellectual qualities to find a proper meaning:

... if we were to seek this credibility of poetry in allegorical meaning, we should be forced to confess that poetry, insofar as it is an imitation, was not given to us as a pastime, as Plato said; since allegory demands acuteness of mind, profundity of learning, variety of knowledge, a most happy memory, and, finally, exquisite judgment in order to fit the allegorical sense to the literal sense. And this effort is fatiguing even to men having these qualities; how much more so will it not be to those who are moderately educated, or to those who are completely ignorant? And that these latter are the audience of the poets is confirmed by Plato in Book II of the *Republic* and by Strabo in the first Book.[85]

Thus the ignorance or the incapacity of the audience, so frequently alleged as an argument against the art as a whole, is here adduced specifically as an argument against allegory.

For the second of the premisses the authority is Aristotle. If poetry is an imitation of an action, one of its conditions is that this action be necessary, probable, credible—and not only in the intrinsic meaning but also in its superficial expression. We cannot, therefore, accept the basic assumption of allegorical writing, that is, that something which appears on the surface as being impossible and untrue should be, within, both possible and true. For the third premiss the authority is partly Aristotle but mainly the reason (thus completing the trilogy of Plato, Aristotle, and the reason, invoked at the beginning). Allegory, say some (and the commentary of Eustathius on the *Iliad* is cited), may be present either in the main plot—which constitutes the soul of the poem—or in the episodes, principal or secondary. But whether it occurs in the one or in the other, it amounts to a second action, and thus the unity of action required by reason is destroyed. Hence it was that Aristotle did not even mention the possibility of allegory in the *Poetics*, and by his silence condemned it. Plato on the audience, Aristotle on credibility, and the reason on unity of action all unite to outlaw a system of interpretation (and perhaps of writing) that is upheld in vain by such critics as Patrizi and Mazzoni, by such poets as Tasso in the *Allegoria* appended to the *Gerusalemme Liberata*.

TORQUATO TASSO (1594)

Tasso himself is the author of a treatise on epic poetry in which many of the problems debated by Possevino, Beltrami, and others of the period are

[85] MS Bibl. Com. Siena D.VII, 10, fols. 64v–65: "quando si ricercasse questo credibile ne senso allegorico, saremmo forzati confessare, che la poesia inquanto è immitatione, non ci fusse stata data per passatempo, si come si diceua da Plat. ricercando l'Allegoria, acutezza d'ingegno, profondità di dottrina, uarietà di scienze, felicissima memoria, e finalmente giuditio esquisito in saper accomodare il senso allegorico al senso letterale; e questo ricerca anco fatica in cosi fatti huomini; quanto maggiore la ricercherà ne' mediocremente letterati, o negl' idioti afatto? e che questi sieno gl'ascoltatori de' Poeti, e Plat. nel 2°. della rep. e Strabone nel primo lo confermano."

treated in some detail. The *Discorsi del poema heroico* was not published until 1594, but it was probably written between 1575 and 1580; it repeats, in many respects, the materials included in the *Discorsi dell'arte poetica* of 1587. The Platonic reference is perhaps most distinct in Tasso's consideration of the ends of poetry. I have already pointed out in Chapter I (p. 32) that in classifying poetry among the arts he subordinated it to politics because he regarded utility as the primary end, pleasure as auxiliary. In a general way, the highest end of poetry is "to benefit men through the example of human actions," and Tasso would therefore define poetry as "an imitation of human actions made for the instruction of life."[86] More particularly, epic poetry instructs great men, who seek to conform to its examples, in "the forms of strength, of temperance, of prudence, of justice, of faith, of piety, and of religion, and of every other virtue."[87] It should thus be defined as "an imitation of an illustrious, great, and powerful action, made by narrating with the highest form of verse, in order to move men's minds through the marvelous and to bring profit in this way."[88] Indeed, the end will be differently stated for each genre: tragedy will purge by means of terror and pity; comedy will use laughter to make men ashamed to do ugly things.

There is a sense, however, in which the functions of the poet are more noble than the mere providing of examples or demonstrating of actions. Like the theologian, he is a maker of images presented for the contemplation of men; this makes of him a kind of theologian—rather of the mystical than of the scholastic strain: "... the act of leading men to the contemplation of divine things and of arousing them in this way by means of images, as the mystical theologian and the poet do, is a much more noble operation than teaching by means of demonstrations, which is the function of the scholastic theologian."[89] For this reason the poet should be held in high esteem, and his art should occupy a more elevated position than that assigned to it by such divines as St. Thomas. His high calling imposes certain obligations. For one, he must treat only the truth, seeking novelty in form and detail rather than in matter. For another, he must avoid the use of the pagan marvelous and employ only that authorized by Christianity. Here again, the close relationships between the poet, the theologian, and the legislator are apparent:

... the most excellent poem is proper only to the most excellent form of govern-

---

[86] *Poema heroico* [1594], pp. 6–7: "giouare à gli huomini con l'essempio dell'attioni humane" and "imitatione dell'attioni humane fatta per ammaestramento della vita."

[87] *Ibid.*, p. 1: "le forme della fortezza, della temperanza, della prudenza, della giustitia, della fede, della pietà, & della Religione, e d'ogni altra virtù."

[88] *Ibid.*, p. 14: "imitator d'attione illustre, grande, e perfetta fatta, narrando con altissimo verso, affine di muouere gli animi con la marauiglia; e di giouare in questa guisa."

[89] *Ibid.*, pp. 29–30: "il conducere alla contemplatione delle cose diuine & il destare in questa guisa con l'imagini come fà il Theologo mistico, & il Poeta è molto più nobile operatione, che l'ammaestrar con le demostrationi com'è officio del Theologo scolastico."

PLATONISM: TRIUMPH OF CHRISTIANITY

ment. This is the monarchy; but the monarchy cannot be properly governed with a false religion. The true religion is therefore proper to the best monarchy, and where there is false piety or false worship of God there can be no perfection in the prince or in the principality. Therefore poems must also participate in this same imperfection, but the fault is not that of the poetic art but of politics, not of the poet but of the legislator. We conclude, therefore, that no poem is to be praised which is excessively full of prodigies.[90]

The only marvelous that is really acceptable is the Christian marvelous, since actions attributed to God and his ministers—even though they are improbable or impossible—become verisimilar through faith. The opinion of the multitude, to whom poetry is addressed, will accept such actions as true: "One and the same action may therefore be both marvelous and verisimilar: marvelous if one consider it in itself and hemmed in by natural limitations, verisimilar if one consider it separated from such limitations with respect to its cause, which is a supernatural force capable of and accustomed to producing such marvels."[91] This credibility of the Christian marvelous is an additional reason why the epic poet—who seeks always credibility—should by preference choose a Christian subject. He must not use the most sacred of these, nor those of recent times. All other conditions of subject matter derive from these original bases. In all this theorizing of Tasso there is, moreover, a hidden Platonism, to the extent to which he sees behind every poem or every part of a poem an Idea which the poet seeks to imitate through the happy combination of matter and form.

Like Tasso's treatise, Sperone Speroni's *Dialogo dell'historia*, published only in 1596, probably goes back to a much earlier date; I have been unable to find any grounds for assigning an approximate date to it. The *Dialogo* also has certain points of doctrine in common with Tasso. One similarity is in the classification of the art, for Speroni too places it, along with logic, grammar, and rhetoric, under rational philosophy. He also sees it as essentially useful to the state and in the service of politics. Most important of all, he insists that the subject of poetry is truth, not falsehood, and that it derives its materials (as does history) from annals:

... a fable is thus not a lie, as it would seem to be from the meaning of the word itself, but without any doubt the truth, not merely natural and pure and simple

---

[90] *Ibid.*, p. 35: "l'eccellentissimo poema è proprio solamente della eccellentissima forma di gouerno. questa è il Regno, ma il Regno non può esser' ottimamente gouernato con falsa religione. Conuiene adunque all'ottimo Regno la vera religione, & oue sia falsa pietà, e falso culto d'Iddio, non può essere alcuna perfettione nel Principe, ò nel Principato: però i poemi ancora participano dell'istessa imperfettione, ma il difetto non è dell'arte poetica, ma della politica, non del poeta, ma de' legislatori, conchiudiamo dunque, che non si debba lodare alcun poema souerchiamente prodigioso."

[91] *Ibid.*, p. 37: "Puo esser dunque vna medesima attione, e merauigliosa, e verisimile, merauigliosa riguardandola in se stessa e circonscritta dentro à i termini naturali, verisimile considerandola diuisa da questi termini nella sua cagione, laquale è vna virtù sopranaturale possente, & vsata à far simili merauiglie."

truth, standing on its own . . . , but the truth adorned and decorated by certain images which are marvelous imitators of the behavior of the reason, or of the ways of saying or believing things common to some part of the world which in other parts would be held as impious or reputed to be impossible.[92]

Simple truth is found in the annals; noteworthy truth is the matter of history; and noteworthy and marvelous truth is the subject of poetry. What is more, this marvelous aspect is less the product of the action itself or of the persons involved in it than the product of the words, metaphors, epithets, and other decorations used to present them. Poetry rapidly becomes a form of rhetoric. We should note, however, that Speroni encounters the Platonic tradition at several points—political usefulness, ends, truthfulness—without specifically calling upon the authority of Plato or discussing his text; rather, the definite references and borrowings involve Aristotle's *Poetics*.

Almost at the end of the century—so healthy is the tradition—Diomede Borghesi supplies us with another example of the extravagant "defenses of poesy" which had been so frequent in the early years of the Cinquecento and which were to continue as a favorite literary exercise in the Seicento as well. This is his *Oratione intorno a gli onori, et a' pregi della poesia, e della eloquenza* of 1596. Borghesi bases his praise of poetry primarily on the fact that the poetic art is a gift of nature and that natural objects are more excellent than all others. It is the divine furor, without which no amount of industry will avail the poet, that constitutes the natural foundation of the art, the divine furor "which is breathed into our souls miraculously by infinite providence."[93] A second source of eulogy is found in the witness of innumerable philosophers, kings, generals, and others who have either practised the art themselves or praised those who did. For poetry, in spite of what the ignorant may think, contains under the beautiful exterior sound counsels and useful instructions. Both poetry and eloquence are joined in a third form of appreciation, the superiority of their language and reasoning to those of the common people. For all these reasons, Borghesi believes that Plato's ban upon the poet was a restricted one and that the whole art was not blamed for the misdeeds of those who practised it badly; these latter are the wicked and unscrupulous versifiers who wilfully corrupt an innocent citizenry. The citation of poets by Christians, even by the church fathers, and the many religious uses of poetry may be taken as proof that this is a proper interpretation of Plato's meaning. Borghesi's paean of praise comes at the end of his oration: "Poetry, by means of which the

---

[92] In *Dialoghi* (1596), p. 394: "fauola adunque non è menzogna, come ella par nel uocabulo, ma uerità senza fallo, non natural solamente, & pura, & semplice, & per se stante . . ., ma uerità lauorata, & intagliata di alcune imagini imitatrice merauigliose del decoro della ragione, ò del usanza del dirsse [sic], & credere uolgarmente in alcuna parte, del mondo cose, che altroue sarebbono empie tenute, ò riputate impossibili."

[93] *Oratione* (1596), p. 10: "il qual ne gli animi nostri dall'infinita prouidenza miracolosamente si spira."

PLATONISM: TRIUMPH OF CHRISTIANITY

mover of the stars is duly celebrated, is the unique imitator of all things, the moderator of unbridled passions, the teacher of high-minded behavior, the producer of noble actions, the arouser of virtue, the dispenser of praise, the guardian of honor, and the immortal conservator of the memories of other men."[94]

It is perhaps fortunate that the last of the texts to be analyzed in this chapter should represent so typically one of the dominant forms of Cinquecento Platonism. The text is Paolo Beni's *Disputatio in qua ostenditur praestare comoediam atque tragoediam metrorum vinculis soluere* (1600), already studied at some length in Chapter VI (p. 244). It is a typical document in the sense that Beni maintains throughout a fundamentally Platonic attitude—considering poetry in the context of ethical and political criteria—while starting always from an opposite assumption: the ethical and political effects will be desirable. A purely personal note is added in the theory that these effects are desirable (at least for tragedy and comedy) as long as the poems are written in prose, but that undesirable consequences result from the writing of the same forms in verse. It is this latter note that constitutes the originality of the work.

I have already indicated that Beni assumes that the real end of poetry is utility through moral instruction and that pleasure is ancillary to this end. To the passages already cited may be added others which clarify and specify the position. The statement on the relationship between pleasure and utility also reveals Beni's conception of the audience to which tragedy and comedy are addressed:

> For honest utility, . . . not pleasure, is the common and proper end of tragic or comic imitation. Pleasure indeed was sought and obtained in tragedy and comedy with this purpose: that, since naked precepts for living joined with philosophical severity are received and borne with difficulty by the people, they should be seasoned and tempered with a kind of pleasure and agreeableness, as if with salt. . . . Thus certainly the good writers of comedy and of tragedy, in imitation of the expert medic who tempers with sweetness the bitterness of a medicine which would otherwise be distasteful to the palate of the patient, season and mix with pleasure the regulations and precepts for life, in order that—by fooling the palate of the masses as it were revolted—they may give them useful lessons in an agreeable way.[95]

---

[94] *Ibid.*, p. 20: "la Poesia, con la qual degnamente si celebra il mouitor delle Stelle, è singolare imitatrice di qualunque cosa, moderatrice di trasandanti affetti, insegnatrice di generosi costumi, producitrice di nobili operationi, solleuatrice di virtù, dispensatrice di lodi, albergatrice d'onore, e dell'altrui memorie immortal conseruatrice."

[95] *Disputatio* (1600), pp. 4–4*v*: "Etenim honesta vtilitas . . . non voluptas est germanus finis ac proprius Comicae aut Tragicae imitationis. Voluptas enim in Tragoedia & Comoedia eo consilio quaesita & comparata est, vt quoniam nuda vitae praecepta philosophicae seueritati admista difficilè excipiuntur a popularibus aut sustinentur, voluptate quadam ac iucunditate tanquam sale condiantur ac temperentur. . . . Sic sanè bonus Comicus & Tragicus periti instar Medici qui Pharmaci amaritudinem dulci temperat, ac fastidiosum aegroti palatum fallit, vitae officia atque praecepta voluptate condit ac temperat, vt vulgi palatum quasi nauseantem fallens, vtilitatem illi cum suauitate propinet."

For such an audience as this, an excess of pleasure can only be dangerous, and Beni takes a stand very close to that of Plato: "They [verses and song] soften our souls and destroy all the sinews of manliness; finally, in the guise of liberal education they can bring us much harm and evil."[96] Thus, the question is raised as to whether the whole art should be condemned because of these potential dangers. Beni cites Cicero's *Pro Archia* for a moderate position and then passes on to a discussion of Plato's banishment of the poets. He believes that if we read Plato well we will find that he disapproves only of certain genres and that in sum his argument authorizes that of Beni himself:

> If one read him more carefully, he will understand that he is not hostile to the lyric poets or to any others who are not bound by the law of imitation, especially since their verses seem to be adapted to singing the praises of the gods. He might easily have restored to his favor Homer and the epic poets, whom indeed he praises on many scores, wherever they had both used imitation more moderately and had corrected certain things which seemed to be in opposition to decency and virtue. In fact, he became so indignant against the tragic and comic writers because they put that constant imitation through verses and songs so completely to the use of voluptuousness and brutality that in the end he both repudiated the poems and ordered that the poets themselves leave his state, as if he intended to put them completely beyond the pale. And this was because they lulled the ear with rhythm and verse and harmony, and delighted the senses deprived of reason, finally exciting to admiration the mob gathered in the theater; but not only did they not direct men's minds towards prudence and temperance, but with such means they were not even capable so to direct them.[97]

This vice is above all apparent in comedy, where a variety of meters and melodies, in combination with all the claptrap and machinery of the stage, leads to ethical results that are directly the opposite of those sought by the art; Comedy herself, in a long soliloquy, confesses her sins and, in essence, blames them upon the use of verse. Beni's is thus a kind of Platonism which holds one attitude toward poetry in verse and the opposite attitude toward poetry in prose, and which thus bends the texts of Plato to its own purposes. This was not by any means an infrequent situation in the Cinquecento.

---

[96] *Ibid.* p. 15v: "sed tamen mollire animos nostros, neruos omnes virtutis elidere: denique per speciem liberalis eruditionis multa nobis afferre mala & detrimenta."

[97] *Ibid.*, pp. 16–16v: "si quis attentiùs eum perlegat, intelliget non lyricis infensum esse aut si qui sunt alii qui imitationi haud astricti sint: cum praesertim horum carmina diuinis laudibus canendis . . . accommodata uideantur. Cum Homero etiam Heroicisque poetis, quos etiam in multis laudat, facilè rediisset in gratiam vbi & temperatiore imitatione vsi essent, & in primis nonnulla quae cum honestate ac virtute pugnare viderentur, emendassent. verùm in Tragicos & Comicos, quoniam perpetuam illam imitationem metris & cantibus ad lasciuiam seuitiamue inflecterent totam, sic exarsit vt tandem & illorum poemata repudiauerit, & poetas ipsos, è sua Rep. excedere iusserit tanquam si aqua illis & igni interdictum vellet: idque quia versu, rythmo & harmonia mulcerent quidem aures, & expertem rationis sensum delectarent, confluentibus denique in theatrum turbis admirationem mouerent; ad prudentiam verò & temperantiam non modò non informarent animos, sed ea ratione ne informare quidem possent."

CONCLUSIONS

During the last thirty years of the Cinquecento, the documents of literary theory belonging to the Platonic tradition show in certain respects striking similarities with those of the preceding years, in other respects innovations and departures. Perhaps the most constant element is the praise or defence of poetry, usually couched in the most general terms and originating in a vague enthusiasm for the art. Such writers as Menechini, Correa, Benci, and Borghesi add little in the way of arguments to those that had been adduced by a Boccaccio two centuries earlier. One might even say that their orations or treatises reflect little of the critical sophistication which had, nevertheless, developed during the intervening years. In spite of the great erudition resulting from the innumerable commentaries, debates, and discussions of the sixteenth century, their own writings display a kind of charming naïveté—which has the one disadvantage of sounding, always, somewhat trite and unoriginal.

As for the particular questions that at all times formed a part of the Platonic attack or the Platonic defence, these change very little. The critics continue to discuss the great issues—imitation, the divine furor, ethical and political ends—in much the same terms. But perhaps here there is a shift in the balance of interests, for the question of imitation (probably under the influence of the abundant discussions of Aristotle's definition and its uses) ceases to be as exciting as it had been to earlier generations of theorists, and the question of the divine furor is either taken for granted or gives way before a more naturalistic conception of the poet's talents and of his modes of operation. Contrariwise, the consideration of poetry in terms of its relationships to the state and to ethical instruction increases rather than decreases. For all these problems, there is much less direct reference to the texts of Plato themselves, to the point that it is sometimes difficult to distinguish whether a critic actually has a Platonic basis for his point of view or whether he starts from vague and anonymous positions of heterogeneous origin. By this late date there comes to be a κοινή of Platonic ideas, present universally but unspecifically in the minds of men; and it is to this common fund that reference is made by the critics rather than to the dialogues themselves. Such references remain fragmentary and scattered, just as the literary citations before them had been, because of the fundamentally unsystematic attitude of the critics. That is, Plato remains a collection of passages concerning the poetic art—passages extracted from many dialogues—rather than a philosopher having a total system in the light of which his various ideas on poetry were developed.

If the ethical and political connotations of the art of poetry tend to predominate in these years, it may be because there is present in the consciousnesses of the critics a stronger idea of the state. It is true that, beginning with the earliest writings that I have considered, there were suggestions that the art of poetry was subordinate to the art of politics and that the politician should exercise a role of direction and censure with respect to the poet. But these were theoretical in tone and showed always the direct impact of the Platonic texts. In such writers as Denores, now, the whole problem has an air of immediacy and of reality not earlier sensible. I hesitate to say that this phenomenon results either from a broader awareness on the part of critics of the contemporary developments in political theory or from their observations of current politics. But the critical treatises themselves, unless I am mistaken, give increasing prominence to political implications and a lesser role to ethical instruction; the emphasis is less on "character building" and more on the consequences to the state of the practice of the art of poetry as a whole or of certain of its forms. As a rather surprising corollary, theorists are now less prone to banish or expel the poet from the state and more prone to seek ways in which the practice of his art can be controlled and turned to the advantage of the body politic. It is only in the cases of the extreme Christian theorists that the wish to condemn and exile the art is expressed with increased vigor.

The Platonic position, as I have already remarked, carried with it from the start admirable possibilities for exploitation by Christian theorists, and the first steps in such exploitation were taken by writers of earlier years. This application of Platonic methods and ideas to the Christian attack upon poetry reaches its culmination in the years after 1570. Gambara, Panicarola, Possevino see the whole art in the theological context of Catholicism—and a brand of Catholicism that condemns all forms of pleasure in the severest terms. Such an art as poetry, combining pleasure with utility or using pleasure as an instrument of utility, is immediately suspect because of the very presence of pleasure. It must either be prohibited *in toto*, or all such parts of it as cannot be salvaged for purposes of Christian indoctrination must be put under the ban. This may mean the exclusion of certain genres or certain poets or of whole ranges of poems having unacceptable subject matters or teaching undesirable lessons. An especially reprehensible body of poetry will be that produced by poets who were themselves not Christians, since in their works will be found not only vicious moral incitements but also the praises and the beauties of false religions. All pagan antiquity is the object of such a condemnation. Even in less rabid theorists, whose point of view is not specifically that of the church, the desirability of reading, consulting, or citing the Greek and Roman poets is brought into question. Giovambattista Strozzi's lecture is an example of this kind of thinking. I wish to emphasize again that such thinking is far from setting the tone for late Renaissance attitudes toward poetry. It exists to its maximum degree in a small number of sectarian theorists; but it has an influence upon others as well and helps determine the general orientations of theory.

Both the school of political reference and the school of Christian interpretation were joined in a common point of departure, their contempt for the public to which they assumed that poetry was addressed. For if poetry is politically dangerous, it is because the men who will read or hear it are disposed rather to act upon its malevolent insinuations than to follow its salutary lessons. And if it carries with it dangers to religion, it is because the men whom it affects are too weak in their faith or too susceptible to the blandishments of other beliefs to remain Christians unscathed. In both cases, these men are presented by the critics as of the lowest classes, hence ignorant and morally weak, hence under the domination of their senses uncontrolled by reason. Far from being the art of the élite, poetry is the art of the masses. It writes the kind of poems it does and in the ways it uses because it wishes to appeal to these masses, to sway them, to pander to their low tastes, to instruct them if it can. But this instruction itself is a doubtful thing, granted the recalcitrance supposed to characterize these men. Even the possibility that they may be appealed to indirectly, through allegory, is now subjected to serious doubt—again because of their weakness of intellect and their lack of education. Here, the Platonic tradition, insofar as it subjects the whole art of poetry to the considerations of a specific audience, comes very close to the tradition of Horace and the rhetoricians. It comes closest of all, probably, in such a writer as Mazzoni, who diversifies his audience into various classes, establishes for each class a special utility to be sought by the poet, and then assigns a given poetic genre to each such utility.

There are, in fact, many other points of contact between the Platonic tradition and those of Horace and Aristotle. The Platonic ends, as these critics see them, are practically indistinguishable from those that they find in Horace's *Ars poetica*. Utility and pleasure, equal or unequal, dominant or subordinate. The tendency of the Platonists is to declare that the two are unequal in importance, that utility is dominant, that pleasure is its instrument; and this is true even for those who believe that the art serves desirable ends in a satisfactory way. With Aristotle, the *rapprochements* become increasingly numerous and distinct. The theory of imitation moves closer to an Aristotelian solution; the question of utility is with greater and greater frequency answered by means of reference to the theory of purgation. Doubts raised by Plato are solved by Aristotle; attacks made in the name of the *Dialogues* produce defences based on the authority of the *Poetics*. If this is the general position of the Platonists, it is because from the very outset it is an intermediate position, both philosophically and in point of time. The position grew and developed in an intellectual milieu that had already fully accepted Horace's dicta on many of the problems of the poetic art. It raises questions which had already been answered to a certain extent, or for which answers might be found by a re-examination of the Horatian text. Moreover, it raises only a limited number of questions —those which I have sought to trace in the last two chapters—and leaves untouched the vast body of accepted doctrine that the Horatians had developed for all the practical aspects of the art. This doctrine will not be easily displaced. As the sixteenth century advances, a younger text, Aristotle's *Poetics*, comes to vie with Plato's dialogues for domination in matters theoretical—at least insofar as the theory of poetry is concerned. This text, like Horace's, is seen to have, above all, practical uses and applications, suggestions for the poet in the practice of his art, for the critic in the practice of his profession, for the public in its reading and understanding of poetry. But it is also seen to supply answers to many fundamental and abstruse problems—problems which had been raised by Plato, answers which in some few cases confirm Plato's own findings but which in most cases contradict and deny them. The weakening of the Platonic tradition is a concomitant of the solidification of Horatian doctrine and of the growing authority of Aristotle's *Poetics*.

CHAPTER NINE. THE TRADITION OF ARISTOTLE'S *POETICS*: I. DISCOVERY AND EXEGESIS

THERE IS NO DOUBT but that the signal event in the history of literary criticism in the Italian Renaissance was the discovery of Aristotle's *Poetics* and its incorporation into the critical tradition. Whereas Horace's *Ars poetica* had continued to influence critical thinking throughout the Middle Ages, and whereas Plato's miscellaneous ideas had entered into consideration with the coming of humanism, the text of the *Poetics* became available only at the very end of the fifteenth century and became generally known only toward the middle of the sixteenth. Thus, it appeared at a time when a way of thinking about literary matters, derived from the texts known earlier and from the whole rhetorical tradition associated with Horace, was firmly established in the minds of men. It was necessarily read and interpreted in keeping with that way of thinking, and in its turn it changed and modified the body of existing attitudes. The history of the Aristotelian tradition in the Cinquecento will thus be a narrative of the give and take between habitual modes of thought and a fresh text presenting extraordinary and surprising ideas.

If the dates themselves are fundamentally important, the states of mind current in the successive periods are of even greater significance. By the turn of the century, several mutations had taken place which throw the appearance of the *Poetics* at that precise moment into peculiar relief. On the one hand, by 1500 the "spirit of the Renaissance" was full blown. Italy had produced remarkable masterpieces in the fields of painting, sculpture, and architecture; and in the special domain of literature she was engaged in active production both in Latin and in the vulgar tongue. These works of original artistry had been accompanied, since around 1450, by a notable activity in the fields of theory and criticism: universities, academies, scholars in their studies, all had addressed themselves to the problem of ascertaining whence these works acquired their beauty or their quality or their worth. Naturally, the answers were first sought in the ancients, and the study of Horace and of Plato was renewed and extended. The arrival of Aristotle among the company, with a text previously unexplored and unexploited, promised new possibilities for solving the remaining problems.

On the other hand, the text of the *Poetics* was published (first in Latin and then in Greek) at a time when Aristotle's repute in the scholarly world was not of the highest. His method, regarded as too severe and too "scholastic" and too closely linked to the medieval tradition of the church, had been abandoned in favor of the more attractive and more facile discoursings of Plato (as he was then interpreted). In any case, the rigorous construction and logic of Aristotle's treatises was neither understood nor esteemed, and few men of the Italian Renaissance would have been capable of analyzing or applying it. To be sure, the vogue of Aristotle (especially of such works as the *Ethics*, the *Politics*, the *De Anima*, the *Rhetoric*, and the treatises on natural history) continued throughout the sixteenth century: witness the large number of editions and commentaries, of university courses devoted to interpreting him, of discussions of all kinds. But he was no longer the Master, the Philosopher, the tyrant who imposed method as well as doctrine. His authority was frequently questioned, he was openly attacked by some, and the methods and conclusions of his rivals were upheld against him. Even more serious was the fact that his best expositors and champions were often men of insufficient training and improper intellectual habits (I have spoken of them in Chapter II), and, hence, the interpretations that they offered were woefully insufficient. Thus the appearance of the *Poetics* was essentially an anachronism: the newest, most exciting, and most promising text of Aristotle came to light at precisely the time when men were least prepared to read and understand it correctly.

It should be said, in defence of the Renaissance reader, that the text of the *Poetics* was not—is not—easy to understand. Incomplete in the form in which we have it, it is highly condensed, and the subtlety and rigorousness of its structure become apparent only after the most searching study and in the light of a method discoverable only through analysis of the whole Aristotelian corpus. For the Renaissance reader, the procedure was even more difficult. He had before him a text in many places corrupt, a text which has been much improved by the labors of modern scholarship but in which conjecture and uncertainty are still present. Moreover, it was a text which borrowed its examples and its illustrations from a literature still very imperfectly known, either as to content or to form, and these examples must have provided little clarification for him. If to these circumstances are added the hazards of badly printed texts and inadequate translations, it will be seen that his difficulties were indeed almost insuperable. Hence the necessity, after discovery, for the tremendous effort of exegesis to which the Cinquecento dedicated itself.

I hesitate, even in our time, to propose an interpretation of the text against which the problems and the solutions of the Renaissance may be reflected; the matter is still in great dispute. But perhaps the following general statement would be acceptable. If there has been, in recent years, a recrudescence of interest in the *Poetics* as a guide to the theory and practice of literary criticism, it is because critics have seen in it, more than in any other theoretical document, a treatise which concentrates its attention upon those qualities of the work of art itself which make it beautiful and productive of its proper effect. Aristotle is at no time neglectful either of the audience in whom this proper effect is produced or of the natural reality which is represented in the artificial work of art. But his aim is neither to analyze audiences nor to study nature. He wishes to discover how a poem, produced by imitation and representing some aspect of a natural object—

its form—in the artificial medium of poetry, may so achieve perfection of that form in the medium that the desired aesthetic effect results. His points of departure are two: one, a general conception of aesthetics which comprises such elements as the end of poetry, the nature of imitation, the relationship of artificial to natural objects, the relationship between the work and its contemplator, and the general criteria for artistic achievement; the other, a body of materials (the literature of Greece as he knew it) which he analyzes in the light of this aesthetic to discover how poets have achieved or have failed to achieve the perfection of which their art is capable, and from which he obtains suggestions as to how, in the past, the various forms and genres have been successfully practised. The analysis of the works thus becomes a verification of the aesthetic, just as the aesthetic had provided the initial means for the analysis. The suggestions with respect to the past are never solidified into rules or dogmas, and hence the critic of the future may find in them guides and indications for the analysis of other poems, differently conceived and executed, but nevertheless relatable to the same aesthetic insofar as they belong to the same art.

In anticipation of the ways in which the Renaissance was to read the *Poetics*, two things should be noted about the theory as I have outlined it: First, as concerns the audience, Aristotle at all times bears in mind the presence of a contemplator who sees or reads and appreciates the poem. Statements about the "effect" of which I have spoken may be made either in terms of the kind of reaction within an audience or of the structural particularities within the work which produce that reaction. In either case, the audience is considered in a general way; it is a general and universal one, and never particularized through race, time, place, class, or personal idiosyncracies. It is composed of men sharing the common feelings and experiences of all mankind, having the common conviction that actions spring from character and that events spring from causes, susceptible of enjoying the pleasures afforded by the imitative arts, and capable through their sensitivity and their habits of reading of distinguishing good works from bad. Otherwise, it has no distinctive qualities as an audience. Hence the position of the *Poetics* is not a rhetorical one, because nowhere is the poem made to be what it is in order to have a particular effect of persuasion upon a particular audience; moreover, nowhere does the "character" of the poet enter as a structural element in the poem.

Second, as concerns natural reality, Aristotle at all times maintains a sense of the relationship between the natural object which lies behind the imitation and the artificial object which is the product of the imitation. But this does not mean that the latter is good as it conforms to the former or bad as it fails so to conform. The criterion is not one of resemblance, of faithfulness, of "realism," of "imitation" in its narrowest sense. This means that the requirements of "necessity" and "probability" are not derived from natural verisimilitude or from the way in which things usually happen in an ordered universe. Rather, they are expressions of relationships of a strictly structural character, which assure the proper integration and order of the component parts of the work. Since they are, in a way, like the laws of nature—wherein actions spring from character and events spring from causes—they on the one hand establish the imitative relationship between the poem and its object in nature and on the other assure the intelligibility of the work to the audience and its capacity to feel the desired effect.[1]

How, then, did the men of the Renaissance, first coming into contact with the text of the *Poetics*, read that text? What kind of text, what kind of translations, what kind of commentaries were first available to them, and what was the nature of their interpretations of these documents?

I do not think it useful here to speak of the existence of a medieval translation of the *Poetics* into Latin, recently published,[2] since as far as we can discover that translation was completely unknown during the Renaissance. Nor is it necessary to retail the first fragmentary and passing allusions to the *Poetics* found in the writings of the humanists,[3] since these display merely a knowledge of the existence of the work without any indication of the way in which it was understood. Instead, I wish to pass immediately to a discussion of Averroës' commentary on the *Poetics*. Written in Arabic in the twelfth century, translated into Latin by Hermannus Alemanus in the thirteenth, it was first published in Venice in 1481 under the title of *Determinatio in poetria Aristotilis*. It was reprinted in 1515 and several times thereafter. It was thus that Averroës' commentary was made available before Giorgio Valla's Latin translation of 1498 or the Aldine Greek text of 1508 and was the first instrument by means of which the scholars of the Renaissance could gain an apprehension of the content of Aristotle's text.

THE AVERROËS PARAPHRASE

It would be difficult for any writer of classical antiquity to be less well served, for his presentation to the modern world, than was Aristotle by Averroës and Hermannus. It is clear, from the printed version of their text as we have it, not only that Averroës had before him a garbled version of the *Poetics* but that he himself was incapable of understanding completely the materials with which he was working. He did not know the Greek works to which Aristotle refers for his examples (only the names of Homer and Aesop, among Greek poets, seem to be familiar to him), and the illus-

---

[1] For fuller statements of this interpretation of the *Poetics*, see various articles in *Critics and Criticism: Ancient and Modern*, ed. R. S. Crane (Chicago: University of Chicago Press, 1952), especially those of R. S. Crane, R. P. McKeon, and Elder Olson. See also Elder Olson, "The Poetic Method of Aristotle: Its Powers and Limitations," in *English Institute Essays, 1951* (New York: Columbia University Press, 1952), pp. 70–94.

[2] *De arte poetica, Guillelmo de Moerbeke interprete*, ed. E. Valgimigli (Bruges-Paris: Desclée de Brouwer, 1953).

[3] Cf. Remigio Sabbadini, *Il Metodo degli Umanisti* (Florence: Le Monnier, 1922), pp. 71–74; also Lane Cooper and Alfred Gudeman, *A Bibliography of the Poetics of Aristotle* (New Haven: Yale University Press, 1928).

trations were meaningless to him. He did not have any idea of the literary forms of which Aristotle speaks, with the possible exception of the epic, and the whole of the treatise must have seemed to him to exist in a kind of vacuum. He did know certain kinds of Arabic poetry, and he saw in them certain similarities to the works which Aristotle was describing. Moreover, he was aware of a rhetorical tradition in his own literature, concerned largely with tropes and figures and rhetorical devices, and these too he assimilated to the text of Aristotle. Indeed, his intention as stated at the outset is to discover to what extent the *Poetics* is applicable to his own literature: "Our intention in this edition is to determine how much of Aristotle's book *On Poetry* is concerned with universal rules common to all nations or to most; for most of what is found in this book either consists of rules proper to their poetry and their usage [i.e., of the Greeks] in Greek poems, or they are not found in Arabic poetry, or they are found in other languages."[4]

The cross between misunderstanding on the one hand and an intention to "Arabize" on the other brings about several immediately visible consequences in Averroës' *Determinatio*. In the first place, it leads him to omit many passages, sometimes fairly long ones, from the translation that forms the basis of the commentary. I think it useful to indicate here which passages are actually translated; to do so, I have numbered the passages in Hermannus' translation and given the equivalents in the *Poetics*.[5] The gaps will speak for themselves:

1	1447a8	16	24–27
2	12–13	17	1449a21–28
3	15–16	18	31–36
4	18–28	19	1449b9–13
5	28–1447b8	20	24–28
6(?)	1447b9–13	21	31–34
7(?)	16–23	22	36–1450a7
8	23–29	23	1450a7–14
9	1448a1–5	24	15–23
10	11–12	25(?)	23–37
11	14	26	37–1450b4
12	24–25	27	1450b4–8
13	1448b4–12	28	8–13
14	12–19	29	13–16
15	20–24	30	16–21

[4] *Determinatio* (1481 ed.), p. f: "Intentio nostra est in hac editione determinare quod in libro poetrie aristotilis de canonibus uniuersalibus comunibus omnibus nationibus aut pluribus cum plurimum eius quod est in hoc libro aut sunt canones proprii poematibus ipsorum & consuetudini ipsorum in ipsis aut non sunt reperta in sermone arabum aut sunt reperta in aliis idiomatibus."

[5] A question mark after the number of a passage indicates that the parallelism is so vague as to make exact identification impossible; after a reference to the *Poetics*, that the limits of the passage being paraphrased are unclear.

POETIC THEORY

31	22–24	70	17–22
32	25–32	71	23–26
33	35–40(?)	72	31–25
34	1451a6–15	73	1455b12–(?)
35	16–19	74	24–29
36	23–24	75	33–1456a3
37	30–35	76	1456a3–7
38	36–1451b11	77	25–(?)
39	1451b15–19	78	33–34
40	27–33	79	35–1456b2
41	33–39	80	1456b2–8
42	1452a12–18	81	8–19
43	22–23	82	20–21
44	29–33	83	22–34
45	33–36	84	35–38
46	36–1452b3	85	38–1457a6
47	1452b9–13	86	1457a6–10
48	14–18	87	10–14
49	25–27	88	1457a14–18
50	30–32(?)	89	18–23
51	1453a7–12	90	23–30
52	22–23	91	31–1457b6
53	23–26	92	1457b6–12(?)
54	30–36	93	33–35
55	1453b1–8	94	1458a1–3(?)
56	8–15	95	18–26(?)
57	15–22	96	1458b1–11
58	27–31(?)	97	11–15
59	1454a13–15	98	1459a15–30
60	16–27	99	1459b8–12(?)
61	33–36	100	17–21(?)
62	1454b1–2(?)	101	1460b2–5
63	8–14	102	6–7(?)
64	15–18	103	13–17(?)
65	19–21	104	23–25(?)
66	30–31	105(?)	1461b16–17
67	1454b36–1455a4	106(?)	1461a16(?)
68	1455a4–6	107	1461b22–25
69	12–15	108	[no equiv.]

A study of the passages in Aristotle omitted by Averroës-Hermannus shows both misunderstanding and "Arabizing" at work. Many of them (more than in any other category) are passages in which Aristotle had cited or analyzed specific works by Greek authors, and these were, of course, incomprehensible to Averroës, especially when Aristotle had spoken of specific details of plot or character (e.g., 6, 7, 9–10, 10–11, 11–12, 16–17, 35–36, 36–37, 38–39, 39–40, 53–54, 54–55, etc.). In another group are passages in which Aristotle had spoken of such specifically dramatic elements

[354]

POETICS: DISCOVERY AND EXEGESIS

of tragedy as the constitution of the plot, the tragic hero, recognition, reversal, the "deus ex machina," the quantitative parts; since Averroës had no notions of dramatic poetry, these sections were completely meaningless for him (e.g., 1–2, 17–18, 32–33, 41–42, 46–47, 48–49, 49–50, 50, 62, 72–73, etc.). A third set is comprised of passages in which Aristotle had treated the very essence of poetry as an art of imitation; since Averroës' conception of poetry (as we shall see later) was an entirely different one, he could have no comprehension of such ideas as that of imitation itself, of necessity and probability, of truth and historical truth as related to imitation, of the distinctions among object, manner, and means (e.g., 3–4, 11–12, 20–21 42–43, 102, 103–4, 104–7). Contrariwise, Averroës felt quite at home in discussions of diction and rhetorical figures, and the most continuous single part of the *Poetics* translated by him is that represented by passages 79 to 91.

The intention to "Arabize" leads, in the second place, to the replacing of Aristotle's examples by examples from Arabic poetry. Besides, many fresh examples are added. It is difficult, from the bare translation, to discover what kinds of Arabic poetry Averroës has in mind. But some of the names mentioned and some of the descriptions help to establish the general categories. It is clear that he excludes the Koran from the general classification of poetry; it is the "liber sanctus" (p. gii) and is carefully differentiated from poetry: "Most hyperbolical figures of this kind are found in Arabic poetry, but in the book of the Most High, that is, the Koran, none such are found."[6] It is also clear that he excludes certain religious writings, called the "Sermones Legales" and apparently very close in content to the Old Testament: "You will find several stories of the kind mentioned here in the Books of Laws, since of this kind are the laudatory tales which incite to praiseworthy actions; for instance, Joseph and his brethren is an example from history and there are other similar incidents as examples in accounts of the past; these are all called hortatory exempla."[7] Once again, the distinction is carefully made: "And you will find many examples of this kind, all of them in the Scriptures of the Laws since poems in praise of virtue [i.e., tragedies] are not to be found among the poems of the Arabs; and they are not found in our times except in the legal writings."[8] If these are excluded specifically, other kinds of writing are excluded merely because they do not exist among the writings of the Arabs: all dramatic genres and

---

[6] *Determinatio* (1481 ed.), p. g*v*: "tales iperbolici sermones quamplurimi inueniuntur in poematibus arabum sed in libro altissimi id est in alkoratio [sic] nihil."

[7] *Ibid.*, p. f vii: "tu reperies plures representationum incidentium in sermonibus legalibus secundum hunc modum cuius fecit mentionem cum talia sint sermones laudatiui instigantes ad opera laudabilia: ut quidem inducitur de historia ioseph et fratrum suorum & alia similia de narrationibus gestorum preteritorum que nominantur exempla exortatiua." Cf. p. f vii*v* on the story of Abraham.

[8] *Ibid.*, p. f vii*v*: "Et tu reperies multa ad modum omnium istorum in scripturis legalibus cum carmina laudatiua uirtutum non inueniantur in poematibus arabum & non inueniuntur in hoc nostro tempore nisi in legibus scriptis."

such lengthy narrative poems as the epic. The poetry which Averroës knew consisted therefore exclusively of shorter works, narrative or lyric in general form and embracing such matters as encomia or eulogies, satires, elegiac or love themes, laments and songs of joy. Within this body of known materials, he tried to find examples of the literary phenomena which he thought Aristotle was describing and discussing, with greater or less success according as parallelisms did or did not exist between Arabic and Greek poetry.

In a positive way, we may say that the theory of poetry found in the *Determinatio* differs from that found in the *Poetics* in three striking ways: (1) Averroës conceives of poetry as a representation or manifestation of the truth, in which the notion of "imitation" is essentially lacking; (2) he thinks of the end of poetry as exclusively ethical, seeking to inculcate virtue or to discourage vice in the reader; (3) he sees this end as achieved specifically through the affective devices of rhetoric—the figures, mainly—rather than through the total effect of a poetic form. I shall expand somewhat on each of these points in order to indicate the precise nature of Averroës' position.

Perhaps the simplest approach to Averroës' general conception of poetry is through his initial statement that "sermones poetici sermones sunt imaginatiui" (p. f). From what follows, it is clear that "imaginatiui" means something like "composed of or productive of images," something like "figurative." The next sentence, "Modi autem imaginationis & assimilationis tres sunt," confirms this through the establishment of the equivalence between "imaginatio" and "assimilatio"; moreover, it indicates without a doubt that these formulas are meant to translate *Poetics* 1447a15–16 and that "imaginatio" and "assimilatio" are translations of μίμησις. But whereas Aristotle had gone on to distinguish three kinds of differences among imitations, according to object, manner, and means, Averroës discerns three kinds of figures: (1) an "assimilatio rei ad rem," which may take the form either of a simile using "quasi" or "sicut" or of a metaphor based on a proportional relationship; (2) an "assimilatio conuersa" in which a comparison is "reversed" (you say that the sun is like a woman rather than that a woman is like the sun); and (3) a combination of the other two. Since synonyms for "assimilatio" are "transumptio," "translatio," and "similitudo," and since Averroës refers the reader to Aristotle's *Rhetoric* for further information, it is clear that the notion of imitation has been reduced to that of figurative expression.

The consequences of this construction put upon the term "imitation" are apparent throughout the work. It should be pointed out that "imitatio" does appear as a term, but always in a meaning consistent with that already given. When Averroës comes, shortly afterward, to a listing of the three means of imitation in poetry, he gives them as "sonus" (harmony), "pondus" (rhythm), and "assimilatio"; the last is equivalent to diction, and an imitation or representation in diction is said to be "in sermonibus representatiuis seu imaginatiuis" (p. fv). When he wishes to state the natural causes of poetry, he gives the first as man's natural practice of "assimilatio rei ad rem: & representatio rei per rem" and he cites as evidence the usefulness in teaching of such "assimilationes" as examples and comparisons (p. f2v). In a more important way, when he is confronted with the necessity of treating the parts of plot (which is a much larger "imitative" form than any he could conceive), he is obliged to replace translation by paraphrase, to substitute for the ideas of the original those which agree with his own conceptions. Reversal and recognition (translated by "circulatio" and "directio") are both figures of speech, both may be found together in a brief narrative passage such as the one cited from a poet called Abyraibi (pp. f vi–f viv). Action or plot itself has no more specific meaning than "res" or subject matter, although the word "actio" is at times used; unity of action is violated in certain Arabic poems of praise, for example, when "some matter worthy of praise presents itself, such as a fast horse or a precious sword, [and] they digress from the main theme and they linger too long on the praises of the matter which has offered itself for praise."[9] Similarly, the notions of knot and denouement (translated by "carmen consecutiuum" and "dissolutio" or "disiunctio") are made to pertain to lyric poetry and may be illustrated by short citations (cf. p. gii).

Further evidence that the concept of imitation has, for Averroës, anything but its Aristotelian meaning is found in his insistence that poetry must treat only what is true. There are echoes here, of course, of Aristotle's ideas on probability and on historical truth; but essentially the ideas are reversed and an opposite conclusion is presented. Thus when he is translating *Poetics* 1451*a*35 ff., he makes this categorical statement:

... representations which are made through untrue and extraordinary figments are not the poet's business. And these are the ones which are called proverbs and exempla, and they are those which are found in the book of Aesop and in similar fabulous writings. For it does not belong to the poet to speak of anything except things which exist or which can possibly exist. . . . For the maker of extraordinary proverbs and fables invents or fabricates entities that simply do no exist as a matter of fact and he gives them names. But the poets give names to things which exist. . . .[10]

The same thesis is developed more specifically with respect to tragedy, which he calls the "ars laudatiua" or the "carmen laudatiuum":

---

[9] *Ibid.*, p. f v: "quando occurrerit eis aliqua materia laudandi: ut aliquis equus strenuus aut ensis preciosus digrediuntur a proposito: et immorantur nimis in laudibus materie que optulit ad laudandum."

[10] *Ibid.*, p. f vv: "representationes que fiunt per figmenta mendosa adinuenticia non sunt de opere poete. Et sunt ea que nominantur prouerbia & exempla: ut ea que sunt in libro Isopi et similibus fabulosis conscriptionibus: ideo quod poete non pertinet loqui nisi in rebus que sunt aut quas possibile est esse. . . . fictor ergo prouerbiorum adinuentiuorum et fabularum adinuenit seu fingit indiuidua que penitus non habent existentiam in re: & ponit eis nomina. Poete uero ponunt nomina rebus existentibus."

... the things from which the imitative representation is selected must be things existing in nature, not things invented or imaginary, for which terms are fabricated. For the songs of praise [i.e., tragedies] have as their intention the improving of those actions which spring from the will; when therefore they are possible and almost real, they contain a greater capacity for persuasion or poetic credibility, which moves the soul to follow something or to reject it. In actions, however, which do not exist in nature, [this capacity] is not present.[11]

Imitation is no longer the process of presenting something that is *like* nature; it is the process of presenting nature.

The reason for this, the greater credibility of that which is and its greater persuasiveness, is contained in the last paragraph quoted; if the poem is to produce ethical action through persuasion of its audience, and if persuasion depends upon a conviction of truth, then only true subjects will be admitted to poetry. The end is action, the means persuasion, the materials truth. We may take this as a statement of Averroës' other two fundamental concepts of the art of poetry. With respect to the end of moral action, his statements are once again unequivocal. Paraphrasing *Poetics* 1448a1, he writes: "Those who represent and those who imitate intend by means of their imitations to instigate to certain actions which spring from the activity of the will and to prevent certain other actions; whence those things which they seek through their imitations will of necessity be virtues and vices."[12]

Later in the same passage he rephrases the intention in such formulas as "propter ostentationem decentis aut indecentis," "assecutio decentis & refutatio turpis," "laus bonorum et uituperatio malorum," "approbatio decentis & detestatio turpis." The various literary genres come to be named and judged in the light of their service of these ends. Tragedy ("ars laudandi") and comedy ("ars uituperandi") will be acceptable forms since both praise and blame contribute to the end of virtuous action; the definition of tragedy, for example, is modified to contain this clause: "It is an imitation, I say, which generates in men's souls certain passions which temper them toward pitying and fearing and to other similar passions, which it induces and promotes through what it makes virtuous men imagine about honesty and moral cleanliness."[13] (It should be remembered that Averroës knew no dramatic literature and conceived of these two forms as

---

[11] *Ibid.*: "ut sint res a quibus sumitur imitatiua representatio res existentes in natura non res adinuenticie siue figmentales quibus ficta sint nomina. Carmina namque laudatiua intentionem habent promouendi actiones uoluntarias: quando ergo fuerint possibiles & quasi reales amplius incidit per eas sufficientia persuasiua seu credulitas poetica motiua anime ad assequendum aliquid aut ad refutandum ipsum. Rebus autem non existentibus in natura non ponuntur. . . ."

[12] *Ibid.*, pp. fv–f2: "representatores et assimilatores per haec intendunt instigare ad quasdam actiones que circa uoluntaria consistunt et retrahere a quibusdam erunt necessario ea que intendunt per suas representationes aut uirtutes aut uicia."

[13] *Ibid.*, pp. f3–f3v: "Representatio inquam que generat in animabus passiones quasdam temperatiuas ipsarum ad miserendum aut timendum aut ad ceteras consimiles passiones quas inducit & promouet per hoc quod imaginari facit in uirtuosis de honestate & munditia."

short poems resembling eulogies and satires.) But love poems, since they lead only to vice, will not be acceptable:

> But the species of poetry which they call elegy is nothing but an incitement to acts of copulation which they conceal and adorn with the name of love. And therefore it is necessary that children should be restrained from the reading of such poems and that they should be instructed and exercised in poems which incite and incline to fortitude and liberality.[14]

After pointing out what virtues are pursued by Arabic poetry, Averroës insists that the Greeks always seek to teach in their poetry and that didactic materials are included in it "insofar as they intend by them [their poems] to convey didactic illustrations and precepts for the following of the virtues and the rejecting of the vices, or for any other good things which may be done or known."[15] The end of poetry is thus instruction—for what may be learned, but especially for the actions that may be taken in the light of learning. Because of this emphasis, it is essentially moral instruction.

With respect to the rhetorical means by which such moral instruction is achieved, we have already seen that the principal one will be figurative language. If we think of poetry as consisting in imitation and of imitation as essentially a process of "assimilatio" or metaphor, then whatever power the art has must be found in the rhetorical effectiveness of such metaphors. Averroës states the case fairly clearly, again deforming the text of Aristotle, in connection with his treatment of recognition and reversal. It will be remembered that he had reduced both to the status of figures of speech; to explain their effectiveness he says this, after pointing out how they should be mixed within the individual poem:

> For it is proper that odes, that is songs of praise [Aristotle's tragedies], through which one seeks the instigation to the virtues, should be made up of representations of the virtues and of representations of things causing fear or bringing sadness, from which follows some emotion, such as the misfortunes falling upon good people without relationship to their merits. Through these indeed the exciting of the soul to the reception of the virtues is made powerful. . . . Certainly these representations stir up men's souls and make them quick to the reception of the virtues.[16]

---

[14] *Ibid.*, p. f2: "Species uero poetrie quam elegiam nominant non est nisi incitatio ad actus cohituales quos amoris nomine obtegunt & decorant. Ideoque oportet ut a talium carminum lectione abstrahantur filii & instruantur & exerceantur in carminibus que ad actus fortitudinis & largitatis incitant & inclinant."

[15] *Ibid.*, pp. f2–f2v: "inquantum intendunt per ea tradere documenta & precepta ad sequendas uirtutes aut respuenda uicia aut quaslibet alias bonitates operabiles aut scientiales."

[16] *Ibid.*, p. f vii: "Oportet enim ut ode id est carmina laudum per que intenditur instigatio ad uirtutes composite sint ex representationibus uirtutum & ex representationibus rerum incutientium pauorem & contristantium ex quibus sequitur perturbatio: ut sunt infortunia incidentia bonis praeter merita ipsorum: per haec enim uehemens fit incitatio anime ad receptionem uirtutum. . . . He nempe representationes exacuunt animas & festinas reddunt eas ad receptionem uirtutum."

Further consequences of this basically rhetorical attitude are seen throughout the work.

We may take as a striking example the handling of the six qualitative parts of tragedy. These are the terms which he uses as equivalent to Aristotle's:

plot	"sermones fabulares representatiui"
character	"consuetudines"
thought	"credulitas"
diction	"metrum"
spectacle	"consideratio"
song	"tonus"[17]

As I have already pointed out, there is in Averroës no conception of plot or action as such; thus "sermones fabulares representatiui" really refers to the whole of the poem rather than to a specific part. The next two parts are for Averroës the most important: "the major parts of laudatory songs are 'consuetudines' and 'credulitates.'"[18] He states the reasons for this judgment: "For tragedy is not a part which represents men themselves as they are individuals present to the senses; but it is representative of their honest ways of living and of their praiseworthy actions and of their beliefs which render them happy. And 'consuetudines' include actions and characters."[19] It is the third of these parts, "credulitas," which has the most specific rhetorical implications. Averroës defines it as "the capacity to represent a thing as being thus or as not being thus." Then he goes on to explain:

And this is similar to that which is attempted in rhetoric in the declaration that a thing exists or does not exist; except that rhetoric seeks to do this through a persuasive composition and poetry through an imitative composition.... And the difference between a preceptive poetic composition which incites to beliefs and a preceptive one which incites to ways of living is that the latter incites to accomplishing and doing something or to renouncing and avoiding something; whereas a composition which incites to belief incites to nothing else but the acceptance or the rejection of the notion that something is or is not, not to the active seeking out or refusal of the thing itself.[20]

[17] *Ibid.*, p. f3v.

[18] *Ibid.*, p. f iiii: "partes maiores carminis laudatiui sunt consuetudines et credulitates."

[19] *Ibid.*: "Tragedia enim non est pars representatiua ipsorummet hominum prout sunt indiuidua cadentia in sensum: sed est representatiua consuetudinum eorum honestarum & actionum laudabilium & credulitatum beatificantium. Et consuetudines comprehendunt actiones & mores."

[20] *Ibid.*: "Et hoc est simile ei quod conatur rethorica in declaratione quod res existat aut non existat nisi quod rethorica conatur ad hoc per sermonem persuasiuum & poetria per sermonem representatiuum.... Et differentia inter sermonem poeticum preceptiuum & instigatiuum ad credulitates & preceptiuum & instigatiuum ad consuetudines est quoniam ille qui instigat ad consuetudines instigat ad operandum & ad agendum aliquid aut ad recedendum & fugiendum. Sermo uero qui instigat ad credulitatem non instigat nisi ad credendum & fugiendum aliquid esse aut non esse sed non ad inquirendum ipsum aut respuendum."

There are many curious things about these statements, but perhaps the most significant aspects are these: (1) "plot," "character," and "thought" are not parts of poems at all, but separate kinds of poetic compositions; (2) these kinds are divided into two larger classes, both of which produce ethical ends through rhetorical means, but one of which leads to knowing while the other leads to doing.

It should by now be clear what the reader of the late fifteenth or early sixteenth century would learn about Aristotle's *Poetics* from reading Averroës' *Determinatio* in the translation of Hermannus Alemanus. He would derive from it only the vaguest notions about the text: some of the main terms (but often misused and misapplied), some of the central ideas (but as frequently as not deformed), the most general theoretical distinctions. He would be led, contrary to the intention of Aristotle himself, to think of poetry as a didactic instrument proceeding to moral instruction through rhetorical devices. Of these, the most important would be the figures of speech and other ornaments. Poetry, in this view, comes to be identical with rhetoric, and with the kind of limitation to diction and figures associated with the Alexandrian rhetoricians. None of the distinctively Aristotelian concepts of poetry remains clear and discernible.

THE VALLA TRANSLATION (1498)

The first great step forward in the presentation of Aristotle's *Poetics* to the modern reader came with the publication, in 1498, of Giorgio Valla's translation into Latin. According to E. Lobel's *Greek Manuscripts of Aristotle's Poetics* (p. 25), Valla used as the basis for his translation the manuscript now in the Biblioteca Estense at Modena, Estensis gr. 100. The translation, which preceded any publication of the Greek text, is in general a good one. For the first time, it gave to a larger public than was able to consult the few available manuscripts of the Greek original an accurate idea of what was contained in the text. It is by no means a perfect translation; it could not be, given the state of the manuscript on which it was based and the state of Greek scholarship at the time. For the modern reader, it offers the additional difficulties of a solid presentation, with no paragraphing or division into chapters, and of a completely capricious punctuation; these are undoubtedly the responsibility of the printer rather than of Valla himself. But still, it is a good translation and, above all, a notable advance over everything that had preceded it. I should like, in the following pages, to emphasize the following points with respect to it: (1) the degree to which it rendered properly the key terms of the *Poetics*; (2) the degree to which it rendered correctly most of the text, including certain central passages; (3) the kinds of errors which it made as a result of the imperfections of the Greek manuscripts; and (4) those errors which were actually errors of translation, and the reasons behind them. Again, my purpose will be to indicate what kind of general idea a reader of this translation might have of Aristotle's *Poetics* during the years from 1498 to 1536 (when Pazzi's translation took its place beside it).

The key terms of the "Poetics." The satisfactory character of Valla's rendering of the key terms is not only apparent but even striking to one who has read the Averroës version. Not only that, but Valla, in a sense, established the tradition of the Latin terms that were to be used in the translations of his successors and by the later commentators. Thus, with respect to the general nature of poetry, μίμησις becomes "imitatio" and μιμοῦνται becomes "imitantur"; the three means ῥυθμῷ καὶ λόγῳ καὶ ἁρμονίᾳ are rendered by "rhythmo & oratione: & harmonia"; the distinction of means, object, and manner of imitation, τῷ ἐν ἑτέροις..., ἢ τῷ ἕτερα, ἢ τῷ ἑτέρως, is translated by "genere in alienis [there is some ambiguity in the translation here], aliena, aliter"; the "effect" of poetry (δύναμις) appears as "vis" and the imitation of characters, passions, and actions (καὶ ἤθη καὶ πάθη καὶ πράξεις) as "mores: & affectus & actiones imitantur." With respect to the qualitative parts of tragedy, the terms used are "fabula" for plot, "mores" for character, "animi sententiae" for thought, "dictio" for diction, "conspectus" for spectacle, and "melopoeia" for song (I shall speak later of the difficulties involved in the use of "animi sententiae" and "conspectus"). One of the parts of plot, ἀναγνώρισις, is expressed as "recognitio" and the effects of pity and fear resulting from tragedy—φοβερά καὶ ἐλεεινά—as "miseratio" or "commiseratio" and "formido." For the "complication" and the "denouement" of plot (δέσις, λύσις), Valla uses "ligatio'" and "solutio."

A certain number of miscellaneous terms are equally well translated: πράττοντας and δρῶντας = "peragentes, agentes"; τὴν σύστασιν... τῶν πραγμάτων (1450*b*23) = "rerum complexum"; θαυμαστόν = "mirificum"; τὰ πάθη = "affectus"; εἰκονογράφους = "pictores simulacrorum"; ἐκ συλλογισμοῦ = "ex ratiocinatione"; τὸ πρέπον = "decorum"; πεπληγμένη = "implexa" and παθητική = "passiva"; φιλάνθρωπον = "humanum"; κατὰ τὸ ἀνάλογον = "iuxta proportionem"; εὐφυΐας = "ingenii"; διηγηματικήν = "expositricem"; ἄλογα = "rationis expertes." And so on for many other felicitous solutions. To have presented in this way, to the reader of the beginning of the Cinquecento, a large number of the Latin terms that were to become standard in the translations and commentaries of the *Poetics* was already a considerable achievement for Giorgio Valla.

The translation in general. But Valla's achievement was more extensive. In most cases, he solved correctly the problems of syntax presented by the original, giving as a result a text which for the most part made sense—and the right sense. This is difficult to demonstrate, except by an extensive comparison of the original and the translation. I can only invite the reader to compare the translation with the original text.

Errors resulting from the text. In spite of these excellences in Valla's translation of 1498, there were a large number of errors and inadequacies. These were of two kinds, those occasioned by the corruptness of the manuscripts which he was using and those resulting from his own misunderstandings. With respect to the manuscripts, they presented many lacunae, haplographies, misreadings, and these were reproduced in the later *editio princeps* (1508); hence we are able to discover the state of Valla's manuscripts through the edition of 1508 as well as through our modern editions. For in many cases, and in spite of the brilliant conjectures and emendations of modern scholars, the text remains imperfect. Indeed, in almost every passage of Valla's translation where major difficulties are found, one may find the explanation in some imperfection of his original text.

1447*a*28. Valla: "Epopoeia orationibus tenuibus: aut metris. Hisque siue inuicem inter se miscendo: siue uno aliquo genere utendo metrorum ad hoc usque tempus." Valla's difficulties come from the presence in the MS of the word ἐποποιία after Ἡ δέ and from the absence after μέτρων of the word ἀνώνυμος, which is a conjecture of Bernays confirmed by the Arabic version.

1448*a*15. Valla: "circa leges pergas." 1508 reads: τοὺς νόμους. ὡς πέργας. The passage gave infinite trouble throughout the sixteenth century. ὥσπερ γάρ is a conjecture of Vahlen.

1448*a*25. Valla: "in quibus & quo modo." καὶ ἅ lacking in the text.

1450*a*16. Valla: "Tragoedia namque est imitatio non hominum sed actionis & uitae & felicitatis & infelicitas in actione est & finis actio quaedam est non qualitas. . . ." Valla's text lacked, after εὐδαιμονίας, the words καὶ κακοδαιμονίας·ἡ δὲ εὐδαιμονία, a Vahlen conjecture.

1452*b*25. Valla: "partes tragoediae quibus utendum: Antea diximus." The words ὡς εἴδεσι were lacking from 1508 (and from Pazzi, 1536); they have been supplied subsequently from other MSS.

1455*b*27. Valla: "unde transitus est ad infortunium." The MSS lacked, after εἰς εὐτυχίαν, the words συμβαίνει ἢ εἰς ἀτυχίαν, supplied by a Vahlen conjecture and from other MSS.

1455*b*31. Valla: "ligatio quidem quae prius gesta & pusionis acceptio rursus ipsorum quod est apetita morte adfinem usque." There is a lacuna in our text which was still longer in Valla's.

1455*b*35. Since ἁπλῆ . . . ἡ δέ was lacking from Valla's text, his kinds of tragedies did not include the "simple."

1456*a*2. Valla: "Quarta porro aequabilis," since 1508 reads τὸ δὲ τέταρτον rather than the modern conjectural reading; the passage is still corrupt.

1457*a*2. Valla: "tam in extremis quam in medio," translating καὶ ἐπὶ τῶν ἄκρων καὶ ἐπὶ τοῦ μέσου, which now is excluded from the text by editors.

1460*b*15. Valla: "duplex error est. unus non recte praeoccupare: sed aequum in utramlibet partem prouoluere quod in qualibet sit arte peccatum." Valla's translation is garbled for two reasons: because certain words now conjectured for the text were lacking and because his text included, after μὴ ὀρθῶς, a repetition of κατὰ συμβεβηκός, thus leading to a haplography.

1461a27. Valla: "unde factum est crus nuper fabrefacti stanni & aereas ferro elaboratas: unde dicitur ganymedes ioui uinum miscere non bibentibus uinum." The garbled translation results from the fact that in Valla's MS, as in 1508, the two phrases beginning with ὅθεν εἴρηται and ὅθεν πεποίηται were inverted.

These are by no means the only cases of imperfect translations ascribable to an imperfect text (others may be found, for example, at 1454b2 and b14, –55b15 and b33, –56a10, 11, and 17, –56b8, –57a7, –60a11, –61b28). But they may serve as examples of the kinds of difficulties which the Greek text presented and of the kinds of confusion and misunderstanding which were necessarily reflected in the Valla translation. For the reader of the time, they merely served to make more difficult and enigmatic a document whose philosophical difficulties were already almost insuperable.

Actual errors of translation. Some of these are of the simplest kind and are easily explained: the terms signified objects which Valla did not know and hence he had no idea as to their proper rendering in Latin. These are mostly technical terms of the poetic art. He did not know what gnomic poetry was and translated τῶν νόμων at 1447b26 as "legum"; πάροδος and στάσιμον as parts of the chorus are given as "accessus" and "statiua" (–52b17). Whereas he consistently gives the proper equivalent for ἀναγνώρισις as "recognitio," he just as consistently mistranslates περιπετεία as "petulantia" (e.g., –52a17) or as "procacitas" (e.g., –59b11). It is not surprising that ἁμαρτία should have troubled him; he translates it as "flagicium & scelus" (–53a16). In other cases, proper names gave him trouble: thus καρκίνῳ (–55a27; preceded by τῷ in 1508) becomes "cancrum," Λάϊος (–60a30) is "iolaus," and Πινδάρου (–61b35) is "darium," giving the completely misleading "talis fuit erga darium opinio."

In another category, and a far more extensive one, come those terms whose general meaning he understood clearly enough but for which, at given places in the text, he gave unacceptable equivalents. That is, he failed to seize the shade of meaning required by the context. This came about for two reasons: one, because he did not fully understand the text at specific points; two, because he lacked a knowledge of the possible range of meanings for a word, of its nuances and its implications. For example: πάθος is usually properly rendered as "affectus"; but it is also so rendered at –52b10, where one needs something equivalent to "pathetic event," and at –53b18, where one needs "actual pain." λύειν is usually correctly given as "soluere"; but at –53b22, it should be "change" or "modify." ἦθος is character; but at –60a10, it needs to be "a person having character," and

POETICS: DISCOVERY AND EXEGESIS

the total phrase "uirum aut foeminam aut morem aliquem" becomes ambiguous. οἱ γραφεῖς may mean "scriptores"; but at –48a5 it means "painters."

Other cases are more serious, since they involve terms whose understanding is essential for the total interpretation of the *Poetics*. Such terms as "necessity" and "probability," for example, are fundamental. Valla regularly gives "necessarium" for ἀναγκαῖον; but he just as regularly gives "aequum" or "aequitas" or even "modestia" for εἰκός (cf. –51a27, –51a36, –51b8), and these do not render the notion of probability. Aristotle's four terms for the four requisites of character are χρηστόν, ἁρμόττον, ὅμοιον, ὁμαλόν. The third and fourth find satisfactory equivalents, I think, in "simile" and "aequabile." But "frugalem" and "concinnum" were hardly capable of giving the reader the notions of "goodness" and "likeness" (I should point out, in passing, that the exact sense of the terms is still in dispute). In discussing the types of action, Aristotle uses the phrase εἰδότας καὶ γινώσκοντας; Valla interprets the first epithet as "idiotas planeque uulgares," thus deforming the sense (–53b28); shortly afterward, he translates εἰδότας ἢ μὴ εἰδότας (–53b37) as "cernentes: aut non cernentes." Numerous other examples of the same kind might be cited.[21]

For another category of "mistranslations" Valla should perhaps not be blamed. For they do not constitute errors of translation. Rather, they consist in the choice of unfortunate Latin equivalents—unfortunate in the sense that they had associations and implications which might lead the reader to assign to Aristotle meanings that he did not intend. Thus for σπουδαίους ἢ φαύλους at –48a2 Valla gives "probos: aut improbos," restricting unnecessarily the distinction of moral character. At –48b25, "speciosas & speciosorum" emphasizes excessively the attitude of others towards actions and persons. At –49b8 and –50b13, the rendering of καθόλου by "in totum" fails to get across the notion of generality which is needed. At –49b17 (cf. the first example above) Valla's translation for τραγῳδίας ... σπουδαίας καὶ φαύλης is "tragedia honesta & uili," which again overemphasizes the moral implications. The use of the word "insignes" at –50a5 adds to the definition of character an inappropriate element, and at –50a19 it introduces an unfortunate distinction of moral merit. At –55a18, the translation of δι' εἰκότων by "per decorem" not only loses the meaning of verisimilitude, but it makes dangerous allusion to a current theory which should not be confused with Aristotle's text.

[21] *Poetica*, tr. Valla (1498). Cf. ψιλομετρίαν (–48a11) = in carminis tenuitate; φθαρτική (–52b11) = corruptiua; ὡς εἴδεσι (–52b14) = tanquam speciebus; ἐπιεικεῖς (–52b34) = modestos & aequos; φιλάνθρωπον (–52b38) = homini amicabile humanumque; χορηγίας δεόμενον (–53b8) = egetque adminiculo uerum; τερατῶδες (–53b9) = monstrosum; μιαρόν (–53b39) = scelestum; δι' ἀπορίαν (–54b21) = ex ambiguitate; σημεῖον (–56a15) = coniectura; ἄνευ διδασκαλίας (–56b5) = citra doctrinam; τὸ κύριον (–58a23) = proprium; ὀγκωδέστατον (–59b35) = turgidissimum; παραλογισμός (–60a20) = absonum; πάθη τῆς λέξεώς (–60b12) = dictionis sunt passiones; ἡμαρτῆσθαι (–60b29) = hallucinari; ἀμιμήτως (–60b32) = sine imitatione.

Finally, one must consider, in addition to the isolated terms already studied, those longer passages which present unsatisfactory translations. There are many of these. They are explained by the presence of the types of words just examined, but also and particularly by deficiencies in Valla's comprehension of construction and of syntactical difficulties. The result is a passage which fails to give a clear and precise meaning. Some of these are fairly short; so the version of −50*b*4, "id autem est uerbis complecti posse agitantia & concinnantia"; of −50*b*35, "item ad honestum & animal"; of −53*b*30, "est sane agere. quidem ignorantes sed ignorantes agere quiduis siue posterius recognoscendo amiciciam"; of −54*a*21, "est quidem mos fortis: sed nec dum mulieri congruus fortem ipsam aut grauem esse"; of −54*b*34, "quia iuxta dictam est hallucinationem. licet namque non nihil est ingerere." Some of them are longer. So for −59*b*26–30, collapsed into the following sentences: "Quantitate & in quae seiuncta diuiduntur. Haec sunt ut uero oportet coniectare: & quae constructas fabulas uereri oporteat & unde fuerit opus tragoediae post haec quae nunc dicta sunt nobis dicendum erit." So also for −59*b*26 ff.: "quod sit expositio est partes multas facere terminatas quibus suis eius aceruus poematis augetur. Proinde id habet bonum ad magnificentiam & mutare auditorem & agressus admittere inaequalibus episodiis." There are, in all, some twenty passages of this kind throughout the translation.[22]

I should not fail to point out that in addition to these "actual errors" of translation, there are many passages in Valla which I should characterize as "questionable" or "doubtful." In these, because of ambiguities of meaning or because of unclear constructions the reader might easily be led to understand the text in a way which was not intended. Or he might not understand it at all. The reader's difficulties would be further enhanced— and his distance from the original text increased—by the fact that in the whole section on diction (chapter 22) the textual examples are omitted and that in the section on replies to criticism (roughly −61*a*12 ff.) the Greek examples are given without translation. Therefore, in spite of Valla's really considerable contribution and of the many qualities of his translation, his reader would not find in it a perfectly satisfactory introduction to Aristotle's *Poetics*. He had the *Poetics* for the first time in a reasonably accurate form; but he also had before him a form which could easily lead to the many problems and discussions and insurmountable difficulties that were to plague the exegetes throughout the sixteenth century.

THE ALDUS TEXT (1508)

In 1508, ten years after the Valla translation, the first Greek text of the *Poetics* appeared, in a volume published in Venice by Aldus and entitled simply *Rhetores in hoc volumine habentur hi*, followed by a listing of the

[22] Cf. also the translations of −53*b*35, −55*a*35, −56*b*3, −56*b*9, −56*b*33, −58*b*12, −59*a*21, −60*a*26, −60*b*3, −60*b*32, −60*b*36, −61*b*13, −62*a*6, −62*a*9, −62*a*17.

texts included. There is no prefatory or explanatory material. The text, based on manuscripts then in Italy, is a reasonably good one, and it was long to remain the basic text for the *Poetics*; it was copied or adapted or corrected by most of the sixteenth-century editors. It is possible that the editor of the text may have been Joannes Lascaris; such, at least, was the thesis of Margoliouth, who credited Lascaris with the greatest single contribution to the editing of the *Poetics*.[23] If one compares this text with a modern edition, one finds many errors of spelling, many lacunae, and of course the same difficulties which have led to the conjectures and the exclusions of recent editors. But these are largely imperfections of the manuscripts and not failures of the editor of the printed text. Essentially, Aristotle's text is presented in a usable form, and to the growing group of humanists and scholars it offered the possibility of controlling Valla's translation, of preparing generally more satisfactory translations, and of proceeding to better editions and to intelligent exegeses.

For the next thirty years, there is practically no activity in the tradition of Aristotle's *Poetics*. Such texts as are found treat the *Poetics* in passing, alluding or referring to it in connection with other problems. It is hardly an exaggeration to say that study of the document, if we are to go by the extant works, was at a standstill for almost a third of a century. An example of the passing references to the *Poetics* may be found in Pomponio Gaurico's commentary on Horace, *De arte poetica* (*ca.* 1510).[24] In a work which is essentially a paraphrase of Horace, we suddenly come upon this phrase in the section on tragedy: "praecipue quum uult spectatores ad misericordiam commouere" (p. Aiii). The phrase, if it refers to Aristotle at all, does so only in the vaguest way and might be the result merely of hearsay rather than of a knowledge of the text. In an almost contemporary work, Vittore Fausto's *De comoedia libellus* (1511), the citations are more specific. Fausto takes directly from the *Poetics* the assertion that comedy imitates the ridiculous ("Hoc etiam Aristoteles comprobauit, inquens, quod in turpitudine ridiculum est comoediam imitare," p. AA3) and he cites it on the origins of comedy ("quemadmodum Aristoteles in poeticis ait: quoniam Epicharmus comicorum antiquissimus poeta illinc [of Sicily] esset oriundus," p. AA4; this refers to *Poetics* 1448*a*33).

In Lodovico Ricchieri's *Lectionum antiquarum libri XXX* (1516), the references are still more extensive.[25] For the most part Ricchieri is working

---

[23] For indications of the basic manuscripts, see D. S. Margoliouth's edition of the *Poetics* London: Hodder and Stoughton, 1911), pp. xv, 95–97; also Vahlen's edition (Leipzig, 1885), p. xi; and E. Lobel, *Greek Manuscripts of Aristotle's Poetics* (London: Oxford Univ. Press, 1933, pp. 31–32. Margoliouth, who ascribes the Aldine text to Lascaris, makes this judgment on it: "Lascaris's emendations constitute an important epoch in the history of the Poetics. ... a number will be retained so long as the Poetics is studied; and it is probable that the contribution of Lascaris to the text is the greatest which any one scholar has made" (p. 97).

[24] See above, chap. iii, pp. 88–90, and n. 41 for a study of this text and for its date.

[25] See above, chap. ii, p. 57 for this work.

in the Platonic tradition. But when he speaks of the origins of poetry, he gives as equivalent to the Latin "ex rudi principio" the Greek ἐκ τῶν αὐτοσχεδιασμάτων, which may derive from *Poetics* 1449*a*9, and then he gives the following explanation, translating fairly closely *Poetics* 1448*b*24 ff.:

> Indeed, from this basis of imitation, whence poetry had its origin, art was disengaged and as an art was subdivided and issued in several component parts. For the inclination to imitate was revealed according to the nature and the character of each writer. The more worthy ones proposed to imitate fine and honorable actions, but the lower and baser ones chose conformably vile and ignoble actions; just as some from the start undertook poems of blame while others sang hymns and praises.

There is also possibly some reflection of *Poetics* 1448*b*9, on the pleasure derived from the imitation of ugly objects, in the following passage:

> For that work of art arouses admiration whose portrayal seems to be coherently handled for the representation and depiction of the images of things. In the same way, indeed, we praise a lizard or a monkey depicted in conformity with the truth, not because of their beauty, which we know to be non-existent in such animals, but because of the resemblance.[26]

Pietro Pomponazzi's *De incantationibus* (1520), first published in the *Opera* of 1567, contains a short passage which cites the Averroës paraphrase of the *Poetics*. It is a defence of poetry as an instrument of education:

> For the mode of expression in the laws, as Averroës says in his *Poetry*, is similar to that used by the poets; for just as the poets do, they invent fables which, according to the literal meaning of the words, are nor possible, but within they contain the truth, as Plato and Aristotle frequently point out. For they tell untruths so that we may arrive at the truth, and so that we may instruct the vulgar crowd, which must be led toward good action and away from wicked action.[27]

Such a passage as this is especially interesting for several reasons: it shows to what extent Aristotle, in these years, was still read through Averroës,[28] and it demonstrates with what ease Plato and Aristotle were spoken of as assigning the same pedagogical role to poetry.

---

[26] *Lectionum* (1516), p. 162: "Ex hac uero imitandi ratione, unde Poesis ortum ducit, diuulsa, disparataq́ue Ars est, ac abiit quodammodo in membra plura. Nam pro cuiusque natura, & moribus imitandi studium proferebatur, honestiores enim pulchras honestasq́ue actiones sibi imitandas proponebant. Tenuiores autem, humilioresq́ue Viles itidem, & ignobiles, & primo quidem uituperationem complexi, Sicuti hymnos alii, & Laudes concinnarunt"; and p. 160: "Verum Artificium parere admirationem, quo expressio congruenter uidetur pertractata adumbrandis, informandisq́ue rerum imaginibus. Nam & eodem ferè modo Lacertam, aut Simiam commode ad Veritatem pictam laudamus, non utique ex pulchritudine, quam esse nullam in eiusmodi animalibus scimus. Sed ob similitudinem."

[27] In *Opera* (1567), p. 201: "Sermo enim legum, ut inquit Auerrois in sua poësi, est similis sermoni poëtarum, nam quanquam poëtę fingunt fabulas, quę, ut uerba sonant, non sunt possibles, intus tamen ueritatem continent, ut multotiens Plato & Aristoteles referunt: nam illa fingunt, ut in ueritatem ueniamus, & rude uulgus instruamus, quod inducere oportet ad bonum, & à malo retrahere."

[28] The Averroës paraphrase and the Valla translation had been reprinted together in 1515.

Apropos of Averroës, it should be mentioned that a new Latin translation of his paraphrase of the *Poetics*, that of Abram de Balmes, was published in 1523. Balmes' translation was based, however, on the fourteenth-century Hebrew translation of Todros Todrosi, and there is not much evidence to indicate that it was used extensively by Italian commentators.

The earliest extensive exploitation of the *Poetics* in Italian among the documents we shall examine is found in Giovanni Giorgio Trissino's dedication of his *Sophonisba* to Pope Leo X, dated 1524. Trissino first calls upon the text of Aristotle for a general distinction between tragedy and comedy:

... knowing also that tragedy, according to Aristotle, is to be preferred to all other poems, since it imitates by means of harmonious language a virtuous and perfect action, which should have magnitude; and just as Polygnotus, an ancient painter, imitating in his works, made the bodies better than they were and Pauson worse, so tragedy as it imitates makes the forms of behavior better and comedy, worse. And therefore this comedy moves to laughter, a thing which is related to ugliness, since what is ridiculous is defective and ugly. But tragedy moves to pity and fear, with which—and along with other teachings—it brings pleasure to the listeners and utility for human living.[29]

At the very end of the passage, inevitably, the Horatian "utile dulci" is introduced. Trissino then proceeds to an apology for his use of Italian rather than Latin and of his use of unrhymed verse; and for both the justification is found in Aristotle. The defence is curious and the interpretation of Aristotle garbled:

... since tragedy has six necessary parts, that is, plot, characters, words, discourse, representation, and verse, it is clear that, having to be presented in Italy, [the Sophonisba] could not be understood by all the people if it were composed in another language than Italian. And furthermore the ways of behavior, the sententiae, and the discourse would not provide universal utility and pleasure if they were not understood by the listeners. Hence, in order not to deprive it of the possibility of representation, which (as Aristotle says) is the first of the parts of tragedy, ... I chose to write it in this language.[30]

[29] *Sophonisba* (1524), p. aijv: "sapendo etiandio, che la Tragedia, secondo Aristotele, è preposta a tutti gli altri poemi, per imitare con soave sermone una virtuosa, e perfetta actione, la quale habbia grandeza; e come Polygnoto antico pictore nele opere sue imitando faceua e corpi di quello che erano migliori, e Pauson peggiori, cosi la Tragedia imitando fa e costumi migliori, e la Comedia peggiori, e per ciò essa Comedia muove riso, cosa che partecipa di brutteza, essendo ciò, che è ridiculo, difettoso, e brutto, Ma la Tragedia muove compassione, e tema, con le quali, e con altri amaestramenti arreca diletto agli ascoltatori, et utilitate al vivere humano."

[30] *Ibid.*, p. Aiij: "hauendo la Tragedia sei parti necessarie, cioè, la favola, e costumi, le parole, il discorso, la rappresentatione, et il verso; Manifesta cosa è, che hauendosi a rappresentare in Italia, non potrebbe essere intesa da tutto il popolo, s'ella fosse in altra lingua, che Italiana composta; & appresso e costumi, le sententie, et il discorso, non arrecherebbono universale utilitate, e diletto, se non fossero intese da gli ascoltanti. Si che per non le torre la rappresentatione, la quale (come dice Aristotile) è la prima parte de la Tragedia ... elessi di scriverla in questo Idioma."

Trissino's confusion springs either from his identification of "plot" with "representation," or more probably from a faulty reading of *Poetics* 1450a14, where "spectacle" is listed first among the qualitative parts. He defends the absence of rhyme, also on the basis of the *Poetics*, declaring that speeches which move to pity must themselves be expressions of suffering, and that such expressions are spontaneous and intolerant of such restrictions as that provided by rhyme (p. Aiij*v*).

Parts I to IV of the *Poetica* of the same Trissino, published in 1529, occupy a remarkable position in the history of Aristotle's *Poetics* (Parts V and VI, based entirely upon the *Poetics*, were published posthumously in 1563, and they will be treated in a later chapter). What is remarkable is that Trissino, knowing the *Poetics* as he did, should have proceeded almost without reference to it in the composition of his own *Poetica*. His sources are, instead, the rhetoricians and such writers on prosody as Antonio da Tempo. He cites the *Poetics* twice, first in a passage preliminary to his study of diction:

> I say then that poetry (as Aristotle said before me) is an imitation of the actions of man, and since this imitation is made by means of words, rhymes, and harmony, just as the painter's imitation is made by means of design and colors, it would be well before coming to this imitation to treat of that with which this imitation is made, that is of words and of rhymes, leaving harmony or song aside, since the others are capable of producing the imitation without song, and since the poet considers these two and leaves song to be considered by the singer.[31]

From then on, Trissino in these four parts treats only diction and rhyme. His second reference to Aristotle, indeed, is occasioned by his treatment of the choice of words, when he speaks of foreign words: "These are especially to be used in heroic poetry, where variety of languages, as Aristotle says, is sought."[32] The allusion is probably to *Poetics* 1459a10.

In Aulo Giano Parrasio's *In Q. Horatii Flacci artem poeticam commentaria* (1531, posthumous) we have the first of those numerous commentaries on Horace which were to develop the parallelisms between the *Ars poetica* and the *Poetics*. In this case (as I have already pointed out[33]), the parallels are few in number, and in most cases the statement of the Aristotelian position is such that one thinks immediately of Averroës rather than of the *Poetics* itself. So, in Parrasio's introduction, for the statement "Obseruauerunt eam mortales, quod harmonia & rythmus natura nobis tributa

---

[31] *La poetica* (1529), p. iiv: "Dico adunque, che la Poesia (come prima disse Aristotele) è una imitazione de le azioni de l'homo; e facendosi questa cotale imitazione con parole, rime, et harmonia, si come la imitazione del dipintore si fa con disegno, e con colori, fia buono, inanzi che ad essa imitazione si vegna, trattare di quello, con che essa imitazione si fà, cioè de le parole, e de le rime; lasciando la harmonia overo il canto da parte; perciò, che quelle ponno fare la imitazione senza esso, e di queste due il Poeta considera, e lascia il canto considerare al Cantore."

[32] *Ibid.*, p. iiiiv: "e queste specialmente stanno bene ad usarsi ne lo heroico, nel quale la varietà di lingue, come dice Aristotele, si ricerca."

[33] Cf. chap. iii, pp. 96–100.

sunt" (p. 1v), which refers to Averroës, p. f2v, and for another, "Erit ergo boni poetae ante omnia ideam futuri sibi poematis statuere, & quod periti faciunt architecti, breui quasi tabella totius operis imaginem ante oculos proponere" (p. 6v), which may refer to Averroës, p. gv. In the same introduction, however, there is at least one passage which seems to go back directly to the *Poetics*. Beginning with a rapid history of poetry before Homer, Parrasio continues:

> The latter [Homer], having put together all that was previously dispersed, gave to poetry a single and definitive body, and it is to be marveled at that no imitation—not even a dramatic representation—might be contrived which did not have a counterpart in his work. With his own might he introduced into his works the subjects of comedies, tragedies, dithyrambs, and of all kinds of poems.[34]

The next statement, however—"All poems are either dramatic, or narrative, or a mixture of these"[35]—could come as well from Plato or from the current Horatian tradition. In the line-by-line commentary on Horace there are no references to Aristotle. But late in the text, in connection with vss. 318 and 408, there are two brief passages which again are closer to Averroës than to the *Poetics*: on p. 68v, Parrasio says, "Nihil enim aliud est poesis nisi imitatio uitae & morum, quae hominis propria est, facitque ut vel hac una differt a caeteris animalibus," with which compare Averroës, p. f2v: "istud proprium est homini respectu ceterorum animalium. Et causa in hoc est quum homo inter cetera animalia delectatur in assimilatione rerum quas iam in sensu percepit & in earum representatione seu imitatione." And on p. 78 he says "Si enim . . . poetica nihil aliud est, quam imitatio naturae," with which compare Averroës, p. fv. As in other contemporary documents, the text of the *Poetics* itself is reflected only slightly; Averroës continues to dominate the scene.

PAZZI'S TEXT AND TRANSLATION (1536)

The general situation will be changed, however, after the publication in 1536 of Alessandro de' Pazzi's Greek text and Latin translation of the *Poetics*. Pazzi's own statements in the dedication indicate that he had prepared the volume in Rome in 1524; the dedication itself is dated 1527, and the publication was posthumous, Pazzi (or Paccius) having died in the intervening years. For the contemporary reader, Pazzi's volume must have had two especially attractive features. For the first time, it offered text and translation together, separated from the other works with which both had previously been printed; and for the first time it presented them in a small, portable, inexpensive format, contrasting with the sizable tomes of earlier

---

[34] *Commentaria* (1531), pp. 2–2v: "Hic complexus quicquid antea diuisum fuerat unum poeticae corpus perfectum fecit, & admirandum, ut nulla imitatio ne ritu quidem dragmatico effingi possit, quę non in illo eluceat, ui sua comediarum, tragoediarum, dythiramborum, omniumque poematum argumenta suis operibus inseruit."

[35] *Ibid.*, p. 2v: "Poemata omnia aut actiua sunt, aut enarratiua, aut ex his mista."

editions. These reasons probably explain why the volume was rapidly reprinted in Basel, in 1527, and in Paris, in 1538. As for the text and translation themselves, both represent advances over their predecessors. The progress is perhaps less notable in the case of the Greek text, where there was little to add, on the basis of available manuscripts, to Lascaris' distinguished contributions in the Aldine edition. Pazzi used three manuscripts, one of them in the Vatican (now Vat. gr. 1400), and from them he derived a certain number of useful emendations to Lascaris' text. But it was the translation which really rendered the greatest service to Pazzi's contemporaries. It is, generally, far superior to Giorgio Valla's. I should not say that it is always and unfailingly better; some of Valla's errors are repeated, some of his correct solutions are spoiled, and the basic difficulties of the available Greek manuscripts still continue to be reflected in the translation. But for the most part, Pazzi's work is more accurate and more readable; it has a much greater clarity of construction and is less dense and elliptical, and its sentence divisions and punctuation assist the reader in making sense out of the *Poetics*. As an example of the kind of improvement achieved, we may compare the two translations of the crucial passage in which tragedy is defined (*Poetics* 1449*b*24):

Valla: Est igitur tragoedia imitatio actionis probae atque consumatae magnitudinem iucunda oratione obtimentis citra quamlibet speciem in particulis agentium nec de comissorum pronuntiatu de miseratione & pauore terminans talium disciplinarum purgationem. suauem ac oblectabilem in quam orationem habentem rhythmum & harmoniam & melos quod autem citra species id per metra quaedam dumtaxat perficitur sicut porro alia per melos. Verum quia faciunt agentes imitationem. primo quidem si particula tragoediae aliqua sit uisus ornamentum esse necesse est inde melopoeiam & dictionem in his siquidem imitationem conficiunt. Dictionem uero ipsam uoco metrorum compositionem ut melopoeiam uim omnem habet manifestam at quia actionis. est imitatio. agitur autem ab aliquibus agentibus. quos qualitate aliqua insignes esse necesse est moribus atque animi sententia propter haec enim quod actiones qualitate insignes esse dicamus uis tulit naturae actionum binas esse causas animi sententiam & morem unde assecuntur & uoti impotes fiunt. est uero actionis fabula imitatio (p. r ii*v*).

Pazzi: Tragoedia est imitatio actionis illustris, absolutae, magnitudinem habentis, sermone suaui, separatim singulis generibus in partibus agentibus, non per enarrationem, per misericordiam uerò atque terrorem perturbationes huiusmodi purgans. sermonem suauem appello, in quo numerus, harmonia, & melos inest: id uerò separatim genere dictinctum: cum metro tantum quaedam absoluantur, quaedam rursum melodia. Quoniam uerò tota imitatio in actione uersatur, primum quidem apparatum ipsum, partem Tragoediae ponere necesse est, mox melodiam, & dictionem; utpote ex quibus imitationem conficiant: dictionem appello illam quidem metrorum compositionem: melodiam, cuius omnino uis per se ipsa satis apparet. Sed quoniam actionis imitatio est, agiturque ab agentibus quibusdam, quos tum moribus, tum sententia tales esse omnino oportet, sicuti quoque & actiones aliquas esse tales dicimus: manifestum est harum actionum duas esse causas, sententiam, & mores: per quas planè uel uoti compotes, uel minime compotes omnes fiunt. Ad haec actionis imitatio fabula est (p. 9v).

Pazzi's translation immediately became standard for the *Poetics*; not only was it reprinted at least a dozen times during the century, in Italy, France, and Switzerland, but it was taken as the basis for such important commentaries as those of Robortello and Maggi.

LOMBARDI AND MAGGI (1541)

The next event in the history of Aristotle's *Poetics* in the Cinquecento involves three men and two important documents. The event is the first public lectures on the *Poetics* of which we have accurate records; the three men are Bartolomeo Lombardi, Vincenzo Maggi, and Alessandro Sardi; and the documents are, first, Sardi's notes on Maggi's lectures, dated 1546, and the *Explanationes* published by Maggi, for himself and Lombardi, in 1550. The story is rather complex; I reconstruct the chronology roughly as follows:

In December, 1541, Bartolomeo Lombardi began the public exposition of the *Poetics* at Padua. But shortly afterward he died, leaving among his papers: (a) a text and translation of the *Poetics*; (b) a "Praefatio" to the work, addressed to the Accademia degli Infiammati of Padua; and (c) extensive notes on the work, later incorporated into the *Explanationes*.[36]

The lectures were continued by Maggi, and apparently with considerable success. As witness, we may consult the letter which Benedetto Varchi received from Cosimo Rucellai on December 17, 1541:

> I am greatly desirous of having those lectures, few or many as they may be, which Maggi gave on Aristotle's *Poetics*; wherefore I pray you, if you have them, to send them to me as soon as you possibly can, and as carefully written as is possible. If you don't have them, try to get a copy of them from some friend of yours, and then send them to me. In a word I desire greatly to have them such as they may be; although I have heard that they are divine.[37]

In 1543, Maggi became professor of philosophy at Ferrara, where he again expounded the *Poetics*.

Among those who heard Maggi's lectures at Ferrara was the young

[36] For the date of Lombardi's lectures, see F. V. Cerreta, "An Account of the Early Life of the Accademia degli Infiammati in the Letters of Alessandro Piccolomini to Benedetto Varchi," *Romanic Review*, XLVIII (1957), 253, 264. See also Maggi's introduction to the *Explanationes* (1550), p. *ij on Lombardi's lectures, interrupted by his death; and p. 27 on Lombardi's contributions to the volume. The "Praefatio" is printed in the same volume, pp. 1–11.

[37] Letter of Cosimo Rucellai (from Florence) to Benedetto Varchi (in Bologna), dated "Di Firenze adì 17. di Dicembre 1541," printed in the *Prose Fiorentine*, Pt. IV, Vol. I (Florence, 1734), p. 42: "io desidero assai di avere quelle o poche, o assai lezioni, che elle fussero, che fece sopra la Poetica d'Aristotile il Maggio; per la qual cosa vi prego, che se l'avete, me le mandiate quanto prima potete, e più diligentemente scritte, che sia possibile; se non l'avete, cerchiate da qualche vostro Amico averne copia, e dipoi me le mandiate. In somma grandemente desidero di averle quali elle si siano, benchè ho inteso son divine."

Alessandro Sardi, who was later to become the author of several erudite works.[38] His notes on these lectures are dated "15 Cal. Februarj MDXLVI" and are preserved in the Biblioteca Estense at Modena as MS.a.Q.6.14. In spite of the late date of these notes, I see no reason for believing that they do not represent the lectures substantially as Maggi began to give them in 1541, since in them Maggi declares that his interpretation is still based on that of Lombardi. Even with their date of 1546, however, Sardi's notes constitute the earliest extant commentary on Aristotle's *Poetics*.

In 1548, before Maggi was able to publish the *Explanationes* on which he had been working, Francesco Robortello published his own *Explicationes*, which thus became the first published commentary. Maggi was of course furious, and he took occasion to attack Robortello in a section of his manuscript entitled "Obiectiones quaedam aduersus Robortelli explicationem in primum Aristotelis contextum," stating his objections and indicating Robortello's errors and omissions.

Finally, in 1550, the joint work of Lombardi and Maggi appeared under the title *In Aristotelis librum de poetica communes explanationes*. I am assuming that this text represents a much later state of Maggi's thinking, and hence I shall discuss it under the date 1550.

Meanwhile, we may suppose that Lombardi's "Praefatio" was published essentially as he wrote it and analyze it at this point. As a preface to a commentary on Aristotle's *Poetics*, these pages are remarkable above all for the fact that they have nothing to do with the text or the ideas of the *Poetics*. Except for a brief passage near the end (p. 10) where Lombardi divides the *Poetics* into "prooemium" and "narratio," indicates its subject matter, and exclaims upon the excellence of the work and its superiority to all others on poetics, the "Praefatio" might just as well serve as an introduction to any other work on the art of poetry. Lombardi's ideas are completely traditional. He is interested in two problems: the relationship of poetry to the other arts and disciplines, and the defence of poetry. With respect to the first, he insists upon the fact that all other disciplines are present in poetry, and he shows one by one how the materials of the other sciences are also the materials of poetry. This is done for grammar and especially for rhetoric, which treats of the same subjects and uses the same devices; Homer and Vergil, for example, are full of rhetorical topoi, just as the works of the rhetoricians are full of examples from the poets. Similarly for logic, all of whose parts are found in the exposition of the poet and in the speeches of his personages, including the syllogism and paralogism. All natural philosophy has been treated by the poets, and indeed philosophy is a necessary appanage of the poet. The demonstration continues for theology, music, astrology, geography, the prophetic arts, physiognomics, moral philosophy, painting, and medicine.

[38] On Sardi, see the life written by Girolamo Ferri and published with Sardi's *Numinum et Heroum Origines* (Rome, 1775).

In another development, Lombardi adopts Averroës' classification of "Demonstrativa, Dialectica, Sophistica, Rhetorica, Poetica" and seeks the distinctions to be made between poetry and each of its sister-disciplines. The five arts are divided into two groups. The first, containing Logic, Dialectic, and Sophistic, produces dissertations which attempt to convince by argumentation and the use of the syllogism; all three are branches of "logic." The second, containing Rhetoric and Poetics, does not really belong to logic; it uses more popular devices, such as the example and the enthymeme, and its materials are largely political. Having accepted this classification, it is not surprising that Lombardi should propose a definition of poetry which is much closer to Aristotle's definition of rhetoric than to anything found in the *Poetics*. "Poetry," he says, "is the faculty of discovering whatever is appropriate to the imitation of any action, passion, or character, by means of harmonious discourse, for the purpose of correcting our way of living and of leading to a good and happy life.[39]

Lombardi's defence of poetry is based in part on the moral utility indicated in this definition. Poetry is superior to philosophy since it proposes, through the imitation of an action, to correct moral behavior by pleasurable means ("morum cum uoluptate correctione," p. 6). Its purpose is to lead us to a good and happy life ("ad bene beateque uiuendum comparatam," p. 9) by teaching us to love the virtues and to hate the vices ("uirtutes ut amplexemur, uitia ut auersemur," p. 8). These considerations lead Lombardi to answer Plato's ban of the poets, and he does so by insisting that Plato had in mind not the art as a whole but only certain passages in Homer. The rest of the defence derives from the universality of subject matter of poetry—and of the poet's knowledge—and from its antiquity. Only in passing does Lombardi mention that it springs from two natural causes (and he cites Aristotle). In general, the whole argument is related to the current discussions in the Platonic tradition, to the conception of the ends as proposed by Horace, and to the ideas of the classical rhetoricians. Aristotle figures only in the most incidental way.

Later in the sixteenth century, it became a commonplace to say—in explanation of the deficiencies of the *Poetics*—that the text represented merely a set of lecture notes by Aristotle; hence its incompleteness, its inconsistencies, its lack of order. The same is really true of those notes which Alessandro Sardi took on Maggi's exposition of the *Poetics* at the University of Ferrara in 1546, except that these are the notes of a student rather than of the lecturer. They must represent only imperfectly the spoken word of the master, still less satisfactorily the written notes from which he was speaking. One senses, in reading them, an abridgment of the numerous quotations, an elimination of much of the source material, many inade-

---

[39] *Explanationes* (1550), p. 9: "Poetica est facultas uidendi quodcunque accommodatum est ad imitationem cuiusque actionis, affectionis, moris, suaui sermone, ad uitam corrigendam, & ad benè beateque uiuendum comparata."

quacies of the language. Nevertheless, these notes are a completely remarkable document in the history of modern literary criticism. Remarkable, first, by its date: as was pointed out, the lectures given in 1546 probably were very close in content to the ones that Maggi began giving in 1541; hence by all odds the earliest extant commentary on Aristotle's *Poetics*. Remarkable, also, by its approaches to the *Poetics* and by its solutions to the problems raised.

The text as we have it in MS.a.Q.6.14 of the Biblioteca Estense at Modena is incomplete; it provides a commentary on the *Poetics* from the beginning through 1453b11 (i.e., to the end of what would later be Maggi's seventy-third "particella"). Whether this is because the lectures themselves stopped at that point, or because Sardi did not hear the rest, or because the remaining notes have not come down to us, we can only surmise.[40] The word-by-word gloss was preceded by a general introduction, devoted by Maggi to a general discussion of the art of poetry, of the nature of Aristotle's treatise, and of the latter's title. At no point is the treatment as complete and extended as it was to be in Maggi's later published *Explanationes* (1550); first, because an Italian student taking notes in Latin on a lecture in Latin was bound to abbreviate and condense as much as possible; second, because Maggi's thought and his erudition were undoubtedly much less fully developed at this point than they were to be almost ten years later. As an example of the differences, we may take Maggi's statements about the word "Dithyrambica" in Pazzi's translation of Aristotle's second sentence (1447a14).

In the notes, folios 8v–9, the whole of the gloss occupies about one small page; I give here the whole of the text:

Dithyrambica. in graeco habetur διθυραμβοποιητική. id est. dithirambopoetica uno uerbo. Ideo interpres non est fidelis. Aristoteles autem miro artificio hoc uerbo composito usus est. quia dithyrambi maxime gaudent nominibus compositis, et nominibus longis. Ideo etiam philosophus de ipsis loquens usus est nomine longo, et composito. Horatius enim tum loqueretur quo pacto nomine nouo uti debemus utitur ipse nouo nomine Inuideo cum loquatur de nouitate. Ita philosophus hic loquens de Dithyrambicis nominauit nomine composito, et longo. Plato L. 7. de legibus dicit ambiguum esse an saltatio Bacchica, quae est

---

[40] In his edition of Sardi's *Numinum et Heroum Origines*, Girolamo Ferri prints two documents of interest for the history of these notes. One of them, a list of unpublished works of Sardi, includes the following passage: "le Lezioni manoscritte del Maggio, del Guarino, e di altri miei precettori in tre Volumi in quarto" (Ferri, p. xlviii). The other, from which the first passage had been quoted, is a testament bequeathing the same works to Gio. Francesco Serragli: "Al Sig. Gio. Francesco Serragli Medico l'opere d'Ippocrate, e di Oribasio, Plinio *de re Medicinali*, l'Istoria Naturale di Plinio *appostillata da me*, il Commento sopra Detti di Stefano Aqueo, e le *Lezioni manoscritte del Maggio, del Guarino*, e di altri miei Precettori, legati alla Romana in tre Volumi in quarto" (Ferri, p. lii). Sardi's handwriting, notorious among scholars at the Estense, is practically undecipherable. To this date, I have succeeded in transcribing only a portion of the MS, and the analysis I give is based on that partial transcription.

ista, sit saltatio: quia [fol. 8v] saltationes erant in duplici differentia, quae imitabantur res bellicas, in quibus ostendebatur agilitas: et etiam saltationes urbanae et modestae ad bonos mores. Et quia saltationes istae in honorem Bacchi erant, propter uinum. nec urbanae, nec militares, ideo inter saltationes eas non rediget. In Phaedro autem de dithyrambis loquitur. et Arist. L. 3. Rhet. ubi dicit proemia esse similia in Dithyrambis demonstratiuis, id est libera quae nihil cum re conueniant. et Diony: Halicarnasseus ubi de mutatione, ubi modos saltandi esse dicit tres, Doricos, lyricos, et Phrigios: quandoque graciles etiam. et quandoque ad imitationem dithyramborum. Et idem fl. 167 examinat dithyrambicum Pindari. In istis transitur ab una musica in aliam musicam. Aristopha. in Nebulis, quo pacto nubes alant aliquos deridet Dithyrambicos poetas Vbi multa de illis agit commentator. et etiam alibi in ornithiis deridet eos Aristophanes quod sint multa uerborum, et nullum sententiarum habeant. Inde uerba Dithyrambicorum diuersa, et absque sententia. De his [illegible] in libro de poetis: et de nomine eorum et quia erant in honorem Bacchi nunc nos iis non utimur (fol. 9).

As against this relatively short passage, the commentary in the 1550 work fills one and one-third closely printed folio pages. Many of the same materials appear, but in a different order (pp. 34–35). Maggi now repeats the explanation of Aristotle's use of a compound noun, so appropriate to the genre which it signifies (omitting, however, the citation of "inuideor" from *Ars poetica* 56); this is much expanded and other examples are offered. Next follows the allusion to *Rhetoric* III, in very similar terms. In place of the brief "In Phaedro autem de dithyrambis loquitur," he quotes two separate passages from the *Phaedrus*. He then gives, in rapid succession, passages from *Rhetoric* III, the *Problemata*, and *Politics* VIII, and references to Lycophron, Dionysius of Halicarnassus, Demetrius of Phaleron, Menander, and the commentator on Aristophanes. Finally, he discusses the relationship between dithyrambic poetry and Bacchus, quoting at length from Book VII of Plato's *Laws*. The purpose of this display of erudition is to define the name of the genre, to describe it as fully as possible, and to collect opinions about it from ancient authors.

Maggi's procedure in this passage is typical of what he does throughout his spoken commentary on the *Poetics*. He brings to bear, upon each word or phrase that merits remark, all the erudition that he has been able to accumulate. His erudition is very extensive, perhaps remarkably so for so early a date in the century; it covers the whole range both of Greek and Latin writers and includes many texts which had been made available only since the beginning of the century—the space of a generation. In the first ten pages of the notes, for example, Sardi records references to authors as diversified as the following: Plato (*Laws, Phaedrus, Cratylus, Sophist, Phaedo, Timaeus*), Aristotle (*Prior Analytics,* both *Rhetorics, Posterior Analytics, De Anima, Physics, Problemata, Ethics,* as well as commentators on several of these texts), Plutarch, Hermogenes, Dionysius of Halicarnassus, Ammonius, Aphthonius, Diomedes, Simplicius, Suidas, Cicero (*De Oratore, De Finibus, Tusculan Orations*), and Quintilian. The list for the whole of the set of notes would be much longer. In using these ancient authors for the exposition of his text, Maggi was merely applying the familiar technique of the scholarly gloss; more specifically, he was adapting to the *Poetics* the devices of elucidation which had been for so long used in connection with the *Ars poetica*.

Throughout, the consideration of the *Poetics* in the light of the *Ars poetica* is completely explicit. In his opening sentence, Maggi declares his intentions; after stating that he means to rely on Lombardi's notes, he continues: "... and we shall observe this order: we shall say how Aristotle and Horace agree between them, and what Aristotle said that Horace omitted, or what Horace said that Aristotle omitted; and who did better."[41] He passes immediately (according to the canonical order) to an examination of the titles of the two works, asking why Aristotle should have called his merely *De poetica* whereas Horace called his *De arte poetica*, and these considerations lead him far into the discovery of the basic difference between the two works. The same is done at other points where a parallel examination of Horace seems appropriate. What Maggi is doing is really very simple: he takes as a basis for his discussion that work of literary theory which his audience knows best, and to it he compares, *pari passu*, another work which he himself is in a sense introducing into the canon of public literary discussion; the reference is from the known to the unknown. In so doing, however, he is making history; he is establishing the tradition of the confronting of Aristotle and Horace which will last to the end of the century and beyond.

This does not mean that Maggi conceives of the two works as identical. Instead, his initial opposition of their titles leads him to discover a fundamental difference between them. Stated in a succinct formula, it is that "the philosopher [Aristotle] treats of the thing in itself and Horace of precepts and almost nothing at all of the thing."[42] Thus Aristotle calls his treatise *De poetica* because "considering the knowledge of poetry, he speaks of poetics so that we may know its parts both quantitative and qualitative." In other words, "because Aristotle's intention was to treat of the knowledge of poetry, since the art is taken from the thing, and because according to nature it [the thing] precedes, he entitled his book for that very same thing."[43] But Horace's title, *De arte poetica*, is a clear recognition of his intention to include those precepts and rules that would teach the poet how to write a poem: "Horace, who writes only a little of the thing and more of the art, justly gave the title 'de arte,' as if he were to

[41] MS Modena, Bibl. Estense, a.Q.6.14, fol. 1: "et hunc ordinem seruabimus. quid concordent inter se Aristoteles et Horatius dicemus: et quid dixerit Aristoteles, quod omisserit Horatius: uel quid dixerit Horatius quod omisserit Aristoteles. Et quis melius fecerit."

[42] *Ibid.*, fol. 3: "philosophus de re in se; et de praeceptis agit Horatius quasi nihil de re."

[43] *Ibid.*, fols. 3–3v: "respiciens ad cognitionem poesis, dixit de poetica, ut cognoscamus partes, quantas, et quales ... quia Aristotelis intentio erat agere de cognitione poesis, quia ars sumitur a re: et quia secundum natura praecedit, de ista re inscripsit librum."

speak of the laws which the poet must observe."[44] The philosopher, in sum, writes a "method" whereas the poet writes an "art." Maggi repeats this opposition, very briefly, when he glosses the first two words of Pazzi's translation (fol. 5).

As a result of the difference in intention, the content of the two works is also different. The *Ars poetica*, adding precept to knowledge and art to method, will comprise a larger variety of materials than the *Poetics*. Maggi divides it into three sections, points out how it treats both poetry and the art of poetry, distinguishes it from the *Poetics*:

> Whence with respect to his book you will see that it is divided into three parts. In the first he writes of what poet [?]; in the second, of poetry; in the third he teaches the precepts of poetry. At the beginning he speaks to him who wishes to be a good poet; Aristotle says nothing about this. Horace, when he says "Pictoribus atque poetis quidlibet audendi semper fuit aequa potestas," is speaking of poetry; because like Plutarch in the book *Quomodo pueri debeant uidere poetas*, he says that poets are like painters. On the other hand, [he speaks] of precepts in "Humano capiti," etc.[45]

The *Poetics*, being a methodical treatise, will be differently composed and will have another kind of order. Maggi sees it as having two parts, which may be designated as the "proemium" and the "tractatus" or as the "principium" and the "narratio." The "proemium," brief as it is (it is made up of only the first sentence), has many functions to perform and is subdivided into many parts:

  A. Genera et partes
   1. Genera
   2. Partes
     a. De poesi in se
     b. De generibus
     c. De fabula
     d. De partibus qualibus et quantis
     e. De omnis quae pertinent ad hanc materiam
  B. Modum quae uult seruare in tractandis propositis (fol. 5)

The "tractatus" is subdivided into only two parts:

  A. De poesi
   1. De conuenientia Epopeiae, Comoediae, et Tragoediae . . . et aliarum artium quae conueniunt in hoc, quod sint imitationes
   2. Differentia tria inter has
   3. De inuentione poesis
  B. [Treatment of the individual kinds] (fol. 7v)

---

[44] *Ibid.*, fol. 3v: "Horatius qui modicum de re, plura de arte scribit, merito inscripsit de arte, quasi diceret de legibus quas seruare poeta debet."

[45] *Ibid.*, fol. 3: "Vnde circa scripta ipsius uidebitis ipsa diuisa in tres partes. in prima quem poetam [illegible] scribit: in 2. poesim: in 3. tradit praecepta poesis. In principio loquitur eum qui uult esse bonus poeta. Aristoteles nihil de hac dicit. Horatius quando dicit pictoribus atque poetis quidlibet audendi semper fuit aequa potestas, loquitur de poesi. quia ut plutarchus in libro quomodo pueri debeant uidere poetas: dicit poetae esse similes pictoribus agit autem de praeceptis Humano capiti etc."

Clearly, and in spite of his designations, Maggi sees in the *Poetics* a philosophical rather than a rhetorical order.

This establishment of differences between Aristotle and Horace and this distinction of Aristotle's method do not, however, prevent Maggi from assigning to his poetic theory the same ends for poetry that might be found in philosophers of widely different approaches. The naming of the ends is found first in Maggi's definition of poetry: "We say consequently upon Aristotle's principles that poetry is an imitation of the actions, passions, and characters of men themselves, in pleasant speech, to the end that men may be led to proper conduct."[46] The "art" will be the art of making the imitation in such a way that "men will be enticed to proper conduct" ("ut homines alliciantur ad bonos mores," fols. 3v–4). Although each of the genres may have a specific end, they have a common end in the production of moral improvement. As Maggi distinguishes the "end" of tragedy from those of comedy, he uses two meanings of "end" as he repeats various medieval commonplaces. First, "end" is taken as equivalent to "denouement": "... for no matter how much tragedy and comedy may seem to differ, they agree nevertheless in the end. Comedy may have a sad beginning and a happy ending, and tragedy just the opposite." The passage continues by distinguishing the other ends: "Yet not for this do they differ in end, because they bring men to proper conduct through divers ways. Comedy laughs at bad and wicked men so that we may flee them; Tragedy extols illustrious men and the best characters so that we may follow them."[47] Sweetness of language is considered a rhetorical device which makes the lessons of poetry acceptable.

It is this same identification of the moral end that enables Maggi to classify poetry under moral philosophy. Antecedent traditions had provided him with two major alternatives for the classification: the medieval logicians and Averroës suggested a subsuming under logic, Plato and Plutarch and Cicero a subsuming under moral philosophy. Maggi accepts both suggestions and tries to reconcile them:

Nevertheless we say that poetics must be classified under moral pholosophy; for Plutarch says that the poet teaches proper conduct, and Cicero also says so. But in what way can it be classified under the moral [philosophy] if Averroës puts it under logic? If poetics be considered according to the way in which it goes about imitating actions, characters, and passions, because it has to do with language and depicts actions, characters, and the passions of men by means of language, it is concerned with logic. Because it is concerned with words and

---

[46] *Ibid.*, fol. 3v: "Nos dicimus consequenter ad principia Aristotelis quod poesis est imitatio actionum, passionum, et morum ipsorum hominum sermone suaui ad hoc ut homines trahantur ad bonos mores."

[47] *Ibid.*, fol. 4: "quia quamuis tragoedia, et comoedia uideantur differre: conueniunt tum in fine licet comoedia principium triste, et laetum finem habere, e contra autem tragoedia. non tamen in fine differunt, quia redducunt homines ad mores bonos per diuersos modos. Comoedia deridet malos, et uiles, ut ab eis effugiamus. Tragoedia uiros extollit claros, et mores optimos, ut eos sequamur."

POETICS: DISCOVERY AND EXEGESIS

λόγος, it is language. But it is under the moral because of this reason, because it considers its end as being conduct; for this reason, it is classified as moral.[48]

Regarding both classifications as justifiable, Maggi goes on to point out that Petrarch is a moral philosopher because he teaches how lovers should love; that poets who treat wicked matters are "cacopoetae" and should not be read ("nec legendi sed cohorrendi," fol. 4v); that Plato's and Cicero's demand for the teaching of good conduct is reflected in Horace's "Aut prodesse uolunt, aut delectare poetae." The Platonic and Horatian traditions of the end of poetry are thus allowed to direct the reading of Aristotle.

In an exactly similar way, this first commentary on the *Poetics* reads into it, from earlier critical positions, the requirement that poetry be in verse. If the object of imitation is actions, passions, characters, the means is sweet language and verse ("sermo suauis" and "carmen," fol. 4). The laws of poetry are reduced to those "which we must use in composing verses" ("quibus uti debemus in componendis carminibus," fol. 5). So, too, the meaning assigned to "fabula" is traditional and rhetorical. Discarding the meanings suggested by Terence, Horace, and Cicero, Maggi adopts the whole of Aristotle's argument from the *Problemata*, assuming that what he says there is applicable to the poetic "fabula":

But now we understand by "fable" that which stands in the place of a true example, which is like a certain exemplum. Aristotle in the *Problemata* (particula 18, probl. 3) asks why in their orations orators take greater pleasure in examples and fables than in enthymemes and reasonings, and he advances these three reasons. Because examples are more familiar and pleasant, they are quickly learned and on that account they are more acceptable. Also because fables are particular things, but reasonings are universal things which are more remote; but fables are closer to us, therefore we learn more speedily. And the second reason, because that thing is said to be more readily believed by us, which is confirmed by judgment, which is present in examples. The third reason, because we learn more readily things that are similar, and because examples and fables are similar. Therefore we enjoy the things more. With respect to this, when Aristotle there says expressly that a fable is like an example, we thus here understand by fable an image of some thing, and thence fables are like a picture of the thing which is being treated.[49]

---

[48] *Ibid.*, fols. 4–4v: "tamen dicimus quod poetica debet reduci sub philosophia morali: quia Plutarchus dicit poetam docere bonos mores. quod etiam Cicero dicit. quo pacto autem debetur [?] redduci sub morali: si Auerrois eam sub logica ponit? Si poetica consideretur ratione qua uersatur ut imitetur actiones, mores, et passiones. quia uersatur circa sermonem et pingit sermone actiones mores et passiones hominum uersatur circa logicam: qui[a] uersatur in uerbis qui est sermo. sub morali autem est quia ea ratione, quia respicit finem mores esse. ea ratione ad moralem redducitur."

[49] *Ibid.*, fols. 5v–6: "Fabulam autem nunc intelligimus id quod est loco exempli ueri, quod est ueluti quoddam exemplum. Aristotel. in problematibus particula 18, probl. 3. quaerit quare in orationibus oratores magis delectentur exemplis et fabulis, quam Entimematibus et rationibus. et has tres rationes affert. Quia exempla sunt magis familiaria, iucundia, cito addiscuntur, ideo gratiora sunt. Etiam quia fabulae sunt res particulares: rationes autem uniuersales quae sunt magis remotae: uiciniores autem fabulae, ideo magis discemus cito. et .2. ratio quia haec res dicitur magis credi a nobis, quae est existimatio confirmata: quod in exemplis est. .3. ratio quia nos addiscimus libentius similia, et quia exempla et fabulae sunt similes. Ideo res magis gaudemus. Quo circa cum Aristoteles ibi exprese dicit quod fabula est uelut exemplum. Ideo hic per fabulam intelligimus imaginem alicuius rei, et ideo fabulae sunt ueluti pictura rei de qua agitur."

[381]

In the first of these cases, the meaning is derived from old ways of thinking about poetry; in the second, from old ways of talking about rhetoric.

Maggi's developments are, indeed, apt to be more extensive on such traditional matters as these than on ideas which are new because they are particularly germane to Aristotle's *Poetics*. For some of the latter, the treatment is brief to the point of being disappointing; topics which later became the great cruxes of Aristotelian discussion are here passed over without a flurry. We may take as an example the definition of tragedy. Maggi states that Aristotle defines tragedy first, before the other genres, because it is the most excellent of all, that he includes its qualitative and quantitative parts as promised in the "proemium," and that the definition meets all requirements by stating genus and differentiae. His glosses on the individual words are extremely short. "Imitatio" is said to indicate the genus, the rest of the definition the differentiae. "Illustris" means merely "ad differentiam uulgarium." (There is no gloss on "actionis," since action had been discussed previously.) "Absolutae" means "perfectae, quia debet esse una tota actio integra." On "magnitudinem," he merely remarks that this is the magnitude of the action, the imitation. For "sermone suaui" and "separatim" he refers to a later commentary. "Enarrationem" is clarified by the phrase "vt in epopeis." The only extensive notes are on "misericordiam," where Maggi compares the purgation of pity and fear to that purgation of which Aristotle speaks in Book VIII of the *Politics*, the purgation of passions from the soul through music. The pleasurable aspects of the effect are indicated in the sentence: "And purgations are exaltations of the soul along with pleasure" ("Et expurgationes sunt sublationes animae cum uoluptate," fol. 44). Maggi interprets the effect of purgation as the driving out from the soul, through the spectacle of strong passions, of those same passions, leaving the soul provided with more desirable ones: "...they are purged and liberated of such passions, and thus they are made strong and constant" ("expurgantur, et liberantur a talibus affectibus, et ita redduntur fortes et constantes," fol. 44). Maggi thinks that this is the best of several suggested interpretations. It might be noted at this point that in the 1550 *Explanationes* he studies the whole matter much more thoroughly, and arrives at an essentially different conclusion.

Even this partial analysis of Sardi's notes on Maggi will serve to show their distinctive features. Maggi begins the long tradition of explicating the *Poetics* by placing it in two contexts, Horace's *Ars poetica* and the rhetorical tradition. He brings to it the same kind of erudition that had long been called upon for the elucidation of other classical texts. But because he does use old methods and refers to old ways of considering poetic problems, he is bound to miss much that might have been new for a fresh reader of the *Poetics*. He sees in it at times distinctions, definitions, and conclusions which belong rather to other systems, even if at other times he is scrupulous about trying to discover Aristotle's own system. He is, of course, faced with insuperable difficulties: a difficult text, philosophically, in poor philological shape, in an only moderately satisfactory translation, full of terms and conceptions that had not previously attracted the attention of the scholars. His great merit, in this situation, was having tackled the problem, pursued it with great diligence through at least a decade, and produced a number of valid conclusions. What he did in his lectures set the pattern for Aristotelian commentary throughout the century and provided for later theorists an initial interpretation on the basis of which they might elaborate their own studies.

All these materials were of course "unpublished" in 1541, the date under which they have been treated. But they were "public" in the sense that Lombardi's "Praefatio" had been delivered as an opening lecture before the Accademia degli Infiammati (Robortello was to make a similar use of his preface, recited before the Accademia Fiorentina in 1548[50]) and that Lombardi's and then Maggi's lectures were actually a form of publication. Between this date and 1548 the uses of the *Poetics* in critical documents are sparse and incidental.

One of these documents is of especial interest since it constitutes an early application of Aristotelian principles and terminology to practical criticism. It is a set of notes on a speech or conversation about Dante by Girolamo Benivieni, preserved in the Biblioteca Marucelliana, MS A.137. The notes are undated; I assign them without proof to *circa* 1540, since Benivieni died in 1542. In them, Benivieni passes judgment on the *Divine Comedy*. First, he praises the unity of structure, and in so doing he uses terms all of which are borrowed from Aristotle's definition of tragedy; I give the text in Italian, italicizing the significant phrases:

... quanto all'*anima di questa compositione* che e, senza dubbio, la inuentione, o, *la fauola*, chi punto sottilmente bada, ageuolmente scorge, hauere Dante *imitato un sol' fatto*, non dico un sogno, anzi uno desto, et auueduto uiaggio, che egli altra uolta hauea trapassato, e fu questo *di conueneuole grandezza, proportionato, e finito*, narrando di se quello, che alcune altre fauole, narrano di altrui, *con ornato parlare*, e profitteuole alli ascoltanti.[51]

Despite such traditional elements as the identification of "favola" with "inventione" and the final "profitable to the listeners," the description has a note of freshness supplied by the intention to apply Aristotle's definition to an actual critical judgment. One other phrase in the notes, "egli tutto Poeticamente passa, per uia d'Imitatione" (fol. 138*v*), may have

[50] See MS BNF II.IV.192.
[51] MS Marucelliana A. 137, fol. 134*v*. In translation: "as for *the soul of this composition* which is, undoubtedly, the invention or *the plot*, he who looks at all carefully will easily discover that Dante has *imitated a single action*, I do not say a dream but rather a voyage made while awake and aware, which he had taken at a previous time; and this was *of proper magnitude, proportioned, and complete*, narrating about himself what certain other plots narrate about others, *with embellished language*, and profitable to the listeners."

Aristotelian origins. For the rest, Benivieni insists on the utility of Dante's poem, which, like those of the best and most ancient poets, "under a pleasant veil, with the beauty of Poetry, ... impresses upon those who enjoy his poem the highest mysteries of Christian philosophy."[52] He praises the variety and multiplicity of ideas in Dante, his treatment of the sciences and the liberal arts, and his many wise sayings, pointing out finally how both Petrarch and Boccaccio had imitated him.

Another contemporary piece in Italian, Giovambattista Giraldi Cintio's dedication to his *Orbecche* (written in 1541 but published in 1543), complains of the impossibility of using the *Poetics* rather than doing so. It may well reflect the attitude of readers in general before the publication of the great commentaries. Giraldi is speaking of the difficulty of writing tragedy in his time:

And although Aristotle gives us the method for composing them, aside from his native obscurity, which, as you know, is extreme, he remains so obscure and full of so many shadows because we do not have the authors from whom he derives his authority and the examples for confirmation of the orders and the laws that he imposes on writers of tragedies, that one understands with difficulty I will not say the art that he teaches but the very definition that he gives of tragedy.[53]

Bernardino Tomitano's *Ragionamenti della lingua toscana* of 1545 makes extensive use of the *Poetics*, but withal it is not an Aristotelian treatise; rather, as has been pointed out, it is a little bit of everything (see Chapter VII, pp. 264-67). Tomitano tends to develop individual sections of his dialogue by paraphrasing earlier works or by translating from them directly; and as Plato, Horace, and various rhetoricians pass through his hands, so also does Aristotle. There is a long section in Book III which follows the *Poetics* closely. It develops the difference between orator and poet as a difference between persuasion and imitation; but then it adds the further differential of verse and rhyme. It lists the kinds of poetry approximately as Aristotle had done and repeats his distinction of object, manner, and means of imitation (p. 226). The poet is defined as "an imitator of human actions who arouses admiration in the listener"[54]—obviously a mixed definition. It is followed by this statement:

In this definition we are led to understand that poetry is an imitation; and since an imitation is related to him who acts in life as a shadow is to bodies, it is necessary that, actions themselves being of two kinds, good and bad (since all human

---

[52] *Ibid.*, fol. 136: "sotto piaceuole uelame, con la uaghezza della Poesia, ne imprime ... in coloro, che sono del suo Poema uaghi, i piu rileuanti misterij della Cristiana filosofia."

[53] *Orbecche* (1543), p. 2: "Et anchora ch'Aristotile ci dia il modo di comporle, egli oltre la sua natia oscuritade, la quale (come sapete) è somma, riman tanto oscuro, & pieno di tante tenebre, per non ui essere gli auttori, de quali egli adduce l'auttoritadi, et gli essempi, per confirmatione de gli ordini, & delle leggi, ch'egli impone à gli scrittori d'esse, ch'affatica è intesa, non dirò l'arte, ch'egli insegna, ma la diffinitione, ch'egli dà della tragedia."

[54] *Ragionamenti* (1545), p. 227: "imitatore de gli atti humani con merauiglia di chi l'ascolta."

actions prove to be distinguished on the basis of vice and of virtue), similarly every imitation should turn out to be like a real action, or better, or worse.[55]

This ethical distinction is what leads to the difference between tragedy and comedy. But when Tomitano wishes to develop the difference, he does so in terms which go back to the rhetorical classification of the literary genres according to subject matters or passions:

> This imitation is based on our common human passions, on the events of fortune, on the qualities of the mind and of the body. As for the passions, tragedy imitates hopes, desires, despair, weepings, memories of deaths, and deaths; comedy, suspicions, fears, sudden passages from good to evil and from evil to good, rescues, happy human lives and human beings. Sapphic poetry brings forth tender thoughts and magnificent eulogies; the hendecasyllable, humble and low concerns; the elegy, tears and signs; odes, precepts, customs, memories, loves, and praise of others; sermons, discourses necessary for happy living; satire, condemnations of vicious living and rewards for virtues; the heroic style, illustrious and magnanimous feats.[56]

Similar distinctions are made for the Italian genres.

When Tomitano develops his ideas on the "manner" of imitation, he follows *Poetics* 1448a25 fairly closely; but when he expands the passage by adding examples of his own, he shows that he has not understood at all the implications of narrative and dramatic "manner": "Thus Michelangelo and Titian," he says, "might possibly imitate the same thing, but nevertheless in different ways; which difference may equally well be seen in Petrarch and in Dante."[57] The section of the *Ragionamenti* based on Aristotle concludes with a passage on the natural causes of poetry. The whole section is of interest since it reveals how a scholar of 1545 used the letter of the text of Aristotle without understanding its spirit, and how he sought elucidation in more familiar texts and traditions.

The same kind of eclecticism is apparent in Lilio Gregorio Giraldi's *Historiae poetarum dialogi*, a set of ten dialogues variously dated from 1541 to 1545 and published in 1545. Giraldi wishes primarily to list the Greek and Latin poets and provide a biographical compendium of the known

[55] *Ibid.*, p. 227: "Nellaqual diffinitione si da à comprendere, che la poesia sia imitatione: & perche l'imitatione è tale rispetto à colui che opera, quale l'ombra à i corpi; per questo è necessario, che operandosi in due maniere ò bene ò male (come che tutte le attioni humane uengono ad esser differenti per conto del uitio & della uirtu) similmente ogni imitatione o simile adiuiene, ò migliore, ò piggiore dell'effetto."

[56] *Ibid.*, p. 228: "E questa imitatione fondata sopra gli affetti della nostra humanita, sopra i casi della fortuna, sopra i beni dell'animo & del corpo. Quanto à gli affetti, imita la Tragedia le speranze, i desii, le disperationi, i pianti, i mor[t]al ricordi, & le morti, La Comedia i sospetti, le paure, i subiti mouimenti dal bene al male, & dal male al bene, le saluezze, le uite & gli humani contenti. Dolci pensieri partorisce & magnifiche lodi il Saphico: humili & basse cure lo Endecasillabo: lagrime & sospiri la Elegia: precetti, costumi, ricordi, amori, & lode d'altrui le Ode: discorsi al uiuere beatamente necessari i sermoni: uituperi del uitioso uiuere, & premi delle uirtu le Satire: gesti illustri & generosi l'heroico stile. . . ."

[57] *Ibid.*, p. 229: "cosi Michel'agnolo & Titiano potranno per auentura imitare l'istessa cosa, nondimeno dissomigliantemente: laqual differenza comprender si puo medesimamente nel Petrarca e in Dante."

facts relating to them. He includes as well the standard defence of poetry, a discussion of the poetic furor, and a certain amount of theoretical material. Plato, Horace, Cicero, Donatus are freely drawn upon, and almost necessarily—at this date—there are a number of references to Aristotle. At the outset, Giraldi lists Aristotle first among the writers "qui de poëtis scripserunt"; he cites him on the origins of poetry (p. 6) and for his insistence that the plot, not verse, makes the poet: "Aristotelis est sententia, poëtam ex fabulis potius esse, quàm ex carminibus" (p. 84). In Dialogue III, he deplores the loss of the original two books of the *Poetics*.[58] It is not, however, until he comes to the discussion of tragedy and comedy, in Dialogue VI, that he makes any substantial borrowings from Aristotle's text. There, after giving Diomedes' and Theophrastus' definitions of tragedy, he cites Aristotle on the antiquity of the genre and then gives his definition, in a translation that does not correspond to any of those published before 1541 and hence may be his own or may represent some manuscript version: "Est ergo Tragoedia imitatio studiosae & perfectae actionis, magnitudinem suaui oratione habentis, separatim ab unaquaque specierum agentium in particularis: & non per annunciationem, sed misericordia quadam & timore perficiens talim affectionum purgationem" (p. 672). There are short quotations from Aristotle's explanation of the definition and a discussion of the qualitative and quantitative parts.

When he comes to comedy, Giraldi again cites first a traditional Greek definition, then those of Donatus and Cicero, finally that of Aristotle: "Comoedia est imitatio improbioris quidem, non ad omnem tamen malitiam, sed turpitudinis quaedam est ridicula particula" (p. 677); the translation is again unknown. Ultimately, after citing Aristotle's definition of the ridiculous, he concludes: "It is seen from these words that the philosopher implies that comedy was invented to give pleasure to the people"[59]—a conclusion by no means justified by the text. Giraldi's method is the same as that of many of his contemporaries. He takes pieces out of the *Poetics*, transports them to his own work; they there stand alongside other pieces borrowed from other works, neither changing them nor changed by them. There is nothing even vaguely suggesting an "interpretation" of Aristotle.

In Parrasio's commentary on Horace of 1531 there had been some introductory allusions to the *Poetics*. Fifteen years later, in 1546, the *Ecphrasis in Horatii Flacci artem poeticam* of Francesco Pedemonte (published posthumously by Puresius) made the first full-scale use of the *Poetics* as a source of parallels to and explanations of the *Ars poetica*. Moreover, it gave fairly extensive quotations of the text in Greek. There are some thirty

[58] *Historiae poetarum* (1545), p. 313: "duo primùm de ea facultate uolumina composuit, quae temporum, ut uidemus, iniuria periere. Mox alterum uolumen edidit, quod dimidiatum imperfectumque nunc in studiosorum manibus habetur."

[59] *Ibid.*, p. 677: "Videtur ex his uerbis Philosophus innuere, Comoediam inuentam esse ad oblectandos populos."

such parallel passages (as I have indicated in Chapter IV). They are drawn from widely separated sections of the *Poetics* and demonstrate a fairly complete knowledge of the text. Pedemonte achieves a better fusion of his borrowed materials than was the case with his immediate predecessors. For example, he assigns to the first thirteen lines of the *Ars poetica* the subtitle "De idea concipienda," suggesting that Horace means to demand that the poet have a conception of his total "form" before setting to work; on the one hand, this conception is likened to a Platonic Idea, and on the other the process of representing it is described by Aristotle in the term "imitation": "This also [the preconception of the Form] comes about in every art, especially in painting, molding, and sculpturing, which indeed seem to Aristotle to proceed in the same way of imitation as does poetry."[60] This same requirement explains why Aristotle demands the complete form having beginning, middle, and end ("miniméue totum ipsum, quod [ut inquit Aristoteles] ex principio, medio, ac fine constat, absoluetur," p. 4), and why he should have proposed Homer as the model most closely resembling nature (p. 4v.) In such a case as this, Pedemonte attempts to clarify a text of Horace by studying what seem to him to be related ideas in Plato and in Aristotle.

In general, the passages from Aristotle which Pedemonte uses fall into categories. First, those of historical interest: he cites numerous texts on the origins and development of tragedy and of comedy, somewhat fewer on the origins of the epic and on the excellence of Homer as an epic poet. These are for the most part without critical interest. Second, those which concern general principles of the poetic art: the notions of necessity and probability and the differences between poetry and history (pp. 52–53); the poet's need for knowledge, especially of a philosophical kind (pp. 36v, 57); the necessity that the poet should himself first feel what he hopes to convey to others (p. 16); the requirement of appropriateness, related to Horace's "decorum" (p. 15v); the conception of the poem as having a proper magnitude and thus of its resemblance to a beautiful animal (p. 16); and the idea of the inevitability of the work's structure, of the presence and place of each of its parts (p. 25). In a third classification come those passages which pertain to the handling of the separate genres. Most of these pertain to tragedy and comedy, although there are a fair number for the epic and some for satire. What Horace has to say about tragedy, for example, is elucidated by citations from the *Poetics* of its definition and explanations of that definition; on the comparison between tragedy and comedy and tragedy and the epic; on the use of iambic verse; on unity through action rather than through the choice of a single hero; on the creation of the tragic effect through reading only, without recourse to spectacle and stage presentation; on the kinds of plot; and on the mixture of tragedy with

[60] *Ecphrasis* (1546), p. 3v: "sic itaque in omni arte, pingendi maxime, fingendi, atque sculpendi; quae quidem eodem imitationis tramite cum poesi Aristoteli incedere uidentur."

satire (mostly, pp. 29–32). What results from all this is undoubtedly a conception of the art of tragedy much richer and much more detailed than the reader might obtain from Horace alone. But it still remains doubtful whether there is any interpretation of Aristotle's text or any awareness of the special character of his theory of tragedy.

Several passages in Pedemonte, finally, should be singled out for the witness they give to the position that Aristotle's *Poetics* was attaining at this state. The first of them, a part of the commentary on *Ars poetica* 179–88, asserts that Aristotle's notions were inferior to Horace's since Horace came at a later date and represented a more refined taste: "Since he [Aristotle] handed down the norms for the poetic art without departing from the models supplied by ancient poetry, whereas this poet [Horace] —and this is a matter of the greatest importance—assessing the poems of his predecessors and contemporaries, accepts certain things while rejecting others."[61] Nevertheless, Aristotle's dicta are to be taken as laws; and, in addition to the usual "asserit" or "inquit" or "autore Aristotele," we find such formulas as "statuisse" and the final categorical statement that the precepts of the art are to be found only in Aristotle and in Horace, "who taught the rules which it would never be possible to transgress" ("qui regulas docuerunt, quas transgredi nequaquam licitum foret," p. 60). Before the time of the great commentaries, then, the *Poetics* had achieved a position of authority equal to that of the *Ars poetica*—and this was no small feat, considering the reverence for the latter document throughout the late Middle Ages and the humanistic period.

ROBORTELLO (1548)

The first of the "great commentaries" to be published was that of Francesco Robortello, the *In librum Aristotelis de arte poetica explicationes* of 1548. Robortello apparently prepared his own Greek text, using as a basis the Aldine text of 1508 but correcting it by consulting manuscripts; two of these were in the possession of the Medici family, and Robortello frequently argues for the superiority of their readings. He used the Pazzi translation; but again he corrected it, and a collation of the two Latin versions shows many slight variations in detail. For the history of literary criticism in the Renaissance, however, Robortello's great importance lies in his commentary, the first extensive one to be printed. It not only was an epitome of the earlier scattered interpretations of the *Poetics*; it also in many ways made new suggestions which determined the future tendencies in the reading of the text.[62]

[61] *Ibid.*, p. 31v: "Quippe ille ab antiqua poesi non discedens artis poeticae normas tradidit; hic autem uates, quod quidem permultam interest, cum maiorum tum iuniorum poemata perpendens quaedam admittit, quaedam uero non probat."

[62] I have given an extensive analysis of the commentary in an article, "Robortello on the *Poetics*," in *Critics and Criticism: Ancient and Modern*, the argument of which is summarized above, chap. ii, pp. 66–68. In the following pages, I extract from the article its essential points.

The essential direction of Robortello's analysis of the *Poetics* results from his conception of the ends of poetry. There seem to be three ends: First, the dual Horatian end of pleasure and utility: "Poetry, if we consider it carefully, bends all its efforts toward delighting, although it also does profit."[63] Besides, there is the Aristotelian end of imitation: "And since this imitation or representation is produced by means of discourse, we may say that the end of poetry is language which imitates, just as that of rhetoric is language which persuades."[64] All the ends are brought together in such a passage as the following (commenting on 1448*b*4): "Poetry thus sets a double end for itself, one of which is prior to the other; the prior end is to imitate, the other to delight."[65] Profit is here included as an unexpressed concomitant of delight.

The nature of the pleasure derived from poetry is specified in a passage from Robortello's prologue:

> There is, indeed, for men no greater pleasure, truly worthy of a man of refinement, than that which is perceived by the mind and by thought; it frequently happens that things which arouse horror and terror in men as long as they are in their own nature, once they are taken out of nature and represented in some form resembling nature, give great pleasure. . . . What other end, therefore, can we say that the poetic faculty has than to delight through the representation, description, and imitation of every human action, every emotion, every thing animate as well as inanimate?[66]

Two salient features of this passage must be emphasized; first, the pleasure is achieved *through* imitation, which thus becomes an intermediate end; second, the imitation is not only of human actions and passions (as in Aristotle) but of all kinds of objects as well. The nature of the utility derived from poetry is much more explicitly indicated; once again, the key passage is found in the prologue:

> For, just as poetic readings and imitations are of various kinds, so they bring to men a multiple utility. If, on the one hand, the reading (or performance) and imitation consist in the virtue and the praise of some excellent man, people are incited to virtue; if, on the other hand, vices are represented, people are strongly

---

[63] *Explicationes* (1548), Prologue, p. 2: "Poëtice, siquis diligenter attendat, omnem suam vim confert ad oblectandum, & si prodest quoque."

[64] *Ibid.*, p. 2: "Et quoniam imitatio, & repręsentatio hęc per orationem fit; dicimus in poëtice finem esse, sermonem imitantem, sicut in rhetorice sermonem persuadentem."

[65] *Ibid.*, p. 30: "Finem enim duplicem habet sibi propositum poëtice, alterum altero priorem: Prior est imitari. Alter vero est, oblectare."

[66] *Ibid.*, p. 2: "Nulla verò inter homines maior voluptas, quae quidem liberali homine digna sit, quàm quae mente, & cogitatione percipitur; imò saepè contingit, vt quae horrorem, & terrorem incutiunt hominibus, dum in propria natura sunt, extrà naturam posita in quapiam similitudine, dum repraesentantur; multum oblectent. . . . Quem igitur alium finem poëtices facultatis esse dicemus, quàm oblectare per repraesentationem, descriptionem, & imitationem omnium actionum humanarum; omnium motionum; omnium rerum tùm animatarum, tùm inanimatarum?"

POETIC THEORY

deterred from those vices, and they are driven away from them with much greater force than if you were to use any other form of persuasion.[67]

From this and other passages[68] it is clear that the utility is essentially an ethical one, achieved through rhetorical means; men discover through poetry man's common fate, they learn what characters and events are worthy of dread and commiseration, and they achieve the capacity to moderate their own passions when adversity strikes.

In these passages on the various ends of poetry, it becomes clear that the end of imitation is an intermediate end, producing beyond itself either pleasure or utility of the moral kind so completely outlined. It is soon clear not only that the different ends of pleasure and utility are achieved by different means but that they result from different parts of the poem itself. Moreover, each separate kind of utility has its source in a separate poetic element. Neither is the pleasure a concomitant of the utility, nor is the utility a resultant of the total structure of the poem. Rather, Robortello proceeds by a fragmentation of the work and an analysis of what each fragment contributes toward one of the separate ends. The case is especially clear with respect to utility. Moral betterment derives from three separate sources: there are lessons from the fortunes of men, there are lessons from the characters of men, there are lessons from maxims or sententiae. Let us take the fortunes of men first. The conclusion that fate strikes all men equally, that men pass quickly from happiness to unhappiness, is deduced not from a study of men's characters but from the contemplation of the actions in which they are involved; hence it is related to the plot or the "fabula" of the play. The representation of such a plot on the stage is a powerful moral instrument: "This representation is very powerful in moving and rousing the souls of men to anger and rage, on the one hand, or, on the other hand, in calling them back to gentleness and in softening them, now exciting them to pity, to sorrow and tears, now to laughter and joy."[69]

The effectiveness of the representation depends, however, upon the resemblance of the imitation to life; if the imitation is "as if it were the thing itself" ("quasi rem ipsam," p. 3), it will produce its full effect. Hence the criterion of truth to life and credibility enters as a fundamental consideration in any discussion of the actions of the poem. The problem is a

―――――――――

[67] *Ibid.*, p. 3: "Recitationes autem, & imitationes poëticae vt sunt multiplices, ita multiplicem afferunt hominibus vtilitatem; Nam si recitatio, atque imitatio virtutum fit, & laudum praeclari alicuius viri; incitantur homines ad virtutem: Si rursus vitia repraesentantur, ab his homines multum deterrentur; maioréque quadam ui repelluntur, quàm si alia quauis hortatione vtaris."

[68] *Ibid.*, pp. 53, 102, 165–66, 211.

[69] *Ibid.*, p. 3: "Magnam autem habet vim huiusmodi repręsentatio in commouendis, & inflammandis hominum animis, tum ad iram, & furorem; tum ad mansuetudinem reuocandis, & emolliendis, tum concitandis ad commiserationem, ad fletum & lacrymas; tum ad risum, & laetitiam."

real one and a difficult one; for, essentially, poetry differs from the other arts of discourse in taking for its subject matter things which are not true:

Since, then, poetics has as its subject matter fictitious and fictional discourse, it is clear that the function of poetics is to invent in a proper way its fiction and its untruth; to no other art is it more fitting than to this one to intermingle lies. ... In the lies used by the poetic art, false elements are taken as true, and from them true conclusions are derived.[70]

If from these fictional elements an impression of truth is to be obtained, the *plot* itself must contain actions belonging to one of three kinds: "For poetics speaks only of those actions which exist, or which can exist, or which do exist according to what men used to think"[71]—i.e., the true, the possible, the traditional. The true is the best: "we should try, if it is at all possible, to treat true actions."[72] The possible or probable is next best—"but, if not, we should invent new ones according to the probable."[73] Insofar as a poet uses a true plot, he does not invent, and hence his work resembles the activity of a historian; his true poetic activity, as we shall see, bears upon elements other than the plot. If he creates in accordance with probability, then he is an inventor on the level of plot as well.

The whole range of possibilities is summarized by Robortello in his commentary on *Poetics* 1460*b*7:

The things, actions, and persons which a poet imitates are either true or invented. If true, they either exist now or did exist, or they are living or died long ago. If they exist and are living, the poet imitates them in two ways, either as they are commonly said to be or as it appears they are. If they are neither living nor exist, but died long ago, they are still imitated in these two ways, either as general opinion reports them to have been or as it appears they were. If the persons are invented by the poet himself, he imitates and expresses them as being what it is fitting and proper that they should be.[74]

It will be noted that Robortello omits, from this apparently exhaustive set of distinctions, the notion of imitation of things as they are. This is not accidental. "True" is equated with "said to be" and "seem to be" rather than with "are" for the simple reason that the realm of the poet is, after all, the fictitious. If he treats things as they are, then he trespasses upon the

---

[70] *Ibid.*, p. 2: "Cum igitur poëtice subiectam sibi habeat pro materie orationem fictam, & fabulosam; patet ad poëticen pertinere, ut fabulam, & mendacium aptè confingat; nulliúsque alterius artis proprium magis esse; mendacia comminisci, quàm huius ... in poëticis mendaciis principia falsa pro veris assumuntur, atque ex his verae eliciuntur conclusiones.'

[71] *Ibid.*, p. 2: "Nam poëtice loquitur de iis tantum rebus, aut quę sunt, aut quae esse possunt. aut quas uetus est apud homines opinio, esse."

[72] *Ibid.*, p. 219: "danda est opera, vt si fieri possit, circa veras actiones versemur."

[73] *Ibid.*, p. 219: "Sin minus, nouas ex verisimili confingamus."

[74] *Ibid.*, p. 290: "res, actiones, & personę quas imitatur, poëta, aut verae sunt, aut fictae. Si verae, aut sunt aut fuerunt, vel enim viuunt; vel iamdiu interierunt. Si sunt, ac viuunt duplici modo has imitatur poëta, aut quales aiunt vulgò esse, aut videntur esse. Si non viuunt, neque sunt; sed iamdiu interierunt, imitatur etiam has duplici modo; aut quales rumor est fuisse, aut quales videntur fuisse. Si personae fictae sunt ab ipso poëta, eas imitatur; exprimitque, quales esse conuenit, & oportet."

domain of the historian. It is by this line of reasoning that Robortello arrives at his interpretation of Aristotle's τὰ δυνατὰ κατὰ τὸ εἰκὸς ἢ τὸ ἀναγκαῖον (1451a38); at his own theory of the possible, the probable, and the necessary; and at his central doctrine of credibility as determining the moral effect of the action. The true is credible, hence moving; the verisimilar is moving only insofar as it resembles the true. The whole argument is presented in the passage expounding 1451b15:

> Tragedy has as its purpose to arouse two of the major passions of the soul—pity and fear. Now it is much more difficult to arouse these than others which agitate in a more pleasant way, such as hope, laughter, and others of this kind. For men by their very nature are prone to pleasant things but averse to unpleasant ones; they cannot, therefore, easily be impelled to sorrow. It is thus necessary for them first to know that the thing actually happened in such and such a way. Thus if a tragic plot contained an action which did not really take place and was not true, but was represented by the poet himself in accordance with verisimilitude, it would perhaps move the souls of the auditors, but certainly less. For, if verisimilar things give us pleasure, all the pleasure derives from the fact that we know these things to be present in the truth; and, in general, to the extent that the verisimilar partakes of truth it has the power to move and to persuade. . . . If verisimilar things move us, the true will move us much more. Verisimilar things move us because we *believe* it to have been possible for the event to come about in the way specified. True things move us because we *know* that it did come about in the way specified. Whatever virtue is thus contained in verisimilitude is derived totally from its relationship to truth.[75]

This passage relates credibility to verisimilitude and verisimilitude to truth.

Other terms relevant to the action in a poem are treated elsewhere. The false and the impossible are never acceptable: "The poetic faculty rejects those things which are absolutely false"; and "as often as poetry errs in its imitation and fails to preserve what is necessarily true, or else verisimilar, and instead tries to express something which is impossible and completely unbelievable."[76] The necessary is the same as the true, consisting of those things which had happened or been done; as a critical term, it must then

---

[75] *Ibid.*, p. 93: "Habet sibi propositum tragoedia mouere duas maximas perturbationes animi commiserationem, & metum; multò verò difficilius est, has mouere, quàm reliquas, quae iucundius perturbant, qualis est spes, risus, & huiusmodi. sunt enim suaptè natura homines ad iucundas res proni; ab iniucundis autem alieni; non facilè igitur ad luctum possunt impelli. necesse est igitur, vt sciant prius rem ita cecidisse; quod si fabula tragica actionem contineat, quae non acta sit, neque sit vera; sed ab ipso poëta fuerit efficta secundum verisimile; commouebit fortasse animos audientium, at minus certè. nam verisimilia si nos oblectant, oblectatio omnis inde prouenit, quòd in veris inesse ea scimus; & omnino quatenus verisimile veritatis est particeps vim habet mouendi, ac persuadendi . . . si nos verisimilia mouent, multo magis vera mouebunt. Verisimilia nos mouent, quia fieri potuisse credimus, ita rem accidisse. Vera nos mouent, quia scimus ita accidisse, quicquid igitur vis est in verisimili, id totum arripit à vero."

[76] *Ibid.*, p. 284: "patet poëticen facultatem . . . reiicere ea, quae prorsus sunt falsa"; and p. 292: "quotiescunque poëtica in imitatione peccat; neque seruat, necessarium, ac verisimile, conaturque exprimere aliquid, quod impossibile sit; praeterque omnem fidem."

have the same meaning as the "true" and refer not to real existence but to possibility and opinion. The possible consists of those things which can be done (τὰ δυνατά) and subdivides into the necessary and the probable. If to this subdivision we add another one, that affecting unnatural and incredible objects (for these in certain circumstances are admissible into certain poems), we get another exhaustive distinction as follows:

Duplici modo fingere, & mentiri poëtas:
1. in rebus secundum naturam (the possible)
   (a) τὸ ἀναγκαῖον (the necessary)
   (b) τὸ εἰκός (the probable)
2. in rebus praeter naturam (the impossible)
   (a) quae receptae iam sunt in opinionem vulgi (the traditional)
   (b) non antè unquam auditis, aut narratis ab alio (the newly invented)

The impossible or the false, because it is incredible, has no place in poetry, no persuasive power, no possible moral effect. But it is occasionally admitted when the poet can succeed in giving it a semblance of credibility (p. 87).

In many of the passages in which Robortello speaks of the utility springing from the actions of poems, he speaks of representation or performance (rather than merely of imitation) and of the effect upon spectators (rather than upon readers). This is because he considers the art of imitation really two arts, a *poetic* art concerned with the writing of poems and a *histrionic* art concerned with their performance. The division of functions is clear in his commentary on *Poetics* 1449b31:

It should be noted, in fact, that the imitation in tragedy may be considered in two ways, either insofar as it is scenic and is acted by the actors or insofar as it is made by the poet as he writes. If you think of it in terms of the poet who writes, then we may say that the principal end of tragedy is to imitate the nature of souls and the characters of men through written words, through which description it is possible to discern whether men are happy or unhappy. If you assume it to refer to the actor as he acts, then we may say that the greatest and most powerful end is that very action as a result of which men are judged to be happy or unhappy. In the writing and the imitation of the poets some such order as the following is established, if you follow nature; *character*, from which comes *happiness* or *unhappiness*. But in the action on the stage of the actor as he recites, in this way: *action*, from which comes *happiness* or *unhappiness*.[77]

---

[77] *Ibid.*, p. 58: "Notandum verò . . . tragoediae imitationem duplici modo considerari; aut quatenus scenica est, & ab histrionibus agitur, aut quatenus à poëta fit scribente. Si quatenus à scribente poëta intelligas, dicimus primarium in tragoedia finem esse imitari, habitum animi, & mores hominum per orationem scriptam; ex qua descriptione homines cerni possunt an felices, an verò infelices sint. Si quatenus histrio agens eam refert, sumas . . . dicimus maximum, ac potissimum finem esse ipsam actionem, ex qua homines diiudicantur aut felices, aut infelices. In scriptione & imitatione poëtarum talis ordo constituitur, si naturam sequaris. MORES, ex quibus FELICITAS, aut INFELICITAS. In actione verò scenica recitantium histrionum, huiusmodi. ACTIO. ex qua FELICITAS, aut INFELICITAS."

In the light of these ideas, one of Robortello's most puzzling statements about poetics becomes significant. In *Poetics* 1450a10, Aristotle indicated that the six parts of tragedy (plot, character, thought, diction, song, and spectacle) might be distributed thus among the constitutive elements of poetry: three to the object, two to the means, and one to the manner of imitation. Robortello provides such a distribution, and in it, plot (which in the Aristotelian text must be one of the objects of imitation) becomes the one part belonging to the manner of imitation; the manner is dramatic, what is acted is the action or plot, hence the plot is the part of tragedy belonging to the manner of imitation. He even goes on to demonstrate how that part of the means especially germane to stage presentation—spectacle or apparatus—is in a sense the end of tragedy and contains all the other parts within itself.[78]

The second kind of moral utility, the lessons learned from the characters of men, comes specifically from the depiction of character. In the distribution of parts already mentioned, Robortello assigns to the object of imitation the three parts of thought, character, and diction. The characters as depicted serve as moral examples to mankind; hence, they must be well chosen, must present no wicked persons except when one means (as in comedy) to expose them to ridicule. These considerations lead him to interpret as he does Aristotle's distinction of "better," "worse," and "like" characters. He takes "better" as meaning "superior to those who live in our times," the heroes of epic and gnomic poetry and the kings and heroes of tragedy. "Like" refers to characters who resemble men of our own times and who appear in dialogues and in epic poems. "Worse" means those who are morally base; but it may also mean those who are of low station in life. Indeed, all along the line the distinction tends to become social rather than moral. The process is especially clear in the case of the tragic hero, who must be of high station if his fall from happiness to unhappiness is to produce the desired effect (pp. 20, 132–33).

Just as in the case of action no moral utility can be achieved unless the action itself is credible or is made credible, so in the case of character a basis of credibility must be established. The problem is perhaps more complicated than it is with action; indeed, all four of the requirements for character that Aristotle indicated in 1454a15 ff. become, in the hands of Robortello, separate means to credibility. "Goodness" becomes conformity to type characteristics; the audience will accept readily only those persons who conform to type. "Appropriateness" is interpreted as the theory of

[78] *Ibid.*, p. 57: "Probat verò alia quadam ratione esse sex, per tres videlicet notas illas differentias, quae in principio libri appositae fuerunt, & declaratae. Sunt autem hae, οἷς. ὡς. ἅ. Per primam differentiam scilicet οἷς, quae instrumentum significat velut quoddam. Per secundam differentiam scilicet ὡς; quae modum significat, ex quo imitatio diuersitatem sumit. Per tertiam differentiam scilicet ἅ quae subiectam materiem significat, in qua versatur imitatio tragoediae. Ex prima differentia duae existunt partes, APPARATVS, MELODIA. Ex secunda vna pars tantum. FABVLA. Ex tertia; tres partes. DICTIO, MORES, SENTENTIA."

decorum, according to which a complex of traits was assigned to each person in accordance with the circumstances surrounding him. Here again, the audience holds these expectations with respect to the person and will find him credible when they are realized. "Likeness" is taken to mean the observance, for traditional or historical persons, of the conception of character established for them. They must conform to the accepted opinion held by the audience. "Consistency" refers especially to persons newly invented by the poet; these must be constant throughout if the audience is to believe in them (pp. 167–69).

This distinction between new and traditional characters is fundamental. We have already seen a similar distinction at work with respect to action: "true" actions, as they should be or seemed to be (note the traditional element), fall into the category of the necessary; "invented" actions into that of the probable or verisimilar. So for character:

> If, therefore, the persons are real and the actions in themselves and the outcome of the deeds related are true, then the characters of the persons must be expressed by the poet according to the necessary, that is (as Averroës correctly explains it), according to truth. If the persons are fictitious, their characters will have to be expressed according to the verisimilar, that is (as the same Averroës interprets it), according to the opinion of the majority.[79]

These various statements about action and character assume that both truth and verisimilitude are within the jurisdiction of the audience, that the individual character or action is submitted to the judgment of the spectator or the auditor. The assumption is made more specific in connection with Robortello's treatment of the passages on the epic. He says:

> In epic poetry, just as in the others, this is the first thing that must be attended to: that the words used should have nothing about them that is incongruous or contradictory, but that they should in every respect agree among themselves and fit properly together. For, whenever either the period of time in which the action is done or the place or the person or the manner is not congruous, these things do not satisfy reason, nor are they acceptable to the mind of the readers or the hearers.[80]

Such a passage as this indicates that the really important consideration in any poem is the relationship among words—rather than among characters and actions—that the goodness of the relationship is determined essenti-

[79] *Ibid.*, p. 175: "Si igitur personae verae sunt, & facta ab ipsis, euentaque rerum, quae narrantur, vera sunt; debent tunc personarum mores exprimi à poëta, secundum necessarium. hoc est (vt aptè declarat Auerroës) secundum veritatem. Si nouae sint personae, illarum mores exprimendi erunt secundum verisimile. hoc est (vt idem interpretatur Auerroës) secundum plurimorum opinionem."

[80] *Ibid.*, p. 286: "In poësi Epica, sicuti etiam in aliis illud in primis videndum, ne sermones habiti absonum aliquid habeant, aut repugnans. Sed ab omni parte consentiant inter se, & quadrent; Quotiescunque enim aut spatium temporis, quo res gesta fuit; aut locus, aut persona, aut modus, non constat; non quadrant rationi, neque cum legentium, aut audientium mente conueniunt."

ally by the reactions of the audience, and that the only internal criterion is one of a vague "fittingness" or "congruity" of all the words in the poem.

It is perhaps in this sense that diction, along with sententiae and character, becomes for Robortello one of the objects of imitation; this is just as remarkable as that plot should be assigned to the manner. The poetic faculty "produces ethical discourse [conficitque orationem moratam]" (pp. 291–92) and both character and thought (sententiae) contribute to the production of this discourse; in this sense it is an end or an object rather than a means of imitation. A special form of diction, the speech made by a character in a poem, is even more clearly an object of imitation for Robortello. As in the cases of action and character, it produces a special kind of effect upon the audience, an effect of persuasion which, in addition, arouses the emotions (p. 198). As for action and character, also, the persuasive and emotional qualities of speeches will depend upon the credibility of these speeches; they must closely resemble "true" speeches made by "real" people. Verisimilitude will bring about credibility.

In summary, then, the various kinds of utility which men derive from poetry come separately from various parts of poems: from plot, the spectacle of man's happiness or unhappiness springing from his actions; from character, the example of man's happiness or unhappiness springing from his character; from sententiae, the statements which will persuade the spectator to action or dissuade him from it, which will demonstrate truths to him and move him to imitation or revulsion. These are not, perhaps, entirely separate, since the sententiae become the final expression of the lessons from both action and character. In all cases, utility will result only from a belief of the audience in the truthfulness of the poem, and that, in turn, will depend upon the degree to which the poem is made probable and verisimilar.

Since Robortello's system is analytical in the sense that specific effects result from separate causes, we may expect that his treatment of pleasure will follow the same pattern. Pleasure itself will not be subdivided into a number of kinds, but separate parts of the poem will be distinguished as providing different aspects of the "voluptas" produced by poetry. Moreover, these will usually be different from the parts providing utility or will be special subdivisions of these parts. The whole problem of pleasure will be complicated by several considerations: (1) it must be derived from subjects which are in themselves not pleasurable (in the case of tragedy); (2) the audience will tend to prefer inartistic to artistic pleasures; (3) the things done for the achievement of utility essentially militate against the achievement of pleasure.

Since truth itself lies outside the domain of poetry, pleasure will be associated with the credible. However, credibility in itself is not enough (as it is for utility); some subjects will readily be "believed" by an audience, but they will not as readily be "liked." Hence there arises a distinction between genres such as comedy, where the subject matter itself is pleasurable, and tragedy, where it is not pleasurable; men will naturally prefer the former to the latter. Hence, also, bad poets will make concessions to the mob in the form of such devices as the happy ending for tragedy (p. 142). The distinction between the pleasure of tragedy and the pleasure of comedy is found in the following passage:

> ... the pleasure which is obtained from tragedy is that which imitation provides. The power that this imitation has in delighting our souls may be sufficiently recognized from the fact that even horrible things, if they present themselves in some imitative expression, attract us to them and bring us delight and pleasure. ... Such is therefore the pleasure that is derived from tragedy. Nor is that which comes from comedy unlike it, insofar as comedy contains imitation. The latter, therefore, pleases because it imitates in a joyous fashion the ridiculous actions of men; the former because it imitates in an artistic fashion the sorrow, the lamentation, and the calamity of mortal men. Now if you should ask which is the greater pleasure of the two, I should dare to affirm that the one deriving from tragedy is much greater, for it pervades our souls more deeply and touches us in a more unusual way, and that imitation is accomplished with somewhat greater effort. Therefore, to the extent that we know it to be more difficult to express that imitation, to that extent—if it be successful—we regard it with greater admiration, and we obtain from it a greater pleasure.[81]

I have cited this passage at length because it contains an elaboration of what are, essentially, the three bases of pleasure for Robortello: imitation, the *difficulté vaincue*, and admiration.

Of these three bases, perhaps the most important is admiration, that feeling of wonder and amazement which comes from the spectacle of the unexpected, the extraordinary, the marvelous. If this is an essential ingredient of pleasure, then a crucial question is raised: Is not the marvelous the exact contradictory of the credible, and would not the pleasure arising from it exclude the possibility of utility? Robortello works out the difficulty in a way entirely consistent with the previous *données* of his system. The marvelous is indeed in conflict with the credible. Hence it must be kept to a minimum in those genres where credibility is most essential (e.g., comedy) and may attain a maximum in other genres, where, because they

---

[81] *Ibid.*, p. 146: "Sed respondeo; voluptatem, quae capitur ex tragoedia, esse eam, quam parit imitatio. quantum verò habeat haec vim ad oblectandos animos, vel inde satis cognosci potest. quòd etiam horribilia, si imitatione aliqua expressa sese nobis obtulerint; delectationem, voluptatémque afferunt. ... Talis est igitur voluptas quae ex tragoedia percipitur. Nec dissimilis huic est, quae ex comoedia prouenit quatenus imitationem continet. Haec igitur oblectat, quòd festiuè imitatur ridiculas actiones hominum, illa quòd artificiosè imitatur moerorem, luctum, calamitatémque mortalium. Quòd si quaeras vtra maior voluptas, ausim affirmare, quae ex tragoedia prouenit maiorem multò. altius enim peruadit animos, rariúsque nobis contingit; maioréque quadam vi fit imitatio illa; quantò igitur difficilius exprimi eam posse scimus, tantò magis, si exacta fuerit, admiramur; maiorémque capimus voluptatem."

are narrative rather than dramatic, credibility is of lesser importance. This is especially true of the epic (cf. p. 87). In such a genre as tragedy, the problem for the poet is to reconcile the credible with the marvelous, and this he does through the use of a number of specific devices (cf. pp. 328, 45, 121). In the last analysis, the poet is virtually permitted to discard all concern for credibility in order to exploit all the available means of achieving the marvelous and the pleasure connected with it.

The pleasures arising from imitation, the *difficulté vaincue,* and admiration are largely attached to parts of the poem different from those which produce utility; they come from episodes, from recognition and reversal rather than from the principal action of the plot, from secondary characters rather than from the hero, from elements of diction independent of the ethical speeches, from gratuitous descriptions. This does not mean that the other "essential" parts of the poem do not give pleasure. It merely means that, in keeping with his analytical tendency, Robortello seeks as often as possible to find separate causes for the pleasure and the utility derived by the audience. Pleasure will contribute to the achievement of the ultimate utilitarian goal of the work (if such a subordination indeed exists) only by making the poem as a whole enjoyable to the audience. The total effect upon the audience will be one of moral betterment accompanied by pleasurable sensations.

The constant conclusion of any individual discussion, in the preceding pages, with such terms as "persuasion," "moral betterment," "effect upon the audience," "pleasurable sensations," should point clearly to the essential character of Robortello's system. It is a rhetorical system, in which Robortello sees the poem as seeking a specific effect of persuasion upon a specified audience and obtaining that effect through the potentiality of each of the parts of the poem to move the audience in a separate way. The character of the audience is thus involved as an ingredient. It is an audience of the élite, not the "vulgus"—not the "rough and ignorant crowd of men" that demands such cheap satisfactions as those found in the double ending of tragedies (pp. 145–46). It is, moreover, an audience made up of good men only, an audience which will sympathize with the tragic hero and will be capable of experiencing the effects of purgation and of moral betterment. Robortello develops his idea at length in the commentary on 1453*a*5, "a man like ourselves":

> Fear is aroused, indeed, when we behold someone like ourselves who has fallen into misery. Aristotle means like the auditors themselves, almost all of whom are judged to be good; or else he speaks only of the good ones. For it is out of their souls that the rule for writing tragedy is derived, nor must any poet ever be mindful of the wicked, but he must adapt everything he writes to the nature of good men. Good men, then, when they see evil things happen to some good man, fear—since they understand that he is like themselves and that they

are like him—lest a like thing at some time befall them, since they live in equivalent circumstances.[82]

Finally, we know that the audience is possessed of a large amount of knowledge and a large number of expectations, all of which contribute to the constitution of its canon of credibility: what is true, what is traditional, what is a matter of opinion, what is probable and verisimilar—all these are known only by reference to the audience, and only by consulting the audience do we know whether they have been achieved.

I have already pointed out, in Chapter II (pp. 66–68), the consequences of this shift from a poetical system to an almost completely rhetorical system and the implications of a methodological order. The reader is referred to that discussion.

THE ROBORTELLO TREATISES (1548)

To his commentary on Aristotle, Robortello added—"so that nothing belonging to the poetic art might be lacking"—a paraphrase of Horace's *Ars poetica* and a group of short treatises on satire, the epigram, comedy, humor, and the elegy; these were published in a separate part of the volume containing the *Explicationes*. The latter group especially would seem to hold great promise of an Aristotelian approach applied to genres not treated fully by Aristotle, for Robortello declares that "in iis scribendis Aristotelis methodum seruauit: & ex ipsius Libello de arte Poetica principia sumpsit omnium suarum explicationum" (half-title page to the separate part). The promise is not, however, fulfilled. Robortello does indeed cite from the translation of the *Poetics* those passages which are pertinent to the particular genre being treated. But for the development of the theory he is usually content to seek elsewhere, in other writers of antiquity, the materials not found in Aristotle. There is, of course, no guarantee that these materials will in any way develop Aristotle's thesis; they merely supplement it with a miscellany of information.

The treatise *De satyra*, first in the group, establishes the pattern. Satire, like all other kinds of poetry, imitates human actions, and it does so by means of rhythm, diction, and harmony. Imitation, not verse, is its distinguishing feature; for a history in verse would still be a history. Paraphrasing Aristotle in this way, Robortello goes on to the distinction between actions which have happened and actions which might happen. But when, soon, he wishes to treat the "manner" of satire (finding no direct indication in the *Poetics*), he shifts to Athenaeus (*Deipnosophistae*, Bk. XIV, §§ 28 ff.), cites his subdivisions of lyric and scenic poetry, and finds satire in the latter

[82] *Ibid.*, p. 128: "Metus verò concitatur, cum intuemur aliquem nobis similem, in miseriam esse lapsum. Similem auditoribus ipsis intelligit Aristoteles; qui ferè omnes boni censendi sunt, vel de bonis tantum loquitur. nam ex eorum animis norma sumitur scribendę tragoediae; neque vllus debet poëta improbos vnquam respicere, sed totam suam scriptionem accommodare ad bonorum naturam. Viri igitur boni, cum immerenti alicui viro bono aliquid mali vident accidisse, metuunt, quòd similem illum sibi, seque illi esse intelligunt, ne idem sibi aliquando accidat, quia pari viuunt conditione."

POETIC THEORY

group. Various authorities are then cited on the antiquity of the form. Satyrs, fauns, and sileni are distinguished, again on the basis of many authorities. Robortello next attacks the problem of the personages of satire; he finds information on satyrs in Julius Pollux and Dionysius of Halicarnassus. As for the subject matter of this genre, Robortello returns to Aristotle, excludes the terrible and the pitiable, decides that satire, like comedy, must treat the ridiculous. The people at whom it pokes its laughter are "ambitiosos, auaros, ingratos, prodigos, periuros, rapaces, adulteros, adulatores, loquaces, stolidos, amatores, ineptos, irreligiosos, parricidas, desides, inertes, parasitos, & qui huiusmodi sunt" (p. 30); the list resembles those traditionally cited in discussions of comedy. Next, the qualifications of the satiric poet: he must be versatile, skillful, keen, sharp-witted, eloquent; but he must also be good and honest: "for seeing that he examines the vices of others, he himself must possess such a way of life as may not justly be criticized by anybody."[83] There follows a long section on "maledicentia" and on the poets of antiquity who have used it well or badly; on the good to be gained by proper use of satirical blame; and on why Horace called his satires "sermones."

In all this, there is occasional quotation of the *Poetics* and an occasional attempt to extend what Aristotle said about comedy to the sister genre of satire. But nowhere is there any intention to apply, in a fundamental way, the principles underlying Aristotle's treatment to a genre which he had not treated.

The procedure in the *De epigrammate*, which follows ("ex Aristotelis Libro de Poetica; magna ex parte desumpta"), is somewhat different. Robortello announces at the beginning that he will treat three subjects: the kind of poetry to which epigrams belong, their subject matter, and what practices are to be followed or avoided in writing them. These subjects are then treated in the order given. For the first, poetic genres are divided into two groups, the longer forms (tragedy, comedy, epic, dithyramb, and "legum poesis" or divine poetry) and the shorter forms (satire, epistle, and sylva). The epigram, in a strange way, may belong to either group; for just as a tragedy or a comedy is a small part of an epic, so the epigram is a small part of any of these forms. The genres may be further divided into those having "imitation" or direct speech and those having no imitation but only "narration." The first section ends with a discussion of the origins and etymology of the epigram. So far, no word of Aristotle. In the second section, Robortello states that the matter of the epigram will in each case be one that would be appropriate to the genre of which it would be a smaller "part." So for the tragic epigram, in a passage where the text of the *Poetics* is reflected indirectly:

It is proper for tragedy to treat serious matters that have about them much to

[83] *Paraphrasis* (1548), pp. 30–31: "qui cum optimè aliorum vitia perspiciat. ipse tamen talem ineat vitae rationem, quae à nullo, iurè reprehendi possit."

evoke pain, pity, and no little wonder, as Aristotle abundantly explains in the *Poetics*. Sorrow is produced by all horrible things, such as floggings, wounds, murders; pity is produced by these same things if they happen to a man who does not deserve them or if they come about between relatives, as between a mother and her son or between brothers. Events arousing admiration are those involving accident, such as when the statue of Mitys at Argos, falling down, killed him who had killed Mitys. All these things are susceptible of the most beautiful descriptions.[84]

Epigrams written on deaths and funerals will belong in this category. For comedy, also, Robortello cites Aristotle (1449a31); the epigram related to it will use a "materia conuitiosa & ridicula" (p. 37) for the purpose of laughing at vice and condemning it. "Nor does the epigram differ from comedy in anything except in the form and in the way of treating the materials; the latter is more diffuse and proceeds by dialogue, the former is shorter and proceeds by a kind of simple narration."[85] Similar comparisons are provided for epigrams related to amatory verse and to the epic. In the third section, the positive recommendations concern such elements of style as "venustas," "suauitas," and acuteness, as well as the kinds of words to be used, while negatively Robortello condemns the use of acrostics and Greek words. Things, in the epigram, should not become the servants of the words, and the poet should never indulge in excess or superfluity. A final sentence urges the poet to follow Robortello's method, to read the ancient poets, and to practise writing.

The treatise *De comoedia* would seem, outwardly, to be more nearly "Aristotelian" than the others, for almost all the materials of which it is made are direct quotations or paraphrases of the *Poetics*. But with few exceptions they are passages from that text dealing with tragedy, in which the word "comedy" has been substituted for the word "tragedy" or in which the passage has been taken over unchanged as equally applicable to both genres. Some adjustments, of course, had to be made. The treatise is most interesting for the light it throws on Robortello's conception of a dramatic genre and for some of its interpretations of the text of Aristotle. Robortello begins by reporting from the *Poetics*, in brief form, the fundamental distinctions with respect to the end of poetry, its three means, its objects, and its manners. For the objects, a first difference: comedy "differs from the others in the subject matter which it treats; for it imitates those actions of men which are more lowly and more common; and in this it

---

[84] *Ibid.*, p. 36: "Tragoediae quidem proprium est tractare res serias, quae in se multum doloris, & commiserationis habeant, neque parum admirationis, sicuti copiosè explicat Arist. in Poët. Dolorem afferunt omnia atrocia, vt verbera, vulnera, caedes; Commiserationem afferunt eadem ipsa, si viro immerenti accidant; aut si inter consanguineos, vtpotè inter matrem, & filium, vel inter fratres. Admirabilia sunt fortuita, vt Argis statua Mityi collapsa eum peremit, qui Mityum peremerat; Recipiunt enim haec omnia pulcherrimas descriptiones."

[85] *Ibid.*, p. 37: "neque vlla in re epigramma differt à comoedia, praeterquàm forma, et ratione tractandarum rerum, Illa enim fusius, ac per collocutionem; Hoc autem breuius, atque simplici quadam narratione."

differs from tragedy, which imitates those which are more excellent."[86] From Aristotle come also the developments on the natural origins of comedy, its history and improvement, supplemented, however, by Plutarch and Donatus on the distinctions between Old and New Comedy. For the discussion of the qualitative parts, Robortello again merely adapts the treatment of tragedy in the *Poetics*. In such a passage as the following, for example (paraphrasing *Poetics* 1449b31 ff.), it is only the substitution or the addition of the word "comoedia" which makes the text in any way especially pertinent to comedy:

> Non potest recitari comoedia vlla, si non adhibeatur Melodia (quia ita obtinuit vsus) & apparatus, vt res in scena, tanquàm in vrbe, aut oppido aliquo geri videatur; Ergo necessariae sunt hae partes. Melodia, Apparatus; multò verò magis necessariae aliae, quia sine iis ne scribi quidem potest comoedia; Nam scripturo comoediam prius necesse est excogitare rem, quae scribenda est; Ea continetur fabula. sed rursus oportet fabulam, quia imitatur esse moratam; & exprimere exactè diuersorum hominum mores; & ideò necessaria altera pars. MORES. nam non omnis oratio Morata; qualis est Mathematicorum, Medicorum, Physiologorum, Dialecticorum. Verùm quia necesse est animi sensa exprimi per orationem; ideò necesse alteram addere partem, quae est. SENtentia. Sed quia sententia verbis constat; ideò necessariò additur etiam alia, quae est. DICTIO" (pp. 44–45).

The central section of the treatise is occupied by an orderly discussion of the "rules" and conditions of the qualitative parts, a discussion which leans heavily upon Robortello's own interpretations in his commentary on the *Poetics*, but which also appeals to later sources such as Horace. For the parts "sententia" and "dictio," most of the materials are drawn from Aristides, and for "apparatus" from a whole series of Latin writers on the theater. Donatus is the authority on the quantitative parts and on the division of comedy into five acts.

The *De comoedia* is in a sense the most disappointing of the supplementary treatises. We would be curious to discover how a theorist of 1548 would have constructed a theory of comedy, but we find instead merely a transfer of familiar ideas and passages, with only the most passing and the most perfunctory adaptations to the special conditions of comedy.

Aristotle's *Rhetoric* and Cicero provide the majority of the materials for the short treatise *De salibus*. As its title suggests, it has no particular reference to any poetic genre; indeed, its interest is rhetorical rather than poetic, as Robortello indicates in his first sentence: "Of the rhetorical faculty, which has many and ample parts, it seems to us that hardly anything remains to be explained except these two matters: first, what aims at delighting and lightening the souls of the listeners, that is, wit and clever sayings; then, those things that aim at a form of discourse and at the embel-

---

[86] *Ibid.*, p. 41: "differt etiam comoedia ab aliis materie rerum subiectarum, quas tractat; nam imitatur actiones hominum humiliores, & viliores; & ideò differt à tragoedia, quae praestantiores imitatur."

lishment of speech."[87] The treatment is thus exclusively rhetorical, except for such kinds of wit as may be used in certain poetic types, and the whole document is unrelated to the fortunes of the *Poetics* in the Renaissance. Indeed, the work seems to be a fragment of a larger treatise on rhetoric.

In the last of the short treatises, *De elegia*, the *Poetics* appears again only in a most incidental way; since Aristotle had not treated the elegy specifically, Robortello was obliged to turn to other sources. Unable to adapt Aristotle's theory to this genre, he took refuge in a conventional treatment of the "origo, finis, materies, artificium" of the elegy. For each topic, he sought solutions in a variety of ancient authors (Athenaeus, Proclus, Cicero, Horace are prominent among them). He sees the elegy as a poem which may treat almost any subject matter and whose kind and category vary with variations in subject matter. A funeral elegy belongs to auletic poetry; one which describes laws belongs to the "poesis legum"; others which treat of war, mores, philosophy are of doubtful classification. In a general way, all elegies are related to the epic since their "imitation" is "mixed," containing both narration and dialogue. They are neither too high nor too low in style, use a variety of devices, create an effect in which the pathetic is accompanied by an air of antiquity.

We may conclude our discussion of the addenda to Robortello's *Explicationes* of 1548—actually it is the first item in the supplementary volume—with his *Paraphrasis in librum Horatii, qui vulgo de arte poetica ad Pisones inscribitur* (see above, Chapter IV, p. 118). Just as the "paraphrase" is little more than that, so the uses of Aristotle's *Poetics* are the traditional ones for the period: Robortello cites the *Poetics* in about a dozen passages, in each case showing how it says the same things that Horace had said or corroborates his statements. The choices seem to be haphazard. Several of the texts concern matters of metrics (1459b31, 1449a23), others refer to the history of tragedy and comedy (1449a2, –19), still others to the treatment of character (1453a17, 1451b11, 1454a16). In the latter connection, Horace's "sibi constet" is explained by the ὁμαλόν of Aristotle (1454a25). Some random distinctions are borrowed from the *Poetics*: the fact that epic is a narrative form (1460a5), the uses of lies and paralogism (1460a18), the interdict on the "deus ex machina" (1454a37). In none of this is there any interpretation of Aristotle, except insofar as the allegation of equivalence is a kind of reading of the text. In one passage of the *Paraphrasis*, Robortello seems to interpret the *Poetics* as saying the opposite of what it says, insisting that meter is necessary for poetry;[88] but this is consonant with

---

[87] *Ibid.*, p. 51: "Ex Rhetorica facultate, quae multas et amplas partes habet; nihil iam ferè nobis videtur reliquum, quod explicemus, praeter duo haec. Primum ea quae ad oblectandos, & releuandos animos auditorum spectat: Sales scilicet & acutè dicta. Deinde, quae ad locutionis genus, & ornamentum sermonis spectant."

[88] *Ibid.*, p. 6: "vt enim poëma aliquod dicatur, non tantum imitatione opus est, sed etiam metro; non quidem quòd metrum absque imitatione poëtam vllum efficiat; Sed & ipsum requiritur tamen, ne nimium soluta sit oratio, sicut etiam in Poët. innuere videtur Aristoteles."

his theory, expressed in the *Explicationes*, that the best kind of poetry is a composite of imitation and verse (cf. p. 90).

THE SEGNI TRANSLATION (1549)

Bernardo Segni had the distinction of publishing, in 1549, the first translation of the *Poetics* in a modern vernacular—his *Rettorica et poetica d'Aristotile*. He paid tribute in his introduction to the recent advances in the understanding of the text, Pazzi's work on the text itself, Robortello's text and commentary. His debt to the latter was probably more considerable than he admitted, since he seems to have based his Italian translation on Robortello's Latin translation rather than on the Greek. In any case, Pazzi was not his source, because passages present in Pazzi and lacking in Robortello are also lacking in Segni's version (cf. Segni, p. 278, Pazzi, p. 6v, Robortello, p. 20). On the whole, Segni's translation is a good one; it is clear and readable, and it is accurate within the limitations of the available texts. He made no effort to correct errors or to supply lacunae, and hence at the really garbled spots in the text he makes no better sense than had his predecessors. But for the unlettered public of his day his contribution must have been most welcome, giving them for the first time the opportunity to read the *Poetics* in Italian. The volume was reprinted at Venice in 1551 and again, in the series of the *Autori del ben parlare*, in 1643.

Besides the translation, Segni provided a brief explanatory introduction and a set of commentaries on the individual chapters. The introduction is concerned with comparing the arts of poetry and of rhetoric, probably because Aristotle's *Rhetoric* occupies the larger part of the volume. But there is nothing Aristotelian about the comparison. Segni finds the two "faculties" alike in that they achieve their ends by using language "which has spoken discourse, and character, and the other desirable features capable of rendering the diction beautiful."[89] Both use the same kinds of arguments—enthymeme, example, and amplification—as means of proof and demonstration, although poetry tends to make greater use of the example. Both are capable of treating any subject, although poetry "imitates more worthy persons and more celebrated actions" than does oratory (p. 273). The ends are the same for both; they are the traditional "to move men's minds" and "to delight them," otherwise stated as "to profit" and "to give pleasure." Segni attempts to evaluate the two arts on their capacity to give pleasure; poetry, because of its beauty, is definitely superior here. This beauty results from imitation "represented to us in action," from a special diction and figurative speech, from meter and verse, from great and delightful materials, from universality in virtue and in vice, and from the general fact that the art is divine and derives all its goodness from nature rather than from art. As for utility, it is difficult to judge of the

[89] *Rettorica et poetica* (1549), p. 272: "che habbia discorso, & costume; & l'altre conuenienze atte à far bella la locutione."

comparative effectiveness of poetry and of rhetoric since, in modern times, we do not see either of them in public performance. Poetry is even less frequently performed than oratory, which may be heard in the pulpit. Hence the effectiveness of purgation, its capacity to bring to our minds "tranquillity and freedom from every perturbation" (p. 275), cannot be properly measured.

In the commentaries on the individual chapters Segni proposes to give brief paraphrases first, "so that those who are less learned may understand some part if not all of it" (p. 280). He will then expound difficult points in the text. Such interpretation as is found here seems again to come largely from Robortello, who, declares Segni, "has in such wise made this work clear that no obscurity now remains in it."[90] But Segni's total theory of poetry is less complete and less systematic than Robortello's. He frequently seeks explanations and parallels in Horace, and he is not averse to citing Italian works to illustrate the theories expounded (thus Boccaccio's stories are given as examples of poems written in prose [p. 281]). His division of the *Poetics* into twenty-two sizable chapters is an improvement over the unbroken texts of Pazzi and Robortello's 270 fragments. It enables the reader to get a much clearer idea of the general order of Aristotle's text.

As for that order, Segni believes that when Aristotle declares that he will treat first things first, he means that he will give definitions of the individual genres before attempting a general definition of poetry and that this determines the general scheme of the *Poetics*. Following the text chapter by chapter, Segni presents a number of separate interpretations which are of interest because of their originality or because they go counter to the accepted tradition. He states, in connection with chapter I, that it is not possible to give a universal definition of poetry for the same reasons that Aristotle adduced for the impossibility of defining the state (referring to the *Politics*). On the moot question of the meaning of λόγοις ψιλοῖς, he offers the correct reading of "prose," whereas many Renaissance commentators refused to admit the possibility of prose as a medium for poetry. Yet he adopts Robortello's conclusion that the best poetry joins verse to imitation. Still relative to the same chapter, he makes significant remarks on the ways in which painting may imitate mores. When, on chapter II, he distinguishes the two natural sources of poetry, he again lists them correctly as imitation and the pleasure derived from imitation, unlike many of his contemporaries who insisted that meter was one of the natural sources. The effect of purgation (chapter V) is said to be a moral and a psychological one:

When we see similar cases which have happened to excellent people, we support our own calamities more easily; or rather we learn how to bear them. And in this way if we are wrathful or intemperate, we come to purge our souls of such

[90] *Ibid.*, p. 280: "di tal' sorte ha fatto aperta questa opera, che nessuna oscurità più ci resti."

passions, considering those perils and those evils which befall him who is wrapped up in vice and him who is involved in the passions; from which consideration it is inevitable that very great pleasure results.[91]

As he passes on to the qualitative parts of tragedy, he adopts for them Robortello's division, assigning "apparatus" and "music" to the instrumental parts, plot to the material, and language, thought, and character to the final. It will be noted, however, that whereas the division is the same as Robortello's, the categories are different, instrumental replacing means, material replacing manner, and final replacing object. By the same token, the division of Aristotle is altered to fit another Aristotelian form of analysis, but not the one being employed at this point in the *Poetics*.

In those sections of his commentary which relate to Aristotle's specific remarks about the tragic form, Segni leans more heavily than elsewhere upon parallels from Horace and upon traditional materials inherited from the Middle Ages. Thus, for example, his commentary on *Poetics* 1453*b*1, ἐκ τῆς ὄψεως, includes a citation of Horace's "Nec pueros coram populo Medea trucidet" (l. 185), and Aristotle's remarks on the "deus ex machina" bring forth the obvious quotation from the *Ars poetica* (l. 191). Similarly, when he discusses the tragic hero, Segni distinguishes him, in conventional fashion, as a "principe" excellent and great for his "beni di fortuna"; tragic heroes would thus be separated from the "privati" of other genres (p. 308). On the whole, however, such references are rare; and because of its brevity and conciseness Segni's commentary seems to be dealing much more directly with the meaning of the text than did the glosses of his contemporaries. For this reason, as well as because it was written in Italian, it must have shed considerable light upon the *Poetics* for a large reading public.

LOMBARDI AND MAGGI (1550)

The second of the great published commentaries was that of Bartolomeo Lombardi and Vincenzo Maggi, *In Aristotelis librum de poetica communes explanationes* (1550). As has already been pointed out, this was a work of long elaboration, in which the role of Lombardi ceased at an early date and for which, in its final form, Maggi was undoubtedly largely responsible. The arrangement is special in the sense that after each section of text and translation (the *Poetics* is divided into 157 sections) there is a paragraph entitled "Explanatio" and then the usual "Annotatio." The text and translation are essentially those of Pazzi; but where the commentators wish to emend the text they place an asterisk before the doubtful passage, and when they

---

[91] *Ibid.*, p. 294: "ueggendo noi simili casi auuenuti in persone eccellenti, più ageuolmente comportiamo le calamità nostre; ò uero impariamo à sopportarle. Et in tal' modo se noi siamo iracundi, ò intemperati uenghiamo à purgar' l'animo di tali affetti; considerando quei pericoli, & quei mali, che incontrano à chi è ne' uitij rinuolto, & à chi è fitto nelle perturbationi: dalla qual' consideratione è forza, che ne risulti piacer' grandissimo."

wish to propose an alteration of the translation they mark both text and translation with a dagger. The same symbols are then used in the annotations to explain the changes that they propose. The "Explanationes" are given as the work of Lombardi and Maggi; they contain first a kind of paraphrase of the preceding text, then a first commentary of a textual and literary character. This commentary is continued in the "Annotationes," prepared by Maggi, usually in a much expanded form. In both explanations and annotations, linguistic matters and questions of translation bulk large; for many sections, indeed, this is the only kind of commentary provided. Nevertheless, there is a very extended treatment of all problems involved in the interpretation of the *Poetics*. Moreover, since Maggi had a thorough knowledge of the other works currently consulted on the art of poetry—Horace, Plato, Aristotle's *Rhetoric*, the other Greek and Roman rhetoricians—and since he himself had some well-developed conceptions of the art, we find in his annotations a completely consistent theory of poetry—not Aristotle's, but his own.

The cornerstone of this theory, as needs must be, is his conception of the end of poetry, a dual end borrowed from Horace: teaching and pleasure. The earliest statements in the "Prolegomena" (an important section for the discovery of Maggi's views) emphasize the utilitarian end. Thus: "The end of poetry itself is, by imitating human actions in delightful discourse, to render the soul refined" ("Finis autem ipsius Poesis est, actiones humanas imitando, suaui sermone animum excultum reddere," p. 13). The utilitarian end is a moral one, variously described in the same "Prolegomena": poetry attempts to embellish the human soul with the best possible moral dispositions ("optimis moribus sibi expoliendum proponit") and to produce proper moral action ("ut bonos mores inducant," *ibid.*). The moral end is variously stated for the various genres—for tragedy, to purge the soul of its passions ("illa nos ab animi perturbationibus expurgari" and "perturbationes ex animis auferendo"); for the epic, to praise the deeds of great men ("praeclara illustrium uirorum gesta uersibus exornando"); for comedy, to make fun of the vices ("uitia irridendo," *ibid.*). In the course of the commentary, these ideas are considerably expanded and clarified. The restatements bring with them the use of terms long associated with other critical traditions. Horace's "Aut prodesse uolunt, aut delectare poetae" is quoted in connection with the pleasure to be derived from recognition and reversal (p. 111), and the meaning of "prodesse" is defined in connection with Aristotle's τὸ φιλάνθρωπον:

By φιλάνθρωπον he means that which expresses good character and which leads to proper living in society.... Thus when Aristotle says οὔτε γὰρ φιλάνθρωπον, οὔτε ἐλεεινὸν, οὔτε φοβερόν ἐστι, it is as if he were to say that it is neither profitable nor does it bring pity or terror. And the poets attempt above all to bring profit to humankind, and those examples of action are useful to the society of men in which the worst men fall from happiness into unhappiness, since through these the human race is taught and abstains from wicked deeds.[92]

Having established the end of moral utility for all poetry, Maggi is careful to seek, in the various parts of tragedy, the particular ways in which that end is achieved. Purgation, as we have already seen, is the particular kind of utility produced by the genre. In discussing its operation, Maggi takes sides on an issue that was beginning to be much debated: whether tragedy, through purgation, actually removes pity and fear from men's souls or whether it removes, through their intermediation, other less desirable passions. Maggi argues for the latter interpretation, holding that men would be worse off if pity and fear were expelled from their souls:

Therefore it is much better, by the intervention of pity and terror, to purge the soul of wrath, through which so many violent deaths come about; of avarice, which is the cause of almost an infinity of ills; of lust, thanks to which the most harmful of wicked deeds must frequently be suffered. For these reasons I have no doubt whatever that Aristotle was unwilling to make the purgation of terror and pity from the human soul the end of tragedy; but rather, to use these for the removal of other disorders from the soul, through which removal the soul comes to be adorned with the virtues. For once wrath is driven out, for example, kindness takes its place.... [93]

Maggi cites the *Politics* in support of his position; he concludes, at a later point, that "the purpose of tragedy is to purge the human soul of disorders; once these are expelled, men emerge at peace and essentially better."[94] The moral utility contained in purgation is a function of plot; other kinds derive from the handling of mores. Of the four requisites of character, Maggi concludes that the first, goodness, has a pedagogic utility. "Good" character in the personages of tragedy will lead to improvement of character in its spectators: "For this reason we judge that in this section Aristotle accorded the first place to goodness of character, so that he might admonish the poets most strongly to be especially attentive to their expression."[95]

[92] *Explanationes* (1550), p. 153: "Per φιλάνθρωπον intelliget idem, quod moratum, quodque ad societatem humanam conducit.... Aristoteles igitur cùm dicit οὔτε γὰρ φιλάνθρωπον, οὔτε ἐλεεινὸν, οὔτε φοβερόν ἐστι, idem est, ac si diceret, nec prodest, nec misericordiam, timoremúe habet. at in primis humano generi poetae prodesse student, Prosunt autem humanae societati exempla, in quibus pessimi uiri ex felicitate in miseriam labuntur; quoniam his instruitur genus humanum, & à sceleribus abstinet."

[93] *Ibid.*, p. 98: "longè igitur melius est misericordiae & terroris interuentu expurgare animum ab Ira, qua tot neces fiunt: ab Auaritia, quae infinitorum penè malorum est causa: à Luxuria, cuius gratia nefandissima scelera saepissime patrantur. His itaque rationibus haudquaquam dubito, Aristotelem nolle Tragoediae finem esse animam humanam à terrore, miscricordiaúc cxpurgare; sed his uti ad alias perturbationes ab animo remouendas; ex quarum remotione animus uirtutibus exornatur. nam ira, uerbi gratia, depulsa, succedit mansuetudo...."

[94] *Ibid.*, p. 110: "Officium uerò Tragoediae... est humanum animum à perturbationibus expurgare: quibus extrusis tranquilli, ac seipsis meliores homines euadunt."

[95] *Ibid.*, p. 170: "hac ratione arbitramur Aristotelem hac in parte primum locum bonis moribus concessisse, ut poetas potissimùm admoneret de illis exprimendis magis esse sollicitos oportere."

Goodness consists in the highest possible degree of manifestation of the virtues (cf. p. 175 on the procedure of painters), in such a way that the actors in a tragedy may serve as models for the audience ("debent exemplar facere," p. 175). In a similar way, that particular kind of tragedy which Aristotle calls ἠθική (1456a1) is taken to mean one "imitating and expressing good mores, and those which contribute to proper living in human society" ("imitans exprimensque bonos, & humanae societati conferentes mores," p. 195); Maggi derives the interpretation from the earlier φιλάνθρωπον. In all these passages, it is difficult to assign an exact meaning to "mores"; but it seems clear that Maggi means by the term, rather than the "character" or the "disposition to moral action" of Aristotle, a form of action itself, judged as "good" according to an accepted ethical code.

A similar set of distinctions and developments is offered by Maggi with respect to the other end, pleasure. The assumption throughout, I believe, is that the "voluptas" afforded by poetry is an intermediate end to the achievement of the moral utility, although there are few specific statements to this effect. Such a clear statement comes near the end, in the commentary to *Poetics* 1462b3:

> But in these words Aristotle seems to say that the function of the poet is to give pleasure, and that this should be considered the end of poetry. Yet since in the definition of tragedy he had said that it purges the disorder of the soul by means of pity and terror, purgation and not pleasure must be considered to be the end. . . . in such matters there may be many ends, of which one is regarded as greater than another. We thus concede that the poets have as their end to produce pleasure, but that they wish in a more important way to bring profit by adorning men with the virtues.[96]

The elements of a poetic work which give pleasure to its audience are mostly the plot and the diction. Hence the necessity that the plot of tragedy should be a known plot, based on the argument that what is known gives greater pleasure than what is unknown. Maggi is explaining *Poetics* 1457b19:

> Just as the image of a thing gives greater pleasure to one who knows the thing previously than to one who does not, since one who knows the thing learns and reasons, so one who knows previously that action which the poet imitates will learn and reason that this is the imitation of that action. . . . thus he who knows the action of which the plot is an imitation experiences a greater pleasure than he who does not know it, since the latter is incapable of deducing [the identification of the action] from it. . . . for those plots which give the greatest pleasure

---

[96] *Ibid.*, p. 299: "his enim in uerbis Aristoteles dicere uidetur, poetae munus esse uoluptatem afferre, eamque poeticae finem statuere. uerum cùm in Tragoediae definitione dicatur, quòd interuentu misericordiae, & terroris animum perturbationibus expurgat: igitur huiusmodi expurgatio finis. non autem uoluptas statuenda erit. . . . rei eiusdem multi possunt esse fines; quorum alter altero magis intenditur. concedimus enim poetas scopum habere uoluptatem inducere, magis tamen uirtutibus exornando prodesse uelle."

(other things being equal) are to be preferred to others which are less enjoyable.[97]

Maggi himself recognizes the contradiction that exists between this statement (pleasure from knowledge) and the earlier statement that recognition and reversal, as parts of plot, produced pleasure out of the unknown (pleasure from ignorance). In this latter connection, he is led to examine the whole question of the derivation of pleasure from the essentially painful events of tragedy. Rejecting the explanation of Alexander of Aphrodisias—that we rejoice at seeing ourselves exempt from the sufferings of others—he proposes rather that the "pleasure" of tragedy results from the fact that it is natural and human for men to feel pity:

> We feel sorrow by reason of the heart, which contracts beyond its normal state at the spectacle of piteous events, but in fact we do [at the same time] feel joy because it is human and natural to have pity.... Since therefore it is human and natural for men to feel pity, it will also be pleasurable and most delightful.... For pleasure and pain concern different objects; pain to be sure will be a pleasure to the heart, since it is a movement contrary to nature precisely towards that which is constrictive; whereas pleasure is a movement of the soul towards that which is natural for it and born with it.[98]

The pleasure associated with tragedy will thus come from certain kinds of plots, from certain parts of plot, such as recognition and reversal, and from the emotion of the spectator involved in his sympathy for the fate of the personages. Maggi takes this last kind as an answer to Plato's condemnation of the "voluptuous" aspects of poetry. Assuming from the start that the *Poetics* is a defence of the art against such attackers as Plato (cf. p. 37), Maggi asserts that the cultivation of "voluptas" is a fault of certain poets, not of the art as a whole, and that Aristotle specifically answers the objection by assigning to the pleasure of tragedy an intermediary role in the achievement of purgation and hence of moral utility (cf. "Prolegomena," p. 13).

Pleasure may come, as well, from other features of the poetic work. From the chorus, which provides the possibility of relaxation ("cantus choricos ad relaxandos animos audientium," p. 149). From the episodes, which are to be considered as ornaments to the plot rather than parts of it. As a matter of fact, it is because of the desirability of such ornamentation that

[97] *Ibid.*, p. 134: "sicut imago rei magis eum delectat, qui rem prius nouit, quàm qui non nouit: quoniam qui rem nouit addiscit, & ratiocinatur: ita quoque qui prius eam actionem nouit, quam imitatur poeta, discet, & ratiocinabitur hanc actionis illius imitationem existere. ... is utique, qui actionem nouit, cuius fabula imitatio est, maiori uoluptate afficietur, quàm is, qui eam ignorat, quoniam de ea ratiocinari non potest. ... nam fabulae, quae magis delectant (caeteris paribus) aliis minus gratis sunt praeferendae."

[98] *Ibid.*, pp. 112–13: "Dolemus itaque ratione cordis, quod à specie rei miserabilis uisae ultra naturam suam constringitur: laetamur uerò, quoniam humanum, ac naturale est miserere.... Cum igitur misereri humanum, atque hominibus naturale sit, uoluptuosum etiam erit, ac periucundum.... Voluptas itaque ac dolor diuersa respicient. nempe dolor gratia cordis erit; quoniam motus praeter naturam est, ad id scilicet, quod angustum est: uoluptas uerò erit animae motus ad id, quod ei naturale connatumque est."

POETICS: DISCOVERY AND EXEGESIS

the poet—as compared with the historian—chooses a relatively meager plot, which he then proceeds to magnify and adorn with episodes.

Since it is the poet's aim to amplify the action and to strengthen it with every ornament, he will adorn the subject most wonderfully with digressions, and he will separate and rejoin one thing with another in such a way that the action, through the episodes, will appear more beautiful and clear. For it is not the poet's end to express the action in an arid and meager way, but to place it before our eyes in an ornate and elegant fashion.[99]

The total conception of the plot—brief in tragedy so as to avoid satiety ("satietatem parit," p. 257), extensive and varied in epic for the pleasures of magnificence ("ad oblectandum varietate accommodatur," *ibid.*)—is itself determined by this end of pleasure. Furthermore, in different genres the plot will end differently—happily or unhappily, similarly for all persons or diversely for the wicked and the good—in order to create different kinds of pleasure: "It is necessary that the pleasures [voluptates] which come from tragedy and from comedy should be different and appropriate to each separately."[100]

Finally, but by no means as a minor cause, pleasure will be provided by the language, the diction of poetry. One of the principal differences between poetry and rhetoric, aside from the fact that the latter persuades while the former imitates, resides in the superior ornateness of poetic diction ("poeticam elocutionem esse pluribus illustratam ornatibus," p. 237). One of the main consequences of this demand for ornament is Maggi's insistence that verse is essential for poetry. Since this runs counter to certain clear affirmations of Aristotle, Maggi is obliged to develop a complicated theory of the ingredients of true poetry. He distinguishes three degrees: (1) the true poets, who both imitate and use verse; (2) those who imitate without using verse, and who are also poets; (3) those who do not imitate, and who are called poets merely because they write in verse (p. 57). Of these, the first are the only real poets. Maggi reinforces his theory by declaring that meter is one of the natural causes of poetry (with the assertion that "cùm ... Poetica ex imitatione & carmine constet," p. 74), and that the phrase "suauem sermonem" in the definition of tragedy is again a demand for the inclusion of verse: "From this text one concludes most clearly that verse is an intimate part of poetry and included in its very nature."[101] Such a conception almost necessarily brings with it the further theory of the appropriateness of verse to subject matter. Each genre will be written in a form of verse light

---

[99] *Ibid.*, p. 251: "cùm poetae propositum sit, quam amplectitur actionem, omnibus eam ornamentis fulcire, egressionibus ueró mirum in modum rem exornet, & rem à re disterminet ac seiungat, iure factum fuit, ut actio episodiorum interuentu pulchrior, ac perspicua magis appareret. non enim poetae munus est aridè ac ieiunè res exprimere, sed ornatè, ac expolitè eas ob oculos ponere."

[100] *Ibid.*, p. 160: "uoluptates, quae ex Tragoedia, Comoediáque proueniunt, diuersas, ac unicuique accommodatas esse oportere."

[101] *Ibid.*, p. 100: "Ex hoc contextu colligitur manifestissimè, carmen esse quid intimum Poesi, in eiusque natura claudi."

POETIC THEORY

or grave according to the nature of the materials treated. In the epic, for example, "the verse must be proportioned to the subject treated, and since heroic matter is grave and magnificent, it requires a meter by its very nature stable and ample."[102]

Having adapted so much of Aristotle's *Poetics* to his own notion of the dual end of poetry, instruction and pleasure, Maggi is inevitably led to develop in considerable detail two further matters, the nature of the audience and the demands which it will make on the poetic work. For Maggi, as later for Castelvetro and other theorists, the poet's audience is not the few but the many, not the élite but the "vulgus." He states so specifically with respect to tragedy:

> Add to this the fact that tragedy is performed for the pleasure of the populace and of the crowd in general, and moreover that such a multitude does not know that sort of plots. For even if they may be known to one or another of the spectators, because the poet has in mind the people in general he will pay no attention to those few, even if he might give them great pleasure.[103]

In a curious way, this "generality" of the audience becomes a basis and a justification for the "universality" of poetic subject matters.

The argument runs thus: If the poem is to have its proper effect, especially as concerns moral instruction, it must be accepted as "true" by its public. Maggi insists upon this on several occasions, and most particularly in connection with Aristotle's remarks on the "impossible probable" (*Poetics* 1460a27):

> ... because his end is to teach proper conduct, whether this be introduced into men's souls by false narratives or by true narratives, his desire is fulfilled. But since a poet cannot accomplish this purpose unless he obtains the belief of his audience, he follows common opinion in this respect.[104]

Acceptability to common opinion, rather than "truth," is the criterion; for the poet may invent things which are essentially "untrue," provided that he does so in a way which makes them seem probable:

> ... falsehoods of the kind that are told by the poets, insofar as they are received in the opinion of the crowd, are held to be verisimilar and true. Therefore if a certain poet were to imagine something new, it will be said to be acceptable to the opinion of the crowd. Since the crowd admits as true similar things and things

---

[102] *Ibid.*, p. 259: "carmen debere rei, qua de agit, proportione respondere. & quoniam heroica materia grauis est, & magnifica, iccirco ex sui natura stabile, atque amplum metrum requirit."

[103] *Ibid.*, p. 135: "Adde, Tragoediam in populi, ac uniuersae turbae gratiam fieri, eiusmodi autem multitudinem fabulas eas ignorare. Quanquam igitur unus, aut alter eas optime calleat, poeta tamen populum respiciens, de paucis illis, etiam si magis eos delectet, non erit sollicitus."

[104] *Ibid.*, pp. 267–68: "quòd ei propositus finis est, bonos mores instituere: quos siue ueris, siue falsis narrationibus in hominum animos inducat, uoti compos efficitur. sed quoniam id poeta praestare non posset, nisi ei fides adhiberetur, iccirco uulgi opinionem sequitur."

which for a long time cannot have been done, then it will accept as true what is but recently invented.[105]

It is thus not necessary that the materials of poetry be "true"; the only requirement is that they be acceptable as such to the common crowd which constitutes the audience of poetry.

Moreover, acceptability may result from various qualities of the materials: (1) From what is "natural." Maggi seems to mean by this those aspects of any action or character which seem to be inherently present in it: "To express things according to verisimilitude and necessity is nothing else but to express them taking into account the nature of those things. Nature indeed is a kind of universal."[106] (2) From what is "verisimilar." This does not always correspond to everyday truth, but it is nevertheless acceptable to the mind. "For many things happen customarily to mortals which are not verisimilar, and every day the senses experience what is contrary to the reason. And still this is reasonable; for since verisimilar things are not necessary, and may come to pass in some other way, it is verisimilar that certain things should happen contrary to verisimilitude."[107] The distinction here is apparently between what reason would demand as constituting normal action and what actually does happen in life—between the "rational" and the "probable."

(3) From what is "necessary." This is an internal factor; according to necessity, certain circumstances of action and of character, presented among the *données* of the poem, must lead to expected consequences in the later development of the work. "This is called the necessary *ex positione*, when one thing being posited, it is necessary that another should follow."[108] But even here a criterion of universality is present, since the consequences "most usually" resulting from the given circumstances are the ones to be used by the poet: "He warns us that we should contrive those conclusions for our plots which follow upon the actions necessarily or for the most part, not those which follow rarely."[109] These somewhat vague distinctions are clarified slightly by the example which Maggi develops. He assumes that

---

[105] *Ibid.*, p. 131: "id genus falsa, quae à poetis dicuntur, quoniam in uulgi opinionem sunt recepta, pro uerisimilibus ac ueris habentur. Quòd si quispiam poeta nouum aliquid finxerit, id etiam uulgi opinione receptum dicetur. quoniam si similia & quae longè minus fieri nequeunt, tanquam uera uulgus, admittit: etiam quòd recenter est fictum, tanquam uerum recipiet."

[106] *Ibid.*, p. 131: "Exprimere autem res secundum uerisimile & necessarium, nil aliud est, quàm eas exprimere habita ratione illarum rerum naturae. natura uero quidpiam uniuersale est."

[107] *Ibid.*, p. 201: "nam multa mortalibus usu uenire non uerisimilia, praeterque rationem omnem in dies ipso sensu comprobatur. idque rationi consonum est. nam cùm uerisimilia necessaria non sint, aliter quoque fieri possunt: igitur uerisimile est, praeter uerisimile nonnulla fieri."

[108] *Ibid.*, p. 126: "Id autem ex positione necessarium dicitur, cùm uno posito, necesse est aliud sequi."

[109] *Ibid.*, p. 121: "nos admonet, ut fines eos fabulis faciamus, qui aut necessariò, aut in plurimis, non autem qui rarò huiuscemodi actiones sequuntur."

we are given certain characters for a father and a son and a proposal for the marriage of the son; certain reactions will have to follow:

We say that such-and-such actions must necessarily follow; for these things which preceded having been established, the poet must see to it that others come about. Otherwise the comedy will not be properly made. ... if the father proposes a marriage to the son, it is verisimilar that the son should consult a household servant or a friend concerning the way to avoid his father's proposal. If, therefore, the poet introduces the son consulting a servant, he will then rest on verisimilitude. ... But if the poet introduces a father, who, in order to bring about the marriage of his son, tries to use the offices of the servant, it will immediately result from necessity that the servant should, for example, necessarily deceive the old man.[110]

But the distinction is still not very useful; at best we see in verisimilitude an approximation of what traditionally happens, in necessity a development from stated *données*. (4) Acceptability depends in part on conformity to the reason. Maggi's commentary is a fairly close paraphrase of *Poetics* 1460a27: "He enjoins that in the total composition of the poem there should be no part which might seem to contain anything absurd or contrary to reason, but that all should be made with a maximum of reason. This is the same as if one were to say that everything should present itself as verisimilar or necessary."[111]

(5) Most clearly and most convincingly, acceptability by the audience will result from the presentation of type characters according to the requirements of decorum. The relationships are fairly simple here: if the audience is to derive from the poem the proper utility in the form of moral instruction, it must be willing to accept as "true" the characters presented, and it will do so if these correspond to recognizable, traditional types. The people presented in poems are exemplars of good behavior: "Since they [the poets] imitate the best people, when they present their behavior they must make exemplars of it, that is, they must express the highest probity of character in those persons whom they undertake to imitate."[112] Maggi relates the παράδειγμα of his text at this point (1454b13) to Platonic Ideas of character, "Nature considered in itself, and not as manifested in this or

[110] *Ibid.*, p. 126: "id sanè dicitur esse necessarium, ut sequatur. constitutis enim illis, quae praecessere, poeta id efficere cogitur: alioqui Comoedia probe facta non esset. ... ut pater filium de nuptiis tentarit, uerisimile sanè est, filium consulere seruum domesticum, uel amicum, quomodo possit patrem eludere. Si igitur poeta filium consulentem seruum inducit, uerisimili tunc innititur. ... Quòd si pater inducatur à poeta, qui ut ad exitum nuptias filii deducat, serui opera uti uelit, hoc statim exoritur necessarium, ut scilicet seruus necessariò senem eludat."

[111] *Ibid.*, p. 267: "Praecipit quoque, ut in uniuersa Poesis constitutione nulla sit pars, quae aliquid absurdi, ac praeter rationem continere uideatur, sed omnia summa cum ratione facta sint. hoc autem perinde est, ac si diceret omnia praeseferre uerisimile, aut necessarium oportere."

[112] *Ibid.*, p. 175: "quoniam praestantiores imitantur cùm mores exprimunt, debent exemplar facere, hoc est in moribus summum probitatis illius personae, quam sibi imitandam proponunt, exprimere."

that particular object" ("natura secundum se consyderata, non ut in hoc, aut in illo reperta," p. 175). These Ideas, however, rapidly become the collections of traits habitually associated with certain types; a servant will be gluttonous and will think only of food; his master will think only of honor and glory (p. 115); a king must do and say those things proper to a king (this constitutes another kind of "universal"). "The meaning is that the poet deals with the universal. For if he introduces a king as saying or doing a given thing, what he says or does must belong to those things which are usually or necessarily attributed to kings."[113] In a still more general way, a man must not have feminine characteristics (Ulysses should not be presented as weeping), and a woman should not show virility of soul (example, Menalippe, p. 171).

Because the ends of pleasure and utility must be achieved in an essentially common audience, and because this audience provides certain criteria of universality, generality, and truth, the activity of the poet in writing the poem comes to be fairly well restricted. The great field of liberty remaining open to him is that of ornamentation through a variety of episodes added to the plot and through ornateness of diction—in a word, the field of the pleasurable elements of the poem. Contrariwise, the plot itself must be one known or acceptable to the audience, the characters must conform to traditional types, and the needs of instruction must be kept constantly in mind. At times, as in the case of necessity, an internal and structural criterion results from these demands of the audience; but more frequently the criterion is imposed from without. Thus Aristotle's remark on the usual time of tragedies is transformed into a rule for both tragedy and comedy ("unico solis circuitu, uel paulò longiore exprimere *debet*," p. 93) on the basis of audience demands for credibility.

Since then tragedy and comedy ... attempt to approach as close to truth as is possible, if we were to hear things done in the space of a month presented in two or at most three hours, in which time certainly a tragedy or a comedy is acted, the thing will absolutely produce an effect of incredibility. [Thus if a messenger is sent to Egypt and he returns within an hour:] what spectator indeed, if after one hour this man returning here is seen introduced on the stage, will not whistle and hiss the actor off the stage and judge that an action lacking in all reason was contrived by the poet?[114]

[113] *Ibid.*, p. 131: "sensus est, poetam circa uniuersale uersari. quoniam si regem quidpiam, aut dicentem, aut facientem inducit, debet id ex iis esse, quae regibus ut plurimum, aut necessariò contingunt." Cf. p. 272: "Poeticae enim scopus est rerum ideas ... exprimere. ueluti si regem exprimit, regis ideam referre, quantumq̀ue in rege desyderari posset, id omne illi tribuere. ... rectitudo enim Poeticae est, quae fieri possunt sectari in quacunque re, qua de agit. quòd si ab eo quod fieri potest recedat, à propria sua rectitudine recedet."

[114] *Ibid.*, p. 94: "Cùm igitur Tragoedia atque Comoedia, ... propè ueritatem quoad fieri potest, accedere conentur, si res gestas mensis unius spatio, duabus, tribusúe ad summum horis, quanto nimirum tempore Tragoedia uel Comoedia agitur, factas audiremus, res prorsus incredibilis efficeretur. ... quis profectò spectator, si post horam hunc redeuntem illinc, in scenam introduci uideat, non exibilabit, explodetq́ue, & rem à poeta omni prorsus ratione carentem, factam praedicabit?"

The system of ideas encountered in Maggi's *Explanationes* shows two complementary tendencies: first, a wish to explain Aristotle's text in terms of its own order and its own intellectual structure; second, an almost inevitable tendency, at this period in criticism, to complete the explanations by reference to other documents and, hence, to give the whole of the theory a decidedly un-Aristotelian cast. With respect to the first, Maggi is at some points more successful than his predecessors. The interpretation of "necessity" may again be cited as an example, since it conceives of the term as designating an internal relationship in the poem, just as Aristotle does. Again, when he assigns the various qualitative parts of tragedy to object, manner, and means, Maggi makes a more correct distribution than Robortello had done: for the means, "melopoeia, dictio"; for the manner, "apparatus"; and for the object, "fabula, mores, sententia" (p. 104). He shows here a much keener apprehension of Aristotle's basic meaning.

On the other hand, he cannot resist the temptation of other ideas current in the thinking of his time. So, as we have seen, he ascribes to the *Poetics* the ends of utility and pleasure, with which he was familiar through Horace, and cites Horace as his authority. From Horace also, and from the long rhetorical tradition associated with him, he borrows the theory of decorum and of the types of character and human behavior. The same rhetorical tradition provides him with a number of remarks on tragedy and comedy which come ultimately from Donatus and Diomedes rather than from Aristotle. Thus the moral distinction between "better" and "worse" forms of character is turned into the familiar social distinction between "reges & heroas" for tragedy and "uiles, moriones, seruos, ancillas, scurras" for comedy (p. 64)—otherwise stated as "uenerandis, atque potentibus" against "humiliores, puta rusticos, seruos, id genus homines" (p. 77)—and the two genres are further differentiated by the unhappy ending of the one and the happy ending of the other (p. 160). Indeed, when Maggi presents a summary of Aristotle's ideas on the qualitative parts of tragedy, he collects a group of terms which might easily be found so assembled in any standard rhetorical treatise: "Dicitur igitur ab Apparatu, uel regia, uel sumptuosa: à Dictione, metrica, elegans, ornata: à Musica, suauis: à Sententia, euidens, grauis, affectibus referta: à Moribus, morata: à Fabula simplex, uel perplexa" (p. 101). The conventional association between poetry and verse leads to the long argument justifying verse that we have already noted. Homer is praised for his proper handling of invention, disposition, and elocution (p. 79). The answers to critical objections are organized around the old "res-verba" distinction. And so on for other rhetorical ideas. From Plato, Maggi derives the conception of character types as παραδείγματα or Ideas, the theory that poetry may serve in the education of youth (he does not fail to explain away Plato's banishment of the poets), certain ideas on the nature of beauty (p. 123).

This is not, however, pure eclecticism. Maggi does have a theory, centering about his notion of the dual end of poetry; and most of what he offers in the way of interpretation tends to orient the *Poetics* in the direction of that theory. He is not led, however, to a total deformation of Aristotle's text, and in at least a few respects his commentary presents the best light on the *Poetics* to date.

In the same volume as the *Explanationes*, Maggi published two other works, his commentary on Horace's *Ars poetica*, called an *Interpretatio* (treated in Chapter IV, pp. 119–22), and his treatise on comedy entitled *De ridiculis*. I have already pointed out that his main interest in the first of these was the establishment of parallels between the texts of Aristotle and of Horace and that his array of such parallels was the most extensive yet prepared. Naturally, some of the theory elaborated in the *Explanationes* is repeated in connection with Horace's text, which Maggi regards as stemming directly from Aristotle. The "res-verba" distinction figures prominently, and Maggi tends—perhaps more than in the *Explanationes*—to identify "res" with elements of plot and with the end of utility and "verba" with diction and with the end of pleasure. Hence, the ends distinguished are also the same and they are similarly related to the various parts of the poem. The essence of character is once more found in decorum. Maggi again interprets necessity as an interconnection of the parts of the poem, and he regards as digressions all those episodes which are meant to give a variety and magnitude to the plot. All these matters are stated more succinctly —and with less philosophical justification—in the *Interpretatio*, which must be considered essentially as an appendix to the commentary on Aristotle.

A similar judgment may be made on the little treatise *De ridiculis* which, in the 1550 volume, comes between the *Explanationes* and the *Interpretatio*. Maggi means it as a supplement to Aristotle, for he notes that comedy requires two elements, a certain kind of plot structure and the ingredient of the ridiculous, and that Aristotle treats only the first of these. Before offering his own theory of the ridiculous, Maggi examines those of Cicero, Quintilian, and Pontano. His own theory, unfortunately, is very unsatisfactory, since it does little more than collect the passages from the *Poetics* which refer to the ridiculous and attempt to explain them by citation of other authors. Thus, after quoting Aristotle's definition, "peccatum, & turpitudinem ac deformitatem quandam esse sine dolore," he points out that the ridiculous may be of the body or of the mind, and he cites examples of the latter from Cicero. A third kind may come from circumstances ("ex rebus"). Plato's *Sophist* is consulted for a definition of "turpitudo." Various examples of the ridiculous springing from "res" and from "verba" (note the persistence of the distinction) are cited. Maggi sees the need in comedy for the same kind of admiration which he had required in tragedy and in the epic, achieved in part through variety and novelty. "Risus à turpitudine citra dolorem cum admiratione dependet," he insists (p. 307).

And as for the various genres treated by Horace, comedy as well requires the gifts of nature and the skills of art on the part of the poet.

GIACOPO GRIFOLI (1550)

The middle year of the century was also marked by the publication of another extensive commentary on Horace, Giacopo Grifoli's *In artem poeticam Horatii interpretatio* (see above, Chapter IV, pp. 122–27). Unlike Maggi, Grifoli is primarily interested in the text of Horace, and he uses Aristotle as a means of clarifying and expounding the *Ars poetica*. In a few places—and a considerable number of Aristotelian passages are used by Grifoli—his remarks and applications constitute an interpretation of the *Poetics* and are hence of interest to us here. Generally, there is the tacit assumption that Aristotle and Horace are not only talking about the same things, but that they are saying the same things. Hence, it is just as proper to read Aristotle in terms of Horace as it is to read Horace in terms of Aristotle. In the second place, since Grifoli seeks in Aristotle primarily a means of discovering the order and sense of Horace's text, he is most attracted by those sections of the *Poetics* which present neat categories and numerical divisions. Two such sets of distinctions appeal to him most forcefully: the six qualitative parts of tragedy and the four requisites of character. Not only does he see in the six parts the essential ordering principle of Horace's text, but he interprets them in the light of that text. Grifoli takes "fabula" to be the whole of the work, and to consist of two elements, "res" or the materials and "verba" or the instruments of expression; the other five parts are then distributed thus:

All these things indeed happen on the stage, whose external presentation does not in any way clash with the materials themselves. Rather is it a kind of instrument, since imitation occurs also in the spectacle and the melody, according to the laws of plot. In truth, diction and character and thought are the materials [res] which are proposed for imitation. Now if we *read* a tragedy, spectacle and melody are no more parts of it than delivery and memory in the orations of the ancients when they are read.[115]

We should note here the crossing of imitation with the "res-verba" distinction, the parallelism with rhetoric, and the strange division which puts melody (considered as actual singing) among the "means" and diction among the objects of imitation (this is the same division suggested by Robortello). The same division is repeated, perhaps more clearly, in connection with lines 319–22 of the *Ars poetica*:

We said from the beginning that there are six parts of tragedy: plot, character,

[115] *Interpretatio* (1550), p. 82: "omnia enim haec versantur in scena, quae quidem speciem habet à rebus nihil abhorrentem: est enim velut instrumentum, nam ex apparatu, & melodia sunt imitationes vt fabulae ratio postulat. dictio verò, mores sententiae res sunt, quae ad imitandum sunt propositae. verum si tragoediam ipsam legamus, non magis apparatus & melodia sunt illius partes, quàm in antiquorum orationibus, quae leguntur, actio, & memoria."

diction, thought, spectacle, and melody. Of these the last two are as it were the instruments of imitation, the middle three are the subjects proposed for imitation. The first, then, contains in itself the manner of imitation, since the plot is a composition of all the things in a tragedy and since the imitation must be made in that manner and in that order in which the plot itself has been composed.[116]

As for the four requisites of character, Grifoli begins by generalizing them into a set of criteria for language ("verba"): "... without language, indeed, it will be difficult to determine whether the moral quality, the appropriateness, the similarity, and the constancy of character have been observed or not."[117] The very terms used indicate Grifoli's understanding of the requisites: "officium," "proprietas," "similitudo," "constantia." He explains them in full at several later points. Commenting on lines 114-18, he cites Aristotle's Greek terms and then proceeds to define them:

This means that we should see to it in the first place that there should be characters which are good, then that they should be appropriate, then that they should be similar, finally that they should be uniform. These qualities are different from one another, for—to speak briefly—the first concerns the moral quality, the second appropriateness, the third similarity, and the fourth constancy of character. In the first, nobody errs except through wickedness; in the second, he errs who goes counter to his own dignity; in the third, he who departs from his proper kind; in the fourth, he who does not remain constant to himself.[118]

Grifoli thus reduces Aristotle's four requisites to (1) a rule of moral goodness, (2) a rule of decorum, (3) a rule of conformity to type or tradition, and (4) a rule of self-consistency. By so doing, he brings them into harmony with his interpretation of the *Ars poetica*. Moreover (pp. 42-43), he especially assigns the fourth quality, τὸ ὁμαλόν, to characters newly invented by the poet, since the nature of traditional characters will have been well established by earlier poets.

These matters of character and the rules associated with them belong to the "res" of poetry; they affect "verba," however, since they are the

---

[116] Ibid., p. 97: "Diximus à principio sex esse partes tragoediae fabulam, morem, dictionem, sententiam, apparatum & melodiam: quarum postremae duae sunt tanquam instrumenta imitationis, tres mediae subiectae sunt, & propositae ad imitandum. Prima verò continet in se modum, cum fabula sit compositio rerum omnium in tragoedia, & eo modo, & ordine imitandum sit, quo composita sit ipsa fabula."

[117] Ibid., p. 12: "officium porro, proprietas, similitudo, constantia morum seruetur nec ne, sine oratione vix constare poterit."

[118] Ibid., p. 39: "id est vt videamus, vt mores primum sint, qui boni sunt, tum qui consentanei, deinde qui similes, postremo qui aequabiles. differunt enim haec inter se, quod ut paucis agamus, primum genus est officij, secundum est decori, tertium similitudinis, quartum constantiae: in primo nemo peccat sine scelere, in secundo qui contra dignitatem suam, in tertio qui à suo genere discrepat, in quarto qui sibi non constat." Cf. p. 40: "τὸ δὲ ἁρμόττον postulat, vt naturae quisque suae consentiat: vt vir, quae sunt viri: mulier, quę sunt mulieris agat. τὸ ὅμοιον δὲ, vt non discrepet à sua conditione, vt seruus seruo non sit dissimilis, neque mercator mercatori. τὸ δὲ ὁμαλὸν vt in omni actione sibi constet."

POETIC THEORY

material for which words are used. Grifoli justifies his insistence on the primacy of "res" by quoting Aristotle to the effect that the poet is a poet through imitation, not through the use of verse. But imitation becomes invention and this in turn becomes plot and character, which are more important than verse because they make a greater appeal to the audience. The whole nature of the transformation of Aristotle's thesis is seen in such a passage as the following: "The poet indeed, as Aristotle himself affirms, insofar as he imitates is a poet of actions, not of meters. Therefore, an excellent invention—and a structure of the plot in which character is diligently observed—holds the audience much more than would verses poor in content and presented on the stage with great solemnity."[119] Moreover, Grifoli sets up a single criterion of Nature for these subject matters, making probability and necessity dependent upon it: "Tragedy cannot support anything which is not appropriate to Nature. And even though it is not the function of the writer of tragedy or of comedy, as Aristotle says, to relate those things which actually happened, nevertheless they must relate them in a way that they might probably or necessarily have come about."[120] Nevertheless, the Nature to be imitated is not a commonplace and visible one; just as Maggi does, Grifoli refers to the Ideas of Plato as the norms which the poet—like the painter—should attempt to represent. Once again, Plato and Aristotle are brought together as providing a single object for the poet's study, the Form or the Idea; and Grifoli also indicates a parallelism between them on the purgation of such passions as pity and fear (pp. 96, 37).

There is, in all this, a kind of total interpretation of the *Poetics*. It becomes a text in which poetry appears as a "natural" object, seeking on the one hand to present the perfection of the highest forms in Nature, the Ideas, and on the other hand to conform to a more commonplace Nature as represented by the traditional practice of the poets and by the laws of decorum. That is, an ideal of beauty is proposed to the poet, but it is accompanied by an ideal of verisimilitude, which prevents any wild flights of the imagination. Everything that he does is reduced to rule and precept.

In 1550, also, Lodovico Dolce published his *Osservationi nella volgar lingua*, of which the first three books are exclusively linguistic and grammatical; the fourth treats of poetry only by way of introducing a lengthy discussion of prosodic questions relevant to the various genres. In the treatment of poetry, one might say that Dolce begins at each step with Aristotle but rapidly moves in the direction of the current rhetorical

[119] *Ibid.*, p. 98: "Poëta enim (vt idem testatur Arist.) quatenus fingit, rerum est poëta, non metrorum. Inuentio igitur insignis, & fabulę constitutio, in qua ratio morum diligens habeatur, magis capit spectatores, quàm versus inopes rerum & magno cum pondere missi in scenam."
[120] *Ibid.*, p. 15: "Atqui Tragoedia ferre nihil potest, quod non sit naturae consentaneum. Et quamuis tragici non sit, vt inquit Aristoteles, nec item comici ea dicere, quę gesta fuerint ea tamen illi dicenda sunt omnino, quae fieri potuisse verisimile sit, aut etiam necessarium."

theory. So for the definition of the art: "That Poetry, a heavenly gift, is nothing else but imitation is taught to us by Aristotle in a single and proper definition; for the function of the poet is to imitate the actions of men; and the end is to delight the soul of the reader under pleasant veils of moral and useful inventions."[121] Here the "slipping" is from imitation to invention and from a notion of imitation as the end to the more readily comprehensible pleasure and utility. So also for the idea that imitation, not verse, makes the poet:

> But let nobody think that all those who write in verse are worthy of this title of Poet. For in addition to the variety of knowledge which this faculty requires, it needs invention, order, artifice, and words; which things—each one by itself and all together—are so difficult and so necessary that they are acquired only with great sweat, and if one of them is lacking, the dignity of the Poet is in large part decreased. But none is more so than imitation, which does more to make him a poet than artifice and words. For it is possible for any mediocre mind to find some noble invention; but to display it with those ornaments and beauties which are proper to the function of the Poet is given to few; and these few are the good Poets.[122]

In this passage, Dolce reduces all his ideas to terms of invention, disposition, and elocution (slightly disguised); and although he seems at first to mean that imitation-invention is the most important ingredient of poetry, he ends up by saying that imitation-elocution is really the crux of poetic excellence. In later passages, he emphasizes increasingly the fact that the real art of the poet lies in his handling of words and of verse; and Dolce is thus justified in devoting his book on poetry to such matters of composition.

In 1550, finally, Jacob Mantino's translation of Averroës' commentary on the *Poetics* was added to the two already available, those of Hermannus Alemanus and of Abram de Balmes. Like the latter, Mantino's was based on the Hebrew translation of Todros Todrosi (1337). Both translations from the Hebrew were to enjoy some circulation during the coming decade, Balmes' being reprinted in 1560 and Mantino's in 1562. The significance of the shift away from Hermannus and toward the new versions lies in the fact that the latter tend to omit most of Averroës' materials based upon Arabic

---

[121] *Osservationi* (1550), p. 87v: "La Poetica, celeste dono, niente altro essere, che imitatione, c'è con propria e una difinitione insegnato da Aristotele: percioche l'ufficio del Poeta è di imitare le attioni de gli huomini: e il fine sotto leggiadri ueli di morali & utili inuentioni dilettar l'animo di chi legge."

[122] *Ibid.*, pp. 87v–88: "Ma non pensi alcuno, che tutti coloro, che uersi scriuono, siano degni di questo titolo di Poeta: percioche oltre la diuersità delle dottrine, che questa faculta ricerca, ella ha mestiero di inuentione, di ordine, d'artificio, e di parole: lequali cose, ciascuna da per se, e tutte insieme, sono tanto difficili e necessarie, che non senza molti sudori s'acquistano: e mancandone l'una, è scemata in gran parte la dignità del Poeta: ma niuna è oltre alla imitatione, che maggiormente lo faccia Poeta di quello che fa l'artificio e le parole. Percioche ad ogni mediocre intelletto è conceduto il poter trouare alcuna nobile inuentione; ma quella spiegar con quegli ornamenti e bellezze, che all'ufficio del Poeta conuengono, è dato a pochi: e questi pochi sono i buoni Poeti."

literature, and the work seems therefore to be closer to its distant Greek original.[123]

CONCLUSIONS

The first half-century—or slightly more—of the history of Aristotle's *Poetics* in modern times is thus a period of tremendous progress in the knowledge and the interpretation of the text. We must constantly bear in mind the fact that as the end of the fifteenth century approached, only a few humanists knew the text at all, having read or consulted the available manuscripts. A somewhat larger group of scholars might have read Averroës' commentary, extant in a number of manuscripts and printed in 1481; but from it they would have obtained a very imperfect idea indeed of the content and orientations of Aristotle's theory. Beginning with Valla's translation into Latin in 1498, a whole series of documents soon became available to the Renaissance reader: the Greek text of 1508, the reprint of Valla and Averroës in 1515, Erasmus' Greek text of 1532, Pazzi's text and translation of 1536 (reprinted 1537 and 1538), and finally Segni's translation into Italian of 1549. With these documents at hand, it was soon possible to undertake the serious study and exegesis of the *Poetics*; especially after the appearance of the Pazzi volume does activity of this kind seem to increase, as witnessed by the public lectures of Lombardi-Maggi beginning in 1541 and by the first two of the great published commentaries, Robortello's in 1548 and Lombardi-Maggi's in 1550.

The first result of this diffusion of texts and commentaries was the increasing number of passing references to the *Poetics* in works of many kinds. It became necessary to consider and cite the dicta of Aristotle on the art of poetry, just as it had long been necessary to reckon with the opinions of Horace, of Plato, and of such rhetoricians as Cicero |and Quintilian. Such consideration of Aristotle was usually brief and fragmentary, tending to limit itself to a few passages which the writers found eminently useful; from it we can derive no general statements about the way in which the *Poetics* was read in this early period. The second result of the diffusion was undoubtedly more significant: Aristotle came to be considered an authority on poetry equal in prestige to Horace. If such "equality" was possible, it was because the cumulative wisdom of the time found in Aristotle's *Poetics* essentially the same theory of the poetic art which it had come to attribute to Horace's *Ars poetica*. Thus, in the period which we have been studying, we discover the growth of a habit and of a procedure, that of establishing parallelism between the two texts. This was done at first for separate passages, in the passing references of which I have spoken; it was

---

[123] For a modern edition of the Mantino translation, see Friedrich Heidenhain, *Jahrbücher für class. Philologie*, Supplementband XVII, 1889, pp. 354–82. See also the discussion by Jaroslav Tkač, "Über den arabischen Kommentar des Averroes zur Poetik des Aristoteles," *Wiener Studien: Zeitschrift für klassische Philologie*, XXIV (1902), 70–98.

later done, and in a constantly more elaborate way, for the totality of the two texts. Naturally, it appears in its most complete form in the successive commentaries on Horace: Parrasio's of 1531, Pedemonte's of 1546, Maggi's and Grifoli's of 1550. In all these, the procedure is to search in Aristotle for clues to the meaning of Horace, whether they be to single lines or passages or whether they be to the general organization of the epistle.

I have studied, in earlier chapters, the effects of this search on the understanding and the elucidation of the *Ars poetica*. As has already been obvious in the present chapter, the partnership with Horace was not without its dangers for Aristotle. For it meant that many readers—specialists in Horace and others—came to the *Poetics* determined to find in it the doctrine which they had long associated with the *Ars poetica*. This they did without difficulty, for there are sufficient similarities of subject matter and enough accidental likeness of detail to facilitate the discovery of "parallels." It should be said, in exculpation of those who yielded too easily to the temptation, that the temptation was very great indeed. The first half of the Cinquecento was deeply concerned with all problems of poetic theory, and the discovery of a new treatise by so revered a writer as Aristotle was bound to elicit much attention. Naturally, the first impulse was to find the known in the unknown, to read Horace into Aristotle. On the other hand, this impulse prevented or delayed for a long time the discovery of what Aristotle was actually doing and saying in the *Poetics*. Even the "great commentaries" on the *Poetics* published during this period (and later as well), directly concerned though they were with the text and its exegesis, show the results of this tendency. They may not specifically seek identity of theory; they may even attempt to read Aristotle for his own sake. But, nevertheless, the old habits of mind and the old accepted ideas are there, and what is produced in the way of theory is much closer to the standard Horatian rhetorical tradition than to any distinctively Aristotelian analysis.

CHAPTER TEN. THE TRADITION OF ARISTOTLE'S *POETICS*: II. THE FIRST THEORETICAL APPLICATIONS

IN THE YEARS following the middle of the century, the tendencies observed in the first half are continued and accelerated. This is generally true in all branches of criticism, for as the documents accumulated, as more new materials became available, as the partisan spirit grew, there was a multiplication of discussions, of pamphlets, of treatises. If one were to prepare a statistical curve of Cinquecento criticism, on a purely quantitative basis, one would note a sharp rise in the years following 1550. The writings relative to Aristotle's *Poetics* would provide no exception. There is no "great commentary" until 1560, when Vettori's appeared. Nevertheless, the editions of and commentaries on Horace, short independent treatises on a variety of poetic matters, and miscellaneous materials become constantly more numerous, and with them the Aristotelian tradition expands and develops.

CONTI AND SPERONI (CA. 1550)

I shall discuss first three documents which are not dated and which I place roughly at the middle of the century for want of better evidence. The first two are by Antonio Maria de' Conti (called Maioragio), who died in 1555. His very brief *De arte poetica* appeared as "Oratio XXIV" in the collected *Orationes et praefationes* of 1582. The oration, as I have pointed out (Chapter VII, p. 267), is primarily devoted to a defence of poetry and a rejection of Plato's ban; but it uses the *Poetics* as a part of this defence and —more important still—derives from it statements about imitation and about the history of poetry. Conti refers to *Poetics* 1447b1 to confirm his defence of poetry: "Aristotle himself intimates that poetry is the same thing as wisdom and philosophy, when he numbers among poems the most learned and most elegant dialogues of Plato, in which are treated the most important matters both divine and human."[1] In a later passage, Conti collapses together a brief early history of poetry. He begins with "imitation" as a "cause" or "origin" (coupling it immediately with meter), proceeds to the division of poetry into species (comic, tragic, epic, melic, and dithyrambic), concludes with the differentiation between poets of high moral character and those of low moral character and between their divergent products.[2] Conti thus chooses some of the ideas from the *Poetics*

---

[1] In *Orationes et praefationes* (1582), p. 145: "quod autem poetica sit eadem quae sapientia seu philosophia, innuit etiam Aristoteles, qui doctissimos & elegantissimos Platonis dialogos, in quibus maximae quaeque res & diuinae, & humanae tractantur, inter poemata connumerat."

[2] *Ibid.*, p. 146v. The full text reads thus: "Aristoteles poesim ex imitatione primo natam fuisse censet, quoniam imitandi studium sit ab ineunte aetate cunctis hominibus innatum, qua in re à belluis homo differat. qui igitur ad metrum natura procliues fuerunt, eos ait poesim primo protulisse, ex quodam imperito rudiḱue principio, atque ex subita ac fortuita

most frequently cited by his predecessors, those which might throw light on the beginnings of the art and its earliest history.

Conti returns to Aristotle and imitation in his *In tres Aristotelis libros, de arte rhetorica explanationes*, published posthumously in 1572. There are a few scattered passages in the commentary on Book III that are of interest for poetic theory. In the first one, Conti argues for the antiquity of poetry and for the fact that it preceded oratory, basing his argument on Aristotle's statement that it is an imitation; this he proceeds to support by citing the *Cratylus* to the effect that words themselves are imitations and that imitation is natural to man. Then, again, the brief history of poetry:

> Whence from the imitation contained in words were born many arts, such as the epic, which expresses in hexametric verse the wars and the deeds of kings, generals, and leaders; and the histrionic art, which includes comedies, tragedies, satires, and mimes, and which represents through the medium of words the characters and the lives of men of every age, class, and condition.[3]

As he had done previously, Conti assimilates Aristotle to Plato; but when he speaks of the literary types he moves in the direction of the medieval definitions and of a theory of literature based above all on decorum. In later passages he states that one of the important differences between oratory and poetry lies in the ornate language of the latter (this is because poetry comes from a divine furor, p. 381A); he repeats his assertion that imitation is the essence of poetry (" & Horatius egregium poetam uocat doctum imitatorem," p. 406A); and he distinguishes those poets who please only on the stage from those who also please when they are read (p. 415B). In all these statements about imitation, Conti shows no understanding of the peculiar meaning given the term in the *Poetics*; he chooses rather a Platonic meaning and one that can be applied to passages separated from the whole of the text.

Sperone Speroni is also concerned with the problem of imitation in his *Discorso dell'arte, della natura, e di Dio*, but in a much broader and more philosophical way. It is difficult to say whether his doctrine is primarily Platonic or Aristotelian, as elements from both seem to be intermingled. Speroni's premiss is that art imitates Nature just as Nature imitates God

---

dictione. sed deinceps ex hac imitandi ratione, quasi in plura membra diuisa poesis multas in species abijt, atque ita poetę dicti sunt alij Comici, alij Tragici, alij Epici, alij Melici, alij Dithyrambici, alij alio nomine. nam pro cuiusque natura & moribus imitandi studium proferebatur. honestiores enim poetae res egregias & praestantes, & laudabiles actiones sibi canendas proponebant. itaque in regum & deorum conuiuijs uirorum excellentium laudes, resque praeclarè gestas heroicis carminibus concinebant, ut ad eas imitandas iuuenes excitarentur, & alacriores redderentur. qui uerò abiectiori essent animo. uiles etiam & humiles actiones canere coeperunt, atque hunc & illum irridere, salibusque inuadere. unde postea comoedia atque Satyra nata est."

[3] *De arte rhetorica* (1572), p. 347A: "quare à uocis imitatione natae sunt artes plurimae, ut epica, quae regum, imperatorum, ducum res gestas & bella carminibus exametris exprimit, & histrionica, quae comoedias, tragoedias, Satyras, mimos amplectitur, & cuiuslibet aetatis, ordinis, conditionis hominum mores & uitas uoce repraesentat."

in operation. He seeks the conditions under which art imitates Nature and finds, first, that art always seeks to resemble Nature as much as possible. But complete resemblance is not possible since the object of art is not the real object.

And this comes about because the subject upon which art operates is an actually true thing; therefore no substantial form can be introduced into it, but everything that is added to it is an accident which resembles the substance as much as it possibly can. . . . Art therefore has for subject the being in action, so to speak, and insofar as it is in action and must remain in action, just as it was before, after the form which the artifex will have impressed upon it.[4]

Consideration of the triple relationship among God, Nature, and art leads Speroni to inquire into their relative nobility and to decide that it follows the order in which they have been named:

Thus since art imitates Nature, but is not Nature herself—for the painting is not a man, but his image and imitation—but imitates her, since it operates in a subject which was made by Nature and in this subject art and Nature are joined, the latter making it, the former presupposing it to be already made; and Nature is more noble than art, since the less noble always seeks to resemble the more noble; the same is to be said about Nature and God.[5]

Speroni is clearly inquiring into a metaphysical and aesthetic problem when he examines imitation, a problem of a far different order than that posed by Conti. The text of the *Poetics*, if it is present at all, is present only in a remote way.

Imitation is once again the subject of discussion in the *Lettione decima*, published by Giovanni Battista Gelli in 1551 in a volume entitled *Tutte le lettioni*. But in Gelli we encounter the same kind of discussion as in Conti. The lecture is devoted to the arts of painting and poetry (it ends with praise for Giotto, Dante, and Petrarch), both of which are arts of imitation. Gelli cites Aristotle (*Poetics* 1448b4) on the reasons why imitation is pleasurable to man, adding to these arguments the notion (from *Rhetoric* III.I) that man imitates by speaking words and by using his voice, "since words are nothing but an imitation of concepts, and since the voice serves for nothing better than for demonstrating the passions of the soul."[6] He

---

[4] *Discorso* (1740 ed.), III, 365: "E ciò avviene, perche il subietto, intorno al quale si adopra l'arte, è cosa vera in effetto; però in essa non può introdursi alcuna forma sustanziale, ma ogni cosa, che vi si aggiunge, è accidente, che alla sostanza, in quanto puote, si rassimiglia. . . . L'arte adunque ha per subietto lo ente in atto, per dir così, ed in quanto egli è in atto, ed in atto de' rimanere, come era prima, dopo la forma, che vi arà impressa l'artefice."

[5] *Ibid.*, p. 366: "Dunque come l'arte imita la natura, ma non è essa natura; perciocchè la dipintura non è uomo, ma sua imagine ed imitazione; ma imita lei, perciocchè ella opera in un subietto, il quale è fatto dalla natura, ed in esso si aggiungono arte e natura, questa facendolo, quella già fatto presupponendolo; e la natura è dell'arte più nobile; perciocchè sempre al più nobile cerca il men nobile di assimigliarsi: così è da dire della natura e di Dio."

[6] *Tutte le lettioni* (1551), p. 358: "Non essendo altro i nomi, che imitation de concetti; ne seruendo la voce a cosa alcuna meglio che a dimostrare gli affetti de l'animo."

POETICS: THEORETICAL APPLICATIONS

then returns to direct translation or paraphrase of Aristotle on the pleasure derived from learning and on the pleasure derived from contemplating representations of essentially unpleasant objects.

Two years later, in 1553, Giason Denores published his *In epistolam Q. Horatij Flacci de arte poetica* (see above, Chapter IV, pp. 128–29). Denores is less interested than were some of his predecessors in the mere listing of parallels between Horace and Aristotle, although there is a small number of cross references in the course of his commentary. Thus, for example, he cites Aristotle on the resemblance of the iamb to common speech (p. 34), on the proper size of animals (p. 69v), on artistic and nonartistic errors (p. 125v). But there are several major questions of poetic theory for which he recurrently appeals to the *Poetics*, and they are the same ones that were troubling his contemporaries. One was the problem of imitation. We see a first reflection of it in his statement that invention is the "soul" of poetry: "de inuentione, hoc est de ipsa quasi anima, & constitutione poematis" (p. 5v). We see it reflected again, in what may seem to be an extraordinary way, in his discussion of figurative language. Denores wonders why metaphors and similes are pleasurable and discovers that it is because they are imitations which teach; Aristotle's whole argument is then brought to bear on the question:

> I should hold then that metaphors produce in all men greater admiration and pleasure than do proper terms for the same reason for which we judge that poetry delights more than history, that is, because poetry imitates. Imitation, moreover, affects and delights all men equally. . . . For, since all receive learning easily, by means of imitation and resemblance, of matters from the knowledge of which they then derive the greatest pleasure, it is certain that metaphors are most pleasurable, not only because they generate knowledge in us via resemblance and imitation, but also because they produce pleasure in us out of that knowledge.[7]

These ideas are not basically different from those expressed by certain writers studied in the last chapter, notably Maggi, Grifoli, and Dolce. The passage just quoted introduces the second of the problems for which Denores consulted Aristotle, that of the relationship between poetry and history. He sees one difference in the distinction between things as they actually happened and things as they might happen ("Non, ut gestae sunt, sed ut geri potuerunt," p. 32), and quotes Aristotle in corroboration. Another distinction is between truth and what may be added to truth—provided that verisimilitude be observed: "For it is not simply that the historian differs from the poet only because one uses verse and the other

---

[7] *In epistolam* (1553), pp. 23–23v: "Ego autem uel ea potissimum ratione existimarem translata maiorem afferre apud omnes admirationem, & uoluptatem, quàm propria, qua etiam magis oblectare poesis historia iudicatur, hoc est, quia imitatur. imitatio autem omnes pariter afficit, atque delectat. . . . Quare cum ex imitatione, & similitudine facile omnes disciplinas percipiant, ex quarum postea cognitione summam capiant iucunditatem: certum est translationes esse gratissimas: tum quia per similitudinem, & imitationem pariunt in nobis cognitionem; tum quia ex cognitione pariunt uoluptatem."

prose, but also in this, that the historian adds nothing to the truth and takes nothing away from it; the poet adds and removes many things, but what he presents is verisimilar."[8] Aristotle is again cited on history and on verisimilitude.

Denores' third problem is that of the end of tragedy and the purgation of pity and fear. It is significant that his problem arises in connection with *Ars poetica* 333, in the gloss on "prodesse." He quotes the definition and then comments:

> For, since the end of tragedy relates to softening and as it were purifying the passions of the soul, because it aims, apparently, at inculcation of the right way of living and [thus] at a practical effect, we must say that it is not only proper for the poet to express things relevant to living, but that this is his main object.... On this subject, when Aristotle says that it is proper to poets to treat above all those matters of a universal kind, so that they will present them not such as events were on a particular occasion but as they should have been, does he not perhaps openly say that this end should be assigned to them—to embrace in their poems the various species and the various functions of daily life? This is nothing other than to express things relevant to living.[9]

The transition is easy, for Denores, from the purgation of pity and fear, to moral usefulness, to the instruction in proper living which constitutes for him the end of poetry. Aristotle is readily reduced to Horace. As for the achievement of this end, the question arises partially in connection with Horace's remarks on off-stage action (ll. 179 ff.). Denores identifies those actions which should not be shown on the stage with those which bring pity and fear to the spectator, which are incredible or miraculous, or which are wicked (p. 64). He summarizes: "Tria igitur sunt tantummodo referenda, non autem agenda in scaena, quae terribilia sunt, & miserabilia; quae fieri non possunt; & quae obscaena sunt" (p. 64v). Rather should pity and terror be produced by the composition of the plot (*Poetics* 1453b1). This consideration leads Denores to conclude that the epic is superior to tragedy as a genre since it requires less in the way of external machinery and appeals to the ear rather than to the eye, and that those tragedies are most perfect which most closely approach the epic form (pp. 65–67).

What is most striking, perhaps, about Denores' use of Aristotle is his wresting of the texts from their original reference and their application to widely different materials. This is evidence not only of a lack of respect

---

[8] *Ibid.*, p. 56v: "Neque enim solum differt à poeta historicus carmine, uel soluta oratione; sed quòd alter ueritati nihil addat, ac nihil detrahat; alter plura addat, ac plura detrahat, uerisimilia tamen."

[9] *Ibid.*, pp. 117–17v: "Quare cum finis tragoediae referatur ad leniendos, & quasi expiandos animorum motus, quod ad recte degendae uitae institutionem, & utilitatem uidetur spectare non solum dicendum est poetis etiam esse proprium idonea uitae afferre, sed hoc maxime.... Ad haec cum Aristoteles in rebus uniuersi generis maxime uersari proprium poetis esse dicat, ut non quales aliqui fuerint, sed quales esse debuerint ab his referantur, nonne aperte indicat munus hoc esse illis assignatum, ut uarias in eorum poematis ciuilis uitae species, & officia complectantur, quod nihil quicquam esse putandum est, quàm idonea uitae dicere."

for the text of the *Poetics*, but of a complete indifference to careful thinking or to proper distinctions. A modicum of similarity—a word—is enough for Denores, not only to establish parallels but to set up elaborate arguments and to reach definite conclusions.

BENEDETTO VARCHI (1553–54)

Benedetto Varchi's *Lezzioni della poetica*, delivered before the Accademia Fiorentina in late 1553 and early 1554 and published in 1590, constitutes a kind of art of poetry. The philosophical derivation of the lectures is complex, but I think it no exaggeration to say that the principal basis of organization is found in the *Poetics*. In a preliminary lecture, Varchi concerns himself first with the classification of the art (see Chapter I, pp. 7–9) and then proceeds to such general matters as the end of poetry. Varchi sees the end of poetry as that shared by all arts and sciences, "to make man perfect and happy" ("fare l'huomo perfetto, e felice," p. 574); but it differs from others in that it uses imitation to achieve this end. We find, therefore, a distinction between "end" and "function": "The end of the poet is thus to make the human soul perfect and happy, and his function is to imitate, that is to invent and represent, things which render men good and virtuous, and consequently happy."[10] The particular objects imitated by the poet are the actions, passions, and moral characters of men (p. 574), and hence the poet must be thoroughly versed in ethics and in politics. Although we begin here with an Aristotelian principle of imitation, it is rapidly reduced from the role of "end" to that of "function"; and since the "end" becomes one of moral improvement, the art is soon identified as a branch of moral and civil philosophy. Nevertheless, it obtains its efficacy from the power of imitation over men's souls (cf. Aristotle), and imitation becomes an essential part of the definition of poetry which Varchi compounds: "Poetics is a faculty which teaches in what ways any action, passion, or character should be imitated; by means of rhythm, discourse, and harmony, all together or separately, in order to remove men from vice and incite them to the virtues, in order that they may achieve their perfection and beatitude."[11] Again the framework of the definition is vaguely Aristotelian; but its content has been so changed as to make of the art of poetry an entirely different one from what Aristotle intended.

Even the meaning of "imitation" becomes fluid, and in his gloss on the above definition Varchi soon gives it another sense. Speaking of art and genius, he declares that genius would not be sufficient for poets "unless

---

[10] *Lezzioni* (1590 ed.), p. 576: "è adunque il fine del Poeta far perfetta, e felice l'anima humana, e l'vffizio suo imitare, cioè fingere, e rappresentare cose che rendono gl' huomini buoni, & virtuosi, e per conseguente felici."

[11] *Ibid.*, p. 578: "La poetica è vna facultà, la quale insegna in quai modi si debbe imitare qualunche azzione, affetto, e costume; con numero, sermone, & armonia, mescolatamente, o di per se, per rimuouere gli huomini da' vizij, & accendergli alle virtù. affine, che conseguano la perfezzione, e beatitudine loro."

they were to make use of imitation, that is, in their own compositions to go about imitating the compositions of good poets, for in that way it would be like using art; indeed, nothing can be done of greater usefulness than to consider the works of the perfect masters."[12] This is imitation in the meaning so frequently given to it in the Renaissance. Nevertheless, its use in this way does not prevent Varchi, almost immediately, from speaking of the kinds of imitation as narrative, dramatic, and mixed (pp. 579-80), of object, manner, and means, and from quoting Aristotle to the effect that imitation, not verse, makes the poet. One sees, in his distinction of the kinds of poets, the same ideas that Maggi had expressed: the poet may be considered "most narrowly" as one who practises both imitation and verse, "properly" as one who uses imitation only, without verse, and "commonly" as one who uses verse only, without imitation. Varchi himself believes that verse is a necessary ingredient of poetry, and he so construes *Poetics* 1448b20 as to make it an argument for his position. In these multifarious ideas on imitation, we note that Varchi, like so many of his contemporaries, had clearly in mind the content of the *Poetics*; but he freely combined it with the content of other texts and other traditions, leading sometimes to patent contradictions.

The ideas presented thus far are contained in the introductory lecture to Varchi's series. In the *Lezzione prima*, of December, 1553, he returns again to the discussion of imitation, this time taking as a point of departure *Poetics* 1448a1 (on the objects of imitation) in order to develop his theory that the poet imitates three objects: actions, passions, characters (pp. 602-3). The *Lezzione seconda*, devoted specifically to epic poetry, raises the question of the relationship between imitation and object, and the answer is found in the demand for the necessary, the possible, or the probable. Here again the utilitarian end directs the poets in their choices:

They are not to write of human actions in the way in which they were done, but in that way in which it was either possible, or verisimilar, or necessary that they might be done. . . . Poets must not consider in the main how things are done by men, but how they should be done, although many things are permitted to them even outside nature; and even outside the reasonable or the verisimilar, so that they may bring not only greater utility for this mortal life but also greater delight and admiration to men.[13]

These general considerations lead to judgments on Homer and Vergil—

[12] *Ibid.*, p. 579: "se già non si seruissero dell'imitazione, cioè andassero ne' componimenti loro imitando i componimenti de' poeti buoni, perche in tal caso è come si seruissero dell'arte, anzi non si può far cosa di maggiore vtilità, che andar considerando l'opere de' maestri perfetti."

[13] *Ibid.*, pp. 616-17: "non hanno à scriuere l'azzioni humane in quel modo, che fatte furono, ma in quel modo, nel quale era o possibile, o verisimile, o necessario, che si facessero. . . . i poeti non deono considerare per lo piu come le cose si fanno da gli huomini, ma come fare si douerebbono, ancora che si conceda loro molte cose, eziandio fuori della natura, non che del ragioneuole; o uerisimile, acciochè possano arrecarne non solo piu vtilità alla vita mortale, ma ancora maggior diletto, e ammirazione a gli huomini."

judgments in which the theoretical positions are almost entirely absent. Homer is great because of his extensive knowledge and because of the good characters and customs he presents; Vergil is great because of his erudition, his eloquence, his gravity (pp. 617–20). The *Lezzione quarta*, on tragedy, quotes Aristotle's definition *in extenso* (reflecting still the imperfect state of text and translations in the transition to the last clause, "non per modo di narrazione, ma mediante la misericordia, e il terrore," p. 657). His commentary on the definition is of interest in many ways. He interprets "graue" as referring to great and illustrious persons—"Kings, Generals, and other such persons" (p. 658)—whose actions are grave, high, worthy, and of great moment, and as distinguishing tragedy from the low persons and ordinary actions of comedy. He gives to "perfetta" the function of distinguishing good tragedies from the earlier imperfect ones and from the action of the epic, which because of its many episodes is less perfect. To "purgazione," of course, he gives the meaning already noted; it indicates the end of tragedy, that of "leading men, through virtue, to their perfection and beatitude" (p. 660); but he takes the clause as referring not only to pity and fear but to all the passions. The commonplace lessons to be learned from tragedy are then retailed. The rest of the lecture treats the qualitative parts in the order listed by Aristotle. With respect to character, he does not fail to add to what he says by way of commentary a complete treatment of the various types and the characteristics which need to be attributed to them according to the laws of decorum.

It is thus apparent that, while Varchi organizes his set of lectures around the *Poetics* and follows its order in many of the detailed developments, he is constantly led away from the position of the *Poetics* by his knowledge of other texts. More frequently than not, he ends up with a theory whose real support would be found in Horace, not in Aristotle. It is for this reason that his lectures are significant. Unlike the official commentaries on Horace or on Aristotle, he is not seeking parallel passages, he is not looking for corroboration of one text by the other. Rather, he is attempting an original treatment whose basic source is Aristotle. But the weight of the established tradition is too heavy, and at every juncture it causes him to veer away in the direction of accepted positions.

Two letters to Varchi from Pietro Angeli, of November and December 1553, return to the question of imitation and challenge particularly Varchi's belief that the dialogue, as a form of imitation, was to be considered a genre of poetry.[14] Angeli believes that to hold this view is to interpret badly the passage in the *Poetics*. Rather, he says, the ends are so different as to separate the dialogue completely from poetic forms. He declares that Pietro Vettori is also of his opinion and that Vettori's interpretation of the *Poetics* will confirm their agreement.[15]

[14] Cf. Varchi, *Della Poetica* (1553), printed in the *Lezzioni* (1590 ed.), pp. 580–82[=81].
[15] In *Prose Fiorentine*, I, 66–68, 68–70.

Like Varchi's *Lezzioni*, Alessandro Lionardi's *Dialogi della inventione poetica* (1554) are an attempt at an original formulation of certain theories with respect to the art of poetry. But whereas Varchi begins with Aristotle, Lionardi begins with Horace and the rhetorical tradition. I have indicated in Chapter IV the kind of theory which he develops. His use of Aristotle is incidental and in most cases reflects the thinking of his contemporaries; it revolves largely about the question of imitation and verisimilitude. As for others, imitation for Lionardi is identified with the "invention" of the rhetorical scheme: "[The poet] is not a poet because of verse, but because of the plot, that is, because of the quality of the invention and imitation."[16] But the meaning of imitation is not clear, especially in such a sentence as this: "It is true that the most perfect poem is the one which is made up of fiction, of imitation, and of verse."[17] Nor is the meaning helped by this statement: ". . . all this [the poet's varied knowledge] belongs to the imitation, feigning, and description of persons, operations, and accidents."[18] The text of Aristotle is more accurately represented in the assertion that "the plot may stand without the characters, since it carries with it the actions,"[19] but this too is obscured by the discovery that "favola" means not only plot but also "fables" or even "falsehoods." This becomes apparent when, after distinguishing three kinds of "favole," Lionardo defines the second kind which is proper to poetry:

That "favola" which is called poetic imitation is a shadow and image of the truth, that is a narration and exposition of verisimilar things. And the tragic or heroic poem is made up of truth and of verisimilitude together. . . . And thus it comes about that the poet relates the causes of events sometimes by means of history, sometimes by means of fable. . . . just as it is vicious for the historian to tell fables or false things, so it is also improper for the poet to depart from imitation and from the use of fable.[20]

Yet, at a later point Lionardi does not hesitate to require of the poet—especially the tragic poet—the use of true materials:

[Tragedy] follows verisimilitude in all things . . . , tries to imitate some other past action described by somebody else. But that imitation will be best which is founded on the truth, and which will be decorated and enriched with many veri-

---

[16] *Dialogi* (1554), p. 14: "non è poeta per li uersi, ma per la fauola, cioè per la qualità dell'inuentione & imitatione." See also p. 30: "essendo lo scriuere poeticamente null'altro, che imitare le attioni de gli huomini, se il Poeta non si servisse ancora di questa guisa di parlare, sarebbe imperfetta la inuentione, ò imitatione."

[17] *Ibid.*, p. 15: "È il uero che piu perfetto poema è quello, che si fa di fintione, d'imitatione, & di uerso."

[18] *Ibid.*, p. 23: "tutto ciò appartiene all'imitatione, fintione, & descrittione delle persone, dell'operationi & accidenti."

[19] *Ibid.*, p. 58: "la fauola puo stare senza i costumi, apportando seco l'attioni."

[20] *Ibid.*, p. 63: "Ombra & imagine di uero poi è quella fauola che è chiamata poetica imitatione, cioè narratione & ispositione di cose uerisimili. Et il poema Tragico & Eroico fassi di uero & di uerisimile insieme. . . . E perciò auiene che il poeta racconta le cause de gli auenimenti, hora per istoria, hora per fauola. . . . come è uitioso all'istorico il narrar fauole ò cose false, cosi ancora al poeta si disconuiene il partirsi dalla imitatione et dalla fauola."

POETICS: THEORETICAL APPLICATIONS

similar things. . . . And just as art succeeds best when it is aided by nature, so the verisimilar is worth much more every time that it has for its assistance and basis the truth.[21]

Aristotle's preference for the impossible probable to the improbable possible is to be taken seriously as a guide to poetic composition (p. 67).

The sequence of ideas associated with imitation and verisimilitude, confused as it may sound, does have a certain consistency. Imitation is invention; as such, it is the invention of what is not true, of fables, and this is the proper domain of the poet. However, the poet will err if he "invents" too freely. The closer he stays to the truth—especially in such serious genres as tragedy and the epic—the better his work will be; and where the truth cannot be strictly observed (historical and actual truth), the verisimilar or the probable should take its place. Such a theory, of course, has only surface similarities with the doctrine of the *Poetics*, and although the latter is frequently cited, its sense is just as frequently distorted and obscured.

GIRALDI AND PIGNA (1554)

A whole group of important documents belonging to the year 1554 is concerned with the controversy between Giovambattista Giraldi Cintio and Giovanni Battista Pigna over the romance form. Pigna's treatise, *I romanzi*, was published first; but Giraldi Cintio answered by publishing his own, in which he declared that Pigna, who had been his pupil, had seen Giraldi's treatise many years before and had plagiarized its ideas. In fact, Giraldi dates his treatise, *Discorso intorno al comporre dei romanzi*, "MDXLIX adi XXIX di Aprile" and the accompanying *Discorso intorno al comporre delle Comedie, et delle tragedie* "In Ferrara a di XX. di Aprile. MDXLIII." (A companion treatise, *Lettera ovvero discorso sopra il comporre le satire atte alle scene* is also dated 1554, although it was not published until the nineteenth century.) There followed letters and denials, accusations and counteraccusations.[22] Without prejudice to either side of the case, I shall treat Giraldi's discourses first because of the earlier dates which they bear—even though these may be falsified dates.

Giraldi's discourses belong to the history of Aristotle's *Poetics* in a rather curious way. Basically, they are modeled upon the *Poetics*, taking their essential points of departure in it; one of them, the discourse on tragedy (dated 1543), even claims to be the first exposition of Aristotle's text. Yet

---

[21] *Ibid.*, p. 64: "segue in tutto il uerisimile . . ., si sforza di imitare qualche altra d'altrui descritta & passata attione. Ma miglior fia quella imitatione, che sara fondata sopra il uero, & che fia ornata, & arricchita di molti uerisimili. . . . Et come l'arte riesce meglio quando ella è aiutata insieme dalla natura, così il uerisimile assai piu uale qualunque uolta ha per suo aiuto & fondamento il uero."

[22] A group of letters relevant to the controversy is to be found in a sixteen-page brochure, without date, title page, or other identifying information (British Museum, 11826.d.42). The third letter, by Giraldi, is dated 1554 and gives the reasons for publishing the others. The pamphlet was apparently prepared by Giraldi to substantiate his case against Pigna. See below, chap. xix, p. 957, on the dates of the first two letters.

[433]

the theory that Giraldi develops with respect to the romance finds itself at every point in overt opposition to Aristotle, and he presents it in three sections devoted respectively to invention, disposition, and elocution. Moreover, the conclusions which he reaches on such matters as the end of poetry are constantly those of the Horatian tradition. Perhaps the fundamental reason for a difference of theory between the *Poetics* and the *Discorso intorno al comporre dei romanzi* is Giraldi's contention that there are two kinds of poems, those in which there is a single unified action (the kind treated by Aristotle) and those in which there is a multiple action unaffected by requirements of unity (as exemplified by the romance). This conception leads to a rephrasing of the definition of plot—and incidentally of poetry—so as to account for the two types: "The plot should be based on one or several illustrious actions, which he [the poet] imitates appropriately by means of pleasant discourse in order to teach men honest living and good character, for this is the end that every good poet must seek";[23] and "since Heroic Poetry is nothing else than the imitation of illustrious actions, the subject of such compositions will be one or more illustrious actions of one or more famous and excellent men, which the poet will imitate by means of words accompanied by rhythm and by sweet language."[24]

The opposition to Aristotle inherent in these definitions is explicitly stated later in the text: "The laws given by Aristotle apply only to the forms of poetry which are of one single action; and . . . all poetic compositions which contain deeds of heroes are not included within the limits that Aristotle has set for poets who write poems having a single action."[25] Giraldi clearly means to separate the romance from the epic. Once he has done so, the way is clear for the establishment of a whole new set of requirements and conditions, and these are such as would not be admissible for the epic. The first is multiplicity of action: the poet may relate many actions of one hero—indeed, all those included in a long lifetime—without making the poem too long for the audience's pleasure (see p. 21). Rather, the multiplication of actions and ornaments will increase the variety of the poem and hence the delight of the audience: "This diversity of actions brings with it variety, which is the condiment of pleasure, and gives a wide field to the writer to add episodes, that is, enjoyable digressions, and to

[23] *Discorso intorno al comporre dei romanzi* (1554), pp. 8–9: "la quale fauola uuole essere fondata soura una o piu attioni illustri, lequali egli imiti conueneuolmente con parlare soaue per insegnare a gli huomini l'honesta uita, et i buoni costumi, che questo si dee preporre per fine qualunque buono Poeta."

[24] *Ibid.*, pp. 10–11: "perche la Poesia Heroica non è altro che imitatione delle attioni illustri, sarà il soggetto di tali componimenti una, o piu attioni illustri, di uno o di piu huomini chiari, & eccellenti, che con le uoci, accompagnate col numero, & con la dolcezza imiterà il Poeta."

[25] *Ibid.*, p. 22: "le leggi date da Aristotile non si stendono, senon alle Poesie, che sono di una sola attione; & . . . tutte le compositioni Poetiche, che contengono fatti di Heroi, non sono chiuse tra i termini, c'ha messo Aristotile a Poeti, che scriuono Poema di una sola attione."

introduce therein events which can never happen (without some suspicion of blame) in poems which are made up of a single action."[26] Another way of obtaining multiplicity of action is by recounting many deeds of many heroes.

As a second general new requirement, the poet will add to the action or actions a large number of ornaments or "fillers" ("riempimenti"). Giraldi gives several lists of such ornaments: on page 26:

> ... amori, odij, pianti, risa, giuochi, cose graui, discordie, paci, bruttezze, bellezze, descrittioni di luochi, di tempi, di persone, fauole finte da se, & tolte da gliantichi, nauigationi, errori, mostri; improuisi auenimenti, morti, essequie, lamentationi, recognitioni, cose terribili & compassioneuoli, nozze, nascimenti, uittorie, triomphi, singolari battaglie, giostre, torneamenti, cataloghi, ordinanze, & altre simili cose.

On page 43: "amori, auenimenti improuisi, cortesie, giustitie, torti, liberalità, uitij, uirtù, offensioni, difese, inganni, insidie, fede, lealtà, fortezze, dapocaggini, speranze, timori, utili, danni"—and the passage continues: "and other such episodes or digressions which are most numerous and which can introduce, along with the linking together and the disposition of the work, so much variety and so much pleasure that the poem will become most lovely and most delightful."[27]

A third general requirement is that the poet interrupt the flow of the action as a means of obtaining suspense and of removing satiety ("leuare la satietà," p. 42) from the reader. Whereas the epic poet may tell his story in a continuous fashion, the writer of romances should break up the narrative as much as possible. The many digressions and disturbances of the natural order will be means to this end.

Any Aristotelian conception of "unity of action" has thus been completely rejected. But Giraldi realizes that some way must be discovered for holding the poem together, and he proposes two devices: verisimilitude and decorum. There is also a general principle of order or disposition, stated in the rhetorical terms of proposition, invocation, and narration. By verisimilitude Giraldi means credibility, by disposition he means a believable order of events; the two are closely linked in such a statement as the following:

> And because poetry is all imitation, and alone imitation and verse make the poet, and because this imitation as far as the subject of the poem is concerned relates to the actions, the poet must be extremely careful that the actions which he takes for subject and foundation of the structure of his work carry with them,

---

[26] *Ibid.*, p. 25: "Però che porta questa diuersità delle attioni con esso lei la uarietà, laquale è il condimento del diletto, & si da largo campo allo Scrittore di fare Episodij, cio è digressioni grate, & introdurui auenimenti, che non possono mai auenire (senon con qualche sospetto di biasimo) nelle Poesie, che sono di una sola attione."

[27] *Ibid.*, p. 43: "& altri tali Episodij, o digressioni, iquali sono piu che molti, & possono indurre insieme con la legatura, & con la dispositione dell'opera tanta uarietà, & tanto diletto, che diuerrà il Poema uaghissimo, & piaceuolissimo."

both in the disposition and in the other parts, so much verisimilitude that it will not be incredible, and that one part of the work will depend from another in such wise that one will come after the other either necessarily or probably.[28]

The same principles of disposition and verisimilitude apply to the digressions as well as to the main subject of the poem:

> And in these digressions the poet must be very watchful to treat them in such a way that one will depend from the other, and that they will be well joined with the parts of the subject which he has undertaken to relate with a continuous thread and a continuous chain, and that they will bear verisimilitude with them (insofar as this is possible in poetic fictions). For if these digressions were made in any other way, the poem would become faulty and displeasing, whereas it delights and pleases when they are seen to come about in a way that they appear to be born along with the subject itself.[29]

There are, of course, no specific recommendations for the achievement of this order, this linking, this over-all disposition. The principle is no more precise than the Horatian dogma which it obviously reflects in such a statement as this: "... giving with these [digressions] to all the parts the proper size and the appropriate ornament, with such proportion that out of it all will come a regulated and well-composed body."[30]

As for the principle of verisimilitude, it will also be related to that of decorum. Just as proper order leads to a kind of credibility, so a proper handling of characters and situations produces another kind of credibility. The problem is complicated, however, by the fact that the poet must relate what is untrue and incredible in order to please his audience; the marvelous is an essential ingredient of his work. Giraldi resolves the difficulty in several ways: first, by a distinction between major subject and digressions —the major subject must be true, the digressions may be false (pp. 50–51); second, by admitting that certain false stories and episodes have come to be accepted as verisimilar through their exploitation by earlier poets (p. 55). Verisimilitude is thus essentially a matter of action or plot; decorum may also be a matter of plot, although primarily it concerns character and thought. Giraldi's description is very broad: "In these things as in the

---

[28] Ibid., p. 54: "Et perche la Poesia è tutta imitatione, & solo la imitatione, & il uerso fa il Poeta, & perche essa imitatione quanto al soggetto del Poema, è intorno alle attioni, deue hauere grandissimo riguardo il Poeta, che le attioni, ch'egli si piglia per soggetto, & per fondamento della fabrica della opera sua, portino con esso loro, & nella dispositione, & nelle altre parti tanto del uerisimile, che non rimanga priua di fede, & che una parte cosi dall'altra dipenda, che o necessariamente, o uerisimilmente l'una uenga dietro l'altra."

[29] Ibid., p. 25: "Et deue in queste digressioni esser molto aueduto il Poeta in trattarle di modo, che una dipenda dall'altra, & siano bene aggiunte con le parti della materia, che si ha preso a dire con continuo filo & con continua catena, & che portino con esso loro il uerisimile (quanto s'appertiene alle fittioni, Poetiche . . .). Perche, se queste digressioni si facessero altrimenti, diuerrebbe il Poema uitioso & increscieuole, come diletta, & piace quando elle si ueggono nascere tali, che paiano nate con la cosa istessa."

[30] Ibid., p. 26: "dando con esse a tutte le parti la debita misura, & il diceuole ornamento, con tale proportione, che se ne ueda riuscire un regolato, & ben composto corpo."

others, the poet must always keep an eye on decorum, which is nothing else but what is proper to places, times, and persons. . . . decorum is merely the grace and the appropriateness of things, and it must be considered not so much with respect to actions as to the speeches and the responses that men make to one another."[31] As such, decorum once again approaches the general Horatian principle of appropriateness. Insofar as it relates to the depiction of character, decorum has a peculiarly normative function. It shows people not as they are, but as they should be; and it provides object lessons by displaying the necessary accompaniments, fair or foul, of virtue and vice:

The poet, imitating illustrious actions in his fictions and visualizing them not as they are but as they should be, and accompanying appropriately the things which vice carries with it with honor and pity (for this belongs no less to the heroic poet than to the tragic poet, when the matter justifies it), purges our souls of similar passions and arouses us to virtue, as we see in the definition that Aristotle gives of tragedy. And thus it is that, in addition to verisimilitude, what is praiseworthy and what is honest must be considered everywhere in the work.[32]

In this passage, two Aristotelian ideas take on new forms. The notion that the poet, unlike the historian, relates such events as *could* happen (*Poetics* 1451b5) is transformed here into an ethical requirement that the poet present what *should* be. And the effect of purgation indicated in the last clause of the definition of tragedy becomes a statement of an ethical end— to make us better by demonstrating the results of vice.

The principle of appropriateness involved in decorum raises the question —a constant one in all theories of decorum—as to the criterion by which appropriateness is judged. Usually, the expectations or the demands of a given audience are involved. Here, Giraldi does not hesitate: the audience is a contemporary one, and Italian. The poet follows the customs and manners of his own time, not those of his model or even those of the period which he is depicting; Vergil's practice may serve as an example here (p. 58). If this is the general rule for poets, it is because they wish to satisfy a contemporary audience, "in order to profit and delight at the same time, satisfying the men of that age in which they are writing."[33] As a matter of

[31] *Ibid.*, p. 63: "Et in queste cose, come nell'altre, il Poeta dee sempre hauere l'occhio al decoro; ilquale non è altro, che quello, che conuiene a i luochi, a i tempi, alle persone. . . . il decoro non [è] altro, che la gratia & il conueneuole delle cose; & si dee egli considerare, non pur quanto alle attioni, ma quanto al parlare, & al rispondere, che fanno gli huomini tra loro."

[32] *Ibid.*, p. 59: "imitando il Poeta, col suo fingere, le attioni illustri, & proponendolesi non quali sono, ma quali esser si debbono, & accompagnando conueneuolemente le cose, che portano con esso loro il uitio, con l'horribile & col miserabile (che ciò non è meno del Poeta Heroica, che sia del Tragico quando la materia il richiede) purga gli animi nostri da simili passioni, & ci desta alla uirtù, come si uede nella difinitione, che da Aristotile della Tragedia. Et di qui è, che oltre il uerisimile è da considerare in tutta l'opera il lodeuole, & l'honesto."

[33] *Ibid.*, p. 58: "per giouare, & dilettare insieme, sodisfacendo a gli huomini di quella età, nella quale scriuono."

POETIC THEORY

fact, the whole difference between Aristotle and the theory of the romance may be stated as a difference of time: Aristotle's *Poetics* is based on the practice of the poets of his time and of earlier centuries; Giraldi's is similarly derived. The rules for the romance

> ... should be left within those limits established by those poets who have, among us, given authority and reputation to that kind of poetry. And just as the Greeks and the Latins have derived the art of which they have written from their poets, so also we must derive it from our own, and follow that form which the best writers of romances have given us.[34]

The poet who writes a romance is thus independent of the rules of Aristotle and of Horace and needs to consider only the practices of his predecessors in the same genre—all of whom are relatively recent. The audience will thus prefer a form which is close to it, within which it will recognize its own mores. Moreover, that form will achieve its ends with special efficacy if it uses as one of its means the religion of its contemporary audience. Giraldi praises Boiardo and Ariosto for having added the embellishment of Christianity,

> ... which arouses a marvelous attention, and causes the reader to be joyous over the fortunate adventures of those who are of the same faith as he is, and to be sorrowful when the contrary happens, and to be always in a state of suspense, waiting for his God to provide relief from the difficulties and the harms which they suffer at the hands of the unfaithful. This is a thing which is also well adapted to the terrible and the pitiful, which two things are not the least in importance in compositions of this kind.[35]

It is difficult to reconcile, with such statements as these, another affirmation of Giraldi: the subject of a poem "must be pleasing in every age, not only to the learned but to all men of that language in which he writes."[36]

In most of the passages previously cited, there are indications of the ends which Giraldi proposes for the poet. These are Horace's ends of utility and pleasure, assimilated to Aristotle's text by the same method that we have seen elsewhere in Giraldi. There is a kind of division of labor among the parts of the poem for the service of these ends; Giraldi states it overtly in his discussion of elocution: "just as utility belongs to the sententiae and to

---

[34] *Ibid.*, p. 45: "ma si deuono lasciare tra que termini, tra quali gli hanno posti, chi ha data tra noi auttorità, & riputatione a queste specie di Poesia. & come i Greci et i Latini hanno tratta l'arte, dellaquale hanno scritto, da i loro Poeti, cosi la debbiamo anco noi trarre da i nostri, & attenersi a quella forma che i migliori Poeti de i Romanzi ci hanno data."

[35] *Ibid.*, p. 11: "laqual cosa desta marauigliosa attentione, & fa che si allegri il lettore de i felici auenimenti di coloro, che sono della medesima fede, della quale egli è: & si dolga de i contrarij, & stia tuttauia con l'animo sospeso in aspettando che dal suo Iddio uenga prouisione alle inconuenienze, & a i danni, che patiscono da gli infedeli. Cosa ch'è anco molto atta al terribile & al compassioneuole, lequali due cose non tengono le ultime parti in simili compositioni."

[36] *Ibid.*, p. 15: "si che possa piacere in ogni tempo, non pure a i dotti, ma a tutti gli huomini di quella fauella, nella quale egli scriue."

[438]

the things which are treated, so the words—in addition to the expression of the idea—entirely serve pleasure and delightfulness."[37] In terms of Aristotle's qualitative parts, utility would come from plot, character, and thought, and pleasure from diction; in terms of the rhetorical division of invention, disposition, and elocution (around which he organizes his own treatise), utility would derive essentially from the first two, pleasure from the third. The latter division really involves also the "res-verba" distinction. Following the total line of relationships, we see that the utilitarian end of moral improvement is achieved by the arousing of pity and fear (even in the romance), which depends for its effectiveness on verisimilitude of subject, upon proper disposition of the parts, and upon a general credibility springing from the audience's sense of contemporaneity, of decorum, and of common interest with the heroes of the poem. Pleasure, on the other hand, depends upon the total composition of the work, upon the marvelous introduced by means of digressions, upon variety resulting from innumerable ornaments, and above all upon diction. (Giraldi regards elocution as the "soul" of the poem; see pp. 160–61.) On the whole, the treatise presents the physiognomy of a work which begins with certain Aristotelian conceptions of the tragedy and the epic, which it treats in the mould of the habitual rhetorical distinctions, and from which it derives conclusions which are primarily Horatian.

At the beginning of his *Discorso intorno al comporre delle comedie, e delle tragedie*, also published in 1554, Giraldi Cintio declares that this is the first vernacular treatise on comedy and tragedy and that thus far "nobody has set his hand to the exposition of Aristotle's *Poetics*."[38] If the date which he gives at the end, "In Ferrara a di XX. di Aprile. MDXLIII," is authentic, his claims are justified, at least insofar as published treatises are concerned. In any case, the treatise follows very closely the order of the *Poetics* and in many places is little more than a translation. The commentary, however, as we should now expect, at every point finds in Aristotle Giraldi's own theory of poetry, which becomes clear as the exposition develops. It consists of little more than an application of the principles already discovered for the romance to the genres of tragedy and comedy. Giraldi's remarks may be divided into two categories, those which concern the common characteristics of the two dramatic genres and those which concern their differences. Of the common characteristics, the most salient is the end pursued; it is in all cases to teach good behavior; "both of them intend to introduce good manners" ("amendue intendono ad introdurre buoni costumi," p. 207). The means to the achievement of this end are two, the imitation of an action and language accompanied by verse; both of these contribute to the moving of the audience's passions, and from this

---

[37] *Ibid.*, p. 99: "come il giouare è delle sentenze, et delle cose, che si trattano; cosi le uoci oltre l'espressione del concetto sono tutte del piacere et della uaghezza."

[38] *Discorso intorno al comporre delle comedie, et delle tragedie* (1554), p. 202: "ne alcuno habbia ancora messo mano ad isporre la Poetica di Aristotile."

movement comes the desired moral effect, "since the power of moving the tragic passions rests only upon imitation, which is not separated from verisimilitude, and since things in themselves cannot move the passions without words which are properly put together and in verse."[39] Apparently the moral lesson results from the sympathy which the audience feels for the actors, from its sense of justice and humanity. But it also results from a reasoning process by which the spectator puts himself in the place, let us say, of Oedipus the King: "The spectator, in an unexpressed deduction, says to himself: 'If this man, because of a fault committed unwittingly, has suffered as much harm as I now see, what would happen to me if I were perchance to commit this sin voluntarily?' and this thought makes him abstain from mistakes."[40]

Imitation is thus equivalent to verisimilitude, and this in turn is necessary for the participation of the audience in the action. The poet presents actions as they should be, as they appropriately come about, as they are in their most general and universal aspects (p. 226). But—as in the case of the romance—verisimilitude is local and contemporaneous: "In selecting or forming for himself these illustrious actions, ... it is good to have them such as the times in which the poet is writing desire them according to verisimilitude, with respect to the reasonings, the mores, the decorum, and the other circumstances relative to persons."[41] The difference between verisimilitude and necessity is indicated by an example: a courageous man will *necessarily* seek to avenge an insult, and it is *verisimilar* (or *probable*) that he will do so in an open, rather than in an underhanded, fashion (p. 245). The ultimate appeal in matters of verisimilitude is to what would happen in everyday life:

Be sure that the persons introduced on the stage do not do or say in public things that they would not verisimilarly do or say at home; and be certain that what would be blameworthy if done at home, according to honest rules of action, is also blameworthy on the stage. ... things must be composed and represented as they would be done according to verisimilitude.[42]

Giraldi, of course, thinks of verisimilitude and decorum in terms of an

[39] *Ibid.*, p. 209: "non stando la forza del mouere gli affetti Tragici, senon su la imitatione, che non si parta dal uerisimile, & non mouendo le cose da se gli affetti senza le uoci acconciamente, & numerosamente insieme giunte."

[40] *Ibid.*, pp. 217–18: "lo spettatore con tacita consequenza seco dice, se questi per errore commesso non uolontariamente, tanto male ha sofferto, quanto uedo io hora, che fia di me, se forse uolontariamente commettessi questo peccato? & questo pensiero il fa astenere da gli errori."

[41] *Ibid.*, p. 218: "nello eleggersi, o formarsi queste attioni illustri, cosi dette, non perche siano lodeuoli, o uirtuose, ma perche uengono da grandissimi personaggi, non è senon bene hauerle tali, quali le ricercano uerisimilmente i tempi, ne iquali scriue il Poeta, quanto a i ragionamenti, a i costumi, al decoro, & alle altre circonstanze della persona."

[42] *Ibid.*, p. 284: "auertiate, che le persone introdutte nella Scena, non facciano, o dicano quello nel publico, che uerisimilemente non farebbono, o non direbbono in casa; & che teniate certo, che quello che in honesta attione sarebbe uituperoso a fare in casa, sia anco uituperoso nella Scena. ... cosi si debbono, & comporre, & rappresentare, come uerisimilmente si farebbono."

audience; he excludes obscene and plebeian matters, which please only "sausage-makers and similar kinds of people" (p. 219), and insists that the poet must try to please only "the good judges" (p. 285). But please the audience he must, since this is one of the fundamental requisites for all poetry; without pleasure, the participation of the audience in the action and the consequent moral instruction are both impossible. When he deems it necessary, Giraldi goes counter to Aristotle in recommending devices that will be more pleasurable to the audience. Thus he does not hesitate to suggest a diluted form of tragedy with a happy ending, designed for presentation to his audience (pp. 221–22).

The other precepts relevant to common characteristics are largely close reflections of the Aristotelian text. Plot in both tragedy and comedy must be complete ("perfetta") and of a proper magnitude ("debita grandezza"); but proper size is quickly translated into length of performance (despite Aristotle's warning), with minima of three hours for comedy and four for tragedy—lest the audience be disappointed (pp. 203–4). Verse is required for both forms, and Giraldi seems to be conscious of no discrepancy between this requirement and Aristotle's theory (p. 205). Both imitate an action and limit the time of that action to a single day (pp. 205–6). In both dramatic genres, the plot is the end toward which the other parts contribute (p. 207); and such parts of the plot as knot and solution must be carefully contrived, without recourse to such artificial means as the "deus ex machina" (pp. 211–13). For both—and here the departure from Aristotle is radical—a double plot is preferable to a single one; the "good" and "bad" characters and their rewards and punishments will provide additional enjoyment to the audience.

It is in the treatment of the difference between the two genres that the force of the antecedent tradition makes itself most clearly felt. Joined to this is the concern for the pleasure of the contemporary audience. We have already seen that Giraldi ascribes to tragedy and comedy the common end of moral instruction. He derives from Aristotle, as well as he can, the different emotional effects by means of which they proceed; tragedy works through terror and pity, comedy through pleasure and merry jokes (p. 208). These are produced by different kinds of action: tragedy presents death and horrible events, comedy the activities of everyday life. The kinds of actions themselves have moral implications:

Tragedy through horror and compassion, showing what we should avoid in life, purges us of the disturbances in which the tragic characters have become involved. But comedy, by setting before us what we should imitate, through passions, through temperate feelings mixed with play, with laughter, with derisive jests, calls us to a proper way of living.[43]

[43] *Ibid.*, p. 219: "la Tragedia coll'horrore, & colla compassione, mostrando quello che debbiam fuggire, ci purga dalle perturbationi, nelle quali sono incorse le persone Tragiche. Ma la Comedia col proporci quello, che si dee imitare con passioni, con affetti temperati mescolati con giuochi, con risa, & con scherneuoli motti, ne chiama al buon modo di uiuere."

But if in Aristotle tragedy and comedy involved particular kinds of plot structure, in Giraldi the differences between those kinds tend to be diminished. Thus the happy ending is recommended for both forms, and Giraldi proudly declares that he has used no other type in his own tragedies. He admits that this goes against Aristotle and that it favors the audience; he has used the happy ending

> ... exclusively to serve the needs of the spectators, and to make them [the tragedies] more pleasing on the stage, and to conform better to the usage of our times. For even if Aristotle says that this is a way of catering to the ignorance of spectators, since the other side nevertheless has its partisans I have thought it better to satisfy him who must listen, at the risk of lesser excellence (supposing that Aristotle's opinion be accepted as the better), than with a little more grandeur to displease those for whose pleasure the plot is put on the stage. For it would be of little use to compose a slightly more praiseworthy plot if it were to be distasteful when acted on the stage. Those terrible plots (if perhaps the minds of people in the theater abhor them) may be used in written works; and those with a happy ending in works to be acted on the stage.[44]

Principle—as he understands it—gives way to expediency.

Just as rapidly and as wittingly, the distinction between "better" and "worse" moral characters is made into a distinction between higher and lower classes; that is, a similar transformation takes place with respect to plot and to character. The personages of tragedy, fitted to an "illustrious and royal" action, are kings, heroes, nobles; those of comedy, participating in a "plebeian and civil" action, are men and women of the people; "and therefore Aristotle said that comedy imitated worse actions; not that he meant that it imitated the wicked and the guilty, but the less illustrious, who are worse insofar as nobility is concerned if they are compared with royal persons."[45] The personages of comedy are even less dignified than the average citizenry; they are "servants, parasites, prostitutes, cooks, pimps, soldiers, and finally almost every kind of plebeian folk who are to be found in the city"[46]—all those who had long figured in the traditional lists.

If these differences are to be found among the objects imitated, there will be corresponding differences among the means of imitation. Tragedy may still use rhythm (bodily motion) and melody (choral song) as means supple-

[44] *Ibid.*, p. 221: "solo per seruire a gli spettatori, & farle riuscire piu grate in Scena, & conformarmi piu con l'uso de i nostri tempi. Che anchora che Aristotile dica, che cio è seruire alla ignoranza de gli spettatori, hauendo pero l'altra parte i difensori suoi, ho tenuto meglio sodisfare a chi ha ad ascoltare, con qualche minore eccellenza (quando fusse accettata per la migliore l'openione d'Aristotile) che con un poco piu di grandezza dispiacere a coloro, per piacere de quali la fauola si conduce in Scena: che poco giouerebbe compor fauola un poco piu lodeuole, & che poi ella si hauesse a rappresentare odiosamente. Quelle terribili (se gli animi de gli spettatori forse le abhoriscono) possono essere delle scritture: queste di fin lieto delle rappresentationi."

[45] *Ibid.*, p. 203: " & però fu detto da Aristotile, che la Comedia imitaua le attioni peggiori. Non che ci uolesse significare, che imitasse le uitiose & le ree, ma le meno illustri, lequali sono peggiori, quanto alla nobilità, se si conferiscono colle reali."

[46] *Ibid.*, p. 215: "serui, parasiti, meretrici, cuochi, ruffiani, soldati, & finalmente quas ogni sorte di gente popolaresca, che si troui nelle città." V. pp. 271-75 for other listings of persons and for the characters to be associated with various types.

mentary to verse; but comedy now uses neither (p. 205). If verse is the universal accompaniment of diction, it is not used in the same way in the two genres. Comedy admits of no rhyme, whereas tragedy should mix rhymed with unrhymed sections, rhyme being useful especially in the choruses and in those "moral" parts where a lesson is specifically stated, "so that they may be more easily received in the mind of the listener" ("accioche piu ageuolmente siano riceuute nell'animo di chi ascolta," p. 234). The diction itself will necessarily be appropriate to the actions and the persons depicted. "The speech of tragedy should be great, royal, and magnificent, and figurative; that of comedy simple, pure, familiar, and appropriate to men of the people."[47] Giraldi develops his ideas on the special circumstances which require a more or less noble diction than that employed for the rest. One senses, throughout the discussion, the presence of the theory of the styles, and also the rules of decorum in character and in diction as they were applied to the examination of Terence's comedies.

The third of Giraldi's treatises, bearing the date 1554 but published much later, is entitled *Lettera ovvero discorso sopra il comporre le satire atte alle scene*. It is relatively short, and its shortness permits one to perceive, even more clearly than in the case of the previous treatise, the extent to which its organization depends upon the outline of the *Poetics*. Giraldi conceives of the dramatic satire, "proper for the stage," as a genre combining the characteristics of both tragedy and comedy. Thus the definition which he gives for it and the detailed remarks on the definition attempt to combine the materials found in Aristotle—and in his own treatise—on the other two dramatic genres: "Satire is an imitation of a complete action, of suitable length, combining the mirthful with the grave, in pleasant language, the components of which are in part combined in a single place, in part divided, presented on the stage in order to move men's souls to laughter and to an appropriate terror and pity." And the gloss; the remarks made on imitation and on the complete action are the same as those on all other kinds of poetry.

"Of suitable length"—separates it from complete works which are short, such as epigrams, odes, elegies. . . . "Mirthful and grave at the same time"—this shows its difference from comedy and from tragedy, of which the first is composed to be pleasing, the other to be serious. . . . "In pleasant language"—this divides it from works written in prose, for it favors verse just as much as do the other two types already mentioned.[48]

---

[47] *Ibid.*, p. 264: "quel parlare della Tragedia uuole esser grande, reale, & magnifico, & figurato: quello della Comedia semplice, puro, famigliare, & conueneuole alle persone del popolo."

[48] *Lettera ovvero discorso*, in *Scritti estetici* (1864), II, 134–35: "La satira è imitazione di azione perfetta di dicevole grandezza, composta al giocoso ed al grave con parlar soave, le membre della quale sono insieme al suo luogo per parte, e per parte divise, rappresentata a commovere gli animi a riso, ed a convenevole terrore e compassione. . . . Di dicevole grandezza—la separa dalle cose perfette, ma che sono picciole, come epigrammi, ode, elegie. . . . Insieme giocosa e grave—la fa diversa dalla comedia e dalla tragedia, delle quali la prima è composta al piacevole, l'altra al grave. . . . di parlar soave—il quale la divide dalle cose scritte in prosa, perchè ella così ama il verso, come l'amano l'altre due già dette."

[443]

The remainder of the gloss explains the appearance of "numero, armonia, canto" together or separately; the dramatic character of the genre; and the "appropriate" terror and pity, to be distinguished from the stronger passions of tragedy. For the satire, Giraldi demands the unhappy ending which he had not deemed necessary for tragedy, an action limited to one day and having the same quantitative and qualitative parts as the other dramatic forms. The qualitative parts are treated in this order: (1) "l'apparato," or spectacle; (2) "il ragionare" (language, including necessarily verse); (3) "melodia," or the music of the choruses; (4) "sentenza" (the verbal expression of concepts); (5) "costume," or character; and (6) "favola." There is very little here that goes beyond the text of Aristotle, although some of the points of view noted in the other treatises reappear here in its interpretation.

Giraldi Cintio's group of treatises is highly representative of the activity around the *Poetics* in these middle years of the Cinquecento. They are original treatises rather than commentaries, treating three dramatic genres which Giraldi regards as traditional and one narrative genre which he considers to be new. They are patterned on the *Poetics*, following its general outline and repeating many passages and many principles. For the traditional genres, they accept without question much of Aristotle's theory; for the new one, they declare the independence of modern forms of the rules established before such forms came into being. Throughout, however, the acceptance of Aristotle is only superficial, for the theorist is constantly led to alter—sometimes drastically—Aristotle's principles by his own adherence to another set of principles which is essentially Horatian and rhetorical.

I romanzi of Giovanni Battista Pigna, also published in 1554, belongs to the group of original treatises based on Aristotle as did Giraldi Cintio's three discourses. Whether Pigna learned what he knew about the romance from Giraldi or whether Giraldi plagiarized Pigna is indifferent; Pigna's work presents an essentially independent theory of the romance. It is based on Aristotle in a somewhat different way from the others. For although Pigna declares that Aristotle has been his guide in everything that he has said on the romanzo (p. 65), he does not follow the order of the *Poetics* as Giraldi had done. He seems to state the problem this way: Given the fact that Aristotle does not treat the genre of the romance, what may one derive from his theories of history, tragedy, comedy, and the epic that will be useful in defining the conditions and the excellences of the new genre? His method everywhere reflects this statement. He proceeds by finding similarities in the romance to one or another of the genres and by transferring to the romance the apposite statements. He must use this method since the only genre closely resembling the romance, the epic, is nevertheless considerably different, and the same rules do not apply to both (p. 68). This is a fundamental tenet of his position: "the rule will be discovered whereby one will be required to write in a way proper to the romance ["Romanzeuolmente"]; and that this kind of writing has a form of its own, in part agreeing with the others [Greek and Latin epics], in part not; and that given this foundation it is not to be blamed for the fact that it is different from the other forms in many respects."[49]

The principal differences between the romance and the epic will be in the object of imitation, which Pigna calls merely "imitazione." The general rules of imitation apply equally to both; but the epic is based on the truth and the romance is not:

> There is this single difference, that the basis of their imitation [i.e., of the romances] is not the same as that of the epic; for the epic uses a true event as the basis for a probable one. By true I mean derived either from history or from fable, that is, true in actuality or supposed to be true. These others [romances] have no concern whatever with the truth.[50]

In this respect—and here the cross reference to other genres appears—the romance is like comedy, which invents its own subjects. But not entirely, since the romance does treat known and "true" subjects. It may mix a large ingredient of falsehood with the true and in any case must make its materials acceptable as verisimilar (pp. 20–21). Next, there is a difference in the kinds of persons selected for treatment. Here, the romance will rather resemble the *Odyssey*, which mixes "high" and "low" (royal and pastoral) personages, than the *Iliad*, which represents only the "high." It will thus have a "mixed" action, accompanied necessarily by a double ending; like the *Odyssey*, "each romance will be such through a great variety of infinite fortunes, and in the rank of the persons it will also be of two kinds, but it will tend toward the highest rather than toward the lowest, and almost every one of its actions will be illustrious."[51]

The general structure of the action will also be different, for whereas the epic presents one action of one man, the romance will relate many actions of one man. The problem of unity of the poem without unity of action necessarily arises, and Pigna solves it in a way which may not be thoroughly satisfactory since it is essentially "impressionistic":

> The romances readily devote themselves to several deeds of several men, but ... they concern especially one man who should be celebrated over all the others. And thus they agree with the epic poets in taking a single person, but not so in

---

[49] *I romanzi* (1554), p. 15: "la regola si scoprirà, con cui Romanzeuolmente scriuer si richieda: & come tale scrittura habbia vna forma da per se, parte con l'altre conueniente, & parte nò: & come per lo posto fondamento non sia degno di biasimo, se in molte cose dall'altre s'allontana."

[50] *Ibid.*, pp. 19–20: "Euui questa sola differenza; che il fondamento della costoro imitatione non è con l'Epico vn' istesso: percioche l'Epico sopra vna cosa vera fonda vna verisimile. & vera intendo ò per historie, ò per fauole: cio è ò in effetto vera, ò vera sopposta. Questi altri alla verità risguardo alcuno non hanno."

[51] *Ibid.*, p. 24: "tale per molta varietà di casi infiniti sarà ciascun Romancio. il quale ne gradi delle persone sarà etiandio di due sorti. ma piu alle supreme mirerà, che all'infime: & quasi ogni sua attione sarà illustre."

[445]

POETIC THEORY

taking a single action; for they take as many of them as seem to be sufficient. The number is "sufficient" when they have put the heroes in all those honorable perils and in all those major actions which are sought in a perfect knight; and in this way endless adventures are avoided. . . . And to finish the poem as soon as we have arrived at that goal which we have selected, the order of nature will help; for when all the attributes are present in matter, motion ceases.[52]

A final difference of subject matter between the romance and the classical epic lies in the use of religion. The gentiles were permitted to invent fables based on their religion and to use them as ornaments for their poems, whereas Christians are not (p. 14). Nevertheless, the Christian poet may use saints and devils, miracles and other supernatural acts, insofar as they agree with the beliefs of his audience, which he is much more apt to please in this way than by the introduction of an antiquated pagan mythology (p. 41).

I have already touched upon the handling and organization of these materials in connection with the problem of unity. Pigna notes other important differences. The epic poet presents a continuous narrative, whereas the poet of romance interrupts his story from time to time, pretending to sing it in portions before his hosts (p. 14). Thus the narrative of the epic will be straightforward and direct, while that of the romance will wander, digress, retrace its steps—just like the knights who are its heroes:

> Even if it does not observe the epic order, this does not mean that it does not have a rule of its own, which is the following: . . . It breaks off the narrative either when the time for an interruption presents itself, or when it does not. When it does, the mind of the reader remains at rest, from which he derives contentment and therefore pleasure, since he remains in presence of a completed action . . . When the time does not present itself, the mind remains in suspense, and from this there arises a desire which is a source of pleasure.[53]

Similarly, the romance will be longer. There is no need for its plot to be perceptible in one glance, and it is better to err by excessive length than to disappoint the reader by excessive shortness. One may even consider that the proper length for each canto is what one may sing or hear in a single sitting. The cantos should be connected to one another by moral discourses.

---

[52] *Ibid.*, pp. 25–26: "i Romanzi si dan bene à piu fatti di piu huomini, ma . . . vn huomo specialmente si propongono: il quale sia soura tutti gli altri celebrato. & cosi con gli Epici concorrono nel pigliare vna sola persona. ma nel prendere vn sol fatto non è cosi: percioche tanti ne trattano, quanto lor pare essere assai. Et assai è, ogni volta che in tutti quegli honorati pericoli, & in tutte quelle maggiori attioni posto gli hanno, che à vn perfetto cauagliere si ricercano. & cosi il gire in infinito si toglie. . . . & quanto al finire il poema tosto che arriuati siamo à quel segno, à che mirauamo; seruasi l'ordine della natura. percioche presenti che sono gli habiti nella materia cessa il moto."

[53] *Ibid.*, p. 45: "se bene l'ordine Epico non osserua, non è che vna sua regola non habbia: la quale è questa. . . . Tralascia ò quando il tempo dà che s'interponga, ò quando nol dà. Quando il dà, l'animo di chi legge, quieto rimane. dal che ha contentezza, & perciò piacere: restando egli con vna cosa compiuta. . . . Quando nol dà, l'animo resta sospeso. & ne nasce perciò vn desiderio che fa diletto."

And this discourse will be moral so that by means of virtue it will invite us to be better, and so that it will serve its purpose, which is to inflame us to praiseworthy action through pleasure; whence arises a certain affection which makes us attentive, and through attention we become capable of absorbing the material, and ultimately benevolent toward the poet.[54]

The romance, generally freer, will use more numerous descriptions and comparisons than the epic (p. 51), and although both are necessarily written in verse, the verse form is not the same (p. 15).

In their totality, these differences between the romance and the epic do not represent merely the adaptation to two sister genres of the same set of principles. Rather, as we pass from Aristotle's theory of the epic to Pigna's theory of the epic and the romance we see certain major changes in orientation—from a theory directed toward the beauty of the work itself to one seeking a particular kind of pleasure and of moral instruction for a given audience; from one concerned with the structural unity of the poem to another recommending variety, multiplicity, diversity, discontinuity; from one deriving its criteria from within to another seeking criteria in a miscellany of external factors. The movement in these directions is even clearer when one considers the broad context of theory in which Pigna places his treatment of the romance. The development of his thought on the dual end of utility and pleasure may be taken as an example. He gives a lengthy explanation of why we derive pleasure from the representation of sad and tearful events, and in this explanation Aristotle's remark about the pleasure accompanying knowledge plays only a minor part:

> The profit arises from learning about the tenor of human life and about how uncertain is prosperity; and it teaches us especially about the opposite fortune. This nevertheless gives pleasure, since knowledge is a perfection, and since therefore the soul rejoices, finding its proper form. And it is a natural thing to wish to know, and that which is natural and which occurs gives us pleasure. And for the same reason we have another delight, which consists in being so moved by these great changes of fortune that we take pity on those who suffer them. For pity comes to man of itself and is therefore natural.

To explain pleasure from painful events, a physico-physiological theory is offered:

> The consideration is diverse, since it is the natural movement of pity which delights us and a movement of the heart that is not natural which saddens us. For when the heart is compressed, sadness results, as dilatation produces joy. If then joy comes about through dilatation, how can pity ever give us pleasure, since it produces the shrinking of the heart in the opposite direction? It is nevertheless necessary that these humors [spiriti] should expand; otherwise they will not comfort us; and this will come about at the very same time in which they are being

---

[54] *Ibid.*, p. 46: "Et sara questo discorso morale; accioche per mezzo della virtù meglio c'inuiti; & accioche stia nel suo proponimento, che è con diletto à lodeuoli cose infiammarne. dal che nasce vna certa affettione, che attenti ne rende: & d'attenti capaci della materia, & finalmente beneuoli verso il poeta."

compressed. For in part restricted and in part set free, they will give us partly pleasure and partly uneasiness. Pleasure, because it is a human thing to have pity on the afflicted, aside from the fact that it consoles us to see that we ourselves are free from the evil, in which there is still another pleasure. Uneasiness, because feeling sorrow is outside of nature, aside from the fact that it disturbs us to transfer to ourselves, by the imagination, the suffering of others.[55]

Pigna presents here a kind of compendium of current thinking on the causes and nature of aesthetic pleasure. In other passages, he studies the artistic devices which may produce that pleasure. The ornateness of the narrative style, for example, produces novelty, hence the marvelous, hence an intense pleasure (p. 17). A strict observance of decorum, presenting to the audience types which it knows and recognizes, makes possible the pleasure of recognition (p. 20). Those plots which teach most about human life will be the most pleasurable, because of the delight accompanying knowledge (p. 24). Verse is required at once because it is more enjoyable than prose, being more artistic, and because it assists in the communication of the moral lesson (pp. 53–54).

Very few of Pigna's statements take issue with Aristotle, since for the most part he believes himself to be in agreement; the differences consist in added ideas which essentially alter Aristotle's thought. So for the distinction between poetry and history:

And although both of them, not without some profit, are delightful, they are nevertheless different and of unequal value. For the historian remains always with the particular, pursuing a perpetual similarity rarely changed; and the poet seeks the universal, removing monotony through constant variety. And there are many other things which make a notable difference between them, so that the poet charms and teaches more than the historian.[56]

[55] *Ibid.*, pp. 28–29: "il giouamento nasce dall'apparare il tenore della vita humana, & quanto instabile sia la prosperità: & dal contrario massimamente c'insegna. Ciò tutta uia fa diletto: essendo la scienza vna perfettione; & rallegrandosi perciò l'anima che il suo sugello ritroui. & natural cosa è il voler sapere: & quello che è naturale & che viene, ne dà piacere. & per questa istessa ragione vn'altro diletto habbiamo, che è nell'essere da questi grandi mutamenti talmente commossi, che pietà ci venga di chi loro sottoposto si troua. percioche la misericordia viene all'huomo da se, & è perciò per natura. . . . il rispetto è diuerso; essendo il moto naturale della misericordia quello che ci diletta; & il moto del cuore che naturale non è, quello che ci attrista: percioche compresso ch'egli è, contristatione ne nasce; come allegrezza dalla dilatatione. Se adunque l'allegrezza è per mezzo della dilatatione, come ci porgerà mai diletto la misericordia, poscia ch'ella ha lo stringimento del cuore in opposito? Bisogna tutta uia che essi spiriti s'allarghino: altramente non ci conforteranno. & ciò auerrà in quel tempo istesso che comprimeransi: percioche parte ristretti & parte slargati, parte piacere & parte noia ne daranno. Piacere, quanto che humana cosa è l'hauer compassione à gli afflitti. senza che ne consola il vedere che siamo fuor del male, in che è vn'altro. Noia, quanto che il rincrescimento è fuor di natura. senza che ne disturba il trasferire con l'imaginatione in noi stessi l'altrui dolore."

[56] *Ibid.*, p. 2: "& quantunque ambe non senza qualche giouamento sien diletteuoli; sono nondimeno diuerse, & di pregio disuguale. percioche l'historico stà in sul particolare con vna perpetua similitudine alterata di rado: & all' uniuersale mira il poeta togliendo col sempre variare la satietà. & molte altre cose vi sono che differenza notabile vi fanno: & tale, che questo alletta & insegna piu che quello."

POETICS: THEORETICAL APPLICATIONS

From the particular and the universal the passage is made to monotony and variety, and thence to greater pleasure and instruction. A more striking case, perhaps, is found in the treatment of the four requisites for character. Pigna assumes immediately that characters are either traditional or new (i.e., invented) and that Aristotle's four requisites are divided between these two types. All four are forms of verisimilitude, but some are natural and others are "by reference." These distinctions give the following schema:

	Verisimilitude		
New characters		Traditional characters	
(*finta*)		(*tolta*)	
Appropriateness		Similarity	
(*convenevole*)		(*simile*)	
By nature	By reference	By nature	By reference
Christón	*Armótton*	*Ómalon*	*Ómion*

The terms "by nature" and "by reference" are explained thus:

> By reference: referring the one whom I am treating to the opinion in which he is held in histories or in fables, I will depict him primarily as fierce or pleasant, as prudent or bold, as deceitful or just. . . . By nature: considering the habits as confirmed dispositions of the soul, I will make any person throughout the work and to the very end such as I have established him to be from the beginning.[57]

Verisimilitude is thus defined in terms of consistency of character ("by nature") or of faithfulness to a tradition ("by reference"), and Aristotle's four requisites are reduced to these terms.

A special feature of *I romanzi* is its insistence on the pleasure that the audience takes in the *difficulté vaincue*. A number of passages point to this. But Pigna notes that it is not always appreciated and that there is perhaps a difference between those who admire ingeniousness—a select group—and the popular taste which is less discriminating. So tragedies will be "demonstrative of greater wit" ("di maggior ingegno dimonstratrici," p. 2), but will appeal less to popular taste than the romance. Still, even in the romance form the difficult solution will be the best. A new subject involving new characters will be less admirable than the traditional ones, since the poet will not, in handling them, be under the constraint of the accepted story and of the decorum of known personages, "which, because it is less easy to do, always shows greater virtuosity."[58] As a general thing, pleasure comes from the spectacle of the poet's triumphs: ". . . the more narrow is the field in which our genius is restricted, the more difficulty is seen there;

---

[57] *Ibid.*, p. 34: "Per relatione; se referendo colui di ch'io tratto, all'opinione in che egli è nelle historie ò nelle fauole, ò fiero ò piaceuole, ò circonspetto ò temerario, ò insidiatore ò giusto principalmente il dipingerò. . . . Per natura; se mirando à gli habiti che sono dispositioni confirmate, tale qual da principio haurò stabilito alcuno, il farò essere per tutta l'opera infino alla fine." See below, p. 468, for a similar schema resulting from the text of Pigna's *Poetica Horatiana* of 1561.

[58] *Ibid.*, p. 20: "che perche disagiosamente si fa, mostra tutta uia piu virtù."

POETIC THEORY

and ... difficult things happen rarely; and they are therefore more beautiful and of greater efficacy, since this grows by opposition to its contrary."[59] It is for this reason—and we may again see an adaptation of Aristotelian principles—that tragedy is to be considered superior to the epic:

> Restriction gives it all its excellence, since it is limited in its action, not disposing of a plot in which great events come together; and in the matter of digressions, since it cannot permit itself many or varied ones, lest the composition turn out to be disproportionate; and in time, having only the space of one day or of a day and a half in which the whole action must be concluded; and in its pleasure, which is deprived of an important element, brought about more easily by a narrator than by a chorus.[60]

Pigna's treatise is significant, finally, for the extensive sections devoted to practical criticism. All of Books II and III is occupied by an examination of Ariosto's works, the comedies as well as the *Orlando Furioso* (although primarily the latter). In this examination, Pigna is not really seeking a judgment of the works, for the judgment is admitted from the start: the *Orlando Furioso* is the best romance ever written, and Ariosto's comedies, especially the *Cassaria*, are the best in the language. Rather, he wishes to discover in the *Orlando* the authority for the precepts he has given in Book I; indirectly, praise will fall upon the *Orlando* as the source of all the best examples and precedents. A certain amount of Pigna's material may be neglected, since it is biographical or deals with Ariosto's fame. But his indication that the form of the plot is determined by the works of Boiardo and Homer needs to be noted. So also the fact that the digressions are in part explained by the wish to glorify the Este family, for it is also a justification; and Pigna takes it for granted that such external reasons do constitute justifications of the form of the plot. He declares that Ariosto is supreme both in the essence and in the accidents, and, from an earlier statement (p. 15), we know that the essence or substance is the plot and the accidents are the digressions. The analysis of plot consists in asking which of the four types of plot are to be found here—and Pigna finds them all—in examining the treatment of the quantitative parts, in studying the use of knot and denouement. It is clear from the analysis that Pigna thinks of the *Orlando Furioso* as made up of many whole plots and that each of the separate "actions" constitutes a "plot." This is consonant with his theory of the multiplicity of plot in the romance. So that while the machinery of

[59] *Ibid.*, pp. 36-37: "quanto piu stretto è il campo, in che l'ingegno nostro è ridotto, che tanta piu difficoltà ui si vede: & ... le cose difficili di rado auengono; & sono perciò piu belle & di maggior virtù, accrescendo ella contra il suo contrario."
[60] *Ibid.*, p. 37: "la strettezza tutta l'eccellenza le dà. essendo ella angusta nell'attione, per non hauere vn fatto, in cui gran fatti concorrano: & nelle digressioni, percioche non può pigliarne molte ne varie, accioche sproportionato non venga il componimento: & nel tempo, hauendo ella solo lo spatio d'un giorno, ò d'un giorno & mezzo, in cui tutta la cosa conchiuda: & nel piacere, che d'una gran parte manca, la quale dal narratore piu commodamente nasce, che dal choro."

POETICS: THEORETICAL APPLICATIONS

the Aristotelian text is applied, the theoretical basis is fundamentally different in Pigna. He applies a criterion of unity to the poem—but only insofar as it is possible or desirable in the romance: "in the end everything is properly conducted with beautiful unity, to the extent that this kind of poetry admits of unity."[61] The problem of unity involves the problem of digressions, and Pigna praises Ariosto for the use of episodes which properly mix the grave and the light, the calm and the disturbed, the active and the passionate. Decorum is everywhere correctly observed, in the transfer to the *Orlando* of traditional materials, in the use of contemporary events, and in the expression. Finally, events and episodes are accompanied by moral overtones and by possibilities of allegorical interpretation which serve the end of utility.

In this discussion of the *Orlando Furioso*, Pigna uses the term "imitation" in three separate senses which demonstrate with especial clarity his habits in the use of terminology. Since the plot depends upon Homer and Vergil, it contains "imitations" of them. A second kind of imitation occurs when men are presented "as they should be," either through narration or through dialogue. Dialogue itself is a kind of imitation, in the Platonic sense which distinguishes imitation from narration (p. 80). The Aristotelian sense appears earlier in the text: "The plot is an imitation of an action" ("Favola è imitatione d'una attione," p. 15); but in the definition which follows, Pigna clearly gives it a restricted meaning: "To imitate is to use the verisimilar according to that form which is most proper in the matter undertaken."[62] Imitation as direct or dramatic representation is also fully treated in the early sections of the text (p. 16). Although he assigns so many meanings to the word, Pigna makes no attempt to define or distinguish, and the reader must derive the proper meaning from the context. A similar case, although not nearly so extensive, is found with respect to the word "favola" (pp. 15, 92).

The examination of Ariosto's comedies (pp. 105 ff.) presents interesting solutions to the question of why one comedy, the *Cassaria*, is superior to another, the *Suppositi*. Seven reasons are offered: (1) the denouement derives more successfully from the preceding action; (2) the denouement does not depend upon external signs; (3) the *Cassaria* is more verisimilar; (4) the comedy succeeds in conducting a more difficult plot; (5) it has more of pleasantness in it and less of sadness; (6) its devices are newer, causing increased admiration and greater pleasure; (7) the episodes are more immediately derived from the knot and solution and more closely linked to them. In these seven points, Pigna once again raises questions found in the *Poetics*, although his applications and conclusions are not necessarily

---

[61] *Ibid.*, p. 101: "alla fine ogni cosa con vaga vnità per quanto questa poesia patisce, è debitamente guidata."

[62] *Ibid.*, p. 15: "Imitare è pigliare il verisimile secondo quella forma, che nella proposta materia piu conuiene."

Aristotelian. But he does more: judging that works may be evaluated by comparison with their contraries, he compares the *Cassaria* with the "best tragedy that one might read." This is the result:

> In this [tragedy], we will see royal life expressed, in the *Cassaria*, the life of the people; the one excellent in long discourses, the other in brief repartees; on the one hand, the operation of fortune, on the other, of cunning; in the former, grave teachings and majesty and sorrows and infinite anguish, in the latter, delight and joy and playfulness and many warnings about private life.[63]

Here, Aristotle is absent, and we return once again to the juxtaposition of tragedy and comedy familiar throughout the Middle Ages. A final reason for preferring the *Cassaria* to the *Suppositi*, and one which should not surprise in the context, is its superior morality (p. 107).

Pigna devotes the third book of *I romanzi* to a study of the style of the *Orlando Furioso*. His method is new and prophetic. He takes one hundred passages from the romance and shows the successive stages in the composition of the text; in each case, he gives the reason why Ariosto preferred the last version. In this study of variants, the comments concern such matters as grammar, phonetics or sound, proportion and symmetry, prosody, clarity, ease of construction, ambiguity, appropriateness to matter and to nature, and ornament. The point of view is thus almost entirely grammatical and rhetorical.

LOVISINI (1554)

The year 1554 was thus extraordinarily rich in short works on the poetic art that bore in one way or another the stamp of Aristotle's *Poetics*. It also was the year of publication of a major commentary on Horace, Francesco Lovisini's *In librum Q. Horatii Flacci de arte poetica commentarius*, which made the customary comparisons between Aristotle and Horace. But in regard to the history of Aristotle's *Poetics* in the Cinquecento, Lovisini's work is much less rewarding than its contemporaries. Although it discovers an extraordinarily large number of parallels between Horace and Aristotle (see Chapter IV, pp. 130–32 above), for the most part it does little else than cite the selected text from the *Poetics* and give a translation of it. Moreover, since by this time many of the parallels have become commonplace and traditional, not much is to be learned from a mere examination of the juxtaposed passages. It would be difficult to say what Lovisini's general interpretation of the *Poetics* was, aside from the fact that he found in it many passages that conveyed the same meaning as Horace's *Ars poetica*, perhaps so many that one might insist that the total meaning of the two texts was the same. There are a few points at which what is said about a

---

[63] *Ibid.*, pp. 106–7: "in essa la vita reale espressa si vedrà; & nella Cassaria la popolaresca. In lunghi discorsi l'una: l'altra in prontezze strette eccellente. Di là la fortuna: di qua l'astutia. In quella documenti graui & maestà & dolori & angoscie infinite: in questa diletto & gioia & piaceuolezze & auertimenti domestici assai."

POETICS: THEORETICAL APPLICATIONS

passage in Aristotle reveals the construction which Lovisini put upon it. So for the early commentary on lines 1–13 of the *Ars poetica*, where we find how Lovisini understands imitation:

> Poets follow the imagination, not opinion, since they call themselves poets not because they write in verse but because of the plot and the fiction, as Aristotle has set it down for us in the *Poetics*. And therefore all those who imitate the image or the appearance of things by means of art, as do many sculptors and painters, are poets, as Plato's Socrates affirms in the *Symposium*, through the fact that they give pleasure by their invention and imitation of things.[64]

The sense of "imitation" is here composed of its meaning in the *Poetics* plus its meaning in Plato, with emphasis on the latter. Furthermore, the Platonic (and Horatian) element is further emphasized in the next sentence: "Indeed, in these matters we must establish a rule: not all poetic figments are to be approved, but only those which derive rather from prudence than from freedom of creation."[65] The presence of prudence, with its moral and political connotations, indicates the direction taken by the interpreter. Lovisini again expresses the same ideas in connection with *Ars poetica* 146–52, when he cites *Poetics* 1451*a*36 (p. 34*v*). For lines 119–27, on character, Lovisini necessarily refers to Aristotle's four requisites: then he makes the following distinction between ὅμοιον and ὁμαλόν: "There is a difference between ὅμοιον, καὶ ὁμαλόν, that is, similar and uniform; for similarity refers to those about whom others had written previously, and uniformity to those about whom we alone are writing. We must observe constant uniformity in a personage whom we are ourselves introducing, so that he will always be himself."[66] This is the distinction between traditional and newly invented characters which we have just seen developed by Pigna, but with differences in the understanding of the requisites. Lovisini also attempts to answer one of the questions about the *Poetics* which was already much debated, the meaning of "one day" in the remark on the duration of the tragic action. Here he accepts Robortello's demonstration that an "artificial day" (i.e., twelve hours) was intended (p. 40).

In a few places at least, Lovisini seems to wish to oppose some point of theory offered by Aristotle. In *Poetics* 1454*a*28, Aristotle had given examples of a number of characters who were improperly treated. Lovisini takes exception to several, claiming that Menelaus seems to him to be an

---

[64] *Commentarius* (1554), p. 4: "Poetae phantasiam, non opinionem sequuntur: quia poetae nomen sibi asciscunt non propter carmen, sed propter fabulam, & fictionem, ut in poetice testatum relinquit Aristoteles. & iccirco quicunque rerum effigiem, & simulacra arte imitantur, ut mechanici plerique artifices faciunt, poetae sunt, quemadmodum in symposio Platonis Socrates affirmat, propterea quòd fictione, & rerum imitatione delectantur."

[65] *Ibid.*, pp. 4–5: "Verum his modus statuendus est: neque enim omnia poetarum figmenta probanda sunt, sed quae à prudentia potius, quàm à sola fingendi libertate proficiscuntur."

[66] *Ibid.*, p. 29*v*: "discrepant inter se ὅμοιον, καὶ ὁμαλόν, idest simile, & aequale, nam similitudo ad eos refertur, de quibus alij etiam scripserunt, aequalitas ad eos, de quibus nos tantum scribimus, perpetuam aequalitatem seruare debemus in ea, quam inducimus, persona, ut sit sibi constans."

example of admirable probity and that Iphigenia does display the necessary uniformity of character. Such differences of judgment might result from the fact that Lovisini had different texts in mind or that he interpreted in a different way Aristotle's requisites (p. 54v). On the subject of necessity and probability, the disagreement apparently springs from the fact that Lovisini believes necessity to be natural necessity, that is, the inevitable realization of events. Hence he says: "Horace required of the poet only the law of verisimilitude, Aristotle that of necessity as well. But it seems to me that our author understood the matter better. Indeed, so far are poets from expressing the law of necessity that sometimes they invent things which are not even verisimilar."[67] It is to be noted that Lovisini in no sense regards Aristotle as an authority whose opinion is to be preferred to that of Horace.

As for the important matter of the end of poetry, finally, Lovisini hides his disagreement under a verbal distinction. Wishing to reconcile Aristotle with Horace, he uses the term "munus" or "finis" for Aristotle and "officium" for Horace:

Munus and *officium*. These two words may either signify the same thing or two different things [so distinguished] that "munus" means the end sought by the poet. Indeed the "finis" and the "officium" are different. The "officium" of the poet is to imitate, since ποίησίς ἐστι μίμησις, as Aristotle says in the *Poetics*. But the "finis" is instead to profit and delight.[68]

The distinction is clearly between function or operation and end, with Horace as providing the real definition of the latter.

Matteo San Martino's *Osservationi grammaticali e poetiche della lingua italiana* of the following year, 1555, belongs primarily to the history of Horace's *Ars poetica*, although certain passages are relevant to the fortunes of Plato's ideas (see above Chapters IV and VII, pp. 138, 275). Only incidentally does it concern Aristotle's *Poetics*, and then almost exclusively for the interpretation of imitation. In his highly heterogeneous definition of poetry, San Martino of course includes imitation as an element; the times would not have permitted him to do otherwise: "Poetry is a beautiful fiction which, restricted within harmonized rhythms and imitating human actions, by means of pleasure brings profit to the listener." In what immediately follows, however, he shows the importance he attributes to

---

[67] *Ibid.*, pp. 66v–67 (the latter page misnumbered 65): "Horatius uerisimile tantum, Aristoteles etiam necessarium poetis proposuit. at melius sensisse uidetur hic n[o]ster. nam tantum abest, ut poetae necessarium exprimant, ut ea aliquando, quae uerisimilia etiam non sunt, comminisci uideantur."

[68] *Ibid.*, p. 61v: "*Munus, et officium.* duae hae dictiones uel idem significant, uel diuersa: ut munus finem poetae innuat. differunt enim inter se finis, & officium. officium poetae est imitari. nam ποίησίς ἐστι μίμησις, ut ait in poetice Aristoteles. finis uero prodesse, & delectare."

POETICS: THEORETICAL APPLICATIONS

imitation: "So that imitation is its secondary and not its principal part."[69] From such a passage as this it would seem that the "principal part" would be the pursuit of pleasure and utility. Yet, at a later point, the writer insists that "the final intention of the poets consists in imitation, and all must practice it according to the doctrine of Aristotle and of Cicero, that is, by means of diction, number, and harmony."[70] Here again there is uncertainty, since one wonders what is meant by the "doctrine of Aristotle and of Cicero." In any case, it is fairly clear that the ends of poetry are Horatian and that imitation has some intermediary function in the achievement of those ends. Further light is thrown on the problem in San Martino's statement on the relationship of poetry to reality:

> He [Aristotle] says also that since the poet is an imitator, or another designer of images, he must always imitate one of three things, either things as they were, or as they appear and are said to be, or as it is proper for them to be, provided that all poets make their imitations, according to what was said, of diction, number, and harmony, either separately or together.[71]

In both these passages, I have translated by "diction" the original "componimento," which is stated to mean something like "the disposition or arrangement of ornate speech" (p. 158). As San Martino uses this and the accompanying terms "numero" and "concento" or "harmonia," not only do they signify the means of imitation indicated by Aristotle, but they also carry with them the stress on rhetoric and on prosody which will be his principal concern in the treatise. Aside from these passages, the *Poetics* is used only rarely.

SIGONIO (1557)

Another kind of activity affecting Aristotle's text is represented, in 1557, by Carlo Sigonio's *Emendationum libri duo*. For besides the editions and commentaries of the text, we frequently find philological and philosophical discussions in shorter critical miscellanies devoted largely to textual exegesis. The sections on the *Poetics* in Sigonio's book are answers to suggestions by Robortello or statements of open disagreement with him. Before proceeding to the study of individual passages, Sigonio expresses his opposition to Robortello's way of dividing the text; his own suggestion is an interesting one for the total conception of Aristotle's plan:

---

[69] *Osservationi* (1555), p. 130: "la Poetica sia una uaga fittione che fra harmonizzati numeri ristretta, imitando l'humane attioni, con diletto gioui a chi l'ascolta; Si che la imitatione è sua parte secondaria, e non principale."

[70] *Ibid.*, p. 146: "consistendo la final intentione de i Poeti nella imitatione, che a tutti exercitarla conuiene secondo la dottrina d'Aristotele, e di Cicerone, cioè con Componimento Numero, & Concento."

[71] *Ibid.*, p. 184: "Dice ancor che essendo il Poeta imitatore, o come aitro disignator de imagini, che una di tre cose conuien che sempre imiti, o le cose come furono, o come appaiono e che si dicono, o come esser gli conuiene, pur che tutti fanno la loro imitatione secondo che è detto, di Componimento, Numero & Harmonia o separatamente o congiuntamente."

In my judgment this book is to be divided not into three parts, but into six. For in the first he treats not only the definition of poetry, but also its origin and its growth. But origin and growth do not belong at all to the definition. There follow then two other parts, one on tragedy, the other on the epic. The fifth part concerns questions and answers about poetry, which comes afterwards in his division since it is a separate subject from tragedy and the epic. In the last book he compares tragedy with the epic; this may properly be called a sixth part because it is detached from the discussion of tragedy and the epic.[72]

For the rest, Sigonio's "emendations" offer his opinion on some of the texts which gave the greatest difficulty to his contemporaries:

On 1447a15, "Quid sit αὐλητική, & κιθαριστική." Sigonio draws three conclusions from the text: (1) there are some kinds of auletic and citharistic poetry which do not imitate at all; (2) they use harmony and rhythm (dance) only for their imitation, excluding speech and meter; (3) Aristotle meant them as examples of kinds of poetry which imitate without speech (pp. 148v–50).

On 1447b24–28, "Quid sit Poesis Nomorum. Persas non esse iocosum comoediae nomen." The text presents two difficulties. First, what is meant by "gnomic" poetry—or, more properly, how should one interpret "νόμος" in the text? Sigonio's suggestion is that it has nothing to do with laws but rather is a counterpart to comedy in the same way that the dithyramb is a counterpart to tragedy. The first two express "little" matters, the last two "great" matters. The νόμος would thus be a form of comic poetry, and Sigonio cites the texts of ancient authors who condemned it as such. The second difficulty comes from Robortello's reading at 1448a15 of νόμους ὡς Πέρσας; hence the statement about "Persas" in the heading of the paragraph. Sigonio uses the term as synonymous with νόμος and offers no emendation to the text (pp. 149v–50v).

On 1448a20, "Quid sit μιμεῖσθαι ἐν τοῖς αὐτοῖς." Sigonio rejects Robortello's explanation that the phrase ἐν τοῖς αὐτοῖς referred to the men whose actions were imitated. He declares that it should rather be interpreted as signifying the means of imitation, discourse, harmony, and the dance. Here as before he uses the word "saltum" as equivalent to Aristotle's ῥυθμός (pp. 150v–51).

On 1448b4 ff., "De causis naturalibus poeseos." Another moot point. Robortello had seen the two "natural causes" of poetry as the instinct toward imitation in man and the pleasure which he derives from imitation.

---

[72] *Emendationum libri duo* (1557), p. 148v: "Meo enim iudicio liber hic non in tres, sed in sex partes distribuendus est. primum enim non solum de definitione poeseos agit, sed etiam de origine eius, & incremento. origo autem, & incrementum nihil ad definitionem pertinent. Sequuntur deinde aliae partes, una de tragoedia, de epopoeia altera. Quinta est de quaestionibus, & dissolutionibus poeticis. quae ab eo in sua diuisione praeterita est, cum tamen à tragoedia, & epopoeia separata materia sit. extremo libro tragoediam cum epopoeia comparat. quae sexta pars appellari, cum à disputatione de tragoedia, & epopoeia auulsa sit, merito potest."

Sigonio chooses rather to adopt the position of Averroës that the two causes are (1) imitation and (2) rhythm plus harmony; one cause would thus be imitation, the other the means of imitation. Rhythm itself is dual, being composed of meter and the dance. Sigonio gives his version of Aristotle's arguments thus:

> The means indeed are three in number, comprising harmony and rhythm; for rhythm is divided into two, dance and meters. Meters, then, he says, are constituent parts of rhythms. He does not offer proof, though, that the means of imitation are natural to us, because he thought this sufficiently clear from the fact that he had proved imitation itself to be natural to us.[73]

On 1449*b*25, "'Ἡδυσμένῳ λόγῳ quid sit, non esse intellectum." Sigonio thinks that λόγῳ should be translated by "Rationem, modum" and that the whole phrase means "modo suauitatis pleno." The means he considers to be music, harmony, and rhythm, with music ("melos") having the special sense of meter (pp. 153*v*–54).

On 1449*b*25, "Quid sit χωρὶς τῶν εἰδῶν non esse intellectum." At this point, Sigonio believes, Aristotle is using "melos" in a broader sense of harmony and rhythm. He thinks that the whole passage in the definition of tragedy is meant to indicate that there were certain parts of a tragedy recited with music and dance, certain others without them (pp. 154–54*v*).

On 1450*a*10, "Partes tragoediae intellectas non esse." Rejecting Robortello's distribution of the six qualitative parts of tragedy among object, manner, and means of imitation, Sigonio proposes his own division which he defends thus:

> For the tragic poets imitate plot, character, and thought as their subject matter; they imitate with diction and song as means, and song includes harmony and rhythm. The third element, manner, is the stage onto which the actors are introduced, which Aristotle calls *ornatus aspectus*. ... the means of imitation are two, diction and song; the manner, one, embellishment of visual spectacle; the objects, three, plot, character, and thought.[74]

It would be difficult to affirm that, on the whole, Sigonio's emendations represent an advance over Robortello for the interpretation of the passages discussed. His over-all division of the text and his distribution of the qualitative parts are superior; but some of the individual exegeses move backward rather than forward.

In 1559, the *Poetics* appears in a role which it frequently played during

---

[73] *Ibid.*, p. 152*v*: "instrumenta uero tria sunt, harmonia, & rhythmus. nam rhythmus in duo diuiditur, in saltum, & metra. metra enim, inquit, particulae sunt rhythmorum. Non probat autem instrumenta imitationis esse nobis naturalia, quia satis perspicuum putauit ex eo, quòd imitationem ipsam nobis esse naturalem probauit."

[74] *Ibid.*, p. 155: "Nam tragici imitantur fabulam, mores, & sententiam, ut materiam, imitantur autem dictione, & melopoeia, ut instrumentis, melopoeia uero harmoniam, & rhythmum comprehendit. Modus autem tertius est scena, in qua agentes inducunt, quem Aristoteles uocat ornatum aspectus. ... quibus imitantur duo sunt, dictio, & melopoeia. quomodo, unum, aspectus ornatus: quae, tria, fabula, mores, & sententia."

the Cinquecento, that of a source of theory on the art of history. The document in question is Dionigi Atanagi's *Ragionamento de la eccellentia et perfettione de la historia*. Atanagi's theoretical treatment of history follows two separate lines, one emphasizing the differences between poetry and history and one displaying their similarities. It is for the first of these that Aristotle is the principal source; for the second, Atanagi refers largely to the tradition of Horace and of the rhetoricians. After a defence of the art as a means to Platonic elevation of the soul, Atanagi defines history as "a narrative of things done as they were done, with praise or with blame, according to persons, places, and times, and including the deliberations, the causes, and the events."[75] Then he proceeds to the comparison with poetry, from which I cite the salient passages:

> History is different from poetry, not because the latter is written in verse and the former in prose, as is commonly believed by those who think that everything that is written in verse is poetry. For although verse is proper to the poetic faculty, nevertheless it is not verse but imitation that makes poetry; and that this is true is shown by the fact that there are also poems which are composed in prose. . . . Therefore the true difference and divergence between them lies in this, that poetry imitates and history does not. . . . Poetry takes a single action of a single man and all its other actions are accidental. History takes several actions of several men; and although it is not denied that history also at times treats a single action . . . , nevertheless its proper function is to treat several and diverse actions. The poet concerns himself with the universal, attending to the simple and pure idea of things; the historian deals with the particular, representing things as they are, like a painter who draws from nature. The historian thus relates things done, as they were done; the poet relates them as they should be done necessarily or as they might verisimilarly and probably be done. The poet, once he has undertaken to imitate somebody, keeps him always and everywhere exactly the same as he was when first introduced. . . . The historian keeps men constant or varies them, as he takes them from life, depending on whether he finds them constant or unstable and varied. The order of poetry is certain, connected, and linked, since because of the interrelationship of its actions it makes one out of many, one toward which it directs all the others as servants and domestics serve a mistress; and this by means of the episodes, which by their nature and property always concern the plot, which is the substantial part and as it were the form and soul of the poem. The order of history is for the most part uncertain, disjoined, and fortuitous, since its actions are not similar and linked but separate and diverse; neither does one depend from another nor do they relate to a single end.[76]

---

[75] *Ragionamento* (1559), p. 3v: "La historia è una narration di cose fatte, come elle son fatte, con laude, ò con uitupero, secondo le persone, i luoghi, e i tempi, co i consigli, con le cagioni, & con gli auenimenti."

[76] *Ibid.*, pp. 4–4v: "La historia è differente de la poesia, non perche questa in uerso, & quella in prosa si scriua, come uolgarmente si crede; stimando, che tutto ciò, che in uerso è scritto, sia poesia. Percioche se bene il uerso è proprio de la poetica facoltà, nondimeno non il uerso, ma la imitatione fa la poesia, & che ciò sia uero, si ritrouano de le poesie anco in prosa tessute. . . . Adunque la uera differenza, & diuersità loro è in questo, che la poesia imita, la historia nò. . . . La poesia prende una sola attione, d'un'huomo solo, l'altre tutte

Back of each one of these comparisons there lies some principle derived from the *Poetics*. If one were to abstract from the passage the sections relevant to poetry alone, one would have a fairly complete statement of Aristotle's basic theory. But in some cases at least, this theory will have taken on a flavor peculiar to Atanagi's text, as in the indication that "necessity" refers to things as they "should be" and probability to things as they "might be." As the process of opposition continues, Atanagi breaks away from the Aristotelian text, and the basic principles become more exclusively Horatian.

It is also Horace who presides over the somewhat lengthy study of the resemblances between the two arts of poetry and history—Horace augmented by general notions derived from the rhetoricians. Both are narrative, but poetry alone uses invocation. Both practise the demonstrative and the deliberative types of rhetoric, and therefore both praise the virtues and blame the vices and both introduce consultations and speeches. Nor is the judicial type excluded, although history uses it more frequently. Both observe prudence and decorum, both wish to teach, delight, and move—and above all to produce utility. They describe many peoples, places, customs, laws, present great variations of fortune, practise digressions and many rhetorical devices. Both must attempt a visual representation of what they are saying, so as to make it live for the audience. Although he disagrees with Robortello on the matter of the classification of history and would make it a part of moral philosophy rather than of rhetoric, Atanagi seems to agree in seeing in history an art prior to poetry—whatever is true in poetry comes to it from history (pp. 4v–7v).

Atanagi's *Ragionamento* is not at all extraordinary, for the times, in its facile combination of various theoretical traditions. It is perhaps unusual in the extent to which it keeps them separate for separate purposes and in the completeness with which each is represented in a small compass.

Like Sigonio's *Emendationes*, Cristoforo Rufo's *Antexegemata*, published in Padua in 1559, is a collection of commentaries on isolated

---

sono per accidente. La historia piu, & di piu huomini; & come che non si nieghi, che la historia, anch'ella tratti alcuna uolta una attion sola . . . nondimeno il proprio officio suo è di trattar piu, & diuerse attioni. Il poeta opera intorno a l'uniuersale attendendo a la semplice, & pura idea de le cose. L'historico intorno al particolare, rappresentando le cose, come elle sono, quasi pittor, che ritragga dal naturale. L'historico adunque narra le cose fatte, come elle son fatte. Il poeta le narra, ò come elle dourebbono necessariamente, ò come elle potrebbono uerisimilmente, & probabilmente esser fatte. Il poeta, poi che s'ha proposto la imitatione d'alcuno, egli il mantien sempre, & per tutto in quel modo stesso, che egli l'ha da prima introdotto. . . . L'historico come prende gli huomini, cosi ò gli mantiene, ò gli uaria, secondo che gli truoua, ò costanti, ò instabili, & uariati. L'ordine de la poesia è certo, congiunto, & concatenato, percioche ella per l'affinità de le attioni ne fa una di molte, a la quale come a donna indirizza tutte l'altre, come ministre, & seruenti, & cio col mezzo de gli episodij, i quali di loro natura, & proprietà sempre riguardano a la fauola, che è la parte sostantiale, & quasi la forma, & l'anima del poema. L'ordine de la historia il più è incerto, disgiunto, & a caso, percioche le attioni in essa non sono simili, nè congiunte, ma separate, & diuerse: ne l'una dipende da l'altra: ne risguardano ad un medesimo fine."

passages. They are largely linguistic and philological in character, although some do represent interpretations of texts. As they relate to the *Poetics*, they state disagreements with such earlier commentators as Robortello and Maggi.

On 1456*b*3, ἀπὸ τῶν αὐτῶν εἰδῶν. The initial difficulty at this point results from the text, which is still defective. For the reading which he had, Rufo disagreed with Robortello's version, "ad naturam rerum," and proposed instead "ex iisdem earum rerum propriis locis." His whole interpretation of the passage reads as follows: "I think that he meant that, whenever the occasion presents itself in tragedies and comedies ... for compassion to be aroused or a certain horror produced or for something to be amplified or proved or made acceptable to the mind, all these things should be derived from the very situations proper to these actions."[77]

On 1456*b*8, εἰ φανοῖτο ἡδέα. Again, difficulties of text, and Rufo supports his own reading against that of Maggi. He interprets the passage (which still gives difficulty) as meaning that there must be a difference between the language of tragedy and that of oratory. His commentary throws light on his conceptions of both arts:

> It has been said, indeed, that in order to arouse the emotions of the soul, the tragic poet may seek his arguments in the same places in which the orator seeks them. But there should be a certain difference between them; for it is indispensable that the art of the tragic poet should be most secret and that his words should not reek of precepts or of doctrine. But in the orator it is proper that the art and the teaching should be clear, in such a way that by the force of oratory what he says has manifest luster and is set out in a clear light. Indeed, what function will the orator be judged to have served if some things seem to be pleasantly and agreeably expressed and delivered, but if his speech nevertheless is not judged to be productive of this pleasure?[78]

The comparison of the two arts and the notion that tragedy secretly works toward the same moral ends are of interest here.

On 1451*b*29, κἂν ἄρα συμβῇ γενόμενα ποιεῖν. The disagreement is again with Robortello, on the question of whether the poet may imitate events which have actually happened and still remain a poet. Rufo judges that he may, providing that such events satisfy his criteria of verisimilitude and probability (p. G7).

---

[77] *Antexegemata* (1559), pp. G5–G5v: "voluisse censeo, si quando contingat, vt in tragoediis & comoediis ... misericordia mouenda sit, aut horror quidam incutiendus, aut amplificandum, aut probandum & suadendum aliquid, ex iisdem earum rerum propriis locis eae res omnes comparandae erunt."

[78] *Ibid.*, p. G6: "Dictum quidem est ad ciendas animi motiones ex iisdem locis peti argumenta posse a tragico, ex quibus a rhetorico petuntur. ceterùm inter vtrunque debet interesse, quòd tragici ars sit occultissima oportet, nec praecepta aut doctrinam aliquam redoleant eius dicta. At in oratore artem & doctrinam conspicuam esse decet, ita vt constet vi denique orationis ea, quae dicat, splendescere atque illuminari. Etenim quodnam munus praestitisse censebitur orator, si suauiter aliqua & iucundè expressa elataque fuisse appareant, eius tamen suauitatis non iudicetur effectrix oratio?"

On 1453a32, καὶ τελευτῶσα ἐξ ἐναντίας τοῖς βελτίοσι καί χείροσιν. Rufo interprets the passage as meaning that the great and praiseworthy men in the *Odyssey* undergo a fate opposite to that of the wicked (p. G7v).

On 1453b13, ἐν τοῖς πράγμασιν ἐμποιητέον. Rufo insists that the pleasure of tragedy must come from the action itself and not from the spectacle (p. G8).

On 1461b23, ἢ ὡς βλαβερά. Robortello is again rejected, since Rufo believes that Aristotle meant by βλαβερά those things which are harmful to morality (p. Hv).

On 1462b13, φανερὸν ὅτι κρείττων ἂν εἴη μᾶλλον. This time it is with Maggi that Rufo disagrees, denying that Aristotle wished to indicate a superiority of tragedy over epic in the achievement of the end proposed (p. H2).

On 1452b11, πάθος δ'ἐστὶ πρᾶξις φθαρτική. Robortello's translation of πάθος as "perturbatio" and his reference of the passage to the spectators are contested. Rufo declares instead that Aristotle meant to refer to the personages of the tragedy and to some extreme ill that they might suffer (p. I3).

On 1453a9, ἀλλὰ δι' ἁμαρτίαν τινά, τῶν ἐν μεγάλῃ δόξῃ ὄντων καὶ εὐτυχίᾳ. Disagreeing again with Robortello, Rufo interprets the passage as meaning that the tragic hero must be of those "who enjoy great fame and a prosperous and abundant fortune" ("qui magna sunt in opinione, lautaque & secunda fortuna," p. I5).

Rufo's work belongs to the long and slow process concerned with improving the text of the *Poetics* and especially with suggesting, passage by passage, better interpretations. His suggestions are sometimes more acceptable than those of his predecessors, and this alone gives him a certain distinction in the elaboration of the process.

VETTORI (1560)

In 1560, Pietro Vettori published the third of the "great commentaries" on the *Poetics*, the *Commentarii in primum librum Aristotelis de arte poetarum*. (The phrase "in primum librum" appeared traditionally in such titles because of the assumption that additional books, now lost, had once existed and had contained Aristotle's theory of comedy and of the other genres.) Vettori's work followed the usual plan: the Greek text, divided into small fragments—there are two hundred and twelve of them in Vettori's division—was given first, followed by a translation into Latin, followed by Vettori's commentary on each fragment. Vettori's Greek text was the best to date, based as it was upon the available editions and upon an ancient manuscript (Vahlen believes that it was the Parisinus gr. 1741[9]); his Latin translation was also his own. In a general way, he was more interested in the philological and textual questions raised by the *Poetics* than his prede-

---

[9] Vahlen (1885 ed.), p. viii.

cessors had been, less interested consequently in imposing a poetic theory of his own upon the reading of Aristotle. Much of the commentary is exclusively linguistic; certain of his questions and suggestions have been taken up by modern editors. For example, his doubts about the position in the text of 1452*b*14–31 were later shared by Ritter and subsequent scholars.

It is perhaps because of this close philological attention to the text that Vettori is frequently more faithful to the spirit of the *Poetics* than were his contemporaries. Early in the text for example, in connection with 1448*b*19 on the natural origins of poetry, he summarizes these two natural sources as (1) the instinct to imitate and (2) the pleasure which men derive from imitation. He makes of the naturalness of rhythm and harmony a third cause (p. 34), whereas Maggi (p. 71) had insisted that this was one of the two sources indicated by Aristotle (Robortello [p. 30] had earlier rejected this last interpretation, which he had found in Averroës). At 1449*a*30, Vettori insists that both comedy and tragedy imitate "the actions of men" (p. 47), departing from the positions of Lombardi and Maggi, who defined imitation as "the expression of the actions, characters, and passions of human beings,"[80] and of Averroës, who held that poetry was an "imitation of Nature" (fol. fv). A really significant difference from Robortello and Maggi is found in Vettori's assignment of the qualitative parts of tragedy to object, manner, and means. It will be remembered that the two earlier commentators had placed plot under manner, spectacle and song under means, and diction, character, and thought under the objects.[81] Vettori, commenting on 1450*a*8, correctly distributes diction and song to the means, spectacle to the manner, and plot, character, and thought to the objects (p. 62). In other less extensive developments, he shows proper insights into the meaning of the text: in connection with the definition of tragedy, 1449*b*23, he sees clearly that the purgation included by Aristotle constitutes the "end" of tragedy (p. 56); in connection with Aristotle's criticism of the character of Menelaus in Euripides' *Orestes* (1454*a*29), he shows correctly that the "plot could very well have been brought to conclusion without the dishonoring of so great a hero; ... indeed, the plot was not established in the beginning in such a way that this would be the necessary consequence."[82] What is interesting here is that Vettori understands clearly Aristotle's criticism as based on structural considerations; he does not criticize the character because it failed to follow the traditional portrayal, as later critics frequently did (cf. Castelvetro [1576 ed.], p. 327). Such passages as these demonstrate a comprehension of some of the basic orientations of the *Poetics*.

All of Vettori's interpretations are not, however, so fortunate as these. In

[80] Maggi and Lombardi, *Explanationes* (1550), p. 34.
[81] See above, chap. ix, pp. 394 and 416.
[82] *Commentarii* (1560), p. 146: "sine tanta nanque clari viri turpitudine fabula ad exitum commodè perduci poterat. ... neque enim à principio res ita constitutae fuerant, vt hoc inde sequi necesse foret."

many cases, the force of the tradition as already established is irresistible, and he makes repeated and ingenious attempts to fit Aristotle's text into that tradition. The most notable example of this effort is found in Vettori's remarks, throughout the commentary, on the relationship between poetry and verse. His basic and immutable contention is that verse is necessary for poetry, and he bends his interpretation of the *Poetics*, at numerous places, to justify that contention. This is done for the first time in the remarks on λόγοις ψιλοῖς at 1447a29; Vettori states his position:

> In order to declare completely how I feel about this matter, I hold that one of those elements which make true poets of some men is metrical discourse. Nobody can call himself a poet in the proper sense of the word, even if he imitates and expresses what he wishes in an excellent fashion, unless he uses this form of discourse.[83]

There would thus seem to be, for Vettori, three indispensable elements of poetry: imitation, verse, and excellent expression. On the basis of this assumption he condemns those modern writers of comedy who have written it in prose (p. 12). Consonant with the same position, Vettori interprets the ἡδυσμένῳ in the definition of tragedy (1449b25) as implying meter—"numerum concentum & metrum" (p. 55). He argues again, in connection with 1450b13, that the passage confirms his earlier thesis that poetic diction necessarily involves verse (p. 77).

A second example of Vettori's yielding to tradition may be found in his wish to reduce poetics to a kind of rhetoric. There are many examples of this, but perhaps the position may be sufficiently clear if we examine those passages treating the end of poetry with respect to its audience. The first occurs in the commentary on the first sentence of the *Poetics*, where Vettori says that the species of poetry were invented "to purge us of the vices and to delight us."[84] The statement becomes more distinctly rhetorical when, in the definition of tragedy, he states that purgation is achieved in tragedy by "putting before our eyes misfortunes which necessarily move our souls."[85] Specifically, purgation is said to be an answer to Plato's banishment of the poets for their moving of the passions:

> Aristotle, on the contrary, judges that these feelings are useful if they are moderated. Nevertheless, since at times they could spill over in such a way as to be completely irrepressible, it is necessary to provide a remedy for this evil. The remedy is found when somebody purges them in advance and takes away from them what is excessive in quantity and dangerous. This is done most conspicu-

---

[83] *Ibid.*, p. 12: "Vt autem penitus, quod sentio, de hac re, testificer, arbitror alterum eorum, quae reddunt aliquos propriè poetas, esse orationem metricam. nec posse quempiam vere vocari poëtam, quamuis imitetur: eximieque exprimat, quod vult, nisi vtatur hac oratione"; cf. p. 18: "primo ipsum λόγον cum dixit, poeticam orationem, id est certis mensuris illigatam intellexisse"; and p. 23, where Vettori claims that prose is not acceptable for the poet: "remotamque ipsam penitus existimo ab officio poëtae." Also p. 52.

[84] *Ibid.*, p. 2: "cum inuentae sint nobis à vitijs purgandis atque oblectandis."

[85] *Ibid.*, p. 56: "ponens ante oculos casus, qui necessario moueant animos nostros."

ously indeed by tragedy, which sets bounds to all the passions and teaches how far one may go. In fact, tragedy devotes itself to this end and heals the violence and the outbreak of all the passions by means of two of them which it arouses and moderates through the actions which it presents on the stage, i.e., by means of pity and fear.[86]

Moreover, the verbs used in later repetitions of these formulas are ones constantly found in rhetorical treatises: "ad timorem *iniiciendum*, & ad misericordiam *mouendam* accommodatos," "ad metum *iniiciendum*, & ad misericordiam in animis spectatorum *excitandam*" (p. 101); "timoremque magnum *incutere* animis eorum" (p. 134). So for the parts of tragedy. Recognition and reversal make for tragedies which "vehementer *capiant* animos hominum, ac *ducant* ipsos *quò velint*" (p. 69); spectacle "*allicit* ad se animos" and has power to "*capere* sine dubio animos spectatorum" (p. 78). The need for verisimilitude is dictated by the fact that both tragedy and comedy must "sumere materiam... *aptam ad persuadendum*" (p. 96); their actions are those which "magis *aptae* sint *ad persuadendum*" (p. 97). Vettori states the whole position very clearly in this passage, again in connection with verisimilitude: "In fact, the end of the poets is to obtain the belief of the listeners; for which reason poets must adapt themselves to their judgment and express those things which are apt to persuade."[87]

These rhetorical orientations are apparent in Vettori's theory of the nature of the poet's audience and of its expectations. The audience of tragedy is made up of "the multitude seated in the theater" (p. 183). The poet must strive to please it: "I say that nothing must be brought upon the stage which would go counter to the wish and the desires of the spectators. Since the poets seek to please them, the very opposite effect would result [from any such unacceptable materials]."[88] The poet must strive to move it in various ways; he will use surprise "to provoke in the minds of those who hear this marveling and this fear";[89] he will use episodes for the sake of elegance and pleasure (p. 244) and especially to avoid monotony and tedium for the spectator (p. 251). Above all, he will use probable materials in order to gain credibility: "For the poetic art is in subjection to the beliefs of the listeners, and it attempts to insinuate itself, with every

---

[86] *Ibid.*, p. 56: "contra vero Aristoteles iudicat motus hos temperatos esse utiles: veruntamen quia aliquando ita effunderentur, vt nulla ui reprimi possent, opus esse huic malo remedium adhibere: remedium autem esse, si quis antea ipsos purget, ac quod nimium importunumque est in illis, tollat. Hoc verò praeclare facere tragoediam, quae modum adhibet omnibus perturbationibus: docetque quatenus progrediendum sit: ipsa enim incumbit huic rei, & curat impetum, exultantiamque perturbationum omnium ope duarum, quas factis, quae in scenam inducit, excitat, moderaturque, id est misericordiae & metus."

[87] *Ibid.*, p. 260: "finis enim poëtarum est adipisci assensum eorum qui audiunt: quare accommodare se debent ad eorum iudicia, & ea proferre, quae sint apta ad persuadendum."

[88] *Ibid.*, p. 122: "nihil inquam afferri debere in scenam, quod contra voluntatem & desideria sit spectatorum: cum enim poëtae placere studeant ipsis, contrarium inde penitus sequeretur."

[89] *Ibid.*, p. 163: "efficere in animis eorum qui audiunt hanc admirationem ac pauorem."

means possible, into their minds, seizing upon all means useful for this purpose and rejecting their opposites."[90]

The rhetorical bent expresses itself, finally, in Vettori's emphasis upon a special poetic diction. We have seen earlier that he regards this as one of the distinguishing features of the art and as necessarily involving the use of verse. In his commentary on 1450*b*13, he specifically states that diction is not the same for prose and for poetry: "... not all words are proper in the same way to both kinds; for the poets have certain words which are properly their own, which are only little used in prose."[91] When this demand for verse and a special diction is reduced to terms of the poet's genius, it becomes its distinctive quality, "since it is proper to the poetic faculty to embellish diction with words and to bring to it all the beauties of this kind."[92] In certain parts of the poem, then, as Aristotle suggests, the poet will cultivate all the "flowers" and "beauties" of diction.

Besides the insistence on verse and the tendency toward rhetorical interpretation, a certain number of miscellaneous elements appear in Vettori as a result of the prevalent critical tradition. For one thing, he interprets Aristotle's "better, like, or worse" as meaning "better than men of our times [nostra aetate], or worse, or similar" (p. 20; cf. "nunc" on p. 22). In connection with character, again, the personages of tragedy are said to be those of highest birth while comic persons are of middling condition (p. 24); the nature of the tragic hero is clarified in this later passage:

... he should not be a man of the people, or some lowly person, but one of the number of those who have a great name and are rich and favored by fortune with all advantages. This is not in opposition to the fact that he [Aristotle] does not wish this same person to be provided with an extraordinary virtue. For he approves his being excellent in praise and in esteem, even though honor and glory are usually the companions of virtue. Indeed, he is speaking in terms of the judgment of the multitudes, who admire the appearance of virtue more than virtue itself and false more than true glory.[93]

Vettori's distinctions among characters are social, whereas Aristotle's had been moral. Similarly, Aristotle's four requisites for character take on the contemporary meaning: "good" becomes morally good ("for this is useful to life, for those who watch, when they see these qualities praised in

[90] *Ibid.*, p. 291: "seruit enim ars poëtarum opinionibus eorum qui audiunt: studetque insinuare se omni ratione, qua potest, in animos ipsorum, captans quidquid ad hoc aptum est, reiiciensque contraria."

[91] *Ibid.*, p. 77: "quamuis non omnia verba eodem pacto conueniant vtrique generi: habent enim poëtae sua quaedam propriaque verba, quae non magnopere vsurpantur in prosa."

[92] *Ibid.*, p. 264: "Cum facultatis poëtarum sit ornare verbis orationem: omnesque huiuscemodi concinnitates adhibere."

[93] *Ibid.*, p. 123: "ut non sit vnus e populo, & obscura aliqua persona, sed è numero eorum aliquis, quorum magnum nomen est: quique opulenti sint, atque à fortuna omnibus commodis ornati. Non repugnat autem, quod ipsum uirtute aliqua praestanti praeditum esse non vult: eundem tamen laude & existimatione excellentem probat, quamuis uirtutis comes honor ac gloria plerunque sit: loquitur enim ex opinione multitudinis, quae admiratur magis imaginem uirtutis, atque inanem, quàm veram gloriam."

POETIC THEORY

the plot and accepted with approval, are impelled to imitate those deeds which spring from these characters, and they try to become just such persons"[94]); "appropriate" refers to decorum and such considerations as the sex of the personage; "like" means like the characters of the century being depicted; and "constant" means self-consistent (pp. 144–45).

For matters other than character, also, Vettori calls upon traditional interpretations. The meanings assigned by Aristotle to "imitation" are crossed with those found in Plato, and true imitation is identified with the dramatic manner (p. 26). Tragedy is said to "purge" other passions besides pity and fear (p. 57), and thus the notion of an effect proper to a given genre is lost. All statements concerning necessity and probability reveal that these are understood in the context of nature; thus a man wounded in the heart "necessarily" dies (p. 81) and things which could "probably" happen are those which common opinion admits to be such (p. 94).

On the whole, while it cannot be said that Vettori presents a general theory of poetics at variance with that of Aristotle—I think indeed that there is no general theory contained in his commentary—it is nevertheless true that many individual interpretations derive from current thinking about poetry rather than from insights into the *Poetics* itself. However, Vettori makes many contributions to the text and to the translation, his remarks are sometimes original and acceptable, and the very fact that he does not impose upon Aristotle a total theory of his own is perhaps a distinguishing quality of his work.

Little need be added to what has already been said (Chapter V, pp. 156–57) about Pietro Angeli's *In Quintij Horatij de arte poetica librum annotationes*, except to put it in chronological place (around 1560) among the commentaries on Horace which made use of the *Poetics*. Angeli, as his references to Aristotle indicate, used one of the editions of Vettori's commentary; but these references do not permit us to determine exactly whether it was that of 1560 or that of 1573. If it were the latter, then of course our treatment of him here and in Chapter V would have to be moved to a later date.

PIGNA (1561)

Like Angeli's work, Pigna's *Poetica Horatiana* of 1561 is a commentary on the *Ars poetica*; but it is a full-scale one, presenting on each one of the eighty "precepts" found in Horace a lengthy explanatory remark. The correspondences which Pigna found between Horace and Aristotle have already been summarized (Chapter V, pp. 160–61); at the present time we may look more closely at the particular construction which Pigna puts upon the *Poetics*. As might be expected, there are many points at which his

---

[94] *Ibid.*, p. 143: "hoc enim uitae prodest, nam qui spectant cum haec in fabulis laudari, plausuque excipi vident, ad ea facta imitanda excitantur, quae ab illis moribus proueniunt: conantúrque & ipsi tales euadere."

references to Aristotle give no hint as to how he understood him. Such, for example, are his remarks on language (pp. 10, 12, 23) and on meter (p. 32) and his distinction between artistic and nonartistic errors (p. 16). But there are three broad subjects on which Pigna offers a rather extensive interpretation of the *Poetics*: (1) imitation, (2) necessity and probability, and (3) character.

The passages on imitation concern everything from the nature of imitation itself to the six qualitative parts of tragedy. Commenting on the first lines of Horace, Pigna avers that poetry and painting are both imitations and that both, seeking beauty, treat the better, the like, and the worse (p. 2). The object of imitation is defined as one action of one man; the reason is that "we must judge in the case of a poem as we do in human affairs, in which our understanding embraces a single action more readily than when it is directed towards several ends."[95] The magnitude of a poem (p. 56) is similarly related to our capacity for understanding—the whole must not surpass our ability to remember—as well as to our willingness to attend to it—the whole must not be negligibly small. In a general way, different objects of imitation produce different effects, and this gives the basis for the distinction among the genres: tragedy produces horror, comedy wit, and the epic admiration. The effect of each genre is proper to itself; but somehow (since this is a commentary on Horace) the effect of tragedy becomes identified with its utilitarian end. Pity and terror are aroused and the minds of the spectators are "purified" of them:

> ... [tragedy] does not purge for the reason that we become [in consequence] more circumspect and that those emotions teach us the tragedy of human life and repress the pride in our individual lives, but rather because, while we are attracted by that spectacle, our wearied mind is refreshed and ceases its burdensome thoughts; so the soul throws off every care and so it is purified.[96]

Whatever Aristotelian elements there might be in these topics related to imitation are stated, more so than in Aristotle, in terms of effects upon the audience.

Much more closely related to the text of the *Poetics* is what Pigna has to say about necessity and probability, although such a reference as the first one—"They [the digressions] will be coherent whenever they are necessary or probable"[97]—is little more than an allusion to a vague current generalization. His main treatment of the matter concerns Horace's "sixtieth precept" (ll. 338–40), where he finds Horace saying that verisimilitude is a

---

[95] *Poetica Horatiana* (1561), p. 8: "Ita uerò in poemate statuendum, vt in rebus humanis, in quibus vna actio contemplatione nostra commodius amplectitur, quàm si plures fines posceret."

[96] *Ibid.*, p. 76: "non purgat, quia cautiores, euadamus: & permotiones illae nos humanae vitae calamitatem edoceant, & superbiam nostrae premant. Sed quia dum illo attrahimur spectaculo, aegra mens reficitur, & cessat à duris cogitationibus: ita vt animus omni solicitudine exuatur: itaque purgetur."

[97] *Ibid.*, p. 5: "Erunt autem cohęrentia, quoties aut necessaria, aut verisimilia."

condition of our pleasure as spectators. This accounts for Aristotle's statement that the impossible verisimilar is preferable to the incredible true. Pigna identifies Aristotle's necessity with Horace's verisimilitude; but his gloss on *Poetics* 1451a37 shows that he himself is thinking of necessary and contingent actions:

> Indeed those words καὶ τὰ δυνατὰ κατὰ τὸ εἰκὸς ἢ τὸ ἀναγκαῖον must be understood in this sense: that εἰκὸς is used for the contingent and ἀναγκαῖον for the necessary; and εἰκὸς is not distinguished because it is verisimilar, but because it is proper to things which may either happen or not happen. Indeed δυνατὰ at that point are verisimilar things, and of these some are contingent, others necessary. For at times the truth is necessary, as in history, at times verisimilitude, as in poetry.[98]

The terms of the *Poetics* are thus interpreted in the light of other theories of Aristotle, not in the light of his poetic theory. It might be appropriate at this point to indicate that Pigna frequently refers to other works of the Aristotelian corpus: to the *Rhetoric*, the *Ethics*, the *Politics*, the *Posterior Analytics*, the *Meteorologica*.

The most extensive and detailed treatment of materials from the *Poetics*, however, is given in connection with character. Following Aristotle, Pigna states that both character and passions are derived from plot; but Aristotle's four requisites for character are justified in terms of verisimilitude, consistent with Pigna's general position. A special schematism is provided for the relationship of the four requisites to verisimilitude and to the separate poetic genres. First, verisimilitude is divided into two kinds, one for things which are easily believed, the other for things which are believed with difficulty. The former includes known things, and the requisite for it is propriety, in itself or by comparison; the latter includes unknown things, and the requisite for it is resemblance, in itself or by comparison. Thus the following diagram results:

	facile		*difficile*	
	quod decet		similitudo	
	(notioris)		(ignotius)	
per se	in collatione		per se	in collatione
χρηστόν	ἁρμόττον		ὁμαλόν	ὅμοιον
	(personarum qualitas)		(similes)	(opinione)

Verisimile

It then follows that Aristotle's χρηστόν would be the appropriateness of a woman's character to her nature as a woman, and his ἁρμόττον would be the appropriateness of the same character as compared with that of a child

---

[98] *Ibid.*, p. 79: "nam verba illa καὶ τὰ δυνατὰ κατὰ τὸ εἰκὸς, ἢ τὸ ἀναγκαῖον ita sunt intelligenda vt εἰκὸς dicatur de contingenti, & ἀναγκαῖον de necessario, atque εἰκὸς non distinguitur; quia sit uerisimile, sed quia sit de eis, quae possint accidere, & non accidere. Siquidem δυνατὰ ibi sunt uerisimilia. quorum alia contingentia alia necessaria: est enim necessarium modo uerum, vt in historia: modo verisimile, ut in poesi."

or of a woman from another country. Aristotle's ὁμαλόν is consistency of character with itself throughout the work, whereas his ὅμοιον demands the resemblance of such a personage as a prince to the character which opinion ascribes to him. Pigna believes that the first quality, χρηστόν, is mentioned only to make the distinction exhaustive, "for we never consider any person in action by himself."[99] With respect to ὁμαλόν and ὅμοιον, Pigna sees them as serving different genres. In such poems as tragedy and the epic, ὅμοιον must be observed, since the heroes are traditional; but this is not true for comedy, where all persons are invented and where hence only ὁμαλόν applies (pp. 46–47). Both qualities, moreover, are needed by the orator and the historian. At a later point, finally, commenting on Horace, lines 153–60, Pigna affirms that ἁρμόττον must be considered especially with respect to the age of characters and that this is the most difficult of all its applications (p. 53).

Many of the same principles appear in Pigna's *Gli heroici*, also published in 1561; indeed, the second work constitutes a clarification of the first insofar as its dealing with concrete cases provides examples of the principles. *Gli heroici* is a short treatise meant to introduce and explain Pigna's own heroic poem on the fall of Alfonso da Este in a tournament; the poem follows in the same volume. His choice of the subject was dictated, he says, by the fact that it contained in their proper form the "seven circumstances of all civil operations": a person, an action, relationship to great persons, an instrument, a place and occasion, a mode for the action, and an end (pp. 9–10). As a heroic poem, or an epic, this work will possess some qualities common to all poetry, some features peculiar to the epic, and some characteristics which it will share with the related form of tragedy. So for the most part the statement that it contains "one single action of one illustrious person" is general in its application, except that the "illustrious" relates it specifically to tragedy and the epic (p. 11). Similarly, the particular relationship of his *Heroico* to truth classes it among the serious genres:

> ... this imitation consists in "coloring" a verisimilar thing upon a true one. In comedy and in certain other poems it is sufficient that the thing should be said in a verisimilar way, even if there is no truth present. But in heroic poetry ... and in tragedy it is necessary to have a foundation of some true thing, since it is not reasonable that a great event should have occurred to some great and famous gentleman without being widely known.[100]

In Pigna's poem, the true event is the fall of Alfonso from his horse; the verisimilar consequence is that the guardian angels, headed by Mars,

---

[99] *Ibid.*, p. 45: "nunquam tamen personam vllam in actionibus solam consideramus."
[100] *Gli heroici* (1561), p. 11: "questo imitare è sopra una cosa uera colorire una uerisimile. nella comedia & in certi altri Poemi basta che la cosa si dica uerisimilmente, ancora che non ui sia uerità alcuna. ma nella Poesia Heroica che in un sol nome è detta Epopeia & nella tragedia è necessario che ui sia il fondamento di cosa uera. non essendo ragioneuole, che sia occorso un gran fatto di qualche gran Signore segnalato che diuolgato non si sia."

POETIC THEORY

should have interceded with God for his life. This latter action constitutes the "imitation." It will be noted that the action as described contains elements both of tragedy and of the epic: first, there is a mutation of fortune which relates it to tragedy; second, there is a perfecting of the actual events which relate them to the epic. The emotional effects are equally mixed: pity and terror accompanied by the desire for honor (on the part of common men) and the desire for magnanimity (on the part of the great). "And thus in addition to the emulation of illustrious actions, which will be the principal passion, pity and fear will touch our hearts every time we read a heroic poem having tragic elements."[101] Finally, the action combines elements of the active and the contemplative lives; the active life is more proper to illustrious persons, the other to private citizens. Thus Pigna's poem leans more towards the active, which is both heroic and tragic (pp. 65–66).

Tragedy differs from epic in the limits of time, and these in turn are imposed by the willingness of the audience to believe:

... the epic is longer than tragedy, since the accidents of things of this world may change all of a sudden, so that these may easily be contained in the space of one day. And they thus become useful for the stage, which does not admit too much passage of time since it is not proper that an action of many days should be represented in four hours.... And since a man may not, in so short a time, show that he has something divine in him, nor can he in one single day give an account of his greatness of soul, not less than a month is required to set forth the life of a great prince. This is not too long, since a composition made in this way is to be read, not to be listened to by a waiting spectator.[102]

The nature of the action itself and the circumstances of its presentation to an audience will thus determine whether it is fit for epic or for tragedy. Regardless of the genre, the poet uses certain devices, common also to the orator, to present his materials; these are such rhetorical means as the enthymeme, the example, the deduction, the conclusion. These are all adapted to the capacities of the audience: "One considers men in general, insofar as these must be able to comprehend what is contained in the poem."[103]

It is clear from what Pigna says in the three books of *Gli heroici* that theory has been made to serve two purposes, to provide the basis of the

[101] *Ibid.*, p. 14: "Et cosi ancora oltre alla emulatione delle attioni illustri, che sarà l'affetto principale, la pietà & lo spauento, ci toccheranno il cuore, ogni uolta che leggiamo una Poesia Heroica, c'habbia del tragico." V. p. 76.

[102] *Ibid.*, p. 14: "è piu lunga l'Epopeia della tragedia: perche gli accidenti delle cose del mondo possono uariare in un subito di modo, che essi si rinchiudono facilmente nello spatio d'un giorno: & uengono a seruire alla scena che non comporta troppo tempo per non essere il douere che una attione di molte giornate sia rappresentata in quattro hore.... Et perche non cosi tosto l'huomo dimostra hauer del diuino, ne puo in un di solo dar conto del suo grand'animo, non ui uuol meno d'un mese a dichiarare la uita d'un sopremo Principe. il che non è di troppo lunghezza douendosi leggere cosi fatto componimento, & non stare ad udirlo come spettatore."

[103] *Ibid.*, p. 23: "si riguarda l'uniuersale de gli huomini: in quanto che essi hanno da esser capaci di cio che si contiene nel Poema."

poem itself and to justify, after the fact, certain features of that same poem. In this way the "theoretical application" of Aristotle's *Poetics* is two-edged. But it is at best a vague and general application, since most of the Aristotelian principles taken over are now hardly recognizable. One is aware of their presence in certain formulas, and one realizes that they are there especially because one has seen them earlier in the *Poetica Horatiana*.

MARANTA (1561)

In 1561 also, but some time after the publication of the *Poetica Horatiana*, Bartolomeo Maranta undertook to expound the *Ars poetica* to the members of the Accademia Napoletana; the lectures are now found in MS R.126.Sup. of the Biblioteca Ambrosiana.[104] If these discourses have a place in the present chapter, it is because Maranta seeks to cast some fresher light on the interpretation of Horace by referring at length to the *Poetics*. He concerns himself only with the first two "precepts" of Horace, which he interprets as treating the relationship between plot and episodes. The interpretations of Robortello, Maggi, Vettori, and Pigna are all rejected as inadequate. Instead, Maranta suggests that we must define carefully the meanings of "plot" ("favola") and "episode." Plot, he says, has three meanings in Aristotle; it is, first,

> ... one formal part among the six. ... it does not differ at all from the universal except in the addition of names; for the universal, the plot, and the principal action of the whole poem are all one and the same thing. ... In the second way, plot is the same thing as the tragedy or the comedy or the epic or any other poem, that is, the whole aggregate of the universal and of the episodes. ... The third way of the plot is that which concerns the action proper ... ; in this meaning plot is restricted solely to the true episodes, that is, to all that part of the poem which begins from the first chorus and ends in the last chorus.[105]

Maranta's disagreement with his predecessors consists in the fact that they regard episodes as external to the action, whereas he can admit of no part of the poem as external to the unifying plot. The distinction he makes is between episodes which belong to the general "story" and those which are integral to the plot; he has this to say about plot and episodes in the *Aeneid*:

> In this way, we can say that the universal contains within itself a sum of epi-

---

[104] See my article, "Bartolomeo Maranta: nuovi manoscritti di critica letteraria," *Annali della Scuola Normale di Pisa*, Serie II, XXIV (1955), 115–25, for the dates of these discourses and the attendant circumstances. The MS now being discussed is No. VI in the article mentioned.

[105] MS Ambr. R.126.Sup., fols. 128v–29: "una parte formale delle sei ... non differisce punto dall'vniuersale se non per la aggiuntione de nomj. perche l'vniuersale la fauola, e la principal attione di tutto il poema sono tutte una cosa medesima. ... Nella 2ª maniera Fauola è quello medesimo che la Tragedia o uero la comedia o la epopeia o altro poema cioè tutto l'aggregato della vniuersale e delli episodij. ... La terza maniera della Fauola e quella che uersa circa la attione propria ... in questo significato la fauola si ristrigne solo nelli ueri episodij cioè in tutta quella parte del poema che comincia dal primo coro et finisce nell'ultimo coro."

sodes, considering, however, those episodes which truly belong to the principal action of the whole poem, but not to the plot which the poet has undertaken principally to write. And these episodes are the most appropriate when taken from within the action for they are like a part of the principal action and they are truly necessary; the others are indeed drawn from within, but they are not considered as parts of the principal action.[106]

In these passages, Maranta seems to be distinguishing one kind of plot which contains the whole of a story in general terms and the episodes proper to it; a second kind which specifies this story in terms of a single action and named characters, and the episodes proper to it; and, finally, plot as a qualitative part of a tragedy or an epic. In the last sense, the "episodes" are the sections between the choruses of a tragedy, for example.

The preceding remarks constitute the substance of Maranta's second discourse. In the third, he repeats Aristotle's recommendation that the poet find the universal plot, the "modello," then add names to it, then supply the episodes. The dominant principle of construction is unity and the plot must be so knit that the removal of any episode would spoil the whole structure. Unity must exist independently of episodes. There seems to be some wavering and inconsistency when, later in the same discourse, Maranta declares that the episode is a quantitative part (adding "volume" to the poem) and that as such its addition to plot constitutes a combining of formal and quantitative elements. In the fourth discourse, Maranta gives further details on the definition and use of episodes. The episode, he says, "does nothing else but extend and augment the plot and the universal by telling how what is summarized in the universal has come about. ... its nature and its end is none other than to tell the way in which the complication and the solution of the plot are brought about."[107] The plot is thus the "immutable, invariable, eternal" story, the episodes are the variations which a poet can bring to that story. It is clear that Maranta is here speaking in terms of traditional, accepted stories and of their particular treatment by successive poets.

The fifth and sixth discourses do little more than repeat and expand the discussion of the same materials. In its totality, the manuscript belabors in a repetitious and monotonous way Maranta's ideas about plot and episode. But this is perhaps its chief worth. For it gives very extended consideration to what he considers to be the most important aspect of the poetic art, and

[106] *Ibid.*, fols. 129v–30: "A questo modo noi potremo dire che l'uniuersale contenghi dentro di se somma di Episodij pigliando pero quelli episodij che sono ben del fatto principale di tutto il poema ma non della fauola presa principalmente a scriuersi dal poeta; Et questi episodij sono gli più proprij presi da dentro l'attione perche sono como parte della attione principale; et sono ueri necessarij: li altri si ducono bene da dentro ma non hanno consideratione di parti della principale attione."

[107] *Ibid.*, fol. 146v: "non fa altro che dilatare et accrescere la fauola et l'universale con dire il modo che quello che nell'universale si dice sia accaduto. ... non sia altro la sua natura et il suo ufficio senon dj dire il modo con el quale si fa la connessione et la solutione della fauola."

it seeks its solutions for this aspect in the text of the *Poetics*. Maranta's reading of Aristotle is frequently closer and more adequate than were his predecessors', although it has some notable failings. At any rate, his presentation of the lectures to the Accademia Napoletana must have seemed new and informative—if boring.

During the same months of 1561, Maranta wrote for Giovanni Villani a clarification of some of the points made in his lectures; the manuscript, in Latin, is now Ambrosianus R.118.Sup., fols. 117–24v. The additions to his statement of theory are significant. Most important of all is his rejection of the usual way of dividing and interpreting the *Ars poetica* by seeking in it the parts corresponding to invention, disposition, and elocution. His rejection is on Aristotelian grounds: "We believe that he who wishes to divide poetics must seek a division proper to it and which does not belong to any other art or any other science."[108] The distinction rejected, belonging to rhetoric, cannot be of any possible use for poetics. In its place, Maranta will try to apply the divisions of the *Poetics* to the *Ars poetica*.

[Aristotle] seems to divide the *Poetics* itself according to the variety of means by which the imitation is made. As for the imitation, indeed, having enumerated the kinds of poems, . . . and omitted the last three of these, . . . we may easily adapt it to the latter three by using a kind of similarity derived from the first three types. He divides the first three very carefully into parts. . . . Then there are two kinds of parts: some, like ideal forms or species, are present in the whole of the poem and can be revealed in it rather in potentiality than in actuality, whence they are properly called "potentials," if I may use that term. . . . The others are the parts which Aristotle calls quantitative because they divide the same poems into parts "actually" existing; these have also come to be called "integrating" parts since by means of them the body of the poem is brought together and made into a whole, just as the body of an animal by means of the members. . . . A perfect master of poets must reveal all these six parts one by one, which is what Horace indeed accomplishes, albeit not in the same order that Aristotle used.[109]

The consideration of the first qualitative part, plot, brings Maranta back to his constant theme: the discussion of "fabula," of the conditions for unity, and of episodes. Here he makes another important remark, too

---

[108] MS Ambr. R.118.Sup., fol. 117v: "Oportere autem eum qui poeticam partiri cupiat propriam, et quae nulli praeterea arti aut scientiae conueniat, diuisionem quaerere existimauimus."

[109] *Ibid.*, fols. 118–18v: "poeticam ipsam a uarietate instrumentorum quibus imitatio perficitur partiri uidetur: imitationem uerò enumeratis poematum speciebus . . . omissis uero tribus posterioribus . . . ex tribus prioribus per similitudinem quandam acceptam facile ipsis accommodare possumus; tria priora diligentius in partes scindit. . . . Sunt autem partium duo genera: aliae quidem ueluti formae siue species sunt in toto poemate quae potentia potius quam actu in ipso ostendi possunt quam obrem potentiales ut hoc verbo utar merito appellantur. . . . Aliae sunt partes quas quantas appellat Aristoteles quia in partes actu existentes eadem poemata diuidunt, has etiam integrantes appellare consueuerunt quia ex ipsis ueluti corpus animalis ex membris poematis corpus coalescit et totum fit. . . . optimus autem poetarum institutor has omnes sex partes sigillatim ostendere debet quod quidem exequitur Horatius tam et si non eodem ordine quo Aristoteles usus est."

frequently missed by his contemporaries: the plot is an imitation not of men but of human actions, of the fortune and misfortune that is found in such actions (fol. 118*v*). Again, the principle for choice and exploitation of a plot is its unity, and Maranta summarizes the three kinds of false unity listed by Aristotle as that of person, of time, and of a single war (fol. 120). Horace's first two "precepts," to return to the original argument, concern unity of plot and its relationship to episodes.

CONCLUSIONS

The years 1550 to 1561 are marked by several developments in the history of Aristotle's *Poetics*. Not many of these are new, since critics and commentators early established the main lines of discussion with respect to the text. But some of the emphases are marked and significant, and the tradition takes on new general lines. These may perhaps be more clearly seen if we consider three questions: (1) the uses to which the *Poetics* was put during these years, (2) the range of problems connected with it, and (3) its relationship to other critical modes.

Some of the "uses" of the *Poetics* are already familiar to us. To seek within it as many passages as one could find to parallel the text of the *Ars poetica* was a game discovered early in the century; in the present period the game continues to be played, although perhaps with less vigor and imagination. The tendency is now less to accumulate increasingly large numbers of parallels and more to investigate in detail the similarities between selected points of theory. Maranta's study of plot and episodes may serve as an example here. Another favorite use is for confirmation or refutation of Plato's ideas, the former for such problems as the meaning of "imitation," the latter for the perennial question of the ban put upon the poets in the *Republic*. Here again there seems to be some slackening of activity—or at least in the texts studied this is an incidental rather than a dominant preoccupation. The procedure, indeed, may be generalized: critics continue to use Aristotle as an incidental authority in the exposition of all kinds of theories; a passage here, a fragment there, will be used for the illustration of specific points in a miscellany of systems, rhetorical, poetical, and historical.

Something newer, something that really gives the tone to this decade, is the exploitation of the *Poetics*—if only occasionally—in original treatments of the art of poetry, themselves based essentially on other principles. When Benedetto Varchi, in his *Lezzioni della poetica*, takes Aristotle as a starting point for a theory which turns out to be of an entirely different kind, he is making just such use of him. Newer still is the type of activity which consists in using the *Poetics* to provide an order and a framework for new theories of the genres. Thus Giraldi's treatises on tragedy, comedy, and satire take their suppositions from the Aristotelian text, on which they frankly admit that they are modeled. Both Giraldi and Pigna do the same thing when they develop their theories of a genre unknown to Aristotle, the romance. But here there is a basic difference of procedure, since they must start with the admission that only a part of Aristotle's theory will be applicable. The extent to which each will depart from the dogma will depend first upon the way in which he reads the *Poetics*, second upon the degree of independence which he is willing to accord to the new genre—an independence involving its fundamental similarity or dissimilarity to the epic. Many factors—some of which were later to constitute arguments in the "quarrel of the ancients and the moderns"—must here be taken into consideration. In any case, the *Poetics* becomes more immediate and more contemporary when used in this way. The same is true whenever it contributes to the theory of a new genre, even though the contribution may take the form only of isolated precepts or miscellaneous remarks.

One should give special attention, finally, to the use of the *Poetics* as a basis for practical criticism. For as the century wears on and as abstract theories become commonplace modes of thought, all kinds of works, both old and new, come to be examined and judged in the light of those theories. In the 1550's, perhaps, the effort is more distinctly toward examination than toward judgment; for the problem is to discover what kinds of statements can be made about works by employing the terminology, the distinctions, and the general approaches of the *Poetics*. These statements are at first largely descriptive. They relate to such matters as the identification of the parts of a poem, the discovery of character, the summation of the plot and its episodes. They make affirmations with respect to the unity of the plot and the decorum of the characters. In a word, critics are at work testing the ways in which the text of the *Poetics* may be useful for practical criticism. It will be some time before evaluations will be attempted on the basis of the same text, since the derivation of criteria from principles is a long, difficult, and subtle process.

By "the range of problems connected with the *Poetics*" I mean, as distinguished from the subjects just discussed, the kinds of treatment to which the text itself was actually subjected. With some of these, again, we are already familiar. There was only one major commentary during these years, that of Vettori in 1560. Aside from it, however, there were the partial examinations of the text by such writers as Sigonio and Rufo. In all these there seems to be increased attention to philological, linguistic, and textual problems, and many useful suggestions are made for the improvement of the text. Both Vettori and Maranta work with the text at close range, the one primarily as an erudite professor concerned with the text itself, the other as a popular expositor (literature was his hobby rather than his profession) interested in correcting interpretations and in restoring the Aristotelian tradition. The latter way of handling the text, in public lectures before an academy of distinguished amateurs, seems also to be one of the newer emphases of this period: from the universities (witness

Lombardi and Maggi in the 1540's) the *Poetics* passes to the academies (witness Maranta and Varchi in the '50's and '60's), thus to a wider and less specifically professional audience.

But while attention on the text becomes fixed more closely and while its audience grows, its universality seems to be contested. This results largely from the attempt to apply it to new genres or to the new exploitation of old ones. The scope of the *Poetics*, for example, is narrowed specifically when such a theorist as Giraldi doubts its applicability to the romance. Such a limitation may have serious consequences, for the authority of Aristotle in matters literary is contested and the probability is suggested that there may be forms for which rules must be sought elsewhere. Likewise, when the same Giraldi declares that the double plot is preferable, in modern tragedy, to the single one demanded by Aristotle, he implies that as art changes the principles of Aristotle may no longer be applicable. Hence the principles themselves come to be linked with certain works and certain times—and cease to be principles. Despite such restrictions, the influence of the *Poetics* continues to grow in certain ways. It still remains the source for much new theory about new poetic genres, and in such a writer as Atanagi its main orientations are applied to the art of history. One should thus not see diminution during these years, but rather a complication of attitudes and the raising of some healthy doubts.

As for the relationship of Aristotle's theories to other critical modes, few changes are to be noted. Horace continues to be the dominant authority on poetic questions, and the most frequent assimilation of Aristotle's text is to the statements of the *Ars poetica*. It would not be an exaggeration to say that in most cases Aristotle is read with Horace in mind and that the uncertainties of the former are solved by reference to the relative certainties of the latter. In some cases the procedure is reversed, and difficult passages in Horace are illuminated by citation of the *Poetics*. As usual, we find that Horace is coupled with—and sometimes not distinguishable from—the rhetorical tradition; I mean, of course, in his bearing upon the interpretation of Aristotle. One still thinks of invention, disposition, and elocution as the essential divisions of the art of poetry, and Maranta's vehement protest against this kind of thinking assures us of its currency. Perhaps this is the most striking way in which the Middle Ages continue to exert an influence upon the interpretation of the *Poetics*. Almost equally prominent, though, is the medieval conception of the literary genres. For many of the commentators, the abstract and partial statements found in Aristotle are "completed" by the addition of the whole collection of medieval precepts for the genres: subject matter, kinds of characters, type of action and of ending, style, tone. Pigna provides us with an example here. Related to the same tendency is the insistence upon decorum, which perhaps combines all of the influences already mentioned. This leads increasingly to an emphasis upon social distinctions when Aristotle had made ethical distinctions, and upon ethical distinctions which derive rather from tradition than from the needs of a particular poem.

Among critical modes which had more recently become current, the one most usually associated with the *Poetics* is that of Plato's ideas on imitation. Since imitation was one of the central doctrines of the work, it was only natural that Plato's texts should be called upon for elucidations and for supplementary ideas. Otherwise, little influence of Plato is felt in the interpretations of Aristotle. Aristotle himself becomes one of the main sources of light on the *Poetics*; the other works, especially the *Rhetoric*, are studied more and more intensively, and some of the theorists present complete sets of cross references to the whole of the Aristotelian corpus. These are not always happy or useful; but they indicate a realization of the usefulness, for an understanding of any one work of Aristotle, of studying his other writings. Finally, during the years under examination, there is an increasing desire to ask questions about the relationship of Aristotle's theory to Christian subject matters and Christian attitudes toward the art of poetry. No polemic is as yet engaged. In the years to come, however, when practical criticism becomes more diversified and when the great literary quarrels develop, these considerations will have significant effects in the whole development of Cinquecento criticism.

CHAPTER ELEVEN. THE TRADITION OF ARISTOTLE'S *POETICS*: III. THE VERNACULAR COMMENTARIES

OF THE VARIOUS TENDENCIES just outlined, those that gained the greatest prominence in the years now to be studied were the newer rather than the older ones. The *Poetics* becomes, in a sense, a more "popular" document; formal and erudite commentaries in Latin, searching linguistic analyses, tend to give way to treatments which will be accessible to a larger and less professional audience. Again, within limits, the older modes will continue to be practised. But there will be more numerous academic discourses, many practical applications, a certain number of vulgarizations. These will culminate in the two great vernacular commentaries, Castelvetro's in 1570 and Piccolomini's in 1575, with Piccolomini's Italian translation coming in the intervening years, in 1572.

TOSCANELLA (1562)

Given these general trends, it is perhaps significant that the first work in the present group should be Orazio Toscanella's *Precetti necessari* of 1562. This is a frank work of vulgarization, as were all those of its author. In his preface, Toscanella states that he is merely presenting simplifications of certain basic texts for the benefit of beginners and students; the printer, Avanzo, makes a similar statement: "ho fatto imprimere l'arte poetica d'Oratio Flacco. L'arte poetica d'Aristotile: L'arte breue del Lullio: Vna parte del poeta del Minturno . . . " (p. *4). The digest of Aristotle's *Poetics*, for it is no more than that, occupies pages 80–89. Toscanella prepares a kind of catechism for the text, mentioning topics and then summarizing—in shorthand form—what Aristotle has to say on those topics. The technique may be seen in these opening lines of the treatment:

> Che cosa sia poesia. La poesia considerata in uniuersale è IMITATIONE: hor con questa, hor con quella cosa secondo la diuersità delle poesie. Che cosa habbia per genere la poesia. La poesia ha per genere l'imitatione. Differenza della imitatione. La Imitatione è differente in tre termini. Nel Modo dell'imitare. Nelle cose, che si imitano. Nelle cose con che si imita (p. 80v).

Moreover, when even so simplified a statement might not be fully understood, Toscanella reduces the ideas to tabular form. On the whole, the digest must have been of no value to the serious Aristotelian; but it is highly interesting as an indication of what the schoolmaster of 1562 would have told his pupils about the *Poetics*.

The digest is interesting for other reasons. We can see in it a typical reading of the *Poetics* for this period, a compendium of the solutions which had been reached for all the difficult problems of the text. There is a kind of scholastic undertone to the treatment, a wish to proceed by way of genus and differentia and to make progressive subdivisions, which Toscanella undoubtedly thought appropriate to the handling of an Aristotelian text. If we merely take the text in the order of presentation, we find some of the typical solutions of which I have spoken. The means of poetry, as exemplified by the epic, may be verse (of one kind or several kinds in the epic) or prose. The objects at times determine the genre, at times do not; thus men "better than others" are found in tragedy and the epic, men "like ourselves" are found in comedy, and the "worst" men in any one of the three (p. 81v). On the natural bases of imitation, Toscanella gives the correct reading: "Imitation, which is most natural. The deriving of pleasure from imitation."[1] His translation of the definition of tragedy displays all the contemporary uncertainty, resulting especially from the imperfect state of the text:

> Tragedy is an imitation of a virtuous perfect action. Which has magnitude, with pleasant speech, separately in each one of its species, in the parts of those, who are performing actions. Pleasant speech is that which has number, harmony, sweetness. Conducting the PASSIONS not by means of narration, as the epic poem does, but by means of pity, fear.[2]

When he comes to distributing the six parts of tragedy among object, manner, and means, Toscanella adopts, if imperfectly, the system of Robortello. Apparatus and music are the "instrumental" parts; character, elocution, and discourse are the "final" parts (i.e., those which are imitated). The plot should represent the means; but Toscanella calls it rather "the subject or material part, since it gives the invention." Its parts, he says, are reversal and recognition—no mention of knot and solution. Definitions of some of the other parts are equally strange: elocution is the "composition of the verses" and discourse is everything which "shows or does not show some 'sentenza'" (p. 83).

The pleasure derived from tragedy, through pity and fear, results from the learning of a moral lesson: "The pleasure of tragedy results from pity and from fear; for when the spectators see such terrible misfortunes happening to such great persons, they learn to suffer patiently their own calamities, or to bear them. So that the pleasure springs from the LEARNING."[3] The treatment of plot and episodes is highly instructive, showing as it does the tendency to think in terms of a theme rather than of an action as constituting the unity of plot. Toscanella uses the example of Vergil, whose single

---

[1] *Precetti necessari* (1562), p. 82: "Imitatione, la quale è naturalissima. Il pigliarsi piacere dalla imitatione."

[2] *Ibid.*, p. 82v: "La Tragedia è Vna imitatione d'attione uirtuosa perfetta. Che habbia grandezza, con parlar soaue, separatamente in ciascuna sua spetie, nelle parti di coloro, che uan negotiando. Parlar soaue è quello, che ha Numero. Armonia. Dolcezza. Conducendo gli AFFETTI non per uia di Narratione, come fà il poema heroico: ma per uia di Misericordia. Timore."

[3] *Ibid.*, p. 83v: "Il piacere della Tragedia risulta dalla misericordia, & dal timore: perche uedendo li spettatori casi cosi terribili, successi in persone cosi grandi; imparano a comportar patientemente le calamità sue, ò a supportarle. Tanto che il piacere nasce dallo IMPARARE."

action is constituted by "the exploits of Aeneas after he came to Italy" (p. 83v); the other matters are said to fall outside the poet's intention and to constitute digressions. These are "all those things which the poet treats when he departs from the matter undertaken, which digressions, however, must not be entirely unrelated to the matter proposed, but must have in part an appropriateness to it."[4] Toscanella's translations of the passages on the tragic hero and on the nature of pity and fear both show a basically sound understanding of the text. (I italicize significant words.) On the tragic hero: "Those pass into misery who are not excellent either for virtue or for justice; not for their vice nor for any iniquity, but *for some error committed by them*; who are placed in glory and in prosperity of fortune."[5] On the effects of tragedy: "Pity concerns him who is not worthy, that is him *who should not fall into misery*, and so forth. Fear concerns him *who is like us*; for we fear lest a similar thing should happen to our own selves."[6]

The solutions with respect to the four requisites for character are less felicitous. The principal difficulty lies in Toscanella's inability to distinguish among them. He says that "goodness" ("bontà") consists in the assigning of good characters to good people; that "appropriateness" ("conuenienza") involves assigning the proper kind of speech to men and to women, according to the characteristics of their sex; that "resemblance" ("similitudine") concerns the passions, which must always express the basic character of the person; and that "constancy" ("ugualità") requires uniform presentation of the person's desires throughout the play (p. 85v).

At the end of the digest we find a number of miscellaneous precepts for tragedy and the epic, some of which reveal essential interpretations. The epic poem, for example, is said to contain numerous plots (p. 87v). The episodes of tragedy must be varied, since satiety would result from too much similarity. Epic verse is characterized by stability, swollenness (but not of the blameworthy kind), a variety of languages, and the use of metaphors. Narrative imitation—and he here opposes Aristotle—is the most excellent kind. All forms of speech must be based upon reason. So far as doctrine is concerned, these remarks are no more miscellaneous than the rest of the work. It presents no organized or systematic interpretation of Aristotle's *Poetics*; but isolated translations and commentaries reveal important interpretations of the passages involved.

While Toscanella's thumbnail summary presents the *Poetics* in a volume

[4] *Ibid.*, p. 84: "tutte quelle cose, che tratta il poeta partendosi dalla materia incominciata; i quai digressi però non uogliono essere in tutto lontani dalla materia propostasi; ma hauere in parte conuenienza seco."

[5] *Ibid.*, p. 84v: "Quei passino in miseria, iquali ne per uirtù, ne per giustitia sono eccellenti: non per uitio loro, o per iniquità; ma per qualche errore commesso da loro, che in gloria, & prosperità di fortuna posti sono."

[6] *Ibid.*, p. 85: "La Misericordia è intorno a chi non è degno; cioè à chi non douerebbe cadere in miseria, &c. La Paura, è intorno à chi ci è simile; perche dubitiamo, che il somigliante non interuenga à noi medesimi."

which also contained the other essential treatises, Bernardo Tasso's *Ragionamento della poesia* (published in 1562, but probably delivered before the Accademia Veneziana in 1560) attempts to combine Aristotle's theory with various others in order to make an elaborate defence of the art. Essentially, Bernardo's sources are these three: the elements of the Boccaccian defence of poesy, the allegations of universal knowledge found in such texts as the *Vita Homeri*, and Plato's ideas on the divine furor (see above, Chapter VII, pp. 282–84). In this context, Aristotle plays only a minor role. He is corrected and clarified with respect to the distinction between poetry and poetics; poetry, says Tasso, is "the universal material of the whole poem," while poetics is "the art which teaches the poet how to arrange well and according to rule this material which in itself is confused."[7] Strictly in passing, Aristotle provides a definition of poetry as "an imitation of human actions" ("una imitatione de le attioni humane," p. 4). He provides, much more extensively, the six poetic genres which Tasso distinguishes: comedy, tragedy, epic, auletic, citharistic, and dithyrambic. But the definitions of these types and descriptive statements about them come from elsewhere. Aristotle is contradicted, again, on the matter of his preference for the tragedy over epic; for Tasso, the epic is to be preferred because its writer never has to suffer from the inadequacies of actors (p. 5). In spite of its limitations for his own purposes, the *Poetics* is regarded by Tasso as eminently useful for the practising poet, especially in this generation. Before its discovery, the art of poetry had to be laboriously deduced from the reading of the poets themselves:

... now the poetics of that most famous philosopher, which teaches the art of writing poetry with such orderliness and in such detail, so long buried in the dark shadows of the world's ignorance, and happily translated into the Latin language and perfectly expounded and interpreted by the erudite Robortello and by our most judicious M. Vincentio Maggio and by the excellent M. Pier Vittorio, conducts us like a sure and dependable escort along the difficult roads of poetry.[8]

The same Bernardo Tasso figures as an interlocutor, as the principal authority on tragedy, and as a subject of praise in the anonymous *Tractatus de tragoedia* found in the manuscript at Perugia, Biblioteca Comunale 985 (M. 8). The praise accrues to him through the character and the recent poetic achievements of his son Torquato. (On the treatise and its date, see above, Chapter V, p. 163 and Chapter VII, p. 282.) As far as Aristotle is

---

[7] *Ragionamento* (1562), p. 3v: "la poesia è la materia uniuersale di tutto il poema: e la poetica l'arte, che a bene, et regolatamente essa materia da se confusa di disporre insegna al Poeta."

[8] *Ibid.*, pp. 9–9v: "hora la poetica di quel famosissimo filosofo, laqual con tanto ordine, et si particolarmente insegna l'arte del poetare tanto tempo ne l'oscure tenebre de l'ignoranza del mondo sepolta, e felicemente ne la latina fauella tradotta, e perfettamente dal Erudito Robortello, dal nostro giuditiosissimo M. Vincentio Maggio, et dal Eccellente M. Pier Vittorio isposta, et interpretata, quasi sicura, e fidata scorta per le difficili strade de la poesia ci ua conducendo."

concerned, the main problems of the treatise are two: How does it happen that we find pleasure in the artistic representation of objects which are themselves distasteful? And how can we justify the practice of an art which was condemned by Plato? Aristotle gives answers to both questions. It should be noted at the outset that, in general, the appeal to Aristotle is understood to be a departure from an earlier way of solving problems about poetry. Trissino (author of the *Sophonisba*) and Bernardo Tasso are assigned the opposing points of view: "the one [Trissino] urges a narrower [definition of poetry, one] scrupulously subjected to the injunctions of Aristotle; while the other thinks, more liberally, that it should be defined according to the judgment of the multitude, its perceptions of nature, and the examples supplied by poets."[9] With respect to the first of the questions the answer is found in the pleasure which men take in imitation. There is no direct reference to the *Poetics* but the position is essentially that of Aristotle:

> For who does not know how much delight is present in the imitation of things! we all drink in with our minds a certain joyfulness that, by nature's principles, is intimately involved with our faculties, so that with incredible pleasure we see the representations of things and the semblances of persons and images of the truth and as it were the forms of actions copied through imitation.... For what extreme of pleasure is it, if not this, that vices bring us when presented in a play and produced on the stage—vices, however, that in the very truth of life are rejected by the most discriminating minds and eyes and ears?[10]

Imitation supplies the answer to the second question as well, for the pleasure that it assures to the contemplation of objects and actions makes it possible to use them as devices of instruction. Imitation coats the pill. One may thus contradict the strictures of Plato and Proclus by emphasizing the usefulness of poetry in education. This, of course, has nothing to do with the *Poetics*, although the anonymous author seems to make a direct transition from Aristotle's views on imitation to these other views on pedagogy.

Carlo Sigonio's *De dialogo* of 1562 is Aristotelian in another of the ways noted in the preceding chapter. It applies what it considers to be the system and the principles of Aristotle to a literary form not treated by him, the dialogue. In so doing, it necessarily reveals a reading of the *Poetics*. Thus, our problem in discussing it is to discover what kind of a reading it implies

---

[9] Perugia, Bibl. Com. MS 985 (M.8), fol. 100: "alter angustiorem, et religiosa cogit praeceptionibus Aristotelis deuinctam, alter dissolutius iudicio multitudinis, naturae sensibus, poetarum exemplis definiendam putat."

[10] *Ibid.*, fols. 103v–4: "Quis autem ignorat quanta insit in rerum imitatione suauitas! omnes iucunditatem quamdam e naturae principijs implicitam sensibus animo imbibimus, ut cum incredibili uoluptate spectemus et exempla rerum, et simulacra personarum, et ueritatis imagines, et actionum quasi figuras imitatione simulatas. . . . Quid enim est illud, nisi hoc est, quod in ludum, et scenam prolata uitia tantum oblectationis afferunt! quae tamen in ipsa uitae ueritate fastidiosissimis animis oculis auribus respuuntur?"

and to summarize the character of the precepts for dialogue ostensibly derived from Aristotle. Having no basic text to work with, Sigonio must proceed by analogy, and he starts from a supposition that the dialogue is like three other forms: poetry, oratory, and dialectic. It is like poetry in that it is an imitation; like oratory in that it uses prose rather than verse; like dialectic in that its "res," "those things which demand reason and inquiry,"[11] is the same.

Before we can proceed with the analysis, we must point out that Sigonio uses "imitation" in several meanings. The first is un-Aristotelian. Imitation is common to the poet and the orator. It consists, basically, in copying the style of another writer. When this consists merely in the imitation of language and figures and a way of speech, it may serve a writer's own ends, but it is an improper pursuit and is to be condemned. When, instead, it makes the writer assume the personality of his model and write in such a way as to be mistaken for the model, it is properly done and is to be praised. Amazingly enough, Sigonio cites Plato's condemnation of the poet who always speaks in his own person and Aristotle's rejection of Empedocles as a poet as arguments in favor of this kind of imitation. The second meaning is Platonic; it refers to the dramatic manner as distinguished from the narrative and the mixed. The third meaning is not clearly defined, but it seems to be related to the sense given it in the *Poetics*. The genus of poetry, oratory, and the dialogue is imitation; other forms, such as history and the epistle, come under the same genus. This would seem to indicate that wherever persons and actions are presented or represented in arts of discourse, imitation takes place. At the same time, the term is roughly equivalent to "feigning" or "invention." Thus Silius Italicus and Lucan may be classified as poets because "they described these wars as poets, not as historians. And they achieved this by feigning episodes at will and by interweaving the deliberations of the gods and goddesses with the meetings and discourse of men, and by seeking elsewhere gay narratives of events and pleasant descriptions of places."[12] The test of good poetry is good imitation; if the poet fails by going "counter to the laws handed down to us by the great master"[13]—for example, by treating all the actions of a whole war rather than a single action of a single man—he will be a bad poet.

Since the dialogue belongs to the same genus as poetry, Sigonio will seek a definition of it by examining the same differentiae as Aristotle had considered for poetry, "a rebus, ab instrumentis, a modis" (p. 10). The "res," as we have seen, are the same as those of dialectic; the "instrumentum" is prose; the "modus" combines narrative, dramatic, and mixed, as one may

---

[11] *De dialogo* (1562), p. 13: "ea, quae ... ratione & disquisitione egent."

[12] *Ibid.*, p. 3v: "bella haec non historicorum, sed poetarum more descripserint. Id quod episodiis pro arbitratu fingendis, & deum, dearumque consiliis, & hominum concionibus intexendis, atque festiuis rerum narrationibus, & iucundis locorum descriptionibus aliunde petendis consequuti sunt."

[13] *Ibid.*, p. 4: "contra leges a summo doctore traditas."

see in Plato's dialogues. The definition thus has but few resemblances to that of poetry, which Sigonio gives as follows:

> The matters which the poets represent by imitating he finds to be the actions of men of grave or of light character or of those in between; the instruments which contribute to the imitation are speech, harmony, and rhythm; the manners of undertaking the imitation: when they use continuous narration, or introduce [the personages] as performing the action, or when they use both manners. And thus, when he [Aristotle] came in turn to the treatment of tragedy, he concluded from these principles that tragedy is an imitation of those actions which are undertaken by grave men, using verse, harmony, and rhythm, conducted by the presentation only of persons in action.[14]

In such a statement as this, Sigonio remains fairly close to the text of the *Poetics*. When he adapts it to his own purposes, he does not attempt to deform it. Indeed, he soon departs from Aristotle, by declaring, for example, that the proper style for the dialogue is the "middle" style of the rhetoricians (p. 14), or that the fundamental problems in the handling of the dialogue are decorum and verisimilitude (p. iii).

Indeed, his total theory of the dialogue is really a theory of decorum. The form is to be praised insofar as it obeys the laws of verisimilitude and of decorum, through the observation of which every form of imitation is made perfect (p. 18). "For in fact, what else need be prescribed with respect to this form besides the fact that it is based at once in observation of persons, times, places, and causes, and in keeping one's attention on them?"[15] Even in his dedication, Sigonio insists that all matters relative to the dialogue "must obey above all else the laws of decorum and of verisimilitude; there was never anything more difficult in all the arts than to accomplish these ends, even in the judgment of the most learned men."[16] Essentially these laws, which reduce to one, have as their end convincing the reader of the truth of what is being said. They concern two elements of the dialogue: the man speaking and the language in which he speaks. For the man speaking, verisimilitude of character according to poetic requirements gives the assurance of truth:

> This poetic verisimilitude is of such power and such a nature that when it is present it causes the thing which is invented not to seem so. Rather will that seem

---

[14] *Ibid.*, p. 10: "Res, quas poetae imitando simularent, aut grauiorum, aut leuiorum hominum, aut qui his interiecti essent, actiones esse inuenit; instrumenta, quae ad imitandum afferrent, orationem esse, concentum, & rhythmum; modos ineundae imitationis, cum iidem aut perpetua uterentur narratione, aut quasi agentes inducerent, aut utrunque. Itaque cum deinceps ad tractationem tragoediae descendisset, ex his principiis tragoediam imitationem esse conclusit earum actionum, quae a grauibus susciperentur hominibus, uersu, concentu, rhythmoque, ac sola personarum inductione initam."

[15] *Ibid.*, p. 18: "Quid igitur hoc de genere praecipiendum est aliud, nisi utrunque in personarum, temporum, locorum, & caussarum consideratione, atque animaduersione esse positum?"

[16] *Ibid.*, p. iii: "quae decoro in primis, & uerisimilitudini seruiant, quibus tuendis officiis nihil in omnibus artibus fuit unquam uel doctissimorum hominum iudicio difficilius."

invented which is in strong contrast to the true and which achieves no resemblance to truth, that is, whatever is in disagreement with persons, times, and places and either contains no causes why it should be done as it is or contains improbable causes.

The same passage contains the explanation of verisimilitude (or decorum) in language: "Just as in fact not every man can do every thing, so it is not verisimilar that any one man should speak in every kind of discourse. And for the reason that there is no action except in time and in place, it is necessary that whatever is the case in given circumstances be also expressed in the manner of speech."[17] The whole position is later summarized in a single formula: "Poetic decorum is involved both in the imitation of the characters of men and in the creation of appropriate speech."[18] This statement is followed immediately by a reference to Aristotle's four requisites for character. In the remainder of the treatise Sigonio seems to pass imperceptibly from "mores" to "morata oratio"—a natural transition since the same basic law applies to both.

What starts as an attempt to apply Aristotelian distinctions to a new genre thus becomes little more than an expression of the current theory of decorum in literature. Clearly, Sigonio still writes at a time when the implications of Aristotle's method are not clear, when it is easy to pass from one critical context to another, when there is no notion at all of methodological rigor.

The next document in our chronology, however, displays rigorous method of another kind, the method of the philologists. This is a letter from Pietro Vettori to Bartolomeo Maranta, dated "Florent. XIIII. Kal. Ianuar. CIƆ IƆ LXII" (i.e., December 19, 1562). It is a reply to an earlier letter in which Maranta, after praising Vettori for his achievement in his commentary on the *Poetics*, expressed disagreement and asked clarification on several points. The passages involved in the discussion, found in chapters I and II, concern the distinctions among the arts as "mimetic" and "poetic"; here are Maranta's questions and Vettori's answers:

Should not all the arts mentioned by Aristotle, such as flute-playing, the dance, painting, sculpture (*Poetics* 1447a13–28), be considered as "poetic" arts? They should not, since although they use one or several of the means used by poetry, they do not use the distinguishing means of discourse.

If they are not "poetic" arts, why does Aristotle include them at this

---

[17] *Ibid.*, p. 18v: "Hoc autem poeticum eius est potestatis, atque naturae, ut cum adest, efficiat, ne res, ut est ficta, sic uideatur. ficta autem uidebitur, quae a uero longe abhorrebit, nec ueritatis ullam similitudinem consequetur, idest, quae cum personis, temporibus, & locis discrepabit, & caussas nullas, cur ita factum sit, aut certe non probabiles continebit. Vt enim non quicunque homo quancunque rem agit, sic non est uerisimile, quencunque hominem in quocunque sermone uersari. et quoniam actio nulla est nisi in tempore, & loco, propterea quod in re est, id etiam oratione exprimatur necesse est."

[18] *Ibid.*, p. 20: "Iam uero decorum poeticum cum in imitandis moribus hominum, tum in conuenienti affingenda oratione uersatur."

point? He does so because, like poetry, they are mimetic arts; and this in spite of the fact that the mere use of one of the means does not necessarily constitute imitation.

Is not the use of any one of the means of poetry in a given work a sufficient reason for classifying it as "poetry"? No; the presence of discourse ("oratio") is absolutely essential. Indeed, if diction is present (accompanied, adds Vettori, by verse) in a work which imitates, we will have a poem.

The crux of the whole matter, says Vettori, is the distinction between μίμησις and ποίησις, between all the arts on one side and the poetic arts on the other. Once we understand the basic difference, the disputed passages in Aristotle become clear; thus a philological distinction provides the basis for important philosophical developments.[19]

MARANTA (1563-64)

Bartolomeo Maranta raised these questions with Vettori at a time when he was himself engaged in a study of Aristotle's *Poetics*, not in order to publish a commentary as Vettori had done, but apparently for a series of lectures which he was preparing. It is quite possible that these were meant for delivery to the Accademia Napoletana, as a pendant to the series on Horace's *Ars poetica*. Four of the lectures (or sketches for them) are preserved in MS R.118.Sup. of the Ambrosiana; they date from the years 1563-64. I shall treat these in their order of generality rather than attempt to discover and observe a chronological arrangement.

The first of the discourses (fols. 125-32v) purports to discover Aristotle's central intention, but it soon drifts into other related problems. Aristotle's purpose, says Maranta, is "to reduce to a method the rules and precepts of the poetic art, by means of which the poet may become perfect."[20] This he attempts for two reasons: because he recognizes the importance of poetry in human life and sees the extent to which the art is badly practised; and because he wishes to complete his philosophical system. Such reflections as these bring Maranta to a study of the relationship between the philosopher and the poet; he finds that they are one and the same thing. The same definition applies to both their pursuits: the science of divine and human things ("scientiam rerum diuinarum et humanarum," fol. 125v). The poet, like the philosopher, treats—and teaches—all manner of arts and sciences, and this is especially true of the moral sciences: "... they omit nothing pertaining to moral precepts, to the art of ruling cities and houses; their works are full of the precepts of prudence, justice, fortitude, and temperance."[21]

[19] In *Epistolarum libri X* (1586), pp. 107-9.
[20] MS Ambr. R.118.Sup., fol. 125: "ad methodum redigere regulas et praecepta artis poeticae, quibus optimus fieri poeta possit."
[21] *Ibid.*, fol. 126: "nihil omittunt quod ad praecepta morum pertinet, quod ad artem regendarum urbium et domuum; plena sunt omnia praeceptorum prudentiae, iustitiae, fortitudinis, temperantiae."

If there is a difference between the two, it is one which redounds to the credit of the poet and makes him superior to the teacher. Since he uses examples rather than naked propositions, his works appeal to the senses rather than to the mind; they are therefore more apt to move the passions and to affect the reader. Maranta summarizes his argument thus:

... not only do they [the poets] teach things as do the others [the philosophers], but they make them more powerful through examples. Indeed, the poets teach them better because more clearly, since, as they move the passions and display the habits, they place the things themselves before our eyes in such a way that we seem to see them and to touch them. But the pure philosophers, when they treat a discipline by abstracting it from its matter, weary the mind and the capacity to understand, whence it comes about that they drive their listeners or their readers away from knowledge. Therefore the ancient sages said that poetry is much more useful for this reason, that by penetrating, through the sweetness of diction, into the soul even of him who does not wish it, it makes itself accessible to a greater number of men; whereas unadorned philosophy reaches few men.[22]

Maranta bolsters his argument that poetry is more useful as an instrument of teaching by citing many ancient authors. In the course of the discussion we learn that poetry is especially apt for appealing to simple men, since it uses—instead of the definitions and demonstrations of philosophy—such readily understandable devices as examples and imitation.

By this time, Maranta has departed considerably from his original project of discussing Aristotle's purpose. The next step in the argument at the same time brings him back to Aristotle and removes him farther in the direction of Plato. The new argument reflects Aristotle's statement (*Poetics* 1451*b*5) that poetry is more philosophical than history. The poet treats the universal, the historian the particular. But Maranta has some difficulty in reconciling this statement with the notion that poetry works through examples, which are always particular. He resolves the difficulty by declaring that the poet really depicts the Idea—the perfect and complete expression of any virtue or vice, for example—by presenting an individual manifestation; thus Achilles displays all possible aspects of strength and fortitude. In so doing, the poet serves the greatest end of poetry, which is the inculcation of the virtues.

In a final step of his argument, Maranta recognizes a conflict between two ends which he has distinguished for the art, that of teaching through examples and that of delighting through diction. Clearly, the double Horatian end has been influencing his thinking throughout. He decides,

[22] *Ibid.*, fol. 126*v*: "cum non solùm res doceant ut illi sed exemplis corroborent. Melius etiam quia significantius cum in mouendis affectibus explicandisque habitibus poetae res ipsas ita ob oculos ponant ut intueri ac tractare illas uideamur. At nudi philosophj cum disciplinam tradant à materia abstrahendo mentem et intelligendi uim fatigant, unde fit ut audientes uel legentes a rerum scientia auersos reddant: quare ob hanc rationem multo utiliorem poeticam esse antiqui sapientes dixerunt quia cum ob dictionis suauitatem in animos uel nolentium illabatur, multo pluribus hominibus communis fit: at simplex philosophia paucorum est hominum."

ultimately, that all traces of contradiction can be removed by distinguishing between poetry and the poet, between the art and the artist. The art and the precepts appropriate to it have as their aim the pleasure of the audience:

In fact, it is Aristotle's purpose in this little book to set down the rules by means of which simple and clear philosophy may be adorned so as to make it seem most pleasurable to all men. Whence we have concluded that we should not expect from the art of the poets philosophical teachings, since these are obtained from philosophy itself, but instead the rules through which we may compose, using the probable lie, little fables in which philosophy itself is hidden; for which reason pleasure itself is the end of the art.[23]

But the poet seeks something else. He wishes to profit men, to teach them virtue, to impress philosophical precepts upon their minds ("imprimere philosophica praecepta in hominum animis," fol. 132). This he does by employing pleasurable devices as instruments for moving their souls, so that they may be purged of the passions, returned to tranquillity, and led thus to the highest degree of happiness. The poet's goal is completely utilitarian.

In the first of these discourses, then, Bartolomeo Maranta finds that the *Poetics* is close to Horace in the ends which it establishes for poetry and close to Plato in its conception of the object of imitation. In the second (fols. 109–14v) he addresses himself to the problem of Aristotle's philosophical method and the general organization of the *Poetics*. He finds that one may describe the philosophical method as an orderly passage from the universal to the particular, and that this in turn determines the organization: Aristotle will treat first those things common to all forms of poetry, then the peculiar features of the individual genres. Again, the terminology used, "communia" and "propria," is vaguely reminiscent of Horace. Maranta thinks that the "communia" may be reduced to four general headings: (1) "... in what ways all species of poems are alike, and in what ways they differ." From these come genus and differentia, which in turn give the definitions. The genus is imitation. (2) "On the origin of poems and why different kinds of them were invented." (3) "On the growth of these poems and how, from a formless state, they reached perfection." (4) "In what way tragedy and the epic are alike or how they differ from each other."[24] After these general statements, Aristotle passes on to the treatment of the individual genres.

---

[23] *Ibid.*, fol. 131v: "Est enim Aristotelis mens in hoc libello tradere regulas quibus philosophia simplex et aperta, ita exornari possit ut iucundissima omnibus uideatur.... Ex quo colligimus ab arte poetarum nos non expectare debere philosophica documenta quia haec habentur à nuda philosophia sed tamen regulas, quibus uerisimili mendacio fabellas componamus in quibus lateat ipsa philosophia: quare finis artis est ipsa oblectatio."

[24] *Ibid.*, fols. 113–13v: "Ac primum eorum est ut doceat in quibus omnes poematum species conueniant, et in quibus differant.... Secundum agit de origine poematum et quam ob rem diuersa eorum inuenta sint genera.... Tertium de incremento horum poematum, ac quomodo ad perfectionem ex informibus deuenerint.... Quartum ac postremum docet in quo tragoedia & epopoeia conueniant in quoúe discrepent inter se."

As he develops this general scheme of the *Poetics*, Maranta makes several distinctions which are of interest for the interpretation of that text. He is very early obliged to decide what is meant by δύναμις (1447a9), and after excluding any reference to the end of poetry ("which is to purge the minds of men of the vices"[25]) he argues that it means

... the formal and, so to speak, the specific nature of each poem, by which one differs from another; indeed, when we know the definition of each, we know wherein consists their proper essence [vis], in virtue of which essence, for example, tragedy is so distinctly tragedy that the name of any other kind of poem would not be fitting for it.[26]

This is, I believe, a fairly keen understanding of the term. Shortly afterward, subsequent to remarks on the importance of plot, he says that Aristotle treats tragic plot in a series of ten precepts. The attempt to reduce Aristotle's discussion to a set of numbered precepts recalls a similar effort on the part of the commentators on the *Ars poetica*, an effort by this time commonplace. It had not yet, however, gained currency among the students of the *Poetics*. Maranta's ten precepts, reduced to their simplest form, concern these topics:

1. Proper magnitude; easy to remember without excessive brevity.
2. Unity; a single action directed to a single end.
3. Universality; verisimilar actions, but not particular ones since these are the object of history.
4. Necessary and verisimilar connection of episodes.
5. Pity and terror, produced by incredible events since these excite greater admiration.
6. Complex rather than simple plot.
7. Quantitative parts of tragedy.
8. The proper character for tragic personages.
9. Simple plot: the passage of a single person from good to bad fortune.
10. Rules for the pitiable and the terrible.

These careful recommendations for plot, says Maranta, are essential since plot is the soul of tragedy and since the slightest error in its handling will mean the ruin of the whole poem.[27] In a final section of the manuscript, separate from the rest, Maranta makes a distinction with respect to the genus of poetry. He had earlier declared that the genus was imitation; but he now realizes that poems are also classified under such terms as "effictio," "poesia," "poetica." Of these, the term which most needs to be separated

[25] *Ibid.*, fol. 110: "δύναμιν hoc loco non puto referri ad finem poeticae artis qui est ut expurget a uitijs animos hominum."
[26] *Ibid.*, fol. 110: "formalem ut sic dixerim ac specificam naturam cuiusque poematis qua alterum ab altero differt; nam cognita uniuscuiusque diffinitione scimus in quo uis propria eorum consistat ob quam uim uerbi gratia tragoedia ita est tragoedia ut aliud ei poematis nomen conuenire nequeat." Note that it would be possible to translate "vis" as *effect*; I have avoided doing so because of the danger of reflecting the spirit of certain modern translations.
[27] *Ibid.*, fols. 110v–11.

from imitation is "effictio," and Maranta separates them on the basis of their generality; every imitation is a "making" but not every "making" is an imitation. Imitation is thus the more "proximate" genus and the one in terms of which kinds of poems are to be defined.

Finally, it should be noted that in several of the marginalia to this manuscript Maranta indicates that his position is opposed to that of Vettori. There are three such places, marked in the margin by the phrase "Contra P. Victor." The first is the discussion of δύναμις already noted (fol. 110); the second, his contention that κατὰ φύσιν refers to the method of exposition, beginning with universals and passing on to particulars (fol. 112); the third refers directly to the correspondence with Vettori (already studied) on Aristotle's reasons for listing various arts at the beginning of the *Poetics*. Maranta contends that two of the kinds of "poetry" enumerated at 1447a13, auletic and citharistic, really belong to poetry—rather than to the more general category of imitations—but that they use rhythm and harmony alone without discourse (fol. 114). Unfortunately, the manuscript ends abruptly shortly after this point, and we are deprived of Maranta's particular views on these genres.

The fragments included in the second discourse seem to be of especial interest for their interpretation of the method and order of Aristotle's text, for their distinctions with respect to several terms, and for the way in which they reflect the philological and philosophical disagreements between two contemporary humanists.

At the beginning of the third discourse (fols. 100–107), Maranta announces that he means to give a brief summary of the contents of the *Poetics*, and that is precisely what he does. Most of the interesting ideas are repeated from the discourses which we have already analyzed. There are occasionally, however, passages which reveal a significant attitude toward the text. After speculating on the probable contents of the missing third book, Maranta sees a five-part division of the first book: poetry in general, tragedy, the epic, resolution of objections, and the relative merits of tragedy and the epic. Somewhat later, Maranta remarks on the way in which the definition of tragedy is constituted and how the genre is treated: "He puts together the definition of tragedy in part out of what he had said about poetry in general, in part from the things that he is about to say; and after having explained the parts and the differentiae of the definition, beginning with the definition itself he seeks out the parts of tragedy, especially those which he calls 'formal.' "[28] As is the case with most of his contemporaries, Maranta provides revealing explanations of the requisites of character. "Goodness" is moral goodness, necessary if the poem is to

---

[28] *Ibid.*, fol. 101: "partim ex his quae in genere de poesi dixerat partim ex his quae mox est dicturus colligit Tragoediae definitionem. rursusque explicatis partibus et differentijs definitionis ex ipsa definitione uenatur partes Tragoediae praecipue illas quas formales appellat."

achieve its utilitarian end of ethical improvement; "likeness" may refer either to the nature and habits of the persons introduced or to a resemblance to the customs of the times involved in the action (fol. 103v). Among the features differentiating tragedy from epic is the fact that the former appeals to the eye, the latter to the ear; hence tragedy must be more verisimilar, less marvelous, "for the eyes consent less readily to those things which are said to be against the reason than do the ears."[29] Otherwise, Maranta repeats such ideas as those already expressed on imitation as the genus of poetry, on the five proofs of the priority of plot, on unity and magnitude, on the universality of poetry (as compared with history), and on the pedagogical uses of purgation.

There is some question as to whether the last of the discourses (fols. 133–39v) really belongs to the same series; for it is in Italian rather than in Latin and makes no claim to being related to the text of the *Poetics*. It treats largely of the form and the excellences of the *Aeneid*. But it does so in Aristotelian terms, repeating many of the ideas found in the other fragments and clarifying some of them. One may consider it as developing Aristotle's—and Maranta's—ideas on the epic just as the other discourses had discussed fully problems relevant to tragedy. Perhaps because it is in Italian, perhaps because it takes into consideration some forms of contemporary Italian literature, this little treatise strays somewhat farther from Aristotle and displays strong leanings toward the current Horatian tradition. The objects of imitation are distinguished on the basis of social classes: "illustrious men, great leaders and princes and kings and such like; or . . . very inconspicuous men and of low condition; or intermediate ones between these two extremes."[30] All these are presented rather as they should be than as they are, in accordance with an Idea of human action. The three objects gave rise, in antiquity, to three groups of poets: those who wrote tragedies and epics, those who wrote comedies, and those who wrote mimes. In modern times, in the Kingdom of Naples itself, all three levels are found; tragedies and comedies are written by recognized authors, while the "low" kind is found in farces, in the "Gianni," "Venetiani," and "Mattoccini," as well as in macaronic prose narratives.

With respect to the epic itself, Maranta thinks that Aristotle is perhaps mistaken in his preference for tragedy. The epic, being more varied in its episodes and its digressions, in its reversals and its recognitions, being longer and more pleasant and more marvelous, is on the whole more difficult to achieve. Hence, it is perhaps better. In any case, Vergil is the greatest of all poets in any language and in any form, with the possible exception of the Prophets. Within the epic form, Maranta sees the same

---

[29] *Ibid.*, fol. 106: "quia oculi non ita assentiuntur his quae praeter rationem dicuntur ut aures."

[30] *Ibid.*, fols. 133–33v: "huominj illustri gran maestri et prencipi et Re et similj ò . . . huomini uilissimi et di bassa conditione. O, tra questi duo estremi, mezzani."

qualitative parts that Aristotle had discerned; its quantitative parts are proposition, invocation, and narration. Its pedagogical ends are achieved on the one hand by the action—"from those heroic deeds one is fired in such a way that he, too, is incited to become like their doer, and thus the fruit of poetry is gathered"[31]—on the other hand by the characters, since these represent the perfect expression of given virtues. Maranta's general conclusion on the *Aeneid* is that it has one plot, of one man, in one time, engaged in one action with a beginning, a middle, and an end, that its separate parts are irremovable and unchangeable. These would seem to constitute Aristotelian criteria applied to a single work, and they are prophetic of some of the arguments which were to be adduced during the literary quarrels of the '70's.

Bartolomeo Maranta's one published work of literary criticism, the *Lucullianae Quaestiones* of 1564, is greater in bulk than all the unpublished writings taken together. Its general orientation is rhetorical and Horatian (see above Chapter V, pp. 171–74), and such Aristotelian elements as there are appear incidentally to a long-winded discussion of stylistics and metrics. They reduce, almost all of them, to considerations relative to the tragic plot, its conditions and effects; but there are some applications to the epic form since Maranta is engaged in the study and praise of Vergil. Again, the interpretations of Aristotle echo those found earlier in the manuscript discourses. But since his problem is Vergil, he concentrates on three essential questions: the comparison of tragedy and the epic; the sources of the tragic effect; and the bases of verisimilitude. On the first, he compares the two genres with respect to their qualitative and quantitative parts, to their length, to their manner (dramatic versus narrative); for all these, Aristotle is the source. On the subject of the marvelous, which is more properly produced by the epic than by the tragedy, he goes considerably beyond the *Poetics*; "admiratio," he says, must be produced by all poets at all times, but it falls especially in the domain of the epic. This is because, as a narrative form, it appeals to the ear rather than to the eye and may thus treat more incredible matters (pp. 88, 133). The need to astonish the audience necessarily involves consideration of the effects of tragedy as compared with those of the epic and, above all, of verisimilitude. Maranta at various times cites Aristotle on pity and fear, and he elaborates on the nature of the tragic plot and the tragic hero (p. 125). In this connection, he makes some important remarks on the nature of "fear." Starting from Aristotle's τὸ ὅμοιον (*Poetics* 1453a5), he sees two kinds of "likeness" to the tragic hero. The first is our common humanity with the persons of tragedy; we think of ourselves as subject to the same calamities and the same death. The second is a resemblance among us on the basis of one or several of the elements which constitute decorum: fortune, age, sex, pro-

[31] *Ibid.*, fol. 135v: "da quelle prodezze si accende di si fatta sorte che si incita anco egli a diuenire simile a quello et cosi si coglie il frutto della poesia."

fession, character, and so forth (p. 124). Here again the transition from the *Poetics* to the rhetoricians is almost imperceptible.

Maranta's study of the tragic hero is important to him insofar as he wishes to discover whether Aeneas does or does not fit Aristotle's description. With it in mind, he attempts to analyze more closely the conditions for the tragic action. If pity and fear are to attend the tragic personage, he must be of high station and enjoy great esteem; otherwise, his misfortunes will not produce the proper effect. Maranta accepts Aristotle's notion of the "intermediate" situation (1453a7) and he properly interprets ἁμαρτία as involving an error; but he adds an idea of his own which he recognizes as being non-Aristotelian: the error may be that of persons other than the hero "qui in magna sunt existimatione, & auctoritate" (p. 126). A number of tragedies are cited in proof. Besides, he introduces a distinction between the action, which may be wicked, and the intention, which may not; an essentially good hero who commits, unwittingly, a wicked deed may thus be considered as "intermediate." As for Aeneas, he would in no wise qualify as a tragic hero because he is perfect and cannot err.

Un-Aristotelian, again, is Maranta's thesis that the effects of tragedy may be achieved not only by the plot and character but by all the lesser elements—diction, sententiae, melody, chorus, setting. For Aristotle, these would contribute to the effect; for Maranta, they may produce it almost independently. In keeping with his rhetorical bent, he asserts that the function of sententiae is to arouse the passions, "such as anger, terror, pity, fear" (p. 18).

These passions will be aroused, however, only if the audience believes, only if verisimilitude is achieved. Aristotle is cited:

> Aristotle wrote that if two actions were to offer themselves to the poet, one of which indeed could happen but was not verisimilar, the other of which could not really happen but was nevertheless credible, the poet would accept and choose the one which had an apparent truth, even though it belonged to the number of those which cannot naturally happen under any circumstances.[32]

One of the interlocutors goes on to explain that verisimilitude is a matter of audience opinion and that the difficulty lies in reconciling this with the marvelous: "The poets seek nothing else but the assent of the listeners and they try with all their energies to force men to give credence to marvelous actions. And herein lies the greatest difficulty for the poet."[33] The solution to the problem lies partly, as it did for Aristotle, in the choice of extra-

---

[32] *Lucullianarum quaestionum libri quinque* (1564), p. 89: "Aristoteles tradit, ut si duae res sese poetae obferant, altera quae fieri quidem possit, sed uerisimilis non sit: altera quae fieri reuerà nequeat, credibilis tamen: capiat atque eligat poeta eam quae apparentem habet ueritatem, etiam si ex eorum numero sit quae naturaliter fieri nullo modo possit."

[33] *Ibid.*, p. 89: "poetae nihil uenantur, praeter assensum eorum qui audiunt: atque omnibus neruis contendunt, ut assentiri homines cogant admirabilibus rebus: atque in hoc uersatur maior poetae difficultas."

ordinary events that really occurred, those catastrophes visited upon certain great and noble families (p. 133).

Maranta's total contribution to literary theory is about equally divided between Horatian and Aristotelian elements. It is Horatian in the lectures devoted to the *Ars poetica* and in the *Quaestiones*; it is Aristotelian especially in the other set of lectures, but also in the *Quaestiones*. Throughout, he establishes and reaffirms the parallelism between the two theorists; or, in any case, he introduces the one into a context primarily reflecting the other. He frequently shows a good understanding of his texts, and his interpretations are sometimes superior to those of most of his contemporaries.

SALVIATI (1564)

While Maranta was preparing (and perhaps giving) his lectures on Aristotle for the Accademia Napoletana, Lionardo Salviati was writing the First Lecture of a series of three to be known, collectively, as the *Trattato della poetica*. The *Lezzion prima* was delivered before the Accademia Fiorentina in December of 1564.[34] It is heavily Aristotelian in tone, not only because of the multiple reference to other works of the Stagirite—the *Metaphysics*, the *Ethics*, the *Topica*, the *Posterior Analytics*, the *Physica*, the *De caelo*—but also because of the method which Salviati everywhere attempts to apply. Salviati believes that answers to his questions are to be found only in Aristotle, and as he traces the early history of the arts he sees the beginnings of order and clarity in Aristotle's works—

> ... until at last Aristotle—descended upon earth, I believe, through divine pity in order to liberate us from the fog of so long ignorance—reduced the truths pronounced at first by those first philosophers, not indeed by chance but confusedly, in a scattered way, and as it were stammeringly, to a marvelous order; and reduced divers members to an incredible clarity, as if to an artful body proportioned with ineffable mastery.[35]

If such answers are to be reached in the realm of poetics, an equally rigorous method must be used.

Salviati conceives of this method as involving, basically, two procedures: the careful use of definitions and the application of the device of the four causes. Everything must be defined, including definition itself. A definition (see the *Metaphysics* and the *Organon*) is "that reply which would be given by whoever was asked, not about the word, but about the essence of some

---

[34] I am indebted, for the indication of the whereabouts of this MS, to Peter Brown's "Il Discorso sopra la Ginnastica degli Antichi attribuito al Cav. Lionardo Salviati," *Annali della Scuola Normale Superiore di Pisa*, Serie II, XXVI (1957), 4; Brown gives a complete description of the MS. The second lecture, as far as I know, was never written. The so-called Third Lecture was merely a copy, made in 1566, of a part of this First Lecture.

[35] MS BNF, Magl. VII, 307, fol. 7: "infino che Aristotile finalmente disceso, credo, in terra per diuina pietà a liberarne dalla nebbia di cosi lunga ignoranza, le uerità da quei primi filosofi, non pure a caso, ma in confuso, e sparsamente, e quasi balbettando prima pronunziate in ordine marauiglioso, et in chiarezza incredibile, quasi in un corpo proporzionato con indicibile maestria et artifizioso diuerse membre ridusse."

Universal and of some universal substance, completely properly, but in such a way that there be no part in it which is not operant, nor any part lacking that might operate in it."[36] The first term of which we need a definition, as we approach the subject of poetry, is art itself, and Salviati (see the *Metaphysics*) defines it as "an external Principle of operation, to be differentiated . . . from Nature; because nature . . . is a principle of action in itself."[37] Otherwise stated, it is a "habit of operating in an external subject by means of the reason."[38] The latter definition requires a full differentiation among the possible kinds of habits and among their sources. Salviati (see the *Ethics*) derives the habits from two kinds of intellect, the higher intellect and the reasoning power, and he classifies them under art, prudence, and science:

. . . he [Aristotle] derives from the former [the higher intellect] all the habits which concern themselves with necessary and eternal things, from the latter [the reason] all those which exert themselves only on contingent things. To this group belong, without any doubt, prudence and art; which two habits are different from one another because prudence treats of those actions whose effect remains in the agent, but art directs those whose effects pass over into some foreign matter.[39]

All the arts, and poetry among them, induce perfection in some object outside of the agent himself.

The introduction of the concept of habit obliges Salviati to pursue two further arguments. First, he must answer the Platonists, who maintain that poetry is not a habit but an inspiration, a product of the divine furor. This he does by presenting various rebuttals—it is philosophically wrong to think that God, completely perfect, would operate in an individual; where furor is present, judgment is lacking; the claims of the poets are not reliable—and by insisting that, in accordance with his method, he is seeking a surer and more predictable origin: " . . . we are looking for the cause, or rather the principle, which most of the time does not fail." And again: "But we are seeking for the principle which, not once in a while, but most of the time is a principle. And this must definitely be habit." [40] Furor, in

---

[36] *Ibid.*, fol. 11v: "la risposta, che si darebbe da chi fosse richiesto, non del uocabolo, ma dell'essenza d'alcuno Vniuersale, e d'alcuna uniuersal sostanza proprijssimamente, ma in tal guisa, che parte alcuna non ui sia che non operi, ne alcuna uene manchi, che operare ui potesse."

[37] *Ibid.*, fol. 15: "Principio esteriore d'operare; a differenza . . . della Natura; percioche la natura . . . è principio d'azzione in se stesso."

[38] *Ibid.*, fol. 14v[2]: "Habito d'operare in subbietto esteriore con ragione." (There are two folios bearing the numbers 14 and 15 each; this is the second 14.)

[39] *Ibid.*, fol. 14[2]: "da quello tutti gli habiti, che sono dietro alle cose necessarie, ed eterne, da questo fa uenire tutti quelli, che nelle contingenti s'adoperano solamente. Ciò sono la Prudenza, et l'Arte senza dubbio ueruno. I quali due habiti perciò sono tra loro differenti, percioche la Prudenza in quelle delle azzioni si raggira, l'effetto delle quali si rimane nell' agente; ma l'Arte dirizza quelle, i cui effetti in alcuna materia forestiera trapassano."

[40] *Ibid.*, fol. 18: "noi cerchiamo della cagione, ò uogliam dir principio, che le piu uolte non falla"; and "Ma noi cerchiamo del principio, che non alcuna uolta, ma le piu uolte è principio. E ciò conuiene, che sia l'habito fermamente."

a word, cannot be accepted into the category of universal causes, whereas habit can. Second, he must discover what kind of habit is present in poetry. To do so, he divides the habits into moral and intellectual, the intellectual into habits of doing and of making, and classifies poetry under the last of these (fol. 29). This makes it possible for him to declare that the art of poetry "is capable of counsels and of precepts, and can very well be acquired by an excellent mind through human industry."[41]

A related argument considers the various other sources to which poetry might be attributed. Salviati makes an exhaustive classification of all operations as coming from nature, art, violence, mind alone, fortune, and chance; then he sets out to show that poetry cannot properly be assigned to any of these except art. Not to nature, since nature has its principle in itself, whereas all poems have their source in the poet. Not to fortune or chance, since the poet makes his poem according to design. Not to violence, since this is always contrary to the will. Not to the mind alone, since this is only rarely the source of poetry; hence it cannot be a principle. Thus poetry is an art: "it has in itself all the qualities which are universally required for the existence of art."[42] As an art, it contains the three necessary operations: speculation, before anything is done: the operation of the artist; and the work itself. Its matter is the matter of art, consisting solely in contingent and corruptible matter.

With respect to that other Aristotelian device, the analysis of the four causes, Salviati makes his own assignment of causes. In so doing, he reveals at once how many of his presuppositions come from sources other than Aristotle and how uncertain is his own method. The final cause, he says, is to "bring profit to our minds through pleasure" ("il giouare a gli animi con diletto," fol. 34); this is identical with what Horace has to say in lines 333 and 343. The efficient cause is "the intellect invested with this habit" (i.e., the habit of the art; "l'intelletto di questo habito riuestito," fol. 34). It is when he comes to the material cause that he finds difficulties. For other critics, such as Vettori, have considered as instruments those elements which he himself regards as the matter, that is, language, harmony, and rhythm. Of these, language is indisputably the most important: "not rhythm and music, but significant words, both according to the truth and according to Aristotle's opinion, are firmly of the essence of poems. Words then . . . , according to the authority of Aristotle, are the most general material of all poetry."[43] Salviati finds no philosophical impropriety in considering a single element as now material, now instrument.

---

[41] *Ibid.*, fol. 29: "d'auertimenti, e di precetti è capace, e con humano studio da eccellente ingegno puo molto bene conseguirsi."

[42] *Ibid.*, fol. 31v: "ha in se tutte le qualità che all'essere dell'Arte in uniuersale sono richieste."

[43] *Ibid.*, fol. 34v: "non il rimmo, e la musica, ma le parole significanti, e secondo la uerità, e secondo l'opinione d'Aristotile, sono della essenza delle poesie fermamente. Sono dunque le parole . . . secondo l'autorità d'Aristotile, materia generalissima di tutta la Poesia."

Finally, the formal cause consists in the "invention"; he takes the *Iliad* as his example: "in that greatest poem, the form is that invention which makes it different from every other poem which is not this very same one."[44] As he recapitulates his findings with respect to the causes, Salviati merely repeats what he had said earlier for three of them; but on the subject of final cause he finds it important to make a further distinction. This consists in differentiating an ultimate from an immediate end. "The end," he says, "is to profit with pleasure; I do not say the most proximate end, because this is without doubt the form and the work itself, . . . but I am speaking of the ultimate end of the poet."[45] The *Physica* and the *De caelo* are cited as the basis for this distinction.

Salviati's ties with an un-Aristotelian critical past are further attested by his repetition of the standard, conventional defence of poetry. He traces the beginnings of society, the civilizing role of the arts, their relationship to the sciences. Among the arts, poetry appeals to the highest faculty, the intellect, and hence is close to the contemplative operations of philosophy (fol. 9). Poetry is, moreover, supreme among the arts because it serves the highest end, the health and the well-being of the mind. Once more, Aristotle confirms the conclusion: his belief that tragedy purges the mind of its disturbances shows that poetry is concerned only with the mind (fol. 35v). On his own, Salviati raises some further interesting questions about the art: whether poetry can exist in the poet's mind without being written down or put into words; whether, if this were true, the real matter of poetry would be the feelings expressed rather than the words used to express them; whether, following the same line of argument, poetry would not pass from the arts of making to the arts of doing, and ultimately become a part of prudence. But the answers, rather than being given here, are promised for the subsequent lectures.

Two treatises of Sperone Speroni, one a set of discourses on Vergil and the other a dialogue on Vergil, probably belong to this same year, 1564.[46] As far as Aristotle is concerned, Speroni finds in the *Poetics* useful suggestions with regard to plot and the unity of plot, to imitation in general, and to verisimilitude. Speroni declares that the *Discorsi sopra Virgilio* will treat its subject "according to the art taught by Aristotle and Plato"[47] and that the first of its teachings establishes the primacy of plot: " . . . it is the first thing made by the poet; . . . and this must be woven in such a way that the events follow on one another in almost a natural order, and one should not see in it the poet's will that it should be made in this way;

---

[44] *Ibid.*, fol. 35: "in quel sommo poema la forma è quella inuenzione, che lo fanno diuerso da ogni altro poema, che esso stesso non sia."

[45] *Ibid.*, fol. 35: "il fine il giouare con diletto; non dico il fine piu propinquo, percioche questo senza fallo è la forma, e l'opera medesima . . . ma parlo dell'ultimo fine del poeta."

[46] See the reasons offered by the editor of the 1740 edition of the *Opere*, II, 419 and 356. Also Fr. Cammarosano, *La Vita e le Opere di Sperone Speroni* (Empoli, 1920), p. 164.

[47] In *Opere* (1740), IV, 425: "secondo l'arte da Aristotile e da Platone insegnata."

for if one does, the poem becomes affected rather than verisimilar."[48] Verisimilitude is thus a product, in part at least, of a seemingly natural order of the events. Although we are not so told, we may perhaps assume that it is this "natural order" itself which guarantees the imitative quality of poetry. Poetry is an imitation, it is the plot which imitates human actions; all parts not belonging to the plot are digressions or accidents. Speroni's reasons for insisting upon the unity of plot are not, however, thoroughly Aristotelian. The first is, for "an imitation must be of one single imitated thing, just as a science is of one subject." The second is not, since Speroni argues that the main reason for requiring unity is to provide, through a highly simple and reduced plot, the occasion for much amplification and ornamentation, "for if the poem consists of unnecessary and superfluous ornament, if the poet were to undertake to imitate poetically more than one action the poem, in order to be perfect, would have to grow to infinite length."[49] A poem constituted of more than one action would be possible but imperfect, for the poet would not be able to "decorate" it completely in every one of its parts without making it over-long and tedious. Hence the preference for the simple over the complex plot: "Thence it arises that double or triple comedies and tragedies are not beautiful, as simple ones are; for they are less ornate and more obscure, and this removes some of the beauty."[50] In such an argument as this, Aristotelian *loci* and terms are present; but the whole tendency and conclusion are different.

Imitation is the topic, once again, of the fragmentary *Dialogo sopra Virgilio*; but it is a strange kind of imitation which becomes farther and farther removed from Aristotle's. The *Poetics* itself is an "imitation" of Homer's two epic poems, which thus become its "nature." A philosopher writing on poetics bases his work on poems just as a poet writing poems bases them on nature. But the poet may also use other poems as his "nature," and Vergil should be praised for "imitating" Homer as he did; indeed, it is better to imitate other poets than to heed the instructions of philosophers in their arts of poetry. Speroni goes so far as to suggest that "imitation," since it is not based on the activity of the mind, is not really a human activity. It is more proper to monkeys and to children than to man. Art, on the other hand, is properly the province of man, for it is the disciple rather than the enemy of reason. Clearly, Speroni is thinking, here,

---

[48] *Ibid.*, p. 425: "Però è la prima cosa fatta dal poeta; ... e questa bisogna che sia in modo tessuta, che le cose succedano quasi per ordine naturale l'una dall'altra, e non vi si veda volontà del poeta, che così li paja di fare: perchè diventa non verisimile, ma affettato il poema."

[49] *Ibid.*, pp. 438–39: "perchè di una imitazione debba essere una cosa sola imitata, come di un soggetto una scienza"; "ma anche perchè se'l poema è ornamento redundante e superfluo, se'l poeta togliesse a imitar più di una azione poeticamente, il poema a volere esser perfetto cresceria in infinito."

[50] *Ibid.*, p. 534: "di qua viene che le commedie e tragedie doppie, o triple, non son belle, come le semplici, perchè son meno ornate, e più oscure; il che lieva della bellezza."

of imitation as a kind of copying or physical mimicry, rather than as the essence of the artistic process.

In the following year, 1565, Speroni discussed another Aristotelian problem, that of purgation, in a letter to Alvise Mocenigo dated February 26, 1565. He recognizes two current interpretations of purgation, one insisting that it concerns only the two passions of pity and fear, the other that it admits other similar passions. He adopts the latter, "ut liberemur ab hujuscemodi facinoribus," and he gives his reasons:

> . . . the Aristotelians must be of this opinion, explaining the definition that Aristotle gives of it in the *Poetics* by using the words spoken to us by Plato in Book VIII of the *Laws*, where in fact he talked of the tragedy of Canace and Macareo. And he says that those dishonest acts, and the death of him who commits them, are shown so that one will learn to avoid them; and this is truly the proper way of understanding Aristotle.[51]

Speroni interprets his opposition as holding that purgation achieves its effect through the forming of habits; thus, it would accustom people to pity and fear through repeated exposure to them. He believes that the latter theory also implies a limited usefulness for tragedy and comedy; both would be acceptable only in a state where the government was popular rather than monarchical. Tragedy, showing the misfortunes of the great, would convince the people that their rulers are not gods and that their own station in life is preferable; comedy would teach other "popular" lessons. Both, in such an analysis, become instruments used by the governors—in an indirect and hidden way—for the good of the governed. Throughout the discussion, Platonic overtones are apparent, and Aristotle is forgotten.

Giovanni Fabrini da Fighine's commentary on Horace's *Ars poetica*, in Italian, appeared in 1566 (see above, Chapter V, pp. 179-83). Like its predecessors, it made numerous comparisons between Horace and Aristotle; like them also, it assumed that Horace was following Aristotle and that the content and order of the two treatises were essentially the same. But whereas some of the other commentaries revealed, incidentally, an interpretation of Aristotle, there seems to be none discernible in Fabrini. His constant practice is merely to cite similar passages, prefacing each quotation from the *Poetics* by some such formula as "questo medesimo dice Aristotile nel testo lvi," or "secondo Aristotile ne la poetica al cxxxi. testo" (references throughout are to Maggi's divisions in the edition of 1550). Nor is one any more rewarded by a quest of the topics in Aristotle that were of especial interest to Fabrini; he was interested in everything. Perhaps the more detailed and practical topics appear with greater fre-

---

[51] In *Opere*, letter CCXLII, V, 175: "di questa opinione deono esser li Aristotelici, esponendo la definizion, che ne dà Aristotile nella poetica con le parole detteci da Platone nell' ottavo *de legibus*; ove appunto egli parla della tragedia di Canace e Macareo; e dice che queste cose disoneste, e la morte di chi le commette, si rappresentano, perchè si impari a lasciarle stare: e questa è veramente la bona intelligenzia di Aristotile."

quency, merely because they are closer to the stuff of Horace's work than the more abstract and theoretical considerations—perhaps, also, because Fabrini's Italian commentary was addressed to a more popular and less erudite audience. At times his translations are interesting, since the terminology reveals the extent to which he is thinking of Horace rather than of Aristotle. Thus, for example, he translates 1451*b*27 with the formula "i poeti sono denominati piu da *l'inuentione*, e da la *perfetta narratione* de le fauole, che dal comporre in uersi" (p. 355, italics mine); and he paraphrases 1455*b*23 thus: "diuide la poesia d'Omero in due parti, in fauola, & episodi. cioè, in *digressioni*" (p. 355v; italics mine). Again, 1448*a*16 is translated: "la comedia, e la tragedia sono differenti tra loro; perche questa imita cose *piu eccellenti*, & quella *piu humili*" (p. 364; italics mine). All in all, Fabrini's commentary has little significance for the history of the *Poetics* in the Renaissance, except as another document relating it to the *Ars poetica* and seeing it essentially in terms of the later work.

To about the same period belongs an anonymous manuscript (Siena, Biblioteca Comunale K.IV.36) ascribed by another hand to "Lottino," dedicated to Giovan Francesco Stella and Dionigi Atanagi, and having as its general theme the one indicated in the title, *Intorno alli episodij de' poeti nelle poesie*. I have placed it *circa* 1566 because it treats of the general relationship between plot and episodes that Maranta had discussed in his lectures and because it seems to share the preoccupations of those authors who, around 1566, were debating the merits and demerits of Terence. Lottino starts from Aristotle, in whose works he finds authority for stating that the episodes are to plot as accidents are to substance:

... in fact, it [plot] is nothing else but the substantial part of the poem. But just as nature in her compounds works in such a way that the substantial parts are served by those which are accidental, so the poet causes his plot to be served by the episodes.... This came to pass because the number of principles from which all things in the world had their origin was so small, that it was necessary that not only the principles but things themselves (by resemblance to the principles) should be mixed and intermingled with one another. None of these things could ever have been truly distinguished from another, nor be called one thing, if all the other parts were not regulated and commanded by one single part, as by its principal form.... In this same way, the good poets have proceeded in the linking of the episodes with their plots, in which no episode is found that is not united to them and derived from them in such a way, that it is not possible to divide it from them effectively or even—except by those who are very expert in the matter—to distinguish it from the plot.[52]

[52] Bibl. Com., Siena, K.IV.36, fols. 1–1*v*: "elle in somma non è altro che la parte sustantiale del poema. Ma si come la natura ne suoi composti fa sempre, che le parti sustantiali siano da quelle seruite, che in esso si ritrouano accidentali; cosi il poeta fa, che la sua fauola sia da gli epissodij seruita.... Il che è auuenuto, percio ch'il numero de principij, da quali tutte le cose del mondo hanno hauuto origine, è stato cosi piccolo; ch'egli è stato di bisogno, che non pure i principij, ma le cose stesse a simiglianza di quelli si siano infra loro mescolate, et

Lottino seems here to be seeking metaphysical justification for the close connection of episodes with plot; at the same time, he states an evaluative principle for that connection. As his argument continues, however, it becomes clear that he means by plot not the assemblage of events peculiar to the individual poem, but rather the whole complex of traditional materials associated with a given story. From these, he says, the poet selects those elements which are "excellent" and "singular," which will give to the poem "efficacy" and "admiration," "clarity" or "beauty." Such a process means a reduction of the basic materials to be included in the poem and the possible danger of meagerness. It is to prevent this that the poet introduces episodes. Harking back to Aristotle again, Lottino declares that the addition of episodes is more feasible in the epic than in tragedy and comedy, since the dramatic forms are more restricted in time—"into their operation they cannot put more space of time than those few hours during which they must be presented to the people."[53] A final theoretical consideration regarding plot is again derived from Aristotle; it concerns the division of the "represented" plot into complication and solution. For Lottino, this plot is itself preceded by another, the "narrated" one, which apparently consists of those expository parts at the beginning of the drama which recount the completed parts of the action.

These principles are carefully applied to the discussion of Terence's *Eunuch*, which is interspersed with the theoretical sections of the short treatise. Episodes were added to the central plot, says Lottino, because without them the comedy would have had insufficient size and insufficient beauty; they augment the plot pleasantly through probable actions (fol. 3v). Several dicta from the *Poetics* are compounded into this conclusion on the episodes: " . . . they are all substantial parts of the plot, no one of which—nor of the others like them—could be transposed or removed without causing damage to the plot; and the poet makes them, through verisimilitude, so necessarily follow one from the other, always observing the decorum of persons, that nothing is left to be desired."[54] Decorum itself is clearly respected in the presentation of all personages and the ordering of all parts of the plot is such that verisimilitude and propriety are at all times respected. Hence, for Lottino the *Poetics* becomes the

---

trapposte: ciascuna delle quali non haurebbe mai potuto uera distintione dall'altra hauere, ne una esser chiamata; se da una sola parte, come da sua forma principale, non fusse stato dato regola all'altre, et comandato. . . . In cotal modo sono i buoni poeti proceduti nel collegamento de gli epissodij con le fauole loro: nelle quali ui se ne troua alcuno per si fatta maniera ad esse unito, et da esse dcriuato; che non che con effetto diuiderlo; ma non si puo pure; senon da quelli, che ne sono ben pratichi, conoscerne la differenza."

[53] *Ibid.*, fol. 2v: "queste nella operation loro non posson mettere più spatio che quelle poche hore, nelle quali elle debbono essere al popolo rappresentate."

[54] *Ibid.*, fol. 4: "son tutte parti sustantiali della fauola: delle quali, et delle altre à lor simiglianti, non si potrebbe trasporre, ò leuar alcuna, che non ne uenisse danno alla fauola: et il poeta le fa con uerisimili così necessariamente seguitar l'una dall'altra; il decoro delle persone sempre seruando; che non si puo piu oltre desiderare."

source for both theoretical and practical statements in criticism and a source from which he makes relatively few departures.

The place of Aristotle in Frosino Lapini's *Letione nella quale si ragiona in universale del fine della poesia* (1567) is quite different. For in this lecture, delivered before the Accademia Fiorentina on May 1, 1567, the dominant influence is Plato; it is he who gives the essential orientation to a work which declares that the end of poetry is the inculcation of virtue in man (see Chapter VII, pp. 290–92). There are some references to Aristotle, but rather to the *Physics* and the *Ethics* than to the *Poetics*. From the Aristotelian approach in general, Lapini derives his identification of the material, formal, and final causes of poetry:

> We conclude therefore that since the material of the poet is the plot, under which are veiled and enclosed all the subjects taken by him for explanation, and since the form is the imitation, it follows that the end must be different from these. Nor is this pleasure alone, which is felt as very great, as accidental, in the outer shell and surface of the beautiful invention of the plot, but mainly the utility enclosed within the meaningful and moral subject, veiled by the plot in the same way that the mysteries were hidden and covered in the sacred ceremonies.[55]

Here, whereas the approach may be Aristotelian, the conclusions are surely not those of the *Poetics*, wherein all the causes are differently defined. The conception of moral utility as the end determines Lapini's interpretation of catharsis; moral betterment is achieved when the soul is purged of its passions (p. C). It also determines how he understands "goodness" of character, which he takes to mean honor and virtue, necessary if the personages are to serve as exemplars for better living. Lapini cites Vettori's gloss as corroborating his own and Horace's "utile dulci" as containing the same conclusion. The need for heightened goodness of character is further emphasized by the nature of imitation itself. Imitation is always meant to be pleasant and beautiful, and these effects are achieved by representing any object—even a low person or action—as more nearly perfect than it would normally be. When a virtuous person is concerned, the heightening will bring him near to moral perfection, and the ends of the poem will be completely realized.

CASTELVETRO (1570)

The year 1570 was marked by the publication of the first of the "great commentaries" in Italian and hence the first in any European vernacular. This was Lodovico Castelvetro's *Poetica d'Aristotele vulgarizzata et sposta*, printed first in Vienna in 1570 and later, in a revised edition, in Basel in

---

[55] *Letione* (1567), pp. Eij–Eijv: "Conchiudiamo adunque che sendo la materia del Poeta la Fauola, sotto la quale sono velati & racchiusi tutti i soggetti presi da lui a dichiararsi, & la forma sendo la imitatione, ne segue che diuerso da queste conuien che sia il fine: ne ciò sia il solo piacere, che per accidente nella scorza, e superficie della vaga inuentione della fauola si sente grandissimo ma l'Vtile principalmente, racchiuso nel sensato, e morale soggetto, velato dalla fauola, non altrimenti che i misterij erano nelle sacre cerimonie ascosi, e coperti."

1576.[56] Castelvetro follows the usual pattern for such commentaries; his work is divided into six major "Parti," each of which is divided into "Particelle," and for each "Particella" we are given a section of the Greek text, a brief statement of the "Contenenza" or content, a "Vulgarizzamento" or translation, and then the long "Spositione" or commentary. The passages themselves are fewer in number and longer than in Castelvetro's predecessors, totaling fifty-six in all. Castelvetro differs from his predecessors, also, in his attitude toward Aristotle and the text of the *Poetics*; whereas they were respectful and subservient, he declares his doubts about the theory and proposes to develop his own. The *Poetics* as we have it, he says, is "a first rough form, imperfect and unpolished, of the art of poetry, which it is probable that the author preserved so that it might serve him as a collection of notations and of brief reminders, in order to have them at hand when he might wish to compile and compose the complete art."[57] His own purpose is more ambitious:

> I have tried ... to render the art of poetry clear, showing and displaying not only what was handed down to us in these few pages by that greatest of all philosophers, but also whatever should or could be written for the full benefit of those who might wish to know how one should go about composing poems correctly and how one should judge properly whether those already written do or do not have what they ought to have.[58]

Aristotle will be used, therefore, partly as a point of departure, partly as an opponent. Our immediate problem, here, is to discover what happens to Aristotle's theory in the process of adaptation and of refutation.

It would perhaps not be too bold to say that, in general, Castelvetro transposes the whole of the analysis from the world of art to the world of reality. Let us say, by way of explanation, that Aristotle in the *Poetics* considers the special qualities of poems as works of art (rather than as natural objects), that he analyzes those characteristics of objects which affect their usability in works of art (rather than their natural qualities), that he takes into consideration only those capacities of men which affect

---

[56] Castelvetro died in 1571, and the second edition is posthumous; it was prepared by friends on the basis of the author's manuscripts. There are numerous variations between the texts, even in the direct translations of Aristotle. Questions arise about the authenticity of the changes and which text to use as a basis for study. I have used the 1576 edition as probably representing Castelvetro's final thinking on the text of Aristotle and on poetic theory.

[57] *Poetica d'Aristotele* (1576 ed.), p.)()(3: "vna prima forma rozza, imperfetta, & non polita dell'arte poetica, laquale è verisimile, che l'autore conseruasse, perche seruisse in luogo di raccolta d'insegnamenti, & di brieui memorie per poterle hauere preste, quando volesse compilare, & ordinare l'arte intera." See my article, "Castelvetro's Theory of Poetics," *Critics and Criticism: Ancient and Modern*, ed. R. S. Crane (Chicago: University of Chicago Press, 1952), pp. 349–71; the present treatment is, in large part, abstracted from the article.

[58] *Poetica d'Aristotele* (1576 ed.), p.)()(3: "ho tentato ... di far manifesta l'arte poetica, non solamente mostrando, & aprendo quello, che è stato lasciato scritto in queste poche carte da quel sommo philosopho, ma quello anchora, che doueua, o poteua essere scritto per vtilita piena di coloro, che volessero sapere, come si debba fare a comporre bene poemi, & a giudicare dirittamente, se i composti habbiano quello, che deono hauere, o no."

the intelligence, the appreciation, and the evaluation of works (rather than all their characteristics as men). That is, works and objects and men are viewed always with respect to the special conditions of the art of poetry. In Castelvetro, any idea of "special conditions" tends to be lost; works are treated as if they were natural objects, objects themselves remain unchanged as they pass into the work, and men are men.

Perhaps the crux of the matter lies in Castelvetro's determination to remove the principal emphasis from the poem to the audience. Such a transformation means that all aspects of poetry are considered not in terms of the artistic exigencies of the poem itself but in terms of the needs or demands of a specifically characterized audience. Castelvetro's audience is thus limited and restricted, and it comes to be composed of the "common people": " . . . poetry was invented for the pleasure of the ignorant multitude and of the common people, and not for the pleasure of the educated."[59] Since the élite and the educated are thus rigorously excluded, certain qualities of mind are denied the audience:

. . . poetry [was] invented exclusively to delight and give recreation, I say to delight and give recreation to the minds of the rough crowd and of the common people, which does not understand the reasons, or the distinctions, or the arguments—subtle and distant from the usage of the ignorant—which philosophers use in investigating the truth of things and artists in establishing the rules of the arts; and, since it does not understand them, it must, when someone speaks of them, feel annoyance and displeasure.[60]

This audience will be almost completely lacking in imagination and will believe only the evidence of its senses: "Nor is it possible to make them believe that several days and nights have passed when they know through their senses that only a few hours have passed, *since no deception can take place in them which the senses recognize as such.*"[61] In matters not reducible to the senses, it will be incapable of going beyond what historical fact it knows—"We cannot imagine a king who did not exist, nor attribute any action to him."[62] It is immediately clear that any poet writing for such an audience would have to select as his objects such actions and characters

---

[59] *Ibid.*, p. 679, l. 35: "la poesia fu trouata per diletto della moltitudine ignorante, & del popolo commune, & non per diletto degli scientiati." For this text, I give page and line numbers, since the lines are numbered by the publisher.

[60] *Ibid.*, p. 29, l. 36: "la poesia sia stata trouata solamente per dilettare, & per ricreare, io dico per dilettare & ricreare gli animi della rozza moltitudine, & del commune popolo, il quale non intende le ragioni, ne le diuisioni, ne gli argomenti sottili, & lontani dall'vso degl'idioti, quali adoperano i philosophi in inuestigare la verita delle cose, & gli artisti in ordinare le arti, & non gli'ntendendo conuiene, quando altri ne fauella, che egli ne senta noia, & dispiacere." See also p. 25, l. 30.

[61] *Ibid.*, p. 109, l. 27: "Ne è possibile a dargli ad intendere, che sieno passati piu di, & notti, quando essi sensibilmente sanno, che non sono passate senon poche hore, non potendo lo'nganno in loro hauere luogo, il quale è tuttauia riconosciuto dal senso" (italics mine).

[62] *Ibid.*, p. 188, l. 25: "non ci possiamo imaginare vn re, che non sia stato, ne attribuirgli alcuna attione."

POETICS: VERNACULAR COMMENTARIES

as would be acceptable to the audience, that the choice of the objects would be determined to a degree by the audience, and that the objects would be chosen on the basis of their natural characteristics.

But that is not all. The physical comfort and the convenience of the audience need to be considered. We are speaking, says Castelvetro (p. 53, l. 27), of poems presented before an assembled crowd; we must not ask the crowd to assemble for a poem so short that it would not be worth its while, nor must we expect it to remain beyond a certain limit of physical endurance:

> ... the restricted time is that during which the spectators can comfortably remain seated in the theater, which, as far as I can see, cannot exceed the revolution of the sun, as Aristotle says, that is, twelve hours; for because of the necessities of the body, such as eating, drinking, excreting the superfluous burdens of the belly and the bladder, sleeping, and because of other necessities, the people cannot continue its stay in the theater beyond the aforementioned time.[63]

Finally, this audience has as one of its characteristics the capacity to be pleased by certain things and to be displeased by others. One of the bases for pleasure and displeasure is knowledge: the audience takes pleasure in learning, "especially those things which it thought could not come about"; contrariwise, it dislikes stories from which it cannot learn anything, those which present commonplace events and rapidly lead to satiety (p. 553, l. 9). Another is its hopes ("volontà"): the audience is pleased by events which happen in accordance with its wishes, displeased by those which do not (*ibid.*). Finally, the audience will relate the events of a poem to the fortunes of its own life; it will enjoy seeing the good happy and the wicked unhappy, since the case of the former will lead it to expect happiness from its own goodness and the case of the latter will give it a sense of security and justice. On the other hand, if the good are unhappy, it will experience fear and pity, and if the wicked are happy, it will feel envy and scorn; but these will be only temporary displeasures, since they will give way to feelings of self-righteousness and of justice, which will be ultimately pleasurable (pp. 121, l. 34; 122, l. 21). These additional characteristics of the audience not only restrict further the poet's choice of objects; they also limit his art, for he must now make plots and conceive of characters in certain ways, conform to certain wishes for the length and ordering of his work.

Throughout the above passages, Castelvetro has taken it for granted that pleasure alone is the end of poetry. This is his explicit position everywhere. He finds Aristotle in agreement with him and sees the utilitarian notion of purgation (as he interprets it) as a contradiction on Aristotle's

---

[63] *Ibid.*, p. 109, l. 21: "il tempo stretto è quello, che i veditori possono a suo agio dimorare sedendo in theatro, il quale io non veggo, che possa passare il giro del sole, si come dice Aristotele, cio è hore dodici. conciosia cosa che per le necessita del corpo, come è mangiare, bere, diporre i superflui pesi del ventre, & della vesica, dormire, & per altre necesstia non possa il popolo continuare oltre il predetto termino cosi fatta dimora in theatro." See also p. 57, l. 11.

part: "For if poetry was invented principally for pleasure, and not for utility, as he demonstrated in the passage where he spoke of the origin of poetry in general, why should he now insist that tragedy, which is a part of poetry, should seek utility above all else? Why should it not seek mainly pleasure without paying attention to utility?"[64] He explains purgation as an answer by Aristotle to Plato's banishment of the poets on moral grounds; here, insists Aristotle, is a moral use for poetry (pp. 9, l. 4; 116, l. 24; 272, l. 15; 697, l. 13). The utility lies in the diminution of the passions of pity and fear in the audience or their expulsion (pp. 117, l. 16; 299, l. 12). But if purgation is admitted as a utility, it is only incidental to the real end of pleasure:

> Those who insist that poetry was invented mainly to profit, or to profit and delight together, let them beware lest they oppose the authority of Aristotle, who here [*Poetics* 1459a21] and elsewhere seems to assign nothing but pleasure to it; and if, indeed, he concedes some utility to it, he concedes it accidentally, as is the case with the purgation of fear and of pity by means of tragedy.[65]

As a matter of fact, Castelvetro believes that purgation itself may be considered as a source of pleasure; thus, he affirms that "Aristotle meant by the word ἡδονήν [1453b11] the purgation and the expulsion of fear and of pity from human souls," and he goes on to explain how it can be pleasurable: " . . . it comes about when, feeling displeasure at the unhappiness of another unjustly suffered, we recognize that we ourselves are good, since unjust things displease us, which recognition—because of the natural love that we have for ourselves—is a source of great pleasure to us."[66] It is significant that in this discussion Castelvetro places the end of poetry within the audience in such a way that the end, too, becomes an external force operating upon the composition of the poem.

If the end of pleasure and its achievement are related to certain characteristics of the audience, the means by which the end is to be achieved are similarly related. Here the main consideration is the lack of imagination on the part of the audience. In sum, the argument runs as follows: the audience will derive pleasure only if it identifies itself with the characters

---

[64] *Ibid.*, p. 275, l. 30: "Percioche, se la poesia è stata trouata principalmente per diletto, & non per vtilita, come egli ha mostrato la, doue parlò dell'origine della poesia in generale, perche vuole egli, che nella tragedia, la quale è vna parte di poesia, si cerchi principalmente l'vtilita? Perche non si cerca principalmente il diletto senza hauer cura dell'vtilita?"

[65] *Ibid.*, p. 505, l. 38: "Coloro, che vogliono, che la poesia sia trouata principalmente per giouare, o per giouare, & per dilettare insieme, veggano, che non s'oppongano all'autorita d'Aristotele, il quale qui, & altroue non par, che le assegni altro, che diletto, &, se pure le concede alcuno giouamento, gliele concede per accidente, come è la purgatione dello spauento, & della compassione per mezzo della tragedia."

[66] *Ibid.*, p. 299, l. 12: "Aristotele intese per la voce ἡδονήν la purgatione, & lo scacciamento dello spauento, & della compassione dagli animi humani . . . è quando noi, sentendo dispiacere della miseria altrui ingiustamente auenutagli, ci riconosciamo essere buoni, poi che le cose ingiuste ci dispiacciono, la quale riconoscenza per l'amore naturale, che noi portiamo a noi stessi ci è di piacere grandissimo." The passage goes on to discuss additional, secondary pleasures.

and the events; this identification is possible only if the audience believes in their reality; its belief in their reality will depend upon the credibility—the verisimilitude—of the presentation. It is here that imagination enters. If the audience were endowed with great capacities of imagination, it would "believe" things far removed from the conditions of "real life"; since it is not, it will "believe" only what seems to it to be in the realm of its own experience, to be "true." It is this general argument which leads Castelvetro to interpret as he does Aristotle's remarks on necessity, probability, and verisimilitude. He divides the whole realm of possible actions according to the following schema (see p. 184, ll. 39 ff.):

I. Possible actions, *which have actually happened*
   A. Natural
      1. According to the course of nature
      2. Contrary to the course of nature (i.e., monstrous or miraculous happenings)
   B. Accidental
      1. Resulting from chance or fortune
      2. Resulting from the will of men
II. Possible actions, *which have not yet happened*
   A. and B. as above

Now Category I, since it includes accomplished actions, is essentially the province of history; it corresponds to Aristotle's τὰ γενόμενα and is limited to particular actions, performed by specific persons. Actions of this kind are essential in tragedy and epic, which, since they deal with royal persons, cannot dispense with a historical basis; the audience is incapable of imagining kings who did not exist, etc. But no poem may be composed entirely of such actions, since it then would be a history and not a poem at all. Comedy, of course, needs no component of historical events, since its persons and their actions are private and obscure.

Category II, on the other hand, is coequal with Aristotle's τὰ δυνατά; it is the realm of the universal, since the actions are possible for many persons; it is thus the realm of poetry. All poems must possess some component of actions which have not actually happened. But whereas in the first category the question of credibility does not arise, in the second it is of primary importance. In order that credibility (and hence verisimilitude) may be assured and that the ingredient of the marvelous, also necessary if any pleasure is to occur, may be present, the following three requisites are established for possible actions:

  (a) They must be similar to those actions which have actually happened.
  (b) They must be similar to those actions which had the least probability of happening, but which did actually happen.
  (c) The parts or parcels of such actions must individually be similar to those parts of actions which happened in various cases to various people.

With respect to credibility, then, it may be assured by several means: first, by the use of a historical basis for the action in certain genres; second, by a close adherence, in invented actions, to the conditions of "real" or "true" actions. At this point, the expectations of the audience again impinge upon the poet in a very important way, for the audience is the touchstone of natural probability, and it will believe whatever conforms to its conceptions of reality. In part, its conceptions are formulated in terms of decorum, of traditional traits to be assigned to characters of given types, and of conventional actions. Castelvetro equates these at once with the ἁρμόττοντα of Aristotle and the Horatian decorum.

All degrees of probability as Castelvetro conceives them are natural probability rather than aesthetic probability; that is, probability in a work is established not by reference to the conditions of the work itself or to preliminary statements within the work, but by reference outside the work to the operations of nature. This is especially clear in the example he uses for distinguishing between necessity and verisimilitude. Actions of both kinds are possible, hence admissible into poetry. If a man is wounded on the head, it is "verisimilar" or probable that he will die; hence the poet may represent his death. If a man is wounded in the heart, it is "necessary" that he die; hence the poet may represent his death (p. 188, l. 1). Similarly for actions springing from character, all of which are really matters of decorum (p. 330, l. 40). In all such considerations of historical truth or natural probability or necessity and verisimilitude, the primary aim is not the imitation of nature for the sake of making the poem resemble nature but rather the resemblance to nature for the sake of obtaining the credence of the audience.

If the problems connected with the objects represented in poetry and with its audience are largely problems of "nature," so—in an indirect way—are the problems connected with the making of the work of art. The challenge is not to produce a beautiful work of art through the ordering of all the parts to an artistically perfect structure. Questions of beauty rarely concern Castelvetro. Rather, it is the task of the poet to find some way of entertaining the audience while he keeps it convinced that what it sees (or reads) is true, that is, some way of striking a proper balance between the probable and the marvelous. As we have seen, the first means to the achievement of this end is the proper selection and assorting of materials. A second means to convincing and amusing the audience is the disposition of these materials in accordance with the unities of time, place, and action. We have already noted that the physical comforts of the audience and its lack of imagination have to be taken into account by the poet; these two factors lead, respectively, to the unities of time and of place. With respect to time, the clearest statement is found in the comparison of tragedy and the epic:

Now, just as the perceptible end of tragedy has found its proper compass within the revolution of the sun over the earth without going beyond this limit, in order to put an end to the discomfort of the audience and the expense of the actors, so the perceptible end of the epic has found its proper compass in being able to be extended over several days, since neither the discomfort of the listener nor harm or expense connected with the reciter took this possibility away from it.[67]

Besides, the action before its eyes will take place on a single spot, the stage. Hence two unities: " . . . tragedy . . . must have as its subject an action accomplished in a small area of place and in a small space of time, that is, in that place and in that time where and when the actors remain engaged in acting, and not in any other place or in any other time."[68] Ideally, the invented action should occupy no more time than a real action, and this time should not exceed the time of performance; the place should remain unchanged and be contained within the space visible to a person who himself did not move.

As for the unity of action, which for Aristotle is the only important one and which for him is the very essence of the work of art, Castelvetro's treatment is highly revelatory of his general attitude toward poetics. To begin with, he denies any necessity—in the nature of things—for limiting a poem to a single action; as so frequently, he takes issue sharply with Aristotle here:

For there is no doubt that, if in history one may relate in a single narrative several actions of a single person, . . . in poetry it will be possible in a single plot to narrate without being blamed for it several actions of a single person, just as similarly in poetry one may relate without being blamed for it a single action of a whole people, for history does this with much praise. . . . And, indeed, in poetry not only a single action of a whole people may be narrated, but even several actions of a people. . . . And even if it were conceded to poetry to relate many actions of many persons or of many peoples, I do not see that any blame should come to it for this reason.[69]

Moreover, the presentation of a double or even a multiple plot would more readily serve the end of pleasure sought by the poet:

---

[67] *Ibid.*, p. 534, l. 1: "Hora, si come il termine sensibile della tragedia ha trouata la sua misura d'vn giro del sole sopra la terra senza passare piu oltre, per cessare il disconcio de veditori, & la spesa de rappresentatori, cosi il termine sensibile dell'epopea ha trouata la sua misura di potere essere tirato in lungo per piu giornate, poi che ne disagio d'ascoltatore, ne danno, o spesa del recitatore non gliele toglieua."

[68] *Ibid.*, p. 109, l. 17: "la tragedia . . . conuiene hauere per soggetto vn'attione auenuta in picciolo spatio di luogo, & in picciolo spatio di tempo, cio è in quel luogo, & in quel tempo, doue, & quando i rappresentatori dimorano occupati in operatione, & non altroue, ne in altro tempo."

[69] *Ibid.*, p. 178, l. 23: "Perche non ha dubbio niuno, che, se nell'historia si narra sotto vn raccontamento piu attioni d'vna persona sola, . . . nella poesia si potra sotto vna fauola narrare senza biasimo piu attioni d'vna persona sola. si come parimente nella poesia senza biasimo si potra narrare vna attione sola d'vna gente, percioche l'historia fa cio con molta lode. . . . Et non solamente pure nella poesia si potra narrare vna attione d'vna gente, ma anchora piu attioni d'vna gente. . . . Et, se le si concedera la narratione di molte attioni di molte persone, o di molte genti, non pero veggo, che biasimo alcuno le debba seguire." The argument rests upon an analogy between poetry and history which Castelvetro develops at great length.

[509]

... we should not marvel at all if several actions of one person or one action of a people or several actions of several persons delight us and make us attentive to listen, since such a plot carries with it, through the multitude of the actions, through the variety, through the new events, and through the multitude of persons and of the people, both pleasure and greatness and magnificence.[70]

Why, then, does Aristotle insist upon unity, and why does Castelvetro recommend it? The reason is different for the different genres. For tragedy and comedy, unity of action is a consequence of the unities of time and of place; it would not be possible to crowd into a restricted space and into twelve hours more than one action; indeed, sometimes one of these plays will contain only a part of an action.[71] For the epic, where this "necessity" does not exist, unity of action is sought for two other reasons: first, because such a unified plot is more "beautiful," less likely to satiate the spectator with an abundance of different things (see pp. 179, l. 16; 514, l. 29), and, second, because such a plot demonstrates the ingenuity and the excellence of the poet (see pp. 179, l. 24; 179, l. 16, and 504, l. 23). What is symptomatic about this position, especially in a commentary on the *Poetics*, is its abandonment of any concern with the structural or formal beauties of the work and its insistence upon two such nonartistic considerations as the comfort and character of the audience and the glory of the poet.

Many of these lines of argument, in fact, point to a conception of the art of poetry essentially different from Aristotle's. A first major difference appears in Castelvetro's assimilation of this art to the art of history. Their kinship is so intimate, he says, that if we possessed an adequate art of history, it would be unnecessary to write an art of poetry, "since poetry derives all its light from the light of history."[72] Indeed, Aristotle's work is to an extent vitiated by the fact that he did not base it upon an adequate art of history, and most of the precepts which he presents would have been more adequately and more appropriately developed in an art of history. The two arts differ in two respects only: history presents events which actually happened, poetry those which have not occurred but which might occur, and poetry uses verse whereas history uses prose (see pp. 115, l. 41; 190, l. 1). Otherwise, they are so much alike that poetry may be defined as "a resemblance or imitation of history" ("similitudine, o rassomiglianza d'historia," p. 28, l. 19). Poetry is certainly more like history than it is like painting, and Aristotle errs with others in making the latter comparison.

---

[70] *Ibid.*, p. 179, l. 18: "non sia punto da marauigliarsi se piu attioni d'vna persona, o vna attione d'vna gente, o piu attioni di piu persone ci dilettassono, & ci rendessono intenti ad ascoltarle, portando seco la fauola per la moltitudine dell'attioni, per la varieta, per gli nuoui auenimenti, & per la moltitudine delle persone, & della gente & piacere, & grandezza, & magnificenza." See also pp. 504, l. 36; 692, l. 31.

[71] *Ibid.*, pp. 179, l. 4; 504, l. 19. Castelvetro thinks of the "action" as the whole of the traditional or historical story, not as the plot of their individual work of art.

[72] *Ibid.*, p. 5, l. 21: "prendendo la poesia ogni sua luce dalla luce dell'historia."

Castelvetro was so completely dedicated to the analogy between poetry and history that he failed to construct, as most of his contemporaries were doing, a parallelism between poetry and rhetoric—and this in spite of the essentially rhetorical character of his own system. Aristotle's notion of imitation as introducing differences between an object in nature and that object as represented in a work of art is completely absent; none of the implications of the Aristotelian concept of imitation is present. For the object in nature is also the object in art, and the art which most readily treats of "nature" by means of words, history, is the one which provides all the essential distinctions.

Some of these matters are further discussed, if briefly, in Castelvetro's *Chiose intorno al libro del Comune di Platone*, a work which dates from the period of the *Poetica*[73] but which was first published in the *Opere varie critiche* of 1727. The sections of the *Republic* which deal with poetics are naturally of unusual interest to Castelvetro. He finds that Aristotle contradicts Plato's statement that poetry is meant to teach by example and that we must of necessity follow its examples. Rather, we are at liberty to accept or reject its teachings, since it teaches "through materials about which we may think, and so that we may have examples of all kinds, both to frighten the wicked and to console the good, and to learn the nature of men and of women." The aim is still to teach, in this context, but the audience may react against the examples rather than follow them blindly. This, in essence, is the meaning of purgation: " . . . therefore Aristotle said that tragedy, by means of fears and injustices, drove out fears and injustices from the hearts of the men listening, refuting what Plato says in this passage."[74] Again on purgation, Castelvetro proposes an alternative theory in which like would purge like: "Perhaps Aristotle . . . said that tragedy purged those same passions by means of those same passions because they constituted a purification and a proving of man, just as Plato relates . . . that the perils proposed are a fire for man."[75] Castelvetro's explanations of Plato depend upon an understanding of Aristotle, as his explanations of Aristotle depend upon an understanding of Plato.

Somewhere between 1570 and 1572 an author variously referred to as Anselmo or as Ridolfo Castravilla wrote an attack upon Dante entitled

---

[73] A passage on p. 215 of the *Opere varie critiche* indicates that the commentary is posterior to that on the *Poetics*.

[74] In *Opere varie critiche* (1727), pp. 215–16: "per materia da farvi pensamenti sopra, & acciocchè abbiamo esempj d'ogni maniera e da spaventare i rei, e da consolare i buoni, e da conoscere la natura de gli uomini, e delle donne. E perciò diceva Aristotele, che la Tragedia con le paure, e con le ingiustizie scacciava le paure, e le ingiustizie dal cuore de gli uomini ascoltanti, riprovando quello, che dice Platone in questo luogo." The reference in Plato is to p. 561 of the Ficino translation in the Basel edition of 1546.

[75] *Ibid.*, pp. 226–27: "Forse Aristotele . . . disse, che la Tragedia purgava quelle medesime affezioni con quelle medesime affezioni, poichè erano affinamento, e paragone dell'uomo, siccome racconta . . . Platone, che i pericoli proposti sono il fuoco dell'uomo."

POETIC THEORY

Discorso nel quale si mostra l'imperfettione della Comedia di Dante. This was the work which started the great controversy over Dante, and I shall treat it in detail in a later chapter. But since the attack is based upon principles which claim to be Aristotelian, it is of interest here to see how Castravilla (who has never been successfully identified) understood the text of the *Poetics*. It is important to note that this is a full-scale examination of a great modern work, an examination that takes its approach and its criteria from Aristotle, and that it is one of the earliest practical studies to do so. Castravilla writes in rebuttal of Benedetto Varchi's claim (in the *Hercolano*, 1570) that Dante's poem was superior to Homer's. He first asks whether the *Divina Commedia* is a poem at all, establishing the principle that a poem must contain a plot which is the imitation of an action—an Aristotelian principle:

> Aristotle declares this in his *Art of Poetry* in several places, and especially in the beginning of that book, where he states that all kinds of poems are imitations, and in the passage below where he adds that those who imitate imitate persons in action: and farther below he says that the plot is an imitation of an action. From this passage one concludes that a poem is a plot . . . , except for the fact that a poem is not a poem until it is expressed in meter, which is its outer garment, and that the plot is an imitation of an action even in the mind of the poet and before it has been expressed. For this reason Aristotle said that the plot was like the soul of tragedy.[76]

Two interesting comments are included here: first, plot as an imitation exists prior to any expression in the form of a "poem"; second, making it into a poem involves necessarily the use of verse. Castravilla next asks whether Dante's work may properly be classed as an epic poem, applying to it Aristotle's yard-stick that an epic poem must be "an imitation of heroes" (fol. 77v). Before he proceeds to an analysis of the *Commedia*, he establishes a set of requisites for a good plot; these are attributed to Aristotle and constitute a digest of parts of the *Poetics*:

> It should be verisimilar: for without this the poem would fall short of its end, and would remain deprived of all force and vigor;
> Second, it should be clear and easily remembered, that is, such that it can be seen at a glance and remembered in a single turn of the memory;
> Thirdly, it must be one, that is, include one single action and that a whole one, that is from the beginning to the end;

---

[76] I quote this treatise from MS Vat. Lat. 6528, fols. 76-84; see fol. 76v: "Ilche declara Aristotele nella sua arte poetica in piu luoghi, e maxime nell'exordio di quel libro, doue pone che tutte le spetie delle poesie sono imitatione, et in quello che poi sogiugnie che quelli che imitano, immitano persone agenti: et più di sotto dice che la fauola e imitatione d'attione. dal qual luogo si ritrae che poema è fauola . . .; senonche il poema non e poema sinòche non è espresso col metro, che e la sua ueste, e la fauola è imitatione d'attione etiam nella mente del poeta, e prima ch'ella sia espressa. Pero dicea Aristotele che la fauola era quasi l'anima della tragedia." There are numerous Latin words and expressions throughout the text.

Plots will be beautiful if they are dramatic, that is if the persons introduced act and are in continuous action;

if they are simple, that is if they contain actions of a single thread;

if they have body and a proper size, for beauty cannot exist in little subjects;

if they have recognition and reversal which break forth from the subject probably or necessarily, in some marvelous fashion;

if they contain within the argument itself the marvelous, the terrible, the pitiable, and the moral;

if they do not have too many episodes, and if these are connected in such a way with the argument that they seem to be members born along with the body, not that were added to it.

if it has a beautiful knotting and a beautiful solution which comes out of the action itself.[77]

Castravilla's idea of plot seems to be a proper one—surely more correct than that of Castelvetro—and his digest of the requisites shows an understanding of the essential problems as Aristotle raises them.

NERONI (CA. 1571)

To approximately the same period (I have assigned them roughly to 1571[78]) belong three discourses by Baccio Neroni, probably prepared for delivery to the Accademia degli Alterati. They all deal with matters discussed in the *Poetics* and at times present interpretations of that text. One of them is entitled *Se il verso è necessario nella poesia*, and Neroni's answer to the question is a strong affirmative. This is of course in opposition to the *Poetics*; the author is therefore obliged to prove his position and to find a suitable interpretation of certain passages in Aristotle. He presents twelve distinct (and numbered) arguments: (1) Verse gives importance to subjects which are in themselves unimportant; it adds majesty, greatness, the marvelous, and by delighting the audience achieves the end of poetry: "This is a manifest sign that poets must necessarily use verse, as men who

---

[77] *Ibid.*, fols. 78v–79: "Che la sia uerisimile. che senza questo il poema caderebbe dal suo fine, e resteria spogliato d'ogni forza e uigore.

"Secondo uuol essere conspicua e ramemorabile cioe tale che si possa uedere in un girare d'un guardo e ricordarsene in una uolutione di memoria.

"Item debbe essere una, cioe comprendere una sola actione, e quella tutta cioe dal principio sino al fine.

"Le fauole saranno belle, se saranno dramatiche, cioè se le persone indotte s'opereranno, e saranno in continua operatione se saranno semplic[i], cioe se conteneranno actioni dun sol filo se haranno corpo e grandezza giusta; perche ne piccoli argumenti non puo esser beltà.

"Se haranno peripetia et agnitione, che erumpino uerisimilmente, o necessariamente dalla cosa in alcun modo amirabile.

"Se haranno nell argumento stesso l'admirabile, il terribile et il misericordieuole, el morale.

"Se non haranno troppi episodij e quelli saranno connexi talmente con largumento che pareranno membri nati col corpo non sutiui apposti.

"Se hara bello nexo e bella solutione che erumpa dalla cosa."

[78] See my "Argomenti di discussione letteraria nell'Accademia degli Alterati (1570–1600)," *Giornale Storico della Letteratura Italiana*, CXXXI (1954), 178.

treat mostly of vain things and of little importance, and such that they need to help them by means of the style, a thing which they cannot better achieve in any way than through verse."[79] (2) Even in poems treating important subjects, such as tragedy and the epic, verse is needed, along with all the ornaments of style; without them: "it is clear that these [poems] will remain a cold thing and a simple narration of a fact, and I am positive that such works will never be read in prose because without verse they would give no pleasure at all."[80] (3) The situation is different for histories, where the reader is interested in learning the facts; but in poems, which are imitations of true things, we need "the sweetness and the pleasantness of verse, by which the readers are most highly attracted."[81] (4) Such imitations of history as the *Amadigi* were neglected because they were in prose; this explains why Bernardo Tasso put this work into verse. (5) Even Aristotle argues for the necessity of verse:

... when Aristotle says that to compose any matter at all in verse does not make the writer become a poet . . . , it is a clear sign that the proper poetic style is that which is contained in verses. Nor are works that are written in prose to be called poetry even if there be imitation in them, which is most important in poems. . . . he [Aristotle] said that if somebody were to write in prose and to imitate some action according to probability, as is required in poems, he should not for that reason be called a poet, as one who understood that in poetry verse is necessarily to be required.[82]

This represents, of course, a considerable twisting of Aristotle's meaning. (6) Were this not true, Boccaccio, who imitates most excellently, would be called a poet. (7) Tragedy is poetry, and it is in verse. (8) Verse is needed in lyric poetry, which would be uninteresting without it. (9) One might think that comedy, which treats of low matters in a low style, might dispense with verse; but comedies having it are always more highly praised. (10) Universal usage has given the name "poet" only to those who write in verse. (11) When Aristotle uses the phrase λόγοις ψιλοῖς in connection

---

[79] MS Laur. Ashb. 559, fol. 1v: "Ilche è segno manifesto, che necessariamente i poeti deuono usare il uerso, come coloro che per lo piu trattano di cose uane, et di poca importanza, talche hanno bisogno di aiutarle con lo stile ilche per altra uia meglio conseguire non possono che mediante il uerso." The folios of the MS are unnumbered, and I have merely given a separate pagination to each of the discourses.

[80] *Ibid.*, fol. 2: "chiaro è che esse rimarranno una cosa fredda, et una semplice narratione d'un fatto, et mi rendo sicuro che tali opere mai saranno lette in prosa, per che senza uerso non darebbono piacere alcuno."

[81] *Ibid.*, fol. 2: "la suauita, et piaceuolezza del uerso dalla quale sono sommamente alletati i lettori."

[82] *Ibid.*, fol. 2v: "dicendo Aristotele che il comporre qualsi uoglia cosa in uersi non fa che il componitore diuenti poeta . . . , è segno manifesto che il proprio stile poetico, è quello che da uersi è contenuto. Ne l'opere scritte in prosa poesia douersi chiamare, ancorche in quelle sia l'imitatione che è importantissima ne poemi. . . . non per questo disse che se alcuno componessi in prosa et imitassi qualche attione secondo il uerisimile come si ricerca ne poemi, egli ne douesse essere chiamato poeta, come quegli che intese necessariamente nelle poesie ricercarsj il uerso."

with the epic (*Poetics* 1447a29),[83] he does not mean prose but rather language without rhythm and harmony. (12) In his definition of tragedy, again, the phrase ἡδυσμένῳ λόγῳ denotes "that language in which were present harmony, rhythm, and verse."[84] Neroni concludes his argument by insisting that if verse is required in tragedy and the epic, it is also to be demanded in all other poetic genres.

It is clear that the principles behind Neroni's argument include the necessity, if poetry is to be pleasurable, of certain stylistic and prosodic ornaments, the traditional identification of poetry with verse, and the conviction that Aristotle is the final authority. This last being true, he must follow the lead of his predecessors in giving to every doubtful passage in the *Poetics* a meaning that fits his own theoretical position. The two passages studied in the last two arguments were among those most frequently debated.

Another of Neroni's discourses is entitled *Che la fauola è di maggiore importanza nella poesia che i costumi*. Once again, the argument is very systematically pursued and Aristotle is the main authority; but this time Neroni agrees throughout with his source—or, rather, his use of it does not involve any extensive deformation. The discussion is repetitive, but one may distinguish these essential points: Plot and character are the most important parts of poetry. Neroni presents a philosophical defence of his contention that plot is the more important of the two: " . . . plot is of greater importance in poems than character because the plot exists in poems as the substance upon which all the other things [*var.*: qualities] rest as accidents, the fact being that the substance is not resident in any other subject but is itself the subject of all the accidents."[85] As Aristotle points out, plot can exist without character but character cannot exist without plot; the plots of *Iphigenia in Tauris* and the *Aeneid* are analyzed in proof. Not only is plot the substance of poetry, it is also the end:

> The plot is the end and the purpose of every poem, for the end of poetry is imitation, but actions are imitated primarily, thus the plot. Besides the end is action and not a quality of action, as is said in the *Poetics* and in the first book of the *Ethics*, and this excludes character which, because it consists of accidents and of qualities, cannot be the end.[86]

It is plot which gives form to any poem—the form which is the end of any maker—and as such it is the most noble and the most important of its

---

[83] See above, p. 363, for the difficulties with the text at this point.

[84] *Ibid.*, fol. 3v: "quella oratione, nella quale era l'Armonia, il ritmo, et il uerso."

[85] MS Laur. Ashb. 559, fols. 1–1v: "la fauola è di maggiore importanza ne' Poemi che i costumi non sono peroche la fauola è ne' Poemi à guisa della sustanza su laquale sono appogiate tutte l'altre cose [*var.*: qualità] come accidenti; sendo che la sustanza non è posta in altro suggetto ma è lei il suggetto di tutti gl'Accidenti."

[86] *Ibid.*, fols. 1v–2: "La fauola è il fine e l'intendimento d'ogni Poema peroche il fine della Poesia è l'imitatione, ma si imitano principalmente le attioni adunche la fauola; oltreche li fine è attione e non qualità d'attione come si dice nella Poetica e nel primo dell'Etica il che esclude i costumi, iquali perche sono accidenti e perche sono qualità non possono esser fine."

parts. Poems are praised or blamed for the success or failure of their plots, as Neroni demonstrates by citations from Aristotle, by references to the condemnation of the *Canace*, to Aristotle's praise of Homer, to the high esteem for Vergil and the contempt in which many critics hold the *Orlando Furioso*. Whereas character is multiple, plot is one and its unity brings it beauty and perfection; these qualities result from the fact that it may be seen in its totality in a single glance, and that it may be easily remembered. It is hence the principal source of pleasure in its reader or audience, and this is because actions are more pleasing than their accompanying circumstances. Besides, it is through the plot that a poem achieves its particular effects: "... the poem achieves its end to the degree to which it has a plot well adapted and proper to the moving of pity or terror or to receiving whatever other thing is desired by the author; for the moving of the passions in every poem is brought about properly by the plot, since this consists in reversal, recognition, and perturbation."[87] Other reasons are suggested for the superiority of plot over character and over all other parts of the poem. Neroni's conclusion presents, suddenly, a striking analogy between his consideration of plot and his conception of the place of poetry as subordinate to politics among the sciences: "in this case, it [plot] is the architectonic part and that which commands all the others, in no wise less than does politics over all the other arts and sciences."[88]

The last of the Neroni lectures, although it bears no title, might well be called *Che ogni fauola ha la peripetia, et la recognitione*, for it is a response to the negative of the same proposition presented by Carlo Rucellai. Neroni's reply is made at the request of the Reggente of the academy. What he has to say about recognition and reversal again represents, if not a distortion, at least a very loose understanding of Aristotle on the subject. If reversal, he says, means a change of status, then all forms of poetry necessarily will have it, since tragedy and comedy and the epic all represent a change of fortune from happiness or unhappiness to its contrary. Likewise, in every poem somebody or something is recognized. Of far greater significance are Neroni's remarks on plot, which in a sense continue those of the preceding discourse. But he now emphasizes a utilitarian end not even suggested in the other writings:

And it is a sure thing that poets, when they compose plots, have as their end either to profit or to delight, and that they expend a great effort for no other reason than to be of some utility to men. Wherefore, when they compose either tragedies or comedies or heroic poems, in all of them they have their eye on this end. To achieve it they use those means which best lead them to it; and to

[87] *Ibid.*, fol. 3: "in tanto ha il Poema conseguito il fin suo quanto ha la fauola ben' accomodata e conueniente à muouer la misericordia od il terrore o à riceuere qual si uoglia altra cosa desiderata dall'Autore percioche il muouer degli affetti in ogni Poema à propriamente cagionato dalla fauola, consistendo cio nella Peripetia Recognitione e perturbatione."

[88] *Ibid.*, fol. 4v: "è in questo caso la Architettonica e quella che comanda a tutte l'altre niente meno che si faccia la ciuile a tutte l'altre arti e scienze."

do this, of the parts which are found in such poems certain ones are powerful over all others: reversal and recognition. These are the ones which are apt, more than anything else, to move the passions, and they seize the minds of persons, delighting them or moving them to contempt or to compassion, depending upon the action which is then being represented.[89]

Like his theory of verse, this passage shows Neroni's adherence to the Horatian tradition. But even here he insists on essentially Aristotelian ideas; and, in general, his faithfulness to the text and the principles of the *Poetics* is exemplary for his time.

PICCOLOMINI'S TRANSLATION (1572)

In 1572 appeared the third of the translations of the *Poetics* into Italian, the second (after Segni's) to be issued separately and independently of a commentary. This was Alessandro Piccolomini's *Il libro della Poetica d'Aristotele*. It had been prepared, Piccolomini tells us, as a part of the work on his annotations to the same text, already completed; but fearing delays (and indeed the *Annotationi* were not to appear until 1575), he publishes his translation alone, accompanied only by a prefatory epistle containing a theory of translation. Piccolomini makes no direct mention of Castelvetro's "vulgarizzamento," although it would be surprising if he did not know it; in fact, one may detect throughout his translation an effort to make it as different as possible from that of his immediate predecessor. When one compares the two, one finds the following essential differences: Piccolomini's translation is always a little longer and more diffuse than Castelvetro's, since he is more intent upon making the meaning clear through translation alone, without relying upon a commentary. For example, his "Particella 5" (he uses Maggi's divisions) as compared with the last sentence in Castelvetro's "Particella Terza" (= *Poetics* 1447a26):

Castelvetro: Ma con lo stesso numero rassomigliano senza harmonia certi ballatori, percioche questi per figurati numeri rassomigliano anchora & costumi, & tormenti, & attioni (p. 15).

Piccolomini: Col ritmo stesso poi disgiunto dalla melodia imitan' alcuni di coloro, che son' instrutti nell'arte del saltare. conciosia cosa che questi tali col mezo di ritmi accompagnati da figurati mouimenti, cerchino d'imitare i costumi, gli affetti, & le attioni de gli huomini (p. 10).

Whereas Castelvetro, in such a passage as this, preserves the denseness of the original, Piccolomini substitutes phrases for words and achieves a

[89] MS Laur. Ashb. 559, fol. 1: "Et è cosa per certa, che i poeti nel comporre le fauole hanno per fine, o di giouare, o dilettare, et che per altro non si muouono ad affaticarsi se non per essere di qualche utilita agli huomini, Onde componendo essi, ò tragedie, ò comedie, ò poemi Heroici in tuttj hanno l'occhio à tal fine, per il quale conseguire adoperano que mezzi, che meglio uegli conducono, alche fare sopra tutte le parti che si trouano in tali poemi sono potentissime la Peripetia. et la recognitione, come quelle che sono piu che altro atte à muouere gli affetti, et pigliano gli animi delle persone, ò dilettando, ò mouendo à sdegno, ò à compassione secondo il fatto, che allora si rappresenta."

clearer final meaning. Moreover, he frequently uses words ("imitare" rather than "rassomigliano," "affetti" rather than "tormenti") that seem to convey a meaning closer to the original. For another example, we may compare his "Particella 11" with Castelvetro's "Particella Sesta" (*Poetics* 1448a1):

> *Castelvetro*: Hora, poi che i rassomiglianti rassomigliano coloro, che fanno, & è di necessita, che questi sieno o buoni, o rei, percioche i costumi quasi sempre accompagnano questi soli, conciosia cosa che tutti *gli huomini* sieno differenti di costumi per maluagita, o per bonta, egli è di necessita rassomigliare i migliori, che noi, o i piggiori, o i cosi fatti, secondo che fanno i dipintori. Et certo Polignoto effigiaua i migliori, & Pausone i piggiori, & Dionigi i simili (p. 34).
>
> *Piccolomini*: Hor perche coloro, che imitano, imitan persone, che qualche cosa facciano, & queste tai persone, ò buone, ò ree fa di mestieri, che siano: conciosia cosa che à queste due sole (si può dir) qualità del buono, & del reo, ogni costume dell' huomo segua, & si riferisca; come che per la virtù, & per il vitio, gli huomini nei lor costumi differiscan tutti: è necessario per questo che ò di persone migliori, ò di peggiori, di quali communemente noi siamo; ò di cosi fatte si faccia l'imitatione; si come vsan di fare li Pittori ancora. posciache Polignoto più belle le persone di quello, ch'ordinariamente sono; & Pausone più brutte, & Dionisio simili ad esse, soleuano depingendo rappresentare (p. 11).

It is certain that the second makes better sense than the first to the reader, who is obliged to a lesser degree to puzzle over terms and constructions. It may also, at certain points, represent the Greek text more accurately. We should find it useful, in this connection, to juxtapose the solutions proposed by the two men for certain crucial passages, i.e., passages which gave the sixteenth century more trouble than the rest of the text:

At 1447a29, the λόγοις ψιλοῖς (so critical because of the debate over prose and verse) is translated by Castelvetro as "con parlari nudi" (p. 17), by Piccolomini as "sciolta da misure di versi" (p. 10); the latter permits us to conclude that poetry may be written in prose.

At 1448a11, for ψιλομετρίαν (related to the same problem) Castelvetro gives "intorno a parlari, & a *nudi versi*" (p. 41) and Piccolomini "intorno al parlare, & *allo stesso verso, da per se solitariamente preso*" (p. 11); the latter is a kind of paraphrase, but it attempts to explain the meaning of "nudi."

At 1448b18, on the pleasure which accompanies imitation, Castelvetro translates badly by "& tutti si ralegrano delle rassomiglianze" (p. 63). Piccolomini expands to "L'altra [cagion] è poi, l'esser parimente naturale all'huomo il sentir piacere, & diletto dell'imitatione (p. 13)." The first version allows Castelvetro to find another factor as the second "natural cause," whereas Piccolomini is committed by his to the more correct interpretation.

At 1449b10, σπουδαίων is translated by Castelvetro as "de nobili" (p. 107), permitting the sociological interpretation; by Piccolomini as "di graui, & illustri persone" (p. 16), in which ethical as well as social elements are present.

At 1452*b*38, φιλάνθρωπον gives Castelvetro's "non è *gratiosa a gli huomini*, ne compassioneuole, ne spauenteuole" (p. 265) and Piccolomini's "ne di *commouimento humano*, ne di compassioneuole, ne di temibile" (p. 27), a better rendering of the much-discussed term.

These few examples show to what extent Piccolomini's translation may claim a greater fidelity to the original than Castelvetro's, which frequently is allowed to take on that form most useful for Castelvetro's private theories about poetry. At times, however, Piccolomini (perhaps because of his wish not to repeat Castelvetro) will adopt a less satisfactory solution—for example, in his translation of μίμοι as "ridicolose imitationi" (p. 10) instead of the more simple "mimi." Both translators, it should be noted in passing, are still faced with the problems of an imperfect text, and here they are almost equally unsuccessful; one may examine their attempts to deal with *Poetics* 1447*a*28 (Castelvetro, p. 17; Piccolomini, p. 10), 1447*b*22 (p. 18 and p. 10), 1449*b*26 (p. 113 and p. 25), and several others.

ELLEBODIUS (CA. 1572)

The date of 1572 is the most exact one that can be assigned to the *In Aristotelis librum de Poetica paraphrasis* of Nicasius Ellebodius (Nicaise Van Ellebode) contained in Ambrosian MS R.123.Sup., fols. 68–91*v* and accompanied by a set of "Notae in primum Aristotelis librum de Poetica" (fols. 92–110). The date results from a letter, apparently accompanying the manuscript, sent from Pressburg on February 22, 1572, asking the correspondent to show the manuscript to Riccoboni and to Paulo Manuzio. Throughout, the manuscript shows Ellebodius' Italian connections. It refers to earlier texts and commentaries printed in Italy, especially the Aldine edition of 1508 and Vettori's *Commentarii* of 1560; it derives many good readings for the text of the *Poetics* from an old codex said to be in the possession of Giovanni Vincenzo Pinelli; and it calls upon the authority of Michael Sophianos of Chios who had studied and later taught in Padua. Indeed, most of Ellebodius' connections are Paduan; he himself had studied there, and in addition to Sophianos his literary relationships seem to have been closest with Vettori, Riccoboni, and Pinelli. This work by a Belgian, probably written in Pressburg, may thus properly be considered to belong to the Italian tradition of the Cinquecento, through its origins, its intellectual ties, and its ultimate destination.[90]

[90] On Ellebode (also written Ellebaudt), see the article in the *Biographie Nationale de Belgique*, VII, 554; also Adolfo Rivolta, *Catalogo dei Codici Pinelliani dell'Ambrosiana* (Milano: Tipografia Pontificia Arcivescovile S. Giuseppe, 1933), pp. xxiv, xlv, lxxxviii. Also Jean Noël Paquot, *Mémoires pour servir à l'histoire littéraire des dix-sept provinces des Pays-Bas* (Louvain: Imprimerie Académique, 1765), I, 659. On Michael Sophianos, whose main published work was a translation of Aristotle's *De anima*, see Emile Legrand, *Bibliographie hellénique (XVe et XVIe siècles)* (Paris: Leroux, 1885), II, 168–76, and the various indices to Legrand's volumes.

Ellebodius' work is remarkable in several ways. In the "Notae" he suggests numerous improvements of the Greek text, either from the Pinelli manuscript or from suggestions by Sophianos, some of which have found their way into the modern text through the conjectures of recent scholars (see, for example, in the edition of J. Hardy, the variants on pages 33, 43, and 53). These are frequently supported by citation of other texts which show a considerable erudition in Greek and Latin sources. The paraphrase itself, which is sometimes merely a running translation, sometimes an expansion and development of the original work, is reasonably accurate and faithful to the intentions of the original. Ellebodius sees these intentions as contained in the following program: ". . . so that we may understand under what genus poetry is placed, what conception we should have of it, both how it differs from other arts in the same genus and how its forms differ among themselves, what were its beginnings and development."[91] He attempts to remain as closely Aristotelian as he can, even to the extent of seeking clarification for both text and ideas in other works of Aristotle, and he refers much less frequently than do his predecessors to the rival critical school of the Horatians. Nonetheless, there are two major points on which he departs quite markedly from what we must now consider to be the meaning of the *Poetics*.

The first of these is on the use of verse in poetry. For Ellebodius, poetry is impossible without verse; and, as so many of his fellow-commentators were doing, he interprets all apposite passages in the *Poetics* to corroborate this view. The initial statement comes in connection with 1447a28:

> The epic uses in imitating only bare language, that is verse without modulated . . . sound, and dancing; and it either mixes with one another several kinds of verse, or it uses one form of verse alone. . . . now this must be conceded, that language limited by poetic numbers cannot be absent from the epic or from any kind of poem; surely without this poetry can in no wise imitate. Moreover, imitation is so essential that the very name of poetry chiefly resides in it, nor indeed can it subsist without it; in the light of which remarks neither can verse without imitation, nor imitation without verse, be made into epic, or into poetry of any sort.[92]

Whenever, later in the text, any crucial phrase appears, he finds authority for giving to it a meaning in keeping with this position. Even the most

---

[91] MS Ambrosianus R.123.Sup., fol. 68: "ut cui generi subijciatur poesis, quae eius sit notio, quo modo cum ipsa a ceteris, quę sunt eiusdem generis, tum eius formę inter se differant, quae initia, progressusque poeseos sint, intelligatur."

[92] *Ibid.*, fol. 68v: "Epopoeia nudam tantum orationem, hoc est uersus sine modulato . . . sono, et saltatione adhibet in imitando, siue misceat inter se plura uersuum genera; siue una carminis forma utatur. . . . nunc hoc concessum sit, orationem quae poeticis numeris adstricta sit, neq. ab epopoeia, neq. ab ullo poematis genere abesse posse. quippe sine qua imitari poesis nullo modo potest. imitatio porrò ita necessaria est, ut in ea potissimum poeseos nomen sit positum, nec sine ea cohaerere sanè possit. quocirca neq. carmen sine imitatione, neq. imitatio sine carmine epopoeiam, aut omnino poesin efficitur." The text of Aristotle is corrupt at this point through the presence of the word ἐποποιία.

[520]

cautious and faithful of Aristotelians were thus unable to shake off the traditional association between poetry and verse.

The second point of distortion (if we may call it that) is Ellebodius' insistence that purgation produces moral instruction, which in turn serves the political ends of those who govern the state. Again, he is far from being alone in this contention, and the effects of both Platonic and Horatian ways of thinking are abundantly apparent. This meaning is first read into the *Poetics* at the point at which the *Paraphrasis* is dealing with the explanation of the definition of tragedy:

> The last part of the definition is formulated in such a way that the usefulness of tragedy is made clear: tragedy brings to the state a utility which indeed is the very greatest, even for those who rule over citizens, and is to be sought out at all costs. For the error must be refuted by those who believe that tragedy was devised for no useful role for the citizenry, but merely for the worthless pleasure of the eyes and the ears.

After arguing that, in general, it is the duty of the rulers to make the citizens morally better, Ellebodius continues:

> Virtue moreover, since its effect is especially to hold in check the turbulent movements of the soul and to restrain them within the bounds of moderation, and since tragedy, more than that, curbs these emotions, it must surely be granted that tragedy's usefulness to the state is extraordinary. For it causes two troublesome passions, pity and fear—which draw the soul away from strength and turn it toward a womanish weakness—to be regulated and governed by the soul with precise moderation.

The way in which this is done and the character of the lessons learned are those consecrated by a long line of texts:

> For when we see repeatedly on the stage the most bitter sorrows of kings and princes and blameless (?) men and other most cruel misfortunes, we observe the fickleness of human affairs, and we are taught how to bear with moderation every change of fortune. And thus the soul is hardened by habituation, and those things which it formerly feared in the highest degree, it begins almost to hold in contempt.[93]

[93] *Ibid.*, fols. 72–72v: "Extrema definitionis pars est posita, ut usus tragoediae ostendatur; quem affert reip. qui quidem maximus est, et ijs qui ciuitates regunt, uehementer expetendus. coarguendus enim error eorum est, qui ad nullam partem utilem ciuitatibus, qui ad inanem dumtaxat uoluptatem oculorum, et aurium tragoediam comparatum putant. . . . uirtus autem, cum potissimum id agat, ut animi motus turbidos ratione coerceat, et mediocritatis regionibus includat, tragoedia porrò hos motus comprimat, concedatur profecto, singularem eius esse in rep. utilitatem. facit enim ut duae affectiones importunae, misericordia, et timor, quae auocant à fortitudine animum, et ad muliebrem ignauiam abjiciunt, temperentur et definita animi moderatione gubernentur. nam spectandis in scena identidem regum et principum uirorum inte... bus, acerbissimis doloribus, et alijs asperrimis casibus perspicitur inconstantia rerum humanarum, et ad omnem fortunae commutationem moderate ferendam erudimur. itaque duratur consuetudine animus, et quae antea summe metuerat incipit penè contemnere." Cf. fols. 77–77v: "est autem munus tragoediae per miserationem, et timorem has ipsas affectiones ex animo abstergere quare fabula ita facienda est ut res formidabiles et miserabiles inducantur. nam hoc tragoediae est proprium."

Ellebodius concludes, therefore, that the Platonic exiling of tragic writers from the city was a mistake, for the pedagogical usefulness of purgation is an answer to any charge of moral harmfulness. Later, in the notes to the same passage (fol. 96), he develops the analogy with the gladiatorial spectacles, used to accustom young men to blood and wounds and to incite them to military valor.

A number of miscellaneous translations or notes in the *Paraphrasis* are of interest as they confirm or contradict current thinking about the matters which they treat. Ellebodius' view both of character and of the effects of tragedy depends upon his conception of catharsis. He translates φιλάνθρωπον as "communis humanitatis sensu" (fol. 77v) and glosses it thus: " . . . it generally means the sorrow by which the soul is affected through the misfortunes of others; for nature causes man, from the mere fact that he is a man, to be sorrowful at the troubles of men."[94] Demosthenes, Cicero, Horace, and Hermogenes are cited as authorities. The accompanying effect of fear gives the usual difficulty; he believes that it takes place when the tragic hero is similar in virtue to the mass of men ("cum is qui uulgo hominum uirtute par est," fol. 77v).

The matter of similarity is again involved in Ellebodius' understanding of the third of the requisites for character, τὸ ὅμοιον (1454a23), translated by "similes." This implies a representation of character either as it actually was in the person imitated or as tradition has made it out to be (fol. 82). The requisite is thus closely related to the general problem of verisimilitude, since here too opinion and current conceptions must be respected: "One must take care lest anything be related which is unacceptable to the opinion of men; wherefore those things should be preferred which cannot be done, if only they are probable, to those which can indeed be done, but do not seem to be credible."[95] In a sentence such as this, the last part is the translation of Aristotle, while the first part adds an interpretation which shows the general critical bent of its author. If now we work backward through these various statements we find that credibility will make possible an identification with the tragic hero, who is like ourselves, that this will enable us to feel the tragic emotions, and that as these latter are purged we will become morally better.

Another concatenation of readings of the same kind occurs in Ellebodius' work on the passages dealing with character. Initially, he uses the terms "probi" and "improbi" to differentiate the objects of imitation at 1448a2. Then, when he comes to the four requisites for character, the same term "probi" is used for the first requisite, "good," in spite of the difference in

---

[94] *Ibid.*, fol. 100: "communiter dolorem significat, quo afficitur animus ob alterius res aduersas. nam natura fert, ut homo hominis ob hoc ipsum, quod homo est, incommodis doleat."

[95] *Ibid.*, fols. 87v–88: "Danda etiam opera est, ne quid afferatur, quod ab hominum opinione abhorreat. quamobrem praeoptanda sunt quae fieri nequeunt, modo probabilia sint, ijs, quae fieri quidem possunt, sed tamen credibilia non uidentur."

the original Greek terms (fol. 82). Moral goodness is taken to be necessary because, in tragedy and the epic, the hero teaches virtue in a positive way through the excellence of his own character. He becomes, in a way, a "specimen" or exemplar. It is for this reason that the commentator adds to Aristotle's idea of the heightening of portrayal the reason already given: "Although characters are to be portrayed as similar, nevertheless it is necessary, like the painters, to add something to them, each in its own kind, whether the poet imitates good or less good characters . . . so that they may appear as examples of the virtues and the vices."[96]

On the whole, the *Paraphrasis* of Ellebodius constitutes an extraordinary example of works of its kind: it shows with what vigor the Italian critical tradition imposed itself upon writers of other countries and how closely they remained linked to it. As far as Aristotelianism is concerned, the work presents some remarkable features in the correction and commentary of the text, along with some cases in which, unfortunately, the vigor of the tradition led to a perpetuation of misreadings and misunderstandings.

GIACOMINI (1573)

Another translation of the *Poetics* into Italian, following closely upon Castelvetro's and Piccolomini's and emphasizing the growing activity in the vernacular, was prepared by Lorenzo Giacomini Tebalducci Malespini in 1573. It was never published and exists today in MS Laur. Ashb. 531, fols. 1–38, written by Giacomini's secretary, Giorgio Bartoli, and dated at the end, "Fine A Laude Di Dio à di 28 d'Ag° 1573."[97] Giacomini was neither a scholar nor a professor; he was a distinguished amateur, most of whose literary activity centered about the meetings and the chores of the Accademia degli Alterati. This fact may account in part for the principal merits of the present translation. Giacomini does not copy any of the earlier vernacular translations, although borrowings from both Castelvetro and Piccolomini—in turn of phrase and in choice of words—are frequent. One might say that he combines the best features of both, the conciseness of Castelvetro (which also brings Giacomini's text closer again to the original) and the superior terminology of Piccolomini. His language is terse and direct and his words seem to the modern ear to be closer to those of common speech than were his predecessors'. His main aim is always simplicity, and he frequently achieves it. It might be instructive to compare him with Castelvetro, using the same passages that were quoted for the comparison with Piccolomini. On *Poetics* 1447a26:

Castelvetro: Ma con lo stesso numero rassomigliano senza harmonia certi

---

[96] *Ibid.*, fol. 104: "Etsi mores affingendi sunt similes; tamen instar pictorum addere illis aliquid in suo cuiq. genere oportet, siue bonos siue minus bonos mores poeta imitetur . . . ut uirtutis, uitijq. specimen appareant."

[97] For a more complete account of this MS, see my "Nuove Attribuzioni di manoscritti di critica letteraria del Cinquecento," *Rinascimento*, III (1952), 245–46.

ballatori, percioche questi per figurati numeri rassomigliano anchora & costumi, & tormenti, & attioni (p. 15).

Giacomini: et il ritmo solo senza armonia usano i ballatori; perche questi mediante i figurati ritmi imitano et i costumi et le passioni et le azzioni (fol. 1*v*).

On *Poetics* 1448*a*1:

Castelvetro: Hora, poi che i rassomiglianti rassomigliano coloro, che fanno, & è di necessita, che questi sieno o buoni, o rei, percioche i costumi quasi sempre accompagnano questi soli, conciosia cosa che tutti *gli huomini* sieno differenti di costumi per maluagita, o per bonta, egli è di necessita rassomigliare i migliori, che noi, o i piggiori, o i cosi fatti, secondo che fanno i dipintori. Et certo Polignoto effigiaua i migliori, & Pausone i piggiori, & Dionigi i simili (pp. 33–34).

Giacomini: Ma perche gli imitanti imitano agenti, et necessario è questi essere, ò buoni, ò cattivi, perche i costumi quasi sempre questi accompagnano soli, perche per la virtu et per il vizio quanto à costumi tutti sono differenti ò migliori che secondo noi ò peggiori, ò ancora tali necessario è imitare: come i pittori Polignoto migliori Pausone peggiori, et Dionisio simili ritraeva (fols. 2–2*v*).

The first of these passages shows the return to brevity and the choice of words which are in almost every case more current; the second, along with the same qualities, some of the confusion which might have been avoided if Piccolomini's suggested versions had been adopted.

Giacomini experiences the same difficulties with the text itself as did his predecessors. But in at least one case, the definition of tragedy, he supplies a word which none of his predecessors had included and which immediately clarifies one of the major problems of the text:

Giacomini: È adunque la tragedia imitazione d'azzione virtuosa [vars.: studiosa; spudea] et perfetta, che habbia grandezza con orazione condita in disparte ciascuna de le specie ne le parti, *di negozianti*, et non per narrazione: ma per misericordia et terrore conducente à fine la purgazione di cotali passioni (fol. 7; italics mine).

The translation is still confused and unclear and on the whole inferior to Piccolomini's; but the inclusion of "di negozianti," furnishing for the first time the proper opposition to "et non per narrazione," is a notable improvement. In a marginal gloss on the same passage, Giacomini also makes a clarifying statement about the meaning of σπουδαίας, for which he had offered three variant translations: "An action which is 'studiosa' or 'spudea' is to be distinguished from that action which is done in play in the reposeful moments of life."[98] In another passage, the best in the *Poetics* for the understanding of necessity and probability (1454*a*34), Giacomini's translation is superior because of its completeness and its clarity:

Castelvetro: Hora fa bisogno cosi ne costumi, come anchora nella constitutione delle cose cercare o quello, che è di necessita, o quello che è di verisimilitudine, &

[98] MS Laur. Ashb. 531, fol. 7: "Azzione studiosa spudea si contradistingue da la azzione che si fa per gioco nel riposo de la vita."

che si faccia questo dopo questo o per necessita, o per verisimilitudine (p. 320).

Piccolomini: Hor' egli fa di bisogno, che nei costumi, si com'ancor nella fauola, & nel connettimento delle cose, si cerchi sempre, ò il necessario, ò il verisimile, & che l'vna cosa segua doppo l'altra ò necessariamente, ò verisimilmente (p. 31).

Giacomini: Ancora bisogna ne' costumi, si come ne la constituzione de fatti sempre cercare, ò il necessario, ò il verisimile, si che il tale tali cose dire ò fare, ò necessario sia ò verisimile, et questo dopo questo farsi, ò necessario, ò verisimile sia (fol. 20).

This is, as far as I know, the best translation of the passage to be found in Italy in the sixteenth century. One should not, however, exaggerate Giacomini's merits; on many of the difficult passages (such as those wherein Piccolomini was better than Castelvetro) he has no contribution whatsoever to make.

On the margins of several folios, Giacomini gives, in addition to alternative translations, notes which tell us how he understood the text; there are only four such places, and we may look briefly at them all.

On folio 3v, a note about the natural causes of imitation. Giacomini tries to reduce to syllogistic form two of the arguments in the text. The first is on pleasure in general, and is presented in tabular form:

Passion	Cause of the passion	Subject
a. pleasure	b. learning	c. seeing the images

"In seeing of images there is learning, in learning there is pleasure; therefore in the seeing of images there is pleasure." The second is on the pleasure deriving from images of objects which are in themselves distasteful:

Passion or predicate	Subject and cause	Effect and sign
a. pleasure	c. things made with imitation	b. images of ugly things

Things made with imitation are the cause why the images of ugly things give us pleasure; and these are a sign of their cause, that is, the things made with imitation give pleasure. This is demonstrated as follows: The images of ugly things give us pleasure, the images of ugly things are things made with imitation; therefore things made with imitation give us pleasure.[99]

---

[99] *Ibid.*, fol. 3v:

"Passione	Causa de la passione	subietto
a. Diletto	b. Imparare	c. veder le imagini

Nel veder l'imagini è l'imparare, nel imparare è diletto. adunque nel veder le immagini è diletto.

Passione ò predicato	Subietto et causa	Effetto et segno
a. Diletto	c. Cose fatte con imitazione	b. immagini de le cose brutte

Le cose fatte con imitazione sono causa che le immagini de le cose brutte ci danno diletto; et queste sono segno de la loro causa, cio è le cose fatte con imitazione danno diletto. dimostrasi cosi Le immagini de le cose brutte ci danno diletto, le immagini de le cose brutte sono cose fatte con imitazione, Adunque le cose fatte con imitazione ci danno diletto." ·

POETIC THEORY

On folio 4, continuing the same discussion, Giacomini analyzes the syllogistic form of the deduction by which we recognize objects as they are represented by images. After reducing the argument to a syllogism, he says: "It is in the second figure, and good because it can be converted, the major premiss saying 'Whoever has these properties is this example . . . ' or without converting as follows: 'This example alone has these properties.' The middle term will thus be the properties common to the image and to the example which alone has all of them."[100] Such passages as these reveal the way in which men of the time were accustomed to practice textual analysis and commentary.

On folio 4v, we find a lengthy discussion of the passage on Homer as the model for the dramatic genres (1448b34). Giacomini is here concerned with clarifying the meaning of the text, its terms and its implications. "When Aristotle says first that Homer imitated virtuous things dramatically, he means that in his imitations of virtuous actions he showed the design for tragedy."[101] "Dramatically" is thus to be taken as meaning "in the way of drama" and is further explained by the formula, "that is, to introduce persons who act among themselves and who talk with one another."[102]

On folio 17, Giacomini reduces to tabular form all the ways in which plot may be constituted:

Plot is divided according to
- the action
  - one
  - many
- the agents
  - simple, if the agents are on one side
  - double, if in the plot there are two sides, contrary and opposed
- fortune
  - simple, if fortune and the state of affairs is the same from the beginning to the end
  - reversed, if it has a mutation of fortune and of state[103]

---

[100] *Ibid.*, fol. 4: "E ne la seconda figura et buono perche si puo convertire, la maggior dicendo Chiunque ha queste proprietà è quello essemplare . . . ò senza convertire cosi Quello essemplare solo ha queste proprietà. il mezzo adunque sarà l[e] proprieta comuni à la immagine et à lo essemplare che solo le ha tutte."

[101] *Ibid.*, fol. 4v: "Dicendo Aristotile prima che Omero imitò le cose virtuose dramaticamente vuole dire che ne le sue imitazioni de le virtuose azzioni mostrò il disegno de la tragedia."

[102] *Ibid.*, fol. 4v: "a uso di drama . . . cio è introdur persone che tra se negozino et parlino l'uno con l'altro."

[103] *Ibid.*, fol. 17:

"la favola si divide o
- da l'azzione
  - una
  - molte
- da gli agenti
  - semplice—se gli agenti sono una parte sola
  - doppia —se ne la favola sono due parti contrarie et nimiche
- da la fortuna
  - semplice—se la fortuna et lo stato de le cose è uno et il medesimo dal principio à la fine
  - piegata —se ha mutazione di fortuna et di stato."

[526]

This is interesting as a synthesis of fairly widely separated passages, and again as an indication of the total approach to the text.

In a general way, Giacomini's translation is symptomatic of the lively interest in getting the *Poetics* into Italian and of the resultant tendencies in technique—tendencies toward greater conciseness, toward simpler language, and toward the use of terms more like those of common speech than like those of the philosophers or the Latinists. In a sense, it is unfortunate that the work was not published, for such later Italian translations as the reprint of Piccolomini's (1575) and even such Latin versions as Riccoboni's (1579) might have been better for having known it.

The same manuscript contains a folio (39–39v) immediately following the translation of the *Poetics* which discusses the meaning of imitation and the definition of poetry (see above, Chapter II, pages 62–63); it may readily be taken as a further note on the text. In it, Giacomini displays some of the less admirable aspects of his literary method. He assimilates Aristotle's imitation to Plato's mythology and fable and extends the parallel to the three forms indicated for each. Similarly, in an interpretation of "favola," he allows the meaning of "lying" found in Plato to color his interpretation of Aristotle, producing thus a definition of poetry in which lying and falseness—in speech at least—are a necessary element.

Another Florentine manuscript, Magl. IX, 125 of the Biblioteca Nazionale, folios 23–26, contains a document by Francesco Bonciani which belongs to the same year and to the activities of the same Accademia degli Alterati. It is his *Parere intorno alla risposta del primo argomento del Castravilla*.[104] Here again the materials are purely theoretical and relate directly to the interpretation of the *Poetics*. For Bonciani is intent upon disproving Castravilla's first argument in the *Discorso*, which for present purposes is reduced to the following form:

> Every poem is a plot;
> Dante's *Commedia* is not a plot;
> Therefore Dante's *Commedia* is not a poem.[105]

The rebuttal involves a close analysis of both terms, poem and plot, as they appear in Aristotle and, hence, some fundamental questions about the total meaning of the *Poetics*. Bonciani offers three arguments in refutation of the statement "Every poem is a plot." (1) Plot cannot be predicated of a poem either as its material or as its form:

> If the plot is to be "said" or (to use the proper terms) predicated of the poem, it must be predicated either as material or as form . . . but it is not predicated as

---

[104] See my "Nuove Attribuzioni . . .," *Rinascimento*, III (1952), 253–54.
[105] MS BNF Magl. IX, 125, fol. 23:
"Ogni Poema è fauola
La Commedia di Dante non è fauola.
Adunque la Comedia di Dante non è Poema."

[527]

material because then the comparison of Aristotle (who says that the plot is the soul of tragedy), derived from a substituted proportion, would be bad. . . . The soul is not the material of the animal, hence neither is the plot the material of the poem. [Nor can it be predicated as the form:] because the form is not predicated substantively but rather by denomination. . . . Just as we cannot say that the animal is a soul, so we cannot say that the poem is a plot.[106]

In this argument, the same kind of logical analysis used by Giacomini is again applied. (2) The second argument depends upon a translation of 1447a13—a bad translation—which Bonciani renders thus: "The epic, tragedy, comedy, dithyrambic poetry, and the greater part [la maggior parte] of the poetry fitted to zithers and to flutes agree in this, that they are imitations."[107] From this use of the phrase "the greater part" Bonciani deduces that there are some parts of some kinds of poems which are not imitations, "and if there is no imitation there is no plot, whence is constituted the following argument: every plot is an imitation, some poems are not imitations, therefore some poems are not plots; or rather, not every poem is a plot."[108] This is the contradictory of Castravilla's original proposition. (3) For his third argument Bonciani refers to *Poetics* 1447b13, which he interprets as meaning that those who use verse alone, without imitation, may also be called poets. "It seems then that Aristotle admits that one may be called a poet even if he does not imitate; therefore not every poem is a plot, contrary to the proposition."[109] In the last two arguments especially, Bonciani's Aristotelianism seems to be shaky, and he surely does not contribute to a better understanding of the text.

Bongianni Gratarolo's *Difesa di Dante* [undated, but *ca.* 1573)[110] relates again to the controversy started by Castravilla; but it is more concerned than was Bonciani's *Parere* with answering specific objections and making a detailed defence. Some of its answers involve denying the authority of Aristotle, upon which Castravilla had based his attack, and Gratarolo finds his best denial in a general question about the worth of the *Poetics*. Fairly early in the manuscript (MS Vat. Lat. 6528) he refers contemptu-

[106] *Ibid.*, fols. 24v–25: "Se la fauola si debbe dire ò (per parlare co' termini proprij) predicare del Poema, ò la si debbe predicare come materia, ò come forma . . . ma la non si predica, come materia, perche cattiua sarebbe la comparatione d'Aristotele (che dice la fauola essere l'anima della tragedia) cauata dalla proportione commutata. . . . l'anima non è materia dell' animale, adunque ne anco la fauola è materia del Poema. . . . perche la forma non si predica in sustantiuo, ma denominatiuamente . . . come . . . non si puo dire l'animale è anima, cosi non si puo dire il Poema è Fauola."

[107] *Ibid.*, fol. 25: "la epopeia, la tragedia, la commedia, la dithyrambica, et la maggior parte della poesia accomodata alle cithare et alle tibie conuengono in questo che sono imitatione."

[108] *Ibid.*, fol. 25v: "e se non u'è imitatione non u'è fauola perche si constituisce questo argomento ogni fauola è imitatione, qualche Poema non è imitatione, adunque qualche Poema non è fauola, o uogliam dire Non ogni Poema è fauola."

[109] *Ibid.*, fol. 26: "Pare adunque, che Aristotele ammetta, che uno si possa chiamare Poeta, ancorche non imiti, et pero non ogni Poema è fauola contra alla Propositione."

[110] See M. Rossi, *Filippo Sassetti* (Città di Castello, 1899), p. 77, n. 4; also below, chap. xvi, pp. 841–42.

[528]

ously to "that little note-taker and paper-spoiler of Aristotle's *Poetics*" ("quel Notaiolo, o sfogliaccio della poetica d'Arist.," fol. 90). Later he defends his remark in a complete statement: "Other universal Aristotelians also, and especially your Castelvetro, confess that this is not a work reduced to perfection by its author, but merely a set of notes in which he put down things as they came to him, in order to treat them fully later with his usual orderliness (in which he surpasses all others) in some perfect book."[111] Gratarolo offers historical and literary proofs of the incompleteness of the *Poetics* and asserts that, because of the many poetical matters that it leaves in doubt, we cannot follow it literally on those that it does treat. He himself makes only one important theoretical statement, which consists in reducing all poetry to two basic types, tragic and comic; the reduction, he says, would be perfectly clear if we possessed the whole of Aristotle's treatise. The raising of one's voice against Aristotle was to become increasingly frequent as the great literary quarrels of the century developed.

SASSETTI (CA. 1573)

Still related to the same controversy and belonging approximately to the same period—these were the years of the initial flush of excitement—is Filippo Sassetti's *Sopra Dante*, found in MS VII, 1028 of the Biblioteca Nazionale, Florence.[112] It is an Aristotelian document in several ways, first because its essential organization follows the order of Aristotle's qualitative parts, second because it presents at the beginning a long discussion of theoretical matters found in the *Poetics*. The examination of the *Divina Commedia* comes only later. Moreover, the discussion has a remarkable feature in that it attempts, from a kind of practical point of view, to see how Aristotle's theories may be adapted to the circumstances of the present time and what modifications must be made when one passes from fifth-century Greece to sixteenth-century Italy. Aristotle is the master, although his teaching is not correctly understood at all times; Plato is called upon for certain ideas; but Horace has disappeared.

Sassetti really has his own theory of poetry, which results in a particular interpretation of the *Poetics* in many places. In general, he believes that the art has two ends, one of them internal—this is the imitation of human actions—the other external—this is the moral usefulness to the audience: "I say an end within the art of poetry because ultimately it seeks the profit

---

[111] MS Vat. Lat. 6528, fol. 92*v*: "anco degli altri Aristotelici catolici, e specialmente il uostro casteluetro, confessano ch'ella non è opera ridotta à perfettione dall'Authore. ma solamente un memoriale nel quale esso metteua giu le cose secondo che gli soueniuano per distenderle poi co' suoi ordini soliti (ne quali soprauanzaua tutti) in alcun libro perfetto." The reference to Castelvetro is to the *Poetica*, p.)()(3 in the 1576 edition; see n. 57 above.

[112] The treatise was published by Mario Rossi in the *Collezione di Opuscoli Danteschi inediti o rari*, Vols. XL–XLI (Florence, 1897), pp. 37–118. On the date, see Rossi, *Filippo Sassetti*, p. 19, n. 6.

of the human species and this is, we might say, the ultimate end which terminates, as in a thing outside the poet's work, in the soul of the readers or of the listeners who are the end to which this utility is ordered."[113] The poet's end is thus succinctly stated as "imitation for profit" ("lo imitare a giouamento," fol. 2v). It should be noted that this is not the Horatian end —pleasure is omitted—but one which seems to be Sassetti's own. In this connection Sassetti makes his first adaptation to modern times. The utilitarian end, he says, will vary according to the needs of different peoples at different times; so at carnival, comedies and masquerades are presented and on holy days one sees representations of the Passion. The poet, then, serves different ends by the choice of different objects, "now grave actions and full of high marvelousness, now light ones worthy of jests."[114] "Grave" and "light" are not absolute qualities of the object, however, since Sassetti thinks that each is magnified in the direction that it takes away from the middle; grave actions are made more grave, low ones more humble and abject. This in a sense constitutes one kind of imitation, the second kind residing in such actions as one sees done every day. Sassetti believes that the former kind is still practised in Italy, and he cites Alamanni's *Avarchide* as an example of "better" actions and Pulci's *Morgante* as an example of the worse; he is unable, however, to discover any case of imitations of the "like." With respect to the "better," finally, Sassetti thinks that one must, almost of necessity, seek such characters in ancient times, "whose men are always magnified and celebrated as more virtuous than those of the present century"[115]—a passage which gives us his interpretation of *Poetics* 1448a18.

Similar considerations lead to Sassetti's redefinition of the epic hero for modern times; and since this is done in terms of virtue rather than of position or of military prowess, we are suddenly brought back to a proper reading of Aristotle on the tragic hero.

> Now if heroic virtue is virtue, generally considered, which in perfection exceeds that which is commonly found, we must believe that, just as extraordinary strength is a heroic virtue, so also is extraordinary prudence; and the same for every other disposition of the mind . . . so that today in the place of the heroes we should not put those of illustrious lineage who are renowned in war, but, wishing to take cognizance of the change, generally those who through their virtue are far and away superior to virtuous men. . . . In a word, let us not be led into thinking that instead of the heroes there come now only men valorous in war, but rather all

---

[113] MS BNF VII, 1028, fol. 2v: "dico fine dentro all arte della poesia percioche egli ultimamente si ricerca il profitto del genere humano e questo è come si dice il fine vltimo il quale termina come in cosa fuori dell opera del poeta nell anima de lettori o degli ascoltanti che sono il fine a cuj è ordinata quella vtilità."

[114] *Ibid.*, fol. 3: "hora attioni graui e piene di alta marauiglia hora le leggieri e degne di beffe."

[115] *Ibid.*, fol. 3v: "gl huomini de' quali sono sempre magnificati e celebrati come piu uirtuosi di quegli del secolo presente."

those who through their virtue, whatever it may be, are greatly admired by other virtuous men.[116]

The same may be said for the epic action. For whereas tragedy presents actions "which happen every day to the human race" ("che auuengono tutto giorno al genere humano," fol. 4), the epic seems to treat only war; but since heroic deeds of the kind treated in ancient epics no longer occur, "we need to find men who could properly accomplish actions similar to those which the ancients supposed to have been done by such heroes [as Achilles, Ulysses, Hector, Aeneas]."[117]

Almost everything that Sassetti has to say about action and plot is in the nature of a commentary on Aristotle, and most of the clarifications tend to show how plot may achieve its proper pleasurable effects. Two ideas seem to be predominant: that of verisimilitude and that of the marvelous. The first is essential: "if one were to recount simply an action which did not bear credence with those who listened to it, it would not in any way move their soul, which is poetry's effect."[118] Sassetti insists on this at various places; ultimately he explains what verisimilitude is and how it is to be obtained:

A probable proposition is verisimilar, so that in order to know the nature of the latter it is necessary to know that of the probable. Those things are probable which are in agreement with the opinion of all men or of most or of the wisest, so that truth is of no concern in this matter of verisimilitude. It is indeed true that false things are lacking in probability, and consequently in verisimilitude, whenever impossibility is made to accompany them. . . . The probable is not determined by the possible because there are many possible things which are not probable. . . . Since, then, verisimilitude depends upon the opinions of men, it is absolutely necessary that, as these change, the probable should also change.[119]

---

[116] *Ibid.*, fols. 4v–5: "Hora se la virtu eroica e uirtu generalmente considerata che di perfettione sourasta a quella che uulgarmente si ritroua, stimar si dee che sicome la sourastante fortezza è eroica uirtu, cosi ancora sia la sourastante prudenza; e dogni altro habito il somigliante . . . in maniera tale che hoggi in luogo degli heroj non si douranno porre da noj coloro che di sangue illustre sono di nome nella guerra, ma uolendo rendere il cambio generalmente coloro che per la uirtu loro sourastanno agl huominj virtuosi di gran lunga. . . . ensomma non ci lasciamo dare ad intendere che in luogo degli eroi succedano solamente gl huominj nella guerra ualorosi ma tutti coloro che per la uirtu loro qualunque ella si sia sono dagl'altri uirtuosi grandemente ammirati."

[117] *Ibid.*, fol. 4v: "percio habbiamo bisogno di trouare huominj da quali stieno bene essere adoperate attioni a quelle somiglianti che gl antichi fingeuano essere fatte da que' tali.'

[118] *Ibid.*, fol. 5: "chi raccontasse semplicemente una cosa laquale non hauesse credenza appresso coloro che lascoltano ella di niente mouerebbe lanimo loro che à leffetto della poesia."

[119] *Ibid.*, fol. 10v: "Verisimile è una propositione probabile di maniera che per sapere la natura desso bisogna sapere quella del probabile. probabili sono quelle cose le quali sono secondo l'oppenione di tutti o de piu o de piu saggi di maniera che la uerita in questo affare del uerisimile non adopera cosa nessuna. egli è ben uero che le cose false mancano del probabile e conseguentemente del uerisimile ogni uolta che in compagnia loro si aggiunga limpossibilità. . . . non si determina giai l probabile dal possibile conciosia cosa che molte cose sieno possibili le quali probabili non sono . . . stando adunque il uerisimile con loppenione degl huomini egli è al tutto di mestieri che secondo che esse si mutano si muti ancora il probabile."

The last sentence transports us again into modern times; just as the superstitions of antiquity have been replaced by the teachings and precepts of Christianity, so the notion of what will be probable and verisimilar in poetry is affected by this change. Again, if what is verisimilar lies within the bounds of credibility, the marvelous lies beyond them. Sassetti discusses the latter largely in connection with the complex plot, which, because it contains recognition and reversal, is more apt than the simple plot to make the audience marvel. Simple plots place before our eyes only such things as anyone might readily imagine to have happened; in complex plots, the human intellect is led to expect one event, but another happens instead. This is a source of pleasure, "because marvelous things as such are pleasing" ("perche le cose marauigliose come tali sono gioconde," fol. 6). The need for these features of plot is more urgent in tragedy than in the epic, since the general conditions of the epic are such as to facilitate the achievement of the marvelous:

> For these [tragedies] are limited to a small action and to one place where it must happen, whereas the epic plot is longer and spreads out over more territory and embraces various sites and places where it occurs; and since it must be narrated and not acted it carries with it greater possibility of moving the passions and of appearing marvelous, because what has really happened, even a thing marvelous in itself, will lose none of its power when it is recounted, whereas when it is acted—since the imitation cannot take place in it without great likelihood of being recognized as false—clearly the deed will leave us cold.[120]

The conclusion would seem to be that circumstances which permit the marvelous to be disguised give to it the kind of credibility that the verisimilar has; but when it must be presented forthright, it is best presented through such acceptable devices as recognition and reversal.

In the last passage cited, Sassetti extends the principle of the unity of action to include a unity of place; the unity of time is stated in Aristotle's terms. But nowhere does he call them "unities" (except of action), nor does he emphasize them to the extent that Castelvetro had done. His notion of unity of action is loose; after excluding the actions of one person, he clarifies thus: "... it is circumscribed by the continuation of one and the same affair, such as a voyage, an acquisition of some thing, or even a war carried to its conclusion by a valorous captain."[121] Aristotle's

---

[120] *Ibid.*, fol. 6: "auuenga che esse si determinano a piccola attione e a un luogo doue ella debba seguire, la doue lepopeia ha la sua fauola piu lunga e piu per costa si distende et abbraccia diuersi siti e luoghi doue ella accaggia e douendo essere raccontata e non rappresentata apporta seco maggior facilita nel muouere e mostrarsi marauigliosa conciosia cosa che quello che ueramente sara accaduto cosa per se marauigliosa nell essere raccontato non perdera niente della sua forza; doue che nell essere rappresentato per non hauerui luogo limitatione, senon con grandissima euidenza dessere falso [cognosciuto manifestamente: added] il fatto cadra nel freddo."

[121] *Ibid.*, fol. 5v: "si circonscriue dalla continouatione dun medesimo negotio come un viaggio, un acquisto di qualunche cosa opure una guerra tratta a fine da un valoroso capitano."

ideas of causality and of inner determination are lacking, as they are in Sassetti's contemporaries. He has some difficulty in deciding to what extent the plot and the poem are consubstantial—this was an issue much debated in the current controversy over Dante—and he concludes that they are not; plot is argument, the bare action summarized in a few words, to which must be added the episodes if one is to have the whole poem (fol. 5). In spite of such looseness, he insists firmly that the important part of any poem is the plot and that this is particularly true of tragedy. As a result he condemns those who, like Seneca, forget that they are poets and become rhetoricians, the danger that threatens epic poets above all others:

... since all their affair consists in a work of words, they come to resemble orators more than do dramatic poets who, if they have fine actions at hand, spend their time uttering many *sententiae*, as Seneca did in his tragedies, and they cover up the main action in such a way that it disappears and is not considered as its proper object (the mind running after the truth of these *sententiae*).[122]

Sassetti's one extensive call upon Plato is on the matter of imitation. He conflates Plato's notion of imitation with the Aristotelian concept—or rather, he replaces the latter by the former, and imitation here comes to have the meaning of dramatic manner. This leads to some confusion in the use of the term. Elsewhere, however, the major guide to the judgments on Dante is Aristotle; we shall see what those judgments were in a later context.

DEL BENE (1574)

Early in 1574, the Accademia degli Alterati, which figures prominently in the literary life of these years, devoted several sessions to a debate over the need for the poet to imitate actions rather than characters or passions.[123] One of the discourses, Giulio Del Bene's *Che egli è necessario à l'esser poeta imitare actioni*, is preserved in MS Magl. IX, 137, folios 69–80r, of the Biblioteca Nazionale in Florence. The debate arose for two reasons: first, because some commentators on Aristotle declared that the three objects, action, character, and passion, were equally important; second, because others declared that a poem might still be a poem even if it imitated only character or passion. Del Bene's stand is clear: the only essential object of imitation is action, and it is essential in all forms, lyric as well as narrative and dramatic. Most of what he has to say is direct quotation or paraphrase of the *Poetics*, accompanied at times by interpretative remarks. His willingness to rely on the *Poetics* stems from his admiration for Aristotle and

[122] *Ibid.*, fol. 24v: "consistendo tutto il caso loro in opera di parole e uengono ad assomigliarsi piu agl oratori che i rappresentatiuj poeti non fanno i quali se hanno belle attionj alle mani e s'occupano in proferire molte sentenze come Seneca fece nelle sue tragedie e ricuoprono lattione principale in guisa che ella sparisce e non è considerata correndo l'intelletto dietro alla verita di quelle sentenze come al proprio oggetto suo."

[123] See my "Argomenti di discussione letteraria," *Giornale Storico della Letteratura Italiana*, CXXXI (1954), 180.

his conception of his method, "since he not only drew the precepts of the art out of nature, as an admirable observer of its secrets, but he also considered it principally in all the poems that had been written up to his time, the best and the most perfect of which were [those of] Homer, no less good as a poet than he [Aristotle] was as a philosopher."[124] The double reference to nature and to the poet-model will be increasingly important in the later Renaissance.

Del Bene's argument is simple and, for the most part, remains close to that of the *Poetics*. He sees the end of poetry as pleasure, but limited to the special pleasure which is proper to each poem ("quella delettatione quale e propria del poema," fol. 71v). Three elements—beauty, purgation, and the marvelous—seem to contribute to pleasure, although this is not clearly stated and we must derive it from such passages as the following: "All the beauties and the delights and the purgations which poems produce, all depend upon the plot and the actions which are contained in it, and by means of which the poet achieves his end"; "The marvelous is a most beautiful part of the poem, when something happens in it beyond the expectations of the listener; for men marvel at new things and at those contrary to their opinion, and they take pleasure in them."[125] The main source of pleasure, however, is the imitation of an action; without it there is no pleasure and no poem. Hence the inevitability of action and of plot: "Poetry in truth will be nothing but the imitation of actions, and it will be necessary for the poet, in order to be a poet, only to imitate actions."[126] These statements lose some of their clarity, however, when we discover what meanings Del Bene associates both with imitation and with plot. The former comes to mean a dramatic representation, as it had in Plato, and the poet is said to be imitating only when he writes in this way (fol. 72v); "plot" takes on some of the overtones of "fiction," and the kinds of action are consequently restricted: "Not of every kind of thing, but of those actions which are not true but verisimilar; and because these are made in this way, being feigned, they merit the name of 'favola'; and therefore little or no difference is found between poetic imitation, fiction, and plot."[127]

---

[124] MS BNF Magl. IX, 137, fol. 71: "il quale hauendo, non solo i precetti di essa tratti dalla natura, come speculatore mirabile de suoi secreti, ma anchora hauendo cio principalmente considerato in tutti i poemi che furono fino al suo tempo, et i migliori et piu perfetti fra i quali fu homero non meno buono poeta che egli filosofo si fosse."

[125] *Ibid.*, fol. 71: "tutte le bellezze, et i diletti, et li purgamenti [corrected to "le purgationi"] che fanno le poesie tutte dependono dalla fauola et dalle actioni che in essa si contengono, et mediante le quali il poeta consegue il suo fine"; and fol. 73: "Bellissima parte è della poesia lo ammirabile quando in essa qualcosa fuori della espettatione di chi lascolta adiuiene, perche gli huomini delle cose nuoue et fuori della loro opinione si marauigliono et ne pigliono diletto."

[126] *Ibid.*, fol. 70: "altro ueramente non sara la poesia che imitatione di actioni; et al poeta sara necessario solo per esser poeta di imitare le actioni." Cf. fol. 69v.

[127] *Ibid.*, fol. 70: "Et non dogni sorte cosa, ma di quelle actioni che uere non sono ma uerisimili; et questa per esser cosi fatte, sendo finte, meritono il nome della fauola, et però poca a nulla differentia si ritroua fra la imitatione poetica, la fintione et la fauola."

We find thus that a poem is an imitation, an imitation is a dramatic representation of a plot, a plot is an unreal but probable action. This goes for all poems, including the less "perfect" ones found in the lyric genres; the difference is that the latter are exclusively "narrative" (the poet recounting the actions of men), whereas the epic is "mixed" and tragedy and comedy are "dramatic." All are alike in that their actions must be at once marvelous and verisimilar; we may suppose that in all of them—although the statement as made is restricted to the dithyramb—the kind of necessity which springs from character will be required: " . . . he feigns and describes and imitates them [actions] not as they were, but as it was necessary that they should be, being done by such men."[128] Del Bene shows how ancient lyric poets and writers of pastoral eclogues really did imitate actions and makes an incidental defence of Dante (who constantly introduced people speaking and acting) and of Ariosto (even though his action is multiple) and of Petrarch (who imitated actions in a different way in each genre that he practised). In the light of these convictions, Del Bene contradicts certain common notions about the arts in general. Not only are all poets necessarily imitators of actions, but so are all other artists. To say that a painter, for example, imitates characters or passions is nonsense, for the latter can be imitated only through action. The historian narrates actions, the painter depicts them, the poet imitates them.

Giulio Del Bene also delivered before the Alterati, in 1574, a lecture entitled *Che la favola de la comedia vuole esser honesta et non contenere mali costumi* (MS BNF Magl. IX, 137, fols. 47–58v).[129] The subject being what it was, he was led much farther afield than in the other lecture, not only into consideration of the ends proposed for poetry by Horace and Plato but also into reflections on the nature of man (both as the object of poetry and as its audience) and on the nature of art. Throughout, however, matters seem to be decided by reference to the *Poetics*. As the object of poetry, man provides more actions and characters for comedy than he does for tragedy and the epic, for low and ordinary men are more numerous than exalted and extraordinary ones. This is the way of nature, which creates more frequently what is commonplace than what is rare and excellent. Hence, there are many more examples of comedy to study, many fewer of tragedy and the epic (fols. 47–47v). As the audience of poetry, however, man seems to demand what is rare and excellent. He prefers what is beautiful to what is ugly, what is honest to what is dishonest. Indeed, he can derive no pleasure from the morally ugly and reprehensible; the actions of comedy, "if they were dishonest, would not move to laughter, but rather to disdain and accusation and shame, because for the most part men are ashamed of dis-

---

[128] *Ibid.*, fol. 74: "non quali furono, ma quale era necessario che elle fussero sendo di cotali huomini le finge et descriue, et le imita."

[129] See note 123 above.

honest things as badly done and by vicious persons."[130] Or again, "a dishonest action does not produce joy, but hatred and shame."[131] Our first conclusion then is that morally dishonest actions will fail to please their audience, specifically because of its nature as an audience.

Similar generalizations result from Del Bene's thoughts on the nature of art. He sees it first as a device by which nature is perfected, a device "to imitate nature and render it more perfect" ("imitare la natura, et quella rendere piu perfetta," fol. 48); this means that whatever the subject matter, humble or exalted, art will depict it in a superior degree. For the subject at hand, comedy, it means that even common objects will be presented "in estremo grado et exquisite" (fol. 55). Moreover, the artist is to blame if he does not treat nature in this way, for he has complete freedom of choice in what he does. This distinguishes the poet from the historian:

And all the more so must the poet do this than the historian, that the latter is really constrained to recount actions just as they happened according to the truth, the former, as they should have been or as it is verisimilar that they must have been; whence he has the choice, and by art and by nature he is driven to what is honest and to virtue, to follow always what is best as the most useful and the most delightful thing, in order best to achieve his end.[132]

The free choice of the poet, in connection with his striving for perfection, is further emphasized in this passage:

And since this art of poetry, so excellent, operates upon its subject not through necessity but through choice, shall we believe that its artist, being able to select an honest subject and one which concerns honest actions, will choose among so great a multitude of subjects as are those of comedy rather one which is dishonest and dishonorable than one which is honest and gentle, having the freedom to take the one and the other?[133]

What subject is ultimately preferred will depend upon the poet's conception of the end of his art. Here he has two alternatives: He may think of the ends proposed by Horace, pleasure and utility; if he does, he will have to choose the honest subject, for its opposite would neither teach the right

---

[130] MS BNF Magl. IX, 137, fol. 53: "se fussero dishoneste, non moverieno a riso, ma si bene a sdegno et a riprensione, et à uergogna auuenga che delle cose dishoneste per lo piu gli huomini si uergognino come cose mal fatte e da persone uitiose."

[131] Ibid., fol. 55v: "la dishonesta, non partorisce allegrezza ma odio et uergogna."

[132] Ibid., fol. 54v: "E tanto maggiormente debbe far questo il poeta che lo Historico, che questi è pur costretto à raccontare le actioni qualli elleno sono state secondo il uero, quelli, quali doueuono essere ò quali è uerisimile che esser debbino, onde egli ha la eletione, et da larte et dalla natura a l'honesto, et alla uirtu e spinto, a seguire sempre il meglio come cosa piu utile et piu diletteuole per meglio conseguire il suo fine."

[133] Ibid., fol. 48v: "Et questa arte tanto excellente della poesia non per necessita ma per eletione operando nel suggetto, crederremo noi che potendo eleggersi lartefice di essa un suggetto honesto et di honeste ationi egli sia per scerne in cosi gran multitudine come son quelli della comedia piutosto [uno] dishonesto, et uituperoso che [uno] honesto et gentile sendo in suo arbitrio di pigliare luno et laltro?"

moral lessons nor (given the nature of man) afford any real pleasure (fol. 51v). The end of teaching, to show men good mores and to induce emulation of them, is constantly repeated through Del Bene's pages. Or the poet may think of the ends proposed by Aristotle, the moving of the audience to pity and fear by tragedy, to laughter and contentment by comedy. Again, only the honest subject will achieve these ends, for the audience will find no pleasure in what is basically immoral.

Difficulties and doubts about these matters are solved by an artistic consideration, the way in which the poet interprets Aristotle's grouping of moral characters. There are three groups, the high, the middle, and the low; the low contains the personages of comedy. But we would err gravely were we to equate "lowness" with vice, "since he himself interprets it, saying that the actions of tragedy are actions of illustrious men, those of comedy not of vicious men, but of men who are humble and low in family and in intellectual capacity; not meaning the 'worst' through some vice that might be in them, but through the low and base concepts of their mind."[134] Another passage from Aristotle may also be appealed to here, the one in which he distinguishes the four requisites of character (*Poetics* 1454a15); the requisite of "goodness" must be taken to mean moral goodness—in every kind of poem, including comedy—"honesty" and "virtue" to the exclusion of ugliness, vice, dishonesty, wickedness (fol. 56). Such characters are excluded, moreover, by the artistic demands for the handling of plot and of character. The argument on plot may be stated thus: To produce joy and contentment in the audience the action of comedy must end happily; but a happy ending for wicked people fails to produce the desired effect; hence the poet, if he wishes his plot to be properly complicated and resolved, must avoid the inclusion of wicked people (fol. 54). If this is unavoidable (e.g., Aeneas' Dido), such persons must be admitted only to the episodes and not to the central plot (fol. 55). Corroboration of this thesis is found in the fact that when poets actually do introduce bad characters, they always punish them in the denouement, thus creating an effect different from that proper to comedy (fol. 50). The argument on character is similar: Since all poets imitate men not as they are but as they should be— Achilles represents the perfect Idea of strength, Ulysses of prudence— character must show an improvement upon nature in the direction of virtue and honesty (fol. 55).

It is only when these artistic conditions are met that dramatic works achieve the end of purgation, which they seek. Del Bene offers several possible interpretations of this effect:

... tragedy arouses fear and pity in the breasts of the listeners, in order to liber-

---

[134] *Ibid.*, fol. 49: "interpretandolo lui stesso, dicendo; queste della Tragedia ationi di huomini illustri, quelle della comedia, non di huomini uitiosi, ma humili et bassi di sangue et di intelletto. non intendendo i peggiori per alcuno uitio ch'in loro sia ma per i bassi et uili concetti d'animo."

ate and purge them of these same passions of fear and pity. . . . it seems that the end of the comic poet is to delight and to move to laughter and gaiety . . . in order to purge them of the pleasure that they take in similar low actions and of the laughter that necessarily arises from them; or perhaps in order to purge them through the laughter and the pleasure that they feel in comic actions, so that when later they see or hear other real ones of the same kind, they will no longer be moved to laughter or take delight in them.[135]

The poet who violates these moral and artistic requirements by treating wicked persons—especially if he treat them publicly on the stage—should suffer the banishment recommended by Plato. In its totality, then, Del Bene's theory goes beyond that of the *Poetics* in seeking elsewhere (in the nature of man, in the nature of art) the principles upon which the poet works; but it returns to Aristotle for such artistic recommendations as will enable him to make poems conforming to those same principles.

In the same year the same academy heard Francesco Bonciani's *Lezione sopra il comporre delle novelle*. This was the kind of Aristotelian exercise of which we have already seen several examples, an attempt to treat a genre not mentioned in the *Poetics* in terms of the same critical system. Bonciani proceeds in an orderly fashion, following Aristotle's text quite closely as he attempts to discover the particular rules and precepts of the novella. And just as Aristotle had appealed constantly to the practice of Homer, so Bonciani uses Boccaccio as his principal model. Certain of Bonciani's presuppositions about poetry in general color the way in which he treats the short story. He turns Aristotle's statement about the delight found in imitation into a statement that imitation removes the pain from learning, relieves the ills of man's life, and allows him to distinguish between true and false pleasures (p. 162). This view will later determine Bonciani's understanding of purgation; since man's life is so full of annoyances and troubles, such literary works as the novella will have as their end to drive out sorrow and replace it by joy (pp. 183–84). I say "literary works" advisedly, since Bonciani refuses to classify the novella as poetry for the simple reason that it is in prose. All poetry, he says, must be in verse; the best interpreters of Aristotle give to the word λόγος the exclusive meaning of verse. Furthermore, far from accepting the theory that imitation is the genus of poetry, he declares that poetry contains imitation as a part, residing in its plot which is the summation of its action (he likens it to an "argument"). Hence we arrive at a definition of poetry in which verse is perhaps

[135] *Ibid.*, fol. 55v: "la tragedia, muoue timore et la misericordia ne petti delli auditori, per questi medesimi liberare et purgarli da questi medesimi affetti di timore et di misericordia. . . . pare che il fine del poeta comico sia, il dilettare et mouere a riso, et allegrezza . . . per purgarli del diletto che in simil[i] ationi uili si piglia, et del riso che da esse necessariamente nasce. o forse perche, purghino per il riso ò per il piacere che essi sentono per le ationi comiche, et altre poi ueramente ueggendone ò udendo, non piu si mouino a riso, ne di esse si rallegrino."

a more essential element than imitation, although this he specifically denies (p. 174).

The novella will differ from other genres in its objects, its manner, and its means. Bonciani's definition of the objects changes as he thinks of one kind of novella or another, and the refined distinctions which he makes tend to obscure the issue. The general object of literary works, of the novella as well as of the epic, tragedy, and comedy, is human actions. But the men who perform these actions are either virtuous or vicious, and virtue or vice may be depicted either as it is or in a supreme degree:

> But because it is seen that people usually maintain a certain middle ground, in virtue as well as in vice, and that nevertheless our mind can conceive the Idea (so to speak) of wickedness or of goodness, never found in their supreme degree in any one person, hence it comes about that not only may we imitate men endowed with that virtue or that vice as we see them every day, but moreover those who exceed them considerably, who for this reason come to be called "better" or "worse."[136]

Aristotle's ethical distinction is thus transformed into a difference of degree, with "better" or "worse" applying either to virtue or to vice and "like" meaning the everyday way in which these manifest themselves. The novella, especially since Boccaccio, imitates any one of these objects. But because its actions, when they resemble those of tragedy and the epic, may be handled in the ways indicated by Aristotle, Bonciani finds no need for discussing them and, instead, concentrates his attention on those stories which are like comedy. These present "light and foolish" actions (p. 176), ones which fall into the general category of the ridiculous (p. 169). Another division must be made here; for anybody may be ridiculous, the great and the poor as well as those in between. Since we should not laugh at the great and should pity the poor, only men of the middle station will be proper objects for this kind of novella. But not all:

> That sort of persons, then, who without being completely crazy smack (rather more than less) of folly, will be imitated by novelle. . . . One should imitate in these men of vulgar stripe not their ordinary actions, since all of theirs are foolish, but those which are completely out of kilter. . . . One may say that all those who, thinking themselves possessed of great wisdom and sagacity, lay themselves open

[136] My references to Bonciani are to the edition published in the *Prose fiorentine* founded by Dati, Pt. II, Vol. I (Florence, 1727). For the present passage, v. pp. 164–65: "Ma perchè e' si veda, le persone ordinariamente osservare una certa mezzanità, così nella virtù come nel vizio: e nondimeno può l'intelletto nostro immaginarsi l'idea (per dir così) della malvagità o della bontà, che in niuno in così supremo grado si ritruovano; di qui è, che non solo si possano imitare gli uomini, di quella virtù o vizio dotati, come tutto il dì si veggiono; ma quegli ancora, che di gran lunga gli trapassano, i quali perciò migliori o peggiori ne vengono a essere chiamati." See also p. 178: "Le azioni . . . sono da due maniere d'uomini adoperate, o da' virtuosi o da' malvagi, i quali in due modi si possono considerare, o con quella bontà e cattività, che sono per l'ordinario, onde simili da Aristotile sono chiamati: o veramente nel supremo grado di ciascuno di questi abiti."

to deception, should be imitated by our novelle; and all the more so when they have greater wit, for the marvelous appears even more in these.[137]

Wickedness and vice must also be excluded; they bring sorrow to men and give examples of bad behavior, and hence they can never produce the laughter that is the end sought.

After some hesitation, the question of the manner is resolved in favor of the "mixed"—narrative interrupted by speeches and dialogues among the personages. The hesitation results from doubts as to whether dialogues which tell a story, such as Lucian's, should properly be considered as belonging to the genre, and hence whether a purely dramatic manner is acceptable. Bonciani decides that it is not (pp. 165–70). As for the means of imitation, his answer is unequivocal. None of the three means proposed by Aristotle, rhythm, harmony, and verse, appears in the novella; it uses instead a fourth means, prose, and thus falls outside the general category of poetry: "For the novelle use discourse which is unmetered and in prose, as is known by the authority of all writers, whereas poems always employ verse."[138]

The specific recommendations for the handling of the form also have the *Poetics* as their admitted source. Definitions of the qualitative parts follow the text closely, except that Bonciani adds to the definition of plot this short clarification: "It is that brief summary which we find written at the beginning" ("è quel brieve raccolto, che nella fronte loro scritto troviamo," pp. 184–85). Magnitude of plot in the novella is contrasted with that of tragedy and comedy, the latter determined by considerations which echo closely those of Castelvetro:

But because tragedy has to be acted, it must in part adapt itself to the spectators, who cannot remain for several days at a time in the theater; nor would it be at all verisimilar that an action which took many days to do should be represented in just one. For these reasons tragic poets are obliged to include the whole action within one revolution of the sun; and it seems that the same must be said about comedies, since these use the same means as tragedies.[139]

[137] *Ibid.*, p. 206: "Quella sorte adunque di persone, che non essendo però pazze affatto, sentiranno, anzi che nò, dello scemo, sarà dalle novelle imitata. . . . Deesi adunque in questi uomini di grossa pasta imitare, non le loro ordinarie azioni, comecchè tutte le loro sieno sciocche, ma quelle, che sono al tutto fuor di squadra"; and p. 208: "si può dire, che tutti coloro, che di molta saviezza e sagacità stimandosi, fanno luogo allo 'nganno; dalle nostre novelle debbono essere imitati: e allora viepiù, che essi maggiore ingegno avranno; imperocchè in questi maggiormente la maraviglia apparisce."

[138] *Ibid.*, p. 173: "imperocchè le novelle si servono dell' orazione sciolta e 'n prosa, siccome per l'autorità di tutti è noto, laddove le poesie adoperano sempre il verso."

[139] *Ibid.*, pp. 186–87: "Ma perchè la tragedia si dee rappresentare, e bisogna ch'ella in parte s'accomodi agli aspettatori, i quali non possono stare parecchi giorni per volta ne' teatri: nè manco averebbe del verisimile, che un opera, in molti dì condotta, in un solo si rappresentasse; onde i tragici sono costretti a chiudere in un girare di Sole l'azione tutta quanta: e 'l medesimo pare, che si debba dire delle commedie, poichè esse adoprano lo stesso modo delle tragedie."

The frank admission, on the one hand that the needs of the spectator must be considered, on the other hand of the poet's "obligations," should be noted. Like the epic, the novella is unlimited in time and hence achieves greater verisimilitude than either of the dramatic forms; at the same time, it more readily admits the marvelous since it is addressed to the ear (p. 188). Its popular actions may be freely invented by the storyteller, who is restricted only by the laws of decorum and of verisimilitude and by the admonition to use only those episodes which are necessary. Bonciani finds in Aristotle a basis for listing nine different kinds of plots, all of which he illustrates by examples from Boccaccio. The style of the short story will be the ἰσχνός, or "humble and minute," because "novelle being in prose and containing actions done by ordinary persons who are somewhat ridiculous, they clearly cannot use appropriately that grandness of speech which tragedy and the epic would use."[140] As for the quantitative parts, they will be three in number (combining various suggestions from Aristotle): a prologue, presenting the characters and the circumstances; an "embroiling" ("scompiglio") or knotting which complicates the action; and an "unfolding" ("sviluppo") or unknotting which brings on the conclusion.

Giovambattista Strozzi delivered a similar lecture, also in 1574, before the Accademia Fiorentina, attempting to apply the principles of the *Poetics* to the lesser form of the madrigal. His *Lettione sopra i madrigali* was published posthumously in 1635. The definitions and the descriptions which he develops are all within an Aristotelian framework, although they frequently record conclusions which we should have to consider as heterodox. After a general definition of poetry as "an imitation of an action in verse" ("Imitatione d'Attione in versi," p. 160), he inquires into the kinds of actions which may constitute the proper subjects for the madrigal. There will be two kinds: human actions, especially those revealing character and passions, and actions attributed to nonhuman or inanimate things. Since human actions are really the more important, the genres which treat them—epic, tragedy, comedy—will be the great poetic genres; such a form as the madrigal, however, may permit itself

... a representation and description of those things which, even if they are lacking in speech, may nevertheless be put before the eyes of others by assigning action to them; and this is the proper function of the poet, for he must not merely describe things as they are in fact (for this is proper to others), but it is necessary for him to imitate them in such a way that he will to a certain extent depart from the truth.[141]

---

[140] *Ibid.*, p. 210: "essendo le novelle in prosa, . . . e contenendo azioni fatte da persone ordinarie, che abbiano del ridicolo; chiara cosa è, che elle non potranno usare acconciatamente quella grandezza del favellare, che la tragedia e l'epopeja userebbono."

[141] In *Orazioni et altre prose* (1635), p. 161: "vna rassomiglianza, e descrittione di quelle cose, che se bene mancano del discorso, si possono tuttauia mettere altrui dauanti à gl'occhi col dargli operatione, il che è proprio offitio del Poeta, perciòche egli non dee semplicemente descriuere le cose come elle stanno appunto, perche questo ad altri appartiene, ma fà à lui di mestiero per sì fatta maniera imitarle, che e' venga in qualche parte à partirsi dal vero."

The apologue and the descriptive poem come to be, in a strange way, the opposites of "things as they are." Lyric poems in general may treat everything in the world; but they tend to leave the grand subjects to the grand genres and to exploit rather those which are "pleasant and small," such as love. This will be the case of the madrigal.

Poetry needs verse as well as imitation; the two are indispensable. Therefore, according to Strozzi, Aristotle requires verse in his definitions of tragedy and the epic. Differences among kinds will relate to subject matter, manner, and the type of verse. On the basis of such differences we may constitute a definition of the madrigal: "The madrigal is an imitation of a pleasant, small action, made by way of narration, with verses in rhyme which are not restricted in their number and kind of rhymes."[142] When it does not imitate human actions, it attributes action to objects through metaphorical description. In any case, it will have a plot (if that be the correct translation for "favola" here) and hence necessarily character and discourse (for διάνοια) and language. Its parts will thus be the same as those of the grand genres, if reduced and less perfect. But their order of importance will be disturbed, even to the extent of introducing a rivalry between plot and language for first place; for "he who would place [language] before it [plot] would perhaps not depart from the truth."[143] Choice of words and texture of verse may thus, in Strozzi's opinion, legitimately be the primary concern of the madrigal poet, especially since the form is so brief that every word must be made to count. So prosodic and rhetorical matters demand close attention, and Strozzi offers specific advice with respect to them. The totality of his theory shows a reorientation away from Aristotle and toward the old-fashioned rules for language and versification.

It is perhaps to the years 1574–75 that we should assign Sperone Speroni's *Apologia dei dialogi* (see Chapter VIII, pp. 304–5), which in addition to defending his dialogues expresses his ideas of the moral and political utility of poetry. These relate to Aristotle in that the purgation clause is interpreted as referring to such moral utility; but it is, according to Speroni, a very imperfect instrument for the purpose. The problem is the correct behavior of the whole citizenry:

Aristotle was well aware of that behavior when in the definition of tragedy, besides certain other pleasurable circumstances which are proper to that poem, he added in opposition that useful component, whence it might be called "civil," saying as follows: *ut purgemur ab huiuscemodi*. . . . This means that on seeing a tragedy man is purged of two passions which are not very useful to citizens, that is, horror and commiseration. . . . But if Aristotle wished to purge two such passions by means of tragedy, passions which seem to have something political

[142] *Ibid.*, p. 172: "Il Madrigale è imitatione d'attione gentile picciola, fatta per via di narratione con versi in rima, non sottoposti à numero, nè à maniera di rimare."
[143] *Ibid.*, p. 173: "e chi ancora glie le antiponesse, non si dipartirebbe forse dal vero."

about them and which are without doubt human, his suggestion was not so good as it should have been.[144]

Speroni objects because he believes that such spectacles as the death of gladiators would serve the same purpose more effectively. He thinks that in fact tragedy was invented for another purpose—"to teach citizens to be quietly content with their humble lot and not to try to elevate it by bringing on the ruin of their fatherland"[145]—and that Aristotle failed to mention this end in his definition of tragedy. For comedy, too, he distinguishes desirable and undesirable ends, by reference always to political criteria:

> If I once said that in the laughter of comedy the wearied mind is rested and that such repose is useful to it, I say it now again; and I say again that it is one thing to laugh in the theater for an hour or two, another to write in order to make people laugh on purpose; the former gives repose and is necessary, the latter is an indecorous labor and an antisocial activity.[146]

I take it that in the latter category Speroni would include satirical and humorous and obscene poetry. Throughout, it is clear that he is carrying over into discussion of Aristotle the general Platonic prejudices that inform his thinking at this point of his career.

PICCOLOMINI'S COMMENTARY (1575)

The second of the "great commentaries" in the vernacular, Alessandro Piccolomini's *Annotationi nel libro della Poetica d'Aristotile*, was published in 1575, although its author had declared in the preface of his translation (1572) that the annotations were already complete. Coming as late as it does, his commentary reflects an advanced state of work on the text, at least in the sense that it can discuss and accept or reject all the multitude of interpretations that had already been suggested. Piccolomini announces that he will say nothing about those passages for which he finds the remarks of Maggi and of Vettori satisfactory; but he frequently disagrees with them, as he does with Robortello and Scaliger and Castelvetro. Indeed, some of his most revealing and original pages were written under the stimulus of such disagreement. This does not mean that his approach is essentially controversial or fragmentary. For he does have a personal inter-

---

[144] In *Opere* (1740), I, 355–56: "Ben si accorse di tal decoro Aristotile, quando nella difinizione della tragedia, oltre alcune altre sue dilettevoli condizioni, che sono proprie di quel poema, soggiunse contra quella dell'utile, onde civile si nominasse, così dicendo: *ut purgemur ab huiuscemodi*. . . . il qual vuol dire che nell'aspetto della tragedia si purgò l'uomo di due affetti non molto utili a' cittadini, ciò sono orrore e commiserazione. . . . Ma se Aristotile purgar volendo colla tragedia due tali affetti, che assai par che abbiano del civile, umani son senza dubbio, non fu sì buono come dovea. . . . "

[145] *Ibid.*, p. 356: "per insegnare alli cittadini di star contenti quietamente alla loro umile condizione, e non tentar d'innalzarla con la ruina della lor patria."

[146] *Ibid.*, p. 357: "se io già dissi, che nelle risa della commedia riposa l'animo affaticato, e che gli è utile un tal riposo; torno anche a dirlo; e ridico che altro è ridere in un teatro una o due ore, ed altro è scrivere per far ridere a bello studio. quello è ozio e necessità; questo è fatica indecora ed incivile operazione."

pretation of the *Poetics*—one might say, even, his own theory of poetry—which determines how individual passages and their commentators will be considered. Some of this theory is explicitly stated in the "Proemio," which precedes the main body of the work; much of it is found in the individual glosses. For these, Piccolomini uses the numbers and the text of Maggi's *Explanationes*. Unlike Maggi and the earlier scholars, however, his interest is almost not at all philological or textual; it lies rather in the production of a consistent and complete reading of Aristotle.

One of the cornerstones of the theory expressed in the "Proemio" is Piccolomini's conception of the ends of poetry. This is stated as early as his announcement of his general program for the work; he will treat poetry's "form, its end, and its material, and the profit and the pleasure which it brings to the world."[147] The relative importance of profit and pleasure is included in the definition which comes soon after: "Poetry is nothing but an imitation, not only of things either natural or artificial, but mainly of human actions, characters, and passions, done mostly by means of language and of diction, taken universally, in order to give pleasure and by giving pleasure ultimately to benefit human life."[148] These ends of pleasure and utility—with the pleasure made to serve the utility—will be explained and developed repeatedly throughout the text. Good poems will be distinguished from those which merit the Platonic charge of effeminacy and corruption, "those imitations so made that they would be made for a single end, either voluptuous and vain pleasure which was its own end and termination and served no purpose, or instead such pleasure as would bring damage to our lives by rendering our manners effeminate and corrupt, or by some other means."[149] Rather than so doing, poetry must be subordinated (according to Aristotle in the *Ethics*) to the architectonic art of politics, and it must serve these various specific ends:

... through the imitation of virtuous men and the expression of their praise, we come to be aroused and excited to virtue, in order to be like those whom we hear celebrated. On the other hand, if we hear vices and wicked actions expressed through poetic imitation and, as they are expressed, reviled and vituperated, we immediately begin to dispose ourselves to flee and to hate vicious actions, much more incited to do so by such imitations than we would be by direct and personal admonition, no matter how effective.

Similarly, if we see horrible tragic events acted on the stage, a great part of our

---

[147] *Annotationi* (1575), p. ††4v: "la forma, il fine, & la materia sua, & il giouamento, & il diletto, ch'ella reca al mondo."

[148] *Ibid.*, p. ††5: "la Poesia non sia altro, che imitatione non solo di cose, ò naturali, ò artifitiose; ma principalmente d'attioni, di costumi, & d'affetti humani: fatta col mezo principalmente del parlare, ò ver della locutione nel lor' vniuersale, à fine di dilettare, & dilettando finalmente giouare alla vita humana."

[149] *Ibid.*, p. ††5v: "quelle così fatte imitationi, che si facessero à solo fine, ò di voluttuoso, & vano diletto, ch'in se stesso finisse, & terminasse, ò non seruisse à nulla; ò ver di diletto tale, che ò con effeminare, & corromper' i costumi nostri, ò in qual si voglia altra maniera, fusse alla nostra vita per recar danno."

insolence, our temerity, our arrogance, our audacity, our pride disappears in us through this means; and seeing the miseries and the perils to which are subject not only men of middle and low condition but even those who through their power and greatness are used to being happy, . . . we come to moderate our sorrow over the misfortunes which do happen and which can happen every day. Likewise the wrath, the envy, and the other passions which usually are fomented in us through the fact that we do not know well the inconstancy of fortune and the fragility of all worldly things, all these come to be tempered within us.[150]

Piccolomini here collects all the uses previously proposed for tragedy. He will frequently make such compendia; and, to a degree, his work presents a summation of ideas about poetry current in his time.

If we follow through the commentary this guiding principle of utility, we shall see how it affects the interpretation of various separate passages. Primarily, it determines how Piccolomini will understand purgation. He states his theory in connection with *Poetics* 1449*b*24, after repeating what he had said about the priority of usefulness:

. . . since man cannot enjoy and obtain any more useful thing than the possession of true tranquillity of the spirit, from which cannot be separated his virtuous living; and moreover, since this tranquillity cannot be spoiled except through the fault of the passions of the soul, hence it arises that on no other thing have the philosophers so exerted themselves, in order to make the soul peaceful, as on the attempt to purge it of those passions.

Developing, then, the theories of the Stoics and the Peripatetics and repeating (from the *Rhetoric*) Aristotle's classification of the eleven passions, all natural and all moderated by reason, he goes on to the specific uses of purgation, which profits men

. . . by means of the compassion and the terror and the fear which it brings to others with those events and those misfortunes which it represents. For when we see the bitter misfortunes and the unhappy accidents with which the world is so full, . . . we come as we see these things to moderate our hopes, and through the vanity that we see in these hopes, we temper also our joys, considering how fragile is their basis. . . . Although tragedy takes into account the nature of the crowd, it has undertaken, for the profit which it intends to bring to it, to purge

---

[150] *Ibid.*, p. ††7: "con l'imitation degli huomini virtuosi; & con la spressione delle lodi loro, veniamo ad infiammarci, & ad escitarci alla virtù, per diuenir simili à quelli, che celebrar' vdiamo. se i vitij, & le scelleratezze dall'altra banda sentiamo con poetica imitation' esprimere, & esprimendo vilipendere, & vituperare; subito cominciamo a disporsi alla fuga, & all'odio delle vitiose attioni; molto più incitati à questo da cotali imitationi, che da quanto si voglia efficace, & aperta particolar' ammonitione.

"Medesimamente se recitarsi in scena veggiamo horribili auuenimenti tragici, vien per questo à mancar' in noi gran parte dell'insolentia, della temerità, dell'arrogantia, dell'audacia, & superbia nostra. & vedendo le miserie, & li pericoli, à che son sottoposti, non solo gli huomini di mediocre, ò di bassa conditione; ma quegli ancora, che per la potentia, & grandezza, soglion' esser felici . . .; veniamo a moderare il dolore negli infortunij, ch'accascano, ò accascar tutto 'l giorno possono. Vien parimente à mitigarsi l'ira, l'inuidia, & gli altri affetti, che dal non ben conoscere l'instabilità della fortuna, & la fragilità delle cose mondane, fomento riceuer sogliono."

the souls mainly of the excess of those passions which have as their object evil and fear, more than all the others, since these more than all others disturb our lives.[151]

The function of such purgation (which is more useful when it relates to fear than to pity) is thus multiple, in line with the multiple usefulness of poetry in general. The theory is completed in the glosses on other passages. On *Poetics* 1453*b*11, two new ideas are offered: pity must not be the pity of the participants in the action, but of the spectators (thus reaffirming the orientation toward the audience); and pleasure accompanies these passions because we learn about man's fate and such learning is delightful (pp. 208, 211). On 1449*b*31, Piccolomini disagrees with Maggi on the meaning of "ethical tragedy"; for him, any poem is "costumato" which is "entirely composed in a way to be instructive and to excite to honesty and to virtue."[152] On 1459*a*27, Piccolomini tells us that any pleasure connected with poetry is extrinsic, its intrinsic end being profit; indeed, pleasure merely serves this ultimate end: "To this utility pleasure is given for company, as a servant and companion, so that man may more willingly allow himself to receive that usefulness."[153] On 1450*b*24, he disagrees with Castelvetro's statement that pity and fear may be produced separately in separate tragedies; when the drama is properly constituted, both will be produced together. Other passages might be cited. Throughout, the conviction that moral instruction is the real end of poetry determines the reading of single passages in the *Poetics*.

Any such idea involves, of course, a definite conception of the nature of the audience. We have already seen it referred to as the "multitude" (a term used repeatedly), and we are ultimately told why poetry appeals especially to the crowd:

... like epic poems, tragedies are written mainly to benefit and to give pleasure to the multitude. For people who are educated and judicious and friends of virtue and all forms of knowledge do not need, in order to be taught and benefited, to

---

[151] *Ibid.*, pp. 101–3: "non potendo l'huomo gustare, & conseguir maggior' vtilità, che in posseder' vna vera tranquillità dell'animo, da cui non può star separata la virtuosa vita sua; & d'altronde non potendo riceuer macchia questa tranquillità, se non per colpa delle passioni dell'animo, di qui è, ch'in cosa alcuna non si son tanto affatigati i Filosofi per render tranquillo l'animo, quanto in cercar di purgarlo da quegli affetti.... col mezo della compassione, & del terrore, & timore, che reca altrui, con quegli auuenimenti, & casi, che rappresenta. Conciosiacosache vedendo noi gli acerbi casi, & gli infelici accidenti, dei quali è ripieno talmente il mondo ...; veniamo in veder queste cose, à moderar le nostre speranze; & per la vanità, che veggiamo in esse, temperiamo ancor le allegrezze, considerando in quanta fragilità sian poste.... quantunque hauendo riguardo la tragedia alla natura della moltitudine, habbia ella nel giouamento, che recarle intende, preso à purgar principalmente gli animi dal souerchio di quegli affetti, che han per oggetto il male, & il timor più di tutti gli altri, si come più di tutti inquieta la vita nostra."

[152] *Ibid.*, p. 107: "tutto composto in modo, che sia atto à instruire, & ad escitare all' honesto, & alla virtù."

[153] *Ibid.*, p. 372: "alquale vtile è dato per compagnia il diletto, come ministro, & compagno, accioche più voluntieri l'huom si ponga à riceuer quel giouamento."

have the teachings and recommendations which are given to them seasoned with pleasure, as must necessarily be done in order to teach the multitude.[154]

The audience is thus the same as Castelvetro's, and indeed we find Piccolomini speaking of the needs of this audience, and of how they affect the conditions of tragedy, in terms almost identical with those of the earlier commentator. Tragedy must be confined within an artificial day "since those three or four hours which are allowed to the imitation and the performance must represent the time of a whole day, in order to free the spectators of the tedium and the boredom and also the discomfort which would result for them if the performance lasted all day."[155] The division into acts is a device for adjusting the time of performance to the time of the action, with the intermissions accounting for the difference; in this way verisimilitude is saved and, incidentally, change of settings and periods of rest for the actors are made possible (p. 182).

But in one important way, Piccolomini's audience is unlike Castelvetro's: it has imagination. It knows that an imitation is not reality and that it should not expect an imitation to be identical with reality. This is perhaps Piccolomini's most original contribution to the theory of poetry.

I suppose . . . that the spectators of tragedies and comedies have an awareness and knowledge of the fact that the things that are done and said on the stage do not happen there and then as true things and without any feigning, but that they are imitations of things which have already happened or which could happen differently. . . . Therefore, we must not imagine that the cause that might diminish the pleasure of the spectators would be the happening, on the stage, of something that would make them realize that it was not really taking place there, but only as a fiction; but the cause would rather be the lack of resemblance which is required of the imitation.

Actors on the stage, as they walk and talk, cover less space than people in real life; asides are not heard by other actors; but these things do not matter:

. . . these and other similar things do not offend the spectators at all, nor do they in any way disturb their pleasure. This is explained simply by the fact that although these things really go beyond verisimilitude, nevertheless they are rendered necessary by art itself. . . . just as imitation is not truth itself, but is lacking in some part of truth (for if it were not so lacking it would not be an imitation, but the real thing), so also it is necessary that in imitating, certain things should be done which do not accord completely with the truth of the things imitated.

[154] *Ibid.*, p. 415: "così le tragedie, come gli epici poemi, si compongon principalmente per giouare, & dar diletto alla moltitudine. Conciosiacosache alle persone perite, & giuditiose, & amiche delle virtù, & delle scientie, non faccia di mestieri per instruirle, & per giouar loro di condire col diletto gli ammaestramenti, & gli auuertimenti, che si dian loro; come è necessario di farlo per instruire la moltitudine."

[155] *Ibid.*, p. 97: "douendo quelle tre, ò quattro hore, che si concedono all'imitatione, & rappresentatione; rappresentar' il tempo di tutto vn giorno, per liberare gli spettatori dal tedio, & dal fastidio, & ancor dall'incommodità, che seguirebbe loro, se tutto 'l giorno durasse la rappresentatione."

... The spectators ... grant and concede to the imitators everything far from the truth that the art of imitation necessarily brings and requires.[156]

We should distinguish several important ideas here: the audience never makes the mistake of thinking that it is seeing reality; it recognizes important differences between the world of reality and the world of art; it admits the necessity of certain unreal things in works of art; and it grants the poet the license of introducing such things. There is thus present a concept of artistic necessity which has nothing to do with the natural necessity which most commentators emphasized. Piccolomini describes it thus in another context:

... if at times the poet should be forced by the course of the plot and by some legitimate consideration not to observe completely some one of the aforementioned conditions [i.e., the requisites of character], being unable to escape such violation in order to achieve something which might be more important, he will deserve pardon and excuse and it will not be counted against him as an error.[157]

An audience so endowed with imagination will be ready to accept the verisimilar instead of the true as the proper subject for poetry. Poetry becomes a kind of leveler of differences among men; for whereas in life a thing may be pleasant to some, unpleasant to others, in poetry it will please all. If pleasure is to ensue from its representation, it is not important that the audience should be convinced of its truth, but it is important that the audience believe in the probability of the action. Resemblance to truth, not truth itself, is the real criterion (pp. 68–71). But there are certain difficulties in this principle. For if we accept the proposition that pleasure is a function of credibility and that credibility, in turn, is a function of closeness to the truth, then we shall soon be driven to the conclusion that true subjects will ultimately be those which are most effective. This is indeed the argument that Piccolomini pursues, and he is led to the inevitable deduction.

---

[156] *Ibid.*, pp. 23–24: "io suppongo ... che gli spettatori delle tragedie, & delle commedie, habbian notitia, & conoscentia, che le cose, che si fanno, ò si dicon nelle scene, non accaschin quiui allhora, come vere, & senza fintione alcuna; ma che siano imitationi delle già accadute, ò che accascar potessero altrimenti. ... La causa dunque, che possa offuscare il piacere degli spettatori, non s'ha da stimar, che sia l'accader qualche cosa in scena, per la quale eglin possin' accorgersi, che ella quiui, non veramente ma fintamente accaschi: ma la causa di questo sarà la mancanza della somiglianza necessaria all'imitatione. ... queste, o altre cosi fatte cose, non offendon punto gli spettatori, ne conturban punto il piacer loro. Il che, non d'altronde procede, senon perche, quantunque queste cose trapassin veramente il verisimile; nondimeno son recate necessariamente dall'arte stessa. ... si come l'imitatione non è lo stesso vero, ma in qualche parte mancante da esso; posciache se punto da quel non mancasse, non sarebbe l'imitatione, ma la cosa vera; cosi parimente fà di mestieri, ch'alcune cose imitando si facciano, le quali con la verità delle cose imitate, pienamente non concordino. ... gli spettatori ... tutto quello, che lontan dal vero reca, & richiede necessariamente l'arte dell' imitare, donano, & concedono agli imitatori."

[157] *Ibid.*, p. 222: "se alle volte il poeta sarà sforzato dal corso della fauola, & da qualche legittimo rispetto, à non osseruar' à punto alcuna delle dette conditioni, non potendo per saluar qualche cosa ch'importi più, fuggir tal' inosseruantia; meriterà egli perdono, & scusa & non gli sarà attribuito per errore."

POETICS: VERNACULAR COMMENTARIES

Much of the discussion occurs apropos of *Poetics* 1451*b*19, on the subjects of tragedy, and is a development of Aristotle's suggestions. Piccolomini establishes a proportion between the degree of our belief and the intensity of our passions: " . . . when the actions of others are offered to our soul and to our knowledge, they are apt to awaken in us passions proportionate to their quality. . . . Hence it is that the degree of vehemence of the passions will correspond to the degree of certainty of such offerings and cognitions."[158] The essential ratio is "certainty : vehemence"; on the basis of it, we may suppose a scale of increasing credibility accompanied by increasing violence of the passions, hence, of increasing delight. Piccolomini explains that a case we know as false will affect us only during the time of reading, as a result of the force of the poet's words or of his appeal to the imagination; intellectual examination will soon banish the impression. One which we know to be true will produce a deeper and more lasting effect. So for tragedy:

. . . if some image of a tragedy were to be based on persons of whom we not only had no certain knowledge or even belief, but held the opinion that they were entirely invented, this tragedy would be placed at so low a level of perfection that only with the greatest difficulty could it legitimately retain the name of tragedy; whereas if it were based on persons known with clear and definite certainty, in this case (as far as its subject matter is concerned) it would be at the highest level of perfection, and would consequently merit the absolute name of tragedy above all others.[159]

Piccolomini therefore leans toward the "known" rather than the "new" subject for tragedy. This is in spite of the fact that the intrinsic truth or falseness of a subject, its possibility or impossibility, are not a proper consideration for the poetic art. But its credibility is, and this depends upon the audience; Piccolomini distinguishes carefully between possibility as a quality of the action itself and credibility as a function of the audience's knowledge and beliefs about it (p. 392).

These considerations lead Piccolomini at times to reject the theories of his predecessors, at times to accept some of the most traditional explanations. He rejects Castelvetro's notion that tragic subjects must be historical and that history is an art prior to poetry. He thinks that Scaliger is wrong in maintaining that the epic poet sets out to depict a hero perfect in some

---

[158] *Ibid.*, p. 150: "nell'offerirsi all'anima nostra, & alla nostra cognitione gli altrui fatti, son' atti, à suegliar' in noi affetti proportionati alla qualità di quelli . . .; di qui è, che secondo il grado di così fatti offerimenti, & cognitioni nella certezza loro, sarà parimente il grado degli affetti nella vehementia d'essi."

[159] *Ibid.*, p. 152: "se sopra persone, delle quali, non solo, non s'habbia notitia, ò creduta, ò certa, ma s'habbia opinione, che sian totalmente finte . . . sarà formata qualche immagin di tragedia; in così basso grado sarà ella collocata di perfettione, ch'à gran fatiga potrà ella ritener legittimamente il nome di tragedia. doue che se sopra di persone, per chiara, & per risoluta certezza note, sarà fondata; in tal caso si trouerà per quanto appartiene alla materia sua, nel supremo grado di perfettione; & meriterà conseguentemente sopra tutte l'altre il nome assoluto di tragedia."

[549]

virtue or other, since this would imply the use of action to demonstrate character—"an opinion that is not very Aristotelian"—whereas character really exists for the purposes of the action (p. 96). One is thus surprised to find that his ideas of verisimilitude involve an expectation on the part of the audience that characters will always behave according to type; the imitation will be lacking in resemblance "if indications of generosity appear in an old man, or signs of temperance in a very low servant, or of shame in a prostitute, or of great knowledge in a maidservant, and so forth."[160] The old laws of decorum are made equivalent to the audience's conceptions of probability. In fact, Piccolomini's explanation of the four requisites of character derives from what he believes about verisimilitude and about the ends of poetry. He is careful to point out that characters are "good" not in order to serve as moral examples to the spectators, but so they may arouse pity and fear; they are "endowed with virtue and with praiseworthy qualities, and deserving of happiness, and consequently unworthy of those misfortunes."[161] But "appropriateness" for the same good characters means that their good qualities are proper to the type which they represent, according to the laws of decorum: "rank, calling, sex, or other circumstance" ("la qualità, la conditione, il sesso, ò altra circonstantia," p. 219). "Similarity" refers to the characteristics commonly assigned to a known personage; it is distinguished from appropriateness in this way:

... the requirement of appropriateness concerns the universal, as if to say that this character belongs to a prince, that one to a subject, this one to a man, that one to a woman, and so forth, without considering this or that particular person; and the requirement of similarity concerns the particular or the singular, as if to say what character it is proper to give to one who has to represent Achilles, . . . seeking to form and to qualify the persons in the plot similar to the character of those who are being represented, according to the knowledge and the reputation associated with them.[162]

"Constancy," for Piccolomini, is not a separate requisite, but merely another aspect of similarity; he considers the possibility of distinguishing between them by saying that similarity applies to characters already treated by earlier poets, constancy to the new ones whom the poet might invent; but he sees difficulties in this theory.

[160] *Ibid.*, p. 23: "se appariranno in vn vecchio inditij di liberalità, ò in vn vilissimo seruo inditij di temperantia, ò in vna meretrice, di pudicitia; ò in vna ancilla, di gran dottrina, ò simili."

[161] *Ibid.*, p. 218: "di virtù, & di lodeuoli qualità dotate, & meriteuoli di felicità, & per conseguente indegne di quelli infortunij."

[162] *Ibid.*, p. 220: "la conditione del conueneuole, riguarda l'vniuersale; com' à dire, che quel costume conuenga ad vn principe, quello ad vn suddito, quello all'huomo, quello alla donna, & simili, senza considerar questa particolar persona, ò quella; & la condition del simile riguarda il particolare, ò ver' il singolare. com' à dire, qual costume conuenga di porre in vno, che habbia da rappresentar' Achille . . . cercando . . . di formare, & qualificar le persone nella fauola simili di costume à quelle, che si rappresentano, secondo la notitia, & la fama, che sene tiene."

A similar persuasion about character produces Piccolomini's stand toward the factors which differentiate literary forms one from another. He takes issue, first, with the commentators who have held that "better" and "worse," relating to the objects of poetry, mean of higher or of lower social station; the distinction is an ethical one: "Aristotle is obviously speaking of goodness and badness with respect to virtue and to vice, whence man obtains absolutely the quality of being good or bad."[163] This difference would in itself be insufficient to constitute two species of poems. Nor would it be adequate to bring into play such factors as age, wealth, health (these are components of decorum), for genres must be differentiated by greater factors still; the only one capable of doing so is social rank or station: "Those qualities are sufficient to do it which diversify man's life and his status from the very foundations, such as the difference between persons of illustrious and dominating station and persons of middling station and of private and subordinate condition; this diversity makes tragedy different from comedy."[164] Thus, on the reading of *Poetics* 1448a1 Piccolomini disagrees with his predecessors; but the necessity of finding a basis for distinguishing among genres ultimately leads him to adopt their essential position. He goes so far as to declare that Aristotle's definition of comedy at 1449a31 is incomplete and imperfect because it includes only one differentia, "the worse," and that not the essential one. A proper definition would call for the imitation of "civil and private persons, and ones placed in a middling station" ("persone ciuili, & priuate, & in mediocre, stato poste," p. 90).

These distinctions are directly related, for Piccolomini, to the ends of purgation and to the whole problem of credibility and of the effect upon the passions. The audience, composed as it is, will not believe in the happiness of heroes unless they are of high estate: " . . . it does not seem to the mass and to the multitude that a person of private and low condition, no matter how virtuous and happy he may be, should be called happy, since they include among the most important parts of happiness the power and the capacity of a man to determine and to be able to do what he wants, and this they believe to be found in princes."[165] Such credibility is essential if the proper effects are to be produced; hence the sharp line drawn between tragic and comic subjects:

. . . those actions which have to draw from our soul the two tragic passions will

---

[163] *Ibid.*, p. 45: "euidentemente parla Aristotele della bontà, & malitia rispetto alla virtù, & al vitio, donde prende assolutamente lo huomo la qualità ò del buono, ò del reo."

[164] *Ibid.*, p. 45: "quelle qualità, che posson dai fondamenti diuersificar la vita sua, & lo stato suo; son bastanti a farlo come à dir, trà persone d'illustre, & signoreggiante stato, & persone di stato mediocre, & di priuata, & soggetta conditione; la qual diuersità rende differente la tragedia dalla commedia."

[165] *Ibid.*, p. 195: "non par' al volgo, & alla moltitudine, ch'vna priuata, & bassa persona, quanto si voglia che virtuosa, & felice sia, si debbi domandar felice; ponendo lor frà le principalissime parti della felicità, la potentia, & facultà di nominare, & di poter fare ciò che l'huom vuole; il che stiman' essi, che sia nei principi."

have need of greater credibility than will those which must elicit such agreeable passions [as those of comedy] and ones which are so close to nature and to our sensibility. . . . since the circumstances and the actions which are imitated in comedies are based on persons of civil and middling status, . . . no sooner have the spectators understood the argument of the plot than they readily believe that it could have taken place. . . . It is necessary, in order to bring credibility to the plots of tragedies, to attribute those imaginary actions to real persons, and the names should be used in order to cause in the minds of the spectators that form of false deduction which we have seen.[166]

For comedy, then—and there is a parallelism here to the decorum of characters—actions will be credible because they are commonplace; in fact, they will be most credible when they are such actions as have frequently been used by poets, "the avarice of old men, the tricks of prostitutes, the prodigality of young men, the cheating of servants, the madnesses of lovers, the boastings of soldiers, the lies of pimps, and so forth";[167] the world, in a word, of Plautus and Terence. For tragedy, the lack of the commonplace quality will be compensated by the knowledge that the persons were real.

Another of the cornerstones of Piccolomini's theory—and this again fixes him firmly in the current tradition—is his insistence that verse is a necessary part of the perfect poem. He remains closer to the letter of the text than did many of his contemporaries on the interpretation of λόγοις ψιλοῖς (1447a28). This means, he says, "speech not measured by verse, but made in prose" ("il parlare non misurato dal verso, ma fatto in prosa," p. 21). Poetry may thus be written in prose, and the presence of imitation will be its distinguishing characteristic. But Piccolomini introduces the matter of the two natural causes of poetry as a means of establishing a hierarchy of perfection. One of these causes is the pleasure which man takes in imitation; the other is the pleasure which he naturally finds in rhythm and song (p. 20). If we interpret the *Poetics* in this way, then it becomes possible to say that the poem which adds verse to imitation will be more perfect than one which does not. Piccolomini takes this position, after Maggi and Vettori, whom he cites; he declares that ποίησις is most properly taken to mean "that imitation . . . which would be made with speech measured by verse" ("quella imitatione . . . che col parlar misurato dal verso, si facesse," p. 20). Verse, as a consequence, becomes "not that element which contributes essentially to the making of the true poet, but

---

[166] *Ibid.*, pp. 142–43: "di maggior credibilità haran bisogno quelle attioni, che han da trar dal nostro animo quei due tragici affetti, che non n'han bisogno quelle, che così piaceuoli affetti, & amici alla natura & al senso nostro, n'han da cauare. . . . essendo i casi, & le attioni, che si fingon nelle commedie, fondate in persone di ciuile, & mediocre stato . . .; non prima gli Spettatori comprendono l'argomento della fauola, che facilmente si fà lor credibile, che possa essere stato. . . . fà di bisogno, che per recar credibilità alle fauole delle tragedie, si attribuischin quelle immaginate attioni à persone vere, & li nomi si prendin di esse, per far nascer negli animi degli Spettatori quelle forma di paralogismo, che hauiam veduto."

[167] *Ibid.*, p. 90: "auaritia di vecchij, inganni di meretrici, prodigalità di giouani, fraudi di serui, pazzie d'innamorati, vantamenti di soldati, bugie di ruffiani, & simili."

only to making him perfectly so."[168] The question arises immediately, as it was to arise with increasing prominence during the latter years of the century, about the use of verse in comedy. Piccolomini's answer contradicts his general position on verse. He thinks that the comic poet (and the dramatic poet in general) can make himself heard, via the actor, through prose as well as through verse; that the example of Greek and Latin drama is inconclusive, since ancient verse was so different from Italian; that there is no Italian verse adapted to comedy; that Italian audiences prefer prose to verse, deriving a greater pleasure from it. Hence, he believes that ultimately tragedy in Italian, as well as comedy, will be written in prose (pp. 25–28).

There are a number of passages, such as the one on prose, in which Piccolomini presents better readings than those of his fellows. He solves correctly the difficulty with respect to the arts of the flute and the zither (1447a15) by pointing out that these are meant to be examples of imitation, not of poetry (p. 8). He shows how wrong Castelvetro was in taking 1447a16 as an indication of the species of poetry, whereas it is really a listing of the differentiae (pp. 9–10). He declares, in connection with 1450a15, that Robortello erred in maintaining that character might be the principal part of the play as read, plot of the play as acted; instead, one must at all times regard plot as the essential form of the imitation (p. 115). With reference to 1450a12, he properly distributes the qualitative parts among the categories of object, manner, and means (p. 120). Castelvetro is taken to task for his whole conception of the unity of plot, both for holding that it was not necessary in the epic and for making it depend upon the auxiliary considerations of time and place (pp. 132–36).

On the negative side, Piccolomini makes his own mistakes. His great difficulties with the manner of imitation spring in part from ambiguities in his use of the term "imitation" (pp. 52–57). He offers debatable ideas about episodes removable without damage to the work (p. 156) and about the relationship of hamartia to ignorance (p. 197). But, on the whole, he makes improvements on his predecessors in the reading of the text, especially on Castelvetro whom he was most eager to controvert. His theory of poetry, although it is independent and frequently far from Aristotle, is less extreme than that of Castelvetro.

SASSETTI ON PICCOLOMINI (1575)

Not long after the publication of Piccolomini's *Annotationi*, Eleonora di Toledo de' Medici, a member of the Accademia degli Alterati, asked the academy to prepare a judgment on the new commentary. The request was made early in August, 1575, and the judgment was presented to the meeting of August 16th; although signed by the "Accademici Alterati," the *Dis-*

---

[168] *Ibid.*, p. 72: "non è quello, che essenzialmente concorre à far' il vero poeta; ma solo à farlo perfettamente tale."

corso containing it was the work of Filippo Sassetti.[169] Sassetti charges Piccolomini with imperfections of translation, with failure to explain certain difficult passages, and with errors of statement. It is interesting to note that in the last category fall some of those items of theory that I have pointed to as most original with Piccolomini. First, Sassetti rejects the hypothesis that the distinction among the genres is essentially one of social status; rather, one must understand Aristotle as establishing the difference on the basis of virtue and vice. But Sassetti has his own way of interpreting "better," "like," and "worse": " . . . if we imitate the good and the bad in the way in which we see them every day, without inventing anything beyond, we will imitate the 'like'; but if we add perfection to the goodness that we find commonly or most frequently, and imperfection to the vices, we will imitate the 'better' and the 'worse.' "[170] There are thus only two kinds of character, good and bad; but either may be imitated in an ordinary or in a superlative degree. Second, Sassetti discards Piccolomini's opinion that verse is not necessary for poetry and that one may admit the existence of "perfect" and "imperfect" poetry, distinguished on this basis. He himself thinks that verse is indispensable, and he reads *Poetics* 1447a28 in the light of this conviction (p. 63). Finally, he disagrees completely on the matter of comedy in prose, citing the practice of the ancients and of Ariosto and insisting that Aristotle demanded verse in all poetic forms.

A much more complete and revealing expression of Sassetti's ideas on Piccolomini—as well as on Aristotle and on the theory of poetry—is found in the marginal notes to his copy of the *Annotationi*, which may be consulted at the Biblioteca Nazionale in Florence. He himself dated the reading of Piccolomini between August 29 and September 18, 1575, just a few weeks after the preparation of the judgment for the Alterati. A few, but not many, of the marginalia concern matters of translation; for example, at 1451b5 Piccolomini has translated in a way which would make it seem that Aristotle is comparing universal things with particular things, rather than poetry with history, and Sassetti claims that the text will not permit this (p. 139). For the most part, however, Sassetti objects to what seem to him to be misunderstandings by Piccolomini, and his objections spring from an essentially different way of reading the *Poetics*. The central question is Aristotelianism. He has certain disagreements with Piccolomini on the nature of the poetic faculty and on what Aristotle was trying to do in the *Poetics*. Whereas Piccolomini had classified it as a "habit" which gives precepts for the poet, Sassetti insists that a habit does not give precepts and that hence it should rather be called a "method" (p. ††7v). Again, he

---

[169] See my "Argomenti di discussione letteraria," *Giornale Storico*, CXXXI (1954), 182–83, and M. Rossi, *Filippo Sassetti*, pp. 98–100.

[170] Ed. F.-L. Polidori, in the *Nozze Riccomanni-Fineschi*, p. 61: "imitando i buoni e' rei in quella guisa che tutto 'l giorno si veggono, senza fingere più oltre, si imiteranno i simili; ma se aggiugneremo alla bontà che comunemente e per lo più si suole ritrovare, perfezione, e imperfezione a i vizii, si imiteranno i migliori e' peggiori."

believes that Piccolomini is wrong in setting out (p. ††5) to treat poetry universally:

... it is nothing unless considered in its species, from each of which in turn the precepts must be derived, and not from that general "poetry" which has no nature of its own. And therefore, Aristotle never used that term, but rather when he wishes to name the genus (so to speak) of poems, he does not say that it is poetry, but imitation.[171]

He takes no exception, however, to Piccolomini's statement that Aristotle meant to give "leggi, precetti, regole, & ammaestramenti" (p. ††7v), and he apparently conceived of the *Poetics* in the same general way (v. p. 28).

These general doubts about method lead Sassetti to disapprove of Piccolomini's definition of poetry and of his conception of its objects, its means, and its manners of imitation. Several things are wrong with the definition: it mentions only one of the means, language, and omits the other two; it includes accidental differences, such as the imitation of natural or artificial objects; it adds to "human actions" the unessential elements of "characters" and "passions," which do not belong in the definition (p. ††5). As for Piccolomini's statement of the end of poetry in his definition, "dilettare, & dilettando finalmente giouare alla vita humana," Sassetti raises no objection at this point; but later, in his own statement of the four causes of poetry, he limits the "final" cause to pleasure:

... considering pleasure also with respect to the imitator, I think that it is necessary to say that it is the final cause, for he who imitates imitates for the pleasure that he takes in doing it, ... whence one might say that the efficient cause of poetry was the poet himself; the formal, imitation; the material, verse; and the final, pleasure.[172]

With respect to these same causes, he challenges Piccolomini's assertion that the actions are the "matter," although not without falling into ambiguity himself; " ... because the imitation of an action is nothing but the plot, which Aristotle said was the soul and the end of tragedy."[173] The problem of the end remains unresolved.

Disagreement on the objects of imitation centers about Piccolomini's repeated stand that "better" and "worse" were not a differentiating factor

[171] All references are to the copy of the *Annotationi* in the Biblioteca Nazionale, Florence, call number Postillati 15. For the present passage, see p. ††5: "ella non è nulla se non considerata nelle sue spetie, dalle quali à una à una si debbono cauare i precetti, e non da questa comune Poesia, che non ha natura propria, e però Aristotile non se ne serui mai, anzi quando uuole nominare il genere (per dir cosi) delle Poesie, non dice, che sia la Poesia, ma l'imitatione."

[172] *Ibid.*, p. 65: "considerato anche il diletto quanto all'Imitante, credo, che sia necessario dire, che egli sia causa finale; auuengache chi imita imita per il diletto, che prende ... onde si potrebbe dire, che la causa efficiente della Poesia fusse lo stesso Poeta la formale l'imitatione la materiale il uerso, e la finale il diletto."

[173] *Ibid.*, p. ††5v: "perche l'Imitatione d'attione non è altro che la fauola, laquale Aristotile disse essere l'anima, e'l fine della Tragedia."

among the genres and that to them must be added the element of social status. This Sassetti denies emphatically, stating that the position of Castelvetro and Piccolomini is completely false (p. 44). In his note to the commentary on 1448*b*24, he says:

> It appears that we may conclude from this text that the difference of characters is an essential difference, and not an accidental one as Piccolomini wishes.... Not only does Aristotle hold this to be an essential difference, but the one which is more important than all the others. Nor can it be said that here the station of the persons is to be understood; for the words of the text are clear, and Piccolomini makes them even clearer through his explanation.[174]

Moreover, these are to be taken as differences in character, in virtue and vice, rather than in degree; when Aristotle compares the poets to the painters, he means that both groups make similar ethical distinctions among their objects (p. 45). On the related question of the "goodness" of character (Piccolomini had limited it to "good" people), Sassetti offers some distinctions of his own. He rejects as artistically unsound the notion that the wicked may be introduced provided that they are punished; at 1454*a*15 Aristotle "speaks in universals, requiring that all the persons who are imitated should be good, each one, however, only as much as his rank permits, with this reservation however that if it were necessary to invent a bad person, he should not be made good"[175]; and in tragedy, where "goodness" must be accompanied by a fall to misfortune, the personage is given only average goodness in the action which the tragedy imitates (p. 218). All in all, on the objects of imitation, Sassetti tries to restore the ethical distinction in place of the social one and to clarify some of the misunderstandings about character.

On the means of imitation, he passes over Piccolomini and returns to the earlier commentators: his general thesis is that verse is a necessary component of poetry. The possibility of greater or less perfection in poetry, depending upon the presence or absence of verse, is denied in a passage which is also interesting for its general remarks on method:

> ... this division of poets into perfect and imperfect seems completely useless and outside Aristotle's intentions; first because the imperfect poets, if they belong under a species of poetry, should have been mentioned by Aristotle, and if they are not, it results that we should not mention them either; next, art never considers any but the perfect form of that thing which it treats; finally, if this same Piccolomini's explanation is correct, that the two universal causes of poetry are

---

[174] *Ibid.*, p. 74: "Da questo testo pare, che si possa cauare, che la diuersita de Costumi è differentia essentiale, e non accidentale, come uuole il Piccolomini.... non solo Aristotile stima questa essere una essentiale differenza, ma quella che piu uaglia, che tutte le altre; Ne si puo dire, che qui s'intenda dello stato delle persone, perche le parole del testo son chiare, e più le chiarisce il Piccolomini con la sua spositione." See also p. 203.

[175] *Ibid.*, p. 221: "parla in uniuersale uolendo che tutte le persone che s'imitano, sieno buone ciascuna però quanto comporta il grado suo, con questo riguardo tuttauia che se fusse necessario fingere vno cattiuo non si faccia buono."

imitation and verse, it follows that no poetry can ever exist without verse, because no effect can ever come into being without all its causes.[176]

The argument runs thus: the means are three, language, rhythm, and harmony, and rhythm includes verse; *Poetics* 1448*b*20 is cited as the authority, although Aristotle's meaning is stretched by the implication that verse is necessarily a part of rhythm (p. 72). Sassetti would thus demand verse in all genres, including comedy; he quotes Castelvetro and Horace against Piccolomini (p. 26), admitting, however, that reason is sufficient without authority; the authorities, he says, are on his side, beginning with Aristotle. He rejects Piccolomini's statement that the imitation is made "con le attioni," since this would make action a means (p. 52). As long as all three means are present in a poem, its basic conditions will be fulfilled; there is no requirement that they all be used simultaneously (p. 39).

The marginalia relevant to the ends of poetry concern two subjects, purgation and credibility. We have already seen that the end of pleasure belongs to Sassetti's definition of poetry; he argues for it, in a roundabout way, by maintaining that Aristotle's remarks on the pleasure found in the imitation of unpleasant objects are meant to stress the greater pleasure to be found in the representation of pleasing objects (p. 69). He does not anywhere indicate specifically that there is an additional end of instruction. But when he comes to speak of purgation, he characterizes it as the end of tragedy, meanwhile correcting Piccolomini (p. 103) on habituation as giving moral effectiveness to tragedy; if purgation is really an intrinsic end, then it must produce its effect through quality and not through quantity. The passions purged by tragedy are pity and fear. But Sassetti contradicts Piccolomini's contention that the more important of the two is fear; this is un-Aristotelian. For Aristotle, he says, frequently speaks of pity without mentioning fear, implying that the former may be produced alone in any given tragedy; this is because it is a passion proper to our feelings about the "better," whereas fear concerns only the "like." The whole argument is given in this passage:

We should note, on this text, that it is not always true that those things which move us to compassion also move us to fear, and this for many reasons. First, because many times we have compassion for one who may have lost a thing which we do not possess, whence we cannot be afraid of losing it ourselves. And another because fear is for those like us . . . , whereas compassion can fall upon those who are not like us. Lastly, because, while we are feeling compassion for the misfor-

---

[176] *Ibid.*, p. 20: "questa diuisione de Poeti in perfetti, et imperfetti pare al tutto uana, e fuor della mente d'Aristotile. prima perche i Poeti imperfetti, se sono sotto una spetie di Poesia, doueuano essere mentouati da Aristotile e se non sono, resta che anche noi non debbiamo farne mentione; di poi l'arte non considera mai se non la perfetta forma di quella cosa, che ella tratta: In ultimo se è buona la spositione del medesimo Piccolomini che uuole che le due cagioni uniuersali della Poesia sieno l'imitare, e'l uerso, ne segue che non possa mai trouarsi la Poesia senza'l uerso perche niuno effetto puo mai nascere senza tutte le sue cause."

tunes of someone, we do not have time to think about our own, but we continue to think about that evil which he is suffering. Therefore, since tragedy must always move compassion, as it seems that Aristotle supposes when he constitutes the personage fitted for tragedy, and since it is not always necessary that fear should follow compassion, one must conclude that tragedy principally arouses and purges compassion.[177]

Sassetti clearly sees factors of personal involvement as influencing the effect of tragedy.

On the other hand, credibility depends rather on the quality of the poem itself than on the knowledge of the audience, and Sassetti attacks Piccolomini's subtle differentiation between comedy and tragedy on this score. His is an interesting position. He sees the situation as distinct from that in painting, where our pleasure is related to the knowledge of the subject, "whereas poetry makes us entirely capable of the things which it recounts, nor is it necessary that we worry our brain to ascribe this action to that given person; for poetry tells us sufficiently who the person is who does that action, whence we derive a universal pleasure not dependent upon individuals."[178] This would make the art more self-sufficient, less rhetorical, in its general operation. However, Sassetti still finds a need for the poet to attend to credibility; in tragedy, he must use known names in order to make the marvelous actions of "better" heroes acceptable to the audience; in comedy, where credibility is just as important, he avoids the use of known names to keep from falling into the kind of personal criticism which is proper to satire (p. 143). Indeed, this matter is related to two essential considerations about art: How much should nature (or history) be allowed to supply to the poet? And how much do particularities of the audience affect the work of the poet? Sassetti tackles these problems in his marginal note to Piccolomini on *Poetics* 1454a10:

... it seems that Aristotle, when he says that the poets derived the plots for their tragedies not from their own art but from fortune, is scolding them as men who are not willing to use the power of their art but have recourse to fortune. When they do so, they submit to a very uncertain thing, because it might be that none of those terrible misfortunes which are demanded in a tragedy have ever happened

---

[177] *Ibid.*, p. 105: "E da notare in questo discorso, che non sempre è uero, che quelle cose che ci muouono à compassione ci muouano à timore per molti rispetti vno perche molte uolte noi habbiamo compassione, che uno habbia perso una cosa, la quale noi non habbiamo, onde non possiamo hauer paura di perderla noi, e l'altro perche il timore è de simili ..., la doue la compassione puo cadere ne non simili, in ultimo perche in mentre che noi habbiamo compassione a' casi d'uno non habbiamo tempo di poter pensare a' nostri, ma perseueriamo in considerare quel male, che colui patisce, perloche douendo sempre la tragedia muouer compassione, come pare che supponga Aristotele quando constituisce la persona atta alla tragedia, e non essendo sempre necessario, che alla compassione seguiti il timore si debbe conchiudere, che principalmente la tragedia ecciti, e purghi la compassione."

[178] *Ibid.*, p. 147: "la doue la Poesia ci fa interamente capaci delle cose che ella racconta ne ci fa di mestiere d'applicare col nostro ceruello questa attione à quella tal persona, perche la Poesia a bastanza ci dice, chi è colui, che faccia quell'attione onde si caua il diletto uniuersale non applicato à indiuiduj."

to those men whom a people consider to be famous. Hence poets, if they wished to follow things which have actually happened, could not compose tragedies. Moreover, it might well not be proper for the poets of all nations to use with equal opportuneness the misfortunes which happened to those ancient Greeks, not only because of the great disparity in time, which is a reason why the customs and the opinions of men vary so greatly, but as well because of the diversity of places and of laws, also a cause of very great difference in humors.[179]

The answer would seem to be that the poet makes his plots, rather than taking them from history or legend, and that when he does so, he takes into account the characteristics and the beliefs of his own potential audience.

In a number of the remaining marginalia Sassetti corrects Piccolomini on specific points of interpretation. These concern largely plot (what is meant by simple plot, p. 166; unity of plot in the epic, p. 377; invention of plot, p. 250; the tragic act on the stage, p. 175) and character (what is meant by σπουδαίας, p. 104; how a tragedy may be "ethical," pp. 114, 115, 116; the real difference between the third and fourth requisites for character, p. 220). These contribute less than do the others to an original Sassettian theory of poetry and an individual interpretation of Aristotle. Nevertheless, theory and interpretation do exist even in these scattered fragments. Sassetti sees the *Poetics* as providing a method that should be used by the poet to the fullest extent. He believes in a strict Aristotelianism of approach, but one contained within the text of the *Poetics* and not dependent upon reference to other works of the corpus; he thus frequently reproaches Piccolomini with erroneous reading. For the art itself, pleasure rather than instruction is the end, and it is achieved by artistic devices (verse is one of them) which themselves produce pleasure, or which operate upon the passions, or which fit the particular needs of the audience. We shall have an opportunity, under a later date, to discover whether these same tendencies manifest themselves in Sassetti's own commentary on the *Poetics*.

CONCLUSIONS

The period from 1562 to 1575 thus presents a fairly distinct character to the student of the Aristotelian tradition during the Renaissance. These are years marked by a growing activity in the translation of and commentary on the *Poetics* in Italian; the major documents are Castelvetro's and Piccolomini's extensive works, and the vernacular translation of Giacomini

---

[179] *Ibid.*, p. 216: "pare, che Aristotile dicendo che i Poeti non dalla propia arte, ma dalla fortuna cauauano le fauole per le loro tragedie gli riprenda, come quegli che non si uoglion ualere della forza dell'arte, ma ricorrono alla fortuna, al che fare si sottopongono à una cosa non ben certa, perche potrebbe essere, che in quegli huomini, che uno popolo stima famosi, non fusse mai accaduto alcuno di questi casi si terribili, che n'una tragedia si ricercano, onde i Poeti se uolesson andar dietro alle cose accadute non potrebbon comporre tragedie; auuenga che possa molto bene non conuenirsi, che i Poeti di tutte le nationi si seruano cosi acconciamente de casi auuenuti à quegli antichi greci; non solo per la disparità dell'età si lunga, che è cagione, che i costumi, e pareri degl'huomini si uarijno tanto, ma ancora per la diuersità de luoghi, e delle leggi, che è anco questa causa di grandissima differenza d'humori."

brings the number to three. Besides, the continued effort toward vulgarization is apparent. Orazio Toscanella presents a digest in his *Precetti necessari* of 1562 and Giovanni Fabrini is much concerned with the *Poetics* in his Italian commentary on Horace. This was in keeping with—and indeed was partly stimulated by—the heightened intellectual life of the Italian academies. In various cities, these groups of gentleman-critics and of amateur literati worked very seriously with literary problems, one of the most prominent of which was the discussion of the *Poetics*. The Accademia degli Alterati stands out among them for the number and the intensity of these discussions, as well as for the quantity of manuscripts which have survived; but one should not overlook the contributions of Maranta to the Accademia Napoletana, of Lapini and Strozzi to the Accademia Fiorentina, of Bernardo Tasso to the Accademia Veneziana. The removal of the *Poetics* from the scholar's study and the university lecture-hall to the open disputes of the academies was a considerable factor in the growth of knowledge about it. One direct consequence is such a work as Giacomini's translation.

There are other consequences. One of them is the repeated attempt to adapt Aristotle's principles to genres which he had not treated or to later works: Bonciani wrote his discourse on the novella and Strozzi his lecture on the madrigal for presentation to academies, as did Maranta his reflections on the *Aeneid* as an epic. Sigonio's Latin treatise on the dialogue is of the same kind, but was not intended for public presentation. Another is the fact that many of the documents coming within this period tend to include consideration of Italian works, and even contemporary ones, as examples or as sources of theory. The most striking case, perhaps, is the *Divina Commedia*; the growing polemic, in its early years, frequently gives rise to academic speeches. Petrarch and Boccaccio are examined, and a certain number of sixteenth-century poems are subjected to analysis. Furthermore, there is an occasional attempt to introduce contemporaneity into the interpretation of the *Poetics* itself, as Sassetti did in several documents.

Concomitant with this growth in activity in the vernacular, there is a decline in the amount of work being done in Latin. No single new Latin translation or commentary is published during these years, although Vettori's compendious volume was republished in 1573. Nicasius Ellebodius was the only writer to attempt a paraphrase and commentary, and this, perhaps significantly, remained unpublished. So did Maranta's lectures, treating both the general content of the *Poetics* and certain specific problems. This does not mean that the scholars were no longer working on Aristotle, for we have traces of correspondence and controversy in the exchanges between Maranta and Vettori and between Ellebodius and Sophianos; but these did not bear fruit as they had in the past.

Perhaps this turn toward the present, toward Italian literature, toward the amateur academies, accounts in part for the fact that Plato and Horace tend less to dominate conversation about Aristotle than they had in previous years. This tendency should not be exaggerated. For our study has shown that comparison among ancient authorities continues to be a favorite form of elucidation, that both Horace and Plato are still called upon constantly for solution of the most difficult problems in the *Poetics*. But the favorite game of parallelism seems to be played less vigorously, and there is a growing desire to find solutions to Aristotle within Aristotle, either within the one central text or by reference to the rest of the corpus. There are, as there had always been, attempts to discover and apply an Aristotelian method, to speak in terms of the four causes and to insist on syllogistic analysis—these not always with great success. One has, however, the sense of a fairly fresh approach, probably because the gentlemen of the academies were less limited by the tradition of the universities than their predecessors had been.

As for the interpretation of the *Poetics* itself, certain problems persist, others tend to disappear, new emphases make themselves felt. Of the old problems, the most perennial is the text, and we may ask whether any forward steps were made by a group of men who were not primarily philologists. I think that the answer is affirmative, especially if we recall some of the excellent conjectures of Ellebodius and his friend Sophianos (unfortunately not published and hence unavailable to the reading public). These men were, of course, philologists connected with universities; but some of their contemporaries also made, on occasion, useful suggestions for the improvement of the text. More important still, they made definite progress in the translation of the *Poetics*. The three successive versions are, I believe, successive ameliorations, if we take as our criteria clarity, concision, and the use of a language which is neither cant nor jargon. In the Latin of Ellebodius as well, we find good solutions, although these are frequently lost in the context of the paraphrase.

The issue of interpretation remains very much alive. In at least two cases, those of Castelvetro and Gratarolo, the authority of Aristotle and the general validity of the *Poetics* are challenged. Do we need, they ask, to take this man and this document as necessarily infallible? And they proceed from there to quite complete rejection. But this is not a general tendency, and without being as explicit in Aristotle's defence as was Giulio Del Bene, most critics of the period still assumed that he was infallible and went on to the important business of discovering what he meant. Part of that discovery consisted in the reiterated controversy over given words and phrases, much of it now conducted in Italian and discussed in public sessions. Such stock passages as those containing the words μίμησις, ποίησις, ἁμαρτία, λόγοις ψιλοῖς, such central notions as purgation, verisimilitude, plot, and the four requisites of character continue to arouse interest and debate: and if they do so, it is because they are regarded by men of this period as the fundamental issues of the *Poetics*. I think that it is possible to generalize with respect to their findings, admitting always that there was never any unanimity and that the generalization represents no single theorist. Poetry comes to be distinguished from imitation as a species from its genus, and the poetic imitations are separated from nonpoetic. But poetry—in spite of a few dissenters and subtilizers—remains inextricably linked with verse, and the argument as to whether verse is required in all genres, especially comedy, is usually decided in the affirmative. There is some clouding of all these terms, especially of imitation, by reference to Plato.

The ends of poetry remain what they have been throughout the century, pleasure and instruction, sometimes with pleasure standing as an end in itself, more usually with pleasure subordinated to the utility of moral exemplification and preachment. Here purgation enters, for, taken as it was to mean the expulsion of undesirable passions—pity and fear and others—it provides the most effective means for achieving usefulness. It is still the answer which Aristotle gave to Plato, but less prominently than before; discussion centers more directly on the passions concerned and the ways in which purgation works. Questions of plot and of character are made to relate to the ends of poetry. For if pleasure is to be given to an unruly audience of the "vulgus," plot must be made of certain known materials and organized in certain convenient ways. It is thought of largely as a kind of scenario or "argument" to which episodes are added for purposes of amplification and adornment—episodes which may be considered integral or removable, depending on the decision of individual theorists. In spite of quotations about the "soul of tragedy," there is no organic conception of plot as the organizing element of the poem, from which nothing can be removed. But we should note in this connection that there is at least one trace (in Piccolomini) of a notion of artistic necessity, which would demand that elements of plot be present or absent for "artistic" rather than for "natural" reasons. Verisimilitude and the marvelous are also related to the capacities of plot to achieve its ends, the first establishing the conditions of belief—hence, of moral effect—in the audience, the second creating the possibility of a strong effect upon the emotions and hence of pleasure. Similar considerations affect ideas about character, and Aristotle's four requisites are studied over and over again in the desire to make them serve the purposes of credibility and moral instruction. So are his "better," "like," and "worse," although in this case there is more controversy, relevant to the decision as to whether these involve an ethical or a social distinction; most critics opt for the latter, but there are many nuances in their reasons for doing so.

Perhaps the most subtle way in which an enduring Horatianism manifests itself is in the twisting of the *Poetics* to make of it a set of precepts for the poet who would amuse and instruct an audience of the multitude.

Castelvetro is, of course, the prime example of this, since his theory is so completely directed to the masses. But he is not alone; in almost every theorist, one may ultimately see the audience as the primary determinant of the poem's content and form. Audiences differ. Piccolomini's is more imaginative and intelligent than Castelvetro's. But all are ever-present in a system that continues to be rhetorical in its essential workings. Once this basic position has been taken, it is less necessary than it had been (not long since) to rise to the defence of poetry or to compare it—and its merits—to the other arts. Utility has by this time been established for each specific audience, and now the job is to see how art may serve this utility. The superior appeal of poetry, because of its accessibility to the senses and the passions, is often stressed; but the defensive, even apologetic tone is no longer needed. From Horace and the rhetoricians, again, stem the complex and numerous components of the theory of decorum, which still informs much of the thinking about character, about plot, and about credibility as related to both.

One has the impression, on the whole, that the total interpretation of Aristotle in these years is less rigid and more fluid, perhaps more vigorous, than it had been in the years immediately preceding. It remains to be seen whether this impression is justified by the events of the following years, when the influence of the current literary polemics made itself strongly felt on the interpretation of Aristotle.

CHAPTER TWELVE. THE TRADITION OF ARISTOTLE'S *POETICS*: IV. THE EFFECT OF THE LITERARY QUARRELS

THE EFFECT of the current literary quarrels upon the interpretation of the *Poetics* had already begun to be perceptible in the materials studied in the last chapter. Only one quarrel had been involved, that over Dante's *Divina Commedia*. In the years to come, this polemic will continue to influence the thinking of the theorists, and to it will be added two other major literary debates: that over Tasso and Ariosto (implicating the whole theory of epic poetry) and that over Guarini's *Pastor Fido* (necessitating a re-examination of the whole theory of dramatic poetry). Immediately after 1575, the most prominent is still, of course, the quarrel over Dante; the others enter the picture at broadly spaced intervals. All this activity reflects increasingly the successive "vulgarization" of the *Poetics*, its spread into constantly broader circles of discussion. From Florence the dialogue ranges outward, as other academies and other cities begin to participate.

To be sure, old problems are not forgotten and traditional solutions continue to be offered. In fact, some of the first documents that we shall have to study in the present chapter will echo the sounds of an earlier generation—works by philologists, in Latin, with rather more interest in Horace than in Aristotle—and such works will appear constantly throughout these years. The only major published commentary of the decade is Riccoboni's, and it is in Latin. Alongside it, we shall find several manuscript translations and commentaries in Italian, manifestations of the growing excitement within the academies.

The old tradition is clearly represented by Franciscus Portus' *In omnes Sophoclis tragoedias* Προλεγόμενα, published posthumously by his son Aemilius in 1584, probably written around 1575. One feels, indeed, that Portus is returning to the early Horatian commentaries of the beginning of the century, in spite of his frequent citation of Aristotle; some of the passages in the *Prolegomena* are direct translations of the *Poetics*, but they are followed by explanations which have a distinctly medieval flavor. We may take as an example his treatment of the *Ajax*. In one paragraph he collapses much of the content of the early chapters of Aristotle:

> Tragedy, comedy, and indeed every form of poetry is derived from nature and from it receives its origin. In fact, man is born for imitation and adapted to it, as can immediately and easily be seen in children themselves, who learn by means of imitation to do whatever they do. Now men imitate either happy or sad things. For human life revolves almost entirely about these two pivots, I mean fortunate and unfortunate events. And thus those first men, some of them applying themselves to the former, others to the latter according to the difference of their talents, tried to express them by means of imitation. This came about at first

by chance, as even Aristotle affirms. Then, the matter having come to the attention of those who were more skilled and more capable through the sharpness of their genius, both comedy and tragedy gradually grew and made progress, first modest, then considerable. It is believed that its origin springs from divine things.

Except for the last sentence, the paragraph is entirely out of Aristotle, and so is the following section on the origins of tragedy and its quantitative parts. But then Portus continues with an array of distinctions that recalls Donatus and Diomedes and Badius:

> While there are other differences between tragedy and comedy, this is the principal distinction: in comedy the circumstances of men are middling, the fears small, small the perils, the endings happy; in tragedy on the other hand the persons are mighty, the fears great, the endings mournful. In the one, the first events are disturbed, the last are serene; in tragedy instead the beginnings are happy and peaceful, the endings are violent and sad. And in tragedy is portrayed the kind of life to be avoided, in comedy the kind to be sought. Lastly, comedy invents its subjects, tragedy often seeks them in historical truth.[1]

In the same prologue, Portus draws up a comparison between Euripides and Sophocles; in it, rhetorical criteria alternate with references to Aristotle. Euripides is praised for being more accessible to the ears of the people, more like an orator, more capable of inducing to action. This is because of the many sententiae and commonplaces which he uses and because of his skill in disputation. It is for his skill in moving the passions that Aristotle calls him τραγικώτατος, taken as meaning "aptissimus ad mouendos affectus." To Sophocles are applied such epithets as "grauis," "tragicus," "sublimis," "grandiloquus"; but he always tempers gravity with gaiety, severity with the sweetness of poetry. This gives pleasure. But he also arouses the tragic emotions of pity and wonder (translating οἶκτος, καὶ θαῦμα) and these vie with pleasure in the general effectiveness of his tragedies (p. 13). The use of the Greek phrase and its translation by "misericordia, & admiratio" (for the two tragic emotions) makes one wonder how clearly Portus, at this point, had the text of the *Poetics* in mind.

---

[1] *Prolegomena* (1584), p. 11: "Tragcedia, Comoedia, atque adeò omnis poësis à natura fluxit: & ab ea suum ortum accepit. homo enim ad imitandum natus, aptúsque est: id, quod etiam in ipsis statim infantibus facilè cerni potest, qui imitatione discunt agere quaecunque agunt, imitantur autem homines res vel laetas, vel tristes. Vita enim hominum in his quasi duobus vertitur cardinibus, secundis (inquam) rebus, vel aduersis. Primi itaque illi homines alij has, alij illas pro diuersitate ingeniorum, sequuti, eas imitando exprimere sunt conati, casu primùm hoc accidit vt Aristoteles etiam testatur: deinde re notata ab iis, qui erant solertiores, & ingenij acumine valebant, vtraque res, Comoedia, Tragoediáque paulatim creuit, & progressus primùm modicos, deinde magnos fecit. Ortus eius à rebus diuinis manasse creditur"; and p. 12: "Inter Tragoediam, & Comoediam cum alia intersunt, tum illud in primis est discrimen. in Comoedia mediocres fortunae hominum, parui metus, parua pericula, exitus laeti sunt. In Tragoedia contrà ingentes personae, magni metus, funesti sunt exitus: in illa, turbulenta prima, tranquilla postrema: in Tragoedia contrà, principia laeta & pacata, exitus turbulenti, & funesti: & in Tragoedia vita fugienda, in Comoedia vita expetenda exprimitur. Denique Comoedia fingit argumenta. Tragoedia saepe ab historica fide petit."

In 1576, the *In Q. Horatii Flacci librum de arte poetica commentarius* of Aldo Manuzio the Younger was added to the long list of such studies. It made the customary allegations of parallelism between Horace and Aristotle, but in surprisingly modest number (see Chapter V, p. 194). In the commentary itself there is very little of interest for the study of Aristotle. Manuzio prefaced it, however, by prolegomena in which he considers essentially one problem—the relationship between imitation and poetry— and here he does draw upon the *Poetics*. After an initial definition of poetry as an imitation using language and the additional means of rhythm, harmony, and meter, singly or together, he states that poetry may exist without verse—thus taking his position in the current quarrel. He thinks that Aristotle admits poetry with and without verse and that Plato's dialogues may thus be called poetry. He finds five genres enumerated by Aristotle, the epic, tragedy, comedy, the dithyramb and the gnome; and the question arises as to whether the last two contain imitation. Manuzio derives the answer from a series of distinctions about the dithyramb; the dithyramb, he says, sings the praises of Bacchus:

... now praises are either true or false; if they are true, it is a history and not an imitation; if they are false, what imitation can there be without the image of truth? A double answer suggests itself. For first, as concerns that part of imitation "which is made through λόγος," I concede that when true things are narrated, there is no imitation; about the false things I do not feel in the same way, For false things are either verisimilar or they are such as cannot happen. Every imitation is drawn from the verisimilar ones, nobody imitates those which cannot be done. But if with verisimilar things true ones are occasionally intermingled, the imitation ceases to exist insofar as true things are being narrated. Still, it does not cease to be poetry because of that, but since it continues to treat verisimilar things, it takes its name from the imitation. The fact is not that in tragedy and the epic there is no place for the true, but verisimilar things are more numerous than true ones. ... I therefore believe that the dithyramb is a poem because it consists of praises of Bacchus, some of which are true but the majority of which are verisimilar.[2]

Other demands of the definition are satisfied because the dithyramb also uses meter, rhythm, and harmony. The same argument is then applied to gnomic poetry. Manuzio reiterates the same ideas on truth and verisimili-

---

[2] *Commentarius* (1576), pp. **–**v: "nam laudes aut uerae sunt, aut falsae. si uerae, historia est, non imitatio: si falsae, quae potest esse sine imagine ueritatis imitatio? Duplex occurrit responsio. nam, quod attinet primum ad eam partem imitationis, quae λόγῳ fit; concedo, cum uera narrantur, imitationem non esse; de falsis, non idem sentio. sunt enim falsa aut uerisimilia, aut quae fieri non possunt. ex uerisimilibus omnis ducitur imitatio: ea, quae fieri non possunt, imitatur nemo. quod si uerisimilibus admiscentur interdum uera; desinit esse imitatio, quatenus uera narrantur; nec tamen poesis non est ob eam caussam, sed, quia uerisimilia persequitur, ab imitatione nomen capit. non enim aut in tragoedijs, aut in epopoeia nihil ueri locum habet: sed uerisimilia plura, quam uera. ... Opinor igitur Poema esse, dithyrambum, quia constet ex Bacchi laudibus nonnullis fortasse ueris, plerisque tamen uerisimilibus."

tude in connection with lines 1–23 of the *Ars poetica*, on imitation as the distinguishing mark of the poet in connection with line 151 (pp. 2 and 35). Throughout, Manuzio reflects the concern of his contemporaries with the problem of truth; but he differs from many of them in admitting the possibility of poetry without verse.

Plato rather than Horace provides the point of departure for Lorenzo Gambara's *Tractatio de perfectę poëseos ratione* (1576). As has already been pointed out (Chapter VIII, pp. 305–8), it is a document which Christianizes Plato in order to make an appeal for a new Christian poetry. Aristotle enters the argument in several capacities. First, he is the authority for the preference for what is verisimilar and necessary to what is true, and this preference is turned by Gambara to his own purposes. Whoever portrays the perfect model of man, he says, departs from the truth and moves in the direction of what might be. The poetic art becomes one of meditation and actions are used as episodes: "A vast field is opened to pious and Christian writers, not for inventing, but for meditating piously many things and for drawing them from the springs of theology—things which are most useful and pleasant for the persuasion of human minds and well adapted moreover to receiving the narration of events inserted as episodes."[3] Aristotle's conception of poetry is thus completely reversed. Second, the *Poetics* gives as the natural causes of poetry the desire to imitate and harmony and rhythm; Gambara uses these as demonstrations of the precedence of Biblical writings over those of the Gentiles. Finally, Aristotelian elements enter prominently into a rather complex statement of the ends and workings of poetry:

... they set down a double end for poetry, the one imitation, the other instruction, so that the poetic power lies in seeing whatever may be adapted to the imitation of any action, passion, character, in pleasant language, for the amendment of life and for the promotion of a good and happy life. But if in imitation we must have regard for what we imitate, and why, and with what means, and in what manner, certainly ... the rule for every proper imitation must be sought in the very truth of the actions, and in actions of men gloriously accomplished, and in solid virtues.[4]

Here Aristotle's distinctions with respect to poetry are deliberately set aside in favor of rules which would further its didactic ends.

---

[3] *Tractatio* (1576), p. 23: "pijs & christianis scriptoribus latissimum patere campum ad multa non confingenda, sed piè meditanda, & ex theologię fontibus haurienda, quae vtilissima, iucundissimaque sint permouendis humanis ingenijs, rerum autem narrationi, interpositis illis tanquam episodijs, valde commoda."

[4] *Ibid.*, p. 24: "Duplicem porro finem Poëtices statuunt, imitationis alterum, alterum Doctrinae: vt poëtica facultas sit videndi quodcunque accommodatum sit ad imitationem cuiusque actionis, affectionis, moris, suaui sermone ad vitam corrigendam, & ad bene beateque viuendum. At si in imitatione spectandum est quid, quare, quo, & quomodo imitemur, sane . . . ex ipsa rerum veritate, & rebus hominum praeclarè gestis, solidisque virtutibus petenda erit omnis rectissimae imitationis ratio."

ORAZIO CAPPONI AND TORQUATO TASSO (1576)

The next set of documents to be examined returns specifically to the *Poetics*. It consists in a set of remarks on Piccolomini and on Castelvetro by two writers, Orazio Capponi and Torquato Tasso, who were engaged in 1576 in a correspondence about these very questions. Of the two manuscripts by Orazio Capponi, the first, his *Censure sopra le annotationi della Poetica d'Aristotele del Rever.mo Monsig.re Alessandro Piccolomini*, is found in the Biblioteca Comunale of Siena, MS C.VI.9, folios 50–53v; I have assigned to it the date of 1576.[5] It contains a series of separate paragraphs on passages in Piccolomini which Capponi refers to by "particella" and page numbers; the general method is similar to that of Sassetti's *Discorso*. Capponi usually rejects Piccolomini's ideas in the particular passages studied, agreeing rather with those of Maggi, Vettori, or Robortello, or proposing his own solutions. Two major topics preoccupy him: whether "good" and "bad" (for persons imitated) constitute specific differences among genres, and whether the plots and characters of tragedy need to be previously known. Both were discussed by Sassetti. On the first, Capponi states firmly that by the distinction between good and bad objects Aristotle meant to establish a specific differentia (fol. 50v). He refers to 1448a16, on tragedy and comedy:

> Why then did Aristotle include it at this place, where it seems indeed that he is treating the specific differences which exist between these imitations? And there is no doubt that these differences of instruments, of things, and of the manner are specific. Why then should we want to say that they do not differentiate these two poems specifically? And if there were another specific difference between them which consisted in the things imitated, why would Aristotle not have mentioned it here?... And if there is another which does not consist in imitating the better or the worse with respect to character, we shall reprove Aristotle as one who enumerated only three of them for us, and not all of those that he should have.[6]

The question of how such goodness or badness is made known to the audience involves Capponi in a discussion of new and traditional plots and characters. He tries to steer a middle course between the conflicting views previously expressed. When both plot and persons are known, he says, the poet must conform in every way to the accepted opinions about them, lest his imitations appear false. When they are newly invented, their goodness or badness of character must be made apparent not only through their

---

[5] See my "Nuove Attribuzioni...," *Rinascimento*, III (1952), 257–59.

[6] MS Bibl. Com. Siena C.VI.9, fol. 51: "Perche dunque l'ha numerata Arist: in questo luogo doue par pur che tratti delle differenze specifiche che si ritrouano fra queste imitationi? e non è dubbio che queste differenze d'istromenti, di cose imitate, e del modo non sieno specifiche. per qual cagione dunque voliam dire che non diuersifichino specificamente questi due poemi? e se altra differenza specifica fusse fra loro che consistessi nelle cose imitate perche non harebbe fatto qui Aris: mentione?... E se altra ce n'è che non consista nell'imitar i migliori o peggiori in quanto a costumi riprenderemo Arist: come quello che n'habbia annouerate solamente tre, e non tutte quelle che deueua."

own choices and actions within the tragedy but also by expository reference to their past actions. Here the various devices of the dramatist's art must be used (fol. 53). Capponi's general position is that if characters are known, their actions must also be known through history. He thinks that Aristotle was arguing inconsistently when, at 1451*b*19, he declared that a tragedy might exist with no known personages in it; such a tragedy would be less perfect than one presenting known persons (fols. 52–52*v*).

Throughout, one of Capponi's main preoccupations is plot. He argues for Robortello and against Piccolomini on the interpretation of "a single action" and on the relationship of episodes to it. Aristotle's statement, at 1451*a*30, that all arts imitate a single thing seems to him to be a cogent refutation of those who would argue for multiplicity of plot or action (fol. 52). He points out, further, that a single episode is of necessity less moving than a whole plot: "If they are moved to compassion on hearing Oedipus' weeping, coming to see through it how he fell from a happy state into misery, they will also purge and diminish the other passions.... It is true that it will move and purge very little, since the interweaving of the whole action is not present."[7] This is a shrewd observation. On other passages his views are less acceptable. So for his agreement with Maggi and Vettori that the "one actor" of early tragedy must have been the one who expounded the plot (fol. 51*v*) and for his misunderstanding of Aristotle on spectacle at 1453*b*1.

The area of discussion is somewhat enlarged in Capponi's letter to Lionardo Salviati, dated September 27, 1576, and now found in the Ambrosian Library, MS Q. 113. Sup., folios 155–58. Capponi is apparently answering a request by Salviati for remarks which he might use in his own commentary on the *Poetics*; hence he remains less closely attached to Piccolomini (although some of the comments are repeated) and expresses more clearly his own opinions about Aristotle. He is also more directly concerned with textual matters (as in his notes on 1453*b*26 and 1448*b*37) and with general questions on the order of parts in the *Poetics* (as in his doubts whether 1454*a*3 ff. should appear where it does in the text). Some of the problems in the *Censure* reappear, approached now from a different angle. So for the question of "goodness" as a requisite of character; Capponi believes, after comparison of passages, that Aristotle means to require it of all characters, not only the one upon whom pity falls. He is willing to admit "bad" characters when they are necessary for the conduct of the tragedy (fol. 156). His discussion of unity of plot in tragedy involves considerations of both time and place in an interesting way. Challenging Aristotle's statement (1459*b*22) that the difference between tragedy and the

---

[7] *Ibid.*, fol. 52: "Se si moueranno a compassione nel sentir il pianto d'Edippo venendo a veder per questo com'egli di stato felice sia caduto in miseria purgheranno ancora gl'altri affetti, e li diminuiranno.... è ben uero che poco si mouerà, e poco si purgherà per non ui essere l'intessimento di tutta l'azzione."

epic in length and complexity of plot results from the difference between a dramatic and a narrative form, he maintains that the tragic plot may be just as complicated, that events which occur off stage may readily be narrated, and that such events are just as much "imitations" as those actually represented. The real difference, he says, is in the length of time involved, and he expresses surprise that Aristotle did not emphasize it further. Moreover, it is probable that the difference in place is also important:

> Perhaps it could be said that, while the epic can contain actions which are done in very remote places, and tragedy on the other hand can contain only those nearby, it would not be verisimilar to receive, within a matter of hours, information about other deeds. Therefore the epic may contain a greater diversity of episodes because in very remote places more diverse actions may take place than in those nearby.[8]

Capponi thus seems to be moving toward Castelvetro's position, if for different reasons. He disagrees with Aristotle, again, on the difficulty of perceiving a very small plot (1450*b*39). The smaller the better, in fact, for a small plot (unlike a small animal) would have fewer parts and their relationship would be easily perceptible. Finally, he thinks that at 1451*a*36 Aristotle is begging the question which he sets out to prove. We should note in this letter the serious attention paid to the text and its interpretation as well as the willingness to question the authority and the method of Aristotle.

In this letter to Salviati, Capponi speaks of having written to Torquato Tasso on the same day. Perhaps the subject was again Aristotle, for we have a letter from Tasso to Capponi, dated 1576, in which he speaks of his objections to Castelvetro, objections which he planned to state in a projected treatise.[9] Tasso's jottings have come down to us in a manuscript which is also at the Ambrosiana, and which was published in 1875 under the title of *Estratti dalla Poetica di Lodovico Castelvetro*. Using his copy of the 1570 edition of Castelvetro, Tasso makes extracts from it and to them appends his expressions of approval or disapproval. Most of these are brief, some are quite pungent; some, also, concern themselves with Aristotle directly. From them emerge Tasso's ideas on a number of central poetic questions. He rejects, first, Castelvetro's thesis that the materials of poetry and history are the same: "If the material of the poem were that of history, it would be the very same thing, and therefore it would not be 'similar.' Answer that one! Besides the poet would deserve no praise for

---

[8] MS Ambrosiana Q.113.Sup., fols. 156*v*–57: "Fortasse dici posset, quod cum epopeia continere possit actiones quae in remotissimis locis gestę sunt. Tragedia autem eas tantum quae in uicinis alias non esset uerisimile spatio horarum resciri. Idcirco maiorem dissimilitudinem episodiorum potest continere cum in remotissimis locis magis diuersae fiant actiones quam in uicinis."

[9] In *Lettere*, ed. Guasti, I, 195–96.

it, since he would have made no effort to invent it. This is a better reason."[10] If one thinks correctly about imitation, one will have the answer about the materials, for "the imitation required of poetry cannot be called imitation directly; but it can be called a rivalry of the poet with the arrangements of fortune or with the course of mundane affairs."[11] As for the end of such imitation, Tasso believes that it is restricted to pleasure (without utility) and that Aristotle meant to treat only such poems as are performed in the public square "for the pleasure of the people" ("per diletto del popolo," p. 285). Hence he quarrels with Aristotle for having introduced the whole question of purgation and for having treated it as he did, without proof and without cogent arguments.

Aristotle contradicts himself; for having said earlier, where he is seeking the origin of poetry, that its end is pleasure, he now directs tragedy toward utility, that is, the purgation of souls; of which utility no account at all must be taken, or at least not so much that because of it all the other kinds of tragedies, which do not have it, will be rejected. And if indeed we are to have some consideration for utility, why not of another kind of utility? as in those tragedies which contain the passage of good men from misery to happiness, which confirm the opinion that the people has about God's providence. And so forth.[12]

The whole argument is quickly summarized in a later passage: "you will see that the end of the poet is pleasure and that poetry is not an imitation of history. Read the text and the commentary; you will find inconsistency in Castelvetro."[13]

Tasso finds Castelvetro most unsatisfactory on matters of unity, especially when he advocates kinds of unity other than that of plot: "Note that it seems that Castelvetro holds that several actions may become one through the unity of time, of place, of person, not merely through dependency. This is most false."[14] The same epithet "falsissimo" is applied to Castelvetro's contention that all tragedies and comedies have double plots; this comes, says Tasso, from a false supposition that a variety of personages necessarily means a multiplicity of plots. He believes that the whole

[10] In *Prose diverse*, ed. Guasti, I, 280: "Se la materia del poema fosse quella dell'istoria, sarebbe quell'istessa, e perciò non sarebbe simile. Rispondi tu a questa. Oltre di ciò il poeta non ne meritarebbe lode, perchè non si sarebbe faticato a trovarla. Questa è miglior ragione."

[11] *Ibid.*, p. 284: "La imitazione richiesta a la poesia non si può chiamare direttamente imitazione; ma si può appellare gareggiamento del poeta e della disposizione della fortuna, o del corso delle mondane cose."

[12] *Ibid.*, pp. 283–84: "Aristotile contraddice a se stesso, perchè avendo detto di sopra, là dove cerca l'origine della poesia, che 'l suo fine è 'l diletto, ora drizza la Tragedia a l'utilità, cioè a la purgazione degli animi; della quale utilità o non si deve tenere conto alcuno, o almeno non se ne deve tener tanto, che per lei si rifiutino tutte l'altre maniere di Tragedie, che ne son prive. E se pur dell'utilità s'ha d'aver considerazione; perchè non d'altra sorte d'utilità? come di quelle Tragedie, che contengono la mutazion de' buoni di miseria in felicità; le quali confermano l'opinione, che ha il popolo, della provvidenza di Dio, ec."

[13] *Ibid.*, p. 290: "vedrai che 'l fine del poeta è 'l diletto, e che la poesia non è imitazion dell'istoria. Leggi il testo e 'l comento: troverai contrarietà nel Castelvetro."

[14] *Ibid.*, p. 282: "Nota, che par che 'l Castelvetro voglia che più azioni possano divenir una per l'unità del tempo, del luogo, della persona, non solo per la dipendenza. Falsissimo."

difficulty may be solved by admitting the possibility of greater or less simplicity within unity and that this will explain why the epic, while still unified, is more complex than other forms (p. 294). On the epic specifically (the form which interested him most personally), he states that it is capable of greater magnificence, of a more marvelous quality, than other forms (p. 289); by "magnificence" he means essentially the ornaments of language, justified in the epic by several of its peculiar conditions. Vergil would thus seem to be superior to Homer as an epic poet: "Homer, particularizing, was concerned with what is proper to poetry in general, that is, imitation; Vergil, universalizing, had in mind what is proper to the epic, that is, the magnificent."[15]

BALDINO (1576)

The most curious document of the year 1576 returns us to Aristotle himself, presenting as it does a translation of the *Poetics* into Latin verse. This is Bernardino Baldino's *Liber de arte poetica Aristotelis versibus fideliter, et latine expressus,* published in Milan. The phrase "Liber de arte poetica" in the title prepares us, in a way, for the general form and tone of the translation; for Baldino makes of the *Poetics* a kind of Horatian art of poetry, complete with an invocation to the muses and not without an occasional anachronism such as reference to a Roman actor. At times the original text is followed fairly closely, at others there are rapid summaries or complete gaps. A general idea of Baldino's technique may be had from the following lines, corresponding to the beginning of Aristotle's text:

> Plura loqui nobis opus est, artemque poesis,
> Et genera, & uires; quo gratas texere pacto
> Fabellas deceat uatem, qui ducitur arte;
> Et quae membra sibi, quas culta poetica dotes
> Vendicet ars; ac cuncta tuo natura tenore
> Educam; notumque prius caput eloquar artis.
> Sunt imitatores alijque, aliique poetae.
> Vt qui cantat epos, tenui nec uoce tragoedus,
> Comicus & tenuis, dithrambique inclytus author;
> Atque alij, quibus est plectrum, queis tibia in usu.
> Vt propriis Helenes expressa coloribus ora
> Sunt Zeusi; caput ut Veneris depinxit Apelles.
> Hique uel à ritu docti, uel ab arte magistra.
> Roscius in scenis ut uerbis, gestibus, ore
> Voces, & gestus effinxit, & ora uirorum,
> Sic rhythmis, sic harmonia, sic uoce canora
> Assimilant aliis alij se, ceu citharoedus,
> Tibicenque aliique uelut queis tibia cordi.

---

[15] *Ibid.*, p. 291: "Omero, particolareggiando, ebbe riguardo a quel che è proprio della Poesia in generale, cioè l'imitare. Virgilio, universaleggiando, mirò al proprio dell'Epopeia, cioè al magnifico."

It is clear that while the meaning of the text is given fairly accurately now and then, the exigencies of the verse and the desire to create a given poetic tone preclude the possibility of any careful distinctions of meanings. Sometimes, instead, the translation reflects all the current misconceptions about the sense of the text. We may take as an example the verses presenting the distinction between tragedy and epic:

> Inter epos, tragicumque poema hoc conuenit; ambo
> Reges, magnanimosque duces, genus atque Deorum
> Complectuntur; epos metris sed pergit eisdem
> Ad calcem: uariique pedes, numerique cothurnis
> Aptantur: tragicosque dies amplectitur una
> Actus: sed plures aeneis tenditur annos:
> Vtraque se quamuis extenderet ante poesis.
> Sed quas coepit epos sublime, recepit & omneis,
> Insuper ac alias inflata tragoedia partes.
>
> (Pp. B2–B2v; for 1449b7)

Or those which translate the definition of tragedy:

> Nunc mihi de tragicis est rebus sermo futurus.
> Nobilis, et nitido spectanda tragoedia cultu,
> Est grauis, egregiique actus imitatio, certos
> Ad fines porrecta, breui neque margine pressa:
> Cui musaea mele, cui mixta locutio rhytmis,
> Addita; quaeque metu, pietateque pectora flectit;
> Fluctibus ut uariis animos exoluat, & aestu.
>
> (P. B2v; for 1449b24)

Baldino's translation may be taken as a curious and unique exercise, reflecting a kind of accumulated popular tradition with respect to the *Poetics*, but making no serious contribution either to the translation or to the exegesis of the text.

SASSETTI (1576)

Filippo Sassetti's earlier work with the *Poetics*, both on Piccolomini's *Annotationi* for the Accademia degli Alterati and in his marginalia to the same book, may be considered as preparation for his own translation and commentary of Aristotle. He began to work on this in 1575 and probably interrupted it the following year; the manuscript (untitled, but commonly called the *Sposizione della Poetica*) is in the Biblioteca Riccardiana, MS 1539.[16] Sassetti made little more than a beginning on what was to have been a compendious volume, for the fragment of forty-five pages which we have goes only from the beginning of the *Poetics* to 1449a2 and includes as well a fairly long preface. Such as it is, it is full of original ideas on the *Poetics* and constitutes a clarification and expansion of what Sassetti had said in his earlier writings. Rather than taking the early commentators as its

[16] See M. Rossi, *Filippo Sassetti*, pp. 25–26.

POETIC THEORY

point of departure, it develops an independent analysis, discussing its predecessors only when necessary.

Perhaps the distinguishing feature of Sassetti's approach is his determination to find an Aristotelian method for the analysis of Aristotle. Whereas others had been content to elucidate the *Poetics* by occasional reference to the *Ethics*, the *Politics*, and the *Rhetoric*, Sassetti goes instead to the *Organon* (and even to the *De partibus animalium*) for statements on such matters as the constitution of definitions, the inductive method, and the criticism of syllogistic structure. Hence, while others had been content with discovering the order of the parts of the text, he wishes rather to determine the philosophical reason for their presence in the treatise. Such a wish may have been prompted by his dissatisfaction with the method of Piccolomini and by his hope of improving upon all his predecessors; Castelvetro, for example, is severely chided for his logical deficiencies (fol. 115v). This does not mean that Sassetti proves in every respect to be a sound Aristotelian, for some of his solutions are doubtful; but his attention to method does result in many excellent interpretations.

This attention allows us to understand why he wrote the kind of preface he did for his commentary. For the preface seems at first reading to be a kind of Platonic statement of the didactic and political ends of poetry. Not only different genres, he says, but poems within each genre are distinguished by the kinds of persons they imitate, and these persons are paradigms of goodness or badness or of the middle state between the two. So for goodness: "one poem will imitate valorous men of high enterprise, placing before us the idea of the proper knight, of the true captain, and the form of the true king and lord, representing in each one of these kinds of men that character from which perfect teachings may be derived, with no possibility of learning any ugly thing from that work."[17] Sassetti maintains that we read all kinds of poetry for the pleasure which they afford; but some make us laugh, others make us weep. We must wonder, then, whether all kinds are good at all times and in all places. Sassetti answers that this depends upon the general state of happiness in the country:

> This matter must be decided according to the various conditions in which men find themselves. For if some country abounds in great happiness, whence the citizens derive the highest joy, and if the souls of the good men must be in such wise habituated that in the midst of joys they realize that they can fall into misery, to such as these it might well not be good to show pleasurable spectacles which would distract their minds so considerably from believing that that good fortune might some time change, as every well prepared heart should do.[18]

[17] MS Riccardiana 1539, fol. 81v: "Iuno imitera huomini ualorosi e dalto affare proponendoci l'idea del propio cauaiere, del vero capitano, e la forma del uero Re e signore; fingendo in ciascuna di queste maniere dhuomini quel costume onde perfetti ammaestramenti possano trarsi; senza che cosa laida possa in quell opera appararsi."

[18] *Ibid.*, fol. 82: "ma in cio debbe deliberarsi secondo i varij stati ne quali gl huomini si ritruouano; peroche abbondando alcuna terra di grandissima felicita donde ne cittadini somma letitia deriua e douendosi talmente assuefare gl animi de buoni che nelle allegrezze

The opposite would hold true for unhappy states. Now while it is the function of the poet to produce the desired effects, he neither decides which effects are wanted nor does he know by what precepts they may be achieved. He therefore needs to receive advice from two experts whose decisions are prior to his own: the magistrate or the prince who will tell him what effects are good for his contemporaries—politics thus becomes the reigning art—and the preceptor of poetics who will tell him how to achieve the effects in exactly the correct degree. Aristotle falls into the third category, and the *Poetics* "contains nothing but the precepts and the instructions to poets on how to compose their poems well."[19] Sassetti establishes a hierarchy among the three arts: "the order among these three arts will be such that politics will be the noblest and the most important, as the one that commands; after it will be poetry; and in the third place will be put that faculty which shows poets in what way they must compose their poems."[20]

The first function of Sassetti's preface is thus to separate the determination of the ends from the writing of poems on the one hand and from the setting down of precepts on the other hand. Its second function is to discover what method Aristotle uses in writing the *Poetics*, and for light on this Sassetti turns to the distinction of methods which he finds in Galen. Galen, he says, had described three possible methods: a method by definition, which defines its object, analyses the definition into parts, and then treats each of the successive parts; a method by composition (the opposite of the first), which by division discovers each of the component parts of an object and then combines them into a conception of the whole; and a method by resolution, which proceeds from the knowledge of an end to the discovery of the means to its achievement. As an example of the first (or analytical) order, Sassetti cites Galen's own works on the medical art; of the second (or synthetic) order, Aristotle's treatises on natural objects and his *Organon*, which moves from nouns and verbs to syllogisms and demonstrations; of the third (or resolutive) order, Galen's writings on the curative art, Aristotle's *Ethics* and certain of the logical treatises which move from a knowledge of the syllogism and of demonstration to a study of their necessary components. The case is thus clear for the *Poetics*:

... since it has no other purpose than to explain the things which are necessary for their composition [i.e., of poems], and since I showed that this is found by means of the method of resolution, it is clear that in this treatise the precepts will

---

stimino di potere cadere nelle miserie a costoro facilmente non istara bene il mostrare i piaceuoli spettacoli i quali tanto maggiormente distrarrebbono lanimo loro dal riputare che possa quella fortuna per alcun tempo cangiarsi come pensare dourebbe ogni bene preparato petto."

[19] *Ibid.*, fol. 82v: "in esso altro non si contiene che precetti e ammaestramenti a Poeti per che bene compongano le loro Poesie."

[20] *Ibid.*, fol. 83: "tale adunque sara lordine tra queste arti che la Politica sara la piu nobile e la principale come quella che comanda; dopo a lei sara la Poesia; e nel terzo luogo si riporrà quella faculta, che dimostra a poeti in che maniera deono comporsi le Poesie."

be given through the method of resolution, insofar as the principal purpose is concerned. But because it is necessary, if we wish to write this or that poem, to know what it is and what it is good for, the demonstration of which is a result of definition, it was therefore necessary in the first part of this book to use the method of definition, which is itself necessarily preceded by the divisive method; for no definition can be obtained without the latter.[21]

As Sassetti sees the *Poetics*, its main problem in the early chapters is that of definition; before giving the precepts for the correct composition of poems, precepts which constitute the "art," it must seek the definition of poetry by inquiring first into its matter and its form, then into the combination of the two. The initial section, up to the definition of tragedy, will treat "of poetry in general and in itself" ("della poesia insomma e di per se," fol. 87v), after which it will discuss the species with respect to their natures, omitting for the time being their subject matter and other differentiating factors. Afterward will come the detailed treatment of each kind. This, says Sassetti, is the same method as that which Aristotle followed in the *Categories*, essentially a search for the genus through induction, passing from less universal to more universal considerations, then a discovery of the differentiae and the constitution of the species. Sassetti keeps this plan constantly in mind as he comments on the successive passages of the treatise. Thus, the first sentence is said to contain the "general proposition" of the work; the second is an indication of the genus; the third lists the three differentiae; the fourth (1447a18), as it distinguishes the three means of poetry, makes possible the later definitions of the separate species. When he comes to the point (1448a24) at which Aristotle summarizes the three differentiae, he digresses from his orderly commentary on passages and reduces the materials to tabular form, as follows:

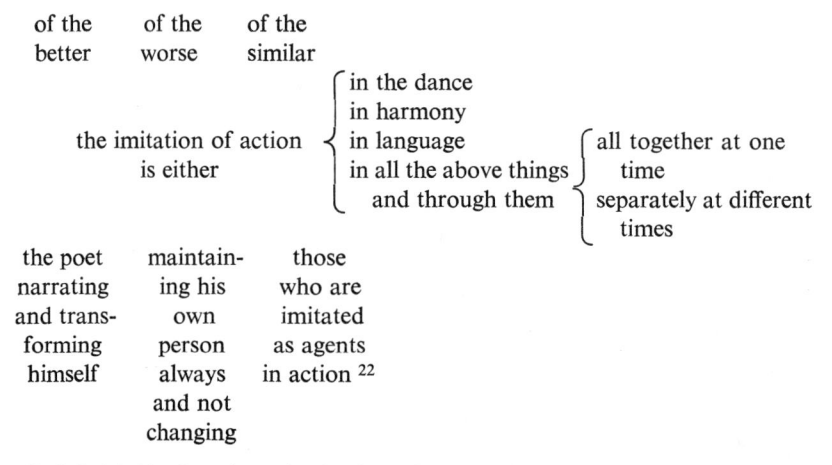

	of the better	of the worse	of the similar		
the imitation of action is either			in the dance in harmony in language in all the above things and through them	all together at one time separately at different times	
the poet narrating and transforming himself	maintaining his own person always and not changing	those who are imitated as agents in action [22]			

[21] *Ibid.*, fol. 84v: "non hauendo altro intendimento che lo spianare le cose che a comporle si ricercano; et hauendo io dimostro che cio si ritroua per mezzo della resolutiua disposizione;

Sassetti maintains that the definition of every poetic species may be derived from this table, and he offers some examples. But he qualifies Aristotle's treatment by insisting that it covered only the "perfect" species: "... it should be clearly noted that since in this book the precepts of true and perfect poems are given, only those things are considered in it which belong to these poems, and the precepts for them are given."[23] Thus Aristotle should not be blamed for his failure to treat so "imperfect" a form as the pastoral.

If he is to treat poetry completely, Aristotle must include in his method a consideration of all four causes. Sassetti believes that he does. The elements entering into the definition provide two of the causes, the material and the formal; the others will come along later, and we shall thus have all four causes

... which (because poems are inventions of our intellect which imitates nature) will be four just as the causes of natural things are four, which are composed of matter and of form and have the efficient cause which made them and the end for which they were made. [These will all be found in poems:] ... since these also have that element which, in proportion, corresponds to matter and that which corresponds to form, which are the imitation common to all kinds and the differences ... these are causes which are in poetry just as matter and form are in natural things.[24]

---

manifesta cosa che in questo trattato i precetti saranno dati con la resolutiua dispositione; quanto appartiene allo intendimento principale; ma perche e bisogna a voler comporre questo o quel poema sapere quello che egli è et a quello che egli è buono il che dimostrare è effetto della diffinitione però e stato di mestieri nella prima parte d'esso libro adoperare la diffinitiua dispositione alla quale necessariamente ua innanzi la diuisiua non si potendo senza essa procacciare alcuna diffinitione."

[22] *Ibid.*, fol. 115: "de migliorj de peggiori de simili

l'imitatione d attione e o
- nel ballo
- nella armonia
- nell oratione
- in tutte le sopradette cose e per queste
  - tutte insieme in vno stesso tempo
  - separatamente en diuersi tempi

| narrando e tramutandosi il poeta | conseruando la sua persona sempre e non si mutando | come adoperanti enfaccendati coloro che simitano." |

[23] *Ibid.*, fol. 108v: "egli si dee bene auuertire che dandosi in questo libro i precetti delle poesie uere et perfette quelle cose solamente in esso si considerano che a queste si appartengono & sene danno i precetti."

[24] *Ibid.*, fol. 118v: "lequali (percioche sono le poesie inuentioni dello intelletto nostro che imita la natura) saranno quattro sicome quattro sono le cagioni delle cose naturali. le quali sono composte di materia e di forma, et hanno la causa efficiente che le fece, el fine per il quale esse furono fatte.... hauendo esse ancora quello che proportionatamente risponde alla materia e quello che alla forma; che sono l'imitatione comune a tutte quante; e le differenze ... lequali sono cagioni che sono nella poesia si come la materia e la forma sono nelle cose naturali."

As for the efficient and the final causes, Sassetti finds them in the paragraph on the natural origins of poetry (1448*b*4). To distinguish them, he must divide the paragraph differently from Maggi (whose divisions he normally follows), breaking it after the parenthetical section ending with πρώτας. In this way the natural disposition to imitation becomes the efficient cause and the pleasure derived from imitation becomes the final cause. The relationship between the two is stated by Sassetti as follows:

> Since this power [of imitation] is one of the cognitive ones, which operate for pleasure or for utility or for what is honest, it follows that one or several or all of these things moved it [the human mind] to generate poetry. But because Aristotle says that the cause was the joy that every man finds in things which imitate, it follows that pleasure is the end which moved the human mind to create poetry, even though this pleasure may be such that it can include the useful and the honest. . . . poems must be used which are composed in such a way that they delight us and bring profit to us honestly.[25]

In the last parts of this passage, Sassetti allows himself to be influenced by the theory which produced his preface, and there may be some doubt about the solidity of his own method at this point.

Applying these various methodological distinctions to the text of the *Poetics*, Sassetti discovers to us his own interpretation of the text. In the light of what earlier commentators had done with it, he is obliged to decide whether imitation is the genus of poems or whether another genus, "poetry," is interposed between imitation and the individual species. He rejects his predecessors and affirms that the genus is imitation; as for poetry, it will be "a name given to its single species considered altogether, without its having any proper differentia or any proper nature which is distinct from each one of these species in a way that they would possess one differentia more than it; and imitation will be the true genus whence the essence of the species is derived."[26] Object, manner, and means are the differentiae which divide the genus. In connection with them, Sassetti makes the following philosophical statement on their function in the "art":

> ". . . but because those things by which one species is different from another are those of which they are composed, and these are the same ones which divide the generic nature, hence it is that one may say that the three differentiae named, through which one kind of poem is different from another, are

[25] *Ibid.*, fol. 119*v*: "essendo questa potenza una delle cognoscitiue lequali si muouono per il diletto o per l utile o per l honesto egli ne seguita che una di queste tre cose o piu o tutte siano state quelle che l hanno mossa allo ingenerare la poesia; ma perche Aristotile dice che questa e stata il rallegrarsi ciascuno delle cose che imitano e ne seguiterà che il diletto sia il fine che mosse l'intelletto humano a creare la poesia auuenga che questo diletto sia tale che e possa comprendere el utile el honesto. . . . adoperare si deono le poesie in maniera disposte che elle ci dilettino e ci giouino honestamente."

[26] *Ibid.*, fol. 89*v*: "uno nome posto alle spetie singolari dessa tutte insieme considerate senza che ella habbia una propia differenza o una propia natura laquale sia diuersa da ciascuna desse spetie perche elleno abbondino duna differenza piu di lei e limitatione sara il vero genere donde lessenza delle spetie si piglia."

the ones which divide the imitation."[27] In such judgments as these the methodological concern is paramount.

When he comes to the actual discussion of the differentiae, Sassetti finds himself on much more controversial ground. Means, object, and manner had been interpreted in many ways, and he must decide among them; and almost everywhere he makes decisions of a partisan nature which are not justified by the *Poetics* itself. So, for example, with respect to the means. He translates the terms for the three means as "nel ballo; nell oratione; e nell armonia" and provides a lengthy discussion of all three. The meaning of λόγος especially troubles him, and after examination of his predecessors, he decides that it must include the concept of verse (fols. 94–94v); no poetry is possible without verse. Hence, at a later point the translation becomes "ballo, melodia, verso" (fol. 100), and all the passages which traditionally aroused dispute—1447a28, 1448a11—are interpreted in such a way as to corroborate his thesis.

The difficulty with respect to the objects of imitation is to know what is meant by "good" and "bad," by "better," "worse," and "like." Sassetti takes a strong position against Piccolomini on this point, insisting that these distinctions do constitute a substantial differentia, capable of distinguishing one genre from another. He proposes his own theory that, however one interprets the terms themselves, they must be taken as referring "to actions, and not to the condition in which men have been placed by fortune."[28] Therefore, any theory which ascribes to them a distinction of status or station or condition will be false, and Sassetti disagrees both with Piccolomini and with the earlier commentators. He finds a solution rather in his contemporary Agnolo Segni, whose lectures he must have heard or read in their original form (1573)—unless, of course, he had access to the revised version before its publication:

I find much more probable the opinion of messer Agnolo Segni, who believes that by the "better" Aristotle here meant the heroes, who are not called "better" because they were masters of the others but because—since it was thought that they descended in some way from those false and lying gods—it was probable that in them were to be found greater vigor both of mind and of body, joined with greater prudence, than were to be found in men of Aristotle's time.[29]

[27] *Ibid.*, fols. 90v–91: "ma perche quelle cose per lequali una specie è dall altra diuersa sono quelle delle quali elle si compongono e questo sono le medesime che diuidono la natura generica di qui è che dire si possa le tre nominate differenze per lequali luna poesia e differente dall altra; sono quelle che diuidono l'imitatione."

[28] *Ibid.*, fol. 107v: "ha riguardo alle attioni; e non allo stato nel quale sono gli huomini stati posti dalla fortuna."

[29] *Ibid.*, fol. 103v: "molto piu uerisimile giudico io che sia loppinione di ms. Agnolo Segni il quale per i migliori crede che fussono intesi qui da Aristotele gl'eroi i quali non sono chiamati migliori perche e fossono signori degl'altri; ma perche stimandosi che e discendessono in qualunque maniera da quegli Dij falsi e bugiardi; uerisimile era che in loro fusse e maggior uigore d'animo e di corpo aggiunta con maggiore prudenza che negl huominj del secolo dAristotile non si ritrouaua." Note that in a letter of 1573 (MS Riccardiana 2438 bis, Pt. III) to Lorenzo Giacomini, Sassetti speaks of Segni's lectures: "egli stesso studia la Poetica leggentela il segni con bella frequenza" (fol. 2).

Social station here seems to be replaced by qualities of body and of soul rather than by the accident of divine descent, although Sassetti does not go so far as to make of it an ethical distinction. "Likeness" would differ from the other two terms by referring to the present century; for it is possible to imitate virtuous and good actions as well as wicked and bad ones in our own time (fol. 104). In any case, Sassetti reiterates his insistence that these differences must be considered in actions (fol. 103v).

On the subject of the manner, Sassetti runs afoul of the old Platonic use of "imitation" to mean dramatic representation, and all his care for method does not enable him to untangle the knot. He discards Castelvetro's notion that there is a "modo similitudinario" in addition to the three manners usually distinguished, as he discards Piccolomini's refinements on the mixed manner. But he cannot see how a poem can be an imitation—and hence a poem—if the poet speaks constantly in his own person. The dithyramb is pure narration; it becomes an imitation only because its other two means, harmony and the dance, are added. And a work such as Vergil's *Moretum*, spoken entirely by the poet, cannot rank either as poem or as epic (fols. 107–112v).

We must regard some of Sassetti's failures as deriving from the deficiencies of his own method and from the pressures of tradition. Others, such as the lengthy wonderings over the use of ἐποποιία at 1447a29, are ascribable to an erroneous reading of the text, which the state of scholarship in his time did not permit him to correct. On the whole, however, his commentary must be regarded as one of the most remarkable of the period—especially because of his careful study of method—and we can only regret that he did not push it beyond the first few chapters of the *Poetics*. His promises to treat utility as an end in connection with purgation and the pure narrative form in connection with the dithyramb remain unfulfilled.

In 1578, Francesco Bonciani delivered before the Accademia Fiorentina his *Lettione della prosopopea*, now found in three manuscripts in the Biblioteca Riccardiana. This differs from other works of its kind in treating, rather than a literary genre, a rhetorical figure used in various genres. Orators, poets, and philosophers alike represent inanimate objects and animals as human beings, and such representations constitute the figure called prosopopoeia. Aside from its connections with Horace and Plato (see Chapter VI, p. 201 and Chapter VIII, p. 310), this lecture belongs to the Aristotelian tradition by virtue of its development of a theory of imitation for this figure. Imitation, according to Bonciani, may be of four classes of objects: the true, the verisimilar, the false, and the impossible; of these, prosopopoeia imitates impossible things and those false things which are not verisimilar. Since this imitation generates pleasure—the marvelous teaches us things we did not previously know—Bonciani is able to constitute thus his definition of prosopopoeia: "An imitation of impossible things, in an appropriate way, made in the simple narrative mode, or the mixed, or the dramatic, in order to teach or to delight or to persuade."[30] He is careful to point out that imitation, here, does not mean dramatic representation but has rather that broader sense given to it elsewhere by Aristotle, especially in the *Rhetoric*: "a person by means of words represents the form and the nature of a thing and gives it motion."[31] The imitation of the impossible itself becomes possible through the workings of the imagination, which combines known parts into an unknown and unnatural whole. "In an appropriate way" in the definition is explained by an example: one must not animate objects which, in their natures, are too far distant from animate things, as Petrarch did with his sighs. Other kinds of appropriateness are demanded within the figure, and they seem to be related either to decorum or to verisimilitude. Of the three ends mentioned in the definition, pleasure is the servant of instruction, although it is sometimes used alone by the poets, as persuasion (by means of prosopopoeia, of course) is by the orators. Bonciani thus constructs a kind of "little poetics" around the figure of speech which he has chosen to elucidate.

All the preliminary materials accompanying the editions of Sforza d'Oddo's comedy, *L'Erofilomachia, ouero Il duello d'amore & d'amicitia*, bear the date of 1572, and the exact date of August 1, 1572 is found at the end of Bernardo Pino da Cagli's *Discorso intorno al componimento della comedia de' nostri tempi*, which is printed with it. I am treating the *Discorso* at the present place, however, because I have found no edition of it earlier than 1578. The *Discorso*, in the midst of a discussion which is essentially Horatian in its sources and theory, calls upon Aristotle for enlightenment on two matters, the distinction between tragedy and comedy and the limitation of the comic subject. For Bernardo Pino, the basic difference between the two dramatic genres lies in the social status of their subjects, and he interprets Aristotle in this light:

> Comedy must not be the imitation of men who are more unfortunate or wicked, as would seem to be indicated by the word φαυλοτέρων which means viler and lower men, but of persons low and abject in comparison with those who are introduced in tragedy; for in tragedy princes and kings and other persons of highest station are introduced . . . and in comedy men of humble condition are introduced, such as gentlemen and private citizens.[32]

---

[30] MS Ricc. 1539. fol. 134: "Imitatione di cose impossibili in maniera conueneuole fatta nel modo narratiuo semplice o misto, o nel rappresentatiuo a fine d'insegnare, o dilettare, o persuadere."

[31] *Ibid.*, fol. 134v: "altri con parole ritragga la forma, e l'abito d'una cosa, e mouimento le dia."

[32] In *L'Erofilomachia* (1578 ed.), p. A9: "non debbe esser la Comedia imitatione de huomini piu tristi, o piu ribaldi, come par, che noti la parola, φαυλοτέρων, che vuol dire huomini piu vili, & piu bassi, ma di persone in comparatione di quelle, che sonno introdotte nella Tragedia, bassi & abietti, essendo in essa Tragedia introdotti, Prencipi & Regi, & altre persone de grandissimi stati . . . & nella Comedia, introducendosi huomini di humile conditione, come sono Gentilhuomini, & Cittadini priuati."

The point is restated later (p. b), and Pino adds the judgment that the actions of tragedy are, in the last analysis, more wicked than those of comedy, whose heroes are not necessarily characterized by greater vices, greater crimes, or worse actions; they are merely of inferior station. The question thus arises with respect to the kind of "badness" to be attributed to comic characters, and again Pino gives Aristotle's answer:

... even if Aristotle in the *Poetics* says, almost openly, that the subject upon which the whole argument of comedy rests is vice (called by him κακία), such vice is not as a result totally that which is the contrary of virtue, but rather that which is opposed to beauty, that is, ugliness or deformity. ... vice cannot, by its nature, generate any praiseworthy or fruitful pleasure.[33]

The nature of this ugliness and a definition of comedy are developed more specifically in the following passage:

Nor by "ugly" are we always to understand what is dishonest and obscene, for by themselves such words as "obscene" and "dishonest" always have the meaning of evil; but we must take as ugly that which does not have its parts in proportion and in a proper relationship. ... Comedy is therefore an imitation of persons and of actions lower and more abject than those which are described in tragedy, and it must move to laughter and to pleasure just as tragedy moves to pity and to terror.[34]

Pino's Aristotelianism is thus mixed; it is fairly correct in its understanding of the ridiculous and the ugly, it is wrong in its affirmation that the differences between tragic and comic characters are exclusively social differences.

RICCOBONI (1579)

Antonio Riccoboni's work on the *Poetics*, constituting in its totality the last of the "great commentaries" in Latin to appear in the Cinquecento, resembles Piccolomini's in that it was published in two stages, translation first, then commentary. Riccoboni had professed the *Poetics* at Padua, and in 1579 he added to a volume which also contained his translation of the *Rhetoric* the following items related to the *Poetics*: a prefatory notice entitled *Quomodo ars poetica sit pars logicae*; a brief set of *Variae quaedam lectiones*; a translation into Latin, accompanied by marginal topical headings; and a treatise *De re comica*. The lengthy commentary was not to appear until 1585. But the preliminary notice of 1579 examines the argu-

[33] *Ibid.*, p. A11: "se bene Aristotile nella Poetica, quasi alla scoperta dice, che'l soggetto in cui s'appoggia tutto l'argomento della Comedia è'l vitio da lui detto κακία, tal vitio non è perciò totalmente quello, che è contrario alla virtù, ma quel che s'appone [sic] alla bellezza, cioè la brutezza, ò deformità. ... il vitio non puo di sua natura generare piacere alcuno lodeuole, & fruttuoso."

[34] *Ibid.*, pp. A9v, A10v: "Ne per brutto si dee sempre intendere il dishonesto & l'osceno, che per se stesse tali parole d'osceno, & di dishonesto, hanno sempre significato di male: ma per brutto l'ha da prendere, quel che non ha le sue parti proportionate, & corrispondenti. ... E adunque la Comedia, vna imitatione da persone & di cose piu vile & piu abiette, che non si descriuono nella Tragedia, & debbe muouere al riso e al piacere, come la Tragedia alla misericordia & a l'errore." The text is very bad throughout and full of typographical errors.

ments of those who had previously studied the relationship of poetry to logic: Bartolomeo Lombardi, who had maintained that poetry uses both the enthymeme and the example, just as rhetoric does; and Iacopo Zabarella, who, in his *Logic*, had held that poetry teaches by using examples of things or actions (rather than words) and that any art which does so belongs to logic. Riccoboni is astonished at the latter argument, since he believes—and he cites Aristotle as his authority—that all argumentation takes place in the words which express things rather than in the things themselves. He agrees with Zabarella on one point—poetry uses syllogism and paralogism—but he would revise the position by saying that its purpose is "to teach the use of reasoning powers in imitation."[35] A comparison with rhetoric helps him to delimit further the role of poetry: "Poetry indeed has certain things in common with rhetoric, certain others proper to itself. The common ones are sententiae, character, and diction; the proper one is plot."[36] One of the functions of sententiae is to present arguments; but according to the *Poetics*, this function is more properly a part of rhetoric, as are the other tasks of appealing to the passions and of augmenting and diminishing. The only way in which poetry will properly belong to logic is through its one distinctive element, plot. Now Aristotle indicates that recognition and reversal are beautiful parts of the plot, that recognition involves a kind of syllogism which is proper to the art of poetry; this art is consequently a part of logic. Riccoboni concludes:

For although it has many things which do not belong to logic, nevertheless it is sufficient that in some outstanding aspect it may be called logic; just as also is the case with rhetoric, which contains not only the demonstrative discourse through which it is assigned to logic but also character and passions and moreover language and the order of its parts; nevertheless it is said to be a part of logic because of one device of demonstration. Similarly poetry, in addition to sententia which it has in common with rhetoric, treats not only plot whose most important part, which is called recognition, needs the syllogism, but also character and diction and harmony and spectacle; nevertheless because of one form of reasoning which is employed in plot construction, and instruction in whose use is pertinent in the extreme to the plot itself, it seemed to the great philosopher Averroës and to others that it should be called a part of logic.[37]

[35] *Aristotelis ars poetica* (1579), p. 378: "docere vsum ratiocinandi in imitatione."

[36] *Ibid.*, p. 378: "Ac Poetica quidem habet quaedam sibi communia cum Rhetorica: quaedam propria. Communia sunt, sententia, mores, & dictio. propria est fabula."

[37] *Ibid.*, pp. 382–83: "Nam tametsi multa habeat, quae non pertinent ad Logicam: tamen sufficit, ut in aliqua re praecipua appellari Logica possit; quemadmodum etiam euenit Rhetoricae, quae non solam continet oratoriam demonstrationem, propter quam reducitur ad Logicam, sed simul mores, & affectus, & praeterea elocutionem, ac partium dispositionem: tamen dicitur pars Logicae propter unum artificium demonstrationis. Sic Poetica praeter sententiam, quam ipsa habet cum Rhetorica communem, non unam fabulam tractat, cuius praecipua pars, quae dicitur agnitio, indiget syllogismo; sed mores quoque, & dictionem, & harmoniam, & apparatum: tamen propter unam ratiocinationem, quae fit in fabula, cuiusque usum docere ad ipsam potissimum spectat, videtur ab Auerroe maximo philosopho, & ab aliis fuisse pars Logicae appellata."

The reference to Averroës indicates his continued influence, even late in the century, on the interpretation of the *Poetics*.

The "variae lectiones" are few in number and not of any great originality. Riccoboni merely justifies his choice, at various difficult points in the text, of one of the solutions proposed by his predecessors, and he does so largely to explain why he translated as he did. Sometimes his decisions are good, as when he discards the troublesome ὡς πέρσας at 1448a15; elsewhere they are bad, as when he adopts ἀμφοτέροις at 1447a20 in place of διὰ τῆς φωνῆς and translates it by "alij autem vtrisque" (p. 386). Their total effect upon the translation is small. Riccoboni's translation is itself characteristic of his times, for it constitutes a kind of vulgarization of the Latin text. He makes every effort to render his version accessible to the reader. Marginal notations summarize the content of the adjacent passages— the kind of notations that readers of earlier translations and commentaries had to write in for themselves—and provide a sort of running index. Moreover, they frequently raise the problems which were most discussed by the commentators; for example, opposite the sentence (at 1447a28) "Epopoeia vero solum sermonib. nudis, vel metris," Riccoboni writes "Quidam exponunt, uel, pro Idest," thus raising the moot question about prose and verse. Immediately afterward, the margin bears this query: "An Epopoeia possit fieri soluta oratione," making the same question even more specific (p. 386). At times conveniently numbered lists are added to the margins, and wherever feasible Riccoboni inserts references to works cited. The text is broken up into major sections, according to Riccoboni's own division, unnumbered but clearly titled. Paragraphs and sentences are also so broken up, sometimes with the addition of numbers, to produce an almost tabular effect. For example, the definition of tragedy appears as follows (p. 392):

1. Est igitur Tragẹdia imitatio.
2. actionis probae,
3. & perfectae,
4. magnitudinem habentis,
5. suaui sermone,
6. separatim singulis formis in partib. agentib.
7. & non per enarrationem,
8. sed per misericordiam, & metum inducens talium perturbationum purgationem.

Many of these mechanical devices were dropped when the text was reprinted in 1587, but some of them were expanded and exploited.

I think that we may state thus Riccoboni's principles for the translation: To achieve a Latin version simpler and more readable than those heretofore available; to adopt, by means of the translation itself, a firm stand on as many of the disputed questions of the text as possible; to render apparent the order, the parts, and the method of the original work. The first of these ends is obtained through a number of devices. Riccoboni simplifies Latin word order in such a way as to make it almost as straightforward as Italian word order; he eliminates all flourishes of style, all farfetched words, all useless attempts at variety and sonority; he adopts a uniform terminology which eliminates ambiguity and doubt. The results of this effort may be seen in a comparison of the following passage (1447*a*18) as it is handled by Maggi and by Riccoboni:

> *Maggi, p.* 39: Vt enim coloribus, atque figuris pleraque quidam aemulantes imitantur, hi quidem arte, consuetudine illi, nonnulli etiam uoce: ita quoque & in dictis artibus accidit. etenim omnes imitationem exercent, numero dico, sermone, harmonia; hisque uel separatim, uel promiscue.
>
> *Riccoboni, p.* 386: Vt enim, & coloribus, & figuris multa imitantur aliqui effigiem exprimentes, partim quidem per artem, partim vero per consuetudinem; alij autem vtrisque: sic in dictis artibus omnes quidem faciunt imitationem in numero, & oratione & harmonia; atq. his separatim, aut mixtis.

Latinity has suffered, but something more palatable to the Italian reader has been achieved. For consistency of terminology, we may take the case of the crucial words βελτίονας and χείρονας, which Aristotle uses for "better" and "worse" at 1448*a*4 and –*a*17. Maggi translates by "meliores" and "deteriores" at the first place, by "praestantiores" and "humiliores" at the second (thereby prejudicing the interpretation); whereas Riccoboni uses "meliores" and "peiores" throughout.

As for the second of the main objectives—to make the translation a kind of interpretation—we have seen that Riccoboni is at times obliged to resort to his marginalia for clarifications. Thus at 1448*a*4, having translated ἢ καθ' ἡμᾶς by "quàm secundum nos," he explains in the margin: "... secundum nos id est quàm homines praesentis aetatis, uel quàm homines communes, quales nos sumus" (p. 387). This, of course, leaves the choice to the reader; at other points the stand is much clearer. On page 405, two of the requisites for character are explained in the margin: "Similitudo refertur ad eos de quibus alij scripserunt," "Aequalitas ad eos, de quibus nos primum scribimus." In the text itself, the renderings may seem unremarkable; but in such a passage as that on the tragic hero, the words that I have italicized constitute decisions on much-debated issues:

> Est autem talis, qui neque virtute praestat, & iustitia. Neque propter vitium, & prauitatem *mutatur in aduersam fortunam,* sed *propter errorem aliquem.* Eorum, qui sunt *in magna existimatione,* & *fortunae prosperitate,* cuiusmodi Oedipus, & Thyestes, & qui *ex talibus familijs* illustres uiri sunt. Necesse enim est egregie se habentem fabulam simplicem esse magis, *quam duplicem,* vt quidam dicunt (p. 401).

The third objective, concerning order and method, is largely reached by means of the mechanical devices already mentioned, the main one of which is the breaking up of the text into short, numbered sentences.

For his *De re comica* (expanded and republished in 1585 as the *Ars comica*), Riccoboni had before him the example of Robortello's *De comoedia*, printed as an adjunct to the 1548 commentary on the *Poetics*; he could also consult, on a more limited subject, the *De ridiculis* which Maggi added to his own volume in 1550. But whereas Robortello spends most of his time in a paraphrase of the *Poetics*, making a few alterations to adapt its principles to comedy, and in a retailing of the traditional saws about the form, and whereas Maggi leaves these things aside in order to write a treatise on laughter, Riccoboni addresses himself to the task of constructing a new art of comedy. He bases it on Aristotle's statements about poetry in general as well as about tragedy and the epic, and it springs from his total conception of Aristotle's method in the *Poetics*. That is, he attempts to apply Aristotle's basic distinctions to the treatment of the comic genre (his statement of intentions is quoted above, Chapter II, p. 53) and to devote a single chapter to each of the major subjects: the origin of comedy, its definition, its qualitative parts, its quantitative parts, and the ridiculous. It should be pointed out here that the conception and the application of the method are less well developed in 1579 than they will be in 1585.

Riccoboni seems to take as his point of departure the "laus : vituperatio" distinction of Averroës, which permits him to classify hymns and encomia, then tragedy and the epic, under "laus," iambic songs and comedy under "vituperatio." Comedy belongs in a subcategory of forms which blame by means of the ridiculous. It is defined in fairly rudimentary terms: "Comedy is defined as an imitation, which is made by means of language, the dance, and harmony, through the mode of action, of a matter consisting of that vice which moves to laughter."[38] As Riccoboni elaborates his gloss on this definition, he reveals his position on one of the current debates, concerning the means of imitation. He states that prose is not acceptable in comedy. Distinguishing between usage, which authorizes prose, and reason, which does not, he argues that verse is necessary in all poetic genres, "not because verse constitutes the nature of poetry, but because it is its proper instrument or vestment."[39] He holds that any poem in prose is a defective poem; for comedy, moreover, prose is too weak an instrument and fails to command an audience assembled in the theater.

Riccoboni's discussion of the qualitative parts revolves largely about plot ("fabula" is defined as "the composition of the materials, which imitates actions performed outside of the stage," "Fabula est rerum compositio, quae actiones extra scenam habitas imitatur," p. 442). And for plot he establishes eight requisites:

[38] *Ibid.*, p. 438: "Definitur Comoedia, vt sit imitatio, quae fit sermone, saltatione, harmonia, per modum actiuum, in materia eius vitij, quod mouet risum."
[39] *Ibid.*, p. 439: "non quòd versus constituat naturam poesis, sed quia sit proprium instrumentum, uel uestimentum eius."

1. Debet esse tota;
2. Debet congruentem magnitudinem habere;
3. Debet esse una;
4. Debet esse verisimilis;
5. Non debet esse episodica;
6. Debet esse admirabilis;
7. Debet esse implexa;
8. Debet esse affecta, vt moueat laetitiam, & molestiam (pp. 442-45).

The list of requisites recalls the lists of criteria for plot currently being applied in the literary quarrels. For Riccoboni, the oneness and the wholeness are among the primary considerations, and they are conceived of in a way which shows his indebtedness to Castelvetro. A comic action may be thought of, he says, as a larger one which contains all the events of many days, or as a smaller one which contains only the events of the last day. The comic plot is restricted to this "totum parvum"—which nevertheless is complete and has a beginning, a middle, and an end (p. 443). It is essentially the audience (and here we recognize Castelvetro's arguments) which imposes these restrictions upon the plot:

It must have a suitable magnitude, in order to be neither too small nor too large but adapted to viewing in that time which the spectators can easily support. For one must take into account the ease of the public, and the people must leave the theater after a number of hours because of their human needs. And thus one must maintain that the time proper to the comic plot is of one or two hours, nor should it exceed twelve hours.

Riccoboni then provides the most succinct statement we have so far encountered of the "three unities"—one which makes unity of action depend upon the other two: "It must be one.... Moreover the time of twelve hours and the narrowness of place does not permit a multitude of actions in comedy."[40] He distinguishes three kinds of verisimilitude: universal verisimilitude (those things which might happen to many persons), particular verisimilitude (which must nevertheless be treated in a universal way), and a verisimilitude which consists in the giving of names befitting the qualities of character. The "admirabilis" or "marvelous," a quality usually associated with tragedy and the epic, has a peculiar function in Riccoboni's conception of comedy; on the one hand, through our marveling at some ridiculous deception, we are purged of that same kind of deception; on the other hand, our marveling at wickedness teaches us not to fall into similar forms of wickedness (p. 445). The dual poetic ends of purgation and moral instruction are thus both served by the marvelous.

[40] *Ibid.*, p. 443: "Debet congruentem magnitudinem habere ut nec perexigua, nec permagna sit, sed accommodata ad eius temporis prospectum, quod fert commodum spectatorum, cum ratio commodi popularis habeatur, & necesse habeat populus post aliquot horas de theatro propter humanas necessitates discedere. Itaque tempus fabulae comicae accommodatum necesse vnius, aut duarum horarum, nec duodecimam praeterire censendum est.... Debet esse una.... Tempus autem duodecim horarum, & angustia loci non permittit in Comędia multitudinem actionum."

Just as the requisites for plot are all drawn from the *Poetics*, so the four requirements for character are adapted to comedy. "Goodness" of character becomes "badness"—such qualities as harshness, obsequiousness, boastfulness. It is apparent that Riccoboni thinks of "goodness" as a general term for the virtues. The second requisite—appropriateness—includes all the usual components of decorum. And the third—likeness—may be understood in two ways: either as meaning a conformity to the literary tradition associated with a given character, or as implying (for present-day personages) a conformity to the conventions of comic types—Pantaleone, Gianni, Graziano. "Consistency" is a warning against any change in character throughout the course of the play (pp. 446–47). Riccoboni represents, regarding character, a kind of average position for the period, with all its doubts and hesitations. What he says about the remaining qualitative parts and about the quantitative parts repeats the *Poetics* without interpreting it.

On the subject of the ridiculous, Riccoboni is somewhat more original. He begins, of course, with Aristotle's statement, to which he adds a definition of laughter derived from a "very learned man": "... it is a sign of joy which the soul makes through the dilatation of the heart coming from the liberation of the spirits, which can no longer be contained as the image of happy things triumphs."[41] Such a definition, of course, departs from the materials of the *Poetics*, and Riccoboni admits that his sources on the ridiculous are Aristotle's *Rhetoric*, Cicero, Maggi, and Castiglione. He finds it useful to enumerate, in a way not unlike that of Aristotle treating the tragic plot, the kinds of wickedness that will arouse laughter in comedy; each springs from a kind of deception:

1. One that comes from ignorance of those things that people ordinarily know;
2. one that comes from false opinion;
3. one that comes from misunderstanding, or from a turning of events against their author;
4. one that comes from the trickery of another or from accident (p. 456).

In spite of such adventures as these into other topics and other sources, Riccoboni follows closely the text of his model, creating thereby the first "ars comica" of the century to be based so closely on Aristotle. For Riccoboni, however, it was merely a first attempt, and just as the translation of 1579 was to be supplemented by the full commentary on the *Poetics* a few years later, so the *De re comica* was at the same time to benefit from his broader understanding of his basic text; the *Ars comica* of 1585 becomes a much more learned document.

DELLA POETICA (CA. 1580)

The Biblioteca Nazionale in Florence possesses, in its manuscript Magliabechi VII, 437, an anonymous translation of and commentary on

[41] *Ibid.*, p. 453: "signum laetitiae quod facit animus per dilatationem cordis ex spirituum resolutione, qui vincente imagine rei laetae contineri non possunt."

the first part of the *Poetics*, entitled simply *Della poetica*. I have not yet been able to assign even an approximate date to the work, although its method of procedure and its central preoccupations would lead me to place it around 1580. It is essentially a paraphrase, giving either parts of the Greek text or sections of an Italian translation followed by more or less extensive explanatory remarks. The fragment covers the text from the beginning to 1450a7, then (since there is apparently one folio missing) from 1450a18 to 1450b4, where it ends abruptly. Such parts of the translation as we have are clumsy and confused, and it would not be unfair to say that its author usually does less well than his predecessors; there are no passages in which he makes a decidedly superior suggestion. On the other hand, his commentary is a very typical one for the period, wrestling with all the current problems; and in many cases his arguments and analyses are original—if not always completely convincing.

Linguistic matters—questions of meaning, of syntax, and of punctuation—occupy a fair proportion of the commentary. The author's speculations about meanings of words reflect the uncertainty which still prevailed, even toward the end of the century, over the sense of the text. Many of the meanings assigned affect directly the interpretation of the *Poetics*. Thus if μιμουμένους at 1448a23 is said to mean "istrioni" (fol. 11v) and if πράττοντες at 1449b31 means "mimi" (fol. 33v), one will necessarily think of the tragedy as acted rather than as written, and the nature of the object of imitation may be misunderstood. Similarly, if αὐτοσχεδιασμάτων at 1448b23 is taken as meaning "in rude verses" ("co' versi rozzi"; the author specifically rejects "allo improviso" as a translation, fol. 21), then the identification of poetry with verse is further stressed. The author's purely lexical difficulties are exemplified by the word λευκογραφήσας at 1450b2, translated by "se dipingesse in bianco" and glossed with "come dipingere in un muro bianco" (fols. 20–20v). Elsewhere in the work interpretations depend upon syntactical matters; so at 1447a29, ἢ is taken to be a "corrective" copulative with the force of "or rather." The author insists at length upon this meaning, citing a passage from the *Nicomachean Ethics* in corroboration; for upon it depends in large part his thesis that verse is indispensable for poetry. At least one excellent suggestion is made for punctuation, that of separating δρώντων at 1449b25 from the rest of the sentence, making possible an independent phrase in the translation, "di coloro che negotiono in scena"; but the author does not go far enough in reorganizing the sentence, and the last part of the definition still reads "et facendo la purgatione di tali passioni non per narratione, ma per misericordia et paura" (fol. 32). The imperfect readings in the Greek text still account for many hesitations, and long passages of the paraphrase are devoted to their explanation.

In a brief prologue, the author of the paraphrase tackles two problems, the old distinction among "poema," "poesia," and "arte poetica," and the essential content and organization of the *Poetics*. The "arte poetica," as a treatise on the art, will have to offer a definition of poetry, one which will define the species by giving the genus and the differentiae; it will also have to analyze completely the differences. The author believes that the task of definition is accomplished in the first part of the *Poetics*, which is to be taken rather as a "propositione" than as a "proemio," since it does not attempt to gain the reader's attention. Because the work fails to define "imitation," an integral part of the later definitions, the author does so himself (relying, he says, upon Plato): "Imitation then is an assimilating of one thing to another and of a false one to a true."[42] In the paraphrase itself, the author (who here resembles Sassetti) is very sensitive to the kind of methodological questions raised in the prologue. He divides the work into a proposition (extending to 1447a28) and a narration and finds that the first part indicates that Aristotle will treat of poetry—rather than of the "art"—and that the whole of the *Poetics* will offer precepts for the poet. It will pass from the universal to the particular, which is the proper order of science as Aristotle himself distinguishes it in the *Posterior Analytics* and the *Physics* (fol. 2v). The universals are ones which are most known to nature, least known to men; but men already know the particulars from which they derive: "Thus if Aristotle begins from universals, he assumes that the reader of the *Poetics* already knows comedies, tragedies, the epic, and dithyrambs and the other species of imitations; whence one concludes that it is necessary to have heard and read the poets, otherwise one cannot approach this study."[43]

The author is especially interested in the constitution of definitions. He points out carefully how Aristotle first establishes the genus of poetry, then its differentiae, and—much later—how the definition of tragedy is derived from preceding universals about genus and differentiae (fols. 4, 30v). He warns the reader against taking Aristotle's statements on comedy at 1449a31 as a definition: "... this can be seen because many things are lacking which should enter into its definition; he does not do this when he defines tragedy, but rather does not omit any single thing."[44] At 1449b31 he calls the attention of the reader to the passage from definition to discussion of the component parts and the reason why Aristotle now proceeds to the latter: "... for we then know well a whole when we know all its parts, which parts make it what it is."[45] Contrariwise, he warns us not to

[42] MS Magl. VII, 437, fol. 1: "L'imitazione dunque è un assimigliare una cosa ad un'altra et una falsa ad una vera."

[43] *Ibid.*, fol. 3: "cosi se Arist: incomincia dagl' uniuersali, presuppone, che allo auditore della Poetica gia siano [note] le comedie, le tragedie, l'epopeia, e dithirambicj, et l'altre specie d'imitatione. onde se ne caua che sia bisogno hauere udito e letto de Poetj, altrimenti non si puo accostare à questa lettione."

[44] *Ibid.*, fols. 26–26v: "questo si puo uedere, perche ci mancono molte cose, le quali douerrebbono entrare nella sua diffinitione, il che quando diffinisce la tragedia non fa cosi, anzi non lascia cosa ueruna indietro." Cf. fol. 31.

[45] *Ibid.*, fol. 33v: "perche all'hora si sa bene un tutto, quando si conoscono tutte le sue parti, le quali parti sono quelle che la fanno quale."

take as a treatment of parts something which is not (fol. 36). Finally with respect to method, he distinguishes between Aristotle's a priori and a posteriori arguments (fol. 19), again with a view to keeping his reader constantly aware of how the text is organized and presented.

As was the case with Sassetti, however, these scruples about method do not prevent the author from reading the *Poetics* pretty much as his predecessors had done. The definition of imitation was, as we have seen, one of the "universals" most needed for the understanding of Aristotle's text; yet he does not hesitate to take it over directly from Plato, without inquiry into its appropriateness to the particular circumstances of the *Poetics*. Moreover, he declares that μῦθος or "favola" is necessary for imitation, and this permits him to identify poetry with mythology (following Plato) and to find in this identification the reason for Aristotle's insistence upon "fiction." He does not, however, fall into the usual confusion over the various possible meanings of the word "imitation," excluding from Aristotle's use the designation of a dramatic manner (fol. 1, margin). He sees imitation as one of the two natural causes of poetry; but the other one, he says, is rhythm, not the pleasure found in imitation. Taking issue with the position (found also in Sassetti's manuscript *Sposizione*) that one of these constitutes the final cause of poetry, the other the efficient, he argues that both of them must be called efficient causes (fol. 14). The case is clear for him: "these two natural causes are made up of imitation and rhythm, because imitation and rhythm are natural in us and poetry is composed of imitation and of rhythm; for rhythm is in verse, which is a part of poetry along with imitation."[46]

The last of the preceding assertions is in line with the author's constant affirmation that poetry and verse are inseparable; every relevant passage in the *Poetics* is interpreted in this sense, as they had so frequently been by his contemporaries. From the very beginning, when the means of imitation are identified, language is said to imply verse: "quando dice oratione intende sempre metrica" (fol. 3v); the phrase later becomes "parlar' metrico" (fol. 5v). If a general statement is needed, we may find one in connection with 1447b14: "But we must not think therefore that the poet can be a poet without verse, because it is one of his differences through which he becomes different from those who imitate without verse."[47] Metrical language thus becomes the means by which poetry is distinguished from kindred imitations.

If the author treats the means in a somewhat conventional way, he is more original in his treatment of the objects of imitation. These are

[46] *Ibid.*, fol. 14v: "queste due cagioni naturali siano fatte dall'imitatione et dal rhithmo, perche l'imitatione e'l rhithmo sono in noi naturali, et la poesia è composta d'imitatione et di rhithmo, perche il rh[i]thmo è nel uerso, che è parte della poesia insieme con l'imitatione."

[47] *Ibid.*, fol. 7v: "Ma non bisogna però pensare che il poeta possa essere poeta senza 'l uerso, perche è una sua differenza per la quale si fa differente da quelli che imitano senza 'l uerso."

identified as "passions, characters, and actions" (fol. 3v). In order that we may know what these are, the author gives us a set of examples: "The passions are fear, hope, love, and the like; the characters, strong, generous, audacious, just, unjust, prodigal, temperate, intemperate; the actions, to perform an act of fortitude, an act of timidity, and the like."[48] Aristotle's three-way division of the objects is interpreted as follows: men "better" than ourselves are "heroes and sons of the gods and semi-gods"; men "worse" than ourselves are "the very avaricious or the very stupid or the very unfortunate" men of comedy (fol. 9); but we are not told who are "like" us.

While purgation is specifically identified as the end of tragedy, no such statement is made about the ridiculous as the end of comedy. On both of them, the author makes fairly extensive remarks. Having said that purgation operates by "putting pity and fear into the souls of the listeners," he is obliged to explain his meaning:

... pity can be good and bad, and so also fear; for we are afraid of certain things which it is a virtue to fear. Tragedy, therefore, puts into our breasts the good pity, by which we drive out pitilessness, cruelty, and other similar passions which are contrary to the good pity. In the same way, by driving out from our breasts certain passions which make us insolent, we get used to being afraid; whence, if terrible and horrible things happen to us, we have formed the habit of being afraid, and so they do not give us so much fear. In the second book of the *Rhetoric*, Aristotle teaches us how to remove bad passions from our breast by putting in good ones.[49]

The effects of purgation are thus indirect, and they make permanent changes in the moral well-being of the spectator. The ridiculous is not considered in terms of its effects—except for the general one of laughter—but the author concerns himself rather with distinctions among the terms used by Aristotle at 1449a33 ff. and with separating the ridiculousness of the spirit from that of the body. The latter opposition is also derived from Plato, in the *Laws* (fol. 27v).

Perhaps the most elaborate set of distinctions in this anonymous paraphrase of the *Poetics* relates to the qualitative parts of character and thought. The initial distinctions will be clearest if we assume, on the part of the author, a separation between the world of reality and the world of

---

[48] *Ibid.*, fol. 5v: "Le passioni sono il timore, la speranza, l'amore et similj: i costumi, forte, liberale, audace, giusto, ingiusto, prodigo, temperato, intemperato: l'ationj operare un'atto di fortezza, uno atto di timidità & simili."

[49] *Ibid.*, fols. 32v-33: "la misericordia puo esser' buona et cattiua, cosi la paura, perche si ha paura d'alcune cose, le qual' temendo è uirtù, la tragedia adunque ci mette nel petto la misericordia buona, con laquale noi scacciamo l'impietà la crudeltà, et simili altre passioni, lequali sono contrarie alla misericordia buona, cosi scacciando dal petto alcune passioni che ci fanno essere insolenti, ci aue[z]ziamo hauer paura onde se ci sopraggiungono cose terribili, et spauenteuoli, habbiamo fatto l'uso nell'hauer' paura, et cosi non ci danno tanto spauento. Nel secondo della Rethorica Aristotile ci insegna cauar' le cattiue passioni del petto, mettendoci le buone."

art, which becomes later a separation between things and words. The true actions of reality are represented by the feigned actions of a tragedy. Actions are performed by agents, and insofar as agents have habits of the soul which determine their actions, they have character; in the work of art, character will be manifested through language, and this is the "character" or "orazione morata" of tragedy. Agents also have habits of the soul which account for their reasoning and their speech, and when these are expressed through language in the work, they become the "thought" or "dianea" of tragedy (marginalia to fols. 34v–35). Another way of making the distinction is to refer character and thought to the appetitive and the intellective principles of the soul, which combine in the production of any action. These principles give, respectively, character and thought (now called "intelligenza") and the author summarizes thus their relationship to action: "The plot is the composite of the actions, intelligence is the act of the intellect, as in speaking and taking counsel, character is in appetite. If there are actions in tragedy, it is necessary that these two principles be there."[50] An agent will be "prudent, imprudent, sagacious, malicious, stupid or wise or ignorant" as these qualities are present in his "intelligence" and manifest in his actions. Throughout the discussion, the author makes underlying assumptions of a philosophical kind which determine his attitudes toward art and nature and toward the specific problems of the *Poetics*.

Plato rather than Aristotle is the main topic of study in Girolamo Frachetta's *Dialogo del furore poetico* of 1581; but since Aristotle is used as a rebuttal to Plato's various charges against the poets, some general ideas about the *Poetics* emerge. Moreover, Frachetta examines and rejects certain interpretations of Castelvetro and Maggi and otherwise shows himself in touch with the Aristotelian tradition. Unlike most of those who pitted Aristotle against Plato, Frachetta's principal concern is not with the uses of poetry for moral education, but rather with its relationship to the truth. Plato had condemned poetry for not representing the truth; Aristotle says that it has no business with the truth. For the poet is supposed to use as his material things as they "should be," not as they "are," and thus "we can in no wise, if we want to rely on Aristotle, designate as a good poet one who undertakes to describe in verse true things exactly as they are."[51] Indeed, we should not call him a poet at all, since truth is different from probability and possibility. This is apparently only a tentative position in the dialogue, for later the interlocutors argue that Aristotle

[50] *Ibid.*, fol. 35: "La fauola è il componimento dell' ationi, l'intelligenza è l'atto dello intelletto, come discorrere consigliarsi. Il costume è nello appetito. Se nella tragedia sono le ationi, è necessario che ci siano questi duoi principij."

[51] *Dialogo* (1581), p. 29: "noi non potiamo in modo niuno, se ci uogliamo appoggiare ad Aristotele, appellar buon poeta colui, che si prende a descriuere in uersi le cose uere per l'appunto come elle sono."

does permit the use of known events and real people in poetry. They go so far as to admit that the completely or even the partially invented plot, in epic or in tragedy, would be less desirable than that which was based on the truth: "... since the material of tragedy is things which can come about, things which have already happened will be by far a more suitable material than those thought up or imagined by the poet"; Aristotle's statements on the epic lead us to conclude that "without doubt it is much better if they are true than if they are not."[52] Thus, the difference between poetry and history resides less in the nature of the matter than in the way of handling it:

... the historian must write of things which happened in that exact manner in which they happened, without altering them in any detail no matter how small or without inserting the slightest bit of his own invention; whereas the tragic or the epic poet, taking an event which occurred, must not recount it in the way in which it happened, but he must strive by means of eliminations and much more of additions and otherwise to polish it up and to make it as noteworthy as he can.[53]

The art of poetry in this way becomes a kind of superior art of rhetoric, whose main function is to adorn and augment.

Frachetta touches, of necessity, upon the ends of poetry as seen by Plato and Aristotle, and here he finds the two authorities in distinct opposition. Aristotle, he says, proposes only one end for poetry and that is pleasure, "to give delight and recreation to the minds of everybody, and especially of the common people; and if the poet sometimes benefits us, he does so by supererogation and as if by accident."[54] He points out (with acute historical insight) that those who have found the double end of pleasure and utility in Aristotle have merely been concerned with making him agree with Horace. If pleasure is the only end for Aristotle, why then does he include purgation in the definition of tragedy? Frachetta's answer is the standard one: this is done in order to contradict Plato, and the very passions which Plato had attacked seem to be recommended by Aristotle:

... as if he wished to say that horrible and pitiful things not only do not make us fearful and pitying, as Plato thinks, but rather bring about the exact opposite. Nevertheless it must be understood that they do this accidentally, since through the events of this kind which are placed before us we become accustomed, and

[52] *Ibid.*, p. 86: "essendo materia della tragedia le cose aueneuoli, di gran uantaggio piu conueneuol materia saranno le cose già state, che le pensate o immaginate dal poeta"; and "senza fallo molto meglio è se son uere, che se non sono."

[53] *Ibid.*, p. 88: "l'histori[c]o dee scriuere le cose accadute in quella istessa guisa per l'appunto, che elle accaddettero, senza uariare in alcuna cosa, da quanto che ella sia; o senza trametterci entro pur un puntino di suo trouato. la oue il poeta tragico, o l'epopeico pigliando un fatto auenuto, non nel modo, che' succedette, dee raccontarlo; ma dee sforzarsi con isminuimenti, & assai piu con aggiunte, & con altro, di ripulirlo, & di renderlo ragguardeuole il piu, ch'ei può."

[54] *Ibid.*, p. 90: "dilettare, & ricrear gli animi di ciascuno, & spetialmente del uulgo. Et che se'l poeta alcuna uolta ci gioua, ciò faccia per sopra derrata, & quasi per accidente."

little by little we free ourselves of such passions. And Aristotle's mind was so intent upon this matter, and he was so preoccupied with it, that he did not take care to include pleasure in that definition, even though he held it to be the principal and almost the only end.[55]

In the light of this interpretation, Frachetta brands as ridiculous Maggi's notion that Aristotle wishes to include the purgation of anger, avarice, debauchery, and so forth. When he comes, finally to consider whether Aristotle would or would not admit the presence of the divine furor in the poet, Frachetta expounds Aristotle's metaphysics to show that he would necessarily think of the poet's operations as natural, linked to the body and to the humors, and susceptible of a "divine" influence only in so far as the heavenly bodies which cause alterations in the humors may be said to be divine.

CARRIERO AND BULGARINI (1582)

The *Breve et ingenioso discorso contra l'opera di Dante* of Alessandro Carriero (1582) is divided into two distinct sections, the first entirely theoretical in nature, the second devoted to a discussion of the *Divina Commedia*. In the first, the *Poetics* supplies not only the essential theoretical basis but also the general plan of organization. However, Plato is frequently consulted on points of detail and the doctrine shows many similarities to the current Horatian mode. Carriero is a lover of distinctions, and he tries everywhere to refine upon the divisions suggested by his authorities. In its general outlines, his treatise examines successively these matters: the ends of poetry; the narrative and dramatic manners, divided respectively into three and four kinds; the qualitative parts; the comparison of poetry with history; the use of verse; comedy and tragedy; the mixed manner, divided into eight kinds; and the comparison of tragedy and epic. The comparison with history serves to place and delimit the art.

Carriero starts from Aristotle's differentiation between truth on the one hand and verisimilitude and necessity on the other; this is accompanied by a difference in order of presentation of the events. The second major difference lies in the treatment by the historian of many actions, by the poet of one only. This does not prevent the poet from being universal; for if he recounts the actions of one man, he does so in such a way as to emphasize the general qualities of that man—for example, Ulysses: "nor indeed should he be considered as he was; but leaving aside the circumstances and the minute particularities of the individual, one should pass

---

[55] *Ibid.*, p. 92: "Quasi dir uolendo, che le cose horribili, & compassioneuoli, non che ci faccino tementi, & misericordiosi, come uuole Platone; ma adoprano innanzi tutto il contrario. Il che non dimeno si dee intendere, che faccin per accidente, in quanto che per i casi di questa fatta, che ci son porti dauanti, noi ci auuezziamo, & a poco a poco ci liberiamo da cotai passioni. Et a questo hebbe tanto Aristotile l'animo inteso, & ne fu in guisa sollecito, ch'ei non si curò di mettere in detta definitione il diletto. tutto che egli lo hauesse per principale, & quasi per solo fine."

on to the universal, in order to make this man prudent and shrewd as he is wont to be perfectly described by the philosophers."[56] The third difference (supplied by Lucian) lies in the writer's attitude toward his subjects; the historian must not indulge in excessive praise, since this would be a departure from the truth, whereas the poet may make any changes he wishes in words or in deeds. Finally, the historian has many actions and hence he does not need to resort to the use of episodes; but the poet, restricted to a single action, must invent and imagine many episodes in order to fill out and adorn his poem. It is here that his admirable genius is displayed (pp. 12–18).

The distinction between truth and verisimilitude accounts, in a way, for the primary end of poetry; for the poet depicts "things as they should be" in order to exert a moral influence on his audience: ". . . whence we understand clearly that this is the function of the poets, i.e., to treat various and divers forms of civil life in their poems; this brings not a little profit to those who read and consider them with care. Indeed, poems are not only profitable to private persons but also to public ones, and to cities themselves."[57] Tragedy may prevent civil wars through the example of the miserable end of wicked persons, comedy maintains the calm and the happiness of the citizenry. In all this, pleasure is the instrument: "Thus the poets, having utility as their aim, in order to lead men to obtain it more easily, first endeavor to give pleasure to the readers and auditors of their poems by means of every grace of poetic ornament."[58] The audience is not otherwise specified than by its designation as the "vulgo" (p. 52).

Kinds of poems are determined jointly, for Carriero, by their audiences and their subject matter and their ends. He divides narrative poetry into three kinds, called historical, moral, and dogmatic. The historical sings the famous deeds of illustrious ancients; the moral treats subjects which have reference to the instruction of the citizenry; and the dogmatic teaches both the divine and the natural mysteries. Of the four kinds of "active" or dramatic poetry, the first, the mime, imitates the thoughts, the actions, and the gestures of any person whatsoever; because of its obscenity, it is not to be tolerated in a republic. Satire scolds wicked people and their vices—essentially unpleasant things—in order to arouse laughter and to generate hatred for these same vices. But comedy imitates pleasant things;

[56] *Breve et ingenioso discorso* (1582), p. 16: "nè già quale egli sià stato considerar si deue, ma tralasciate le circostanze, & minute particolarità dell'indiuiduo passar si deue all'uniuersale, per formar quest'huomo prudente, & accorto, quale egli suole esser descritto perfettamente da i Filosofi."

[57] *Ibid.*, pp. 1v–2: "da che chiaramente si comprende questo esser l'ufficio de Poeti, cioè di trattar uarie, & diuerse guise della uita ciuile ne i lor poemi: il che apporta non mediocre giouamento à chi con diligenza li legge, & li considera: Anzi le Poesie non solamente giouano alle persone priuate, ma anco alle publiche, & alle Cittadi stesse."

[58] *Ibid.*, p. 2v: "Cosi i Poeti hauendo per suo scopo l[']utile, per indur' à conseguirlo più facilmente gli huomini, prima s'ingegnano con ogni uaghezza d'ornamenti Poetici di porger diletto à Lettori, & Auditori de i lor Poemi."

its purpose is to make people laugh; and it may be defined as "an imitation of the worst men, which by discovering their uglinesses and their obscenities induces laughter in the spectators."[59] Its subjects are common people of ordinary condition, city dwellers, peasants, soldiers; they are never illustrious or heroic. The latter characteristics are reserved for tragedy, defined by Aristotle as "the imitation of a great and illustrious action, made completely, and sweetly written with its parts separate and distinct, setting forth and calming the troublesome accidents which happen in it, not through narration but by means of pity and of despair."[60] (The translation of the definition illustrates how completely it still baffled those who were not expert Aristotelian scholars.) When, much later, he comes to the subdivisions of the mixed manner he finds that it contains eight kinds: epic, melopoeia, elegy, dithyramb, iamb, epigram, hymn, and epithalamium. Of these, only the epic is treated at length, and that for two reasons, because Carriero could find much material on it in Aristotle and because it was pertinent to his discussion of Dante. Its essential characteristic, as compared with tragedy, is its length and complexity; through the variety of its episodes and the pleasantness of its digressions, it prevents the boredom and the lassitude of the reader (p. 50).

For the handling of the qualitative and the quantitative parts, Carriero has little to suggest besides what he had found in the *Poetics*. He does insist that verse is necessary in all forms of poetry—a commonplace in his day—if perfection is to be achieved; poems which imitate without verse are of an inferior order (pp. 18–19). The general rhetorical turn of his theory becomes apparent in the handling of the parts of poetry. Plot is more important than character because to it belong such elements as recognition and reversal, "which are wont in the highest degree to move within our souls various and divers passions, and to fill them with wonder, and at times to affect them violently and to carry them away in any direction whatsoever."[61] Sententiae are of two kinds; some of them relate directly to the central subject, and these follow political precepts; others are outside the subject, and these are handled rhetorically. In comedy, sententiae concern matters of "economy," the government of one's possessions and one's family. If decorum is needed in character (in all forms of poetry) and if all parts of the plot require verisimilitude, it is because the achievement of the ends of poetry, "the teaching of good manners and of refined character,"[62] depends upon the belief of the audience. The poet must, therefore,

[59] *Ibid.*, p. 9: "una imitatione de gli huomini peggiori, che co'l iscoprir le loro brutture, et oscenità s'induca il riso ne gli Spettatori."
[60] *Ibid.*, pp. 27–28: "è imitatione d'un' attione grande, & illustre, compitamente fatta, e dolcemente descritta con le sue parti separate, e distinte, dichiarando, & acquetando i trauagliosi accidenti, che ui concorrono non per uia di narratione, ma per mezzo di misericordia, e di sgomento."
[61] *Ibid.*, p. 10: "i quali massimamente sogliono muouer ne gli animi uarii, e diuersi affetti, e di merauiglia ingombrarli, e tall'hora uiolentarli, & rapirli in qual si uoglia parte."
[62] *Ibid.*, pp. 51–52: "il documento di buone creanze, e di costumi gentili."

at all times follow the opinions of the people. In this way, Carriero's theory is just as Horatian in its theory of the achievement of the ends of poetry as it is in the statement of those ends.

The copy of Carriero's *Breve et ingenioso discorso* which belonged to Bellisario Bulgarini is now in the library of Harvard University; it contains Bulgarini's marginal notations, some of them expressing ideas that he was later to develop in his attack on Carriero. His marginalia seem to have two purposes: to condemn some of Carriero's theoretical conclusions and to state some of Bulgarini's own positions. He blames Carriero for not considering Plato's banishment of the poets and for trying to reconcile Plato with Aristotle (p. 2). Referring to Carriero's three subdivisions of narrative poetry, he believes that they tend to make a poet of any versifier, "against Aristotle's opinion and against reason" ("contra l'opinion d'Aristo: e contra la ragione," p. 3). Carriero's statements about the effects of recognition and reversal, which "carry the soul away," would be more appropriate to the orator than to the poet (p. 10) and his distinction between the poet and the historian with respect to the expression of praise is a false one. For if the poet were to reveal his own feelings about a character he would on the one hand destroy the verisimilitude of his poem, on the other he would speak in his own person and would thus cease to imitate (p. 16). On more specific matters, Carriero completely mistranslates and misunderstands Aristotle's definition of tragedy (p. 28), and his own definition of comedy is false because it misconstrues the meaning of "worse" (p. 9).

A few of Bulgarini's own suggestions refer to general matters of poetic theory, such as his insistence that certain poetic genres, like the lyric, the elegy, the epigram, do not need to have a plot (p. 10). But for the most part he is interested in correcting Carriero on the three major forms, tragedy, comedy, and the epic. He agrees that the poet should not invent new plots for tragedy out of whole cloth, truth being a necessary ingredient; but it is possible to think of "new" plots as those which are true, but which the tragic poets have not previously treated. These are permitted to the poet. When old plots are used, the complication and denouement must be altered according to Aristotle's recommendation (p. 34). Bulgarini admits the possibility of tragedies with happy endings and says that some do exist (p. 39). He has doubts about Aristotle's requirement of the unified plot:

> Nor must the poet be prevented from including in his poem several and divers actions, provided that they are well interconnected and interdependent; let Ovid's *Metamorphoses* be an example of this, which although they are of many and divers actions are still praised. But Aristotle approves principally the poem in which the single plot is found, because the genius of the poet who has undertaken to imitate such a plot is perhaps demonstrated more fully as he varies it and conducts it pleasurably to a proper size.[63]

[63] Harvard copy of Carriero, *Breve et ingenioso discorso* (1582), p. 15: "Nè al Poeta si

Multiplicity of plot is especially desirable in comedy, where the double plot is to be preferred to the single; example, Terence's *Andria*. Carriero errs when he uses Plautus' *Amphytrion* as an example of a double comedy; Bulgarini cites the opinion of those who regard this play as a monster because it combines tragic and comic characters and actions, and of those who think it is a tragedy (p. 21). His main concern with comedy centers about its end and its object. He would distinguish comedy, which moves to laughter, from satire, which moves to indignation (p. 4). The objects of comedy are not, as Carriero wishes, obscene and wicked persons, but rather good men of middling condition; Aristotle's "worse" should be understood as meaning the condition of fortune, not the quality of the mind—or at least, he says, this is the opinion of the best interpreters of the *Poetics* (p. 9). He thinks that the happy ending of comedy will be much more pleasurable if it is preceded by grave disturbances and not merely by ridiculous events (p. 22). Concerning the epic, Bulgarini speaks only of its greater length, which results from the fact that it may be recited in a number of sittings and does not depend upon the comfort of an assembled audience, and of the fact that it is not necessarily better adapted to the production of the marvelous than is tragedy (pp. 50–51).

There is little pertinent to the present discussion in Giordano Bruno's *De gl'heroici furori* (1585), since it is essentially a set of dialogues devoted to the amatory poets and to an analysis of the various passions of love. But in the first Dialogue his interlocutors digress to make an attack upon the "regolisti di Poesia" who examine and reject the great poets according to the rules of Aristotle. Bruno holds that those rules were meant only to give a representation of Homer's poetry or of epic poetry like Homer's, "and not to teach others who could well be different in talent, art, and inspiration, equal, similar, and greater, of diverse genius."[64] Poetry does not spring from the rules, he says, but rather the rules from poetry; Homer does not follow them, he is their source. Moreover, such rules are good only for those who are more capable of "imitating" than of inventing, and they were set down by one who was not a poet at all. (It is interesting to see this meaning given to the verb "imitate.") They are useful only for those who have no individual genius. It is not by setting up criteria of this kind that we recognize the true poet, but rather through his singing in verse, by means of which he comes to delight or profit or to do both at

---

dee uetare il comprender nel suo poema più, e diuerse azzioni, purche se sieno infra di loro ben colligate, e dependenti; siancene essempio le Trasformazioni d'Ouidio: che pur essendo di molte, e diuerse azzioni uengon lodate. Ma Aristotile approua maggiormente il Poema, nel qual si troua la fauola una, perche, nel uariarlo, e condurlo con delettazione a conueneuol grandezza, si dimostra perauentura più l'ingegno del Poeta, che una tal fauola s'è presa ad imitare."

[64] *De gl'heroici furori* (1585), p. A.2.v: "et non per instituir altri che potrebbero essere con altre vene, arti, et furori; equali, simili, et maggiori, de diuersi geni."

once (p. A.3). There follows an attack upon the "poor pedants" of the time who exclude certain writers from the ranks of the poets because they have failed to observe one of the prescribed rules. Bruno's stand is of course anti-Aristotelian, and it has traces both of Platonic and of Horatian influences.

PATRIZI AND TASSO (1585)

Another anti-Aristotelian document of the same year (1585) is Francesco Patrizi's *Parere in difesa dell'Ariosto*; but this time the attack upon Aristotle is the direct result of the publication of the first work in a new literary polemic, Camillo Pellegrino's *Carrafa*. We can thus see the immediate impact upon Aristotelian theory of one of the great literary quarrels. If it is a negative impact, it is because Pellegrino had used Aristotle's rules to attack Ariosto's *Orlando Furioso*; now, rather than interpreting the rules in another way in order to defend and justify Ariosto, Patrizi says that the rules themselves are without value. His conclusion involves a general reappraisal of the *Poetics*—and, incidentally, of Horace. The point of view is unequivocally stated; Pellegrino was wrong

... in taking the poetical teachings of Aristotle as comparable, in this matter, to the clear, proper, and firm principles of the sciences; for those of Aristotle are neither proper, nor true, nor sufficient to constitute a scientific art of poetry, nor to form any poem whatsoever, nor to judge it; nor are they made according to the practice of either the Greek or the Latin poets.[65]

Having made this comprehensive statement, Patrizi proceeds to attack Aristotle on three grounds: his failure to make proper distinctions, his failure to produce proper definitions, and the lack of conformity between his precepts and the practice of the best poets. Other arguments appear with lesser emphasis. The best example of Aristotle's insufficiencies in the field of distinctions is his failure to treat adequately the term "imitation," because the meanings which he and Plato assign to the term amount to four or more, and his first task should have been to discover the meaning proper to poetry. Since he did not do so, how can he pretend to have developed a useful and scientific approach to the art (pp. L8v–M)? Another example is the confusion among the terms used to designate epic poetry; Aristotle does nothing about it, and this is a sign both that his knowledge of Greek was imperfect and that he did not actually know the whole of Greek epic literature (pp. L6–L7). The inadequacy of definitions is a corollary of the lack of distinctions. Since the prior definitions of imitation, of poetry, and of the heroic poem have not been supplied, we can make no sense of such a definition as this: "The epic poet was an imitator of the

[65] *Parere* (Ferrara, 1585), p. L5v: "in prendere gli insegnamenti poetici d'Aristotele pari in questo affare, a i principi chiari, e propri, e fermi delle scienze; non essendo questi di Aristotele, ne propri, ne ueri, ne bastanti à constituire arte scienziale di poetica, ne à formar poema alcuno, nè à giudicarlo. nè sono fatti secondo l'uso de' poeti nè Greci, nè Latini."

actions of illustrious persons" (p. M); for we know neither what a poet is nor what an imitation is.

Patrizi sees Aristotle as having formed for himself an Idea of epic poetry; unfortunately, it is one which is in no way related to the epics that we know. He says that all poems are imitations; but this is obviously not true. For the works of Orpheus, of Homer, and of Hesiod contained no imitations, and indeed none were to be found before the advent of tragedy, comedy, and the other dramatic genres. (It is clear that Patrizi is using "imitation" in one of the Platonic senses, that of dramatic representation.) Moreover, Aristotle asserts that plot, not verse, makes the poet; whereas it is clear from the practice of the poets themselves that there are many poems which have no plots and many plots which are not poems (p. M). In the case of the epic, if we were to apply the definition just given along with the restriction to a single action, we should get very strange results indeed:

> ... if a poet were to take for imitation not actions, as it says, but one single action ... of Caligula the Emperor, a most illustrious person, who, having led his army in formation to the shore of the ocean, had the signal for battle given by the trumpets and shouted that they should gather all the shells and shellfish that were on the shore; or when Domitian caused the flies that were going through the air to be captured and shut up in a paper prison; I do not know, I say, whether these poets and poems should be called "heroic."[66]

This is, of course, a *reductio ad absurdum*, as well as a misunderstanding of what is meant by a single action. Patrizi challenges the necessity for unity of plot and even the requirement that poems must in all cases have plots; the practice of Lucretius, of Vergil in the *Georgics*, of Lucan—all epic poets—is cited in support of his thesis. More damagingly still, Homer's great epics have no central unified action, but are composed rather of a multitude of episodes. Similarly, Patrizi calls into question everything that Aristotle has to say about the requisites for character. In the first place, these are not only common to all poetic genres, but they are even the same requirements as those set up for the historian and the panegyrist. In the second place, they are false. Goodness? But Homer, the perfect example, presents many wicked people, and of all his gods and heroes only one, Nestor, is absolutely good. He also violates in many places the demand for appropriateness. Likeness? The precept, which is both Aristotelian and Horatian, is very shaky; for it requires the likeness of persons to their counterparts in history or reputation, and how are we to establish the character of the counterparts when history is so uncertain and public

---

[66] *Ibid.*, pp. M–M*v*: "s'un poeta togliesse a poetare, non azioni, come ella dice, ma azione vna sola ... di Caligola Imperadore, illustrissima persona, il quale condotto l'essercito suo in sul lito dell'Oceano in ordinanza, fece dar nelle trombe il segno di battaglia, e gridare che si raccogliessero tutte le conchiglie, e calcinegli ch'erano in sù'l lito. ò quando Domiziano facea a prendere le mosche che per l'aria andauano, e a chiuderle in vna prigion di carta; non sò, dico, se questi poeti, e poemi, sariano Eroici da chiamarsi."

opinion so variable? Finally, the demand for constancy (Horace's "sibi constet") is belied by our common human nature and is everywhere violated by Homer, from whom Aristotle derived his theory (pp. M7–M8v).

Aristotle's Idea of the epic poem is thus without basis in any such poems existing before him. It will not stand the examination of the reason, and, hence, there is no reason why it should be set up as a standard for later epic poets. Patrizi's rejection is complete; it prepares, in a way, the development of his own theories at a later date.

Patrizi's objections were answered, point for point and with great firmness, by Torquato Tasso in his *Discorso sopra il Parere fatto dal Sig. Francesco Patricio, in difesa di Lodouico Ariosto* (1585). What Tasso most objected to in Patrizi was the general anti-Aristotelian position, and hence his own *Discorso* becomes a serious defence of Aristotle. Starting with Patrizi's initial statement (quoted above), he affirms that the opposite is true: "Aristotle's principles are proper, and true, and sufficient to teach us the art of poetry and to form poems, and to show us the way in which to judge them."[67] Then he proceeds to show in what ways the principles are "proper," "true," and "sufficient." They are proper in the sense that they are not common to any of the other imitative arts (such as painting and sculpture) or to any of the other arts of discourse (such as dialectic and rhetoric). "Besides this, they have those conditions which are appropriate to proper ones, since they are the first by nature and the clearest; and they are those by which all the other propositions of poetry may be demonstrated, and they are capable of separating poetry from every other species or genus of imitation."[68] The argument on "truth" is less cogent. Poetry, says Tasso, is not concerned with distinguishing true from false (this is the field of dialectic), but rather with imitating truth; or rather, it imitates verisimilitude which is itself a kind of truth. Aristotle's principles are not false since they consider verisimilitude and truth. As for their being "sufficient," Tasso insists that "no other one is needed, nor is there any species of good poetry which cannot be discovered through the differentiae that Aristotle sets down and for which correct judgment cannot be given in the way that he teaches us."[69] He insists, moreover, that it is not the business of the preceptor of the art to derive his precepts from usage, but rather "by considering the reasons why some of the things used merit praise and others blame, to separate the ones from the others, and to teach how to choose

[67] *Discorso* (1585), pp. 100–101: "i principij d'Aristotele sono proprij, e veri, e bastanti ad insegnarci l'arte della Poesia, & à formar i poemi, & a mostrarci la maniera di giudicarne."

[68] *Ibid.*, p. 101: "hanno oltre di ciò quelle conditioni, che si conuengono a' proprij, percioche sono primi per natura, e sono piu chiari. E son quelli, co' quali si posson dimostrare tutte l'altre propositioni della Poesia, e possono separar la Poesia da ciascuna altra specie, ò genere d'imitatione."

[69] *Ibid.*, p. 102: "non ce n'è necessario alcuno altro, ne c'è alcuna specie di buona poesia, che non possa ritrouarsi con le differenze, le quali pone Aristotele, e darsene dritto giudicio in quel modo, ch'egli c'insegna."

the good from the bad in the same way that this has come about in medicine."[70]

As for the principles themselves, Tasso re-establishes poetry under the genus imitation, for all its species imitate, even those which do not have plots, and the name of "poet" itself means "imitator." A part of his argument here consists in removing poetry from the genus music, where others might wish to put it because of its use of verse. But verse is not an adequate basis for distinction among genres, the poet is a poet through imitation, and even if both genera were possible places of classification, imitation, as the more noble and the more necessary one, should be chosen. For the rest, Tasso defends both the definitions and the distinctions which he finds in Aristotle, and he defends Homer's epics. Patrizi's attacks seem to him unjustified, his readings of the *Iliad* and the *Odyssey* incorrect. Tasso's own final estimate of Homer reveals in a significant way his attitudes toward the art of poetry: "... all his poetry is nothing else but a praise of virtue, according to the testimony of the great Basil himself; whence he has risen above death and above envy."[71]

RICCOBONI (1585)

The skirmish between Patrizi and Tasso over the position of Aristotle, as I have just outlined it, may serve as a prelude to the publication in 1585 of Antonio Riccoboni's "great commentary" on the *Poetics*. After having published in 1579 a first set of materials on the *Poetics*, including a translation into Latin and the *De re comica* (see above, pp. 582-88), Riccoboni added to these a full-scale commentary and a revised version of the treatise on comedy. These appeared separately, without the translation, in a volume entitled *Poetica Antonii Riccoboni poeticam Aristotelis per paraphrasim explicans, & nonnullas Ludouici Casteluetrij captiones refellens. Eivsdem ex Aristotele ars comica.* The volume contained, in addition to the works, only a dedication and a very brief index. After a short introductory section, "De natura poeticae," the commentary itself presented (in fifty numbered paragraphs) a much briefer analysis of the *Poetics* than those of Riccoboni's immediate predecessors; he wished to treat Aristotle's ideas in general rather than philological questions of the text.

To a degree, Riccoboni's commentary is polemical in tone, since he reacts not so much against Castelvetro's errors of interpretation as against the general tone of disparagement with which Castelvetro had treated the Aristotelian text. His own commentary is written in the spirit of one who believes that the text provides the ultimate answers on all matters related to the art of poetry. Before embarking on an analysis of the in-

[70] *Ibid.*, p. 102: "considerando le cagioni per le quali alcune delle cose vsate meritano lode, altre biasimo, separar l'vne dall'altre, & insegnar à scegliere il buono dal cattiuo in quel modo, ch'è auenuto nella medicina."
[71] *Ibid.*, pp. 116-17: "tutta la sua poesia, altro non è, ch'una lode della virtù per testimonio del gran Basilio istesso: la onde hà superata la morte, e l'inuidia."

dividual passages, however, Riccoboni presents his general ideas on the art (in the section called "De natura poeticae"), and these, for the most part, have nothing to do with Aristotle. He means to treat of the art of making poems rather than of poems themselves. For when he seeks the genus of "poetics," he says that it is either an art or a faculty or an organic habit ("organic" is taken as equivalent to "instrumental"): an art in the general sense that it seeks, in a given matter, the causes through which an end may be achieved; a faculty insofar as it is a discipline; and an organic habit because it serves something else as an instrument. In the last sense, it belongs to rhetoric, both because it makes use of sententiae and because one of its most beautiful devices, recognition, is produced by enthymeme or syllogism. The differentiae of the art are four in number: its end, its function, its subject matter, and the way in which the subject is treated. As he discusses the differentiae, the reason for the multiple genus becomes apparent; and as he works especially with the end, the solutions of other philosophers are rejected in favor of Aristotle's.

Surveying the various ends proposed for poetry, Riccoboni concludes that they are five in number: (1) utility, (2) pleasure, (3) utility and pleasure jointly, (4) imitation, (5) the plot. The first three are found in Horace; arguments in support of the first are found in Zabarella, who makes pleasure an instrument of utility, and in those critics who interpret Aristotle's purgation as a form of utility; common opinion, corroborated by statements of Cicero, approves the second. The fourth is argued most effectively by Scaliger; but it is the fifth which is in Aristotle, and which Riccoboni adopts. Against the other positions, Riccoboni maintains that the first, utility, is proper to the philosopher as an end and is sought by the poet only *per accidens*; that the second, pleasure, leads to such extremes as Plato's ban on the poets, since it may fly in the face of good mores and may justify wickedness and obscenity; that the third, utility and pleasure jointly, is impossible because the two ends are mutually exclusive; that the fourth, imitation, fails to account for many poems which have no imitation. Only the fifth, plot, is fully acceptable; for this is an internal end, common to all poems, and having as a necessary consequence the pleasure which is always attributed to poetry. Hence, one may properly state the end as "fabulosa delectatio" (p. 4).

When, however, Riccoboni attempts to show how the fifth end agrees or disagrees with each of the others, his distinctions lose their sharpness. There is agreement with the first insofar as the plot may be useful through its moral lessons; disagreement, because this is a utility *per accidens*. Good poetry need not be useful. In this connection, he studies the question of purgation in Aristotle, with some interesting results. His general conclusion is that whatever is useful in purgation is an end *per accidens*, for the following reasons:

For tragedy in itself leads men to pity and to fear, and by the very structure of the events it causes the spectators, who feel discomfort as they see misery unjustly visited upon others, to recognize that they themselves are good, and they learn that no hope is to be placed in the course of human affairs; and we shall understand that this is the pleasure appropriate to tragedy. But at the same time, through frequent example and by placing before their eyes many cases of misfortunes, it causes the spectators to become strong and magnanimous, and in this way they also derive utility. Indeed, by habituation to pity and terror, they purge pity and terror, that is, they temper and moderate them. And in this way they become, not excessively pitying and timid as Plato believed, . . . but rather magnanimous and strong.[72]

The construction of the plot has, *per se*, pleasurable consequences; the utilitarian results are accidental. Riccoboni's thesis agrees with the second proposal for the end, since the plot is followed by pleasure; but rather than expressing the end of pleasure overtly, it includes it tacitly. Moreover, since other things beside poetry give pleasure, to say that pleasure is the end is not sufficiently specific and proper. On the third proposal, agreement insofar as plot gives both utility and pleasure, the one *per accidens*, the other *per se*; disagreement, because Riccoboni's thesis makes a distinction between them. On imitation, finally, a similar acceptance of plot as an imitation; but again he distinguishes, saying that imitation is a genus which includes many other species besides poetry, whereas plot is a single species.

The other three differentiae are treated summarily. The "munus" or function is to imitate in verse, the subject matter is human actions, and these are handled in such a way as to become useful for the plot. Having made these various distinctions, Riccoboni is now in a position to define poetics as an art, as a faculty, and as an organic habit: "Poetics is the art of executing plots; or the faculty of imitating in verses; or the organic habit of seeing, in human actions, whatever is suitable for fashioning a plot."[73]

Most of the significant passages in the commentary itself are developments of the principles stated in this introductory section. If we take the end of "fabulosa delectatio," we find important glosses concerning both the origins of poetry and the nature of plot. In connection with his second chapter (1448*b*4 ff.), Riccoboni separates the origins of poetry into divine

---

[72] *Poetica* (1585), p. 5: "Etenim Tragoedia per se adducit homines ad misericordiam, & metum, atque ipsa rerum constitutione efficit, vt spectatores ex alterius miseria iniuste exorta molestiam percipientes se bonos agnoscant, & in rebus humanis spem ponendam non esse condiscant; quam esse propriam voluptatem Tragoediae intelligemus: sed simul fit, vt frequenti exemplo, & crebra miseriarum ante oculos subiectione spectatores magnanimi, & fortes efficiantur, atque hoc modo adiuuentur. Nam per consuetudinem misericordiae, & terroris, perpurgant misericordiam, & terrorem, id est, temperant, & moderantur. Itaque non nimis misericordes, & timidi, vt Plato existimabat, . . . sed potius magnanimi, & fortes efficiuntur." References to the commentary are to the second pagination of the volume; the first, in smaller type, is used for the translation.

[73] *Ibid.*, p. 7: "vt Poetica sit ars fabularum conficiendarum; vel facultas versibus imitandi: vel habitus organicus videndi in actionibus humanis, quod appositum est ad fabulam conformandam."

and natural (or human), and further subdivisions give the following schema:

Origins

Divine   Human

"furor divinus"   "natura"   "ars"

(cf. Plato)

"imitatio" "harmonia"   "ars poetica"

Now in this schema all the elements under human origins are productive of pleasure: "imitatio," because it is the genus under which plot is found, "harmonia," because it supplies verse and the other pleasurable accompaniments, and the "ars poetica" (as we have seen), because it furnishes the way of making the plot correctly. In a general way, harmony "was given to men by nature so that they might bear the labors of human life."[74] We may even ask, therefore, whether there is not here a suggestion of one of the utilities springing from artistic pleasure. This would be perfectly consistent with Riccoboni's usual derivation of utility, naturally but *per accidens*, from the pleasure of poetry. So much for the end of "delectatio." But since this is "fabulosa," and since the plot is the internal end of the poem, the excellence and pre-eminence of plot among the qualitative parts must be established. This is, of course, done by Aristotle; Riccoboni, as he comments on 1450*a*15, multiplies the arguments, and among others he insists that that part of a poem which most vigorously attracts our minds is the most excellent. Plot satisfies this criterion since it contains the elements of recognition and reversal. If we remember that the same elements are at once the most beautiful and the most pleasurable, we may then establish some such series of effects as the following: the plot (because of recognition and reversal), gripping the soul most effectively, hence producing the greatest pleasure, hence achieving the proper end of the art.

Consideration of plot always involves consideration of the objects imitated insofar as these are human actions. Riccoboni, on this matter, makes several departures from the thinking of his contemporaries. First, he declares that the action of tragedy need not be based upon history or upon legend; it is sufficient that some similar example be found among events which have occurred (p. 52). This is a sort of verisimilitude. Next, he constructs (in various passages) an elaborate system of verisimilitude, which we may again represent by a schema:

Objects of
Imitation

Natural   Supernatural

"facta"   "ut fieri   contrary to   according to

(= history)   potuerint"   common opinion   common opinion

according to   according to

necessity   verisimilitude

[74] *Ibid.*, p. 19: "data est hominibus à natura ad humanae vitae labores tolerandos."

In each major category, one of the alternatives is eliminated; history, not poetry, treats those events which have actually happened; and supernatural events which have no acceptance in public opinion are not usable. Of natural objects, those "which could come about" are the proper province of the art; they are divided, in turn, into necessary objects and verisimilar objects, and Riccoboni explains the distinction by examples. A man wounded in the heart must die: the cause-and-effect relationship is, in nature, necessary and inescapable. A man wounded in the head may die: there is a probability, but no necesssity, that the effect will follow on the cause. Of actions which run counter to nature, the poet will choose only those which most men would believe. It should be noted that belief includes traditional belief, perhaps as its main ingredient. For a poet must present the characters and actions of great heroes as tradition has brought them down to his public; otherwise he sins against verisimilitude. Finally, with respect to the objects, the poet treats them universally and thus achieves another kind of verisimilitude:

> Poetry treats universal things; that is, it considers single facts universally or as they might have come about through many causes and in many ways. For instance, the deed of Orestes when he killed his mother Clytemnestra, was a particular deed; nevertheless, the poet considers it in a universal way, as it might have happened through numerous causes and in numerous ways. And poetics is concerned precisely with this universality, in order to invent causes and ways at discretion according as they seem capable of providing greater pleasure.[75]

Consistently with the general position, universality itself is regarded as a source of pleasure, and the end of pleasure directs its operation.

It would seem, then, that the actions chosen and represented in a poem are above all such as will contribute to the pleasure of its audience. But this is not exclusively true; for in Riccoboni's view, the pleasures of plot are always followed by some utility. Various moral lessons are learned. Above all, actions which are terrible and pitiable will bring about the purgation of fear and pity, itself an accompaniment of the correct pleasure: "In fact, in tragedy one must not seek every pleasure, but the proper one; and since the poet must bring about pleasure through imitation, out of pity and fear, this must be achieved by the actions."[76] However, utility seems to spring more directly from another part of the object, character. That is why the poet must have an eye to the beauty of the characters (the phrase "de spectanda morum pulchritudine" appears in the title of Section

---

[75] *Ibid.*, p. 44: "Poesim tractare vniuersalia, id est, in vniuersum considerare singularia, quatenus scilicet plurimis de caussis, & plurimis modis euenire potuerunt; vt singulare factum fuit Orestis, cum Clytemnestram matrem interfecit. id tamen in vniuersum consideratur à poeta, quatenus plurimis de caussis, & plurimis modis potuit euenire; & in hoc vniuersali versatur poetica, vt caussas, & modos ex arbitrio fingat, prout affere posse maiorem delectationem videantur."

[76] *Ibid.*, p. 66: "Non enim omnem in Tragoedia oportere voluptatem quaerere, sed propriam; &, quoniam ex misericordia, & metu per imitationem poetam efficere oportet voluptatem, id in rebus efficiendum esse."

XVIII), which means that each passion must be represented in its best, or most complete, or supreme manifestation. For each passion is to serve as an example for the men who witness it, and the role of imitation is to embellish and enhance (p. 80). Of the four requisites for character, Riccoboni singles out propriety for special recommendations which are no more than the standard rules of decorum. Presumably, a kind of verisimilitude is obtained by giving to each personage the characteristics of his type. One of the kinds of tragedy, the "morata," is actually written for the purpose of presenting good characters, and in it character is more important than action.

Although the greater part of Riccoboni's commentary centers about the objects of imitation, he does have some things to say about the means. Here it would appear that his concern is with pleasure rather than with utility. With most of his contemporaries, he proclaims the necessity of verse in poetry; but his reasons are somewhat different. Verse, he says, is the proper instrument of poetry because it contributes to verisimilitude:

> That this has the greatest importance for the verisimilitude of poetry is seen in this fact: since poetry itself requires an ample and elevated tone of voice, in order that the audience may hear it readily (because it is scarcely probable that men should speak to one another in prose in a tone so high and so ample as to be intelligible to the spectators—unless those who speak be either deaf or stupid, and thus obliged to raise their voices), verse then is particularly adapted to this purpose, because it is proffered with elevation and amplitude of the voice, almost half sung, and is the opposite of the low and humble tone of prose.[77]

If verse is "verisimilar" in tragedy because it lends itself to the loud recitation of a public performance, Riccoboni does not tell us how it would be justified in other more intimate genres; he merely calls upon Aristotle, who authorizes it as the proper instrument of all poetry (p. 13). Of the three means, only "oratio" (or metrical language) will appear in all genres; "saltatio" (or the dance) will appear in some, "harmonia" (or choral music) in the same ones or in others.

Riccoboni's commentary reintroduces a certain amount of restraint into the study of the *Poetics*. It is the shortest of the great commentaries for two reasons: it eliminates all the philological and most of the historical materials which had cluttered up its predecessors. In a way, this makes it less useful. Secondly, it insists on removing the oversubtleties of a Castelvetro, on returning to the text, and on reading it fairly simply and directly. To be sure, this is frequently done by referring to outside sources, especially

---

[77] *Ibid.*, pp. 13-14: "quodque valere plurimum ad verisimilitudinem Poesis ex eo perspicitur, quia cum ipsa vocis postulet elationem, & amplitudinem, vt commode à populo audiri queat, quemadmodum parum verisimile est, vt homines soluta oratione tam elate, & ample inter se colloquantur, vt à spectatoribus intelligantur, nisi illi, qui loquuntur, aut surdi, aut stulti sint, qui vocem extollere necesse habeant: sic ad eam rem maxime accommodatus est versus qui cum elatione, & amplitudine vocis, ac dimidio quodam cantu profertur, & submissioni, atque humilitati solutae orationis oppositus est."

Horace, for clarification. But in certain notable aspects it does return to Aristotle. The most striking of these is the attempt to re-establish the plot as the end of the poem, according to Aristotle's own statement, and to combat the specious arguments of those who argued otherwise. This attempt is spoiled somewhat by Riccoboni's eagerness to reconcile his own position with all the others. Such a preoccupation is, of course, typical of the thinkers of his century.

SALVIATI (1586)

In 1586, Lionardo Salviati completed his work on the first of four parts of a major translation and commentary of the *Poetics* in Italian. He had been engaged on the project for at least ten years by this time. The manuscript, some of it in two copies or drafts, is in the Biblioteca Nazionale in Florence. Of the sections for which we have two copies, one is a short note entitled *Delli interpetri di questo libro della Poeticha*; we may regard it as a kind of prolegomenon to the rest, since in it Salviati examines the earlier scholarship on the *Poetics*. Beginning with Averroës' commentary, which suffers from the differences between Greek and Arab customs, he reviews the translations of Valla and Pazzi and then the later commentaries. Of these he thinks that Vettori's is the best—"it seems that little more light can be desired on this work"[78]—and that Castelvetro's is not entirely acceptable, although he does credit Castelvetro with the best translation into Italian. Throughout his own commentary he finds many occasions to reject Castelvetro's solutions, whereas he frequently praises those of Robortello, Maggi, and Vettori.

Salviati's translation and commentary (a title-page added later calls it *Poetica d'Aristotile parafrasata e comentata*) extends from the beginning of the text through 1449b9, thus treating most but not all of the first five chapters of modern editions. All the initial definitions and distinctions are handled, but unfortunately the commentary stops before the definition of tragedy and its development. Salviati divides the text into short sections, numbering 320 in all; only the first fifty are covered in the extant manuscript. For each "particella" he gives the Greek text, then a translation into Italian, then a "parafrasi," which is an extended and expanded translation, and finally the "comento." Index reference numbers are generously interspersed in the translation, providing the link with sections of the commentary bearing the same numbers. The translation is Salviati's own. It is closer to Castelvetro than to Piccolomini, especially in its conciseness and in the use of certain constructions. But Salviati, who seems to be using Castelvetro as a starting point, attempts to find more current and more accurate terms and in general to achieve a clearer version. We may compare their versions of Aristotle's statement on the object of comedy, both to

---

[78] MS BNF II, II, 11, fol. 372: "poco piu auanti pare che di lume a questo libro possa desiderarsi."

indicate how Salviati works and to show what difficulties were still besetting the translators. The passage is *Poetics* 1449a31:

Castelvetro: Hora la comedia è, come dicemmo, rassomiglianza de piggiori, non gia secondo ogni vitio. Ma il rideuole è particella della turpitudine. Percioche il rideuole è vn certo difetto, & turpitudine senza dolore, & senza guastamento, come, per non andare lontano per essempio, Rideuole è alcuna faccia turpe, & storta senza dolore (1576 ed., p. 91).

Salviati: Ma la commedia è si come habbiam detto imitazione di piu cattiui certamente non gia secondo ogni cattiuità, ma del brutto è il ridicolo parte, percioche il ridicolo è una certa fallenza, et bruttezza senza dolore et non corruttiua, come di fatto il ridicolo uiso brutto alcuno, e trauolto senza dolore (fol. 350).

Since he has tried to be brief in the translation and to remain as close as possible to the Greek text, Salviati uses the paraphrase as a means to clarification; thus the above passage is expanded as follows:

Parafrasi: Ma la commedia, come addietro dicemmo è imitazione di persone piu cattiue che le moderne comunali non sono. Cattiue dico non però in ogni maniera di cattiuità: percioche non ogni maniera di cattiuità è ridicola, come uuole essere quella della commedia: ma solamente alcuna parte della bruttezza, o uogliam dir la cattiuità è ridicola: percio che il ridicolo tra le cose, che stanno male, e tra le cose brutte è solamente quell'errore, e quella bruttezza, che non arrecano, ne dolore, ne graue danno a chi l'ha, come, per darne pronto esempio, è ridicolo alcun uiso brutto, a trauolto, che sia senza dolore (fol. 350v).

The commentary itself is quite extensive, perhaps as extensive as Castelvetro's. Frequently, it calls upon examples from contemporary Italian literature, discusses the opinions of earlier scholars, attempts to point out the major divisions and subdivisions of the *Poetics* as well as to provide glosses on individual words and phrases.

In the preliminary materials as well as in the commentary itself, Salviati reveals fully his attitude toward the text on which he is writing. It is a curious and complicated one. Rather than sharing the skepticism of some of his contemporaries, he judges the *Poetics* to be

... a precious book, and not only most useful but necessary to anyone who wishes to write poetry properly; for in it there are most wonderful teachings and most subtle considerations, compressed in marvelous brevity; whence, as Maggi says so well, one may derive greater benefit from this book alone—so small and so ill-treated—than from all the volumes which have been written about this art by the ancients or by the moderns up to our day.[79]

But one must not take it to be a perfect book, for it is limited both in method and in content. In method, by the fact that Aristotle is not writing

---

[79] *Ibid.*, fols. 6v–7: "prezioso libro e non solo utilissimo, ma necessario a chiunque uoglia dirittamente poetare. Peroche ci hanno bellissimi ammaestramenti, e sottilissime considerazioni, ristretti in marauigliosa breuità. Onde, come ben dice il Maggio, maggior profitto si puo ritrarre da questo cosi picciolo, e mal trattato libro solo, che da tutti i uolumi, che d'antichi, o moderni dietro a questa arte infino a hoggi sono stati composti."

about a science and hence does not need to observe the same rigor of exposition that would be required in a scientific treatise. Thus in the very first sentence he speaks of the composition of the plot, which is only one part of a poem, whereas a "proem" of this type should treat only general matters (fols. 30v–32). In content, by the fact that Aristotle does not mean to treat the whole of the art of poetry but only those parts of it which pertain to six genres: epic, tragedy, comedy, dithyramb, and auletic and citharistic poetry. His principles would therefore not be applicable to such kinds as the mask, the epithalamium, the parody, the satire, and to such poems as Petrarch's *Trionfi* and Boccaccio's *Amorosa Visione* (fol. 252). This means that he did not consider all the possible differentiae of imitations, and his art remains a partial one. Moreover, Aristotle based what he had to say upon the literature available in his time; he studied only a part of that literature, for he wanted to investigate two kinds of poetry, the magnificent as represented by the epic and tragedy, the low as represented by comedy.

All these restrictions mean that if we are to make of the *Poetics* a useful art of poetry we must supplement it in various ways. We must appeal to usage, to authority, and to reason. "Usage, again, when it does not cause any harm, brings with itself not a little authority, and it must be revered and observed as law, especially if it is confirmed by a very long period of time and by the authority of wise men."[80] Usage is invoked as one of the justifications for the insistence upon verse in all forms of poetry. Authority, in this same statement, is of two kinds: it is the practice of the poets and it is the theory of the "wise men," undoubtedly the writers of arts of poetry and the critics. Reason tells us what is "reasonable"; for example, if rhyme is an accompaniment of song, it must not be used in those parts of poetry which are not sung; hence, it would not be reasonable to include it in the spoken parts of a tragedy (fol. 345v).

Finally, by way of reservation, Salviati occasionally points to the corrupt state of the text and its incompleteness. He thinks that some passages have been interpolated by a "corrector" (e.g., 1448a1), that others are not in their proper place (e.g., 1448b4), that in still others the disagreements among the manuscripts make the determination of the proper text impossible. The text he used was, of course, less satisfactory than our own, and in many cases he devotes lengthy discussions to problems which have since been solved or eliminated by better readings.

Salviati distinguishes three major divisions in the *Poetics*, the prologue or proposition, the treatise itself, and the epilogue. The treatise in turn subdivides into four major sections as it examines four problems: poetry in general; two special kinds of discourse (I presume that he means the

---

[80] *Ibid.*, fols. 137–37v: "L'usanza ancora, quando alcun male non cagioni, porta seco medesima non picciola autorità, e si dee riuerirla, e come legge osseruarla massimamente se da molto lungo spazio, e dall'autorità de' saui huomini è confermata."

magnificent and the low); criticisms and defences of the poet; the priority of tragedy over the epic (fol. 15). The end of Aristotle in this work is "to teach how to make the poem and to give its rules; since he wishes to derive these rules from the definitions of the species of poems—and will do so, as will be clearly seen in the course of the work—he will give the latter [definitions] first."[81] In the achievement of this end, one may distinguish, as it were, qualitative parts of Aristotle's presentation; these are "demonstrative or declarative," "narrative," "definitive," "instructive," "dubitative," and "confirmative." For example, the narrative parts will be those in which he traces the origins and development of the divers species; the "definitive," such sections as the definition of tragedy; the "instructive," all the parts containing precepts; the "dubitative," those in which accusations and defences are offered; the "confirmative," ones in which "the precepts are reinforced through the comparison of tragedy with heroic poetry."[82] Such an enumeration of parts implies an analysis of Aristotle's method and order, which Salviati approves in a general way in the following statement: "And this is the order which may be required of a book which does not treat the secrets of philosophy, not only the resolutive, definitive, compositive, and divisive methods over which Robortello exerts himself so much without advantage for the present work."[83] These are the same distinctions of method that we discovered in Sassetti a decade earlier; they appear early in Robortello (pp. 4–5), who attributes them to Philoponus' commentary on *Posterior Analytics* II.

To the interpretation of the *Poetics* Salviati brings three basic suppositions, and these color everything that he has to say in his commentary. (1) Poetry is an imitation of verisimilar objects; this supposition involves him in a lengthy debate over the nature of imitation, over verisimilitude, and over the identification of the objects. (2) It is an imitation in verse; this supposition requires much sleight of hand in the reading of Aristotle. (3) Its ends are to profit and to please; this supposition introduces many extraneous elements into the consideration both of matter and of form in poetry. As we examine these suppositions in turn, we shall discover to what an extent Salviati departs from Aristotle in his attempt to use them as a basis for understanding the *Poetics*.

(1) For Salviati a poem is "an imitation of the verisimilar expressed through ornamented language" ("imitazione del uerisimile espresso col fauellar condito," fol. 10). But to define imitation is not so easy a matter,

[81] *Ibid.*, fols. 41–41v: "d'insegnarne fare il poema, e di darne le regole, le quali regole percioche dalle difinizioni delle spezij del poema uuol ritrarre, e farallo, si come nel processo dell'opera si uedrà manifesto, prima quelle ne darà."

[82] *Ibid.*, fol. 42v: "i precetti si fortificano col paragone della tragedia per rispetto all' heroico."

[83] *Ibid.*, fol. 42v: "E questo è l'ordine, che da un libro, che non tratti i segreti della Filosofia puo richiedere, non i cotanti metodi risolutiui, diffinitiui, compositiui, e diuisiui, ne' quali il Rubertello senza pro di questa opera cotanto s'affatica."

POETICS: EFFECT OF LITERARY QUARRELS

since he finds many meanings and much confusion both in Plato and in Aristotle. He thinks that the meanings in Aristotle reduce to two. The first attaches to simple narration, wherein "the poet imitates, that is, expresses or represents continuously anything whatsoever, either actions, or characters, or persons, or places, or seasons, or tempests, or battles or anything else that can fall under imitation; and he does this without introducing anybody who speaks."[84] This is an acceptable form; what is not acceptable is for the poet to intervene himself, giving judgments and making speeches, for here no imitation is present. The second kind is present when persons are introduced as actors and speakers; this is imitation in the Platonic sense. Further light is thrown upon the term by the comparison which Salviati makes between poetry and history. History is an imitation, for it represents the kinds of things listed; but it is less an imitation than poetry because it does so less vividly. We may thus distinguish, within poetry itself, between two kinds of imitation, one of which represents the principal action in a general way (this is universal), the other of which is found in particular parts:

> Then it receives particular imitations especially in the parts in which either bodies, or sounds, or times, or movements or other things compounded of these are feigned by the poet; in which either characters or thoughts of the mind or passions which are not true but verisimilar are depicted in this special way; wherever by comparison, diminution, augmentation, distinct narration, we are made almost to touch with our hands the things invented by the poet, and they almost to appear visibly in their verisimilar form.[85]

These kinds of partial imitation are found separately in different poets: Dante imitates by descriptions, Petrarch by character, Euripides and Vergil by thoughts of the mind, Vergil by passions, Homer by comparison, Terence by diminution, Lucan by augmentation, Ariosto by distinct narration. In the latter contexts, imitation seems to consist in the enhancing or the heightening of the materials by the use of rhetorical devices.

This impression is confirmed by Salviati's remarks on imitation in the lyric. Since the lyric has no action or plot, it will not display that kind of imitation which accompanies narration; hence, it will not conform to the requirement that a "poem" be imitative throughout. But that is not necessary, for "poetry is present whenever one makes with verse any poetic imitation whatsoever, no matter how brief and compressed, as a part or a

---

[84] *Ibid.*, fol. 68: "il poeta imiti, cioè esprima, o rappresenti sempre mai che che sia, o azzioni, o costumi, o persone, o luoghi, o stagioni, o tempeste, o battaglie, o cheunque altro cader possa sotto l'imitazione. E questo faccia senza indurr' alcuno a parlare."

[85] *Ibid.*, fols. 70v–71: "Appresso particolari imitazioni riceue spezialmente nelle parti, ouunque, o corpi, o suoni, o tempi, o mouimenti, o altre cose di queste mescolate dal poeta si fingono, ouunque ò costumi, o concetti di mente o passioni non uere, ma uerisimili in un cotal modo si dipingono: ouunque comparando, diminuendo, accrescendo, partitamente recitando, ci si fanno le cose trouate dal poeta quasi toccar con mano, quasi nella lor forma uerisimile uisibilmente apparire."

parcel of a composition which may not be a poem."[86] It will thus be possible to find imitation, and hence poetry, even in the minute sections—words or phrases—of works which are not imitations in the more general sense. Salviati here comes close to the position of Averroës, who saw imitation essentially in the rhetorical figure; and he departs radically from the position of Aristotle. He expresses the same idea in a modified way when he says that "imitation is thus only of appearances, of appearances I say which are the objects of those same senses to which imitation has as its end to show itself."[87] If we compare poetry with nature, then, we find that in nature the cause-and-effect relationship is as follows:

$$\text{objects} > \text{senses} > [\text{pleasure}]$$

whereas in poetry it is as follows:

$$\text{objects} > \text{appearances} > \text{imitation} > \text{senses} > [\text{pleasure}].$$

The objects may be actions, in which case the imitation informs the whole work and makes it a poem; or they may be things, in which case the imitation is fragmentary and partial and produces poetry only occasionally.

There are two further consequences of this theory of imitation. First, on the general relationship between imitation and poetry, Salviati holds that imitation is essential and that we have poems or parts of poems according as we have one or the other kind of imitation. But imitation itself is not sufficient. He discusses Aristotle's statement that imitation makes the poet: "For if one had to take that statement absolutely, it would follow that every imitator should be called a poet and every imitation a poem. Similarly, painters and monkeys would be poets, and statues, masks, and puppets would be poems." What must be added is verse, which does not in itself make the poet but which is a necessary adjunct to imitation: "Nor is it enough to say that imitation is the form of the poem; for in order to make the composite, form in itself is not sufficient, but there must also be the matter and not every matter but the proper matter which (speaking of the extrinsic one) in poetry is verse."[88] Second, in any conception of the ends of poetry, imitation must be reduced to its proper importance. Salviati finds that there are four ends for poetry, stated in ways which come closer and closer to the definition of the art as he sees it:

[86] *Ibid.*, fols. 244v–45: "ogni hora si poeti, che si faccia col uerso qualunque poetica imitazione, sia pur quanto si uoglia breue, e compresa, come parte, o come particella da un componimento, che poema non sia."

[87] *Ibid.*, fol. 276: "È adunque l'imitazione solamente dell'apparenze, delle apparenze dico, che oggetti sono di quei sensj, a i quali ell'ha per fine il mostrarsi."

[88] *Ibid.*, fol. 131v: "Percioche se assolutamente douesse prendersi quella sentenzia, ne seguirebbe che ogni imitatore poeta, et ogni imitazione poema dir si douesse. Cosi poeti sarebbono i dipintori, e le scimie, e poemi le statue, le maschere, e i fraccurradi. . . . Ne uale il dire l'imitazione è la forma del poema: percioche a fare il composto non è la forma da per se stessa sofficiente, ma ui uuol la materia, e non ogni materia. ma la materia propria, la qual (parlando dell'estrinseca) nella poesia si è'l uerso."

POETICS: EFFECT OF LITERARY QUARRELS

Artists have two ends: one of them proximate, and that is the work itself; the other ultimate, and that is what follows upon it. The proximate end of the poet is truly to imitate, the ultimate to bring profit and pleasure, which is the same as saying to offer utility and enjoyment by imitating. ... The poem, therefore, has mainly four ends: To imitate; to imitate with verse; to profit and delight by imitating; to profit and delight by imitating with verse. The first is the proximate general end, the second the proximate special, the third the ultimate general, the fourth the ultimate special.[89]

In this analysis, imitation becomes an element in a composite of ends rather than a simple end in itself.

Poetry is an imitation, but of verisimilar objects. Its objects, we have seen, are not merely actions or characters but also a large variety of things, animate and inanimate. We have seen what some of these things are (compare also fol. 202v). It is possible, moreover, to classify them, and Salviati's classification gives a first answer to the relationship between objects and imitations. The poet may imitate objects which are true or false, and in the latter category those which are probable or improbable. But true objects are improper to poetry, since they come from nature and do not demand invention; the poet cannot be a poet without invention. Those which are false and improbable are also excluded, because they prevent the poet from achieving his end, "which is to move the passions along with profit and delight; this cannot be achieved by the imitation of the improbable."[90] The assumption is that emotion depends upon belief and belief upon probability. Hence the third category, of false (or invented) objects which are probable, is the only one left for the poet, and it is this one which Aristotle considers exclusively (fol. 77). Salviati also suggests the sources of our notions of the probable: "It cannot be denied that the probable is found either in nature, or in the sempiternal Idea, or in the mind of the poet, or in the universal, and being found there it is clear that it can be imitated."[91] The poet invents his subject by taking probable materials and fashioning them into a likeness of truth; he disposes them in a proper order; and he expresses them in words (the rhetorical elements of invention, disposition, and elocution are clearly present). Of all these things he is—unlike the historian—maker and creator:

... the poet in his work makes everything himself. ... the poet, inventing what does not exist, and in such a way that it is formed equal to that which exists or

---

[89] *Ibid.*, fols. 151–51v: "gli arteficj hanno due fini, un vicino, e cio è l'opera stessa, uno ultimo, che è cio che ne segue. Prossimo fine del poeta è ueramente l'imitare: ultimo l'arrecar giouamento, e piacere, che il medesimo uiene a dire, che porgere utilità, e dilettazione imitando. ... Ha adunque il poema quattro fini massimamente. Imitare. Imitar col uerso. Giouare, e dilettare imitando. Giouare, e dilettare imitando col uerso. Il primo si è prossimo fine generale, il secondo prossimo speziale, il terzo, ultimo generale, il quarto, ultimo speziale."

[90] *Ibid.*, fol. 76: "il quale è di commuouere con profitto, e diletto il che l'imitazione del non uerisimile non puo adoperare."

[91] *Ibid.*, fol. 76v: "negar non si puo, che'l uerisimile, o uogliam dir nella natura, o nell'Idea sempiterna, o nella mente del poeta, o nell'uniuersale non si ritruouj, e ritrouandosi è manifesto, che si puo imitare."

even better, by himself makes the matter, by himself disposes it; and not content with this, since he must make it appear as it were in the mantle of speech, he does not wish to borrow the latter, either, from somebody else; but he forms a new and excellent one by himself, so that no part shall find a place in his work that he himself has not made.[92]

Verisimilitude is the resemblance of what the poet produces to the world of reality; insofar as it is "better," it resembles the world of Ideas; and the process of creating or inventing such resemblance is called imitation.

(2) Poetry is an imitation in verse. Salviati has established, in passages already examined, the necessity for verse as the proper matter of poetry (and he has called this the "extrinsic" matter to separate it from the "intrinsic" matter or "subject matter" or the objects as imitated). He recognizes the philosophical (and Aristotelian) principles concerning form and matter in imitation:

... the imitation is of the form alone; so long as this is expressed by the imitator, it is of no importance through what matter or with what instrument he presents it to us. And since the matter of the thing imitated and the matter of that which imitates must be different, this difference ought to be, as the logicians say, not specific but of number. For it would be important not that the same sort of language, but that the same words arranged in the same way, should not be used.[93]

But his argument for verse is not based on principle; it consists in a triple appeal to artifice, to pleasure, and to usage. By "artifice" he means the skilful use of the potentialities of language; this is pleasurable because it reveals the greatness of the poet's genius, and moreover it serves to "magnify" the poem. Pleasure itself is a part of the end—or one of the ends—and insofar as verse adds an element of pleasure to the poem it is desirable. The usage of the best poets in the past should convince the poet that verse is indispensable.

These arguments are not without their difficulties. On the one hand there are such works as Sannazaro's *Arcadia*, which is to be blamed for not being entirely in verse rather than for mixing verse with prose. On the other hand, Boccaccio's *Decameron*, although it is a plot and should require verse, is so good in prose that one would not wish it otherwise: "... perchance no composition either of the moderns or of the ancients

---

[92] *Ibid.*, fol. 167: "il poeta nella sua fabbrica fa da se ogni cosa. ... il poeta fingendo quel che non è, et in maniera, che al par di quel, ch'è, o ancor meglio è formato, da se medesimo fabbrica la materia, da se medesimo la dispone, ne contento di cio, quella douendo fare quasi col manto della locuzione apparire, ne anche quella uuol da altrui torre in presto, ma una nuoua, et eccellente se ne forma da per se, acciò niuna parte nella sua fabbrica non da lui fatta, habbia luogo."

[93] *Ibid.*, fol. 136v: "l'imitazione è della forma solamente, la qual pur che dall'imitatore uenga espressa, nulla rilieua per uia di qual materia, o di quale strumento auanti ce l'appresenti. E posto che la materia della cosa imitata, e di quella che imita esser douesse differente, si fatta differenza harebbe a essere, come dicono i loici, non ispecifica, ma di numero: che importerebbe non che la stessa maniera di locuzione, ma le medesime parole nel medesimo modo ordinate non si douessero adoperare."

was ever made so graceful and so beautiful: and woe to the author if he had made it in verse!"[94] Salviati solves the dilemma by stating that the fault is with respect to the species, but that the particular work is excellent; nevertheless, one senses the ascendency of taste and preference over the dictates of principle and argument. The problem of comedy is especially thorny. If it is a poem, it must have verse: Aristotle never permits, in any passage of the *Poetics*, the use of prose. One might think that the popular actions of comedy and its homespun conversations would demand the medium of prose; but instead, poets have invented a kind of verse particularly suited to its needs, and this always appears. Piccolomini's arguments for prose are rejected, and Salviati develops a thorough case for the use of Italian verse in Italian comedy. He summarizes it thus:

> The law that it must be made in measured language is given to all comedy, not to the Greek language or any other; and the reason on which the aforementioned law is based is common to all languages: this is artifice, which, even if it did not afford utility and profit to the listener, if only it did not bring harm and damage to him, should not be neglected, lest the author be deprived of praise and of the privilege of his title. And if one makes verse in the way that has been indicated, it will bring no unpleasantness and no harm to the ears and to the mind of the spectator.[95]

Salviati obviously has in mind not only his principle about verse but also his conviction (stated in another context) that "Art is one and has a certain form of its own and a firm essence from which it must not be removed."[96] In a perfectly consistent way, he maintains that verse does not necessarily involve rhyme. There is no justification for rhyme in Italian tragedy, and, indeed, reason tells us that the use of rhyme in any spoken verse is an improbability (fol. 345v).

(3) The ends of poetry—its ultimate ends—are utility and pleasure. In his initial statement about the four causes (see Chapter II, p. 49 above), Salviati declares that the final cause "is concerned with mores" ("è intorno a' costumi," fol. 13). Nevertheless, he neither subordinates pleasure to utility nor does he insist that utility must always be present. Instead, he seems to neglect the "concern with mores" almost completely and to talk largely about the pleasure to be found in the various genres. Two considerations relate to the kind of pleasure resulting from a given literary

---

[94] *Ibid.*, fol. 140v: "niun componimento ne da' moderni, ne da gli antichi si grazioso, e si bello fu fatto per auuentura: e guai all'Autore, se l'hauesse fatto in uersj."

[95] *Ibid.*, fol. 189v: "La legge, che in legata locuzione debba farsi è data alla commedia non alla greca lingua, o ad altra: e la ragione sopra la quale la predetta legge è fondata a tutte le lingue è comune: cio si è l'artifizio, il quale, come che utile, o giouamento all'uditore non recasse, solo, che noia, o disutile non gli arrechi, per non ispogliar l'autore della lode, e del priuilegio del suo titolo non douerrebbe trascurarsi. E chi farà il uerso nella guisa, che s'è detto, niun fastidio, e niun danno all'orecchia, et all'animo dello spettatore porterà."

[96] *Ibid.*, fol. 69: "L'arte è una, et ha una sua certa forma, et una ferma essenza, onde trarla non conuiene."

form: the audience for which it is written and the objects which it represents. The end of comedy, for example, is pleasure alone—the pleasure which comes from laughter (fols. 146, 200). It has nothing to do with teaching, with using other people's lives to better our own, although this has sometimes been ascribed to it as an end; at best, it avoids presenting positively harmful examples (fol. 355). Its audience is of two kinds: some men (the common people) care only about their laughter and their pleasure; others (the educated men) are more discriminating:

> ... since pleasure is sufficient for men, they care about nothing else, nor are they bothered by the obscenities, or the lack of verisimilitude, or the other errors of the art, or the improprieties and the impertinences of which these plots [in the "commedie di zanni"] are everywhere full, so long as the laughter and the pleasure last continuously. Grave men also find extreme pleasure in them, because of their admirable imitation; but on the other hand, they feel greater annoyance at the absurdities and the other defects than if this were not so. From the striving for pleasure nothing but praise can come to these plots, because pleasure must be said without any doubt to be the end of comedy.[97]

The same is true for certain "joyous writers" in Italian, such as Berni, whose works give even greater pleasure to the "giudiziosi" and the "discreti" than they do to ordinary men: "... they are heard with greater pleasure by men of merit because they recognize in them, better than the multitude, the beauty of the sayings, the grace of the witticisms, the sharpness of the conceits, and the appropriateness of the language."[98]

In order to achieve this effect, to please this audience, comedy must treat men of low social station. Salviati insists throughout that the difference between comedy and tragedy is not a difference between vice and virtue, or badness and goodness, but uniquely between common and illustrious people. This is the "specific" difference:

> For the fact that the persons are good or bad in a given tragedy or comedy will make them more or less commendable, indeed, or more or less perfect; but it will not make them change species. For if popular subjects were taken, no matter how much "better" the persons of such a story were made to be, we should not have a tragedy; and on the contrary, if kings were taken for the imitation, even if their actions were as abominable and as wicked as possible, from such a

---

[97] *Ibid.*, fols. 145v–46: "gli huomini bastando loro il diletto, di niente altro hanno cura ne fa lor noia le sconce cose, ne'l mancamento del uerisimile, ne gli altri errorj dell'arte, ne le sconueneuolezze, e le scede, di che per tutto ripiene sono quelle fauole: pur che continuo il riso duri, e'l piacere, il quale eziandio i seueri huominj grande ui gustano oltr'à misura, per l'ammirabile imitazione di coloro: ma degli assurdi all'incontro, et degli altri difetti senton maggior la noia, che se questo non fosse del cercare il diletto, altro, che lode a quelle fauole non potrebbe uenire: imperciocbe il diletto il fine della commedia senza alcun fallo è da dire."

[98] *Ibid.*, fol. 298: "sono ... da' ualent' huomini con piu diletto ascoltate, quanto eglino meglio, che'l uolgo la bellezza de' mottj, la grazia degli scherzi, l'acutezza de concettj, e la proprietà della fauella dentro ui riconoscono."

plot—provided it were set forth as a dramatic representation—no other poem than a tragedy would ever result.[99]

Hence, all the passages in Aristotle that make an ethical distinction between goodness and badness are explained away or are interpreted in such a way as to justify Salviati's basic contention. Unfortunately, we do not have his remarks on tragedy, on the effect of purgation, and on the specific pleasure to be obtained from that form. But his judgment of Dante is revealing; he holds that Dante writes for "wise men" rather than ordinary ones, that he therefore chooses a highly noble subject, magnifies it in every way, and by so doing gives to his audience marvelous and extraordinary pleasure (fol. 168v). We do know that the effects of compassion and terror result from the spectacle of the misfortunes of illustrious men, just as those of laughter are produced by the spectacle of men who are "ridiculous through their condition" ("ridicoli per la loro condizione," fol. 209).

Salviati's definitions of poetry and of its kinds reflect his attitudes toward imitation and its objects, toward the use of verse, and toward the essential end of pleasure. We have already seen poetry defined as "an imitation of the verisimilar expressed through ornamented language" (fol. 10). The presence of verisimilitude and the use of language both establish a relationship between poetry and rhetoric, since rhetoric treats of both; some knowledge of rhetoric is thus prior to the practice of poetry. Besides, insofar as "costumi" are involved, there will also be a link with moral philosophy. But Salviati refuses to follow Castelvetro in establishing a priority of history over poetry. The reasons are clear: although history is also an imitation, if to a lesser degree than poetry, its object is the true and not the verisimilar; neither the imitation of the truth nor the use of prose would satisfy the basic conditions of poetry, and hence history is essentially different from it. The notion of fiction, of falsehood, of the lie is contained in such terms as μῦθος and λόγος, and these inevitably accompany poetry (fols. 70–70v, 76v). By definition, then, poetry is more closely akin to rhetoric and to moral philosophy than to history. The definition of comedy is modeled on Aristotle's definition of tragedy: "Comedy is a representation of a low subject, having a happy ending and magnitude, with ornamented language, with the ornaments sometimes separated, giving recreation to the soul by means of laughter and of witticisms."[100] It is

---

[99] *Ibid.*, fol. 200v: "Percioche l'essere, o buoni i personaggi, ò cattiui d'una qualche tragedia, o commedia, le farà bene piu, o meno commendabili, o piu, o men perfette, ma cangiare spezie non gia. Conciosia cosa, che se soggetti si prendano popolareschi, facciansi quanto si uuol migliori le persone di cotale argomento tragedia mai non s'haurà, et all'incontro tolgansi Re ad imitare, sien pur quanto si uogliano abbomineuoli, e scelerate le loro operazioni, di cotal fauola, se per maniera di rappresentazione si distenda, altro poema, che tragedia non uscirà giamai."

[100] *Ibid.*, fol. 351: "La commedia è rappresentazione di basso, e sollazzeuole auuenimento hauente fine, e grandezza con fauellar condito, coi condimenti alcuna uolta in disparte, per uia del riso, e delle piaceuolezze l'animo ricreante."

notable that no ethical end is here stated for comedy, as was so frequently done in this period; but otherwise the definition shows many incomprehensions of the *Poetics*.

Throughout his commentary as we have it, Salviati indicates his independence of the earlier students of the text. He examines their positions in the light of his own theory, accepting or rejecting accordingly. That theory is difficult to describe succinctly. It has some elements of a rhetorical theory, such as the concern for the audience and for certain problems of language; but it is not completely oriented in these directions. It discards the contemporary supposition that poetry has moral instruction as its end; hence, the Platonic or the Horatian element is much reduced. It remains close to Aristotle on some points, but frequently—as on the matter of verse, of imitation, of the objects—is far distant from him. One can only regard it as highly eclectic, as perhaps not fully achieved, but as seeking nevertheless a clarification of Aristotle's text and a removal of accumulated error.

One should not conclude, from Salviati's position, that it represented a general tendency in the period. For the next document to be studied, a short pamphlet by Lorenzo Parigiuolo entitled *Questione della poesia* (1586), takes a clearly anti-Aristotelian stand. Its central thesis is that verse makes the poet. We have seen most of the apologists of recent years maintaining that verse was an essential ingredient of poetry, along with imitation, but we have not seen them discarding imitation. That is precisely what Parigiuolo does. He rejects Aristotle's proposition that imitation, not verse, makes the poet, and this constitutes the first point in his program for the work:

> We shall therefore first deny Aristotle's proposition. In addition to this we shall prove that verse makes poetry, not imitation. From this it will follow that the writers of verses without imitation are true poets, contrary to Aristotle's deduction. Finally, we shall remove the accessory that is made to all this, that when the poet speaks in his own person he is not a poet and that one who speaks through the mouth of another is a poet.[101]

"Aristotle's proposition" is disposed of rapidly, merely by saying that he offered no proof for it and that of all the writers of antiquity, only Plutarch accepted it. For the rest, the basic distinction is Cicero's: oratory is in prose, poetry is in verse. Parigiuolo states only one condition: "I do not say, though, that the poet (by which I mean the good poet) is made by verse alone . . . ; but by good verse, which can be written only through

---

[101] *Questione della poesia* (1586), pp. 6–7: "Si neghera dunque prima la proposta d'Aristotele. Oltre accio si prouera che il verso fa la poesia non la imitatione. A questo seguitara che i compositori di versi senza imitatione sono veri poeti contra la consequenza di Aristotele. Vltimamente si torra via la giunta, che vi si fa, che il poeta fauellando in persona sua non sia poeta, e sia quello che per bocca d'altri fauella."

miracles of nature, not without art, and eloquence, and a knowledge of universal things."[102] Imitation may also be included in the poetic faculty; but it is accidental, its use depending upon the ends sought by the poet. The ends are simply stated: all composers of poetry "have directed their road to the end of profiting others, but along different routes according as certain things were pleasant to and appropriate to their minds and their powers."[103]

In many other ways Parigiuolo returns to the tradition of the beginning of the century. Etymologizing on the principal terms connected with the art, he finds that one of them is "fingo" and that this means both "to feign" and "to form"; hence the question of fiction, which brings on a consideration of allegory in poetry: " . . . for the poet, this will be 'to feign' and simulate parables and stories and other similar things in order to delight and profit others with those fictions, under which are always hidden a thousand fine secrets about nature and about customs."[104] This, of course, repeats one of the essential arguments in the early defences of poetry. But Parigiuolo adds the caution that one must introduce no such fictions into religious, Christian poetry, with which fables of the pagan gods must not be intermingled: Horace, in his *Ars poetica*, forbids such monstrous compositions. Many others of the standard arguments for poetry are introduced. Indeed, the extent to which Parigiuolo is retrogressing to a distant time is indicated by his final use, as a definition for poetry, of the Latin formula, "Poesis est cuiuslibet rei versibus comprehensa dictio" (p. 19). All these arguments, it should be noted, are offered as contradictions to Aristotle and as proofs that the concept of imitation is unnecessary in any consideration of the art of poetry.

DENORES (1586)

The position of Aristotle in Giason Denores' *Discorso intorno à que' principii, cause, et accrescimenti, che la comedia, la tragedia, et il poema heroico ricevono dalla philosophia morale, & civile, & da' governatori delle republiche* (1586) is indeed a curious one. As we have already seen (Chapter VIII, pp. 316–19), Denores is primarily concerned with the relationship between poetry and moral and civil philosophy and with the various pedagogical ends served by poetry. To this extent he is a Platonist. He believes that the end of pleasure, everywhere present, is auxiliary and accessory—that instruction follows upon pleasure. Insofar as he holds that the devices capable of producing pleasure are defined and described in the *Poetics*, he

---

[102] *Ibid.*, p. 8: "Non dico pero che semplicemente il verso basti a fare il poeta intendendo del buon poeta . . . ma il buon verso, il quale far non si puo se non per miracoli di natura, senza arte, & eloquenza, e cognitione delle cose vniuersali."

[103] *Ibid.*, p. 9: "hanno . . . drizzato il lor camino al fine di giouare altrui, ma per diuersa strada, secondo che piu le cose a gli animi, & alle forze loro aggradano, e si confanno."

[104] *Ibid.*, p. 13: "per la parte del poeta, sara fingere, e simulare parabole, e nouelle, & altre simili cose per dilettare e giouare altrui con quelle fittioni sotto le quali stanno sempre coperti mille bei secreti & ammaestramenti di natura, e di costumi."

is an Aristotelian. This means that he goes to Plato for a statement of the ends of poetry, to Aristotle for information about its means. The means themselves work in two ways: some of them, such as character and sententiae, produce instruction directly; others, such as plot and diction, produce pleasure directly and instruction ultimately. One may summarize the total situation in this way: The poet himself, wishing to benefit mankind, seeks as his goal instruction about ethics or about nature; hence he turns to Plato for an indication of the proper ends. But realizing that his audience, which seeks only pleasure, must be moved and delighted before it will learn, he turns to Aristotle for precepts of the art.

If pleasure is the means, or at best an intermediate end, all matters pertaining to it will be fully discussed in the *Poetics*. For according to Aristotle, one of the two bases (and the earliest) for the origin of poetry was the wish to give pleasure through imitation; the other (coming later) was the wish to be useful to the public (p. 1v). Art itself is the reduction to method and precept of those devices by which poets have succeeded in pleasing their audiences. For Denores, as he considers the sources of pleasure, all reduce to one word, the marvelous—"la marauiglia." Each of the devices used in the poem must be capable of causing wonder and admiration in the audience. "Therefore every poem is founded on the marvelous. For if this were not so, it would not engender in our minds that pleasure which the audience desires."[105] The marvelous depends, in part, upon the selection of the materials by the poet; to achieve it, he must avoid all those matters which are well worn, familiar, commonplace. But it depends, in greater part, upon how they are handled, for therein lies the artistry of the poet. First and foremost, of course, is the handling of plot, and Denores sees each element of plot-construction, as well as the totality of its form, as contributing to the arousing of admiration. Every plot consists in a change of fortune (the two poles being prosperity and adversity), and this change must be contrived in an unexpected and extraordinary way; for example, in comedy: "it consists in this, that a man of low estate finds himself in some predicament, and it does not seem that he can ever get himself out of it; nevertheless, the poets, following the orders of the law-givers, arrange this kind of poem in such a way, through their inventions, that although in the beginning he is in trouble, at the end however he achieves a most happy conclusion."[106] Wonder grows as the audience sees these things accomplished within the limited time of twelve hours. For tragedy, the conditions are almost identical, even if the situation is reversed:

[105] *Discorso* (1586), p. 16: "Pertanto è fondato ogni poema nella marauiglia. Percioche se non è tale, non partorisce negli animi nostri quel diletto, che si propone l'auditore."

[106] *Ibid.*, pp. 16–16v: "consiste in questo, che trouandosi un huomo di bassa fortuna in vna qualche molestia, non pare, che possa mai rileuarsi da quella, nondimeno i poeti, seguendo gli ordini de' legislatori, acconciano con le loro inuentioni si fattamente questa tal poesia, che se ben nel principio egli è in disturbo, all'vltimo tuttauia sortisce felicissimo fine."

... while some powerful man is in a state of the highest happiness, it does not seem, because of his great power and authority, that he can ever fall into misery. Nevertheless, the poets, through their most skilful plots, weave the tragedy in such a way that although in the beginning he is in a state of extreme contentment and prosperity, at the end, however, he falls into many misadventures. Such marvelousness is rendered even greater by the very brevity and shortness of time, since it is necessary that the poet bring about this great transmutation from good to bad fortune within one revolution of the sun.[107]

In the epic, similarly, a great prince is returned to a state of good fortune.

A plot will be still more marvelous if, to the kinds of "revolution" already indicated, it adds the devices of recognition and reversal. For both of these go counter to our expectations, surprise us, fill us with wonder not only at the turn of events itself, but at the poet's skill in putting them together in this way. The episode may also be added to the list of marvelous devices; for the poet displays both his genius and his inventiveness when he "finds" those episodes which, in a verisimilar way, extend a plot to its correct proportions (pp. 17v–21). Verisimilitude and the proper handling of time are two considerations which must everywhere be observed in these matters. From such passages as his discussion of Vergil, it is apparent that Denores gives to "verisimilitude" the meaning of "natural probability"; such phrases as "per natura" and "contraria alla ragione" are used as criteria for actions. As for time, not only does the limitation for tragedy and comedy permit the display of the poet's powers while the freedom of the epic gives scope to his invention, but somehow the varying lengths are adapted to the differing moral lessons. The king in a tragedy may quickly fall into misery; but it will take a long time for the hero of an epic to regain his lost position. Indeed, since the moral lesson is the ultimate end, it will never be omitted from judgments on the effectiveness of plot. Denores' way of combining means and end may be exemplified by his remarks on the usefulness, for tragedy, of Boccaccio's novella on Rosciglione's wife (*Decameron* IV, 9); it has a plot

... which can equally well receive both the change of fortune, and the reversal, and the recognition, and the revolution of one single day, and the morality; by which it is demonstrated that these furtive and illegitimate loves are discovered at last and receive as punishment, through these secret ways from eternal providence, desperation and death.[108]

[107] *Ibid.*, pp. 16v–17: "essendo qualche potente huomo in vna somma felicità non pare per la sua gran potenza, & signoria, che possa mai trabocar in miseria, nondimeno i poeti, hauendo la mira alle cose predette, tessono con le loro prudentissime fauole la tragedia in tal guisa, che quantunque nel principio egli sia in vna supprema contentezza, & prosperità, all'vltimo nondimeno cade in molte disauenture. Vna tal marauiglia si rende ancho maggiore dalla medesima breuità, e strettezza di tempo, essendo necessario, che il poeta faccia risultar questa gran tramutatione dalla buona fortuna alla cattiua in vn giro di Sole."

[108] *Ibid.*, p. 29v: "laquale parimente puo riceuer, & la tramutation di fortuna, & la peripetia, & l'agnitione, & il giro di vn sol giorno, & la moralità, per la quale si dimostra, questi amori furtiui, & non legitimi essere finalmente discoperti, & riceuer per queste occulte vie dalla prouidentia eterna per castigamento la desperatione, & la morte."

The devices of the marvelous contribute to the achievement of the pedagogical ends.

Diction and verse constitute another qualitative part capable of producing the marvelous. In comedy and tragedy the audience is astonished by the fact that verse can so completely resemble prose and that it can so well be adapted to the conditions of the personages. In any genre, the use of figures of speech will in itself be pleasurable. Denores thinks of diction in terms of the "figures," or the traditional styles, each of which is adapted to particular kinds of subject matters.

The marvelous of words in all these poems, but especially in the heroic and the tragic, consists in this, that they are accompanied by poetic figures and forms of speech and raised above the way of speaking of private persons, so that the language appropriate to the condition of their illustrious persons has in itself a certain royal dignity and grandeur which stems from the choice of the words and from the artful ordering and succession of the same. The figure of lowness, next, must be used for comedy, since it is the imitation of the actions of private citizens.[109]

It is interesting to note that whereas on matters of plot Denores appeals to the authority of Aristotle, on questions of style he attaches himself to the medieval tradition.

The two remaining qualitative parts, character and what Denores calls "sententia," present their moral lessons in an even more direct way. He speaks of character and decorum as affording great delight because the poet presents, via imitation, all the imaginable types and nationalities and the good and the bad in each. He does so specifically in order that his audience may obtain knowledge of the various types, each of which will be delineated in accordance with the laws of decorum. The special language to be used for this delineation is called "oration morata." Here it is another tradition—the rules of decorum of the rhetoricians—that is called upon to provide a basis of procedure for the poet. The rhetorician is also uppermost in Denores' mind when he considers the utility of sententiae, for these arguments and appeals to the emotions are no more than so many lessons in eloquence (p. 32v).

If such parts as plot and diction are marvelous and hence produce delight, and such others as character and thought achieve a moral end more directly, there is no formal or structural criterion which would determine the relationship among all these parts. Aristotle's "if one wishes the poetic composition to be beautiful" (1447a10) is not represented in any

---

[109] *Ibid.*, pp. 35–35v: "La marauiglia delle parole in tutti questi poemi, ma sopratutto nell'heroico, & nel tragico, consiste in questo, che siano con figure, & con maniere di dir poetiche, & inalzate dal modo di ragionar delle persone priuate, a tal che il parlar secondo la conditione delle sue persone illustri habbia in se una certa dignità regia, & grandezza, che deriua dalla eletion delle parole, et dalla prudente ordination, & continuation delle medesime. La figura poscia dell' humilta douera essere accommodata alla comedia, essendo ella imitation delle attion de' priuati."

way, and there is no substitute for it. The only general conception that would permit one to see a given poem as a totality is the conception of its moral lesson, and indeed genres themselves are distinguished on the basis of such a conception. Tragedy, for example, must teach an ethical lesson of a specific kind, having the required social and political implications. Hence, whatever the particular form of its plot might be—revolution, recognition, reversal—its general form must always be the same: it must have an unhappy ending, else the lesson will not be taught. In the same way, its personages must be public figures of illustrious rank; social position, not character, is the only basis of distinction which Denores finds in Aristotle, and he believes that Aristotle also meant to imply the necessity of the unhappy denouement. Moral character enters, to be sure, but because it is an accompaniment to the social station necessary to arouse the proper passions. Moderately good men, in high station, who fall rapidly into misery and a final state of misfortune will arouse the passions of pity and terror; and these were the only ones useful and necessary for Greek tragedy, which aimed at preparing the citizens for military life and for the defence of their country (pp. 10–14v). Hence, purgation itself, as a pedagogical instrument, takes the form required by the lesson.

The definitions of poetry itself and of the various genres (some of which we have already seen in Chapter VIII) are little more than combinations of the various elements that produce the moral lesson—although they have the external form of Aristotelian definitions. One need only compare them with such definitions as we have in the *Poetics* to discover how basically different is Denores' total orientation. His general definition of poetry is modeled on that of tragedy found in the *Poetics*:

Poetry, then, is an imitation of some human action, marvelous, complete, and sizeable, which has in itself a change of fortune either from prosperous to adverse or from adverse to prosperous, which is presented to the listeners through language in verse, either in narration or in dramatic form, in order to purge them by means of pleasure of the most important passions of the soul, and to direct them toward good living, toward the imitation of virtuous men, and toward the conservation of good republics.[110]

The same general pattern is followed in the definition of comedy. By the very abundance of elements which he includes, and by their specificity, Denores shows on the one hand the eclecticism of his sources, on the other his failure to grasp the essence of an Aristotelian definition:

Comedy therefore will be the representation of a pleasant action of private persons, between the good and the bad; which through some human error of

[110] *Ibid.*, p. 36: "E dunque la poesia rassomiglianza di vna qualche attion humana, marauigliosa, compita, & grande, che habbia in se tramutation di fortuna; ò dalla prospera nell' auuersa; ò dall'auuersa nella prospera, che si propone agli ascoltanti con parlar in versi; ò narrando; ò rappresentando, per purgargli col mezzo del diletto da' piu importanti affetti dell'animo, & per indrizzargli al ben viuere, alla imitation degli huomini virtuosi, & alla conseruation delle buone republiche."

stupidity, beginning from hardship, ends in laughter and happiness; in the space of one revolution of the sun; composed in short verses and with low words; in order to purge the spectators, by means of pleasure and of the ridiculous, of those hardships which disturb their calm and tranquillity, through the love affairs of wives and daughters and sons, through the deceits and treacheries of servants, pimps, nurses, and others of that kind; in order to make them become enamoured of private life; for the conservation of that well-regulated popular republic in which they will find themselves.[111]

In such a definition as this, one may work back from the Platonic statement of the ends, through the medieval enumeration of the kinds of subjects, through rhetorical elements of verse and style, to certain Aristotelian requirements for the constitution of the poem; but even these latter are warped by extraneous considerations. In this sense, the definitions of Denores are symptomatic of his total method: a generous eclecticism in which all other ingredients are made to serve two general aims, the achievement of ends whose statement derives from Plato, through means whose conditions are outlined in Aristotle's *Poetics*.

There are striking affinities between Denores' general point of departure and that of Lorenzo Giacomini in his lecture *Sopra la purgazione della tragedia*, delivered before the Accademia degli Alterati in 1586. For Giacomini also, there is a duality of ends, consisting in an immediate end of beauty and pleasure and an ultimate end of Platonic instruction (on the latter, see Chapter VIII, pp. 315–16). Giacomini himself states it this way:

The end of the poet, as a poet, is to construct the poem correctly according to the rules, and the end of the tragic poet is to form the tragedy according to the general idea of the art—the tragedy which, like any poem, may be used for many ends, whose consideration with respect to their causes belongs to the politician who forms the city or who governs it.[112]

The first of these is the proper end of the art, "which is the poem itself" ("il quale è lo istesso poema," p. 33); as he deals with it further, Giacomini indicates that it is also the formal end. He defines poetry as "an imitation, in figurative language reduced to verse, of a human action; ... made

[111] *Ibid.*, pp. 36–36v: "Sara per tanto la comedia rappresentation di una ation piaceuole di persone priuate fra buone, & cattiue, che per qualche errore humano di sempietà, cominciando da trauaglio, finisce in riso, & in allegrezza nello spacio di un giro di Sole, composta con uersi corti, & con parole humili, per purgar gli spettatori col mezzo del diletto, & del ridicolo da que' trauagli, che turbano la loro quiete, & tranquilità per gl'inamoramenti delle mogli, delle figliole, de' figlioli, per gl'inganni, & tradimenti de' seruitori, de' ruffiani, delle nutrici, & di altri simili, & per fargli inamorar della vita priuata a conseruation di quella tal ben regolata republica populare, nella quale si troueranno."

[112] *Orazioni e discorsi* (1597), p. 33: "il fine del poeta in quanto poeta, è il fabricare il poema con retta ragione, & il fine del poeta Tragico è secondo l'idea del arte formare la Tragedia, la quale si come ogni poema per molti fini può essere adoperata, la considerazione de quali per le loro cagioni pertiene al politico, che forma la Città, overo la gouerna."

according to the poetic art; proper for purging, for teaching, for giving recreation or noble diversion."[113] Now the human action imitated, in terms of the four causes, is the formal cause, the material cause is language, the efficient cause is the poetic art, the final cause is that indicated in the last part of the definition. The form itself must be beautiful and pleasurable, and indeed it achieves directly one of the ends, that of "recreation or noble diversion." Hence it is that "the poet always aims to make the work delightful, and therefore he invents the plot out of marvelous things ... , he forms the verse which flatters our ear, he uses chosen words, he adorns the diction with strange and wonderful forms of speech."[114] There is thus, for Giacomini, a proper area for the operation of an art of poetry—based on the *Poetics*, we may assume—and this is the creation of the beautiful form according to the rules.

But Aristotle also provides for him the best statement of the pedagogical ends, and this is in the purgation clause, which is the subject of his lecture. He is moved to consider it at length because of the many difficulties of interpretation and because of the three alternative meanings proposed by earlier commentators. The first theory holds that tragedy purges only the two passions of pity and fear, causing the men in its audience to be less fearful and less pitying. The second theory holds, instead, that the opposites of these passions are purged—envy, hate, wrath, joy, confidence. According to the third theory, tragedy moderates all the passions through the spectacle that it gives of the instability of human affairs, makes us accept our own misfortunes with greater equanimity. Giacomini's theory is none of these. He believes, in a general way, that the passions are purged by exteriorization, that a man who suffers any given passion within his soul will suffer it less as he gives it outward expression, as, for example, through weeping. Moreover, this lightening or purgation of the soul is accompanied by a feeling of pleasure. A tragedy presents just such an opportunity for exteriorization. Giacomini likens its effect to that of medicinal purgatives which drive out certain humors from the body, provided that the purgatives have some natural appropriateness to the humors. Tragedy presents vividly before our eyes the spectacle of terrible and pitiable events. As we see misfortunes impending over men like ourselves, we fear for their safety; when misfortune actually occurs, we are compassionate. Hence as we feel these passions in sympathy with others, our souls are relieved of them (pp. 36 ff.). At the same time, the spectacle is full of moral teachings.

To this seemingly divided poetics, divided between two ends of pleasure and utility, between a formal cause and a final cause, Giacomini gives

---

[113] *Ibid.*, p. 33: "imitazione con parlare fauoloso ridotto in versi di azzione humana ... fatta secondo l'arte poetica, atta a purgare, ad ammaestrare, a dar riposo, o nobile diporto."

[114] *Ibid.*, p. 35: "il poeta intende sempre far l'opera dilettevole, e perciò finge la favola di cose maravigliose, ... forma il verso, che ci lusinga l'orecchio, usa sceltezza di parole, adorna la favella di maniere di dire pellegrine e mirabili."

unity by making pleasure a necessary condition of purgation. That is, the form of the poem itself produces not only the pleasure but also the utility. He expresses this notion elaborately in a passage which offers at once a psychology of aesthetic pleasure and a statement of utilitarian ends:

> ... the spectator of the tragic act, although he knows as long as he has recourse to his intelligence for assistance that what is represented is not true, nevertheless fooled by the artful imitation accompanied by flattering sweetness, especially when present objects strike his view and create within his imagination phantasms capable of moving it, feels within himself fear and compassion and weeping, and in addition to the pleasure coming from the lightening of his spirit which he achieves while it is operating according to these passions, he feels still other pleasures. First, tragedy pleases by teaching the action represented, since learning is among the things which are joyful by their nature; it pleases through the marvelous, demonstrating that a thing not believed can readily come to pass; it is delightful through the imitation. . . . To these delights it is not improper that we should add in order three others, even though they are somewhat external and remote. One is that since compassion is an act of virtue, and since every operation according to virtue or resembling virtue is by its nature joyful, the compassion of tragedy can bring delight also in this respect. . . . The second is, that it informs us that we indeed are free from such grave misfortunes, which cannot do otherwise than give us pleasure and joy. The last is the learning of salutary lessons. . . . [115]

Giacomini's ideas on purgation are not derived exclusively, it will be clear, from the *Poetics*; he refers also to the *Politics* on the effects of music, to Plato on poetry in general, and to a theory of the passions and of their effects upon the soul. These elements are welded into a doctrine which uses Aristotle to defend the poet against Plato, and which achieves an almost complete identification of the pleasures and the utilities of poetry.

TASSO (1586-87)

It is another of the questions raised by Aristotle in the *Poetics*, that of truth and verisimilitude, that occupies Torquato Tasso in his *Risposta al Discorso del Sig. Oratio Lombardelli*, also of 1586. And although this work sets out to contradict Lombardelli, essentially it develops a thesis of its own

---

[115] *Ibid.*, pp. 240-41: "lo spettatore dell'atto tragico benchè conosca quello, che si rappresenta, non esser vero, mentre all'intelletto ricorre per aiuto, nondimeno ingannato dall'artifiziosa imitazione da lusinghevole dolcezza accompagnata, massimamente quando oggetti presenti feriscon la vista, e crean nella fantasia fantasmi possenti ad alterarla, sente in se timore, e compassione, e pianto, ed oltre la compiacenza dell'alleggerimento dell'animo, che mentre secondo questi affetti opera, egli consegue, prova ancora altri diletti. Primieramente piace la tragedia insegnando l'azione rappresentata, poichè lo imparare è tralle cose per natura gioconde, aggrada colla maraviglia, proponendo la cosa non creduta poter agevolmente avvenire; è dilettevole per l'imitazione. . . . A questi diletti non è disdicevole, che accompagniamo in ischiera tre altri benchè alquanto esterni, e remoti. Uno è, che essendo il compatire atto di virtù, essendo ogni operazione secondo la virtù, o alla virtù somigliante, per natura gioconda, può anche per questo riguardo la compassione della tragedia apportar diletto. . . . L'altro è, che ne fa conoscere, che pur da sì fiere disavventure siamo liberi noi, il che non può non ci porgere piacere, e gioia. L'ultimo è l'apprendere documenti salutevoli. . . ."

with respect to necessity, probability, credibility, and the marvelous. Much of what Tasso has to say is of course influenced by his intention to defend his own poem, and the thesis becomes a justification of his own practice. Throughout his argument, he uses the art of history as a point of comparison with the art of poetry (answering Lombardelli's views), and the following conclusions result from the comparison: History and poetry differ essentially in the absence and presence of imitation. Tasso has some difficulty with the term, since, at times, he tends to use it as meaning dramatic representation. But in a broader sense it seems to mean the vivid placing of things and actions before our eyes, and this occurs in poetry; whereas history gives merely a simple narrative of events. One consequence of this distinction is that the customary statement to the effect that history treats the truth and poetry treats verisimilitude is not valid. For Tasso, both arts are equally concerned with the truth. In fact, he sees truth as a necessary foundation for poems in whatever genre, and the hierarchy which he establishes descends from genres which are based entirely on the truth to those which represent it only slightly. He puts it this way:

... all poems have some foundation of truth, some more and some less, according as they participate more or less in perfection. We must nevertheless note that just as the whole structure is not the foundation, so perchance the whole action does not need to be true, but it must leave its part to the verisimilar, which is proper to the poem.[116]

Thus tragedy and the epic would be the highest genres, being wholly founded on the truth; comedy and the pastoral would be the lowest, since they have no foundation in truth. Tasso thinks little of poems whose only truth is a truth (or reality) of cities and countries; somewhat more of those which present true (or real) persons as well; and most of those whose actions are true in the sense that they are historically verifiable.

Since poetry is not merely a retailing of historical facts—or a falsification of them—other elements must be added. The "mode" and not the "matter," he says, distinguishes poetry from history (p. 9). For one thing, the poet must organize his materials according to necessity and probability; for another, he must give them a proper form. Perhaps Tasso reduces both of these to one procedure: "That is not a poem to which form is lacking, in which things and events are not well composed together."[117] We are not told of what necessity and probability consist. But we do know that the poet must add something to the truth (otherwise there would be no opportunity for his "invention") and that the marvelous is a necessary ingredient. "The poem reaches the highest degree of perfection when these

---

[116] *Risposta* (1586), p. 18: "tutti i poemi habbiano qualche fondamento della uerità, chi piu, e chi meno, secondo che piu, e meno participano della perfettione; dee nondimeno hauersi auertenza, che si come tutta la fabrica non è fondamento, cosi per auentura tutta l'attione non dee esser uera, ma lasciarsi la sua parte al uerisimile, il quale è proprio del poema."

[117] *Ibid.*, p. 10: "quello non è poema, à cui manchi la forma, nel quale le cose, e gli auenimenti non siano ben composti insieme."

two things [the marvelous and verisimilitude] are joined together, and they may be conjoined in various ways."[118] He thinks of the marvelous as consisting of those events which do not enter into natural probability. How, then, can they be credible and acceptable in the poem? The answer is in the beliefs, even the faith, of the audience. For Christians believe the miracles of the Bible, know them to be true even though they are improbable. This is the only kind of credibility which the poet seeks:

> ... from Cicero we may deduce that the credible belongs rather to the orator, because it is a part of the probable; but the verisimilar belongs to the poet, who frequently does not seek to persuade, if only he can please, nor does he care whether things are believed, but that they should give pleasure; nor does he so much avoid lying as the inappropriateness which may be in the lie, and he seeks to hide it or at least to color it in many ways, so that even if it is known, at least it will not be blamed; and if the poet ever takes the credible into consideration, I believe that he does not consider it *per se* but *per accidens*.[119]

There seems to be much confusion in these terms and in the general position. Perhaps we can clarify it in this way: The poet, at his best, takes a historically true subject. He develops it by the addition of elements that seem to flow "necessarily" and "probably" from the given materials. These may be inconsistent with natural probability and with normal credibility; but to the extent to which they contribute to the totality and the beauty of the poetic form, and hence give pleasure, they will be acceptable. In spite of Tasso's protestations, the element of belief in the audience seems to remain an important factor, and "truth" may as well be something which the audience believes to be true as something for which there is historical evidence.

Some further clarification of these points is given by Tasso in his little pamphlet entitled *Delle differenze poetiche*. It was written sometime after 1585, in response to Orazio Ariosto's *Difese dell'Orlando Furioso dell' Ariosto*, but was not published until 1587. In the final pages of the work, where he is discussing the relationship of episodes to plot, Tasso throws light on the meanings which he attaches to necessity and verisimilitude. He does so by proposing an analogy to nature, in which there are no "episodes" but in which everything is necessary, i.e., in which all the parts have a fixed order and interdependency. A similar order would be desirable in poetry, but it is impossible:

[118] *Ibid.*, pp. 14–15: "all'hora il poema è nella somma perfettione, che queste cose insieme s'accoppiano, e si possono in piu modi congiungere."
[119] *Ibid.*, p. 19: "da Cicerone si può raccorre, che'l credibile appartenga piu all'Oratore; perche egli è parte del probabile, ma il uerisimile è del poeta, il quale molte uolte non cerca di persuadere, pur che diletti, nè si cura, che le cose sian credute; ma che elle piacciano: nè tanto fugge la menzogna; quanto la sconueneuolezza, ch'è nella menzogna; e cerca d'occultarla, ò almeno colorirla in molti modi: accioche, s'ella è pur conosciuta, non sia almeno biasimata: e se'l poeta hà mai consideratione al credibile, io stimo, ch'egli no'l consideri per se, ma per accidente."

... art also would like to demonstrate conclusively its riches and its ornaments and reduce all the parts of the poem to an almost certain order and give to each one the necessary disposition and dependency. But not being able to attain such perfection, it sometimes does in a verisimilar way that which it is not permitted to it to do necessarily.[120]

Verisimilitude, in this context, appears to imply a looser connection of parts than that required by necessity; but it must not be so loose that removal of the part could be effected without spoiling the whole structure.

Tasso's concern with these matters is incidental in the pamphlet. His main problem is twofold: to justify the value and the usefulness of the *Poetics* in a general way, and to insist that Aristotle's ways of distinguishing between genres (these are the "differenze poetiche") are the only proper ones. On the first score, he denies all of Orazio Ariosto's assertions; here is his total estimate of the *Poetics*:

... we do not have, in any work which has been written in any of the three finest languages, any greater light on the art of poetry than in this one. We must not take poetic teachings more willingly from any other, nor allow ourselves to be deceived by false persuasions or by apparent reasons; for every little error that is committed in the principles, as we go beyond, becomes very great toward the end. Thus, Aristotle's principles remain sound and not thrown to the ground.[121]

The principles of which he speaks are the definitions, the bases of similarity, and the differentiae of the species—primarily, the distinction of the object, manner, and means of imitation.

On the interpretation of this distinction, Tasso is usually more rigorist than his contemporaries. For whereas they are frequently willing to admit that objects may be distinguished on a number of bases—rank of persons, or their moral character, or the way in which they are intermingled—and that a number of genres is possible within each manner, Tasso reduces severely the possibilities: the only valid basis of characterizing objects is the general nature of the total action, as illustrious or as popular, and hence only two genres are possible under each manner of imitation. As a consequence, for example, tragedy will present an illustrious action, and even if popular persons take part in it, it will still be a tragedy. The dramatic manner will admit of only two genres, tragedy and comedy; any mixture of the two in a tragicomedy or a comitragedy would be impossible, since it

---

[120] *Delle differenze poetiche* (1587), p. A7: "l'arte vorrebbe anch'ella dimostrar à proua le sue ricchezze, & gli ornamenti; & ridurre tutte le parti del Poema sott'ordine quasi certo; & dare à ciascuna dispositione, & dependenza necessaria ma non potendo peruenir à tanta perfettione; fà verisimilmente alcuna volta quel, che non l'è conceduto di fare necessariamente."

[121] *Ibid.*, pp. A4v–A5: "non habbiamo in opera, che sia stata composta in alcuna delle tre lingue più belle, maggior luce dell'arte Poetica, che in questa: non debbiamo prendere gli ammaestramenti Poetici più volentieri da alcun' altro, ne lasciarsi ingannare da false persuasioni; ò da ragioni apparenti: imperoche ogni piccolo errore, che si commette ne' principij, procedendo oltre, diuiene grandissimo verso il fine: rimangano dunque i principij d'Aristotele saldi, & non gettati in terra."

would violate the essential nature of either action. The narrative manner will also give two forms, serious epics like the *Iliad*, the *Odyssey*, and the *Aeneid*, and comic epics like the *Margites* and the *Moretum*; again, mixtures of the two are unthinkable in Aristotelian terms. This integrity of the essential action is a condition of and product of the unity of plot. But Tasso insists that unity does not mean singleness of action; rather, unity implies a multiplicity of things to be unified, and in a poem this multiplicity is constituted by all the various elements which contribute to the realization of the central action.

In some ways, Tasso's view represents a return to Aristotelianism. It sets aside some of the irrelevant subtleties on which others were insisting, it proclaims the primacy of unity of plot and the adequacy of Aristotle's distinctions with respect to object, manner, and means of imitation. In other ways, it is less sound methodologically. For the dictum against mixture of different kinds of actions is little more than Cicero's principle of the purity of styles; and the notion of unity out of multiplicity goes back to certain ideas of Plotinus on harmony in music. Tasso admits his use of some of these external sources, which are basically irreconcilable with the stern Aristotelianism that he is advocating.

CONCLUSIONS

During the years we have been discussing, the effect of the literary quarrels made itself felt upon the Aristotelian tradition in a real if only an occasional way. I mean that there was no continuous and growing body of polemical materials whose vital arguments involved interpretation and reinterpretation of the *Poetics*; yet in such works as those by Bulgarini, Carriero, Patrizi, and Tasso the current literary quarrels brought about fresh and significant appraisals of what Aristotle had said. In fact, these works make more of a contribution to the study of Aristotle than they do to the furthering of the literary debates.

Something of the polemic spirit manifested itself in the estimates of Aristotle's worth as a writer on the art of poetry. Once Aristotelian arguments had been used in defence of Dante or of Ariosto, it was natural that those who wished to attack these Italian poets should, as at least a part of their attack, deny the validity of Aristotle's principles. Such was the case with writers like Patrizi and Lombardelli. They were answered, in turn, by the vigorous defences of a Tasso or a Salviati. The importance of the whole procedure is that, as in the preceding decade, the question of Aristotle's merits leads to a much more searching analysis of his text, in the broadest terms. The minute exegeses of earlier times—which had already accomplished most of what they were to achieve in this century—tend to be replaced by the over-all view of the text, its principles, its arguments, its relationship to poetical realities. Two broad orientations with respect to the text now result. First, the attention to Aristotle's method (we have seen examples of it in Chapter XI) continues to provide some of the most original ideas. As it motivates Riccoboni, Sassetti, or the anonymous writer of the Magliabechi MS VII, 437, it leads to fruitful discoveries of principle and useful interpretations of detail. Second, a new criterion appears with frequency: How useful is the *Poetics* as a guide to the poet who wishes to write today? The theoretical approach, perhaps under the impact of the quarrels, gives way to a much more practical attitude. Should Ariosto, one asks, have followed the demands of Aristotle in the *Poetics*? To what extent? Are ancient principles valid for modern times? Will Tasso be well- or ill-advised to respect these principles? And what about a man who wishes to write a tragicomedy? The questions are put on two levels, on the level of theory (as we have seen in recent pages) and on the level of actual performance (as we shall see in the later chapters on the quarrels).

These diversified orientations may account in part for the nature of the documents written during these years. Certain types of work are conspicuously absent; there is only one major commentary in Latin among the printed volumes of the period, none in Italian. Three lesser commentaries are written in Italian—two of them never continued beyond the early chapters—but none is published. These seem to be the result of the great academic activity of the '70's; but not only has public interest waned, the authors themselves lose courage and enthusiasm—or go off into other adventures. Riccoboni is the only universitarian to publish a Latin translation of the *Poetics*; no new one appears in Italian. In a similar way, the academic discourse or lecture is much less often encountered. So is the commentary on Horace, in which discussion of Aristotle might play a secondary part; I think only of Aldo Manuzio the Younger, in whose work Aristotle's part is very secondary indeed. What we do have is a highly miscellaneous group of works, some of them connected with the polemics, others presenting independent views of highly varied subjects.

Since the great commentaries are few in number, we find in this period, rather than total analyses of the text, discussions of detailed points isolated from their context in the *Poetics*. In this sense, Lorenzo Giacomini's lecture on purgation is typical. The main problems discussed continue to be the same ones—after all, it is still the same text—but some new suggestions are made for interpretation. Theorists still have great difficulty with the notion of imitation; but although many meanings are given the term, Aristotle's are not so often confused with Plato's. Increasingly, writers see as one of the necessary components of imitation a kind of heightened and vivid portrayal which appeals to the senses rather than to the intellect. The complicated matter of the interrelationship of truth, verisimilitude, and necessity draws much attention. Most critics believe that the object must be a true one if credibility is to result, that verisimilitude is a kind of second-best truth. But they interpret necessity variously as referring to a cause-and-effect sequence in nature, or as indicating an artistic quality of poems which justifies the way in which certain devices are handled. Aristotle is sometimes challenged on his requirement that plots be unified; but more usually the problem is how they should be unified—to what extent "double" and "multiple" plots are permissible, in what way episodes may be integrated into the whole. Such theorists as Tasso, in their insistence on a high degree of unity, are perhaps most representative of the period. There is at least one statement, by Riccoboni, which recognizes the existence of three unities.

On some major issues there is relative unanimity of attitude. Almost everybody thinks that verse is inseparable from poetry, and (just as before) many ingenious interpretations of the *Poetics* are offered to prove it. In the same way, almost all the critics are in agreement that the ends of poetry, either immediately or ultimately, are utilitarian. The moral intention of the poet may be realized in the general form which he gives to his story, in the characters he presents, or in the dicta which constitute the sententiae. This theory determines, for the most part, the way in which the four requisites of character are understood; or at least the first, that of "goodness," is generally given an ethical meaning. Aristotle is juxtaposed to Plato on this matter of moral instruction, and both the statements of the ends of poetry and the discussions of purgation are seen as answers to Plato's banishment. None of these is a new idea; all echo the earliest expressions of the Aristotelian tradition in the sixteenth century.

More generally, Plato seems to be less omnipresent than he was in former times. So do Horace and Cicero and the rhetoricians. For the documents studied here, while they make the customary references to other authorities, are more closely concerned with the problem of interpreting Aristotle in and for himself. This may result in part from the fact that the work of comparison and conflation has long since been done, in part from the concentration upon specific passages of the *Poetics* itself. The question now is agreement or disagreement with Aristotle's principles—and the element of disagreement should not be overlooked in such writers as Capponi and Parigiuolo—for the purpose of discovering the truth about the art of poetry. Aristotle is the guide. But he is not infallible, and writers now feel justified in setting up their own theories against those of the master. The commentary on commentaries is much less conspicuous, the study of Aristotle himself more direct. It is perhaps this kind of spirit which gives rise to the last great defences of Aristotle in the closing years of the century.

S.O.